Like species in a jungle, retailers face a dynamic, highly competitive environment. New retail formats arise complementing and, in some cases, replacing traditional formats.

The world has certainly changed a lot since Audrey Hepburn looked at the window display in the classic film *Breakfast at Tiffany's*. F.W. Woolworth's Five and Dime stores have disappeared from the retail landscape. Wal-Mart has grown to become the largest retailer and the largest nongovernment employer in the world. Category killers like Circuit City now dominate the market for a variety of merchandise types ranging from pet supplies to office supplies. Traditional retailers like Home Depot have responded to the emergence of electronic retailers like Garden.com by becoming "clicks and mortar" retailers.

To survive and prosper in the retail jungle, retailers must build a path based on well-developed strategic plans and use state-of-the-art information and distribution systems to implement them. This Fourth Edition of *Retailing Management* by Michael Levy and Barton Weitz is an effective guide for finding your way through the 21st century retailing jungle.

FOURTH EDITION

Retailing Management

FOURTH EDITION

Retailing Management

MICHAEL LEVY, PH.D.
Babson College

BARTON A. WEITZ, PH.D.
University of Florida

Boston   Burr Ridge, IL   Dubuque, IA   Madison, WI
New York   San Francisco   St. Louis
Bangkok   Bogotá   Caracas   Lisbon   London   Madrid   Mexico City
Milan   New Delhi   Seoul   Singapore   Sydney   Taipei   Toronto

McGraw-Hill Higher Education

A Division of The **McGraw-Hill**

RETAILING MANAGEMENT

Published by McGraw-Hill/Irwin, an imprint of The McGraw-Hill Companies, Inc. 1221 Avenue of the Americas, New York, NY, 10020. Copyright © 2001, 1998, 1995, 1992, by The McGraw-Hill Companies, Inc. All rights reserved. No part of this publication may be reproduced or distributed in any form or by any means, or stored in a database or retrieval system, without the prior written consent of The McGraw-Hill Companies, Inc., including, but not limited to, in any network or other electronic storage or transmission, or broadcast for distance learning.

Some ancillaries, including electronic and print components, may not be available to customers outside the United States.

This book is printed on acid-free paper.

domestic   1 2 3 4 5 6 7 8 9 0 VNH/VNH 0 9 8 7 6 5 4 3 2 1 0
international 1 2 3 4 5 6 7 8 9 0 VNH/VNH 0 9 8 7 6 5 4 3 2 1 0

ISBN 0072315776

Publisher: *David Kendric Brake*
Sponsoring editor: *Rick Adams*
Senior development editor: *Nancy Barbour*
Marketing manager: *Kimberly Kanakes*
Senior project manager: *Pat Frederickson*
Production supervisor: *Rose Hepburn*
Senior designer: *Jennifer McQueen Hollingsworth*
Cover images: *"Breakfast at Tiffany's" by Photofest; "Woolworth's" © Corbis Images; "Circuit City" and "Wal-Mart" © 2000 Susan Holtz; The Home Depot and Garden.com websites with courtesy; and Background image © Photodisc*
Supplement coordinator: *Cathy L. Tepper*
Media technology producer: *Burke Broholm*
Compositor: *Shepherd, Incorporated*
Typeface: *10.5/12 Janson*
Printer: *Von Hoffmann Press, Inc.*

Library of Congress Cataloging-in Publication Data

Levy, Michael.
    Retailing management/Michael Levy, Barton A. Weitz—4th ed.
        p. cm.
    Includes index.
    ISBN 0–07–231577–6 (alk. paper)
    1. Retail trade—Management. I. Weitz, Barton A. II. title.

    HF5429 .L4828 2001
    658.8′7--dc21

                                                                                00–033526

www.mhhe.com

To my wife, Marcia, and my daughter, Eva
Michael Levy

To my wife, Shirley
Barton Weitz

Michael Levy, Ph.D.
Babson College

MICHAEL LEVY PH.D. is the Charles Clarke Reynolds Professor of Marketing at Babson College. He received his Ph.D. in business administration from The Ohio State University. He taught at Southern Methodist University before joining the faculty as professor and chair of the Marketing Department at the University of Miami. He has taught retailing management for 22 years.

Professor Levy has developed a strong stream of research in retailing, business logistics, financial retailing strategy, pricing, and sales management that has been published in over 30 articles in leading marketing and logistics journals including the *Journal of Retailing, Journal of Marketing*, and *Journal of Marketing Research*. He currently serves on the editorial review board of *Journal of Retailing, Journal of the Academy of Marketing Science, International Journal of Logistics Management*, and *International Journal of Logistics and Materials Management*.

Professor Levy has worked in retailing and related disciplines throughout his professional life. Prior to his academic career, he worked for several retailers and a housewares distributor in Colorado. He has performed research projects with many retailers, including Andersen Consulting, Burdines Department Stores, Mervyn's, Neiman Marcus, and Zale Corporation.

Barton A. Weitz, Ph.D.
University of Florida

BARTON A. WEITZ, PH.D. received an undergraduate degree in electrical engineering from MIT and an MBA and Ph.D. in business administration from Stanford University. He has been a member of the faculty at the UCLA Graduate School of Business and the Wharton School at the University of Pennsylvania. He is presently the JCPenney Eminent Scholar Chair in Retail Management in the College of Business Administration at the University of Florida.

Professor Weitz is the executive director of the Center for Retailing Education and Research at the University of Florida. The activities of the center are supported by contributions from 20 national and regional retailers, including JCPenney, Sears, Burdines, Wal-Mart, Home Depot, Rich's, Office Depot, Bealls, and Electronic Boutique. Each year the center places over 150 undergraduates in paid summer internships with retail firms and funds research on retailing issues and problems.

Professor Weitz has won awards for teaching excellence and has made numerous presentations to industry and academic groups. He has published over 40 articles in leading academic journals on electronic retailing, salesperson effectiveness, sales force and human resource management, and channel relationships. He is on the editorial review boards of the *Journal of Retailing, Journal of Marketing, Journal of Interactive Marketing, International Journal of Research in Marketing*, and *Journal of Marketing Research*. He is a former editor of the *Journal of Marketing Research* and is presently co-editor of *Marketing Letters*.

Professor Weitz is a member of the board of directors of the National Retail Federation, the National Retail Foundation, and the American Marketing Association.

I N THIS FOURTH EDITION OF *RETAILING MANAGEMENT*, we have focused on describing and examining the implications of the evolution of retailing into a global, high technology industry. Technological developments have affected the way consumers buy products and services and the way retailers run their businesses. A growing number of consumers now shop the world through the Internet. Sophisticated information systems turn purchase transactions into orders and eventual store deliveries ensuring the right products are in the right place at the right time. Retailers use decision support systems to develop merchandise assortments, evaluate retail sites, schedule sales associates, and target promotions to customers.

The competitive landscape of the retail industry is going through a period of dramatic change. Electronic retailers with stock market capitalization greater than most store-based retail chains have emerged to satisfy the needs of these cybershoppers. Store-based retailers are expanding beyond their local markets to become global businesses. Innovative retail entrepreneurs are taking advantage of these new opportunities to build the next generation of industry giants. Traditional retailers must adapt or go out of business.

Our objective in preparing this fourth edition is to capture this excitement and challenge in the retail industry as we inform students about the state-of-the-art management practices of these important institutions in our society.

NEW FEATURES IN THE FOURTH EDITION

In preparing the fourth edition, we have made a number of changes to reflect the evolving nature of retailing.

Electronic Retailing   The growth of electronic retailing in the United States is dramatic. In response to the emergence of electronic retail entrepreneurs like Amazon.com, most major traditional store-based retailers have launched electronic retail offerings, shifting from "bricks-and-mortar" to "clicks-and-mortar" retailers.

The fourth edition addresses the emergence of this new retail format in two ways. First, we have devoted most of Chapter 3 to providing an overview of electronic retailing. In this chapter, we review the factors affecting the growth of electronic retailing and the impact of this format on traditional store-based retailers. The chapter addresses issues such as

* Will shoppers abandon the mall to surf the Net?
* Will consumers buy products with important "touch-and-feel" attributes (e.g., apparel) over the Internet?
* Which retailers will be winners and which will be losers?
* Will manufacturers sell directly to consumers, thus bypassing retailers?
* Will electronic shopping increase price competition and reduce retail profits?

In addition to the overview chapter, we examine issues related to electronic retailing throughout the textbook—for example,

- The relative advantages of shopping on the Internet and in stores (Chapter 5).
- The financial implications of electronic retailers compared to store-base retailing (Chapter 7).
- The prospects for virtual malls (Chapter 8).
- Systems for dealing with the high returns experienced by electronic retailers (Chapter 11).
- Assortment decisions in a virtual world (Chapter 14).
- Pricing merchandise using electronic auctions (Chapter 15).
- Attracting customers to electronic retail websites using affiliate programs (Chapter 16).
- Designing retail websites (Chapter 18).

Amazon.com, eBay, Bluefly.com, Garden.com, and other electronic retailers are used throughout the text to illustrate retailing concepts and how they apply or do not apply to electronic retailers.

Retailing and the Internet   In addition to selling merchandise and services over the Internet, retailers are using the Internet to run their businesses more effectively. Internet applications we review in the fourth edition include

- Communicating with employees to implement human resource management policies (Chapter 10).
- Managing the supply chain (Chapter 11).
- Communicating with vendors (Chapter 14).
- Targeting promotions and managing frequent shopper programs (Chapter 16).
- Providing customer service (Chapter 19).

The Internet is also an important source of information about retailing and retailers. In each chapter of the text, we have included Internet exercises indicating useful Internet sites and issues that can be addressed with information in these sites. Some examples of these exercises are

- The new NAICS system for classifying retailers (Chapter 2).
- Comparison of shopping bots (Chapter 3).
- Information on the latest fashion trends (Chapter 5).
- SAP and Oracle websites describing information systems they offer for retailers (Chapter 11).
- Websites for retail trade publications and news (Chapter 1).
- Information on comparison of assortments offered by electronic retailers (Chapter 12).
- Illustrations of delivering coupons over the Internet (Chapter 16).
- Descriptions of affiliate programs available to electronic retailers (Chapter 16).
- Evaluations of electronic retail shopping experiences and customer service (Chapter 19).

Profile of Retail Managers   To illustrate the challenges and opportunities in retailing, each chapter in the fourth edition begins with a brief profile of a manager or industry expert whose job or expertise is related to the material in the chapter.

These profiles range from Cole Peterson, senior vice president of Wal-Mart, to Ron Stoy, the owner and founder of a two-store chain in Tampa, Florida, selling used music CDs. They include people who have extensive experience in a specific aspect of retailing like Jeff Baird (vice-president of distribution for Electronic Boutique, a clicks-and-mortar retailer with 500 mall-based specialty stores) and Juli Johnson (who is managing a Walgreens store in Houston, Texas, several years after graduating from college).

These profiles illustrate both how senior executives view the industry and the career opportunities for college students. They provide students with first-hand information about what people in retailing do and what are their rewards and challenges. For example, Chris Manning (a buyer at Rich's, an Atlanta-based department store chain) equates his job to surfing.

Utilization of Information, Communications, and Decision Support Systems   Information, communications, and decision support systems are playing an increasing role in the management of retail businesses. Thus we have expanded the discussion of these systems in the fourth edition. For example,

- Strategic and implementation issues involving information, communication, and distribution systems appear in Chapters 6 and 11.
- The use of geographic information systems for evaluating store locations is discussed in Chapter 9.
- The use of customer information to target promotions and the development of frequent shopper programs are discussed in Chapters 11 and 16.

Globalization of Retailing   In recognition of the increasing globalization of retailing, the fourth edition includes expanded treatment of non-U.S. global retailers such as Ahold, Carrefour, and IKEA as well as discussions of issues confronting U.S. retailers as they expand from their domestic base. For example, we explore

- Keys to success in global retailing (Chapter 6).
- Evaluation of international expansion opportunities (Chapter 6).
- Global sourcing of merchandise (Chapter 14).
- Consumer behavior (Chapter 5), employee management (Chapter 17), and customer service (Chapter 19) in international markets.

Reader-Friendly Textbook   In the fourth edition, we have continued to interest and involve students in the course and the industry by making the textbook a "good read." For example, we have

- Added more interesting facts about retailing, called Refacts, in the margin of each chapter. Did you know that a Montgomery Ward buyer created Rudolph, the Red-Nosed Reindeer as a Christmas promotion in 1939? Or that the teabag was developed by a Macy's buyer and the pantyhose were developed by a JCPenney buyer?
- Provided new and updated vignettes called Retailing Views in each chapter to relate concepts to activities and decisions made by retailers. These vignettes include major retailers like Sears, Wal-Mart, JCPenney, Taco Bell, and Home Depot that interview students on campus for management training positions; innovative retailers like REI, Starbucks, The Container Store, Sephora, and The Bass Pro Shop; and retail entrepreneurs like Bluefly.com and Sheetz.

Website for Students and Instructors   (www.mhhe.com/business/levyweitz/retail) Just as retailers are using the Internet to help their customers, we have developed a website to help students and instructors use the fourth edition of this textbook effectively. Some of the features on the website are

- News articles about current events in retailing.
- PowerPoint slides summarizing key issues in each chapter.
- Hot links to retailing news sites and sites associated with the Internet exercises in the textbook.
- Additional cases about retailers.
- Sample test questions for each chapter.

BASIC PHILOSOPHY

The fourth edition of *Retailing Management* maintains the basic philosophy of the previous three editions. We continue to focus on the broad spectrum of retailers, both large and small retailers selling either merchandise or services. The text examines key strategic issues with an emphasis on the financial considerations and store management issues. We include descriptive, how-to, and conceptual material.

Broad Spectrum of Retailing   In this text, we define retailing as the set of business activities that adds value to the products and services sold to consumers for their personal or family use. Thus, in addition to the products in stores, this text examines the issues facing service retailers like Travelocity, Starbucks, and Marriott and nonstore retailers like Lands' End, eBay, and Avon.

Critical Issues in Retailing   Strategic thinking and the consideration of financial implications are critical for success in the present dynamic, highly competitive retail environments. In addition, operations and store management are playing an increasingly important role.

Strategic Perspective   The entire textbook is organized around a model of strategic decision making outlined in Exhibit 1–5 in Chapter 1. Each section and chapter is related back to this overarching strategic framework. In addition, the second section of the book focuses exclusively on critical strategic decisions such as selecting target markets, developing a sustainable competitive advantage, and building an organizational structure and information and distribution systems to support the strategic direction.

Financial Analysis   The financial aspects of retailing are becoming increasingly important. The financial problems experienced by some of the largest retail firms like Kmart and Montgomery Ward highlight the need for a thorough understanding of the financial implications of retail decisions. Financial analysis is emphasized in selected chapters such as Chapter 7 on the overall strategy of the firm and Chapter 13 on retail buying systems. Financial issues are also raised in the sections on negotiating leases, bargaining with suppliers, pricing merchandise, developing a communications budget, and compensating salespeople.

Operations and Store Management   Traditionally, retailers have exalted the merchant prince—the buyer who knew what the hot trends were going to be. This text, by devoting an entire chapter to information systems and supply chain management and an entire section to store management, reflects the changes that have occurred over the past 10 years—the shift in emphasis from merchandise management to the block and tackling of getting merchandise to the stores and customers and providing excellent customer services and an exciting shopping experience. Due to this shift toward store management, most students embarking on retail careers go into store management rather than merchandise buying.

BALANCED APPROACH The fourth edition continues to offer a balanced approach for teaching an introductory retailing course by including descriptive how-to, and conceptual information in a highly readable format.

Descriptive Information   Students can learn about the vocabulary and practice of retailing from the descriptive information throughout the text. Examples of this material are

- Management decisions made by retailers (Chapter 1).
- Types of store-based and nonstore retailers (Chapters 2 and 3).
- Changing demographics and values of retail customers (Chapter 4).
- Approaches for entering international markets (Chapter 6).
- Locations (Chapter 8).
- Organization structure of typical retailers (Chapter 10).
- Flow of information and merchandise (Chapter 11).
- Branding strategies (Chapter 14).
- Methods for communicating with customers (Chapter 16).
- Store layout options and merchandise display equipment (Chapter 18).
- Career opportunities (Appendix 1A to Chapter 1).

How-to Information   *Retailing Management* goes beyond this descriptive information to illustrate how and why retailers, large and small, make decisions. Step-by-step procedures with examples are provided for making the following decisions:

- Comparison shopping (Appendix 2A to Chapter 2).
- Attracting customers to your website (Chapters 3 and 16).
- Scanning the environment and developing a retail strategy (Chapter 6).
- Analyzing the financial implications of retail strategy (Chapter 7).
- Evaluating location decisions (Chapter 9).
- Developing a merchandise assortment and budget plan (Chapters 12 and 13).
- Negotiating with vendors (Chapters 14).
- Pricing merchandise (Chapter 15).
- Recruiting, selecting, training, evaluating, and compensating sales associates (Chapter 17).
- Designing an electronic retailing website (Chapter 18).

Conceptual Information   *Retailing Management* also includes conceptual information that enables students to understand why decisions are made as outlined in the text. As Mark Twain said, "There is nothing as practical as a good theory." Students need to know these basic concepts so they can make effective decisions in new situations. Examples of this conceptual information in the fourth edition are

- Retail evolution theories (Appendix 2B to Chapter 2).
- Customers' decision-making process (Chapter 5).
- Market attractiveness/competitive/position matrix for evaluating strategic alternatives (appendix to Chapter 6).
- Activity-based costing analysis of merchandise categories (appendix to Chapter 7).
- The strategic profit model (Chapter 7).

- Price theory and marginal analysis (Chapters 15 and 16).
- The Gaps model for service quality management (Chapter 19).

Supplemental Materials   To improve the student learning experience, the fourth edition includes new cases and videos illustrating state-of-the-art retail practices, a computer exercise package for students, and a comprehensive instructor's manual with additional cases and teaching suggestions.

Cases   Electronic retailers (eBay, Garden.com, Webvan, and Peapod); traditional store-based retailers (Abercrombie & Fitch, Old Navy, Neiman Marcus, Wolf Camera, and Borders); and service retailers (Starbucks, Marriott, and Cleveland Clinic) are presented in the new and significantly revised cases. New international cases examine the issues faced by supermarket retailers in the UK; a hypermarket-type retailer in Singapore; and a computer retailer in Canada.

Videos   Ten new video segments on Starbucks, AOL, Papa John's, Walgreens, Circuit City, L.L. Bean, HomeGrocer.com, and the Pebble Beach Resort complement 15 updated videos featuring Home Depot, JCPenney, Sears, Burdines, Rainforest Cafe, Wal-Mart, Fiesta Markets, and Southwest Airlines.

ACKNOWLEDGMENTS

Throughout the development of this text, several outstanding individuals were integrally involved and made substantial contributions. We wish to express our sincere appreciation to Carolyn Gurney (Babson College) for her assistance throughout the development of the fourth edition and the *Instructor's Manual* as well as to Thomas K. Pritchett and Betty M. Pritchett of Kennesaw College for their comprehensive *Manual of Tests*. The CD-ROM included with each copy of *Retailing Management* includes an exciting array of tutorials and exercises prepared by Hal Koenig of Oregon State University. Kathy Brown and Margaret Jones (Center for Retailing Education and Research, University of Florida) provided invaluable assistance in preparing the manuscript.

The support, expertise, and occasional coercion from our development editor at McGraw-Hill/Irwin, Nancy Barbour, are greatly appreciated. The book would also never have come together without the editorial and production staff at McGraw-Hill/Irwin: Michael Hruby, Bruce Sylvester, Cathy Tepper, Jennifer Hollingsworth, Rose Hepburn, and Rick Adams.

Retailing Management has also benefited significantly from contributions by several leading executives and scholars in retailing and related fields. We would like to thank

William Alcorn
JCPenney

Marty Anderson
Babson College

Douglas Bailey
Bailey and Associates

Robert Beall
Beall's Inc.

Tim Bolton
Home Depot

Cynthia Cohen
Strategic Mindshare

David Doub
Dillard's Department Stores

Joseph Firestone
Electronic Boutique

Joan Fox
Host Marriott

David Fuente
Office Depot

Deanne Gipson
Holiday Inn

Coleman Peterson
Wal-Mart

Erik Gordon
University of Florida

Ann Rupert
Burdines

John Gremer
Walgreens

Carol Sanger
Federated Department Stores

Tom Harden
Send.com

Kathleen Seiders
Babson College

Debbie Herd
JCPenney

Kris Spain
Ernst & Young LLP

Steven Kirn
Sears

Terry Stickler
E3 Corporation

Keith Koenig
City Furniture

Dan Sweeney
IBM

John F. Konarski III
International Council
of Shopping Centers

John Thomas
Pinch-A-Penney

Jim McAbee
ESRI

Suzanne Voorhees
The Grapevine Group

Kathleen McManus
Rich's/Lazarus/Goldsmith's

Petey Wasserman
Bloomingdales

Tracey Mullins
National Retail Federation

Bruce Weinberg
Boston University

Larry Negrich
JDA Software Group

Jeffrey Wells
Circuit City

Edward Nolan
Eckerd

Bruce Zarkowsky
Walgreens

The fourth edition of *Retailing Management* has benefited from the reviews of several leading scholars and teachers of retailing and related disciplines. Together, these reviewers spent hundreds of hours reading and critiquing the manuscript. We gratefully acknowledge

Lance A. Bettencourt
Indiana University

David M. Georgoff
Florida Atlantic University

Nick Saratakes
Austin Community College

Kim McKeage
University of Maine

Irene J. Dickey
University of Dayton

Michael D. Hartline
Louisana State University

We also thank the following reviewers for their diligence and insight in helping us prepare previous editions:

Mary Barry
Auburn University

George W. Boulware
Lipscomb University

Jeff Blodgett
University of Mississippi

Leroy M. Buckner
Florida Atlantic University

David J. Burns
Purdue University

Lon Camomile
Colorado State University

J. Joseph Cronin, Jr.
Florida State University

Ann DuPont
The University of Texas

Chloe I. Elmgren
Mankato State University

Richard L. Entrikin
George Mason University

Kenneth R. Evans
University of Missouri–Columbia

Richard Feinberg
Purdue University

Kevin Fertig
University of Illinois

Peter Gordon
Southeast Missouri State University

Larry Gresham
Texas A&M University

Tom Gross
University of Wisconsin

Tony L. Henthorne
University of Southern Mississippi

Eugene J. Kangas
Winona State University

Herbert Katzenstein
St. John's University

Terrence Kroeten
North Dakota State University

Elizabeth Mariotz
Philadelphia College of Textiles
and Science

Harold McCoy
Virginia Commonwealth University

Robert Miller
Central Michigan University

Mary Anne Milward
University of Arizona

John J. Porter
West Virginia University

Laura Scroggins
California State University–Chico

Shirley M. Stretch
California State University–LA

William R. Swinyard
Brigham Young University

Janet Wagner
University of Maryland

Ron Zallocco
University of Toledo

We received cases from professors all over the world. Although we would like to have used more cases in the text and the *Instructor's Manual*, space was limited. We would like to thank all who contributed but are especially appreciative of the following authors whose cases were used in *Retailing Management* or in the *Instructor's Manual*:

Ronald Adams
University of North Florida

Laura Bliss
Stephens College

James Camerius
Northern Michigan University

David Ehrlich
Marymount University

Ann Fairhurst
Indiana University

Linda F. Felicetti
Clarion University

Joseph P. Grunewald
Clarion University

K. Douglas Hoffman
University of North Carolina–
Wilmington

Laura Kellogg
Scotty's

Kirthi Kalyanam
Santa Clara University

Dilip Karer
University of North Florida

Hean Tat Keh
National University, Singapore

Robert Kenny
Saint Michael's College

Alison T. Knott
University of Florida

Evan Koenig
University of Miami

Nirmalya Kumar
International Institute of
Management, Switzerland

Robert Letovsky
Saint Michael's College

Debra Murphy
Saint Michael's College

Pirkko Peterson
University of Florida

Jan Owens
University of Wisconsin

Michael Pearce
University of Western Ontario

Catherine Porter
University of Massachusetts

Richard Rausch
Hofstra University

William R. Swinyard
Brigham Young University

William Walsch
University of Florida

Vidya Sundari
National University, Singapore

Irvin Zaenglein
Northern Michigan University

Heather Zuilkoski
University of Florida

BRIEF CONTENTS

CONTENTS

Customer Buying Behavior   137

SECTION TWO   Retailing Strategy   169

Retail Market Strategy   171

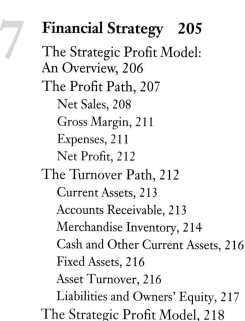

Financial Strategy 205

Retail Locations 233

13 Buying Systems 383

14 Buying Merchandise 415

19 Customer Service 585

SECTION FIVE   ## Cases

FOURTH EDITION

Retailing Management

Introduction to the World of Retailing

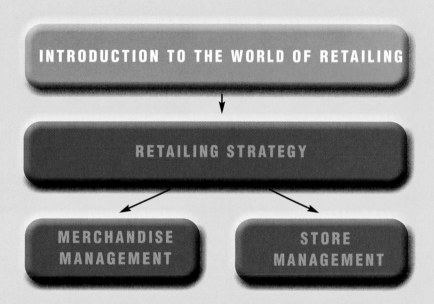

THE CHAPTERS IN THIS FIRST SECTION provide the background information about retail customers and competitors needed to understand retailing and develop and effectively implement a retail strategy. ● Chapter 1 describes the functions retailers perform and the variety of decisions they make to satisfy customers' needs in a rapidly changing, highly competitive environment. The remaining chapters in this section give you background information to understand the retail environment. ● Chapters 2 and 3 cover different types of retailers, both in-store and electronic retailers. ● Chapter 4 details how retailers are reacting to changing consumer demographics, lifestyles, and values. ● Chapter 5 discusses factors consumers consider when choosing stores and buying merchandise. ● Section II outlines the strategic decisions retailers make. ● Sections III and IV explore tactical decisions concerning merchandise and store management.

Keith Spurgeon
Chairman and CEO
Zany Brainy

RETAILING IS AN INDUSTRY of opportunities. Toy retailing is very competitive with Toys "R" Us offering broad assortments and Wal-Mart and Target offering low prices. But, David Schlessinger had a vision for a new kind of toy store—one that sold safe, nonviolent toys in a playful, kid-friendly, interactive environment. In 1991, he opened the first Zany Brainy store in Wynnewood, Pennsylvania. We now have 103 stores in 28 states and are selling products over the Internet at www.ZanyBrainy.com. Our mission statement still reflects David's vision: • To provide a unique retail environment where Inter-Activity reigns . . . where connections flourish. Between parents and children. Kids and toys. Staff and families. Store and community. Friends and peers. And most importantly, between the ZANYNESS of play and BRAINYNESS of learning. Through the experience of Inter-Activity, we spark the imagination and nurture the sense of accomplishment so vital to every child's future. • But having an exciting vision is not enough. Execution is critical. We design our stores to be bright, colorful, and inviting for children and adults. They are fully carpeted with low shelving to encourage children to see, touch, and play with the products. We have a play center in the middle of the store surrounded with large red pillars so children can locate it easily. We also provide seating in the play center so adults can comfortably play with their children. • Special events play an important role in making our stores an attractive destination for children and adults. These "free fun every day" events include creative arts and crafts activities, character and author appearances, and miniconcerts by children's performers. In addition, we host an exclusive Summer Reading Club that now has a growing membership of more than 30,000. • Our superior customer service complements our store design and merchandising. We actively recruit educators, childcare providers, and back-to-work parents as store employees. These people have a respect and affection for children. They know how they can learn through play. New sales associates get about 25 hours of training during their first month and must pass a test before they become a "certified kidsultant." • There is also a lot that goes on behind the scenes. Our buyers are always looking for high-quality, innovative products. Frequently we work with suppliers to first introduce their products in our stores. Excluding books and multimedia, less than 30 percent of Zany Brainy's merchandise is available at the largest toy chain. Our management information systems and distribution center operations are critical for making sure the products that customers want are in the stores.

1

Introduction to the World of Retailing

QUESTIONS

- What is retailing?

- What do retailers do?

- Why is retailing important in our society?

- What career and entrepreneurial opportunities does retailing offer?

- What types of decisions do retail managers make?

RETAILING IS EVOLVING into a global, high tech business. McDonald's has over 23,000 outlets in 109 countries with over 2,500 in Japan alone. Wal-Mart operates stores from Brazil to China. Some of the largest retailers in the United States, such as A&P, Food Lion, Stop & Shop, and 7-Eleven, are owned by companies with headquarters in Europe and Japan.

Refact Wal-Mart is the largest retailer in the world.[1]

Retailers are using sophisticated communication and information systems to manage their businesses. For example, when you buy something at a JCPenney store, you trigger a sequence of electronic communications and decisions that determine what merchandise will be shipped to the store the next day. Over 500 gigabytes of data are transmitted daily via satellite from the point-of-sale (POS) terminals in JCPenney's 1,150 department stores in the United States and Mexico, to its corporate headquarters in Dallas. Computer programs analyze this data and then automatically transmit orders to Penney's vendors, designating what merchandise should be shipped to each of its stores.

Amazon.com maintains a data warehouse with information about what each customer has bought. With this information, customers returning to its website (www.amazon.com) are immediately recognized and suggestions based on past purchases are made. E-mails are sent to the customers when new books in their area of interest are published.

Consumers interested in buying freshwater fishing flies or dried peppers can use electronic agents to shop around the world and find out who is selling this merchandise over the Internet. These electronic agents can also provide side-by-side comparisons of the quality and price of merchandise sold by different retailers.[2] Retailing View 1.1 illustrates how the Internet is changing the way people buy records.

IN ANCIENT TIMES, BEFORE THE INTERNET, high school kids looked for cool new tunes by searching through the racks in their local record shops. With an Internet technology called MP3, high schoolers now can listen to the hottest recording artists using their computers. CD tracks can be converted into MP3 digital files using a personal computer and free software available from a number of Internet sites. The MP3 files can be stored on a server connected to an Internet; anyone with Internet access can use search engines to local specific tracks and download them onto their computers in minutes. People can then listen to the MP3 file using free software available on the Internet.

A student in the heart of Silicon Valley says, "Buying CDs just isn't useful anymore. I can get any CD I want on the Internet." A popular gift at high school birthday parties in that part of the country is a personalized CD with a collection of tracks from different artists and albums. These personalized CDs are made by burning the MP3 files into a disk using an accessory that can be purchased from most retailers selling computers.

The explosion of MP3 files on the Internet is having a dramatic effect on the recording industry and music retailing. Many MP3 files violate copyright laws. They are created and made available for distribution without paying royalties to the artists creating the material. However, other sites (for example, www.MP3.com, www.amplified.com, and www.reel.com) operate legally and charge to download tracks. While companies (www.liquidaudio.com and www.a2bmusic.com) are developing technologies that are piracy proof, music retailers are concerned about their role when their customers can acquire music directly without visiting a store.

Source: Patrick Reilly, "Old Dancer, New Beat," *The Wall Street Journal,* July 12, 1999, pp. R39, R50; Les Gomes, "Free Tunes for Everyone!" *The Wall Street Journal,* June 15, 1999, pp. B1, B4; and Jan Ozer, "Net Tunes: Online Music Services Changes the Face of the Music Retail Industry," *PC Magazine,* February 23, 1999, pp. 239–40.

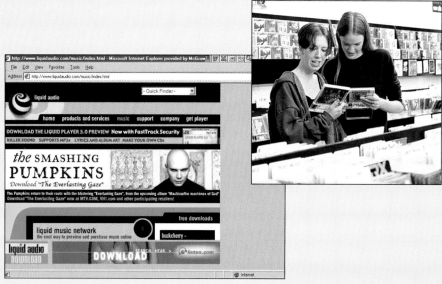

People are turning from buying recorded music in stores (right) to downloading it from Internet sites like Liquid Audio (left).

To attract customers, store-based retailers are providing compelling experiences in their stores like Eatzi (top), REI (lower left), and Niketown (lower right).

Refact More than 4.5 million people annually visit the Potomac Mills outlet center in Dade City, Virginia, making it the number one tourist attraction in the state—ahead of Williamsburg, Arlington National Cemetery, and Mount Vernon.[4]

To compete against nonstore retailers, stores are becoming more than just a place to buy products. They are offering entertaining and educational experiences for their customers.[3] Niketown on Michigan Avenue is the most popular tourist attraction in Chicago. The Discovery Channel's new Washington, DC, store includes educational displays of a life-size tyrannosaurus rex and a virtual dinosaur dig. MARS in Fort Lauderdale allows budding musicians to try instruments and sheet music, and offers lessons, a recording studio, and a service that puts musicians together. MARS also allows them to perform in-store. REI stores have a climbing wall to give customers an opportunity to try their gear before buying it.

In this dynamic environment, entrepreneurs are launching new companies and concepts and becoming industry leaders, while traditional firms have had to rethink their business or go bankrupt. Thirty years ago, some of the largest retailers in the United States—Wal-Mart, The Gap, Home Depot, and Circuit

City—either were small start-ups or did not even exist. Unprofitable Internet retailers have market values greater than profitable, store-based retailers with 100 times greater annual sales. Over the past 10 years, a number of retailers with over $1 billion in annual sales—Revco, Macy's, Zales, Service Merchandise, and Montgomery Wards—filed for bankruptcy.[5]

Retailing is such a part of our everyday lives that it's often taken for granted. Customers aren't aware of the sophisticated business decisions retail managers make and the technologies they use to provide goods and services. Retail managers must make complex decisions in selecting target markets, determining what merchandise and services to offer, negotiating with suppliers, training and motivating sales associates, and deciding how to price, promote, and present merchandise. Considerable skill and knowledge are required to make these decisions effectively. Working in this highly competitive, rapidly changing environment is challenging and exciting and offers significant financial rewards.

This book describes the world of retailing and gives principles for effectively managing businesses in this challenging environment. Knowledge of retailing principles and practices will help you develop management skills for many business contexts. For example, Procter & Gamble and Hewlett-Packard managers need to have a thorough understanding of how retailers operate and make money so they can get their products on retail shelves and work with retailers to sell them to consumers. Financial and health care institutions are using retail principles to develop assortments of services, improve customer service, and make their offers available at convenient locations. Thus students interested in professional selling, advertising, and many other retail-related careers will find this book useful.

WHAT IS RETAILING?

Retailing is the set of business activities that adds value to the products and services sold to consumers for their personal or family use. Often people think of retailing only as the sale of products in stores. But retailing also involves the sale of services: overnight lodging in a motel, a doctor's exam, a haircut, a videotape rental, or a home-delivered pizza. Not all retailing is done in stores. Examples of nonstore retailing are Internet sales of record albums by CDNOW (www.cdnow.com), the direct sales of cosmetics by Mary Kay, and catalog sales by L.L. Bean and Patagonia.

A Retailer's Role in Distribution Channels

A **retailer** is a business that sells products and services to consumers for their personal or family use. Retailers are the final businesses in distribution channels that link manufacturers with consumers.[6] Exhibit 1–1 shows the retailer's position within the distribution channel.

Manufacturers typically make products and sell them to retailers or wholesalers. When manufacturers like Dell Computer and Mary Kay Cosmetics sell directly to consumers, they are performing both the production and retailing business activities. Wholesalers buy products from manufacturers and resell these products to retailers, while retailers resell products to consumers. Wholesalers and retailers may perform many of the same functions described in the next section. But wholesalers satisfy retailers' needs, while retailers direct their efforts to satisfying needs of ultimate consumers. Some retail chains (like Home Depot and Sam's Wholesale Club) are both retailers and wholesalers. They're performing retailing activities when they sell to consumers and wholesaling activities when they sell to other businesses like building contractors or restaurant owners.

EXHIBIT 1–1

Distribution
Channels

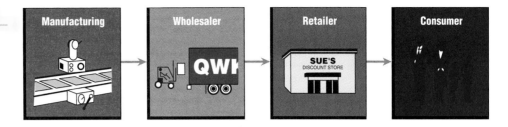

Functions Performed by Retailers

Retailers undertake business activities and perform functions that increase the value of the products and services they sell to consumers. These functions are

1. Providing an assortment of products and services.
2. Breaking bulk.
3. Holding inventory.
4. Providing services.

Providing Assortments   Supermarkets typically carry 15,000 different items made by over 500 companies. Offering an assortment enables their customers to choose from a wide selection of brands, designs, sizes, colors, and prices in one location. Manufacturers specialize in producing specific types of products. For example, Campbell makes soup, Kraft makes dairy products, Kellogg makes breakfast cereals, and McCormick makes spices. If each of these manufacturers had its own stores that only sold its own products, consumers would have to go to many different stores to buy groceries to prepare a single meal.

All retailers offer assortments of products, but they specialize in the assortments they offer. Supermarkets provide assortments of food, health and beauty care (HBC), and household products, while The Gap provides assortments of clothing and accessories. Most consumers are well aware of the product assortments retailers offer. Even small children know where to buy different types of products. But new types of retailers offering unique assortments appear each year, such as Play It Again Sports (used sporting goods), HotHotHot! (hot sauces at www.hothothot.com), and Mini Maid (home cleaning services).

Refact The word *retail* is derived from the French word *retaillier*, meaning to cut a piece off or to break bulk.

Breaking Bulk   To reduce transportation costs, manufacturers and wholesalers typically ship cases of frozen dinners or cartons of blouses to retailers. Retailers then offer the products in smaller quantities tailored to individual consumers' and households' consumption patterns. This is called **breaking bulk.**

Holding Inventory   A major function of retailers is to keep inventory so that products will be available when consumers want them. Thus, consumers can keep a small inventory of products at home because they know the retailers will have the products available when they need more. By maintaining an inventory, retailers provide a benefit to consumers—they reduce the consumer's cost of storing products. The investment to store products ties up consumers' money that could go into an interest-earning bank account or some other use.

Providing Services   Retailers provide services that make it easier for customers to buy and use products. They offer credit so consumers can have a product now and pay for it later. They display products so consumers can see and test them before buying. Some retailers have salespeople on hand to answer questions and provide additional information about products.

The retailers provide valuable services to their customers like helping a customer buy the right ladder.

Increasing the Value of Products and Services By providing assortments, breaking bulk, holding inventory, and providing services, retailers increase the value consumers receive from their products and services. To illustrate, consider a door in a shipping crate in an Iowa manufacturer's warehouse. The door won't satisfy the needs of a do-it-yourselfer (DIYer) who wants to replace a closet door today. For the DIYer, a conveniently located home improvement center like Home Depot or Lowe's sells one door that is available when the DIYer wants it. The home improvement center helps the customer select the door by displaying doors so they can be examined before they're purchased. An employee is available to explain which door is best for closets and how the door should be hung. The center has an assortment of hardware, paint, and tools that the DIYer will need for the job. Thus, retailers increase the value of products and services bought by their customers. Retailing View 1.2 illustrates how retailers provide value to their communities as well as their customers.

Organization of Distribution Channels

In some distribution channels, the manufacturing, wholesaling, and retailing activities are performed by independent firms. But most distribution channels have some vertical integration.

Vertical integration means that a firm performs more than one set of activities in the channel such as investments by retailers in wholesaling and/or manufacturing. For example, most large retailers—such as Kmart, Safeway, Wal-Mart, and Office Depot—do both wholesaling and retailing activities. They buy directly from manufacturers, have merchandise shipped to their warehouses for storage, and then distribute the merchandise to their stores. Other retailers, such as The Gap and Victoria's Secret, are even more vertically integrated. They design the merchandise they sell and then contract with manufacturers to produce it exclusively for them.

Refact The tea bag was developed by a Macy's buyer. A JCPenney buyer developed panty hose.

Structure of Retailing and Distribution Channels around the World

The nature of retailing and distribution channels in the United States is quite unique. Some critical differences between United States, European, and Japanese retailing and distribution systems are summarized in Exhibit 1–2.

The U.S. distribution system has the greatest retail density with the greatest concentration of large retail firms. Some people think that the United States is overstored. Ten percent of its food and general merchandise retail firms account for over 40 percent of all retail sales. Many U.S. retail firms are large enough to operate their own warehouses, eliminating the need for wholesalers. The fastest growing types of U.S. retailers sell through large stores with over 20,000 square feet. The combination of large stores and large firms results in a very efficient distribution system.

In contrast, the Japanese distribution system is characterized by small stores operated by relative small firms and a large independent wholesale industry. To efficiently make daily deliveries to these small retailers, merchandise often might pass through three distributors between the manufacturer and retailer. This differ-

EXHIBIT 1-2   Comparison of Retailing and Distribution Channels across the World

CHARACTERISTIC	U.S.	EUROPE NORTHERN	EUROPE SOUTHERN	EUROPE CENTRAL	JAPAN
Concentration (% of retail sales in category by top three firms)	High	High	Low	Very low	Medium
Number of outlets per 1,000 people	Medium	Medium	High	Low	High
Retail density (sq. ft. of retail space per person)	High	Medium	Low	Low	Medium
Store size (% of retail sales made in stores over 10,000 sq. ft.)	High	Medium	Low	Low	Low
Role of wholesaling (wholesale sales as a % of retail sales)	Low	Medium	Medium	High	High
Distribution inefficiency (average maintained markup—distribution costs as a % of retail price)	Low	Medium	High	High	High

ence in efficiency results in 20 percent of the Japanese labor force being employed in distribution and retailing, compared to only 10 percent of the U.S. labor force.[7]

The European distribution system falls between the United States and Japanese systems on this continuum of efficiency and scale, but the northern, southern, and central parts of Europe have to be distinguished with Northern European retailing being the most similar to the U.S. system. In Northern Europe concentration levels are high—in some national markets 80 percent or more of sales in a sector such as food or home improvements are accounted for by five or fewer firms. Southern European retailing is more fragmented across all sectors. For example, traditional farmers' market retailing is still important in some sectors, operating alongside large "big-box" formats. In Central Europe the privatization of retail trade has resulted in a change from a previously highly concentrated structure to one of extreme fragmentation, with a big increase in kiosk-based retailing but a small overall increase in retail floor space.

Some factors that have created these differences in distribution systems in the major markets are (1) social and political objectives, (2) geography, and (3) market size. First, a top priority of the Japanese economic policy is to reduce unemployment by protecting small businesses like neighborhood retailers. The Large Scale Retail Stores Law regulated the locations and openings of stores of over 5,000 square feet. Several European countries have also passed laws protecting small retailers. For example, in 1996, France tightened its existing laws to constrain the opening of stores of over 3,000 square feet.

Second, the population density in the United States is much lower than in Europe and Japan. Thus Europe and Japan have less low-cost real estate available for building large stores. On the other hand, European governments have passed strict zoning laws to preserve green spaces, protect town centers, and inhibit the development of large-scale retailing in the suburbs.

Third, the U.S. retail market is larger. In Europe, distribution centers and retail chains typically operate within a single country and are therefore not able to achieve the scale economies of U.S. firms serving a broader customer base.

WHEN JONATHAN JOHNSON WAS GROWING UP in Richmond, Virginia, his neighbors took great pride in their homes and community. Now the neighborhood bears the scars of economic hardship, crime, and drugs. Johnson started Community Pride Food Stores in 1992 with the objective of developing a new spirit of community in Richmond's inner city.

Community Pride has seven clean, well-managed stores in urban Richmond that offer affordable, quality products. Eighty percent of its employees live within three miles of the store where they work. Each store has two vans providing rides to customers who aren't mobile. Customers can also cash checks, pay utility bills, and buy bus tickets, postage stamps, and money orders at the stores.

Johnson stresses the importance of education. Employees are encouraged to enroll in many structured training programs. Also, $5,000 scholarships are awarded to employees who pursue college education. Families of high school students who earn all As and Bs and don't miss more than one day of classes per month get a 10 percent discount on food.

Source: Derek Dingle, "Architects of the New Millennium," *Black Enterprise,* June 1998, pp. 93–98; and "Retail Entrepreneur of the Year," *Chain Store Age Executive,* December 1995, pp. 74, 78.

Jonathan Johnson of Community Pride stores is a community leader in Richmond, Virginia.

Reducing distribution costs may be one of the major benefits of the single-market initiative of the European Union and this has become understood in recent years with almost all of the major retailers now operating in more than one country but few operating across all of Europe.

ECONOMIC SIGNIFICANCE OF RETAILING

Because activities performed by retailers are important to consumers, retailing is a significant economic institution and a big business in our society.

Retail Sales

Retailing affects every facet of life. Just think of how many contacts you have with retailers when you eat meals, furnish your apartment, have your car fixed, and buy clothing for a party or job interview. U.S. retail sales in 1997 were $2,566 trillion.[8] These official statistics include only store and catalog sales; they don't include other types of nonstore retail sales, such as Internet sales to consumers, TV home shopping, and sales of services to consumers such as movie tickets, hotel rooms, and legal assistance.

Contrary to popular belief, most retail firms are not large businesses. In 1992, there were 1.1 million U.S. retail firms, but only 6.3 percent of them had more than one store. Of the retail firms in the United States only 7.4 percent of them have annual sales over $2.5 million dollars.[10]

Refact In 1999, total expenditures on goods sold by retailers were greater than expenditures on medical care, housing, and recreation combined.[9]

EXHIBIT **1–3**

Employment by
Industry, 1997

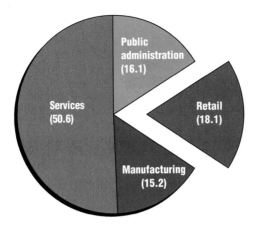

Source: U.S. Department of Commerce.

Employment   Retailing also is one of the nation's largest industries in terms
of employment. As Exhibit 1–3 shows, 22 million people are
employed in retailing—approximately 18 percent of the U.S. workforce. Exhibit 1–4 illustrates the growth in employment in the major sectors of the U.S.
economy. Over the next 10 years, it is estimated that employment in retail
trades will grow by 2.25 million jobs, while there will be a loss of 0.3 million
jobs in manufacturing. Note that these figures understate the impact of retailing
as an employer because many of the 11.3 million service jobs involve firms retailing services to consumers.

Refact One out of every
five U.S. workers is employed
in retailing.[11]

The Top 25 U.S. Retailers   Exhibit 1–5 lists the 25 largest U.S. retailers, revealing the
diverse and dynamic nature of retailing as well as its eco-
nomic importance. The list includes companies that sell a few categories of
merchandise (Toys "R" Us and McDonald's) as well as companies that sell a
wide variety of merchandise through different retail formats, such as
JCPenney (department stores, drug stores, and catalog and Internet sales) and
Dayton Hudson (department and discount stores). Seven firms on the list

EXHIBIT **1–4**   Projected Job Gains, 1996–2006

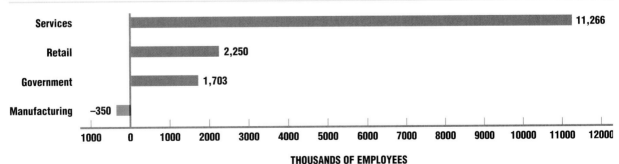

Source: U.S. Department of Labor, Bureau of Labor Statistics.

EXHIBIT 1–5

The 25 Largest
U.S. Retailers

RANK	COMPANY (HEADQUARTERS)	1998 SALES ($ MILLIONS)	1998 PROFITS ($ MILLIONS)	RANK (ALL U.S. FIRMS)
1	Wal-Mart Stores	139,208	4430	3
2	Sears Roebuck	41322	1048	15
3	Kmart	33674	568	21
4	Dayton Hudson	30951	935	30
5	JCPenney	30678	594	31
6	Home Depot	30219	1614	32
7	Kroger	28203	411	36
8	Safeway	24484	807	48
9	Costco	24270	460	49
10	American Stores	19867	234	67
11	Albertsons	18005	567	92
12	Federated Department Stores	15833	662	95
13	Walgreens	15307	511	98
14	CVS	15274	396	99
15	Fred Meyer	14879	−163	104
16	Winn-Dixie Stores	13617	199	115
17	May Department Stores	13413	849	120
18	McDonald's	12421	1550	134
19	Lowe's	12245	482	137
20	Publix Super Markets	12067	378	139
21	Rite Aid	11375	378	149
22	Toys "R" Us	11200	−132	151
23	Limited	9347	2054	169
24	The Gap	9054	825	174
25	Office Depot	8998	233	176

OTHER FIRMS WITH SIGNIFICANT RETAIL SALES

State Farm	48113	New York Life	18848
Prudential	34427	UAL	17561
Metropolitan Life Insurance	26735	Northwestern Mutual	14844
Allstate	25879	Time Warner	14682
Walt Disney	22976	Delta	14138
Pepsico	22348	Nationwide Life	13105
Cigna	21137	Viacom	12096
Aetna Life and Casualty	20604	Northwest Airlines	9044
AMR	19205		

Source: "Fortune 500 Largest U.S. Corporations," *Fortune,* April 27, 1999, pp. F1–F19. © 1999 TIME Inc., Reprinted by permission.

(Wal-Mart, Home Depot, Lowe's, Costco, Toys "R" Us, The Limited, and Office Depot) have developed into major retailers during the past 30 years.

Some of the top 25 retailers have completely changed their retailing approach over this period. For example, Kmart (Kresge) began as a variety store but became a leading discount store operator.[12] Sears began as a catalog retailer, expanded to be a national chain of retail stores, diversified into financial services and insurance, and is now refocusing on in-store retailing.

While people in the United States are familiar with these retailers, some of the large retailers in Europe and Japan are described briefly in Exhibit 1–6.

EXHIBIT 1–6

Large European and
Japanese Retailers

- **METRO Holding** is the largest retailer in Europe with over 3,400 locations including home improvement centers, hypermarkets, electronics stores, cash-and-carry wholesalers, and department stores (Kaufhof, Kaufhalle, Galeria). In 1997, METRO Holding's sales were $39.7 billion. The company mainly markets to Germany, but has stores located elsewhere in Western Europe as well as in Eastern Europe, North America, North Africa, and Asia. The company is also moving into telecommunications and electronic commerce.

- **ALDI Group** is one of the world's largest grocery store chains, with 4,000 stores in Europe and over 500 in the U.S. The company's unique methods consist of no credit cards, no checks, no coupons, and bagging your own groceries. The company deeply discounts prices on about 500 high-volume food items. To cut down on expenses, ALDI purchases cheap land, builds cheap warehouses, keeps a small staff, stocks mostly off-brand products, and displays products on boxes instead of shelves. The company relies on word of mouth rather than expensive marketing efforts. ALDI's sales for 1997 were about $33.0 billion.

- **Carrefour** operates nearly 325 hypermarkets in France, Spain, South America, Asia, and Mexico. These stores carry food, clothing, appliances, computers, and financial and insurance services. The company owns most of Comptoirs Modernes, which runs about 800 supermarkets in France. Carrefour also operates nearly 370 Ed l'Epicier and Ed le Marche Discount stores and has a majority interest in Picard Surgeles in France with over 320 chain stores selling frozen foods. Carrefour is France's largest hypermarket with $32.0 billion in sales in 1998.

- **Tengelmann Group** consists of 7,700 supermarkets, drugstores, and general stores (predominantly in Europe) along with 900 A&P-owned stores in the U.S. Tengelmann also has grocery and discount shops in Italy through a partnership with the PAM group of Venice. In addition, the company manufactures candy and chocolate, and it operates a wholesale division. The company is family owned and produced sales of $29.4 billion in 1998.

- **E. Leclerc** operates over 500 hypermarkets, predominantly in France but also in Portugal, Spain, and Poland. The outlets are grouped in 16 regions in France for economic and logistical reasons, and are individually owned. Many of the stores are located in low-income neighborhoods where owners hire local workers and give a quarter of pretax profits to employees. One of the interesting features of E. Leclerc is the native ethnic music that it plays for shoppers. The company's sales were $27.0 billion in 1997. It is planning to form an alliance with Systeme U.

- **Daiei** is Japan's largest retailer, with over 170 companies. Daiei has ownership in 6,700 Lawson convenience stores (second behind 7-Eleven in Japan). The company also owns supermarkets, discount stores, and specialty stores carrying thousands of private-label goods. Over 45 of the company's subsidiaries and joint ventures are held by K.K. Daiei Holding Corporation; these consist mainly of restaurants, hotels, and real estate businesses. A women's magazine called *Orange Page* and Wendy's restaurants are among the other interests of Daiei. Daiei has had to close stores, restructure management, and sell off assets in order to deal with Japan's faltering economy. The company's sales were $25.1 billion in 1998.

- **Ito-Yokado** is one of Japan's largest retailers, operating over 7,600 7-Eleven stores and over 400 hypermarkets, supermarkets, discount stores, and specialty stores. The company owns 65 percent of 7-Eleven, Inc. with over 10,000 outlets throughout the world. Convenience stores provide a third of Ito-Yokado's sales. However, the stores bring in two-thirds of the company's income. The company holds franchises for Oshman's sporting goods stores, Robinson's department stores, and Denny's restaurants in Japan. The company is planning to open a chain of superstores in China. Ito-Yokado's sales were $24.8 billion in 1998.

OPPORTUNITIES IN RETAILING

Management Opportunities

To cope with a highly competitive and challenging environment, retailers are hiring and promoting people with a wide range of skills and interests. Students often view retailing as a part of marketing because management of distribution channels is part of a manufacturer's marketing function. But retailers undertake most of the traditional business activities. Retailers raise capital from financial institutions; purchase goods and services; develop accounting and management information systems to control operations; manage warehouses and distribution systems; and design and develop new products as well as undertake marketing activities such as advertising, promotions, sales force management, and market research. Thus, retailers employ people with expertise and interest in finance, accounting, human resource management, logistics, and computer systems as well as marketing.

Retail managers are often given considerable responsibility early in their careers. Retailing View 1.3 illustrates the career opportunities in retailing. Retail management is also financially rewarding. After completing a management trainee program in retailing, managers can double their starting salary in three to five years if they perform well. The typical buyer in a department store earns $50,000 to $60,000 per year. Store managers working for department or discount store chains often make over $100,000. (See Appendix 1A at end of this chapter.)

Entrepreneurial Opportunities   Retailing also provides opportunities for people wishing to start their own business. Many retail entrepreneurs are among the Forbes 400 wealthiest people in the United States. Highly successful retail entrepreneurs include Jeffrey Bezos (Amazon.com), Dave Thomas (Wendy's), Tvon Chouinard (Patagonia), and Donald Fisher (The Gap).

After his research uncovered that Internet usage was growing at a 2,300 percent annual rate in 1994, Jeffrey Bezos, the 30-year-old son of a Cuban refugee, quit his job on Wall Street, leaving behind a hefty bonus to start an Internet business. While his wife MacKenzie was driving their car across country, Jeffrey pecked out his business plan on a laptop computer. By the time they reached Seattle, he had rounded up the investment capital to launch the first Internet book retailer. The company, Amazon.com, is named after the river that carries the greatest amount of water, symbolizing Bezos's objective of having the greatest volume of Internet sales. He drew on his electrical engineering and computer sciences degrees from Princeton to implement a vision of an electronic retailer that could offer 4 million titles, make email recommendations based on past purchases, and keep customers loyal by making it easy to buy books. While Bezos had the vision for Amazon.com and his managers had technical skills, the firm hired senior retail executives to provide the critical database and supply chain management skills needed to guide the company toward profitability. Bezos's Amazon.com stock is now worth over $10 billion.[13]

Refact Wendy's International was named after one of Dave Thomas's daughters, Melinda Sue, whose nickname is Wendy. She graduated from the University of Florida with a major in psychology.[15]

Dave Thomas of Wendy's International has appeared in over 300 television commercials and has become the best known restaurateur. His unassuming persona conveys an image that the chain is owned by a caring grandfather rather than a faceless corporation, a lesson he learned from Colonel Sanders, founder of KFC. Thomas never knew his parents. His adoptive mother died when he was five. His involvement in the restaurant business began at the age of 12. After dropping out of high school and completing service in the army, he bought a run-down KFC franchise. At the age of 35, he became a millionaire when he sold his KFC franchises. He decided to open some fast-food restaurants to pay for his children's college educations. Wendy's success is attributed to his focusing on young adults and offering them sandwiches made to order with the condiments selected by the customer.[14]

Tvon Chouinard is a legendary extreme adventurer and environmentalist. He started his business career selling hand-made mountain climbing equipment from his car. In 1974, he founded Patagonia, the California-based retailer

THROUGH THE CENTER FOR RETAILING EDUCATION and Research at the University of Florida (www.cba.ufl.edu/CRER), I was able to participate in the internship program and had my first summer internship after my sophomore year at a Wal-Mart store in Johnson City, Tennessee. The following summer, after gaining store operations experience, I interned at the corporate headquarters in Bentonville, Arkansas, in the merchandising division. After I graduated in 1995, I accepted a position in merchandising in the general office. Today, I am one of seven buyers for the toy department. The categories that I am responsible for are large dolls, plush stuffed animals, junior electronics, and miscellaneous rack toys. These categories will produce over $450 million in sales for Wal-Mart this year. In managing these categories, I am responsible for sourcing new products that will drive sales, promoting the product, getting it to the right stores at the right times, and managing the assets like a portfolio. Buying merchandise is like making a series of investments; I have to make the same risk–return trade-offs that a portfolio manager makes, and I have to watch the performance of my portfolio. At all times, I attempt to maximize my assets by buying more of what's hot, and by marking down and getting rid of items that have not met my expectations.

I also need to be a visionary reacting to current trends and translating them into merchandise that will bring people into our store. For example, several years ago a toy with new technology was introduced at the toy show in New York. It allows a child to "raise" a virtual pet. After working with senior management and deciding that we wanted to strongly support this item, as the buyer for this category, I put together a plan to ensure that Wal-Mart would be among the first to have this product in significant quantities. I worked with the manufac-

Laura Harvey manages a $450 million "investment portfolio" of merchandise for Wal-Mart.

turer to secure large quantities for an early promotion and then worked with marketing to develop a signing concept, information packet, and flyers to hand out at the stores so that we could create excitement at store level about this new item. Since this was a completely new concept and item, we were taking a large risk, but so far the investment has paid off! Although buyers must always take risks, the returns must always outweigh the risk. However, large rewards can only be reaped when large calculated risks are taken.

and manufacturer of high-quality outdoor clothing. The firm's catalog is known for its breathtaking images of high-risk sports activities in exotic locations. Chouinard's values are reflected in the company's policies. One percent of the company's sales are donated annually to environmental causes. In 1996, Patagonia began using 100 percent organic cotton for all its cotton apparel. It was one of the first companies to offer on-site day care. Employees can work up to one month a year for a nonprofit organization with full pay from Patagonia.[16]

Donald Fisher was a finance major and a star swimmer at the University of California at Berkeley. After graduating in 1950, he entered his family's real estate development business. He cofounded The Gap with his wife in 1969 out of his frustration at not being able to find blue jeans that would fit his normally

Retailing offers many opportunities for entrepreneurs like Tvon Chouinard, founder of Patagonia, a catalog retailer of outdoor clothing.

Alpine Shells

Our alpine shells have always been lighter, more compressible and sparer in design than other suppliers'. But this season we take enlightenment a step further. Check out our new, superlight **Stretch Light** and **Direct-X** gear on pp. 16-17.

For alpine use, we approach product enlightenment in three basic ways:

DESIGN We place stretch panels where you need to bend, twist and extend; we contour arms and legs to eliminate excess fabric and prevent binding.

SYSTEMS The key to comfort, whether for a third class jog or 8,000-meter expedition, is balance. We design interactive layers that provide the right balance of weather protection and freedom to move.

FABRICS Must weigh no more than is absolutely necessary for their intended use. And they must also be strong, to withstand the ravages of talus, crampons and years of heavy use.

Deluge DWR Finish

Deluge DWR Finish   Standard DWR Finish

(Water repellency testing results after extended washings and usage.)

We have improved the comfort and breathability of many of our alpine shells by upgrading their fabrics to our HB (highly breathable) standard. We have also upgraded the finish of many of our shells to our advanced Deluge DWR (durable water repellent) finish. Even though rain or snow can't penetrate a waterproof barrier, it can wet out the surface of a garment treated with a conventional DWR; this blocks breathability and creates a clammy feeling inside the shell. The Deluge finish doesn't wet out – increasing breathability and comfort by eliminating this Achilles' heel of waterproof/breathable garments.

QUICK GUIDE TO OUTERWEAR PERFORMANCE

Levels of Protection

To help you choose the best product for the most appropriate use, we have sorted our alpine shells into three broadly defined performance groups: Storm, Vario and Pneumatic®.

STORM

CONDITIONS:	Absolute waterproof protection in snow and rain
FABRICS:	Waterproof, breathable and windproof
DESIGN:	Fully seam-sealed, storm-coverage hood, weatherproof closures

VARIO

CONDITIONS:	Snow and light rain protection over a wide range of activities
FABRICS:	Highly water resistant, very breathable and windproof
DESIGN:	Critical seams sealed, protective hood, weather-resistant closures

PNEUMATIC

CONDITIONS:	Protection during high-exertion activities in cold, wind and light precipitation
FABRICS:	Water resistant, extremely breathable and windproof
DESIGN:	Minimalist features for light weight and compressibility

Refact After working with consultants to develop a name for his new retail concept, Mickey Drexler settled on Old Navy after seeing it on a building during a walk around Paris.[18]

proportioned six-foot-one, 34-inch–waist frame. The Gap stores were unique in offering every size and style of Levis, arranged by size for convenience. When the teen-jean craze slowed in the mid-1970s, stores were repositioned for a more mature customer. Now The Gap sells only private-label merchandise under its own brand name. Reminiscent of the founding of The Gap, GapKids was started when chief operating officer Mickey Drexler couldn't find comfortable clothing for his children. Drexler also developed Old Navy to cater to the new lifestyle when being hip is not to spend money on clothing.[17]

THE RETAIL MANAGEMENT DECISION PROCESS

This book is organized around the management decisions retailers make to provide value to their customers and develop an advantage over their competitors. Exhibit 1–7 identifies chapters in this book associated with each type of decision.

The success of a small entrepreneurial retailer or a major retail corporation, in making these decisions, depends largely on how much it embraces the retailing concept. The **retailing concept** is a management orientation that focuses a retailer on determining its target market's needs and satisfying those needs more effectively and efficiently than its competitors.[19]

The retailing concept emphasizes that high-performance retailers must be strong competitors. They can't achieve high performance by simply satisfying customers' needs. They must also keep a close watch to ensure that competitors don't attract their customers.

Understanding the World of Retailing—Section I

The first step in the retail management decision process, as Exhibit 1–7 shows, is getting an understanding of the world of retailing. Retail managers need a good understanding of their environment, especially their customers and competition, before they can develop and implement effective strategies. The first section of this book provides a general overview of the retailing industry and its customers. Then Chapter 6 describes how an individual retailer performs a situation audit as part of a strategic planning process.

EXHIBIT 1–7

Retail Management Decision Process

THE WORLD OF RETAILING
1. Introduction to the World of Retailing
2. Store-Based Retailing
3. Electronic and Nonstore Retailing
4. The Retail Customer
5. Customer Buying Behavior

RETAILING STRATEGY
6. Retail Market Strategy
7. Financial Strategy
8. Retail Locations
9. Site Selection
10. Organization Structure and Human Resource Management
11. Information Systems and Supply Chain Management

MERCHANDISE MANAGEMENT
12. Planning Merchandise Assortments
13. Buying Systems
14. Buying Merchandise
15. Pricing
16. Retail Communication Mix

STORE MANAGEMENT
17. Managing the Store
18. Store Layout, Design, and Visual Merchandising
19. Customer Service

The critical environmental factors in the world of retailing are (1) the macroenvironment and (2) the microenvironment. The impacts of the macroenvironment—including technological, social, and ethical/legal/political factors on retailing—are discussed throughout the book. For example, the impact of the Internet on retailing is reviewed in Chapter 3; the effects of social trends in Chapter 4, and the use of new information and distribution technologies in Chapters 11, 13, and 16.

Ethical standards and legal and public policy are critical macroeconomic factors affecting retail decisions. Strategy development and implementation must be consistent with corporate values, legal opinions, and public policies. Federal, state, and local laws are enacted to ensure that business activities are consistent with society's interests. These laws define unfair competitive practices related to suppliers and customers; regulate advertising, promotion, and pricing practices; and restrict store locations.

Retailers rely on ethical standards to guide decision making when confronting questionable situations not covered by laws. For example, retail salespeople may wonder if they should use high-pressure, manipulative sales techniques to sell merchandise that seems inappropriate for a customer. Buyers may have to decide whether to accept a supplier's offer of free tickets to a football game. Some retailers have policies that outline correct behavior of employees in these situations, but in many situations people must rely on their own code of ethics. Due to the importance of these issues, we discuss ethical and legal considerations throughout this book and relate them to each retail management decision area.[20]

The introductory section on the world of retailing focuses on the retailer's microenvironment—the retailer's competitors and customers.

Competitors   At first glance, identifying competitors appears easy. A retailer's primary competitors are those with the same format. Thus, department stores compete against other department stores and supermarkets compete with other supermarkets. This competition between the same type of retailers is called **intratype competition.**

To appeal to a broader group of consumers and provide one-stop shopping, many retailers are increasing their variety of merchandise. By offering greater variety in one store, retailers can offer one-stop shopping to satisfy more of the

Refact Fred Lazurus Jr., founder of the Lazurus department stores, promoted the idea of fixing Thanksgiving on the fourth weekend of November to expand the Christmas shopping season. Congress adopted his proposal in 1941.[21]

This supermarket engages in intertype competition with service retailers by offering dry cleaning and coffee.

needs of their target market. For example, clothing and food are now available in grocery, department, discount, and drugstores. The offering of merchandise not typically associated with the store type, such as clothing in a drugstore, is called **scrambled merchandising.** Scrambled merchandising increases **intertype competition**—competition between retailers that sell similar merchandise using different formats, such as discount and department stores.

Increasing intertype competition has made it harder for retailers to identify and monitor their competition. In one sense, all retailers compete against each other for the dollars consumers spend buying goods and services. But the intensity of competition is greatest among retailers located close together with retail offerings that are viewed as very similar.

Since convenience of location is important in store choice, a store's proximity to competitors is a critical factor in identifying competition. Consider two videotape rental stores, Blockbuster and Harry's Video, in two suburbs 10 miles apart. The stores are the only specialty videotape rental retailers within 50 miles, but a grocery store also rents a more limited selection of videotapes in the same strip center as Blockbuster. Due to the distance between Blockbuster and Harry's Video, they probably don't compete against each other intensely. Customers who live near Harry's Video will rent tapes there, while customers close to Blockbuster will rent tapes at Blockbuster or the grocery store. In this case, Harry's major competitor may be movie theaters and cable TV because it's too inconvenient for customers close to Harry's to rent videotapes elsewhere. On the other hand, Blockbuster competes most intensely with the grocery store.

Management's view of competition also can differ, depending on the manager's position within the retail firm. For example, the manager of the Saks women's sportswear department in Bergen County, New Jersey, views the competition as women's sportswear specialty stores also in the Riverside Square mall (www.shopriverside.com) as her major competitors. But the Saks store manager views the Bloomingdale's store in a nearby mall as her strongest competitor. These differences in perspectives arise because the department sales manager is primarily concerned with customers for a specific category of merchandise, while the store manager is concerned with customers seeking the selection of all merchandise and services offered by a department store.

On the other hand, the CEO of a retail chain views competition from a much broader geographic perspective. For example, Nordstrom identifies its strongest competitor as The Bon Marche in the Northwest, Macy's in northern California, and Bloomingdale's in Northern Virginia.

The CEO may also take a broader strategic perspective and recognize that other activities compete for consumers' disposable income. For example, Blockbuster Video's CEO takes the consumer's perspective and recognizes that videotape rental stores are competing in the entertainment industry with other videotape rental stores, other retailers who rent videotapes (such as grocery and convenience stores), movie theaters, regular and cable TV, WebTV, theater, opera, ballet, nightclubs, and restaurants.

Retailing is intensely competitive. Understanding the different types of retailers and how they compete with each other is critical to developing and implementing a retail strategy. Chapters 2 and 3 discuss various types of retailers and retail strategies.

Customers   The second factor in the microenvironment is customers. Customer needs are continually changing at an ever increasing rate. Retailers need to respond to broad demographic and lifestyle trends in our society, such as the growth in the elderly and minority segments of the U.S. population and the importance of shopping convenience to the rising number of two-income families. Retailing View 1.4 illustrates how a corner drugstore evolved into a mail order retailer worth over $400 million by responding to the needs of its customers. Chapter 4 deals with the broad consumer trends facing retailers.

To develop and implement an effective strategy, retailers also need to know the information in Chapter 5 about why customers shop, how they select a store, and how they select among that store's merchandise.

Developing a Retail Strategy—Section II

The next stages in the retail management decision-making process, formulating and implementing a retail strategy, are based on an understanding of the macro and microenvironments developed in the first section. Section II focuses on decisions related to developing a retail strategy. Sections III and IV concern decisions implementing the strategy.

The **retail strategy** indicates how the firm plans to focus its resources to accomplish its objectives. It identifies (1) the target market toward which the retailer will direct its efforts, (2) the nature of the merchandise and services the retailer will offer to satisfy needs of the target market, and (3) how the retailer will build a long-term advantage over competitors.

The nature of a retail strategy can be illustrated by comparing strategies of Wal-Mart and Toys "R" Us. Initially Wal-Mart identified its target market as small towns (under 35,000 in population) in Arkansas, Texas, and Oklahoma. It offered name-brand merchandise at low prices in a broad array of categories, ranging from laundry detergent to girls' dresses. While Wal-Mart stores have many different categories of merchandise, selection in each category is limited. A store might have only three brands of detergents in two sizes, while a supermarket carries eight brands in five sizes.

In contrast to Wal-Mart, Toys "R" Us identified its target as consumers living in suburban areas of large cities. Rather than carrying a broad array of merchandise categories, Toys "R" Us stores specialize in toys, games, bicycles, and furniture for children. While Toys "R" Us has limited categories of merchandise, it has almost all the different types and brands of toys and games currently available in the market.

Both Wal-Mart and Toys "R" Us emphasize self-service. Customers select their merchandise, bring it to the checkout line, and then carry it to their cars. Customers may even assemble the merchandise at home.

Since Wal-Mart and Toys "R" Us emphasize low price, they've made strategic decisions to develop a cost advantage over competitors. Both firms have sophisticated distribution and management information systems to manage inventory. Their strong relationships with suppliers enable them to buy merchandise at low prices.

Strategic Decision Areas   The key strategic decision areas involve determining a market strategy, financial strategy, location strategy, organizational structure and human resource strategy, and information systems strategy. Chapter 6 discusses how selection of a retail market strategy is based on analyzing the environment and the firm's strengths and weaknesses. When major environmental changes occur, the current strategy and the reasoning behind it are reexamined.

FIFTEEN YEARS AGO, IN A PITTSBURGH suburb Stadtlanders was a struggling drugstore with a soda fountain competing unsuccessfully against large national drugstore chains and deep discounters. However, the company had a reputation in the community for tracking down hard-to-find medications. One day, a regular customer who had undergone a kidney transplant at the University of Pittsburgh Medical Center (a leading transplant center) came into the drugstore and asked for a rare and expensive drug that would reduce organ rejection. Gregg Perelman, the owner of the store, was able to provide a regular supply for the customer and offered her substantial store credit while she awaited payment from her insurer. Eventually, Perelman contacted the insurer for direct payment.

Through word of mouth, Stadtlanders developed a reputation for supplying drugs to people who had had organ transplants and helping them with payment assistance. When patients returned home, often to places where the medications were unavailable, they called Perelman and asked him to ship the medications to them.

Stadtlanders is now a sophisticated mail-order retailer offering over 4,000 hard-to-locate pharmaceuticals plus an array of services from counseling to social service referrals. The firm has grown in annual sales from $16 million in 1988 to $500 million in 1999, when it sold over 1.2 million prescriptions to its 77,000 customers. In 1999, the company was acquired by Bergen Brunswig for over $400 million.

Source: "Bergen Brunswig Agrees to Acquire Stadtlanders Drug Company," *Drug Store News,* December 14, 1998, p. CP22; and Matt Murray, "From Soda Fountain to Mail-Order Drugs," *The Wall Street Journal,* May 29, 1997, pp. B1, B6.

The retailer then decides what, if any, strategy changes are needed to take advantage of new opportunities or avoid new threats in the environment.

The retailer's market strategy must be consistent with the firm's financial objectives. Chapter 7 reviews how financial variables such as sales, costs, expenses, profits, assets, liabilities, and owner's equity are used to evaluate the market strategy and its implementation. Decisions concerning location strategy (reviewed in Chapters 8 and 9) are important for both consumer and competitive reasons. First, location is typically consumers' top consideration when selecting a store. Generally consumers buy gas at the closest service station and patronize the shopping mall that's most convenient to their home or office. Second, location offers an opportunity to gain long-term advantage over competition. When a retailer has the best location, a competing retailer has to settle for the second-best location.

A retailer's organization design and human resource management strategy are intimately related to its market strategy. For example, retailers that attempt to serve national or regional markets must make trade-offs between the efficiency of centralized buying and the need to tailor merchandise and services to local needs. Retailers that focus on customer segments seeking high-quality customer service must motivate and enable sales associates to provide the expected levels of service. The organization structure and human resources policies discussed in Chapter 10 coordinate the implementation of the retailing strategy by buyers, store managers, and sales associates.

Retail information and supply chain management systems will offer a significant opportunity for retailers to gain strategic advantage in the coming decade. Chapter 11 reviews how some retailers are developing sophisticated computer and distribution systems to monitor flows of information and merchandise from vendors to retail distribution centers to retail stores. Point-of-sale (POS) terminals read price and product information that's coded into Universal Product

Codes (UPCs) affixed to the merchandise. This information is then transmitted to distribution centers or directly to vendors electronically, computer-to-computer. These technologies are part of an overall inventory management system that enables retailers to (1) give customers a more complete selection of merchandise and (2) decrease their inventory investment.

JCPenney Moves from Main Street to the Mall   The interrelationships among these retail strategy decisions—market strategy, financial strategy, organization structure and human resource strategy, and location strategy—are illustrated by a major strategic change JCPenney made in the early 1960s.[22]

In the late 1950s, Penney was one of the most profitable national retailers. Its target market was small towns. In its Main Street locations, Penney sold staple soft goods—underwear, socks, basic clothing, sheets, tablecloths, and so forth—at low prices with minimal service. All sales were cash; the company didn't offer credit to its customers. Penney had considerable expertise in the design and purchase of soft goods with private labels—brands developed by the retailer and sold exclusively at its stores.

Organization structure was decentralized. Each store manager controlled the type of merchandise sold, the pricing of merchandise, and the management of store employees. Promotional efforts were limited and also controlled by store managers. Penney store managers were active participants in their community's social and political activities.

Although Penney was a highly successful retailer, there was a growing awareness among company executives that macroenvironmental trends would have a negative impact on the firm. First, as the nation's levels of education and disposable income rose, consumers grew more interested in fashionable rather than staple merchandise. Second, with the development of a national highway system, the growth of suburbs, and the rise of regional malls, small-town residents were attracted to conveniently located, large, regional shopping malls. Third, Sears (the nation's largest retailer) was beginning to locate stores and auto centers in regional malls. These trends suggested a decline in small-town markets for staple soft goods.

In the early 1960s, Penney undertook a new strategic direction that was consistent with changes it saw in the environment. All new Penney stores were located in regional malls across the United States. Penney opened several mall

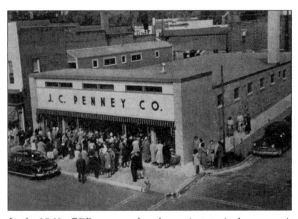

In the 1960s, JCPenney made a dramatic stategic change moving from main street (left) to malls (right) in response to changes in the macroenvironment.

locations in each metropolitan area to create significant presence in each market. The firm began to offer credit to its customers and added new merchandise lines: appliances, auto supplies, paint, hardware, sporting goods, consumer electronics, and moderately priced fashionable clothing.

Besides altering its merchandise and locations, Penney made its organization structure more centralized. Store managers continued to have considerable responsibility for selecting merchandise and managing store operations, but advertising was done centrally, using national print and TV media. Penney emphasized a consistent presentation and similar merchandise in all locations. Buyers at corporate headquarters had more responsibility for providing the general merchandise direction the firm would pursue.

To effectively control its 1,150 department stores, Penney installed a sophisticated communication network. Each store manager can monitor daily sales of each type of merchandise in her store and every other store in the chain. Buyers at corporate headquarters in Dallas communicate daily with merchandise managers in each store over a satellite TV link.

To respond to the increased time pressure on two-income and single–head-of-household families, Penney launched its catalog operation and now is the largest catalog retailer in the U.S. More recently, Penney has used its catalog distribution capability to aggressively move into selling merchandise over the Internet (www.jcpenney.com).

Now JCPenney is facing a new challenge. Middle-market department stores such as Penney's are caught in the middle between higher-priced, fashion-oriented department store chains like Macy's that are lowering their prices through sales and, at the other end of the spectrum, lower-priced, discount stores such as Target that are offering more fashionable merchandise.

This illustrates how retailers must respond continually to a changing environment. These changes often result in new strategic directions that must be supported by new locations, new organization design, and new information and communication systems.

Implementing the Retail Strategy—Sections III and IV

To implement a retail strategy, management develops a retail mix that satisfies the needs of its target market better than its competitors. The retail mix is the combination of factors retailers use to satisfy customer needs and influence their purchase decisions. Elements in the **retail mix** (Exhibit 1–8) include the types of merchandise and services offered, merchandise pricing, advertising and promotional programs, store design, merchandise display, assistance to customers provided by salespeople, and convenience of the store's location. Section III reviews the implementation decisions made by buyers, while Section IV focuses on decisions made by store managers.

Managers in the buying organization must decide how much and what types of merchandise to buy (Chapters 12 and 13), the vendors to use and the purchase terms (Chapter 14), the retail prices to set (Chapter 15), and how to advertise and promote merchandise (Chapter 16).

Store managers must determine how to recruit, select, and motivate sales associates (Chapter 17), where and how merchandise will be displayed (Chapter 18), and the nature of services to provide customers (Chapter 19).

Whole Foods Market: An Organic and Natural Food Supermarket Chain   Whole Foods Market, one of the fastest growing supermarket chains, illustrates the use of merchandise and store management activities to implement a

EXHIBIT **1–8**

Elements in the
Retail Mix

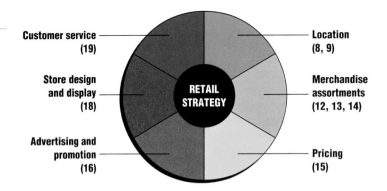

Customer service (19)

Store design and display (18)

Advertising and promotion (16)

RETAIL STRATEGY

Location (8, 9)

Merchandise assortments (12, 13, 14)

Pricing (15)

retail strategy. It is easy to mistake John Mackey for an aging hippie rather than the founder and CEO of a Whole Foods Market with over $1.5 billion in annual sales. At the University of Texas in Austin, Mackey developed a passion for philosophy and religion. When he found that textbooks weren't going to provide the answers he was looking for, he dropped out of college, lived in a vegetarian housing co-op, worked in an Austin natural food store, and eventually opened his own health food store and restaurant. Unlike other veggie joints, Mackey's store catered to a broad clientele by carrying items typically not found at health food stores like refined sugar and eggs. Then he teamed up with a local organic grocer to open the first Whole Foods, which was an instant success.

Whole Foods stores, at 25,000 square feet, are much larger and carry a much broader assortment than the typical natural and organic grocery store. The stores sell vegetarian no-nos, such as red meat and coffee, so that health-conscious nonvegetarians can have a one-stop shopping experience. The assortment includes two lines of private-brand products that are free of artificial sweeteners, colorings, artificial flavorings, and preservatives. Buyers work with artisan food producers and organic farmers for products sold under the Whole Foods™ premium label. The 360 Day Value™ line provides natural products at value prices. To ensure the quality of its private labels, three inspectors fly over 100,000 miles a year visiting farms and checking the crops.

Whole Foods has a FreshShopper Rewards program to increase customer loyalty and reward its best customers. Shoppers get a point for every dollar spent. Their point totals are printed on each receipt. When they accumulate 600 points, they get a 10 percent discount on all merchandise bought in a department of their choice for a year.

The flower power of the 60s is reflected in Mackey's guiding management principles: love, trust, and employee empowerment. All employees are organized into self-managed teams. The teams meet regularly to discuss issues and solve problems. Almost all team members have stock options in the firm. To ensure that employees are compensated equi-

This juice counter at Whole Foods Market is part of the firm's retail mix.

tably, the company has a cap on salaries so that no employee's total compensation can be more than 10 times the average compensation of all employees.[24]

Mackey has a 60s mentality about equality, but he also has an old-fashioned competitive drive to dominate Whole Foods' segment of the supermarket industry. When Whole Foods opened a store in Boulder, Colorado (headquarters of rival Wild Oats), Mackey sent Wild Oats CEO Michael Gilliland the game Risk with a note: "Forewarned is forearmed."

SUMMARY   An important institution in our society, retailing provides considerable value to consumers while giving people opportunities for rewarding and challenging careers. Due to significant shifts in consumers' needs and technology, the retail industry too is changing. Retail formats and companies that were unknown 30 years ago are now major factors in the industry.

The key to successful retailing is offering the right product, at the right price, in the right place, at the right time and making a profit. To accomplish all this, retailers must understand what customers want and what competitors are offering now and in the future. Retailers' wide range of decisions extends from setting a brown wool sweater's price to determining whether a new multimillion-dollar store should be built in a mall. This book is written to provide insights and directions for making such decisions. Some publications for retail managers are listed in Appendix 1B.

KEY TERMS

breaking bulk, *9*

intertype competition, *21*

intratype competition, *20*

providing assortments, *9*

retail mix, *25*

retail strategy, *22*

retailer, *8*

retailing, *8*

retailing concept, *19*

scrambled merchandising, *21*

vertical integration, *10*

SUGGESTED READINGS

Alexander, Nicholas. *International Retailing*. Cambridge, MA: Blackwell, 1997.

"The Annual HFN State of the Industry Survey." *HFN*, March 15, 1999.

Crispell, Diane, and Henry Miller. "Retailing's Next Decade." *American Demographics*, May 1997, pp. 4, 6–10.

De Kare-Silver, Michael. *E-Shock: The Electronic Shopping Revolution*. New York: AMACOM, 1999.

Kahn, Barbara, and Leigh McAllister. *The Grocery Revolution*. Reading, MA: Addison-Wesley, 1997.

Koloszyc, Ginger. "Transforming the Store." *Stores*, May 1999, pp. 22–26.

Kumar, Nirmalya. "The Revolution in Retailing: From Market Driven to Market Driving." *Long Range Planning* 30, no. 6 (1997), pp. 830–35.

Marcus, Bernard, and Arthur Blank. *Built from Scratch: How a Couple of Regular Guys Grew the Home Depot from Nothing into $30 Billion*. New York: Random House, 1999.

Matthews, Ryan. "A Look Back over 90 Years." *Progressive Grocer*, July 1998, pp. 8–14.

Schultz, Howard, and Dori Jones Lang. *Pour Your Heart into It: How Starbucks Built a Company One Cup at a Time*. New York: Hyperion, 1997.

Spector, Robert, and Patrick McCarthy. *The Nordstrom Way: The Inside Story of America's #1 Customer Service Company*. New York: Wiley, 1995.

"State of the Industry." *Chain Store Age Supplement*, August 2000.

Swinyard, William. "Retailing Trends in the USA: Competition, Consumers, Technology and the Economy." *International Journal of Retail & Distribution Management* 25 (August 1997), pp. 244–56.

APPENDIX 1A

Careers in Retailing

Retailing offers exciting and challenging career opportunities. Few other industries grant as many responsibilities to young managers. When students asked Dave Fuente, CEO of Office Depot, what they need to become a CEO someday, he responded, "You need to have profit and loss responsibility and the experience of managing people early in your career." Entry-level retail jobs for college graduates offer both of these opportunities. Most college graduates begin their retail careers as assistant buyers or department managers. In these positions, you will have responsibility for the profitability of a line of merchandise or an area of the store and you will be managing people who work for you.

Even if you work for a large company, retailing provides an opportunity for you to do your own thing and be rewarded. You can come with an idea, execute it almost immediately, and see how well it is doing by reviewing the sales data at the end of the day.

Retailing offers a variety of career paths such as buying, store management, sales promotion and advertising, personnel, operations/distribution, loss prevention, and finance in several different corporate forms such as department stores, specialty stores, food stores, and discount stores.

In addition, retailing offers almost immediate accountability for talented people so they can reach key management positions within a decade. Starting salaries are competitive, and the compensation of top management ranks among the highest in any industry.

Career Opportunities   In retail firms, career opportunities occur in the merchandising/buying, store management, and corporate staff functions. Corporate positions are found in such areas as accounting, finance, promotions and advertising, computer and distribution systems, and human resources.

The primary entry-level opportunities for a retailing career are in the areas of buying and store management. Buying positions are more numbers-oriented, while store management positions are more people-oriented. Entry-level positions on the corporate staff are limited. Retailers typically want all of their employees to understand their customers and their merchandise. Therefore, most managers on the corporate staff begin their careers in store management or buying.

Store Management   Successful store managers must have the ability to lead and motivate employees. They also need to be sensitive to the customers' needs, making sure that merchandise is available and neatly displayed. Store management involves all the disciplines necessary to run a successful business: sales planning and goal setting, overall store image and merchandise presentation, budgets and expense control, customer service and sales supervision, personnel administration and development, and community relations.

Store managers work directly in the retail environment—often at quite a distance from the home office. Thus they have limited direct supervision. Their hours generally mirror their store's and can therefore include some weekends and evenings. In addition, they spend time during nonoperating hours tending to administrative responsibilities.

The typical career path begins as a department manager with responsibility for merchandise presentation, customer service, and inventory control for an area of the store. Next, you advance to a position known as area or group manager with responsibility for executing merchandising plans and achieving sales goals for several areas, as well as supervising, training, and developing department managers. After these positions, you might become a store manager and then a district manager or move into a merchandising or staff position in the corporate office.

Merchandise Management Merchandise management attracts people with strong analytical capabilities, an ability to predict what merchandise will appeal to their target markets, and a skill to negotiate with vendors as well as store management to get things done. Recently, many retailers have broken the merchandising/buying function into two different yet parallel career paths: buying and merchandise planning.

Buyers are responsible for knowing customers' needs and wants, monitoring competition, and working with vendors to select and purchase merchandise. They must constantly stay in contact with their stores by visiting them, by talking to sales associates and managers, and by monitoring the sales data available on their merchandise management systems.

Planners have a more analytical role than buyers do. Their primary responsibility is to determine how many styles, colors, sizes, and individual items to purchase. Planners also are responsible for allocating merchandise to stores. Once the merchandise is in the stores, planners closely monitor sales and work with buyers on decisions such as how much additional merchandise to purchase if the merchandise is doing well, or when to mark down merchandise if sales are below plan.

Corporate Staff These areas provide opportunities for individuals with specific skills and interests. Thus career opportunities in these areas are more difficult to break into.

Computer Systems Experience with computer applications is an important plus when looking for a career in retailing. Such areas as data capture and application, Quick Response (QR) inventory systems to minimize inventory costs and ensure product availability, expedient point-of-sale (POS) systems, and electronic data interchange (EDI) ensure retailers of an efficient merchandise flow.

Operations/Distribution People in this area oversee the movement of merchandise in an accurate, efficient, and timely manner. They are responsible for operating and maintaining the store's physical plant, for providing various customer services, for the receipt, ticketing, warehousing, and distribution of a store's inventory, and for buying and maintaining store supplies and operating equipment.

Promotions/Advertising Promotion's many aspects include public relations, advertising, visual merchandising, and special events. The creative people in sales promotion departments try to presell the customer on the assumption that the best way to generate sales is to encourage people to want new merchandise.

Loss Prevention Loss prevention people provide asset protection for associates, facilities, and merchandise. They are responsible for developing and maintaining loss prevention systems and controlling internal and external theft.

Finance/Control Financial management specialists and top financial officers are among the most highly paid people in retailing. Many retailers have been involved in complicated corporate restructuring leading to high levels of debt. Most retailers also operate on a tight net profit margin. With such a fine line between success and failure, retailers continue to require top financial experts—and they compensate them generously.

The finance/control division is responsible for the financial soundness of the company. This involves preparing the financial reports for all aspects of the business, including long-range forecasting and planning, economic trend analysis and budgeting, shortage control and internal audit, gross and net profit, accounts payable to vendors, and accounts receivable from charge customers.

Real Estate   People in the real estate division are responsible for selecting locations for stores, negotiating leases and land purchases, and managing the leasehold costs.

Store Design   Retailers are finding that clearly defined, comfortable, and visually pleasing stores give them that extra edge over competition. Key elements of store design in the future include easy-to-shop, easy-to-maintain, and flexible store layouts. Talented, creative students in business, architecture, art, and other related fields will have innumerable opportunities for growth in the area of retail store design.

Human Resource Management   Human resource management is responsible for the effective selection, training, placement, advancement, and welfare of employees. Because there are seasonal peaks in retailing (such as Christmas when many extra people must be hired), human resource personnel must be flexible and highly efficient.

Is Retailing for Me?   One of the most important decisions a student must make is what career to pursue. In deciding on careers, you need to pick a career that involves doing things you like to do and are good at doing. Every career has its pros and cons. Finding the best fit, however, takes considerable thought and planning.

Responsibility   Retailing is for people who like responsibility. Starting management trainees are given more responsibility more quickly than in other industries. Buyers are responsible for choosing, promoting, pricing, distributing, and selling millions of dollars worth of merchandise each season. The department manager, which is generally the first position after a training program, is often responsible for merchandising one or more departments as well as for managing 10 or more full- and part-time sales associates.

Career Advancement   Many opportunities for rapid advancement exist simply because of the sheer size of the retail industry. There are millions of retail establishments, and the larger ones have many different positions and multiple managerial levels. Yet in choosing a particular retailer, take care to choose a growth firm. Firms that have recently undergone corporate restructuring may have a glut of middle-management positions. If store operations is an appealing career area, pursue chains with multiple outlets. But these stores don't present particularly good opportunities for people who seek a buying career, because they have relatively small buying staffs compared to the number of outlets. If buying is your primary career interest, choose a firm with a relatively large buying staff (e.g., a department store) or a firm with more decentralized purchasing (e.g., Nordstrom).

Compensation and Benefits   Retailing can be both financially and personally rewarding. Careers in retailing combine continuous personal development with almost immediate responsibility and new challenges. Each day is different, so sales associates and executives are rarely bored. Starting salaries are competitive, and the compensation of top management ranks with the highest in industry. For example, store managers with only a few years of experience can earn up to $100,000 or more, depending on bonuses. Top buyers, systems professionals, and other technical experts may earn just as much.

Compensation varies by amount of responsibility. Specialty store managers are generally paid less than department store managers because their annual sales volume is lower. But advancements can be faster. Aggressive specialty store managers often are promoted to district managers and run 8 to 15 units after a few years so they quickly move into higher pay brackets. Typical compensation for management trainees ranges from $22,000 to $32,000. A senior buyer for a department store earns from $50,000 to $90,000 or more. A department store manager can earn from $50,000 to $150,000; a discount store manager makes from $70,000 to $100,000 or more; and a specialty store manager earns from $35,000 to $60,000 or more.

Because sales can be related to specific managers, retailers typically see a link between performance and compensation. A recent survey found, for example, that 95 percent of retail CEOs were eligible for incentives, which on average represented 61 percent of their salaries. Similarly, about 83 percent of the retailers' top store and merchandising executives were eligible for incentives, although bonuses represented only a little less than 30 percent of their compensation. The survey also found evidence of the spread of incentive plans to other retail ranks. Even at the lower pay levels studied, roughly 82 percent of buyers and store managers, for example, were eligible for incentives.

A compensation package consists of more than salary alone. In retailing, the benefits package is often substantial. It may include a profit-sharing plan; savings plan; stock option plan; hospital, major medical, and dental insurance; life insurance; long-term disability protection and income protection plans; paid vacations and holidays; and bonus potential. Two additional benefits of retailing careers are that most retailers offer employees valuable discounts on the merchandise that they sell, and some buying positions include extensive foreign travel.

Working Conditions   Retailing has an often exaggerated reputation of demanding long and odd hours. Superficially, this reputation is true. Store managers do work some evenings and weekends. But many progressive retailers have realized that if the odd hours aren't offset by time off at other periods in the week, many managers become inefficient, angry, and resentful—in a word, burned out. It's also important to put the concept of long hours into perspective. Most professional careers require more than 40 hours per week for the person to succeed. In a new job with new tasks and responsibilities, the time commitment is even greater.

People shouldn't go into retailing if they like a calm, orderly, peaceful work environment with no surprises. Retailing is for those who like having exciting days, making quick decisions, and dealing with a variety of assignments, tasks, and people—often all at once.

Job Locations   Depending on the type of retailer and the specific firm, retailing enables executives to change locations often or not at all. In general, a career path in store management has more opportunity for relocation than paths in buying/merchandising or corporate. Because buying and corporate offices are usually centrally located, these positions generally aren't subjected to frequent moves.

Women and Minorities in Retailing   Many people consider retailing to be among the most racially and gender-blind industries. Retailers typically think that their manager and executives will make better decisions if they mirror their customer. Since most purchases are made by women and because minorities are becoming an increasingly important factor in the market, most retailers have active programs designed to provide the experiences and support that will enable women and minorities to be promoted to top management positions.

Getting Ready for an Interview with a Retailer   Here are some things you need to do to make a good impression in an interview with a retailer:

- **Visit the retailer's stores before the interview.** Actually seeing the store can give you insight for discussing the company intelligently throughout the interview process. Well-stocked and orderly departments (with the exception of deep-discount stores that sometimes purposely maintain a disorderly look) suggest (but don't prove) that the company is in good health. Signs of decay either could mean the store is planning a relocation or a massive renovation, or could indicate poor management or financial problems.

- **Read about the retailer.** In conjunction with store visits, read the retailer's annual report to stockholders; examine reports from Value Line and other investment service firms; study trade publications such as *Discount Store News, Chain Store Age Executive,* and *Stores;* and visit its website on the Internet.

- **Find out whether the retailer is hiring primarily for store or merchandise management positions.** For example, if you're interested in fashion, a career in a department store or national off-price chain like T.J. Maxx or Marshalls may be the way to go. Be certain that its needs coincide with your goals.

- **Determine whether there have been recent changes in ownership or top management.** A change isn't necessarily bad, but it does add some uncertainty—and therefore risk—to the decision.

- **Research the retailer's strategy and growth potential.** Has it been expanding? Is it in strong markets? How strong and innovative are its competitors? Successful retailers in the new millennium will increase their emphasis on marketing to satisfy customer needs by focusing heavily on service. Moreover, by employing creative organizational and management strategies, retailers will concentrate on giving buyers and store managers greater responsibility, while supporting them with logistics and systems specialists.

- **Determine whether the retailer is known for innovation.** An innovative retailer has a greater chance of long-term success than a stodgy one. To measure innovativeness, look at its stores and promotions. Are they modern? Do the stores and promotions reflect the times? Do they appeal to their target markets?

- **Find out about the retailer's computers and distribution systems.** Highly sophisticated retail technology symbolizes a view toward the future. Technology, if used properly, makes firms more efficient and therefore profitable. Finally, Quick Response inventory management systems, EDI, and sophisticated POS terminals relieve managers from much of the tedious paperwork previously associated with careers in retailing.

Exhibit 17–4 lists some questions frequently asked during interviews. Advance knowledge of some of the questions that may arise should boost your confidence, reduce your anxiety, and improve the interviewer's impression of you.

SUMMARY

Retailing isn't for everyone. This appendix has provided a framework for considering a career in retailing. A variety of careers available in the retail industry have been described. Advantages and disadvantages of a retailing career have been presented. The characteristics necessary to become a successful retail executive were examined. The appendix concluded with the answers to some commonly asked questions about a career in retailing and discussed how to get ready for an interview.

APPENDIX 1B

Trade Publications for Retailers

American Bookseller. Monthly magazine for book retailers covers buying, advertising and promotion, inventory control, display techniques, and publisher–bookseller relations. www.bookweb.org

Apparel Merchandising. Monthly magazine for retail buyers forecasts and interprets apparel merchandising trends and strategies in women's, men's, and children's wear. www.lf.com/pubs/amseg.htm

Chain Store Age. Monthly magazine for retail headquarters executives and shopping center developers. Deals with management, operations, construction, modernization, store equipment, maintenance, real estate, financing, materials handling, and advertising. More oriented to operations than stores. www.chainstoreage.com

CS News. Monthly magazine for convenience store and oil retailing executives, managers, and franchisees. Covers industry trends, news, and merchandising techniques. www.csnews.com

Daily News Record. Daily newspaper on retail fashion, product, merchandising, and marketing for men's and boy's wear. Geared to retailers, wholesalers, and manufacturers. www.dailynewsrecord.com

Dealerscope. Monthly publication for retailers of consumer electronics, appliances, and computers. www.dealerscope.com

Discount Store News. Biweekly national newspaper describing marketing developments and productivity reports from executives in full-line discount stores, catalog showrooms, warehouse clubs, and specialty discount chains. www.discountstorenews.com

Drug Store News. Biweekly publication covering chain drug and combination store retailing. www.drugstorenews.com

Furniture/Today. Weekly newspaper for retail executives in furniture and department stores and for executives in manufacturing firms. www.brcb.com/mainmag/ft.htm

HFD. Weekly newspaper for retailers and manufacturers in the home products industry including furniture, bedding, decorative accessories, lamps, home electronics, major appliances, tabletop, domestics, bath shop, and giftware. www.homefurnishingsnews.com

Hobby Merchandiser. Monthly publication for suppliers and retailers in the model hobby industry. www.hobbymerchandiser

Home Improvement Centers. Monthly magazine for full-line and specialty retailers and wholesale distributors of home improvement products. Covers systems and products to sell to customers ranging from do-it-yourselfers to professional remodelers.

Hotel and Motel Management. Bimonthly magazine reports news and trends affecting the lodging industry.

Internet Retailer. Monthly magazine devoted to electronic retailing issues. www.internetretailer.com

Mass Market Retailers. Biweekly newspaper for executives in supermarket, chain drug, and chain discount headquarters. Reports news and interprets its effects on mass merchandisers.

Modern Grocer. Weekly newspaper covers regional and national food retailing.

Modern Jeweler. Monthly magazine for jewelry retailers looks at trends in jewelry, gems, and watches.

Outfitter. Monthly publication for retailers and manufacturers of outdoor apparel, footwear, equipment, and accessories. www.outfittermag.com

Private Label Product. Bimonthly magazine for buyers, merchandisers, and executives involved in purchasing private, controlled packer, and generic-labeled products for chain supermarkets and drug, discount, convenience, and department stores.

Progressive Grocer. Monthly magazine reporting on the supermarket industry. Original research and analysis includes industry data, special product category reports, tracking studies of trade and consumer trends, and retailer and wholesaler case histories. www.pgshowdaily.com

Retail Info Systems News. Monthly magazine addressing system solutions for corporate/financial, operations, MIS, and merchandising management at retail. www.risnews.com.

RT. Monthly magazine reporting on and interpreting technologies available for all levels of the fashion distribution chain from manufacturers to retailers. Includes computers, retail point-of-sales systems, computer-aided design and manufacturing, software, electronic retailing, credit systems, visual merchandising, and factory automation. www.retailtech.com

Shopping Center World. Monthly magazine providing news, statistical analyses, and feature articles on new-center developments and leasing, redevelopments and releasing, management, operations, marketing, design, construction, and financing of shopping centers. www.internetreview.com/pubs/scw.htm

Store Planning Design and Review. Monthly technique describing new trends and techniques in store design and merchandise presentation. www.retailreporting.com

Stores. Monthly magazine published by the National Retail Federation (NRF), formerly the National Retail Merchants Association. Aimed at retail executives in department and specialty stores, it emphasizes broad trends in customer behavior, management practices, and technology. www.stores.org

Upscale Discounting. A monthly merchandising magazine for catalog showrooms, discount department stores, hypermarkets, specialty discounters, home shopping/TV/mail order, and warehouse clubs in the upscale discount market.

VM/SD (Visual Merchandising/Store Design). Monthly magazine for people involved in merchandise display, store interior design and planning, and manufacturing of equipment used by display and store designers. www.visualstore.com

Women's Wear Daily. Daily newspaper reports fashion and industry news on women's and children's ready-to-wear, sportswear, innerwear, accessories, and cosmetics. www.wwd.com

Ron Stoy
Founder and CEO
Sound Exchange

I GRADUATED FROM COLLEGE with majors in economics and computer sciences and worked in the computer industry in engineering, sales, and marketing positions for 15 years. I became increasingly unhappy with the corporate environment—the politics and bureaucracy. My daughter's softball coach, an industrial psychologist, confirmed my suspicions that my personality just didn't fit with my job. I needed to be in a more entrepreneurial environment. So I decided to stop climbing the corporate ladder and do something that would make me happy.   •   I have always been interested in music and started collecting recordings in the 60s. I bought collections from people and then sold the recordings I didn't want at record shows. From this experience, I learned a lot about what people wanted and how much they would pay for it.   •   I developed a business plan and opened Sound Exchange in 1987. We now have two stores on the West Coast of Florida (one in Tampa and the other in Bradenton), selling new and used entertainment media, primarily recorded music in different formats. Retail music specialty stores have had big financial problems due to the price competition from discount stores and category killers like Best Buy and Circuit City. But our sales are growing at double digits annually and we are quite profitable.   •   Our success is based on doing everything we can to satisfy the needs of our target market—people who really know and love music and have more money than time to spend. They want a broad assortment so they can find that special recording, customer service from knowledgeable store employees, and a fair price. They don't waste their time looking for the lowest price. Consequently we don't stress price and haven't advertised a sale in the past 10 years.   •   All of our policies are geared toward our target market. We focus on used recordings, but offer new recordings to fill the gaps and provide a complete assortment for one-stop shopping. Our customers don't come to our stores for Top 40 music, but we stock some so they can buy it when they are in the store. We spend 50 percent more on payroll than the typical specialty stores, and the tenure of our employees is measured in years, not months. On the other hand, our location costs are low. Due to our unique merchandise and customer service, we are a destination. Our customers know where we are.   •   To be a successful retailer, you need to use both the left and right brains—you need to be creative and analytical.

2

Store-Based Retailing

QUESTIONS

- What are the different types of store-based retailers?
- How do retailers differ in terms of their retail mixes?
- What are the trends in the structure of the retail industry?
- How do services retailers differ from merchandise retailers?
- What are the types of ownership for retail firms?

YOU WANT TO HAVE A CUP of real coffee in the morning, not instant, but you don't want to bother with boiling water, pouring it through ground coffee in a filter, and waiting. You decide to buy an automatic coffee maker with a timer so your coffee will be ready when you wake up. Think of all of the different retailers you could buy the coffee maker from. You could buy the coffee maker at a discount store like Wal-Mart or Kmart, a department store like Macy's, a drugstore like Walgreens, or a category specialist like Circuit City; you could also order a coffee maker from the JCPenney catalog; or you could go to www.shopping.yahoo.com, search for "coffee maker," and review the information on over 300 models sold by more than 50 Internet retailers. All of these retailers are competing against each other to sell you a coffee maker. Many of them are selling the same brands, but they offer different services, prices, atmospheres, and convenience.

To develop and implement a retail strategy, you need to understand the nature of competition in the retail marketplace. The next two chapters describe different types of retailers. Retailers differ in terms of the types of merchandise and services they offer to customers, the nature of the retail mixes used to satisfy customer needs, the degree to which their offerings emphasize services versus merchandise, and the ownership of the firm. This chapter focuses on retailers offering merchandise and services in a store environment. Chapter 3 examines electronic and other nonstore retailers that sell to consumers using the Internet and catalogs.

TYPES OF RETAILERS

The 1.4 million U.S. store-based retailers range from street vendors selling hot dogs to large corporations such as Sears that have become an integral part of American culture. Each retailer survives and prospers by satisfying a group of consumers' needs more effectively than its competitors. Over time, different types of retailers have emerged and prospered because they have attracted and maintained a significant customer base.

Nature of the Retail Mix

The most basic characteristic of a retailer is its retail mix—the elements used by retailers to satisfy their customers' needs. (See Exhibit 1–6.) Four elements of the retail mix are particularly useful for classifying retailers: the type of merchandise sold, the variety and assortment of merchandise sold, the level of customer service, and the price of the merchandise. Retailers often shop at their competitors' stores to compare their retail offering with the competition. Appendix 2A describes the elements involved in a comparison shopping exercise.

Price–Cost Trade-off As you read about the different types of retailers, notice how patterns among retail mix elements arise. For example, department stores appeal to consumers looking for fashionable apparel and home furnishings. Typically department stores have higher prices because they have higher costs due to stocking a lot of fashionable merchandise, discounting merchandise when errors are made in forecasting consumer tastes, providing high levels of service with considerable personal selling, and having convenient but expensive mall locations. On the other hand, discount stores appeal to customers who are looking for lower prices and are less interested in services and a wide range of merchandise sizes and colors.

This difference between the retail mix of department and discount stores illustrates the trade-off retailers make between the price and assortment of merchandise they sell and the services they offer to their customers. Offering more sizes, colors, and brands; making the store atmosphere more attractive and entertaining; and increasing the staff of knowledgeable sales associates raises the retailer's costs. To make a profit and provide these additional benefits to its customers, department stores have to increase the prices of their merchandise to cover the additional costs.

Refact Almost 40 percent of all U.S. retail sales are for automobiles, gas, and food. Department and discount stores only account for 10 percent of U.S. retail sales.[1]

Type of Merchandise The U.S. Bureau of the Census uses a classification scheme to collect data on retail activity in the United States. It classifies all retail firms into a hierarchical set of four-digit Standard Industrial Classification (SIC) codes (Exhibit 2–1). Each of the exhibit's eight two-digit categories is broken down further into three-digit categories. For example, food retailers (SIC 54) are divided into grocery stores (SIC 541), meat and fish markets (SIC 542), fruit and vegetable markets (SIC 543), and so forth. Exhibit 2–2 shows the annual sales of the larger categories as reported in the Census of Retail Trade.

While a retailer's principal competitors may be other retailers with the same SIC code, there are many exceptions. For example, convenience stores (such as 7-Eleven and Circle K), traditional supermarkets, and warehouse grocery stores are all classified as SIC 541. These food stores all sell the same type of merchandise, but they satisfy different consumer needs and thus appeal to different market segments. The convenience store caters to customers who value convenience

EXHIBIT 2–1

Standard Industrial
Classification System
for Retailers

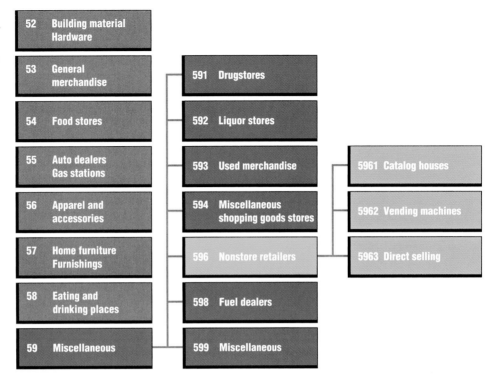

but don't seek low prices or a broad selection. The warehouse grocery store, on
the other hand, caters to customers who want low prices and don't place much
importance on service or store atmosphere.

EXHIBIT 2–2   Retail Sales by SIC Category

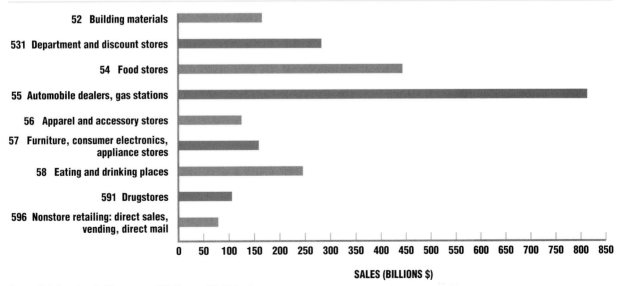

Source: U.S. Department of Commerce, 1998 *Census of Retail Trade.*

INTERNET EXERCISE   Data on U.S. retail sales are available at the U.S. Bureau of the Census Internet site at www.census.gov/mrts/www/mrts.html. Look at the unadjusted monthly sales by SIC. Which categories of retailers have the largest percentage of sales in the fourth quarter (the Christmas season)?

To address some of these problems and develop economic statistics similar to those of our international trading partners, the U.S. Bureau of the Census, along with Mexico and Canada, adopted a new classification system. Reports based on the new system, called the North American Industrial Classification System (NAICS), started to appear in 1999. The conversion from SIC to NAICS will be completed in 2004. The NAICS system recognizes the growth in services and specialty store retailing by assigning numbers to categories such as nail salons and pet supply stores.[2]

INTERNET EXERCISE   At www.census.gov/epcd/www/naics.html you will find a description of the new NAICS system with tables comparing the SIC and NAICS categories. Look through these comparison tables and summarize which categories are changed and which are not.

The degree to which retailers compete against each other isn't simply based on the similarity of their merchandise. The variety and assortment of the merchandise they offer and the services they provide must also be considered.

Variety and Assortment   **Variety** is the number of merchandise categories a retailer offers. **Assortment** is the number of different items in a merchandise category. Each different item of merchandise is called an **SKU (stock keeping unit).** For example, a 32-ounce box of Tide laundry detergent or a white, long-sleeved, button-down–collar Tommy Hilfiger shirt, size 16–33, is an SKU.

Department stores, discount stores, and toy stores all sell toys. However, department stores sell many other categories of merchandise in addition to toys. (They have greater variety.) Stores specializing in toys stock more types of toys (more SKUs). For each type of toy, such as dolls, the specialty toy retailer will

The local bike shop (left) offers a deeper assortment of performance bicycles and different brands than Toys "R" Us (right).

offer more assortment (more models, sizes, brands and deeper assortment) than general merchants such as department or discount stores.

Variety is often referred to as the **breadth of merchandise** carried by a retailer; assortment is referred to as the **depth of merchandise.** Exhibit 2–3 shows the breadth and depth of bicycles carried in a local bicycle shop (a specialty store), in Toys "R" Us (a category specialist), and in Wal-Mart (a full-line discount store) in Gainesville, Florida. Toys "R" Us only carries two types and has a narrower variety than the bicycle shop (four types), but Toys "R" Us has the greatest depth of assortment in children's bicycles. Wal-Mart has the lowest

EXHIBIT 2–3

Variety and Assortment of Bicycles in Different Retail Outlets

	ADULT ROAD	ADULT HYBRID	MOUNTAIN	CHILD
Bicycle shop	Le Tour Ross Schwinn Scott 10 SKUs, $299–$1,000	Schwinn 10 SKUs, $279	Dyno Schwinn 82 SKUs, $199–$1,399	Dyno GT Haro Schwinn 57 SKUs, $99–$599
Toys "R" Us			Magna Mistic Mongoose Pacific Cycle Rallye Roadmaster	AMX Barbie HotWheels Huffy Kent Little Mermaid Magna Mongoose Nice Cycle Pacific Cycle Paragon PlaySchool Pro XTR PT1 Rallye Rand Rhino RideHard Royce Union Sparkle Spice Girls StarWars Viken WildCat
			32 SKUs, $55–$499.99	108 SKUs, $29.99–$199.95
Wal-Mart	Mongoose 1 SKU, $200		Huffy Mongoose Murray Next Roadmaster 14 SKUs, $69.96–$200	Huffy Mongoose Murray Next Roadmaster StarWars 17 SKUs, $39.98–$78.88

number of SKUs (32) compared to 140 at Toys "R" Us and 159 at the bicycle shop. Note that Wal-Mart and Toys "R" Us have some of the same brands, but the bicycle shop offers a completely different set of brands.

Customer Services   Retailers also differ in the services they offer customers. For example, the bicycle shop offers assistance in selecting the appropriate bicycle, adjusting bicycles to fit the individual, and repairing bicycles. Toys "R" Us and Wal-Mart don't provide any of these services. Customers expect retailers to provide some services: accepting personal checks, providing parking, and displaying merchandise. Some retailers charge customers for other services, such as home delivery and gift wrapping. Retailers that cater to service-oriented consumers offer customers most of these services at no charge.

Cost of Offering Breadth and Depth of Merchandise and Services   Stocking a deep assortment like the Toys "R" Us offering in bicycles is appealing to customers but costly for retailers. When a retailer offers customers many SKUs, inventory investment increases because the retailer must have backup stock for each SKU.

Similarly, services attract customers to the retailer, but they're also costly. More salespeople are needed to provide information and assist customers, to alter merchandise to meet customers' needs, and to demonstrate merchandise. Child care facilities, rest rooms, dressing rooms, and check rooms take up valuable store space that could be used to stock and display merchandise. Offering delayed billing, credit, and installment payments requires a financial investment that could be used to buy more merchandise.

A critical retail decision involves the trade-off between costs and benefits of maintaining additional inventory or providing additional services. Chapters 7 and 12 address the considerations in making this trade-off.

TRENDS IN THE RETAIL INDUSTRY

As we discussed in the first chapter, the retail industry is changing rapidly. Some of the most important changes discussed in this section involve (1) the greater diversity of retailers, (2) increasing industry concentration, and (3) globalization.

Growing Diversity of Retail Formats

Over the past 20 years, many new retail formats have been developed. Consumers now can purchase the same merchandise from a wider variety of retailers as illustrated by the coffee maker example at the beginning of this chapter. The initial category specialists in toys, consumer electronics, and home improvement supplies have been joined by a host of new specialists including MARS (musical instruments), Zany Brainy (educational toys and games), Bed Bath and Beyond (home furnishings), and PETsMART (pet supplies). Wal-Mart is closing some of its traditional discount stores to open supercenters—large stores combining a discount store with a supermarket. Carmaxx competes with automobile dealers selling used cars using traditional retailing methods. The Internet has spawned a new set of retailers offering consumers the opportunity to buy merchandise and services at fixed prices (www.amazon.com), participate in an auction (www.ebay.com), or submit a "take-it-or-leave it" bid (www.priceline.com).

Tesco's development of new food retailing formats in the U.K. targeting different market segments illustrates the trend toward increasing diversity. The

SEPHORA, FRANCE'S LEADING PERFUME and cosmetic chain—a division of luxury-goods conglomerate LVMH (Louis Vuitton-Moet Hennessy)—is changing the way cosmetics are sold in the United States. In the United States prestige cosmetics are sold in department stores. Each brand has a separate counter with a commissioned salesperson stationed behind the counter to help customers.

Sephora is a cosmetic and perfume specialty store offering a deep assortment in a self-service 9,000–square-foot format. The 50 U.S. stores have over 13,000 SKUs including 365 different, private-label lipsticks. Merchandise is grouped by product category with the brands displayed alphabetically so customers can locate them easily. Video walls and interactive kiosks provide extensive product and use information.

Customers are free to shop and experiment on their own. Sampling is encouraged. Salespeople, wearing a single black glove (to better display stylish perfume boxes), are available to assist customers. However, the salespeople are paid a flat salary by Sephora, not a commission by the manufacturer. The low-key atmosphere results in customers spending more time shopping.

Sephora developed the concept of open floor selling of cosmetics.

Source: "Selling Open Sell," *Women's Wear Daily Eye on Fragrance Supplement*, June 1999, pp. 4, 6; Phyllis Berman and Katherine Bruce, "Makeover at the Makeup Counter," *Forbes*, April 19, 1999; and "Stores with Sizzle," *Chain Store Age*, September 1998, p. 74.

superstore is the main format. The new formats are Tesco Metro as a city center format, Tesco Compact for smaller towns, Tesco Hypermarket with a bigger nonfood assortment and Tesco Express as a convenience store. Retailing View 2.1 describes how a French retail chain is changing the way cosmetics are sold in the United States.

These new types of retailers coexist with traditional retailers. Each type of retailer offers a different set of benefits, thus consumers patronize different retailers for different purchase occasions. For example, a consumer might purchase a pair of cargo pants from a catalog as a gift for a friend in another city, and then visit a local store to try on and buy the same pants for himself. The greater diversity of retail formats increases competition in the industry and also enables consumers to buy merchandise and services from a retailer who better satisfies their needs for the specific purchase occasion.

Increasing Industry Concentration

While the number of different retail formats has grown, the number of competitors within each format is decreasing. A few national retailers dominate most formats. For example, Wal-Mart, Kmart, and Target account for over 85 percent of the sales in full-line discount stores and Walgreens, CVS, Eckerd, and Rite-Aid represent 56 percent of the drugstore sales.[3] In the United States, there are now only two major category specialists left in consumer electronics (Circuit City and Best Buy) and three in office supplies (Office Depot, Staples, and OfficeMax). The supermarket industry, long dominated by strong regional firms like Publix (Florida), HEB (Texas), and Dominicks (Chicago) is going through a period of consolidation.

Four chains—Albertsons, Safeway, Kroger, and Ahold USA—now account for one-third of the supermarket sales in the United States.[4]

Much of this consolidation has occurred through acquisitions and mergers. For example, Ahold is a Dutch company that has acquired a number of East Coast supermarket chains including Giant Food (Washington, D.C. and Pennsylvania), Pathmark (New Jersey), Stop & Shop (New England), Tops (upstate New York), and BI-LO (the Carolinas). Fred Meyer acquired Smith Food and Drug, Ralph's Grocery, and Quality Food Centers and then was acquired by Kroger. In 1998, Autozone acquired Chief Auto Parts, TruckPro, ADAP Auto Palace, and American Discount Auto Parts. Proffits (renamed Saks) acquired a number of department store chains including Saks and Parisian.[5]

Historically, retailing was a local business. Stores were owned and operated by people living in the community and patronized by local residents. However, the development of efficient distribution and communication systems meant that large national firms could gain substantial cost advantages over smaller regional and local retailers. It is no longer necessary for local managers to make decisions on what merchandise is needed in the store. These decisions can be made at a national headquarters by managers monitoring sales using information systems linked to POS terminals in stores across the world.

Globalization

Many retailers are becoming global firms as they pursue expansion opportunities beyond their domestic markets. Some factors stimulating this globalization of retailing are the maturation of domestic markets, the development of skills and systems to effectively manage global operations, and the removal of trade barriers.

Maturation of Domestic Markets   Most large retailers have saturated their domestic markets. For example, in the United States, as the amount of retail space per capita has grown over the past 10 years, the sales per square foot has declined by 50 percent. Thus opening additional stores in the United States results in limited additional sales, leading large United States retailers to look for growth opportunities in international markets.[7]

Skills and Systems   Retail firms are better prepared now to effectively manage stores in nondomestic markets. Many of the companies have international knowledge and experience since they acquire merchandise through buying offices located across the globe.[8] To facilitate this global sourcing of merchandise, they operate global information and distribution systems. These systems that are critical for the operations of national and international retailers are discussed in Chapter 11.

Trade Barriers   Finally, the relaxation of trade barriers makes global expansion easier. NAFTA (North America) countries, ASEAN (Southeast Asia) countries, and the European Common Market have taken significant steps to lower the barriers to international trade.

While there are millions of retailers across the globe, there are a limited number of retail institutions. The following sections discuss some common types of store-based retailers: food and general merchandise retailers. Appendix 2B, at the end of the chapter, outlines some theories about the evolution of retail institutions.

FOOD RETAILERS

Exhibit 2–4 shows the sales revenues and retail mixes for different types of food retailers.

Conventional Supermarkets

Prior to 1930, most food was purchased in small neighborhood markets referred to as mom-and-pop stores because they were family-owned and -operated. These have been replaced by larger self-service supermarkets, which offer considerably lower prices. Societal changes stimulating the development of supermarkets include the widespread use of cars, improved road systems, development of national mass media, rise of national brands, consumers' growing sophistication, and improved packaging and refrigeration. These changes made it easier for consumers to go to a store beyond the walking distance from their home. Also as a result of these changes, consumers have information that lessens their need for store employees' assistance when they make purchase decisions.[9]

A **conventional supermarket** is a self-service food store offering groceries, meat, and produce with limited sales of nonfood items, such as health and beauty aids and general merchandise. Half of the conventional supermarkets are very promotional. One day each week, they advertise that week's sale items in local papers. These promotion-oriented supermarkets also offer their own coupons and may agree to reimburse customers double or triple the face value of manufacturer coupons. This is called a hi–lo pricing strategy.

The other half of conventional supermarkets use very few promotions and sell almost all merchandise at the same price every day. This is called an everyday low pricing (EDLP) policy. Typically, everyday prices in these supermarkets are lower than regular prices in promotional supermarkets. For example, Food Lion (a Salisbury, North Carolina-based chain that uses an EDLP strategy) keeps costs low by offering a "no-frills" shopping experience. By adopting everyday low pricing, Food Lion reduces advertising costs to 25 percent of typical advertising expenses for a supermarket. Cereal and pet food are sold at cost to draw people into the store. The company philosophy is to do "1,000 things 1 percent better" than competitors.[11] Hi–lo and EDLP strategies are discussed in detail in Chapter 15.

Refact The first self-service grocery store was opened in 1930 by King Kullen in Jamaica, New York.[10]

EXHIBIT 2–4   Types of Food Retailers

	CONVENTIONAL SUPERMARKET	SUPERSTORE COMBINATION	SUPERCENTER	WAREHOUSE CLUB	CONVENIENCE STORE
Sales ($ billions)*	143	158	45	22	28
Number of Stores	18,200	9,200	3,300	750	57,000
Sales/Store ($ millions)	7.9	17.2	13.6	29.3	0.5
Size (000 sq. ft)	20	20–50	100–150	100–150	2–3
SKUs (000)*	20	30	30	20	2–3
Variety	Average	Broad	Broad	Broad	Narrow
Assortment	Average	Deep	Deep	Shallow	Shallow
Services	Average	Average	Average	Low	Average
No. of Checkout lines	6–10	10–20	20–30	10–15	1–2
Prices	Average	Low	Low	Low	High

*Supermarket items only.

Source: "66th Annual Report of the Grocery Industry," Supplement to *Progressive Grocer*, April 1999.

Big-Box Food Retailers

Over the past 25 years, supermarkets have increased in size and have begun to sell a broader variety of merchandise. In 1979, conventional supermarkets accounted for 85 percent of supermarket sales. By 1998, only 41 percent of U.S. supermarket sales were in conventional supermarkets due to the growth of "big-box" food retailing formats: superstores, combination stores, warehouse clubs, and supercenters.[12]

Superstores are large supermarkets (20,000 to 50,000 square feet). **Combination stores** are food-based retailers of 30,000 to 100,000 square feet that have over 25 percent of their sales from nonfood merchandise such as flowers, health and beauty aids, kitchen utensils, film developing, prescription drugs, and videotape rentals.

Refact When Wal-Mart converts a general merchandise discount store into a supercenter by adding groceries, sales of nongrocery items go up 30 to 50 percent.[15]

Supercenters

Supercenters are 150,000-to-200,000–square-foot stores that combine a superstore (a large supermarket) and a full-line discount store. Supercenters are the fastest growing retail category. Wal-Mart's sales in supercenters have grown from $4.6 billion from 143 stores in 1994 to $36.6 billion from 564 stores in 1998. The largest supercenter chains in the United States are Wal-Mart Supercenters (1998 annual sales of $36.6 billion), Fred Meyers ($14.9 billion), and Super Kmart Centers ($4.6 billion).[13]

The supercenters and full-line discount stores sell groceries at low prices to build store traffic. Almost all consumers in the United States shop at supermarkets with the typical household making 2.4 trips a week. However, only 68 percent shop at discount stores, making 1.3 trips per week.[14]

By offering broad assortments of grocery and general merchandise under one roof, supercenters provide a one-stop shopping experience. Customers will typically drive farther to shop at these stores than to visit conventional supermarkets (which offer a smaller selection). General merchandise items (nonfood items) are often purchased on impulse when customers' primary reason for coming to the store is to buy groceries. The general merchandise has higher margins, enabling the supercenters to price food items more aggressively. However, since supercenters are very large, some customers find them inconvenient because it can take a long time to find the items they want.

Warehouse Club

A **warehouse club** is a retailer that offers a limited assortment of food and general merchandise with little service at low prices to ultimate consumers and small businesses. Stores are large (about 100,000 square feet) and located in low-rent districts. They have simple interiors and concrete floors. Aisles are wide so forklifts can pick up pallets of merchandise

Supercenters, like this one in China, are very popular in Asia and South America.

and arrange them on the selling floor. Little service is offered. Customers pick merchandise off shipping pallets, take it to checkout lines in the front of the store, and pay with cash. The largest warehouse club chains are Costco Club (annual sales of $24.3 billion); Sam's Warehouse Club, a division of Wal-Mart (annual sales of $22.9 billion); and BJ's Wholesale Club ($3.6 billion).[16]

Merchandise in warehouse clubs is about half food and half general merchandise. Specific brands and items may differ from time to time because the stores buy merchandise available on special promotions from manufacturers. Warehouse clubs reduce prices by using low-cost locations and store designs. They reduce inventory holding costs by carrying a limited assortment of fast-selling items. Merchandise usually is sold before the clubs need to pay for it.

Most warehouse clubs have two types of members. Wholesale members are small-business people and individual members who purchase for their own use. For example, many small restaurants are wholesale customers buying their supplies, food ingredients, and desserts from a warehouse club rather than from food distributors.

Some clubs require individual members to have an affiliation with a government agency, utility, or credit union. Typically members must pay an annual fee of $25 to $35. In some stores, individual members pay no fee, but pay 5 percent over an item's ticketed price. Wholesale members typically represent less than 30 percent of the customer base, but account for over 70 percent of sales.

Convenience Stores

Convenience stores provide a limited variety and assortment of merchandise at a convenient location in a 2,000-to-3,000–square-foot store with speedy checkout. They are the modern version of the neighborhood mom-and-pop grocery store.

Convenience stores enable consumers to make purchases quickly, without having to search through a large store and wait in a long checkout line. Over half the items bought are consumed within 30 minutes of purchase. Due to their small size and high sales, convenience stores typically receive deliveries every day.

Convenience stores only offer a limited assortment and variety; they charge higher prices than supermarkets. Milk, eggs, and bread once represented the majority of their sales. Now almost all convenience stores sell gasoline, which accounts for over 55 percent of annual sales. Dairy and baked goods represent less than 20 percent of in-store sales. The major in-store merchandise categories are

Refact "Uncle Johnny" Jefferson Green, owner of Southland Ice, opened the first convenience store in 1927 on the corner of 12th and Edgefield in Dallas, Texas.[17]

Food retailers like this Wegman's supermarket, are placing more emphasis on meal solutions—pre-packaged meals that can be served with minimum preparation.

tobacco products (29 percent of annual sales), food service (14 percent), beer (13 percent), and packaged soft drinks (12 percent).[18]

Issues in Food Retailing

Two forces affecting traditional food retailers (supermarket and convenience store chains) are the changing consumer consumption patterns for food and increased competition from discount store chains.

Adapting to Changing Food Consumption Patterns   Due to the time pressures on two-income families and favorable economic conditions, consumers are cooking meals at home less than before. In the United States, 8.2 percent of disposable income is spent on food consumed at home and now 4.0 percent is spent on food consumed at home.[19] When meals are consumed at home, increasingly often they are pre-prepared, either purchased at a store or delivered, and then reheated.[20]

To gain a greater share of food expenditures, supermarkets have made significant investments in providing meal solutions, either hot food or partially cooked entrees. Take, for example, Wegman's Food Market's 50-store chain based in Rochester, New York. Wegman's has chefs in white hats tossing fresh pasta, with dining areas in the stores offering Sunday brunch and chilled wine. The chain offers an extensive variety of prepared meals ranging from Caesar salads to Chinese food made by chefs in full view of its customers. A satisfied customer says, "They have the drama. I ask for a fresh salmon sautéed with a little lemon, browse 10 minutes in the store, and take it home to my wife for dinner."[21]

However, the response to these food service investments by supermarkets has been disappointing. Only 15 percent of supermarket customers are loyal purchasers of these products and 43 percent never buy prepared foods at supermarkets.[22]

Convenience stores are also developing new concepts emphasizing prepared meals. For example, EatZi's, a Dallas-based chain, combines a convenience store and takeout restaurant in an 8,000–square-foot location. EatZi's has ready-to-heat meals, sandwich bar, salads, and a ready-to-eat section. It also offers fresh produce, beverages, snacks, and other food. Customers can park, walk in, pick up tonight's dinner and tomorrow's breakfast, and be back in their cars in 10 minutes.[23]

Competing Effectively against Discount Stores   Traditional supermarket chains are facing increased competition from discount chains.[24] In response to inroads made by supercenters and warehouse clubs, supermarket chains are reducing their costs. The industry consolidation reduces costs by increasing buying power and reducing overhead. However, the major cost reduction effort focuses on more efficient supply chain management.

Discount store chains were able to undercut supermarket prices because their distribution systems were more efficient, and they focused on reducing inventory investments by selling fast-moving items. A study of supermarket distribution costs found that chains could save $30 billion if they did a better job of managing store and warehouse inventory and reduced the number of SKUs in the stores. These cost-cutting initiatives are referred to as ECR (efficient consumer response).

In a continuing effort to reduce cost, supermarket chains are working with vendors on a process called CPFR (collaboration, planning, forecasting, and replenishment). The CPFR process involves developing more accurate store-level sales and order forecasts incorporating historical sales patterns and the upcoming marketing and merchandising activities of the retailer and its vendors. By increasing the forecast accuracy, the inventory levels can be reduced. These initiatives are discussed in more detail in Chapter 11.

In addition to reducing costs, supermarkets are placing more emphasis on perishables and meal solutions (prepared meals and side dishes). Supermarkets continue to sell over 75 percent of the produce, meat, dry/canned goods, frozen food, dairy, bakery, and seafood. However, the big-box food retail formats now account for over 50 percent of the sales of pet food, paper products, beer, and personal care products.[25] In addition to focusing on perishables, supermarkets are offering the larger pack sizes that attract family shoppers to the warehouse clubs.

Convenience stores are also facing significant competition both from full-line discount stores (Wal-Mart and Kmart) with areas near the store front devoted to convenience store merchandise and from the new, enlarged drugstore formats at stand-alone locations. Costs of operating convenience stores are also rising. Recently convenience stores were forced to make significant investments to conform to Environmental Protection Agency regulations governing underground gas storage tanks. In addition, convenience stores are facing increasing labor costs to control losses due to crime.

GENERAL MERCHANDISE RETAILERS

The major types of general merchandise retailers are department stores, full-line discount stores, specialty stores, drugstores, category specialists, home improvement centers, and off-price retailers. Exhibit 2–5 summarizes characteristics of general merchandise retailers that sell through stores. Internet and other nonstore retailers are discussed in the next chapter.

Department Stores

Department stores are retailers that carry a broad variety and deep assortment, offer considerable customer services, and are organized into separate departments for displaying merchandise.[26] The largest department store chains in the United States are Sears ($33.5 billion annual sales),

EXHIBIT 2–5   Characteristics of Different General Merchandise Retailers

TYPE	VARIETY	ASSORTMENT	SERVICE	PRICES	SIZE (000 SQ. FT.)	SKUS (000)	LOCATION
Department stores	Broad	Deep to average	Average to high	Average to high	100–200	100	Regional malls
Discount stores	Broad	Average to shallow	Low	Low	60–80	30	Stand alone, power strip centers
Specialty stores	Narrow	Deep	High	High	4–12	5	Regional malls
Drugstores	Narrow	Very deep	Average	Average to high	3–15	10–20	Stand alone, strip centers
Category specialists	Narrow	Very deep	Low to high	Low	50–120	20–40	Stand alone, power strip centers
Home improvement centers	Narrow	Very deep	Low to high	Low	80–120	20–40	Stand alone, power strip centers
Off-price stores	Average	Deep but varying	Low	Low	20–30	50	Outlet malls
Hypermarkets	Broad	Average	Low	Low	200	50–75	Stand alone

JCPenney ($19.3 billion), Federated Department Stores ($15.8 billion), and The May Company ($13.1 billion).[27]

Each department within the store has a specific selling space allocated to it, a POS terminal to transact and record sales, and salespeople to assist customers. The department store often resembles a collection of specialty shops. The major departments are women's, men's, and children's clothing and accessories; home furnishings and furniture; and kitchenware and small appliances. Since women's wear typically accounts for over half the sales volume, women's merchandise is divided into departments based on size (petite, full-figure), usage occasion (sportswear, business attire, evening wear), lifestyle (conservative, traditional, up-date), or age (juniors, misses).

In some situations, departments in a department store or discount store are leased and operated by an independent company. A **leased department** is an area in a retail store that is leased or rented to an independent firm. The lease holder is typically responsible for all retail mix decisions involved in operating the department and pays the store a percentage of its sales as rent. Retailers lease departments when they feel they lack expertise to efficiently operate the department. Commonly leased departments in U.S. stores are beauty salons, pharmacies, shoes, jewelry, furs, photography studios, and repair services. While relatively few departments are leased in U.S. stores, most of the departments, even men's and women's apparel, are leased in Japanese department stores.

Department stores are unique in terms of the shopping experience they offer—the services they provide and the atmosphere of the store. They offer a full range of services from altering clothing to home delivery. To create excitement, apparel is displayed on mannequins; attention is drawn to displays with theatrical lighting; and sales associates are frequently stationed throughout the store demonstrating products. Department stores also emphasize special promotions such as elaborate displays during the Christmas season.

Some department stores such as Neiman Marcus and Saks Fifth Avenue are referred to as **specialty department stores** because they use a department store format but focus primarily on apparel and soft home furnishings. However, the nature of traditional department stores has changed considerably over the years,

This department store provides an attractive environment for displaying apparel.

so the distinction between traditional and specialty stores has blurred. With few exceptions, traditional department stores have eliminated many of the departments they originally had. No longer can a customer buy a new outfit and then walk to the next aisle for a record album, refrigerator, best-selling book, or toy. Traditional department stores are concentrating more on apparel and soft home furnishings (sheets, bedspreads, pillows) and cutting back or eliminating toys and games, furniture, and consumer electronics. Some department store chains have opened specialty furniture stores and no longer sell furniture in their department stores. Thus, traditional and specialty department stores are offering similar merchandise mixes.

Issues in Department Store Retailing Department stores' overall sales have stagnated in recent years due to increased competition from discount stores and specialty stores. Discount stores offer lower prices and are beginning to sell more fashionable apparel. On the other hand, many customers now feel that specialty stores provide better service and merchandise assortments than department stores.

The initial response to the discount store competition 20 years ago was to reduce costs and prices. Department stores reduced labor costs by cutting back on the number of sales associates in the stores and reduced prices by increasing the frequency of promotional sales. This response decreased the service quality and consumers' perceived fairness in merchandise prices. Many consumers now wait to buy merchandise when it goes on sale rather than buying it at the initial retail price. Sixty to 80 percent of all merchandise sold by department stores is on sale.[30]

Now department stores are taking a different approach to competing against discount and specialty stores. They are altering their merchandise mix, improving their in-stock position on fashion merchandise, and improving their customer service. Besides focusing more on apparel, department stores are developing unique, private-label merchandise that consumers can buy only at their stores. For example, strong private-label jeans have been developed by JCPenney (Arizona) and Sears (Canyon River Blues).

Department store retailers are working closely with their vendors to ensure better in-stock positions for fashion merchandise and still reduce average inventory levels. These initiatives, referred to as Quick Response (QR), are similar to the ECR and CPFR programs undertaken by supermarkets. For example, at the beginning of a season, a department store chain that has a QR relationship with a vendor will commit to buy 120,000 sweaters, but will only specify the sizes and colors for the initial shipment of 2,500 sweaters. The vendors and retailer will closely monitor initial sales and use this information to knit and dye the sweaters in sizes and colors that will match customer demand for the rest of the season.

Refact Consumers go to discount stores an average of 4.7 times per month and visit department stores 2.7 times per month.[29]

Refact Private-label merchandise accounts for 25 percent of Nordstrom's sales.[31]

Discount Stores A **full-line discount store** is a retailer that offers a broad variety of merchandise, limited service, and low prices. They offer national brands, but these brands are typically less fashion-oriented than brands in department stores. The "big three" full-line discount store chains—Wal-Mart Stores (with 1998 annual sales of $58.8 billion), Kmart ($29.1 billion), and Target, a division of Dayton Hudson ($22.5 billion)—account for over 85 percent of the U.S. sales made by full-line discount stores.[32]

Refact Hudson's Bay Company, the oldest retailer in North America, conquered the Canadian wilderness by trading furs over 300 years ago. Today one of it divisions, Zellers, is one of the largest full-line discount chains in Canada.[33]

Issues in Full-Line Discount Store Retailing   Just as department stores face intense competition from specialty stores that focus on a single category of merchandise, the category specialists and home improvement centers such as Circuit City, Sports Authority, and Home Depot compete intensely with full-line discount stores. (Category specialists are described in a subsequent section.) To respond to category specialists' domination of hard goods (appliances, consumer electronics, automotive, hardware, sporting goods, etc.), full-line discount retailers are creating more attractive shopping environments, placing more emphasis on apparel, developing private-label merchandise, and increasing store visits by offering easily accessible convenience-store merchandise. For example, Wal-Mart and Kmart are following the lead of Target, the only full-line discount store with significant sales growth. They are remodeling their stores with wider aisles and better lighting; upgrading the quality and fashion of their apparel; and developing private brands such as Martha Stewart home furnishings at Kmart. Kmart has introduced a Big K store with a "convenience-store" department at its entrance.[34]

Specialty Stores

A traditional **specialty store** concentrates on a limited number of complementary merchandise categories and provides a high level of service in an area typically under 8,000 square feet. Exhibit 2–6 lists some of the largest U.S. specialty store chains.

Issues in Specialty Store Retailing   Sales in apparel specialty stores grew rapidly in the 1970s and 1980s, but by the mid-90s, their sales growth slowed to below the growth rate for total U.S. retail sales. The limited growth in apparel specialty store sales reflects a general lack of growth in women's apparel sales. A number of reasons have been proposed for this malaise in women's apparel. Women, and consumers in general, are becoming more value-oriented. They are buying apparel in more traditional styles that can be worn for several years rather than choosing fashion-forward merchandise that is out of style at the end of the season. The general emphasis is a casual lifestyle as reflected in conservative companies such as IBM switching to a casual work dress code, reduces the need for expensive, fashionable, work-related outfits. Finally, some people feel that apparel designers just have not developed new concepts that stimulate an interest in apparel.

In response to the declining interest in high-fashion apparel, specialty stores are adopting a concept called lifestyle retailing. **Lifestyle retailing** tailors merchandise to the lifestyle of a specific group of customers. For example, Philadelphia-based Urban Outfitters targets teenagers by offering a continuous flow of new merchandise in stores with an urban atmosphere. Stores' wood-planked floors and brick walls are complete with graffiti. In addition to T-shirts and jeans, 30 percent of the merchandise is nonapparel items like makeup, jewelry, candles, and picture frames.

Hard goods (consumer electronics, appliances, sporting goods) specialty retailers have been particularly hard hit by the growth in category specialist chains. Retailing View 2.2 describes how RadioShack changed its strategy to deal with the competition from category specialists.

Drugstores

Drugstores are specialty stores that concentrate on health and personal grooming merchandise. Pharmaceuticals often represent over 50 percent of drugstore sales and an even greater percentage of their profits. The largest drugstore chains in the United States are Walgreens ($15.3 billion in annual sales), CVS ($15.3 billion), Rite Aid ($12.7 billion), and Eckerds, a division of JCPenney ($10.3 billion).[35]

EXHIBIT 2–6

Largest Specialty
Store Chains

COMPANY	SALES, 1998 (MILLIONS)	% CHANGE IN SALES, 1997–98	EARNINGS (MILLIONS)	EARNINGS CHANGE, 1997–98	NO. OF STORES, 1998
APPAREL					
The Limited	$9,346	1.7%	$2,053	845.0%	3,492
The Gap	9,054	39.3	824	54.4	2,428
Intimate Brands	3,885	7.4	400	38.5	1,890
American Retail Group	1,400	7.7	NA	NA	1,200
Spiegel/Eddie Bauer	1,331	1.6	11	—	1,200
SHOES					
Venator	4,550	–1.2	(136)	—	6,002
Payless	2,620	12.3	135	25.3	4,570
Footstar	1,829	1.9	33	–58.1	3,110
CONSUMER ELECTRONICS					
Tandy/Radio Shack	3,591	8.7	245	14.3	7,030
AUTO PARTS					
Autozone	3,242	20.5	228	16.9	2,700
Pep Boys	2,399	16.6	5	—	638
FURNITURE					
Helig-Meyers	2,726	10.4	(21)	—	1,249
Pier 1 Imports	1,138	8.9	80	3.0	807
MUSIC					
Musicland	1,846	4.4	38	172	1,346
Tower Records	1,500	20.0	NA	NA	218
FOOD SUPPLEMENTS					
General Nutrition	1,417	18.8	90	–12	4,091
JEWELRY					
Zales	1,313	4.8	69	36.4	1,140
Tiffany	1,169	14.9	90	23.7	120
Sterling Jewelers	1,057	11.3	129	23.7	788
OPTICAL					
Cole National	1,068	6.8	14	—	2,874
Lenscrafters	1,046	2.0	NA	NA	853
ACCESSORIES					
Claire's Stores	662	23.3	62	3.8	2,027
Sunglass Hut	602	4.9	20	—	2,003

Source: "Top 100 Specialty Stores," *Stores,* August 1999, pp. S1–S23; and "The DSN Annual Industry Report," *Discount Store News,* July 12, 1999, pp. 61–62. Reprinted by permission from *Discount Store News,* July 1999. Copyright Lebhar-Friedman, Inc. 425 Park Avenue, New York, NY 10022 from *Stores* Magazine © NFR Enterprises, Inc.

Issues in Drugstore Retailing   Drugstores are facing considerable competition from discount stores and supermarkets adding pharmacies as well as from mail order retailers filling prescriptions. While the profit margins for prescription pharmaceuticals continue to be higher than other for general merchandise, these margins are shrinking due to government health care policies and HMOs.

In response, the major drugstore chains are building larger stand-alone stores offering a wider assortment of merchandise, more frequently purchased food items, and drivethrough windows for picking up prescriptions.[36] To build customer loyalty, the chains are also changing the role of their pharmacists from dispensing pills (referred to as count, pour, lick, and stick) to providing health care assistance such as explaining how to use a nebulizer.

RADIOSHACK, A DIVISION OF THE TANDY CORPORATION, was an innovative retailer selling consumer electronics and home computers. It was one of the first retailers to sell and service home computers, offering a line of computers designed and manufactured by its parent company, Tandy. When category specialists with broader assortments and lower prices entered the market, Tandy responded by opening its own category specialist chains: Computer City and Incredible Universe. Both of these chains were unsuccessful. Tandy closed both chains, exited the computer manufacturing business, and has repositioned RadioShack to build on its its 7,000 stores conveniently located in neighborhoods.

Rather than selling computers and home entertainment systems, RadioShack is emphasizing making it easier for a technology-savvy household to integrate its Internet, cable or satellite TV, and local and long-distance telephone service. Leonard Roberts, the CEO, says, "Everyone's building the big engines, but no one is building the tracks." RadioShack is focusing on selling the accessories to enable consumers to get the most out of their equipment and providing installation and repair services for home electronics.

In addition to selling hardware and installation and repair services, RadioShack is offering services such as Sprint PCs and Primestar satellite services. When RadioShack sells these services, it gets a percentage of the initial sale plus a percent-

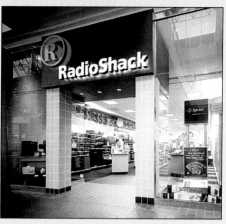

RadioShack is repositioning its stores to help customers exploit home electronics opportunities.

age of the customer's monthly bill. And RadioShack is in the right place to sell the hardware and provide these services. Its 7,000 stores are located within five minutes of 94 percent of the U.S. population.

Source: Stephanie Forrest, "Cable, Phone, Internet—Who Ya Going to Call?" *Business Week,* March 1, 1999, p. 64; and Ed Lieber, "RadioShack Set to Expand Store-within-a-Store Concept," *HFN,* January 25, 1999, p. 50.

Drugstore retailers are using systems to allow pharmacists time to provide personalized service. For example, at Walgreens, customers can order prescription refills via touch-tone phone. Based on the time they plan to pick up the prescription, a computer system automatically schedules the work load in the pharmacy. The systems also monitor the frequency of refilling prescriptions so the pharmacist can make phone calls or send e-mails to monitor patient drug compliance.[37]

Refact Americans rate pharmacists as the most trusted profession.[38]

Category Specialists

A **category specialist** is a discount store that offers a narrow variety but deep assortment of merchandise. These retailers are basically discount specialty stores. Most category specialists use a self-service approach, but some specialists in consumer durables offer assistance to customers. For example, Office Depot stores have a warehouse atmosphere, with cartons of copying paper stacked on pallets plus equipment in boxes on shelves. However, some merchandise, such as computers, is displayed in the middle of the store, and salespeople in the display area are available to answer questions and make suggestions.

By offering a complete assortment in a category at low prices, category specialists can "kill" a category of merchandise for other retailers and thus are frequently called "category killers." Because category specialists dominate a category of merchandise, they can use their buying power to negotiate low prices, excellent terms, and assured supply when items are scarce. Department stores

EXHIBIT 2–7

Largest Category
Specialists

RETAILER	SALES 1998 ($ MILLIONS)	% CHANGE, 1997–98	98 EARNINGS ($ MILLIONS)	% CHANGE, 1997–98	NO. OF STORES, JAN. 1999
CONSUMER ELECTRONICS					
Best Buy	$10,078	20.6%	$365	95%	311
Circuit City	9,340	16.8	235	48	587
Good Guys	928	4.2	(13)	NA	72
OFFICE SUPPLY					
Staples	7,123	24.3	185	10.1	916
Office Depot	5,129	(8.7)	399	1.5	702
OfficeMax	4,338	15.2	87	(40.6)	702
TOYS					
Toys "R" Us	6,581	(3.4)	501	(24.0)	703
COMPUTERS					
CompUSA	5,286	14.6	57	(63.5)	162
BOOKS					
Barnes & Noble	2,515	12.0	189	28.6	1009
Borders	1,564	23.7	167	21	250
PET SUPPLIES					
PetsMART	2,109	17.8	59	NA	423
Petco	840	12.0	4	(16)	476
SPORTS EQUIPMENT					
Sports Authority	1,600	9.2	(89)	NA	200
Gart Sports	658	188.7	3	(72.7)	125
HOME					
Bed Bath & Beyond	1,397	30.1	158	32.8	185
Pier 1 Imports	1,139	6.0	135	10.7	751
Linens N' Things	1,066	22.0	62	36.3	196
IKEA	609	9.7	NA	NA	14
CRAFTS					
Michaels	1,574	8.0	89	29.0	574
Hobby Lobby	665	24.1	NA	NA	177
Frank's Nursery	512	(3.4)	28	660.0	254
APPAREL					
Kids "R" Us	779	(2.0)	NA	NA	212
Mens Wearhouse	768	21.7	72	38.5	431
BABY					
Babies "R" Us	814	44.1	NA	NA	118

Source: "The DSN Annual Industry Report," *Discount Store News*, July 12, 1999, pp. 61–70. Reprinted by permission from *Discount Store News*, April–May 1999. Copyright Lebhar-Friedman, Inc. 425 Park Avenue, New York, NY 10022.

and full-line discount stores located near category specialists often have to reduce their offerings in the category because consumers are drawn to the deep assortment and low prices at the category killer. Exhibit 2–7 lists the largest category specialists in the United States. Retailing View 2.3 describes Bass Pro Shop,
a category specialist targeting fishing and hunting enthusiasts.

Issues for Category Specialists   Most category specialist chains started in one
region of the country and saturated that region before expanding to other

BASS PRO SHOPS OUTDOOR WORLD OFFERS a shopping adventure for the 35 million U.S. fishers and 13 million hunters. The 170,000–square-foot flagship store in Springfield, Missouri, has a four-story waterfall, rifle and archery ranges, four aquariums, an indoor driving range, a putting green, and a 250-seat auditorium and conference room for fish feeding shows and workshops. Visitors can also get a haircut or dine at McDonald's or Hemingway's Blue Water Cafe, which has a 30,000-gallon salt water aquarium. The store and accompanying wildlife museum attract over 3.5 million visitors a year, ranking as Missouri's largest tourist attraction. Slightly smaller stores (150,000 square feet) that are still very interactive and entertaining are located in the suburbs of Atlanta, Fort Lauderdale, and Chicago. There are plans for opening stores in the Detroit, Charlotte, Dallas, Houston, and Orlando markets.

The store offers everything a person needs for hunting and fishing—from 27-cent plastic bait to boats and recreational vehicles costing $45,000. The merchandise and service include fishing tackle, shooting and hunting equipment, camping gear, boats and marine accessories, taxidermy studio, cutlery shop, rod and reel repair, gifts, outdoors-related books and videos, and sportswear and footwear.

Sales associates are knowledgeable outdoor people. Each one is hired for a particular department that matches that person's expertise. All private-branded products are field tested by Bass Pro Shops' professional teams: Redhead Pro Hunting Team and Tracker Pro Fishing Team.

Fishing exhibition in a Bass Pro Shops Outdoor World.

The retailer and the sports are promoted through a syndicated radio show, *Bass Pro Shops Outdoor World,* heard on 450 radio stations in 48 states and 139 foreign countries. A magazine of the same name is available by subscription and at newsstands throughout the country. Bass Pro Shops also puts on a Fall Hunting Classic and Spring Fishing Classic. The events are essentially trade shows with manufacturer and service booths, professional sports persons, demonstrations, hot air balloon rides, NASCAR race cars, and thousands of dollars in prizes.

Source: Edwin McDowell, "Adventures in Retailing," *The New York Times,* April 3, 1999, pp. B1, B14; and Mary Ellen Vander Linden, "Big Fish Story," *Shopping Center World,* October 1998, p. 10.

regions. For example, Office Depot started in Florida and expanded through the Southeast and Southwest, while Staples started in Boston and expanded through New England and the Midwest. During this period of expansion competition between specialists in a category was limited.

Now competition between specialists in each category is very intense as the firms expand into the regions originally dominated by another firm. In many merchandise categories, the major firms are now in direct competition across the nation. This direct competition focuses on price, resulting in reduced profits because the competitors have difficulty differentiating themselves on other elements of the retail mix. All the competitors in a category provide similar assortments since they have similar access to national brands. They all provide the same level of service.

In response to this increasing competitive intensity, the category killers continue to concentrate on reducing costs by increasing operating efficiency and acquiring smaller chains to gain scale economies. In addition, the national chains are expanding into less competitive international markets.

Home Improvement Centers

A **home improvement center** is a category specialist offering equipment and material used by do-it-yourselfers and contractors to make home improvements. It focuses on providing material and information that enable consumers to maintain and improve their homes. The largest U.S. home improvement chains are Home Depot ($30.2 billion in annual sales), Lowe's Companies ($12.2 billion), Menard ($4.0 billion), Hechinger/Builders Square ($3.4 billion), and Payless Cashways ($1.9 billion).[39] While merchandise in home improvement centers is displayed in a warehouse atmosphere, salespeople are available to assist customers in selecting merchandise and to tell them how to use it. For example, most Home Depot stores have a licensed electrician. Experts in specific areas lead workshops to show customers how to do things themselves. All Home Depot salespeople are required to attend "product knowledge" classes and are paid for the time they spend learning about water heaters and power tools.

Refact Women make over 50 percent of the purchases at home improvement centers.[40]

Issues for Home Improvement Centers Home improvement centers are not facing the same level of competitive intensity as other category specialists. The two major chains, Home Depot and Lowe's, only account for 24 percent of home improvement merchandise sales. The needs for home improvement merchandise vary considerably across the country and there are opportunities for differentiating on customer service. As Home Depot saturates the United States with its present format, it is launching new formats including Expo Design and Villager's Hardware. Expo Design targets women in higher-income families. Its stores feature low, painted ceilings and track lights with individually designed display rooms highlighting possibilities for kitchens, baths, lighting, and appliances once available only through a decorator. Certified designers are on staff and ready to assist for a fee. Villager's Hardware is positioned as a "fill-in" store for DIYers (do-it-yourselfers) who normally shop at the company's large stores. The stores also target women by using improved housekeeping and signage and devoting a significant amount of selling space to merchandise similar to that in Bed Bath & Beyond or Crate & Barrel.[41]

Off-Price Retailers

Off-price retailers offer an inconsistent assortment of brand-name, fashion-oriented soft goods at low prices. America's largest off-price retail chains are T. J. Maxx/Marshalls (1998 annual sales of $7.8 billion), Ross Stores ($2.2 billion), and Burlington Coat Factory ($1.8 billion).[42]

Off-price retailers can sell brand-name and even designer-label merchandise at low prices due to their unique buying and merchandising practices. Most merchandise is bought opportunistically from manufacturers or other retailers with excess inventory at the end of the season. This merchandise might be in odd sizes or unpopular colors and styles, or it may be irregulars (having minor mistakes in construction). Typically, merchandise is purchased at one-fifth to one-fourth of the original wholesale price. Off-price retailers can buy at low prices because they don't ask suppliers for advertising allowances, return privileges, markdown adjustments, or delayed payments. (Terms and conditions associated with buying merchandise are detailed in Chapter 15.)

Refact Selling overstocks out of her Brooklyn home in 1920, Frieda Loehmann started the first off-price retail business.[43]

Due to this pattern of opportunistic buying, customers can't be confident that the same type of merchandise will be in stock each time they visit the store. Different bargains will be available on each visit. To improve their offerings' consistency, some off-price retailers complement opportunistically bought merchandise with merchandise bought at regular wholesale prices. Three special types of off-price retailers are outlet, closeout, and single-price stores.

Outlet Stores   **Outlet stores** are off-price retailers owned by manufacturers or by department or specialty store chains. Outlet stores owned by manufacturers are frequently referred to as **factory outlets.** Many manufacturers have one or two outlet stores. Manufacturers with a significant number of outlets include Warnaco (manufacturer of Hathaway shirts and Warner's lingerie), Reebok (athletic shoes), Van Heusen (men's shirts), Palm Beach (manufacturer of Evan Picone women's wear), and Ralph Lauren (men's and women's clothing).

Manufacturers view outlet stores as an opportunity to improve their revenues from irregulars, production overruns, and merchandise returned by retailers. Outlet stores also allow manufacturers some control over where their branded merchandise is sold at discount prices.

Retailers with strong brand names such as Saks (Saks Off Fifth) and Brooks Brothers operate outlet stores too. By selling excess merchandise in outlet stores rather selling it at markdown prices in their primary stores, these department and specialty store chains can maintain an image of offering desirable merchandise at full price.

Closeout Retailers   **Closeout retailers** are off-price retailers that sell a broad but inconsistent assortment of general merchandise as well as apparel and soft home goods. The largest closeout chains are Consolidated Stores (Odd Lots/ Big Lots, Mac Frugal's) ($5.5 billion in annual sales) and Tuesday Morning ($396 million).[44]

Single-Price Retailers   **Single-price retailers** are closeout stores that sell all their merchandise at a single price, typically $1. The largest single-price retailers are Dollar Tree ($919 million in annual sales) and 99 Cents Only ($323 million).[45]

Refact Consumers rate SteinMart, an off-price retailer, the second highest, following Nordstrom, in consumer satisfaction for an apparel retailer.[46]

Issues for Off-Price Retailers   Over the past several years, the sales growth of off-price retailers has slowed. With the increase in sales and promotions in department stores, consumers often are able to get fashionable, brand-name merchandise in department stores at the same discounted prices offered by off-price retailers. In addition, more sophisticated inventory management systems have reduced the amount of excess production that can be bought by off-price retailers. In response to these conditions, off-price retailers are buying more current merchandise to complement the excess merchandise bought at the end of a fashion season.[47]

Hypermarkets   A **hypermarket** is a very large retail store offering low prices. It combines a discount store and superstore food retailer in one warehouselike building. Hypermarkets can be up to 300,000 square feet—larger than six football fields—and stock over 50,000 different items. Hypermarkets are unique in terms of store size, low operating margins, low prices, and the size of the general merchandise assortment. Annual revenues are typically over $100 million per store.

CARREFOUR, A FRENCH RETAILER, refined the hypermarket concept in the late 60s and currently operates 324 hypermarkets in 16 countries across Europe, Latin America, and Asia. The store sells a broad variety of basic merchandise ranging from food to consumer electronics. Daniel Bernard, the chairman and CEO, emphasizes that Carrefour is a " 'glo-cal' company . . . a global group with a local approach to its markets."

The initial impetus for Carrefour's global expansion was the lack of shopping centers, severe zoning restrictions, and high taxation in France. However, early efforts in international markets were not successful. Carrefour no longer operates in three-quarters of the countries into which it has ventured. Bernard attributes these failures to lack of understanding of cultural differences between France and some new markets.

But Carrefour is now a global retail power. All of its hypermarkets are based on three concepts: one-stop shopping, ample free parking, and a discount pricing strategy. Carrefour is using a common centralized system across the globe, yet the system "allows for local differences, but speaks a common language." It spends two years learning about a culture and its

Carrefour is a hypermart retailer with stores around the world, like the one in Kuala Lumpur.

consumers before opening a store in a new country. However, once it enters a country, it opens 5 to 10 stores in a short time period to get distribution efficiencies.

Source: "Carrefour: Global Group with a Local Approach," *Stores,* September 1998, p. 25; and "Asian Retailing. Going Cheap," *The Economist,* August 15, 1998, p. 55.

Hypermarkets were created in France after World War II. By building large stores on the outskirts of metropolitan areas, French retailers could attract customers and not violate strict land use laws. While hypermarkets are quite successful in Europe, Latin America, and Asia, they haven't been very successful in the United States. Land use laws are much less restrictive in the United States than in Europe so American consumers can conveniently shop elsewhere for merchandise sold in hypermarkets. Discount stores often are located at three-mile intervals in metropolitan areas, and supermarkets appear at even closer intervals. While shopping for groceries and general merchandise in the same store appeals to some consumers, many U.S. consumers find that shopping in stores of over 200,000 square feet is too time-consuming. It's hard to find merchandise, and checkout lines can be very long. Retailing View 2.4 describes the global expansion of the hypermarket format by Carrefour, the third largest retailer in the world.

INTERNET EXERCISE Four large associations of retailers are the National Retail Federation (www.nrf.org), the Food Marketing Institute (www.fmi.org), the National Association of Chain Drug Stores (www.nacds.org), and the National Association of Convenience Stores (www.nacs.org). Visit these sites and report the latest retail developments and issues confronting the industry.

SERVICES RETAILING

The retail firms discussed in the previous sections sell products to consumers. However, **services retailers,** firms selling primarily services rather than merchandise, are a large and growing part of the retail industry. Consider a typical Saturday. After a bagel and cup of coffee at a nearby Einstein's Bagels, you go to the laundromat to wash and dry your clothes, drop a suit off at a dry cleaner, leave film to be developed at a Walgreens drugstore, and make your way to the Jiffy Lube to have your car's oil changed. Since you are in a hurry, you drive through a Taco Bell so you can eat lunch quickly and not be late for your haircut at 1 P.M. By midafternoon, you're ready for a swim at your health club. After stopping at home for a change of clothes, you're off to dinner, a movie, and dancing with a friend. Finally, you end your day with a caffe latte at Starbucks, having interacted with 10 different services retailers during the day.

Refact Services account for 58 percent of the U.S. Gross Domestic Product (the value of goods and services produced) and 81 percent of the nonfarm employment.[48]

Types of Services Retailers

In Chapter 4, we discuss trends that suggest considerable future growth in services retailing. For example, the aging of the population will increase demand for health services. Younger people too are spending increasing amounts of time and money on health and fitness. Parents in two-income families are willing to pay to have their homes cleaned, lawns maintained, clothes washed and pressed, and meals prepared so they can spend more time with their families.

Exhibit 2–8 shows the wide variety of services retailers along with the national companies that provide these services. These companies are retailers because they

EXHIBIT **2–8**

Examples of Services Retailers

TYPE OF SERVICE	SERVICE RETAIL FIRMS
Airlines	American, Delta, British Airways, Singapore Airways
Automobile maintenance and repair	Jiffy Lube, Midas, AAMCO
Automobile rental	Hertz, Avis, Budget, Enterprise
Banks	Citibank, NCNB, Bank of America
Child care centers	Kindercare, Gymboree
Credit cards	American Express, VISA, MasterCard
Education	Babson College, University of Florida
Entertainment parks	Disney, Universal Studios, Six Flags
Express package delivery	Federal Express, UPS, U.S. Postal Service
Financial services	Merrill Lynch, Dean Witter
Fitness	Jazzercise, Bally's, Gold's Gym
Health care	Humana, HCA, Kaiser
Home maintenance	Chemlawn, Mini Maid, Roto-Rooter
Hotels and motels	Hyatt, Sheraton, Marriott, Days Inn
Income tax preparation	H&R Block
Insurance	Allstate, State Farm
Internet access/electronic information	America Online, Mindspring
Long-distance telephone	AT&T, MCI, Sprint
Movie theaters	AMC, Odeon/Cineplex
Real estate	Century 21, Coldwell Banker
Restaurants	TGI Friday's, Wendy's, Pizza Hut
Truck rentals	U-Haul, Ryder
Weight loss	Weight Watchers, Jenny Craig
Video rental	Blockbuster
Vision centers	Lenscrafters, Pearle

sell goods and services to consumers. However, some of these companies are not just retailers. For example, airlines, banks, hotels, and insurance and express mail companies sell their services to businesses as well as consumers. Also, a large number of services retailers such as lawyers, doctors, and dry cleaners are not in the exhibit because they focus on local markets and do not have a national presence.

Many organizations such as banks, hospitals, health spas, legal clinics, entertainment firms, and universities that offer services to consumers traditionally haven't considered themselves as retailers. Due to increased competition, these organizations are adopting retailing principles to attract customers and satisfy their needs. For example, banks are following the practices of retailers by emphasizing the need to deliver products and services conveniently, quickly, and knowledgeably to consumers. They are placing branches in convenient locations, switching from "banker hours" to "retail hours," and adapting services offered and branch design to the needs of the local communities.[49]

All retailers provide goods and services for their customers. However, the emphasis placed on the merchandise versus the services differs across retail formats, as Exhibit 2–9 shows. On the left side of the exhibit are supermarkets and warehouse clubs. These retail formats consist of self-service stores that offer very few services. However, these formats do offer a few services such as check cashing and some assistance from store employees. Moving along the continuum from left to right, we find category specialists, which also emphasize self-service, but have employees who can answer questions, demonstrate merchandise, and make recommendations. Next, department and specialty stores provide even higher levels of service. In addition to assistance from sales associates, these stores offer services such as gift wrapping, bridal registries, and alterations.

Optical centers and restaurants lie somewhere in the middle of the merchandise/service continuum. In addition to selling frames, eyeglasses, and contact lenses, optical centers also provide important services like eye examinations and fitting eyeglasses. Similarly, restaurants offer food plus a place to eat, music in the background, a pleasant ambiance, and table service. As we move to the right end of the continuum, we encounter retailers whose offering is primarily services. However, even these retailers have some products associated with the services offered, such as a meal on the airplane or a check book. Services retailers

EXHIBIT **2–9**   Merchandise/Service Continuum

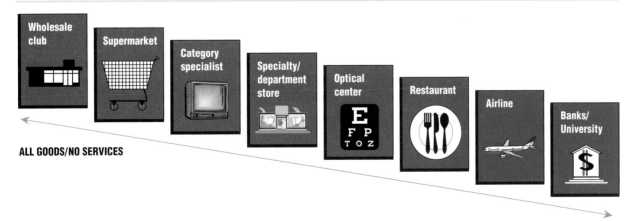

ALL GOODS/NO SERVICES

ALL SERVICES/NO GOODS

are defined as retailers for which the major aspect of their offerings is services versus merchandise.

Differences between Services and Merchandise Retailers

As a retailer falls more to the right on the merchandise/service continuum, services become a more important aspect of the retailer's offering. Four important differences in the nature of the offering provided by services and merchandise retailers are (1) intangibility, (2) simultaneous production and consumption, (3) perishability, and (4) inconsistency of the offering to customers.[50]

Intangibility   Services are generally intangible—customers cannot see, touch, or feel them. They are performances or actions rather than objects. For example, health care services cannot been seen or touched by a patient. Even after diagnosis and treatment, the patient may not realize the full extent of the service that has been performed.

Intangibility introduces a number of challenges for services retailers. First, since customers can't touch and feel services, it's difficult for customers to evaluate services before they buy them or even after they buy and consume them. Due to the intangibility of their offering, services retailers often use tangible symbols to inform customers about the quality of their services. For example, lawyers frequently have elegant, carpeted offices with expensive antique furniture. The design of service retailing outlets is discussed in Chapter 18.

Services retailers also have difficulty in evaluating the quality of services they are providing. For example, it's hard for a law firm to evaluate how well its lawyers are performing their jobs. To evaluate the quality of their offering, services retailers emphasize soliciting customer evaluations and complaints.

Since it is difficult to judge service quality, services retailers like the Ritz-Carlton, London, (left) and a bank (right) provide tangible cues of service quality in the design of the lobby and offices.

Simultaneous Production and Consumption   Products are typically made in a factory, stored and sold by a retailer, and then used by consumers in their homes. Service providers, on the other hand, create and deliver the service as the customer is consuming it. For example, when you eat at a restaurant, the meal is prepared and consumed almost at the same time.

The simultaneity of production and consumption creates some special problems for services retailers. First, the customers are present when the service is produced, may even have an opportunity to see it produced, and in some cases may be part of the production process, as in making their own salad at a salad bar. Second, other customers consuming the service at the same time can affect the quality of the service provided. For example, an obnoxious passenger next to you on an airline can make the flight very unpleasant. Finally, the services retailer often does not get a second chance to satisfy the needs of its customers. While customers can return damaged merchandise to a store, customers that are dissatisfied with services have limited recourse. Thus it is critical for services retailers to get it right the first time.

Because services are produced and consumed at the same time, it is difficult to reduce costs through mass production. For this reason, most services retailers are small, local firms. Large national retailers are able to reduce costs by "industrializing" the services they offer. They make substantial investments in equipment and training to provide a uniform service. For example, McDonald's has a detailed procedure for cooking french fries and hamburgers to make sure they come out the same whether cooked in Paris, France, or Paris, Illinois.

Perishability   Because the creation and consumption of services are inseparable, services are perishable. They can't be saved, stored, or resold. Once the airline takes off with an empty seat, the sale is lost forever. This is in contrast to merchandise that can be held in inventory until a customer is ready to buy it.

Due to the perishability of services, an important aspect of services retailing is matching supply and demand. Most services retailers have a capacity constraint, and the capacity cannot be changed easily. There are a fixed number of tables in a restaurant, seats in a classroom, beds in a hospital, and electricity that can be generated by a power plant. To increase capacity, services retailers need to make major investments such as buying more airplanes or building an addition to increase the size of the hospital or restaurant.

In addition, demand for service varies considerably over time. Consumers are most likely to fly on airplanes during holidays and the summer, eat in restaurants at lunch and dinner time, and use electricity in the evening rather than earlier in the day. Thus services retailers often have times when their services are underutilized and other times when they have to turn customers away because they can't accommodate them.

Services retailers use a variety of programs to match demand and supply. For example, airlines and hotels set lower prices on weekends when they have excessive capacity because businesspeople aren't traveling. To achieve more capacity flexibility, health clinics stay open longer in the flu season, while tax preparation services are open on weekends during March and April. Restaurants increase staffing on weekends, may not open until dinner time, and use a reservation system to guarantee service delivery at a specific time. Finally, services retailers attempt to make customers' waiting time more enjoyable. For example, videos and park employees entertain customers while they wait in line in Disney theme parks.

Inconsistency   Merchandise is often produced by machines with very tight quality control so customers are reasonably assured that all boxes of Cheerios will be identical. Because services are performances produced by people (employees and customers), no two services will be identical. For example, tax accountants can have different knowledge and skills for preparing tax returns. The waiter at the Olive Garden can be in a bad mood and make your dining experience a disaster.

Thus an important challenge for services retailers is providing consistently high-quality services. Many factors determining service quality are beyond the control of the retailers; however, services retailers expend considerable time and effort selecting, training, managing, and motivating their service providers.

TYPES OF OWNERSHIP

The first three sections of this chapter discussed how retailers are classified in terms of the merchandise they sell (food, general merchandise, and specific categories of merchandise), their retail mix (the variety and depth of merchandise and services offered to customers), and the relative importance of merchandising and services in their offering. Another way to classify retailers is by their ownership. The major classifications of retail ownership are (1) independent, single-store establishments, (2) corporate chains, and (3) franchises.

Independent, Single-Store Establishments

Retailing is one of the few sectors in our economy where entrepreneurial activity is extensive. In 1998, over 60,000 new retail businesses were started in the United States.[51] Many such stores are owner-managed. Thus, management has direct contact with customers and can respond quickly to their needs. Small retailers are also very flexible. They aren't bound by bureaucratic rules that restrict store location or types of merchandise sold.

While single-store retailers can tailor their offering to their customers' needs, corporate chains can more effectively negotiate lower prices for merchandise and advertising due to their larger size. In addition, corporate chains have a broader management base, with people who specialize in specific retail activities. Single-store retailers typically have to rely on owner-managers' capabilities to make the broad range of necessary retail decisions.[52]

To better compete against corporate chains, some independent retailers join a retail-sponsored cooperative group or wholesale-sponsored voluntary chain. A **retail-sponsored cooperative** is an organization owned and operated by small, independent retailers to improve operating efficiency and buying power. Typically, the retail-sponsored cooperative operates a wholesale buying and distribution system and requires its members to concentrate their purchases from the cooperative's wholesale operation.

A **wholesale-sponsored voluntary cooperative group** is an organization operated by a wholesaler offering a merchandising program to small, independent retailers on a voluntary basis. Independent Groceries Alliance (IGA) and Ace Hardware are wholesale-sponsored voluntary cooperative groups. In addition to buying, warehousing, and distribution, these groups offer members services such as store design and layout, site selection, bookkeeping and inventory management systems, and employee training programs.

Corporate Retail Chains

A **retail chain** is a company operating multiple retail units under common ownership and usually having some centralization of decision making in defining and implementing its strategy. Retail chains can range in size from a drugstore with two stores to retailers with over 1,000 stores such as Safeway, Wal-Mart, Kmart, and JCPenney. Some retail chains are divisions of larger corporations or holding companies. For example, Venator owns Foot Locker, Lady Foot Locker, Champs, Afterthoughts, and Northern Reflections; Intimate Brands owns Victoria's Secret, Cacique, and Bath & Body Works; and Dayton Hudson Corporation owns Dayton's, Hudson's, Marshall Field's, Mervyn's, and Target.

There has been considerable concern that corporate retail chains will eventually drive independent retailers out of business. For example, Wal-Mart and other discount store chains have pursued a strategy of opening full-line discount stores and supercenters in the outskirts of small towns. These stores offer a broader selection of merchandise at much lower prices than previously available from local retailers. Due to scale economies and an efficient distribution system, corporate chains can sell at low prices. This forces some directly competing local retailers out of business and alters the community fabric.

On the other hand, local retailers offering complementary merchandise and services can prosper. When large chain stores open, more consumers are attracted to the community from surrounding areas. Thus the market for the local stores expands. While chain stores may have cost advantages over local retailers, large retail chains can be very bureaucratic, stifling managers' creativity with excessive rules and procedures. Often, all stores in the chain have the same merchandise and services, while local retailers can provide merchandise compatible with local market needs. Finally, the chain stores do employ 200 to 300 people from the local community.[53]

Trends in Corporate Retail Chains   In addition to the mergers and acquisitions leading to consolidation, the retail chains are focusing their expertise on managing a specific retail format rather than operating as a holding company for a diverse set of retail formats. For example, TJX is focusing on off-price retailing, CVS (originally named Melville) on drugstore retailing, May Company on department stores, and Kmart on full-line discount stores. By focusing their efforts, they are in a better position to develop a strategic advantage and increase their profitability, as Chapters 6 and 7 relate.

Franchising

Franchising is a contractual agreement between a franchisor and a franchisee that allows the franchisee to operate a retail outlet using a name and format developed and supported by the franchisor. Approximately one-third of all U.S. retail sales are made by franchisees. Exhibit 2–10 lists some retailers governed by franchise agreements.

In a franchise contract, the franchisee pays a lump sum plus a royalty on all sales for the right to operate a store in a specific location. The franchisee also agrees to operate the outlet in accordance with procedures prescribed by the franchisor. The franchisor provides assistance in locating and building the store, developing the products and/or services sold, management training, and advertising. To maintain the franchisee's reputation, the franchisor

EXHIBIT 2–10

Franchise Retailers

NAME	TYPE	NUMBER OF OUTLETS*	START-UP COST ($000)	ROYALTY (% OF SALES)
FAST FOOD/RESTAURANTS				
McDonald's	Hamburgers	25,336	$434K–1.4M	12.5% and up
Subway	Sub sandwiches	13,892	66K–175K	8.0
KFC	Chicken, fast food	9,835	1.1M–1.7M	4.0
Pizza Hut	Pizza	7,067	268K–1.4M	6.5
Dairy Queen	Ice cream	5,892	170K–622K	4.0–5.0
Taco Bell	Mexican food	4,947	191K–470K	5.5
Dunkin' Donuts	Donuts	5,144	132K–881K	4.9
Denny's	Restaurant	1,760	392K–711K	4.0
Long John Silver's	Seafood, fast food	1,262	500K–800K	4.0
MERCHANDISE RETAILERS				
7-Eleven	Convenience stores	18,154	12K+	Varies
GNC	Health food	4,289	125K–268K	6.0
Medicine Shoppe	Pharmacy	1,292	67K–117K	2–5.5
SERVICES RETAILERS				
Mail Boxes Etc.	Postal services	3,811	118K–199K	5.0
Coldwell Banker	Real estate services	2,998	23K–477K	Up to 6.0
Carlson Wagonlit	Travel services	2,456	3K–151K	$1.2K–6K
Merry Maids	House cleaning	1,165	27K–44K	5–7
Budget	Auto rental	3,138	166K–449K	7.5
Jazzercise	Fitness	5,171	1.5K–20K	Up to 20

Source: "21st Annual Franchising 500," *Entrepreneur*, January 2000, pp. 195–295. Reprinted with permission of Entrepreneur Magazine, 2000, www.entrepreneur.com.

*Company-owned and -franchised.

also makes sure that all outlets provide the same quality of services and products.

The franchise ownership format attempts to combine advantages of owner-managed businesses with efficiencies of centralized decision making in chain store operations. Franchisees are motivated to make their store successful because they receive the profits (after the royalty is paid). The franchisor is motivated to develop new products and systems and to promote the franchise because it receives a royalty on all sales. Advertising, product development, and system development are efficiently done by the franchisor, with costs shared by all franchisees.

Other Forms of Ownership
Some retail outlets are owned by their customers; others are owned by government agencies. In **consumer cooperatives,** customers own and operate the retail establishment. Customers have ownership shares, hire full-time managers, and share in the store's profits through price reductions or dividends. The best-known consumer cooperatives are credit unions that provide financial services. Retailing View 2.5 describes a unique cooperative selling outdoors equipment.

Local, state, and federal government agencies sometimes own retail establishments. For example, the Army and Air Force Exchange Service, with sales over $7 billion, provides retail services for military personnel at 24,000 retail outlets on military bases in 24 countries.

RECREATIONAL EQUIPMENT INC. (REI) IS ONE of the largest outdoor specialty retail chains and also the United State's largest consumer cooperative. By paying a $15 one-time fee, customers become members and co-owners of the company. Their share in the company profits is based on the amount of their purchases. REI's goal is to refund 10 percent of purchases to members in the form of dividends that can be used to make future purchases at REI or redeemed for cash.

REI's 48 stores generate over $475 million annually. The company is noted for its commitment to high-performance mountain climbing and outdoor gear. Julie Writing, REI merchandise manager for footware and apparel, asserts, "People know they can walk into REI and see the best hiking boot wall in the U.S."—an assertion most people in the industry support. REI works closely with its vendors to improve the performance of the products it sells. For example, REI consulted with a vendor to reengineer a hiking boot for women. The hiking boot buyer says, "We don't jump on trends. We have been selling hiking boots for 58 years. That's the core of our business and that will never change." And employees are encouraged to try out REI merchandise on their outdoor adventures supported by the company's REI Employee Challenge Grant program.

In the face of growing competition in the outdoor market, REI is transforming itself into a hipper retailer. Its Seattle flagship store is an exciting shopping experience with a huge 65-foot–high, freestanding climbing rock, mountain bike paths, and "rain rooms" so customers can test all their equipment before buying it. Use of materials such as raw wood, unpainted steel, and concrete reflects REI's core val-

This climbing wall in REI's flagship Seattle store gives customers an opportunity to try out equipment.

ues of honesty, authenticity, and straightforwardness. Within a year, this redesigned store environment boosted REI's sales significantly.

Source: Bruce Nussbaum, "Blueprint for Business," *Business Week,* November 3, 1997, p. 112; Mark Tedeschi, "2 Ways Out: Managing the Outdoor Market," *Footwear News,* April 1994, p. 12; and company documents.

SUMMARY This chapter explained different types of retailers and how they compete with different retail mixes to sell merchandise and services to customers. To collect statistics about retailing, the federal government classifies retailers by type of merchandise and services sold. But this classification method may not be useful in determining a retailer's major competitors. A more useful approach for understanding the retail marketplace is classifying retailers based on their retail mix, the merchandise variety and assortment, services, location, pricing, and promotion decisions made to attract customers.

Over the past 30 years, U.S. retail markets have been characterized by the emergence of many new retail institutions. Traditional institutions (supermarkets and department, discount, and specialty stores) have been joined by category specialists, superstores, convenience stores, home improvement centers, warehouse clubs, off-price retailers, catalog showrooms, and hypermarkets. In addition, there has been substantial growth in services retailing. The inherent differences between services and merchandise result in services retailers emphasizing store management while merchandise retailers emphasize inventory control issues.

Traditional retail institutions have changed in response to these new retailers. For example, department stores have increased their emphasis on fashion-oriented apparel and improved the services they offer. Supermarkets are focusing more attention on meal solutions and perishables. Appendix 2A provides guidelines for comparing competing retailers' retail mixes and Appendix 2B describes theories of retail change.

KEY TERMS

assortment, *40*

breadth of merchandise, *41*

category specialist, *54*

closeout retailer, *48*

combination store, *46*

consumer cooperative, *66*

convenience store, *47*

conventional supermarket, *45*

department store, *49*

depth of merchandise, *41*

drugstore, *52*

factory outlet, *58*

franchising, *65*

full-line discount store, *51*

home improvement center, *57*

hypermarket, *58*

leased department, *50*

lifestyle retailing, *52*

off-price retailer, *57*

outlet store, *58*

retail chain, *65*

retailer-sponsored cooperative, *64*

services retailer, *60*

single-price retailer, *58*

SKU (stock keeping unit), *40*

specialty department store, *50*

specialty store, *52*

supercenter, *46*

superstore, *46*

variety, *40*

warehouse club, *46*

wholesale-sponsored voluntary cooperative group, *64*

DISCUSSION QUESTIONS AND PROBLEMS

1. Distinguish between variety and assortment. Why are these important elements of retail market structure?

2. How can small independent retailers compete against the large national chains?

3. What do off-price retailers need to do to compete against other formats in the future?

4. Compare and contrast the retail mixes of convenience stores, traditional supermarkets, superstores, and warehouse stores. Can all of these food retail institutions survive over the long run? Why?

5. How can retailers that emphasize low price (such as discount stores and category specialists) improve customer service without increasing costs and, thus, prices?

6. The same brand and model personal computer is sold in specialty computer stores, discount stores, category specialists, and warehouse stores. Each type of retailer offers a different retailing mix for selling it. Why?

7. Since the 1970s, U.S. department store sales haven't kept pace with overall retail sales growth. Internet retailers,

specialty stores, category specialists, and mail order firms have captured American consumers' interest, reducing traditional department stores' market share and profits. Will this trend continue and eventually cause the department store as we now know it to become extinct. Why? How might department stores reverse this trend?

8. A chef wants to open an Italian restaurant and plans to do an analysis of the competition. Besides other Italian restaurants in town, what types of retailers might be considered competition for her restaurant?

9. Which of the store-based retail formats discussed in this chapter is most vulnerable to competition from Internet retailers? Why? Which is least vulnerable? Why?

10. Many experts believe that customer service is one of retailing's most important issues in the new millennium. How can retailers that emphasize price (such as discount stores, category specialists, and off-price retailers) improve customer service without increasing costs and, thus, prices?

SUGGESTED READINGS

Andersen, Arthur. *Small Store Survival: Success Strategies for Retailers.* New York: J. Wiley, 1997.

Crispell, Diane, and Henry Miller. "Retailing's Next Decade." *American Demographics*, May 1997, pp. 4, 6–10.

"The DSN Top 200." *Discount Store News*, July 2000.

Elango, B., and Vance Fried. "Franchising Research: A Literature Review and Synthesis." *Journal of Small Business Management* 35 (July 1997), pp. 68–81.

"Global Powers in Retailing." *Stores Special Supplement*, February 1999.

Michman, Ronald, and Alan Greco. *Retailing Triumphs and Blunders.* Westport, CT: Quorum, 1995.

"Reinventing the Discount Store." *Discount Store News*, May 15, 1995, pp. 37–71.

Schroeder, Carol. *Specialty Shop Retailing.* New York: Wiley, 1997.

Sheridan, Mike. "Keeping an eye on the Future." *Shopping Center World*, November 1998, pp. 1–3.

"69th Annual Report of the Grocery Industry." *Progressive Grocer*, April 2000.

"Top 100 Retailers." *Stores*, August 2000.

"The State of the Industry." *Chain Store Age Executive*, August 2000.

Zeithaml, Valarie, and Mary Jo Bitner. *Services Marketing.* New York: McGraw-Hill, 1996.

APPENDIX **2A**

Comparison Shopping

All retailers learn about their competitors through comparison shopping. Comparison shopping might be as informal as walking through a competitor's store and looking around. But a structured analysis is more helpful in developing a retail offering that will attract consumers from a competitor's store.

The first step in the process is to define the scope of the comparison. For example, the comparison might be between two retail chains, two specific stores, two departments, or two categories of merchandise. The appropriate scope depends on the responsibilities of the person undertaking the comparison. For example, CEOs of retail chains would be interested in comparing their chain with a competitor's. Comparisons might focus on chains' financial resources, inventory levels, number of stores and employees, store locations, merchandise sold, employee compensation programs, and return policies. Thus, CEOs would examine factors for which the corporate office is responsible.

On the other hand, store managers would be interested in comparing their store with a competing store. For example, department store managers would want to know more about other department stores anchoring the mall where they're located. Buyers and department managers would focus on specific areas of merchandise for which they're responsible.

Exhibit 2–11 lists questions to consider when comparison shopping. Exhibit 2–12 suggests a format for comparing merchandise, in this case lug-sole shoes in JCPenney and a men's shoe store.

EXHIBIT 2–11

Examples of Issues
to Address in
Comparison
Shopping

MERCHANDISE PRESENTATION

1. How is the selling floor laid out? What selling areas are devoted to specific types of merchandise? How many square feet are devoted to each area?
2. Where are the different selling areas located? Are they in heavy traffic areas? By restrooms? On the main aisle? On a secondary aisle? How does this location affect sales volume for merchandise in the area?
3. What kind of fixtures are used in each selling area (faceouts, rounders, cubes, bunkers, tables, gondolas)?
4. Are aisles, walls, and columns used to display merchandise?
5. What is the lighting for sales areas (focus, overhead, bright, toned down)?
6. How is the merchandise organized in the selling areas (by type, price point, vendor, style, color)?
7. Evaluate the housekeeping of the selling areas. Are they cluttered or messy? Are they well maintained and organized?
8. What's the overall atmosphere or image of the selling areas? What effect does the lighting, fixturing, spacing, and visual merchandising have on customers?
9. What type of customer (age, income, fashion orientation) would be attracted to the store and each selling area within it?

SALES SUPPORT/CUSTOMER SERVICES

1. How many salespeople are in each department? Is the department adequately staffed?
2. How are salespeople dressed? Do they have a professional appearance?
3. Do salespeople approach customers promptly? How soon after entering a selling area is a customer greeted? How do customers respond to the level of service?
4. Evaluate salespeople's product knowledge.
5. Do salespeople suggest add-on merchandise?
6. Where, if applicable, are fitting rooms in relation to the selling floor? In what condition are they? Are they supervised? Are there enough fitting rooms to meet demand?
7. How many registers are on the selling floor? Are they well staffed and well stocked with supplies?
8. What services (credit charges acceptance, gift wrapping, delivery, special ordering, bridal registry, alterations, other) does the store offer?
9. What level of customer service is provided in the selling area?

MERCHANDISE (EACH CATEGORY)

1. Who are the key vendors?
2. How deep are the assortments for each vendor?
3. What are the private labels and how important are they?
4. What are the low, average, and top prices for merchandise in the category?

SUMMARY AND CONCLUSIONS

1. Who is the store's target customer?
2. What are the competitor's strengths and weaknesses?
3. How can we capture more business from the competitor?

APPENDIX 2B

Theories of Retail Evolution

A number of theories have been developed to explain the present structure of the retail industry and predict how the structure will change. No individual theory explains all of the changes in the retailing environment. Yet as a whole, the theories provide insights for understanding the evolution of retail institutions.[54]

Four theories of retail evolution are the wheel of retailing, accordion theory, dialectic process, and natural selection. The first two theories are cyclical theories. These theories suggest that retail institutions go through cycles, beginning with one state and then returning to that state at some time in the future. The last two theories, dialectic process and natural selection, are evolutionary theories suggesting that changes in retail institutions are similar to patterns observed in biological evolution.

EXHIBIT 2–12 Format for Merchandise Comparisons

Retailer	Factors	Lug sole casual shoes			Comments
JC Penney	Style	3 eyelet oxford			
	Brands	St. Johns Bay (private)			
	Price	$35			
	% mix	5%			
	Depth	36 pair			
	Breadth	4 colors			
Father/Son Shoes	Style	3 eyelet oxford	Tie suede	Chakka suede	
	Brands	British Knights Private	Private	Private	
	Price	$38.99–39.99	$29.99	$37.95	
	% mix	10%	5%	5%	
	Depth	24 pairs	36 pairs	12 pairs	
	Breadth	3 colors	3 colors	2 colors	
Harwyns	Style	2 eyelet oxford	Tie suede		
	Brands	British Knights	Private		
	Price	$39.99	$29.95		
	% mix	5%	5%		
	Depth	36 pairs	36 pairs		
	Breadth	3 colors	3 colors		

Style For clothing, style might be the fabric or cut. For example, sweater styles might be split into wool, cotton, or polyblend and V-neck, crewneck, or cardigan.

Brands The identifying label. Indicate whether or not the brand is a national brand or store brand.

Price The price marked on the merchandise. If the item has been marked down, indicate the original price and the marked-down price.

Percent mix The percentage of the total assortment devoted to this style of merchandise.

Depth The amount of inventory for this style. The amount on display is one indicator of inventory depth. Another indicator is the amount of space devoted to the style.

Breadth The number of SKUs in this style.

The Wheel of Retailing One of the first and most famous frameworks for explaining changes in retailing institutions is the wheel of retailing (Exhibit 2–13). The wheel represents phases through which some types of retailers pass.[55] The cycle begins with retailers attracting customers by offering low price and low service. Over time, these retailers want to expand their market and they begin to stock more expensive merchandise, provide more services, and open more convenient locations. This trading-up process increases the retailers' costs and the prices of their merchandise, creating opportunity for new low-price retailers to enter the market.

The evolution of the department store illustrates the wheel of retailing theory. In its entry phase, as Exhibit 2–13 shows, the department store was a low-cost, low-service venture. After World War II, department stores moved into the trading-up phase. They upgraded their facilities, stock selection, advertising, and service. Today, department stores are in the vulnerability phase. They're

EXHIBIT 2-13

The Wheel
of Retailing

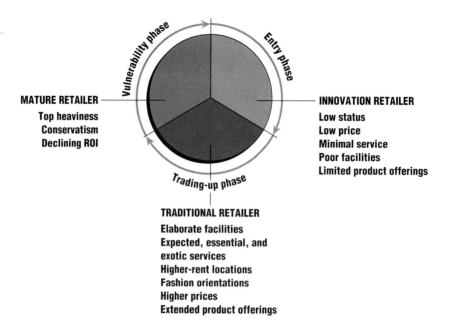

MATURE RETAILER

Top heaviness
Conservatism
Declining ROI

INNOVATION RETAILER

Low status
Low price
Minimal service
Poor facilities
Limited product offerings

TRADITIONAL RETAILER

Elaborate facilities
Expected, essential, and
exotic services
Higher-rent locations
Fashion orientations
Higher prices
Extended product offerings

vulnerable to various types of low-cost, low-service formats such as full-line discount stores and category specialists.

The first phase of full-line discount stores was the national mass merchandise chains such as Sears and JCPenney. But over the years, these retailers have also succumbed to the turning of the wheel of retailing. Both of these retailers have made a concerted effort to upgrade their stores and merchandise. For instance, it is now hard to distinguish between a new Penney store and a department store at the same mall, so Sears and Penney became vulnerable to new forms of low-price, low-service retailers just like other department store chains.

Now these low-cost, low-service full-line discount stores such as Target, Kmart, and Wal-Mart stores offer credit, more fashionable merchandise than before, some carpeted departments, and limited service. One could view these discount stores as beginning to enter the trading-up phase of the wheel of retailing.

The new entry in the low-status/low-price arena is the warehouse club. These stores, such as Sam's Wholesale Club and Costco, require customers to become members and are a cross between wholesale warehouses and discount stores. The question remaining for warehouse clubs is whether they'll proceed to the trading-up phase on the wheel of retailing. This question raises a general criticism of the wheel. Some types of retailers never trade up. A corollary criticism is that some institutions don't begin as low-price/low-service entrants. Upscale fashion specialty stores, for instance, have never fit the wheel of retailing pattern.

The Accordion Theory   The Accordion Theory, the second cyclical theory, proposes that the retail institutions fluctuate from the strategy of offering many merchandise categories with a shallow assortment to the strategy of offering a deep assortment with a limited number of categories. This expansion and contraction calls to mind an accordion. During this nation's early development, relatively small general stores succeeded by offering rural Americans many categories of merchandise under one roof. As towns grew, they were able to support retail specialists like shoe, clothing, drug, and food stores. Department stores de-

EXHIBIT 2–14

The Dialectic
Process

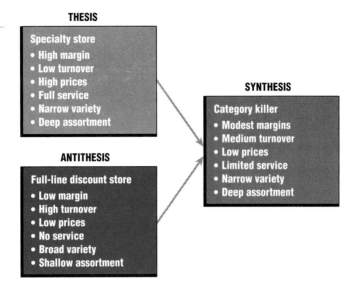

THESIS

Specialty store
- High margin
- Low turnover
- High prices
- Full service
- Narrow variety
- Deep assortment

ANTITHESIS

Full-line discount store
- Low margin
- High turnover
- Low prices
- No service
- Broad variety
- Shallow assortment

SYNTHESIS

Category killer
- Modest margins
- Medium turnover
- Low prices
- Limited service
- Narrow variety
- Deep assortment

veloped during the next expansion of the accordion. Department stores, somewhat like giant general stores, again offered customers multiple merchandise categories under one roof. This time, however, the depth of selection improved as well. The next contraction of the retail accordion results from specialty stores' tendency to have become even more specialized in the past two decades. These retail formats known as category killers or category specialists (such as Toys "R" Us, Circuit City, and Sports Authority) offer consumers deep selections in a limited number of merchandise categories.[56]

Dialectic Process   The first of the two evolutionary theories of change in retail institutions is the dialectic process of thesis, antithesis, and synthesis (Exhibit 2–14). This theory implies that new retail institutions result from stores borrowing characteristics from other very different competitors, much like children are a combination of the genes of their parents. The established retail institution, known for relatively high margins, low turnover, and plush facilities, is the specialty store—the thesis. Discount stores in their early form were the antithesis of service-oriented specialty stores. That is, they were characteristically low-margin, high-turnover, Spartan operations, with broad variety. Over time, characteristics from both department stores and discount stores were synthesized to form category specialist stores like Best Buy and Sports Authority.[57]

Natural Selection   A final theory, natural selection, has the strongest intuitive appeal for explaining change in retailing institutions. It follows Charles Darwin's view that organisms evolve and change on the basis of survival of the fittest. In retailing, those institutions best able to adapt to changes in customers, technology, competition, and legal environments have the greatest chance of success. For instance, the increased number of women in the workforce and America's interest in physical fitness have made salad bars successful in some grocery stores. Video stores appeared in virtually every neighborhood in America only a few years after videocassette recorder technology was developed. Department stores have tried to battle specialty stores' competitive inroads by creating small specialty stores or boutiques within their stores.[58]

Dionn Schaffner
Vice President of Marketing
Garden.com, Inc.

WHEN I CAME TO GARDEN.COM as vice president of marketing, I never dreamed it would be such a creative endeavor. I guess I was lucky. My undergraduate degree in computer science coupled with an MBA, both from Stanford, have enabled me to deal with the technical side of this business and at the same time tackle the complex marketing issues surrounding building a brand in an e-retailing environment. • Let me explain why we think we can get and keep customers better than our bricks-and-mortar competition (the local nursery and the mail order catalog). We have always strived to be the entire solution for everyone's gardening needs. • Suppose you have never planted a garden and you just moved into your first house. At Garden.com, we can help you plan your garden. We can tell you what will grow well in particular locations—sun versus shade, north versus south. You can even allow our garden planner software to plot out the garden so you can see exactly what it will look like. If you have specific questions, you can send e-mails to our garden doctors. They can answer anything from "How do I start?" to "What do I do about those little white funny things crawling around on my gardenias?" • Once you buy from us, you don't even need to worry about when to plant particular plants or seeds. Since we know where you live, we arrange for your plants or seeds to be delivered at ideal times. After all, if you live in Minnesota, you don't want to plant strawberries until May. Since many of our customers purchase months ahead of delivery, we include a Care Guide with each plant. You can also go to our website and access articles about the plants in your garden, planting tips, and idiosyncrasies about your region—basically anything you need to be a better gardener. • Our relationship with our customers doesn't stop when the products are delivered, however. If you like, we'll send you reminders about how to prepare your plants for winter or when to prune or fertilize. Since we are dealing with living things, we want to do everything we can to help our customers throughout the lives of their plants. • Because gardening is so seasonal, we do all we can to keep our customers coming to our site throughout the year. We have a great gift line, for instance. One of our biggest sellers is a culinary herb wreath. It is a decorative living herb wreath that is typically hung in the kitchen. If you want birdhouse earrings, we have those too! • You can take advantage of a lot of our services even if you don't buy anything. Our feeling is that we want to give every potential Garden.com customer a really good reason for coming to our web page. They might not buy this time, but if they feel good about us, chances are they will buy next time. We believe this is the way to get and keep loyal customers—one at a time.

3

Electronic and Nonstore Retailing

QUESTIONS

- What are the different types of nonstore retailers?

- What factors will affect the growth of electronic retailing?

- Will consumers buy merchandise with important "touch-and-feel" attributes over the Internet?

- What types of companies are well positioned to become leaders in electronic retailing?

- Will the Internet lead to manufacturers bypassing retailers to sell directly to consumers?

JUDY JAMISON WANTS to buy a present for her son Dave, whose birthday is in several weeks. She goes to her home computer, accesses her personal shopper program called FRED, and has the following interactive dialog:

Fred: Do you wish to browse, go to a specific store, or buy a specific item?
Judy: Specific item
Fred: Occasion? [Menu appears and Judy selects.]
Judy: Gift
Fred: For whom? [Menu appears on screen.]
Judy: Dave
Fred: Type of gift? [Menu appears.]
Judy: Toy/Game
Fred: Price range? [Menu appears.]
Judy: $75–$100
[Now FRED goes out and literally shops the world electronically, visiting the servers for companies selling toys and games in Europe, Asia, Africa, Australia, and North and South America.]
Fred: 121 items have been identified. How many do you want to review?
[Menu appears.]
Judy: Just 5
[Fred selects the five best alternatives based on information about Dave's age and preference for toys and Judy's preference for nonviolent, educational toys. The

five toys appear on the screen with the price, brand name, and the retailer listed beneath each one. Judy clicks on each toy to get more information about the toy. With another click, she sees a full-motion video of a child Dave's age playing with the toy. She selects the toy she finds most appealing.

Fred: How would you like to pay for this? [Menu appears.]

Judy: American Express

Fred: Etoys [the firm selling the toy Judy selected] suggests several books that appeal to children who like the toy you have selected. Do you want to review these books?

Judy: Yes

[The books are displayed on the screen. Judy reviews each of the books and decides to order one.]

Fred: Would you like this gift wrapped?

Judy: Yes

[The different designs for wrapping paper are displayed on the screen and Judy selects paper with a baseball motif.]

Fred: Just a reminder. You have not purchased hosiery in 30 days. Do you wish to reorder at this time?

Judy: Yes

Fred: Same shades?

Judy: Yes

Shopping electronically is very convenient for this two-income, time-pressured family.

This scenario illustrates the benefits electronic retailers can offer their customers. In addition to the convenience and security of shopping from home, electronic retailers can tailor their offering to individual customers and provide the information customers need to make satisfactory purchase decisions.

In this chapter, we review the growing interest in retailing over the Internet as well as other non-store retailing formats: catalog and direct-mail retailing, direct selling, TV home shopping, and vending machines. While only 10 percent of retail sales are made through nonstore channels, sales in nonstore formats are growing faster than store sales. New computer and communication technologies now make it possible for consumers to shop the world from their homes. Although only in its infancy, electronic retailing has the potential to fundamentally change the way people shop as well as the structure of the consumer goods and retail industries.

NONSTORE VERSUS STORE-BASED RETAILERS

Nonstore retailing is a form of retailing in which sales are made to consumers without using stores. The various types of nonstore retailers are defined in terms of the medium they use to communicate with their customers. As Exhibit 3–1 shows, electronic retailers use an interactive computer or computerlike interface to communicate with customers; catalog and direct-mail retailers communicate

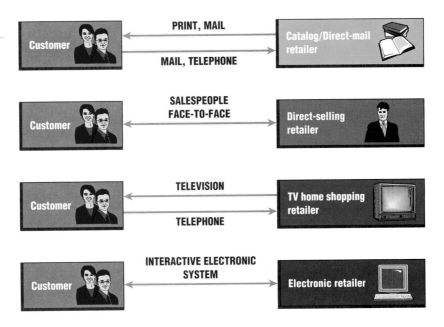

EXHIBIT 3–1

Types of Nonstore
Retailers

using printed material distributed through the mail; direct-selling retailers communicate with customers through a personal, face-to-face contact by a salesperson; TV home shopping retailers use television; and vending machine retailers have limited communications through the display of the merchandise in the machine.[1]

The nature of the communications between the retailer and its customers differs for the various nonstore retailing formats. Communications in direct selling are highly interactive. The salesperson responds immediately to customer comments and questions; responses are tailored to the needs of each customer. Electronic retailing has the potential for providing this same high level of interactivity. On the other hand, the communications in TV home shopping, vending machines, and catalog retailing are not very interactive. All customers get the same information from these nonstore retailers and responses to customer inquiries are delayed.

The annual sales made by the nonstore format are shown in Exhibit 3–2. More than 90 percent of all retail sales are made in stores. However, nonstore sales now are growing at a rate of 11 percent a year, while sales in retail stores are increasing at only 3.5 percent per year. The high growth rate for nonstore retailing is primarily due to the growth of electronic retailing. The growth of catalog retail sales is slowing and sales in other nonstore retailing formats such as TV home shopping, direct selling, and vending machines are stagnant.

Refact Wal-Mart's sales in 1999 were greater than all U.S. nonstore retail sales.

Most nonstore retailers offer consumers the convenience of selecting and purchasing merchandise at a time (typically 24 hours a day, seven days a week) and location of their choosing. Usually, after the choice is made and the order placed, the merchandise is delivered a few days later to the customer's home. But nonstore retailing transactions also take place at work or at a neighbor's house.

EXHIBIT **3–2**

Sales by Nonstore
Format

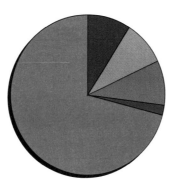

Sales by Nonstore Format—2000

- ▨ **Catalog and direct mail $186 million (71%)**
- ▪ **Electronic retailing $24 million (9%)**
- ▨ **Vending machines $24 million (9%)**
- ▨ **Direct selling $24 million (9%)**
- ▪ **TV home shopping $4 million (2%)**

TOTAL = $262 million

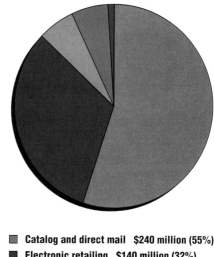

Sales by Nonstore Format—2003 (projection)

- ▨ **Catalog and direct mail $240 million (55%)**
- ▪ **Electronic retailing $140 million (32%)**
- ▨ **Vending machines $30 million (6%)**
- ▨ **Direct selling $30 million (6%)**
- ▪ **TV home shopping $4 million (1%)**

TOTAL = $444 million

Source: "State of the Industry: Nonstore Retailing: Nonstore Retailing Gains Favor with Consumers,"*Chain Storage Age*, August 1999, pg. 29A; *Statistical Fact Book*. New York: Direct Marketing Association, 2000; *2000 Direct Selling and Growth Outlook Survey*. Washington, DC: Direct Selling Association, 2000; Forrester Research; and Dataquest.

As we will discuss in Chapter 4, these benefits of nonstore retailing are very appealing to time-conscious consumers and consumers who can't easily go to stores, such as the handicapped, the elderly, mothers with young children, and rural residents.[2]

Nonstore retailing can involve highly personalized services (such as those provided by Mary Kay beauty consultants) or the very impersonal interactions associated with a vending machine. The merchandise offered by a nonstore re-tailer ranges from the broad assortment found in the 1,000-page JCPenney catalog and at its Internet site (www.jcpenney.com) to narrow product lines such as Dilmah's teas from plantations in the highlands of Ceylon (www.dilmahtea.com), mustards (www.mustardstore.com), or steel drums (www.steelofthenight.com). Retailing View 3.1 describes a nonstore retailer that revolutionized the retail bedding industry.

While nonstore retailing provides unique convenience benefits over store-based retailing, store-based retailers provide some benefits not available from nonstore retailers. For example, customers ordering over the Internet or from a catalog can't touch and feel the merchandise, try it on, attend sessions on how to use it, or have it altered prior to purchase. If customers are dissatis-fied with the merchandise, they can't simply go to a store and return it. When

BY USING MANY OF THE DIRECT MARKETING, order fulfillment, and customer techniques now employed by electronic retailers, 1-800-Mattress, a 25-year-old retailer based in New York City, has changed the nature of bedding retailing. Napoleon ("Nap") Barragan, the founder and CEO, believes in the principle that the three most important factors in retailing are location, location, and location—and the best location is inside the customer's mind and home.

Through customer referrals and advertising on television and radio, 1-800-Mattress generates 3,000 inbound phone calls daily, 365 days a year. These calls are converted into 500 sales daily—a volume that enables 1-800-Mattress to turn its 2,500-SKU inventory 50 to 60 times a year.

Barragan was one of the first retailers to recognize the time pressures facing households. He implemented a delivery system that enables customers to choose the time when their mattress is delivered. Customers can select delivery times within a two-hour window for any day or night of the week, in-

cluding the day the order is placed. "We were the first to have round-the-clock service, delivery, and a 30-day comfort guarantee," says Barragan.

Barragan's success has bred a host of competitors. With over 80 toll-free numbers for bedding retailers (including Macy's) in the New York City metropolitan area, price competition is keen. For example, Sleepy launched a full-scale advertising attack against 1-800-Mattress, promising a free mattress and $500 to any customer who brings in an ad with a price lower than Sleepy's price.

In response, 1-800-Mattress uses an extensive database of mattress model numbers, brands, and current competitor prices. With this database, its telephone salespeople can match competitor prices and suggest comparable models when the requested model is not in stock.

Source: "Bedtime Story," *Chain Store Age,* July 1999, pp. 50–52; and Leslie Walker, "Losing Sleep in a Mattress War," *The Washington Post,* April 1, 1999, p. E01.

---

returning merchandise to a nonstore retailer, customers have to repackage the merchandise and send it to the retailer, often at their own expense. The following sections discuss each of the major nonstore forms of retailing.

ELECTRONIC RETAILING

Electronic retailing (also called e-tailing and Internet retailing) is a retail format in which the retailer and customer communicate with each other through an interactive electronic network. In response to the customer's inquiries, the electronic retailer transmits information and graphics to the customer's computer or TV. After an electronic dialog between the retailer and customer, the customer can order merchandise directly through the interactive network or by telephone; the merchandise then is typically delivered to the customer's home.

The scenario portrayed at the beginning of this chapter illustrates some of the unique properties of the Internet: interactivity, information intensity, and global reach. In the scenario, Judy specifies the type of merchandise sought and then FRED, an electronic agent, communicates with retailers around the world, locating a large group of alternatives. Using information about Judy's personal tastes, FRED reduces the large number of alternatives down to a small set that are of most interest to Judy. Then Judy has access to extensive information about each alternative. After Judy selects the merchandise she wants to buy, the retailer suggests accessories. Again the presentation of these accessories is personalized to Judy.

Mustardstore.com offers a deep assortment of merchandise in one product category.

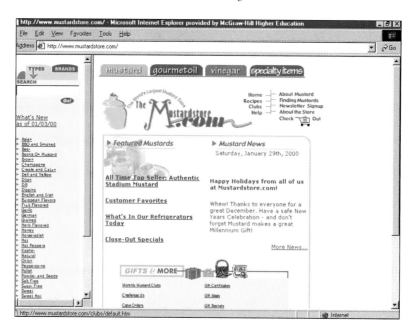

INTERNET EXERCISE   Go to the following retail sites and shop for a pair of pants.

JCPenney, www.penney.com
Wal-Mart, www.walmart.com
L.L. Bean, www.llbean.com
Lands' End, www.landsend.com

How do you compare your experience shopping for pants on the Internet to shopping in a local store? What are the advantages and disadvantages of the Internet shopping experience? How does your shopping experience differ from the scenario at the beginning of the chapter?

Current electronic retailing sites are not like the scenario at the beginning of the chapter. Shopping at many current retail sites is like looking through a lot of catalogs. Most of the present Internet retail sites do not offer you extensive information about the merchandise or the opportunity to tailor the selection and presentation of merchandise to your interests and needs.

The bandwidth of the Internet connection into most households limits the interactivity as well as the amount and quality of information that can be presented. Bandwidth is basically the size of the electronic pipe bringing information on the web to you. When the bandwidth increases, more information can be downloaded quicker from the web to your home computer.

Most household computers are connected to the Internet through small pipes—standard telephone lines. It would take a long time for Judy Jamison to download the short full-motion videos showing children playing with the five toys selected for her by FRED through this small pipe. However, AT&T, regional Bell operating companies, and satellite communications firms are making substantial investments in a number of different technologies to provide broad-band Internet connection (big pipes) into households. Experts predict that a large percentage of U.S. households will have this broadband service by 2002.[3] Thus, over the next few years, the quantity and quality of information you get from electronic retailers will improve dramatically.

Factors Affecting the Growth of Electronic Retailing

Electronic retailing is less than 1 percent retail sales in the United States and even a smaller percentage of retail sales in Europe and Asia. However, the annual growth of U.S. electronic retail sales is over 100 percent. If this growth continues, electronic retailing will have a major impact on the retail industry, significantly decreasing retail sales in stores.[4] Retailing View 3.2 describes eToys, an electronic retailer, that is already making a significant impact on the toy industry and toy retailing.

Three critical factors affecting the adoption of a new innovation such as shopping electronically are (1) the ease with which customers can try the innovation, (2) the perceived risks in adopting the innovation, and (3) the benefits offered by the innovation compared to the present alternatives.[6]

Trying Out Electronic Shopping   To experience electronic shopping, consumers need to have access to the Internet and be able to communicate with electronic retailers through the Internet using a computer. In 1999, over 180 million people around the world had access to the Internet with a majority of these web surfers living in North America. (See Exhibit 3–3.) While the early users of the Internet were mainly male, educated, and with higher income than the general U.S. population, as this innovation diffuses, the demographics of Internet users are beginning to reflect the general population. Women now comprise slightly less than half of all Internet users in the United States, which is important for electronic retailers because women do most of the shopping.

The substantial Internet usage by Generation Y (see Chapter 4) suggests a bright future for electronic retailing. Teenagers and children constitute one of the fastest growing Internet populations, with 77 million people under 18 expected to be online globally by 2005. Surfing the Net is a highly regarded activity

Refact In 1999, 45 percent of U.S. households had Internet access and 57 percent of them had bought something over the Internet. Of the consumers making Internet purchases, 80 percent planned to spend more on the Internet in the next year and 57 percent planned to spend less in stores.[5]

Refact In 1999, 58 percent of U.S. Internet shoppers were men compared to 78 percent in 1998.[7]

EXHIBIT **3–3**

Number of Internet Users across the Globe

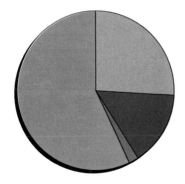

- North America   102 million (57%)
- Europe   47 million (26%)
- Asia/Pacific   27 million (15%)
- Other (Latin America, Near East, and Africa)   4 million (2%)

Source: "How Many People Are On-Line?" Nua, June 1999, www.nua.ie/surveys/how_many_online/index.html.

eToys: Winning the Toy War in Cyber Space

FOUNDER AND CEO TOBY LENK, a former VP for strategic planning for Disney's theme parks, did not start eToys until he understood the toy industry and what customers wanted when buying toys over the Internet. Even though eToys' annual sales are about 1 percent of industry giant Toys "R" Us's, its stock value is 50 percent higher. eToys achieved this success by providing a broad assortment, offering outstanding customer service, and paying attention to the little things that satisfy its customers.

The company has a cleanly designed, easy-to-use website that provides a welcome contrast to some pitfalls of shopping in stores: crowded parking lots, poor service, desired toys that are not in stock, and accompanying children who want to buy expensive or inappropriate merchandise. Online shoppers can focus their search through 15,000 SKUs on toys recommended by parenting magazines, or the best-sellers in different categories, or items costing under $20.

The company's culture stresses the importance of customer service. Signs in the gift wrapping station at the warehouse say FOR THE KIDS. Customer service employees are available to answer questions by phone or e-mail. They have access to samples of toys so they know how the toys are assembled and operated. E-mails are sent to customers informing them about where their order is in the shipping process.

But eToys goes beyond just shipping toys out the door. Customers can select gift wraps and dictate personalized cards to accompany a gift. The invoice sent with gifts does not include the price but has a personalized "to–from" tags on each gift. That way, multiple gifts to and from different people

eToys provides the convenience of shopping at home plus information and services not available from store-based competitors.

can be sent to the same address in one box. The company has a parent-password–protected gift registry as well as spare parts and repair services for toys.

eToys hired the president of operations from L.L. Bean to make sure that it has a cost-effective distribution system centered around its 1.5 million square feet of distribution centers in Utah and Virginia.

Source: Larry Armstrong, "The Toy War Is No Game," *Business Week,* August 9, 1999, p. 86; Jason Fry, "eToys Story," *The Wall Street Journal,* July 12, 1999, p. R38; and Adam Bryant, "A Lot of Play-Dough," *Newsweek,* May 31, 1999, p. 54.

---

by this age group. A study in Britain reports Internet users are described as clever, friendly, cool, trendy, and rich by both users and nonusers. As one would expect, entertainment products such as games, music, tickets, and videos are the most common purchases by these young consumers.[8]

However, the younger brothers and sisters of these young adults often cannot shop electronically because they do not have the credit cards required for payment by electronic retailers. Several Internet shopping sites are offering a way around this problem. IcanBuy.com (www.IcanBuy.com), DoughNET.com (www.DoughNET.com), and RocketCash (www.RocketCash.com) now let parents establish an account for their children using a credit card to set the initial balance. The teenager logs onto the site using a password, browses the site's electronic retailer partners, selects desired merchandise, and puts it in an electronic shopping cart. The shopping site takes care of the payment. Using their own passwords, parents can check up on the teen's buying habits and balance.[9]

But it's not just teenagers and young adults surfing the web. In the United States, adults over 50 years old are the fastest growing market going online, now comprising almost 20 percent of the Internet users. Seventy percent of Americans in this age group have home access to the Internet. Studies have found that older people are receptive to new technology and have the time, money, and enthusiasm to surf the web regularly. They spend an average of 130 minutes a day online, almost 50 percent more than any other age group. Their primary attraction to the Internet is the use of e-mail to stay in touch with long-distance family and friends. Older people tend to buy merchandise and services online because shopping in stores can be difficult for them.[10] Some websites providing services to this market segment are ThirdAge (www.ThirdAge.com) and SeniorNet (www.SeniorNet.org).[11]

> **Refact** Each month, 89 percent of the Internet users send e-mail and access information about a product or service.[12]

INTERNET EXERCISE   NUA Limited (www.nua.ie/surveys) compiles studies on electronic retailing. Go to the site, read the results of some of the studies, and make a list of some critical issues affecting the growth of electronic retailing.

Internet usage and electronic shopping is much less common in Europe than in the United States. This is due, in part, to differences in the payment systems for local telephone connections. In the United States, most people pay a flat rate for local telephone service, while Europeans typically are charged by the minute. Thus surfing the web for an extended period of time is much more expensive in Europe. In addition, Europeans tend to see shopping as a social activity while U.S. consumers often view shopping as a necessary activity to purchase needed merchandise. Some other obstacles to the growth of electronic shopping and other forms of nonstore retailing in Europe are the unreliable postal service in some countries, the tax differences across countries, and a greater concern about credit card security among Europeans.[13]

Perceived Risks in Electronic Shopping   A critical concern of consumers is that credit card transactions are not secure when shopping on the Internet. But these security risks have not arisen in actual usage because almost all electronic retailers use sophisticated technologies to encrypt communications. The perception of risk is diminishing as credit card companies promote the use of their cards on the Internet and inform customers that the customers will not be responsible for security lapses.[14]

Thus, a significant number of consumers in North America have Internet access now and Internet access is growing around the world. Technological developments are reducing the risk of electronic shopping by enabling secure transactions and increasing the amount and quality of information available to electronic shoppers by providing broadband connections to households. The primary factor determining the growth of electronic retailing will not be Internet access or technological limitations, but whether this new format can provide sufficient benefits over existing retail format to interest customers in surfing the Net rather than going to stores. In the next section, we compare the benefits offered by store-based and catalog retailers with those offered by electronic retailers.

> **Refact** Seventy-three percent of U.S. consumers are uncomfortable disclosing credit card and other financial details online to electronic retailers, while 62 percent feel secure about conducting bank transactions and paying bills online.[15]

Benefits of Shopping on the Internet

Although the electronic shopping experience described at the beginning of the chapter is appealing, current retail formats effectively satisfy most consumer needs. A wide variety of stores are convenient to most consumers in the United States. Just think of the number of stores you could go to in 15 minutes to buy a VCR, a shirt, or milk. And consumers who can't get to a store easily have a wide selection of catalogs they can order from. Electronic retailing sales will grow only if the format offers consumer advantages over other existing retail formats.

Exhibit 3–4 compares the benefits and costs to consumers of six retail formats: three store-based formats (described in Chapter 2) and three nonstore formats (the traditional catalog, the present electronic retailing offering, and the highly personalized and interactive electronic retailing offering described at the beginning of the chapter).[16]

Entertainment and Social Experience   In-store retail formats provide more benefits to consumers than simply having merchandise readily available and helping them buy it. For example, in-store shopping can be a stimulating experience for some people, providing a break in their daily routine and enabling consumers to interact with friends. Mall developers and in-store retailers place considerable emphasis on attracting customers by satisfying these needs.

All nonstore retail formats are limited in the degree to which they can satisfy these entertainment and social needs. Even the most attractive and inventive web pages and video clips will not be as exciting as the displays and activities in a Disney or Niketown store. Note that Exhibit 3–4 indicates that supermarkets are less effective at providing these entertainment and social benefits than other store-based retail formats because most people view grocery shopping as a chore to be accomplished as quickly as possible.[17]

EXHIBIT **3–4**   Dimensions Affecting Relative Attractiveness to Consumers of Alternative Retail Formats

BENEFIT TO CUSTOMERS	STORE-BASED RETAIL FORMATS			NONSTORE RETAIL FORMATS		
	SUPERMARKET	DEPARTMENT STORE	CATEGORY SPECIALIST	CATALOG	ELECTRONIC RETAILER (CURRENT)	ELECTRONIC RETAILER (FUTURE)
Entertainment	Low	High	Medium	Low	Low	Medium
Social interaction	Medium	High	Medium	Low	Low	Low
Personal security	Low	Low	Low	High	High	High
ORDERING AND GETTING MERCHANDISE						
Locations for placing orders	Few	Few	Few	Everywhere	Many	Many
Delivery time	Immediate	Immediate	Immediate	Days	Days	Days
NUMBER OF ALTERNATIVES						
Number	Medium	Medium	Low	Low	Medium	High
ASSISTANCE IN SCREENING ALTERNATIVES						
Assistance	Low	High	Medium	Low	Low	High
MERCHANDISE INFORMATION						
Quantity of information	Medium	Medium	Medium	Medium	Medium	High
Side-by-side comparisons	Medium	Low	Medium	Low	Low	High
FACTORS AFFECTING COST OF MERCHANDISE						
Retailers cost of operating stores	High	High	High	Low	Low	Low
Customer time cost	High	High	High	Low	Low	Low
Shipping costs	None	None	None	High	High	High

Safety   Security in malls and shopping areas is becoming an important concern for many shoppers. Nonstore retail formats have an advantage over store-based retailers by enabling customers to review merchandise and place orders from a safe environment—their homes.[18]

Ordering and Getting Merchandise   Electronic retailing, like most nonstore retail formats, enables consumers to order merchandise from many locations at any time of the day. However, consumers usually have to wait several days to get the merchandise. Thus, all nonstore retailers suffer in comparison to stores on this dimension.

The importance of getting merchandise to customers immediately depends on the type of buying situation and merchandise. For example, Hispanics typically buy wedding gifts just before they attend the ceremony and reception. Thus, they would be unlikely to buy wedding presents from nonstore retailers. Many items bought in a supermarket are perishable and must be taken home and stored in a refrigerator or consumed shortly after they are purchased. Thus an electronic supermarket retailer must be able to deliver orders to customers shortly after they are picked from a store or warehouse.

Number of Alternatives   As Exhibit 3–4 shows, a potential benefit of electronic retailing compared to other retail formats is the vast number of alternatives that become available to consumers. A person living in Columbus, Ohio, can shop electronically at Harrod's in London in less time than it takes to visit the local supermarket.

However, having a lot more alternatives to consider might not be that much of a benefit. Consumers rarely visit more than two outlets even when buying expensive consumer durables.[19] While it is easy to go from one web site to another, finding what you want is not so easy because each web site has a different interface that you have to learn to get the information you want.

Consider Judy Jamison's search with FRED. Does Judy really care if FRED found 10 or 121 toys initially? Having identified 121 Internet retail sites selling a product you might like, how many sites would you take the time to visit? The advantages of having a lot of alternatives is only meaningful if you have FRED to search through them and find a few items you might like to look at in detail.

Assistance in Screening Alternatives   A more significant potential benefit of electronic retailing is the ability to have an electronic agent like FRED search through a wide range of alternatives and select a small set for the customer to look at in detail. As indicated in Exhibit 3–4, service-oriented retailers like department and specialty stores also have this capability. Often sales associates in these stores know what their preferred customers want, select a few outfits, and arrange to show these outfits before the store opens or even take the outfits to the customer's office. FRED provides the same service as these super sales associates; however, FRED never is in a bad mood, is not paid anything to do its job, and is always available.

FRED is called an electronic agent. An **electronic agent** is a computer program that locates and selects alternatives based on some predetermined characteristics.[20] **Shopping bots** or **search engines** are computer programs that simply search for and provide a listing of all Internet sites selling a product category and/or brand with the price of the merchandise offered.

Using MySimon, a shopping bot, a customer can easily compare the prices for a Canon digital camera from different electronic retailers.

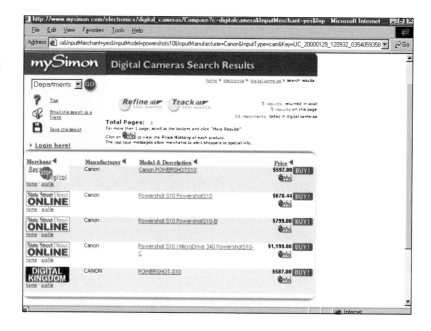

In the future, electronic agents may be computer software programs bought by consumers. The program could learn about a consumer's tastes by asking questions when it's installed on the consumer's computer. For example, when Judy adds the FRED software to her home electronic systems, the software asks her questions to learn about her tastes and preferences.

Electronic retailers may incorporate electronic agents as part of their websites. The agents would function as a super sales associate in a department store, helping customers locate merchandise they might like. For example, the CDNow site (www.cdnow.com) has an electronic agent that recommends albums based on your responses to some questions and your past purchases. Retailing View 3.3 illustrates how a retailer of high-fashion apparel tailors the presentation of its merchandise for each customer. Finally, electronic agents are operated by independent companies to help consumers locate merchandise.

INTERNET EXERCISE   A listing and description of shopping bots is at www.botspot.com and some specific sites are www.mysimon.com, www.pricescan.com, www.bottomdollar.com, www.20-20consumer.com, and www.shopping.yahoo.com. Go to the sites and search for this textbook, a particular video and brand of athletic shoes. How useful was the information returned by the shopping bot? How could the information be improved to be more useful to you?

Providing Information to Evaluate Merchandise   An important service benefit offered by retailers is providing information that helps customers make better purchase decisions. The retail formats shown in Exhibit 3–4 differ in terms of how much information they provide and whether customers can easily make side-by-side comparisons of different brands.[21]

Bluefly.com—Selling Designer Apparel on the Net

NOT EVERYONE WILL BUY A $295 Gianni Versace jacket without being able to try it on first—even if it has been marked down from $1,400. But enough people will do so that Bluefly.com has trouble keeping them in stock.

Bluefly.com is an electronic off-price retailer selling end-of-season and excess production designer clothing from such elite design houses as Donna Karan and BCBG at discounts up to 75 percent. It uses the Net to reach a broader audience than store-based retailers. In addition to selling fashionable apparel, the site offers fashion tips and personalized "shopping carts" that make suggestions based on a customer's size, complexion, and designer preferences.

Bluefly.com exploits the ability of an electronic retailer to personalize its offering and overcome the common frustration of the size-12 off-price shopper finding a garment she really wants and finding out it is only available in a size 3. Its "MyCatalog" service allows customers to enter their sizes and preferences. When they go to the site, the clothing they view is preselected. They don't have to look through pages of merchandise that they don't like or that isn't available in their size. The 75,000 registered users are also notified by e-mail when their favorite clothing is posted on the site. In addition to providing a service to its customers, the e-mail notifications help Bluefly.com move merchandise faster.

Rather than serving as a clearinghouse for manufacturers, Bluefly.com owns its inventory. Thus it can ensure that all orders are reliably filled. By buying the merchandise from manufacturers, consolidators, and retailers clearing out end-of-season merchandise, Bluefly.com develops strong relationships with its suppliers.

tuesday, 11:15 p.m.
buying a new dress.

www.bluefly.com
the outlet store in your home

Women's, men's and kid's designer fashions.
Save up to 75%. 90-day money back guarantee.

Bluefly.com personalizes its website so that customers will only see apparel they like, in sizes that are available.

Source: Jean Thilmany, "Bluefly.com: The Pains and Gaines," *WWD,* July 26, 1999, p. 25; Marcia Stepanek, "Closed, Gone to the Net," *Business Week,* June 7, 1999, p. 113; and Elizabeth Gardner, "Selling Designer Brands at a Discount," *Internet World,* May 24, 1999, p. 23.

Retailers vary in the sheer amount of information provided about their merchandise. For instance, some catalogs provide only a few specifications for each item, such as price, weight, and brand/model. Other catalogs offer much more detail about each item carried. For many clothing items, Lands' End not only provides color pictures but often gives extensive detail about the construction process, stitching, and materials.

Store-based retailers also differ in the information they make available to consumers. Specialty and department stores typically have trained, knowledgeable sales associates, while most discount stores do not. Customers for durable goods such as appliances report that salespeople are the most useful information source, more useful than *Consumer Reports,* advertising, and friends.[22]

Knowledgeable sales associates are able to dramatically increase the usefulness of the information they provide through their face-to-face interaction with customers. They ask questions about a customer's needs and provide specific information the customer seeks. However, the personal knowledge of sales associates working for store-based retailers is typically limited and the space available for self-service, store-based, and catalog retailers to provide information is limited to a printed page, a sign, and the package on a shelf.

Electronic retailers have the opportunity to provide more information to their customers than specialty and department store retailers—they have the capability of providing as much information as each customer might want.[23] Using an interactive electronic communication channel, retailers can respond to customers' inquiries just like a sales associate would. Customers shopping electronically can drill down through web pages until they have enough information to make a purchase decision. In addition, the information in the electronic retailer's database can be frequently updated and will always be available. Store-based retailers may have a difficult time retaining knowledgeable sales associates, and in many cases it is not cost-effective for them to do so. The cost of adding information to an electronic retailer's database is likely to be far less than the cost of continually training thousands of sales associates.

When making product choices, it is useful to have side-by-side comparisons of alternatives. Exhibit 3–5 illustrates how electronic retailers can easily provide information in this format. However, customers in stores usually have to inspect each brand, one at a time, and then remember the different attributes to make a comparison. Many category specialists display brands in a category next to each other to make it easier for customers to compare them. Even though the brands and models are next to each other, it is still easier to make the comparisons when they are presented in a tabular format shown in Exhibit 3–5.

Cost of Merchandise   Some experts suggest that electronic retailers will have much lower costs, as much as 25 percent lower than in-store retailers, because electronic retailers do not have to spend money building and operating stores at

EXHIBIT 3–5

Information Presented by an Electronic Retailer to Compare Alternatives

Product Name	TOSHIBA 2615DVD	COMPAQ 1692	COMPAQ 1930
Price	$1,799.95	$1,899.95	$2,399.95
Online Purchase	BUY	BUY	BUY
Warranty Labor Months	12	12	12
Warranty Parts Months	12	12	12
Item Height in Inches	1.9	2.0	1.9
Item Width in Inches	12.4	12.2	11.6
Item Depth in Inches	10.3	10.1	9.3
Processor Brand	Intel®	AMD	Intel®
Processor Type	Celeron™ Processor	K6®-2 with 3D Now!™ Technology	Celeron™ Processor
Processor Speed (MHz)	433	433	433
Screen Size (Inches)	12.1	12.1	13.3
Frontside Bus Speed (MHz)	66	96	
Level 2 Cache (KB)	128	512	128
RAM (MB)	64	64	64
RAM Expandable To (MB)	192	160	192
Type of RAM	SDRAM	SDRAM	SDRAM

convenient locations.[24] However, electronic retailers, or their customers, will have higher costs to get merchandise to homes, deal with the high level of returns, and attract customers to their websites.

It is quite costly to deliver merchandise in small quantities to customers' homes. Customers presently incur these costs when they spend their time and money going to stores to pick out and take home merchandise and then going back to the stores to return merchandise they don't want.

Even though sales by electronic retailing are small now, electronic retailing has the potential to be a major retail format and realize optimistic sales estimates in the future, because the format can offer consumers superior benefits to those offered by present in-store and nonstore formats. Due to the interactive nature of the electronic retail format, customers can have a selection of merchandise and information about the merchandise tailored to their needs. In effect, the electronic format has the potential for preparing an individually tailored catalog for the customer each time the customer goes shopping. Using this individually tailored shopping experience, customers will be able to make more satisfying selections of merchandise using the electronic format compared to other formats. The key to providing these individually tailored catalogs is the availability of electronic agents like FRED described at the beginning of the chapter.

What Types of Merchandise Will Be Sold Effectively by Electronic Retailers?

In addition to the amount and presentation of information, retail formats also differ in the type of information they can present effectively. For instance, when you purchase apparel, some critical information might be "look-and-see" attributes like color and style, as well as "touch-and-feel" attributes like how the apparel fits. Customers can get both the look-and-see and touch-and-feel information when they buy merchandise in a store. When buying merchandise electronically, touch-and-feel information isn't available. Customers' ability even to assess color depends on the adjustment of a computer monitor. Fit cannot be predicted well, unless the electronic retailer has consistent sizing and the consumer has learned over time what size to buy for a particular brand. It is impossible to feel the fabric in a dress, taste a sample of an ice cream flavor, or smell a perfume before buying the product from a nonstore retailer.

Based on the difficulty of providing touch-and-feel information electronically, one might conclude that electronic retailers will not be able to successfully sell merchandise such as clothing, perfume, flowers, and food with important touch-and-feel attributes.[25] However, this type of merchandise is presently sold by other nonstore retailers such as catalogers. Branding overcomes many of the uncertainties in purchasing merchandise without touching and feeling it.

Consider branded merchandise like Nautica perfume or Levi's 501 jeans. Even though you can't smell a sample of the perfume before buying it, you know that it will smell like your last bottle when you get it from an electronic retailer because the manufacturer of Nautica makes sure each bottle smells the same. Similarly, if you wear a size 30-inch waist/32-inch inseam Levi's 501 jean, you know it will fit when you buy it from an electronic retailer.

In some situations, electronic retailers might even be able to provide superior information, compared to store retailers. For example, Judy, before she started to shop electronically, wanted to see toys before buying one for her son Dave. So she went to toy stores to look at the toys. But in the stores, the toys

Branding enables electronic retailers such as Perfumania.com to sell merchandise electronically that has important "touch and feel" attributes.

were not displayed, so she could only see a picture on the side of the box containing the toy. Now that Judy shops electronically, she can get superior information from the full-motion video clip showing a child playing with the toy.

In other situations, touch-and-feel information might be important, but the information in a store is not much better than the information provided by an electronic retailer. For example, suppose you're buying a bottle of perfume for your mother. Even if you go to the store and smell the samples of all the new scents, you might not get much information to help you determine which one your mother would like. In this situation, store-based retailers offer little benefit over electronic and other nonstore retailers in terms of information about the merchandise. But, buying gifts from electronic retailers offers the benefit of saving you the time and effort in packaging and sending the gift to your mother. For this reason, gifts represent a substantial portion of sales made by present electronic retailers.

Some services retailers have been very successful over the Internet, because the look-and-see attributes in their offering can be presented very effectively over the Internet. For example, Travelocity (www.travelocity.com) is an Internet travel planning service. After you go to the Internet site and fill in an online form indicating your destination and preferred departure time, the electronic agent locates the lowest-cost fare for the flight. To purchase a ticket, you simply click on the purchase ticket icon, enter your credit card information, and get an eticket confirmation number. Travel service providers like Travelocity, Preview (www.previewtravel.com), and Expedia (expedia.msn.com) provide detailed information about destinations like the locations of hotels on a map. Chat rooms provide an opportunity for travelers to share their experiences in hotels and restaurants.[27] Due to the appeal of the Internet for providing services, many banks are making major investments to provide banking services over the Internet.[28]

Thus the critical issue determining what types of merchandise can be sold successfully by electronic retailers is whether the electronic retailer can provide enough information prior to the purchase to make sure customers will be satisfied with the merchandise once they get it. There are many buying situations in which electronic retailers can provide sufficient information even though the merchandise has important touch-and-feel attributes.

Will Electronic Retailing Lead to More Price Competition?

Many store-based retailers offer similar assortments of branded merchandise and thus have difficulty differentiating themselves on the basis of their merchandise offering. However, price competition between these store-based retailers offering the same merchandise is reduced by geography. Consumers typically shop at the stores and malls closest to where they live and work. With electronic retailing, consumers can search for merchandise across the globe at low cost. The number of stores that a consumer can visit to compare prices is no longer limited by physical distance.[29]

To limit price comparisons, many present electronic retailers make it hard for customers to go from one Internet site to another. These electronic retailers use different interfaces so customers need to learn how to search through the offerings at each new site they visit. In addition, Internet retailers electronically prevent shopping bots from accessing their sites and collecting information about the products sold at the site, and from using this collected data to compare the prices offered at different electronic retailing sites.[30]

As mentioned previously, one key benefit of the electronic format is the ability to shop the world and easily compare alternatives from different retailers. Thus by making these comparisons difficult, electronic retailers are limiting the attractiveness and growth of the format. However, consumers eventually will insist on making these comparisons and will reward electronic retailers that offer this service by going to their sites. If FRED is not allowed in at a site, FRED's owner will buy from competing sites that let FRED in.

INTERNET EXERCISE   Visit two Internet Sites, www.compare.net and productreviewnet.com, providing side-by-side comparisons of brands in a product category. Look for information on toaster ovens and digital cameras. How useful is this information?

While consumers shopping electronically can collect price information with little effort, they can get a lot of other information about the quality and performance of products at a low cost. For instance, an electronic retailer of custom oriental rugs can clearly show real differences in patterns and materials used for construction. An electronic grocery service such as Peapod can allow the customer to sort cereals by nutritional content, thus making it easier to use that attribute in decision making.

Electronic retailers will reduce the emphasis on price by providing better services and information. Because of these services, customers might be willing to pay higher prices for the merchandise. For example, Amazon.com provides customers with table of contents and synopses of books as well as book reviews and comments by the authors and people who have read the book. When you find an interesting book, its system is programmed to suggest other books by the same author or of the same genre. Finally, you can tell Amazon about your favorite authors and subjects and then receive e-mail on new books that might be of interest. The classic response to the question, "What are the three most important things in retailing?" was "location, location, location." In the world of electronic retailing, the answer will be "information, information, information."

Keys to Success in Electronic Retailing

Some critical resources needed to successfully sell merchandise electronically are (1) strong brand name and image, (2) customer information, (3) complementary merchandise and services, (4) unique merchandise, (5) the ability to effectively present information on web pages, and (6) a distribution system to efficiently ship merchandise to homes and receive return. Exhibit 3–6 lists these critical resources with an assessment of the degree to which electronic-only retailers (such as Amazon.com and eToys), catalog, traditional store-based retailers, and merchandise manufacturers possess them.

Strong Brand Name and Image   The retailer's brand name and image are important for two reasons. First, most shoppers only know the limited number of stores they patronize in their local area. However, Internet shoppers have access to over 100,000 locations they can visit. It is very expensive for electronic retailers to develop a high level of awareness to attract customers to their websites.

Second, a trustworthy reputation is important for an electronic retailer. Buying merchandise over the Internet is risky because customers cannot see the merchandise before they buy it. Thus, electronic shoppers need to believe the retailer will provide secure credit card transactions, deliver the quality of merchandise described on its web pages, and maintain privacy of any information revealed by the customer. When asked what attributes are critical in selecting a website for shopping, 25 percent said credit card security, 22 percent cited fast download speed, 20 percent named the availability of customer service, 7 percent answered deep price discounts, and 7 percent said privacy.[31] To reduce risks for customers, most Internet and catalog retailers offer money-back guarantees. Some electronic retailers even pay for the return mailing cost.[32]

Refact Electronic-only retailers spend $42 to acquire a customer, while multichannel retailers (those with both stores and electronic offerings) spend only $22 to acquire a customer.[33]

EXHIBIT 3–6

Capabilities Needed for Success in Electronic Retailing

CAPABILITIES	ELECTRONIC-ONLY RETAILERS	CATALOG RETAILERS	STORE-BASED RETAILERS	MERCHANDISE MANUFACTURERS
Strong brand name and image to build traffic and reduce customers' perceived risk	Low	Medium to high	High	Medium to high
Availability of customer information to tailor presentations	Medium to high	High	Medium to high	Low
Complementary merchandise and services to efficiently solve customer problems	High	High	High	Medium
Unique merchandise	Low	Medium to high	Medium to high	High
Presentation of merchandise information in electronic formats	High	High	Medium to high	Medium
Efficient distribution system to deliver merchandise to homes and accept returns	Low	Medium to high	High	Low

Large store-based retailers and national brand manufacturers have high awareness and strong reputations. On the other hand, only a few catalog and Internet-only retailers are well known and respected by consumers. Thus, electronic retailers spend 65 percent of revenues on marketing and advertising.[34]

INTERNET EXERCISE   Bizrate.com (www.bizrate.com) and eTRUST (www.eTRUST.com) provide information to help consumers patronize trustworthy electronic retailers. Visit their sites and check out the ratings and evaluations for electronic retailers. How valuable are these services and ratings to you? Would they affect your choice of electronic retailers to patronize? How could the benefits of this service be improved?

Refact Ninety-three percent of Internet sites collect information from people visiting their sites.[35]

Customer Information   As mentioned previously, an important benefit provided by electronic retailers is tailoring their presentations to the needs of specific customers. Electronic retailers have the opportunity to exploit this unique interactive feature of the Internet using information such as demographics, past purchase histories, and preferences of each customer. With this customer information, electronic retailers can target promotions to specific customers and suggest appropriate merchandise.

An extensive customer database is a critical asset for building loyalty with electronic shoppers for two reasons. First, using the database, electronic retailers will increase customer satisfaction with the shopping experience at their site. Second, each time a customer patronizes a particular electronic retailer, more information is collected and the electronic retailer gets to know the customer better. Thus, a cycle is created—customer satisfaction provides the opportunity to learn how to provide greater satisfaction. If customers break this cycle by switching to another electronic retailer, they will experience a decrease in satisfaction while the new electronic retailer learns more about their needs and preferences.

While the use of this information provides benefits for customers, it also raises privacy concerns. To reduce these concerns, almost all Internet retailers post information about their privacy policies on their sites and most offer customers a choice about how their information is used.[36]

Catalog retailers, and to a lesser extent store-based retailers, have considerable information about their customers that they can use to provide this personalized service. Due to their brief time in business, most electronic-only retailers have limited customer databases. Since manufacturers sell to retailers, they have even less information about specific customers who buy their products.

Complementary Merchandise and Services   The opportunity for an electronic retailer to make multiple-item sales is important for two reasons. First, when making multiple-item purchases from an electronic retailer, customers reduce their shipping costs. Second, the electronic retailer is in an ideal position to make recommendations to a customer based on the customer's primary purchase and to offer a set of items that solves a customer's problem. Remember how the electronic retailer at the beginning of the chapter suggested gift wrapping and a book to go with the toy Judy ordered.

The Internet provides an opportunity to go beyond the traditional merchandise assortments offered by store-based retailers and provide tools and information to assist consumers in solving a problem. Virtual communities are examples

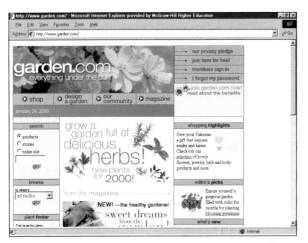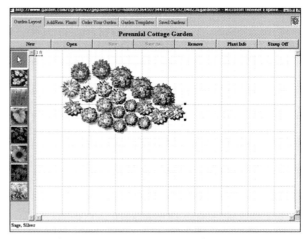

Garden.com (left) is a virtual community for gardeners offering a wide variety of products and services such as software programs to help gardeners plan their gardens (right).

of solution-oriented ebusinesses. A **virtual community** is a network of members that communicate with each other electronically.[37] For example, Garden.com (www.garden.com) is a virtual community for gardeners. The website includes a computer program that allows customers to develop plans for next year's garden and store and update the plans on the website. When the plans are finalized, the customer can place an order for the plants and have them shipped by overnight delivery when they should be planted in the customer's climate zone. The site also offers gardening tools, articles written by well-known gardeners, books on gardening, and a chat room in which customers can state their views on issues and ask and answer questions.[38] The use of chat rooms by electronic retailer is discussed in Chapter 19. A virtual community for people planning weddings is discussed in Retailing View 3.4.

Retailers are ideally suited to offer these problem-solving websites for their customers. They are skillful at putting together merchandise assortments, a skill that most manufacturers lack. In addition, retailers typically have more credibility than manufacturers when suggesting merchandise since they offer an assortment of brands from different suppliers.

Unique Merchandise   By offering unique merchandise, electronic retailers differentiate themselves from competition and reduce the potential price competition. Basically, if a firm is the only retailer selling a specific model or brand, customers cannot easily compare its price with the prices offered by other electronic retailers.

Three approaches for offering unique merchandise are (1) private-label merchandise, (2) branded variants or co-branded merchandise, and (3) prepackaged assortments. Electronic retailers can differentiate themselves by developing their own private-label merchandise that they sell exclusively. For example, the merchandise sold at The Gap, Victoria's Secret, and Lands' End can only be bought from these retailers.

Electronic retailers can also work with manufacturers to provide "branded variants" that they sell exclusively.[39] For example, Sony sells VCRs at Wal-Mart and Circuit City that look the same but have different model numbers and slightly different features.

WEDDING-RELATED INTERNET SITES are popular and creative virtual communities to help couples and families cope with a traditionally stressful experience. The Knot (www.theknot.com) offers a searchable database of gowns and a wedding-centric bookstore. Each month over 2 million wedding gowns are viewed on its site. WeddingChannel.com (www.weddingchannel.com) offers couples personal websites and, through its relationship with Federated Department Stores, a gift registry that is broadcast to guests through e-mail. The sites also offer planning guides, tips, and an opportunity to chat with other couples getting married.

The typical engagement/wedding planning process lasts for 14 months and costs almost $20,000. The process involves many emotionally charged decisions such as how many people and whom to invite, what print style to use on the invitations, where to hold the reception, what music to play during the ceremony, and what gifts to list in a registry. Wedding sites offer the couple and their families an opportunity to collect information in their home rather than by making appointments with different suppliers. Potential places for the reception can be ruled out by looking at photos on the web. Instead of going to hear different bands, audio clips can be downloaded from the web. Hotel reservations for out-of-town

The Knot provides solutions to the problems couples have planning a wedding.

guests can be made over the Internet and maps can be created showing how to get to the hotel and reception.

Source: Eric Wilson, "Bridal Firms Waltz with the Net," *WWD*, August 10, 1999, pp. 10–11; and Ellen Neuborne, "Weddings and the Web: A Marriage Made in Cyber Heaven," *Business Week*, February 15, 1999, p. 45.

Finally, electronic retailers can offer unique merchandise by selling unique bundles of complementary products. For example, an electronic retailer could sell gift baskets with branded wines, cheese, fruit, crackers, and utensils. While the components of the bundle could be acquired from different retailers and manufacturers, the bundle would be a unique product.

As indicated in Exhibit 3–6, manufacturers and some catalog and store-based retailers presently sell unique merchandise. Typically, electronic-only retailers have not developed this capability.

Presentation in Electronic Formats   Traditionally, some store-based retailers have used store design and atmosphere to differentiate their offerings from competing retailers'. For example, Target's wide, uncluttered aisles and attractive merchandise displays provide a superior shopping experience for some customers compared to Wal-Mart and Kmart. The design of websites in terms of the download time, ease of navigating through the site, and sensory experiences may play a similar role for electronic retailers.[40]

Electronic retailers, having been immersed in Internet technology, have considerable skills in this area. Catalog retailers and some store-based retailers engaged in direct mail and catalog activities have presentation skills similar to those needed in electronic retailing.

Efficient Distribution   As mentioned previously, when customers shop at retail stores, they bear the cost of transporting merchandise from stores to their homes and bringing unsatisfactory merchandise back to the store. When buying from an electronic retailer, the cost of home delivery can significantly increase the total cost incurred by the customer.[41]

Catalog retailers have very efficient systems for taking orders from individual customers, packaging the merchandise ordered for shipping, and delivering it to homes. Electronic-only retailers lack the infrastructure that store-based and catalog retailers have. Recognizing the importance of these distribution systems, they are hiring executives from traditional retailers to build their own systems.[42]

Manufacturers and most store-based retailers lack the appropriate systems for shipping individual orders to households. Their warehouse systems are designed to fill large orders from retail firms or stores and deliver truckloads of goods to retailers' warehouses or stores. However, store-based retailers with broad market coverage can use their stores as convenient places for electronic shoppers to pick up their merchandise and return unsatisfactory purchases.

Some merchandise such as computer software and games and recorded music can be delivered electronically to homes over the Internet. Clearly, these digital products will be sold and distributed electronically in the future—a conclusion that motivated Egghead (www.egghead.com) to close its stores and sell software exclusively over the Internet.[43]

Distribution costs and systems play a particularly important role in the growth of electronic grocery shopping. Since many items sold in supermarkets are perishable, deliveries must be made when someone is at home to put the perishables in a refrigerator or freezer. Some electronic supermarkets such as NetGrocer (www.netgrocer.com) avoid the problem by only selling nonperishable merchandise and shipping it via standard package delivery firms. Peapod (www.peapod) and Webvan.com (www.webvan.com) commit to making deliveries within a 30-to-120–minute window and charge extra for this service. Streamline (www.streamline.com) addresses this problem by installing refrigerated storage boxes with touch-pad security, enabling deliveries to garages and other secure locations outside the home.

Providing delivery services to households is costly. The charge of $5 to $10 a delivery probably does not cover the actual cost of picking the groceries, loading them in a truck, driving to the customer's house, and unloading the order. In addition to the labor costs for delivering the merchandise, electronic grocers need to construct specialized warehouses for efficiently picking individual household orders.[44]

Potential Winners and Losers in Electronic Retailing

In this section, we examine the degree to which retailers using different formats have the resources outlined in Exhibit 3–6 to effectively compete in cyberspace.

Catalog Retailers As indicated in Exhibit 3–6, catalog retailers are best positioned to exploit electronic retailing. They have order fulfillment systems and database management skills needed for effective electronic retailing. Also, the visual merchandising skills necessary for preparing catalogs are similar to those needed in setting up an effective website.

For example, Lands' End maintains a mailing list of 9 million people, 45 percent of whom have purchased merchandise from the firm in the previous 36 months. In 1999, it mailed out 150 million catalogs, which generated annual sales of over $1 billion. When customers call the toll-free number to place orders, Lands' End operators can access information about their past purchases and address, making it easy for customers to order. Operators can also access infor-

Imagine being able to shop with a friend 3,000 miles away.

Only landsend.com lets you shop online with someone else, anywhere else. We call it Shop With A Friend.™ And it lets each of you, at your own computer screen, simultaneously flip through our web site. Compare selections together, look at different colors, different outfits. Try it with a friend, or family, or anyone.

www.landsend.com

Lands' End has the resources to be a successful electronic retailer.

mation about merchandise and provide detailed information about measurements for a garment and its fabrication. Ninety percent of all orders are mailed to the customer within 24 hours.[45]

However, catalog retailers vary in the uniqueness of their merchandise. For example, Lands' End has a big opportunity for profitable electronic retailing because it sells high-quality, private-brand merchandise that can't be bought elsewhere. On the other hand, Spiegel's opportunities may not be great because it sells primarily branded merchandise that is susceptible to price comparisons.

Store-Based Retailers   The Internet provides an attractive opportunity for some store-based retailers to expand their customer base with relatively low cost and risk. Local and regional retailers can become national and international retailers overnight by simply putting up a website. Electronic retailing is particularly attractive to firms with strong brand names but limited locations and distribution. For example, retailers such as Harrod's, Gumps, Saks, Bloomingdale's, and Neiman Marcus are widely known for offering unique, high-quality merchandise but require customers to travel to England or major U.S. cities to buy many of the items they carry. Interestingly, most of these stores currently possess an effective mail order catalog operation.[46]

On the other hand, some store-based retailers with extensive market coverage are cautious about selling merchandise over the Internet because they believe their electronic offering might cannibalize their in-store sales. Store-based retailers view electronic retailing as a college football coach would view an inquiry by the NCAA Infractions Committee. It is something they prefer to avoid but find too dangerous to ignore. Thus many large store-based retailers are just "putting a toe in the water" and establishing Internet sites with a limited number of offerings; such sites don't have the features and merchandise assortments to attract a large number of customers. Many of the sites are used to support their in-store business rather than develop new substantial sales. However, in response to the growth of Internet access and usage in the United States and the success of Internet retailers such as Amazon.com and eToys, most store-based retailers are aggressively selling merchandise over the Internet or at least considering it.[47]

Self-service, store-based retailers such as some category specialists and general merchandise discount stores compete primarily on price and depth and breadth of assortments. These retailers are more vulnerable to competition from electronic retailers. They offer few informational benefits and sell branded merchandise. However, the vulnerability of these self-service, store-based retailers depends on their strategy and merchandise offering.

For example, Toys "R" Us has extensive coverage nationally (and increasingly internationally). Toys "R" Us' electronic sales have cannibalized its in-store sales, making electronic retailing less attractive to it than to an entrepreneur such as eToys or even a store-based retailer with less market coverage such as FAO Schwarz. However, when an electronic toy retailer entered the market,

Toys "R" Us needed to react quickly because eToys offers a wider selection at lower prices.[48] In addition, toys are ideally suited for sales over the Internet because electronic retailers can provide information superior to the information provided in a store as illustrated by the scenario at the beginning of the chapter.

Home Depot is similar to Toys "R" Us in terms of national coverage but it's less vulnerable to an electronic home improvement center because its customers frequently want immediate delivery and specialized advice from experts. Customers often go to a home improvement center for specific parts that are difficult to match from a distance or for a product like paint colors that must match something they have. The hand-holding services from Home Depot's expert sales associates cannot be duplicated electronically. Finally, bulky do-it-yourself merchandise is expensive to ship directly to homes.

In conclusion, some store-based retailers are more vulnerable to competition of electronic retailers than others. The impact of electronic retailing on the various retail formats depends on the nature of the merchandise sold and the needs of customers.

Electronic-Only Retailers   While electronic-only retailers such as Amazon.com have been highly valued by investors, Exhibit 3–6 suggests that they presently do not possess some of the resources needed for long-term success. As mentioned previously, most of the major retailers have not actively sold merchandise electronically, largely due to their concern over cannibalizing in-store sales. However, if and when they decide to exploit this channel, store-based retailers have some significant resources that can be used to compete effectively in the emerging channel. National chains such as Barnes & Noble have strong brand names and reputations, relationships with vendors, skills in editing assortments, and local stores for displaying merchandise and providing information and services.

Refact The electronic-only retailers with the highest brand name awareness are Amazon.com (60.1 percent), Priceline.com (55.4 percent), Ebay (46.4 percent), and Etrade (43.8 percent).[49]

For example, investors are very excited about electronic drugstores such as Drugstore.com (www.drugstore.com), PlanetRx (www.planetrx.com), Rx (www.rx.com), and Soma (www.soma.com).[50] However, consider the resources that Walgreens has supporting its entry into electronic retailing:

"Clicks and mortar" drugstores such as Walgreens have an advantage over electronic-only drugstores retailers because they offer customers the choice of picking up merchandise at the store or having it delivered to their homes.

- Three thousand conveniently located stores in the United States with drive-in windows for picking up prescriptions and merchandise.

- A distribution system in place for picking, packing, and shipping prescription pharmaceuticals and merchandise presently ordered by phone.

- A strong reputation for being trustworthy and helping customers on health-related decisions.

- Agreements in places with third-party payers (HMOs and insurance companies) to accept and provide pharmaceutical benefits for its customers.

Recognizing these synergies between store-based and electronic retailing, CVS acquired Soma.com and Rite-Aid bought a 25 percent interest in Drugstore.com.[51] While electronic-only retailers have pioneered selling merchandise and service over the Internet, they may have a difficult time defending their initial success when store-based retailers become "click and mortar" retailer by launching an electronic retail offering.

Manufacturers and Disintermediation   **Disintermediation** occurs when a manufacturer sells directly to consumers, bypassing retailers. Retailers are concerned about disintermediation because manufacturers can get direct access to consumers by establishing a retail site on the Internet. But, as indicated in Exhibit 3–6, manufacturers lack some of the critical resources to sell merchandise electronically. Retailers are more efficient in dealing with customers directly than manufacturers. They have considerably more experience than manufacturers in distributing merchandise directly to customers, providing complementary assortments, and collecting and using information about customers. Retailers also have an advantage since they can provide a broader array of product and services to solve customer problems. For example, if consumers want to buy a dress shirt and tie directly from the manufacturers, they must go to two different Internet sites and still can't be sure that the shirt and tie will go together. Finally, if manufacturers start selling direct, they risk losing the support of the retailers they bypass.[52]

CATALOG AND DIRECT-MAIL RETAILING

Catalog retailing is a nonstore retail format in which the retail offering is communicated to a customer through a catalog, while **direct-mail retailers** communicate with their customers using letters and brochures. Historically, catalog and direct-mail retailing were most successful with rural consumers, who lacked ready access to retail stores. With the rise of dual-income families and other people with limited time for shopping in stores, catalog retailing has grown in popularity and now appeals to a broad cross section of consumers.

In 1997, $169 billion of merchandise and services were sold to consumers through catalogs and direct mail. Approximately 60 percent of the sales were for merchandise with the remaining 40 percent for services such as insurance. Catalog and direct mail accounted for 4 percent of the U.S. sales of general merchandise but only 2 percent of all U.S. retail sales. Clothing accounts for 32 percent of all catalog sales followed by home furnishings (9.4 percent), housewares (7 percent), and toys and games (7 percent).[54]

Over two-thirds of all U.S. adults (107 million people) made a purchase in response to catalogs and direct mail with 20 percent buying from catalogs 3 to 5 times during 1997. The average U.S. household receives 1.9 catalogs and a similar number of direct-mail solicitations per week. However, households that patronize catalog retailers receive three times as many catalogs as the average household.[55]

Refact In 1489, Aldus Manutius of Venice, Italy, offered the first catalog, listing 15 books written in Latin and Greek. The first American catalog, produced in 1744 by Benjamin Franklin, sold scientific instruments and academic books.[53]

Types of Catalog and Direct-Mail Retailers

Two types of firms selling products through the mail are (1) general merchandise and specialty-catalog retailers and (2) direct-mail retailers. General merchandise catalog retailers offer a broad variety of merchandise in catalogs that are periodically mailed to their customers. For example, JCPenney distributes a 1,000-page catalog with over 50,000 SKUs to its customers twice a year. Besides its general merchandise catalog, Penney distributes 70 specialty catalogs each year. Specialty-catalog retailers focus on specific categories of merchandise, such as fruit (Harry and David), gardening tools (Smith & Hawken), and seeds and plants (Burpee).

Direct-mail retailers typically mail brochures and pamphlets to sell a specific product or service to customers at one point in time. For example, USAA sells automobile insurance and a division of JCPenney sells life insurance through the mail. In addition to the focus on a specific product or service, most direct-mail retailers are primarily interested in making a single sale from a specific mailing, while catalog retailers typically maintain relationships with customers over time.

Exhibit 3–7 lists the nation's largest catalog and direct-mail retailers and illustrates the variety of products and services sold directly to customers through impersonal methods. About two-thirds of the sales are for merchandise; one-third are for services.

Issues in Catalog Retailing

Similar to electronic retailing, direct-mail and catalog retailing are attractive business opportunities, because the start-up costs are relatively low. An entrepreneur can launch a direct-mail business with minimal inventory and can use her garage as a warehouse and office. There is no need to rent a store in a high-rent location, use expensive fixtures, create an attractive shopping environment, or hire salespeople. Mailing lists tailored for a target market can be purchased inexpensively. Retailing View 3.5 describes two neighbors who started a successful catalog retail business.

On the other hand, catalog and direct-mail retailing can be very challenging. Mailing and printing costs are high since catalog retailers mail out 10 to 20 catalogs for each order they receive. It is increasingly hard to capture consumers' attention as they receive so many catalogs in their mail each year. Second, costs of paper and third-class mail have been increasing 20 to 25 percent per year. Third, some direct-mail retailers' misleading and deceptive practices have led to government regulations concerning return policies and notification of delays in delivery. Finally, the length of time required to design, develop, and distribute catalogs

EXHIBIT 3–7

Leading U.S. Catalog and Direct-Mail Retailers

COMPANY	1998 SALES ($ MILLION)	OFFERING
Dell Computer	18,243*	Computer hardware, software, and peripherals
JCPenney	3,929	General merchandise
Office Depot	2,699*	Office supplies
Micro Warehouse	2,200*	Computer hardware, software, and peripherals
CDW Computer Centers	1,734*	Computer hardware, software, and peripherals
Fingerhut	1,609	General merchandise
Global DirectMail	1,435*	Computers, industrial, equipment and office supplies
Spiegel	1,384	General merchandise
Lands' End	1,371	Apparel and home goods
Brylane	1,328	Apparel and home goods
Micron Electronics	1,300*	Computer hardware, software, and peripherals
L.L. Bean	1,030	Outdoor gear, apparel, and home goods
Insight Enterprises	1,002*	Computer hardware, software, and peripherals
Staples	825*	Office supplies
Intimate Brands (Victoria's Secret)	759	Women's apparel
PC Connection	732*	Computer hardware, software, and peripherals
Creative Computers	690*	Computer hardware, software, and peripherals
CompUSA	646*	Computer hardware, software, and peripherals
Hanover Direct	546	General merchandise

*Includes sales to commercial customers

Source: "The Catalog Age 100," *Catalog Age*, August 1999, pp. 68–78.

Starting a Catalog Retail Business

JOANN MARTIN MET VICKIE HUTCHINS when she moved in next door in Delaware, Ohio. Sharing a love of decorating and antiques, they spent weekends together shopping at flea markets and auctions. Then they decided to go into the catalog retail business, putting up $5,000 apiece and naming the business Gooseberry Patch. Their first catalog featured craft items they would like to have: a $195 Redware punch bowl, a $75 handmade mohair teddy bear, and a $400 hand-crafted chair. Sales from their glossy, full-color, 12-page catalog were disappointing. They got only $27,000 in orders and lost $20,000. However, they discovered that the best-selling items were inexpensive country-style crafts with a touch of nostalgia.

They got rid of the slick catalog and expensive items, shifting from country expensive to country whimsical. Their next catalog had a folksier flavor. It was printed on heavy brown paper stock with illustrations by a local artist rather than photos. The second catalog did much better, generating sales of $85,000.

Gooseberry Patch now mails out 2 million catalogs a year, generating $7 million in sales. Price points are $5 to $100. The catalogs feature decorating and party ideas, recipes, as well as updates on the private lives of the owners. The all-time best-seller is a $13 "heart-in-hand" cookie cutter, which creates a heart-shaped cookie with a heart-shaped hole in the middle. Cinnamon is the top-selling fragrance with nut-meg a close second.

Gooseberry Patch increased its catalog sales when it adopted a more folksy presentation of merchandise and information.

The company builds loyalty by involving customers, inviting them to submit ideas and recipes. The response was so good that Gooseberry Patch puts these contributions in its catalogs, giving clients an emotional stake in the company. Its customers—mostly middle-class, Midwestern baby boomers—supply ideas and family stories through the mail, a toll-free hotline, and a website, www.gooseberrypatch.com.

Source: James Ott, "Warm-and-Fuzzy to Cold Hard Cash," *Business Week,* December 7, 1998, p. 10; Marla Matzer, "Selling Smells," *Forbes,* January 16, 1995, pp. 89–90; and "Retail Entrepreneur of the Year," *Chain Store Age Executive,* December 1995, pp. 56–57.

makes it difficult for catalog and direct-mail retailers to respond quickly to new trends and fashions.[57]

DIRECT SELLING

Direct selling is a retail format in which a salesperson, frequently an independent distributor, contacts a customer directly in a convenient location, either at the customer's home or at work, and demonstrates merchandise benefits, takes an order, and delivers the merchandise to the customer. Direct selling is a highly interactive form of retailing in which considerable information is conveyed to customers through face-to-face discussions with a salesperson. However, providing this high level of information, including extensive demonstrations, is costly. Retailing View 3.6 describes an entrepreneur who started a direct-selling retail business and now focuses on helping others.

Annual U.S. sales for direct selling total $23.7 billion. The largest categories of merchandise sold through direct selling are cosmetics, fragrances, decorative accessories, vacuum cleaners, home appliances, cooking and kitchenware, jewelry, food and nutritional products, and encyclopedias and educational materials.

JOE DUDLEY, SR., ONE OF 11 CHILDREN, grew up in a three-room farm house in a small North Carolina town. Labeled mentally retarded, he was held back in first grade. Today he is the owner and founder of a multimillion-dollar hair care and cosmetics company.

Dudley Products is one of the largest minority-owned businesses in the Southeast. Dudley got his start in retailing by selling Fuller Brush products door-to-door while he was a student at North Carolina A&T. Since 1967, when he and his wife began making their own hair care products, Dudley Products has used direct selling to distribute its products to consumers and beauty salons throughout the United States.

Dudley achieved his personal goal of making $1 million by his 40th birthday. Since that time, he has devoted much of his effort to helping others. Dudley Products initiated a high school mentor program. Students meet bimonthly with Dudley executives and get a firsthand view of what it takes to succeed. Dudley and his company were honored with the North Carolina Governor's Business Award in Education and designation as one of the 1,000 points of light by former President Bush.

Source: Company documents.

Joe Dudley, the founder of a successful direct selling retailer, was one of the 1,000 points of light honored by President Bush.

Refact Annual sales by direct selling are almost twice as high in Japan as in the United States. About one-half of new automobile sales are made by door-to-door salespeople in Japan.[59]

For these products, the benefits of the information provided by direct selling outweigh the cost of providing the information. About 69 percent of all direct sales are made in the home, with 11 percent in the workplace, and 11 percent over the phone.[58]

Almost all of the 9.7 million salespeople who work in direct sales are independent agents. They aren't employed by the direct sales firm but act as independent distributors, buying merchandise from the firms and then reselling it to consumers. Eighty-three percent of the salespeople work part-time (less than 30 hours per week). In most cases, direct salespeople may sell their merchandise to anyone. But some companies (such as Avon) assign territories to salespeople who regularly contact households in their territory.

Two special types of direct selling are party plan and multilevel selling. About 15 percent of all direct sales are made using a party plan system. In a **party plan system,** salespeople encourage customers to act as hosts and invite friends or co-workers to a "party" at which the merchandise is demonstrated in a partylike atmosphere. Sales made at the party are influenced by the social relationship of the people attending with the host. The host or hostess receives a gift or commission for arranging the meeting.

Almost two-thirds of all direct sales are made through multilevel sales networks. In a **multilevel network,** people serve as master distributors, recruiting other people to become distributors in their network. The master distributors either buy merchandise from the firm and resell it to their distributors or receive a

Direct selling retailers such as Mary Kay provide personalized information to their customers.

commission on all merchandise purchased by the distributors in their network. In addition to selling merchandise themselves, the master distributors are involved in recruiting and training other distributors.

Some multilevel direct selling firms are illegal pyramid schemes. A pyramid scheme develops when the firm and its program are designed to sell merchandise and services to other distributors rather than to end users. The founders and initial distributors in pryamid schemes profit from the inventory bought by later participants but little merchandise is sold to consumers who use it.

TELEVISION HOME SHOPPING

Television home shopping retailing is a retail format in which customers watch a TV program demonstrating merchandise and then place orders for the merchandise by telephone.[60] The three forms of electronic home shopping retailing are (1) cable channels dedicated to television shopping, (2) infomercials, and (3) direct-response advertising shown on broadcast and cable TV. **Infomercials** are TV programs, typically 30 minutes long, that mix entertainment with product demonstrations and then solicit orders placed by telephone. **Direct-response advertising** includes advertisements on TV and radio that describe products and provide an opportunity for consumers to order them.

Refact The typical person watches 36 hours of programming on QVC before making a purchase.[61]

More than 60 million American consumers now have access to a television shopping channel network; however, only 20 percent of the potential viewing audience even watches. To increase the audience, the shopping channels have increased the level of entertainment included in the programs. For example, QVC has 4 million customers, but 50 percent of the purchases are made by its top 300,000 customers. TV home shopping sales in 1998 were $4.0 billion and not growing. The two largest networks with dedicated channels are The Home Shopping Network and QVC.[62]

The major advantage of TV home shopping compared to catalog retailing is that customers can see the merchandise demonstrated on the TV screen. However, customers can't look at a particular type of merchandise or a specific item when they want to, as they can with catalogs. They have to wait for the time when the merchandise will be shown. To address this limitation, home shopping networks schedule categories of merchandise for specific times so customers looking for specific merchandise can plan their viewing time.

TV home shopping retailers appeal primarily to lower-income consumers. Forty percent of TV home shopping sales are inexpensive jewelry. Other major categories are apparel, cosmetics, and exercise equipment.

VENDING MACHINE RETAILING

Vending machine retailing is a nonstore format in which merchandise or services are stored in a machine and dispensed to customers when they deposit cash or use a credit card. The vending machines are placed at convenient, high-traffic locations such as in airports for selling travel insurance, in factory and office work areas for snacks, and near university classrooms for soft drinks. Since the transaction can be completed without personal interaction, customers can acquire merchandise or services at any time during the day.

While $23.3 billion in goods is sold annually through vending machines in the United States, almost all products sold are hot and cold beverages, food, and candy. Vending machine sales have experienced little growth over the past five years largely due to changes in the workplace. Employment growth has been limited, and the largest growth in the workforce is white- and pink-collar employees rather than the blue-collar workers who buy most heavily from vending machines. In general, consumers are reluctant to buy expensive merchandise from vending machines due to the limited information provided by the machine and the difficulty of returning unsatisfactory merchandise.[63]

Technological developments in vending machine design may result in long-term sales growth. New video kiosk vending machines enable consumers to see the merchandise in use, get information about the merchandise, and use their credit cards to make a purchase.

The new vending machine designs also enable the retailers to increase the productivity of the machines. Electronic systems in the machine keep track of inventory, cash, and other operating conditions. Then radio devices transmit data back to a host computer. This data is analyzed and communications are sent to route drivers telling them when stockouts and malfunctions occur.[64]

SUMMARY   Sales by electronic retailers are a small percentage of total retail sales now but have substantial growth potential. Nonstore retailing is a small but growing sector in the retail industry. The major nonstore retailing formats are electronic retailing, catalog and direct-mail retailing, direct selling, TV home shopping, and vending machines. Each of these formats communicates with customers using different media and offers different levels of interactivity.

The growth of electronic retailing depends on whether or not electronic retailers provide superior benefits over existing retail formats. The critical benefit that electronic retailers can offer is the opportunity for consumers to search across a broad range of alternatives, develop a smaller set of alternatives based on their needs, and get the specific information about alternatives they want. Current Internet retailers are just beginning to provide these benefits. Present offerings on the Internet are very attractive, but in the future Internet retailers will give customers the chance to shop the world and use electronic agents to help them sift through the information quickly to locate what they want.

The type of merchandise sold by electronic retailers depends on delivery costs, the consumer's need for immediacy, and the degree to which electronic retailers can provide prepurchase information that helps customers determine whether they will be satisfied with the merchandise. Successful electronic retailers will overcome the limitations of collecting touch-and-feel data by offering testimonials from other buyers, providing video information about the experience with the merchandise, or using information about brand-size combinations that fit specific members of the household. For experienced consumers, brand name alone may be enough information to predict satisfaction with the purchase decision.

Some critical resources needed to successfully sell merchandise electronically are (1) strong brand name and image, (2) customer information, (3) complementary merchandise and services, (4) unique merchandise, (5) ability to present information on web pages, and (6) a distribution system to efficiently ship merchandise to homes and receive returns. Catalog retailers possess most of these resources and thus are well positioned to exploit electronic retailing opportunities. While store-based retailers lack home distribution systems, they have an opportunity to use their locations as delivery and return points.

Disintermediation by manufacturers is unlikely because most manufacturers do not have the capability to efficiently distribute merchandise to individual consumers, provide assortments, and use information about specific consumers to develop individual catalogs for specific customers.

KEY TERMS

catalog retailing, *99*

direct-mail retailing, *99*

direct-response advertising, *103*

direct selling, *101*

disintermediation, *99*

electronic agent, *85*

electronic retailing, *79*

infomercial, *103*

multilevel network, *102*

nonstore retailing, *76*

party plan system, *102*

search engine, *85*

shopping bots, *85*

television home shopping retailing, *103*

vending machine retailing, *103*

virtual community, *93*

DISCUSSION QUESTIONS AND PROBLEMS

1. What are the five different nonstore retail formats? Which format has the greatest annual sales? Which format has the greatest annual growth rate?

2. Do you think electronic retailing will eventually have annual sales greater than catalog sales? Why or why not?

3. Why are electronic retailers and catalogers frequently patronized for gift giving?

4. Which of the following categories of merchandise do you think could be sold effectively by electronic retailers: jewelry, TV sets, computer software, high-fashion apparel, pharmaceuticals, and health care products such as toothpaste, shampoo, and cold remedies? Why?

5. What is an electronic agent? What benefit does it offer to consumers?

6. If consumers dramatically increase their electronic shopping, which store-based retailers will be most adversely affected? Why?

7. Assume you are interested in investing in a virtual community targeting people interested in active outdoor recreation such as hiking, rock climbing, and kayaking. What merchandise and information would you offer on the site? What type of a company do you think would be most effective in running the site: a well-known outdoors person, a magazine targeting outdoor activity, or a retailer selling outdoor merchandise. Why?

8. Compare catalog, Internet, and TV home shopping from the customer's perspective. What are the advantages and disadvantages of each retail format? Will the electronic retailers replace TV home shopping and catalog retailers? Why or why not?

9. Which of the following retail formats are most vulnerable to losing sales to electronic retailers: catalog and direct-mail retailers, supermarkets, category specialists, home improvement centers, and drugstores?

10. Outline a strategy for an electronic business that is involved in selling merchandise or services in your college town. Outline your strategy in terms of your target market and the offering at your Internet site. Who are your competitors in providing the merchandise and/or service? What advantages and disadvantages do you have over your competitors?

SUGGESTED READINGS

Aron, Laurie. "Delivering on E-Commerce." *Chain Store Age*, June 1999, pp. 6, 130.

Bartlett, Richard. *The Direct Option.* College Station, TX: Texas A&M University, 1994.

Daniel, Elizabeth, and George Klimis. "The Impact of Electronic Commerce on Market Structure: An Evaluation of the Electronic Market Hypothesis." *European Management Journal,* June 1999, pp. 318–26.

The Digital Channel Continues to Gather Steam: The Second Annual Ernest & Young Internet Shopping Survey. Washington, DC: National Retail Federation, 1999.

D'Innocenzio, Anne. "Getting Booked: Coping with a Catalog Crunch." *WWD*, December 9, 1998, p. 8.

Doherty, N.F., F. Ellis-Chadwick, and C.A Hart. "Cyber Retailing in the UK: The Potential of the Internet as a Retail

Channel." *International Journal of Retail & Distribution Management* 27 (January 1999), p. 22.

Global On-Line Retailing: An Ernst & Young Special Report, Stoves, Section 2, January 2000.

Nevens, T. Michael. "The Mouse That Roared: On-line Retail Sales Might Be Modest, but Don't Underestimate the Broader Impact of the Internet." *The McKinsey Quarterly*, Winter 1999, pp. 145–9.

Peterson, Robert, and Gerald Albaum. "What Is Direct Selling? Definition, Perspectives, and Research." *Journal of Personal Selling and Sales Management* 16 (Fall 1996), pp. 1–16.

Schwartz, Evan. *Digital Darwinism.* New York: Broadway Books, 1999.

Seybold, Patricia. *Customers.Com.* New York: Random House, 1998.

APPENDIX

Retail Internet Sites

SOURCES OF INFORMATION ABOUT INTERNET USAGE	
hotlinks to studies on electronic commerce	cyberatlas.internet.com
information on Internet usage worldwide	www.glreach.com/globstats
summaries of electronic commerce studies	www.nua.ie/index.html
summary of Internet surveys conducted by Georgia Institute of Technology	www.gvu.gatech.edu/user_surveys
collection of statistics from industry reports	www.computerworld.com/home/Emmerce.nsf/All/stats

SOURCES OF CURRENT NEWS ON ELECTRONIC COMMERCE AND RETAILING	
site operated by Ziff-Davis, a publisher of niche magazines	www.zdnet.com/enterprise/e-business
technical, IT-oriented news	ecommerce.internet.com
New York Times. Monday issue has a special technology section.	www.nytimes.com
The Economist, European business magazine	www.economist.com
CIO Magazine with associated research center	www.cio.com
Advertising Age articles on e-commerce	www.adage.com
Internet World magazine	www.webweek.com
Computerworld magazine, IT-oriented	www.computerworld.com
Business Marketing magazine, business-to-business e-commerce	www.netb2b.com
Wired Daily News, Internet-related business and technology news	www.wired.com/news
TechWeb, technical information about computing and the Internet	www.techweb.com
CNET e-commerce news	news.cnet.com/news/0–1007.html
Business 2.0 site. Interesting magazine devoted to e-commerce, business issues.	www.business2.com
The Industry Standard magazine site. Another interesting magazine devoted to e-commerce business issues.	www.thestandard.com
site collecting news releases on Internet and e-commerce issues	www.internetnews.com/ec-news
magazine devoted to retailing over the Internet	www.internetretailer.com

RETAIL TRADE ASSOCIATIONS	
Direct Marketing Association	www.the-dma.org
Food Marketing Institute	www.fmi.org
Grocery Manufacturers Association	www.gmabrands.org
National-America Wholesale Grocers Association	www.nawga-ifda.org
National Association of Convenience Stores	www.cstorecentral.com
National Grocers Association	www.onetoone.com/nga
National Retail Federation	www.nrf.com
National Retail Hardware Association	www.nrha.org
Shop.Org (Association of Internet Retailers)	www.shop.org

SPECIALTY RETAILERS	
Autozone	www.autozone.com.
Banana Republic	www.bananarepublic.com
Body Shop (UK)	www.the-body-shop.com
Borders Books and Music	www.borders.com
Burlington Coat Factory	www.coat.com
Container Store	www.containerstore.com
Delias	www.delias.com
Disney Store	www.store.disney.com
Express	www.express.style.com
Eddie Bauer	www.eddiebauer.com
FAO Schwarz	www.faoschwarz.com
Fogdog	www.fogdog.com
Foot Locker	www.footlocker.com
FragranceNet.com	www.fragrancenet.com
The Gap	www.gap.com
The Nature Company	www.natureco.com
Payless Shoes	www.payless.com
Pep Boys	www.pepboys.com
Pier 1 Imports	www.pier1.com
Radio Shack	www.radioshack.com
Roots	www.roots.com.
Sephora	www.sephora.com
Warner Brothers Store	www.studio.warnerbrothers.com
Western Auto	www.westernauto.com
Wolf Camera	www.wolfcamera.com

DRUGSTORE RETAILERS	
CVS	www.cvs.com
Eckerd	www.eckerd.com
Osco	www.americandrugstores.com
Rite-Aid	www.riteaid.com
Vitamins.com	www.vitamins.com
Walgreens	www.walgreens.com

CATEGORY SPECIALISTS	
Best Buy	www.bestbuy.com
Blockbuster	www.blockbuster.com
Circuit City	www.circuitcity.com
CompUSA	www.compusa.com
Media Play	www.mediaplay.com
Office Depot	www.officedepot.com
OfficeMax	www.officemax.com
PETsMART	www.petsmart.com
Petstore	www.petstore.com
Sports Authority	www.sportsauthority.com
Staples	www.staples.com
Toys "R" Us	www.toysrus.com

OFF-PRICE RETAILERS	
Bluefly.com	www.bluefly.com
Ross Stores	www.rossstores.com
Tuesday Morning	www.tuesdaymorning.com

FOOD RETAILERS	
A&P	www.aptea.com
AUCHAN (France)	www.auchan.com
Food Lion	www.foodlion.com
Fred Meyer	www.fredmeyer.com
Hannaford	www.hannaford.com
H.E. Butt	www.heb.com
Home Grocer	www.homegrocer.com
IGA (Independent Grocers Alliance)	www.igainc.com
Peapod	www.peapod.com
Ralphs	www.ralphs.com
J. Sainsbury (UK)	www.sainsbury.co.uk
Shoplink	www.shoplink.com
Streamline	www.streamline.com
Tesco (UK)	www.tesco.co.uk
Trader Joe's	www.traderjoes.com
Wegmans	www.wegmans.com
Whole Foods Market	www.wholefoods.com
Wild Oats	www.wildoats.com

CONVENIENCE STORE RETAILERS	
RaceTrac	www.racetrac.com
7-Eleven	www.7elevenusa.com

GENERAL MERCHANDISE RETAILERS	
Bloomingdale's	www.bloomingdales.com
Carrefour	www.carrefour.fr
Costco	www.costco.com
Dillards	www.dillards.com
Galeries Lafayette	www.galerieslafayette.com
Gottschalks	www.gotts.com
JCPenney	www.jcpenney.com
Kmart	www.kmart.com
Macy's	www.macys.com
Marks & Spencer (UK)	www.marks-and-spencer.co.uk
Neiman Marcus	www.neimanmarcus.com
Nordstrom	www.nordstrom.com
Printemps	www.printemps.fr
Sears Roebuck	www.sears.com
Target	www.target.com
Wal-Mart	www.wal-mart.com
Zellers	www.zellers.co

HOME AND IMPROVEMENT RETAILERS	
Bombay Company	www.bombayco.com
Crate & Barrel	www.crateandbarrel.com
Home Depot	www.homedepot.com
Lowe's	www.lowes.com
Our house.com	www.ourhouse.com
CATALOG RETAILERS	
Lands' End	www.landsend.com
L.L. Bean	www.llbean.com
Patagonia	www.patagonia.com

Cynthia Cohen
President, Strategic Mindshare

AFTER A CAREER IN A LARGE management consulting firm, Deloitte & Touche, I was bitten by the entrepreneurial bug. In 1990, I recognized that there was a vacuum in the retail industry for a niche consulting firm. My vision was to establish a premier firm to develop creative strategies, thought leadership, and action-oriented business plans for growing companies in the face of changing consumer behavior. Strategic Mindshare was founded from this vision.

• Every retailer recognizes the importance of continually growing the business. Without growth, you risk losing market share and competitive advantages. Growth comes from increasing penetration in your target markets. To do that, you must understand not only what makes your customers buy in your store, but also what makes them tick. We've learned that people have a certain propensity to buy products or to select a brand based on the behavioral aspects of their lives. For instance, people who wear heavy boots and outdoor clothing don't necessarily spend all their leisure time hiking. Yet, they identify with this outdoor image and are therefore likely to also purchase a sports utility vehicle. Once you identify the psychographic profile of your customers, it is easy to zero in on their demographic profile—age, income. Then you can readily target the true sweet spot of high-probability buyers of your product. • Over the years, my firm has studied a lot of companies. We found that focusing on brand awareness doesn't necessarily lead to actual product purchases. After all, everyone knows about AT&T and Levi Strauss & Co., but their market share have still fallen in recent years. So, instead, we concluded that retailers should concentrate on improving their "mindshare." Mindshare is how well your brand is ingrained in the consumers' subconsciousness—the degree to which your brand is the intuitive choice to fulfill consumers' needs in your category. Mindshare, not awareness, is what builds customer loyalty and market share. Our goal is to instill this concept with every client that we work with. • Most recently we've concentrated our research on a highly influential group of consumers, Generation Y—people between the ages of 14 and 24. Demographically, they represent the largest collection of potential consumers since the baby boomers (ages 37 to 55). Generation Y has significant buying power as well as unprecedented influence over spending in the entire household. Some retailers have already figured out the true potential of this group, while others are just coming to grips with how to target this broad, yet sophisticated young generational cohort.

The Retail Customer

CONSIDER THREE RETAILERS, each capable of fulfilling any and all prescriptive drug needs of a consumer; yet, each serves different types of customers and each has realized varying levels of success. Danny's Drugs, family-owned and in business since 1952, is located downtown at the corner of Ash and Main. The poorly lit store is filled with a random assortment of somewhat dusty merchandise. It's 5:00 P.M., and business is slow as usual. One teenage clerk behind a cash register ponders why he took such a boring job, while the 60-year-old owner/pharmacist is wondering where all of his customers from years ago have gone. He'll worry about it tomorrow; the store closes at 5:30, just as always.

Meanwhile, the scene is quite different at a new Walgreens drugstore located in a stand-alone location next to a strip shopping center in a nearby suburb. Walgreens prefers stand-alone locations to shopping centers to facilitate its convenient drive-through pharmacy. The strip center has a Safeway and Blockbuster Video as well as other local and national retailers. The parking lot is jammed with men and women coming home from work. Since they're in a hurry to do some errands before they get dinner on the table for their families, they do one-stop shopping to save time. They can go to either the supermarket or drugstore to pick up milk and a prescription. Although Blockbuster has a broader selection, they could also rent a film at Safeway. Both stores are open late, seven days a week. Walgreens is open 24 hours a day!

Walgreens' part-time pharmacist is a man in his 70s who retired from his own drugstore a few years ago. It's not unusual for retailers to seek out older part-time workers since they're experienced and reliable, and there's a shortage of young workers. He's filling a prescription for a tourist from New Jersey. The pharmacist can get the tourist's prescription information from a Walgreens in the tourist's hometown via satellite. Customers don't just wander aimlessly through aisles of cluttered merchandise as they might at Danny's Drugs. Walgreens has an in-store computer terminal for customers to place special orders plus databases that they can use to get information on products and health-related matters. Some products, as well as the music, are geared to the store's primarily Hispanic–American clientele. Most employees are bilingual, announcements are made in both English and Spanish. The store is readily accessible to the handicapped. Signs use large, easy-to-read lettering, and employees are trained to cater to special needs of the elderly.

Walgreens employees are encouraged to participate in civic events and charities. The store manager is a Girl Scout leader; one pharmacist coordinates a food drive for the homeless with other area retailers and restaurants. Recycling bins are found in the parking lot. The store also attempts to purchase products that are ecologically safe.

Meanwhile there isn't a single customer in sight at Drugstore.com. Business, however, is booming (even though its revenues are only a small fraction of Walgreens' revenues). Andy Stergachis and Steven P. Hall will be working through the night to fill prescriptions for some of their customers. In fact, Federal Express has just arrived at its usual pickup time.

Customers place prescription orders through Drugstore.com's innovative website. The website, however, offers much more. For instance, customers can ask pharmacists questions about their health. Health tips are provided along with in-depth information about specific drugs. Importantly, customers can purchase almost anything that is available at Walgreens or Danny's from the privacy of their own home.

The difference between Walgreens and Danny's Drugs is that one anticipated and reacted to the profound demographic trends of today's population, while the other tried to resist them and ended up losing. Drugstore.com has integrated an understanding of how potential customers' needs are changing by embracing the new technology that many believe will have a profound effect on consumer behavior. Walgreens is currently more profitable than Drugstore.com, at least in the short term. Although some consumer segments may always prefer brick-and-mortar drug retailers like Walgreens, others will seek out the convenience of Internet providers like Drugstore.com. As a result, Walgreens has developed its own Internet channel that competes directly with Drugstore.com.

INTERNET EXERCISE   Go to Drugstore.com and Walgreens.com on the Internet. Compare their retail offering: their product offering, prices, website features, design, and ease of use. Which one of these sites would you use?

This chapter is the first of two that focuses on the customer. In this chapter, we examine several consumer trends and how retailers are reacting to them. Next, Chapter 5 concentrates on customer needs, buying behavior, and how retailers segment their markets. This chapter begins with four sections that describe important shifts in consumer **demographics** (vital statistics about populations): generational cohorts, ethnic diversity, income and consumers' use of the Internet. The fifth section discusses the changing American family. Specifically it examines how the women's market has changed and how our time-poor society has created opportunities for many retailers. The last section looks at changes in consumer values. Embracing technology, the metamorphosis of American culture, social consciousness, environmental sensitivity, the value-oriented customer, and dress-down fashions are discussed.

INTERNET EXERCISE   *American Demographics* is an interesting magazine with articles on changing U.S. lifestyles. Go to www.demographics.com, select an article in an issue of the magazine, and discuss how the information in the article can help retailers better understand and appreciate the needs of their changing customer base. What should retailers do based on the information in this article to improve their performance?

GENERATIONAL COHORTS

Retailers and their vendors find it useful to group people into generations and then market to them differently. In general, a **generational cohort**—people within the same generation—have similar purchase behaviors because they have shared experiences and are in the same stage of life. For instance, although baby boomers (people born after World War II, 1946 through 1964) and Generation Xers (people born between 1965 and 1976) gravitate toward products and services that foster a casual lifestyle, they tend to do so for different reasons. Baby boomers are often trying to maintain their youth. Having grown up in jeans and khakis, they tend to continue this practice and have brought casual dressing into their businesses. Xers typically wear jeans and khakis because they are less impressed with symbols of conspicuous consumption than their parents.

Although there are many ways to cut the generational pie, we will discuss four major groups. Also, the exact definitions for these groups shift as time goes by. For instance, older baby boomers have become young seniors. Meanwhile, the youngest group—Generation Y—gets bigger with each new birth. Finally, we do not include our youngest consumers, children aged zero to five, since most still have little control over their shopping behaviors. The four generational cohorts are found in Exhibit 4–1.

Generation Y   At 60 million in the United States alone, this group is more than three times the size of Generation X (whom we discuss next) and the biggest thing to hit since the original baby boom (whom we examine later in this section). The cohort spans so many years, however, that it makes sense to break it down into children (ages 6 to 14), and young adults (ages 15 to 24). Although these two groups have many things in common, they do approach the marketplace somewhat differently.

EXHIBIT 4–1

Generational Cohorts

GENERATIONAL COHORT	RANGE OF BIRTH YEARS	AGE IN 2001
Generation Y	1977–95	6–24
Generation X	1965–76	25–36
Baby boomers	1946–64	37–55
Seniors	Before 1946	56 and older

If you could sum up **Generation Y** in a single word, the word would be *diverse*.[1] First, the original baby boomers are 75 percent non-Hispanic white, compared to less than 67 percent in this group. As a result, many retailers and their vendors develop products and promotions with much broader appeal than in the past. For instance, Fisher-Price (a major supplier of toys to retailers like Toys "R" Us) has Dream Doll House families that are African American, Hispanic, Asian, and Caucasian. Some retailers shoot different versions of the same ad using rap, alternative rock, and even country music to reach different groups of teens and children.

Generation Y exhibits many paradoxical behavior patterns.[2] First, although many want to achieve a high "quality of life," they tend to put themselves under a lot of stress by participating in a variety of activities. Second, although they do healthy things, many also live a fast life with drug use rising. Finally, although they don't tend to want to adapt their parents' "live to work" credo, many crave shopping and recognize they need lots of money to satisfy their consumption fix.

Generation Y has a tendency to show similar attitudes and shopping patterns throughout the world.[3] They watch MTV and *Dawson's Creek*, drink Coke, eat Big Macs, view the same movies, surf the Internet, and wear jeans, T-shirts, and sneakers. Most experts believe that the reason for the similarities is that this is the first generation tied together by a worldwide media web. The influence has a strong American flavor. Although the emergence of the European Union (EU) has brought teens from those countries closer together, these teens tend to embrace products and fashions made in Europe.

Refact Within a couple of years, kids will be spending $35 billion of their own money and $300 billion of their parents'. The marketers' motto in this decade is "If you don't have a kid's product, get one."[4]

The opportunity for marketing to these children and young adults is threefold. First, they have their own money to spend. And they have more money than that age group did in the past. For instance, the aggregate spending by or on behalf of children ages 4 to 12 roughly doubled every decade in the 1960s, 1970s, and 1980s. It has tripled so far in the 1990s.[5] Second, children and young adults influence household purchases through their requests to parents or by shopping themselves. This trend has also accelerated as dual-career parents allow and encourage their children to make choices about everything. Finally, and possibly most important, children are a future market for all goods and services.[6]

Many retailers have realized the gigantic opportunity to sell goods and services to children and their baby boomer parents. For instance, Abercrombie and Fitch Co., Gap Inc.'s Gap Kids, and Gymboree Corp. have launched or expanded stores for 6-to-12–year-olds. Children and young adults are a growing market for fitness clubs and personal trainers in big cities. Delta Airlines and the Canadian discounter Zellers have designed loyalty programs for them.[7] dELiA*s began targeting teen girls in 1993 by distributing 1.7 million catalogs. In 1998 it distributed 55 million

Generation Y presents an incredible selling opportunity for retailers, both in stores and over the Internet. This group is large, has money to spend, and influences household purchases.

*dELiA*s successfully sells to Generation Y girls using catalogs, stores, and the Internet.*

Refact By 1998, between 75 and 90 percent of teens had a computer at home and about half had access to the Internet.[10] Ninety-six percent of consumers age 16 to 22 use the Internet for e-mail, while only 40 prcent use it to purchase products.*

*"Just Surfin' Through," *American Demographics,* January 2000, p. 12, research attributable to Forrester Research.

copies of nine different versions of its dELiA*s catalog and 6 million copies of its TSI soccer catalog. The company also hosts several popular websites: www.delias.com, www.gurl.com and www.screem.com. Other retailers targeting the teenage girl market are Hot Topics, Pacific Sunwear, Gadzooks, and Wet Seal.

Retailers try to react quickly and decisively to reach this group.[8] Like Generation X, they are skeptical about advertising. Although they will watch ads, they typically don't buy until products are "legitimized" by their peers. Not only does this group desire frequent style changes, but brands rise and crash quickly. The "look" also changes depending on the situation—jeans work in the day, exotic at night.

Reaching today's young adults through the media is easier than it was for their older brothers and sisters in Generation X. Although they watch slightly less television than the same age group 10 years before, the tube tends to be more influential. While the Internet is still not an important method for the youngest consumers to shop because many don't yet have credit cards, retailers believe it is an important format by which they can explore new products and trends.

Nonetheless, Generation Y enjoys shopping in malls and department stores. They want their senses excited by the product: sight, sound, and touch.[9] Retailers are planning more multipurpose, entertaining stores with features such as Barnes & Noble's reading chairs and coffee bars and Tower Records' Listening Kiosks. Department and specialty stores are expected to increase their use of fragrance and music, not as products to sell, but as image enhancers. Retailers that offer multiple products and activities—such as gyms that sell sporting goods or PETsMART where you can get a pet vaccinated—will be particularly appealing to Generation Y.

Additional strategies that retailers are using to appeal to Generation Y include

- *Getting young people involved in the store.* Genuardi's Family Markets in Pennsylvania has created a vegetable club for kids. Since children love to collect things, they're given cards of the vegetables they buy and try each time they visit the store.[11] Some stores arrange MTV-inspired fashion shows or other promotional ideas to get children and their parents through their doors.

- *Being conscious of the environment, animal rights, and other social issues.* Young people respond to such issues through personal actions such as vegetarianism or recycling and by avoiding products or companies that do not meet their criteria for responsible social behavior.[12]

- *Being honest.* Retailers will have a greater chance to relate to teens if they emphasize their strengths and face their weaknesses by poking good-humored fun at them.[13]

- *Tying advertising and promotions in with sports and music events.* The objective is to get customers talking about the products and store.

- *Getting stores involved in community service.* McDonald's hopes to make a sick child's stay in the hospital less frightening, while creating brand loyalty, by placing its mascot's image on pediatric hospital gowns.[14]

Strategies retailers use to meet children's special needs include

- *Developing partnerships with schools.* For instance, Pizza Hut offers grade-school children free food if they read at least 20 minutes a day.[15]
- *Presenting merchandise in manageable groupings to eliminate the feeling of having too many choices.* Delias.com, for example has relatively few categories and relatively few SKUs within those categories.
- *Creating "touchy-feely" departments.* A computer store, for instance, might have a children's learning section with working computers and video games that children can play with.

Refact Teenagers spend almost $49 billion in grocery stores, which is more than 10 percent of total grocery industry sales.[16]

Generation X   The next oldest group is **Generation X** (**Xers**). Born between 1965 and 1976, Xers represent some 41 million Americans. This group is very different from their baby boomer parents. For instance, they're the first generation of **latchkey children** (those who grew up in homes where both parents worked) and, as with Generation Y, over 50 percent of their parents' marriages ended in divorce. Whereas their parents were an optimistic group who became unified on many issues such as Vietnam and Civil Rights, the Xers are often pessimistic about their future and not as unified as their parents. Many Xers have different values, shopping habits, and income levels than their parents. On the average, members of Generation X have about one less year of college education than baby boomers. Even those with the same education tend to earn much lower salaries than boomers did at the same age.

Although smaller in number than Generation Y and baby boomers, they possess considerable spending power—about $125 billion per year in the United States.[17] This relatively high affluence is attributed to the fact that Xers get married later in life, buy houses later, and are living with parents longer than previous generations. From a retailer's perspective, they're much less interested in shopping than their parents. They demand convenience. They don't want to wait. For instance, to satisfy these harried customers, grocery stores are attempting to provide total-meal solutions with quick checkout stations.

Xers are generally considered to be astute consumers, more cynical than their boomer parents. They tend to be less likely to believe advertising claims and what salespeople tell them. Xers are inclined to develop shopping savvy at an early age because many grew up in dual-career households where the parents didn't have much time for shopping. As a result, as teenagers many Xers learned how to make shopping decisions, so they grew more knowledgeable about products and more risk-averse than other shoppers. Finally, Xers are much less interested in status products than older generations. It is not that they can't afford luxury brands—they just don't see the point. They ask, "Why buy Calvin Klein jeans when Levi's look just as good?"

To effectively target the valuable Generation X market, many companies have revised their ad campaigns to adapt to the more knowledgeable, cynical group. Gone are the days of ads portraying luxury items. Today's retailers of athletic shoes, cosmetics, fashion, and fast food (who flourish because of Xers) are making their ads more candid, while not pushing the actual

Retailers can appeal to children by getting them involved in the shopping decision.

product too hard on the customer. For instance, drugstore chain Rite-Aid developed an extensive advertising campaign encouraging consumers to buy a new lipstick, knowing that they can return it if they don't like it. The chain believes this strategy appeals to this group because they like to try new things, they buy products to enhance themselves, and they are extremely price-sensitive.[18]

Other strategies retailers are using to appeal to Generation X include

- *Not rushing customers to buy.* They don't like pushy salespeople. For instance, the Speakeasy Café, a cybercafe in Seattle targeting Generation X, has salespeople behind a counter. They only approach customers when they are totally lost or a customer approaches them about buying services to set up a home page.
- *Presenting a lot of options and product information.* IKEA, for instance, is very successful with Xers. It sells low-cost, unassembled furniture with tags indicating by whom it was made. Borders sells CDs by allowing customers to hear music before buying.
- *Using technology whenever and however possible.*

Baby Boomers

After World War II, the birth rate rose sharply, giving rise to a group known as the **baby boomers**—the 78 million Americans born between 1946 and 1964. This huge generation spans 18 years, so it's almost impossible to fit them into one group. The older baby boomers were 17 to 23 years old during a time of economic prosperity and political tumult (the Vietnam War and the Civil Rights movement). Younger boomers were still growing up during Watergate, the oil embargo, and a contracting economy. These vastly different experiences of the two groups during their coming-of-age years has affected their outlook toward life in general and consumption behavior in particular. Further, many older baby boomers are quickly reaching a stage in their family life cycle called empty nest where their families have grown up and left home. Younger boomers, on the other hand, are in the throes of childrearing. As a result, many older boomers have more disposable income and time than the younger boomers.

Despite the differences between older and younger boomers, experts agree that they share several traits that set them apart from people born before World War II.[20] First, they are individualistic. Second, leisure time is a high priority for them. Third, they believe that they can always take care of themselves. They have a feeling of economic security, even though they are a little careless about the way they spend their money. Fourth, they

Refact A "boomer bummer"—as the baby boomer population ages, per capita retail spending will fall, a pattern that will begin with a fractional decrease in 2005 and approach double-digit declines from 2020 to 2025.[19]

The challenge facing retailers who target baby boomers is to sell them merchandise designed for older people while letting them think that they are still young.

have an obsession with maintaining their youth. Finally, they will always love rock and roll.

Although significant in size and wealth, aging baby boomers pose significant challenges to retailers. First, unlike busters, they don't need to make those first-time purchases of furniture, appliances, or business attire. Further, as people reach middle age, they're thought to become less materialistic. For instance, The Sharper Image based its success in the 1980s on providing expensive toys to yup-pies (young urban professionals). In the 1990s, it had to redefine its merchandis-ing strategy to provide more practical products and lower price points.

What will boomers buy? Vitamins, travel, home improvement products, new experiences, and nostalgia are safe bets. Retailers like GNC, Restoration Hard-ware, Crate & Barrel, and REI should capture this market. Experts disagree about boomers' propensity to buy apparel. Some think that they will buy less be-cause they have everything and many fashions are not designed to flatter middle-aged physiques. Others insist that apparel will continue to be important to boomers as they travel more and move back into urban settings. As with Genera-tion X, home-meal–replacement products—with a healthy slant—are an impor-tant opportunity for food retailers and restaurants.[21]

How are retailers reaching this large group? By selling nostalgia, selling nat-ural, and selling youth and fitness.

Selling Nostalgia Many retailers and their suppliers have found that one of the best ways to grab baby boomers is to make them dream about what they re-member to be the care-free days of their youth.[22] The Gap, for instance, launched the Old Navy casual clothing chain with a series of old-timey black-and-white ads and store decor that recalled the 50s. Although Old Navy has modernized its marketing with new advertising campaigns emphasizing value and fashion, many of the original decor touches remain, including 50s Chevy pickup trucks. A&W Restaurants Inc., once famous for carhops on roller skates, is attempting to reverse more than two decades of decline by overhauling its restaurants in a 1950s rock 'n' roll image. Restoration Hardware specializes in selling nostalgia to baby boomers. (See Retailing View 4.1.)

Selling Natural They believe "natural" is better.[23] While the term *natural* means different things to different people, retailers and their vendors will con-tinue to design and sell products that are perceived to be natural to their baby boomer customers. Boomers also respond well to firms with a social consciousness.

At Restoration Hardware, buyers search for products that appeal to their baby boomer customers.

Selling Youth and Fitness Another boomer characteristic that's consistent with their desire to maintain their youth is their obsession with exer-cise and diet. Experts believe that this is more than a fitness fad. As boomers watch their parents grow old, they're seeing that they have to keep them-selves fit to stay out of the nursing home. Retailers of exercise equipment, sports apparel, and sports-related foods such as Gatorade will continue to benefit from boomers' passion for fitness. Service providers such as exercise clubs, personal trainers, diet clinics, and plastic surgeons will also benefit.

Knob Appeal: Restoration Hardware Appeals to Baby Boomers

4.1

IT WAS 1979 WHEN STEPHEN GORDON, then 26, began scouring hardware and antique stores for vintage items. But antique doorknobs, turn-of-the-century light fixtures, and special knickknacks true to the character of the home were scarce. So, the next year, Gordon opened his own retail store in Eureka, California, specializing in hard-to-find interior building and decorative materials to help other home restoration fanatics.

In 1999, his dream is no longer a little shop of knobs and handles. With 65 locations throughout the United States and British Columbia, a catalog division with a circulation of 4 million, and $200 million in sales in 1998, Restoration Hardware is a formidable player in the highly profitable realm of eclectic home decorating chains. That circle includes Pier 1 Imports, Cost Plus, Crate & Barrel, and Williams-Sonoma owned Pottery Barn.

Integrating turn-of-the-century charm with modern tastes and baby boomer nostalgia, Restoration Hardware offers home furnishings, door pulls, bath items, cleaning supplies, and even fun days-of-yore items such as a wind-up tin robot. The focus remains on upscale furnishings, however.

When you walk through one of the Restoration Hardware stores, it is easy to see how the growth and profits have come about. Shoppers can find a deep brown leather chair for $1,395 and a swing-arm floor lamp for $225, for instance. Most merchandise is modern instead of turn-of-the-century retro.

Their customers are baby boomers, just like the management. Their buying strategy tries to determine what their customer wants. But rather than do market research, they just buy what they think they themselves would like in their own homes.

Finding unusual merchandise to keep those boomers and their dollars flowing into stores is a time-consuming safari for Restoration's product development team. Because they use their instincts rather than market research as guidelines, the developers are likely to bring back anything from kitchen tables to a bathroom cleaner when on a buying trip.

Source: Teena Massingill, "Knob Appeal: Restoration Hardware Chain Cashes in on Upscale Decorating Items," *Houston Chronicle,* May 23, 1999; and Heather Chaplin, "Past? Perfect!" *American Demographics,* May 1999, pp. 68–69.

Seniors   This is America's fastest-growing group. Between 1996 and 2010, the number of people age 55 to 64 will grow 65.2 percent, mostly as a result of aging baby boomers.[24]

Refact Seventeen percent of web users are over 50 years old.[26]

Are they an important market segment for retailers to pursue? The American Association of Retired Persons (AARP) reports that they're more likely to complain, need special attention, and take time browsing before making a purchase, and that they don't like changes, compared to other age groups.[25] On the other hand, they have time to shop and money to spend. Although their household income is lower than other groups, the income is likely to be from one individual.

In the past, seniors were very conservative with their savings. They wanted something to pass on to their children. But that attitude is changing. Older people seem to be buying goods and services at the same pace as younger generations. What do they spend this money on? Travel, second homes, luxury cars, electronic equipment, investments, home furnishings, and clothing are frequent purchases. Gifts, particularly to grandchildren, are especially popular among seniors. Genesis Direct, for example, produces a catalog called *Gifts for Grandkids.*

Seniors tend to like "made in the USA" items, natural fibers, recognizable brand names (but generally not designer labels), value, quality, and classic styles. They're typically loyal and willing to spend, but are extremely quality-conscious and demand hassle-free shopping. Since most mature customers don't need basics, they would prefer to buy a few high-quality items rather than a larger number of low-quality items. Convenient locations are a major consideration for them. They also don't like long checkout lines—but who does?

EXHIBIT 4–2

Retailing to Seniors

BETTER SERVICE

Retailers are making shopping easier for older people.

1. Have someone available who knows where things are to help older shoppers find things in the store.

2. Train all people to understand older citizens' needs, including simple, clear explanations and reassurance.

3. Employ older people. They can help other older people. They can reduce shoplifting losses because it is harder to steal from nice older people than from huge impersonal corporations. Wal-Mart hires older people as greeters to make customers of all ages feel welcome.

4. Encourage older people to order things by telephone or mail when they wish.

5. Provide places for them to sit down in different parts of the store.

6. Put up plenty of signs with big print and contrasting colors.

7. Don't move products to new locations all the time.

8. Have good lighting. Make sure lighting changes gradually, especially from the outside.

9. Locate restrooms in the front of the store for convenience and security.

10. Post directories throughout the store as convenient points of reference.

11. Don't put products that older shoppers tend to buy on the very top or bottom shelves.

12. Make store, mall, and parking lot security prevalent and visible.

13. Provide product information, such as information cards and brochures.

BETTER VALUE

Older people are often retired and on fixed (sometimes limited) incomes so retailers targeting these customers provide them with good value for their money.

1. Offer senior citizen discount days.

2. Have special "savings for seniors" sales that go beyond senior citizen discount days and feature products for older people.

Source: Paco Underhill, "Seniors in Stores." *American Demographics,* April 1996, pp. 44–48. "Marketing to Older Shoppers Makes Good Sense," *Discount Store News,* June 20, 1994, pp. 23, 28.

Refact Women over the age of 55 spend $21 billion annually on apparel (25 percent of total apparel sales). These women spend more than other age groups in department stores versus discount stores.[28]

Some retailers have created special programs for the mature segment of their customer base. Ames, for example, offers consumers age 55 or older a card giving them a 10 percent discount on Tuesdays. The card provides the company with information about their older shoppers. Even their stores are designed to appeal to seniors. Smaller than most other discount stores, they're known for their friendly, customer-oriented service.[27] Exhibit 4–2 describes how some retailers are providing strong service and value to older consumers.

ETHNIC DIVERSITY

America has become ethnically diverse due to immigration and increasing birth rates for various ethnic and racial groups.[29] Approximately 80 percent of all population growth for the next 20 years is expected to come from the African, Hispanic, and Asian communities. Minorities now represent about a quarter of the population; by 2050 they will represent about 47 percent. They are also spending at a higher rate than white households.[30] Most of the foreign-born population and recent immigrants are concentrated in a handful of states and metropolitan areas, primarily on the East and West coasts and along the U.S.–Mexican border. Some retailers are correctly

In Ethnic Marketing, Sears Stands Alone

INTERVIEW A DOZEN OR SO MULTICULTURAL marketing executives and ask them to name a retailer that does it successfully, and more than likely each one will respond, "Sears." From top executives to hourly wage employees, diversity is part of the corporate culture. With nearly 200 of its 850 stores in heavily ethnic markets, it has made a point of targeting each and every one. Sears even micromarkets to the subgroups within certain ethnic populations.

Sears began targeting Hispanics in the late 1980s and the program has evolved into a very powerful tool. The chain advertises 52 weeks per year in Spanish-language media and uses a two-pronged approach. For its primary marketing program, Sears uses a generic form of Spanish that all nationalities can understand and then more specifically targets distinct groups. For example, in Los Angeles Sears adopts a Mexican accent, while on the East Coast it has a more Caribbean flavor.

In 1993, Sears launched *Nuestra Gente,* a proprietary Spanish-language publication with a circulation of 800,000. The magazine averages 70 pages and is published four times a year to coincide with peak selling times: Easter, Fathers' Day, back-to-school, and the winter holidays.

Nuestra Gente not only advertises for the chain while attracting ads from manufacturers such as Procter & Gamble, Ford, and Toyota that also target this market; in addition it contains pertinent editorial content. For instance, articles cover everything from health and personal finance to childhood development and entertainment—all adapted to the interests of the various Hispanic cultures.

Sears actively sponsors community events such as the Callo Ocho, which attracts 1.5 million to 2 million people in Miami each year; the Fiesta del Sol in Chicago; the 116th Street Festival in New York; and Puerto Rican Independence Day festivals. And its Fiesta Mobile, a customized Winnebago, travels the country, making appearances at stores and festivals.

Sears also targets African Americans. Sears uses its Softer Side tag line in the African American market, but showcases different color schemes and products than they do in their regular stores. It also gives generously to community groups such as the National Urban League's youth programs.

Marketing to the Asian American population is a bit more challenging for Sears due to its fragmented composition. For instance, Chinese and Vietnamese consumers look for good product value and tend to be more loyal than other segments of this group. Koreans have a higher-end brand focus and therefore are more difficult for Sears to attract. Nonetheless, Sears is a heavy sponsor of events in the Asian American community. It recently ran a promotion in its California stores celebrating the Moon Festival and sponsored the Lunar New Year parade in San Francisco.

When it comes to fostering diversity and implementing truly effective multicultural marketing, Sears really gets it.

Source: "In Ethnic Marketing, Sears Stands Alone," *Discount Store News,* October 16, 1998, pp. 110, 112 (copyright 1998 Lebhar-Friedman, Inc.); Debby Garbato Stankevich, "Marketing to Hispanics: Beyond the Obvious," *Discount Merchandiser,* July 1, 1998, pp. 25–27; and Margaret White Blackburn, "Work × Shop = Profit Measuring Change at Sears," *Diversity Factor* 7, no. 1 (Fall 1998), pp. 7–10.

focusing on the large and growing middle and affluent classes of these minorities. Minorities also make up a bigger share of the retail work force than in the past. Immigrant entrepreneurs have revitalized neighborhoods and small towns. Food stores, restaurants, and service retailers such as dry cleaners and gas stations are particularly attractive to these entrepreneurs. Retailing View 4.2 examines ethnic marketing at Sears.

African Americans

As of 1997, there were 34 million African Americans in the United States.[31] That number is projected to grow to 45 million by 2020. The African American population tends to be younger than the rest of the population, and half of the households have single heads, compared to a third of white households.

Estimates of the group's buying power vary from approximately $350 to $500 billion per year. The average African American household income is

$21,100 compared to $32,300 for all U.S. households. But they spend about 5 percent more than whites on an average trip to a mall. Unlike many other consumer groups, the majority of African Americans believe it's "fun and exciting" to shop for clothes.

Although African American households are less affluent than other groups, they're some retailers' best customers. For instance, African Americans spend more on women's dress shoes, teen clothing, jewelry, women's athletic wear, and children's shoes. Retailers providing products and services that enhance personal appearance should take special note of this market. In general, African Americans spend more than their white counterparts on big-ticket items such as cars, clothing, and home furnishings. Many also have an affinity to brand-name products because they equate them with quality.

Retailers have seized the opportunity of targeting directly to African Americans. For instance, JCPenney has opened boutiques that sell authentic African clothing, housewares, and art. Spiegel Inc. (the giant mail order company) and *Ebony* magazine have successfully targeted blacks with *E Style*, a quarterly fashion, accessories, and home-decor catalog for black women. Kmart and Toys "R" Us have used minority advertising agencies to develop campaigns designed specifically for African American customers. In Atlanta, the South DeKalb Mall has repositioned itself as an "Afrocentric retail center." Several retailers in the mall have tried to orient their goods to blacks. Camelot Music more than doubled its selection of gospel, jazz, and rhythm and blues. Foot Locker stocks styles that do well in black markets, such as suede and black athletic shoes and baseball shirts from the Negro League of the 1930s.

What can retailers do to appeal to African American shoppers?

At the South DeKalb Mall in Atlanta, several retailers have tried to orient their goods to appeal to their African American customers.

- Have a wide selection of nationally recognized brands of clothing.
- Have helpful, friendly, and knowledgeable sales associates. But leave the customer alone until she needs assistance.
- Maintain everyday low prices.

Hispanic Americans

Many retailers see the Hispanic market's worth. JCPenney, for instance, spends about $6 million on Hispanic marketing per year. Why is there all this interest? About 350,000 Hispanic immigrants come to the United States every year. They and their U.S.-born children should increase the number of Hispanic Americans from just under 17 million in 1995 to over 52.7 million in 2020.[32] Hispanic households tend to be larger than other groups. Hispanics represent a $171 billion annual market. Forty-one percent of Hispanic households have annual incomes of at least $25,000, with Cubans having a much higher income than either Mexican or Puerto Rican consumers. Importantly, there's little difference in education, employment, and income between whites and Hispanics who were born in the United States or have lived here at least five years. The Hispanic market is particularly large in certain states and cities, such as California, Arizona, New Mexico, Texas, Miami, New York City, and Chicago.

T. J. Maxx ilumina
esta época con
calidad y ahorros.

Y lucir elegante y a la moda es más fácil que nunca en T.J. Maxx... Donde encontrarás las últimas modas e increíbles regalos para tus seres queridos, como ropa con las marcas de renombre favoritas y los diseñadores más famosos. Además, hay una variedad de accesorios para decorar tu hogar con el alegre ambiente de las fiestas.

Todo con el 20% al 60% menos que en las mejores tiendas por departamento.

Así que estas Navidades brilla de alegría con el estilo y los ahorros de T.J. Maxx. ¡Felices Fiestas!

TJ-maxx

Modas, Calidad y Ahorros.™

Many retailers, like T.J. Maxx, see the Hispanic market's worth by developing entire marketing programs for them.

Like many ethnic markets, the Hispanic market isn't homogeneous. Spanish-speaking people include Cubans, Mexicans, Puerto Ricans, and Central and South Americans—each with their own traditions and cultural backgrounds. Also, some Hispanics are quite affluent and have had roots in the United States for centuries, while others have more recently emigrated, are less affluent, and have limited English-language skills. As in any family, there can be significant generation gaps between grandparents, parents, and children. Hispanics tend to be very loyal to both national brands and to stores.[33] They tend to be attracted to the store because of established brands. And if the store makes them feel comfortable, they are likely to keep coming back. Finally, retailers must be very careful not to alienate their assimilated Hispanic customers by targeting them differently from their Anglo clientele. After all, most Hispanics choose to embrace aspects of both cultures. Given this diversity, retailers say the secret to successfully marketing to Hispanics is to pay attention to the specific characteristics of the clientele of every store—applicable advice for any retailer in any market.

Asian Americans

Although Asian Americans comprise only about 3 percent of the U.S. population, they're the fastest-growing minority population. They also earn more, have more schooling, and are more likely to be professionally employed or own a business than whites. But as with Hispanics, retailers shouldn't assume that they can target all Asians with one strategy. The Chinese, Japanese, Indian, Korean, and southeast Asian subgroups such as Vietnamese and Cambodian all speak different languages as well as come from different cultures.

The Aberdeen Centre near Vancouver, British Columbia, Canada, has targeted the large Asian market in its area. Nearly 80 percent of the merchants and customers are Chinese Canadians. The mall has shops with Hong Kong–made clothing and traditional Chinese medicines. Chinese movies, kung fu martial arts demonstrations, and Chinese folk dances help make this mall an important destination for its customers.

Refact One out of seven Californians speaks a language other than English at home.

INCOME

Income distribution in the United States is becoming more polarized—the highest-income groups are growing, while some middle- and lower-income groups' real purchasing power is declining. Polarization of income has helped to polarize retail institutions. Many retailers have increasingly targeted upscale customers, while others have found success with middle- and lower-income groups.

In the 1990s, the richest 20 percent of the households in the country accounted for nearly half of the nation's income. The top 5 percent had 21 percent of the income. The bottom 20 percent of the households, on the other hand, accounted for just 3.6 percent of the income.[34] There are more wealthy families than in the past because the general population is maturing, there is an increase in dual-income households, and the overall level of education is higher.

The Upscale Customer

Twenty percent of all U.S. households in 1995 are considered to be affluent, with an annual income of at least $70,000 a year.[35] This broad group encompasses enormous lifestyle and behavioral differences. At the lower end are two-earner households whose combined income barely reaches the $70,000 threshold. The superaffluents' existing wealth in some cases does all the earning for them. Clearly, people along the wealth continuum will spend their money differently.

Hammacher Schlemmer in New York City caters to wealthy individuals who are willing to pay top dollar for exclusive, high quality merchandise, and excellent customer service.

Retailers have adapted to meet the needs of the better-educated, high-income customer by adjusting their market strategies. Some middle-market retailers—particularly specialty stores—have upgraded their stores and merchandise. The Williams-Sonoma chain of cooking utensil stores, for instance, caters specifically to upscale customers.

Rich people are willing to pay top dollar for merchandise and services, but they also want exclusivity, high quality, and excellent customer service. Hammacher Schlemmer, for instance, specializes in this market. Its buyers go to great lengths to find exclusive, one-of-a-kind products, sometimes without regard to practicality. The Bionic Dolphin, a watercraft that can reach speeds of 85 miles an hour on the surface and up to 35 miles an hour underwater, can be had for $139,000. A London taxi cab was available for $43,000.

Not all wealthy people shop in upscale stores, however. Target Stores attract a more upscale customer than rivals Wal-Mart and Kmart, for instance. Furniture store IKEA and The Gap's Old Navy are attracting these customers as well.[36] The country that brought the world Chanel, champagne, and chic is now giving the world Tati. France's bargain-basement store has opened an outpost down the street from Saks Fifth Avenue in New York. The mink-and-pearl set rummages through Tati's bins alongside the traditionally low-income clientele. Young hipsters have made toting Tati's pink-and-white–check shopping bags fashionable.[37]

The Mass-Middle and Lower-Income Markets

The mass-middle and lower-income markets are more appealing markets today than ever before. The lower-income market represents consumers with household incomes below $25,000, whereas the mass-middle market includes households between $25,000 and $70,000.

Why are customers searching for value more today than in recent decades? For the first three decades after World War II, most American families experienced real income growth. But in the late 1970s through the 1990s, that growth began to stagnate. Some economists believe that all wage increases accruing in the United States in the past 20 years have gone to the top 20 percent of the population.[38] Family incomes have stayed slightly ahead of inflation, while health care costs, property taxes, and tuition bills have risen much faster than inflation.

To compound the problem of income stagnation, the recession and resulting increased unemployment of the late 1980s and 1990s profoundly affected both consumers and retailers. But retailers appealing to the lower-income group may see their fortunes change as blue-collar employment increases.[39]

The 1980s were the heyday for upscale retailers. Many department stores including JCPenney upgraded their stores and merchandise. But the 1990s were different. Notably, Penney scaled back its fashion image by searching for products offering customers better value—more quality for less money. In 1994, The Gap opened Old Navy Clothing Company that competes directly with discount stores on price, but offers more distinctive clothes made with higher-quality fabrics and attention to detail. Wildly successful, Old Navy draws customers from across the income spectrum.

Another venue for lower-income customers involves used, distressed, or odd-lot merchandise at rock-bottom prices. Companies such as Dollar General, Grow Biz International, and Consolidated Stores have done well by dispensing with many of the shopping amenities found even at traditional discounters. (See Chapter 2.)

Traditional choices for the lower-income groups are Mervyn's, Wal-Mart, Kmart, and Target. These stores have three key success factors in common. First, their atmosphere communicates value. They're nice, but not too nice. If fixtures and lighting are too plush, it implies expensive merchandise. Second, the merchandise assortment is credible. These stores carry a mix of moderately priced national brands that people recognize as well as quality, lower-priced private-label merchandise. Finally, the stores relentlessly promote both sale merchandise and everyday low prices. Retailing View 4.3 describes the "King of Catalogs" for this income group, Fingerhut.

INTERNET USAGE

Throughout *Retailing Management*, we discuss the many ways in which the Internet impacts the world of retailing. In this section, we describe the degree to which the Internet is changing the way customers shop for goods and services.

The Internet is experiencing astounding growth. In the middle of 1996, the online population of the United States was 35 million. By the middle of 1998, the population became 72.6 million. And by April of 1999, there were more than 83 million users online above age 16.[40]

Use of the Internet as an option to bricks and mortar stores has grown in the same fashion. In 1998, 18.6 million people bought goods over the Internet for a total of over $26 billion. By 2002, this number is expected to increase to 64 million people and $268 billion.[41]

In the late 1990s, men were using the Internet more than women. In 1997, about 37 percent of males in the United States were using the Internet, compared to only 17 percent of females. By mid-1998, the gap had tightened to 46.0 percent of males and 37.8 percent of females online. Experts believe that the gender split will be nearly even by 2001.[42]

Of course, some merchandise categories are purchased more often than others over the Internet. The most popular categories listed in order of sales are: software, hardware, books, travel, music, and clothing. There are, however, some gender differences. For instance, 27 percent of male Internet purchasers buy computer software compared to 10 percent of females. Also, 19 percent of

A ONE-TIME BOOKKEEPER AT A CAR DEALERSHIP, Mr. Fingerhut about 50 years ago began selling vinyl car-seat covers through the mail, using lists of car buyers he got from auto dealers. The company he founded, Fingerhut Corp., now has its own list of 30 million names. Through its catalog and almost entirely on credit, Fingerhut sells everything from cookware to coveralls. Little-known outside low-income groups, its customers have an average household income of $27,700. The company sold $1.5 billion in goods in 1997, ranking it number 2 behind JCPenney among companies peddling general merchandise by catalog. It is considered to be so good at what it does that it was acquired by Federated Department Stores, Inc., to collaborate with Macy's.com and Macy's by Mail—wholly owned subsidiaries of Federated—to expand its Internet and direct-mail businesses.

A free trial with monthly payments appeals to people without the money or credit to shop elsewhere. Producing profits at the lower-income end of the retail and loan markets, however, involves considerable wear and tear on the company and the customer.

In 1998 Fingerhut mailed 472 million catalogs featuring prices that typically are far higher than Wal-Mart's and a payment plan with a hefty 24.9 percent interest rate. About 8 million people ordered from Fingerhut, often more than once, in 1997 and 1998. Fingerhut sent out 21 million packages in 1997, making it the number 1 parcel customer of the U.S. Postal Service.

Unfortunately, marketing to this low-income group has its risks. Each of 220 Fingerhut debt collectors calls as many as 35 delinquent customers an hour, asking them for overdue payments as small as $6. About 11 million customers at one time or another have stiffed the catalog company. In 1998, about 22 percent of its merchandise loans were delinquent—compared with about 7 percent at Sears, a level Sears considers too high.

Prices and the interest rate are set to absorb such losses. An eight-piece Revere cookware set that sells for $69.97 at Wal-Mart goes for $129.99 in the Fingerhut catalog. But nearly all Fingerhut's customers choose the payment plan, and 18 installments of $11.49 each bring the out-of-pocket total to $206.82.

To be sure, Fingerhut is sometimes cheaper. Rugrats stuffed dolls go for $29.99 upfront, $5 less than Toys "R" Us is charging. Theoretically, a customer using a credit card for the Wal-Mart purchase and making only the minimum monthly payment could end up paying far longer—and maybe even more—than a Fingerhut customer.

Source: Joseph B. Cahill, "Credit Companies Find Tough Rivals at Bottom of Consumer Market," *The Wall Street Journal*, December 29, 1998, pp. A1, A4; and Whit Andrews, "How a Retailing Stalwart Plans to Apply Precision of Direct Marketing to the Web," *Internet World*, June 14, 1999.

males purchase computer hardware as opposed to 8 percent of females. Although more female Internet purchasers buy clothing at 26 percent compared to 7 percent of male purchasers.[43]

People all over the world are using the Internet for a variety of reasons besides purchasing goods and services, and the reasons differ among men and women of different ages. The primary uses of the Internet, in order of greatest to least, are for personal information, work, education, entertainment, shopping, time wasting, and communication. Females use the Internet more for personal information, education, and communication, though males also show significant usage in these categories. Males use the Internet more for work, entertainment, shopping, and time wasting. People from age 11 to 20 use it mainly for entertainment, education, and time wasting. While people age 21 to 25 use it for these same reasons, they also use it greatly for personal information and work. People age 26 to 50 use the Internet mainly for personal information and work, and those above 50 primarily access personal information.[44]

A study by Roper Starch Worldwide indicates that 25 percent of all users in the world are using the Internet for information on products, 25 percent for information on companies, 22 percent for travel, 18 percent for finances and investments, 10 percent for buying, and 7 percent for banking.[45]

THE CHANGING AMERICAN FAMILY

When baby boomers were growing up in the 1950s and 60s, it wasn't unusual for women to be at home raising a family. That scenario has changed! More women are working and more households are headed by single women. Teenagers and men have taken on more household responsibilities, including purchasing groceries. Unfortunately, women's changing roles in the family coupled with the career pressures on all adults have resulted in a society that's short on time. These shifts have created significant opportunities for retailers, however. Let's look at the changing women's market and implications for the time-poor society.

Gone are the days when Mom is the only one who does the family's grocery shopping.

The Changing Women's Market

From cars to copiers, from sweaters to sweeteners, women make the majority of purchasing decisions and influence most of the rest. For instance, they purchase about 80 percent of men's merchandise in department stores and over 50 percent of merchandise bought at Home Depot. Further, women now head almost 30 percent of American households. Clearly, the working women's segment is a large, complex, lucrative market for retailers.

One of the most challenging issues in retailing today is how women's apparel retailers are dealing with their changing customers. Women of every generation appear to have less need and interest in apparel. Baby boomers with children have more pressing uses for their disposable income. **Empty nesters**—households whose children are grown and have left home—are saving for retirement. In general, older women are less swayed by fashion trends than younger women. They buy less, they buy classics, and they look for value.

Cultural trends are reinforcing a disinterest in fashion. Business dress is becoming more casual (a phenomenon explored later in this chapter). Increasingly women find that one relaxed, stylish wardrobe can fit almost all situations. Also, an environment of everyday low pricing (at discounters and off-price outlets) and continuous sales (at department and specialty stores) encourages women to never pay "full retail."

Retailers are fighting back with a vengeance. Retailers competing at the lower price points (e.g., discounters) continue to provide their customers with value—better merchandise at lower prices. They have also increased their assortment of women's apparel. Department stores have expanded their private-label lines to keep their prices down (see Chapter 14), are mixing apparel categories to help women put together new ways of dressing for work and play, and offer the high-end market an array of designer boutiques. Specialty stores are expanding their product lines into footwear and personal care, and expanding their traditional merchandising focus. For example, Banana Republic has added more careerwear, while Talbots and Ann Taylor are bringing in more leisurewear.

Refact The number of hours spent shopping in stores per month has declined significantly: from an average of 4.8 hours in 1993 to 3.3 hours in 1997. Internet sales are expected to significantly reduce store shopping even further.[46]

The Time-Poor Society

When both husband and wife work while still raising a family, leisure time is in short supply. In the past, shopping provided an opportunity for social interaction and entertainment. Today, shopping takes time away from other activities that many customers either must do or would prefer to

Working mothers around the world no longer have the luxury of being able to shop for food everyday. In some markets, families are able to order groceries and other necessities of modern life over the Internet.

be doing. To succeed in this environment, retailers are adopting some of the following strategies.[47]

Being Available When the Customer Needs Them   Selling to a family that includes a working woman calls for adaptive strategies that weren't necessary in previous generations. To accommodate time-sensitive consumers, retailers are trying to be there when the customer wants to shop. Office Depot and Staples, for instance, open at 7 A.M. because many of their customers want to shop before they start their own business day. If that isn't good enough, customers can always purchase over the Internet.

Improving Customer Service   Many retailers recognize the opportunity to serve the short-on-time customer by providing strong customer service. For instance, numerous department stores are again attempting to provide the benefits that originally attracted customers to the stores. To economize in previous decades, they eliminated services such as gift wrapping, valet parking, and alterations, and they cut their sales staffs. In response, customers who sought the service traditionally offered in department stores began to shop more at specialty stores providing such service.

Many department stores, such as Nordstrom and Neiman Marcus, are famous for their attention to customer service. They use more full-time salespeople than other department stores and offer higher compensation to attract better people. Some discount and off-price retailers now provide services formerly reserved for their more upscale competition. Most now accept discount cards, have salespeople in some departments such as consumer electronics and jewelry, and offer **layaway**—a method of deferred payment in which a store holds merchandise for a customer until it's completely paid for. Wal-Mart employs a **greeter**—a person who greets customers when they enter the store and provides information and/or assistance. Dell allows customers to track the construction and delivery of their computer on the Internet.

Another strategy for improving customer service is to empower salespeople to make decisions. Customers don't like to wait for authorization for check approval, merchandise returns, or other interactions with store staff. Retailers from Montgomery Ward to Neiman Marcus authorize sales associates to make these decisions without managerial approval.

Giving Information   Providing customers with important information can reduce their shopping time. Many specialty stores keep track of their good customers' sizes and preferences so that they can call them up when appropriate merchandise arrives. Informative signage and coordinated merchandise can also speed shopping. For instance, Crate & Barrel places small, tasteful, informative signs beside merchandise to act as a "silent salesperson." Some fashion stores, like Saks Fifth Avenue, offer personalized salespeople who can help speed the decision process. These fashion consultants may even meet with customers in their home or office. Internet retailers have learned that providing customers with additional information garners customer loyalty. Garden.com allows potential customers to plan a garden right on their computer screen, with no strings attached.

FOR TIME-PRESSED PEOPLE, SHOPPING FROM HOME can be a big help. And in this age of technology, there is a growing list of services accessed by the Internet that permit shoppers to order everything from groceries to cars with a valid credit card and the click of a mouse.

Many deliver those products to a customer's doorstep, but relatively few companies deliver fresh groceries with the evening's precooked meal and the week's dry cleaning, home video rental selections, and photo developing services on the same trip—and even fewer do it as well as Streamline. Based in Westwood, Massachusetts, Streamline is a home delivery company formed in 1993 to make life easier for harried families.

Unique to Streamline is its delivery system. All Streamline customers are furnished with a pantrylike storage unit into which their orders are delivered. Placed in the customer's garage, this unit contains a refrigerator and freezer plus storage space so that all delivered items are kept at their appropriate temperature.

Streamline's customers help dictate the merchandise assortment. Slow-moving items are weeded out, and the offerings are constantly reviewed to keep them fresh and relevant. Streamline's grocery list includes about 10,000 items, up from 3,000 a few years ago. Marquee food labels include Starbucks Coffee in six varieties, 15 varieties of fresh bagels, gourmet bakery items, and meats. Other food services include prepared-meal offerings for singles and families plus kids' meals. Streamline also offers dry cleaning pickup and delivery, Kodak film processing, and Blockbuster video rental. The base price for home delivery is $30 per month plus the cost of whatever is purchased.

To help a family establish a relationship with Streamline, the online retailer visits the customer's home, scans the products in the pantry, and talks to the family to understand its eating preferences and to help form a workable shopping list.

As part of Streamline's service, the retailer has what it calls a DRO (don't run out) program. Each personal shopping list features about 175 items, 250 on the high side, with a certain core group of products families determine they must never be without. Those items are placed on a 1-to-12–week order cycle, depending on need and usage, and are automatically part of any order, even when they are not specifically ordered each week. Since 80 percent of purchases are replenishment purchases, customers should never be without such items as bananas, boneless and skinless chicken breasts, and apples.

Source: "Home Shopping Eases Time Strain," *Discount Store News*, October 26, 1998, pp. 98+ (copyright Lebhar-Friedman, Inc.); and Robin Lee Allen, "When Baby Makes Three, HMR and Takeout Set Mom Free," *Nation's Restaurant News*, May 29, 1999, p. 98.

If they decide to make a purchase, the plants, garden tools, and so on are scheduled for delivery based on the optimal planting time determined by ZIP code and light exposure.

Automating Processes   Automated selling or service processes can help save customers time. For instance, A&P, Shop Rite, and Publix are experimenting with automated grocery checkout systems that reduce waiting time in checkout lines. Another supermarket chain, Wegmans, has computerized its deli department. The customer simply enters the order and picks up the items on the way out of the store. Electronic kiosks for information and special-order purposes, inventory control, and customer-directed ad programs are available at some retailers.

Offering Opportunities for One-Stop Shopping   Finally, retailers are offering customers opportunities to make multiple purchases in one location. For instance, some grocery stores have videotape rentals and branches of traditional banks within their stores. Retailers and shopping center developers can create partnerships in which several retailers are strategically clustered together to facilitate time-saving shopping. A shopping center specializing in services—such as a packaging and mail service, dry cleaner, shoe repair store, and printer—would boast significant customer convenience. Streamline.com delivers groceries, prepared meals, dry cleaning, film processing, and video rentals to its customers. See Retailing View 4.4 for details.

Providing Alternatives to Store Visits   Nonstore retailing has expanded in many directions, as Chapters 2 and 3 said. The Gap, for instance, has equipped some of its stores with computers that allow customers to "model" different clothing options, thus saving time in the dressing room. Specialty catalogs such as L.L. Bean and Lands' End as well as traditional retailers such as JCPenney and Neiman Marcus have expanded their use of catalogs. Advances in the development and use of customer databases have enabled these retailers to more accurately target specific customers. (See Chapter 11.) If you have purchased home furnishings from L.L. Bean in the past, for instance, you will probably get its special home furnishings catalog. Finally, traditional bricks-and-mortar retailers are scrambling to offer their customers Internet shopping.

CHANGES IN CONSUMER VALUES

The previous section examined retail customers' changing demographic makeup. As a result of these changes and other environmental factors, consumer values are also changing. For instance, Americans are becoming more worldly, resulting in more sophisticated demand for products and services, while Europeans' shopping behavior is expected to change as a result of the introduction of the euro. Certain demographic groups (notably baby boomers and their children: Generations X and Y) respond well to retailers with a strong social consciousness. Dual-income families and older Americans appear to be searching for convenience and value. This section examines changing consumer values and retailers' reactions to them.

Metamorphosis of American Culture

Americans have become more educated, wealthy, and exposed to different cultures and, as a result, more sophisticated.[48] They are flying more and are discovering more cultures through the Internet and the proliferation of cable television. Besides buying more serious books, they are going to more theater, opera, and art films. They are eating at fine restaurants and drinking specialized beers, better wines, and Starbucks lattes.

There has been a partial reversal of the mass-merchandising phenomenon that characterized the U.S. economy for much of the century. The rise of uniformity-driven retailers put many family-owned retailers out of business. Today, however, chain stores of every type increasingly offer a broad range of niche products aimed at exploiting the very individuality of tastes that those neighborhood stores once fostered.

New bookstore chains like Barnes & Noble, with their coffee bars, convey a sense of eclectic intimacy even though they are almost the same in every location. Grocery chains aggressively promote a diverse range of ethnic, regional and once-uncommon specialties: Tony Chachere's Creole Seasoning, long available only in the southernmost parishes of Louisiana, now sits on store shelves in Nebraska. Fresh sushi is available in regular supermarkets across the country. Outlet malls in remote locations have become the purveyors of designers Liz Claiborne, Geoffrey Beene, and Jones New York. Pottery Barn units in regional malls reintroduce Craftsman-style furniture at middle-class prices. The newest units of Wal-Mart Stores Inc. dedicate significant shelf space to fashionable clothing, cutting-edge kitchen appliances, 230–thread-count sheets, and newly released books.

Refact   Nearly 27 million people attended theatrical stage shows during the 1997–98 season—almost 60 percent of them outside New York—for a record $1.3 billion in ticket sales. Meanwhile, the number of nonprofit, professional theater companies in the United States has grown to more than 800 today, compared with fewer than 60 in 1965.[49]

"Redneckism" still thrives in certain circles, however. Auto racing pulled in nearly 17 million ticket buyers in 1997, up 29 percent in five years. Nude dancing clubs have proliferated; the 1998 *Exotic Dancer* directory lists 2,200 adult entertainment clubs in the United States, an estimated 15 percent more than a decade ago. Wonder remains the single biggest-selling bread brand. On the media front, per capita hours of television watched—an estimated 1,610 hours in 1997—continues to increase.

The Euro's Impact on European Shoppers

With the introduction of the euro in Europe, retailers and their vendors will have to think beyond national borders, something they haven't been forced to do in the past.[50] There are the obvious logistics issues about merchandise going across country borders without the previous bureaucratic red tape. Then there will be less obvious things like the way products are marketed to consumers.

In the past, retailers and their vendors stressed how different the consumers in each country are. Under the euro, the similarities rather than the differences are expected to be the focus, and these similarities will be exaggerated over time. Also, many European marketers believed that people in one country would like a certain color, while people in a second country would like a different color. As a result, merchandise was typically produced locally or in smaller batches for different countries, which drives up prices. Further, with country tariffs, trade barriers, and different currencies, prices varied significantly from country to country, making it difficult for consumers to price compare.

With the euro, companies are expected to be more focused on achieving economies of scale and will begin to pass the savings on to consumers. Further, with one currency, consumers can more easily compare prices in different locales. Experts believe that Europeans will embrace lower prices even if it means they have to accept slight adjustments in the preferences for the products they buy. For instance, people may have a fixed idea of what a light bulb or a battery should be like, but for the right price they could change their mind. With some merchandise (clothing, for example), there will continue to be regional differences just like in the United States. For instance, a European chain like Benneton of Italy would produce one line of sweaters for Northern France and Belgium, while producing another line for Southern France, Italy, Spain, and Portugal.

Social Consciousness

Retailers and their employees play an important role in their communities. A retail manager's influence extends beyond the business world and into the society in which she lives. In other words, a manager's business actions often may have serious repercussions—for good or bad—on society at large. Because companies often directly or indirectly affect our society's mores, they must look beyond the bottom line and factor in societal needs. For example, Kmart, in partnership with local schools and law enforcement agencies, uses its stores as "safe havens" where children can go if they're ever in trouble; here they will be assisted by a caring adult who will help them and/or call their parent, guardian, or the police for assistance. Also, because nutrition is so vital in everyone's life, many fast-food retailers have added healthy items to their menus and made nutritional information readily available. Retailers that are perceived to actively improve citizens' lives are, in turn, esteemed by society.

Refact Patagonia, the purveyor of upscale sporting apparel and equipment, gives 10 percent of pretax profits to saving places that its customers like to climb to and survive in.

The Value-Oriented Customer

Stagnation in real household income growth, baby boomers with families, and Generation Xers with little disposable income have forced retailers to take a hard look at offering their customers a better value than they did in the past.[51] For example, during the 1980s, JCPenney became more fashion-forward and higher-priced as it pushed more national brands like Oshkosh B'Gosh and Levi's. But in the 1990s, it returned to its moderately priced roots. Now Penney sells an $84 suit that is similar to a $600 St. John Knit at Saks Fifth Avenue. Although Penney's model is made of a synthetic fabric instead of wool, other details make it look remarkably like the original.

Fashionable clothing at budget prices has become a priority for other retailers as well. At Wal-Mart, the Kathie Lee Gifford line of women's apparel is displayed in an in-store boutique similar to what you would find in a department store. Wal-Mart salespeople are trained to help women put together outfits.

Manufacturers cut corners in ways that are imperceptible to most customers. For instance, a men's dress shirt manufacturer can make a shirt that will retail for $9.99 instead of $25 for a department store shirt simply by making the shirt a little shorter, using fewer stitches per inch, and putting just one button on the cuff. Retailers like JCPenney and Target subject garments to tough quality control tests. It's often hard for consumers to tell the difference. *Consumer Reports* ranked a $26 woman's sweater from Sears on par with a $340 sweater from Barney's New York.

In their search for bargains, value-oriented customers often sacrifice the perceived safety of purchasing national brands for merchandise offered on sale, through coupons, or by manufacturers' rebates. (See Chapters 14 and 15.) In fact, many retailers have increased their budgets for such promotions, often at the expense of more traditional advertising. Special promotions (such as frequent shopper plans, Discover Card cumulative discounts, magazine subscriptions, gifts, and sweepstakes) are expected to become even more popular in the future.

Dress-Down Fashion

Refact More than 40 million office workers (53 percent) now have the option to dress casually every day, including at IBM and Ford Motor Company.[52]

Gone are the men in their gray flannel suits of the 1950s and 60s.[53] As baby boomers enter the boardrooms and Generation Xers enter the workplace, their khakis and sneakers are coming with them. This important fashion trend creates significant opportunities for retailers and their vendors. Full-time casual dress at work is equivalent to as many as 65 million more wearing occasions each week.[54] Many workers are purchasing a third wardrobe somewhere between business suits and jeans and a T-shirt. Retailers at both ends of the fashion/price spectrum stand to gain. Lower-priced stores benefit because people can go to work in casual pants and a shirt rather than a $500 suit. Other customers are devoting their suit budget to upscale designer fashions.

Some workers, particularly men, have had trouble learning what's appropriate casual business attire. So, smart retailers and their vendors are attempting to educate them. Men's Wearhouse offers the "V.I.P. Corporate Program" in which companies with at least 50 employees work with fashion consultants to help their employees achieve a more professional business casual look. Saks Fifth Avenue's corporate casual campaign includes videos, seminars, and consultations between Saks fashion directors and corporate senior executives.

Most believe that a casual workplace is here to stay. Once people get used to the comfort and functionality of casual clothing, they will not go back. There are rumblings, however, that some people miss getting dressed up, and the pendulum is starting to swing back to more formal attire.

INTERNET EXERCISE   Go to menswearhouse.com and click on "V.I.P. Corporate Program." Evaluate if this site would be helpful to you if you were trying to plan your corporate wardrobe after graduation.

SUMMARY   Not many years ago, customers had relatively few choices. They could choose among department and specialty stores for clothing, appliances, and home furnishings; discount stores for housewares, tools, and bargain clothing; grocery stores for food; and convenience stores for a candy bar or pack of cigarettes. Successful retailers have adapted to changes in their customer base to improve their previous offerings. Others have opened new retail formats, especially over the Internet.

Some retailers target the affluent youth market; others concentrate on older groups. Yet one of the hardest groups to reach is Generation X—those born between 1965 and 1976. Since the United States is becoming more ethnically diverse, and assorted ethnic groups are growing larger and more economically viable, several retailers have specific marketing programs to meet their needs. The number of women in the work force and the fact that they make the majority of purchasing decisions provide interesting challenges to retailers. To meet upscale, dual-income, well-educated, time-poor customers' needs, department and specialty stores have rediscovered how to provide excellent service. Retailers that offer Internet sites and mail order catalogs are prospering as their customers want to spend less of their limited leisure time shopping.

Retailers are also responding to changes in consumer values. Many have found that a strong social consciousness is good not only for society, but also for business. Many consumers have had to adjust to lower real incomes than previous generations enjoyed. Retailers who've developed strategies to attract and maintain more price-sensitive, value-oriented customers have thrived. Others have become more environmentally conscious. Fashion retailers are providing customers in all categories with functional clothing that can be used for both work and play.

KEY TERMS

baby boomers, *117*

demographics, *112*

empty nesters, *127*

Generation X (Xers), *116*

Generation Y, *114*

generational cohort, *113*

greeter, *128*

latchkey children, *116*

layaway, *128*

seniors, *119*

DISCUSSION QUESTIONS AND PROBLEMS

1. Choose a store that you believe successfully caters to Generation X and another that appeals to Generation Y. Based on the differences between the two generational cohorts described in this chapter, what makes them so successful?

2. What is your favorite retailer of luxury products? What makes people willing to pay extra dollars to acquire its merchandise?

3. Explain why wealthy individuals are spending more and more money at stores that traditionally appeal to the mass-middle and lower-income markets.

4. Some service retailers such as Streamline.com that provide home delivery service (e.g., groceries, dry cleaning, and Blockbuster videos) have been very successful in recent years. How do such companies benefit consumers? For what markets are they positioning themselves?

5. Assume that Kmart is opening three new locations in the New York City area. Location A's area is 75 percent African American. Location B's trade area is 80 percent Hispanic; of those, half are Cuban and half are Mexican. Location C is in Chinatown. How can Kmart target each ethnic group in each area? Discuss potential marketing problems.

6. To remain competitive, retailers and their employees must play an important part in their communities at both local and national levels. Give examples of how various companies can give back to the community and respond to America's environmental concerns.

7. What tips could you give Walgreens to help it cater to its large and growing group of elderly customers?

8. How does your favorite clothing store address the trend of wearing casual clothing to the office?

9. How has American culture changed in the past 30 years? How have these changes impacted the goods and services available in today's retailing environment?

SUGGESTED READINGS

Discount Store News, October 26, 1998. (The entire issue is devoted to marketing to generational cohorts and ethnically diverse Americans.)

Dortch, Shannon. "Rise and Fall of Generations." *American Demographics*, July 1996, pp. 6–7, 43.

Emondson, Brad. "Hispanic Americans in 2001." *American Demographics*, January 1997, p. 17.

Fisher, Christy. "Black, Hip, and Primed (to Shop)." *American Demographics*, September 1996, pp. 52–58.

Franey, Eric. *Black America: An Economic Powerhouse in the Dark*. Nova Kroshka Books, 1996.

McNeal, James U. "Tapping the Three Kids' Markets." *American Demographics*, April 1998, pp. 37–41.

Mitchell, Susan. *The Official Guide to the Generations*. New Strategist, 1995.

Moschis, George P. "Life Stages of the Mature Market." *American Demographics*, September 1996, pp. 44–47.

Roberts, D.A. "Exploring The Subtle Relationships between Environmental Concern and Ecologically Conscious Behavior." *Journal of Business Research* 40, no. 1 (July 1997).

Rubin, Rose M., and Michael L. Nieswiadomy. *Expenditures of Older Americans.* Praeger, 1998.

Smith, J. Walker, and Ann Clurman. *Rocking the Ages: The Yankelovich Report on Generational Marketing.* Harperbusiness, 1998.

Underhill, Paco. "Seniors in Stores." *American Demographics,* April 1996, pp. 44–48.

Zill, Nicholas, and John Robinson. "The Generation X Difference." *American Demographics,* April 1995, pp. 24–33.

Paco Underhill
CEO
Envirosell

WHAT IS THE "BUTT–BRUSH EFFECT," and how is it important to the retail environment? My firm, Envirosell (www.envirosell.com), discovered the butt–brush almost accidentally. As part of a study for Bloomingdale's in New York City, we observed shopper dynamics at the entrance and main aisles. A rack of neckties was positioned just off a main aisle near the entrance. Supposedly prime real estate, right? However, something strange was happening. Shoppers would approach it, shop, get bumped once or twice by people heading into or out of the store, and leave. After watching this over and over, we realized that shoppers—women especially—don't like being brushed or touched from behind. They'll move away from appealing merchandise to avoid it. We called in a Bloomingdale's exec to have the tie rack moved several feet out of the main aisle. Sales off that fixture improved instantly. • After college I went to work for an organization founded by William Whyte, the urban geographer who studied how people use public spaces. I realized the same method could be applied to retail. One of my first projects was a study of usage and circulation patterns of the underground concourse at The Lincoln Center. So, I recruited a few students to help and we took some cameras, staked out observation spots, and went to work counting and mapping. Based on observation, we made recommendations to the board of directors of The Lincoln Center and its constituent houses on the viability of a complex of shops and services in the underground concourse. It prospers to this day. • More than 20 years later, my company films, records, and follows 50,000 to 70,000 shoppers each year through their retail experiences in stores, banks, restaurants, and trade shows. We've been very fortunate. Envirosell advises a collection of Fortune 100 companies seeking to understand the behavior and motivation of the contemporary consumer.

5

Customer Buying Behavior

QUESTIONS

- What stages do customers go through when selecting a retailer and purchasing merchandise?

- What information do customers consider when they decide to visit a store, scan a catalog, or surf the Internet?

- How can retailers get customers to visit their stores more frequently and buy more merchandise during each visit?

- Why and how do retailers group customers into market segments?

THE RETAILING CONCEPT (discussed in Chapter 1) emphasizes that an effective retail strategy satisfies customer needs better than competitors' strategies. Thus, understanding customer needs and buying behavior is critical for effective retail decision making. When Dennis President (co-founder and CEO of Coldwater Creek, a Northern Idaho catalog retailer) was asked about his company being the highest performing retailer in a Management Horizon study, he responded, "Our success has everything to do with our intense customer focus. We have never allowed ourselves to think that we are smarter than the customer is and can anticipate what she wants. We take all our cues from her."[1]

Chapter 4 reviewed retail implications of some broad consumer trends, such as the aging population, the increase in ethnic diversity, and the growth in two-income families. This chapter focuses on the needs and buying behavior of individual customers and market segments. It describes the stages customers go through to purchase merchandise and the factors that influence the buying process. We then use the information about the buying process to discuss how consumers can be grouped into market segments.[2] The appendix to this chapter examines special aspects of consumer behavior that concern retailers selling fashion merchandise.

TYPES OF BUYING DECISIONS

Retailing View 5.1 describes how Jennifer Chen, a student, bought a new suit for job interviews. Such purchases typically involve several stages. The **buying process** begins when customers recognize an unsatisfied need. Then they seek information about how to satisfy the need: what products might be useful and how they can be

JENNIFER CHEN, AT SAN FRANCISCO STATE UNIVERSITY, is beginning to interview for jobs. For the first interviews on campus, Jennifer had planned to wear the blue suit her parents bought her three years ago. But looking at her suit, she realizes that it's not very stylish and that the jacket is beginning to show signs of wear. Wanting to make a good first impression during her interview, she decides to buy a new suit.

Jennifer surfs the Internet and looks through some catalogs to see the styles being offered. But she decides to buy the suit in a store so she can try it on and have it for her first interview next week. She likes to shop at the Express and The Gap, but neither sells business suits. She remembers an ad in the *San Francisco Chronicle* for women's suits at Macy's. She decides to go to Macy's in the mall close to her apartment and asks her friend Brenda to come along. Jennifer values Brenda's opinion, because Brenda is a clothes horse and has good taste.

Walking through the store, they see some DKNY suits. Jennifer looks at them briefly and decides they're too expen-

sive for her budget and too stylish. She wants to interview with banks and thinks she needs a more conservative suit.

Jennifer and Brenda are approached by a salesperson in the career women's department. After asking Jennifer what type of suit she wants and her size, the salesperson shows her three suits. Jennifer asks Brenda what she thinks about the suits and then selects one to try on. When Jennifer comes out of the dressing room, she feels that the shoulder pads in the suit make her look too heavy, but Brenda and the salesperson think the suit is attractive. Jennifer decides to buy the suit after another customer in the store tells her she looks very professional in the suit.

Jennifer doesn't have a Macy's charge card, so she asks if she can pay with a personal check. The salesperson says yes, but the store also takes VISA and MasterCard. Jennifer decides to pay with her VISA card.

As the salesperson walks with Jennifer and Brenda to the cash register, they pass a display of scarves. The salesperson stops, picks up a scarf, and shows Jennifer how well the scarf complements the suit. Jennifer decides to buy the scarf also.

Refact Women annually spend $50 billion on work apparel. Sixty percent of purchases are made in department and specialty stores, 17 percent in off-price outlets, 12 percent in discount stores, and 7 percent through mail order.[3]

bought. Customers evaluate the various alternative sources of merchandise such as stores, catalogs, and electronic retailers and choose a store or Internet site to visit or a catalog to review. This encounter with a retailer provides more information and may alert customers to additional needs. After evaluating the retailer's merchandise offering, customers may make a purchase or go to another retailer to collect more information. Eventually, customers make a purchase, use the product, and then decide whether the product satisfies their needs.

In some situations, customers like Jennifer spend considerable time and effort selecting a retailer and/or evaluating the merchandise. In other situations, buying decisions are made automatically with little thought. Three types of customer decision-making processes are extended problem solving, limited problem solving, and habitual decision making.

Extended Problem Solving

Extended problem solving is a purchase decision process in which customers devote considerable time and effort to analyzing alternatives. Customers typically engage in extended problem solving when the purchase decision involves a lot of risk and uncertainty. There are many types of risks. Financial risks arise when customers purchase an expensive product. Physical risks are important when customers feel a product may affect their health or safety. Social risks arise when customers believe a product will affect how others view them.

Consumers engage in extended problem solving when they are making a buying decision to satisfy an important need or when they have little knowledge about the product or service. Due to high risk and uncertainty in these situations,

TEN YEARS AGO, IF SOMEONE WANTED to buy a car, they would visit several dealers, look at different models, test drive the car of choice at a dealer, and then negotiate price and financing with the dealer. Many consumers view this traditional process of buying a car as being about as pleasurable as going to the dentist. But now the Internet is changing this experience as well as the nature of automobile retailing.

The Internet is putting consumers in control of the car buying process. Consumers can access from their homes a wealth of information about automobile specifications plus the dealer's costs for cars and options, reviews of the car's performance are available from websites such as Edmund's (www.edmunds.com) or Autosite (www.autosite.com). This information enables consumers to walk into a dealership knowing as much or more than the dealer's salespeople.

If consumers want to buy a car without visiting a dealer and bargaining over price, they can submit a request for the car they want through a buying service such as Autobytel (www.autobytel.com) or CarPoint (www.carpoint.msn.com). Nearby dealers can respond by telephone or e-mail within 24 hours, offering a car similar to the desired model, and close the deal in a day. Other sites (www.carddirect.com and www.driveoff.com) provide price quotations to consumers and complete the purchase transaction with them. However, state laws require that these electronic retailers actually buy the cars from a franchised dealer rather than from the manufacturer.

Sites like www.fincenter.com help you figure out how much you can afford to spend on a car, whether you should buy a new car or used car, and whether you should lease or buy. The sites feature calculators to walk you through ques-

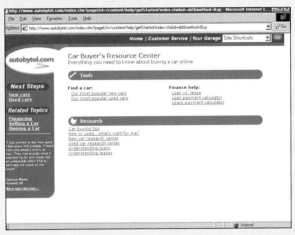

Consumers use websites such as Autobytel.com when engaged in the extensive problem solving of buying a car.

tions like is it better to use a home equity loan or take the $1,500 rebate or take the 1.9 percent finance charge offered by the dealer?

In the future, consumers might be able to specify to the manufacturer the exact car they want and then have the car built to their specifications and delivered to their doorstep.

Source: Larry Armstrong, "Kicking Tires on the Web," *Business Week,* April 26, 1999, p. 121; Sanjiv Gossin and Gajen Kandiah, "Reinventing Value," *Strategy and Leadership* 26 (November 1998), pp. 26–40; and Fara Warner, "Racing for a Slice of a $350 Billion Pie, Online Auto-Sales Sites Retool," *The Wall Street Journal,* January 24, 2000, pp. 131, 136.

customers go beyond their personal knowledge to consult with friends, family members, or experts. They may visit several retailers before making a purchase decision. Retailing View 5.2 describes how the Internet is changing the way people engage in the extended problem solving associated with buying an automobile.

Retailers influence such decisions by providing the necessary information in a manner that customers can understand and easily use and by offering money-back guarantees. For example, retailers that sell merchandise involving extended problem solving provide brochures describing the merchandise and its specifications; have informational displays in the store (such as a sofa cut in half to show its construction); and use salespeople to make presentations and answer questions.

Limited Problem Solving   **Limited problem solving** is a purchase decision process involving a moderate amount of effort and time. Customers engage in this type of buying process when they have had some prior experience with the

Supermarkets use a variety of approaches to increase impulse buying including in-store coupons, end-aisle displays, and point-of-sale advertising.

product or service and their risk is moderate. In these situations, customers tend to rely more on personal knowledge than on external information. They usually choose a retailer they have shopped at before and select merchandise they have bought in the past. The majority of customer decision making involves limited problem solving.

Retailers attempt to reinforce this buying pattern when customers are buying merchandise from them. If customers are shopping elsewhere, however, retailers need to break this buying pattern by introducing new information or offering different merchandise or services.

Jennifer Chen's buying process illustrates both limited and extended problem solving. Her store choice decision was based on her prior knowledge of the merchandise in various stores she had shopped in and an ad in the *San Francisco Chronicle*. Considering this information, she felt the store choice decision was not very risky and she engaged in limited problem solving when deciding to visit Macy's. But her buying process for the suit was extended. This decision was important to her, and she spent time acquiring information from a friend and the salesperson to evaluate and select a suit.

One common type of limited problem solving is **impulse buying.** Impulse buying is a buying decision made by customers on the spot after seeing the merchandise.[4] Jennifer's decision to buy the scarf was an impulse purchase.

Retailers encourage impulse buying behavior by using prominent displays to attract customer attention and stimulate a purchase decision based on little

Refact Seventy percent of all supermarket buying decisions are unplanned, impulse purchases.[5]

analysis. For example, sales of a grocery item are greatly increased when the item is featured in an end-aisle display, when a BEST BUY sign is placed on the shelf with the item, when the item is placed at eye level (typically on the third shelf from the bottom), or when items are placed at the checkout counter so customers can see them as they wait in line. Supermarkets use these displays and prime locations for the profitable items that customers tend to buy on impulse, such as gourmet food, rather than commodities such as flour and sugar, which are usually planned purchases. Electronic retailers stimulate impulse purchases by putting special merchandise on their home page and by suggesting complementary merchandise.[6]

Habitual Decision Making

Habitual decision making is a purchase decision process involving little or no conscious effort. As Chapter 4 said, today's customers have many demands on their time. One way they cope with these time pressures is by simplifying their decision-making process. When a need arises, customers may automatically respond with, "I'll buy the same thing I bought last time from the same store." Typically, this habitual decision-making process is used when decisions aren't very important to customers and involve familiar merchandise they have bought in the past.

Brand loyalty and store loyalty are examples of habitual decision making. **Brand loyalty** occurs when customers like and consistently buy a specific brand in a product category. They are reluctant to switch to other brands if their favorite brand isn't available. Thus, retailers can only satisfy these customers' needs if they offer the specific brands desired.

Refact The typical supermarket customer spends 15 seconds and looks at only one brand when buying laundry detergent.[7]

Brand loyalty creates both opportunities and problems for retailers. Customers are attracted to stores carrying popular brands. But, since retailers must carry the high-loyalty brands, they may not be able to negotiate favorable terms with the supplier of the popular national brands. Chapters 12 and 14 cover buying and stocking branded merchandise.

Store loyalty means that customers like and habitually visit the same store to purchase a type of merchandise. All retailers would like to increase their customers' store loyalty. Some approaches for increasing store loyalty are selecting a convenient location (see Chapters 8 and 9), offering complete assortments and reducing the number of stockouts (Chapter 13), rewarding customers for frequent purchases (Chapters 11 and 16), and providing good customer service (Chapter 19).

Refact The grocery product categories with the highest brand loyalty are cigarettes, mayonnaise, and hot cereal. Milk, cookies, and cold cereal have the lowest brand loyalty.[8]

THE BUYING PROCESS

Exhibit 5–1 outlines the buying process—the stages in selecting a retailer and buying merchandise. Understanding the steps of the buying process is helpful in developing and implementing a retailing strategy. Each stage in the buying process is addressed in the following sections.

As the stages in the buying process are discussed, you should recognize that customers may not go through the stages in the same order shown in Exhibit 5–1. For example, a person might see an ad for Jiffy Lube, go to the nearest Jiffy Lube for an oil change, encounter a long line, leave the Jiffy Lube, and drop his car off at a gas station near work. Here the customer decides what service he wants and selects the specific retailer at the same time. In addition, the amount of time spent at each stage may differ depending on the type of decision being

EXHIBIT 5–1

Stages in the Buying Process

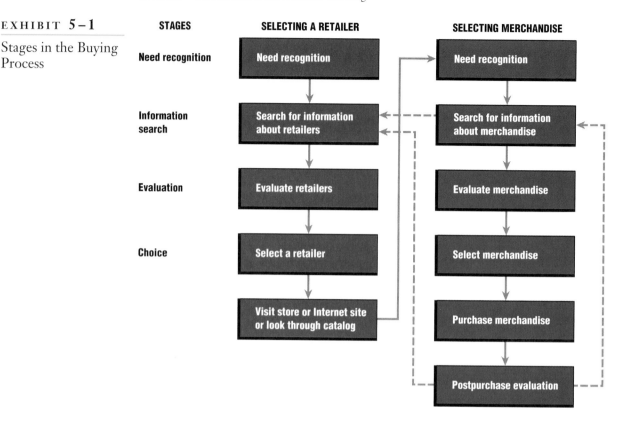

made. For example, customers engaged in habitual problem solving spend very little time making decisions.

Need Recognition   The buying process is triggered when people recognize they have an unsatisfied need. Unsatisfied needs arise when a customers' desired level of satisfaction differs from their present level of satisfaction. For example, Jennifer Chen recognized that she had a problem when she considered interviewing for jobs in her blue suit. She needed a suit that would make a good impression and realized her worn, outdated blue suit wouldn't satisfy this need.

Need recognition can be as straightforward as discovering there's no milk in the refrigerator or it can be as ambiguous as feeling the need for an uplifting experience after a final exam. Visiting stores, surfing the Internet, and purchasing products are approaches to satisfying different types of needs.

Types of Needs   The needs motivating customers to go shopping and purchase merchandise can be classified as functional or psychological.[9] **Functional needs** are directly related to the performance of the product. For example, people who need to style their hair might be motivated to purchase a hair dryer. This purchase is based on the expectation that the hair dryer will assist the customer in styling hair.

Psychological needs are associated with the personal gratification customers get from shopping or from purchasing and owning a product. For example, a Tommy Hilfiger shirt may not serve the function of clothing any better than a knit shirt from Kmart, but the Hilfiger shirt may also satisfy the cus-

This skateboarding park in a California mall provides a stimulating experience for shoppers.

tomer's need to be perceived as a fashionable dresser. When products are purchased to satisfy psychological needs, the product's functional characteristics are typically less important.

Many products satisfy both functional and psychological needs. The principal reason for purchasing a Tommy Hilfiger shirt may be to enhance one's self-image, but the shirt also satisfies the functional need for clothing. Most Americans have more income than they require to satisfy their functional needs for food, liquid, clothing, and shelter. As disposable income rises, psychological needs become increasingly important.[10] Thus, store ambiance, service, and fashionable merchandise are more important to American retail customers than to customers in countries with less-developed economies.

Functional needs are often referred to as rational, while psychological needs are called emotional. These labels suggest that visiting stores or buying products to satisfy psychological needs is irrational. But is it really irrational for people to buy designer clothing because it makes them feel more successful? Anything customers do to improve their satisfaction should be considered rational, whether the action satisfies a functional or a psychological need. Successful retailers attempt to satisfy both the functional and psychological needs of their customers. Psychological needs that can be satisfied through shopping and purchasing merchandise include stimulation, social experience, learning new trends, self-reward, and status and power.[11]

- *Stimulation.* Retailers and developers use background music, visual displays, scents, and demonstrations in stores and malls to create a carnival-like, stimulating experience for their customers.[12] These environments encourage consumers to take a break in their daily environment and visit these sites. Catalog and Internet retailers also attempt to stimulate customers with exciting graphics and photography.
- *Social experience.* Marketplaces have traditionally been centers of social activity, places where people could meet friends and develop new relationships.[13] Regional shopping malls in many communities have replaced open markets as social meeting places, especially for teenagers. Mall developers satisfy the need for social experiences by providing places for people to sit and talk in food courts. Barnes & Noble bookstores have cafes where customers can discuss novels while sipping a latte. Some Internet retailers provide similar social experiences through chat rooms for people visiting their sites. For example, visitors to the Amazon.com electronic bookstore (http://www.amazon.com) share information and opinions about books with other visitors.
- *Learning new trends.* By visiting stores, people learn about new trends and ideas. These visits satisfy customers' needs to be informed about their environment. For example, record stores use displays to show shoppers what new trends and artists are emerging.

- *Status and power.* Some customers have a need for status and power that's satisfied through shopping. When shopping, a person can be waited on without having to pay for the service. For some people, a store is one of the few places where they get attention and respect. Ralph Lauren's store on Madison Avenue satisfies this need by creating an atmosphere of aristocratic gentility and the good life in a refurbished mansion in New York City. The store is furnished with expensive antiques. Cocktails and canapés are served to customers in the evening.
- *Self-reward.* Customers frequently purchase merchandise to reward themselves when they have accomplished something or want to dispel depression. Perfume and cosmetics are common self-gifts. Retailers satisfy these needs by "treating" customers to personalized makeovers while they are in the store.[15]

Refact Ralph Lauren has established the world's most successful designer brands, generating over $5 billion in annual sales for his firm, including $1 billion in royalties from 26 licensees.[14]

Conflicting Needs   Most customers have multiple needs. Moreover, these needs often conflict. For example, Jennifer Chen would like to wear a DKNY suit. Such a suit would enhance her self-image and earn her the admiration of her college friends. But this need conflicts with her budget and her need to get a job. Employers might feel that she's not responsible if she wears an expensive suit to an interview for an entry-level position. Typically customers make trade-offs between their conflicting needs. Later in this chapter we will discuss a model of how customers make these trade-offs.

Often a consumer's needs cannot be satisfied in one store or by one product. Retailing View 5.3 describes how consumers are engaging in more cross-shopping to satisfy their needs for value and self-esteem.

Stimulating Need Recognition   As we have said, customers must recognize unsatisfied needs before they are motivated to visit a store and buy merchandise.[16] Sometimes these needs are stimulated by an event in a person's life. For example, Jennifer's department store visit to buy a suit was stimulated by her impending interview and her examination of her blue suit. An ad motivated her to look for the suit at Macy's.

Retailers use a variety of approaches to stimulate problem recognition and motivate customers to visit their stores and buy merchandise. Advertising, direct mail, publicity, and special events communicate the availability of merchandise or special prices. Within the store, visual merchandising and salespeople can stimulate need recognition. For example, a salesperson showed Jennifer a scarf to stimulate her need for an accessory to complement her new suit.

One of the oldest methods for stimulating needs and attracting customers is still one of the most effective. The Saks Fifth Avenue store in Manhattan has 310 feet of store frontage along 49th and 50th streets and the famed Fifth Avenue. Each day at lunchtime, about 3,000 people walk by the 31 window displays. Saks has 1,200 different window displays each year, with the Fifth Avenue windows changing each week. These displays can dramatically impact sales. For example, when Donna Karan clothes were featured in window displays, they sold over five times better than comparable designer lines.[17]

Information Search

Once customers identify a need, they may seek information about retailers and/or products that might help them satisfy the need. Jennifer's search was limited to the three suits shown her by the

MANY CONSUMERS APPEAR TO BE INCONSISTENT in their shopping behavior. For example, an executive might own an expensive Mercedes-Benz auto and buy gas from a discount service station. A grocery shopper might buy an inexpensive store brand of paper towels and a premium national brand of orange juice. The pattern of buying both premium and low-priced merchandise or patronizing expensive, status-oriented retailers and price-oriented retailers is called **cross-shopping.**

Cross-shopping is of particular concern to department stores because 70 percent of department store customers shop in discount stores but only 47 percent of discount store shoppers shop in department stores. Thus, the growth in cross-shopping is drawing more consumers to discount stores. The middle-class cross-shopper has the profile of a department store customer but is seeking more value through cross-shopping.

While cross-shoppers are seeking value, their perception of value varies across product classes. Thus, a cross-shopper might feel it is worth the money to buy an expensive sweater

in a boutique, but feel there is little quality difference between jeans at Kmart and designer brands at the boutique. Similarly, consumers may cut back on dining at an expensive restaurant but still want to treat themselves to expensive, high-quality jams, mustards, and olive oils in the supermarket. While retailers might think the buying patterns for cross-shopping do not make sense to them, it makes sense to their customers.

Americans place a premium on self expression, in everything from the dishes on the table to the lamp in the living room. As the baby boomers move into a different life stage with kids grown up and mothers returning to work, they have more to spend on home furnishings—and it doesn't hurt knowing that the kids won't trash the house.

Source: Lisa Vincenti, "Fashion-Forward Discounters Score," *HFN,* July 20, 1998, pp. 9, 59; Michelle Morganosky, "Retail Market Structure Change: Implications for Retailers and Consumers," *International Journal of Retail & Distribution Management* 25 (August 1997), pp. 269–84; and "Cross-Shopping," *Women's Wear Daily,* April 26, 1995, section II.

salesperson at Macy's. She was satisfied with this level of information search because she and her friend Brenda had confidence in Macy's merchandise and pricing, and she was pleased with the selection of suits presented to her. More extended buying processes may involve collecting a lot of information, visiting several retailers, and deliberating a long time before making a purchase.[18]

Amount of Information Searched   In general, the amount of information search depends on the value customers feel they'll gain from searching versus the cost of searching. The value of the search is in how it improves the customer's purchase decision. Will the search help the customer find a lower-price product or one that will give superior performance? The cost of search includes both time and money. Traveling from store to store can cost money for gas and parking, but the major cost incurred is the customer's time. Electronic retailing can dramatically reduce the cost of information. Consumers can collect information about merchandise sold across the world by "surfing the Net" from their home computer. However, electronic agents like FRED described in Exhibit 3–4 are needed to make it easier to search electronically across the globe.

Factors influencing the amount of information searched include (1) the nature and use of the product being purchased, (2) characteristics of the individual customer, and (3) aspects of the market and buying situation in which the purchase is made.[19] Some people search more than others. For example, customers who enjoy shopping search more than those who don't like to shop. Also, customers who are self-confident or have prior experience purchasing and using the product tend to search less.

Marketplace and situational factors affecting information search include (1) the number of competing brands and retail outlets and (2) the time pressure under which the purchase must be made. When competition is greater and there are more alternatives to consider, the amount of information searched may increase. The amount decreases as time pressure increases.

Sources of Information   Customers have two sources of information: internal and external. **Internal sources** are information in a customer's memory such as names, images, and past experiences with different stores. For example, Jennifer relied on an internal source (her memory of an ad) when choosing to visit Macy's. **External sources** are information provided by ads and other people. Customers see hundreds of ads in print and the electronic media; they notice signs for many retail outlets each day. In addition, customers get information about products and retailers from friends and family members. External sources of information are particularly important in the selection of fashion merchandise.

A major source of internal information is the customer's past shopping experience. Even if they remember only a small fraction of the information they are exposed to, customers have an extensive internal information bank to draw upon when deciding where to shop and what to buy.[20]

If customers feel that their internal information is inadequate, they may turn to external information sources. Remember how Jennifer Chen asked a respected friend to help her make the purchase decision.[21] External sources of information play a major role in the acceptance of fashions, as discussed in the appendix to this chapter.

Reducing the Information Search   The retailer's objective at this stage of the buying process is to limit the customer's information search to its store. Each element of the retailing mix can be used to achieve this objective.

First, retailers must provide a good selection of merchandise so customers can find something to satisfy their needs within the store. Providing a wide variety of products and a broad assortment of brands, colors, and sizes increases the chances that customers find what they want. For example, Circuit City uses in-store kiosks to increase the selection of merchandise available to customers by giving them the opportunity to purchase merchandise not available in the store such as custom-designed computers and appliances.

Services provided by retailers can also limit search. The availability of credit and delivery may be important for consumers who want to purchase large durable goods such as furniture and appliances. And salespeople can provide enough information to customers so they won't feel the need to collect additional information by visiting other stores. For example, mail order retailer of sportswear and sports equipment L.L. Bean gives employees 40 hours of training before they interact with their first customer. Due to this extensive training, people across the United States call L.L. Bean for advice on such subjects as what to wear for cross-country skiing and what to take on a trip to Alaska. If the employee answering the phone can't provide the information, the customer is switched to an expert within the company. Thanks to L.L. Bean's reputation for expertise in sportswear and sporting goods, customers feel they can collect all the information they need to make a purchase decision from this one retailer.[22]

Everyday low pricing is another way retailers increase the chance that customers will buy in their store and not search for a better price elsewhere. Since Wal-Mart and Circuit City have everyday-low-pricing policies, customers can feel confident that they won't find that merchandise at a lower price in the future. Many stores with everyday low pricing offer money-back guarantees if a competitor offers the same merchandise at a lower price. Chapter 15 talks about benefits and limitations of various pricing strategies.

Evaluation of Alternatives: The Multiattribute Model

Customers collect and review information about alternative products or retailers, evaluate the alternatives, and select one that best satisfies their needs. A multiattribute attitude model provides a useful way to look at the customer's evaluation process. We will discuss it in detail since it offers a framework for developing a retailing strategy.[23]

A **multiattribute attitude model** is based on the notion that customers see a retailer or a product as a collection of attributes or characteristics. The model is designed to predict a customer's evaluation of a product or retailer based on (1) its performance on several attributes and (2) those attributes' importance to the customer. Retail buyers can also use the multiattribute model to evaluate merchandise and vendors. (See Chapter 14.)

Beliefs about Performance   To illustrate this model, consider the store choice decision confronting a young single professional woman who needs groceries. She considers three retailers: a supercenter in the next suburb, the local supermarket, and an Internet grocery retailer such as Peapod (www.peapod.com). They're compared in Exhibit 5–2.

The customer mentally processes Exhibit 5–2A's "objective" information about each food retailer and forms an impression of the benefits the stores provide. Exhibit 5–2B shows her beliefs about these benefits. Notice that some benefits combine several objective characteristics. For example, the convenience

EXHIBIT 5–2

Information Used to Evaluate Retailers

A. INFORMATION ABOUT STORES SELLING GROCERIES			
STORE CHARACTERISTICS	**SUPERCENTER**	**SUPERMARKET**	**INTERNET GROCER**
Grocery prices	20% below average	average	10% above average
Delivery cost ($)	0	0	10
Total travel time (minutes)	30	15	0
Typical checkout time (minutes)	10	5	2
Number of products, brands, and sizes	20,000	15,000	5,000
Fresh produce	Yes	Yes	Yes
Fresh fish	Yes	Yes	No
Ease of finding products	Difficult	Easy	Easy
Ease of collecting nutritional information about products	Difficult	Difficult	Easy

B. BELIEFS ABOUT STORES' PERFORMANCE BENEFITS*			
PERFORMANCE BENEFITS	**SUPERCENTER**	**SUPERMARKET**	**INTERNET GROCER**
Economy	10	8	6
Convenience	3	5	10
Assortment	9	7	5
Availability of product information	4	4	8

*10 = Excellent; 1 = Poor.

benefit combines travel time, checkout time, and ease of finding products. Grocery prices and delivery cost affect the customer's beliefs about the economy of shopping at the retail outlets.

The degree to which each retailer provides the benefit is represented on a 10-point scale: 10 means the retailer performs well in providing the benefit; 1 means it performs poorly. Here no retailer has superior performance on all benefits. The supercenter performs well on economy and assortment, but is low on convenience. The Internet grocer offers the best convenience but is weak on cost and assortment.

Importance Weights The young woman in the preceding example forms an overall evaluation of each store based on the importance she places on each benefit the stores provide. The importance she places on a benefit can also be represented using a 10-point rating scale, with 10 indicating the benefit is very important and 1 indicating it's very unimportant.[24] Using this rating scale, the importance of the store benefits for the young woman and a parent with four children are shown in Exhibit 5–3, along with the performance beliefs previously discussed. Notice that the single woman values convenience and the availability of product information much more than economy and assortment. But the parent places a lot of importance on economy, assortment is moderately important, and convenience and product information aren't very important.

Customers have a unique set of needs when they are about to go shopping. The importance of a store's benefits differs for each customer and may also differ for each shopping trip.[25] For example, the parent with four children may stress economy because food expenditures are high. Since the parent has a baby-sitter for the children during the weekly shopping trip, convenience is not that important. On the other hand, the single woman is very concerned about the nutritional quality and fat content of food she eats, and thus places a high weight on the availability of product information.

In Exhibit 5–3, the single woman and parent have the same beliefs about each store's performance, but they differ in the importance they place on benefits the stores offer. In general, customers can differ on their beliefs about the stores' performance as well as on their importance weights.

Evaluating Stores Research has shown that a customer's overall evaluation of an alternative (in this situation, a store) is closely related to the sum of the

EXHIBIT 5–3

Information Used in Evaluating Stores

CHARACTERISTIC	IMPORTANCE WEIGHTS		PERFORMANCE BELIEFS		
	YOUNG SINGLE WOMAN	PARENT WITH FOUR CHILDREN	SUPERCENTER	SUPERMARKET	INTERNET GROCER
Economy	4	10	10	8	6
Convenience	10	4	3	5	10
Assortment	5	8	9	7	5
Availability of product information	9	2	4	4	8
OVERALL EVALUATION					
Young single woman			151	153	221
Parent with four children			192	164	156

performance beliefs multiplied by the importance weights.[26] Thus, we calculate the young single woman's overall evaluation or score for the supercenter as follows:

$$
\begin{array}{rcl}
4 \times 10 & = & 40 \\
10 \times 3 & = & 30 \\
5 \times 9 & = & 45 \\
9 \times 4 & = & \underline{36} \\
& & 151
\end{array}
$$

Choice of Alternatives

Exhibit 5–3 shows the overall evaluations for the three retailers using the importance weights of the single woman and the parent. For the single woman, the Internet grocer has the highest score, 221, and thus the most favorable evaluation. She would probably select this retailer for most of her grocery shopping. On the other hand, the supercenter has the highest score, 192, for the parent, who'd probably buy the family's weekly groceries there.

When customers are about to select a store, they don't actually go through the process of listing store characteristics, evaluating stores' performance on these characteristics, determining each characteristic's importance, calculating each store's overall score, and then visiting a store with the highest score! The multiattribute attitude model doesn't reflect customers' actual decision process, but it does predict their evaluation of alternatives and their choice.[27] In addition, the model provides useful information for designing a retail offering. For example, if the supermarket here could increase its performance rating on assortment from 8 to 10 (perhaps by adding a bakery and a wide selection of prepared meals), customers like the parent might shop at the supermarket more often than at the supercenter. Later in this chapter we'll discuss how retailers can use the multiattribute attitude model to increase their store's evaluation.

The application of the multiattribute attitude model in Exhibit 5–3 deals with a customer who's evaluating and selecting a retail store. The same model can also be used to describe how a customer evaluates and selects merchandise in a store. For example, Exhibit 5–4 shows Jennifer Chen's beliefs and importance weights about the three suits shown to her by the salesperson in Retailing View 5.1. Jennifer didn't evaluate suits A and B on fit because she didn't try them on. She bought suit C because it was good enough. Its overall evaluation passed some minimum threshold (which in terms of this multiattribute attitude model might be a score of 320). Retailing View 5.4 describes how Land's End provides an opportunity for customers to replicate Jennifer Chen's shopping trip in virtual reality.

EXHIBIT 5–4

Information Jennifer Chen Used in Buying a Suit

BENEFITS PROVIDED BY SUITS	IMPORTANCE WEIGHTS	BELIEFS ABOUT PERFORMANCE		
		SUIT A	SUIT B	SUIT C
Economy	6	6	5	5
Quality	6	10	7	8
Conservative look	8	6	6	10
Complement to wardrobe	8	7	6	9
Fashion	4	7	10	5
Fit	10	?	?	8
Overall evaluation				380

Trying on Clothes in a Virtual Reality at Lands' End's Website

AT THE LANDS' END WEBSITE (www.landsend.com), women can enter information about their body types, including hair color, height, weight, and shoulder and waist descriptions, such as narrow or generous. Based on their responses, a three-dimensional model resembling their body type appears on the screen. Then customers are provided with suggestions of appropriate apparel for their body type. These suggestions are offered for four apparel styles: dressy office attire, casual office, after-work and very casual. Using a click-and-drag interface, customers can electronically "try on" different outfits and accessories and see how they look.

In the future, this virtual shopping experience at the Lands' End site will be made even more realistic by enabling customers to see clothing on their actual body and view the fit from all angles by rotating the three-dimensional picture.

Source: Marcia Stepanek, "Take That Dress into a Web Dressing Room," *Business Week*, June 14, 1999, p. 122A; and Valerie Seckler, "The Shopping Click: The Time Has Come for Apparel to Be a Major Player in Internet Selling," *WWD*, March 24, 1999, p. 23.

The use of virtual models at some websites lets customers "try on" apparel.

Customers often make choices as Jennifer did. They don't thoroughly evaluate each alternative as suggested in the multiattribute attitude model. They simply buy merchandise that's good enough or very good on one particular attribute. In general, customers don't spend the time necessary to find the very best product. Once they've found a product that satisfies their need, they stop searching.[28]

INTERNET EXERCISE McGraw-Hill (the publisher of this textbook and *Business Week*) maintains an Internet site with information about personal computers. Go to the site, www.maven.businessweek, and look for information to purchase a laptop computer for yourself. How does this experience compare to shopping for a computer in a store?

Implications for Retailers How can a retailer use the multiattribute attitude model to encourage customers to shop at its store more frequently? First, the model indicates what information customers use to decide which store to visit. Thus, to develop a program for attracting customers, the retailer must do market research to collect the following information:

1. Alternative stores that customers consider.
2. Characteristics or benefits that customers consider when making their store evaluation and choice.
3. Customers' ratings of each store's performance on the characteristics.
4. The importance weights that customers attach to the characteristics.

Armed with this information, the retailer can use several approaches to influence customers to select its store.

Getting into the Consideration Set   The retailer must make sure that its store is included in the customer's consideration set. The **consideration set** is the set of alternatives the customer evaluates when making a selection.[29] To be included in the consideration set, the retailer must develop programs to increase the likelihood that customers will remember its store when they're about to go shopping. The retailer can influence this top-of-the-mind awareness through advertising and location strategies. Heavy advertising expenditures that stress the store's name increase top-of-the-mind awareness. When a retailer locates several stores in a geographic area, customers are exposed more frequently to the store name as they drive through the area.[30]

After ensuring that its store is in the consideration set, the retailer can use four methods to increase the chances that its store will be selected for a visit:

1. Increase the belief about its store's performance.
2. Decrease the performance belief for competing stores in the consideration set.
3. Increase customers' importance weights.
4. Add a new benefit.

Changing Performance Beliefs   The first approach involves altering customers' beliefs about the retailer's performance by increasing the retailer's performance rating on a characteristic. For example, the supermarket in Exhibit 5–3 would want to increase its overall rating by improving its rating on all four benefits. The supermarket could improve its rating on economy by lowering prices and could improve its rating on assortment by stocking more gourmet and ethnic foods.[31]

It's costly for a retailer to improve its performance on all benefits. Thus, a retailer should focus efforts on improving performance on benefits that are important to customers in its target market. For example, 7-Eleven's market research found that women avoid convenience stores because they view them as dingy and unsafe. To attract more women, 7-Eleven has improved the shopping environment in a number of its stores. To create a sense of space, brighter lighting was installed and aisles were widened. Cigarette racks and other clutter were cleared off checkout counters, and colorful signage was used to designate merchandise areas.[32]

A change in the performance belief concerning an important benefit results in a large change in customers' overall evaluation. In Exhibit 5–3's situation, the supermarket should attempt to improve its convenience ratings if it wants to attract more young single women who presently shop on the Internet. If its convenience rating rose from 5 to 8, its overall evaluation for young single women would increase from 153 to 183 and thus be much higher than the young women's evaluation of supercenters. Note that a larger increase in rating from 6 to 10 on both less-important benefits such as economy or assortment would have no great effect on the store's overall evaluation. The supermarket might try to improve its rating on convenience by increasing the number of checkout stations, using customer scanning to reduce checkout time, or providing more in-store information so customers could locate merchandise more easily.

Another approach is to try to decrease customers' performance ratings of a competing store. This approach may be illegal and usually isn't very effective, because customers typically don't believe a firm's negative comments about its competitors.

Changing Importance Weights   Altering customers' importance weights is another approach to influencing store choice. A retailer would want to increase the importance customers place on benefits for which its performance is superior and decrease the importance of benefits for which it has inferior performance.

For example, if the supermarket in Exhibit 5–4 tried to attract families who shop at supercenters, it could increase the importance of assortment. Typically changing importance weights is harder than changing performance beliefs because importance weights reflect customers' values.[33]

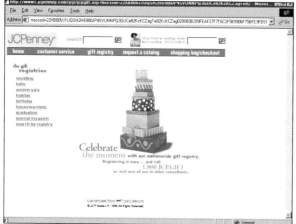

JCPenney, as a national department store chain, offers an unusual benefit. Customers from around the world can use its registry on the Internet to order gifts. The recipient can then return merchandise to any store location.

Adding a New Benefit   Finally, retailers might try to add a new benefit to the set of benefits customers consider when selecting a store. Since JCPenney is America's only national department store, a customer can purchase a gift at a local Penney store or from its website and send it to a person in another part of the country knowing that, if necessary, the recipient can exchange it at her local Penney store. Normally, customers wouldn't consider this when selecting a retailer. This approach of adding a new benefit is often effective because it's easier to change customer evaluation of new benefits than old benefits.

Purchasing the Merchandise

Customers don't always purchase a brand or item of merchandise with the highest overall evaluation. The item offering the greatest benefits (having the highest evaluation) may not be available in the store or the customer may feel that the risks outweigh the potential benefits. Some of the steps that retailers take to increase the chances that customers can easily convert their positive merchandise evaluations into purchases at the cash register are

- Have a complete assortment of sizes and colors in stock.
- Reduce the risk of purchasing merchandise by offering liberal return policies and refunds if the same merchandise is available at a lower price from another retailer.
- Offer credit.
- Make it easy to purchase merchandise by having convenient checkout terminals.
- Reduce the actual and perceived waiting time in lines at checkout terminals.[34]

Refact The key factors that get women to turn away from a store are loud music and messy displays.[35]

Postpurchase Evaluation

The buying process doesn't end when a customer purchases a product. After making a purchase, the customer consumes or uses the product and then evaluates the experience to determine whether it was satisfactory or unsatisfactory. **Satisfaction** is a postconsumption evaluation of how well a store or product meets or exceeds customer expectations.[36]

This **postpurchase evaluation** becomes part of the customer's internal information that affects future store and product decisions. Unsatisfactory experiences can motivate customers to complain to the retailer and to patronize other stores.[37] Consistently high levels of satisfaction build store loyalty—an important source of competitive advantage for retailers. Chapters 17 and 19 discuss means to increase customer satisfaction such as offering quality merchandise, providing accurate information about merchandise, and contacting customers after a sale.

FACTORS INFLUENCING THE DECISION PROCESS

The previous section described the process that customers go through in selecting a retailer to visit and then deciding on what merchandise to buy from the retailer. In this section, we discuss how this decision-making process is influenced by the customer's family, reference groups, and cultural environment.

Family

To develop effective retail programs, retailers must understand how families make purchase decisions and how various family members influence these decisions.

Family Decision Making   The previous discussion of the consumer decision-making process focused on how one person makes a decision—how Jennifer purchases a suit for herself. When families make purchase decisions, they often consider the needs of all family members.[38] In a situation such as choosing a vacation site, all family members may participate in the decision-making process. In other situations, one member of the family may assume the role of making the purchase decision. For example, the husband might buy the groceries, while the wife uses them to prepare their child's lunch, and the child consumes the lunch in school. In this situation, the store choice decision might be made by the husband, while the brand choice decision might be made by the mother but greatly influenced by the child.

Children play an important role in family buying decisions. It's estimated that children between ages 4 and 12 themselves spend or influence their parents' purchases of $135 billion in merchandise. Satisfying the needs of children is particularly important for many baby boomers deciding to have children late in life. They often have high disposable income and want to stay in luxury resorts, but they still want to take their children on vacations. Resort hotels now realize they must satisfy children's needs as well as adults. For example, Hyatt hotels greet families by offering books and games tailored to the children's ages. Parents checking in with infants receive a first-day supply of baby food or formula and diapers at no charge. Baby-sitting and escort services to attractions for children are offered.[39]

Retailers can attract consumers who shop with other family members by satisfying the needs of all family members. For example, IKEA, a Swedish furniture store chain, has a "ball pit" in which children can play while their parents shop. Nordstrom has sitting areas in its store and pubs where men can have a beer and watch a football game while their wives shop. By accommodating the needs of men and children who might not be interested in shopping, the family stays in the stores longer and buys more merchandise.[41]

Refact Shopping ranks among the top seven interests and activities of American youth.[40]

Reference Groups

A **reference group** is one or more people whom a person uses as a basis of comparison for beliefs, feelings, and behaviors. A consumer might have a number of different reference groups, although the most important reference group is the family, as we discussed in the previous section. These reference groups affect the buying decision process by (1) providing information, (2) administering rewards for specific purchasing behaviors, and (3) enhancing a consumer's self-image.

Reference groups provide information to consumers directly through conversation or indirectly through observation. For example, Jennifer received valuable information from her friend about the suits she was considering. On other occasions, Jennifer might look to women like soccer player Mia Hamm and tennis player Martina Hingis to guide her selection of athletic apparel. The role of reference groups in creating fashion is discussed in the appendix to this chapter.

Some reference groups influence purchase behaviors by rewarding behavior that meets with their approval. For example, the reference group of employees in a company might define the appropriate dress style and criticize fellow workers who violate this standard.

By identifying and affiliating with reference groups, consumers create, enhance, and maintain their self-image. Customers who want to be seen as members of an elite social class may shop at prestige retailers, while others who want to create an image of an outdoors person might buy merchandise from the L.L. Bean website.

Department stores use their teen boards to provide a reference group influence on teenage shoppers. The teen board members are selected because they are a group of students that other students would like to emulate. By buying apparel worn by teen board members, other students can identify with these student leaders.

Culture

Culture is the meaning and values shared by most members of a society. For example, core values shared by most Americans include individualism, freedom, mastery and control, self-improvement, achievement and success, material comfort, and health and fitness.[42]

Many retailers are selling merchandise and providing services to satisfy the needs of specific subcultures.

As retailers expand beyond their domestic markets, they need to be sensitive to how cultural values affect customer needs and buying behavior. For example, gift giving plays a much more important role in Japanese than American culture. Each Japanese person has a well-defined set of relatives and friends with whom they share reciprocal gift giving (*kosai*). Most Japanese feel a need to bring gifts for family and friends when they return from a trip. In one study, about half of the Japanese tourists returning home from Los Angeles bought gifts for over 15 family members and friends. They spent as much on gifts for others as on merchandise for their own use. Gift packaging and wrapping offered by retailers is particularly important to Japanese consumers because gifts aren't opened in front of the gift giver. Thus, the gift's appearance is particularly important to the giver.[43]

Subcultures are distinctive groups of people within a culture. Members of a subculture share some customs and norms with the overall society but also have some unique perspectives.[44] Subcultures can be based on geography (Southerners), age (baby boomers), ethnicity (Asian Americans), or lifestyle (punks). Chap-

Refact In 1994, furniture retailer IKEA aired the first mainstream TV ad targeted toward the gay subculture by featuring a gay relationship.[45]

ter 4 addresses how retailers adapt to the effects of subculture on shopping behaviors and decision making.

MARKET SEGMENTATION

The preceding discussion focused on (1) how individual customers evaluate and select stores and merchandise and (2) factors affecting their decision-making processes. To increase their efficiency, retailers identify groups of customers (market segments) and target their offerings to meet the needs of typical customers in that segment rather than the needs of a specific customer. A **retail market segment** is a group of customers whose needs are satisfied by the same retail mix because they have similar needs and go through similar buying processes. For example, families traveling on a vacation have different needs than executives on business trips. Thus, Marriott offers hotels with different retail mixes for each of these segments.

Criteria for Evaluating Market Segments

Customers are grouped into segments in many different ways. For example, customers can be grouped based on the fact that they live in the same city, have similar incomes and education, or barbecue at their homes twice a week or more. Exhibit 5–5 shows different methods for segmenting retail markets. There's no simple way to determine which method is best. Four criteria for evaluating whether a retail segment is a viable target market are actionability, identifiability, accessibility, and size.

Actionability   The fundamental criteria for evaluating a retail market segment are (1) customers in the segment must have similar needs, seek similar benefits, and be satisfied by a similar retail offering and (2) those customers' needs must be different from the needs of customers in other segments. Actionability means that the definition of a segment must clearly indicate what the retailer should do to satisfy its needs. Based on this criterion, it makes sense for Lane Bryant (a division of The Limited catering to full-figure women) to segment the apparel market based on the demographic characteristic physical size. Customers who wear large sizes have different needs than customers in small sizes, so they are attracted to a store offering a unique merchandise mix. In the context of the multi-attribute attitude model discussed previously, women who wear large sizes place more importance on fit and fashion because it's relatively hard for them to satisfy these needs. They should also feel that Lane Bryant performs better on these characteristics than retailers such as JCPenney, Macy's, and Target that don't carry as wide an assortment of large sizes.

It wouldn't make sense for a supermarket to segment its market based on customer size. Large and small men and women probably have the same needs, seek the same benefits, and go through the same buying process for groceries. They have similar importance weights for store attributes. This segmentation approach wouldn't be actionable for a supermarket retailer because the retailer couldn't develop unique mixes for large and small customers. Thus, supermarkets usually segment markets using demographics such as income or ethnic origin to develop their retail mix.

Identifiability   Retailers must be able to identify the customers in a target segment. Identifiability is important because it permits the retailer to determine (1) the segment's size and (2) with whom the retailer should communicate when promoting its retail offering.

EXHIBIT 5-5 Methods for Segmenting Retail Markets

SEGMENTATION BASES/DESCRIPTORS	ILLUSTRATIVE CATEGORIES
GEOGRAPHIC	
Region	Pacific, Mountain, West North Central, West South Central, East North Central, East South Central, South Atlantic, Middle Atlantic, New England
Size of city, country, or standard metropolitan statistical area (SMSA)	Under 5,000, 5,000–19,999, 20,000–49,999, 50,000–99,999, 100,000–249,999, 250,000–499,999, 500,000–999,999, 1,000,000–3,999,999, 4,000,000 or over
Population density	Urban, suburban, rural
Climate	Warm, cold
DEMOGRAPHIC	
Age	Under 6, 6–12, 13–19, 20–29, 30–39, 40–49, 50–59, 60–70, 70+
Gender	Male, female
Family size	1, 2, 3–4, 5+ persons
Family life cycle	Young, single; young, married, no children; young married, youngest child under 6; young, married, youngest child 6 or over; older, married, with children; older, married, no children under 18; older, single, other
Income	Under 10,000, 10,000–14,999, 15,000–24,999, 25,000–34,999, 35,000–49,999, 50,000–74,999, over 75,000
Occupation	Professional and technical; manager, official, and proprietor; clerical, sales; craftsperson, foreperson; operative; turner; retired; student; housewife or househusband; unemployed
Education	Grade school or less; some high school; graduated from high school; some college; graduated from college; some graduate work; graduate degree
Religion	Catholic, Protestant, Jewish, other
Race	White, Asian, African American, Hispanic American
NATIONALITY	
	U.S., British, French, German, Italian, Japanese
PSYCHOSOCIAL	
Social class	Upper class, middle class, working class, lower class
Lifestyle	Traditionalist, sophisticate, swinger
Personality	Compliant, aggressive, detached
FEELINGS AND BEHAVIORS	
Attitudes	Positive, neutral, negative
Benefits sought	Convenience, economy, prestige
Readiness stage	Unaware, aware, informed, interested, desirous, intention to purchase
Perceived risk	High, moderate, low
Innovativeness	Innovator, early adopter, early majority, late majority, laggard, nonadopter
Involvement	Low, high
Loyalty status	None, some, total
Usage rate	None, light, medium, heavy
User status	Nonuser, exuser, potential user, current user
Usage situation	Home, work, commuting, vacation

Source: *Consumer Behavior and Marketing Strategy*, 5th Ed., 1999, by J. Paul Peter and Jerry C. Olson, Irwin/McGraw-Hill Companies, Inc. Reproduced with permission of McGraw-Hill Companies, Inc.

Accessibility   Once a segment is identified, retailers must be able to deliver the appropriate retail mix to the customers in it. Customers for Marriott convention hotels and resort hotels are accessed in different ways because they use different sources to collect information about products and services. Convention hotel customers are best reached through newspapers such as *USA Today* and *The Wall Street Journal*, while resort hotel customers are best reached through ads on TV and in travel and leisure magazines.

Size   A target segment must be large enough to support a unique retailing mix. For example, in the past, health food and vitamins were found primarily in small, owner-operated stores that catered to a relatively small market. In the wake of a higher consciousness about exercise and nutrition, health food stores like General Nutrition have flourished. Supermarkets have also expanded their offering of health foods and vitamins to meet this substantial market segment's needs.

On the other hand, the number of consumers in a target segment may not be a good indicator of potential sales. For example, international retailers are very interested in China because it has 1.2 billion consumers. Although many consumers in China's coastal cities have considerable disposable income, 70 percent of all Chinese live in rural areas with minimal incomes. Even in the urban areas, many Chinese consumers are in their twenties and live with their parents in an apartment.[46]

Approaches to Segmenting Markets   Exhibit 5–5 illustrates the wide variety of approaches for segmenting retail markets. No one approach is best for all retailers. They must explore various factors that affect customer buying behavior and determine which factors are most important. Now we'll discuss methods for segmenting retail markets.

Geographic Segmentation   **Geographic segmentation** groups customers by where they live. A retail market can be segmented by countries (Japan, Mexico) and by areas within a country such as states, cities, and neighborhoods. Since customers typically shop at stores convenient to where they live and work, individual retail outlets usually focus on the customer segment reasonably close to the outlet.

In the U.S., many food retailers concentrate on regions of the country. For example, HEB concentrates on Texas, while Wegmans concentrates on Western New York. However, in the U.K., supermarket retailing is dominated by national firms such as Sainsbury and Tesco.

Even though national retailers such as The Gap and Sears have no geographic focus, they do tailor their merchandise selections to different regions of the country. Snow sleds don't sell well in Florida and surfboards don't sell well in Colorado. Even within a metropolitan area, stores in a chain must adjust to unique needs of customers in different neighborhoods. For example, supermarkets in affluent neighborhoods typically have more gourmet foods than stores in less affluent neighborhoods.

Segments based on geography are identifiable, accessible, and substantial. It's easy to determine who lives in a geographic segment such as the Paris metropolitan area and to target communications and locate retail outlets for customers in Paris.

When customers in different geographic segments may have similar needs, it would be inappropriate to develop unique retail offerings by geographic markets. For example, a fast-food customer in Detroit probably seeks the same benefits as a fast-food customer in Los Angeles. Thus, it wouldn't be useful to segment the fast-food market geographically. Even though Target and The Gap vary some merchandise assortments geographically, the majority of their merchandise is identical in all of their stores because customers who buy basic clothing (underwear, slacks, shirts, and blouses) have many of the same needs in all regions of the United States. On the other hand, Home Depot and many supermarket chains have significantly different assortments in stores located in the same city.

React Across the United States, vanilla is the number one ice cream flavor and chocolate is number two; however, Häagen-Dazs coffee is most popular in New York, butter pecan elsewhere in the East, and chocolate chip in California.[47]

Demographic Segmentation   Demographic variables are the most common means to define segments because such customer segments can be easily identified and accessed. The media used by retailers to communicate with customers are defined in terms of demographic profiles. Chapter 4 discussed special demographic segments retailers focus on such as African Americans, Hispanic Americans, the elderly, and baby boomers.

Gender is a good predictor of shopping behaviors. Men show little ability or interest in honing their shopping skills, while women view the supermarket as a place where they can demonstrate their expertise in getting the most value for their money. Rather than looking for items on sale or making price comparisons, men tend to select well-known brands. They also tend to not pay attention at the checkout register, while women watch the cashier to be sure they're charged the right price. Men and women even buy different merchandise. Women buy more health-oriented foods (such as cottage cheese and refrigerated yogurt) and household essentials (such as cleaning and personal health products). Men's shopping baskets contain more beer, cupcakes, ice cream, and hot dogs. Men also do less planning and make numerous last-minute grocery trips. Single men visit supermarkets 99 times a year, while single women make 80 trips a year. These 11th-hour trips make men more susceptible to impulse purchases such as potato chips and cookies.[48]

While segments based on demographics are easily identified and accessed, demographics aren't always related to customer needs and buying behavior. Thus, demographics may not be useful for defining segments for some retailers. For example, demographics are poor predictors of users of active wear such as jogging suits and running shoes. At one time, retailers assumed that active wear would be purchased exclusively by young people, but the health and fitness trend has led people of all ages to buy this merchandise. Relatively inactive consumers find activewear to be very comfortable. Initially, retailers felt that VCRs would be a luxury product purchased mainly by wealthy customers. But retailers found that low-income customers and families with young children were strongly attracted to VCRs because they offered low-cost, convenient entertainment.

Lifestyle Segmentation   **Lifestyle** refers to how people live, how they spend their time and money, what activities they pursue, and their attitudes and opinions about the world they live in. The segments are identified through consumer surveys that ask respondents to indicate whether they agreed or disagreed with statements such as "My idea of fun in a national park would be to stay in an expensive lodge and dress up for dinner" and "I could not stand to skin a dead animal." Retailers today are placing more emphasis on lifestyles or psychographics than on demographics to define a target segment.

In Chapter 9, PRIZM™, a widely used segmentation scheme based on geographic, demographic, and lifestyle characteristics, is described with an illustration of its use in evaluating store locations.

Buying Situation Segmentation   Buying behavior of customers with the same demographics or lifestyle can differ depending on their buying situation. For example, in Exhibit 5–3, the parent with four children evaluated the supercenter higher than the Internet grocer or supermarket for weekly grocery purchases. But if the parent ran out of milk during the week, he'd probably go to the convenience store rather than the wholesale club for this fill-in shopping. In terms of

Exhibit 5–3's multiattribute attitude model, convenience would be more important than assortment in the fill-in shopping situation. Similarly, an executive will stay at a convention hotel on a business trip and a resort on a family vacation.

Benefit Segmentation Another approach for defining a target segment is to group customers seeking similar benefits. In the multiattribute attitude model, customers in the same benefit segment would have a similar set of importance weights on the attributes of a store or a product. For example, customers who place high importance on fashion and style and low importance on price would form a fashion segment, while customers who place more importance on price would form a price segment.

Benefit segments are very actionable. Benefits sought by customers in the target segment clearly indicate how retailers should design their offerings to appeal to the segment. But customers in benefit segments aren't easily identified or accessed. It's hard to look at a person and determine what benefits she's seeking. Typically, the audience for media used by retailers is described by demographics rather than by the benefits sought.

Composite Segmentation Approaches

As we've seen, no one approach meets all the criteria for useful customer segmentation. For example, demographic and geographic segmenting are ideal for identifying and accessing customers, but these characteristics are often unrelated to customers' needs. Thus, these approaches don't indicate the actions necessary to attract customers in these segments. On the other hand, knowing what benefits customers are seeking is useful for designing an effective retail offering, but presents a problem in identifying which customers are seeking these benefits. For these reasons, composite segmentation plans use multiple variables to identify customers in the target segment. They define target customers by benefits sought, lifestyles, and demographics.

JCPenney's Segmentation of the Women's Apparel Market The market for women's apparel is typically segmented into five categories: conservative, traditional, update, bridge, and designer or fashion-forward. The conservative segment is the most price-conscious and least fashion-oriented. The designer segment seeks just the opposite: fashion and style with little regard for price.

Penney customers are in the first three segments, but the firm is targeting its offering to customers in the traditional and updated segments. Exhibit 5–6A shows characteristics of each women's apparel segment. Note how these descriptions include segment size, customers' values, benefits they seek, and demographic information. Penney has different departments within each store and different private labels tailored to meet each segment's needs. Exhibit 5–6B lists Penney's retail offerings directed toward these segments.

SUMMARY

To satisfy customer needs, retailers must thoroughly understand how customers make store choice and purchase decisions and the factors they consider when deciding. This chapter describes the buying process's six stages (need recognition, information search, evaluation of alternatives, choice of alternatives, purchase, and postpurchase evaluations) and how retailers can influence each stage. A stage's importance depends on the nature

EXHIBIT 5-6   JCPenney Segments for Women's Apparel

A. SEGMENT DESCRIPTION		
	CONSERVATIVE	**TRADITIONAL**	**UPDATE**
Size	23% of population	38% of population	16% of population
	16% of total sales	40% of total sales	24% of total sales
Age	35–55 years old	25–49 years old	25–49 years old
Values	Conservative values	Traditional values	Contemporary values
	Satisfied with present status	Active, busy, independent, self-confident	Active, busy, independent, very self-confident
Employment	Has job, not career	Family- and job/career-oriented	Family- and job/career-oriented
Income	Limited disposable income	Considerable income	Considerable income
Benefits sought	Price-driven, reacts to sales	Quality-driven, will pay a little extra	Fashion-driven, expresses self through apparel
	Wants easy care and comfort	Wants traditional styling, seeks clothes that last	Wants newness in color and style
	Not interested in fashion	Interested in newness	Shops often
	Defines value as price, quality, fashion	Defines value as quality, fashion, price	Defines value as fashion, quality, price

B. RETAIL OFFERING		
RETAIL MIX	**CONSERVATIVE**	**TRADITIONAL**	**UPDATE**
Pricing	Budget	Moderate	Moderate to better
Merchandise	Basic styles, easy-care fabrics	Traditional styling, good quality	Fashion-forward, more selection, comfortable fit, tailored look, newer colors
Brands	Miss Ericka	Lee	Joneswear
	Sag Harbor	Worthington (career)	Crazy Horse
	Cabin Creek	St. John's Bay	Evan Picone
		Hunt Club	Jacqueline Ferrar
Merchandising approach	Price signing, "save stories," stack-out tables	Well-coordinated merchandise, collections, uncluttered displays, knowledgeable salespeople	Color statements, mannequins, theme areas

of the customer's decision. When decisions are important and risky, the buying process is longer; customers spend more time and effort on information search and evaluating alternatives. When buying decisions are less important to customers, they spend little time in the buying process and their buying behavior may become habitual.

The buying process of individual consumers is influenced by their families, reference groups, culture, and subcultures. The largest ethnic subcultures in the United States (African American and Hispanic) have their own values and needs.

To develop cost-effective retail programs, retailers group customers into segments. Some approaches for segmenting markets are based on geography, demographics, lifestyles, usage situations, and benefits sought. Since each approach has its advantages and disadvantages, retailers typically define their target segment by several characteristics.

KEY TERMS

benefit segmentation, *159*

brand loyalty, *141*

buying process, *137*

buying situation segmentation, *158*

composite segmentation, *159*

consideration set, *151*

cross-shopping, *145*

culture, *154*

demograhic segmentation, *158*

extended problem solving, *138*

external sources of information, *146*

fashion, *162*

functional needs, *142*

geographic segmentation, *157*

habitual decision making, *141*

impulse buying, *140*

information search, *144*

internal sources of information, *146*

knock-off, *164*

lifestyle, *158*

lifestyle segmentation, *158*

limited problem solving, *139*

mass market theory, *164*

multiattribute attitude model, *147*

postpurchase evaluation, *153*

psychological needs, *142*

reference group, *153*

retail market segment, *155*

satisfaction, *152*

store loyalty, *141*

subculture, *154*

subculture theory, *164*

trickle-down theory, *164*

DISCUSSION QUESTIONS AND PROBLEMS

1. Does the customer buying process end when a customer buys some merchandise? Explain your answer.

2. What would get a consumer to switch from making a habitual choice decision to eat at Burger King to making a limited or extended choice decision?

3. What actions can an electronic retailer take to ensure that customers have a satisfactory experience when visiting and placing orders from its website?

4. Reflect on your decision process in selecting a college. (Universities are nonprofit service retailers.) Was your decision-making process extensive, limited, or habitual? Did you go through all of Figure 5–1's stages?

5. Any retailer's goal is to get a customer in its store to stop searching and buy a product at its outlet. How can a record retailer ensure that the customer buys a CD at its outlet?

6. What advantages and disadvantages do consumers receive by purchasing from an Internet retailer rather than from a store? What type of merchandise do consumers prefer to purchase in a store? From the electronic retailer? Why?

7. Develop a demographic profile for two different target market segments for a hardware store. Outline the difference in the retail mixes that would be most appealing to each of these target markets.

8. How would you expect the buying decision process to differ when shopping at an electronic retailer on the Internet compared to shopping in a store?

9. A family-owned bookstore across the street from a major university campus wants to identify the various segments in its market. What approaches might the store owner use to segment its market? List the potential target market segments based on this segmentation approach. Then contrast the retail mix that would be most appropriate for two potential target segments.

10. Using the multiattribute attitude model, identify the probable choice of an auto repair outlet for a young single businesswoman and for a retired couple with limited income.

CHARACTERISTICS	IMPORTANCE WEIGHTS		PERFORMANCE BELIEFS		
	YOUNG SINGLE	RETIRED COUPLE	LOCAL GAS STATION	NATIONAL SERVICE CHAIN	LOCAL CAR DEALER
Price	2	10	9	10	3
Time to complete repair	8	5	5	9	7
Reliability	2	9	2	7	10
Convenience	8	3	3	6	5

SUGGESTED READINGS

Birstwistle, Grete, Ian Clarke, and Paul Freathy. "Customer Decision Making in Fashion Retailing: A Segmentation Approach." *International Journal of Retail & Distribution Management* 26 (April–May 1998), pp. 147–55.

Carsky, Mary, Roger Dickenson, and Mary Smith. "Toward Consumer Efficiency: A Model for Improving Buymanship." *Journal of Consumer Affairs* 29, no. 2 (1995), pp. 442–58.

"The Devotion CYCLE: A Model for Helping Retailers Profit from Changing Consumer Values." *Chain Store Age*, January 1999, pp. 52–65.

Earl, Peter, and Simon Kemp, eds. *Consumer Research and Economic Psychology.* Northampton, MA: Edward Elgar, 1999.

Pegler, Martin, Arthur Winters, and Peggy Winters, eds. *Retail Entertainment.* New York: Visual Reference Publications, 1998.

Peter, J. Paul, and Jerry Olson. *Consumer Behavior and Marketing Strategy,* 5th ed. Burr Ridge, IL: Irwin/McGraw-Hill, 1999.

"Retail Shopping: Profiling Fashion Innovators' Favorite Haunts." *WWD,* November 6, 1997, pp. 2–3.

Sheth, Jagdish, Banwari Mittal, and Bruce Newman. *Consumer Behavior.* Fort Worth, TX: Dryden, 1999.

Solomon, Michael. *Consumer Behavior,* 4th ed. Englewood Cliffs, NJ: Prentice-Hall, 1999.

Sullivan, Pauline, and Ronald Savitt. "Store Patronage and Lifestyle Factors: Implications for Grocery Retailers." *International Journal of Retail & Distribution Management* 25 (August–September 1997), pp. 351–65.

Taubes, Gary. "Confessions of a Shopper." *Forbes,* April 6, 1998, pp. S66–70.

Underhill, Paco. *Why We Buy: The Science of Shopping.* New York: Simon & Schuster, 1999.

APPENDIX

Consumer Behavior Toward Fashion

Many retailers, particularly department and specialty stores, sell fashionable merchandise. To profitably sell this type of merchandise, retailers need to (1) understand how fashions develop and diffuse through the marketplace and (2) use operating systems that enable them to match supply and demand for this volatile merchandise. This appendix reviews the consumer behavior aspects of fashion. The operating systems for matching supply and demand for fashion merchandise are discussed in Chapter 13.

Fashion is a type of product or a way of behaving that is temporarily adopted by a large number of consumers because the product or behavior is considered to be socially appropriate for the time and place.[49] For example, in some social groups, it is or was fashionable to have brightly colored hair, play golf, wear a coat made from animal fur, have a beard, or go to an expensive health spa for a vacation. In many retail environments, however, the term *fashion* is associated with apparel and accessories.

Customer Needs Satisfied by Fashion   Fashion gives people an opportunity to satisfy many emotional and practical needs. Through fashions, people develop their own identity. They can use fashions to manage their appearance, express their self-image and feelings, enhance their egos, and make an impression on others. Through the years, fashions have become associated with specific lifestyles or roles people play. You wear different clothing styles when you are attending class, going out on a date, or interviewing for a job.

Fashion also can be used to communicate with others. For example, you might wear a classic business suit when interviewing for a job at Sears but more informal attire when interviewing for a job with The Gap. These different dress styles would indicate your appreciation and understanding of the differences in the cultures of these firms.

People use fashions both to develop their own identity and to gain acceptance from others. These two benefits of fashion can be opposing forces. If you choose to wear something radically different, you will achieve recognition for your individuality but might not be accepted by your peers. To satisfy these conflicting needs, man-

Fashions provide an opportunity for consumers to express their self-image and feelings.

ufacturers and retailers offer a variety of designs and combinations of designs that are fashionable and still enable consumers to express their individuality.

What Creates Fashion?   Fashion is affected by economic, sociological, and psychological factors.

Economic Factors   Fashion merchandise is a luxury. It includes design details that go beyond satisfying basic functional needs. Thus, demand for fashion merchandise is greatest in countries with a high level of economic development and in market segments with the greatest disposable income.

Sociological Factors   Fashion changes reflect changes in our social environment, our feelings about class structure, the roles of women and men, and the structure of the family. For example, time pressures arising from the increased number of women in the workforce have led to the acceptance of low-maintenance, wrinkle-resistant fabrics. Rising concern for the environment has resulted in natural fibers becoming fashionable and fur coats going out of fashion. Interest in health and fitness has made it fashionable to exercise and wear jogging clothes, leotards, and running shoes.

Psychological Factors   Consumers adopt fashions to overcome boredom. People get tired of wearing the same clothing and seeing the same furniture in their living room. They seek changes in their lifestyles by buying new clothes or redecorating their houses.

How Do Fashions Develop and Spread?   Fashions are not universal. A fashion can be accepted in one geographic region, country, or age group and not in another. In the 1970s, the fashion among young women was ankle-length skirts, argyle socks, and platform shoes, while older women were wearing pantsuits, double-breasted blazers, and midheeled shoes. During the 1970s, natural hairstyles were fashionable among African Americans, while cornrow hairstyles became fashionable in the early 1980s.

The stages in the fashion life cycle are shown in Exhibit 5–7. The cycle begins with the creation of a new design or style. Then some consumers recognized as fashion leaders or innovators adopt the fashion and start a trend in their social group. The fashion spreads from the leaders to others and is accepted widely as a fashion. Eventually the fashion is accepted by most people in the social group and can become overused. Saturation and overuse set the stage for the decline in popularity and the creation of new fashions.

Creation   New fashions arise from a number of sources. Couture fashion designers are only one source of the creative inspirations. Fashions are also developed by creative consumers, celebrities, and even retailers. Courtney Cox and Jennifer Anniston, two actors in the TV program *Friends*, created an interest in wearing hair accessories such as banana clips and scrunchies. The Sungil baby carrier was designed by American Ann Moore based on slings she saw African women use.[50]

Courtney Cox Arquette and the cast of Friends *created new fashions for hair accessories.*

EXHIBIT 5–7

Stages in the Fashion
Life Cycle

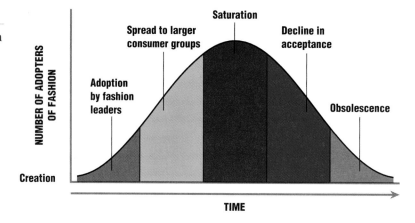

Adoption by Fashion Leaders   The fashion life cycle really starts when the fashion is adopted by leading consumers. These initial adopters of a new fashion are called fashion leaders or innovators. They are the first people to display the new fashion in their social group. If the fashion is too innovative or very different from currently accepted fashion, the style might not be accepted by the social group, thus prematurely ending the life cycle.

Three theories have been proposed to explain how fashion spreads within a society. The **trickle-down theory** suggests that the fashion leaders are consumers with the highest social status—wealthy, well-educated consumers. After they adopt a fashion, the fashion trickles down to consumers in lower social classes. When the fashion is accepted in the lowest social class, it is no longer acceptable to the fashion leaders in the highest social class.

Manufacturers and retailers stimulate this trickle-down process by copying the latest styles displayed at designer fashion shows and sold in exclusive specialty stores. These copies, referred to as **knock-offs,** are sold at lower prices through retailers targeting a broader market. For example, a bamboo-handle bag that Tom Ford, a designer, showed at Gucci one season year for $640, was similar to the bag offered the next season at Sears for $20. The leopard print of Diane Von Furstenberg's new $190 wrap dresses was reinterpreted at Sears as a wrap blouse with matching black pants and sold for $69.[53]

The second theory, the **mass-market theory,** suggests that fashions spread across social classes. Each social class has its own fashion leaders who play a key role in their own social networks. Fashion information "trickles across" social classes rather than down from the upper classes to the lower classes. Department stores use teen boards to stimulate diffusion of fashion across social classes. Social leaders are selected to be members of the board and promote the retailer and the merchandise sold in its stores.

However, consumers often can distinguish between hype and buzz. Buzz is genuine, street-level excitement about a hot new product; while hype is artificially generated word of mouth, manufactured by public relations people. Sometimes hype and buzz converge. For example, shortly after the launch of the "Yo Quiero Taco Bell!" advertising campaign featuring the talking Latino Chihuahua, the dog started showing up on skateboards in Venice Beach, California, and on black-market T-shirts.[54]

The third theory, the **subculture theory,** is based on the development of recent fashions. Subcultures of mostly young and less affluent consumers, such as motorcycle riders and urban rappers, started fashions for such things

ALEX BAJRECH, IS VICE PRESIDENT and fashion director for the Wet Seal, a specialty store chain headquartered in Foothill Ranch, California. Mr. Bajrech's job is predicting the next teen fashion trend so that it appears in the company's 456 Wet Seal and Contempo Casual stores just as its popularity is rising. "We don't look like a Gap or Old Navy," says Mr. Bajrech. "There is no room for another one like that. We need to have an edge." Four other chains targeting fashion markets are Delia's, Hot Topics, Urban Outfitters, and Gadzooks.

To find that edge Mr. Bajrech reads *Seventeen* magazine and watches *Dawson Creek* on television. He listens to Crystal Method and Transglobal Underground and spends his working days stopping and talking to teens on streets in Manhattan, London, and Tokyo. He goes to fashion shows in Milan and Paris and visits Wet Seal stores to get feedback from the store managers.

Mr. Bajrech started working at The Wet Seal in 1994 when it seemed like the grunge look might take over teen fashion. Young trendsetters were shopping at the Salvation Army store rather than the mall. At that time, The Wet Seal was a Southern California retail chain offering surfer styles. The company decided that it needed to grow beyond its Southern California roots to survive. "A lot of trends used to start in Southern California. Now a lot of trends start in other parts of the country or world," says Ed Thomas, Wet Seal president and chief operating officer.

As a fashion predictor, Mr. Bajrech has learned that not every prediction is on target. Four years ago, he saw teens wearing dark denim jeans in London's Camden Market and in

The Wet Seal needs to keep on top of the latest fashions to satisfy the needs of the teen market.

Osaka, Japan. He persuaded Wet Seal to introduce them in the U.S. "It was a complete bomb," he says. "Everyone was into stone wash and vintage." But Wet Seal prides itself on its ability to move quickly to correct the inevitable mistakes in predicting fashion. The firm never commits too much to one item. Merchandise that does not sell gets marked down in four weeks and again after six weeks so Wet Seal has an annual inventory turn of nine compared to its competitors' five turns.

Source: Rusty Williamson, "Tracking the Teen Shopper: Turf War Heats Up as Retailers Vie for Piece of Growing Junior Market," *WWD*, February 25, 1999, p. 2B; and Emily Nelson, "The Hunt for Hip: A Trend Scout's Trail," *The Wall Street Journal*, December 9, 1998, B1, B4.

---

as colorful fabrics, T-shirts, sneakers, jeans, black leather jackets, and surplus military clothing. These fashions started with people in small, lower income consumer groups and "trickled up" to mainstream consumer classes. Nike employs "cool-hunters" to canvas subcultures and find out what will be the next hot sneaker. (Unfortunately for Nike, the answer was New Balance.)

The Goth scene is an example of a subculture that has developed a unique style. It revolves around dark fashion and even darker, moody music performed by artists like Marilyn Manson. Hot Topics, a Pomona-based mall retailer, is the Goth Gap selling clothing and accessories to hip-hop kids, punks, and lounge rats. Some goth fashions are black lipstick, nail polish, and eyeliner as well as silver bracelets and earrings, black rubber pants, hooded capes, black fishnet leggings, and fitted, square-neck velvet gowns. Popular item at Hot Topics are two dolls, Misery and Tragedy, dressed in goth fashion—the Ken and Barbie dolls of goth.[55]

These theories of fashion development indicate that fashion leaders can come from many different places and social groups. In our diverse society, many types of consumers have the opportunity to be the leaders in setting fashion trends. Retailing View 5A.1 describes how the Wet Seal predicts teen fashions.

Spread to Large Consumer Groups   During this stage, the fashion is accepted by a wider group of consumers referred to as early adopters. The fashion becomes increasingly visible, receives greater publicity and media attention, and is readily available in retail stores.

The relative advantage, compatibility, complexity, trialability, and observability of a fashion affect the time it takes the fashion to spread through a social group. New fashions that provide more benefits have a higher *relative advantage* compared to existing fashions, and these new fashions spread faster. Fashions are often adopted by consumers because they make people feel special. Thus more exclusive fashions like expensive clothing are adopted more quickly in an affluent target market. On a more utilitarian level, clothing that is easy to maintain, such as wrinkle-free pants, will diffuse quickly in the general population.

Compatibility is the degree to which the fashion is consistent with existing norms, values, and behaviors. When new fashions aren't consistent with existing norms, the number of adopters and the speed of adoption are lower. Since the mid-1960s, the fashion industry has repeatedly attempted to revive the miniskirt. It has had only moderate success because the group of women with the most disposable income to spend on fashion are baby boomers, many of whom no longer find the miniskirt a relevant fashion for their family-oriented lifestyles.

Complexity refers to how easy it is to understand and use the new fashion. Consumers have to learn how to incorporate a new fashion into their lifestyle. For example, at times, tie manufacturers have tried to stimulate sales of bow ties but were unsuccessful because men had difficulty tying the knot.

Trialability refers to the costs and commitment required to initially adopt the fashion. For example, when consumers need to spend a lot of money buying a new type of expensive jewelry to be in fashion, the rate of adoption is slower than if the fashion simply requires wearing jewelry that the consumer already owns on a different part of the body.

Observability is the degree to which the new fashion is visible and easily communicated to others in the social group. Clothing fashions are very observable compared to fashions for the home, such as sheets and towels. It is therefore likely that a fashion in clothing will spread more quickly than a new color scheme or style for the bedroom.

Fashion retailers engage in many activities to increase the adoption and spread of a new fashion through their target market. Compatibility is increased and complexity is decreased by showing consumers how to coordinate a new article of fashion clothing with other items the consumer already owns. Trialability is increased by providing dressing rooms so customers can try on clothing and see how it looks on them. Providing opportunities for customers to return merchandise also increases trialability. Retailers increase observability by displaying fashion merchandise in their stores and advertising it in newspapers.

INTERNET EXERCISE   The Internet enables people around the world to see the latest fashion. Visit the following sites displaying fashionable merchandise: www.boo.com, www.widemedia.com/fashionuk, www.fashiontrip.com, and www.bluefly.com.

Saturation   In this stage, the fashion achieves its highest level of social accept-ance. Almost all consumers in the target market are aware of the fashion and have decided to either accept or reject it. At this point, the fashion has become old and boring to many people.

Decline in Acceptance and Obsolescence   When fashions reach saturation, they have become less appealing to consumers. Because most people have already adopted the fashion, it no longer provides an opportunity for people to express their individuality. Fashion creators and leaders are beginning to experiment with new fashions. The introduction of a new fashion speeds the decline of the preceding fashion.

Retailing Strategy

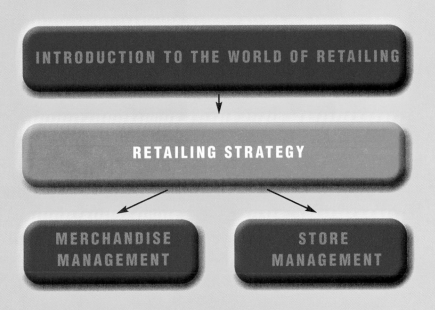

SECTION I DESCRIBES RETAIL MANAGEMENT decisions; the different types of retailers; the changing nature of retailing in terms of consumer needs and technology; and factors that affect consumers' choice of retailers and merchandise. This broad overview of retailing provides the background information needed to develop and implement an effective retail strategy. ● Section II discusses strategic decisions made by retailers, including development of a retail market strategy (Chapter 6), the financial strategy associated with the market strategy (Chapter 7), the location strategy for retail outlets (Chapters 8 and 9), the firm's organization and human resource strategy (Chapter 10), and systems used to control the flow of information and merchandise (Chapter 11). As outlined in Chapter 1, these decisions are strategic rather than tactical because they involve committing significant resources to developing long-term advantages over competition in a target market segment. ● Sections III and IV review tactical decisions concerning merchandise and store management to implement the retail strategy. These implementation or tactical decisions impact a retailer's efficiency, but their impact is shorter term than the strategic decisions reviewed in Section II.

Dave Fuente
CEO
Office Depot

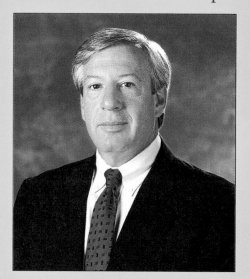

WHEN I STARTED WITH OFFICE DEPOT in 1987, the retail office supply business primarily consisted of family-owned businesses in Main Street locations that were open between 9 A.M. and 5 P.M., sold merchandise with a 40 percent markup, and had a relatively limited stock selection. Our strategy in those days was fairly simple: Open stores in lots of locations, be open when our primary customer (the small business owner) can come to shop, lower the price, have a large variety of merchandise, and never be out of stock on items small businesses need every day. In those early years, there were lots of office supply superstores. Now there are only three major players. So, our strategy worked very well. • I've always believed that one cannot be complacent when it comes to being on top. The business world changes, and so has Office Depot. We now have 850 superstores and 30 warehouses. We are the largest office supply retailer on the Internet, with $350 million in sales in 1999. Unlike high-flying web-based companies that have yet to turn a profit, officedepot.com has been profitable from virtually the day we opened. We believe that the success of brick-and-mortar retailers like us will be based on our ability to leverage the strengths of our stores' systems, our relationship with our vendors, our local distribution system, and our strong brand in cyberspace. • Office Depot has integrated the Net into the heart of its operations. Focusing primarily on business-to-business, we have set up customized web pages for 37,000 corporate clients. For each customer, we design a site with parameters that allow different employees various degrees of freedom to buy supplies. That way, a stockroom clerk might only be able to order pencils, paper, and a few other things, but the CEO could order anything, including a Mont Blanc pen. Customers can also use the Net to check up-to-the-minute inventory at the nearest store or warehouse to see what's available for delivery the next day. These services make Office Depot and officedepot.com top-of-mind for any customer with office supply needs.

6

Retail Market Strategy

QUESTIONS

- What is a retail strategy?

- How can a retailer build a sustainable competitive advantage?

- What steps do retailers go through to develop a strategy?

- What different strategic opportunities can retailers pursue?

THE GROWING INTENSITY of retail competition due to the emergence of new formats and technology plus shifts in customer needs is forcing retailers to devote more attention to long-term strategic thinking. As the retail management decision-making process indicates, retailing strategy (Section II) is the bridge between understanding the world of retailing—the analysis of the retail environment (Section I) and the more tactical merchandise management and store operations activities (Sections III and IV) undertaken to implement the retail strategy. The retail strategy provides the direction retailers need to take to deal effectively with their environment, customers, and competitors.[1]

The first part of this chapter defines the term *retail strategy* and discusses three important elements of retail strategy: the target market segment, retail format, and sustainable competitive advantage. Next, we outline approaches for building a sustainable competitive advantage. The chapter concludes with a discussion of the strategic retail planning process.

Refact The word *strategy* comes from the Greek word meaning the "art of the general."[2]

WHAT IS A RETAIL STRATEGY?

The term *strategy* is frequently used in retailing. For example, retailers talk about their merchandise strategy, promotion strategy, location strategy, and private-brand strategy. In fact, the term is used so commonly it appears that all retailing decisions are now strategic decisions. But retail strategy isn't just another expression for retail management.

Definition of Retail Market Strategy

A **retail strategy** is a statement identifying (1) the retailer's target market, (2) the format the retailer plans to use to satisfy the target market's needs, and (3) the bases upon which the retailer plans to build a sustainable competitive advantage.[3] The **target market** is the market segment(s) toward which the retailer plans to focus its resources

Starbucks has developed several bases of competitive advantage, one of which is the service provided by this barista.

and retail mix. A **retail format** is the retailer's mix (nature of merchandise and services offered, pricing policy, advertising and promotion program, approach to store design and visual merchandising, and typical location). Here are examples of retail strategies.

- **Starbucks,** a national chain of gourmet coffee cafes, generates annual sales over $1 billion. The cafes provide an opportunity for people to take a break from their busy lives to savor specialty coffee drinks in a relaxing atmosphere. Friendly, knowledgeable counter servers, called *baristas* (Italian for bartenders), educate customers about Starbucks' products. The company has entered into some creative partnerships to put its cafes in Nordstrom and Barnes & Noble stores and serve its coffee on United Airlines. Licensing the brand name for other food products such as ice cream and soft drinks increases its brand awareness[4]

- **Fingerhut** is a billion-dollar retailer that is unknown to most consumers because it uses many different catalogs to sell a wide variety of merchandise ranging from flowers to $2,000 home entertainment centers. Each year, it mails out over 500 million catalogs to its primary customer base, households with annual income between $15,000 and $35,000. To meet the needs of these lower income customers with limited credit histories, Fingerhut gives its customer the opportunity to make monthly payments for merchandise over a year or two. The company maintains a database of 30 million customers with up to 1,400 pieces of information about each customer. A critical component in this database is the names of 11 million customers who failed to pay for merchandise purchased. Sophisticated database management techniques are used to target marketing activities and minimize credit risks. In 1999, Federated Department Stores acquired Fingerhut for $1.7 billion.[5]

- **Autozone,** a Memphis-based auto parts retailer with annual sales exceeding $3 billion, is the largest auto supply retailer in the United States. Its target market is lower-income people who repair their cars themselves out of economic necessity since they can't afford to have their cars repaired by others. Autozone builds loyalty in this segment by providing exceptional convenience and service. Stores are located in neighborhoods near their customers and stay open until midnight. Almost all employees (called Autozoners) have prior automotive repair experience. They're encouraged to go out to the store parking lot with a customer to check on the exact part needed and even help the customer install simple items like headlights and hoses.[7]

- **Ukrop's** is a family-owned supermarket chain with 26 stores in Virginia centered around its corporate headquarters in Richmond. The chain dominates its market by providing outstanding value-added services for its customers. It was one of the first supermarket chains to offer its customers meal solutions—imaginative, healthy, freshly prepared ready-to-go meals—and a frequent shopper program to reward its loyal customers. An exciting store atmosphere is created by stations for coffee, bagels, yogurt, made-to-order Caesar salad, and sushi as well as the Meal Idea Center demos plus its bakery department chefs and decorators.[8]

Each of these retail strategies involves (1) selecting a target market segment and retail format and (2) developing sustainable competitive advantage that enables the retailer to reduce the level of competition it faces. Now let's examine these central concepts in a retail strategy.

INTERNET EXERCISE Visit the Autozone homepage (www.autozone. com) and Ukrop's (www.ukrops.com). Do these Internet sites reflect the retail strategies for the companies as discussed here?

TARGET MARKET AND RETAIL FORMAT

The retailing concept (discussed in Chapter 1) emphasizes that retailers must consider both their customers and their competitors when developing a retail strategy. Successful retailers satisfy the needs of customers in their target market segment better than the competition does. The selection of a target market focuses the retailer on a group of consumers whose needs it will attempt to satisfy. The selection of a retail format outlines the retail mix to be used to satisfy needs of customers in the target market.

The retail strategy determines the markets in which a retailer will compete. Traditional markets, like a farmers' market, are places where buyers and sellers meet and make transactions—say, a consumer buys six ears of corn from a farmer. But in modern markets, potential buyers and sellers aren't located in one place. Transactions can occur without face-to-face interactions. For example, many customers contact retailers and place orders over the Internet using a computer.

We define a **retail market,** not as a specific place where buyers and sellers meet, but as a group of consumers with similar needs (a market segment) and a group of retailers using a similar retail format to satisfy those consumer needs.[9]

Exhibit 6–1 illustrates a set of retail markets for women's clothing. A number of retail formats are listed down the left-hand column. As Chapter 2 said, each format offers a different retail mix to its customers. Customer segments are listed in the exhibit's top row. As mentioned in Chapter 5, these segments can be defined in terms of the customer's demographics, lifestyle, buying situation, or benefits sought. In this illustration, we divide the market into three fashion-related segments: conservatives who place little importance on fashion, traditional who want classic styles, and fashion-forwards who want the most fashionable merchandise. Each square of the matrix shown in Exhibit 6–1 describes a potential retail market where two or more retailers compete with each other. For example, Wal-Mart and Kmart stores in the same geographic area compete with each other using a discount store format targeting conservative customers, while Saks and Neiman Marcus compete against each other with a department store format targeting the fashion-forward segment.

The women's clothing market in Exhibit 6–1 is just one of several representations that could have been used. Retail formats could be expanded to include outlet stores and electronic retailing. Rather than being segmented by fashion orientation, the market could have been segmented using the other approaches described in Chapter 5. While Exhibit 6–1 isn't the only way to describe the women's retail clothing market, it does illustrate how retail markets are defined in terms of retail format and customer market segment.

EXHIBIT 6-1   Retail Market for Women's Apparel

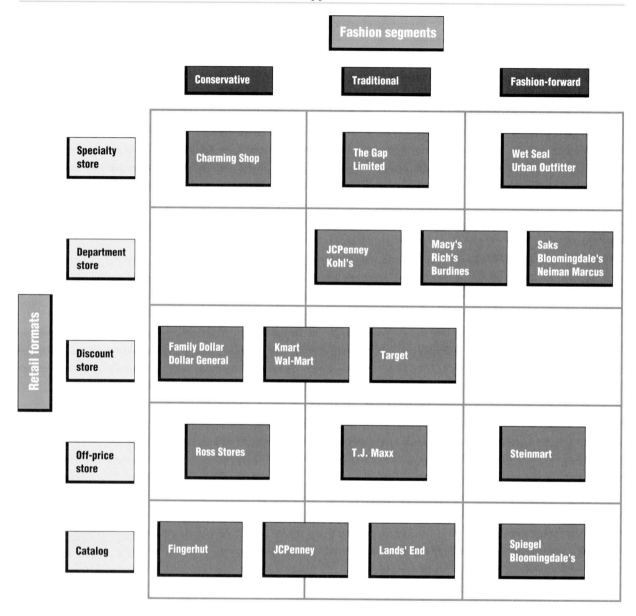

Basically, Exhibit 6–1's matrix describes the battlefield where women's clothing retailers compete. The position in this battlefield indicates the first two elements of a retailer's strategy: its target market segment and retail format. Consider the situation confronting The Gap as it develops a retail strategy for the women's clothing market. Should The Gap compete in all 25 retail markets shown in Exhibit 6–1, or should it focus on a limited set of retail markets? If The Gap decides to focus on a limited set of markets, which should it pursue? The Gap's answers to these questions defines its retail strategy and indicates how it plans to focus its resources.

BUILDING A SUSTAINABLE COMPETITIVE ADVANTAGE

The final element in a retail strategy is the retailer's approach to building a sustainable competitive advantage. A **sustainable competitive advantage** is an advantage over competition that can be maintained over a long time. Exhibit 6–2 shows some approaches a retailer can use to gain an advantage over its competitors. The list isn't exhaustive. Any business activity that a retailer engages in can be a basis for a competitive advantage.[10]

But some advantages are sustainable over a long period of time, while others can be duplicated by competitors almost immediately. For example, it would be hard for Jiffy Lube to get a long-term advantage over Pep Boys Automotive Center by simply offering an oil change at a lower price. If Jiffy

Ukrop's meal solutions are the basis for a sustainable competitive advantage because it is difficult for competitors to copy this special offering.

Lube's price reduction was successful in attracting customers, Pep Boys would know what Jiffy Lube had done and would match the price reduction within hours. Similarly, it's hard for retailers to develop a long-term advantage by offering broader or deeper merchandise assortments. If broader and deeper assortments attract a lot of customers, competitors will simply go out and buy the same merchandise for their stores.

Establishing a competitive advantage means that a retailer builds a wall around its position in a retail market. This wall makes it hard for competitors outside the wall to contact customers in the retailer's market. If the retailer has built a wall around an attractive market, competitors will attempt to break down the wall. Over time, all advantages will be eroded due to these competitive forces; but by building high, thick walls, retailers can sustain their advantage, minimize competitive pressure, and boost profits for a longer time. Thus, establishing a sustainable competitive advantage is the key to long-term financial performance.

EXHIBIT **6–2**

Methods for Developing Competitive Advantage

SOURCES OF ADVANTAGE	SUSTAINABILITY OF ADVANTAGE	
	LESS SUSTAINABLE	MORE SUSTAINABLE
Location (Chapters 8, 9)		Convenient locations
Customer relationships (Chapters 4, 5)		More loyal customers Extensive customer database
Vendor relationships (Chapter 14)		Close vendor relationships
Operations (Chapter 11)	Bigger and faster computers	Better information systems More efficient distribution
Human resource management (Chapter 10)	More employees	Committed, knowledgeable employees
Merchandise management (Chapters 12 to 16)	More merchandise Greater assortment Lower price Higher advertising budgets More sales promotions	Exclusive merchandise Lower merchandise cost due to more buying power
Store management (Chapters 17 to 19)	Better visual merchandising Cleaner stores	Superior customer service Committed, motivated, knowledgeable sales associates

Five important opportunities for retailers to develop sustainable competitive advantages are (1) customer loyalty, (2) location, (3) vendor relations, (4) effective, committed employees, and (5) low-cost operations. Let's look at each of these approaches.

Customer Loyalty

Customer loyalty means that customers are committed to shopping at the retailer's locations. Loyalty is more than simply liking one retailer over another.[11] Loyalty means that customers are committed. For example, loyal customers will continue to shop at the Circuit City store even if Best Buy opens a store nearby and provides a slightly superior assortment or slightly lower prices. Some ways that retailers build loyalty are (1) positioning, (2) customer service, (3) database retailing, and (4) unique merchandise.[12]

Positioning   A retailer builds customer loyalty by developing a clear, distinctive image of its retail offering and consistently reinforcing that image through its merchandise and service. **Positioning** is the design and implementation of a retail mix to create an image of the retailer in the customer's mind relative to its competitors.[14]

Positioning emphasizes that the image in the customer's mind (not the retail manager's mind) is critical. Thus, the retailer needs to research what its image is and make sure that its image is consistent with what customers in its target market want. A perceptual map is frequently used to represent the customer's image and preference for retailers.

Exhibit 6–3 is a hypothetical perceptual map of retailers selling women's clothing in the Washington, DC, area. The two dimensions in this map, fashion style and service, represent the two primary characteristics that consumers in this example use in forming their impression of retail stores. Perceptual maps are developed so that the distance between two retailers' positions on the map indicates how similar the stores appear to consumers.[15] For example, Neiman Marcus and Bloomindale's are very close to each other on the map because consumers in this illustration see them as offering similar service and fashion. On the other hand, Nordstrom and Kmart are far apart, indicating consumers think they're quite different. Note that stores close to each other compete vigorously with each other because consumers feel they provide similar benefits.

Based on this example, The Limited has an image of offering moderately fashionable women's clothing with good service. T.J. Maxx offers more fashionable clothing with less service. Sears is viewed as a retailer offering women's clothing that's not fashionable with poor service.

The ideal points (marked by green dots on the map) indicate characteristics of an ideal retailer for consumers in different market segments. For example, consumers in segment 3 prefer a retailer that offers high-fashion merchandise with low service, while consumers in segment 1 want more traditional merchandise and aren't concerned about service. The ideal points are located so that the distance between the retailer's position (marked with a blue "x") and the ideal point indicates how consumers in the segment evaluate the retailer. Retailers that are closer to an ideal point are evaluated more favorably by the consumers in the segment than retailers located further away. Thus, consumers in segment 6 prefer The Gap to Sears because The Gap is closer to their image of their ideal retailer.

In the beginning of the 1990s, Sears fell on hard times because it had failed to adapt to changing customer tastes. Mall shoppers were mostly in segments 4, 5, and 6 in Exhibit 6–3. They sought fashionable clothing from retailers in re-

EXHIBIT 6–3   Hypothetical Perceptual Map of Women's Apparel Market in Washington, DC

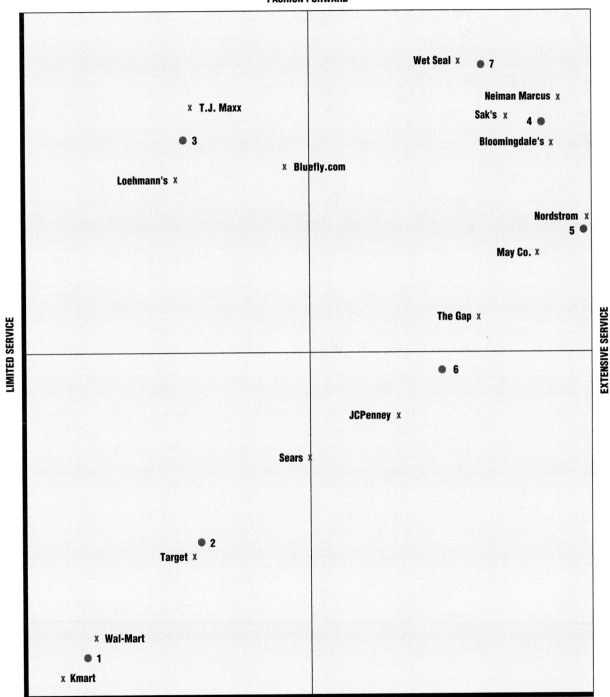

AMERICAN EAGLE OUTFITTERS, a specialty apparel retailer with over 400 mall-based stores, originally targeted young men with a rugged, outdoor lifestyle. The stores featured national brands such as Patagonia and Timberland. When sales and profits deteriorated, American Eagle undertook a repositioning strategy to move from a traditional to a more fashionable image. It sought to appeal to a 16-to-34–year-old customer base, both males and females who desire fashionable, yet affordable, all-American, casual lifestyle apparel.

To attract this customer, American Eagle altered its merchandising and marketing. On the merchandising front, the company developed fashionable interpretations of fundamental wardrobe items such as graphic T-shirts, dungarees, flannel shirts, and khakis. It reinforced this more fashionable image by reaching an agreement with the producers of *Daw-son Creek,* the popular Warner Brothers TV program. The actors in the program wear American Eagle apparel, appear in company ads, and do special in-store promotions. Presently, women's merchandise accounts for about 25 percent of stores' sales, but they are striving for a 50–50 balance in the future.

New stores have flat screen monitors flashing seasonal fashion themes and athletes participating in extreme sports. Tall glass windows are used with unusual blends of materials such as dark woods combined with stainless steel and aluminum.

Source: Vicki Young, "American Eagle Builds New Nests," *WWD,* August 18, 1999, pp. 12–13; and Jean Palmieri, "American Eagle Makes a Name for Itself," *WWD,* December 9, 1998, p. 4.

gional malls and went to category specialists for car batteries, hardware, and refrigerators. But Sears was continuing to sell basic apparel alongside its Craftsman tools and Kenmore appliances in its mall stores. Sears' new CEO Arthur Martinez decided to rekindle growth in its mall locations by emphasizing fashion apparel at value prices. The "Softer Side of Sears" advertising campaign communicated this new positioning to Sears' customers. These changes in Sears' retail mix were designed to move Sears' image closer to the ideal point of segment 6.[17] Retailing View 6.1 describes American Eagle Outfitters' approach for repositioning its store's image.

Service Retailers also build loyalty by offering excellent customer service.[18] But offering good service consistently is difficult. Customer service is provided by retail employees—and humans are less consistent than machines. Retailers that offer good customer service instill its importance in their employees over a long period of time.[19]

It takes considerable time and effort to build a tradition and reputation for customer service, but good service is a valuable strategic asset. Once a retailer has earned a service reputation, it can sustain this advantage for a long time because it's hard for a competitor to develop a comparable reputation. Chapter 19 discusses how retailers develop a service advantage.

Database Retailing **Database retailing** is the development and implementation of retailing programs to build loyalty utilizing a computerized file (**data warehouse**) of customer profiles and purchase patterns.[20] Retailing View 6.2 describes how a Canadian menswear chain uses customer information to build store loyalty by service and targeting its promotional activities to improve customer satisfaction. Database retailing is discussed in more detail in Chapters 11 and 16.

Unique Merchandise Typically it is difficult for retailers to develop store loyalty through merchandise because competitors can purchase and sell the same

HARRY ROSEN, A 19-STORE CANADIAN MENSWEAR retailer with annual sales of $135 million, Canadian, uses information to improve customer service and build long-term relationships. Each Harry Rosen salesperson can access the firm's data warehouse with customer information from any POS terminal in any store. The database tells what the customer has bought in the past and also provides personal information. All sales associates are urged to contribute to the database. If a wife buys a birthday gift for her husband, salespeople are encouraged to find out his birthday and how old he is and include this information in the system rather than in their personal notebook.

The information system improves customer service and targeting of retail promotions. For example, when garments are left in the store for alterations, the system tracks their progress and electronically notifies the salesperson of any delay so the salesperson can relay this information to the customer. Heavy spenders are easily identified and invited to special promotional events. The system is also used to sell slow-moving merchandise. For example, a store may have too many size-44–short suits. A salesperson can go to a terminal, generate a list of all customers who have bought 44–short suits in the past month, and offer them a discount if they make a purchase now. When new merchandise arrives, the salesperson can identify customers who have bought that type of merchandise in the past and inform them of the new merchandise.

Source: "State of the Industry: Customer Management," *Chain Store Age*, August 1998, pp. 20–24; and "RITA '96," *Chain Store Age*, September 1996, pp. 50–52.

popular national brands. But many retailers realize a sustainable competitive advantage by developing store brands—brands that are only available at their stores.[21] For example, if you want to buy a Kenmore washer and dryer, you have to buy it from Sears. Issues concerning the development of store-branded merchandise are discussed in Chapter 14. As discussed in Chapter 3, the low search associated with electronic shopping increase the importance of unique merchandise as a competitive advantage.

Location The classic response to the question "What are the three most important things in retailing?" is "location, location, and location." Location is the critical factor in consumer selection of a store. It is also a competitive advantage that is not easily duplicated. For example, when a Holiday Inn motel occupies the best location on a highway, competing motels are at a disadvantage. Days Inn and LaQuinta can overcome this disadvantage only if Holiday Inn abandons its location. Chapters 8 and 9 discuss this approach to developing a sustainable competitive advantage. However, the use of the Internet for shopping makes it more difficult to build a locational advantage.

Vendor Relations By developing strong relations with vendors, retailers may gain exclusive rights (1) to sell merchandise in a region, (2) to buy merchandise at lower prices or with better terms than competitors who lack such relations, or (3) to receive popular merchandise in short supply. Relationships with vendors, like relationships with customers, are developed over a long time and may not be easily offset by a competitor.[22]

For example, JCPenney's extranet, SupplierNet, lets 3,000 registered merchandise vendors receive orders, check on payment status, and see results for their products, but not for their competitors' goods. By developing computer links with its vendors, JCPenney increases its opportunity to have the right merchandise at the right store when the customer wants it.[23] Chapter 11 discusses the technological side of building vendor relationships through electronic data interchange (EDI), while Chapter 14 examines how retailers work with their vendors.

Effective, Committed Employees

Retailing is a labor-intensive business. Employees play a major role in providing services for customers and building customer loyalty. Knowledgeable and skilled employees who are committed to a retailer's objectives are a critical asset supporting the success of retailers such as Southwest Airlines, Whole Foods, Home Depot, and Men's Wearhouse.[24] Chapter 10 examines how these retailers gain a sustainable competitive advantage through effective human resource management.

Low-Cost Operations

All retailers are concerned about the costs of providing their retail offering. Costs are important even to retailers such as Tiffany's selling high-priced jewelry to customers who aren't very price-sensitive. If Tiffany's can offer the same merchandise quality and service as its competitor at a lower cost, then Tiffany's will either make a higher profit margin than its competitors or invest the profits from the higher margins to attract more customers and increase sales. It may decide to use the additional margin to attract customers from its competitors by offering even better service, merchandise assortments, and visual presentations rather than lowering its prices.

Family Dollar is a discount retailer that has gained a competitive advantage through efficient, low-cost operations. The firm has over 3,000 stores generating $2.3 billion in annual sales by targeting families with incomes between $15,000 and $25,000. Family Dollar keeps prices low for families with limited disposable income by operating a no-frills discount retail format. The format is a cross between a discount store and a convenience store. Stores are small (6,000 to 8,000 square feet); have limited service, few employees, and cash-and-carry sales; and are located in low-cost, neighborhood centers.[25]

Efficient supply chain management plays an important role in developing a sustainable low-cost advantage. For example, Wal-Mart's expansion strategy across the United States was based on reducing distribution costs by locating multiple stores around each warehouse. Chapter 11 discusses operating (distribution and information) systems and shows how some retailers have developed sustainable competitive advantages through them.

Multiple Sources of Advantage

To build a sustainable advantage, retailers typically don't rely on a single approach such as low cost or excellent service.[26] They need multiple approaches to build as high a wall around their position as possible. For example, McDonald's' success is based on developing loyal customers, maintaining good vendor relations, having excellent information and distribution systems, and controlling costs.

The McDonald's target market segment doesn't expect a lot of customer service. Customers know they will not get a meal prepared to their specific tastes. But customers do expect that the food will be hot, available with a minimal wait, and reasonably priced. McDonald's has developed a loyal group of customers by meeting these expectations every time a customer visits a store.

To consistently meet customer expectations, McDonald's has developed capabilities in a number of areas. Its relationships with vendors ensure that it will always have quality ingredients. Its distribution and inventory control systems enable it to make sure that the ingredients are available at each location. By de-

The Container Store—Building a Competitive Advantage in Selling Products to Make Life Simpler

GARRETT BOONE AND KIP TINDELL DEVELOPED the concept for The Container Store after seeing a Swedish-designed modular shelving system called Lundia in a home improvement show in Dallas. After looking at the Lundia display, they thought, "Wouldn't it be neat to have a store with home organization products? We fell in love with the products and sensed that people need and want them."

An initial challenge was finding products to sell. Most of the manufacturers focused on commercial customers—offices, factories, and hospitals. So, at first, Boone and Tindell had to settle for selling commercial products that would work in the home. Eventually they convinced manufacturers to supply them with merchandise designed for homes.

The Container Store sells products to organize people's lives. Multipurpose shelving and garment bags are available to organize closets. Portable file cabinets and magazine holders create order in the home office. Backpacks, modular shelving, and CD holders can make dorm rooms less cluttered. Recipe holders, bottles, jars, and recycling bins bring harmony to kitchens.

When asked how The Container Store has maintained its leadership in a retail segment it pioneered 20 years ago, Boone replied, "We have a collection of products that takes extreme effort to select and buy merchandise properly. It's a combination of products that are hard to sell, such as closet systems and modular shelving. It can only be sold by people who know how this stuff works and can work with customers to get it right."

To get it right, The Container Store places a lot of emphasis on customer service. Considerable time is spent educating

The Container Store spends considerable time educating this sales associate about its unique merchandise that simplifies its customers' lives.

sales associates about the store's merchandise. Then sales associates are empowered to use their own intuition and creativity to solve customer problems. The company's supportive corporate culture results in an annual turnover rate for sales associates of less than 15 percent, considerably less than the industry average of 50 to 100 percent.

Sources: Jennifer Karas, "Independent Retailer of the Year," *Stores,* January 1999, pp. 106–7; and Barbara Thau, "Organized Living Stresses Solutions," *HFN,* September 21, 1998, p. 34.

veloping a system for producing its food and using extensive training for store managers, McDonald's reduces customers' waiting time. This training also means that customers will be handled quickly and courteously. By developing unique capabilities in a number of areas, McDonald's has built a high wall around its position as a service retailer, using a fast-food format directed toward families with young children.

Each of the retail strategies outlined at the beginning of the chapter involves multiple sources of advantage. For example, Starbucks has developed a strong competitive position through its unique locations, strong brand name, and high-quality service provided by committed employees. Retailing View 6.3 describes The Container Store, a retail chain that built a sustainable competitive advantage through unique merchandise, excellent customer service, and effective, committed employees.

GROWTH STRATEGIES

Four types of growth opportunities that retailers may pursue (market penetration, market expansion, retail format development, and diversification) are shown in Exhibit 6–4.[27] The vertical axis indicates the synergies between the retailer's present markets and growth opportunity's markets—whether the opportunity targets markets the retailer is presently pursuing or new markets. The horizontal axis indicates the synergies between the retailer's present retail mix and the growth opportunity's retail mix—whether the opportunity exploits the retailer's present format or requires a new format.

Market Penetration

A **market penetration opportunity** involves directing investments toward existing customers using the present retailing format. Examples are attracting consumers in the retailer's target market who don't shop at its outlets and attempting to increase sales by inducing current customers to visit the store more often or buy more merchandise on each visit.

Approaches for increasing market penetration include attracting new customers by opening more stores in the target market and keeping existing stores open for longer hours. Other approaches are displaying merchandise to increase impulse purchases and training salespeople to cross-sell. **Cross-selling** means that sales associates in one department attempt to sell complementary merchandise from other departments to their customers. For example, a sales associate who has just sold a dress to a customer will take the customer to the accessories department to sell her a handbag or scarf that will go with the dress. More cross-selling increases sales from existing customers.

> **Refact** A 4 percent increase in weekly store visits by customers can result in a 58 percent increase in profits for a typical grocery store.[28]

Market Expansion

A **market expansion opportunity** employs the existing retail format in new market segments. For example, The Gap's strategy is using a specialty store retail format to sell updated, private-brand sportswear to upscale men and women between ages 20 and 45. Banana Republic was a market

EXHIBIT 6–4

Growth
Opportunities

Old Navy (left) is an example of a retail format development growth strategy, while Babies "R" Us (right) is an example of a market development growth strategy.

expansion opportunity in which the same specialty store format for private-label apparel is directed toward a different segment–more fashion-oriented, young adults. Another example is the opening of Toys "R" Us stores in Japan and Germany. This opportunity involved entering a new geographic market segment with the same retail format.

Retail Format Development

A **retail format development opportunity** involves offering customers a new retail format—a format involving a different retail mix—to the same target market. For example, Barnes & Noble, a specialty book store retailer, exploited a format development opportunity when it sold books to its present target market over the Internet (www. barnesandnoble.com). Another example of a retail format development opportunity is a retailer's adding merchandise categories such as Amazon.com selling CDs, videos, pet supplies, and gifts in addition to books. Adjusting the type of merchandise or services offered typically involves a small investment, while providing an entirely different format (such as a store-based retailer going into electronic retailing) requires a much larger and riskier investment.

Diversification

A **diversification opportunity** involves a new retail format directed toward a market segment that's not presently served. Diversification opportunities are either related or unrelated.

Related versus Unrelated Diversification   In a **related diversification opportunity,** the present target market and/or retail format shares something in common with the new opportunity. This commonality might be purchasing from the same vendors, using the same distribution and/or management information system, or advertising in the same newspapers to similar target markets. In contrast, an **unrelated diversification** lacks any commonality between the present business and the new business.

Old Navy was viewed by The Gap as a related diversification because it targeted a different market—a lower-income, older market—and used a different

This kiosk in a Circuit City store is an example of a "clicks and mortar" retailer using its store and Internet offering synergistically.

Refact Brooks Brothers, a men's specialty store chain, sold the rights to the Polo brand name to Ralph Lauren.[31]

retail format—larger stores in strip mall locations versus mall locations. However, the Old Navy concept did build on The Gap's skill in developing and merchandising private-label, casual apparel. While Old Navy was positioned toward a different market segment, when the stores were opened, The Gap discovered that many customers were shopping at both Old Navy and Gap stores.[29] On the other hand, synergy between Dayton Hudson's mall-based department stores and its discount stores (Target) is limited. Due to the unrelated nature of this diversification, investors have devalued the company's stock.

Vertical Integration   **Vertical integration** is an example of diversification involving investments by retailers wholesaling and/or manufacturing merchandise.[30] Examples of vertical integration are The Limited's acquisition of Mast Industries (a trading company that contracts for private-label manufacturing) and Zales' manufacturing of jewelry. Backward integration into manufacturing represents diversification because manufacturing merchandise requires different operating skills than retailing merchandise. In addition, retailers and manufacturers have different customers—the immediate customers for a manufacturer's merchandise are retailers, while the retailer's customers are consumers. Thus, a manufacturer's marketing activities are very different from a retailer's. Note that some manufacturers and designers like Nike and Ralph Lauren forward-integrate into retailing. However, when manufacturers open retail stores, they are often more interested in building brand image than selling merchandise.

Strategic Opportunities and Competitive Advantage   Typically, retailers have the greatest competitive advantage in opportunities that are very similar to their present retail strategy. Thus, retailers would be most successful engaging in market penetration opportunities that don't involve entering new, unfamiliar markets or operating new, unfamiliar retail formats.

When retailers pursue market expansion opportunities, they build on their strengths in operating a retail format and apply this competitive advantage in a new market. A retail format extension opportunity builds on the retailer's reputation and success with present customers. Even if a retailer doesn't have experience and skills in operating the new format, it hopes to attract its loyal customers to it.

For example, many store-based retailers are now offering merchandise and services from their websites—a retail format extension growth strategy. These retailers are referred to as **multi-channel** or **"clicks and mortar" retailers.** Store-based retailers may have less skills than pure electronic retailers in developing website and the associated communication and information systems. However, as discussed in Chapter 3, store-based have some important resources including a high level of awareness and customer loyalty and considerable information about their present customer base. In addition, clicks and mortar retailers have an opportunity to exploit synergies between their electronic and store-based retail operations. Signs in stores, advertising for store events, and shopping bags distributed in stores promote their websites. Kiosks with Internet access in the stores enable customers to order merchandise not stocked in stores such as unusual sizes for apparel. The stores are also convenient places to pick and return merchandise ordered from the website. The website is used to provide information about the location of stores, the availability of merchandise in stores, and special events occurring in stores.

Retailers have less competitive advantage when dealing with opportunities that involve new markets or new retail formats. But retailers must often consider market expansion or retail format extension opportunities. For example, Kmart felt it had saturated its U.S. target market using a general merchandise discount format and decided to pursue (1) a market expansion strategy by opening discount stores in Eastern Europe and Mexico and (2) a retail format expansion strategy by opening category specialist stores (Sports Authority, Pace Warehouse, and Builders Square) in the United States. Both of these growth strategies diverted Kmart's attention from its core discount business. To refocus its strategy on the U.S. discount store market, Kmart divested the category specialist businesses and the international expansion plans.

Retailers have the least competitive advantage when they pursue diversification opportunities. Thus, these opportunities are very risky. In part, Sears' financial problems resulted from its diversification into insurance, real estate, and consumer financial services.

INTERNATIONAL GROWTH OPPORTUNITIES

International expansion is one form of a market expansion strategy. Some of the most aggressive U.S. retailers pursuing this growth opportunity are Wal-Mart, The Gap, Blockbuster, Toys "R" Us, and Home Depot. However, large European retailers such as Carrefour, Ahold, and Metro/Makro embraced international expansion before these U.S. retailers because they saturated their domestic markets earlier. The most commonly targeted regions are Mexico, Latin America, Europe, China, and Japan. International expansion is risky because retailers using this growth strategy must deal with differences in government regulations, cultural traditions, and language.[32]

Global Retailing Opportunities

Retailers—particularly specialty store retailers with strong brand names such as The Gap and Zara and category killers such as Toys "R" Us—may have a strong competitive advantage when competing globally. More affluent consumers in most developed countries share the same important characteristics. Specifically, they enjoy a relatively high level of disposable income due, in part, to having fewer children per household than in the past, being dual-income families, and enjoying generous benefits from employers and governments.

Refact Only 4 percent of Wal-Mart's annual sales are nondomestic while the nondomestic sales of Metro/Makro are 68 percent, Ahold 51 percent, and Carrefour 38 percent.[33]

U.S. retailers may have a competitive advantage in international markets. The American culture is emulated in many countries, particularly among young people. Due to the rising prosperity and rapidly increasing access to cable TV with American programming, fashion trends in the United States are spreading to young people in emerging countries. The global MTV generation prefers Coke to tea, athletic shoes to sandals, Chicken McNuggets to rice, and credit cards to cash. Surveys of youth around the world found that 87 percent watch music videos, basketball has replaced soccer as most popular sport, and 98 percent of the teenagers in Thailand watch MTV. Extended families across the world are spending money on these young people. For example, the average child between 7 and 12 in a Chinese family in large city has $182 to spend annually, compared to $377 in France and $493 in the United States.[34]

Successful European retailers like Makro (left) and IKEA (right) are opening stores around the world.

On the other hand, some large European and Japanese retailers have considerably more experience operating retail stores in nondomestic markets. For example, Carrefour of France has been operating stores in nondomestic markets for over 25 years. It is very good at adapting its hypermarket format to local tastes. The company buys many products locally and hires and trains local managers, passing the power and authority to them quickly. Even though Wal-Mart has a more efficient distribution system, Carrefour has competed effectively against Wal-Mart in Brazil and Argentina.[35]

Category killers and hypermarket retailers may be particularly suited to succeed internationally because of the expertise they've already developed at home. First, these retailers are leaders in the use of technology to manage inventories, control global logistical systems, and tailor merchandise assortments to local needs. For instance, firms such as Home Depot provide consumers with an assortment of brand-name merchandise procured from sources around the world. This advantage is particularly valuable if brand-name merchandise is important to consumers. Second, retailers like Wal-Mart and Carrefour have become the low-price provider in every market they enter because of their buying economies of scale and efficient distribution systems. Third, despite idiosyncrasies in the international environment, category killers and hypermarket retailers have developed unique systems and standardized formats that facilitate control over multiple stores. These systems and procedures should work well regardless of the country of operation. Fourth, because of the category killer's narrow assortment and focused strategy, communications across national boundaries and cultures are specifically focused, which improves management coordination. Finally, at one time, people felt that consumers outside the United States were used to high levels of personalized service and would not accept the self-service concept employed by category killers and hypermarket retailers. However, a substantial number of international consumers are willing to forgo the service for lower prices.[36]

Refact Of the 35 retailers identified as being the most global, 9 are headquartered in the United States, 23 in Europe, and 3 in Asia.[37]

Keys to Success   Five characteristics of retailers that have successfully exploited international growth opportunities are (1) domestic market leadership, (2) strategic consistency, (3) adaptability, (4) global systems, and (5) long-term commitment.[38] A hypothetical evaluation of international growth opportunities is described in the appendix to this chapter.

Domestic Market Leadership   Retailers pursing international opportunities need the cash flow generated from a secure and profitable position in their domestic markets to make the necessary investments in global markets. Successful entry into international markets requires a long-term investment in developing systems to support global retailing and learning how to adapt the firm's retail mix to the needs of nondomestic markets.

Strategic Consistency   Entry into nondomestic markets is most successful when the expansion opportunity is consistent with the retailer's overall strategy and core competencies—bases of competitive advantage. Some core competencies for global retailers are shown below:

CORE COMPETENCY	GLOBAL RETAILER
Low cost, efficient distribution	Wal-Mart, Carrefour
Strong private brands	Marks & Spencer, The Gap, IKEA
Fashion reputation	The Gap/Banana Republic, Zara, Hennes & Mauritz
Category dominance	Toys "R" Us, Office Depot, Home Depot, Blockbuster
Image	Disney, Warner Brothers

Thus, Wal-Mart and Carrefour are successful in international markets where price plays an important role in consumer decision making and distribution infrastructure is available to enable these firms to exploit their logistical capabilities. On the other hand, The Gap and Zara are successful in international markets valuing fashionable merchandise.

Adaptability   While successful international retailers build on their core strengths, they also recognize cultural differences and adapt their core strategy to the needs of local markets.[39] Color preferences, the preferred cut of apparel, and sizes differ across cultures. For example, in China, white is the color of mourning and brides wear red dresses. Food probably has the greatest diversity of tastes. When Domino's Pizza opened its first outlet in Japan, it needed to educate Japanese consumers about the toppings on American pizzas. In this educational process, Domino's learned that it needed to develop new toppings like apple, rice, burdock root, and squid to please the Japanese palate.[40]

Refact The most popular topping for Domino's pizzas in Iceland is reindeer sausage.[41]

Selling seasons vary across countries. The Gap's major U.S. selling season is back-to-school in August; however, this is one of the slowest sales periods in Europe because most people are on vacation. Back-to-school in Japan is in April.

Store designs and plan-o-grams need to be adjusted. In American supercenters, fruit and vegetables are typically located in the back of the store. But this merchandise is considered staples in Latin America and commonly placed in the front of the store. In some cultures, social norms dictate that men's and women's clothing cannot be displayed next to each other. In the United States, the standard practice is to place low-priced, private-label merchandise on the shelf to the right of national brands, assuming that customers' natural eye movement is from left to right. This merchandising approach does not work in cultures where people read from right to left or up and down. IKEA initially tried to sell its Scandinavian beds in the United States before discovering they were the wrong size for American bed linens.

Government regulations and cultural values also affect store operations. Some differences such as holidays, hours of operation, and regulations governing part-time employees and terminations are easy to identify. Other factors require a deeper understanding. For example, the Latin American culture is very family oriented. Thus U.S. work schedules need to be adjusted so that employees can have more time with their families. Boots, a U.K. drugstore chain, has the check-out clerks in its Japanese stores standing up because it discovered that Japanese shoppers found it offensive to pay money to a seated clerk. Retailers in Germany must recycle packaging materials sold in their stores.[42]

Global Systems   Significant investments are often needed to develop systems that account for different operating procedures across markets. For example, in many international markets, micromarketing (adapting the merchandise assortments for each store in a market) is difficult to implement due to the lack of a well-developed, logistical infrastructure.

Long-Term Commitment   Expansion into international markets requires a long-term commitment and considerable upfront planning. Retailers find it very difficult to generate short-term profit when they make the transition to global retailing. Carrefour's operating margins are 6 percent of sales in France, but it loses money in Asia and Latin America. Wal-Mart's return on investment from its international business is 5.8 percent, far less than the return it realizes in the U.S. Even for the largest and most successful retailers, it takes time to develop relationships with a new set of customers, employees, and vendors.[43]

Entry Strategies   Four approaches that retailers take when entering nondomestic markets are direct investment, joint venture, strategic alliance, and franchising.[44]

Direct Investment   **Direct investment** involves a retail firm investing in and owning a division or subsidiary that builds and operates stores in a foreign country. This entry strategy requires the highest level of investment and exposes the retailer to significant risks, but has the highest potential returns. One advantage of direct investment is that the retailer has complete control of the operations. For example, McDonald's chose this entry strategy for the U.K. market, building a plant to produce buns when local suppliers could not meet its specifications.

Joint Venture   A **joint venture** is formed when the entering retailer pools its resources with a local retailer to form a new company in which ownership, control, and profits are shared. Examples of successful joint ventures are Wal-Mart and CIFRA in Mexico, Price/Costco and Shinsegae in Korea, and Crabtree & Evelyn and Daiei in Japan.[45]

Establishing a joint venture reduces the entrant's risks. In addition, the local partner provides understanding of the market and access to resources—vendors and real estate. Many foreign countries require joint ownership. Problems with this entry approach can arise if the partners disagree or the government places restrictions on the repatriation of profits.

Strategic Alliance   **Strategic alliances** are collaborative relationships between independent firms. For example, a foreign retailer might enter an international market through direct investment but develop an alliance with a local firm to perform logistical and warehousing activities.

Refact Due to concerns about investing in physical assets, more than half of all U.S. retailers plan to expand internationally using nonstore formats: the Internet or catalogs.[46]

Franchising Franchising offers the lowest risk and requires the least investment. However, the entrant has limited control over the retail operations in the foreign country, potential profit is reduced, and the risk of assisting in the creation of a local domestic competitor is increased.

Marks & Spencer, a U.K.-headquartered department store chain, has three of these approaches. It has 260 wholly owned stores in the U.K. plus wholly owned stores in Belgium, France, Germany, the Netherlands, Ireland, Hong Kong, and Canada. It formed a joint venture when it entered Spain and has 85 franchised stores in 20 countries including the Czech Republic, Hungary, Israel, Turkey, Portugal, and Greece.

The rest of this chapter outlines steps in developing a retail strategy.

THE STRATEGIC RETAIL PLANNING PROCESS

The **strategic retail planning process** is the set of steps a retailer goes through to develop a strategic retail plan.[47] (See Exhibit 6–5.) It describes how retailers select target market segments, determine the appropriate retail format, and build sustainable competitive advantages. The planning process can be used to formulate strategic plans at different levels within a retail corporation. For example, American Express's corporate strategic plan indicates how resources are to be allocated across the corporation's various businesses such as credit cards and travel services. Each business within American Express has its own strategic plan, and then strategies are developed for products in a business such the American Express Gold card.

EXHIBIT **6–5**

Steps in the Strategic Retail Planning Process

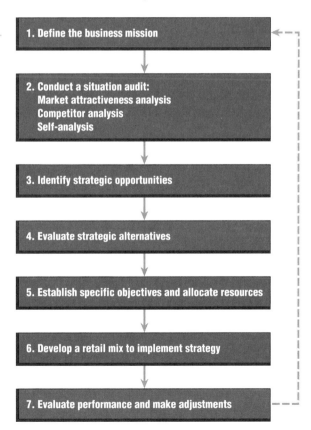

1. Define the business mission

2. Conduct a situation audit:
   Market attractiveness analysis
   Competitor analysis
   Self-analysis

3. Identify strategic opportunities

4. Evaluate strategic alternatives

5. Establish specific objectives and allocate resources

6. Develop a retail mix to implement strategy

7. Evaluate performance and make adjustments

As we discuss the steps in the retail planning process, we will apply each of these steps to the planning process Kelly Bradford is undertaking. Kelly owns Gifts To Go, a small, two-store chain in the Chicago area. One of her 1,000–square-foot stores is in the downtown area; the other is in an upscale suburban mall. The target market for Gifts To Go is upper-income men and women looking for gifts in the $50-to-$500 price range. The stores have an eclectic selection of merchandise, including handmade jewelry and crafts, fine china and glassware, perfume, watches, writing instruments, and a variety of one-of-a-kind items. The stores have developed a number of loyal customers who are contacted by sales associates when family anniversaries and birthdays come up. In many cases, customers have a close relationship with a sales associate and have enough confidence in the associate's judgment that they tell the associate to pick out the gift. The turnover of Gifts To Go sales associates is low for the industry, because Ms. Bradford treats associates as part of the family. The company pays for medical and dental insurance for all associates. Sales associates share in the profits of the firm.

Step 1: Define the Business Mission

The first step in the strategic retail planning process is to define the business mission. The **mission statement** is a broad description of a retailer's objectives and the scope of activities it plans to undertake.[48] The objective of a publicly held firm is to maximize its stockholders' wealth by increasing the value of its stock and paying dividends.[49] Owners of small, privately held firms frequently have other objectives such as providing a specific level of income and avoiding risks rather than maximizing income.

The mission statement should define the general nature of the target segments and retail formats that the firm will consider. For example, the mission statement of an office supply category specialist, "Serve the customer, build value for shareholders, and create opportunities for associates," is too broad. It does not provide a sense of strategic direction.

In developing the mission statement, managers must answer five questions: (1) What business are we in? (2) What should be our business in the future? (3) Who are our customers? (4) What are our capabilities? (5) What do we want to accomplish? Gifts To Go's mission statement is "The mission of Gifts To Go is to be the leading retailer of higher-priced gifts in Chicago and provide a stable income of $100,000 per year for the owner."

Since the mission statement defines the retailer's objectives and the scope of activities it plans to undertake, Gifts To Go's mission statement indicates its management won't consider retail opportunities outside the Chicago area, won't consider opportunities for selling low-priced gifts, and won't consider opportunities that would jeopardize its ability to generate $100,000 in annual income.[50]

Step 2: Conduct a Situation Audit

After developing a mission statement and setting objectives, the next step in the strategic planning process is to do a situation audit. A **situation audit** is an analysis of the opportunities and threats in the retail environment and the strengths and weaknesses of the retail business relative to its competitors. The elements in the situation analysis are shown in Exhibit 6–6.[51]

Market Factors   Some critical factors related to consumers and their buying patterns are market size and growth, sales cyclicality, and seasonality. Market

EXHIBIT **6-6**

Elements in a Market Analysis

MARKET FACTORS

Size
Growth
Seasonality
Business cycles

COMPETITIVE FACTORS

Barriers to entry
Bargaining power of vendors
Competitive rivalry
Threat of superior new formats

ENVIRONMENTAL FACTORS

Technology
Economic
Regulatory
Social

ANALYSIS OF STRENGTHS AND WEAKNESSES

Management capabilities
Financial resources
Locations
Operations
Merchandise
Store management
Customer loyalty

size, typically measured in retail sales dollars, is important because it indicates a retailer's opportunity for generating revenues to cover its investment. Large markets are attractive to large retail firms. But they are also attractive to small entrepreneurs because they offer more opportunities to focus a market segment.

Growing markets are more attractive than mature or declining markets. For example, retail markets for specialty stores are growing faster than those for department stores. Typically, margins and prices are higher in growing markets because competition is less intense than in mature markets. Since new customers are just beginning to patronize stores in growing markets, they may not have developed strong store loyalties and thus might be easier to attract to a new store.

Firms are often interested in minimizing the business cycle's impact on their sales. Thus, retail markets for merchandise affected by economic conditions (such as cars and major appliances) are less attractive than retail markets unaffected by economic conditions (such as food). In general, markets with highly seasonal sales are unattractive because a lot of resources are needed to accommodate the peak season, but then resources are underutilized the rest of the year. For example, to minimize these problems due to seasonality, ski resorts promote the summer vacations to generate sales during all four seasons.

To do an analysis of the market factors for Gifts To Go, Kelly Bradford went to the library to get information about the size, growth, cyclicity, and seasonality of the gift market in general and, more specifically, in Chicago. Based on her analysis, she concluded that the market factors were attractive. The market for more expensive gifts was large, growing, and not vulnerable to business cycles. The only negative aspect was the seasonality with peaks at Valentine's Day, Easter, June (due to weddings), and Christmas.

Competitive Factors The nature of the competition in retail markets is affected by barriers to entry, bargaining power of vendors, competitive rivalry, and threat of superior new formats.[52] Retail markets are more attractive when competitive entry is costly. **Barriers to entry** are conditions in a retail market that make it difficult for firms to enter the market. These conditions include scale economies, customer loyalty, and availability of locations.

Scale economies are cost advantages due to a retailer's size. Markets dominated by large competitors with scale economies are typically unattractive. For example, a small entrepreneur would avoid becoming an office supply category specialist because the market is dominated by three large firms: Staples, Office

SMALL RETAILERS CAN EFFECTIVELY COMPETE head-to-head against industry giants like Wal-Mart and Home Depot. These large retailers with buying power can sell merchandise at lower prices than small retailers. However, small retailers can compete effectively by (1) offering unique merchandise tailored to the local community, (2) giving customers a personal touch, and (3) developing ties with the local community. For example, Toys "R" Us and Wal-Mart are primarily interested in selling well-known toys and games at low prices and letting their manufacturers advertise how the toys work. But many toys are too complicated to explain in a 30-second commercial. Playmobil construction toys are only sold through independent toy stores, because these stores are interested in setting up Playmobil playpens on their floors so parents and children can have "an out-of-box experience."

At Classic Creations (a Venice, Florida, jewelry shop) owners of the store rather than a commissioned salesperson wait on customers. By offering personal attention they build customer loyalty. For example, a man recently bought a $4,000 engagement ring based on a recommendation he received from his parents, who had their wedding bands redesigned there several years ago.

Independent fishing tackle shops compete against discount giants like Wal-Mart and Sports Authority by offering special services. In Sarasota, Florida, Mr. CB's Bait & Tackle teams up with local charter boat captains to offer seminars and discounted trips. The captains get the fishing trips and Mr. CB's sells the fishing gear. K & K True Value Hardware in Bettendorf, Iowa, focuses on fishing experts who want to make their own lures. The store stocks the raw materials: spinner blades in 14 sizes, tinsel in 40 colors, chicken feathers, deer fur, weights, and hooks.

Independent retailer Abt Electronics and Appliances effectively competes against national chains like Circuit City and Best Buy by offering unique high-end merchandise and impeccable customer service.

Bookseller's in Fridley, Minnesota, competes against Barnes & Noble by specializing in books on Christianity. Customers include pastors, Sunday school teachers, and people who need spiritual guidance. For example, the owner suggested some books for a mother concerned about her son's drug problems. The son is now an honors student in college. A pet store builds its reputation among children by inviting classes from the local school to visit the store and learn about pets.

Source: Elaine Schmidt, "Finding Their Niche," *Milwaukee Journal Sentinel,* May 2, 1999, pp. 1, 4; Alina Matus, "Taking on the Retail Giants," *Miami Herald,* May 22, 1995, pp. 12–13; Kenneth Stone, *Competing against the Giants* (New York: Wiley, 1995); and Michael Sele, "Small Retailers Fare Well Despite Chains' Onslaught," *The Wall Street Journal,* September 12, 1994, p. B2.

Depot, and OfficeMax. These firms have a considerable cost advantage over the entrepreneur because they can buy merchandise cheaper and operate more efficiently by investing in the latest technology and spreading their overhead across more stores. Retailing View 6.4 discusses how some small retailers develop sustainable advantages over national chains with larger-scale economies.

Similarly, retail markets dominated by a well-established retailer that has developed a loyal group of customers offer limited profit potential. For example, Home Depot's high customer loyalty in Atlanta makes it hard for a competing home-improvement center to enter the Atlanta market.

Finally, the availability of locations may impede competitive entry. Retailing is a different business in Asia than in the United States. For example, in Asia, most retailing occurs in densely populated urban areas. Real estate for locating stores is costly and scarce. Thus, retailers entering Asian markets typically are at a disadvantage unless they have a partnering relationship with a local tenant management firm.

Entry barriers are a two-edged sword. A retail market with high entry barriers is very attractive for retailers presently competing in that market, because those barriers limit competition. However, markets with high entry barriers are unattractive for retailers not already in the market. For example, the lack of good retail locations in Hong Kong makes this market attractive for retailers already in the region, but less attractive for retailers desiring to enter the market.

Another competitive factor is the **bargaining power of vendors.** Markets are unattractive when a few vendors control the merchandise sold in it. In these situations, vendors have an opportunity to dictate prices and other terms (like delivery dates), reducing retailer's profits. For example, the market for retailing fashionable cosmetics is less attractive because two suppliers, Estée Lauder (Estée Lauder, Clinique, Prescriptive, Aramis, Tommy Hilfiger, and Donna Karan brands) and L'Oréal (Lancombe, L'Oréal, and Ralph Lauren brands), provide the most desired premium brands. Since department stores need these brands to support a fashionable image, these suppliers have the power to sell their products to retailers at high prices.[53]

The final industry factor is the level of competitive rivalry in the retail market. **Competitive rivalry** is the frequency and intensity of reactions to actions undertaken by competitors. When rivalry is high, price wars erupt, employee raids occur, advertising and promotion expenses increase, and profit potential falls. Conditions that may lead to intense rivalry include (1) a large number of competitors that are all about the same size, (2) slow growth, (3) high fixed costs, and (4) the lack of perceived differences between competing retailers.

When Kelly Bradford started to analyze the competitive factors for Gifts To Go, she realized that identifying her competitors wasn't easy. While there were no gift stores carrying similar merchandise and price points in the Chicago area, there were a number of other retailers where a customer could buy these types of gifts. She identified her primary competitors as department stores, craft galleries, catalogs, and Internet retailers. Kelly felt there were some scale economies in developing customer databases to support gift retailing. The lack of large suppliers meant that vendors' bargaining power wasn't a problem and competitive rivalry was minimal because the gift business was not a critical part of the department store's overall business. In addition, merchandise carried by the various retailers offered considerable opportunity to differentiate the retailers.

Environmental Factors Environmental factors that affect market attractiveness span technological, economic, regulatory, and social changes.[54] When a retail market is going through significant changes in technology, present competitors are vulnerable to new entrants that are skilled at using the new technology. For example, JCPenney, a late entrant into the catalog retail market, adopted new data processing and communication technology faster than Sears, which had 50 years more experience in catalog retailing.

Some retailers may be more affected by economic conditions than others. For example, Neiman Marcus and Nordstrom employ many well-paid salespeople to provide high-quality customer service. When unemployment is low, their costs may increase significantly, as salespeople's wages rise due to the difficulty in hiring qualified people. But retailers like Wal-Mart that provide little service and have much lower labor costs as a percentage of sales may be less affected by low unemployment.

Refact Sears started in business when it launched its first catalog in 1888 and closed its catalog division in 1993.[55]

Government regulations can reduce the attractiveness of a retail market. For example, regulations make it costly for retailers in Europe to build stores (due to zoning laws) and hire employees (due to limitations on terminating employees). These regulations may serve as barriers to entry. They may make a market more attractive to retailers already in the market and less attractive to potential new entrants.

Finally, trends in demographics, lifestyles, attitudes, and personal values affect retail markets' attractiveness. Chapter 4 covered many of these changes and their implications. Retailers need to answer three questions about each environmental factor:

1. What new developments or changes might occur, such as new technologies and regulations or different social factors and economic conditions?
2. What is the likelihood that these environmental changes will occur? What key factors affect whether these changes will occur?
3. How will these changes impact each retail market, the firm, and its competitors?

Kelly Bradford's primary concern when she did an environmental analysis was the potential growth of traditional catalog and electronic retailers in the gift business. Gifts seem to be ideal for electronic retailing. Typically, customers don't get much benefit out of visiting the store, because they aren't buying the merchandise for themselves. Even when they see and touch the merchandise, they don't know how the recipient will feel about it. In addition, many Gifts To Go customers have the store ship the present rather than taking the present with them. Finally, Kelly felt that electronic retailers could effectively collect information about customers and then target promotions and suggestions to them when gift-giving occasions arose.

Strengths and Weaknesses Analysis   The most critical aspect of the situation audit is for a retailer to determine its unique capabilities in terms of its strengths and weaknesses relative to the competition.[56] These strengths and weaknesses indicate how well the business can seize opportunities and avoid harm from threats in the environment. Exhibit 6–7 outlines issues to consider in performing a self-analysis.

Here is Kelly Bradford's analysis of Gifts To Go's strengths and weaknesses:

Management capability	**Limited.** Two excellent store managers and a relatively inexperienced person who helped Kelly with buying merchandise. An accounting firm kept the financial records for the business, but had no skills in developing and utilizing customer databases.
Financial resources	**Good.** Gifts To Go had no debt and a good relationship with a bank. Kelly had saved $255,000 that she had in liquid securities.
Operations	**Poor.** While Kelly felt Gifts to Go had relatively low overhead, the company did not have a computer-based inventory control system or management and customer information systems. Her competitors (local department stores and catalog and Internet retailers) certainly had superior systems.
Merchandise capabilities	**Good.** Kelly had a flair for selecting unique gifts and she had excellent relationships with vendors providing one-of-a-kind merchandise.
Store management capabilities	**Excellent.** The store managers and sales associates were excellent. They were very attentive to customers and loyal to the firm. Employee and customer theft were kept to a minimum.
Locations	**Excellent.** Both of Gifts To Go's locations were excellent. The downtown location was convenient for office workers. The suburban mall location was at a heavily trafficked juncture.
Customers	**Good.** While Gifts To Go did not do the sales volume in gifts done in department stores, the company had a loyal base of customers.

EXHIBIT **6–7**

Strenghts and
Weaknesses Analysis

In performing self-analysis, the retailer considers the potential areas for developing a competitive advantage listed below and answers the following questions:
- At what is our company good?
- In which of these areas is our company better than our competitors?
- In which of these areas does our company's unique capabilities provide a sustainable competitive advantage or a basis for developing one?

 MANAGEMENT CAPABILITY
Capabilities and experience of top
management
Depth of management—capabilities of
middle management
Management's commitment to firm

 MERCHANDISING CAPABILITIES
Knowledge and skills of buyers
Relationships with vendors
Capabilities in developing private brands
Advertising and promotion capabilities

 FINANCIAL RESOURCES
Cash flow from existing business
Ability to raise debt or equity financing

 STORE MANAGEMENT CAPABILITIES
Management capabilities
Quality of sales associates
Commitment of sales associates to firm

 OPERATIONS
Overhead cost structure
Quality of operating systems
Distribution capabilities
Management information systems
Loss prevention systems
Inventory control system

 LOCATIONS

 **CUSTOMERS**
Loyalty of customers

Step 3: Identify Strategic Opportunities

After completing the situation audit, the next step is to identify opportunities for increasing retail sales. Kelly Bradford presently competes in gift retailing using a specialty store format. The strategic alternatives she is considering are defined in terms of the squares in the retail market matrix shown in Exhibit 6–1 and the growth strategies in Exhibit 6–4.

Market penetration	**1. Increase size of present stores and amount of merchandise in stores.**
	2. Open additional gift stores in Chicago area.
Market expansion	**1. Open gift stores outside the Chicago area (new geographic segment).**
	2. Sell lower-priced gifts in present stores or open new stores selling low-priced gifts (new benefit segment).
Retail format development	**1. Sell apparel and other nongift merchandise to same customers in same or new stores.**
	2. Sell similar gift merchandise to same market segment using the Internet.
Diversification	**1. Manufacture craft gifts.**
	2. Open apparel stores targeted at teenagers.
	3. Open a category specialist selling low-price gifts.

Note that some of these growth opportunities involve a redefinition of her mission.

Step 4: Evaluate Strategic Opportunities

The fourth step in the strategic planning process is to evaluate opportunities that have been identified in the situation audit. The evaluation determines the retailer's potential to establish a sustainable competitive advantage and reap long-term profits from the opportunities under evaluation. Thus, a retailer must focus on opportunities that utilize its strengths and its area of competitive advantage. For example, expertise in developing private-label apparel is one of The Gap's sources of competitive advantage. Thus, The Gap would positively evaluate opportunities that involve development of private-label merchandise. Some areas retailers consider when evaluating new opportunities, are shown in Exhibit 6–7.

Both the market attractiveness and the strengths and weaknesses of the retailer need to be considered in evaluating strategic opportunities. The greatest investments should be made in market opportunities where the retailer has a strong competitive position. A formal method for performing such an analysis is described in the appendix to this chapter. Here's Kelly's informal analysis:

OPPORTUNITY	MARKET ATTRACTIVENESS	COMPETITIVE POSITION
Increase size of present stores and amount of merchandise in stores.	Low	High
Open additional gift stores in Chicago area.	Medium	Medium
Open gift stores outside the Chicago area (new geographic segment).	Medium	Low
Sell lower-priced gifts in present stores or open new stores selling low-priced gifts (new benefit segment).	Medium	Low
Sell apparel and other nongift merchandise to same customers in same or new stores.	High	Low
Sell similar gift merchandise to same market segment using the Internet.	High	Medium
Manufacture craft gifts.	High	Low
Open apparel stores targeted at teenagers.	High	Low
Open a category specialist selling low-price gifts.	High	Low

Step 5: Establish Specific Objectives and Allocate Resources

After evaluating the strategic investment opportunities, the next step in the strategic planning process is to establish a specific objective for each opportunity. The retailer's overall objective is included in the mission statement. The specific objectives are goals against which progress toward the overall objective can be measured. Thus, these specific objectives have three components: (1) the performance sought, including a numerical index against which progress may be measured, (2) a time frame within which the goal is to be achieved, and (3) the level of investment needed to achieve the objective. Typically, the performance levels are financial criteria such as return on investment, sales, or profits. Another commonly used objective, market share, is becoming more popular because it's easier to measure and often more objectively assessed than financial measures based on accounting information (which can be dramatically affected by accounting rules). Research indicates that market share is a good surrogate for long-term profitability in many businesses.[57]

Step 6: Develop a Retail Mix to Implement Strategy

The sixth step in the planning process is to develop a retail mix for each opportunity in which investment will be made and to control and evaluate performance. Decisions related to the elements in the retail mix are discussed in Sections III and IV.

IN TODAY'S BOWLING CENTER, LASER LIGHTS, neon, glow-in-the-dark alleys, fog machines, and a top-quality sound system are as important as bowling balls and pins. Turn down the lights, and turn on the special effects, and the center is transformed into a night club. DJs with portable microphones work the crowd. Video cameras are installed so customers can see all the action by watching monitors placed throughout the center, or the monitors can show music videos.

Changing consumer entertainment profiles are prompting bowling centers to rethink their marketing strategies and target new customers. Faced with a 40 percent decline in league bowling (the primary source of bowling center revenues and profits), Brunswick developed the Cosmic Bowling concept to attract young people to its centers.

The target market for cosmic bowling is Generation Yers and Xers, people in the 18-to-34 demographic group; however, the retail concept works for youngsters and even senior citizens. The nightclub atmosphere draws lots of high school students who aren't old enough to attend clubs. Theme nights can be developed for different segments by varying the type of music played such as retro, rap, and country.

Refact Bowling is the number one participant sport in the United States.[58]

The increased revenues from Cosmic Bowling are due to more efficient space utilization as well as attracting a new market segment. Typically bowling centers have few customers from 10:00 P.M. to 2:00 A.M. Cosmic bowling enthusiasts fill the centers during this dead time with people who pay a premium to party.

Source: Cindy Guier, "Cosmic Bowling Strikes at Whole New Audience," *Amusement Business,* May 18, 1998, pp. 20–24; and Jonathan Burton, "Up Periscope: Brunswick Chairman and CEO Peter N. Larson," *Chief Executive,* December, 1998, pp. 22–23.

Brunswick developed cosmic bowling to attract a younger generation to bowling when its target market of league bowlers declined.

Step 7: Evaluate Performance and Make Adjustments

The final step in the planning process is evaluating the results of the strategy and implementation program. If the retailer is meeting or exceeding its objectives, changes aren't needed. But if the retailer fails to meet its objectives, reanalysis is needed. Typically, this reanalysis starts with reviewing the implementation programs; but it may indicate that the strategy (or even the mission statement) needs to be reconsidered. This conclusion would result in starting a new planning process, including a new situation audit. Retailing View 6.5 illustrates how changes in the environment forced bowling alley operators to reevaluate their strategy, target a new market segment, and tailor their offering to meet the needs of this new segment.

Strategic Planning
in the Real World

The planning process in Exhibit 6–5 indicates that strategic decisions are made in a sequential manner. After the business mission is defined, the situation audit is performed, strategic opportunities are identified, alternatives are evaluated, objectives are set, resources are allocated, the implementation plan is developed, and, finally, performance is evaluated and adjustments are made. But actual planning processes have interactions among the steps.[59] For example, the situation audit may uncover a logical alternative for the firm to consider, even though this alternative isn't included in the mission statement. Thus, the mission statement may need to be reformulated. Development of the implementation plan might reveal that resource allocation to the opportunity is insufficient to achieve the objective. In that case, the objective would need to be changed or the resources would need to be increased, or the retailer might consider not investing in the opportunity at all.

SUMMARY

Strategic planning is an ongoing process. Every day, retailers audit their situations, examine lifestyle trends, study new technologies, and monitor competitive activities. But the retail strategy statement isn't changed every year or every six months. The strategy statement is reviewed and altered only when major changes in the retailer's environment or capabilities occur.

When a retailer undertakes a major reexamination of its strategy, the process for developing a new strategy statement may take a year or two. Potential strategic directions are generated by people at all levels of the organization. These ideas are evaluated by senior executives and operating people to ensure that the eventual strategic direction is profitable in the long run and can be implemented.

A retailer's long-term performance is largely determined by its strategy. The strategy coordinates employees' activities and communicates the direction the retailer plans to take. Retail market strategy describes both the strategic direction and the process by which the strategy is to be developed.

The strategic planning process consists of a sequence of steps including a detailed analysis of (1) the environment in which the retailer operates and (2) the retailer's unique capabilities. Based on this analysis, the retailer can evaluate alternatives using financial theory and a market attractiveness/competitive position matrix.

The retail strategy statement includes identification of a target market and the retail offering to be directed toward the target market. The statement also needs to indicate the retailer's methods to build a sustainable competitive advantage.

KEY TERMS

bargaining power of
vendors, *193*

barriers to entry, *191*

clicks and mortar
retailers, *184*

competitive rivalry, *193*

cross-selling, *182*

customer loyalty, *176*

data warehouse, *178*

database retailing, *178*

direct investment, *188*

diversification
opportunity, *183*

joint venture, *188*

market
attractiveness/competitive
position matrix, *200*

market expansion
opportunity, *182*

market penetration
opportunity, *182*

mission statement, *190*

multi-channel retailers,
184

positioning, *176*

related diversification
opportunity, *183*

retail format, *172*

DISCUSSION QUESTIONS AND PROBLEMS

1. For each of the four retailers discussed at the beginning of the chapter, describe their strategy and basis of competitive advantage.

2. What approaches can a retailer use to develop a competitive advantage?

3. Give an example of a market penetration opportunity, a retail format extension, and a market extension opportunity for Circuit City.

4. Draw and explain a positioning map like Exhibit 6–3's for the retailers and customer segments (ideal points) for the bicycle market in your town.

5. Do a situation analysis for McDonald's. What is its mission? What are its strengths and weaknesses? What environmental threats might it face over the next 10 years? How could it prepare for these threats?

6. Give an example of a retailer using the retail format development growth strategy.

7. Assume you are interested in opening a restaurant in your town. Go through the steps in the strategic planning process shown in Exhibit 6–5. Focus on doing a situation audit of the local restaurant market, identifying alternatives, evaluating alternatives, and selecting a target market and a retail mix for the restaurant.

8. Disney decided to expand its retail operations by opening specialty stores in malls. What are the advantages and disadvantages of Disney's pursuing this opportunity?

9. Many retailing experts have suggested that improving customer service is the basis for capturing a sustainable competitive advantage in the 1990s. What practical changes can a food/grocery retailer make to improve customer service?

10. Evaluate the strategic alternatives being considered by Gifts To Go as outlined in the chapter. Which do you think the company should pursue and why?

11. Amazon.com started as an Internet retailer selling books. Then it expanded through acquisitions to sell CDs, videotapes, and gifts and to operate an Internet drugstore. Evaluate these growth opportunities in terms of the probability that they will be profitable businesses for Amazon.com. What competitive advantages does Amazon.com bring to each of these new businesses?

SUGGESTED READINGS

Aaker, David. *Strategic Market Management*, 5th ed. New York: Wiley, 1998.

Alexander, Nicholas. *International Retailing*. Cambridge, MA: Blackwell, 1997.

"Global Retailing: Global Uncertainties." *Chain Store Age*, December 1998, pp. 132–41.

"Global Retailing Supplement." *Chain Store Age*, December 1997.

Goldbrick, Peter, and Gary Davies. "International Retailing: Trends and Strategies." *Journal of Retailing and Consumer Services* 5 (June 1998), pp. 23–32.

Lang, James, Roger Calantone, and Donald Gudmundson. "Small Firm Information Seeking as a Response to Environmental Threats and Opportunities." *Journal of Small Business Management*, January 1997, pp. 11–29.

Lehmann, Donald, and Russell Winer. *Analysis for Marketing Planning*, 5th ed. Burr Ridge, IL: Irwin/McGraw-Hill, 2000.

Madigan, Charles, and Arthur Martinez. *Hard Road to the Softer Side: Lessons from the Transformation of Sears.* New York: Times Books, 1999.

Peppers, Don, and Martha Rogers. *Enterprise One to One: Tools for Competing in the Interactive Age.* New York: Doubleday, 1999.

Porter, Michael. *Competitive Advantage.* New York: Free Press, 1985.

Samli, A. Coskun. *Strategic Marketing for Success in Retailing.* New York: Quorum Books, 1998.

Woodruff, Robert. "Customer Value: The Next Source of Competitive Advantage." *Journal of the Academy of Marketing Science* 25 (Spring 1997), pp. 139–53.

APPENDIX

Using the Market Attractiveness/Competitive Position Matrix

The following example illustrates an application of the market attractiveness/competitive position matrix.[60] The **market attractiveness/competitive position matrix** (Exhibit 6–8) provides a method for analyzing opportunities that explicitly considers both the retailer's capabilities and the retail market's attractiveness. The matrix's underlying premise is that a market's attractiveness determines its long-term profit potential for the opportunity, and the retailer's competitive position indicates the profit potential for the opportunity. The matrix indicates that the greatest investments should be made in opportunities where the retailer has a strong competitive position.

There are six steps in using the matrix to evaluate opportunities for strategic investments:

1. Define the strategic opportunities to be evaluated. For example, a store manager could use the matrix to evaluate departments in a store; a vice president of stores for a specialty store chain could use it to evaluate stores or potential store sites; a merchandise vice president could use it to evaluate merchandise categories sold by the retailer; or a retail holding company's CEO could use it to evaluate international growth opportunities.

2. Identify key factors determining market attractiveness and the retailer's competitive position. Factors that might be selected are discussed in the

EXHIBIT 6–8

Evaluation of International Growth Opportunities

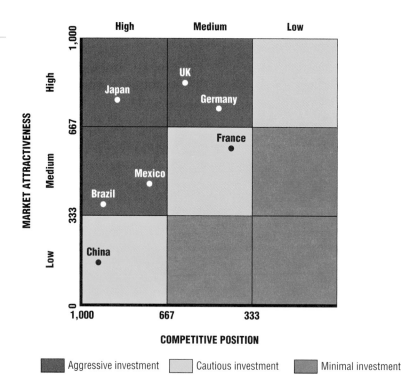

market attractiveness, competitor analysis, and self-analysis sections of the situation audit.

3. Assign weights to each factor used to determine market attractiveness and competitive position. The weights assigned to each factor indicate that factor's importance in determining the market attractiveness and competitive position. Typically, weights are selected so that they add up to 100.

4. Rate each strategic investment opportunity on (1) the attractiveness of its market and (2) the retailer's competitive position in that market. Typically, opportunities are rated on a 1-to-10 scale, with 10 indicating a very attractive market or very strong competitive position and 1 indicating a very unattractive market or very weak competitive position.

5. Calculate each opportunity's score for market attractiveness and competitive position. Scores are calculated by (1) multiplying the weights by each factor's rating and (2) adding across the factors.

6. Plot each opportunity on the matrix in Exhibit 6–8.

In this example, a fashion-oriented U.S. women's apparel retailer is evaluating seven countires for international expansion: Mexico, Brazil, Germany, France, the U.K., Japan, and China. Some information about the markets is shown in Exhibit 6–9.

EXHIBIT 6–9   Data on International Markets

	U.S.	MEXICO	BRAZIL	GERMANY	FRANCE	U.K.	JAPAN	CHINA
Population (millions)	266	95	160	82	59	59	126	1,239
Population's projected annual growth rate (%)	0.78	1.43	0.94	–0.10	0.13	0.15	.09	0.62
GDP (billion $)	8,111	403	749	2,084	1,380	1,290	4,187	902
Projected GDP annual growth rate (%)	2.3	4.0	3.0	2.1	2.3	1.9	0.2	7.3
Per capita GDP ($)	29,300	3,700	2,576	28,725	26,780	21,205	43,455	635
Retail sales per capita ($)	6,320	906	1,364	5,683	5,601	5,236	10,390	272
% of retail outlets nonfood vs. food	61	54	60	81	70	38	61	94
% of consumer expenditures on clothing	5	6	4	7	6	6	6	8
% of wealth in top 20% of population	42	55	67	40	42	44	38	44
Population density (per sq. km.)	30	50	20	230	110	240	330	130
% living in urban areas	74	73	76	84	74	89	77	26
Business Climate Index	3	29	37	10	11	2	24	43
Sales per retail outlet ($M)	1.50	0.89	0.14	0.80	0.81	1.00	0.61	0.03
Retail industry concentration	High	Avg.	Low	High	High	High	Avg.	Low
Logistical infrastructure	Exc.	Avg.	Avg.	Good	Good	Good	Avg.	Poor
Local vendors	Exc.	Avg.	Avg.	Exc.	Exc.	Exc.	Avg.	Poor

Source: "Global Powers of Retailing," *Stores Supplement,* February 1999; and "Retailing's Great Global Gold Rush," *Chain Store Age Gobal Retailing Supplement,* December 1997.

EXHIBIT 6–10   Market Attractiveness Ratings for International Growth Opportunities

	WEIGHT	MEXICO	BRAZIL	GERMANY	FRANCE	U.K.	JAPAN	CHINA
Market size	20	2	2	7	6	5	10	4
Market growth	10	10	7	3	3	3	2	6
Economic stability	15	2	2	10	9	9	5	2
Business climate	25	4	2	7	7	10	6	2
Attitude toward U.S.	30	7	5	8	3	10	10	2
	100	480	340	735	550	815	745	280

Refact The 10 major Asian countries have over one-half of the world's population.[61]

To evaluate each country's market attractiveness, management identified five market factors, assigned a weight to each factor, rated the markets on each factor, and calculated a market attractiveness score for each alternative (Exhibit 6–10). Here management assigned the highest weight to the attitude that consumers in the country have to the United States (30) and save the lowest weight to economic stability (15). Ratings for market size and market growth are based on country data; the firm had to consider size of it target market—middle-class women between the ages of 25 and 50. For this reason, Brazil, Mexico, and China had low ratings on market size. These countries are also low on economic stability; however, the retailer did not think that factor was particularly important because the buying power of its target segment is relatively insensitive to the country's economy. The business climate factor includes an assessment of the degree to which the government supports business and foreign investment. The European countries and Japan are high on this dimension.

Exhibit 6–11 shows the factors, weights, and ratings used to evaluate the retailer's position in each country versus the competition. In evaluating the competitive position, management felt that brand image was the most critical aspect of competitive position because image is particularly important in selling fashionable merchandise. Since cost was viewed as the least important factor in determining the competitive position of a high-fashion retailer, it received a weight of only 10.

In terms of the retailer's competitive position within each country, the firm felt its brand name was very well known in Japan and Brazil, but not well known in France and Germany. Brazil, Mexico, and China offer the best opportunities to operate efficiently due to the low labor costs in these countries.

EXHIBIT 6-11   Competitive Position for International Growth Opportunities

	WEIGHT	MEXICO	BRAZIL	GERMANY	FRANCE	U.K.	JAPAN	CHINA
Cost	10	9	10	5	5	5	7	10
Brand name	30	8	10	4	3	7	9	6
Vendor relations	20	7	7	4	4	3	8	8
Locations	20	6	8	6	5	7	6	10
Marketing	20	8	8	6	3	6	8	10
Total	100	750	860	490	380	630	780	840

Evaluations of each of the countries are plotted on Exhibit 6–8's business attractiveness/competitive position matrix. Based on the recommended investment level and objectives associated with each cell in the exhibit, the retailer should invest substantially in Japan, the U.K., Germany, Mexico, and Brazil and be cautious about investments in China and France.

Gary Schrodt
Chief Financial Officer
Burdines

INVENTORY IS ONE OF THE THREE big investments that a store-based retailer makes. The other two are "bricks and mortar" and people. Managing our inventory investment is like managing a portfolio of stocks. In fact, it might even be more challenging for a fashion forward department store chain like Burdines because fashion changes more quickly than the valuation of dot.com stocks. I am basically the custodian for our investments. • My group keeps track of the health of our investments. I am not involved in finding promising merchandise opportunities or getting out of bad merchandise investment. But I work with the CEO, president, and merchants of Burdines to analyze the returns we are getting from our investments and decide where to make investments in the future. • In the last ten years, we have become much more sophisticated in understanding the factors that contribute to our financial performance. We used to concentrate on sales growth and EBIT (earnings before interest and taxes). But now we emphasize return on investment. We use a measure called GoRI (gross return on investment) that tells us if a merchandise category gives a good return on the inventory and the space investments we have made in it. When you use this criterion, some mundane categories like mattresses are very attractive because they have a high inventory turn and don't take up much space. • I meet people who go into retailing because they like to shop. They are attracted by the glamour of traveling the world to find the best bargains and hot fashions. But a good shopper is not necessarily a good buyer. To be a good buyer, you need to get into the numbers and be a financial analyst. • After graduating from California State University—Northridge with a major in finance, I went to work for Bullocks, a department store chain in Southern California that was acquired by Federated. When I initially interviewed with Bullocks, I was interested in a position in the credit department, but after talking with various managers during the interview process, I decided to work in data processing. Shortly after turning 30, I was promoted to vice-president of Merchandise Processing and Information Systems. When the president of Bullocks became chairman of Burdines, he asked me to come to Burdines to consolidate their distribution system with two other chains merged into Burdines and automate the distribution centers. Seven years ago, I became CFO of Burdines.

7

Financial Strategy

QUESTIONS

- How is retail strategy reflected in retailers' financial objectives?
- Why do retailers need to evaluate their performance?
- What measures do retailers use to assess their performance?
- What is the strategic profit model and how is it used?

FINANCIAL DECISIONS ARE an integral component in every aspect of a retailer's strategy. In Chapter 6, we examined how retailers develop their strategy for sustaining a competitive advantage. In this chapter, we look at financial tools retailers use to measure and evaluate their performance.

Kelly Bradford, owner of the Gifts To Go store we described in Chapter 6, needs to know how well she is doing because she wants to be successful and stay in business. She sees how many customers enter her store and counts up the receipts at the end of the day to see how much she has sold. Unfortunately, these simple measures aren't enough. For instance, sometimes she finds that sales are good, but she still can't afford to buy new merchandise. When things are good, she doesn't need to think about her strategy. But when things go bad, she thinks about nothing else.

Based on the strategies Bradford set, it is important to establish quantifiable performance objectives. If she is achieving her objectives, changes in strategy or implementation programs aren't needed. But if the performance information indicates that objectives aren't being met, she needs to reanalyze her plans and programs. For example, after reviewing her accountant's financial report, Kelly might conclude that she's not earning a fair return on the time and money she's invested in the store. Based on this evaluation, she might consider changing her strategy by appealing to a different target market and lowering the average price point of the gifts that she carries.

We'll first show how financial information taken from standard accounting documents can be used to plan and evaluate strategies. Specifically, retailers have two paths available to achieve a high level of performance: the profit path and the turnover path. Different retailers, however, pursue different strategies, resulting in different types of financial performance. The two paths are combined into the strategic profit model to illustrate that retailers using very different strategies and financial performance characteristics can be financially successful. As a vehicle for discussion, we'll compare the financial performance of two very different retailers: Tiffany & Co. (a national jewelry store chain) and Wal-Mart (the world's largest retailer).

Then we will discuss how retailers set performance objectives and how different performance measures are used throughout the organization. The chapter concludes with an appendix that describes activity-based costing and how it is used to make retailing decisions.

We begin our examination of corporate-level performance measures by looking at the strategic profit model.

THE STRATEGIC PROFIT MODEL: AN OVERVIEW

Every retailer wants to be financially successful. One important financial goal is to achieve a high return on assets. For instance, Kelly Bradford invested $174,000 in setting up her store and buying merchandise to sell. At the end of the year, she made $33,000 in profit, a 19 percent return on her investment ($33,000 ÷ 174,000). This ratio, net profit ÷ total assets, is called return on assets. To determine whether 19 percent is a good return on her investment, Bradford compares it with what she thinks she could make on another investment with similar risk.

Return on assets can be divided into two paths: the profit path (which is measured by net profit margin) and the turnover path (which is measured by asset turnover). Net profit margin is simply how much profit (after tax) a firm makes divided by its net sales. Asset turnover is used to measure the productivity of a firm's investment in assets. It is expressed as net profit ÷ total assets. When you multiply net profit margin times asset turnover, the net sales cancels out of the equation and you get return on assets:

$$\text{Net profit} \quad \times \quad \text{Asset turnover} \quad = \quad \text{Return on assets}$$

$$\frac{\text{Net profit}}{\text{Net sales}} \quad \times \quad \frac{\text{Net sales}}{\text{Total assets}} \quad = \quad \frac{\text{Net profit}}{\text{Total assets}}$$

To illustrate how the strategic profit model works, consider the two very different hypothetical retailers in Exhibit 7–1. La Madeline Bakery has a net profit margin of 1 percent and asset turnover of 10 times, resulting in a return on assets of 10 percent. The profit margin is low due to the competitive nature of this commodity-type business. Asset turnover is relatively high, because the firm doesn't have its own credit card system (no accounts receivable). Also, it rents its store, so fixed assets are relatively low, and it has a very fast inventory turnover—in fact, its inventory turns every day!

EXHIBIT 7–1

Return on Assets Model for a Bakery and Jewelry Store

	NET PROFIT MARGIN	×	ASSET TURNOVER	=	RETURN ON ASSETS
La Madeline Bakery	1%		10 times		10%
Kalame Jewelry	10%		1 time		10%

Jewelry stores typically have a higher net profit margin than bakeries, but their asset turnover is much lower. How can return on assets of a jewelry store and a bakery be the same?

On the other hand, Kalame Jewelry Store has a net profit margin of 10 percent and an asset turnover of one time, again resulting in a return on assets of 10 percent. The difference is that even though the jewelry store has higher operating expenses than the bakery, its gross margin is much more—it may double the cost of jewelry to arrive at a retail price. Kalame's asset turnover is so low compared to the bakery's because Kalame has very expensive fixtures and precision jewelry-manufacturing equipment (fixed assets), offers liberal credit to customers (accounts receivable), and has very slow inventory turnover—possibly only one-half to one turn per year. In sum, these two very different types of retailers could have exactly the same return on assets.

Thus, La Madeline is achieving its 10 percent return on assets by having a relatively high asset turnover—the *turnover path*. Kalame Jewelry, on the other hand, achieves its return on assets with a relatively high net profit margin—the *profit path*.

In the next three sections we will take a close look at these three financial ratios. Specifically, we will examine the relationship between these ratios and retailing strategy, and describe where the information can be found in traditional accounting records.

One way to define financial success is to provide the owners of the firm with a good return on their investment. Although retailers pursue similar financial goals, they employ different strategies. For instance, Tiffany & Co., described in Retailing View 7.1, has broad assortments of jewelry and gifts, exceptionally high levels of service, and opulent surroundings. Tiffany & Co. concentrates on the profit path. Wal-Mart, described in Retailing View 7.2, takes the opposite approach. It concentrates on the turnover path. Wal-Mart has narrow assortments, relatively little service, and functional decor. Based on this description, why would anyone shop at Wal-Mart? The answer is that Wal-Mart strives for and maintains everyday low prices. The strategic profit model is used to evaluate the performance of different retailers that, like Tiffany and Wal-Mart, may employ very different strategies.

THE PROFIT PATH

The information used to analyze a firm's profit path comes from the income statement. The income statement summarizes a firm's financial performance over a period of time.

OF ALL THE GREAT AMERICAN BRANDS, Tiffany, which has been around over 160 years, is among the best known. Tiffany is more than a retailer; it's a tourist attraction, an American icon that has worked its way into movies and songs.

Such reputations can be profitable. It has grown aggressively—from $230 million in sales in 1987 to more than $1 billion in 1997—by opening new retail locations, expanding its direct-mail operations, restructuring its corporate sales division, and gaining popularity overseas. (International sales account for 42 percent of the company's total revenues.)

Marketers get the Tiffany message across in all the expected ways: employing ever-consistent communications (such as advertising, brochures, and catalogs) and training retail and corporate salespeople to provide superior customer service. And then there are the not-so-noticeable ways: pricing a few products to be affordable for the average consumer, positioning the company as an authority.

In some ways, the custodians of the Tiffany brand image at the New York headquarters have been blessed by the company's strong beginnings. In 1837 founder Charles Lewis Tiffany understood the principles of branding. He was one of the great entrepreneurs of the mid-19th century, one of those responsible for developing the luxury goods market in the United States That the founder had a vision—distinctive product, distinctive store, distinctive color (it was he who introduced robin's-egg blue, universally recognizable as the trademark Tiffany blue)—has made sustaining the brand a lot easier—not to mention the good fortune of the regal-sounding name, Tiffany.

Charles Lewis Tiffany's legacy was he made his firm to be the authority on gems, jewlery, and watches. He was interested in making sure that people understood what they were looking at. For instance, Tiffany was the first company to hire a gemologist, George Kunz, who went on expeditions to different parts of the world seeking rare gemstones. While he was abroad, he would often freelance for other organizations, like the U.S. Geological Service, sharing his knowledge when he returned. Even Walter Hoving, the chairman of the company from 1955 to 1981, penned a book, *Tiffany's Table Manners for Teenagers,* which is still available. The firm's mission has always been educational, which is unusual for a store.

In keeping the rest of us up-to-date on how to behave, and by setting itself as the ultimate authority, Tiffany reinforces its image of quality and builds trust in its products. Today, the company produces simple, easy-to-read brochures such as "How to Buy a Pearl" and "How to Buy a Diamond," which explain the qualities of each stone that the untutored should consider before making a significant purchase.

In the past, most people would agree that there was a certain degree of intimidation associated with Tiffany. Today, however, it tries to reach out to mall habitues in Guess jeans, without sacrificing Ladies Who Lunch in Chanel suits. Just look at its new website where an Etiquette Quiz instructs the insecure on questions such as "How do I eat asparagus?" (Answer: It is perfectly acceptable to pick up asparagus with your fingers.) Tiffany, whose average sale is actually only around $250, is also pointing out that the authority it offers is surprisingly affordable. Ads for engagement rings now stress a price range "from $950 to $950,000." Tiffany always had some relatively inexpensive rings; it's just that people didn't know it.

Source: Erin Kelly, "Tiffany—My Gawd—Prospers With a Mall-Rat Strategy," *Fortune,* June 21, 1999, pp. 40–44; and Sarah Lorge, "A Priceless Brand," *Sales and Marketing Management,* October 1998, pp. 102–10.

Exhibit 7–2 shows income statements adapted from corporate reports of Wal-Mart and Tiffany & Co. The profit path portion of the strategic profit model that utilizes such income statement data appears in Exhibit 7–3. Let's look at each item in the income statement.

Net Sales   The term **net sales** refers to the total number of dollars received by a retailer after all refunds have been paid to customers for returned merchandise:

Net sales = Gross amount of sales – Customer returns – Customer allowances

Customer returns represents the value of merchandise that customers return because it's damaged, doesn't fit, and so forth. Customer allowances represents any additional price reduction given to the customer. For instance, if an

Refact Ninety percent of the purchases of Avon products in Patrocino, Brazil, are made with gold dust.[1]

HOW BIG IS WAL-MART? Its sales equate to the GDP of countries such as El Salvador, Kenya, and Iceland! Although Wal-Mart began as a discount operation in rural U.S. towns, it has expanded to urban locations both in the United States and abroad. Further, by 2004, Wal-Mart plans to have approximately 1,400 supercenters operating in the United States. These supercenters carry not only the usual Wal-Mart merchandise but groceries as well. Wal-Mart also expects to have a large presence in e-commerce. It has combined forces with Fingerhut Business Services to provide it with order fulfillment capabilities for its online business. Fingerhut, a subsidiary of Federated Department Stores, is known for its successful catalog operation geared to low-income customers. Wal-Mart has even gotten into the banking business by buying a small bank in Oklahoma.

How big is Wal-Mart? Its sales equate to the GDP of countries such as El Salvador, Kenya, and Iceland. They employ over 825,000 people.

Most experts agree that Wal-Mart's amazing results are based on three simple principles. First, it provides customers with everyday low prices—the lowest aggregate market basket price in each market in which it competes. Second, it strives to give customers good-quality merchandise and third a level of service that is somewhat unusual for discount stores. Randy Mott, Wal-Mart's senior vice president and CIO, puts it this way: "[our goal is] not to be the best national or global retailer [but] to be the best retailer in every community we're in, on a store by store basis."

How is this done exactly? Wal-Mart's success in executing its promise to customers is generally thought to be supported by its ability to gain economies of scale and an efficient distribution and information system. The company's attitude toward information technology was summed up by founder Sam Walton: "People think we got big by putting big stores in small towns. Really we got big by replacing inventory with information."

More specifically, Wal-Mart has used information technology to enable store managers to alter suggested product assortments to meet local tastes. At the same time, they are able to continually decrease their inventory levels while maintaining product availability to the customer. For instance, while sales were up by 17 percent in 1999, inventories only increased by 3.5 percent.

Wal-Mart is also continually working on improving its communication ability. For instance, radio frequency handsets communicate directly with the data warehouse at the head office so all price and item information is in real time. In the buying division, the company provides suppliers with access to sales and in-stock information and has developed a process known as Collaborative Planning, Forecasting and Replenishment (CPFR), which is fast becoming the standard production planning procedure between merchants and suppliers. Its distribution centers use state-of-the-art techniques such as cross-docking to get merchandise onto the shelf as quickly as possible. (See Chapter 11 for details on CPFR and cross-docking.)

Wal-Mart also believes in investing in people. For instance, sales associates are indoctrinated with the "10-foot attitude" that requires all employees coming within 10 feet of customers to make eye contact and greet and ask the customer if any help is needed. To maintain high loyalty among associates, all staff with over one year of service are entitled to stock options which, given Wal-Mart's stunning growth, has made millionaires out of many long-time Wal-Mart employees.

Source: Lawrence J. Ring; Douglas J. Tigert; and Ray Serpkenci, "Supermarkets at Risk," July 1, 1999, *Chain Store Age Executive with Shopping Center Age,* pp. 56+; Emily Nelson, "Wal-Mart, Widening Its Focus, to Buy Tiny Bank," *The Wall Street Journal,* June 30, 1999, p. A4; David Moin Thomas Cunningham, "Fingerhut to Service Wal-Mart," *WWD,* June 22, 1999, p. 1; and Michael Brewis-Levie, "Marketing Is Meaningless without Operational Back-up," *Brand Strategy,* July 23, 1999, p. 10.

Income Statements for Wal-Mart Stores, Inc., and Tiffany & Co. and Subsidiaries, 1999 ($ in Millions)

	WAL-MART	TIFFANY
Net sales	139,208	1,173
Less: Cost of goods sold	108,725	515
Gross Margin	30,483	658
Less: Operating expense	22,363	493
Less: Interest expense	950	9
Total expense	23,313	502
Net profit, pretax	7,170	156
Less: Taxes*	2,740	66
Tax rate	38.21%	42.31%
Net profit after tax	4,430	90

*Effective tax rates often differ among corporations due to different tax breaks and advantages.
Source: Annual reports via Edgar SEC website.

item at Gifts To Go regularly retails for $5 but is sold for $4.50 because it's scratched, the 50-cent difference is the customer allowance.

Sales are an important measure of performance because they indicate the activity level of the merchandising function. Retailers are particularly interested in sales growth due to its direct link to the firm's overall profitability. Chapters 12 and 13 cover sales forecasting techniques.

EXHIBIT 7–3   Profit Margin Models for Wal-Mart Stores, Inc., and Tiffany & Co. and Subsidiaries, 1999 ($ in Millions)

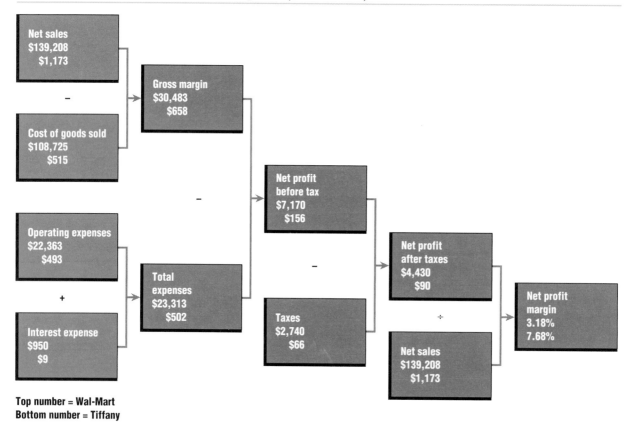

Top number = Wal-Mart
Bottom number = Tiffany

Gross Margin   Gross margin = Net sales − Cost of goods sold

Gross margin, also called **gross profit,** is an important measure in retailing. It gives the retailer a measure of how much profit it's making on merchandise sales without considering the expenses associated with operating the store.

Gross margin, like other performance measures, is also expressed as a percentage of net sales so retailers can compare (1) performances of various types of merchandise and (2) their own performance with other retailers.

(Gross margin   ÷ Net sales) = Gross margin %
Wal-Mart: ($30,483 ÷ $139,208) = 21.90%
Tiffany: ($658   ÷ $1,173)   = 56.10%

Grocery stores attempt to increase their average gross margin by emphasizing high-margin departments like produce.

(Throughout this chapter, dollar figures are expressed in millions.)

Superficially, Tiffany appears to outperform Wal-Mart on gross margin. However, further analysis will show that other factors interact with gross margin to determine overall performance. But first, let's consider the factors that contribute to differences in gross margin performance.

Discount stores like Wal-Mart generally have lower gross margins than jewelry stores because discount stores pursue a deliberate strategy of offering merchandise at everyday low prices with minimal service to several cost-oriented market segments. Discount stores have tried to increase their average gross margin by adding specialty products and departments like gourmet foods and jewelry. But Wal-Mart's overall average gross margin lags behind Tiffany's. Chapters 12, 13, and 15 explore the use of gross margin in merchandise and pricing decisions.

Expenses   **Expenses** are costs incurred in the normal course of doing business to generate revenues. One expense category in Exhibit 7–3, operating expenses, is further defined in Exhibit 7–4.

Another major expense category, interest, is the cost of financing everything from inventory to the purchase of a new store location. For instance, if a bank charges Tiffany 10 percent interest, Tiffany pays $49 million in interest to borrow $490 million.

Tiffany has significantly higher total expenses as a percentage of net sales than Wal-Mart. Like gross margin, total expenses are also expressed as a percentage of net sales to facilitate comparisons across items and departments within firms.

(Total expenses   ÷ Net sales) =Total expenses/Net sales ratio
Wal-Mart: ($26,053 ÷ $139,208) = 18.72%
Tiffany: ($568   ÷ $1,173)   = 48.42%

EXHIBIT **7–4**

Types of Retail
Operating Expenses

Selling expenses	= **Sales staff salaries + Commissions + Benefits**
General expenses	= **Rent + Utilities + Miscellaneous expenses**
Administrative expenses	= **Salaries of all employees other than salespeople + Operations of buying offices + Other administrative expenses**

The total expenses/net sales ratio is only approximately 19 percent for Wal-Mart; at Tiffany, it's over 48 percent. This difference is to be expected. Discount stores have relatively low selling expenses. They're also typically located on comparatively inexpensive real estate so rent is relatively low. Finally, discount stores operate with a smaller administrative staff than a store like Tiffany's. For instance, buying expenses are much lower for discount stores. Their buyers don't have to travel very far, and much of the purchasing consists of rebuying staple merchandise that's already in the stores. On the other hand, a jewelry store's total expenses are much higher because its large, experienced sales staff requires a modest salary plus commission and benefits. Unlike Wal-Mart stores' locations that are usually suburban or in rural areas, Tiffany's stores are in some of the most expensive malls in the country, not to mention its flagship store on Fifth Avenue in New York. Tiffany's locations therefore command high rent and incur other expenses.

Net Profit   **Net profit** is a measure of the firm's overall performance:

$$\text{Net profit} = \text{Gross margin} - \text{Expenses}$$

Refact The most profitable retailers in 1998 were Wal-Mart ($4.43 billion), Home Depot ($1.614 billion), and Dell Computer ($1.46 billion).[2]

Net profit can be expressed either before or after taxes. Generally, it's more useful to express net profit after taxes, since this is the amount of money left over to reinvest in the business, disburse as dividends to stockholders or owners, or repay debt.

Net profit margin, like gross margin, is often expressed as a percentage of net sales:

$$\text{Net profit margin} = (\text{Net profit} \div \text{Net sales})$$

However, net profit measures the profitability of the entire firm, while gross margin measures the profitability of merchandising activities. In Exhibit 7–3, the after-tax net profit margin is 3.18 percent for Wal-Mart and 7.68 percent for Tiffany. From a profit perspective alone, Tiffany is outperforming Wal-Mart. Even though Tiffany has a higher total expenses/net sales ratio, its gross margin percentage is so large compared to Wal-Mart's that it still surpasses the discount store's profit performance.

THE TURNOVER PATH   The information used to analyze a firm's turnover path primarily comes from the balance sheet. While the income statement summarizes the financial performance over a period of time, the balance sheet summarizes a retailer's financial position at a given point in time, such as the last day of the year. The balance sheet shows the following relationship:

$$\text{Assets} = \text{Liabilities} + \text{Owner's equity}$$

Assets are economic resources (such as inventory or store fixtures) owned or controlled by an enterprise as a result of past transactions or events. **Liabilities** are an enterprise's obligations (such as accounts or notes payable) to pay cash or other economic resources in return for past, current, or future benefits. **Owners' equity** (owners' investment in the business) is the difference between assets and liabilities. It represents the amount of assets belonging to the owners of the retail firm after all obligations (liabilities) have been met.

EXHIBIT 7–5

Balance Sheets for
Wal-Mart Stores,
Inc., and Tiffany &
Co. and Subsidiaries
($ in Millions)

	WAL-MART (AS OF 1/31/99)	TIFFANY (AS OF 1/31/99)
ASSETS		
Current assets		
Accounts receivable	$ 1,118	$ 108
Merchandise inventory	17,076	481
Cash	1,879	189
Other current assets	1,059	37
Total current assets	21,132	816
Fixed assets		
Building, equipment, and other		
Fixed assets, less depreciation	28,864	241
Total assets	$49,996	$1,057
LIABILITIES		
Current liabilities	$16,762	$ 293
Long-term liabilities	9,607	194
Other liabilities	2,515	53
Total liabilities	$28,884	$ 541
OWNERS' EQUITY		
Common stock	$ 445	$ 0
Retained earnings	20,667	516
Total owners' equity	$21,112	$ 516
Total liabilities and owners' equity	$49,996	$1,057

Exhibit 7–5's balance sheet for Tiffany and Wal-Mart continues the comparison between them. The turnover path portion of the strategic profit model is shown in Exhibit 7–6's asset turnover model. The remainder of this section covers elements of the balance sheet.

Current Assets   By accounting definition, **current assets** are those that can normally be converted to cash within one year. In retailing,

Accounts receivable + Merchandise inventory + Cash + Other current assets = Current assets

Accounts Receivable   **Accounts receivable** are monies due to the retailer from selling merchandise on credit. This current asset is substantial for some retailers. For example, Wal-Mart's investment in accounts receivable is proportionately much smaller than Tiffany's due to Wal-Mart customers' high propensity to pay cash or use third-party credit cards like VISA or MasterCard. Here are their accounts receivable:

Wal-Mart: $1,118 or .8 percent of sales

Tiffany: $108 or 9.2 percent of sales

From a marketing perspective, the accounts receivable generated from credit sales may be the result of an important service provided to customers. The retailer's ability to provide credit, particularly at low interest rates, could

EXHIBIT 7–6

Asset Turnover
Model for Wal-Mart
Stores, Inc., and
Tiffany & Co.
and Subsidiaries
($ in Millions)

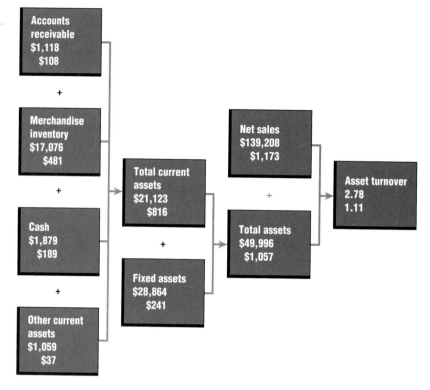

Top number = Wal-Mart
Bottom number = Tiffany

make the difference between making or losing a sale. Paying cash for a sizable purchase like a diamond engagement ring or car may be difficult for many people!

Unfortunately, having a large amount of accounts receivable is expensive for retailers, who of course would like to sell a product for cash and immediately reinvest the cash in new merchandise. When merchandise is sold on credit, proceeds of the sale are tied up as accounts receivable until collection is made. The money invested in accounts receivable costs the retailer interest expense and keeps the retailer from investing proceeds of the sale elsewhere. To ease the financial burden of carrying accounts receivable, retailers can use third-party credit cards such as VISA or MasterCard, give discounts to customers who pay with cash, discourage credit sales, and control delinquent accounts.

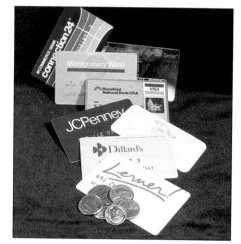

To ease the burden of carrying accounts receivable, retailers use third-party credit cards such as VISA or MasterCard.

Merchandise Inventory   Merchandise inventory is a retailer's lifeblood, representing approximately 34.15 percent of total assets for Wal-Mart and 45.51 percent of total assets for Tiffany. An exception to this generalization is service retailers such as Sears Pest Control Service, Marriott Hotels, and your local barber shop/beauty salon, which carry little or no merchandise inventory.

Think of inventory as "merchandise in motion." The faster it moves through the store, the greater the inventory turnover.

(Inventory ÷ Total assets)

Wal-Mart:	($17,076 ÷ $49,996)	= 34.15%
Tiffany:	($481 ÷ $1,057)	= 45.51%

Inventory turnover is used to evaluate how effectively managers utilize their investment in inventory. Inventory turnover is defined as follows:

Inventory turnover = (Net sales ÷ Average inventory)

Note that average inventory is expressed at retail rather than at cost.

Think of inventory as a measure of the productivity of inventory—how many sales dollars can be generated from $1 invested in inventory. Generally, the larger the inventory turnover, the better. Exhibit 7–7 illustrates the concept of inventory turnover. Inventory is delivered to the store, spends some time in the store, and then is sold. We can think of inventory turnover as how many times, on average, the inventory cycles through the store during a specific period of time (usually a year).

Wal-Mart's inventory turnover is almost six times Tiffany's: 6.35 compared to 1.07.[3]

(Net sales	÷ Average inventory)	= Inventory turnover
Wal-Mart: ($139,208	÷ $21,906)	= 6.35
Tiffany: ($1,173	÷ $1,094)	= 1.07

Refact Inventory turnover at Zale Corporation, the largest specialty retailer of fine jewelry in the United States, is 1.43, about 40 percent higher than at Tiffany. Inventory turnover at Kmart is 4.03, about 42 percent less than at Wal-Mart.

Wal-Mart's faster inventory turnover is expected due to the nature of discount and grocery stores. First, most items in Wal-Mart are commodities and staples such as batteries, housewares, and basic apparel items. Its new superstores carry grocery products such as baked goods, frozen meat, and produce. Tiffany, on the other hand, specializes in unique luxury items. Second, since Wal-Mart–type merchandise is available at other discount and grocery stores, it competes by offering lower prices, which results in rapid turnover. Third, discount stores carry a simpler stock selection than jewelry stores do. In a Wal-Mart store,

EXHIBIT 7–7

Inventory Turnover

for example, there may be only two brands of ketchup, each in two sizes, which represents four inventory items. Jewelry stores, on the other hand, may stock 100 distinctly different types of necklaces. Finally, due to Tiffany's unique positioning strategy, much of its inventory, particularly the jewelry, is made especially for it in other countries, requiring buyers to place orders several months in advance of delivery. Discount stores, on the other hand, order items daily or weekly. These factors, when taken together, explain why Wal-Mart has a faster inventory turnover than Tiffany.

Management of this aspect of retailing permeates most retailing decisions. Chapters 12 and 13 address the crucial subject of merchandise inventory management.

Cash and Other Current Assets

Cash = Monies on hand

+ Demand and savings accounts in banks to which a retailer has immediate access

+ Marketable securities such as Treasury bills

Other current assets = Prepaid expenses + Supplies

Wal-Mart reports cash of about 1.35 percent of sales, whereas Tiffany's cash percentage is 16.11 percent.

Fixed Assets

Fixed assets are assets that require more than a year to convert to cash. In retailing,

Fixed assets = Buildings (if store property is owned rather than leased)

+ Fixtures (such as display racks)

+ Equipment (such as computers or delivery trucks)

+ Long-term investments such as real estate or stock in other firms

Fixed assets represent 57.73 percent and 22.80 percent of total assets for Wal-Mart and Tiffany, respectively. Wal-Mart's fixed assets are relatively higher than Tiffany's because they have vast real estate holdings in stores and distribution centers, whereas Tiffany typically rents space in malls and has direct store delivery.

Fixed assets = Asset cost – Depreciation

Since most fixed assets have a limited useful life, those assets' value should be less over time—in other words, they're depreciated. For instance, Tiffany stores require refurbishing every few years due to general wear-and-tear. So, carpet and some fixtures are depreciated over 3 to 5 years, whereas a building may be depreciated over 25 years.

Mannequins are fixed assets that are depreciated over three to five years.

Asset Turnover

Asset turnover is an overall performance measure from the asset side of the balance sheet.

Asset turnover = (Net sales ÷ Total assets)

Although fixed assets don't turn over as quickly as inventory, asset turnover can be used to evaluate and compare how effectively managers use their assets. When a retailer redecorates a store, for example, old fixtures, carpeting, and lights are removed and replaced with new ones. Thus, like inventory, these assets cycle through the store. The difference is that the process is a lot slower. The life of a fixture in a Tiffany's store may be five years (instead of five months, as it might be for a diamond ring in the store's inventory), yet the concept of turnover is the same. When a retailer decides to invest in a fixed asset, it should determine how many sales dollars can be generated from that asset.

Suppose that Tiffany needs to purchase a new fixture for displaying dinnerware. It has a choice of buying an expensive antique display cabinet for $5,000 or having a simple plywood display constructed for $500. Using the expensive antique, it forecasts sales of $50,000 in the first year, whereas the plywood display is expected to generate only $40,000. Ignoring all other assets for a moment,

$$\text{(Net sales} \div \text{Total assets)} = \text{Asset turnover}$$

Antique cabinet: ($50,000 ÷ $5,000)   = 10
Plywood cabinet: ($40,000 ÷ $500)   = 80

The antique cabinet will certainly help create an atmosphere conducive to selling expensive dinnerware. Exclusively from a marketing perspective, the antique would thus appear appropriate. But it costs much more than the plywood shelves. From a strict financial perspective, Tiffany should examine how much additional sales can be expected to be generated from the added expenditure in assets. Clearly, by considering only asset turnover, the plywood shelves are the way to go. In the end, a combination of marketing and financial factors should be considered when making the asset purchase decision.[5]

Wal-Mart's asset turnover is 2.5 times Tiffany's. The asset turnover is 2.78 for Wal-Mart and 1.11 for Tiffany. This finding is consistent with the different strategies each firm is implementing. We saw earlier that Wal-Mart has a higher inventory turnover. Its other assets are relatively lower than Tiffany's as well. For instance, the fixed assets involved in outfitting a store (such as fixtures, lighting, and mannequins) would be relatively lower for a discount store than a jewelry store.

The other side of the balance sheet equation from assets involves liabilities and owners' equity. Now let's look at the major liabilities and components of owners' equity.

Liabilities and Owners' Equity

Current Liabilities   Like current assets, **current liabilities** are debts that are expected to be paid in less than one year. The most important current liabilities are accounts payable, notes payable, and accrued liabilities. Current liabilities as a percentage of net sales is 12.04 percent for Wal-Mart and 24.98 percent for Tiffany.

Accounts Payable   **Accounts payable** refers to the amount of money owed to vendors, primarily for merchandise inventory. Accounts payable are an important source of short-term financing. Retailers buy merchandise on credit from vendors. The longer the period of time they have to pay for that merchandise, the larger their accounts payable—and the less they need to borrow from financial institutions (notes payable), issue bonds or stock, or finance internally through retained earnings. Since retailers normally don't have to pay interest to vendors on their accounts payable, they have strong incentive to negotiate for a long time period before payment for merchandise is due. (See Chapter 14.)

Notes Payable   **Notes payable** under the current liabilities section of the balance sheet are the principal and interest the retailer owes to financial institutions (banks) that are due and payable in less than a year. Retailers borrow money from financial institutions to pay for current assets, such as inventory.

Accrued Liabilities   **Accrued liabilities** include taxes, salaries, rent, utilities, and other incurred obligations that haven't yet been paid. These are called accrued liabilities because they usually accumulate daily but are only paid at the end of a time period, such as a month.

Long-Term Liabilities   **Long-term liabilities** are debts that will be paid after one year. The notes payable entry in the long-term liability section of the balance sheet is similar to the one in the current liability section except that it's due to be paid in more than one year. Other long-term liabilities include bonds and mortgages on real estate.

Owners' Equity   Owners' equity, also known as **stockholders' equity,** represents the amount of assets belonging to the owners of the retail firm after all obligations (liabilities) have been met. In accounting terms, the relationship can be expressed as

Owners' equity = Total assets – Total liabilities

Although there are several entries in the owners' equity category, two of the most common are common stock and retained earnings.

Common stock is the type of stock most frequently issued by corporations.[6] Owners of common stock usually have voting rights in the retail corporation. They also have the right to share in distributed corporate earnings. If the firm is liquidated, common stock owners have the right to share in the sale of its assets. Finally, they have the right to purchase additional shares to maintain the same percentage ownership if new shares are issued.

Retained earnings refers to the portion of owners' equity that has accumulated over time through profits but hasn't been paid out in dividends to owners. The decision of how much of the retailer's earnings should be retained in the firm and how much should be returned to the owners in the form of dividends is related to the firm's growth potential. Specifically, retailers with a propensity toward and opportunities for growth will retain and reinvest their profits to fund growth opportunities. For example, a high-growth retailer such as Wal-Mart retains most of its earnings to pay for the new stores, inventory, and expenses associated with its growth.

Total owners' equity is over $21,112 million for Wal-Mart and over $516 million for Tiffany.

THE STRATEGIC PROFIT MODEL

The previous sections defined the most important balance sheet and income statement entries as well as the most useful performance ratios. Yet many of these items are interrelated, and when examined alone they can be confusing. More importantly, it's hard to compare the performance of retailers with different operating characteristics, such as Tiffany and Wal-Mart. The strategic profit model (Exhibit 7–8)

EXHIBIT 7–8   The Strategic Profit Model

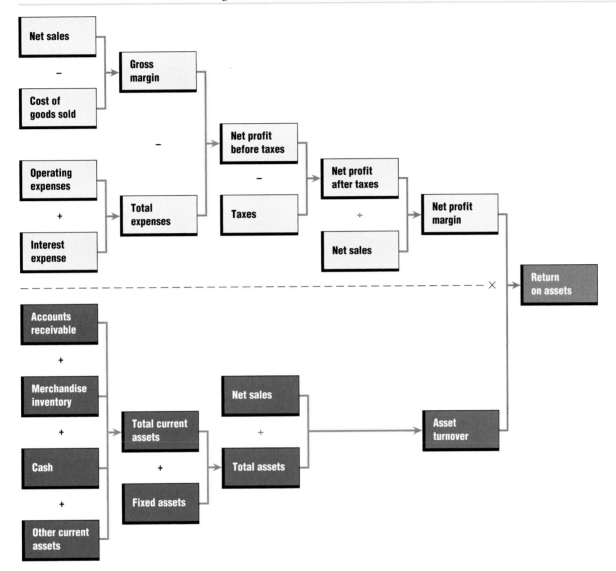

combines the two performance ratios from the income statement and balance sheets: net profit margin and asset turnover. By multiplying these ratios together, you get return on assets.

INTERNET EXERCISE   Go on the Internet to the Wal-Mart site (www.wal-mart.com and take the link to "Newsroom") and use the financial information from the most recent annual report to update the numbers in the profit margin model in Exhibit 7–3 and the asset turnover model in Exhibit 7–6. Use these two models to develop the strategic profit model in Exhibit 7–8 for the two companies. Do the same for Tiffany at the Tiffany website (www.tiffany.com and take the links to "About Tiffany," "Shareholder Information," and "Financial Highlights") and compare the two companies.

Return on Assets

Return on assets = Net profit margin × Asset turnover

= (Net profit ÷ Net sales) × (Net sales ÷ Total assets)

= (Net profit ÷ Total assets)

Return on assets determines how much profit can be generated from the retailer's investment in assets. (Note that when we multiply net profit margin by asset turnover, net sales drops out of the equation.)

The most important issue associated with return on assets is that the money that would be invested in retailing could also be invested in any other asset, such as a CD or Treasury bill. For instance, if a retailer can achieve 9 percent return on assets by opening a new store, and 10 percent by investing in a nearly risk-free Treasury bill, the retailer should take the higher-yield, lower-risk investment. In fact, should the return on assets of another investment with similar risk be greater, it would be the manager's fiduciary duty to invest in the other asset. In general, return on assets is effective in evaluating the profitability of individual investments in assets because it can easily be compared with yields of other investments with similar risk. It has also been shown to be an effective predictor of business failures.[7]

	(Net profit ÷ Total assets)	= Return on assets
Wal-Mart:	($4,430 ÷ $49,996)	= 8.86%
Tiffany:	($90 ÷ $1,057)	= 8.51%

Return on assets for Tiffany and Wal-Mart is almost identical! Tiffany generated a larger net profit margin, 7.68 percent, compared to 3.18 for Wal-Mart (Exhibit 7–3). But Wal-Mart outperformed Tiffany on asset turnover, 2.78 compared to 1.11, respectively (Exhibit 7–6).

Exhibit 7–9 shows strategic profit model (SPM) ratios for a variety of retailers. In the next section, we continue the strategic plan developed for Kelly Bradford in Chapter 6. Retailing View 7.3 looks at the strategic profit model of an online jewelry retailer and compares it to Tiffany & Co.

INTEGRATING MARKETING AND FINANCIAL STRATEGIES FOR KELLY BRADFORD'S GIFT STORES

Recall from Chapter 6 that Kelly Bradford owns Gifts To Go, a two-store chain in the Chicago area. She's considering several growth options, one of which is to open a new Internet store called Giftstogo.com. She determined that the market for such a store is high but very competitive. Now she needs to do a financial analysis for the proposed online store and compare the projections with Gifts To Go.

We'll first look at the profit path, followed by the turnover path. Then we'll combine the two and examine the stores' return on assets. Exhibit 7–10 shows income statements for one of her Gifts To Go stores and her projections for Giftstogo.com.

Profit Path

Gross Margins We expect Giftstogo.com to have about the same gross margin as Gifts To Go because it will carry a similar but more extensive assortment.

	{Gross margin ÷ Net sales}	= Gross margin %
Gifts To Go:	{$90,000 ÷ $200,000}	= 45 %
Giftstogo.com:	{$90,000 ÷ $200,000}	= 45 %

EXHIBIT **7–9**

Strategic Profit
Models for Selected
Retailers

	(1) NET PROFIT MARGIN (NET PROFIT ÷ NET SALES) (%)	(2) ASSET TURNOVER (NET SALES ÷ TOTAL ASSETS)	(3) RETURN ON ASSETS (NET PROFIT MARGIN × ASSET TURNOVER) (%)
DISCOUNT STORES			
Costco Companies, Inc.	1.45	3.92	5.70
Kmart Corporation	0.77	2.37	1.84
Best Buy Co., Inc.	1.13	4.06	4.59
GROCERY STORES			
Food Lion, Inc.	1.69	2.95	4.98
The Kroger Company	1.55	4.22	6.53
Safeway Inc.	2.48	2.65	6.56
DEPARTMENT STORES			
The May Department Stores Company	6.11	1.28	7.80
Dillard Department Stores, Inc.	3.90	1.19	4.62
Federated Department Stores, Inc.	3.42	1.14	3.90
SPECIALTY STORES			
Circuit City Stores, Inc.	1.18	2.74	3.23
The Limited, Inc.	2.37	2.14	5.05
The Gap, Inc.	8.20	1.95	16.00
Nordstrom, Inc.	3.84	1.69	6.50
Service Merchandise Company, Inc.	−2.64	1.78	−4.69
CATALOGS			
Spiegel, Inc.	−1.08	1.57	−1.69
Lands' End, Inc.	5.08	2.92	14.80

Total Expenses/Net Sales Ratio   You might think that the total expenses/net sales ratio would be lower for Giftstogo.com because it doesn't have to maintain stores with highly trained salespeople. Actually, the total expenses/net sales ratio is projected to be much higher for Giftstogo.com because it must hire people and have space to maintain the website, process orders, and get them ready for shipment. Also, Gifts To Go has an established clientele and a great location. Although the new website may attract some of their current customers, there is a lot of competition for gifts on the Internet. Kelly must invest a lot of money to establish awareness for her new brand—Giftstogo.com—to people who are unfamiliar with her store.

EXHIBIT **7–10**

Income Statements
for Gifts To Go
and Giftstogo.com

	GIFTS TO GO	GIFTSTOGO.COM (PROJECTED)
Net sales	$200,000	$200,000
Less: Cost of goods sold	110,000	110,000
Gross margin	90,000	90,000
Less: Total expenses	30,000	50,000
Net profit, pretax	60,000	40,000
Less: Taxes	27,000	18,000
Tax rate	45%	45%
Net profit after tax	$33,000	$22,000

ASHFORD.COM IS A LEADING INTERNET RETAILER of luxury and premium products, including new and vintage premium watches and fine writing instruments. The company's e-commerce site, located at www.ashford.com, offers an extensive selection of more than 7,000 new and vintage watches from more than 70 of the finest brands. The site also offers more than 600 different styles of fine writing instruments from 12 leading brands. Its assortment now includes more than 60 of the finest brands of fragrances, along with the latest styles of sunglasses and leather goods.

Its offering is targeted toward hardworking, upscale professionals who appreciate fine products, but lack the time and patience to visit brick-and-mortar stores. As a result it has built several features into its website to encourage customers to browse and buy. For instance, the Ashford.com A+ Program is a registry that lets customers register their designer and product preferences and schedule reminders of their special dates and anniversaries.

Like many Internet retailers, Ashford.com is not as profitable as one would hope. In fact, it had a negative profit for the year prior to March 31, 1999. Why? Let's look at the rest of Ashford.com's profit path and compare it with Tiffany & Co. Its gross margin is 14.1 percent, compared to 56.10 percent for Tiffany. Ashford.com is living up to its claim of offering customers good value with low margins. Operating expenses as a percentage of sales is 35.3 percent compared to 42 percent for Tiffany. You would expect Ashford.com's expenses to be relatively lower since it doesn't incur expenses in stores as Tiffany does. Instead, their expenses come from their Internet technology investment coupled with the high cost of establishing a new brand. In the end, even though its operating expenses were a little lower than Tiffany's, its gross margin was much lower, resulting in a negative net profit of 21.2 percent, compared to a positive 7.68 percent for Tiffany.

The turnover path also contains some interesting differences. Ashford.com's accounts receivable represent only 2.7 percent of sales, compared to 9.2 percent for Tiffany. Most of Ashford.com's sales are by cash, check, or third-party credit card such as VISA or MasterCard. Ashford.com's inventory as a percentage of total assets is 64 percent compared to 45.51 percent for Tiffany. Tiffany has significant investments in its stores, manufacturing facilities, and administrative offices—an investment that shows up as fixed assets. Ashford.com, on the other hand, has no stores and buys rather than makes its merchandise, which keeps fixed assets relatively low. Neither Ashford.com nor Tiffany has a rapid inventory turnover compared to Wal-Mart. Wal-Mart's inventory turnover is 6.35, compared to 1.56 and 1.07 for Ashford,com and Tiffany, respectively. Even though the ratios leading up to asset turnover are different, and reflect the stores' different retail formats, the asset turnovers are relatively similar: 1.16 and 1.11 for Ashford.com and Tiffany, respectively.

Turning to return on assets, Ashford.com is the clear loser. A negative net profit margin must result in a negative return on assets. The return on assets was −24.7 percent and 8.51 percent for Ashford.com and Tiffany & Co., respectively.

Source: Edgar-online.com, form S-1/A for Ashford Com Inc filed on August 3, 1999; Melanie Kletter, "E-tailer Ashford.com Planning an IPO," *WWD*, July 19, 1999, p. 25.

{Total expenses ÷ Net sales} = Total expenses/Net sales ratio

Gifts To Go: {$30,000   ÷ $200,000} = 15%
Giftstogo.com: {$50,000   ÷ $200,000} = 25%

Net Profit Margins   Although the gross margins for the two stores are projected to be the same, since Giftstogo.com is projected to have higher expenses than Gifts To Go is projected to have, Giftstogo.com is expected generate a lower net profit margin, at least in the short term.

{Net profit ÷ Net sales} = Net profit margin

Gifts To Go: {$33,000   ÷ $200,000} = 16.5%
Giftstogo.com: {$22,000   ÷ $200,000} = 11%

EXHIBIT 7-11

Balance Sheets for
Gifts To Go and
Giftstogo.com

	GIFTS TO GO	GIFTSTOGO.COM
ASSETS		
Current assets		
Merchandise inventory	$ 44,000	$22,000
Cash	2,000	0
Other current assets	3,000	2,500
Total current assets	49,000	24,500
Fixed assets	$125,000	$70,000
Total assets	$174,000	$94,500
LIABILITIES		
Current liabilities		
Accounts payable	$ 35,000	$30,000
Notes payable	7,000	5,000
Total current liabilities	$ 42,000	$35,000
Long-term liabilities	$ 10,000	$12,000
Total liabilities	$ 52,000	$47,000
OWNERS' EQUITY		
Owners' equity	$122,000	$47,500
Total liabilities and owners' equity	$174,000	$94,500

Turnover Path   Now let's compare the two stores using the turnover path. Exhibit 7–11 shows balance sheets for Gifts To Go and Giftstogo.com.

Accounts Receivable and Inventory Turnover   Like Gifts To Go, Giftstogo.com would have no accounts receivable due to taking credit cards like VISA, MasterCard, and American Express.

Giftstogo.com should have a faster projected inventory turnover than Gifts To Go because it will consolidate the inventory at one centralized distribution center that services a large sales volume, as opposed to Gifts to Go that has inventory sitting in several stores with relatively lower sales volume.

$$\{\text{Net sales} \div \text{Average inventory}\} = \text{Inventory turnover}^9$$

Gifts To Go   = {$200,000 ÷ $80,000}   = 2.5
Giftstogo.com = {$200,000 ÷ $40,000}   = 5

Fixed Assets   Gifts To Go and Giftstogo.com rent their space. Thus, their fixed assets consist of the fixtures, lighting, and other leasehold improvements in their store as well as equipment such as point-of-sale terminals and computers. Gifts to go has more invested in assets that make their store aesthetically pleasing, whereas Giftstogo.com has its investment in computer and distribution systems.

Asset Turnover   As we would expect, Giftstogo.com's projected asset turnover (2.12) is significantly higher than Gifts To Go's (1.15). Giftstogo.com is projected to have a higher inventory turnover. Its other current assets and fixed assets should be lower as well.

$$\{\text{Net sales} \div \text{Total assets}\} = \text{Asset turnover}$$

Gifts To Go   = {$200,000 ÷ $174,000}   = 1.15
Giftstogo.com = {$200,000 ÷ $94,500}   = 2.12

Return on Assets   {Net profit ÷ Total assets} = Return on assets

Gifts To Go: {$33,000   ÷ $174,000}   = 19%

Giftstogo.com: {$22,000   ÷ $94,500}   = 23%

Although Gifts To Go's net profit margin is much higher than that projected for Giftstogo.com (16.5 percent versus 11 percent), Giftstogo.com's asset turnover should be greater than Gifts To Go's (2.12 versus 1.15). When we multiply the asset turnovers by the net profit margins, the resulting return on assets ratios are similar: 19 percent for Gifts To Go and 23 percent projected for Giftstogo.com.

If Kelly believes she's receiving an acceptable return on her investment with Gifts To Go, then based on this financial analysis alone, Giftstogo.com becomes a very viable alternative. She must, however, combine this financial analysis with her findings from the strategic audit described in Chapter 6 before determining whether to proceed.

RECAP OF THE STRATEGIC PROFIT MODEL

The strategic profit model is useful to retailers because it combines two decision-making areas—margin management and asset management—so managers can examine interrelationships among them. The strategic profit model uses return on assets as the primary criterion for planning and evaluating a firm's financial performance.

The strategic profit model can also be used to evaluate financial implications of new strategies before they're implemented. For instance, suppose Kelly Bradford wishes to increase sales by 10 percent at Gifts To Go. Using the strategic profit model, she can estimate this action's impact on other parts of the strategic profit model. For instance, to increase sales, she may choose to have a sale. Lowering prices will reduce gross margin. She would have to advertise the sale and hire additional sales help, thus increasing operating expenses. So, although she may be able to achieve the 10 percent sales increase, net profit margin might go down.

Looking at the turnover path, increasing sales without an appreciable change in inventory will increase inventory turnover. Assuming other assets aren't affected, asset turnover will also increase. When she multiplies the lower net profit margin by the higher asset turnover, the resulting return on assets may remain unchanged. Retailing View 7.4 looks at the very different strategic profit model of a service retailer.

We'll look at another method of evaluating strategic options in this chapter's appendix on activity-based costing. First, however, let's see how financial performance objectives are set in retailing organizations.

SETTING PERFORMANCE OBJECTIVES

Setting performance objectives is a necessary component of any firm's strategic planning process. How would a retailer know how it has performed if it doesn't have specific objectives in mind to compare actual performance against? Performance objectives should include (1) the performance sought, including a numerical index against which progress may be measured, (2) a time frame within which the goal is to be achieved, and (3) the resources needed to achieve the objective. For example, "earning reasonable profits" isn't a good objective. It

The Strategic Profit Model of a Service Retailer: HealthSouth

HEALTHSOUTH IS THE LARGEST PROVIDER of outpatient surgery and rehabilitation health services in the United States. Now in 50 states, the United Kingdom, and Australia, HealthSouth boasts over 1,900 locations.

HealthSouth isn't just any health care provider, however. It has become the leader in outpatient rehabilitation and sports medicine centers. It provides sports medicine coverage for 2,000 high schools and 125 university and college teams, 40 to 50 professional teams, the Professional Golf Association, the Senior Professional Golf Association, the Ladies' Professional Golf Association, the Southeastern Conference, USA Hockey, USA Wrestling, and USA Volleyball. The Richard M. Scrushy/HealthSouth Sports Medicine and Sport Science Center at the Colorado Springs Olympic Complex was established by HealthSouth and the United States Olympic Committee to provide advanced training and sports medicine care to Olympic athletes.

The firm's strategic profit model seems quite different from those of the merchandise retailers we've looked at in this chapter. Let's first examine HealthSouth's profit path. It has no gross margin per se because it has no cost of goods sold. It sells only service! Operating expenses as a percentage of sales is 65 percent, compared to almost 16 and 42 percent for Wal-Mart and Tiffany, respectively. HealthSouth's net profit in 1998 was about 1 percent of sales.

The turnover path is just as different. Its accounts receivable represents 13.26 percent of total assets, compared to 3 and 28 percent for Wal-Mart and Tiffany, respectively. But inventory as a percentage of total assets is only 1.15 percent, compared to 34.15 for Wal-Mart and 54.51 percent for Tiffany. Clearly, a service provider like HealthSouth has little need for inventory.

HealthSouth's asset turnover is only .59, compared to 2.78 and 1.11 for Wal-Mart and Tiffany, respectively. So, although a service provider like HealthSouth doesn't have to maintain a heavy inventory position, it does maintain a heavy investment in the long-term assets necessary to run these facilities, that is, the real estate investment and medical equipment. For instance, the cost of a Gamma Knife used to remove brain tumors without invasive surgery is about $3 million—HealthSouth currently owns three!

HealthSouth achieved a .69 percent return on assets in 1998, compared to 8.86 for Wal-Mart and 8.52 for Tiffany. Relatively low asset turnover combined with a small net profit margin adversely affected its return on assets. One should not infer from these financial results that all service providers don't achieve high returns compared to merchandise retailers. We can see, however, why some of the strategic profit model's component ratios are different.

Source: Courtesy of HealthSouth.

doesn't provide specific goals that can be used to evaluate performance. What's reasonable? When do you want to realize the profits? A better objective would be "earning $100,000 in profit during calendar year 2002 on $500,000 investment in inventory and building."

Top-Down versus Bottom-Up Process
Setting objectives in large retail organizations entails a combination of the top-down and bottom-up approaches to planning. **Top-down planning** means that goals are set at the top of the organization and filter down through the operating levels.

In a retailing organization, top-down planning involves corporate officers developing an overall retail strategy and assessing broad economic, competitive, and consumer trends. Armed with this information, they develop performance objectives for the corporation. This overall objective is then broken down into specific objectives for each merchandise category and each region or store.

The overall strategy determines the merchandise variety, assortment, and product availability plus store size, location, and level of customer service. Then the merchandise vice presidents decide which types of merchandise are expected to grow, stay the same, or shrink. Next performance goals are established for each

Top-down planning means that goals are set at the top of the organization and filter down through the operating levels.

category manager or buyer. A category manager, discussed in Chapter 12, is like a "superbuyer" in many retail organizations.

The director of stores works on the performance objectives with each regional store manager. Next these regional managers develop objectives with their store managers. The process then trickles down to department managers in the stores.

This top-down planning is complemented by a **bottom-up planning** approach. Buyers and store managers are also estimating what they can achieve. Their estimates are transmitted up the organization to the corporate planners. Frequently there are disagreements between the goals that have trickled down from the top and those set by lower-level employees of the organization. For example, a store manager may not be able to achieve the 10 percent sales growth set for the region because a major employer in the area has announced plans to lay off 2,000 employees.

These differences between bottom-up and top-down plans must be resolved through a negotiation process involving corporate planners and operating managers. If the operating managers aren't involved in the objective-setting process, they won't accept the objectives and thus will be less motivated to achieve them.

Accountability

At each level of the retail organization, the business unit and its manager should be held accountable only for revenues and expenses it directly controls. Thus, expenses that benefit several levels of the organization (such as the labor and capital expenses incurred in operating a corporate headquarters) shouldn't be arbitrarily assigned to lower levels. In the case of a store, for example, it may be appropriate to set performance objectives based on sales and employee productivity. If the buyer lowers prices to get rid of merchandise and therefore profits suffer, then it's not fair to assess a store manager's performance based on the store's profit. (Activity-based costing, discussed in this chapter's appendix, provides a vehicle for allocating costs.)

Performance measures should only be used to pinpoint problem areas. Reasons why performance is above or below planned levels must be examined. Perhaps the people involved in setting the objectives aren't very good at making predictions. If so, they may need to be trained in forecasting. Also, a manager may misrepresent a business unit's ability to contribute to the firm's financial goals in order to get a larger inventory budget than is warranted. In either case, funds could be misallocated.

Actual performance may be different than the plan due to circumstances beyond the manager's control. For example, there may have been a recession. Assuming the recession wasn't predicted, or was more severe or lasted longer than anticipated, there are several relevant questions: How quickly were plans adjusted? How rapidly and appropriately were pricing and promotional policies modified? In short, did the manager react to salvage an adverse situation or did those reactions worsen the situation?

Performance Measures

Many factors contribute to a retailer's overall performance. Thus, it's hard to find one single measure to evaluate performance. For instance, sales is a global measure of how much activity is going on in the store.

EXHIBIT 7-12   Examples of Performance Measures Used by Retailers

LEVEL OF ORGANIZATION	OUTPUT	INPUT	PRODUCTIVITY (OUTPUT/INPUT)
Corporate (measures of entire corporation)	Net sales Net profits Growth in sales, profits	Square feet of store space Number of employees Inventory Advertising expenditures	Return on assets Asset turnover Sales per employee Sales per square foot
Merchandise management (measures for a merchandise category)	Net sales Gross margin Growth in sales	Inventory level Markdowns Advertising expenses Cost of merchandise	Gross margin return on investment (GMROI) Inventory turnover Advertising as a percentage of sales* Markdown as a percentage of sales*
Store operations (measures for a store or department within a store)	Net sales Gross margin Growth in sales	Square feet of selling areas Expenses for utilities Number of sales associates	Net sales per square foot Net sales per sales associate or per selling hour Utility expenses as a percentage of sales*

*These productivity measures are commonly expressed as an input/output.

However, a store manager could easily increase sales by lowering prices, but the profit realized on the merchandise (gross margin) would suffer as a result. Clearly, an attempt to maximize one measure may lower another. Managers must therefore understand how their actions affect multiple performance measures. It's usually unwise to use only one measure since it rarely tells the whole story.

The measures used to evaluate retail operations vary depending on (1) the level of the organization where the decision is made and (2) the resources the manager controls. For example, the principle resources controlled by store managers are space and money for operating expenses (such as wages for sales associates and utility payments to light and heat the store). Store managers focus on performance measures like sales per square foot and employee costs.

Types of Measures   Exhibit 7–12 breaks down a variety of retailers' performance measures into three types: output measures, input measures, and productivity measures. **Input measures** assess the amount of resources or money used by the retailer to achieve outputs. These inputs are used by the retailer to generate sales and profits. **Output measures** assess the results of a retailer's investment decisions. For example, sales revenue results from decisions on how many stores to build, how much inventory to have in the stores, and how much to spend on advertising. A **productivity measure** (the ratio of an output to an input) determines how effectively a retailer uses a resource.

Exhibit 7–13 shows productivity measures used at different levels of a retailing organization. This chapter has concentrated on productivity measures used at the corporate level since they are most closely tied to a retailer's overall strategy. Productivity measures used to evaluate merchandise are discussed in Chapters 12 and 13, whereas we look at productivity measures for evaluating the space in stores in Chapter 18.

In general, since productivity measures are a ratio of outputs to inputs, they can be used to compare different business units. Suppose Kelly Bradford's two stores are different sizes: One has 5,000 square feet and the other has 10,000 square feet. It's hard to compare stores' performances using just output or input

EXHIBIT 7–13   Illustrative Productivity Measures Used by Retailing Organizations

LEVEL OF ORGANIZATION	OUTPUT	INPUT	PRODUCTIVITY (OUTPUT/INPUT)
Corporate (chief executive officer)	Net profit	Owners' equity	Net profit/owners' equity = return on owners' equity
Merchandising (merchandise manager and buyer)	Gross margin	Inventory*	Gross margin/inventory* = GMROI
Store operations (director of stores, store manager)	Net sales	Square foot	Net sales/square foot

*Inventory = Average inventory at cost.

measures. The larger store will probably generate more sales and have higher expenses. But if the larger store generates $210 net sales per square foot and the smaller store generates $350 per square foot, Kelly knows that the smaller store is operating more efficiently even though it's generating lower sales.

SUMMARY This chapter explains some basic elements of retailing financial strategy and examines how retailing strategy affects the financial performance of a firm. We used the strategic profit model as a vehicle for understanding the complex interrelations between financial ratios and retailing strategy. We found that different types of retailers have different financial operating characteristics. Specifically, jewelry store chains like Tiffany generally have higher profit margins and lower turnover than discount stores like Wal-Mart. Yet, when margin and turnover are combined into return on assets, we showed that it's possible to achieve similar financial performance.

We also described some financial performance measures used to evaluate different aspects of a retailing organization. Although the return on assets ratio in the strategic profit model is appropriate for evaluating the performance of retail operating managers, other measures are more appropriate for more specific activities. For instance, gross margin return on investment (GMROI) is appropriate for buyers, whereas store managers should be concerned with sales or gross margin per square foot.

The chapter concludes with an appendix describing the use and benefits of activity-based costing. Based on contribution analysis, activity-based costing is a method of allocating the cost of all major activities a retailer performs to products, product lines, SKUs, and the like. Using activity-based costing, retailers can make more informed and profitable decisions, since they have a clear understanding of the costs associated with the different activities involved in making those decisions.

KEY TERMS

accounts payable, 217

accounts receivable, 213

accrued liabilities, 218

activity-based costing (ABC), 230

assets, 212

bottom-up planning, 226

current assets, 213

current liabilities, 217

customer returns, 208

expenses, 211

fixed assets, 216

gross margin, 211

gross profit, 211

input measure, 227

liabilities, 212

long-term liabilities, 218

net profit, 212

net sales, 208

notes payable, 218

output measure, 227

owners' equity, 212

productivity measure, 227

retained earnings, 218

stockholders' equity, 218

top-down planning, 225

DISCUSSION QUESTIONS AND PROBLEMS

1. Why must a retailer use multiple performance measures to evaluate its performance?

2. Describe how a multiple-store retailer would set its annual performance objectives.

3. Buyers' performance is often measured by their gross margin. Why is this figure more appropriate than net profit or loss?

4. How does the strategic profit model (SPM) assist retailers in planning and evaluating marketing and financial strategies?

5. Nordstrom Department Stores (a chain of high-service department stores) and Price/Costco (a chain of warehouse clubs) target different groups of customers. Which should have the higher asset turnover, net profit margin, and return on assets? Why?

6. Given the following information, construct an income statement for the Neiman Marcus Group, Inc., and determine if there was a profit or loss in 1997. (Figures are in $000.)

Sales	$2,209,891
Cost of goods sold	1,504,858
Operating expenses	524,051
Interest expense	26,330
Taxes	63,407

7. Using the following information taken from Sharper Image Corporation's 1998 balance sheet, determine the asset turnover. (Figures are in $000.)

Net sales	$215,193
Total assets	78,662
Total liabilities	49,506

8. Using the following information taken from the 1998 balance sheet and 1998 income statement for Lands' End, Inc., develop a strategic profit model. (Figures are in $000.)

Sales	$1,263,629
Cost of goods sold	675,138
Operating expenses	489,923
Interest expenses	(1,995)
Inventory	241,154
Accounts receivable	15,443
Other current assets	42,549
Accounts payable	83,743
Notes payable	0
Other current liabilities	98,270
Fixed assets	133,409
Long-term liabilities	0

9. Assume Sears is planning a special promotion for the upcoming holiday season. It has purchased 2.5 million Santa Bears, a stuffed teddy bear dressed like Santa Claus, from a vendor in Taiwan. The GMROI for the bears is expected to be 144 percent (gross margin = 24 percent and sales-to-stock ratio = 6), about average for a seasonal promotion. Besides the invoice cost of the bears, Sears will incur import fees, transportation costs from Taiwan to distribution centers and then to stores, and distribution center and store costs such as marking and handling. Since the bears arrived early in April, additional storage facilities are needed until they are shipped to the stores the first week of October. Is GMROI an adequate measure for evaluating the performance of Santa Bears? Explain your answer.

SUGGESTED READINGS

Activity-Based Costing for Food Wholesalers and Retailers. Ernst & Young LLP and the Joint Industry Project on Efficient Consumer Response, 1994.

Cokins, Gary. *Activity-Based Cost Management Making It Work: A Manager's Guide to Implementing and Sustaining an Effective ABC System.* Burr Ridge, IL: Irwin, 1996.

Compton, Ted R. "Implementing Activity-Based Costing." *The CPA Journal,* March 1996, pp. 20–27.

Fairchild's Retail Stores Financial Directory 1999. Tampa, FL: Business Guides, Inc.

Hicks, Douglas T. *Activity-Based Costing: Making It Work for Small and Mid-Sized Companies.* New York: John Wiley & Sons, 1999.

Kerin, Roger A., and Raj Sethuraman. "Exploring the Brand Value–Shareholder Value Nexus for Consumer Goods Companies." *Journal of the Academy of Marketing Science* 26, no. 4 (Fall 1998), pp. 260–73.

Lambert, Douglas M., and James R. Stock. *Strategic Logistics Management,* 3d ed. Burr Ridge, IL: Irwin, 1993.

Mecimore, Charles D., and Alice T. Bell. "Are We Ready for Fourth-Generation Activity-Based Costing?" *Management Accounting,* January 1995, pp. 22–26.

Rappaport, Alfred. *Creating Shareholder Value: The New Standard for Business Performance.* New York: Macmillan, 1986.

Raz, Tzvi, and Dan Elnathan. "Activity Based Costing for Projects." *International Journal of Project Management,* February 1999, pp. 61–67.

Ring, Lawrence J., Douglas J. Tigert, and Ray Serpkenci. "Supermarkets at Risk." *Chain Store Age,* July 1999, pp. 56–62.

Srivastava, Rajendra K., Tasaddq A. Shervani, and Liam Fahey. "Market-Based Assets and Shareholder Value: A Framework for Analysis." *Journal of Marketing* 62, no. 1 (1998), pp. 2–18.

Weigel, John R. "An Integrative Financial Statement Approach to the Strategy Value Chain." *Journal of Financial Statement Analysis* 4, no. 2 (1999), pp. 41–59.

APPENDIX

Activity-Based Costing
by Professor Kathleen Seiders,
Babson College

Activity-based costing (ABC) is a financial management tool that has been recently adopted by many retail companies.[10] This accounting method is superior to traditional methods in that it enables retailers to better understand costs and profitability. Retailers that adopt ABC gain an information-based means of improving financial analysis and performance.

In activity-based costing, all major activities within a cost center are identified and the costs of performing each are calculated. The resulting costs are then charged to cost objects, such as stores, product categories, product lines, specific products, customers, and suppliers. Using ABC to plan and evaluate merchandising performance provides an alternative to the standard gross margin and inventory turnover measures. As discussed in this chapter, maximizing these traditional measures may produce less than optimal results.

Although ABC uses general ledger data, it differs from other costing methods in that it assigns all expenses—all sales, marketing, administrative, financing, and operating costs. The process of assigning all these costs is difficult because they are typically not easily identified.

Retailers have focused on improving costing analyses for some time. For example, the direct product profit (DPP) accounting system was developed and used by food and general merchandise retailers beginning in the mid-1970s to permit the calculation of product profitability. Activity-based costing represents a more comprehensive approach because, unlike DPP, it recognizes overhead and administrative expenses as well as direct product costs.

Implementation of Activity-Based Costing   The five-step process used to conduct activity-based costing is as follows:

1. *Summarize the resources.* Organize costs by grouping those that are related. For example, people-related costs could be grouped as wages and benefits.

2. *Define the activities.* Identify the activities performed in the key departments or cost centers that represent significant work.

3. *Define the resource drivers.* Convert general ledger costs into activity costs by quantifying the relationship between resources and activities.

4. *Specify the cost objects.* Identify the focus of the profitability assessment. For example, the cost object could be a product category such as paper goods, health and beauty aids, or gourmet foods.

5. *Identify the activity drivers.* Measure the amount of activity performed in servicing the cost object. These drivers are aspects of the activity that are highly correlated with the activity cost.

An Illustration of ABC   Consider the following hypothetical example illustrated in Exhibit 7–14. Safeway is considering reducing the amount of shelf space dedicated to Pepperidge Farm's line of premium cookies in order to expand Safeway's own private-label cookie line. The company is performing an ABC analysis to evaluate the profitability of the two lines. Based on past experience, Safeway believes that, in general, private-label, ("store-brand") items offer higher profits.

Suppose Safeway's cost is $2 per unit ($24 per case of 12) for each variety of Pepperidge Farm cookies. The retail selling price is $2.60 ($31.20 per case), so

EXHIBIT 7–14

Activity-Based
Costing Profitability
Statement for
Pepperidge Farm
and Private-Label
Cookies at Safeway

	PEPPERIDGE FARM	PRIVATE-LABEL COOKIES
Retail price per case	$31.20	$27.00
Cost per case	24.00	18.00
Gross margin	7.20	9.00
Other "relevant" costs	1.50	5.00
Operating margin	5.70	4.00

the gross margin (per case) is $7.20, or 23 percent. Safeway pays $1.50 per unit ($18 per case of 12) for its private-label cookies, which retail for $2.25 ($27 per case). The gross margin per case is $9, or 33.33 percent.

The traditional gross margin measure of profitability suggests that the private-label cookies are Safeway's most attractive option. However, the "real" profit picture may be obscured because all relevant costs have not been applied directly to the products.

The cost of handling the private-label cookies must be considered because there are no distribution costs related to the Pepperidge Farm cookies, which are delivered directly to each Safeway store by the vendor (a direct-store-delivery (DSD) approach). Pepperidge Farm allows 30 days for payment and gives immediate credit for any damaged merchandise. The private-label cookies are shipped to a Safeway distribution center, stored, and then shipped to individual stores. The private-label vendor demands payment in 10 days, rather than 30, and is not responsive to damaged-goods claims. Safeway's ABC analysis, which followed the steps outlined above, included an examination of the warehouse costs related to the company's private-label cookies.

1. *Summarize the resources.* The accounts identified for this analysis included warehouse expenses related to (1) wages and benefits, (2) equipment depreciation, and (3) occupancy (depreciation and utilities).

2. *Define the activities.* The key warehouse activities identified were receiving, storing, shipping, and quality control.

3. *Define the resource drivers.* Wages were assigned based on the number of workers performing the activity. Depreciation was allocated based on each activity's use of the equipment. Occupancy costs were assigned based on square footage used by the activity.

4. *Specify the cost objects.* The cost objects in this case were initially specified as Safeway's private-label cookie line and Pepperidge Farm's cookie line.

5. *Identify the activity drivers.* Receiving was based on number of receipt transactions; storing on number of pallet positions; shipping on number of cases shipped; and inspection on a complexity factor.

The total costs (classified as operating expenses) of receiving, inspection, storage, and shipping Safeway's private-label cookie line were calculated to be $5 per case. The cost for Pepperidge Farm (primarily for receiving) was calculated at $1.50 per case. Operating margins are $5.70 per case (or 18.3 percent) for Pepperidge Farm and $4 per case (14.8 percent) for Safeway private label. The ABC analysis, unlike the traditional gross margin analysis, suggests that it would not be optimal for Safeway to expand its private-label cookie line by reducing Pepperidge Farm's shelf space.

John Konarski III, PhD
Senior Staff Vice President
of Research
International Council of
Shopping Centers

THERE'S A REASON THEY'RE called "fundamentals." It's because that's what they are: necessary to the business! Retailing and retailers have been operating under a set of fundamentals since the marketplaces of ancient Roman times up to, and including, the onslaught of the Internet. • Early in my career, when I was a professor of retailing, we stressed to our students the notion of getting merchandise to the ultimate consumer at the right place, at the right time, in the right quantities, and at the right price. Although it sounded good at the time, it meant little more to me than it did to my students. Little did I know how this one phrase would be central to what I do as senior vice president of research for the International Council of Shopping Centers, the trade group representing the shopping center industry in the United States. • During the past 100 years, and particularly during my life, retailing has undergone dramatic and, at times, overwhelming change. We've seen endless fads and fashions, designed and redesigned our stores and shopping centers, experimented with various management strategies, and employed a constant new supply of technological inventions to help us better serve our customers. • Now we struggle with trying to figure out how the Internet will change the way customers shop and how it will affect bricks-and-mortar retailers and shopping centers. Everyone connected with retailing is focused on this situation. The press constantly writes about it, retail analysts speculate about it, and retailers of all kinds search for the perfect model for this new distribution channel. • Despite these changes over time, and despite our current predicament, the answers still can be found by going back to the fundamentals: What is the best way to get merchandise to the customer at the right place and so on? Technology helps us do our jobs better, but it doesn't replace the fundamentals. No matter how "friendly" the Net becomes, no matter how many consumers have computer access, and no matter what the next technological breakthrough is, unless we focus our efforts on the fundamentals of the business, we will fail. • As increasing sophistication and rate of change become the hallmarks of retailing in the 21st century, it's important not to get caught up in the hype of technology advancement and forget what retailing is really about. Actually, the retail business doesn't change that much over time. Save this book. Later on in your career, every once in a while, take out your old Levy and Weitz textbook, open up to the first chapter, and read about the fundamentals of this great business. They still, and will, guide everything we do.

CHAPTER EIGHT

Retail Locations

QUESTIONS

- What types of locations are available to retailers?
- What are the relative advantages of these types of locations?

FOR SEVERAL REASONS, store location is often the most important decision made by a retailer. First, location is typically the prime consideration in a customer's store choice. For instance, when choosing where you're going to have your car washed, you usually pick the location closest to your home or work.

Second, location decisions have strategic importance because they can be used to develop a sustainable competitive advantage. As Chapter 6 said, retailers can change their pricing, service, and merchandise assortments in a relatively short time. However, location decisions are harder to change because retailers frequently have to either make substantial investments to buy and develop real estate or commit to long-term leases with developers. It's not unusual, for instance, for a national chain store to sign a lease for 7 to 10 years. Thus, retailers with excellent locations have a strategic advantage competitors can't easily copy.

Location decisions have become even more important in recent years. First, there are more retailers (particularly national chains like The Gap and Toys "R" Us) opening new locations, making the better locations harder to obtain. This problem is made more complex by a slowdown in both population growth and new shopping center construction. A retailer may find a suitable location, but high rent, complicated leases, and expensive fixturing and remodeling can make it very costly.

This chapter describes the types of locations available to retailers and the relative advantages of each. We then examine factors that retailers should consider when choosing a particular site within a shopping center. In the next chapter, the topic of location continues. Chapter 9 examines issues in selecting appropriate regions of the country and trade areas for locating retail stores. (A **trade area** is a geographic sector that contains potential customers for a particular retailer or shopping center.) Specifically, we examine the qualitative and quantitative issues that define the sales potential for a retail location. As such, Chapters 8 and 9 are designed to be studied together. The information box on the next page examines issues that are particularly salient to service retailers.

HAVING A GOOD LOCATION MAY BE even more important for a service retailer than it is for a merchandise retailer. After all, services are a perishable commodity. If it isn't available when the customer wants it because of a bad location, there is no second chance. A sustainable competitive advantage will accrue to those service retailers who maintain convenient locations.

Consider, for instance, automatic teller machines (ATMs). Not too many years ago, the only way a bank customer could get cash or make a withdrawal was via a face-to-face interaction with a teller during the bank's limited hours. Interestingly, many banks are still closed during the hours that people have time to go to the bank such as early morning, evenings, and weekends. Not only have ATMs partially solved the "bankers' hours" problem by being open 24 hours a day, but they are conveniently located virtually everywhere in the Western world.

For other service providers, however, their physical location is unimportant or even "virtual." Dog groomers, lawn care specialists, pest exterminators, and delivery services like UPS and Federal Express go to their customers. Thousands of firms perform their services over the Internet. For instance, one can find help doing research for school (lexis-nexis.com/universe), evaluating a car purchase (Kelly Blue Book at kbb.com), or selecting a retail site (claritas.com).

TYPES OF RETAIL LOCATIONS

Many types of locations are available for retail stores—each with its own strengths and weaknesses. Choosing a particular site involves evaluating a series of trade-offs. These trade-offs generally concern the cost versus the value of the site for a particular type of retailer. For instance, the best location for a 7-Eleven convenience store isn't necessarily—or usually—the best location for a Saks Fifth Avenue specialty store.

Retailers have three basic types of sites to choose from: a central business district (CBD), a shopping center, or a freestanding location. They can also choose kiosks, which are selling spaces typically found in mall common areas. Finally, retailers can locate in a mixed-use development. The following sections describe each type of location and present criteria for choosing a particular site.

Central Business Districts (CBDs)

The **central business district** is the traditional downtown business area in a city or town. Due to its business activity, it draws many people into the area. Also, people must go to the area for work. The CBD is also the hub for public transportation, and there is a high level of pedestrian traffic. Finally, the most successful CBDs for retail trade are those with a large number of residents living in the area.[1]

But central business district locations in the United States have their drawbacks. Retailers can be dubious about CBDs because high security may be required, shoplifting can be especially common, and parking is often a problem. High crime rates, urban decay, and no control over the weather can discourage shoppers from the suburbs. Shopping in the evening and on weekends can be particularly slow in many CBDs. Also, unlike modern shopping centers, CBDs tend to suffer from a lack of planning. One block may contain upscale boutiques while the next may be populated with low-income housing, so consumers may not have enough interesting retailers that they can visit on a shopping trip.

Some central business districts have undergone a process of **gentrification** in which old buildings are torn down or restored with new offices, housing developments, and retailers.[3] Why is it happening?

Refact The annual cost for The Gap's 19,000–square-foot flagship store on the Champs-Elysées in Paris is over $10 million.[2]

- Gentrification is part of a natural evolution in retailing. Starting in the 1950s, retailers followed their customers to the suburbs by locating in suburban shopping centers. As cities restored their urban areas, people began to move back. Retailers simply continue to follow their customers to where they live and work.

- Developers aren't building as many malls as before, and it's often hard to find a good location in a successful mall.

- Successful national chain stores like The Gap, The Limited, and Starbucks need these locations to fuel their expansion.

- These same chains are finding that occupancy costs in CBDs compare favorably to malls.

- Cities often provide significant incentives to locate in urban centers. Shopper's World in Detroit, for instance, is a discount department store that successfully targets the urban poor. A significant property tax incentive was provided to the landlord as an inducement to enter a neighborhood in the urban core. Not only is the store very successful, but it has generated employment for 200 people—most from the immediate vicinity.

Many cities use entertainment to attract people to the gentrified CBD. Craft and cooking fairs, horse-drawn carriages, sidewalk cafes, and historical points of interest draw people to downtown shopping areas in cities like San Francisco, New Orleans, San Antonio, Denver, Cincinnati, and Orlando.

Central business district gentrification in larger cities isn't always successful. It's hard to get people to drive in from the suburbs just to find merchandise similar to what they can find at a shopping center close to home. Also, today's value-oriented, back-to-basics customer isn't likely to be attracted to these redeveloped areas since many are populated by high-end retailers.

Another side of retailing in the central business district is the opportunities found in the inner city. The inner city is typically a high-density area consisting of apartment buildings populated primarily by ethnic groups: African Americans, Hispanics, and Asians. Although many national chains have a strong presence in inner cities, experts believe that there is an unmet annual demand of close to $100 billion.[4] Importantly, these customers "desire to buy branded merchandise from nationally recognized retailers in the neighborhoods where they live."[5] Although income levels are lower in inner cities than in other neighborhoods in a particular region, most inner-city retailers achieve a higher sales volume and often higher margins, resulting in higher profits.

Successful operations in inner cities, however, require special attention.[6] Senior management must be committed to inner-city initiatives. Retailers must do their marketing research and real estate homework before entering these markets. The best, most experienced, and culturally sensitive managers should be used in these locations. The stores, their managers, and employees should be integrally involved in the community. Finally, assortments must be customized to the specific needs of the trade area. Retailing View 8.1 describes how former basketball star "Magic" Johnson is investing in urban retailing.

The gentrification process on "Main Street" appears to be more successful, however. **"Main Street"** is the CBD located in the traditional shopping area of smaller towns, or a secondary business district in a suburb or within a larger city. Main Streets share most of the characteristics of the primary CBD. But their

Refact What are the most expensive shopping streets in the world? Fifth Ave. (48th to 58th St. in New York City) costs $580 per square foot, 57th St. (5th Ave. to Madison Ave. in New York City) costs $500, Oxford St. (London) costs $400, Madison Ave. (57th to 72nd St. in New York City) costs $375, and Ave. des Champs-Elysées (Paris) costs $360.[7]

IN 13 UNPARALLELED YEARS IN THE National Basketball Association, Earvin "Magic" Johnson rewrote the record books and dazzled fans with his no-look passes and gorgeous perimeter jump shots. He also led the Los Angeles Lakers to five championships. After he announced to the world in 1991 that he had contracted HIV, many thought that was the end. Instead, for Johnson, that was just the beginning. "People thought I was going to go away," he says. "But I never planned on going anywhere."

Rather, he took his game to a different arena, one where the obstacles are higher and the challenges greater. His new career began with a relatively modest partnership with Loews Cineplex Entertainment, formerly Sony Retail Entertainment. After doing some research, Magic and his partners realized that approximately 32 to 35 percent of the movie audience is minority, but there are generally few theaters in minority neighborhoods. They were driving 30 to 40 minutes to get to a theater. So it seemed natural to build movie theaters in urban neighborhoods across the country.

With the theaters in place, the next step was finding other businesses that would complement the theme. Johnson and his partners didn't have to look far. They built theaters and waited for quality sit-down casual restaurants to follow. What they found was an industry that was very much like the theater industry. Either through the franchise holders or the compa-

No longer on the basketball court, Magic Johnson now spends much of his time investing in urban retailing.

nies in charge, eateries weren't willing to commit to urban locations. They had customers coming in saying they loved the theaters, but they had to go all the way across town if they wanted to get something to eat. So, next Magic collaborated with Starbucks and TGI Fridays.

Source: Eric L. Smith, "The Magic Touch!" *Black Enterprise*, May 1999, pp. 74–82; and Gersh Kuntzman, "Earvin's Magic Bullet: Johnson Is Showing Big Chains They Can Be Profitable in Harlem," *New York Post*, May 9, 1999, p. 62.

---

occupancy costs are generally lower than a primary CBD's. They do not draw as many people as the primary CBD because fewer people work in the area, and fewer stores generally mean a smaller overall selection. Finally, Main Streets typically don't offer the entertainment and recreational activities available in the more successful primary CBDs.

Main Street isn't new to national retailers.[8] Woolworth, Kresges, and McCrory's were Main Street's mainstays in the past. Today, however, Main Street locations across the United States have The Gap, Crate & Barrel, J. Crew, The Limited, Sunglass Hut, and garden emporium Smith & Hawken interspersed with local, independent merchants as tenants. Even General Cinema Theaters, normally found in malls, are returning to Main Street. Saks Fifth Avenue is opening small stores in several Main Street locations. These Saks stores carry an edited stock selection from full-line Saks stores with an emphasis on frequently purchased categories such as cosmetics, shoes, and intimate apparel. Why does Saks find Main Streets so appealing? Because that's where its core customers—affluent women and men between 35 and 45 years old—live and shop already.

Some drawbacks of CBDs and Main Streets in the United States are not found in cities and towns in other industrialized countries, particularly in Europe. Retailing View 8.2 examines how Main Street locations in Europe are fighting to maintain their traditional advantage over the encroachment of large retailers.

Refact Home Depot is launching Villager's Hardware stores, while Staples is opening Express Staples stores. These smaller versions of their "regular" stores are designed to compete with local retailers in downtowns and strip centers.[9]

DURING THE 1990S EUROPEAN RETAILING HAS been changing at the expense of the traditional mom-and-pop retail stores. In the past, mom-and-pop stores were the town or village meeting place. The locals would shop at these stores for convenience and service and because the owner was their neighbor.

Yet in most of Europe, the number of small and medium-size stores has fallen drastically over the past several years. Downtown and corner stores are threatened with extinction as suburban superstores selling everything under one roof—from food and cosmetics to clothing and electronics—become more popular. For example, in Italy, the number of superstores doubled between 1988 and 1993. The two countries experiencing the largest expansion of superstores are Germany (in particular, what was East Germany) and the Commonwealth of Independent States (formerly the USSR).

In countries where this change has been occurring steadily over the past few years, local governments have tried to restrain superstores' growth by limiting their size, thus helping local entrepreneurs compete. For instance, in metropolitan Norwich, England, a horse trots down a dirt lane. It may sound sleepy and pastoral, but this is all happening only three miles from the center of this county capital of 250,000. The nearby downtown has more than 500 shops and 200 restaurants, an open-air market, and a new mall that lures a quarter of a million shoppers into the city center each week.

Were this an American city of similar size, the dirt lane no doubt would be replaced by a highway, the plowed field by a Wal-Mart, and the meadows by a multiplex cinema. European cities such as Norwich like to do things differently, partly because they have less space and partly because they take great pride in their heritage. Strict planning and greenbelt laws force a sharp division between town and country. Suburbs are few. There is no place for the urban area to sprawl.

The efforts help Main Streets thrive and protect the underdeveloped countryside. The London-based Association of Town Center Management says 80 percent of United Kingdom retail sales are still conducted in towns, despite a crusade by food superstores, mall developers, and other big retailers that want to locate outside downtown. In the United States, only 4 percent of the retail market is still downtown, according to the International Downtown Association in Washington D.C.

But preservation comes at a cost for Europe. The limits on out-of-town retailing reduce competition and retailing efficiency, causing higher prices. Looking for a Trivial Pursuit game? It will cost about $55 in downtown Norwich. A short-sleeve Polo shirt from Ralph Lauren? $90.

What's more, the protection of town centers may also be a culprit behind Europe's chronic unemployment woes. A McKinsey & Co. study said policies such as strict zoning laws "represent the most obvious and easily correctable barriers to increased employment" in retail.

Toys "R" Us, which has located 41 of its 49 U.K. stores out of town, has tried repeatedly to build a store in the Norwich area that would bring 150 new jobs. But it has been consistently rejected by Norwich and its neighbors. Phillip Kerrigan, after buying a toy for his daughter at Langleys (a pricey shop in town), says he isn't sorry the Toys "R" Us application was rejected. "I'd come into the city anyway. I want it to be a going concern, not a row of empty shops."

The rewards of Norwich's efforts: It has kept 95 percent of nonfood sales in the town center. The retail store occupancy rate is 95 percent as well.

Source: Cacilie Rohwedder, "Europe's Smaller Food Shops Face Finis," *The Wall Street Journal*, May 12, 1993, pp. B1, B7; Dana Milbank, "Guarded by Greenbelts, Europe's Town Centers Thrive," *The Wall Street Journal*, May 3, 1995, pp. B1, B9; and "Global Trends Suggest Large Retailers Will Dominate," *National Home Center News*, September 21, 1998, p. 21.

Shopping Centers

From the 1950s through the 1980s, retailing declined in many central business districts, while suburban shopping centers grew as populations shifted to the suburbs. Life in the suburbs has created a need for stores a short drive from home. Large shopping centers provide an assortment of merchandise that often exceeds the CBD's. Combining many stores under one roof creates a synergy that attracts more customers than if the stores had separate locations. It's not uncommon, for instance, for one department store's sales to increase after a competing store enters a shopping center.

The term *shopping center* has been evolving since the early 1950s.[10] A **shopping center** is a group of retail and other commercial establishments that is planned, developed, owned, and managed as a single property. The two main

EXHIBIT **8–1**   Shopping Center Definitions

TYPE	CONCEPT	SQ. FT. INCLUDING ANCHORS	NUMBER OF ANCHORS	TYPE OF ANCHORS	TRADE AREA*
STRIP CENTERS Neighborhood	Convenience	30,000–150,000	1 or more	Supermarket	3 miles
Community	General merchandise; convenience	100,000–350,000	2 or more	Discount dept. store; supermarket; drug; home improvement; large specialty discount apparel	3–7 miles
Power	Category-dominant anchors; few small tenants	250,000–600,000	3 or more	Category killer; home improvement; discount department store; warehouse club; off-price	5–10 miles
SHOPPING MALLS Regional	General merchandise; fashion (typically enclosed)	400,000–800,000	2 or more	Full-line department store; junior department store; mass merchant; discount department store; fashion apparel	5–15 miles
Superregional	Similar to regional but has more variety and assortment	800,000+	3 or more	Full-line department store; junior department store; mass merchant; fashion apparel	5–25 miles
Fashion/ specialty	Higher-end, fashion-oriented	80,000–250,000	N/A	Fashion	5–15 miles
Outlet	Manufacturers' outlet stores	50,000–400,000	N/A	Manufacturers' outlet stores	25–75 miles
Theme/festival	Leisure; tourist-oriented	80,000–250,000	N/A	Restaurants; entertainment	N/A

*The area from which 60 to 80 percent of the center's sales originate.

Source: International Council of Shopping Centers.

configurations of shopping centers are strip centers and malls. **Strip centers** usually have parking directly in front of the stores. Open canopies may connect the store fronts, but a strip center does not have enclosed walkways linking the stores. **Malls,** on the other hand, have a pedestrian focus. Customers park in outlying areas and walk to the stores. Traditional malls are enclosed, with a climate-controlled walkway between two facing strips of stores.

The International Council of Shopping Centers has defined eight principal shopping center types, as shown in Exhibit 8–1.[11]

Strip Shopping Centers   There are three types of strip shopping centers: the neighborhood center, the community center, and the power center. Strip centers have been successful in the United States because they offer customers convenient locations, easy parking, and relatively low rents for retailers. The neighborhood centers of today have fewer mom-and-pop stores than in the past. Instead, there are more national tenants like Blockbuster Video, Little Caesars, and Walgreens. National specialty store chains like Payless Shoe Source are able to compete effectively in strip centers against their rival stores in malls. They can offer lower prices, partly because of the lower rents incurred by being in a community center, plus their customers can drive right up to the door. Strip centers have started to take on nontraditional service-oriented tenants. (See Retailing View 8.3).

THE INNOVATIVE TENANT MOVING INTO SPACE formerly oc-cupied by Laneco Department Store in Allentown, Pennsylva-nia's Trexler Mall is not a multiscreen theater or bookstore that serves cups of caffe latte with its literature. Rather, the new tenant in this supermarket-anchored strip center will be the Wellness Place, a 50,000–square-foot medical facility with outpatient services provided by a local hospital. The Wellness Place is not just another medical building. It will also contain retail and food shops.

Medical and other service tenants are hardly as sexy as entertainment retail, which gets most of the credit for breath-ing new life into today's shopping centers. But service should not be overlooked. Many strip developers say nontraditional tenants are quickly and quietly becoming a greater part of a strip's landscape.

The increase in these types of tenants, particularly health care and financial services, can be traced to changes in their respective industries as well as to retail trends affecting unen-closed shopping centers. Category killers such as Staples are expanding to larger prototypes and supermarkets are opening more boutique shops within their stores. Thus, there is less room—and less need—for small specialty shops. That leaves holes for nontraditional retailers such as check-cashing stores.

Strip center developers also report doing more deals with chains of orthodontics practices. One prominent company is Orthodontics Centers of America. Because 80 percent of its patients are children, it looks to locate in strip centers or pro-fessional buildings near retailers with a complementary con-sumer base, such as Toy "R" Us and Home Depot.

Another trend bringing more health care facilities to shopping centers is the aging population. By 2000, people 50 years and older will account for about 29 percent of the popu-

This Loyola Family Health Center is located in an untraditional location—a strip center.

lation, according to the U.S. Bureau of the Census. This mar-ket not only needs medical attention, but wants it close to home. As a result, it seems only natural to revamp unused re-tail space in community centers to house medical practices that cater to this powerful demographic.

On another front, hospitals needing more convenient and cost-effective ways to reach out and treat people are opening more outpatient, satellite facilities in locations like community shopping centers, where space and parking already exist. By locating away from a medical campus, hospitals can cut over-head costs, increase visibility, and improve access.

Source: Joanne Gordon, "The Service Side of Strips," *Chain Store Age,* February 1998, pp. 136–38; and "Renovation Case Study: Spruced Up by Office Space," *Shopping Center World,* May 30, 1999.

Neighborhood Centers A neighborhood center is designed to provide conven-ience shopping for the day-to-day needs of consumers in the immediate neigh-borhood. Roughly half of these centers are anchored by a supermarket, while about a third have a drugstore anchor. These anchors are supported by stores of-fering sundries, food, and a variety of personal services such as barber shops and dry cleaners.

Community Centers A community center typically offers a wider range of ap-parel and other soft goods than the neighborhood center does. Among the more common anchors are supermarkets, super drugstores, and discount department stores. Community center tenants sometimes include off-price stores or category killers selling such items as apparel, home improvement/furnishings, toys, shoes, pet supplies, and electronics and sporting goods.

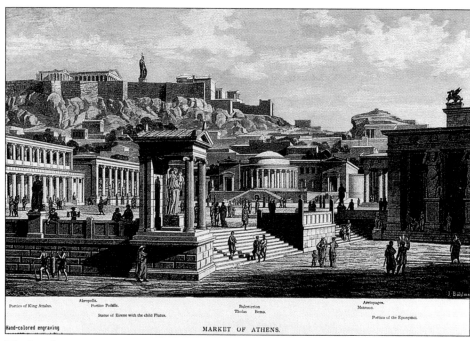

The first shopping center, a marketplace with retail stores, was the Agora at the foot of the Parthenon in Athens in 600 B.C. It was the center of all commerce, politics, and entertainment in ancient Greece.
Source: John Fleischman, "In Classic Athens, a Market Trading in Currency of Ideas," Smithsonian 24 (July 1993), pp. 38–47.

Of the eight center types, community centers encompass the widest range of formats. For example, certain centers that are anchored by a large discount department store refer to themselves as discount centers. Others with a high percentage of square footage allocated to off-price retailers can be termed off-price centers.

Power Centers   This type of center is dominated by several large anchors, including discount department stores (Target), off-price stores (Marshalls), warehouse clubs (Costco), or category killers (also known as "big-box" stores) such as Home Depot, Office Depot, Circuit City, Sports Authority, PETsMART, and Toys "R" Us. Unlike the centers previously discussed, a power center often includes several freestanding (unconnected) anchors and only a minimum number of small specialty tenants. They are typically unenclosed in a strip center configuration, or they can be arranged in a "village" cluster.

Power centers were virtually unknown a decade ago, but have become the mainstay of shopping center development activity. The typical new power center has increased in size throughout the 1990s. Many are now larger than some regional malls. Why have they become so popular? First and foremost, their tenants have experienced tremendous growth and prosperity, and there are new entries into the category killer arena all the time. A power center is a natural location for these large tenants. They don't want to pay the high rents of regional shopping malls and they benefit from the synergy of being with other big-box stores. Also, shoppers are seeking "value" alternatives to the stores found in shopping malls.[12]

Refact The first power center featuring a general merchandise discount store, category specialists, off-price retailers, and warehouse clubs was opened in Coloma, California, in 1986.[13]

Shopping Malls Shopping malls have several advantages over alternative locations. First, because of the many different types of stores, the merchandise assortments available within those stores, and the opportunity to combine shopping with entertainment, shopping malls have become the Main Street for today's shoppers. Teenagers hang out and meet friends, older citizens in Nikes get their exercise by walking the malls, and families make trips to the mall an inexpensive form of entertainment (as long as they don't buy anything). To enhance the total shopping experience, many malls incorporate food and entertainment.

The second major advantage of locating in a shopping mall is that the tenant mix can be planned. Shopping mall owners control the number of different types of retailers so that customers can have a one-stop shopping experience with a well-balanced assortment of merchandise. For instance, it's important to have several women's clothing stores in a major mall to draw in customers. Yet, too many such stores could jeopardize any one store's success. Mall managers also attempt to create a complementary tenant mix. They like to have all stores that appeal to certain target markets (such as all upscale specialty clothing stores) located together. Using this approach, customers know what types of merchandise they can expect to find in a particular mall or location within a mall. Managers also strive for a good mix between shopping and specialty goods stores. A strong core of shopping goods stores, like shoe stores, brings people to the mall. Specialty stores, like computer software stores, also bring shoppers to the mall. While specialty store customers are in the mall, they'll likely be attracted to other stores.

The third advantage of planned shopping malls is that individual retailers don't have to worry about their external environment. The mall's management takes care of maintenance of common areas. Mall tenants can look forward to a strong level of homogeneity with the other stores. For instance, most major malls enforce uniform hours of operation. Many malls even control the external signage used for window displays and sales.

Although planned shopping centers are an excellent site option for many retailers, they have some disadvantages. First, mall rents are higher than those of some freestanding sites and many central business districts. As a result, retailers that require large stores, such as home improvement centers, typically seek other options. Second, some tenants may not like mall managers' control of their operations. They can, for instance, dictate store hours and window displays. Finally, competition within shopping centers can be intense. It may be hard for small specialty stores to compete directly with large department stores. In the past few years, some shopping centers have had a particularly hard time keeping their space rented. Retailing View 8.4 shows how they've addressed this problem.

Regional Centers This type of center provides general merchandise (a large percentage of which is apparel) and services in full depth and variety. Its main attractions are its anchors: traditional, mass-merchant, or discount department stores or fashion specialty stores. A typical regional center is usually enclosed with an inward orientation of the stores connected by a common walkway, while parking surrounds the outside perimeter.

Superregional Centers Similar to a regional center, but because of its larger size, a superregional center has more anchors and a deeper selection of merchandise, while it draws from a larger population base. As with regional centers, the typical configuration is an enclosed mall, frequently with multilevels. Exhibit 8–2 lists the biggest shopping centers in the United States.

Refact Thirty-four percent of U.S. consumers indicated they shop less in malls than the previous year and only 11 percent said they shopped more frequently. They noted three reasons for fewer mall visits: "merchandise too expensive," "don't need to buy as much as I used to," and don't "have enough time to shop in malls." The average number of trips to a mall per month was 1.97.[14]

Refact Marshall Field's opened the first suburban department stores in Evanston, Lake Forest, and Oak Park, Illinois, in 1930.[15]

SHOPPING MALLS ARE FACING COMPETITION from power centers, outlet centers, catalogs, the Internet, and other retail locations. Many of today's shoppers are looking for "value" alternatives to stores found in shopping malls. Also, the apparel business, which makes up a large percentage of mall tenants, has continued to be weak, causing some specialty store chains to close. The result is lots of empty space in America's shopping malls.

What are they doing about their problem? Mall owners are turning their centers into traditional town squares with lots of entertainment opportunities. They believe if they can encourage people to spend more time in the mall, people will spend more money there. The owners are renting to nontraditional mall tenants like dry cleaners, doctors' offices, and even chapels—everything that you would have found in a Town Square in the 1950s. Others are forging links to their communities by opening wellness centers, libraries, city halls, and children's play areas. Some malls view their new role as a family entertainment center.

For example, the new Circle Center mall in Indianapolis has no shops on the fourth floor. Instead, you can play virtual reality games like throwing "virtual" grenades at your friends wearing Space Age wraparound goggles. If you don't want to play games, you can go to a movie, theme restaurant, or bar.

But some industry professionals warn that not enough thought is given to the costs and sometimes less desirable impact of entertainment tenants. Some don't consider, for instance, how existing customers and tenants will be affected. Some entertainment formats, after all, can be teen magnets, and these sometimes do not coexist with older apparel customers, who have always been the industry's bread and butter. Careful attention also must be paid to where entertainment is placed to make sure it helps, rather than hinders, existing tenants.

Although some entertainment providers are proven traffic draws, many lack the resources to pay the high rents paid by their apparel retailer predecessors. Does this mean they should be viewed as loss leaders? Not necessarily, as long as they draw some people who otherwise wouldn't come to the mall, the other mall tenants should be willing to supplement the cost of having them there.

To help keep their parents shopping, some malls provide entertainment for their kids.

A more extreme approach to revitalizing a mall is known as demalling. **Demalling** usually involves demolishing a mall's small shops, scrapping its common space and food courts, enlarging the sites once occupied by department stores, and adding more entrances onto the parking lot. For example, Anaheim Plaza was one of the first enclosed malls in Orange County, California, near Disneyland. During the 1980s, it had lost most of its original glamour. Its owner bulldozed most of the mall and built in its place a string of stores, opening onto a parking lot. The new tenants include a Wal-Mart, CompUSA, Old Navy, RadioShack, Petco, and Payless Shoes.

Source: Kevin Kenyon, "Entertainment's Not Fun for Everyone," *Shopping Centers Today,* April 1998, p. 5–6; James R. Lowry, "The Life Cycle of Shopping Centers," *Business Horizons,* January–February 1997, pp. 77–86; Mitchell Pacelle, "The Aging Shopping Mall Must Either Adapt or Die," *The Wall Street Journal,* April 16, 1996, pp. B1, B16; Sharon Edelson, "Regional Malls Borrow Town Square Concept as Apparel Sales Fall," *Women's Wear Daily,* May 8, 1996, pp. 1, 8–9; and Mitchell Pacelle, "Malls Add Fun and Games to Attract Shoppers," *The Wall Street Journal,* January 23, 1996, pp. B1–B9.

EXHIBIT 8–2

The Largest U.S.
Shopping Malls

NAME	LOCATION	GROSS LEASABLE SPACE IN SQUARE FEET
Mall of America	Bloomington, MN	4,200,000
Del Amo Fashion Center	Torrance, CA	3,000,000
South Coast	Costa Mesa, CA	2,900,000
Plaza/Crystal Court Woodfield Mall	Schaumburg, IL	2,700,000
Sawgrass Mills	Sunrise, FL	2,300,000

Source: "The List: Shop City," *Business Week,* July 28, 1997, p. 23.

Refact On any given day, Mall of America has enough people in it to qualify as the third largest city in the state. It has more than 42 million visitors each year—more than Disney World, the Grand Canyon, and Graceland combined.[17]

Near Minneapolis, Minnesota, Mall of America—the largest superregional shopping center in the United States—is designed to appeal to all of the people all of the time. Hence the name, Mall of America. It has an interesting combination of upscale and off-price retailers geared to provide one-stop shopping for consumers with various sizes of pocketbooks. Inside are 4.2 million square feet, 2.5 million of which are devoted to retail space! This is equivalent to four regional shopping centers connected together. It houses four department stores, over 400 other shops, 45 restaurants, nine nightclubs, 14 cinema screens, 12,750 on-site parking spaces, a roller coaster, a seven-acre Knott's Camp Snoopy theme park, Lego City, and a synthetic rain forest.[16]

INTERNET EXERCISE   The largest mall in the United States is the Mall of America in Minnesota. Go to mallofamerica.com and take a tour. Do you think retailers in the mall complement each other? Why?

Mall of America in Minnesota is America's largest shopping mall—4.2 million square feet, including a seven-acre Knott's Camp Snoopy Theme Park.

Fashion/Specialty Centers   A fashion/specialty center is composed mainly of upscale apparel shops, boutiques, and gift shops carrying selected fashions or unique merchandise of high quality and price. These centers need not be anchored, although sometimes gourmet restaurants, drinking establishments, and theaters can function as anchors. The physical design of these centers is very sophisticated, emphasizing a rich decor and high-quality landscaping.

Fashion/specialty centers usually are found in trade areas having high income levels, in tourist areas, or in some central business districts. These centers' trade area may be large because of the specialty nature of the tenants and their products. Customers are more likely to travel great distances to shop for specialty products sold at nationally known shops such as Neiman Marcus and Ralph Lauren/Polo than for other types of goods.

A great example of a fashion/specialty center is the newly renovated Sommerset Collection in the wealthy Detroit, Michigan, suburb of Troy. Although the mall is over 25 years old, it has recently become the fashion focus of Michigan and Western Ontario. The owners believed that their upscale customers were traveling to trendy shops in New York and Chicago, so they expanded the mall and brought in anchor stores like Neiman Marcus, Hudson's, Nordstrom, and Saks Fifth Avenue as well as specialty shops like F.A.O. Schwarz, Crate & Barrel, and Rand McNally. Mall management offers customers a variety of services, including free valet parking and car washes, as well as complimentary beverages from a cafe in the mall.

Outlet Centers   Outlet centers consist mostly of manufacturers' outlet stores selling their own brands, supposedly at a discount. These centers also sometimes include off-price retailers such as T.J. Maxx and Burlington Coat Factory or retailer clearance centers like Neiman Marcus' Last Call or Saks Fifth Avenue's Off Fifth. As a result of the shifting tenant mix in some of these centers, various industry experts now refer to outlet centers as value centers or value megamalls. Similar to power centers, a strip configuration is most common, although some are enclosed malls, and others can be arranged in a "village" cluster.

Refact Vanity Fair opened its first store exclusively for their employees in Reading, Pennsylvania, in 1970, starting the factory outlet concept.[18]

At outlet malls like this, value retailers are keeping customers on-site two to three times longer than their full-price counterparts.

Outlet centers have progressed rather quickly from no-frills warehouses to well-designed buildings with landscaping, gardens, and food courts that make them hard to distinguish from more traditional shopping centers. The newest outlet centers have a strong entertainment component, including movie theaters and theme restaurants, comprising about 15 to 20 percent of the leasable area.[19] Mall developers believe that these entertainment concepts help keep people on the premises longer. Outlet center tenants have also upgraded their offerings by adding credit, dressing rooms, and high-quality fixtures and lighting. There are now more than 10,000 outlet stores in the United States.

Manufacturers have opened so many such stores that they can no longer fill them with irregulars and overruns. So outlet tenants now offer first-quality, full-line merchandise. Although outlet-mall developers typically require their tenants to cut at least 20 percent off the suggested retail price, many shoppers are finding that they can do just as well or better at the regional mall closer to home.[20]

Outlet centers are often located some distance from regional shopping centers so outlet tenants don't compete directly for department and specialty store customers, although outlet mall developers and their tenants are becoming less sensitive to the wishes of traditional regional mall tenants. For instance, Prime Outlets in Hagerstown, Maryland, is a short distance from Baltimore and Washington D.C.[21] Outlet centers can be located in strong tourist areas. For instance, since shopping is a favorite vacation pastime, and Niagara Falls attracts 15 million tourists per year, the 1.2 million–square-foot Factory Outlet Mega Mall in Niagara Falls, New York, is a natural location for an outlet center. Some center developers actually organize bus tours to bring people hundreds of miles to their malls. As a result, the primary trade area for some outlet centers is 50 miles or more.

The future of outlet centers in the United States is uncertain.[22] After years of growth, recent trends are down. From 1988 to 1997, the number of outlet centers roughly tripled from 108 to 329. By the end of 1998, there were only 301. Also, many big-name designers whose stores often anchor these malls have been having mixed results. Reasons for the downturn in popularity are building in less productive locations, growing competition from other retail venues, and consumers' increasing sophistication.

While there may be a downturn in outlet centers in the United States, their popularity is beginning to take off in other areas like Japan (see Retailing View 8.5) and Europe. Some believe that in the EU, even the bad centers make money. In some centers, off-price apparel must be reduced by at least 30 percent and high fashion clothes must be cut by a minimum of 50 percent. Low price is not the only driving force for expansion of outlet malls in Europe. There these centers play an important role in brand promotion. For instance, brand recognition was a key motive when Reebok opened outlets in Europe. Reebok's stores are quite successful there, enjoying about 60 percent more sales than a typical American store has.[23]

Refact Customers typically spend two to three times longer in a value center than in a regional mall primarily because of the deep assortment of particular brands.[24]

INTERNET EXERCISE The Mills Corporation is the largest developer of outlet malls in the United States Go to Millscorp.com. Determine the similarities and differences between the Mill's outlet centers. Which is nearest to you?

ON ANY GIVEN SATURDAY more than 20,000 people venture into an industrial district of the port city of Yokohama, Japan, and converge on a fake New England fishing village named Sawtucket.

Sawtucket has a clock tower, quaint storefronts, and windmills. But the big lure isn't ersatz Americana. It's shopping. Within the Sawtucket complex, which opened in September 1998, is Yokohama Bayside Marina Shops and Restaurants, a factory outlet mall offering famous brands—J. Crew, Eddie Bauer, Reebok, and the like—at bargain prices. Crowds of yen-pinching consumers are heeding the call.

A familiar retail format in the United States, the outlet mall is a revolutionary retailing concept in Japan. For decades, Japanese retailers had assumed, with considerable reason, that consumers wanted only the newest versions of products. And manufacturers avoided selling leftovers openly, often destroying inventory so as not to risk hurting their brand images or annoying department stores that sold at list price.

Then came national economic distress, overturning the assumptions of retailers and altering the attitudes of consumers, who increasingly patronized second-hand stores and discounters. Today, factory outlet malls can be found in or near Japan's big cities and are increasingly popular with shoppers.

In the past, Japanese tourists by the busload descended on American outlet malls armed with the floor plans of stores and Japanese translations of important English phrases like "Buy one, get one free." The mall developers wanted to have consumers experience an American outlet mall without ever getting on an airplane. So they courted 50 outlet tenants, including U.S. outlet regulars such as Nike, Levi's, Guess, and Coach. It was much harder attracting Japanese tenants, many of whom worried about backlash from the department stores.

Some Japanese companies that agreed to open a store in the Yokohama mall are still reluctant to describe just what they're doing. Some insist that its products are ones that were on regular store shelves just a few weeks ago and aren't the season's leftovers. In many stores, big banners on the walls assure customers that the discounted products are legitimate. Products marked "second-class," one banner explains, are items that are slightly damaged and thus can't be sold in regular stores.

Source: Yumiko Ono, "Once-Proud Japanese Discover Outlet Malls," *The Wall Street Journal*, December 30, 1998, p. B1; Sandra Sugawara, "U.S. Developer Learning to Adapt While Doing Business with Japan," *Houston Chronicle*, April 18, 1999, p. 29.

Theme/Festival Centers These centers typically employ a unifying theme that is carried out by the individual shops in their architectural design and, to an extent, in their merchandise. The biggest appeal of these centers is to tourists. These centers typically contain tenants similar to those in the specialty centers, except that there are usually no large specialty stores or department stores. They can be anchored by restaurants and entertainment facilities. Because they lack traditional anchor stores and are often perceived as being trendy, these centers are viewed by some industry experts as being risky, unstable investments.

A theme/festival center can be located in a place of historical interest such as Faneuil Hall in Boston or Ghirardelli Square in San Francisco. Alternatively, they can attempt to replicate a historical place (such as the Old Mill Center in Mountain View, California) or create a unique shopping environment (like MCA's CityWalk in Los Angeles).

A new type of mall can be found on the Internet. Retailing View 8.6 examines its relative merits.

INTERNET EXERCISE Faneuil Hall and CityWalk are two very different theme/festival centers. Go to their websites (faneuilhallmarketplace.com and mca.com/citywalk) and compare them.

A VIRTUAL MALL IS A GROUP of retailers and service providers that can be accessed over the Internet at one location. Like bricks and mortar malls, virtual malls offer consumers one-stop shopping and include nationally recognized stores. For instance, mall.com features Gap, Neiman Marcus, J. Crew, and Disney Store. Other virtual malls are Yahoo!'s viamall.com, internetmall.com, and choicemall.com. Retailers affiliated with virtual malls give a percentage of their sales generated through the mall to the mall operator. Other retailers pay a flat fee.

The concept of a virtual mall is an example of a business model that may not translate well from the physical world to the virtual world. Bricks and mortar malls provide consumers with a one-stop shopping experience. They park the car once and visit many conveniently packaged stores, entertainment, and food options. Retailers benefit because the mall location brings them customers.

In the virtual world, customers have many alternatives to virtual malls. They can move from store-to-store quickly on their own. Bookmarks can be used to build their own personal mall.

They can go to websites like MySimon www.mysimon.com and other shopping bots discussed in Chapter 3 to "shop" for specific products or services. Also, the large portals like Yahoo.com, Altavista.com, Lycos.com, or Excite.com have their own shopping services.

Retailers may prefer shopping bots or the portals to virtual malls because there is typically no charge to be listed. On the other hand, like a physical mall, competition—particularly price competition—can be limited at a virtual mall. The more powerful retailers can dictate that no competing retailers can be in the mall. It is more difficult, therefore, for consumers to "shop around" in a virtual mall than it is using a shopping bot.

Virtual malls do have a niche in the electronic world under some specialized situations. Smaller retailers in a specific locale, such as a Main Street location, could benefit from a virtual mall. Customers could order merchandise over the Internet and either go pick it up or have it delivered. Customers around the world interested in shopping an Internet mall featuring unique products made in the Republic of Ireland can visit www.celticlinks.com.

Freestanding Sites

Although most retailers locate in strip centers or planned shopping malls, a frequent option for large retailers is a freestanding site. A **freestanding site** is a retail location that's not connected to other retailers, although many are located adjacent to malls. Retailers with large space requirements, such as warehouse clubs and hypermarkets, are often freestanding. Category killers such as Toys "R" Us also utilize freestanding sites. Advantages of freestanding locations are greater visibility, lower rents, ample parking, no direct competition, greater convenience for customers, fewer restrictions on signs, hours, or merchandise (which might be imposed in a shopping center), and ease of expansion. The most serious disadvantage is the lack of synergy with other stores. A retailer in a freestanding location must be a primary destination point for customers. It must offer customers something special in merchandise, price, promotion, or services to get them into the store.

Many retailers (e.g., Sports Authority and Walgreens) report freestanding stores perform better than stores in malls. Specifically, the 70-plus Walgreens stores that have moved to freestanding sites attract 10 percent more customers and achieve 30 percent higher revenues than they did in their previous mall locations.[25] Walgreens and other drugstore chains have shifted their emphasis to freestanding locations because supermarkets, traditionally the other anchor store in neighborhood and community shopping centers, have added their own pharmacies.[26]

Refact Freestanding sites are popular with retailers. They accounted for more than half of the retail construction in the United States in 1996 and 1997.[27]

Other Retail Location Opportunities

Kiosks are a popular location alternative within malls. Mixed-use developments and other nontraditional retail sites are also examined in this section.

Will bookstores become mere showrooms for titles to be ordered on the Net? At Borders, Title Sleuth kiosks give browsers instant access to an entire online catalog.

Kiosks   **Kiosks** are selling spaces typically found in mall common areas. These selling spaces are typically between 40 and 500 square feet, and can be in prime mall locations. They're relatively inexpensive compared to a regular store. For instance, a cart called The Sportsman's Wife at Mall of America was started with $15,000 ($10,000 of which was for inventory). They usually have short-term leases, shielding tenants from the liability of having to pay long-term rent in case the business fails. Of course, vendors also can be evicted on little notice. These alternatives to regular stores are often a great way for small retailers to begin or expand.

Mall operators see these alternative selling spaces as an opportunity to generate rental income in otherwise vacant space. Some of the nation's biggest mall developers are installing kiosks in every available space. These electronic kiosks sell everything from concert tickets to gift certificates. They also can generate excitement, leading to additional sales for the entire mall. For instance, Woodbridge Center in Woodbridge, New Jersey, typically has several kiosks selling ethnic merchandise such as clothing and art made by Africans and Native Americans. Mall operators must be sensitive to their regular mall tenants' needs, however. These kiosks can block a store, be incompatible with its image, or actually compete with similar merchandise.

Mixed-Use Developments (MXDs)   **Mixed-use developments (MXDs)** combine several different uses in one complex, including shopping centers, office towers, hotels, residential complexes, civic centers, and convention centers. MXDs are popular with retailers because they bring additional shoppers to their stores. Developers like MXDs because they use space productively. For instance, land costs the same whether a developer builds a shopping mall by itself or builds an office tower over the mall or parking structure.

A good example of an MXD is found in Seattle's central business district. Metropolitan Plaza is an eight-acre pocket of luxury stores and restaurants. The developers have created a special human feeling by concentrating on small things like wide sidewalks, generous display windows, plush carpeting in interior hallways, and an open arcade that welcomes people the way an Italian courtyard offers a visual invitation to leave the intensity of the street. The retail offering focuses on owner-operated stores rather than on franchised chains.

Nontraditional Locations   Retailers and service providers are also looking for new ways to expand their markets. One important high pedestrian area that has become more popular with national retail chains is airports. After all, what better way to spend waiting time than to have a Starbucks coffee or stop into Victoria's, Secret? Sales per square foot at airport malls are often three to four times as high

Retailers are experimenting with nontraditional locations, like this Eight O'clock Coffee Shop in an A&P supermarket.

as at regular mall stores.[28] However, rents are at least 20 percent higher than at malls. Also, costs can be higher—hours are longer and since the location is often inconvenient for workers, the businesses have to pay higher wages. The best airport locations tend to be ones where there are many layovers (Pittsburgh) and international flights (Miami). The best-selling products are those that make good gifts, necessities, and easy-to-pack items.

Another nontraditional location for retailers is within other, larger stores. Retailers, particularly department stores, have traditionally leased space to other retailers such as sellers of fine jewelry or furs. Grocery stores have been experimenting with the store-within-a-store concept for years with service providers like banks, film processors, and Blockbuster video. Wal-Mart had been putting McDonald's and independently owned coffee shops in some of its new stores.[29]

LOCATION AND RETAIL STRATEGY

Now that we've examined the types of locations available to retailers, let's see why some retailers choose the locations they do. Exhibit 8–3 reviews relative advantages of the major retail locations. In this section, we'll examine the location strategies of department stores, specialty apparel stores, category killers, grocery stores, and an independent optical boutique.

Department Stores

Department stores—like those owned by May Department Stores Company (Foley's) or Federated Department Stores (Bloomingdale's)—are usually located in central business districts and regional or superregional shopping centers. Department stores have historically been the backbone of CBDs. Since the 1950s, they have become the anchors for most regional and superregional shopping centers.

EXHIBIT 8–3

Relative Advantages
of Major Retail
Locations

LOCATION ISSUES	CBD	NEIGHBORHOOD CBD	STRIP CENTER	SHOPPING MALL	FREESTANDING
Large size draws people to area	+	–	–	+	–
People working/living in area provide source of customers	+	+	+	–	–
Source of entertainment/recreation	?	–	–	+	–
Protection against weather	–	–	–	+	–
Security	–	–	–	+	–
Long, uniform hours of operation	–	–	+	+	+
Planned shopping area/balanced tenant mix	–	–	–	+	–
Parking	–	–	+	?	+
Occupancy costs (e.g., rent)	?	+	+	–	+
Pedestrian traffic	+	+	–	+	–
Landlord control	+	+	+	–	+
Strong competition	+	+	+	–	+
Tax incentives	?	?	?	?	?

CBDs and shopping centers are a natural location for department stores. These locations draw a large number of people due to their large size and merchandise selection. Of course, the department stores create their own traffic for the CBD or mall. CBDs have the advantage of having potential customers working in the area. Most malls and some CBDs are a source of entertainment and recreation. Some cities in the United States and around the world have CBDs where residents can enjoy a leisurely stroll. In Italy, for instance, it is customary to take a walk through the shopping district every night before dinner between 6 and 8 P.M. As we noted earlier, malls have become America's Main Street where people gather, walk, and simply hang out.

It is not difficult to understand why the regional and superregional shopping centers are the location of choice for department stores. Since they're enclosed, they protect shoppers against the weather. Most people would rather stroll around the climate-controlled malls during Minnesota's winters than venture out to the CBDs. Malls also afford customers the feeling of a secure environment. Department stores appreciate malls' uniform and long hours of operation. Also, better malls design their tenant mix so that stores appealing to certain target markets are located together. For instance, upscale specialty stores will tend to be clustered near Neiman Marcus or Nordstrom, while more moderately priced stores will be near Sears.

Refact Malls in Southern Europe are typically anchored with supermarkets instead of department stores because people in Southern Europe spend half their income on food compared to one-third in the U.K. and United States.[30]

Specialty Apparel Stores

Specialty apparel stores like The Limited or The Gap thrive in central business districts, neighborhood CBDs, and most types of malls including regional and superregional shopping centers, fashion/specialty centers, and theme/festival centers. These locational venues appeal to these specialty stores for the same reasons that they are popular with department stores. These locations are all capable of drawing large numbers of people, and provide entertainment and recreational opportunities for their customers. Shopping centers also provide security, uniform and long hours of operation, protection against weather, and a balanced tenant mix that is consistent with their target market.

Specialty apparel stores carry **shopping goods**—products for which consumers spend time comparing alternatives. It's not uncommon, for instance, for a woman to go from The Limited to The Gap and on to other apparel stores during one shopping trip. Malls and to some extent CBDs facilitate this type of shopping behavior by having several stores with the same types of merchandise so that customers can compare across stores.

Category Killers

Category killers like Home Depot, Sports Authority, and Toys "R" Us are likely to be found in power centers or in freestanding locations. Category killers have different locational needs than department stores or specialty apparel stores. Category killers choose power centers or freestanding locations for several reasons. First, such stores typically compete on price, and these locations cost less than CBDs or malls. Second, easy access to parking is important to customers of category killers since purchases are often large and difficult to carry. Finally, category killers are **destination stores.** A destination store is one in which the merchandise, selection, presentation, pricing, or other unique features act as a magnet for customers. As such, it is not as important for these stores to be located adjacent to stores selling similar merchandise or in areas that have a natural customer draw. People in the market for a kitchen faucet or a child's birthday present will seek out Home Depot or Toys "R" Us, irrespective of the store's location.

Grocery Stores

Grocery stores are typically located in neighborhood strip centers. Like category killers, grocery stores are price competitive, and neighborhood strip centers have relatively inexpensive rent. These centers' readily accessible parking is also important to grocery store customers. People generally aren't willing to travel long distances to shop for groceries. Grocery stores carry **convenience goods**—products consumers aren't willing to spend effort to evaluate prior to purchase, such as milk and bread. The location success factor that's critical to stores carrying convenience goods is being readily accessible to customers. Neighborhood strip centers meet these criteria.

Wholesale clubs, like Sam's Wholesale Club and Costco, are stores that carry food, but aren't located in neighborhood strip centers. Like other category killers, these stores are very price competitive. Their customers are willing to give up some of the convenience of shopping at their neighborhood grocery store for lower prices. So wholesale clubs are typically located in freestanding sites.

Optical Boutique

Let's examine the location options for Mr. I's Optical Boutique, a South Miami, Florida, store specializing in upper-end high-fashion eyewear. Mr. I's has chosen a Main Street location. Although Main Street location does not draw from a trade area as large as a CBD or a shopping center, it serves the people working and living in the area.

The retailers in this Main Street location recognize that their location lacks the entertainment and recreation found in shopping centers, so they sponsor art and music festivals to bring people to the area. On Halloween, each store provides candy to its future customers and their parents.

Mr. I's recognizes other issues that make the South Miami Main Street location less than perfect. There's no protection against the heavy rains that characterize this subtropical climate. Security also could be an issue, but most stores are

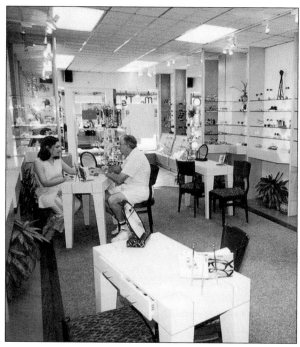

Mr. I's Optical Boutique, a store in a South Miami, Florida neighborhood, specializes in upper-end, high-fashion eyewear.

closed at night (when most of their customers have the time to shop). Although most of the stores cater to upscale customers living in surrounding neighborhoods, the tenant mix isn't always balanced. For instance, Mr. I's shares its block with a secondhand clothing store and an inexpensive diner. Finally, parking is often a problem.

In general, though, Mr. I's finds this Main Street location attractive. The rent is much less expensive than it would be in a shopping mall. There is usually good pedestrian traffic. Since the properties in the Main Street location are owned by several individuals, the landlords have less control over the tenants than they would in a shopping mall. Finally, although there are other optical stores in the area, the competition is not intense due to the exclusive lines Mr. I's carries.

SUMMARY

Decisions about where to locate a store are critical to any retailer's success. A clear, coherent strategy should specify location goals. A location decision is particularly important because of its high cost and long-term commitment. A location mistake is clearly more devastating to a retailer than a buying mistake, for instance.

Retailers have a plethora of types of sites to choose from. Many central business districts and Main Street locations have become a more viable option than in the past due to gentrification of the areas and lack of suburban mall opportunities. Retailers also have many types of shopping centers from which to choose. They can locate in a neighborhood, community, or power strip center, or they can go into a mall. We examined the relative advantages of several types of malls including regional and superregional centers, fashion/specialty centers, theme/festival centers, and outlet centers. We also examined the viability of freestanding sites, kiosks, mixed-use developments, and other nontraditional locations.

Retailers have a hard time finding a perfect site. Each site has its own set of advantages and disadvantages. In assessing the viability of a particular site, a retailer must make sure the store's target markets will patronize that location. The location analyst's job isn't finished until terms of occupancy and other legal issues are considered. (See this chapter's appendix.)

Chapter 9 continues the discussion of how to locate a retail store by examining the issues used to determine which region, trade areas, and sites are best and how to obtain and analyze data for making these decisions.

KEY TERMS

central business district (CBD), *234*

convenience goods, *251*

demalling, *242*

destination store, *251*

escape clause, *256*

exclusive use clause, *255*

fixed-rate lease, *255*

freestanding site, *247*

gentrification, *234*

graduated lease, *255*

kiosk, *248*

lessee, *255*

lessor, *255*

Main Street, *235*

maintenance-increase–recoupment lease, *255*

mall, *238*

mixed-use development (MXD), *248*

net lease, *255*

outparcel, *255*

percentage lease, *254*

percentage lease with specified maximum, *254*

percentage lease with specified minimum, *254*

prohibited use clause, *255*

shopping center, *237*

shopping goods, *251*

sliding scale, *254*

strip center, *238*

trade area, *233*

virtual mall, *247*

DISCUSSION QUESTIONS AND PROBLEMS

1. Why have location decisions become more important in recent years?

2. Pick your favorite store. Explain why you believe it is (or isn't) in the best location, given its target market.

3. Home Depot, a rapidly growing chain of large home improvement centers, typically locates in either a power center or a freestanding site. What are the strengths of each location for a store like Home Depot?

4. What are the advantages and disadvantages of a retailer's leasing space in a shopping center in an area with extensive zoning restrictions?

5. Retailers have a tradition of developing shopping centers and freestanding locations. These stores are often located in neighborhoods or central business districts that have suffered decay. Some people have questioned the ethical and social ramifications of this process, which is known as gentrification. What are the benefits and problems associated with gentrification?

6. What is the best location option for a Tommy Hilfiger outlet store? Justify your answer.

7. In many malls, fast-food retailers are located together in an area known as a food court. What are this arrangement's advantages and disadvantages to the fast-food retailer?

8. Why would a Payless ShoeSource store locate in a neighborhood shopping center instead of a regional shopping mall?

SUGGESTED READINGS

Braun, Raymond. "Exploring the Urban Entertainment Center Universe." *Urban Land*, August 1995 Supplement, pp. 11–17.

Buckner, Robert W. *Site Selection: New Advancements in Methods and Technology*, 2d ed. New York: Lebhar-Friedman Books, 1998.

"Changing Retailer Needs and Preferences: Implications for Strip Centers." *ICSC Research Quarterly* 2, no. 4 (Winter 1995), pp. 4–8.

Davies, R.L., and D.S. Rogers, eds. *Store Location and Store Assessment Research*. New York: John Wiley & Sons, 1984.

Drezner, Tammy. "Optimal Continuous Location of a Retail Facility, Facility Attractiveness, and Market Share: An Interactive Model." *Journal of Retailing* 70 (Spring 1994), pp. 49–64.

Finn, Adam, and Jordan Louviere. "Shopping-Center Patronage Models: Fashioning a Consideration Set Segmentation Solution." *Journal of Business Research*, November 1990, pp. 259–75.

Ghosh, Avijit, and Sara L. McLafferty. *Location Strategies for Retail and Service Firms*. Lexington, MA: D.C. Heath, 1987.

Ghosh, Avijit, and Sara McLafferty. "The Shopping Center: A Restructuring of Post-War Retailing." *Journal of Retailing* 67 (Fall 1991), pp. 253–67.

Howard, Elizabeth, "The Management of Shopping Centres: Conflict or Collaboration?" *International Review of Retail, Distribution and Consumer Research* 7, no. 3 (1997), pp. 143–56.

ICSC Research Quarterly. New York: International Council of Shopping Centers.

Lowry, James R. "The Life Cycle of Shopping Centers," *Business Horizons*, January–February 1997, pp. 77–86.

Tayman, Jeff, and Louis Pol. "Retail Site Selection and Geographic Information Systems." *Journal of Applied Business Research* 11, no. 2 (Spring 1995), pp. 46–54.

"Turning a Retail Center Inside Out." *Urban Land*, April 1995, pp. 26–27.

Wakefield, Kirk L., and Julie Baker. "Excitement at the Mall: Determinants and Effects on Shopping Response." *Journal of Retailing* 74, no. 4 (Fall 1998), pp. 515–39.

APPENDIX

Terms of Occupancy and Location Legal Issues

Refact The Port Authority of New York and New Jersey, developer of New York City's World Trade Center office/hotel/retail complex, requires all of its 70 stores to open at 7:30 A.M. on weekdays to serve office workers and commuters on their way to work.

Terms of Occupancy   Once a particular site is chosen, retailers still face a multitude of decisions, including types of leases and terms of the lease.

Types of Leases   Most retailers lease store sites. Although there are advantages to owning a store site (such as stable mortgage payments and freedom from lease covenants), most retailers don't wish to tie up their capital by owning real estate. Also, most of the best locations—such as in shopping malls—are only available by leasing.

There are two basic types of leases: percentage and fixed-rate leases.

Percentage Leases   Although there are many combinations within each type of lease, the most common form is a **percentage lease,** in which rent is based on a percentage of sales. In addition to the percentage of sales, retailers also typically pay a maintenance fee based on a percentage of their square footage of leased space. Most malls use some form of percentage lease. Since retail leases typically run from 5 to 10 years, it appears to be equitable to both parties if rents go up (or down) with sales and inflation.

A **percentage lease with specified maximum** is a lease that pays the lessor, or landlord, a percentage of sales up to a maximum amount. This type of lease rewards good retailer performance by allowing the retailer to hold rent constant above a certain level of sales. A similar variation, the **percentage lease with specified minimum,** specifies that the retailer must pay a minimum rent no matter how low sales are.

Another type of percentage lease uses a **sliding scale** in which the percentage of sales paid as rent decreases as sales go up. For instance, a retailer may pay 4 percent on the first $200,000 in sales, and 3 percent on sales greater than

$200,000. Like the percentage lease with a specified maximum, the sliding scale rewards high-performing retailers.

Fixed-Rate Leases   The second basic type of lease is a **fixed-rate lease.** These leases are most commonly used by community and neighborhood centers. Here a retailer pays a fixed amount per month over the life of the lease. With a fixed-rate lease the retailer and landlord know exactly how much will be paid in rent, but, as noted earlier, this type doesn't appear to be as popular as the various forms of percentage leases.

A variation of the fixed-rate lease is the **graduated lease.** Here rent increases by a fixed amount over a specified period of time. For instance, rent may be $1,000 per month for the first three years and $1,250 for the next five years.

A **maintenance-increase–recoupment lease** can be used with either a percentage or fixed-rate lease. This type of lease allows the landlord to increase the rent if insurance, property taxes, or utility bills increase beyond a certain point.

Finally, a **net lease** is a popular form of leasing arrangement. In a net lease, the retailer is responsible for all maintenance and utilities. Thus the landlord is freed from these responsibilities. A net lease can also be used with either a fixed-rate or percentage lease.

Terms of the Lease   Although leases are formal contracts, they can be changed to reflect the relative power and specific needs of the retailer.[31] Recognize that since most leases' basic format is developed by the **lessor** (the property's owner), the lease's terms may be slanted in favor of the lessor. It's up to the **lessee** (the party signing the lease, in this case the retailer) to be certain that the lease reflects the lessee's needs. Let's look at some clauses retailers may wish to include in a lease.

Prohibited Use Clause   A **prohibited use clause** limits the landlord from leasing to certain kinds of tenants. Many retailers don't want the landlord to lease space to establishments that take up parking spaces and don't bring in shoppers—for example, a bowling alley, skating rink, meeting hall, dentist, or real estate office. Retailers may also wish to restrict the use of space to those establishments that could harm the shopping center's wholesome image. Prohibited use clauses often specify that bars, pool halls, game parlors, off-track betting establishments, massage parlors, and pornography retailers are unacceptable.

Exclusive Use Clause   An **exclusive use clause** prohibits the landlord from leasing to retailers selling competing products. For example, a discount store's lease may specify that the landlord can't lease to other discount stores, variety stores, dollar stores, or discount clothing outlet stores.

Some retailers are particular about how the storefront appears. For instance, a women's specialty store may specify that the storefront must have floor-to-ceiling glass to maximize window displays to improve customers' ability to see into the store. Other retailers believe it's important that nothing blocks the view of the store from the street, so they specify that the landlord can't place any outparcels in the parking lot. An **outparcel** is a building (like a bank or McDonald's) or kiosk (like an automatic teller machine) that's in the parking lot of a shopping center but isn't physically attached to the shopping center.

It's crucial to some retailers that they be in shopping centers with specific types of tenants. For instance, a chain of moderately priced women's apparel shops benefits from the traffic flow of Kmart and Wal-Mart stores. It therefore specifies in its leases that if the major retailer leaves the shopping center, it has the option of canceling its lease or paying a reduced rent.

Escape Clause   An interesting feature that any retailer would want to have in a lease, if it could get away with it, is an **escape clause.** An escape clause allows the retailer to terminate its lease if sales don't reach a certain level after a specified number of years, or if a specific co-tenant in the center terminates its lease.

Finally, retailers must attempt to protect themselves from legal actions by citizens or government agencies that result from a landlord's action or inaction. Clauses may be inserted into leases that protect retailers from these legal problems. The next section looks at some of these legal issues.

Legal Considerations   Laws regarding how land is used have become so important that they should be a retailer's first consideration in a site search. Legal issues that affect the site decision include environmental issues, zoning, building codes, signs, and licensing requirements.

Environmental Issues   The Environmental Protection Agency plus state and local agencies have become increasingly involved with issues that could affect retail stores.[32] Two environmental issues have received particular attention in recent years. First is "above-ground risks" such as asbestos-containing materials or lead pipes used in construction. These materials can be removed relatively easily.

The second issue is hazardous materials that have been stored in the ground. This can be particularly important for a dry cleaner because of the chemicals used, or an auto repair shop because of disposal of used motor oil and battery fluid. The costs of cleaning up hazardous materials can range from $10,000 to over $6 million.

Real estate transactions almost always require an environmental impact statement on the property. But relying on past public filings of buried tanks and other potential hazards can be unreliable and not a protection in court. Retailers have two remedies to protect themselves from these environmental hazards. The best option is to stipulate in the lease that the lessor is responsible for removal and disposal of this material if it's found. Alternatively, the retailer can buy insurance that specifically protects it from these risks.

Zoning and Building Codes   Zoning determines how a particular site can be used. For instance, some parts of a city are zoned for residential use only; others are zoned for light industrial and retail uses. Building codes are similar legal restrictions determining the type of building, signs, size and type of parking lot, and so forth that can be used at a particular location. Some building codes require a certain size parking lot or architectural design. In Santa Fe, New Mexico, for instance, building codes require buildings to keep the traditional mud stucco (adobe) style.

Signs   Restrictions on the use of signs can also impact a particular site's desirability. Size and style may be restricted by building codes, zoning ordinances, or even the shopping center management. At the Bal Harbour Shops in North

Miami Beach, for example, all signs (even sale signs) must be approved by the shopping center management.

Licensing Requirements   Licensing requirements may vary in different parts of a region. For instance, some Dallas neighborhoods are dry, meaning no alcoholic beverages can be sold; in other areas, only wine and beer can be sold. Such restrictions can affect retailers other than restaurants and bars. For instance, a theme/festival shopping center that restricts the use of alcoholic beverages may have limited clientele at night.

Legal issues such as those mentioned here can discourage a retailer from pursuing a particular site. These restrictions aren't always permanent, however. Although difficult, time-consuming, and possibly expensive, lobbying efforts and court battles can change these legal restrictions.

Kenard E. Smith, PhD
Vice President, Area Research
The May Department
Stores Company

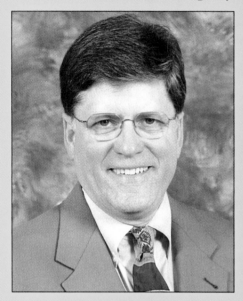

THE BUSINESS OF FORECASTING department store sales and determining store expansion strategy has changed a lot in the last 20 years. For 12 years, I have led the Area Research Department at The May Department Stores Company. • I originally went to work for Dayton Hudson Corporation (now Target Corp.) after getting a PhD in geography and teaching for a few years. At the time I thought I'd be a professor again in a few years, but I wanted to work in the retail trenches, doing applied research first. In those days, we would emphasize the qualities of the retail site as well as demographics of the population living near the site. But things were different then. There were still lots of available locations and competition wasn't nearly as saturated as it is today. There were scores of markets with high growth potential. Most department stores could go into growing areas and be successful. • Now, most markets are saturated with competitors of all kinds. As a result, chains have to be much more strategic in developing their store expansion plans. Today we still study demographics and sometimes psychographic profiles of potential customers in a trade area. But competition, their store locations, strengths, weaknesses, and strategies are increasingly important. • 1. We evaluate competitor strengths and weaknesses, and try to predict where they plan to open stores in the future. We learn about our competitors from fieldwork, real estate developers, mall operators, directories, and company websites. • 2. Another change is the way we define our competition. We used to think of our competition as mall-based department and specialty stores plus discounters, and we defined our customer as a "department store customer." Today, we compete not only with mall-based stores, but also with a wide range of off-price stores (e.g., Linens N' Things, Kohl's, and outlet stores in "Mills-type" centers). The effects of e-commerce remain to be seen. • 3. We also have to be concerned about overcrowded markets. Not all markets can absorb an unlimited supply of traditional and discount department store companies. • As we evaluate markets, we ask ourselves how might we be positioned in a market in, say, five years? Who is the market leader? What new markets do we want to enter?. We may even ask what stores we might acquire to get a better position in a market. • Doing site location/market analysis for a living is challenging, fascinating, and fun. We utilize top analytical tools. We travel across the United States, which for market analysts, is a large field laboratory. But at the end of the day, we still have to sit down and decide, will this location be a good site for a May Department Store or not?

Site Selection

QUESTIONS

- What issues should be considered when determining in which region or trade area to locate a store?
- What factors should retailers consider when deciding on a particular site?
- What is a trade area, and why should a retailer choose one over another?
- How can retailers forecast sales for new store locations?

CHAPTER 8 EXAMINED different types of locations available to retailers and why certain types of retailers gravitate toward particular types of sites. In this chapter, we take a closer look at how retailers choose specific locations.

Retail site selection is a very strategic decision. First, a location is generally one of the most important factors customers use in choosing a store. Second, a site is expensive and, once chosen, a retailer must live with it for many years. Finally, it is often difficult to find great sites—most are already taken by other retailers.

Exhibit 9–1 breaks the location decision into three levels: region, trade area, and specific site. The **region** refers to the country, part of the country, a particular city, or **Metropolitan Statistical Area (MSA).** An MSA is a city with 50,000 or more inhabitants or an urbanized area of at least 50,000 inhabitants and a total MSA population of at least 100,000 (75,000 in New England). A **trade area** is a contiguous geographic area that accounts for the majority of a store's sales and customers. A trade area may be part of a city, or it can extend beyond the city's boundaries, depending on the type of store and the density of potential customers surrounding it. For instance, a video rental store's trade area may be only a few city blocks within a major metropolitan area. On the other hand, a Wal-Mart store's trade area in the rural South may encompass 50 square miles.

In making store location decisions, retailers must examine all three levels simultaneously. For instance, suppose Taco Bell is expanding operations in the Pacific Northwest. Its research indicates that competition in the Tacoma, Washington, market is relatively weak, making it an attractive region. But maybe it can't find a suitable site in Tacoma, so it must temporarily postpone locating there.

EXHIBIT 9–1   Three Levels of Spatial Analysis

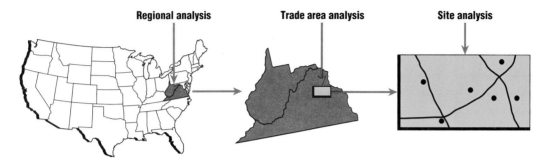

The remainder of the chapter examines these three location decisions sequentially. First, we look at the factors that affect the attractiveness of a particular region and trade area. Then we examine what retailers look for in choosing a particular site. Of course, the most important factor in choosing a site is the amount of sales it can generate. Thus, we will examine several methods of predicting the amount of sales.

FACTORS AFFECTING THE DEMAND FOR A REGION OR TRADE AREA

The best regions and trade areas are those that generate the highest demand or sales for a retailer. Although the regional analysis is distinct from the trade area analysis, the factors that make them attractive are the same. To assess overall demand in a particular region/market or trade area, the retail analyst considers the population's demographic and lifestyle characteristics, the business climate, competition from other retailers in the area, the retailer's propensity to manage multiple stores, and economies of scale versus cannibalization. (See Exhibit 9–2.)

Demographic and Lifestyle Characteristics

In most cases, areas where the general population is growing are preferable to those with declining populations. Some retailers, such as Subway Sandwich & Salad Shops, often go into new strip shopping centers in anticipation that the surrounding suburban area will eventually be built up enough to support demand. Yet population growth alone doesn't tell the whole story. Mr. I's Optical Boutique (discussed in Chapter 8), for example, is in a "Main Street" location in a mature neighborhood with a stable population. A reason for the success of this store and similar independently owned retailers in the area is that household income in the trade area is relatively high.

Size and composition of households in an area can also be important success determinants. For instance, Ann Taylor (a chain specializing in traditional and business apparel for women) generally locates in areas with high-income households and in tourist areas; household size, however, isn't a particularly critical issue. Toys "R" Us, on the other hand, is interested in locations with heavy concentrations of families with young children.

Some retailers, such as Subway Sandwich & Salad Shops, often go into new strip shopping centers in anticipation that the surrounding suburban area will eventually be built up enough to support demand.

EXHIBIT **9–2**

Factors Affecting
the Demand
for a Region
or Trade Area

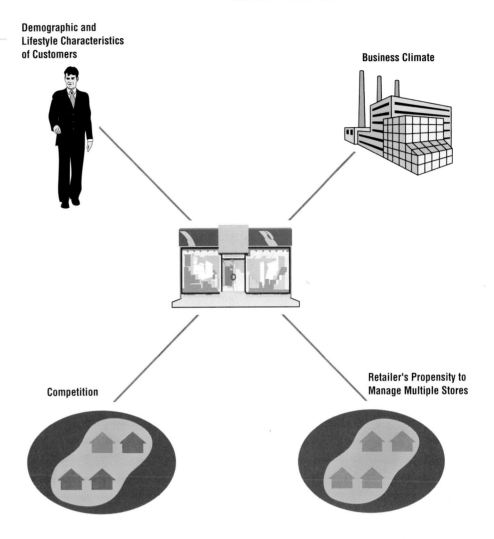

Finally, lifestyle characteristics of the population may be relevant, depending on the target market(s) a particular retailer is pursuing. Many college students, for instance, have relatively low incomes. However, they may come from well-to-do families and, by the fact that they are in college, they're relatively educated. Their lifestyles more closely resemble those of recent college graduates in professional jobs making a good income than they do people with similar incomes working odd jobs on a ranch in a rural area. Thus the way people spend their money is often as important as how much money people make.

Business Climate   It's important to examine a market's employment trends because a high level of employment usually means high purchasing power. Also, it's useful to determine which areas are growing quickly and why. For instance, the east side of Seattle, Washington, has become a desirable retail location because of its proximity to Microsoft's corporate headquarters. Retail location analysts must determine how long such growth will continue and how it will affect demand for their merchandise. For instance, the economies of some Rustbelt cities like Flint, Michigan, experience greater peaks and valleys due to their dependence on specific industries such as automobiles.

Employment growth in and of itself isn't enough to ensure a strong retail environment in the future. If growth isn't diversified in a number of industries, the area may suffer from adverse cyclical trends. For instance, many towns with military bases are expected to decline in population in the new millennium as the military downsizes and bases close in towns like Plattsburgh, New York, and Moreno Valley, California.

Competition

The level of competition in an area also affects demand for a retailer's merchandise. The level of competition can be defined as saturated, understored, or overstored. A **saturated trade area** offers customers a good selection of goods and services, while allowing competing retailers to make good profits. Since customers are drawn to these areas because of the great selections, retailers who believe they can offer customers a superior retail format in terms of merchandise, pricing, or service may find these areas attractive. Some restaurants such as Burger King seek locations where their major competition—McDonald's—has a strong presence. They believe that it's important to go head-to-head with their strongest competitors so that they can develop methods and systems that will allow them to successfully compete with them. They contend that locating in areas with weak competition allows them to become complacent. The strongest competitor will eventually enter the trade area. By then, however, it will have lost its competitive edge.[1]

Another strategy is to locate in an **understored trade area**—an area that has too few stores selling a specific good or service to satisfy the needs of the population. Wal-Mart's early success was based on a location strategy of opening stores in small towns that were relatively understored. Now these stores experience high market share in their towns and draw from surrounding communities.

In effect, these areas have gone from being understored before Wal-Mart arrived to being **overstored**—having so many stores selling a specific good or service that some stores will fail. Unable to compete head-to-head with Wal-Mart on price or breadth of selection, many family-owned retailers in those towns have had to either reposition their merchandising and/or service strategies or else go out of business.

Span of Managerial Control

Some retailers focus on certain geographic regions or trade areas. For instance, Davenport, Iowa-based Von Maur is a regional department store chain that has 14 stores. Although it can compete with larger, national chains on several dimensions, one of its advantages stems from its regional orientation. It can maintain a loyal customer base by remaining a regional chain. It has excellent visibility and is well known throughout the area. Second, its merchandising, pricing, and promotional strategies specifically target the needs of a regional market rather than a national market. For instance, Von Maur knows that merchandise that's popular in Davenport will also sell in Des Moines. Finally, the management team can have greater locus of control over a regional market. Managers can easily visit the stores and assess competitive situations.

Economies of Scale versus Cannibalization

At first glance, you would expect that a retailer should choose the one best location in a given trade area. But most chains plan to go into an area with a network of stores. After all, promotion and distribution economies of scale can be achieved with multiple locations. The total cost is the same to run a newspaper ad for a retailer with 20 stores in an area as it does if the retailer has only one store. Likewise, chains like Wal-Mart only expand into areas where they have a distribution center designed to support the stores.

The question is, what is the best number of stores to have in an area? The answer depends on who owns the stores. For company-owned stores, the objective is to maximize profits for the entire chain. In this case, the retailer would continue to open stores as long as the marginal revenues achieved by opening a new store is greater than the marginal costs. Home Depot subscribes to this fundamental axiom of site selection: It is better to have two stores producing $75 million each than one store producing $100 million. The company believes that a store can do too much business. The store might be overcrowded, offer poor service, have a hard time staying in stock, and actually be underperforming. Home Depot believes that the solution to an underperforming store is to build another store in the same trade area. Although this strategy may sound illogical at first glance, it works for Home Depot.[2]

Starbucks subscribes to the same strategy. It saturates a market with stores before new markets are entered. For example, there were over 100 Starbucks outlets in the Seattle area before the company expanded to a new region. Having several stores in close proximity to each other generally increased overall revenues although slowed growth in comparable store sales in saturated markets suggests cannibalization of existing businesses.

For franchise operations, however, each individual franchise owner wants to maximize his or her profits. Some **franchisors** (owners of the franchise) grant their **franchisees** (owners of the individual stores) an exclusive geographic territory so that other stores under the same franchise do not compete directly with them. In other franchise operations, the franchisees have not been afforded this protection and often have been involved in very antagonistic negotiations with the franchisors in an attempt to protect their investment.

Retailing View 9.1 examines some of the factors that make global site selection such a challenge.

FACTORS AFFECTING THE ATTRACTIVENESS OF A SITE

Now let's look at the issues that make a particular site attractive. Specifically, we'll examine the site's accessibility and locational advantages within the center.

Accessibility

The **accessibility** of a site is the ease with which a customer may get into and out of it. The accessibility analysis has two stages: a macro analysis and then a micro analysis.

Macro Analysis The macro analysis considers the primary trade area, such as the area two to three miles around the site in the case of a supermarket or drugstore. To assess a site's accessibility on a macro level, the retailer simultaneously evaluates several factors, such as road patterns, road conditions, and barriers.

In the macro analysis, the analyst should consider the **road pattern.** The primary trade area needs major arteries or freeways so customers can travel easily to the site. A related factor is the **road condition** (including the age, number of lanes, number of stoplights, congestion, and general state of repair of roads in the primary trade area). For instance, a location on an old, narrow, congested

MANY OF THE ISSUES AND PROCEDURES used for making global location decisions are the same as we have discussed throughout this and the last chapter. The retailer needs to decide on a region, a trade area within that region, and a specific site. The retailer still needs to examine competition, the population characteristics, traffic patterns, and the like. What makes global location decisions more difficult and potentially interesting is that those in charge of making these decisions are typically not as familiar with the nuances of the foreign location issues as they are with the same issues in their home country. Further, national chains in the United States typically have a close working relationship with a handful of major developers. Developers work with retailers on a strategic level while the malls are still on the drawing board.

While similar developer–retailer relationships are growing worldwide, often retailers must deal with landlords directly—and cope with a confusing world of site requirements, red tape, and restrictions. For example, a retailer may be surprised to learn that the local government requires a $1 million key payment upfront. A landlord may demand a 25-year lease. And if there's to be construction, it's likely to be a slow, politically charged process.

Real-estate selection is where many grand global designs ultimately succeed or fail. A retailer may devote months to targeting a region—Latin America, for instance—before choosing a country to enter. From that point, a city must be chosen.

But when it comes to picking an exact site within that city—a decision that often demands knowing local traffic flows, the most desirable side of a street, or urban development patterns—the decision is sometimes rushed and made without the right knowledge. As with many locations in the United States, particularly congested urban areas, if the retailer chooses the wrong side of the street, it may fail.

Costs can also be troublesome. Compared to U.S. locations, occupancy costs in cities like London, Paris, or Tokyo are extremely high. Retailers have to be extremely high-volume to survive. Real estate rental costs are 30 percent more in the U.K. than they are in Germany, which are 30 percent more than they are in the United States, which are 30 percent more than they are in Canada.

Real estate restrictions also complicate international location decisions. For instance, tough European laws make it difficult for big-box retailers to open large stores that have historically required a large piece of property. Solutions occasionally demand a little ingenuity and flexibility. Costco Wholesale's solution, for example, has been to modify store formats in some overseas markets—most notably, the adoption of two-level operations in Korea and Taiwan.

Source: Erik Gordon, "Taking the Plunge?" *Chain Store Age Global Retailing Supplement* (Ernst & Young), December 1997, pp. 14–23.

secondary road in disrepair with too many stoplights wouldn't be a particularly good site for a retail store.

Natural barriers (such as rivers or mountains) and **artificial barriers** (such as railroad tracks, major highways, or parks) may also impact accessibility. These barriers' impact on a particular site primarily depends on whether the merchandise or services are available on both sides of the barrier. If, for instance, only one supermarket serves both sides of a highway, people on the opposite side must cross to shop.

Micro Analysis   The micro analysis concentrates on issues in the immediate vicinity of the site such as visibility, traffic flow, parking, congestion, and ingress/egress.

Visibility refers to customers' ability to see the store and enter the parking lot safely. Good visibility is less important for stores with established and loyal customers and for stores with limited market areas because customers know where the store is. Nonetheless, large national retailers like Kmart insist that there be no impediments to a direct, undisturbed view of their store. In an area with a highly transient population (such as a tourist center or large city), good visibility from the road is particularly important.

When doing a micro analysis of a potential site, retailers look at many factors. The Kmart store on the left is clearly visible from the street and is easily accessible. At the Gurnee Mills mall in Gurnee, Illinois (right), there is plenty of parking available.

The success of a site with a good **traffic flow** is a question of balance. The site should have a substantial number of cars per day but not so many that congestion impedes access to the store. To assess the level of vehicular traffic, you can usually obtain data from the regional planning commission, county engineer, or state highway department. But you may have to adjust the data for special situations. As a result, it's sometimes easier and more accurate to do the analysis in-house. For instance, the analyst must consider that the presence of large places of employment, schools, or big trucks may lessen a site's desirability. Also, areas congested during rush hours may have a good traffic flow during the rest of the day when most shopping takes place. Finally, some retailers might wish to adjust the raw traffic counts by excluding out-of-state license plates or counting only homeward-bound traffic.

The **amount and quality of parking facilities** are critical to a shopping center's overall accessibility. If there aren't enough spaces or if they're too far from the stores, customers will be discouraged from entering the area. On the other hand, if there are too many open spaces, the shopping center may be seen as a failure or as having unpopular stores. It's hard to assess how many parking spaces are enough, although location analysts use parking ratios as a starting point. A standard rule of thumb is 5.5:1,000 (five and a half spaces per thousand square feet of space).[3] Nevertheless, there's no good substitute for observing the shopping center at various times of the day, week, and season. You must also assess the availability of employee parking, the proportion of shoppers using cars, parking by nonshoppers, and the typical length of a shopping trip. One retailer examines outlying parking spaces for engine grease. If there's a lot of grease, he assumes that the parking lot is often filled and therefore the site is successful.

An issue that's closely related to the amount of available parking facilities, but extends into the shopping center itself is the relative congestion of the area. **Congestion** can refer to the amount of crowding of either cars or people. There's some optimal range of comfortable congestion for customers. Too much congestion can make shopping slow, irritate customers, and generally discourage sales. On the other hand, a relatively high level of activity in a shopping center creates excitement and can stimulate sales.[4]

The last factor to consider in the accessibility analysis is **ingress/egress**—the ease of entering and exiting the site's parking lot. Often, medians or one-way streets make entering or exiting difficult from one or more directions, limiting accessibility.

Locational Advantages within a Center

Once the center's accessibility is evaluated, you must evaluate the locations within it. Since the better locations cost more, retailers must consider their importance. For instance, in a neighborhood shopping center, the more expensive locations are closest to the supermarket. A liquor store or a flower shop that may attract impulse buyers should thus be close to the supermarket. But a a shoe repair store (which shouldn't expect impulse customers) could be in an inferior location because customers in need of this service will seek out the store.

The same arguments hold for regional multilevel shopping centers. It's advantageous for shopping goods stores like The Limited or Ann Taylor to be clustered in the more expensive locations near a department store in a mall. Women shopping for clothing may start at the department store and naturally gravitate to stores near it. Yet a store such as Foot Locker—another destination store—needn't be in the most expensive location, since many of its customers know they're in the market for this type of product before they even get to the center.

Another consideration is to locate stores that appeal to similar target markets close together. In essence, customers want to shop where they'll find a good assortment of merchandise. This is based on the principle of **cumulative attraction** in which a cluster of similar and complementary retailing activities will generally have greater drawing power than isolated stores that engage in the same retailing activities. This is why antique shops, car dealers, and shoe and clothing stores all seem to do better if they're close to one another. Of course, an area can become overstored when it has too many competing stores to profitably satisfy demand.

The principle of cumulative attraction applies to both stores that sell complementary merchandise and those that compete directly with one another. Consider Exhibit 9–3's map of Dallas's North Park Center. The more fashion-forward, higher-income customers will find stores like Alfred Dunhill of London and other exclusive boutiques between Neiman Marcus and Lord & Taylor. Some stores sell exactly the same merchandise categories, while others sell complementary products, such as perfumes in one store and lingerie in another. A similarly healthy tenant mix is found in the more moderately priced wing between Dillard's and JCPenney. Customers can buy shoes at Penney or a Kinney Shoe store. At the same time they can find a gift at Dillard's and a card at Bolen's Hallmark Shop. Thus a good location is one whose tenant mix provides (1) a good selection of merchandise that competes with itself and (2) complementary merchandise.

ESTIMATING DEMAND FOR A NEW LOCATION

Retailers estimate the demand for a new location by defining its trade area and then estimating how much people within the trade area will spend. In this section we will take a close look at how retailers delimit their trade areas and the factors they consider when defining trade area boundaries. Then we describe the types of information and techniques retailers use to estimate demand.

EXHIBIT 9–3

Map of Dallas's
North Park Center

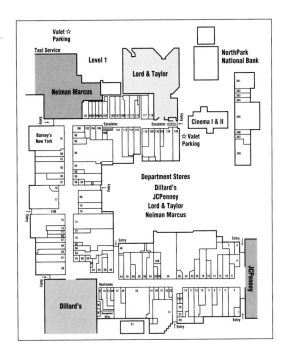

Trade Area   A trade area is a contiguous geographic area that accounts for the majority of a store's sales and customers. Trade areas can be divided into two or three zones, as depicted by Exhibit 9–4's concentric polygons. Such trade areas are called **polygons** because their boundaries conform to streets and other map features. The zones' exact definitions should be flexible to account for particular areas' nuances.

The **primary zone** is the geographic area from which the store or shopping center derives 60 to 65 percent of its customers. The **secondary zone** is the geographic area of secondary importance in terms of customer sales, generating about 20 percent of a store's sales. The **tertiary zone** (the outermost ring) includes customers who occasionally shop at the store or shopping center. There are several reasons for the tertiary zone. First, these customers may lack adequate retail facilities closer to home. Second, there are excellent highway systems to the store or center so customers can get there easily. Third, customers may drive near the store or center on the way to or from work. Finally, customers are drawn to the store or center because it is in or near a tourist area.

Factors Defining Trade Areas   The actual boundaries of a trade area are determined by the store's accessibility, natural and physical barriers, type of shopping area, type of store, and competition. Exhibit 9–4 illustrates the trade area for Mr. I's Optical Boutique, a store in South Miami, Florida, specializing in upper-end high-fashion eyewear. The map, generated by ESRI's ArcView GIS system, is based on drive times: 5 minutes for the primary trade area (blue), 10 minutes for the secondary trade area (red), and 20 minutes for the tertiary trade area (yellow).

Note that the trade area boundaries are oblong. This is because the major highways, especially U.S. 1, run north and south. Not only do the north–south highways bring traffic to the area, but heavy traffic often makes them difficult to

EXHIBIT 9–4

Oblong Trade Area
Caused by Major
Highways and
Natural Boundaries

Source: ESRI's ArcView GIS
System.

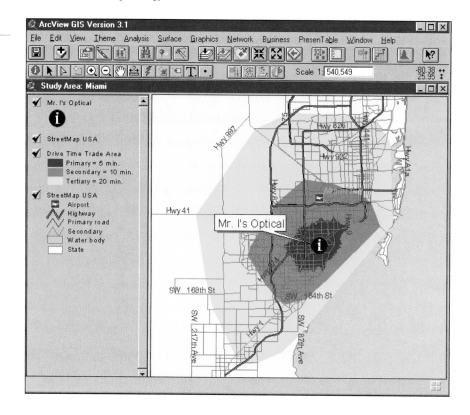

cross. Biscayne Bay also limits the trade area on the east. Other barriers (such as a river, mountain range, or high-crime area) may also influence the shape and size of a trade area.

Trade area size is also influenced by the type of store or shopping area. A 7-Eleven convenience store's trade area, for example, may extend less than one mile, whereas a category specialist like Toys "R" Us may draw customers from 20 miles away. The difference is due to the nature of the merchandise sold and the total size of the assortment offered. Convenience stores succeed because customers can buy products like milk and bread quickly and easily. If customers must drive great distances, the store's no longer convenient. Category specialists offer a large choice of shopping and specialty products that customers are willing to put forth additional effort to shop for. Thus customers will generally drive some distance to shop at a category specialist. Mr. I's Optical Boutique is located in a "Main Street" location rather than a major shopping center. Thus, its trade area is smaller than it would be if it were located in a regional shopping center.

Another way of looking at how the type of store influences the size of a trade area is whether it's a destination or a parasite store. A **destination store** is one in which the merchandise, selection, presentation, pricing, or other unique features act as a magnet for customers. In general, destination stores have larger trade areas than parasite stores—people are willing to drive further to shop there. Mr. I's Optical Boutique would qualify as a destination store due to the exclusive nature of its merchandise. Other examples of destination stores are anchor stores in shopping centers such as grocery stores or department stores; certain specialty stores such as RadioShack, Cartier, and Polo/Ralph Lauren; category killers such

This dry cleaning shop is in a strip mall in Grayslake, Illinois. A Walgreens drug store anchors the center. Which is the parasite and which is the destination store?

as Sports Authority and Toys "R" Us, and some service providers such as movie theaters.

A **parasite store** is one that does not create its own traffic and whose trade area is determined by the dominant retailer in the shopping center or retail area. A dry cleaner would qualify as a parasite store to a Wal-Mart store. People tend to stop at this cleaner on the way to or from Wal-Mart and other stores. Its business is thus derived from Wal-Mart and other businesses in the area. Some retail experts have noted that Wal-Mart can be a destructive force to competition in a trade area because it's so fiercely competitive. Yet, some parasite stores and stores that have learned to provide product/service offerings that complement, rather than compete with, Wal-Mart actually benefit from its presence. Other examples of parasite stores are food court restaurants and kiosks in a mall.

The level of competition also affects the size and shape of a trade area for a particular store. If two convenience food stores are too close together, their respective trade areas will shrink since they offer the same merchandise. On the other hand, Mr. I's Optical Boutique is one of several optical shops in this business district. Having similar shopping goods stores in the same vicinity generally expands the trade area boundaries; more people are drawn to the area to shop because of its expanded selection. Additionally, Mr. I's Optical Boutique's trade area is limited on the south by a large regional shopping center that has several stores carrying similar merchandise.

Sources of Information

Three types of information are required to define a trade area. First, we must determine how many people are in the trade area and where they live. For this, retailers use a technique known as customer spotting. Second, retailers use demographic and GIS (geographic information systems) data, the *Decennial Census of the United States* published by the U.S. Department of Commerce, and *Demographics USA*'s Buying Power Index to describe their potential customers in an attempt to assess how much they will buy in the proposed trade area. Finally, retailers use the Internet and other published sources to assess their competition. In strongly competitive trade areas, a retailer can expect to achieve a smaller piece of the total market potential for a particular type of merchandise or store.

Customer Spotting The purpose of the customer spotting technique is to spot, or locate, the residences of customers for a store or shopping center.[5] Data specific to a retailer's customers are usually obtained from information obtained from credit card or check purchases, or from customer loyalty programs. They are accessible from data warehouses described in Chapter 11. Retailers can also collect this information manually as part of the checkout process. Another method is by collecting automobile license plates in the parking lot and tracing them to the owner by purchasing the information from state governments or private research companies. A word of caution, however: This method is not thought to be very accurate and is illegal in some states. Experts believe that at least 500 plates are necessary to provide a good sample. The Motor Statistical Division of R.L. Polk and Co.[6] in Detroit can match the plates against its national vehicle registration database and summarize where the vehicles originate. This approach is particularly useful for understanding the trade area of competitors.

The data can be processed in two ways: by manually plotting the location of each customer on a map or by using a GIS system like those described later in this chapter.

Once the customers are spotted, we delineate the trade area like the one in Exhibit 9–4. Since this process involves a lot of subjectivity, follow the guidelines presented earlier in this chapter.

Demographic Data and GIS Vendors   There are hundreds of private companies specializing in providing retailers with information that will help them make better store location decisions.[7] Some, known as demographic data vendors (such as Claritas[8]), specialize in repackaging and updating census-type data in a format that's easy to understand, easy and quick to obtain, and relatively inexpensive. Since the data from the census can be dated, these firms construct computer models to generate estimates of current and future population and demographic characteristics.

Other firms, such as ESRI, Inc.,[9] specialize in geographic information systems (GISs). A **Geographic Information System (GIS)** is a computerized system that enables analysts to visualize information about their customers' demographics, buying behavior, and other data in a map format.[10] In many ways it resembles a database program because it analyzes and relates information stored as records. Additionally, however, each record contains information used to draw a geometric shape—usually a point, a line, or a polygon—and represents a unique place on earth to which the data corresponds. As such, GIS is a spatial database, a database that stores the location and shape of information. Using GIS, analysts can identify the boundaries of a trade area and isolate target customers groups. Data for GIS is collected at the point of sale and stored in data warehouses and combined with the type of information that is available from the demographic data vendors.

INTERNET EXERCISE   ESRI and Claritas both provide the types of information and maps described in this section. Go to their websites at www.esri.com and www.claritas.com and compare their product/service offerings. Which company would you call first?

Refact The worldwide market for GIS software, hardware, and services is greater than $6 billion.[11]

Like most industries, these data providers have their own niche specialties. However, the major players now offer a full-service array of information in both table and map formats. A retailer can obtain this information on an annual licensing basis for as little as $1,000; here the retailer is equipped with annually updated computer disks or CD-ROMs, or given data on a site-by-site basis for as little as $100 per report, based on requests by retailers. An analyst can choose from an unlimited array of area sizes and shapes, such as concentric rings (or bands), neighborhood sectors, polygons, or travel-time contours (rings around a particular site based on travel time instead of distances); there are also reports by state, county, city, and ZIP code. See Retailing View 9.2 to see how Domino's uses GIS to slice up a pizza market.

DOMINO'S PIZZA CORP. IN ANN ARBOR, MICHIGAN, once relied on 4,300 paper maps to analyze pizza delivery zones and based most site selection on intuition, backed up with a few facts. In 1995, it decided it needed well-defined delivery areas for maximum market penetration as well as hard demographic and geographic data for sound location and relocation decisions.

Domino's contracted with Thompson Associates in Ann Arbor to map the delivery zone of each Domino's in Chicago and Ann Arbor. This process identified several overlapping delivery areas and unserved areas. By using GIS, Domino's was able to look at a large area quickly. In a major market like Chicago, it could spend days or weeks becoming familiar with an area. Using a GIS map, it can see all stores, delivery areas, and markets at once.

Thompson Associates also performed site analysis in unserved areas. By combining demographic data with mapping analysis, the consultants identified potential growth areas, profiled an area's customers, analyzed the competition, and determined road access.

Once it knew the demographic profile of a given area and how well the area matched its target markets, it was able to rank unserved areas and potential sites within those areas. Then, the most efficient delivery zones were determined for each area. Domino's goal is to have a store within eight minutes of every household in a market. So a drive-time algorithm was created to identify a network serving the most households in the least time. A polygon based on the drive time is then plotted on a map.

Source: *Business Geographics,* March 1997, p. 11.

Decennial Census of the United States The *Decennial Census of the United States* is a complete source of information for making location decisions. But as the name implies, it's taken only once every 10 years so it's often out of date and requires supplementary reports and updates by government agencies and private firms. In the census, each household in the country is counted to determine the number of persons per household, household relationships, sex, race, age, and marital status. Additionally, a report on each building identifies the number of housing units at the address, the status of plumbing facilities, the number of rooms, whether the dwelling is owned or rented, whether the dwelling is owner-occupied, the housing value, the rent, and the vacancy status. Additional information is obtained for approximately one-sixth of U.S. households.

The decennial census data is available in many formats. Data can be obtained for areas as small as a city block or as large as the entire country. One of the most useful designations for regional evaluations is the Metropolitan Statistical Area (MSA). Census tracts are subdivisions of an MSA with an average population of 4,000. Because of their smaller size, they are more useful than MSAs for doing trade area or site analyses.

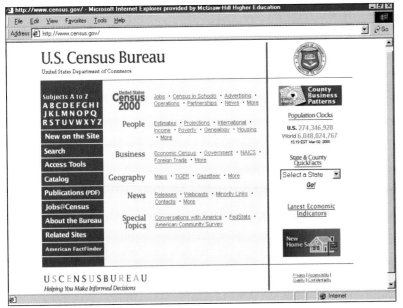

At *www.census.gov* retailers can access the Decennial Census of the United States for a wealth of useful information for making location decisions.

Not only is the census taken only once a decade, but also the information is not totally published for up to three years after the census has been conducted. Fortunately, the Bureau of the Census does release preliminary reports in the interim. It also publishes a variety of supplementary reports that the analyst can use as an update even after the census is published. The census, supplementary reports, and maps are usually available in public libraries, from state data centers that operate in conjunction with the Bureau of the Census; or directly from the U.S. Government Printing Office in Washington, DC.

Some information from the census is also available through vendors, regional planning commissions, and state, local, and county agencies.[12] Caution should be exercised when using some vendors and local sources, however, since an optimistic bias may be built into the data.

Buying Power Index   The Buying Power Index (BPI) published annually in *Demographics USA*[13] is a measure of a given market's ability to buy, and is expressed as a percentage of the total U.S. potential. The basic BPI is created by weighting and combining three significant factors that exist in every market and are used to determine the population of each market's ability to buy: total income, total retail sales, and total population. It is thus a combination of the peoples' ability to buy merchandise, their access to outlets where the transaction can be made, and the number of people who can purchase a product or service.

The standard formula for BPI is

$$BPI = .5 \times (\text{Percentage of U.S. effective buying income})$$
$$+ .3 \times (\text{Percentage of U.S. retail sales})$$
$$+ .2 \times (\text{Percentage of U.S. population})$$

For instance, the BPI for New England is calculated as follows:

$$BPI = .5 \times (255,823,658 \div 4,399,998,035)$$
$$+ .3 \times (134,588,046 \div 2,546,287,000)$$
$$+ .2 \times (13,404.3 \div 270,253.5)$$
$$= .291 + .159 + .099 = 5.49$$

This BPI for New England means that 5.49 percent of the buying power of the United States is concentrated in the New England states. By comparison, the highest BPI of any census region is in the South Atlantic states, which represent 18.38 percent of national buying power.

The rationale for this weighted average is that an area's income level has the largest impact on retail sales and thus should receive the highest weight (.5). The preceding year's retail sales total receives the second highest weight (.3), followed by population size (.2). Users are encouraged, however, to customize these weights and/or the three components depending on their particular application. For example, if the retailer is selling video games, the 18-and-under age segment is a better indicator of market potential than total population.

BPIs for regions and states will not be broken down enough for specific location decisions. Fortunately, though, BPIs are available for counties, metropolitan areas, cities, and TV viewing areas. Also, the BPI reports provide indices for different types of products such as food, eating and drinking places, general merchandise, furniture/home furnishings and appliances, automotive, and drugs.

The BPI is one piece of information, used in conjunction with others, to help make location decisions. In general, retailers want to have stores in locations with high buying power. Thus, a region with a high BPI is preferable to a low-BPI area, all other factors held constant.

Measuring Competition   Estimating the demand for a retailer's products is a critical success factor, but it only tells half the story. It's equally important to determine the level of competition in the trade area. Earlier in this chapter, we concluded that either a saturated or an understored trade area offers a potentially good location opportunity, but that retailers should avoid trade areas that are overstored. How can a retailer like Mr. I's Optical Boutique determine the level of saturation of the trade area for a potential new location? In other words, what's the level of trade area competition?

One of the most powerful methods of measuring competition is over the Internet.[14] Most websites list not only all current locations, but future sites as well. Demographic information for prospective sales in other countries might eliminate the need for an in-person visit. A more traditional method of accessing competitive information is through the Yellow Pages of the telephone book. This information is also available on CD-ROM. Other sources of competitive information are

- Directories published by trade associations.
- Chambers of commerce.
- *Chain Store Guide* (published by CSG Information Services).
- International Council of Shopping Centers (shopping centers).
- Urban Land Institute (shopping centers).
- Local newspaper advertising departments.
- Municipal and county governments.
- Specialized trade magazines.
- List brokers.

A relatively easy way to determine level of competition is to calculate total square footage of retail space devoted to a type of store per household. From published sources, Mr. I's can estimate the total square feet devoted to optical retailers in its trade area and divide it by the number of households. The higher the ratio, the higher the level of competition will be. Of course, there's no substitute for personal visits to stores to assess competition.

To illustrate the process of measuring competition, consider the situation in which Mr. I's Optical is assessing the relative level of competition for four potential new sites using Exhibit 9–5's information.

Based on the information in Exhibit 9–5, Mr. I's Optical should locate its new store at site B. The trade area potential is high and competition is relatively low. Of course, relative competition is only one issue to consider. Later in this chapter we'll consider competition along with other issues to determine which is the best new location for Mr. I's Optical Boutique. (See Exhibit 9–10.)

Other types of retailers could perform a similar analysis. Competitive analyses are easiest for large chains selling commodity-type merchandise, like grocery stores. First, they have information on sales and competition for all of the trade areas in which they have stores. The data are readily available and can be used to estimate what sales would be for a new store. Second, it is relatively easy to determine how much people spend on food or other commodities in a trade area and how much of the demand is being adequately satisfied by stores in the area.

EXHIBIT **9–5**   Competitive Analysis for Mr. I's Optical Boutique

TRADE AREA (1)	EYEGLASSES/ YEAR/ PERSON (2)	TRADE AREA POPULATION (3)	TOTAL EYEGLASSES POTENTIAL (4)	ESTIMATED EYEGLASSES SOLD (5)	TRADE AREA POTENTIAL UNITS (6)	TRADE AREA POTENTIAL PERCENTAGE (7)	RELATIVE LEVEL OF COMPETITION (8)
South Miami	0.2	98,291	19,658	7,550	12,158	61.85%	Low
Site A	0.2	91,683	18,337	15,800	2,537	13.83	Medium
Site B	0.2	101,972	20,394	12,580	7,814	38.32	Low
Site C	0.2	60,200	12,040	11,300	740	6.15	High
Site D	0.2	81,390	16,278	13,300	2,978	18.29	Medium

*Column 2: To perform analysis, estimate the number of eyeglasses sold per year per person. This information could be obtained from industry sources.[a]

*Column 3: Trade area population is taken from information provided by Urban Decision Systems (Exhibit 9–6).

*Column 4: The total trade area potential for eyeglasses is column 2 times column 3.

*Column 5: Estimates of the number of eyeglasses sold in the trade areas are taken from industry sources, from customer surveys, and/or from visits to competitive stores.

*Column 6: The unit sales potential for eyeglasses in the trade areas is column 4 minus column 5.

*Column 7: The trade area potential percentage is column 6 divided by column 4. For instance, since the total eyeglasses potential for the South Miami store trade area is 19,658 pairs, and we estimate that an additional 12,158 pairs could be sold in that trade area, 61.85 percent of the eyeglasses market in this area is left untapped. The bigger the number, the lower the competition. We could also say that 38.15 percent of the market is saturated (100 − 61.85 percent).

*Column 8: The relative level of competition is subjectively estimated based on column 7. Remember, unlike other optical stores in the trade area Mr. I's Optical carries a very exclusive merchandise selection. In general, however, the higher the trade area potential, the lower the relative competition will be.

[a]The appropriate ratio will vary depending upon the situation. For instance, a retailer may use average sales per square foot of selling space average sales per household, or number of persons in the target market per store.

On the other hand, these analyses are more difficult for retailers with few outlets that carry exclusive merchandise. As we have seen from our analysis, Mr. I's Optical doesn't have data from multiple trade areas from which it can derive its analysis. Also, since it carries exclusive merchandise, defining its competition can be difficult.

Methods for Estimating Demand

A number of complementary analytical methods are used to estimate the demand for a new store. One of the most widely used techniques—the analog approach—was first developed by William Applebaum for the Kroger Company in the 1930s. A more formalized statistical version of the analog approach uses multiple regression analysis. A third approach, known as Huff's model, is based on Newton's law of gravity. We discuss these location analysis methods below.

The Analog Approach   The analog approach could just as easily be called the "similar store approach." Suppose Mr. I's Optical Boutique wants to open a new location. Since its present location in South Miami has been very successful, it would like to find a location whose trade area has similar characteristics. We would estimate the size and customer demographic characteristics of its current trade area and then attempt to match those characteristics to new potential locations. Thus, knowledge of customer demographics, the competition, and sales of currently operating stores can be used to predict the size and sales potential of a new location.

The analog approach is divided into three steps.[15] First, the current trade area is determined by using the customer spotting technique described earlier in the chapter. Second, based on the density of customers from the store, the pri-

EXHIBIT 9–6

Income Distribution
of Three-Mile Ring
Surrounding Mr. I's
Optical Boutique

	1990 CENSUS		1998 ESTIMATE		2003 PROJECTION	
Population	89,952		94,574		98,291	
In group quarters	4,236		3,389		3,395	
Per capita income	$26,395		$35,414		$41,917	
Aggregate income ($mil)	2,374		3,349		4,120	
Households by income	34,277		35,909		37,282	
Less than $5,000	1,753	5.1%	1,221	3.4%	971	2.6%
$5,000–$9,999	1,905	5.6	1,854	5.2	1,909	5.1
⋮						
⋮						
$40,000–49,999	3,101	9.1	3,098	8.6	3,275	8.8
$50,000–59,999	2,430	7.1	2,813	7.8	2,484	6.7
$60,000–74,999	2,766	8.1	2,983	8.3	3,169	8.5
$75,000–149,999	5,968	17.4	6,968	19.4	7,238	19.4
$150,000+	3,192	9.3	5,450	15.1	7,127	19.1
Median household income	40,729		50,817		54,914	
Average household income	68,864		92,957		110,217	

Source: Claritas Inc., www.claritas.com.

mary, secondary, and tertiary trade area zones are defined. Finally, we match the
characteristics of our current store with the potential new stores' locations to determine the best site.

Steps 1 and 2: Define Current Trade Area   Based on customer spotting data
generated from its data warehouse of current customers, Exhibits 9–6, 9–7, and
9–8 describe the primary trade area (three-mile ring) for Mr. I's Optical Boutique
in South Miami, Florida.[16] Claritas' Income Distribution Report (Exhibit 9–6)
contains detailed household income figures as well as growth projections. With
the estimated year 2003 average household income at $110,217 and 19.4 percent
of the households with incomes between $75,000 and $149,000 and 19.1 percent
with incomes over $150,000, the three-mile ring surrounding Mr. I's Optical is
very affluent.

Claritas' demographic trends report (Exhibit 9–7) includes data on population,
households by number of persons, race, ethnic origin, and age by sex. An interesting characteristic of the area surrounding Mr. I's Optical is that an estimated 48.2
percent of the population will be of Hispanic descent by 2003.

INTERNET EXERCISE   In *Business Geographics* you can find many interesting articles about retail location analysis, demographic data, and GIS vendors. Go to
its website at www.geoplace.com/bg/ and click on *QUICKSCAN* **Software Reviews** to see the variety of software available for doing location analysis.

As we said earlier in this chapter, it is just as important to look at consumer
lifestyles or psychographics as it is to examine their demographics. We know
that Mr. I's' trade area is generally affluent, but are the residents the kind of
people who would appreciate its upscale fashion eyewear? Developed by Claritas,
the Potential Rating Index for Zip Markets (PRIZM) is one of several commercially

EXHIBIT 9–7

Demographic Trends for Three-Mile Ring Surrounding Mr. I's Optical Boutique

	1990 CENSUS		1998 ESTIMATE		2003 PROJECTION	
Population	89,952		94,574		98,291	
Households	34,277		35,909		37,282	
Average household size	2.50		2.54		2.55	
Race						
White	79,650	88.5%	83,275	88.1%	86,159	87.7%
Black	8,268	9.2	8,420	8.9	8,627	8.8
Asian/Pacific Islander	1,907	2.1	2,651	2.8	3,221	3.3
American Indian	131	0.1	223	0.2	285	0.3
Hispanic origin	31,649	35.2	40,331	42.6	47,367	48.2
Median Age	35.9		39.4		41.4	
Males	43,375		45,590		47,377	
0–20	11,880	27.5	11,596	25.4	11,623	24.5
21–44	16,989	39.1	16,560	36.3	16,061	33.9
45–64	9,340	21.5	11,560	25.4	13,464	28.4
65–84	4,825	11.1	5,395	11.8	5,670	11.9
85+	341	0.8	479	1.1	559	1.2
Females	46,570		48,979		50,905	
0–20	10,998	23.6	11,006	22.4	11,061	21.7
21–44	17,753	38.1	16,842	34.4	16,114	31.7
45–64	10,220	21.9	12,531	25.7	14,640	28.7
65–84	6,829	14.7	7,479	15.2	7,816	15.3
85+	770	1.7	1,121	2.3	1,274	2.5

Source: Claritas Inc., www.claritas.com.

available services that combine census data, nationwide consumer surveys, and other statistics as well as information from 1,600 municipal and regional agencies to provide lifestyle descriptions of geographic clusters. This information is analyzed by social rank, mobility, ethnicity, family life cycle, and housing. The PRIZM system categorizes the nation's neighborhoods into 62 types. PRIZM is based on the old adage, "Birds of a feather flock together." Specifically, people like to live in neighborhoods with their peers, and people in a neighborhood tend to have similar consumer behavior patterns.[17]

Exhibit 9–8 summarizes the most prominent PRIZM lifestyle report for the three-mile ring surrounding Mr. I's Optical. These segments, described in Exhibit 9–9, indicate an interesting mix of potential customers. "Blue Blood Estates" and "Pools & Patios" both represent affluent, older groups—perfect for Mr. I's Optical. "Young Influentials" will also be drawn to Mr. I's' high-fashion product lines. "Upstarts & Seniors," however, are not a perfect fit with Mr. I's' target market because of their middle-income designation. Generally, though, the PRIZM reports mirror the income and demographic trends reports—the area is affluent and is therefore ideal for selling exclusive and expensive eyewear.

Which PRIZM cluster do you think these people best represent: "Pools and Patios" or "Young Influentials"?

EXHIBIT 9–8

PRIZM Neighborhood Lifestyle Clusters for Three-Mile Ring Surrounding Mr. I's Optical

CLUSTER	POPULATION	PERCENTAGE
Blue Blood Estates	18,457	19.5
Pools & Patios	11,279	11.9
Young Influentials	12,163	12.9
Upstarts & Seniors	10,416	11.0

Source: Claritas Inc., www.claritas.com.

INTERNET EXERCISE   Claritas' PRIZM clusters is only one type of commercially available geodemographic data. Go to www.natdecsys.com; next click on "NDS Website" and then "fun stuff." Play the Lifestyle Game. To see how the MicroVision Segmentation Systems works, try it with your home ZIP code. Do you fit one of the segments?

Step 3: Match Characteristics of Current Store with Potential New Store's Location to Determine the Best Site   Now that we have defined the trade area for Mr. I's' existing store, we can use the information to choose a new store location. The trick is to find a location whose market area is similar or analogous to its existing store.

Based on the factors affecting demand that we described earlier in the chapter, we conclude that the five factors that contribute most to the success of Mr. I's' current location are high income, predominantly white-collar occupations, relatively large percentage of older residents, upscale PRIZM profile, and relatively low competition for expensive, high-fashion eyewear. Exhibit 9–10 compares Mr. I's' current location with four potential locations on these five factors.

EHXIBIT 9–9

Descriptions of Largest PRIZM Clusters Surrounding Mr. I's Optical

BLUE BLOOD ESTATES

Blue Blood Estates are America's wealthiest socioeconomic neighborhoods, populated by upper-class, established managers, professionals, and heirs to "old money." They are accustomed to privilege and living in luxurious surroundings. One in 10 millionaires can be found in Blue Blood Estates, and there is a considerable drop from these heights to the next highest level of affluence.

UPSTARTS & SENIORS

Upstarts & Seniors includes both youths and seniors. It shows that, if employable, single, and childless, they have much in common. They share average educations and incomes in several fields, such as business, finance, retail, health, and public service. This group lives in condos and apartments, and prefers the nation's retirement areas in the Sunbelt and West. This group is middle income, predominantly white, and either under 24 or 65 and older.

POOLS & PATIOS

Pools & Patios are found in upscale green-belt suburbs. Most of their children have grown and departed, leaving aging couples and aging nests too costly for young homemakers. Good education, high white-collar employment levels, and double incomes ensure "the good life" in these neighborhoods.

YOUNG INFLUENTIALS

Young influentials are young metropolitan sophisticates with exceptional high-tech, white-collar employment levels. Double incomes afford high spending. Lifestyles are open, with singles, childless couples, and unrelated adults predominating in expensive one- and two-person homes, apartments, and condos.

EXHIBIT 9-10   Descriptions of Mr. I's Optical Boutique and Four Potential Locations' Trade Areas

STORE LOCATION	AVERAGE HOUSEHOLD INCOME	WHITE COLLAR OCCUPATIONS	PERCENTAGE OF RESIDENTS AGE 45 AND OVER	PREDOMINANT PRIZM PROFILE	LEVEL OF COMPETITION
Mr I's Optical	$110,217	High	44%	Blue Blood Estates	Low
Site A	$60,000	High	25	Young Suburbia	Medium
Site B	$70,000	Low	80	Gray Power	Low
Site C	$100,000	High	30	Young Literate	High
Site D	$120,000	High	50	Money and Brains	Medium

Average household income is taken from Exhibit 9–6 year 2003 projections. Level of white-collar occupations is estimated from PRIZM data in Exhibit 9–8. Percentage of residents 45 years old and over is estimated from Exhibit 9–7. Level of competition was subjectively determined.

Although the potential customers of site A typically have white-collar occupations, they have relatively low incomes and are comparatively young. Young Suburbans also tend to have young families, so expensive eyewear may not be a priority purchase. Finally, there's a medium level of competition in the area.

The Gray Power residents surrounding site B have moderate incomes and are mostly retired. Even though competition would be low and most residents need glasses, these customers are more interested in value than in fashion.

Site C has strong potential since the Young Literati residents in the area have high incomes and are a mix of executives, professionals, and students living near an urban university. They would appreciate Mr. I's' fashionable assortment. Unfortunately, other high-end optical stores are entrenched in the area.

Site D is the best location for Mr. I's. The residents are older professionals with high incomes. Money and Brains are sophisticated consumers of adult luxuries like high-fashion eyewear. Importantly, this PRIZM cluster is similar to Blue Blood Estates but not as wealthy.

Unfortunately, finding analogous situations isn't always as easy as in this example. The weaker the analogy, the more difficult the location decision will be. When a retailer has a relatively small number of outlets (say, 20 or fewer), the analog approach is often best. Even retailers with just one outlet like Mr. I's Optical can use the analog approach. As the number of stores increases, it becomes more difficult for the analyst to organize the data in a meaningful way. More analytical approaches such as multiple regression analysis are necessary.

Multiple Regression Analysis   Multiple regression analysis is a common method of defining retail trade area potential for retail chains with greater than 20 stores.[18] Although multiple regression analysis uses logic similar to that of the analog approach, it uses statistics rather than judgment to predict sales for a new store.

The best location for Mr. I's Optical Boutique should contain many older professionals with high incomes.

Family income is a good predictor (independent) variable to use in a regression analysis to predict sales for a new jewelry store.

The initial steps in multiple regression analysis are the same as those in the analog approach. First, the current trade areas are determined by using the customer spotting technique. Second, the primary, secondary, and tertiary zones are determined by plotting customers on a map. But then the multiple regression procedure begins to differ from the analog approach. Instead of matching characteristics of trade areas for existing stores with a potential new store by using the location analyst's subjective experience, a mathematical equation is derived.

Using "canned" statistical packages, three steps are followed to develop the multiple regression equation:

1. Select appropriate measures of performance, such as per capita sales or market share.
2. Select a set of variables that may be useful in predicting performance.
3. Solve the regression equation and use it to project performance for future sites.

Steps 1 and 2: Select Store Performance Measure and Variables Used to Predict Performance   Sales or per capita sales is the store performance measure most often used in location regression analyses.

Potential variables used to predict performance include demographic and lifestyle composition of the individual store trading areas; business climate; specific information on the location; image of the store; strength of each potential competitor; and site-related real estate variables such as visibility, access, or other types of tenants at the site. The predictor variables should differ, depending on the type of store being analyzed. For instance, household income may be an important variable when predicting sales of a new Peoples Jewelry store, whereas the number of school-age children per household would be appropriate for predicting sales of a McDonald's restaurant.

Step 3: Solve the Regression Equation and Use It to Project Performance for Future Sites   Data for each store's performance measure and predictor variables are input to a computerized regression program. The end result of the regression analysis is an equation that can be used to predict sales of a new store, given data on the predictor variables for that store. A simple example illustrates how the multiple regression procedure works.[19] Exhibit 9–11 provides data for 10 hypothetical home improvement centers. (The example has been simplified considerably; simple regression should not be performed without at least 30 stores. Also, only one predictor variable is used: population within a three-mile radius of the store. Normally, the analyst would utilize several predictor variables.)

Exhibit 9–12 plots yearly sales and population data from Exhibit 9–11. A regression line has been drawn on the plot that best describes the relationship between sales and population. Specifically, the regression line is statistically defined

EXHIBIT **9–11**

Yearly Sales, Population, and Income for 10 Home Improvement Centers

STORE	YEARLY SALES ($000)	0-TO-3–MILE RADIUS POPULATION
1	$402	54,000
2	367	29,500
3	429	49,000
4	252	22,400
5	185	18,600
6	505	61,100
7	510	49,000
8	330	33,200
9	210	26,400
10	655	83,200

Source: Reprinted by permission of *Site Selection*, 1982. Copyright Lebhar-Friedman, Inc. 425 Park Avenue, New York, NY 10022.

as that which minimizes the squared distances from the points to the line. (The exact form of this line can be determined by any statistical package designed for personal computers as well as some handheld calculators.) The closer the points are to the line, the better the fit and, therefore, the better the sales forecast. As indicated by the line, as population increases, so do sales. Assume a proposed site had a zero-to-three–mile radius population of 40,000. To estimate sales, extend a vertical line from the 40 mark on the horizontal axis of the graph to the regression line, and then extend it horizontally to the vertical axis. (See the dotted line in Exhibit 9–12.) Sales would be approximately $366,000.

EXHIBIT **9–12**

Regression of Population on Sales

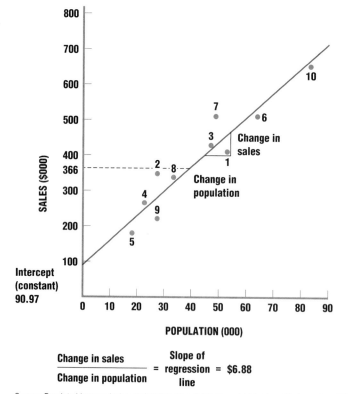

Source: Reprinted by permission of *Site Selection*, 1982. Copyright Lebhar-Friedman, Inc. 425 Park Avenue, New York, NY 10022.
Note: Each number on the graph corresponds to the store number on Exhibit 9–11.

The regression line is derived from the equation

Sales = $a + b_1 x_1$

where

- a = A constant derived by the regression program; a also defines where the regression line in Exhibit 9–12 intercepts the y-axis and is therefore also known as the y-intercept.
- b_1 = A number derived by the regression program that defines the relationship between sales and the predictor variable(s); it is also the slope of the regression line.
- x_1 = The predictor variable (zero-to-three–mile population).

Continuing with the example,

Sales = $91,000 + ($6.88 × 40,000)
        = $366,200

In this case, the regression-derived b indicates that sales will increase positively at a rate of $6.88 for every person in the zero-to-three–mile population. Since the zero-to-three–mile population is 40,000 people, and a is derived as $91,000, the sales total is forecast as $366,200. Note that the mathematical and graphic approaches give the same answer (within one's ability to read the graph).

This simplified illustration used only one predictor variable. Assume that other predictor variables were tested and that average family income was also shown to have a strong and statistically significant relationship to sales. (The number of predictor variables is limited to two in this example for simplification purposes.) The new regression equation is

Sales = $a + b_1 x_1 + b_2 x_2$

where

- a, b_1, and x_1 are as previously defined.
- b_2 = A number derived by the regression program that defines the relationship between sales and average family income.
- x_2 = The predictor variable (average family income).

Assume the new store has a zero-to-three–mile radius population of 55,000, and average family income is $28,000. After solving the regression equation,

$a = -144,146$
$b_1 = 6.937$
$b_2 = 10.132$

Substituting these values into the equation, the new sales forecast is derived:

Sales = −144,146 + (6.937 × 55,000) + (10.132 × 28,000)
        = $521,085

Using the multiple regression method, then, a retailer can predict sales of a new store if variables that have been successfully used to predict sales in other stores are known. Regression analysis does have limitations, however. First, to be reliable, a large database is required. Second, the analyst must be properly trained and must adhere to strict statistical procedures. Finally, since regression is an averaging technique, it seldom identifies extremely good or extremely poor potential locations.

Huff's Gravity Model   Huff's model,[20] loosely based on Newton's law of gravity, is based on the premise that the probability that a given customer will shop in a particular store or shopping center becomes larger as the *size* of the store or center grows and the *distance* or *travel time* from customers to the store or center shrinks. Huff's model is derived from earlier research by Reilly,[21] Converse,[22] and Christaller[23] dating back to the early 1930s.

The objective of Huff's model is to determine the probability that a customer residing in a particular area will shop at a particular store or shopping center. To forecast sales, the location analyst multiplies the probability that the customer will shop at a particular place by an estimate of the customer's expenditures. Then, all the estimated expenditures in an area are aggregated to estimate sales from the area. To begin the process of estimating sales using the Huff method, the general model is defined as follows:

$$P_{ij} = \frac{S_j \div T_{ij}{}^b}{\sum\limits_{j=1}^{n} S_j \div T_{ij}{}^b}$$

where

P_{ij} = Probability of a customer at a given point of origin i traveling to a particular shopping center j

S_j = Size of shopping center j

T_{ij} = Travel time or distance from customer's starting point to shopping center

b = An exponent to T_{ij} that reflects the effect of travel time on different kinds of shopping trips

The model indicates that the larger the size (S_j) of the shopping center compared to competing shopping centers' sizes, the larger the probability that a customer will shop at the center. A larger size is generally better in the customer's eye because it means more assortment and variety. Travel time or distance (T_{ij}) has the opposite effect on the probability that a customer will shop at a given shopping center. The greater the travel time or distance from the customer compared to competing shopping centers, the smaller the probability that the customer will shop at the center. Generally, customers would rather shop at a close center than a distant one.

The exponent $T_{ij}{}^b$ reflects travel time's effect on different kinds of shopping trips. The larger the value of b, the larger the effect of travel time or distance (T_{ij}) on the probability that a customer will shop at a given center. Travel time or distance is generally more important with convenience goods than with shopping goods—people are less willing to travel a great distance for a quart of milk than for a new pair of shoes. Thus a larger value for b is assigned if the store or shopping center being studied specializes in convenience goods rather than shopping goods. b is usually determined through surveys of shopping patterns or from previous experience.

The Huff model is currently being used by retailers to define their trade areas and forecast sales. To illustrate the use of Huff's model, examine Exhibit 9–13. Assume a local shoe store is thinking of opening a new store at the University Park Center shopping center. Two major shopping centers—The Falls and Old Town—provide competition for women's shoes.

SHOPPING CENTER	SIZE (000 SQ. FT.)	DISTANCE FROM UNIVERSITY (MI.)
University Park Center	1,000	3
The Falls	500	5
Old Town	100	1

(The exponent, *b*, is assumed to be 2.)

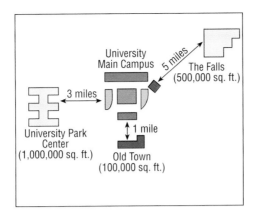

EXHIBIT **9–13**

University and
Shopping Centers:
Gravity Model
Illustration

The following four steps are repeated for each area surrounding the shopping center. Since University Park Center will draw heavily from a nearby university, the process for determining a sales forecast from the university students is described.

1. Determine the probability that a student at this university will shop at University Park Center. Using the formula for Huff's model and data for the centers,

$$P_{ij} = \frac{1{,}000 \div 3^2}{(1{,}000 \div 3^2) + (500 \div 5^2) + (100 \div 1^2)}$$

Probability = .48

2. Determine the number of students who will buy their shoes at University Park Center. The probability is multiplied by the number of students:

.48 × 12,000 students = 5,760 customers

3. Determine the sales forecast. Assuming each customer will spend an average of $150 on shoes, the forecasted sales will be

5,760 customers × $150 = $864,000

4. Estimate sales for the entire trade area. The university population represents only part of the trade area for University Park Center. To estimate sales for the entire trade area, repeat steps 1 to 3 for the remaining areas and then sum them.

Choosing the Best Method(s)   In any decision, the more information that's available, the better the outcome is likely to be. This is true for research in general and location analysis in particular. Therefore, if a combination of the techniques is applied and the same conclusion is reached, the retailer should have more confidence in the decision.

Some methods used for analyzing trade areas are better in certain situations, however. The analog and Huff approaches are best when the number of stores with obtainable data is small, usually fewer than 30. These approaches can also be used by small retailers. The regression approach, on the other hand, is best when there are multiple variables expected to explain sales, since it's hard to keep track of multiple predictor variables when using a manual system like the analog approach. Also, the Huff gravity model explicitly considers the attractiveness of competition and customers' distance or travel time to the store or shopping center in question. Finally, since Huff's gravity model usually does not utilize demographic variables, it's particularly important to use it in conjunction with the analog or regression methods.

SUMMARY   There are three trends that will shape site selection research in the next few decades.[24] First, it will be easier to collect and store data on customers in data warehouses. (This topic will be explored in Chapter 11.) Second, advanced statistical modeling techniques, such as CHAID (Chi Square Automatic Interaction Detection) and spatial allocation models, will become more popular. Finally, GIS will become more sophisticated and at the same time more accessible to users.

Retailers consider several issues when assessing the attractiveness of a particular region, market, or trade area. They want to know about the people living in the area. What are their lifestyles? How wealthy and large are the households? Is the area growing or declining? Does it have a favorable business climate? Importantly, what is the level of competition? Retailers should only locate in areas with heavy competition if they believe their retailing format is superior to their competition's. A safer strategy is to locate in an area with little competition. Of course, in today's overbuilt retail environment, such areas are nearly impossible to find. Does a retailer have the ability to manage multiple stores in an area or in multiple areas? What is the most profitable number of stores to operate in a particular area?

Retailers have a hard time finding a perfect site. Each site has its own set of advantages and disadvantages. In assessing the viability of a particular site, a retailer must consider the location's accessibility as well as locational advantages within the center.

Trade areas are typically divided into primary, secondary, and tertiary zones. The boundaries of a trade area are determined by how accessible it is to customers, the natural and physical barriers that exist in the area, the type of shopping area in which the store is located, the type of store, and the level of competition.

Retailers have three types of information at their disposal to help them define a trade area. First, they use a customer spotting technique to determine how many people are in their trade area and where they live. Second, they use demographic data and GIS firms, the U.S. Census, and the Buying Power Index to describe those customers and assess how much they will buy. Finally, to assess their competition they use the Internet, other sources of secondary information, and a good old-fashioned walk through the neighborhood.

Once retailers have the data that describes their trade areas, they use several analytical techniques to estimate demand. The analog approach—one of the easiest to use—can be particularly useful for smaller retailers. Using this method, the retailer makes predictions about the sales of a new store based on sales in stores in similar areas. Multiple regression analysis uses the same logic as the analog approach but is statistically based and requires more objective data. Finally, we showed how Huff's model is used to predict the probability that a customer will frequent a particular store in a trade area. It is based on the premise that customers are more likely to shop at a given store or shopping center if it's conveniently located and offers a large selection.

KEY TERMS

accessibility, *263*	franchisor, *263*	parasite store, *269*	secondary zone, *267*
amount and quality of parking facilities, *265*	geographic information system (GIS), *270*	polygon, *267*	tertiary zone, *267*
artificial barrier, *264*	ingress/egress, *266*	primary zone, *267*	trade area, *259*
congestion, *265*	MSA (Metropolitan Statistical Area), *259*	region, *259*	traffic flow, *265*
cumulative attraction, *266*		road condition, *263*	understored trade area, *262*
destination store, *268*	natural barrier, *264*	road pattern, *263*	
franchisee, *263*	overstored, *262*	saturated trade area, *262*	visibility, *264*

DISCUSSION QUESTIONS AND PROBLEMS

1. What are the shape and size of the trade area zones of a shopping center near your school?

2. When measuring trade areas, why is the analog approach not a good choice for a retailer with several hundred outlets?

3. True Value Hardware Stores plans to open a new store. Two sites are available, both in middle-income neighborhood centers. One neighborhood is 20 years old and has been well maintained. The other was recently built in a newly planned community. Which site is preferable for True Value? Why?

4. Geographic Information Systems (GIS) have become readily available to even the smallest retailers in the past few years. Why do you think the use of GIS is growing so quickly?

5. Marisol Perez is a graduate student at Florida State University. She is supporting herself by working at a mental hospital. Mary Petrey also lives in Tallahassee, Florida, but never went to college and works in a factory. Both make $20,000 per year, are single, and 21 years old. Would they be in the same PRIZM cluster? How do you think they spend their disposable income?

6. How is the Buying Power Index used in location analysis?

7. Burdines (a division of Federated Department Stores, Inc.) has made a strategic decision to only operate stores in Florida. In fact, it's known as "the Florida store." Evaluate this strategy.

8. Some specialty stores prefer to locate next to or close to an anchor store. But Little Caesars, a take-out pizza retailer typically found in strip centers, wants to be at the end of the center away from the supermarket anchor. Why?

9. Retailers have a choice of locating on a mall's main floor or second or third level. Typically, the main floor offers the best, but most expensive locations. Why would specialty stores such as RadioShack and Foot Locker choose the second or third floor?

10. A drugstore is considering opening a new location at shopping center A, with hopes of capturing sales from a new neighborhood under construction. Two nearby shopping centers, C and E, will provide competition. Using the following information and Huff's probability model, determine the probability that residents of the new neighborhood will shop at shopping center A:

SHOPPING CENTER	SIZE (000 SQ. FT.)	DISTANCE FROM NEW NEIGHBORHOOD (MILES)
A	2,500	3
C	1,250	3
E	250	2

(Assume that $b = 2$.)

SUGGESTED READINGS

Benoit, D., and G.P. Clarke. "Assessing GIS for Retail Location Planning." *Journal of Retailing and Consumer Services* 4, no. 4 (1997).

Birkin, M., G.P. Clarke, M. Clarke, and A. Wilson. "Intelligent GIS: Location Decisions and Strategic Planning." *Journal of Retailing and Consumer Services* 5, no. 4 (June 1998).

Buckner, Robert W. *Site Location: New Advancements in Methods and Technology*, 2d ed. New York: Lebhar-Friedman Books, 1998.

Business Geographics. Ft. Collins, CO: GIS World.

Castle, Gilbert H. *GIS in Real Estate*. The Appraisal Institute, 1998.

Harder, Christian. *GIS Means Business*. Redlands, CA: Environmental Systems Research Institute, Inc., 1997.

Jones, Ken, and Michael Pearce. "The Geography of Markets: Spatial Analysis for Retailers." *Ivey Business Journal* 63, no. 3 (Mar.–Apr. 1999), pp. 66–70.

Jones, Ken, and Jim Simmons. *The Retail Environment*. New York: Rutledge, Chapman and Hall, 1990.

Mitchell, Susan. "Birds of a Feather." *American Demographics*, February 1995, pp. 40–48.

Salvaneschi, Luigi, and Camille Akin, eds. *Location, Location, Location: How to Select the Best Site for Your Business"* Psi Successful Business Library, 1996.

Tayman, Jeff, and Louis Pol. "Retail Site Selection and Geographic Information Systems." *Journal of Applied Business Research* 11, no. 2 (Spring 1995), pp. 46–54.

Weiss, Michael J. *The Clustering of America*. New York: Harper & Row, 1988.

Cole Peterson
Senior Vice President
People Division
Wal-Mart

SAM WALTON STRESSED that the key to our success is our people—our associates and our customers. Supporting and reinforcing this perspective is a challenge for the People Division as Wal-Mart expands globally and continues to experience significant growth. Each year we have to pass along our unique corporate culture to over 50,000 new sales associates we hire. • An important aspect of our culture is a willingness to try new things, to adapt to the changing world around us. We are always experimenting with new products, services, and formats. There is a natural tendency for successful companies like ours to become complacent. But we continue to innovate, to encourage our people to take risks. We recognize that some of these experiments will be successful and some will not. But some failures are bound to occur. The failures simply demonstrate that we are trying new things. • I am responsible for the human resource management policies and practices at Wal-Mart. With over 1.2 million associates, Wal-Mart is the largest nongovernment employer in the world. After graduating from Loyola University, I began my retailing career at Jewel Companies in Chicago, Illinois. I eventually moved to the May Department Store Company, where I became Senior Vice President for Human Resources at their Venture Store Division, before joining Wal-Mart. • Listening is really a critical skill needed to adapt to the environment. Our job in the home office is to support our associates in our stores. Senior executives and management at all levels need to listen to what the front line associates and our customers have to say. Sam Walton called this coaching by walking around (CBWA). • One of our most important challenges is finding enough talented managers to maintain our growth. As retailing becomes a high tech, global business, the demands on our management increase. They need both people and analytical skills. Our store managers work with a diverse group of associates and customers. They also need to be good with numbers, to understand what's working and what is not from a business perspective, and to make the appropriate changes. • Retailing offers exciting and rewarding career opportunities for college students. But many students, and their parents, still think that if they go into retailing, they will be working as a sales associate—the same job they had during their Christmas vacation. They don't realize that they will be responsible for managing business within our company shortly after they graduate.

10

Organization Structure and Human Resource Management

QUESTIONS

- Why does the management of human resources play a vital role in a retailer's performance?

- How do retailers build a sustainable competitive advantage by developing and managing their human resources?

- What activities do retail employees undertake and how are they typically organized?

- How do retailers coordinate employees' activities and motivate them to work toward organization goals?

- What are the human resource management programs for building a committed workforce?

- How do retailers manage diversity among their employees?

RETAILERS ACHIEVE THEIR financial objectives by effectively managing their four critical assets: their locations, merchandise inventory, stores, and employees. This chapter focuses on the organization and management of employees—the retailer's human resources.[1]

Human resource management is particularly important in retailing because employees play a major role in performing critical business functions. In manufacturing firms, capital equipment (machinery, computer systems, robotics) often is used to perform jobs employees once did. But retailing and other service businesses remain labor-intensive. Retailers still rely on people to perform the basic retailing activities such as buying, displaying merchandise, and providing service to customers.

Two chapters in this text are devoted to human resource management because it's such an important issue in the performance of retail firms. This chapter focuses on the broad strategic issues involving organization structure, the general approaches used for motivating and coordinating employee activities, and management practices for building an effective, committed workforce and reducing turnover. Retailing View 10.1 describes how Taco Bell used these approaches to dramatically improve performance.

IN THE EARLY 1980s, TACO BELL was losing money. It had such a weak reputation that people in the eastern United States thought it was a Mexican telephone company. Prices were rising and a typical family of four was reluctant to spend $25 for a fast-food dinner.

A new management team, headed by John Martin, was brought in to reengineer the business, reduce costs, and improve customer service. Business activities were reorganized so centralized sites were set up to perform a lot of slicing, dicing, and cooking formerly done at the back of each restaurant. This centralization of food preparation reduced cost, improved food quality and safety, and increased restaurants' space for servicing customers.

The team concept was introduced to extend the notion of ownership and responsibility to the people who interact with the 50 million customers Taco Bell serves weekly. Restaurants were organized as team managed units (TMUs). Instead of having a full-time manager, the crews work together as a TMU to run the restaurant. To reduce the 16 hours a week being spent on administrative tasks, Taco Bell developed a computerized system for employee scheduling and food ordering. Front-line crew members are given responsibility for hiring and training other crew members, handling customer requests and complaints, and even reviewing the financial statements to see how well the restaurant is doing. They decide among themselves about what can be done to improve performance.

Taco Bell's reengineering efforts have built the chain from 1,500 restaurants with less than $600 million in sales in

Effective human resource management played an important role in the success that Taco Bell has achieved.

1982 to over 20,000 locations with $5 billion annual sales. Taco Bell feels that benefits of the TMU concept go beyond improving restaurant performance. For many people, Taco Bell is their first real job. The TMU experience introduces them to the notion of accepting responsibility and developing a work ethic that can serve them throughout their lifetime.

Source: Tim Durnford, "Redefining Value: For Whom the Taco Bell Tolls," *Cornell Hotel & Restaurant Administration Quarterly* 38 (June 1997), pp. 74–81; and Roger Hallowell, Leonard Schlesinger, and Jeffery Zornitsky, "Internal Service Quality, Customer and Job Satisfaction: Linkages and Implications for Management," *Human Resource Planning* 19, no. 2 (1996), pp. 20–31.

Refact Labor costs typically are over 25 percent of sales and 50 percent of operating costs in service-oriented department and specialty stores.[2]

The activities undertaken to implement the retailer's human resource strategy including recruiting, selecting, training, supervising, evaluating, and compensating sales associates are typically undertaken by store management. We discuss these operational issues in more detail in Chapter 17 on store management.

HUMAN RESOURCE MANAGEMENT OBJECTIVES

The strategic objective of human resource management is to align the capabilities and behaviors of employees with the short-term and long-term goals of the retail firm.[3] One human resource management performance measure is **employee productivity**—the retailer's sales or profit divided by its employee costs. Employee productivity can be improved by increasing the sales generated by employees and/or reducing labor costs. While employee productivity is directly related to the retailer's short-term profits, other

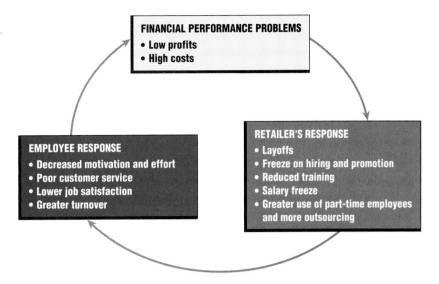

Downward
Performance Spiral

performance measures such as employee and customer satisfaction have important effects on long-term performance.

A failure to consider both long- and short-term objectives can result in a mismanagement of human resources and a downward performance spiral shown in Exhibit 10–1. Often, when retailers' sales and profits decline due to increased competition, they respond by decreasing labor costs. They reduce the number of sales associates in stores, hire more part-timers, and spend less on training. While these actions may increase short-term profits, they have an adverse effect on long-term performance because employee morale and customer service decrease.[4] Retailing View 10.2 describes how Sears broke this downward spiral by placing more emphasis on its human resources.

This chapter examines two important human resource strategies that affect employee productivity: the design of the organization structure and the programs used to develop a coordinated, committed, motivated workforce. The first part of the chapter describes how retail firms are typically organized—how authority and responsibility for doing tasks is assigned to people and business units. Then we discuss the retailers' approaches to improve coordination between departments and employees. The last sections review human resource programs used to motivate employees to work toward achieving company goals and build employee commitment to the firm.

DESIGNING THE ORGANIZATION STRUCTURE FOR A RETAIL FIRM

The **organization structure** identifies the activities to be performed by specific employees and determines the lines of authority and responsibility in the firm. The first step in developing an organization structure is to determine the tasks that must be performed. Exhibit 10–2 shows tasks typically performed in a retail firm.

These tasks are divided into four major categories: strategic management, administrative management (operations), merchandise management, and store management. The organization of this textbook is based on these tasks and managers who perform them.

THE YEAR 1992 WAS THE WORST in the history of Sears. The company's net loss was almost $2 billion because it failed to adapt to changing consumer tastes. Consumers were going to the mall to buy fashionable merchandise from department and specialty stores and going to category killers for car batteries, hardware, and appliances.

Under the direction of Arthur Martinez, the CEO, five task forces—customers, employees, financial performance, innovations, and values—were formed to develop a strategy for Sears' turnaround. To clearly communicate its new direction both internally and externally, Sears adopted the three C's as its objectives—compelling place to shop, to work, and to invest—and the three P's—passion for the customer, our people add value, and performance leadership—as its core values.

Sears undertook a number of human resource management programs to make the company a compelling place to work including increasing the training for sales associates, using learning maps and monthly town hall meetings in the stores to improve employee knowledge of retailing economics and the company's strategy, establishing Sears University to train managers, developing a compensation system emphasizing performance-based financial and nonfinancial rewards, and instituting a 360-degree performance appraisal systems including feedback from subordinates and supervisors.

Sears also undertook a program to measure its performance toward achieving each of the three C's. By analyzing the relationships between the measures, Sears found that an improvement of five points on the measure of employee satisfaction resulted in a 1.3-point increase in the measure of cus-

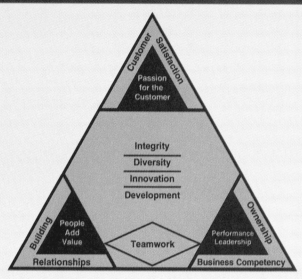

One of the three critical elements in Sears' strategy is making Sears' a compelling place to work.

tomer satisfaction, which led to 0.5 percent improvement in sales growth. Thus Sears' effort to make the company a compelling place to work increased customer satisfaction and financial performance.

Source: Arthur Martinez, "Sears' Strategy for Continuing Renewal," *Chain Store Age*, July 1999, pp. 64–74; and Anthony Rucci, Steven Kirn, and Richard T. Quinn, "The Employee–Customer–Profit Chain at Sears," *Harvard Business Review*, January–February 1998, pp. 82–97.

Section II of the text focuses on the strategic and administrative tasks. The strategic market and finance decisions (discussed in Chapters 6 and 7) are undertaken primarily by senior management: the CEO, COO, vice presidents, and the board of directors representing shareholders in publicly held firms. Administrative tasks (discussed in Chapters 8 through 11) are performed by corporate staff employees who have specialized skills in human resource management, finance, accounting, management information systems, site location, and distribution. These administrative activities develop plans, procedures, and information to assist operating managers in implementing the firm's strategic plans.

In retail firms, the primary operating managers are involved in merchandise management (Section III) and store management (Section IV). These operating managers implement the strategic plans with the assistance of administrative personnel. They make the day-to-day decisions that directly affect the firm's performance.

EXHIBIT 10–2 Tasks Performed in a Retail Firm

STRATEGIC MANAGEMENT
- Develop a retail strategy
- Identify the target market
- Determine the retail format
- Design organizational structure
- Select locations

MERCHANDISE MANAGEMENT
- Buy merchandise
  - Locate vendors
  - Evaluate vendors
  - Negotiate with vendors
  - Place orders
- Control merchandise inventory
  - Develop merchandise budget plans
  - Allocate merchandise to stores
  - Review open-to-buy and stock position
- Price merchandise
  - Set initial prices
  - Adjust prices

STORE MANAGEMENT
- Recruit, hire, train store personnel
- Plan work schedules
- Evaluate performance of store personnel
- Maintain store facilities
- Locate and display merchandise
- Sell merchandise to customers
- Repair and alter merchandise
- Provide services such as gift wrapping and delivery
- Handle customer complaints
- Take physical inventory
- Prevent inventory shrinkage

ADMINISTRATIVE MANAGEMENT (OPERATIONS)
- Promote the firm, its merchandise, and services
  - Plan communication programs
  - Develop communication budget
  - Select media
  - Plan special promotions
  - Design special displays
  - Manage public relations
- Manage human resources
  - Develop policies for managing store personnel
  - Recruit, hire, train managers
  - Plan career paths
  - Keep employee records
- Distribute merchandise
  - Locate warehouses
  - Receive merchandise
  - Mark and label merchandise
  - Store merchandise
  - Ship merchandise to stores
  - Return merchandise to vendors
- Establish financial control
  - Provide timely information on financial performance
  - Forecast sales, cash flow, profits
  - Raise capital from investors
  - Bill customers
  - Provide credit

To illustrate the connection between the tasks performed and the organization structure, the tasks are color coded. Red is used to represent the strategic tasks, blue for the administrative tasks, gold for the merchandising tasks, and green for the store management tasks.

Organization Design Considerations

Once the tasks have been identified, the retailer groups them into jobs to be assigned to specific individuals and determines the reporting relationships.[5]

Specialization Rather than performing all the tasks shown in Exhibit 10–2, individual employees are typically responsible for only one or two tasks. **Specialization** enables employees to develop expertise and increase productivity. For

The strategic decisions discussed in Chapters 6 and 7 are undertaken primarily by the senior management in a retail firm.

example, a real estate manager can concentrate on becoming expert at selecting retail sites, while a benefit manager can focus on becoming expert in developing creative and cost-effective employee benefits. Through specialization, employees work only on tasks for which they were trained and have unique skills.

But employees may become bored if they're assigned a narrow set of tasks such as putting price tags on merchandise all day long, every day. Also, extreme specialization may increase labor costs. For example, salespeople often don't have many customers when the store first opens, mid-afternoon, or at closing. Rather than hiring a specialist for stocking shelves and arranging merchandise, many retailers have salespeople perform these tasks during slow selling periods.

Responsibility and Authority   Productivity increases when employees have the proper amount of authority to effectively undertake the responsibilities assigned to them. For example, buyers who are responsible for the profitability of merchandise in a category have the authority to make decisions that will enable them to fulfill this responsibility. They should have the authority to select and price merchandise for their category and determine how the merchandise is displayed and sold.

Sometimes the benefits of matching responsibility and authority conflict with benefits of specialization. For example, buyers rarely have authority over how their merchandise is sold. Other employees, such as store managers who specialize in management of salespeople, have this authority.

Reporting Relationships   After assigning tasks to employees, the final step in designing the organization structure is determining the reporting relationships. Productivity can decrease when too many or too few employees report to a supervisor. The effectiveness of supervisors decreases when they have too many employees reporting to them. On the other hand, if managers are supervising very few employees, the number of managers increases and costs go up.

The appropriate number of subordinates ranges from 4 to 12, depending on the nature of their tasks, their skills, and their location. The number of subordinates is greater when they perform simple standardized tasks, when they're well trained and competent, and when they perform tasks at the same location as the supervisor. Under these conditions, supervision isn't as difficult, and the supervisor can effectively manage more people.

Matching Organization Structure to Retail Strategy   The design of the organization structure needs to match the firm's retail strategy. For example, category specialists and warehouse clubs such as Circuit City and Costco target price-sensitive customers and thus are very concerned about building a competitive advantage based on low cost. They minimize the number of employees by having decisions made by a few people at corporate headquarters. These centralized organization structures are very effective when there are limited regional or local differences in customer needs.

On the other hand, high-fashion clothing customers often aren't very price-sensitive, and tastes vary across the country. Retailers targeting these segments tend to have more managers and decision making at the local store level. By having more decisions made at the local store level, human resource costs are higher, but sales also increase since merchandise and services are tailored to meet the needs of local markets.

RETAIL ORGANIZATION STRUCTURES

Retail organization structures differ according to the type of retailer and the size of the firm. For example, a retailer with a single store will have an organization structure quite different from a national chain.

Organization of Single-Store Retailers

Owner-managers of a single store may be the entire organization. When they go to lunch or go home, the store closes. As sales grow, the owner-manager hires employees. Coordinating and controlling employee activities is easier in a store than in a large chain of stores. The owner-manager simply assigns tasks to each employee and watches to see that these tasks are performed properly. Since the number of employees is limited, single-store retailers have little specialization. Each employee must perform a wide range of activities, and the owner-manager is responsible for all management tasks.

Refact Over 95 percent of all U.S. retailers own and operate a single store, but single-store retailers account for less than 50 percent of all retail store sales.[6]

When sales increase, specialization in management may occur when the owner-manager hires management employees. Exhibit 10–3 illustrates the common division of management responsibilities into merchandise and store management. The owner-manager continues to perform strategic management tasks. The store manager also may be responsible for administrative tasks associated with receiving and shipping merchandising and managing the employees. The merchandise manager or buyer may handle the advertising and promotion tasks as well as the merchandise tasks. Often the owner-manager contracts with an accounting firm to perform financial control tasks for a fee.

Refact Mellerio dits Meller, the French jeweler founded in 1591, is one of the oldest family-owned retail chains still operating[7]

EXHIBIT 10–3   Organization of a Small Retailer

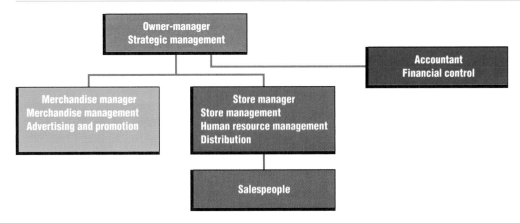

Organization of a Regional Department Store Chain

In contrast to the management of a single store, retail chain management is complex. Managers must supervise units that are geographically distant from each other. In this section, we use Rich's/Lazarus/Goldsmith's (a regional department store chain headquartered in Atlanta, Georgia, and owned by Federated Department Stores) to illustrate the organization of a large, multi-unit retailer.

The Rich's/Lazarus/Goldsmith's division was formed in 1995 when Federated Department Stores merged three regional department store chains. While the stores in each region continue to carry the name of the regional chains, there's only one headquarters office. Rather than using the full name of the division, we'll refer to it as Rich's in the following discussion.

Traditionally, department stores were family-owned and -managed. Organization of these firms was governed by family circumstances. Executive positions were designed to accommodate family members involved in the business. Then, in 1927, Paul Mazur proposed a functional organization plan that has been adopted by most retailers.[9] The organization structures of retail chains, including Rich's, continue to reflect principles of the Mazur plan such as separating merchandising and store management tasks into separate divisions.

Exhibit 10–4 shows Rich's organization. Most retail chains such as The Gap, Home Depot, and T.J. Maxx have similar organization structures. Vice presidents responsible for specific merchandise categories, stores, and administrative tasks report to the chairperson and president.

In most retail firms, the chairperson and president work closely together in managing the firm. They are frequently referred to as principals or partners. One member of the partnership is primarily responsible for the merchandising activities of the firm—the merchandise, stores, and marketing divisions. The other partner is primarily responsible for the human resource, distribution, information systems, and finance divisions. For example, James Zimmerman and Terry Lundgren are CEO and president, respectively, of Federated Department Stores. While they share a lot of responsibilities for developing and implementing Federated's strategy, Lundgren is primarily concerned with merchandising while Zimmerman is more involved in operations.

Most managers and employees in the stores division work in stores located throughout the geographic region. Merchandise, planning, marketing, finance, visual merchandising, and human resource managers and employees work at corporate headquarters.

Merchandise Division   The merchandise division is responsible for procuring the merchandise sold in the stores and ensuring that the quality, fashionability, assortment, and pricing of merchandise is consistent with the firm's strategy. Chapters 12 through 15 discuss major activities performed in the merchandise division.

Exhibit 10–5 shows a detailed organization structure of Rich's merchandise division. Each senior vice president/general merchandise manager (GMM) is responsible for specific categories of merchandise. GMMs report directly to the chairperson and CEO, the partner in charge of the merchandising activities.

The organization structure of the merchandising division in retail chains has changed significantly over the past 10 years. Previously, the buyer was the key operating manager in the merchandising division. Each buyer was responsible for a specific category of merchandise (such as bed sheets and comforters) and

EXHIBIT   10–4   Organization of a Regional Department Store: Rich's

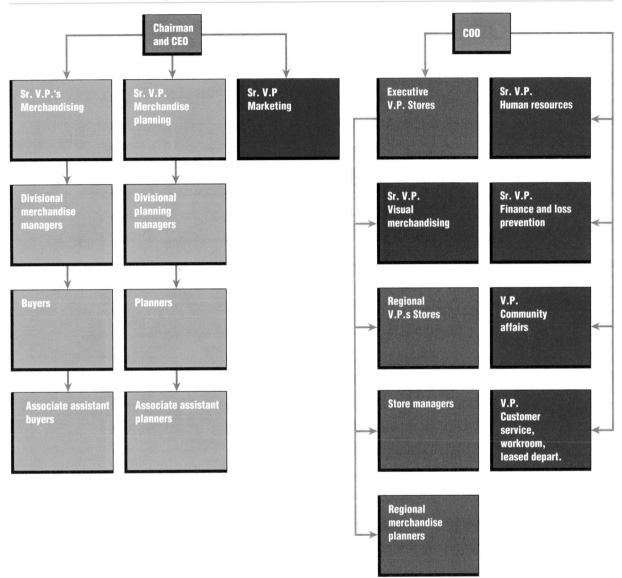

managed that category as if it were a separate business. Buyers selected merchandise and priced it. They determined what merchandise was stocked and sold in each store and managed their business with profit-and-loss responsibility.

Giving this much responsibility and authority to buyers can cause problems. First, the merchandise strategy across categories might not be consistent. For example, the buyer for preteens' accessories might select merchandise that wasn't compatible with the merchandise bought by the preteen's apparel buyer. Second, the allocation of merchandise to specific stores wasn't coordinated. For example, some buyers might allocate more expensive merchandise to stores in high-income areas, while others wouldn't make this adjustment.

EXHIBIT **10–5**   Merchandise Division Organization: Rich's

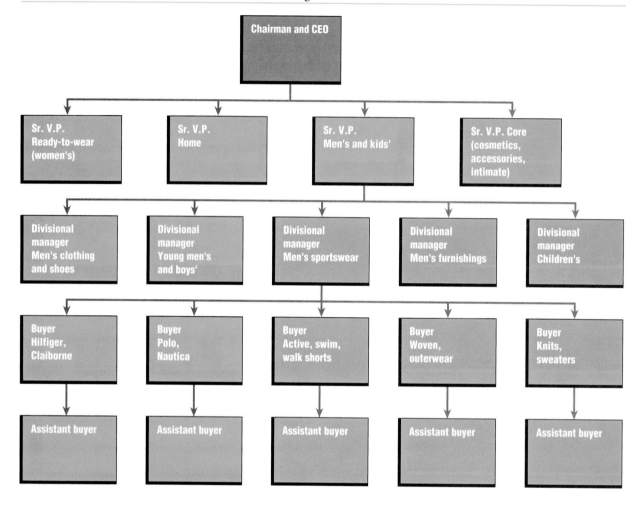

To address these problems, most retail chains created a merchandise planning group, with a Senior VP of planning and distribution who is often as important as the merchandise managers in the buying organization. Each merchandising planner is responsible for tailoring the assortment in several categories for specific stores in a geographic area. For example, the planner at The Gap would alter the basic assortment of sweaters for the different climates in South Florida and the Pacific Northwest.

Stores Division   The stores division is responsible for the group of activities undertaken in stores. Each vice president is in charge of a set of stores. A store manager, often called a general manager, is responsible for activities performed in each store.

Exhibit 10–6 shows the organization chart of a Rich's store. General managers in large stores have three assistant store managers reporting to them. The assistant store manager for sales and merchandising manages the sales associates and presentation of the merchandise in the store. The assistant manager for human resources is responsible for selecting, training, and evaluating employees.

EXHIBIT 10-6

Store Organizations:
Rich's

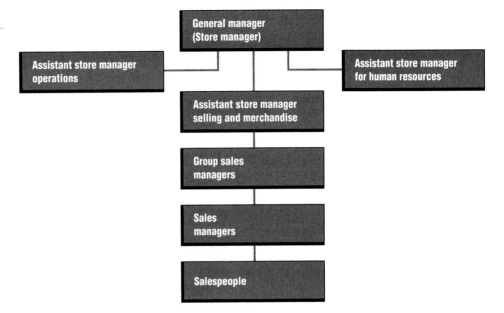

The assistant store manager for operations is responsible for store maintenance; store security; some customer service activities (such as returns, complaints, and gift wrapping); the receiving, shipping, and storage areas of the store; and leased areas including the restaurant and hair styling salon. In smaller stores, for example, the general manager may perform the tasks done by an assistant store manager for merchandise.

Group sales managers, sales managers, and the salespeople work with customers in a specific area of the store. For example, a sales manager might be responsible for the entire area in which kitchen appliances, gifts, china, silver, and tableware are sold, while a group sales manager might be responsible for an entire floor of the store.

As Federated Department Stores, Inc. focuses its strategy on its department store chains, it is reengineering itself to instill a "customer-first" mentality throughout the corporation.

Corporate Organization of a Regional Department Store Chain

As mentioned in Chapter 2, many regional chains such as Rich's are owned by retail corporations. Exhibit 10–7 shows the organization chart of Federated's corporate headquarters in Cincinnati, Ohio. Retailing View 10.3 reviews the evolution of Federated Department Stores into one of the world's largest department store chain.

The decisions made at the corporate office involve activities that set strategic directions and increase productivity by coordinating the regional chains' activities. For example, having one corporate management information system and one private-brand merchandise program is much more efficient and effective than having separate systems and programs in each regional chain.

EXHIBIT **10-7**

Corporate
Organization of
Federated
Department Stores

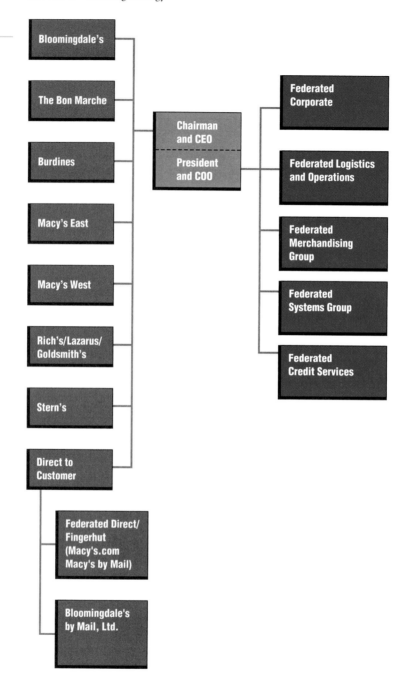

Corporate Functions   Activities performed at the Federated corporate office,
rather than at the regional chain level, include

- Corporate (Cincinnati, Ohio): Support services cover tax, audit, accounting,
  cash management and finance, internal audit, planning, insurance, economic
  forecasting, law, corporate communications, purchasing, store
  design/construction, and real estate.

FEDERATED DEPARTMENT STORES WAS FOUNDED IN 1929 as a holding company by several family-owned, regional department store chains including Shillito's founded in 1830 in Cincinnati, Ohio; Bloomingdale's in New York founded in 1885; Jordan Marsh founded in 1841 in Boston; F&R Lazarus founded in 1851 in Columbus, Ohio; and Abraham & Strauss founded in 1865 in New York. Over the next 30 years, Bon Marche (Seattle), Rike's (Dayton, Ohio), Goldsmith's (Memphis), Burdines (Miami), and Rich's (Atlanta) joined Federated. In addition, the company started Filene's Basement (an off-price retailer) and Gold Circle (a full-line discounter) and acquired Ralph's (a West Coast supermarket chain). Each of these chains was operated as an independent division with its own buying office, distribution center, corporate offices, and human resource policies. While the divisions were profitable, the stock price was low.

In 1986, Robert Campeau, a successful Canadian real estate developer, felt that the stock for retail conglomerate companies like Federated was low and he bought Allied, a similar holding company, for $3.5 billion. In April 1988, he bought Federated for $6.6 billion. To finance these acquisitions, he sold off over 25 chains owned by the two holding companies (including Brooks Brothers, Ann Taylor, Ralph's, Filene's, Joske's, Miller's, Bonwit Teller, and Gold Circle) and attempted to cut operating costs. However, most of the acquisition was financed by issuing bonds and taking out loans. On January 15, 1990, the retail subsidiaries could not pay the interest on its debt and filed for bankruptcy, the largest bankruptcy in U.S. history at that time.

Under the protection of the bankruptcy court, Federated's new management team closed unprofitable stores, sold divisions unrelated to its core department store activities, and reduced operating costs dramatically by developing information, distribution, and buying systems used by most of the department store divisions. In 1992, Federated emerged from bankruptcy as one of the largest and best managed retail chains. The company has since acquired three department store chains—Macy's, Horne's (Pittsburgh), and The Broadway (Los Angeles)—and Fingerhut, an Internet and catalog retailer, but it maintains its focus on developing synergies between its department store divisions. Federated appears to have a long-term strategy of operating two national retail chains (Bloomingdale's, and Macy's) positioned at different points on the price/quality continuum. The Bullock's and Broadway stores in Southern California and the Jordan Marsh stores in New England were converted to the Macy's nameplate in 1995 and 1996.

Source: *Reflections: 1999 Fact Book,* Federated Department Stores; and Linda Grant, "Miracle or Mirage on 34th Street," *Fortune,* February 1996, pp. 84–91.

- Merchandising and Product Development (New York): Development of merchandising strategies, coordinating relationships with vendors, designing and sourcing private-label merchandise, and managing marketing programs for private-brand merchandise. Among Federated's private brands are Charter Club, I.N.C. International Concepts, Arnold Palmer, Club Room, Tools of the Trade, Badge, Style & Co., and Alfani.

- Financial Credit Services Group (Mason, Ohio): This group provides proprietary credit card and services for each regional department store chain. Federated has over 58 million credit card holders. The group also is responsible for payroll and benefits processing.

- Federated Systems Group (Norcross, Georgia): This division designs, installs, and manages the information system used by all divisions.

- Federated Logistics and Operations (Secaucus, New Jersey): Logistics coordinates and manages the logistics and distribution functions as well as accounts payable, purchasing, store planning, vendor technology, and energy management and expense control.[10]

Most retail chains have an organization structure very similar to Rich's structure in Exhibit 10–4 with people in charge of the merchandising, store management, and administrative tasks reporting to the CEO and president. Only corporations that operate several different chains such as Dayton Hudson, Intimate Brands, and The Gap have the overarching corporate structure shown in Exhibit 10–7. Large supermarket chains such as Safeway and Kroger are often organized geographically, like Federated Department Stores, with each region operating as a semi-independent unit having its own merchandise and store management staff.

Organization Structure of Other Types of Retailer

The primary difference between the organization structure of a department store and other retail formats is the numbers of people and management levels in the merchandising and store management areas. Many national retailers such as The Gap, Sears, and Circuit City centralize merchandise management activities at corporate headquarters and have fewer buyers and management levels in the merchandise group. On the other hand, these national retailers have many more stores than a regional department store chain like Rich's; thus they have more managers and management levels in the stores division. For example, one person is responsible for stores and operations at The Gap, in contrast to the six regional chain and one national chain (Bloomingdale's) executives for stores and operations in the decentralized Federated Stores organization. But The Gap, with over 900 stores, needs more levels of store management (14 zone vice presidents, 18 regional managers, and 195 district managers) than Rich's, which only has 76 stores.

RETAIL ORGANIZATION DESIGN ISSUES

Federated Department Stores, Inc., is an example of a retail corporation with a geographically decentralized organization structure. Many retailing decisions are made by the regional department store chains, not by corporate managers.

Centralized versus Decentralized Decision Making

Centralization is the degree to which authority for retailing decisions is delegated to corporate managers rather than to geographically dispersed regional, district, and store managers. Retailers reduce costs when decision making is centralized in corporate management. First, overhead falls because fewer managers are required to make the merchandise, human resource, marketing, and financial decisions. For example, Federated has both regional women's blouse buyers and corporate buyers coordinating the regional chains and buying private-label blouses. The Gap has one buyer for women's blouses at the corporate headquarters.

With annual sales of about $2.2 billion, Rich's has over 90 people in its buying organization. The Gap has about twice those annual sales and only half as many buyers. Centralized retail organizations can similarly reduce personnel in administrative functions such as marketing and human resources.

Second, by coordinating its efforts across geographically dispersed stores, the company achieves lower prices from suppliers. Finally, centralization provides an opportunity to have the best people make decisions for the entire corporation. For example, in a centralized organization, people with the greatest expertise in areas such as MIS, buying, store design, and visual merchandise can have all stores benefit from their skills.[11]

Most centralized retail organizations emphasize efficiency. Standard operating policies are used for store and personnel management; these policies limit the decisions made by store managers. Often their stores are similar physically and carry similar merchandise. Corporate merchandisers do considerable research to determine the best method for presenting merchandise. They provide detailed guides for displaying merchandise to each store manager so that all stores look the same throughout the country. Because they offer the same core merchandise in all stores, centralized retailers can achieve economies of scale by advertising through national media rather than more costly local media.

While centralization has advantages in reducing costs, it can be hard for the centralized retailer to tailor its offering to the needs of local markets. However, retailers are relying more on their information systems to react to local market conditions. For example, American Drug Stores use data collected by point-of-sale terminals to understand local conditions. Most drugstore chains are cutting back on the space devoted to automotive supplies. But American Drug sales data indicated that people in the inner city are more likely to change their own oil so it maintained its automotive supply offering in these stores.[12]

In addition to problems with catering to local needs, the centralized retailer may have difficulty responding to local competition and labor markets. Since merchandise mix and pricing are established centrally, individual stores may not be able to respond quickly to competition in their market. Finally, centralized personnel policies can make it hard for local managers to pay competitive wages in their area or to hire appropriate types of salespeople.

Coordinating Buying and Store Management

Small independent retailers can effectively coordinate their stores' buying and selling activities. Owner-managers typically buy the merchandise and work with their salespeople to sell it. Being in close contact with customers, they know what their customers want.

This store owner does not have a problem coordinating employee activities because she has daily, face-to-face contact with her employees and her customers.

On the other hand, large retail firms organize the buying and selling functions into separate divisions. Buyers specialize in buying merchandise and have limited contact with the store management responsible for selling it. While this specialization increases buyers' skills and expertise, it makes it harder for them to understand customers' needs. Four approaches large retailers use to coordinate buying and selling are (1) improving communications between buyers and sellers, (2) making store visits, (3) assigning employees to coordinating roles, and (4) decentralizing the buying decisions.

Improving Communications Fashion-oriented retailers use several methods to increase buyers' contact with customers and to improve informal communication between buyers and store personnel who sell the merchandise they buy. Management trainees, who eventually become buyers, are required by most retailers to work in the stores before they enter the buying office. During this 6-to-10–month training period, prospective buyers gain appreciation for the activities performed in the stores, the problems salespeople and department managers encounter, and the needs of customers.

Making Store Visits   Another approach to increasing customer contact and communication is to have buyers visit the stores and work with the departments they buy for. At Wal-Mart, all managers (not just the buyers) are required to visit stores frequently and practice the company philosophy of CBWA (coaching by wandering around). Managers leave corporate headquarters in Bentonville, Arkansas, Sunday night and return to share their experiences at the traditional Saturday morning meetings.[13]

This face-to-face communication provides managers with a richer view of store and customer needs than they can get from impersonal sales reports from the company's management information system. Spending time in the stores improves buyers' understanding of customer needs, but this system is costly because it reduces the time the buyer has to review sales patterns, plan promotions, manage inventory, and locate new sources of merchandise.

Assigning Employees to Coordinating Roles   Some retailers, like Rich's, have people in the merchandise division (the planner/distributors who work with buyers) and the stores (the managers of operations who work for the store managers) who are responsible for coordinating buying and selling activities. Most national retail chains have regional and even district staff personnel to coordinate buying and selling activities. For example, Target's regional merchandise managers in Chicago work with stores in the North Central region to translate plans developed by corporate buyers into programs that meet the regional needs of consumers.

Involving Store Management in Buying Decisions   Another way to improve coordination between buying and selling activities is to increase store employees' involvement in the buying process. Nordstrom has buyers who live in each geographic region and buy merchandise for that region. For example, much of the merchandise for the four Nordstrom stores in northern California is bought by buyers in San Francisco. Because these buyers work with a limited number of stores in close proximity to their offices, they're in the stores frequently.

JCPenney had a tradition of decentralized store management. **Decentralization** is when authority for retail decisions is made at low levels in the organization. Management in each JCPenney store determined what merchandise that store would sell. Each season, buyers at corporate headquarters in Dallas selected merchandise and presented it to managers in all Penney stores using CD-ROMs and closed-circuit TV. Store managers were given an order planning form with retail prices, margins, and suggested quantities and assortments for their store size. Store merchandise managers then place their orders for the merchandise presented through computer terminals linked to the Penney management information system. Recently, JCPenney shifted to centralized buying.

Using regional buyers and involving store managers in buying decisions enables Nordstrom to better tailor their merchandise to local markets. But Nordstrom loses some buying efficiency; re-

JCPenney uses satellite communication system and Internet to communicate with its employees.

gional buyers only place orders for four stores. They can't use the chain's entire buying power to get prices as low and delivery as quick as comparably sized competing chains can get.

While the buying decisions were made by Penney merchandise managers who interact daily with their customers, these managers had limited buying expertise. Frequently, they've just completed a management training program after graduating from college. Corporate buyers with significant experience and expertise were often frustrated because the store merchandise managers weren't quick to adapt to fashion trends that buyers see coming. Finally, merchandise managers in the stores only saw the merchandise on TV or from CD-ROMs. They couldn't feel the merchandise or see its true colors.

In conclusion, each approach for coordinating buying and selling has limitations. Retail firms constantly make trade-offs between the efficiency gained through centralized buying and the greater sales potential obtained through decentralized buying decisions that tailor merchandise to local markets.

Trends in Retail Organization Designs

To improve financial performance in the face of increased competition, retailers are changing their organizations. These changes reduce cost by centralizing, flattening the organization structure, outsourcing, and improving employee productivity using the Internet.

Centralization Retailers are using sophisticated information systems to make more decisions at corporate headquarters rather than by division staffs or store managers. For example, retailers with long histories of decentralized merchandise buying, such as JCPenney and Nordstrom, are buying more merchandise at the corporate level. The corporate staff at Federated is taking responsibility for operational activities such as distribution, information systems, private-brand merchandise, and human resource management policies that were formerly made in the regional divisions. However, each Federated division is still responsible for the management of merchandise.[14]

Flattening the Organization **Flattening the organization** means reducing the number of management levels. For example, the Rich's merchandise department in Exhibit 10–4 has five levels: partner, Senior Vice President, divisional merchandise manager, buyer, and associate buyer. A flatter organization structure might have three levels: partner, divisional manager, and buyer. Using this structure, there might be more buyers and divisional merchandise managers, but the general merchandise manager and associate buyer levels would be eliminated.

Cutting management levels reduces the total number of managers and increases the organization's responsiveness to customers and competitors. Higher-level managers then become closer to the customer. Fewer levels of approval are needed to make changes and implement new programs. On the other hand, in a flatter organization, managers have more subordinates reporting to them so they can't supervise them closely. They must trust their subordinates to do their jobs well.

Outsourcing Retailers, like other businesses, are reviewing the activities performed by company employees and deciding if these activities can be performed more efficiently by other companies.[15] **Outsourcing** is purchasing from suppliers services that previously had been performed by company employees. For example, many retailers outsource logistical services, store maintenance, and management of their information systems. These retailers find that companies specializing in providing these business services perform them at a lower cost due to their scale economies and use of up-to-date technologies. Another example of outsourcing is having vendors rather than retail employees put labels and price tags on merchandise. This example of outsourcing is discussed in more detail in Chapter 11.

While outsourcing these services can reduce costs, some retailers are concerned that outsourcing may result in loss of a strategic advantage. As Chapter 6 said, retailers can develop competitive advantages based on their distribution and information systems. If these activities are outsourced, competitors can achieve similar performance levels by using the same vendors. Even a mundane activity like cleaning the store can be a source of strategic advantage that retailers are reluctant to outsource. The Bloomingdale's flagship store on 59th St. in New York City is known for its exciting store atmosphere. When asked about outsourcing the maintenance of the store, the store's operations manager responded, "There is so much that is unique about this store . . . I don't believe any outsider would bring the same sense of passion to the job we do in house."[16]

Using the Internet   Retail chains are using intranets to automate and streamline human resource operations. For example, Penney's 150,000 employees use kiosks in the 1,200 Penney stores to make changes in their personnel records, request time off, register for training classes, review the company's policies and procedures manual, and request services such as direct-deposit of their paychecks. These self-service kiosks are also used by job applicants to review open positions, submit applications, and take prescreening tests. The use of these kiosks, connected through an intranet to a centralized base, dramatically reduces the time human resources administrators spend on paper works.[17]

In the following sections of this chapter, we examine some of the unique human resource problems confronting retailers and how they address these problems through programs to motivate and coordinate these activities.

SPECIAL ISSUES IN RETAIL HUMAN RESOURCE MANAGEMENT

Human resource management in retailing is very challenging. Most retailers are open long hours and weekends to respond to the needs of family shoppers and working people. In addition, peak shopping periods occur during lunch hours, at night, and during sales. To deal with these peak periods and long hours, retailers have to complement their one or two shifts of full-time (40-hours-per-week) store employees with part-time workers. Part-time workers can be more difficult to manage than full-time employees. They often are less committed to the company and their jobs, and they're more likely to quit than full-time employees.

Retailers must control expenses and thus are cautious about paying high wages to hourly employees who perform low-skill jobs. To control costs, retailers often hire people with little or no experience to work as sales associates, bank tellers, and waiters. High turnover, absenteeism, and poor performance often result from the use of inexperienced, low-wage employees.

The lack of experience and motivation among many retail employees is particularly troublesome because these employees are often in direct contact with customers. Unlike manufacturing workers on an assembly line, the lowest-paid retail

Refact Thirty-five percent of all retail employees work part-time; 3.3 million of these part-time workers are enrolled in high school or college.[18]

employees work in areas that are highly visible to customers. Poor appearance, manners, and attitudes can have a negative effect on sales and customer loyalty.

The changing demographic pattern outlined in Chapter 4 will result in a chronic shortage of qualified sales associates. To satisfy their human resource needs, retailers are increasing the diversity of their workforces, employing more minorities, handicapped people, and the elderly.

Finally, the work values of 23-to-32–year-old Generation Xers is quite different than those of their baby boomer supervisors. Many older managers feel that younger employees have poor work ethics. Younger employees respond by saying, "Get a life," and strive to balance their personal and professional lives. Managing this growing diversity and changing values in the retail workforce create opportunities and problems for human resource managers.[19]

MOTIVATING AND COORDINATING EMPLOYEES

A critical task of human resource management is to motivate and coordinate employees to work toward achieving the firm's goals and implementing its strategy. The task is often difficult because employees' goals may differ from the firm's. For example, a sales associate might find it more personally rewarding to finish arranging a display than to help a customer. Retailers generally use three methods to motivate and coordinate their employees' activities: (1) written policies and supervision, (2) incentives, and (3) organization culture.[20]

Policies and Supervision

Perhaps the most fundamental method of coordination is to (1) prepare written policies that indicate what employees should do and (2) have supervisors enforce these policies. For example, retailers may set policies on when and how merchandise can be returned by customers. If employees use the written policies to make these decisions, their actions will be consistent with the retailer's strategy.

But strict reliance on written policies can reduce employee motivation. Employees might have little opportunity to use their own initiative to improve performance of their areas of responsibility. As a result, they eventually might find their jobs uninteresting.

Relying on rules as a method of coordination leads to a lot of red tape. Situations will arise that aren't covered by a rule. Employees will need to talk to a supervisor or wait for a new policy before they can deal with a new situation.

Incentives

The second method of motivating and coordinating employees uses incentives to motivate them to perform activities consistent with the retailer's objectives. For example, buyers will be motivated to focus on the firm's profits if they receive a bonus based on the profitability of the merchandise they buy.

Types of Incentives Two types of incentives are commissions and bonuses. A commission is compensation based on a fixed formula such as 2 percent of sales. For example, many retail salespeople's compensation is based on a fixed percentage of the merchandise they sell. A bonus is additional compensation awarded periodically based on an evaluation of the employee's performance. For example, store managers often receive bonuses at the end of the year based on their store's performance relative to its budgeted sales and profits.[21] Chapter 17 details advantages and disadvantages of compensation plans.

Besides incentives based on individual performance, retail managers often receive additional income based on their firm's performance. These profit-sharing arrangements can be offered as a cash bonus based on the firm's profits or as a grant of stock options that link additional income to performance of the firm's stock.

Refact An employee who paid $1,650 for 100 shares of Wal-Mart stock when the company went public in 1970 would now have stock worth over $5 million.

A number of retailers such as Wal-Mart, Home Depot, and Toys "R" Us use stock incentives to motivate and reward all employees including sales associates. Employees are encouraged to buy shares in their companies at discounted prices through payroll deduction plans. Stores compete to have the highest percentage of employee stockholders. These stock incentives align employees' interests with the company's and can be very rewarding when the company does well. However, if growth in the company's stock price declines, employee morale declines too, corporate culture is threatened, and demands for higher wages and more benefits develop.[22]

Drawbacks of Incentives   Incentives are very effective in motivating employees to perform the activities on which the incentives are based. But incentives may cause employees to ignore other activities. For example, salespeople whose compensation is based entirely on their sales may be reluctant to spend time arranging merchandise. Excessive use of incentives to motivate employees also can reduce employee commitment. Company loyalty falls because employees feel that the firm hasn't made a commitment to them (since it's unwilling to guarantee their compensation). Thus if a competitor offers to pay a higher commission rate, they'll feel free to leave.[23]

Organization Culture

The final method for motivating and coordinating employees is to develop a strong organization culture. An **organization culture** is the set of values, traditions, and customs in a firm that guides employee behavior. These guidelines aren't written in a set of policies and procedures, but are traditions passed along by experienced employees to new employees.[24]

Many retail firms have strong organization cultures that give employees a sense of what they ought to do on their jobs and how they should behave to be consistent with the firm's strategy. For example, Nordstrom's strong organization culture emphasizes customer service, while Wal-Mart's organization culture focuses on reducing costs so the firm can provide low prices to its customers.

An organization culture often has a much stronger effect on employees' actions than rewards offered in compensation plans, directions provided by supervisors, or written company policies. Retailing View 10.4 describes how JCPenney's partnership program reinforces the values of the company when its managers qualify for profit sharing.

Nordstrom emphasizes the strength of organization culture in the policy manual given to new employees. The manual has one rule: Use your best judgment to do anything you can to provide service to our customers. Lack of written rules doesn't mean that Nordstrom employees have no guidelines or restrictions on their behavior. Its organization culture guides employees' behavior. New salespeople learn from other employees that they should always wear clothes sold at Nordstrom, that they should park their cars at the outskirts of the parking lot so customers can park in more convenient locations, that they should approach customers who enter their department, that they should accept any merchandise returned by a customer even if the merchandise wasn't purchased at a Nordstrom store, and that they should offer to carry packages to the customer's car.

IN 1902, THOMAS CALLAHAN AND WILLIAM GUY JOHNSON opened a new store in Kemmerer, Wyoming. When they invited James Cash Penney to manage the store and become a one-third partner, a retailing tradition was launched. Mr. Penney has said that this simple act was the key to his success. Becoming a partner fired his ambition to succeed, and he made it a cornerstone in the company he built.

Presently, all JCPenney managers who've been promoted to profit-sharing status with the firm for five years are inducted into the partnership program. Entering the partnership program is a milestone in a Penney manager's career. In October 2000, over 1,000 new partners were inducted.

Mr. Penney made the following comment about the significance of being a partner at the 1942 induction meeting. "When the JCPenney Company is faced with the opportunity of choosing partners . . . I say partners because we believe that all our associates work together as partners . . . we make our selection of partners according to the character qualities that best fit into our business, that build rapidly into the principles of our business: Honor, Confidence, Service, and Cooperation (HCSC)."

At the first induction meeting in 1913 in Salt Lake City, the following HCSC company motto was outlined:

- Honor is the fundamental ingredient of character. It confers respect and esteem, because it is a constant guide to what is right and true. Our sense of honor will continue to ensure our customers' respect for us. May your every thought and your every act be prompted by that which is honorable.
- Confidence is important. We must have confidence in ourselves and confidence in others in order to inspire confidence. May your conduct and your influence be such that you inspire confidence at all times in yourself and in this Company.

JCPenney's profit-sharing program has its roots in James Cash Penney's concept of partnership developed 100 hundred years ago when he opened the first JCPenney store.

- Service is the keynote of success; it attracts customers. Service is the art of making ourselves useful to our jobs, to our associates, and to our communities.
- Cooperation is the fourth essential of the Penney partnership. The goals toward which we all strive can be reached only through cooperation with each other and with all those with whom we deal.

Source: Company documents. Courtesy of JCPenney.

Developing and Maintaining a Culture Organization cultures are developed and maintained through stories and symbols.[25] Values in an organization culture are often explained to new employees and reinforced to present employees through stories. For example, Nordstrom's service culture is emphasized by stories describing the "heroic" service undertaken by its salespeople. Salespeople will relate how a fellow salesperson went across the mall and bought a green extra-large Ralph Lauren/Polo shirt for a customer who was upset because Nordstrom didn't have the shirt in his size. Department sales managers encourage story telling by holding contests in which the salesperson with the best hero story for the day wins a prize.

The Container Store emphasizes the importance of add-on sales using the "man in the desert" story. A man crawling through the desert, gasping for water, is offered water by a retailer at the oasis. But if a Container Store was at the oasis, the salesperson would have said, "Here's some water but how about some food? I see you're wearing a wedding ring. Can we call your family to let them know you are here?"[26]

Using symbols is another technique for managing organization culture and conveying its underlying values. Symbols are an effective means of communicating with employees because the values they represent can be remembered easily.

Wal-Mart makes extensive use of symbols and symbolic behavior to reinforce its emphasis on controlling costs and keeping in contact with its customers. Photocopy machines at corporate headquarters have cups on them for employees to use to pay for any personal copying. At a traditional Saturday morning executive meeting, employees present information on cost-control measures they've recently undertaken. Managers who've been traveling in the field report on what they've seen, unique programs undertaken in the stores, and promising merchandise.[27] Headquarters are Spartan. Founder Sam Walton (one of the world's wealthiest people before he died) lived in a modest house and drove a pickup truck to work.

Finally, the CEO's philosophies and actions play a major role in establishing corporate culture. Herbert Kelleher, CEO of Southwest Airlines, the world's fastest growing and most profitable airline, built his company's corporate culture on two principles: (1) people are important—each person makes a difference—and (2) work should be fun. Humor plays an important role at Southwest because it encourages the frank expression of ideas and feelings without making people uncomfortable. Kelleher hires people with a sense of humor—people who don't take themselves too seriously but don't use humor to make others uncomfortable.

Herbert Kelleher, CEO of Southwest Airlines, the world's fastest growing and most profitable airline, built his company's corporate culture on his principles that people are important and each person makes a difference.

The importance of people at Southwest is expressed through its altruistic values. The airline emphasizes that its employees must be motivated to help others. Southwest employees treat each other as family. When a Midland, Texas, agent's son was dying of leukemia, 3,000 Southwest employees (60 percent of its employees at the time) sent cards to him on their own.[28]

BUILDING EMPLOYEE COMMITMENT

As mentioned previously, an important challenge in retailing is to reduce turnover.[29] **Turnover** is the number of positions divided by the number of employees occupying a set of positions during a period (usually a year) minus 100 percent. High turnover reduces sales and increases costs. Sales are lost because inexperienced employees lack the skills and knowledge about company policies and merchandise to effectively interact with customers. Costs increase due to the need to continually recruit and train new employees.

Consider what happens when Bob Roberts, meat department manager in a supermarket chain, leaves the company. His employer promotes a meat manager from a small store to take Bob's position, then promotes an assistant department manager to the position in the small store, promotes a meat department trainee to assistant

Refact The typical annual turnover among hourly retail employees approaches 100 percent.[30]

manager's position, and hires a new trainee. Now the supermarket chain needs to train two meat department managers and one assistant manager, and hire and train one trainee. The estimated cost for replacing Bob Roberts is almost $10,000.[31]

To reduce turnover, retailers need to build an atmosphere of mutual commitment in their firms. When a retailer demonstrates its commitment, employees respond by developing loyalty to the company. Employees improve their skills and work hard for the company when they feel the company is committed to them over the long run, through thick and thin. Some approaches that retailers take to build mutual commitment are (1) developing employee skills through selection and training, (2) empowering employees, and (3) creating a partnering relationship with employees.[32] Research indicates that engaging in these human resource management practices increases the firm's financial performance.[33]

Developing Skills

Two activities that retailers undertake to develop knowledge, skills, and abilities in their human resources are selection and training. Retailers building a competitive advantage through their human resources are very selective in hiring people and make significant investment in training.

Selective Hiring The first step in building a committed workforce is recruiting the right people. Singapore Airlines, one of Asia's most admired companies, is consistently ranked among the top airlines in terms of service quality. Since its flight attendants are the critical point of contact with its customers, senior management is personally involved in their selection. Only 10 percent of the applicants make the initial screen and 2 percent are eventually hired.[34]

The job requirements and firm strategy dictate the type of people hired. Simply seeking the best and the brightest often is not the best approach. For example, at Recreational Equipment Inc., a category killer in outdoor gear, the motto is "You live what you sell." Outdoor enthusiasts are hired as sales associates so they can help customers and serve as a resource for the buying staff. Borders Books and Music wants avid readers in its workforce.[35]

Training Training is particularly important in retailing because more than 60 percent of retail employees have direct contact with customers. They are responsible for helping customers satisfy their needs and resolve their problems. A key to the success of the Men's Wearhouse is how it treats its employees and its emphasis on training. All wardrobe consultants and store management go through a five-day training program at "Suits University," the company's 35,000–square-foot training center in Fremont, California. The training program emphasizes clienteling, a process designed to

More relaxing, comfortable seats, with footrests and winged headrests. More than 60 choices in KrisWorld, the world's most advanced personal inflight entertainment system. More wines and, for the first time, champagne. More enticing dishes created by our world renowned chefs. More truly affordable Asian tour packages. Call your Travel Agent or Asian Affair Holidays at 800.742.3133 for details. Welcome to a new travel experience. Singapore Airlines' new Economy Class. Now more than ever, a great way to fly. **SINGAPORE AIRLINES**

BALI SPECTACULAR roundtrip airfare plus 5 nights at select 5-star resorts from just $928

Selective hiring plays a key role in the success of Singapore Airlines.

Starbucks Captures the Romance of Italy

THE INSPIRATION FOR STARBUCKS CAME TO Howard Schultz (founder and CEO) as he wandered through the ancient piazzas of Milan. Passing the cheerful espresso bars, he realized that Americans lacked the opportunity to savor a good cup of coffee in a pleasant atmosphere. "I saw what Italy had captured was the romance of the beverage." He opened his first Starbucks in Seattle in 1988 and built a chain of 1,000 coffee bars across the United States with over $500 million in annual sales.

Starbucks develops a passion for coffee in its customers by providing the perfect cup in an entertaining atmosphere. Recognizing that its front-line employees are critical to providing the perfect cup, the company has built an organization culture based on two principles: (1) strict standards for how coffee should be prepared and delivered to customers and (2) a laid-back, supportive, empowering attitude toward employees.

All new hires go through a 24-hour training program that instills a sense of purpose, commitment, and enthusiasm. The new staff are treated with dignity and respect that go along with their title as baristas (Italian for bartender). To emphasize their responsibility in pleasing customers, they're presented with a scenario in which a customer complains that a pound of beans was ground incorrectly. The preferred response is to replace the beans on the spot without checking with the manager or someone with greater authority.

So the firm can hold on to these motivated, well-trained employees, all are eligible for health benefits and a stock option plan called "Bean Stock." Baristas know about and are encouraged to apply for promotion to store management positions. Due to the training, empowerment, benefits, and opportunities, Starbucks' turnover is only 60 percent of its store employees, considerably less than similar food service firms' rates.

Source: Naomi Weiss, "How Starbucks Impassions Workers to Drive Growth," *Workforce,* August 1998, pp. 60–65; Ben Van Houten, "Employee Perks," *Restaurant Business,* May 15, 1997, pp. 85–88; and Howard Schultz, "Starbucks: Making Values Pay," *Fortune,* September 29, 1997, pp. 261–66.

foster a strong relationship between the wardrobe consultants and their customers. Periodically, experienced store personnel come back to the training center for three- and four-day retraining. The employee commitment Men's Wearhouse builds through its training investment is reflected in its low inventory shrinkage rate. Its employees watch out for the company. They don't steal and they stop others from shoplifting.[36]

Investing in developing employee skills tells employees that the firm considers them important. In response to the difficulty in finding qualified service workers, Marriott has made a considerable investment in recruiting and training entry-level workers. The training goes beyond the basics of doing the job to include grooming habits and basic business etiquette like calling when you can't come to work.

Employees involved in this program have a strong commitment to Marriott. For example, Sara Redwell started working at Marriott as a housekeeper after emigrating from Mexico. She's now a housekeeping manager supervising 20 employees and mentoring other Mexican immigrants. "What Marriott gave to me, I want to give to others," she says. Tom Lee (a bartender at the Seattle Marriott) proudly proclaims, "Every day I put on this uniform just like an NBA player."[37] Walgreen's, Wal-Mart, and T.J. Maxx have active programs for hiring people who do not possess entry-level skills.

By investing in employees, companies are able to hire better employees and reduce turnover. Retailing View 10.5 illustrates how Starbucks created strong commitment in its employees.

Empowering Employees

Empowerment is the process of managers sharing power and decision-making authority with employees. When employees have the authority to make decisions, they are more confident in their abilities, have

Retailers recognize that the diversity among the firm's employees needs to match the diversity of their customers.

greater opportunity to provide service to customers, and are more committed to the firm's success.

The first step in empowering employees is to review employee activities that require a manager's approval. For example, Parisian, a regional department chain owned by Saks, changed its check authorization policy, empowering sales associates to accept personal checks of up to $1,000 without a manager's approval. Under the old policy, a customer often had to wait more than 10 minutes for the sales associate to locate a manager. Then the busy manager simply signed the check without reviewing the customer's identification. When the sales associates were empowered to make approvals, service improved and the number of bad checks decreased because the sales associates felt personally responsible and checked the identification carefully.

Each store in the Whole Foods chain is a profit center with the store employees organized in 10 self-managed teams. The teams are responsible and accountable for the store's performance. For example, the store manager recommends new hires. It takes a two-third vote of the team to actually hire the candidate. The team members pool their ideas and come up with creative solutions to problems.

Empowerment of retail employees transfers authority and responsibility for making decisions to lower levels in the organization. These employees are close to the retailer's customers and in a good position to know what it takes to satisfy customers. For empowerment to work, managers must have an attitude of respect and trust, not control and distrust.[38]

Creating a Partnering Relationship with Employees

Three human resource management activities that build commitment through developing partnering relationships with employees are (1) reducing status differences, (2) promoting from within, and (3) enabling employees to balance their careers and families.

Reducing Status Differences   Many retailers attempt to reduce status differences among employees. With limited status differences, employees feel that they play an important role in the firm achieving its goals and that their contributions are valued.

Status differences can be reduced symbolically through the use of language and cut substantively by lowering wage differences and increasing communications between managers at different levels in the company. For example, hourly workers at JCPenney are referred to as associates while managers are called partners, a practice that Sam Walton adopted when he started Wal-Mart.

Whole Foods has a policy of limiting executive compensation to less than eight times the compensation of the average full-time salaried employee. When Herb Kelleher, the CEO of Southwest Airlines, negotiated a five-year wage freeze for his employees in exchange for stock options, he agreed to freeze his base salary at $380,000. Sam Walton was typically on lists of the most underpaid CEOs.

Promotion from Within   **Promotion from within** is a staffing policy that involves hiring new employees only for positions at the lowest level in the job hierarchy and then promoting employees for openings at higher levels in the hierarchy. Nordstrom, Home Depot, JCPenney, and Wal-Mart have promotion-from-within policies, while others frequently hire people from competitors when management positions open up.

Promotion-from-within policies establish a sense of fairness. When employees do an outstanding job and then outsiders are brought in over them, employees feel that the company doesn't care about them. Promotion-from-within policies also commit the retailer to develop its employees.[39]

Balancing Careers and Families   The increasing number of two-income and single-parent families makes it difficult for employees to effectively do their jobs and manage their households. Retailers build employee commitment by offering services like job sharing, child care, and employee assistance programs to help their employees manage these problems.

Flextime is a job scheduling system that enables employees to choose the times they work. With **job sharing,** two employees voluntarily are responsible for a job that was previously held by one person. Both programs let employees accommodate their work schedules to other demands in their life such as being home when children return from school.[40]

Many retailers offer child care assistance. Sears corporate headquarters near Chicago has a 20,000–square-foot day care center. At Eddie Bauer (a catalog retailer in Seattle), the corporate headquarters cafeteria stays open late and prepares take-out meals for time-pressed employees. Some companies will even arrange for a person to be at an employee's home waiting for the cable guy to come or to pick up and drop off dry cleaning.[41]

All Home Depot senior executives—including company co-founders Bernie Marcus and Arthur Blank—spend time in the stores, wearing the orange apron, talking with customers and employees. This "management by walking around" makes employees feel that their inputs are valued by the company and reinforces the customer service culture at Home Depot.

In the next section, we discuss another critical issue facing retailers building a diverse workforce to sell merchandise and services to increasingly diverse consumers.

MANAGING DIVERSITY

Managing diversity is a human resource management activity designed to realize the benefits of a diverse workforce. Today diversity means more than differences in skin color, nationality, and gender. Diversity also includes differences in religion, age, disability status, and sexual orientation.

Managing a diverse workforce isn't a new issue for retailers. In the late 1800s and early 1900s, waves of immigrants entering America went to work in retail stores. The traditional approach for dealing with these diverse groups was to blend them into the "melting pot." Minority employees were encouraged to adopt the values of the majority, white, male-oriented culture. To keep their jobs and get promoted, employees abandoned their ethnic or racial distinctiveness.

But times have changed. Minority groups now embrace their differences and want employers to accept them for what they are. The appropriate metaphor now is a salad bowl, not a melting pot. Each ingredient in the salad is distinctive, preserving its own identity, but the mixture of ingredients improves the combined taste of the individual elements.[42]

Some legal restrictions promote diversity in the workplace by preventing retailers from practicing discrimination based on non–performance-related employee characteristics. But retailers now recognize that promoting employee diversity can improve financial performance.

As Chapter 4 said, retail customers' racial and ethnic backgrounds are increasingly diverse. To compete in this changing marketplace, retailers need management staffs that match the diversity of their target markets. For example, 85 percent of the men's clothing sold in department stores is bought by women, while over 50 percent of Home Depot's sales are made to women. To better understand customer needs, department store and home improvement retailers feel that they must have women in senior management positions—people who really understand their female customers' needs. Besides gaining greater insight into customer needs, retailers must deal with the reality that their employees will become more diverse in the future. Many retailers have found that these emerging groups are more productive than their traditional employees.

After renovating its national reservation center to accommodate workers with disabilities, Days Inn found that turnover among disabled workers was only 1 percent annually compared with 30 percent for its entire staff. Lowe's, a home improvement center chain, changed floor employees' responsibilities so they wouldn't have to lift heavy merchandise. By assigning these tasks to the night crew, the firm was able to shift its floor personnel from male teenagers to older employees who provided better customer service and had personal experience with do-it-yourself projects.[43] Effectively managing a diverse workforce isn't just morally correct. It's necessary for business success.[44]

Programs for Managing Diversity

The fundamental principle of managing diversity is the recognition that employees have different needs and require different approaches for accommodating those needs. Managing diversity goes beyond meeting equal employment opportunity laws. It means accepting and valuing differences. Some programs that retailers use to manage diversity involve offering diversity training, providing support groups and mentoring, and managing career development and promotions.[45]

Diversity Training   Toys "R" Us has all employees attend a diversity training program so they can identify and reduce their biases and develop skills to manage a diverse workforce. The program begins by creating an awareness of employees' different needs and expectations; it includes developing skills to effectively deal with other employees and customers who aren't like them.

Support Groups and Mentoring   **Mentoring programs** assign higher-level managers to help lower-level managers learn the firm's values and meet other senior executives.[46] Many retailers help form minority networks to exchange information and provide emotional and career support for members who traditionally haven't been included in the majority's networks. In addition, mentors are often assigned to minority managers. At Giant Foods, a Maryland-based supermarket chain, the mentoring program has reduced turnover of minorities by making them more aware of the resources available to them and giving them practical advice for solving problems that arise on their jobs.

Career Development and Promotions   While laws provide entry-level opportunities for women and minority groups, these employees often encounter a glass ceiling as they move through the corporation. A **glass ceiling** is an invisible barrier that makes it difficult for minorities and women to be promoted beyond a certain level. To break through this glass ceiling, JCPenney monitors high-potential minorities and women employees and makes sure they have opportunities for store and merchandise management positions that are critical for eventual promotion to senior management.

Refact In 1866, Macy's employed the first female executive in retailing when Margaret Getchell was promoted to the position of store superintendent.[47]

Similarly, women in the supermarket business have traditionally been assigned to peripheral departments like bakery and deli, while men were assigned to the critical departments in the store: meat and grocery. Even in the supermarket chain corporate office, women traditionally have been in staff-support areas like human resource management, finance, and accounting, while men are more involved in store operations and buying. To make sure that more women have an opportunity to break through the glass ceiling in the supermarket industry, firms are placing them in positions critical to the firm's success.[48]

SUMMARY   Human resource management plays a vital role in supporting a retailing strategy. The organization structure defines supervisory relationships and employees' responsibilities. The four primary groups of tasks performed by retailers are strategic decisions by the corporate officers, administrative tasks by the corporate staff, merchandise management by the buying organization, and store management.

In developing an organization structure, retailers must make trade-offs between the scale economies gained through centralized decision making and the benefits of tailoring the merchandise offering to local markets—benefits that arise when decisions are made in a decentralized manner.

Besides developing an organization structure, human resource management undertakes a number of activities to improve employee performance. Retailers motivate employees and direct their efforts in a manner consistent with the retailer's strategy through supervision, policies and procedures, compensation programs, and organization culture. Effective human resource management uses all of these approaches to ensure that the firm's retail strategy is effectively implemented.

Two critical human resource management issues are the development of a committed workforce and the effective management of a diverse workforce. Building a committed workforce is critical in retailing because high turnover has a major impact on profitability. A key factor in reducing turnover is developing an atmosphere of mutual commitment. Managing diversity is important in retailing because customers are becoming more diverse and new entrants into the retail workforce will come largely from the ranks of women and minorities. Programs for managing diversity include diversity training, support groups and mentors, and promotion management.

KEY TERMS

centralization, *300*

decentralization, *302*

employee productivity, *288*

empowerment, *310*

flattening the organization, *303*

flextime, *312*

glass ceiling, *313*

job sharing, *312*

managing diversity, *312*

mentoring program, *313*

organization culture, *306*

organization structure, *289*

outsourcing, *303*

promotion from within, *312*

specialization, *291*

turnover, *308*

DISCUSSION QUESTIONS AND PROBLEMS

1. Why is human resource management more important in retailing than in manufacturing firms?

2. What are the positive and negative aspects of employee turnover? How can a retailer reduce the turnover in its sales associates?

3. Three approaches for motivating and coordinating employee activities are policies and supervision, incentives, and organization culture. What are the advantages and disadvantages of each?

4. Some retailers have specific employees (merchandise assistants) assigned to restocking the shelves and maintaining the appearance of the store. Other retailers have sales associates perform these tasks. What are the advantages and disadvantages of each approach?

5. How can national retailers like Circuit City and The Gap, which both use a centralized buying system, make sure that their buyers are aware of the local differences in consumer needs?

6. To motivate employees, several major department stores are experimenting with incentive compensation plans. Frequently compensation plans with a lot of incentives don't promote good customer service. How can retailers motivate employees to aggressively sell merchandise and at the same time not jeopardize customer service?

7. Describe the similarities and differences between the organization of small and large retail companies. Why do these similarities and differences exist?

8. Assume that you're starting a new restaurant catering to college students and plan to use college students as waiters and waitresses. What human resource management problems would you expect to have? How could you build a strong organization culture in your restaurant to provide outstanding customer service?

9. Why should retailers be concerned about the needs of their employees? What can retailers do to satisfy the needs of employees?

10. You've been promoted to manage a general merchandise discount store. Your assistant managers are a black male, an Hispanic, a white female, and a 65-year-old veteran of the Vietnam War. What are the strengths of your management group, and what problems do you see arising?

SUGGESTED READINGS

Galbraith, J.R. *Designing Complex Organizations: An Executive Briefing on Strategy, Structure, and Process.* San Francisco: Jossey-Bass, 1995.

Hammonds, Keith. "Balancing Work and Family." *Business Week,* September 16, 1996, pp. 74–80.

"HR at the Forefront of Change Management at L.L. Bean." *International Journal of Retail & Distribution Management* 26 (April–May 1998), pp. 192–95.

Kabachnick, Terri. "Retailers Need to Be Aware of the Trends Transforming Today's Workforce." *WWD, Chicago Supplement,* May 1999, p. 28.

Kraut, Allen, and Abraham Korman, eds. *Evolving Practices in Human Resource Management: Responses to a Changing World of Work.* San Francisco: Jossey-Bass Publishers, 1999.

"Labor Shortages/Retention: Employers Work toward Being Employee-Friendly." *National Home Center News,* August 10, 1998, pp. 79–83.

Luthans, Kyle. "Using HRM to Compete in the 21st Century." *Management Quarterly* 38 (Winter 1998), pp. 17–23.

Pfeffer, Jeffrey. *The Human Equation.* Boston: Harvard Business School Press, 1998.

Potochny, Don. "Employee Empowerment Key to Efficient Customer Service." *Nation's Restaurant News,* August 10, 1998, pp. 46–47.

Rucci, Anthony, Steven Kirn, and Richard Quinn. "The Employee–Customer–Profit Chain at Sears." *Harvard Business Review,* January–February 1998.

"State of the Industry: Operational Management." *Chain Store Age,* August 1, 1998, pp. 16A–24A.

Jeff Baird
Vice President, Distribution
Electronics Boutique

JEFF BAIRD IS THE VICE PRESIDENT, distribution, for Electronics Boutique (EB). Electronics Boutique is the leading specialty retailer of computer software, accessories, and video games. EB stores offer over 2,000 software titles and a wide variety of brand-name and private-label accessories in 500 stores in the United States, Canada, Puerto Rico, Ireland, United Kingdom, and Korea. Its state-of-the-art distribution centers, with computerized restocking, enable EB to be the first retailer to have new releases in its stores. Electronic Boutique also sells merchandise electronically (www.ebworld.com). Baird is responsible for getting products for vendors to its two distribution centers and then to its stores and Internet customers. • "Getting merchandise to the right place at the right time is critical in our business. The life cycle of our products is short—most of the sales occur in the first six weeks after introduction. If we don't have products when people want them, we lose a sale forever. Most of our stores are located in malls where space is too costly to store merchandise. So we use centralized distribution and frequent replenishment • We have a hierarchy of distribution costs—inventory holding, freight, labor, and supplies (packaging material)—driven by the nature of products. Software and accessories have a high unit cost per pound. Our primary objective is to move costs down the hierarchy. We will pay more in freight costs to reduce inventory and incur more labor costs to reduce freight costs. For example, we pay more for bubble pack material versus paper fill, increasing supplies cost to reduce package weight and save on freight costs. • Because we use a piece pick distribution system to support our stores, we were in a good position to support our electronic retailing venture, ebworld. The big change was in the packaging we use. I am really proud that we were able to make deliveries before Christmas on all orders we received before 10 P.M. on December 23. • When I graduated from college 20 years ago, distribution was not a very appealing career. Now it's critical to the performance of retailers. We've gotten our distribution system to the point where our inventory turns match our payment cycle. So we don't need to make inventory investments to finance our expansion. But the whole approach has changed. When I started, the objective was to make boxes in truckloads. Now we are focusing on making truckloads into 100,000 single unit shipments."

CHAPTER ELEVEN

Information Systems and Supply Chain Management

QUESTIONS

- How do merchandise and information flow from vendor to retailer to consumer and back?
- How are some retailers using data warehouses to develop a more loyal customer relationship?
- What are quick response delivery systems?
- Which type of retailer is better prepared to compete in an Internet environment: bricks-and-mortar retailers or Internet-only retailers?

WHEN YOU WALK into a Walgreens store to buy a tube of Colgate toothpaste, your transaction triggers a series of information flows that result in merchandise replenishment. Your toothpaste is scanned at the point of sale (POS). The information on the black-and-white bar code (UPC or Universal Product Code) goes directly to a computer at Walgreens' regional distribution center and, importantly, to Colgate–Palmolive's computer as well.

A replenishment order is automatically generated from the POS data and shipped to Walgreens' distribution center. There is a bay waiting for it when it arrives at the distribution center because it was assigned a specific time slot. If it's late, it gets a fine and loses the time slot. Colgate–Palmolive merchandise is unloaded, combined with merchandise from other vendors, and immediately loaded onto Walgreens' trucks. This method of distribution, known as crossdocking, eliminates the need to store merchandise. Once at the store, the merchandise is immediately placed on the shelf. A source tag—an electronic theft prevention device—and Walgreens' price label were affixed to the package by Colgate–Palmolive to save time and effort at the store.

As a result of this immediate access to information, both Walgreens and Colgate–Palmolive know exactly what, where, and when something is being sold. Additionally, Walgreens stores purchase information on customers to be used to plan promotions and to merchandise their stores. By sharing this information, Walgreens and Colgate–Palmolive have become partners in this supply chain. Everyone benefits. Colgate–Palmolive can plan its production and distribution activities, and Walgreens doesn't have to worry about keeping its stores in stock because Colgate–Palmolive shares in the distribution activities.

IN THE EARLY 1990S, PROCTER AND GAMBLE (P&G) studied the impact that promotions were having on its prices and the efficiency of its distribution system. Promotions were seen as a way of gaining rapid market share but they led to wholesalers and retailers ordering up to three months' supply of some products to take advantage of the favorable prices. P&G estimated that as much as one-third of its total inventory was being held in the pipeline between its factories and the customer. Because of the promotions there were peaks and valleys in demand. During the promotions there was plenty of inventory. But during the off-promotion periods, the inventory just sat there. To make matters worse, the promotions brought about an explosion in the number of products, labels, and packages that the retailers had to carry.

P&G responded by setting up a system of using retailers' data to assess shipping needs and supplying them on a just-in-time basis. The number of product variations at the special price was reduced and promotions were cut back in favor of regular lower prices. This led to an initial dip in revenues, but supply chain savings led to increased profitability.

P&G was able to reduce product costs by more than $2 a case between 1990 and 1997, a total of $2.5 billion. The company's total market share rose from 24.5 percent in 1992, when the supply chain reengineering began, to nearly 28 percent in 1997.

Source: Charles Batchelor, "Buzzword—or the Way of the Future?" *Financial Times*, December 1, 1998, p. 3; and M. Eric Johnson, "Giving 'em What They Want," *Management Review*, November 1, 1998, pp. 62–71.

If you think Walgreens' bricks-and-mortar distribution system is slick, consider Walgreens.com. The customer Internet order is immediately filled at Walgreens.com's distribution center and shipped within hours via UPS, Federal Express, or the U.S. Postal Service. Walgreens.com does not need to stock every item demanded. If a customer orders an unusual prescription, for instance, the order would be sent directly to a wholesaler or the manufacturer and shipped directly to the customer.

In this final chapter of the "Retailing Strategy" section, we describe how retailers can gain a strategic advantage through supply chain management. We then examine supply chain *information* flows, with an emphasis on how retailers employ huge databases of information to accurately target their customers and how they communicate with their vendors using electronic data interchange (EDI). We then examine how *merchandise* flows from the point of sale at the store, to distribution centers, and on to vendors. The quick response delivery system (QR) is one of the most important trends in this merchandise flow. With quick response, retailers are developing strategic alliances with vendors to get merchandise to the stores quickly, with less inventory investment, and with a higher level of service than was ever possible in the past. Examine Retailing View 11.1 to see how Procter and Gamble redesigned its supply chain in the grocery industry.

STRATEGIC ADVANTAGES GAINED THROUGH SUPPLY CHAIN MANAGEMENT

Supply chain management is the integration of business processes from end user through original suppliers that provides products, services, and information that add value for customers.[1] Retailers may be the most important link in the supply chain. They connect customers to the rest of the supply chain. It is the retailers' responsibility to gauge customers' wants and needs and work with the other members of the supply chain—wholesalers, manufacturers, transportation companies, and so on—to make sure the merchan-

EXHIBIT 11–1

A Simplified Supply
Chain

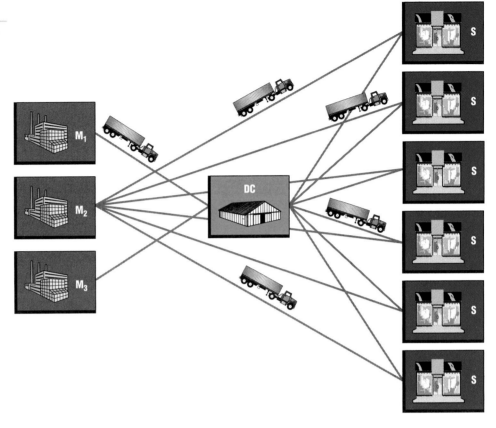

dise customers want is available when they want it. A simplified supply chain is
illustrated in Exhibit 11–1. Manufacturers ship merchandise either to a distribution center operated by a retailer (as is the case for manufacturers M_1 and M_3) or
they ship directly to stores (as is the case for manufacturer M_2). The relative advantages of shipping directly to stores versus to distribution centers are discussed
later in the chapter.

Retailers have increasingly taken a leadership position in their respective
supply chains. Clearly this is not always the case. Small, family-owned retailers
continue to thrive even though they are often at the mercy of their larger suppliers. But over the past 30 years, national chains such as Wal-Mart, Kroger, Safeway, Toys "R" Us, The Gap, and Federated Department Stores have grown to
dominate and control their supply chains. Not only does size generate power, but
knowledge about their customers plays a vital role as well. As a result of their position in the supply chain, retailers are in the unique position to collect purchase
information customer-by-customer, transaction-by-transaction. This information can be shared with suppliers to plan production, promotions, deliveries, assortments, and inventory levels.

Improved Product
Availability   An efficient supply chain has two benefits for customers:
(1) fewer stockouts and (2) assortments of merchandise that customers want. These benefits translate into greater sales and lower
markdowns for retailers. Leda Perez recently went to her local department store
on a Saturday afternoon when she saw an ad for silk blouses. Unfortunately the

store was out of her size in all the colors she liked. The store gave her a rain check so she could come back and still pay the sale price when it received a new shipment. Perez wasn't impressed. She had fought the traffic, waited in line, and generally wasted her afternoon. In the end, Perez never returned to the store and she told all of her friends about her problems there. The problem could have been avoided since the merchandise was available in the distribution center, but it hadn't been delivered to the store on time.

Consumer wants and tastes are changing more rapidly today than ever before. Retailers are attempting to meet these demands by carrying more stock keeping units (SKUs). For instance, only a few years ago a bath department consisted of three sizes of towels in five colors. Now there are twice as many SKUs in towels plus rugs, shower curtains, wastebaskets, toothbrush holders, and other accessories—all in matching colors and patterns. This SKU explosion means that additional inventory must be carefully managed and distributed, or the associated costs will far outweigh the profits generated by the additional sales.

Improved Return on Investment

One measure of retailing performance is the ability to generate a target return on investment (ROI). (See Chapter 7.) Consider the commonly used return on investment measure, return on assets:

$$\text{Return on assets} = \text{Net profit margin} \times \text{Asset turnover}$$

$$\frac{\text{Net profit}}{\text{Total assets}} = \frac{\text{Net profit}}{\text{Net sales}} \times \frac{\text{Net sales}}{\text{Total assets}}$$

An efficient supply chain can increase net profit and net sales, while at the same time reducing total assets. Net sales can increase by providing customers with better assortments. Consider the silk blouse that Perez was trying to purchase. Another retailer with a strong consumer database would have information about the group of customers who like silk blouses including their color and style preferences. That retailer would not only try to stay in stock on these items, but would entice this group into the store with promotions designed for them and announcements sent directly to them. It would merchandise the silk blouses with other items it knows Perez and customers like her purchase.

Net profit can increase by either raising gross margin or lowering expenses. An information system between buying staffs and vendors could take advantage of special buying opportunities and obtain the silk blouses at a low cost—thus improving the gross margin. This same retailer can lower operating expenses by coordinating deliveries, thus cutting transportation expenses. The retailer's distribution center is so efficient that merchandise can be received, prepared for sale, and shipped to stores with minimum handling.

Its inventory management system, which is directly linked to the vendor's computer, is so sophisticated that the retailer needs to carry relatively little backup inventory to stay in stock. Thus, since inventory investment is low, the total assets are also low. In sum, there's untapped opportunity for many retailers to improve their performance through better supply chain management.

Exhibit 11–2 shows the complexities of the merchandise and information flows in a typical multistore chain. Although information and merchandise flows are intertwined, in the following sections we describe how information on customer demand is captured at the store and then triggers a series of responses

EXHIBIT **11–2**

Information and
Merchandise Flows

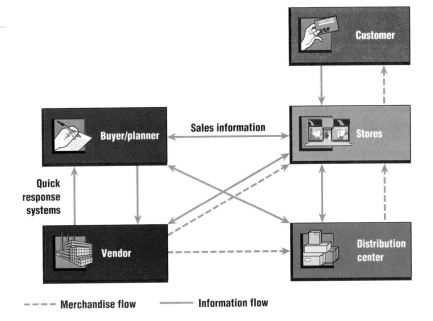

EXHIBIT **11–2**

Information and
Merchandise Flows

- - - - - **Merchandise flow** ────── **Information flow**

from the buyer, distribution center, and vendor that are designed to ensure that merchandise is available at the store when the customer wants it.

THE FLOW OF INFORMATION

The flow of information is complex in a retail environment. Although Leda Perez is disappointed that the store is out of the silk blouse that she wants, she's successful in purchasing a new pair of Guess? jeans. This purchase triggers a series of information messages throughout the system (depicted in Exhibit 11–3).

1. The sales associate scans the UPC tag on the jeans. A sales receipt is created for Perez.

EXHIBIT **11–3**

Information Flows

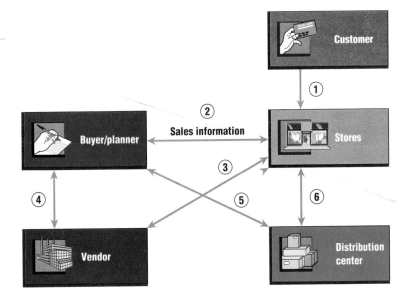

2. The purchase information is recorded in the POS terminal and sent to the buyer/planner. The buyer/planner uses this information to plan additional purchases (Chapter 12 and 13), make markdown decisions (Chapter 15), and make other marketing decisions described in the next two sections on data warehousing and loyalty programs.

3. The purchase information can go directly to the vendor using a system called **electronic data interchange (EDI)**—the computer-to-computer exchange of business documents from retailer to vendor, and back. Issues surrounding EDI are also discussed later in this section.

4. The buyer/planner communicates with the vendor regarding the purchase order for the merchandise. At this point they often negotiate shipping dates and terms of purchase (Chapter 14).

5. The planner communicates with the distribution center to coordinate deliveries from the vendor and to the stores, check inventory status, and so on.

6. Store managers also communicate with the distribution center to coordinate deliveries and check inventory status.

In the next sections of this chapter, we will explore three uses of information flows: data warehousing, customer loyalty programs, and EDI.

INTERNET EXERCISE   Oracle Corporation is the world's second-largest independent software company and the information management company of choice for 70 percent of the Fortune 500 and 64 percent of the Fortune 100. Oracle uses Internet technology to help businesses manage information so that it is reliable, secure, and accessible to the right people, at the right time. Go to www.oracle.com/seetrybuy/ and see how it can help manage retailers' information flow.

Data Warehousing

Purchase data collected at the point of sale goes into a huge database known as a data warehouse. (See flow number 2 in Exhibit 11–3.) A **data warehouse** is the coordinated and periodic copying of data from various sources, both inside and outside the enterprise, into an environment ready for analytical and informational processing.[2] Analysts use various processes[3] to extract information from the data warehouse for making a plethora of marketing decisions from how to target promotions for specific customers to how to group product categories together in a store to increase purchases. Data warehousing goes hand in hand with customer loyalty programs. Purchase data is typically collected from customers participating in the loyalty program via an identifying card. Such data is stored in the data warehouse and used to directly target the loyal customers.

Retail data warehouses are usually comprised of information specific to each store. They typically include (but aren't limited to) customer information such as transaction data, address, phone, demographics, psychographics, and lifestyle. (See the discussion of PRIZM in Chapter 9.) They may also include competitive and trade area information.

Wal-Mart, for instance, makes good use of its data warehouse.[4] It should. Experts estimate that it is second in size only to that of the U.S. government.

Among other things, Wal-Mart mines the data to make merchandising and store layout decisions. The problem is its stores are so big that customers sometimes have trouble finding things. Along with raw sales, profit margin, and inventory numbers, Wal-Mart also collects market-basket data from customer receipts at all its stores. A **market-basket analysis** is one in which retailers use data mining techniques to determine what predominant categories individual customers are buying. They then group these customers into clusters based on their purchases. Market-basket analysis is used for store layout and promotion decisions.

Based on these analyses, Wal-Mart changed the traditional location of several items.

- Since bananas are the most common item in America's grocery carts, Wal-Mart Supercenters sell bananas next to the corn flakes (to help sell more cereal) as well as in the produce section.
- Kleenex tissues are in the paper-goods aisle and also mixed in with cold medicine.
- Measuring spoons are in housewares and also hanging next to Crisco shortening.
- Flashlights are in the hardware aisle and also with the Halloween costumes.
- Little Debbie snack cakes are next to the coffee.
- Bug spray is merchandised with the hunting gear.

Williams-Sonoma, the San Francisco-based mail order giant and retailer of upscale home products, uses its database to precisely target its best customers.[5] It discovered that 30 percent of its customers account for most of its business. It then targets those customers with special promotions. For example, prior to the Christmas season, the company identified select customers from the previous Christmas and offered a free gift if they made a purchase before the holiday rush. This strategy allowed William-Sonoma to increase business during a normally slow period and reduce holiday pressure on the direct-mail warehouse.

Williams-Sonoma also examines its database customer list to segment customers by name and likelihood of specific catalog purchases. The company can determine which customers are most likely to buy specific kinds of merchandise during specific times of the year. It also can learn whether sales are higher for items in large catalogs or smaller, more focused catalogs, as well as how long to keep a nonbuying prospect on the mailing list.

Retailers aren't the only ones who are mining powerful data warehouses. Retailing View 11.2 tells how MasterCard International and Simmons Market Research have teamed up to provide retailers with information.

Customer Loyalty Programs

One of the most important uses of data warehouses is to develop a loyal customer base through loyalty programs. **Loyalty programs** are set up to reward customers with incentives such as discounts on purchases, free food, gifts, or even cruises or trips in return for their repeated business. Retailers have loyalty programs for two reasons: to retain loyal customers and to collect information about them and what they buy.

Loyalty programs have become more prevalent and elaborate than in the past because retailers have discovered how important their loyal customers are to their bottom line. For instance, a grocery store chain in Wisconsin learned from its database that 25 to 30 percent of its shoppers are responsible for 70 percent of

TRANSACTIONAL DATA SOLUTIONS (TDS) is a joint venture between MasterCard International and Symmetrical Resources, parent company of Simmons Market Research Bureau. Both parties bring powerful resources to the table—MasterCard has a huge data warehouse and Symmetrical knows how to analyze the data

Here's how it works. First, TDS generates a panel of 670,000 randomly selected MasterCard users and tracks their buying habits. To protect consumer privacy, the company never knows any individual's name or address. By analyzing the panel's aggregated transactions, TDS clusters consumers by shopping behavior—what they buy, where they shop, how much they spend, and so on. One cluster, for instance, might be 25-to-35–year-old women who shop at upscale department stores. TDS can then "mine" Simmons data to define this cluster even further by looking at its media habits, brand preferences, and lifestyle choices. It might find, for instance, that this group of women often reads fashion magazines and listens to top-40 radio stations on their commute to work.

Armed with this data, retailers can target shopper clusters most important to their bottom line. A national restaurant chain, for example, could see which clusters spend the most in its restaurants and how much they spend in the restaurant category overall. If cluster number 20 represents 15 percent of the chain's sales, but 22 percent in their restaurant category, the chain is probably missing out at the cash register. TDS can also identify, among many factors, which clusters visit the merchant most and spend the most, the extent to which the retailer "shares" consumers with competitors, and the composition of new and repeat customer segments.

Merchandising and advertising teams can glean how to target these attractive consumers most effectively too. Using TDS reports, clients can pinpoint which media are popular with particular shopper clusters and then focus advertising in those particular outlets.

Source: Jennifer Lach, "It's in the (Credit) Cards," *American Demographics,* April 1999, p. 43; and Kelly Shermach, "MasterCard to Leverage Information Found in Cardholder Transactions," *Business and Industry,* March 1999, pp. 6–9.

---

its sales.[6] Some thoughtful marketers not only realize that loyal customers are important, but actually view them as a measurable asset.[7] For instance, the famous consultant Tom Peters calculated the value of his company's business with Federal Express to be $360,000 over an estimated lifetime of 10 years.[8] He also found that the selling costs for existing customers are much lower (on average 20 percent as much) as costs of selling to new customers.[9] Bain & Co., another consulting firm, estimated that the profit impact of a 5 percent increase in customer retention is dramatic—from 35 percent in the software industry to 95 percent for an advertising agency.[10] Another study provided evidence from multiple companies in different industries that customer loyalty can produce profit increases from 24 percent to 85 percent.[11] Clearly, it is easier and more profitable to maintain current customers than to get new ones.

Retailers use the information obtained from the programs for closely targeting their best customers with promotions and appropriate merchandise assortments. The information can even be used to suggest merchandise, given past purchases, and in trade area analysis. Loyalty programs are not new in retailing. Grocery store customers used to receive stamps for purchases from companies like S&H Green Stamps that were redeemable for merchandise. Today, loyalty programs range from the simple (getting one free meal after buying 10) to the complex (frequent flyer programs offered by most airlines).

As technology becomes more sophisticated, so do loyalty programs.[12] The best programs begin with a customer filling out a questionnaire tailored to meet the retailers' needs. Most have demographic questions (name, address, occupation, and income) plus consumer preference questions; other personal information may include birthdays.

Customers are given a personalized card with a magnetic stripe. When a customer makes a purchase, it is recorded by scanning the card. Earned points are added to the customer's account and ideally printed on the customer's receipt.

Let's examine how some retailers get the most out of their loyalty programs. San Francisco's Macy's West, for example, uses its data warehousing techniques to identify its best customers and offer them exclusive extras.[13] It's able to project spending trends down to the specific customer who expects a life-changing event such as marriage or a new child. It then offers these customers special promotions.

Wild Oats Markets, the second largest whole foods supermarket chain in North America, has put a unique spin on its loyalty program.[14] Individual customers can create and modify the electronic profiles Wild Oats keeps on them through e-mail. The company estimates that it's communicating via e-mail with about 22 percent of its loyal customers—an amazing accomplishment considering that in the late 1990s only about 30 percent of American households had modem-equipped PCs, a necessary prerequisite for e-mail. These customers receive monthly newsletters and occasional special deals.

The information taken from loyalty programs can also be used to define trade areas. As we discussed in Chapter 9, customer addresses in a geographic information system (GIS) provide retailers with an instant view of their trade area. Income, PRIZM, or other information about a customer can be superimposed on the same map. Retailers can therefore see exactly where their customers are coming from and what they are like.

Possibly the most powerful method of maintaining loyal customers is through **mass customization.** See Retailing View 11.3.

Now let's take a look at how information flows back and forth from retailer to vendor. (See flow numbers 3 and 4 in Exhibit 11–3.)

Electronic Data Interchange (EDI)

Electronic data interchange (EDI) is the computer-to-computer exchange of business documents from retailer to vendor, and back. In addition to sales data, purchase orders, invoices, and data about returned merchandise are transmitted from retailer to vendor. Many retailers now require vendors to provide advanced shipping notices through EDI. An **advanced shipping notice (ASN)** is an electronic document received by the retailer's computer from a supplier in advance of a shipment. It tells the retailer exactly what to expect in the shipment. If accurate, the retailer can dispense with opening cartons and checking in merchandise. Information about on-hand inventory status and price changes can be transmitted from vendor to retailer too. It's also possible to exchange information about purchase order changes, order status, and transportation routings by EDI. EDI is part of the quick response inventory system that will be discussed later this chapter.

Refact You don't want to be a vendor who tries to deliver to Federated Department Stores without an advanced shipping notice (ASN). It will either send the truck away until the ASN comes in or it will unload the merchandise and send it to a staging area affectionately called the black hole.[15]

There are a variety of ways in which EDI data can be transmitted. (See Exhibit 11–4.) EDI data can be transmitted through **proprietary EDI systems** that are owned and operated by either a retailer, a vendor, or a third-party provider known as a value added network (VAN). Increasingly, EDI data is transmitted over the Internet through extranets. An **extranet** is a collaborative network that uses Internet technology to link businesses with their suppliers, customers, or other businesses. Extranets are typically private and secure in that they can be accessed only by certain parties.[16] For example, several global retailers, including

MASS CUSTOMIZATION IS THE PRODUCTION of individually customized products at costs similar to mass-produced products. Some experts estimate that more than half of all people do not fit well into standard clothing sizes. Levi Strauss, for instance, has been successfully making made-to-order clothing for several years through its own stores. Brooks Brothers and Hart Schaffner & Marx clothing manufacturers are experimenting with electronic mass customization programs.

Mass customization isn't limited to clothing. In its optical stores in Washington state, the Japanese-based retailer Paris Miki creates custom-shaped eyeglass lenses attached to a rimless frame. After reading a person's "facial dynamics" from a photograph, the computer is fed some descriptive words selected from a list by the customer. The computer goes through 5.2 billion patterns to come up with a lens shape that suits the customer's face and personality.

A company known as [TC]2 (Textile/Clothing Technology Corp., www.tc2.com is introducing a body scanning device. Here is how it works. A young woman enters a darkened chamber, steps onto white footprints, and grips the bars beside her. Black curtains close, a Motown song blasts, and discolike light beams flash for eight seconds. It's no amusement park ride, but a body scanner, recording precise body measurements for a made-to-fit garment. The 3-D body scanner is 12 feet wide and 20 feet long. Six cameras mounted on towers in a triangle capture flashes of white light to map a 3-D "point cloud"—300,000 data points in space defining the body's skin. In 53 seconds, a computer program interprets the data points, displays an image, and prints out detailed measurements under a 3-D picture of the human form. The scanner can help predict what could fit best or can tell if a garment will never fit no matter what size it is. This technology is available in stores in Europe and Japan.

Mass customization generates loyal customers in two ways. First, and obviously, customers get exactly what they want. Second, no other retailer can duplicate the customized product! The challenge for the retailer is to ensure that the customer can't walk away with the measurement data and give it to a competitor.

Source: Denis Flaim, "Clothing That Fits—Concept of the Future? Body Scanners Could Make It Profitable Enough to Be Practical," *The Kansas City Star*, May 30, 1999, p. G8; Anne Eisenberg, "If the Shoe Fits, Click It Scans May Make Shopping a Science," *The Denver Post*, August 31, 1998, p. E-07; and Natalia Brubaker, "3-D Body Scanner Records Size Measurements in Seconds," Associated Press Newswires, August 28, 1999.

Refact According to supply chain specialists, $200 billion to $300 billion in excess inventory and missed sales in the United States could be eliminated through closer collaboration between retailers and their suppliers.[18]

PETsMART and France's Carrefour, are using a supplier–buyer extranet network. Suppliers can feature their products, buyers can issue requests for proposals, and then the two parties can electronically negotiate an order and product development.[17]

Also available over the Internet are **intranets,** which are secure communication systems that take place *within* one company. For instance, in Exhibit 11–3, communications from stores to buyer (flow 2), buyer to distribution center (flow 5), and distribution center to store (flow 6) could all be accomplished through intranets. When the general public accesses the Internet to purchase merchandise or services, the transactions often do not require a password to access the site. We will therefore limit our Internet EDI discussion to extranets.

In the next few paragraphs, we discuss the different systems used to transmit EDI data. Then we examine an advanced form of EDI called CPFR that is popular in the grocery and drug industries.

Retailers today have multiple options to communicate directly with their vendors through electronic data interchange (EDI). There are proprietary systems, systems provided by third-party vendors, and extranets. Some retailers simply use e-mail.

Proprietary EDI Systems Some retailers and/or vendors operate their own EDI system. Wal-Mart, for instance, has spent millions of

EXHIBIT 11-4   Methods of Transmitting EDI Data

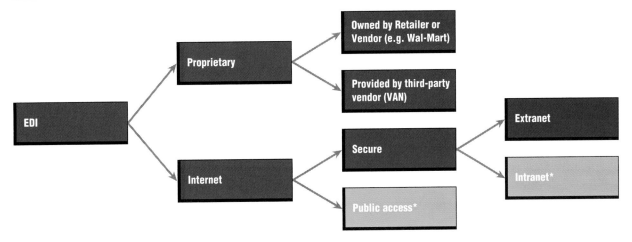

*Public access Internet and intranets are typically not used to transmit information between vendors and retailers.

dollars and several years developing one of the most advanced EDI systems in retailing. It has worked with its vendors to develop systems compatible with theirs. Vendors who are unable or unwilling to adopt these systems no longer sell to Wal-Mart.

Sometimes it is too difficult and expensive for retailers or vendors to develop systems that are compatible with their trading partners. Value added networks (VANs) solve this problem. **Value added networks** are third-party logistics companies that facilitate electronic data interchange (EDI) by making computer systems between vendors and retailers compatible. Suppose Toys "R" Us has contracted with a manufacturer in Mexico to supply toys. Since Toys "R" Us insists that its vendors utilize an EDI system, and their computer systems may be incompatible, it might contract with a VAN like General Electric Information Services to provide the communications link. Computer files would be sent to the VAN via EDI, translated to Toys "R" Us's format, and sent on to Toys "R" Us's computer.

Internet EDI   Wouldn't it be much simpler if retailers didn't have to develop their own proprietary system or go through a VAN? The Internet is revolutionizing the way retailers conduct EDI with their vendors. A buyer sits down at her desk, ready to purchase goods from abroad.[20] Instead of picking up the telephone or sending a fax, she issues a request for a price quote through a website. Not long afterward, she receives a reply and executes an order with the click of a mouse. While the largest retailers and their vendors have embraced EDI for some time, the Internet empowers smaller concerns—particularly international vendors—who could not afford to implement the systems necessary to participate in VANS to become players.

Dayton Hudson Corporation (DHC)—the parent company of Target, Mervyn's, Dayton's, Hudson's, and Marshall Field's—has extended its traditional EDI program to an extranet system called Partners Online.[21] DHC is making some time-sensitive procedures, confidential information, and general supplier

Refact   Most of us think of the Internet as the place to go to buy things for ourselves, get information, and waste time surfing. In fact, 1999 business-to-business sales over the Internet were about five times the consumer online market, Forrester Research predicts that business-to-business sales will reach $1.3 trillion, or 9.4 percent of corporate purchases, by 2003.[19]

ALTHOUGH MANY FIRMS ARE UTILIZING EXTRANET SYSTEMS in lieu of VANs for electronic data interchange, Esprit is thrilled to utilize a fairly simple e-mail system to help source merchandise from other countries. The San Francisco-based women's apparel firm e-mails patterns and specifications to suppliers in Hong Kong, China, and Indonesia. The process, which costs Esprit less than $200 and the supplier nothing, has improved time to market and enhanced accuracy.

Since most of its merchandise is sourced globally from many different companies, communications can sometimes be challenging. Prior to using e-mail, it incurred substantial cost shipping patterns and specifications to overseas suppliers. Language issues often made things worse. To help solve the problem, Espirit began using standard forms that are eas-

ily recognizable to suppliers, and concentrating heavily on visual instructions. Typically the supplier opens the e-mail and forwards it to everyone involved in a matter of hours.

Vendors are responsive if they have a PC, but not all do. In Hong Kong and China, patterns are transmitted via the Internet to a central office in Hong Kong and in turn delivered to the factories daily. In Indonesia, there is usually no problem. In the eastern European nation of Moldova, however, it may be two or three years before factories are equipped with computers.

Source: "Esprit Cuts Communications Static with International E-Mail," *Stores,* June 1999, pp. 22, 24; and Bruce Einhorn, Manjeet Kripalani, and Michael Shari, "ASIA LOGS ON across the Region, More and More Businesses are Discovering That They Ignore the Net at Their Peril," *Business Week,* February 1, 1999, pp. 34–39.

information such as shipping requirements and prerequisites for packing cartons available via the extranet. Retailing View 11.4 examines how women's apparel manufacturer and retailer Esprit uses e-mail to communicate with overseas vendors.

INTERNET EXERCISE Go to www.manugistics.com/ and see how this firm helps retailers develop Internet solutions for EDI.

Collaboration, planning, forecasting, and replenishment (CPFR) takes EDI to a new level.[22] Popular in grocery and drug industries, CPFR is an inventory management system in which a retailer will send information to a manufacturer and the manufacturer will use the data to construct a computer-generated replenishment forecast that will be shared back with the retailer before it's executed. Using CPFR, manufacturer and retailer jointly decide on replenishment issues.

CPFR is a more sophisticated initiative than EDI because it includes upcoming marketing and merchandising plans that can be used to develop more effective forecasts. Using real-time Internet communication between retailer and vendor, CPFR generates exception reports that spit out unusual sales patterns. Then, when authorized by both the retailer and the vendor, the computer makes automatic changes in the amount of merchandise going to the stores or distribution center based on the changes in the forecasting plan. The data in a CPFR system can be concentrated into a common pool that can be accessed by multiple vendors, as well as by multiple users within the retail chain, including the retailer's transportation specialists, replenishment buyers, merchandisers, logistics specialists, and store operations people.

THE PHYSICAL FLOW
OF MERCHANDISE—
LOGISTICS

Logistics is the organized process of managing the flow of merchandise from the source of supply—the vendor, wholesaler, or distributor—through the internal processing functions—warehousing and transportation—until the merchandise is sold and delivered to the customer. Most experts agree that logistics is only part, albeit the most important part, of supply chain management.[24] For instance, supply chain management would include new product development because it should involve all aspects of business development, including marketing for the concept, research, and development. For instance, when Ford Motor Company's engineers design a new component for its cars, they attempt to get all divisions, including Jaguar and Mazda, involved. The entire supply chain would be more efficient if newly designed parts could be used globally. In this section, however, we will concentrate on issues limited to the physical flow of merchandise.

Refact Logistics represents 10.5 percent of U.S. gross domestic product. For North America, Europe, and Asia/Pacific the percentages are 10.77, 11.79, and 11.64, respectively.[23]

Examine Exhibit 11–5.

1. Merchandise flows from vendor to distribution center.
2. Merchandise then goes from distribution center to stores.
3. Alternatively, merchandise can also go from vendor directly to stores.

THE WALL STREET JOURNAL

Sometimes merchandise is temporarily stored at the distribution center; other times it's immediately prepared to be shipped to individual stores. This preparation may include breaking shipping cartons into smaller quantities that can be more readily utilized by the individual stores, as well as tagging merchandise with price stickers, UPC codes, and the store's label. A **UPC code** (the black-and-white bar code printed on the package of most products) is illustrated in the cartoon. UPC stands for Universal Product Code. Later in this chapter we'll discuss why some retailers use distribution centers, while others have vendors ship directly to stores.

EXHIBIT 11–5

Merchandise Flows

Refact Almost all food items are marked with a UPC bar code. In fact, Wal-Mart's buying office has a sign reading, IF YOUR PRODUCT DOESN'T HAVE A BAR CODE, DON'T BOTHER TO TAKE A CHAIR IN OUR WAITING ROOM.

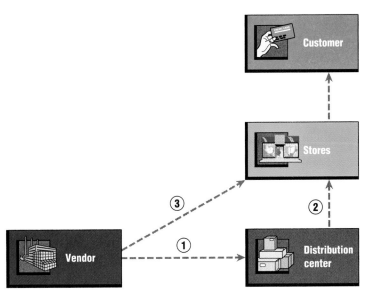

IN THE EARLY 1990s, SEARS, ROEBUCK & Co. was dismissed as a retail dinosaur with its earnings and customer base dwindling. Chief executive officer Arthur Martinez has been credited with the turnaround. Martinez hired the three-star Army general who was chief of logistics for the entire U.S. military during the Gulf War, William G. Pagonis.

Prior to Martinez's and Pagonis's arrivals, Sears had multiple channels of distribution operating separately under different lines of authority, with no effort to cooperate to get savings or delivery speed. The size of the logistics operation is intimidating, even for a general. Sears has 600,000 truckload shipments a year from 160 warehouses and distribution centers to 800 stores, plus home deliveries of about 4 million items a year.

From total logistics spending of about $1.3 billion in 1995, Pagonis cut about $45 million in one year, contributing to a companywide 1.2 percent reduction in sales, general, and administrative expense as a percentage of domestic sales. Let's see how Pagonis did it:

- **Simplified and sped up Sears' distribution system.** Store managers who had to order products through as many as 12 different channels soon dealt with only four. That helped increase the average load of delivery trucks from 60 to 90 percent of capacity.

- **Dictated how and when suppliers make deliveries.** Financial penalties are now imposed on suppliers that fail to meet delivery deadlines or pack and label boxes according to Sears' standards. In 1995, these penalties amounted to $2 million.

- **Reduced delivery times.** Apparel now takes 7 instead of 14 days to get to stores. Home appliances can now be delivered in 24 hours in 70 percent of its markets; a year ago, the company took 48 hours.

- **Reduced inventories.** Faster deliveries from suppliers enabled Sears to reduce its inventory by $10 million in 1995, while 1995 domestic sales increased 7.2 percent.

Source: Jules Abend, "Behind the Scenes at Sears: Pagonis' Rules of Logistics Engagement," *Bobbin*, June 1, 1998, pp. 22–24; and Robert Berner, "Retired General Speeds Deliveries, Cuts Costs, Helps Sears Rebound," *The Wall Street Journal*, July 16, 1996, pp. A1, A7.

Retailing View 11.5 discusses how Sears has saved about $45 million by improving its logistics system.

The Distribution Center   To fully understand the logistics function within a retailing organization, consider a shipment of Hanes hosiery and underwear arriving at a Sears distribution center. The distribution center performs several functions for Sears: coordinating inbound transportation, receiving, checking, storing and crossdocking, ticketing, marking, filling orders, and coordinating outbound transportation.

Management of Inbound Transportation   Examine flow number 1 in Exhibit 11–5. Merchandise flows from vendor to distribution centers. Buyers have traditionally worked with vendors to determine merchandise assortments, pricing, promotions, and the terms of purchase such as discounts to take for early payment. Now, however, buyers and their staffs get much more involved in coordinating the physical flow of merchandise to the stores. The Hanes buyer has arranged for a truckload of hosiery and underwear to be delivered to the Detroit distribution center on Monday between 1 and 3 P.M. The truck must arrive within the specified time because the distribution center has all of the receiving docks allocated throughout the day, and much of the merchandise on this particular truck is going to be shipped to stores that afternoon. Unfortunately the truck was delayed in a snow storm. The **dispatcher**—the person who coordinates deliveries to the distribution center—reassigns the Hanes truck to a Wednesday morning delivery slot and fines the firm several hundred dollars for

Refact A typical Wal-Mart distribution center is approximately 1.2 million square feet under one roof and would hold 24 football fields or approximately 10 Wal-Mart stores.

missing its delivery time. Although many manufacturers pay transportation expenses, some retailers negotiate with their vendors to absorb this expense. These retailers believe they can lower net merchandise cost and better control merchandise flow if they negotiate directly with truck companies and consolidate shipments from many vendors.

Receiving and Checking   **Receiving** refers to the process of recording the receipt of merchandise as it arrives at a distribution center. **Checking** is the process of going through the goods upon receipt to make sure they arrived undamaged and that the merchandise ordered was the merchandise received.

In the past, checking merchandise was a very labor-intensive and time-consuming process. Today, however, many distribution systems using electronic data interchange are designed to minimize, if not eliminate, these processes. The advance shipping notice (ASN) tells the distribution center what should be in each box. A UPC-coded label on the shipping carton that identifies the carton's contents is scanned, and it is automatically counted as being received and checked.

Storing and Crossdocking   Since the Hanes shipment is two days late, it has to be temporarily stored rather than shipped immediately to stores. The merchandise is loaded onto forklift trucks that carry it to prespecified locations in the distribution center.

In the past, distribution centers' primary function was to store merchandise received by vendors until it was needed in the stores. Although the Hanes shipment was stored, many retailers are using distribution centers and designing logistics systems around crossdocking. **Crossdocking** is a system in which vendors ship merchandise to a distribution center prepackaged in the quantity required for each store. The floor-ready merchandise is then transferred to the other side of the distribution center for delivery to a store. Crossdocking distribution centers are less costly than traditional centers because there is little or no

Refact Twenty-five percent of grocery products never see the inside of a warehouse. Several retailers are working with suppliers to eliminate the back door traffic by encouraging them to bring the goods, already sorted by store, to a central distribution center. The retailer can then crossdock the products to a designated truck.[25]

Unlike a traditional distribution center that stores merchandise, in this crossdocking distribution center, merchandise is received from vendors' trucks on one side of the building, moved to the other side of the building, aggregated with merchandise from other vendors, and shipped off to stores—all in a matter of hours.

WHEN SHIPMENTS ARRIVE AT THE RECEIVING DOCK at Children's Place distribution center, nearly 75 percent of the goods bypass storage, circumvent the pick-and-pack area, and move directly to the shipping dock in a matter of hours.

Part of the reason why crossdocking works for Children's Place is that the company is 100 percent private-label, with 80 percent of the goods produced in Asia. Although such international sourcing is far from an exact science, it gives the company a sense of control on the receiving end. In order to facilitate crossdocking, for example, it specifies to suppliers that cartons be packed by SKU and color and filled with a predetermined assortment of sizes. The company believes that a large part of its success with crossdocking is linked to the relationships it has built with suppliers and to open lines of communication.

Children's Place receives full containers almost daily, and using the advance shipping notices (ASNs), the company can predict with 99 percent accuracy what's scheduled to arrive. When the containers land at the receiving dock, crossdocking shifts into high gear. Goods are received onto a conveyor belt and the appropriate shipping label is automatically applied. Cartons are then automatically sorted and sent to the appropriate shipping dock.

An integral component in the Children's Place crossdocking initiative is the company's partnership with United Parcel Service. Once the goods are ready to be shipped, they are loaded onto trucks and moved to a UPS hub facility. There, cartons are sorted by region and ZIP code and delivered within three days. Looking to ensure that fashion merchandise designed to hang as a coordinated group arrived at the stores at the same time rather than piecemeal, Children's Place worked out a plan under which it uses UPS containers for short-term storage. Once a grouping is complete, a release date is set and all the stores receive the complete merchandise group the next day.

Source: "Crossdocking Initiative Brings Sweet Rewards to Children's Place," *Stores,* November 1998, pp. 42–44; and Burt Schaffer, "Cross Docking Can Increase Efficiency," *Automatic I.D. News,* July 1998, pp. 34–35.

storage required, processing at the distribution center is minimal, and the centers can be much smaller than traditional centers.

Had the Hanes shipment been delivered on time, it could have been immediately moved to the shipping area, combined with merchandise from other vendors, and immediately shipped to stores. Retailers want to move merchandise through the inventory pipeline as quickly as possible. After all, retailers can't sell merchandise in a distribution center.

Crossdocking isn't only used for basic merchandise. Retailing View 11.6 describes how crossdocking is used at the apparel chain, Children's Place.

INTERNET EXERCISE SAP, a German firm, is the world's fourth-largest independent software supplier. It specializes in integrated software solutions. Go to www.sap.com/products/industry/retail/index.htm and see what it's doing to help retailers.

Ticketing and Marking In a traditional distribution center, **ticketing and marking** refers to making price and identification labels and placing them on the merchandise. In the past, retailers like Sears have ticketed and marked merchandise on the store's selling floor. Unfortunately the selling process is disrupted if new merchandise is scattered throughout the store and retail salespeople spend their time ticketing and marking price labels. Thus it's more efficient to ticket and mark price labels at a distribution center. Identification labels using universal product codes or other identifiers also facilitate the smooth flow of merchandise

At Amazon.com, an Internet order is filled using sophisticated material handling equipment.

to the stores. These labels can be affixed to shipping cartons and then scanned at the store to quickly check them in.

Of course, the best approach from the retailer's perspective is to get vendors like Hanes to ship the merchandise floor-ready by ticketing and marking their merchandise and shipping cartons at the factory, thus totally eliminating this expensive, time-consuming process for Sears. Floor-ready merchandise is discussed later in the chapter.

Filling Orders   Point-of-sale terminals in a Sears store in East Lansing, Michigan, record each purchase. Data is transmitted to buyers and their staffs so they may formulate replenishment orders for Hanes underwear and hosiery as well as for all other items in the store. (Chapters 12 through 14 detail how merchandise is purchased.) The order for the East Lansing store is transmitted computer-to-computer to the distribution center. The computer at the distribution center creates a **pick ticket** (a document that tells the order filler how much of each item to get from the storage area). The pick ticket is printed in warehouse location sequence so the order fillers don't waste time crisscrossing the distribution center looking for merchandise. The computer knows which items are out of stock so it doesn't even print them on the pick ticket. Order fillers take the merchandise to a staging area where it's consolidated with other merchandise and loaded onto trucks.

In two ways, retailers and their vendors have improved the efficiency of the order-filling function over what we just described. First, using a quick response inventory system that we describe later in the chapter, retailers may turn over the inventory management function to their vendors. The POS sales data is transmitted directly to the vendor, who ships an appropriate amount of floor-ready merchandise directly to the stores, thus bypassing the distribution center entirely. Second, if the retailer chooses to use a crossdocking distribution center, the floor-ready merchandise can be moved from the vendor's to the retailer's truck without going through all the steps involved in filling orders.

Management of Outbound Transportation   Examine flow number 2 in Exhibit 11–5. Due to increased use of distribution centers by retailers, the management of outbound transportation from distribution center to stores has become increasingly complex. The Sears distribution center runs almost 100 routes in one day. To handle its complex transportation problem, the center uses a sophisticated routing and scheduling computer system. This system considers customer service levels, road conditions, and transportation operating constraints to develop the most efficient routes possible. As a result, stores are provided with an accurate estimated time of arrival and vehicle utilization is maximized.

Another challenge to multistore chains is the transportation problems associated with interstore transfers. For instance, Leda Perez may not have been disappointed if the silk blouse she wanted was properly transferred to the store. Buyers and their staffs can balance stocks by shifting sizes or colors to stores where they're needed. In an era of ever more demanding customers, special orders are on the rise. Buying staffs must handle these important but time-consuming orders through interstore transfers or special orders from vendors. Finally, buying staffs at some retail firms consolidate all sale merchandise into one location, like the Neiman Marcus Last Call Clearance stores, resulting in a giant interstore transfer. Buyers may incur additional outbound transportation expenses when merchandise is returned to a vendor because it's damaged or defective merchandise, unsold consigned merchandise, or unsold merchandise that has been authorized by the vendor to be returned.

Reverse Logistics   Although not shown in Exhibit 11-2 or 11-5, sometimes merchandise has to flow back through the channel, from the customer to the store, distribution center, and vendor. Reverse logistics is a more serious problem with catalog and Internet retailers than bricks and mortar-only retailers because returns from customers can average as high as 25 percent. Reverse logistics systems have never been simple or inexpensive. The items may be damaged, and without the original shipping carton, thus causing special handling needs. Transportation costs can be high because items are shipped back in small quantities. Retailers and their vendors usually wish returns to vendors would just disappear.

Fortunately, thereturnexchange.com, a new Internet firm may help retailers and their vendors solve these problems by providing three services. First, they utilize a national database of returns by retailers that assist vendors in making more informed return decisions. Second, they help retailers and their vendors process returns at regional centers strategically located in major shipping hubs around the country. Each center is capable of processing returns from multiple retailers and is therefore more efficient than any single retailer could be on its own. They are able to restore returns rapidly to new, resellable conditions so that they quickly re-enter normal merchandising channels. Merchandise not restored is returned to the manufacturer (particularly defective merchandise) or liquidated through auction—the third service. This worldwide business-to-consumer auction is for nondefective, returned merchandise that cannot be sold as new or returned to the manufacturer.

INTERNET EXERCISE   Go to thereturnexchange.com to learn more about an innovative method of handling reverse logistics.

Now we will look at some additional logistics issues facing retailers today. First, probably the most important development in supply chain management in the past 10 years is the advent of quick response delivery systems. Second, traditional bricks-and-mortar retailers are finding that distribution to Internet customers requires a different logistics system than they are used to. Third, retailers are outsourcing many functions. **Outsourcing** is obtaining a service from outside the company that had previously been done by the firm itself. Fourth, the relative advantages of delivering merchandise directly to stores or using a distribution center are examined. Finally, we will look at the conditions under which it's best to use a pull versus a push logistics strategy.

Quick Response (QR)
Delivery Systems

There are only two groups of retail businesses today: the quick and the dead.[26]

Quick response (QR) delivery systems are inventory management systems designed to reduce the retailer's lead time for receiving merchandise, thereby lowering inventory investment, improving customer service levels, and reducing logistics expenses. The concept of quick response systems is similar to efficient consumer response (ECR) in the grocery industry.[27] QR is the integrating link between the information flows and the merchandise flows depicted in Exhibit 11–2 at the beginning of this chapter.

To illustrate a QR system, consider how the system works at Wal-Mart using its Retail Link system: On Monday afternoon, a customer buys a denim shirt manufactured under a private label for the chain by Americo Group Inc.[29] Every day, Retail Link downloads information from Wal-Mart's computers to Americo's computer. Information includes point-of-sale data by stock keeping unit and by store, warehouse movement, forecast analysis, electronic mail, and remittance advice. A decision support system gives the vendor 100 weeks of product sales history and tracks products' performance globally and by market. Specific sales information on a product is available only to that vendor.

Americo picks the order, affixes Wal-Mart's price label, UPC code, and source tag for shrinkage protection to the merchandise, places it on hangers, and ships it to Wal-Mart's distribution center on Tuesday. Using a crossdocking system described earlier in the chapter, the merchandise is unloaded and sent immediately to a Wal-Mart truck on the other side of the distribution center. By Wednesday, the shipment is in the store, ready for purchase by another customer. Three days to get the merchandise ready for sale may not seem that amazing, except for the fact that in the mid-1980s the process would have taken a month.

Wal-Mart and its customers aren't the only ones to benefit from this QR system. With sales information on an individual store and SKU level, Americo can customize assortments according to region and climate, and plan more accurately. For example, tracking denim shirt sales (which were high in early summer) will allow Americo to beef up stock for back to school. Analysis of sales data leads to more frequent changes in color palettes and concentration in specific sizes in certain stores.

Originally, quick response delivery systems seemed better suited to basic items, such as underwear, paper towels, or toothpaste, than to high fashion. By its nature, fashion dictates being able to quickly adjust to seasons as well as to new colors and styles. Yet quick response is as important in managing fashion inventories as in managing basic-item inventories. Fashion retailers need to determine what's selling (so it can be reordered quickly) and what isn't selling (so it can be marked down). For instance, Saks Fifth Avenue has been using quick response for basics like Coach handbags since the early 1990s. In the mid-1990s, Saks began to develop quick response systems with vendors of fashion merchandise like Donna Karan.

Benefits of a QR System

Reduces Lead Time   By eliminating the need for paper transactions using the mail, overnight deliveries, or even fax, EDI in the QR system reduces lead time. (**Lead time** is the amount of time between the recognition that an order needs to be placed and its arrival in the store, ready for sale.) Since the vendor's computer

Refact Research shows that quick response is exactly what it is cracked up to be. In-store levels are much better than they were 10 years ago, with out-of-stocks having been cut by 60 percent. Additionally, stores using QR offer a greater merchandise selection that, without the cost reduction of QR, would not be possible.[28]

acquires the data electronically, no manual data entry is required on the recipient's end. As a result, lead time is reduced even more, and vendor recording errors are eliminated. Thus use of EDI in the QR system can cut lead time by a week or more. Shorter lead times further reduce the need for inventory because the shorter the lead time, the easier it is to forecast demand; therefore the retailer needs less inventory.

Increases Product Availability and Lowers Inventory Investment   In general, as a retailer's ability to satisfy customer demand by being in stock increases, so does its inventory investment. (This concept is explored in Chapter 12.) Yet with QR, the ability to satisfy demand can actually increase while inventory decreases! Since the retailer can make purchase commitments closer to the time of sale, its inventory investment is reduced. Stores need less inventory because they're getting less merchandise on each order, but they receive shipments more often. Inventory is further reduced because the retailer isn't forecasting sales so far into the future. For instance, in the past, retailers may have made purchase commitments six months in advance and received merchandise far in advance of actual sales. QR systems align deliveries more closely with sales.

The ability to satisfy customer demand by being in stock also increases in QR systems as a result of the more frequent shipments. For instance, if a Wal-Mart store is running low on a medium kelly-green sweater, its QR system will ensure a shorter lead time than that of more traditional retailers. As a result, it's less likely that the Wal-Mart store will be out of stock before the next sweater shipment arrives.

Reduces Logistics Expenses   QR systems also have the potential to significantly reduce logistics expenses. Many retailers receive merchandise in their distribution centers, consolidate shipments from multiple vendors, attach price labels, and then reship the merchandise to stores. Until retailers started using QR systems, the use of a distribution center lowered inventory in the store and raised customer service levels. With QR systems, retailers can negotiate a direct store delivery system in which the vendors deliver floor-ready merchandise to each store rather than to the distribution center. The costs of a distribution center (DC) and transportation from the DC to stores are eliminated. Since the merchandise is floor-ready, there's no need to devote expensive retail space for receiving and processing merchandise in the store—space that can be more productively used to sell merchandise.

Costs of a QR System   Although retailers achieve great benefits from a QR system, it's not without its costs.[30] The logistics function has become much more complicated with more frequent deliveries. With greater order frequency come smaller orders, which are more expensive to transport. The greater order frequency also makes deliveries and transportation more difficult to coordinate. Computer hardware and software must be purchased by both parties. Retailers attempt to get their vendors to absorb many of these expensive logistics costs.

The Logistics of E-Retailing   Fulfilling Internet orders from customers is very different than distributing merchandise to stores.[31] Retailers with stores are concerned with moving a large amount of merchandise from dis-

Refact Traditional retailers that move into e-retailing attract twice the consumer click rate as do Web-only retailers.[32]

tribution centers to individual stores. These distribution centers typically have automated material-handling equipment and warehouse-management software linked to store POS terminals. Internet retailers, on the other hand, have outbound shipments averaging 1.8 items per order that are shipped to addresses all over the world.

So how do traditional retailers with a successful Web presence handle these two disparate distribution tasks? Some, like booksellers Barnes & Noble, Toys "R" Us, and The Gap have set up separate distribution systems. Sharper Image, which started as a catalog merchant, now operates almost 100 stores in the United States and has a fast-growing website. One distribution center serves all three retail formats. Catalog and Web orders are treated identically, but are separated from the store-based distribution system.

Experts believe that traditional retailers that move into e-retailing have the potential to be significantly more successful than Web-only retailers. Bricks-and-mortar retailers already have distribution systems in place, even though they operate differently for their Internet orders. Also, these stores often have significant brand equity. Customers know and feel comfortable shopping in certain stores. It is relatively easy for them to move to an e-retail venue. Finally, there are synergies involved in the marketing of products through both traditional stores and over the Internet. Customers can "discover" a product over the Internet and then purchase it in a store, or vice versa. See Chapter 3 for more details on retailing on the Internet.

Outsourcing

To streamline their operations and make more productive use of their assets and personnel, retailers are constantly looking to outsource logistical functions if those functions can be performed better or less expensively by someone else. Sometimes these functions are passed back to the vendor, as is the case with floor-ready merchandise. Other times retailers contract with third-party logistics companies.

Retailers are demanding and receiving "floor-ready" merchandise from their vendors.

Floor-Ready Merchandise **Floor-ready merchandise** is merchandise that's ready to be placed on the selling floor. Prior to the advent of a floor-ready merchandise system, each carton had to be unpacked and its contents checked to make sure the merchandise received was the merchandise ordered. Price labels and security devices used to prevent shoplifting were generated and attached to each item. Bar codes were attached to shipping labels. Garments were placed on appropriate hangers. Shipments were checked before they were sent to stores.

The following example illustrates how Hanes provides Sears with floor-ready merchandise. The Hanes shipment is received and checked in using scanners. Hanes marks the boxes with unique identifying bar codes. The person on the receiving dock simply scans the bar-coded boxes, and the merchandise is automatically checked in. Unless the merchandise appears to be damaged, there's no need to break open cartons and count merchandise, since the contents have been electronically recorded.

All merchandise inside the boxes are marked with Sears' retail price, other identifying information, and UPC bar codes so it can be read by the point-of-sale scanners in the stores. Also, apparel is on hangers, if appropriate. Finally, every item has a source tag. A **source tag** is a very small electronic device that is unobtrusively affixed to merchandise to prevent shoplifting and provide retailers with merchandise movement information. (Source tagging is explored in Chapter 17.)

Having floor-ready merchandise provides the retailer with several benefits. The cost of making the merchandise floor-ready is passed on to vendors. Large vendors, like Hanes, have developed their own systems to meet their customers' demands. Some smaller vendors, however, have decided it's too costly to provide floor-ready merchandise and have decided to concentrate on smaller specialty stores.

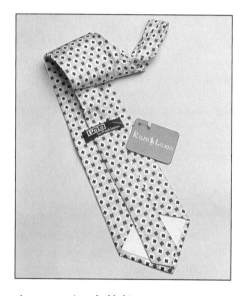

A source tag is embedded in the cardboard hangtag attached to this tie. This electronic device can be used to prevent shoplifting and provide retailers with merchandise movement information.

Third-Party Logistics Companies   Many retailers are outsourcing logistics functions to **third-party logistics companies.** These firms facilitate the movement of merchandise from manufacturer to retailer, but are independently owned. Specifically, they provide transportation, warehousing, consolidation of orders, documentation, and facilitation of EDI orders through VANs (value added networks, which were discussed earlier in this chapter), or a combination of several of these services.

Transportation   Retailers must choose their shippers carefully and demand reliable, customized services. After all, to a large extent, the retailer's lead time and the variation in lead time are determined by the chosen transportation company. Also, many retailers are finding that airfreight is worth the added costs. Some retailers mix modes of transportation to reduce overall cost and time delays. For example, many Japanese shippers send Europe-bound cargo by ship to the U.S. West Coast. From there, the cargo is flown to its final destination in Europe. By combining the two modes of transport, sea-air, the entire trip takes about two weeks, as opposed to four or five weeks with an all-water route, and the cost is about half of an all-air route.[34]

Warehousing   To meet the increasingly stringent demands retailers are placing on their vendors to meet specific delivery times for floor-ready merchandise, many vendors must store merchandise close to their retail customers. Rather than owning these warehouses themselves, vendors typically use **public warehouses** that are owned and operated by a third party. By using public warehouses, vendors can provide their retailers with the level of service demanded without having to invest in warehousing facilities.

Freight Forwarders Freight forwarders are companies that purchase transport services. They then consolidate small shipments from a number of shippers into large shipments that move at a lower freight rate. These companies offer shippers lower rates than the shippers could obtain directly from transportation companies because small shipments generally cost more per pound to transport than large shipments.[35]

One of the most daunting tasks for a retailer involved in importing merchandise to the United States is government bureaucracy. International freight forwarders not only purchase transport services, but also prepare and expedite all documentation, such as government-required export declarations and consular and shipping documents.

Integrated Third-Party Logistics Services Traditional definitions distinguishing between transportation, warehousing, and freight forwarding have become blurred in recent years. Some of the best transportation firms, for example, now provide public warehousing, freight forwarding, and VANs. The same diversification strategy is being used by the other types of third-party logistics providers. Retailers are finding this "one-stop shopping" quite useful.

Store versus Distribution Center Delivery

More and more national and regional chains like The Limited and Toys "R" Us are doing their own distribution. Many of these chains have developed sophisticated logistics systems for bringing merchandise into central distribution centers and then reshipping it to stores. As Exhibit 11–5 shows, they are following merchandise flows 1 and 2. Yet others prefer to have merchandise delivered directly to stores (merchandise flow 3 in the exhibit).

To determine which distribution system—distribution centers or direct store delivery—is better, the retailer must consider the total cost associated with each alternative versus the customer service criterion of having the right merchandise at the store when the customer wants to buy it. What are the advantages of using a distribution center?

- More accurate sales forecasts are possible when the retailer does a combined forecast for all stores that draw from a distribution center rather than doing a forecast for each store. Consider, for instance, a chain with 10 stores, each carrying a Black & Decker toaster oven. Each store normally stocks five units for a total of 50 units in the system. By carrying the item at each store, the retailer must develop 10 individual forecasts, each with the possibility of error resulting in either too much or too little merchandise. Alternatively, by carrying most inventory in a distribution center and feeding the stores toaster ovens as they need them, only one forecast is required, reducing the forecast error.

- Distribution centers enable the retailer to carry less merchandise in the individual stores, resulting in a lower inventory investment systemwide. If the stores get frequent deliveries from the distribution center, they need to carry relatively little extra merchandise as backup stock.

- It's easier to avoid running out of stock or having too much stock in any particular store since merchandise is ordered from the distribution center as needed.

- Retail space is typically much more expensive than space at a distribution center, and distribution centers are better equipped than stores to prepare merchandise for sale. As a result, many retailers find it cost-effective to store merchandise and get it ready for sale at a distribution center rather than in individual stores.

But distribution centers aren't viable for all retailers. If a retailer has only a few outlets, then the expense of a distribution center is probably unwarranted. Also, if many outlets are concentrated in metropolitan areas, then merchandise can be consolidated and delivered by the vendor to all the stores in one area. In some cases, it's quicker to get merchandise to stores by avoiding the extra step of shipping to a distribution center. Finally, if the vendor pays freight charges, then direct store delivery will probably result in a lower total merchandise cost.

What type of retailer should use a distribution center?

- Retailers with wildly fluctuating demand for specific items at the store level, like CDs, since more accurate sales forecasts are possible when demand from many stores is aggregated at distribution centers.

- Stores that require frequent replenishment (like grocery stores) because a direct store delivery system would require stores to spend too much time receiving and processing orders from many vendors. There wouldn't be enough hours in the day to process that many trucks.

- Stores that carry a relatively large number of items or order in less than full-case quantities.

- Retailers with a large number of outlets that aren't geographically concentrated within a metropolitan area, but are within 150 to 200 miles of a distribution center.

Pull versus Push Logistics Strategies

As retail operations become more complex and the information systems described at the beginning of the section become more prevalent, more retailers will utilize a pull logistics strategy instead of a push one. With a **pull logistics strategy,** orders for merchandise are generated at the store level on the basis of demand data captured by point-of-sale terminals. With a **push logistics strategy,** merchandise is allocated to stores based on historical demand, the inventory position at the distribution center, as well as the stores' need.

A pull strategy is the embodiment of the marketing concept in that stores can order merchandise based on their customers' needs. Further, since inventory at the store is based on consumer demand, there's less likelihood of being overstocked or out of stock. There's also less need for store-to-store transshipments to balance inventories.

Pull logistics strategies can't be used by all retailers, however. It's harder to forecast sales for each store than for a distribution center. Therefore, retailers with less sophisticated forecasting and information systems should probably use a push strategy. Also, a push logistics strategy works well for retailers whose merchandise isn't too desirable but still must be sold. An example of a push strategy that's still used by one of the world's largest firms is found at General Motors. As sophisticated as General Motors is, it still allocates cars and trucks to its retail dealers based on its production instead of consumer demand.

 INTERNET EXERCISE   The Council of Logistics Management is the premier industry organization in the logistics area. Go to its site on the Internet (www.clm1.org) and find out about new trends in logistics.

SUMMARY

Supply chain management and information systems have become an important method of achieving a sustainable competitive advantage. Customers are demanding better product availability and broader assortments than in the past. There are simply more retail outlets for chains to service. Many retailers can no longer count on double-digit annual sales increases to sustain growth in profits. Developing more efficient methods of distributing merchandise creates an opportunity to reduce expenses and improve customer service levels in an era of slow growth—or even no growth—in sales.

The systems used to control the flow of information to buyers and onto vendors have become quite sophisticated. Retailers have developed data warehouses that provide them with intimate knowledge of who their customers are and what they like to buy. These data warehouses are being used to strengthen the relationship with their customers and improve the productivity of their marketing and inventory management efforts. Importantly, data warehouses work hand in hand with customer loyalty programs. The loyalty programs provide data for the warehouses, while the warehouses provide information for strengthening the loyal relationship. Electronic data interchange (EDI) enables retailers to communicate electronically with their vendors. Experts believe the Internet will accelerate the adoption of EDI, especially among smaller, less sophisticated vendors.

Retailers are reacting to today's environmental opportunities and threats by changing the way they distribute merchandise. Quick response delivery systems represent the nexus of information systems and logistics management. QR systems reduce lead time, increase product availability, lower inventory investment, and reduce overall logistics expenses. Some retailers are using distribution centers for crossdocking instead of for storing merchandise. Others are forcing their vendors to supply them with floor-ready merchandise and adhere to strict delivery schedules as part of their quick response delivery system. Other retailers are having vendors deliver merchandise directly to their stores and are using pull logistics strategies that base inventory policy on consumer demand. Retailers are outsourcing many of these logistics functions to third-party logistics companies.

KEY TERMS

advanced shipping notice (ASN), *325*

checking, *331*

collaboration, planning, forecasting, and replenishment (CPFR), *328*

crossdocking, *331*

data warehouse, *322*

dispatcher, *330*

electronic data interchange (EDI), *322*

extranet, *325*

floor-ready merchandise, *337*

intranet, *326*

lead time, *335*

logistics, *329*

loyalty programs, *323*

market-basket analysis, *323*

mass customization, *325*

outsourcing, *334*

proprietary EDI systems, *325*

pick ticket, *333*

public warehouse, *338*

pull logistics strategy, *340*

push logistics strategy, *340*

quick response (QR) delivery system, *335*

receiving, *331*

reverse logistics, *334*

source tag, *338*

supply chain management, *318*

third-party logistics company, *338*

ticketing and marking, *332*

UPC code (universal product code), *329*

value added network (VAN), *327*

DISCUSSION QUESTIONS AND PROBLEMS

1. Retail system acronyms include QR, EDI, POS, and UPC. How are these terms related to each other?

2. It's often hard to introduce new technology such as EDI in retail operations. What practical steps can a manager take to ensure that the introduction of EDI will be successful?

3. Explain how QR systems can increase a retailer's level of product availability and decrease its inventory investment.

4. Design a loyalty program for an owner-operated retailer in your neighborhood.

5. This chapter has presented trends in logistics and information systems that benefit retailers. How do vendors benefit from these trends?

6. Would you buy stock in a VAN?

7. What would you include in the ideal retailing data warehouse? Why would you include it?

8. The vice president of logistics and information systems for Pearle Vision Centers has been assigned to improve the time it takes to get hard-to-fit eyeglasses and contact lenses. What would you advise him to do?

9. Explain the differences between pull and push logistics strategies.

10. Why is global logistics much more complicated than domestic logistics?

SUGGESTED READINGS

Bechtel, Christian, and Jayanth Jayaram. "Supply Chain Management: A Strategic Perspective." *The International Journal of Logistics Management* 8, no. 1 (1997), pp. 15–34.

Buzzell, Robert D., and Gwen Ortmeyer. "Channel Partnerships Streamline Distribution." *Sloan Management Review* 36, no. 3 (March 22, 1995), pp. 85–97.

Cooper, Martha C., Douglas M. Lambert, and Janus D. Pagh. "Supply Chain Management: More than a New Name for Logistics." *The International Journal of Logistics Management* 8, no. 1 (1997), pp. 1–14.

Heskett, James L., W. Earl Sasser, Jr., and Leonard A. Schlesinger. *The Service Profit Chain: How Leading Companies Link Profit and Growth to Loyalty, Satisfaction, and Value.* New York: The Free Press, 1997.

Koloszyc, Ginger. "Transforming the Store." *Stores*, May 1, 1999, pp. 22–26.

Lambert, Douglas M., Martha C. Cooper, and Janus D. Pagh. "Supply Chain Management: Implementation Issues and Research Opportunities." *The International Journal of Logistics Management* 9, no. 2 (1998), pp. 1–18.

Lambert, Douglas M., James R. Stock, and Lisa M. Ellram. *Fundamentals of Logistics Management.* Burr Ridge, IL: Irwin/McGraw-Hill, 1998.

Reichheld, Frederick F. "Learning from Customer Defections." *Harvard Business Review*, March–April 1996, pp. 56–61.

Kurt Salmon Associates, Inc. *Efficient Consumer Response: Enhancing Consumer Value in the Grocery Industry.* Washington, DC: Food Marketing Institute, January 1993.

Simon, Alan R. *Data Warehousing for Dummies.* Foster City, CA: IDG Books Worldwide, 1997.

Sullivan, Pauline, and Jikyeong Kang. "Quick Response Adoption in the Apparel Manufacturing Industry: Competitive Advantage of Innovation." *Journal of Small Business Management*, January 1999, pp. 1–24.

Merchandise Management

INTRODUCTION TO THE WORLD OF RETAILING

RETAILING STRATEGY

MERCHANDISE MANAGEMENT

STORE MANAGEMENT

CHAPTERS 6 AND 7 ("Retail Market Strategy" and "Financial Strategy") provided an overall framework for making the tactical decisions that will be examined more closely in Section III. In Sections III and IV, we offer tactical solutions to the strategic problems posed in Section II. ● Section III provides an in-depth discussion of the activities involved in the basic functions of merchandise management. ● Chapter 12 discusses how retailers develop profitable assortments and forecast sales. The buying systems used to make these decisions are examined in Chapter 13. ● No treatise on merchandise management is complete without an examination of processes involved in buying merchandise. ● Chapter 14 explores branding options, sourcing internationally, and establishing and maintaining a competitive advantage by developing long-term relationships with vendors. The important question of how to set and adjust retail prices is the subject of Chapter 15. ● Chapter 16 looks at the relative advantages of various promotional vehicles available to retailers. In addition it considers how promotion affects the consumer decision-making process. The chapter also describes how to develop a promotion program and how to set a budget.

Jennifer Nichols
Buyer
JCPenny

I JUST LOVE MY JOB. I get to travel to Hong Kong and Taiwan to work with our private-label vendors developing new merchandise for our Arizona and City Streets brands. Then I work with some exciting national brands like ODO, YMLA, Pop Icon, and Wood Dog. • Last year, I decided to buy a real fashion-forward shirt from ODO. When the stores received the shirts, I got a lot of calls questioning the buy. People wondered how I could buy something so "ugly." It really felt good when they called in a week, apologized, and asked me to get them more shirts because they were blowing out of the stores. The people in stores know what's selling today, but they don't have a good feel for what's going to sell in the future. • My retailing career started when I was an undergraduate at the University of Toledo in Ohio. I worked for several retailers. I went to work for JCPenney after I graduated as a merchandise assistant in a store and eventually transferred to the home office in Dallas. • Now I am responsible for buying young men's sport shirts for our stores, catalog, and electronic retailing site. My open-to-buy is about $300 million annually and I have three assistants working for me. • I spend a lot of time keeping track of what is hot—what our target market is wearing and doing. I'm always checking out what's on MTV, BET, and WB, programs like *Dawson's Creek*, and what's selling at Gadzook's, Hot Topics, Pac Sun, and Millers Outpost. Our customers are looking for and buying hot merchandise at our stores. • My staff and I are continually analyzing our business. With our systems, we can track the daily sales of each item compared to plan. If the sales are significantly below plan, we take a markdown to sell it and get something new into the stores. If the sales are above plan, we need to scramble to get more merchandise. • The sales in my department were so good that I was one of several buyers recognized for outstanding performance by Penney's top management. When I was introduced to them, Jack Fleischer, former president of the Men's Division, said, "She doesn't accept things because that's the way they are done. And she's not afraid to stick out her chin and make an unpopular decision if it's the right thing to do for the company." • To see what's happening at JCPenney in young men's shirts, go to www.jcpenney.com.

12

Planning Merchandise Assortments

QUESTIONS

- How is the buying process organized?

- How do retailers determine the profitability of their merchandising decisions?

- How do retailers forecast sales for merchandise classifications?

- What trade-offs must retailers make to ensure that stores carry the appropriate type and amount of merchandise?

- How do retailers plan their assortments?

MOST RETAILERS' PRIMARY GOAL is to sell merchandise. Nothing is more central to the strategic thrust of the retailing firm. Deciding what to buy and how much is a vital task for any retailer.

This is the first of five chapters that deal with merchandise management. **Merchandise management** is the process by which a retailer attempts to offer the right quantity of the right merchandise in the right place at the right time while meeting the company's financial goals. This chapter examines strategic and planning issues that lay the foundation for the merchandise management process shown in the top portion of Exhibit 12–1. The issues examined in this chapter are used as input into the buying systems described in Chapter 13, as shown in the bottom portion of Exhibit 12–1. As such, Chapters 12 and 13 are integrally related and are designed to be studied together.

Small and large retailers are required to make decisions about thousands of individual items from hundreds of vendors. If the buying process is not organized in a systematic, orderly way, chaos will result. Thus, in the first section we describe how and why merchandise is organized by categories for buying purposes.

As in any business, a retailer's ultimate objective is to achieve an adequate return on the investment to the owners. In Chapter 7 we looked at how retailers set and evaluate their financial objectives. In this chapter, we show how these financial objectives trickle down the merchandising organization, and how these objectives are used to make buying decisions. Specifically, we look at how gross

EXHIBIT 12–1

Merchandise
Management Issues

PLANNING MERCHANDISE ASSORTMENTS (CHAPTER 12)

Organize the Buying Process by Categories

Set Merchandise Financial Objectives

Develop an Assortment Plan

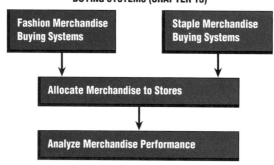

BUYING SYSTEMS (CHAPTER 13)

Fashion Merchandise Buying Systems

Staple Merchandise Buying Systems

Allocate Merchandise to Stores

Analyze Merchandise Performance

margin and inventory turnover merge together into a merchandise-specific return on investment measure called gross margin return on investment (GMROI). We also describe how retailers forecast sales.

Once the financial objectives are set, the retailer starts the task of determining what to buy. Superficially, one would think this would be easy. If the store is a women's clothing store, then the retailer would purchase women's clothing. Unfortunately, it isn't that simple. The retailer is limited by the amount of money available for merchandise and the space in the store. He must decide whether to carry a large variety of different types of clothing (categories)—for example, dresses, blouses, and jeans—or carry fewer categories but a larger assortment of more styles and colors within each category. To complicate the situation, he needs to decide how much backup stock to carry for each item. The more backup stock, the less likely he is to run out of a particular item. On the other hand, if he decides to carry a lot of backup stock, he will have less money available to invest in a deeper assortment or in more categories. The process of trading off variety, assortment, and backup stock is called assortment planning.

The culmination of planning the financial and merchandising objectives for a particular merchandise category is the assortment plan. An **assortment plan** is a list of merchandise that indicates in very general terms what should be carried in a particular merchandise category. For instance, an assortment plan for girls' jeans would include the average number and percentage of each style/fabric/color/size combination that the retailer would have in inventory.

From the assortment plan, we move to the more formal buying systems described in Chapter 13.

ORGANIZING THE BUYING PROCESS BY CATEGORIES

The category is the basic unit of analysis for making merchandising decisions. In this section we define the category, examine the process of category management, and describe where the category fits into the buying organization.

The Category

It would be virtually impossible to keep the buying process straight without grouping items into categories. In general, a **category** is an assortment of items that the customer sees as reasonable substitutes for each other. Girls' apparel, boys' apparel, and infants' apparel are categories. Each of these categories has similar characteristics. For instance, girls' jeans are purchased from a set of vendors that are similar to each other. Also, the merchandise is priced and promoted to appeal to a similar target market. The price promotions are timed to occur at the same times of the year, such as back-to-school in August.

Retailers and their vendors might begin with different definitions of a category.[1] A vendor might assign shampoos and conditioners, for example, to different categories, on the basis of significant differences in product attributes. The category manager for a grocery store, however, might put them and other combination shampoo–conditioner products into a single category on the basis of common consumers and buying behavior. Paper towels could be assigned to a "paper products" category or combined with detergent, paper tissues, and napkins in a "cleaning products" category.

Women's shoes are a merchandise category. The customer sees women's shoes as reasonably substitutable. They are purchased from vendors that are similar to each other. Women's shoes are priced and promoted to appeal to a similar target market.

In some retail segments, such as department stores, the category should be defined in terms of consumer segments. Tommy Hilfiger is one category and Polo/Ralph Lauren is another. Each cosmetics vendor is its own category. Why? Because a "Tommy" customer buys Tommy and not Ralph. Also, it is easier for the buyer to purchase merchandise and plan distribution and promotions if the entire line is coordinated. No matter how the category is defined, supply chain members must agree on the category definition, and it must be based on what is logical to the consumer.

Category Management

As we discussed in Chapter 10, many retail organizations divide responsibility for buying merchandise between a buyer or category manager and a merchandise planner. Although a category manager is more than a buyer in the traditional sense, we will interchange the terms. Since the merchandise planning function is a relatively new concept, it's handled in various ways by different retailers. In some organizations, the category manager or buyer supervises the planners, while in others they're equal partners.

Category management is the process of managing a retail business with the objective of maximizing the sales and profits of a category. This sounds simple. But many retailers organize their merchandising activities around products or vendors. For instance, in a grocery store chain there might be three buyers for breakfast cereal: Kellogg's, General Mills, and General Foods. If all three buyers have merchandise on the same gondola, they will be, in essence, competing with one another. Further, the salespeople for the three vendors will each be vying for the same shelf space. Importantly, smaller vendors that may appeal to special target markets may be squeezed off the shelf altogether.

The category management approach to managing breakfast cereals would be to have one buyer who oversees every aspect of the merchandising function.[2] For instance, the buyer is responsible for working with vendors, selecting merchandise, pricing merchandise, and coordinating promotions with the advertising department and stores. The planner's role is more analytical. She's responsible for buying the correct quantities of each item, allocating those items to stores, monitoring sales, and suggesting markdowns. Together, the buyer and planner are the merchandising team. This team attempts to maximize the sales and profits of the entire category, not just a particular brand.

The merchandising process can be very inefficient for retailers who don't embrace category management. Without a buyer who serves as a category manager, no one individual is totally responsible for the success or failure of a category. It's also harder to identify the source of a problem and solve it without category management. Suppose, for instance, an ad is placed in the newspaper for a Memorial Day sale, but the store doesn't receive the merchandise. Who caused the problem? Was it because the buyer didn't order the merchandise in time? Did the advertising manager fail to inform the buyer or the logistics manager that the ad was going to run? Did the distribution center fail to get the merchandise to the stores? Importantly, without the emphasis on category management, the buyer doesn't have the power to solve the problem. By using category management, all of the activities and responsibilities just mentioned come under the control of the buyer and her staff.

The importance of establishing strategic partnerships with vendors has been stressed throughout *Retailing Management*. (See especially Chapters 6, 11, and 14.) Since retailers and their vendors share the same goals—to sell merchandise and make profits—it's only natural for them to share the information that will help them achieve those goals. Since vendors can develop systems for collecting information for all of the areas that they service, they can provide buyers with valuable information.

Refact Almost 90 percent of all consumer packaged goods companies say they are engaged in some level of category management.[3]

Some retailers turn to one favored vendor to help them manage a particular category. Known as the **category captain,** this supplier forms an alliance with a retailer to help gain consumer insight, satisfy consumer needs, and improve the performance and profit potential across the entire category.[4]

Anheuser-Busch acts as a category captain by working with key retailers to help balance assortments.[5] In a project with a large convenience store chain, Anheuser suggested a program that would optimize the sales of beer by reallocating shelf space. The chain refocused on core SKUs that were driving its sales, but allowed some flexibility for items that were driven by certain demographics. Before category management, shelves were originally set based on quantitative objective criteria, but the shelves were changed over time based upon which vendor was able to get the most space from the store manager. The chain's results were favorable: Beer category sales increased 12.5 percent in reset stores, while total-chain (300 stores) beer sales grew just 10 percent. Anheuser attributes the sales growth to making the shelves more efficient, reducing out-of-stocks, and ensuring that the right products were in the right stores.

A potential problem with establishing a category captain, however, is that vendors could take advantage of their position. It's somewhat like letting the fox

EXHIBIT 12–2   Standard Merchandise Classification Scheme and Organizational Chart

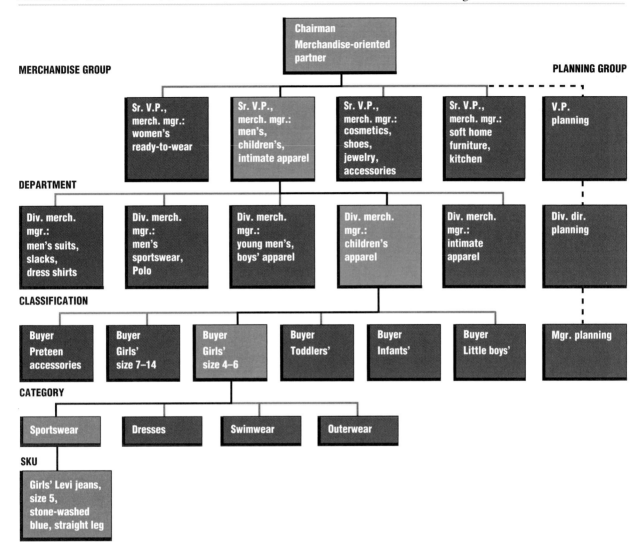

into the henhouse. Suppose, for example, that Anheuser-Busch chose to maximize its own sales at the expense of its competition.

The Buying Organization   All retailers—even those with only one buyer, who may also be the owner–operator of the store—should organize their buying activities around categories to maintain an orderly buying process. Although each retailer has its own system of categorizing merchandise, we have chosen the standard merchandise classification scheme used by the National Retail Federation (NRF) for illustrative purposes. Exhibit 12–2 shows how the NRF scheme is used at major department store chains like Federated Stores, Inc. (Bloomingdale's, Lazarus, and others). In Exhibit 12–2, we have concentrated on the buyer. Recall from Chapter 10, there is a merchandise planning group

How many SKUs are there in this picture?

that works with the buying organization. (See Exhibits 10–4 and 10–5.) Similar schemes are used by other types of stores such as specialty chain stores (The Gap), power retailers (Toys "R" Us), and discount stores (Wal-Mart). These stores typically carry fewer items and have fewer buyers than department stores.

Recall from Chapter 10 that the largest classification level is the **merchandise group.** The merchandise group is managed by the senior vice presidents of merchandise, also called general merchandise managers or GMMs (Exhibit 12–2). These merchandise managers are responsible for several departments. For instance, the second senior vice president on the chart in the exhibit is responsible for men's, children's, and intimate apparel.

The second division in the classification scheme in the exhibit is the **department.** These departments are managed by divisional merchandise managers who report to the vice presidents. For example, the vice president of merchandising for men's, children's, and intimate apparel has responsibility for five divisional merchandise managers. Each divisional merchandise manager is responsible for a department. For example, the divisional merchandise manager highlighted in red in Exhibit 12–2 is responsible for children's apparel.

The classification is the third level in the exhibit's classification scheme. Each divisional merchandise manager is responsible for a number of buyers. The children's apparel divisional merchandise manager here is responsible for six buyers. Each buyer purchases a **classification**—a group of items or SKUs for the same type of merchandise (such as men's pants as opposed to men's jackets or suits) supplied by different vendors. The exhibit highlights the one buyer responsible for girls' apparel sizes 4 to 6. In some cases, a buyer is responsible for several classifications.

Categories are the next level in the classification scheme. Each buyer purchases a number of categories. So, the men's pants buyer might buy jeans, khakis, and dress slacks. The girls' size 4 to 6 buyer in Exhibit 12–2 purchases several categories, such as sportswear, dresses, swimwear, and outerwear. A category like swimwear may be made up of merchandise from one or several manufacturers.

A **stock keeping unit (SKU)** is the smallest unit available for keeping inventory control. In soft goods merchandise, for instance, a SKU usually means size, color, and style. For example, a pair of girls' size 5, stone-washed blue, straight-legged Levis is one SKU.

Now that we've examined how and why retailers manage their merchandise by categories, let's consider the financial implications of their actions.

SETTING MERCHANDISE FINANCIAL OBJECTIVES

Retailers cannot hope to be financially successful unless they pre-plan the financial implications of their merchandising activities. Financial plans start at the top of the retail organization and are broken down into categories, while buyers and merchandise planners develop their own plans and negotiate up the organization. Top management looks at the big merchandising picture. They set the merchandising direction for the company by making (1) projections about how the company will do overall and (2) decisions about which areas deserve more or less emphasis. Buyers and merchandise planners, on the other hand, take a more micro approach. They study their categories' past performance, look at trends in the market, and try to project their merchandise needs for the coming seasons. The financial planning process is similar for smaller retailers. Although there aren't as many layers of management involved in planning and negotiations, they still start with the firm's overall financial goals and break them down into categories.

The resulting merchandise plan is a financial buying blueprint for each category. It considers the firm's financial objectives along with sales projections and merchandise flows. The merchandise plan tells the buyer and planner how much money to spend on a particular category of merchandise in each month so that the sales forecast and other financial objectives are met. Once the merchandise plan is set, the buyers and planners develop the assortment plan. The buyers work with vendors choosing merchandise, negotiating prices, and developing promotions. The merchandise planners break down the overall financial plan into how many of each item to purchase and how they should be allocated to stores. In Chapter 13 we'll describe specific systems used for merchandise and assortment planning.

As you can imagine, there's a great deal of negotiating at each step. Merchandise managers and buyers compete for large sales forecasts because the forecast determines how much money they'll have available to spend on merchandise. Buyers and merchandise managers have to plan elaborate presentations to convince their superiors to increase their sales forecast. Of course, they must be honest with themselves. If they succeed in having a larger sales forecast approved, and the merchandise doesn't sell, their profitability—and their performance evaluation—will suffer.

The next section examines the important merchandise performance measure GMROI and its component ratios: inventory turnover and gross margin percentage. The section concludes with a discussion of how retailers forecast sales.

Putting Profits, Sales, and Turnover Together: GMROI

At the corporate level, return on assets is used to plan and evaluate performance of overall retail operations. (See Chapter 7.)

$$\text{Return on assets} = \text{Net profit margin} \times \text{Asset turnover}$$

$$= \frac{\text{Net profit}}{\text{Net sales}} \times \frac{\text{Net sales}}{\text{Total assets}}$$

$$= \frac{\text{Net profit}}{\text{Total assets}}$$

Using the strategic profit model, we found that we could use return on assets to plan and compare the performance of store managers and other operating executives since they have some control over how assets are employed to produce profits in their store.

But at the merchandise management level, not all components of return on assets are important. Buyers generally have control over gross margin but not operating expenses. Likewise, they have control over their inventory investment but not other assets. As a result, the financial ratio that is important to plan and measure merchandising performance is a return on investment measure called gross margin return on inventory investment (GMROI).[6] It measures how many gross margin dollars are earned on every dollar of inventory investment.

GMROI is a similar concept to return on assets, only its components are under the control of the buyer rather than higher-level executives. Instead of combining net profit margin and asset turnover, GMROI uses gross margin percentage and the sales-to-stock ratio (which is similar to inventory turnover).

$$\text{GMROI} = \text{Gross margin percentage} \times \text{Sales-to-stock ratio}$$
$$= \frac{\text{Gross margin}}{\text{Net sales}} \times \frac{\text{Net sales}}{\text{Average inventory}}$$
$$= \frac{\text{Gross margin}}{\text{Average inventory}}$$

Average inventory in GMROI can be expressed at retail or at cost. Some retailers use retail inventory since it closely reflects the market price of their goods. The preferred method of calculating GMROI is to express average inventory at cost, however, because inventory in the denominator of a return on investment is measured at cost. A retailer's investment in inventory is the cost of the inventory, not its retail value. This measure is called the sales-to-stock ratio.

$$\text{Sales-to-stock ratio} = \frac{\text{Net sales}}{\text{Average cost inventory}}$$

So if sales = \$100,000
and average cost inventory = \$33,333

$$\text{then sales-to-stock ratio} = \frac{\$100,000}{\$33,333} = 3$$

Thus,

Inventory turnover = Sales-to-stock ratio × (100% − Gross margin %)[7]

Continuing the example, if gross margin = 40 percent, then

Inventory turnover = 3 × (100% − 40%) = 1.8

Like return on assets, GMROI combines the effects of profits and turnover. It's important to use a combined measure so that departments with different margin/turnover profiles can be compared and evaluated. For instance, within a supermarket, some departments (such as wine) are high margin/low turnover, whereas other departments (such as dairy products) are low margin/high turnover. If the wine department's performance was compared to that of dairy products using inventory turnover alone, wine wouldn't fare well. On the other hand, if only gross margin was used, wine would be the winner.

Consider the situation in Exhibit 12–3. Here a supermarket manager wants to evaluate performance of two classifications: milk and wine. If evaluated on

The GMROI for low margin/high turnover products like milk can be the same as high margin/low turnover products like wine.

gross margin percentage or sales alone, wine is certainly the winner with a 50 percent gross margin and sales of $300,000 compared to milk's gross margin of 1.333 percent and sales of $150,000. Yet wine turns (sales-to-stock ratio) only four times a year, whereas milk turns 150 times a year. Using GMROI, both classifications achieve a GMROI of 200 percent and so are equal performers from a return on investment perspective.

GMROI is used as a return on investment profitability measure to evaluate departments, merchandise classifications, vendor lines, and items. It's also useful for management in evaluating buyers' performance since it contains both the gross margin ratio and the inventory turnover ratio. As we just demonstrated,

EXHIBIT **12–3**

Illustration of GMROI

				MILK	WINE		
		Gross margin		$2,000	$150,000		
		Sales		$150,000	$300,000		
		Average inventory		$1,000	$75,000		
	GMROI	=	$\dfrac{\text{Gross margin}}{\text{Net sales}}$	×	$\dfrac{\text{Net sales}}{\text{Average inventory}}$	=	$\dfrac{\text{Gross margin}}{\text{Average inventory}}$
MILK	GMROI	=	$\dfrac{\$2,000}{\$150,000}$	×	$\dfrac{\$150,000}{\$1,000}$	=	$\dfrac{\$2,000}{\$1,000}$
		=	1.333%	×	150 times	=	200%
WINE	GMROI	=	$\dfrac{\$150,000}{\$300,000}$	×	$\dfrac{\$300,000}{\$75,000}$	=	$\dfrac{\$150,000}{\$75,000}$
		=	50%	×	4	=	200%

EXHIBIT 12–4

Gross Margin
Percentage,
Inventory Turnover,
and GMROI
for Selected
Departments in
Discount Stores

TYPE OF DISCOUNT STORE ITEM	GROSS MARGIN %	INVENTORY TURNOVER	GMROI
Apparel	36.62%	4.18	241.51
Housewares	34.98	3.41	183.45
Food	20.08	6.8	170.85
Jewelry	37.86	1.89	115.15
Furniture	30.97	2.49	111.71
Health and beauty aids	22.20	3.91	111.57
Consumer electronics	20.89	3.68	97.18

Source: "The DSN Annual Productivity Report," *Discount Store News,* August 9, 1999, pp. 73–91.

merchandise with different margin/turnover characteristics can be compared. Exhibit 12–4 shows GMROI percentages for selected departments from discount stores. The range is from 241 percent (for apparel) to 97.18 percent (for consumer electronics). It's no wonder that discount stores devote so much space to apparel! They continue to carry consumer electronics because they have traditionally brought customers into the store. While there, they hopefully purchase higher-GMROI items.

Although GMROI is a composite of gross margin and inventory turnover, gross margin plays a more important role in pricing decisions. (See Chapter 15.) But inventory turnover is more important when making decisions about merchandise. The following section explains how we measure inventory turnover and the advantages and disadvantages of a rapid rate of inventory turnover.

Measuring Inventory Turnover

The notion of inventory turnover was introduced in Chapter 7 as "merchandise in motion." Jeans are delivered to the store through the loading dock in the back, spend some time in the store on the racks, and then are sold and go out the front door. The faster this process takes place, the higher the inventory turnover will be. We thus can think of inventory turnover as how many times, on average, the jeans cycle through the store during a specific period of time, usually one year. It's a measure of the productivity of inventory—that is, how many sales dollars can be generated from a dollar invested in jeans.

Inventory turnover is defined as follows:

$$\text{Inventory turnover} = \frac{\text{Net sales}}{\text{Average inventory at retail}}$$

or

$$\text{Inventory turnover} = \frac{\text{Cost of goods sold}}{\text{Average inventory at cost}}$$

Since most retailers tend to think of their inventory at retail, the first definition is preferable. Arithmetically there's no difference between these two definitions, and they yield the same result.[8] Be careful, however, since both the numerator and denominator must be at retail or at cost.

Retailers normally express inventory turnover rates on an annual basis rather than for parts of a year. Suppose the net sales used in an inventory turnover calculation is for a three-month season. If turnover for that season is calculated as 2.3 turns, then annual turnover will be four times that number (9.2). Thus, to convert an inventory turnover calculation based on part of a year to an annual figure, multiply it by the number of such time periods in the year.

Exhibit 12–4 shows inventory turnover ratios for selected departments from discount stores. The range is from 6.8 (for food) to 1.89 (jewelry). There are no real surprises in this data. One would expect food and apparel to have the highest turnover. Food spoils and fashion apparel either sells quickly or gets marked down. By their very nature these categories are perishable. By the same token, being a luxury item, jewelry turns relatively slowly. Furniture achieves a relatively low turnover because a relatively large assortment of expensive items is needed to support the sales level. This data supports the decision of many discount stores to remove furniture from their assortment.

Calculating Average Inventory   Average inventory is calculated by dividing the sum of the inventory for each of several months by the number of months:

$$\text{Average inventory} = \frac{\text{Month}_1 + \text{Month}_2 + \text{Month}_3 + \ldots}{\text{Number of months}}$$

But how many months should be used? How could we determine the inventory for the month? One approach is to take the end-of-month (EOM) inventories for several months and divide by the number of months available. For example,

MONTH	RETAIL VALUE OF INVENTORY
EOM January	$22,000
EOM February	$33,000
EOM March	$38,000
Total inventory	$93,000
Average inventory = $93,000 ÷ 3 = $31,000	

This approach is adequate only if the end-of-month figure doesn't differ in any appreciable or systematic way from any other day. For instance, January's end-of-month inventory is significantly lower than the other two since it represents the inventory position at the end of the winter clearance sale and before the spring buildup.

Most retailers no longer need to use physical "counts" to determine average inventory. Point-of-sale (POS) terminals capture daily sales and automatically subtract them from on-hand inventory. Retailers with POS systems can get accurate average inventory estimates by averaging the inventory on hand for each day in the year.

Advantages of Rapid Turnover   Retailers want rapid inventory turnover—but not too rapid, as we'll soon see. Advantages of rapid inventory turnover include increased sales volume, improved salesperson morale, more money for market opportunities, decreased operating expenses, and increased asset turnover.[9]

Increased Sales Volume   A rapid inventory turnover increases sales volume since fresh merchandise is available to customers, and fresh merchandise sells better and faster than old, shopworn merchandise. Notice the produce next time you're in a less-than-successful supermarket. Brown bananas! Since turnover is slow, the produce is old, which makes it even harder to sell.

Recall from Chapter 11 that quick response (QR) delivery systems are inventory management systems designed to reduce retailers' lead time for receiving merchandise. Retailers order less merchandise, more often, so merchandise supply is more closely aligned with demand. As a result, inventory turnover rises since inventory investment falls, and sales climb since the retailer is out of stock less often.

Less Risk of Obsolescence and Markdowns   The value of fashion and other perishable merchandise is said to start declining as soon as it's placed on display. When inventory is selling quickly, merchandise isn't in the store long enough to become obsolete. As a result, markdowns are reduced and gross margins increase.

Improved Salesperson Morale   With rapid inventory turnover and the fresh merchandise that results, salesperson morale stays high. No one likes to sell yesterday's merchandise. Salespeople are excited over new merchandise, the assortment of sizes is still complete, and the merchandise isn't shopworn. When salespeople's morale is high, they try harder so sales increase—increasing inventory turnover even further.

More Money for Market Opportunities   When inventory turnover is high, money previously tied up in inventory is freed to buy more merchandise. Having money available to buy merchandise late in a fashion season can open tremendous profit opportunities. Suppose Levi Strauss overestimates demand for its seasonal products. It has two choices: (1) holding the inventory until next season and (2) selling it to retailers at a lower-than-normal price. If retailers have money available because of rapid turnover, they can take advantage of this special price. Retailers can pocket the additional markup or choose to maintain their high-turnover strategy by offering the special merchandise at a reduced cost to the consumer. In either case, sales and gross margin increase.

Decreased Operating Expenses   An increase in turnover may mean that a lower level of inventory is supporting the same level of sales. And lower inventory means lower inventory carrying costs. In this case there are lower interest costs on money borrowed for inventory. Inventory insurance and taxes are also lower.

Increased Asset Turnover   Finally, since inventory is a current asset, and if assets decrease and sales stay the same or increase, then asset turnover increases. This directly affects return on assets, the key performance measure for top management.

Disadvantages of Overly Rapid Turnover   Retailers should strike a balance in their rate of inventory turnover. An excessively rapid inventory turnover can hurt the firm due to a lower sales volume, an increase in the cost of goods sold, and an increase in buying and order-processing time.

Lowered Sales Volume   One way to increase turnover is to limit the number of merchandise categories or the number of SKUs within a category. But if customers can't find the size or color they seek—or even worse, if they can't find the product line at all—a sale is lost. Customers who are disappointed on a regular basis will shop elsewhere and will possibly urge their friends to do the same. In this case, not only is a sale lost, but so are the customers and their friends.

Increased Cost of Goods Sold   To achieve rapid turnover, merchandise must be bought more often and in smaller quantities, which reduces average inventory without reducing sales. But by buying smaller quantities, the buyer can't take advantage of quantity discounts and transportation economies of scale. It may be possible, for instance, to buy a year's supply of Levis at a quantity discount that offsets the high costs of carrying a large inventory.

Retailers who pay transportation costs must consider that the more merchandise shipped and the slower the mode of transportation, the smaller the per-unit transportation expense. For instance, to ship a 10-pound package of jeans from Dallas to Denver, overnight delivery, would cost about $50 ($5 per pound). If the retailer could order 50 pounds of jeans at the same time and could wait 5 to 10 days for delivery, the cost would be only about $30 (60 cents per pound). In this example, it costs over eight times more to ship small packages quickly.

Increased Operating Expenses   Economies of scale can also be gained when a retailer purchases large quantities. A buyer spends about the same amount of time meeting with vendors and writing orders whether the order is large or small. It also takes about the same amount of time, for both large and small orders, to print invoices, receive merchandise, and pay invoices—all factors that increase merchandise's cost.

In summary, rapid inventory turnover is generally preferred to slow turnover. But the turnover rate can be pushed to the point of diminishing returns—a key concern for merchandise managers in all retail sectors.

Sales Forecasting

An integral component of any merchandising plan is the sales forecast. Without knowing how much is forecast to be sold, you can't determine how much to buy. Inaccurate sales forecasts can also cause return goods problems with vendors. See Retailing View 12.1.

We begin the sales forecasting section by (1) discussing category life cycles and (2) then developing a forecast based on historical sales data and other sources.

Category Life Cycles   When developing a sales forecast, you must be able to predict how well product categories will sell over time. Product categories typically

OVER THE PAST DECADE, EXPERTS CONTEND, product returns have mutated from a necessary cost of doing business to an epidemic problem hemorrhaging red ink. For examples of the scale of the problem,

- At Federated Department Stores, a total of 25 million units amounting to $820 million in merchandise goes back to the vendors annually.

- At Estée Lauder, which does $4 billion in sales worldwide, returns, excess, obsolescence, and destruction amounts to $190 million on an annual basis.

- In the consumer electronics industry, product returns cost more than $15 billion a year.

Analysts say returns started spinning out of control back in the late 1980s, when many retailers began using returns as a competitive weapon in the battle to win market share. Consumers quickly latched onto liberal, no-hassle return policies and retailers perpetuated them, often taking back items they knew were older than their return policy allowed. In some cases, retailers took back products that they didn't even sell—all in the name of keeping customers happy. Meanwhile, manufacturers, who were on the receiving end of this mass of product returns, became increasingly bitter.

Today, retail attitudes toward returns have begun to change. While merchants acknowledge that there's a lot of gray area between the two extremes of completely warranted and completely fraudulent returns, many have begun setting up programs that enable them to draw a line in the sand.

One vendor that has worked closely with its retailers to lessen the returns problem is Nintendo. Retailers electronically register a product's serial number at the point of sale. After entering the product UPC code, a store associate is prompted by a signal built into the POS software to enter the product's serial number. The data is then stored in the retailer's database and transmitted to Nintendo for future reference.

When a customer brings a product back to the retailer for return or exchange, the store associate can instantly access the purchase information from the retailer's database or from Nintendo via a dial-up modem. Electronic registration eliminates the need for the customer to present a receipt at the service desk and prevents the return of a product that is beyond the retailer's policy or Nintendo's terms and conditions. Since introducing electronic registration, return rates have been significantly reduced.

Source: Susan Reda, "Getting a Handle on Returns," *Stores*, December 1998, pp. 22–26; and Harvey Meyer, "Many Happy Returns," *Journal of Business Strategy*, July 1999, pp. 27–31.

follow a predictable sales pattern—sales start off low, increase, plateau, and then ultimately decline. Yet the shape of that pattern varies considerably from category to category. This information enables buyers to understand what customer groups will be buying the products, the variety of products that customers will expect, the nature of competition, and the appropriate type of promotion and level of prices. Knowing whether merchandise is a fashion, a fad, a staple, or seasonal merchandise is equally important for developing a sales forecast and other aspects of a category's merchandise strategy.

This section describes the most fundamental form of sales pattern, the category life cycle. Using the category life cycle as a basis, we'll examine some commonly found variations on it: fad, fashion, staple, and seasonal.

The category life cycle describes a merchandise category's sales pattern over time. The category life cycle (Exhibit 12–5) is divided into four stages: introduction, growth, maturity, and decline. Knowing where a category (or specific item within a category) is in its life cycle is important in developing a sales forecast and merchandising strategy. Specifically, the stage a particular category is in impacts target market, variety, distribution intensity, price, and promotion.

The target market for newly introduced categories is often high-income innovators. For instance, when 3Com's Palm Pilot handheld personal computer

EXHIBIT **12–5**

The Category
Product Life Cycle

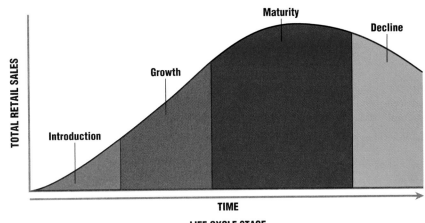

Strategy variable	INTRODUCTION	GROWTH	MATURITY	DECLINE
Target market	High-income innovators	Middle-income adopters	Mass market	Low-income and laggards
Variety	One basic offering	Some variety	Greater variety	Less variety
Distribution intensity	Limited or extensive	More retailers	More retailers	Fewer retailers
Price	Penetration or skimming	Wide range	Lower prices	Lower prices
Promotion	Informative	Persuasive	Competitive	Limited

was first introduced in 1996, its target market was high-use customers like high tech aficionados, who were willing to pay for the convenience of having a very small computer.[10] It was very expensive compared to paper address and appointment books, and not available at all stores that normally sell office supplies and/or computers. As categories reach the growth and maturity stages, they usually appeal to more middle-income, mass market customers—discount store and category killer customers in the case of handheld PCs. Finally, as categories eventually go into decline, they're made available to low-income customers who follow rather than lead fashions. Some new merchandise categories gain popularity in unlikely places, however. In the case of handheld computers, Palm Pilots were next marketed to doctors, stockbrokers, and business executives, who use the products for access to medical databases, stock markets, and e-mail.

The variety available for newly introduced categories is typically fairly small, but grows through maturity and then is cut back as the category goes into decline. For example, pagers were initially available in black, but as the category grew and approached maturity, they became available in a multitude of colors—even Day-Glo. As demand for a category declines, retailers will again reduce the variety to better control inventory costs.

Distribution intensity refers to the number of retailers carrying a particular category. In the introductory stage, categories can be distributed more or

3Com's Palm Pilot handheld personal computer, introduced in 1996, was targeted to high-use customers like high-tech aficionados, who were willing to pay for the convenience of having a very small computer.

less intensely, depending on the type of category and its availability. A high-tech category like handheld computers would initially be available from relatively few retailers. A manufacturer of a new hand tool, on the other hand, would want its category distributed intensively—through as many retailers as possible. As a category gains popularity in the growth and maturity stages, distribution intensity usually increases. Thus, handheld computers have become available at many retailers. But when a category goes into decline, fewer retailers will be interested in stocking it because of decreased demand.

The pricing strategy for newly introduced categories can be either high (**skimming**) or low (**penetration**), depending on the type of category and the level of distribution intensity.

A skimming policy is typically used with categories that are in short supply and available through a limited number of retailers. Handheld computers were originally very expensive when they were available from relatively few retailers. A new grocery store item, on the other hand, would initially use a low price to achieve high market penetration as soon as possible. As a category moves through growth into maturity and decline, the price generally decreases since the category becomes readily available and demand falls.

Promotion in a new category's introductory stage is designed to inform the customer about the category. With a high-tech item like handheld computers, ads show pictures of the category, where it was available, and its cost. But as a category goes into the growth and maturity stages, promotions become much more competitive and are designed to persuade customers to shop at a particular store or buy a particular brand. Retailers limit their promotion for categories in the decline stage and divert those funds to categories that can generate more sales.

Knowing where a category is in its life cycle is useful for predicting sales. For instance, the choice of a penetration or skimming pricing strategy in the introductory stage will influence whether the product will have high or modest sales. Care must be taken, however, that use of the category life cycle as a predictive tool does not adversely affect sales. If a product is classified as being in decline, it's likely that retailers will stock less variety and limit promotions. Naturally, sales will go down. Thus, the "decline" classification may actually become a self-fulfilling prophesy. Many products have been successfully maintained at the maturity stage because their buyers have maintained innovative strategies that are consistent with a mature product. For instance, Kellogg's Frosted Flakes continues to be successful over many decades because it has innovative advertising and is priced competitively.

Variations on the Category Life Cycle   Most categories follow the basic form of the category life cycle: sales increase, peak, and then decline. Variations on the category life cycle—fad, fashion, staple, and seasonal—are shown in Exhibit 12–6. The distinguishing characteristics between them are whether the category lasts for many seasons, whether a specific style sells for many seasons, and whether sales vary dramatically from one season to the next.

A **fad** is a merchandise category that generates a lot of sales for a relatively short time—often less than a season. Examples are Pogs, Furbys, Pokémon, butterfly hair clips, and some licensed characters like Star Wars action figures. More

EXHIBIT **12–6**

Variations on the
Category Life Cycle

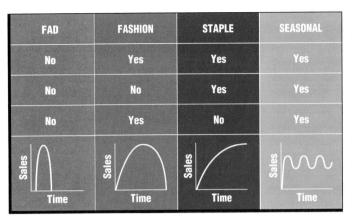

	FAD	FASHION	STAPLE	SEASONAL
Sales over many seasons	No	Yes	Yes	Yes
Sales of a specific style over many seasons	No	No	Yes	Yes
Sales vary dramatically from one season to the next	No	Yes	No	Yes
Illustration (Sales against Time)				

mainstream examples are certain computer games, new electronic equipment, and some apparel, such as cropped and flared jeans. Fads are primarily the providence of children and teens. Fads are often illogical and unpredictable. The art of managing a fad comes in recognizing the fad in its earliest stages and immediately locking up distribution rights for merchandise to stores nationwide before the competition does. Marketing fads is one of the riskiest ventures in retailing because even if the company properly identifies a fad, it must still have the sixth sense to recognize the peak so it can bail out before it's stuck with a warehouse full of merchandise.

Unlike a fad, a **fashion** is a category of merchandise that typically lasts several seasons, and sales can vary dramatically from one season to the next. A fashion is similar to a fad in that a specific style or SKU sells for one season or less. A fashion's life span depends on the type of category and the target market. For instance, double-breasted suits for men or certain colors in domestic goods (sheets and towels) are fashions whose life may last several years. On the other hand, fashions like see-through track shoes may last only a season or two.

Items within the **staple merchandise** (also called **basic merchandise**) category are in continuous demand over an extended period of time. Even certain brands of basic merchandise, however, ultimately go into decline. Most merchandise in grocery stores, as well as housewares, hosiery, basic blue jeans, and women's intimate apparel, are considered to be staple merchandise.

Which of these products is a fad? Which is a fashion?

DUE TO THE PERISHABLE NATURE of services, service retailers can't stockpile as merchandise retailers can. Instead they must have extra equipment (e.g., ski lifts) or additional service providers (telephone repair people) to meet surges in demand. Of course, having idle equipment and service providers is a waste of resources. So service retailers have devised strategies for handling surges in demand.

Many service retailers attempt to match customers with service providers by taking reservations or making appointments. Physicians are notorious for making their patients wait, but patients are fighting back—they walk out and don't come back. Other service retailers use different strategies for lessening the impact of having to wait for service. Sticking a television in front of customers is a simple, inexpensive method used by service providers from airlines to barbershops. Distracting customers by allowing them to watch the service being performed is a strategy used by car washes, photo finishers, and restaurants.

The most innovative service retailers, however, actually devise methods to perform the service better. United Parcel Services of America, Inc. (UPS) and Federal Express (FedEx) now guarantee overnight delivery of packages and letters by 8 A.M. This service isn't inexpensive, however. Delivery of a letter, for instance, costs $37.50 for UPS and $38.75 for FedEx, about three times the price of a letter delivered at 10:30.[11] Finally, some retailers have devised innovative pricing strategies that entice customers to utilize service during off-peak times. (See Chapter 15.)

Refact Even toilet paper has seasonal influences. Fancy toilet paper sells better during the holiday season between Thanksgiving and New Year's, since people have guests in their homes.

Seasonal merchandise is inventory whose sales fluctuate dramatically according to the time of the year. Both fashion and staple merchandise usually have seasonal influences. For instance, fashionable wool sweaters sell better in fall and winter, while staples like lawn mowers and garden tools are more popular in spring and summer. Retailers carefully plan their purchases and deliveries to coincide with seasonal demand.

Fad, Fashion, or Staple? When pagers were first introduced, no one knew if they would be a fad, a fashion, or a staple. Buyers in electronics stores purchased the category carefully at first. They bought small quantities to see how they would sell. As they began to sell, they reordered throughout the season and into the next. Had the merchandise sold briskly for a few months and then died, it would have been considered a fad. Now pagers are increasingly popular. Considered a staple, they've become available in a large variety of colors through many retail outlets at competitive prices. Ultimately, however, with today's technological breakthroughs, the pager will go the way of other staples like rotary phones and vinyl-disc record players—they'll be readily available only at your local secondhand store.

The inventory management systems used for fads and fashion merchandise are very different than those used for staples. Managing fashion merchandise can be tricky. Since there is little or no history for specific SKUs, buyers forecast sales by category rather than by item. Then skill, experience, and creativity enable the buyer to select quantities for specific SKUs.

On the other hand, managing staple merchandise is fairly straightforward. Since there's a rich sales history for each SKU, SKU-based inventory management systems are readily available that forecast future sales using information from the past. Chapter 13 examines these systems.

Armed with information about where an item or a category is in its life cycle, retailers develop their sales forecast.

Developing a Sales Forecast   We develop a sales forecast by adjusting a category's past sales to make projections into the future. Buyers utilize a variety of sources in making these decisions. We divide the discussion into examining previous sales volume, published sources, and customer information, by shopping at the competition, as well as by utilizing vendors and buying offices.

Previous Sales Volume   Exhibit 12–7 shows Levi sales by season over a 10-year period. Sales have been increasing by about 25 percent per season for several years. The exhibit illustrates a strong seasonality pattern. Typically 40 percent of the annual sales occur in fall, 30 percent in winter, and 15 percent each in spring and summer. In the eighth year, the fall season was unusually strong due to early cold weather, whereas spring sales were particularly weak because of a temporary turndown in the local economy. For fashion merchandise, where styles change from year to year, sales figures older than three years probably aren't very useful. When forecasting sales, we must identify real trends (either up or down) and try to isolate a real change in demand from random occurrences. Thus, the unusually high and low sales in the eighth year should be ignored when trying to forecast sales for the current season. The "More Information" box on page 366 shows a simple method of forecasting sales, using Exhibit 12–7's data. Chapter 13 covers more sophisticated methods to forecast sales of staples at the SKU level. Retailing View 12.2 describes how retailers should take weather into consideration when forecasting sales.

Published Sources   Adjustments to sales trends are based on economic trends in the geographic area for which the forecast is developed. For example, a buyer for The Gap would consider national economic indicators such as Gross National Product (GNP), interest rates, and employment rates, whereas an independent local clothing store would primarily consider local conditions. Even if national

Refact Men in New York get inspired to buy a winter coat when the temperature drops to 51 degrees Fahrenheit. But in Chicago, it has to drop to 41![12]

EXHIBIT **12–7**

Sales for Levi Jeans at Trendsetters Department Store

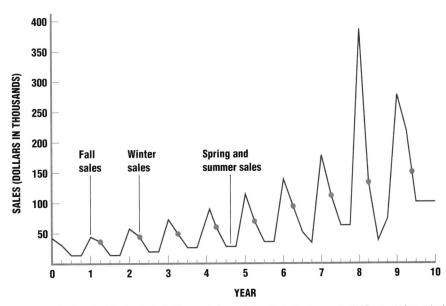

Note: The peaks show the fall sales, typically 40 percent of annual sales; the horizontal lines typify 15 percent of annual sales each in spring and summer; and the dots (the winter sales) are typically 30 percent of annual sales. These data are for illustrative purposes only. They do, however, represent typical growth patterns for a category like jeans.

More Information about Forecasting Sales for Levi Jeans

THE PROCEDURE FOR FORECASTING sales by season is accomplished in two steps. First, we determine a sales forecast for the entire year. Then we consider seasonal sales patterns for each season.

The accompanying exhibit summarizes sales by season for Levi jeans for years 6 through 9 from Exhibit 12–7. For instance, during the fall season of year 6, the store sold $152,587 in jeans, which represents 41.9 percent of the total sales for year 6 ($152,587 ÷ $364,247 = 41.9 percent). The last column indicates the percentages of the increases for the previous three years: 30.1, 48.5, and 5 percent. The 30.1 percent increase from year 6 to year 7 was calculated as follows: ($364,247 − $476,835) ÷ $364,247. Unfortunately the data doesn't show a consistent pattern due to unusually high sales in year 8. The buyer should probably discount the impact of year 8 sales on the forecast and examine sales increases from

earlier years as well as more qualitative factors. The average sales increase over the previous nine years has been 25 percent, general economic indicators in the area are strong, and top management sees an opportunity to "grow" this classification, so the buyer estimates the sales increase for year 10 to be 30 percent. Thus, the sales forecast for year 10 is [($745,056 × .3) + $745,056] or $968,573.

The second step is to apply the seasonal sales pattern to the annual sales forecast to determine sales for each season. The percentage of annual sales occurring in each season has been fairly stable except in year 8. Thus, the buyer decides to apply the same percentages as those in years 7 and 9. To forecast sales for each season, the buyer multiplies the annual sales by each of the seasonal sales percentages. For instance, fall sales for year 10 should equal ($968,573 × .4) or $387,429.

| YEAR | SEASON | | | | TOTAL | PERCENTAGE INCREASE |
	FALL	WINTER	SPRING	SUMMER		
6	$152,587	$114,440	$57,220	$40,000	$364,247	
	41.9%	31.4%	15.7%	11.0%	100%	
7	190,734	143,051	71,525	71,525	476,835	30.1%
	40.0%	30.0%	15.0%	15.0%	100%	
8	400,000	178,813	40,000	89,406	708,219	48.5%
	56.5%	25.3%	5.6%	12.6%	100%	
9	298,023	223,517	111,758	111,758	745,056	5.0%
	40.5%	30.0%	15.0%	15.0%	100%	
6–9 (total)	1,041,344	659,821	280,503	312,689	2,294,357	
	45.4%	28.2%	12.2%	13.6%	100%	
10 (forecast)	387,429	290,572	145,286	145,286	968,573	

unemployment rates are low, they may be significantly higher where a particular retailer has a store. If so, people may spend less money on fashion in this region than in other areas.

The Buying Power Index (BPI) published annually in *Demographics USA*,[13] gives demographic and annual sales data by major line of merchandise broken down into geographic units as small as cities of more than 25,000 people. (See Chapter 9 for more details.) Similar data on a monthly basis is obtainable from the *Monthly Retail Trade Report* published by the U.S. Department of Commerce. These two sources of information cover general trends, but may not be particularly helpful for a buyer forecasting sales for a particular merchandise category.

OF ALL THE FACTORS THAT DRIVE sales in retailing, probably none is more significant than the weather. For instance, when early warm weather drives sales of spring and summer apparel, or when a mid-September heat wave dampens sales of fall fashions, it's weather that gets the blame or credit in the monthly sales reports of chain retailers.

For all this talk about the weather, as the old saying goes, "Nobody does anything about it." Certainly in the world of retailing, the traditional tendency has been to regard weather, when it's regarded at all, as a great unknown factor. Merchandise allocation plans tend to be based on the previous year's sales, which means they assume that the previous year's weather conditions will be repeated.

But according to Frederick D. Fox, President and CEO of Planalytics (formerly Strategic Weather Services), weather only repeats itself from year to year about 35 percent of the time. Thus, retailers who assume a repeat of the previous year's weather will be wrong two seasons out of three.

The result can be devastating. For example, consumers coming into a department store in the Northeast looking for wool socks and thermal underwear during a brutally cold late February may find none to be had, as the store is all decked out with spring merchandise.

Fox's company is a supply chain planning firm that has an extensive track record applying its proprietary long-range weather forecasting technologies, called Weathernomics™, to industries such as agriculture, energy, and film production. In 1993, it began advising the retail industry on how to apply future weather to decisions in receipt timing, merchandise allocation and distribution, advertising, promotions, and markdowns. Today, some of the biggest names in retailing— including Sears, Wal-Mart, Kmart, Target, The Home Depot,

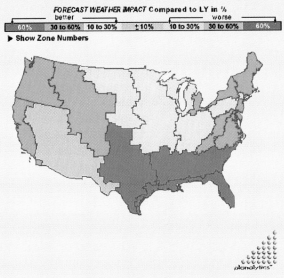

Planalytics forecasts the weather impact on consumer demand for women's shorts compared to last year. It looks like retailers in the Southeastern portion of the U.S. should stack up.

Lowe's, Ross Stores, Charming Shoppes, and Nordstrom— routinely factor the effects of future weather into their plans in order to increase sales and profits. The company claims its Weathernomics technologies have resulted in sales gains of as much as 30 percent as a result of their recommendations.

Source: Rebecca Winters, "Weathering the Business Climate," *TIME*, Feb. 21, 2000, pp. B18–19; and Jennifer Goldblatt, "Winter Clothing Is Scarce as Retailers Think Spring," *The Virginian-Pilot*, Jan. 27, 2000. For more information, contact Planalytics, 1325 Morris Drive, Suite 201, Wayne, PA 19087, telephone (610)640–9485.

Retailers and their vendors can also buy data from private firms like InfoScan. InfoScan buys information from individual supermarkets on price and promotion activity that has been scanned through their POS terminals, and aggregates the data by region, chain, or market area. Information on customer demographics and psychographics as well as competitive information is available from firms like Claritas.[14] (Chapter 9 gives details.) Finally, general retail trade publications such as *Stores*, *WWD*, *Chain Store Age*, and *Discount Store News* analyze general retail trends.

INTERNET EXERCISE InfoScan's website is located at www.infores.com. Go to its site and describe the services it offers retailers.

Customer Information   Customer information can be obtained either by measuring customer reactions to merchandise through sales, by asking customers about the merchandise, or by observing customers and trendsetters. Knowing what customers want today is very helpful in predicting what should be purchased in the future.

Obtaining market information about the merchandise directly from the customer is probably the easiest yet most underused method. For example, a cashier at a restaurant may ask how a customer liked a meal, but not record the answer in any systematic way. Another excellent source of customer information is retail salespeople. They have the direct contact with the customer necessary to determine customer attitudes in depth. Unless the store is owner-operated, however, this information doesn't filter in to the buyer automatically. Salespeople require both training and incentives to pass customer information on to buyers. Some retailers maintain a **want book** in which salespeople record out-of-stock or requested merchandise. This information is collected by buyers for making purchasing decisions.

Customer information can be collected through traditional forms of marketing research like depth interviews and focus groups. The **depth interview** is an unstructured personal interview in which the interviewer uses extensive probing to get individual respondents to talk in detail about a subject. For example, one grocery store chain goes through the personal checks they've received each day and selects all customers with large purchases of groceries and several with small purchases. They call these customers and interview them to find out what they like and don't like about the store.

A more informal method of interviewing customers is to require buyers to spend some time on the selling floor waiting on customers. In most national retail chains, buyers are physically isolated from their customers. For example, buying offices for Mervyn's and The Gap are both in northern California, yet their stores are throughout America. It has become increasingly hard for buyers in large chains to keep a pulse on local customer demand. Frequent store visits help the situation. Some retailers require their buyers to spend a specified period of time, like a day a week, in a store.

A **focus group** is a small group of respondents interviewed by a moderator using a loosely structured format. Participants are encouraged to express their views and to comment on the views of others in the group. To keep abreast on the teen market, for instance, some stores have teen boards comprised of opinion leaders that meet to discuss merchandising and other store issues.[15]

One of the most useful methods of spotting new fashion trends is to observe trendsetters. Where in the past, designers dictated fashions, today's fashions are often discovered by observing cool city kids. By definition, fashion is fickle. Yet, retailers and their vendors need time, usually several months, to bring new fashions to market. Unless they can spot these trends in advance of the typical mall shopper, their opportunity will have passed. So they hire research firms, like Sputnik, that specialize in spotting fashion trends. See Retailing View 12.3.

Shop Competition   Buyers need to observe their competition. They need to remain humble and keep in mind that, no matter how good they are, their competition and similar stores in other markets may be even better. Shopping at local competition helps buyers gauge the immediate competitive situation. For instance, a Macy's buyer shopping at a Nordstrom store may determine that Macy's prices on a particular line of handbags are too high. With the popularity of the Internet, the local competition may not be the most important competition to

WANT A COOL JOB? How about becoming a coolhunter like Ejiro Ejoh. For her, a day at the office means taking her video camera to the streets and immersing herself in youth culture research. The aim is to uncover "the next big thing" that will eventually take the masses by storm.

Being a full-time music student at Westminster University and surrounded by youth, Ms. Ejoh, 30, is the London coolhunter for New York–based trend forecaster Sputnik Inc. Ms. Ejoh's assignments include interviewing emerging makeup artists and fashion designers to find out what colors they believe will be popular in the upcoming season; she's talked to London's up-and-coming DJs and pop groups to get insight into the underground music scene. Staying one step ahead of mainstream trends and finding the next cool thing before competitors do has become imperative for those involved in retailing, product development, marketing, and advertising. Although the youth market is more lucrative than ever, it is also more fickle, cynical, and elusive. Failing to speak their language or meet their demands can mean million-dollar losses.

To get in touch with what's cool and what's not, many retailers (such as Federated Department Stores, Inc., and Niketown) and their vendors are turning to trend predictions companies such as Sputnik, which has an army of young correspondents in London, Tokyo, Berlin, Brazil, Australia, New Zealand, and Ireland as well as the United States.

They analyze the fringe cultures of today's fragmented youth market and provide interpretations to their clients. Sputnik's correspondents are given a list of specific questions that target a particular topic, and are asked to videotape interviews with the movers and shakers in this field. The interviews are sent back to New York where they are edited into a video magazine for corporate clients.

But the job is more demanding than it sounds. Finding the right people who are at the vanguard of progressive thinking and not just following trends is essential. It is about finding people who are progressive, who are moving and tapping into things all the time, and who also are very streetwise. By the time Ms. Ejoh finds the right people to interview, 75 percent of her work is already done.

Source: Jody Scott, "Life at the Cutting Edge of Culture and the Queen of Coolhunters," *The Times of London,* January 23, 1999, p. 27; and "Study Hall: Research Firms are Lining up to Analyze the Spending Habits and Lifestyle Trends of the Increasingly Powerful, Quickly Growing Teen Market," *Footwear News,* February 1, 1999, p. 26.

shop. Retailers must therefore be constantly aware of all of their competitive venues. Shopping markets in buying centers such as New York, Milan, London, and Paris provides information on trends.

Vendors and Resident Buying Office   Buyers musk seek information from vendors and resident buying offices. **Resident buying offices** either are independent organizations or are directly associated with particular retailers that offer a number of services associated with the procurement of merchandise. (Chapter 14 gives details.) Vendors and resident buying offices are excellent sources of market information. They know what's selling in markets around the world. Buyers, vendors, and buying offices must share such information if all are to succeed.

Now that we have set the financial and sales goals for a merchandise category, we can begin to look at what type of merchandise to buy.

THE ASSORTMENT PLANNING PROCESS

All retailers face the fundamental strategic question of what type of retail format to maintain to achieve a sustainable competitive advantage. (See Chapter 6.) A critical component of this decision is determining what merchandise assortment will be carried. Merchandise decisions are constrained by the amount of money available to spend on inventory and the amount of space available in the store. The space constraint is not as binding on e-retailers, however. Based on the financial objectives that have been set at the top and have trickled through the retail organization, decisions regarding variety, assortment, and product availability must be made.

The Chippery in Vancouver rates high on assortment and low on variety. It is THE place to get fresh potato (or beet, or yam) chips, a selection of gourmet dips and fruit smoothies. That is it!

In this section we first define variety, assortment, and product availability. Then we examine the strategic trade-offs between them and the special issues faced by e-retailers. In the next section, we zero in on the assortment plan itself.

Variety **Variety** is the number of different merchandising categories within a store or department. Stores with a large variety are said to have good breadth—the terms *variety* and *breadth* are often used interchangeably. Some stores, like Banana Republic, carry a large variety of categories of sportswear to meet all the needs of their target customers. Banana Republic carries updated slacks, sweaters, shirts, outerwear, and other categories for both men and women. Levi Strauss & Co. stores, on the other hand, carry a much more limited number of categories (variety): jeans and related apparel. Retailing View 12.4 considers Costco's unusual approach to achieving variety.

Assortment **Assortment** is the number of SKUs within a category. Stores with large assortments are said to have good depth—the terms *assortment* and *depth* are also used interchangeably. Levi Strauss & Co. stores, for instance, carry a large assortment of jeans and accessories, such as shirts and belts, that complement jeans. Banana Republic, on the other hand, has a narrow assortment of jeans because it appeals to a more narrowly defined target market and doesn't have the space to devote to jeans due to its emphasis on variety.

INTERNET EXERCISE Go to Macys.com and JCPenney.com. Which seems to have the largest variety? Choose a merchandise category and determine which retailer contains the largest assortment.

Refact JCPenney has its entire catalog, 140,000 SKUs, on the Internet. Now that's assortment![16]

Product Availability **Product availability** defines the percentage of demand for a particular SKU that is satisfied. For instance, if 100 people go into a Levi Strauss & Co. store to purchase a pair of tan jeans in size 33–34, and it sells only 90 pairs before it runs out of stock, its product availability is 90 percent. Product availability is also referred to as the **level of support** or **service level.**

Refact Macy's has roughly 250,000 SKUs on its Internet site, while a typical Macy's store has 2 million to 3 million SKUs.[17]

Assortment Planning for Service Retailers Consider health clubs. Some offer a large variety of activities and equipment from exercise machines to swimming, wellness programs, and New Age lectures. Others, like Gold's Gym, don't offer much variety, but have an excellent assortment of body building equipment and programs. Some hospitals, such as big municipal hospitals found in most urban areas, offer a large variety of medical services. Smaller private hospitals often specialize in physical rehabilitation or psychiatry. For service retailers, the level of product availability is a sales forecasting issue. (See the "More Information" box on page 364.)

Costco Goes for Variety, or Does It?

THE LARGEST WAREHOUSE CLUB CHAIN IN THE UNITED STATES, Costco keeps customers on their toes by offering a wide variety of merchandise. Don't try to guess what you will find there on any particular day, because you might be surprised. Costco is the place where individual and business customers, paying $35 to $100 per year for "membership," buy 24 rolls of toilet paper or none at all. This is where laundry detergent and Italian olive oil come in drums big enough to dunk a toddler, and where a 1,000-piece lot of Ralph Lauren golf jackets, selling 75 percent below retail at $19.99 each, will vanish in an afternoon. In its three-acre stores, you can also splurge on $20,000 engagement rings. They are so popular that waiting lists are often required.

All these disparate categories provide an illusion of expansive variety. A Wal-Mart Supercenter carries as many as 125,000 items; a grocery store stocks roughly 40,000. Not so at Costco, where you'll find just 4,000 carefully chosen products. This makes it easier for the company to manage inventory and to obsessively monitor prices. Three-quarters of the merchandise is "basic," like tuna fish and paper towels; the other items are discretionary, often with high-end names such as Godiva chocolates and Waterford crystal. The store's periphery offers a variety of services: film developing, a pharmacy, and a tire shop. Crazy product juxtapositions—face creams next to crackers—are all part of a selling formula that hones in on the middle-class tastes for cross-shopping and impulse purchases.

Source: Shelly Branch, "Inside the Cult of Costco," *Fortune*, September 6, 1999, pp. 184–90; and Debra Chanil, "Fine-tuning the Wholesale Club Industry," *Discount Merchandiser*, November 1995, pp. 56–59.

Trade-offs between Variety, Assortment, and Product Availability: A Strategic Decision

How do retailers make the trade-off between variety, assortment, and product availability? It depends on their particular marketing strategy. Recall from Chapter 6 that a retail strategy identifies (1) the target market toward which a retailer plans to commit its resources, (2) the nature of the retail offering that the retailer plans to use to satisfy the target market's needs, and (3) the bases upon which the retailer will attempt to build a sustainable competitive advantage.

As a specialty store, Banana Republic tries to be the one-stop shopping alternative for its target markets. It carries a large variety of merchandise categories for both men and women. As a result, it can't physically or financially carry either gigantic assortments within each category or sufficiently high backup stock so as never to be out of stock. Alternatively, Levi Strauss & Co. stores have developed a marketing strategy around a target market of people who are particularly interested in buying jeans. As a result, they provide a large assortment of a limited number of categories. At Levi stores product availability is high; they don't want to miss a sale because they don't have the right size. If any of these three elements—variety, assortment, or product availability—aren't what the customer expects or needs, a retailer will likely lose the sale and possibly the customer.

The trade-offs between variety, assortment, and product availability are strategic issues. Of the three issues, variety is the most strategic. Variety is most important in defining the retailer in the customer's eyes. For instance, is the retailer perceived to be a category specialist like Toys "R" Us or a generalist like a department store? Variety also defines the retailer's vendor structure. Does it purchase from many different types of manufacturers or just a few? Finally, decisions regarding variety are typically made less often and at higher levels in the organization than decisions regarding assortment or product availability. Top managers, for instance, make decisions about whether to delete categories or even departments from the store. Since these decisions have important ramifications, they're made only after serious consideration.

Refact Lack of inventory and high prices are why customers don't buy. In every category, out of stock, wrong size, or wrong brand items or insufficient advertised items in stock account for 33 percent of failed food shopping trips and 40 percent of apparel and home goods shopping trips not resulting in a purchase.[18]

Determining Variety and Assortment

In attempting to determine the variety and assortment for a category like jeans, the buyer would consider the following factors: profitability of the merchandise mix, the corporate philosophy toward the assortment, physical characteristics of the store, layout of the Internet site, and the degree to which categories of merchandise complement each other.

Profitability of Merchandise Mix   Since retailers are constrained by the amount of money they have to invest in merchandise and space to put the merchandise in, they're always trying to find the most profitable mix of products. Thus, for a chain of stores like Levi Strauss & Co. to add a category like shoes to the assortment, a reduction must be made elsewhere. It would attempt to take the inventory investment that it's been making in a less profitable merchandise category (flannel shirts in which it's invested $1 million to generate $2 million in sales) and shift it to shoes, which it hopes will generate $2.5 million.

Corporate Philosophy toward the Assortment   The corporate philosophy toward the assortment helps the buyer determine the number of styles and colors to purchase. To illustrate, let's again consider the hypothetically different philosophies of Levi Strauss & Co. stores and Banana Republic. Both chains have a merchandise budget of $150,000 to spend on jeans that retail for $50. Thus, both stores can purchase 3,000 pairs. The Levi stores purchase 30 different style/color combinations (100 units per combination); Banana Republic purchases 10 (300 per combination). Similar to a portfolio of stocks, the Levi Strauss & Co. stores, with 30 styles and colors, are more diversified than Banana Republic.

As with stocks, the more diversified the portfolio, the less risk of large losses. With Levi Strauss & Co. stores, since there are so many style/color combinations, on average the category will perform adequately even if a few don't sell. But by spreading the 3,000 pairs across so many style/color combinations, the buyer runs the additional risk of **breaking sizes,** which means running out of stock on particular sizes. Typically, retailers take markdowns on assortments with broken sizes since they become harder to sell. Additionally, a large assortment of styles and colors won't enable the buyer to maximize profits by investing a large portion of the budget on the big winners.

Another issue is whether top management wants to grow or shrink a particular merchandise category. Some department stores, for instance, have dropped furniture and major appliances altogether because of low turnover, low profit margins, or lack of space. Many stores, however, have taken a fairly aggressive stance on men's sportswear in recent years. So even if a category is shrinking, if the retailer's overall strategy is to enlarge the department, the category could be expanded.

Physical Characteristics of the Store and Layout of the Internet Site   Retailers must consider how much space to devote to the category—in terms of both physical space and space on their Internet site. If many styles and colors are in the assortment, much space will be required to properly display and store the merchandise. The display area's physical characteristics are also important in the case of bricks-and-mortar retailers. A rack, for instance, may hold 300 pairs of jeans. It wouldn't be aesthetically pleasing to display only 100 units on the rack or to mix the jeans with another merchandise category. By the same token, websites must be designed so that the customer can easily navigate through them. If there are too many choices, if the merchandise is organized in a less than obvious fashion, if the customer perceives the site to be cluttered, or if the checkout process is difficult, customers click and are off to another site.

Retailers typically divide their chain into A, B, and C stores on the basis of their ability to generate sales. Not only will A stores get the largest total inventory allocation, but they can also handle the largest assortment. C stores, for instance, may not receive the extreme sizes or the more avant-garde styles or colors. It's important, however, to assign merchandise that's expected to be best-sellers to the C stores and to judiciously add assortment to the larger A and B stores. Chapter 13 discusses how retailers assign merchandise to stores. Chapter 18 examines how retailers assign space to merchandise.

Complementary Merchandise   When retailers plan to add to their assortment, they must consider whether the merchandise under consideration complements other merchandise in the department. For instance, Dockers may stimulate the sale of plaid shirts and belts, and vice versa. Further, retailers may decide to carry other merchandise, such as men's underwear and socks, as a service because their customers expect it. Internet retailers have the advantage of being able to easily suggest complementary products. For instance, after selecting a book, Amazon.com suggests books that have been purchased by other customers who purchased that book. At landsend.com, each shirt is shown with a tie and several other shirt/tie combinations in smaller boxes on the same page.

Determining Product Availability

The third dimension of the assortment planning process is product availability. Recall that product availability defines the percentage of demand for a particular SKU that is satisfied. The higher the product availability, the higher the amount of backup stock necessary to ensure that the retailer won't be out of stock on a particular SKU when the customer demands it. Choosing an appropriate amount of backup stock is critical to successful assortment planning because if the backup stock is too low, the retailer will lose sales—and possibly customers too—due to stockouts. If the level is too high, scarce financial resources will be wasted in needless inventory that could be more profitably invested in more variety or assortment.

Exhibit 12–8 shows the trade-off between inventory investment and product availability. Although the actual inventory investment varies in different situations, the general relationship is that a very high level of service results in a prohibitively high inventory investment. This relationship can be explained by the relationship between cycle stock and backup stock.

Cycle stock, also known as **base stock,** is inventory that results from the replenishment process and is required to meet demand when the retailer can predict demand and replenishment times (lead times) perfectly, as depicted in green in Exhibit 12–9. In this case, 96 units of an SKU are ordered. During the next two weeks, much of the inventory is sold. But before the store is out of stock, the next order arrives. The cycle then repeats in this typical zigzag fashion.

EXHIBIT 12–8

Relationship between
Inventory
Investment and
Product Availability

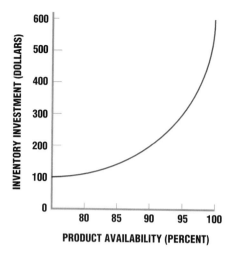

Unfortunately, most retailers are unable to predict demand and replenishment times without error. As a result, retailers carry **backup stock,** also known as **safety stock** or **buffer stock,** as a safety cushion for the cycle stock so they won't run out before the next order arrives. Backup stock is depicted in orange in the exhibit.

Several issues determine the level of required backup stock. First, since every SKU shows a unique demand and lead time pattern, inventory management systems should calculate safety stock requirements for each SKU. That way, SKUs with smooth demand won't be overstocked, and the retailer won't constantly be out of stock on SKUs with erratic demand.

Second, backup stock and, therefore, overall inventory investment depend on the product availability the retailer wishes to provide. If, for instance, Levi Strauss & Co. stores want to satisfy almost all its customers who wish to purchase a pair of Levi's 501 jeans in size 31–32, it must carry a great deal of backup stock compared to what it needs if it decides to satisfy only 75 percent of the demand for the SKU.

EXHIBIT 12–9

Cycle and Backup
Stock

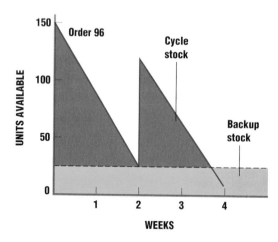

Third, the higher the fluctuations in demand, the greater the need for backup stock. Suppose a Levi Strauss & Co. store sells an average of 100 pairs of Levi's 501 jeans in size 31–32 in two weeks. Yet in some weeks, sales are greater or less than the average. When sales are less than average, the retailer ends up carrying a little more merchandise than it needs. But if sales are more than average, there must be some backup stock to ensure that the retailer doesn't go out of stock. Note in Exhibit 12–9 that during week 4, sales were greater than average so the retailer had to dip into backup stock to avoid a stockout.

Fourth, the amount of backup stock also depends on lead time from the vendor. **Lead time** is the amount of time between recognition that an order needs to be placed and the point at which the merchandise arrives in the store and is ready for sale. If it took two months to receive a shipment of Levi's Dockers, the possibility of running out of stock is greater than if lead time were only two weeks because the Levi Strauss & Co. stores would have to forecast for a longer period. The shorter lead times inherent in quick response inventory systems (described in Chapter 11) result in a lower level of backup stock required to maintain the same level of product availability.

Fifth, fluctuations in lead time also affect the amount of backup stock. If the Levi Strauss & Co. stores know that lead time for Dockers is always two weeks, plus or minus one day, it can more accurately plan its inventory levels. But if lead time is plus or minus one day on one shipment and then plus or minus five days on the next shipment, the Levi Strauss & Co. stores must carry additional backup stock to cover the uncertainty in lead time. Many retailers using quick response inventory systems are forcing their vendors to deliver merchandise within a very narrow window—sometimes two or three hours—to reduce the fluctuations in lead time and thus the amount of required backup stock.

Finally, the vendor's product availability also affects the retailer's backup stock requirements. For example, the Levi Strauss & Co. stores can more easily plan its inventory requirements if Levi normally ships every item that the Levi Strauss & Co. stores order. If, on the other hand, Levi only ships 75 percent of the ordered items, the Levi stores must maintain a higher backup stock to be certain that the jeans' availability to its customers isn't adversely affected.

Internet Assortment Planning Issues

Retailers doing business on the Internet face most of the same assortment planning issues as do bricks-and-mortar retailers. But being a very different type of marketing channel, there are some topics that must be addressed differently. Specifically, what types of products are expected to sell well online, and how is assortment strategy different in an Internet environment?

What Sells over the Internet?   What sells well in the brick-and-mortar world won't necessarily sell online. By the same token, products and services that wouldn't be able to find a substantial market in a regular store may be tailor-made for the Web. In choosing products to successfully sell on the Web, consider the following:

- *Who will buy it?*[19] Every retailer must ask this simple question. If the target market for a retailer isn't likely to shop on the Web, then it is likely to fail. Over time this issue may be ameliorated as more people become comfortable shopping on the Internet. Yet the cardinal rule of traditional business formation should apply to the virtual world: Know your audience.

- *Who is your competition?* As in the traditional retail world, if a retailer plans to compete in an already crowded or highly competitive market, such as books, computers, or toys, it will probably fail. On the other hand, the Internet is perfect for niche players. It can easily link people who want to sell and those who seek hard-to-find and obscure items. The Internet makes it easy to market items that otherwise wouldn't have a large audience. It would be difficult, for instance, for a store selling unusual men's boxer shorts to survive in a mall. But over the Internet, it would have a fighting chance.

- *Will it look good?* In the virtual store, looks are everything. Since a consumer cannot touch it, try it on, sit on it, or walk around it, the way a product is presented on a Web page is crucial. That leaves an online retailer with two options: choose a product whose looks and texture don't matter, or one that can be well presented given the confines of the Web. The first scenario is seeing the most success on the Web so far. Items like books, CDs, software, and financial and travel services—which are heavy on content and don't lean on looks—are the easiest to sell. Consumers can read a book review or sample a track on a CD. They can buy and sell stock, make hotel and airline reservations, and order roses for Valentine's Day—all from the comfort of their computers, without missing out on any aspect of the product. Other products, however, don't translate so naturally online. So retailers need to determine whether the Web has the capability to present their products to their full potential. Apparel and furniture are items whose purchases are often based on physical attributes. You buy the scarf because it will look great with your new suit. Or you purchase the armchair because you love the feel of the leather. To successfully sell such items online, e-retailing experts say, you have to present them so well that they almost sell themselves.

- *Does it ship well?* While getting the product to the customer is the final step in an online transaction, it should be one of a retailer's first considerations. How easily an item can be sent and received—as well as returned—will go a long way toward determining repeat business. Selling puppies online, for instance, may sound like a great idea until you start to think about the logistics of shipping live animals around the country.

The Internet Retailer's Assortment Planning Dilemma   Internet-only retailers face a very different set of issues than traditional bricks-and-mortar retailers with an Internet presence. First, Internet-only retailers are not constrained by their investment in stores. They must, however, contend with different and sometimes sizable costs associated with operating through the Internet such as information technology, distribution centers designed to handle small orders, and premium transportation services. Second, Internet-only retailers do not have to stock every item that they sell. They can, for instance, stock their best-selling items in distribution centers and have other items shipped directly from wholesalers or manufacturers. If done properly, the customer would not know or care about the shipping point of origin because the item would be delivered in the same amount of time regardless of who is the shipper.

Finally, and most importantly, because the size of store and level of inventory investment constraints are relaxed, Internet-only retailers can provide a wider variety, deeper assortment, and higher level of product availability more easily than bricks-and-mortar retailers can. Herein lie several issues in terms of making variety and assortment decisions. An important function of retailers has been to provide a carefully edited selection of merchandise that meets the needs of their target customers. dELiAs, for instance, is a catalog and Internet retailer that targets teenage girls. Its brand equity is very strong for that target market. Now, suppose that dELiAs began to expand its variety and assortment on its Internet site. It decides to offer six casual dress styles instead of three, for instance. In the past, buyers were able to choose the products they believed were the very best choices for their customers. As they venture into new categories and deeper assortments, they may begin to lose their focus by choosing items that don't have the same appeal to their target customer. They may, for instance, begin to lose their customer base if they start carrying new categories like athletic apparel or sweater colors that are not their top choices. Increasing their assortment could adversely affect their customers in two ways. First, customers may become confused by the additional choices, resulting in lost sales. Second, a diluted product selection may cause customers to lose sight of what dELiAs is all about. It may no longer be the top-of-mind place for these customers to shop. The business would, in essence, have lost its distinctive competence.

Officedepot.com, on the other hand, would view the assortment flexibility available through its Internet operation as a way to solve *all* of the purchasing needs of its target customers—small businesses. As a result it carries significantly more items than bricks-and-mortar Office Depot stores. It even carries soft drinks!

In the end, the assortment decision for Internet retailers will depend on several factors. First, what does the target market expect? Is it to provide them with a carefully edited assortment (dELiAs) or one-stop shopping (Officedepot.com)? Second, how effective is the Internet retailer in guiding customers through the site with tailored and adaptive search engines? If, for example, retailers can develop a search engine that is good at suggesting additional purchases given past purchase behavior, then expanded assortments should have a positive benefit.

THE ASSORTMENT PLAN

After setting financial goals and determining the relative importance of variety, assortment, and product availability, the retailer is ready to determine what merchandise to stock using an assortment plan. An assortment plan describes in very general terms what should be carried in a particular merchandise category. The assortment plan for fashion merchandise doesn't identify specific SKUs since fashions change from year to year. The more fashion-oriented the category, the less detail will be found in the assortment plan because the merchandise planner requires more flexibility to adjust to fashion changes.

Historical precedence is the starting point for developing the assortment plan for the current season. The merchandise planner uses the sales, GMROI,

EXHIBIT 12–10   Assortment Plan for Girls' Jeans

STYLES	TRADITIONAL	TRADITIONAL	TRADITIONAL	TRADITIONAL	TRADITIONAL	TRADITIONAL
Price levels	$20	$20	$35	$35	$45	$45
Fabric composition	Regular denim	Stone-washed	Regular denim	Stone-washed	Regular denim	Stone-washed
Colors	Light blue Indigo Black	Light blue Indigo Black	Light blue Indigo Black	Light blue Indigo Black	Light blue Indigo Black	Light blue Indigo Black

STYLES	BOOT-CUT	BOOT-CUT	BOOT-CUT	BOOT-CUT
Price levels	$25	$25	$40	$40
Fabric composition	Regular denim	Stone-washed	Regular denim	Stone-washed
Colors	Light blue Indigo Black	Light blue Indigo Black	Light blue Indigo Black	Light blue Indigo Black

and turnover forecast along with the assortment plan from the previous season to develop the plan for the current season. Adjustments are then made based on the merchandise planner's expectations for what items or fashions will be important in the coming season. For instance, if a particular style, such as boot-cut jeans, is expected to be especially popular in the coming season, the merchandise planner will use more of the merchandise budget for that style and cut back on traditional jeans.

Exhibit 12–10 shows an abbreviated assortment plan for girls' jeans. This assortment plan identifies general styles (traditional five-pocket straight-leg jeans and boot-cut jeans), general price levels ($20, $35, and $45 for traditional jeans; $25 and $40 for boot-cut jeans), composition of fabric (regular denim and stone-washed), and colors (light blue, indigo, and black).

Assortment plans for apparel and shoes also typically include a size distribution. To illustrate, Exhibit 12–11 breaks down size and length for the 429 units for girls' traditional $20 denim jeans in light blue. Thus, the store wants to have nine units of size 1–short, which represent 2 percent of the 429 total. Note that the size distribution approximates a normal distribution or bell-shaped curve. The buyer buys less of the small and large sizes, and more of the middle

EXHIBIT 12–11

Size Distribution for Traditional $20 Denim Jeans in Light Blue for a Large Store

LENGTH	SIZE 1	2	4	5	6	8	10	12	14	
Short	2	4	7	6	8	5	7	4	2	%
	9	17	30	26	34	21	30	17	9	units
Medium	2	4	7	6	8	5	7	4	2	%
	9	17	30	26	34	21	30	17	9	units
Long	0	2	2	2	3	2	2	1	0	%
	0	9	9	9	12	9	9	4	0	units
								Total		100%
										429 units

sizes. However, for some fashion-oriented Internet retailers, the number ordered in different sizes is more evenly distributed. This is because customers requiring the smaller and larger sizes are able to find what they want over the Internet, but are often disappointed when trying to shop in bricks-and-mortar stores because they do not stock the extreme sizes. The process of applying the size distribution is repeated for each style/color combination for each store.

The development of an assortment plan can be complicated. In an actual multistore chain, the process is even more complex than in our example. A good assortment plan requires a good forecast for sales, GMROI, and inventory turnover along with a mix of subjective and experienced judgment. A good inventory management system that combines these elements is also critical to successful merchandise management. These systems are described in the next chapter.

SUMMARY This chapter was the first of five on merchandise management. As such, it examined basic strategic issues and planning tools for managing merchandise. First, merchandise must be broken down into categories for planning purposes. Buyers and their partners, merchandise planners, control these categories, often with the help of their major vendors. Without a method of categorizing merchandise like the one described here, retailers could never purchase merchandise in any rational way.

Tools to develop a merchandising plan include GMROI, inventory turnover, and sales forecasting. GMROI is used to plan and evaluate merchandise performance. The GMROI planned for a particular merchandise category is derived from the firm's overall financial goals broken down to the category level. Gross margin percentage and inventory turnover work together to form this useful merchandise management tool.

Calculating inventory turnover and determining inventory turnover goals are important. Retailers strive for a balanced inventory turnover. Rapid inventory turnover is imperative for the firm's financial success. But if the retailer attempts to push inventory turnover to its limit, severe stockouts and increased costs may result.

When developing a sales forecast, retailers must know what stage of the life cycle a particular category is in and whether the product is a fad, fashion, or staple so they can plan their merchandising activities accordingly. Creating a sales forecast involves such sources of information as previous sales volume, published sources, customer information, and shopping at the competition as well as utilizing vendors and buying offices.

The trade-off between variety, assortment, and product availability is a crucial issue in determining merchandising strategy. Examining this trade-off helps retailers answer the important question of what type of store to be: a specialist or generalist.

The culmination of planning the GMROI, inventory turnover, sales forecast, and assortment planning process is the assortment plan. The assortment plan supplies the merchandise planner with a general outline of what should be carried in a particular merchandise category. Yet the merchandise planner's repertoire of tools is still incomplete. In the next chapter, we show how GMROI, inventory turnover, and the sales forecast are integral components to (1) the merchandise budget plan used for fashion merchandise and (2) inventory management systems used for staple products.

KEY TERMS

assortment, *370*

assortment plan, *348*

backup stock (safety stock, buffer stock), *374*

breaking sizes, *372*

category, *348*

category captain, *350*

category management, *348*

classification, *352*

cycle stock (base stock), *373*

department, *352*

depth interview, *368*

distribution intensity, *361*

fad, *362*

fashion, *363*

focus group, *367*

lead time, *375*

level of support (service level), *370*

merchandise group, *352*

merchandise management, *347*

penetration, *362*

product availability, *370*

resident buying office, *369*

seasonal merchandise, *364*

service level, *370*

skimming, *362*

staple merchandise (basic merchandise), *363*

stock keeping unit (SKU), *352*

variety, *370*

want book, *368*

DISCUSSION QUESTIONS AND PROBLEMS

1. What are the differences between a fashion, fad, and staple? How should a merchandise planner manage these types of merchandise differently?

2. How and why would you expect variety and assortment to differ between different retail formats? In particular, compare a bricks-and-mortar retailer and an Internet-only retailer.

3. Simply speaking, increasing inventory turnover is an important goal for a retail manager. What are the consequences of turnover that's too slow?

4. What does an 85 percent product availability mean from a practical point of view?

5. An assortment plan indicates that a buyer can purchase 1,000 units of fashion wristwatches. The buyer must choose between buying 20 styles of 50 units each or 5 styles of 200 units each. In terms of the store's philosophy toward risk and space utilization, how does the buyer make this decision?

6. A buyer has had a number of customer complaints that he has been out of stock on a certain category of merchandise. The buyer subsequently decides to increase this category's product availability from 80 percent to 90 percent. What will be the impact on backup stock and inventory turnover?

7. Variety, assortment, and product availability are the cornerstones of the assortment planning process. Provide examples of retailers who have done an outstanding job of positioning their stores based on one or more of these issues.

8. The fine jewelry department in a department store has the same GMROI as the small appliances department even though characteristics of the merchandise are quite different. Explain this situation.

9. Calculate GMROI and inventory turnover given

Annual sales	$10,000
Average inventory (at cost)	$5,000
Gross margin	40%

10. Calculate GMROI and inventory turnover given

Annual sales	$25,000
Average inventory (at cost)	$10,000
Gross margin	32%

SUGGESTED READINGS

Blattberg, Robert C., and Edward J. Fox. *Category Management.* Washington, DC: Food Marketing Institute and the Center for Retail Management, Northwestern University, 1995.

Category Management: Positioning Your Organization to Win. Chicago: NTC Business Books, Nielsen Marketing Research, and the American Marketing Association, 1992.

Marks, Steven. *EDI Purchasing: The Electronic Gateway to the Future.* PT Publications, 1997.

Mentzer, John T., Carol C. Bienstock, and Kenneth B. Kahn. "Benchmarking Sales Forecasting Management." *Business Horizons* 42, no. 3 (1999), pp. 48–56.

NACS Category Management Handbook. The National Association of Convenience Stores, telephone (703) 684-3600.

Oliver, Richard W. "The End of Inventory?" *Journal of Business Strategy*, January 1, 1999.

Rawwas, Mohammed Y.A., Scott J. Vitell, and James H. Barnes. "Management of Conflict Using Individual Power Sources: A Retailers' Perspective." *Journal of Business Research*, September 1, 1997, pp. 49–55.

Kim Orcutt
Vice President, Planning and Inventory Management
Circuit City

THE PERFORMANCE OF MY GROUP is measured by our ability to both hit our in-stock goals and improve our overall inventory turns. Our objective is to make sure that Circuit City customers find what they want on the shelf when they come into a store. But we also need to minimize the inventory investment needed to have this in-stock position. It requires a lot of analysis and creativity to manage these conflicting objectives. • I am the vice president of planning and inventory management for Circuit City Stores. After graduating from the University of Virginia, I went to work in public accounting and joined Circuit City's accounting group. Several years ago, I moved from there to the Merchandising department's inventory management team and was recently promoted to my present position. • My area takes over after the buyers develop their strategies for vendors and merchandise assortments. They select the products and negotiate price and delivery terms with the vendors. My team is responsible for managing both the warehouse and store-level inventories. One group works with vendors to forecast sales and inventory needs and use our systems for replenishing our warehouses. Another group is responsible for allocating merchandise to each store. These store planners work with another set of systems to make sure that we have the right products in the right stores and that we have enough product on hand to support our promotional strategies and new product introductions. The last piece of the team is focused on improving our overall supply chain management and logistics systems. All of these groups work very closely together to take care of our customers. • Efficient inventory management is critical to financial performance in retailing. People who aren't in the business think the trick is figuring out what will be the hot products and getting on the bandwagon early. But the real key to success is the "blocking and tackling" of managing the level of inventory in the supply chain. To manage our supply chain, we work with our suppliers, providing sales forecasts and up-to-date sales information that they can use in their production planning. The vendors share with us their new product development plans and so we can coordinate our activities when these products are introduced. • We work very hard on developing partnering relationships with our vendors. These relationships and the sharing of information is key to success for both Circuit City and our vendors. If we work together, we can create win–win solutions. • The inventory management systems we are using now are revolutionizing retailing and achieving much higher levels of efficiency. It's exciting to be part of these new developments.

13

Buying Systems

QUESTIONS

- What are a merchandise budget plan and open-to-buy, and how are they prepared?
- How does a staple merchandise buying system operate?
- How do multistore retailers allocate merchandise to stores?
- How do retailers evaluate their merchandising performance?

"Selling generates revenue, but buying right generates profit."

IN CHAPTER 12, we examined the assortment plan, which indicates in very general terms what should be carried in a particular merchandise category. As Exhibit 13–1 shows, this chapter continues the merchandise management process by showing how retailers utilize many principles and tools introduced in Chapter 12 into formal buying systems. Specifically, these systems help buyers and merchandise planners determine how much to buy. Retailers use two distinct types of buying systems: (1) a merchandise budget for fashion merchandise and (2) a staple merchandise buying system for basics.

While the assortment plan provides a general outline of what types of merchandise should be carried, the merchandise budget plan is used to determine how much money to spend in each month on a particular category of fashion merchandise, given the sales forecast, inventory turnover, and GMROI goals. It's not a complete buying guide because it doesn't indicate how much of a particular SKU should be purchased. To forecast sales for a particular SKU, buyers must know how much was sold in the past. Yet there's little or no sales history for fashions at the SKU level. For instance, even though dresses are purchased year after year, their styles and fabrics change. Buyers must determine the quantity of specific SKUs to purchase based on many of the issues described in Chapter 12.

Forecasting sales is much more straightforward for staples than for fashion merchandise. Since there's an established sales history for each staple SKU, standard statistical techniques are used to forecast sales.

The chapter begins with buying systems for fashion merchandise: the merchandise budget plan and an ancillary system known as open-to-buy. Buying systems for staple merchandise are examined next. The chapter then discusses how

EXHIBIT **13–1**

Merchandise
Management Issues

PLANNING MERCHANDISE ASSORTMENTS (CHAPTER 12)

BUYING SYSTEMS (CHAPTER 13)

multistore retailers allocate merchandise among stores. At the end of this chapter, Appendix 13A describes the retail inventory method (RIM), while Appendix 13B provides alternatives to the stock-to-sales ratio (an integral part of the merchandise budget plan). Retailing View 13.1 provides a glimpse of how not to order merchandise.

MERCHANDISE BUDGET PLAN

The merchandise budget plan's aims are to set up specific merchandise objectives (in dollars) and to plan the financial aspects of the merchandise side of the business. The merchandise budget plan isn't a complete buying plan since it doesn't indicate what kind of merchandise to buy or in what quantities. The plan just specifies how much money should be spent each month to support sales and achieve turnover and GMROI objectives.

Exhibit 13–2 shows a six-month merchandise budget plan for men's tailored suits at a national specialty store chain. For a category like this, the buyer is probably doing the plan for the spring season sometime in the summer. She needs to plan how much merchandise should be delivered in each month to achieve her financial goals for the period.

A merchandise budget plan has no guarantee that what actually sells during the period will coincide with the plan, however. But without the plan, merchandise would be delivered haphazardly over the season. Demand for merchandise would not be coordinated with supply—either too much or too little would be ordered. Importantly, there would be no coordination between categories or buyers. There would be too much merchandise in some categories and not enough in others. From a global perspective, the merchandise assortment could become off-balance and therefore confuse customers.

- The salesperson shows the merchandise to the buyer in a cramped, noisy stockroom.

- The buyer assumes that there's enough money in the budget to make the purchase, without really checking. The buyer doesn't stipulate when the merchandise should be delivered.

- The salesperson submits the order to the vendor without checking its accuracy.

- The vendor receives the order, but can't read it clearly. The vendor doesn't bother to confirm the order with the retailer.

- The order is delayed while a credit check on the retailer is performed. The buyer receives a "request for information" from the vendor's credit department. The buyer turns the request over to the accounting department. They put it into a "to do" file.

- Time passes.

- Business at the store has been great and this order is really needed.

- The buyer calls the salesperson to ask where the order is.

- The salesperson calls the vendor to ask where the order is.

- The vendor checks with its credit department to ask where the approval is.

- The credit department calls the retailer to ask where the credit information is.

- The credit information is faxed to the credit department, which immediately releases the order.

- The vendor finds that 40 percent of the order isn't available so it substitutes six styles for the unreadable and unavailable merchandise.

- The retailer receives the shipment, checks in goods, but can't find the original purchase order, so it has no idea which items have been substituted.

- The buyer inspects the shipment and finds partial shipment and substitutions, so she holds the merchandise off the selling floor.

- More time passes.

This nightmarish scenario is unfortunately more common than you would expect. However, at least some of the situations outlined above can be avoided, or their negative effects can be mitigated with proper planning and recordkeeping.

Source: Bill Pearson, "Playing Hard-Ball with Your Orders . . . It's the Follow Through That Counts," *Stores*, November 1993, pp. 73–74. Reprinted from *Stores* Magazine, © NRF Enterprises, Inc. 1993.

Take a close look at Exhibit 13–2's last line, line 8, "Monthly Additions To Stock." In the next few pages we will systematically work through Exhibit 13–2 on our way to the last line. "Monthly Additions To Stock" tells the buyer how much money to spend in each month, given the category's sales forecast, GMROI, inventory turnover, and the monthly fluctuations in sales. As such, the merchandise budget plan coordinates purchases to coincide with the category's financial goals.

This chain uses Arthur, a strategic merchandise system available through JDA Software Group of Phoenix, Arizona. Available around the world, Arthur is currently used by over 300 retailers including Wal-Mart, Kay-Bee Toy Stores, Saks Inc., Pier 1 Imports, Carrefour, Victoria's Secret, Best Buy, Littlewoods, and VF Corporation. Even relatively small stores now use advanced computer technologies like Arthur to plan merchandise budgets. Retailing View 13.2 shows how Arthur was successfully used at Pier 1 Imports.

INTERNET EXERCISE More information on the Arthur product line can be found through the JDA Software Group's website at (www.jda.com). To see all that Arthur can do and learn how retailers around the world have embraced Arthur's power, go to its site.

WITH MORE THAN 800 STORES, the $1.4 billion Pier 1 Imports offers over 5,000 items of culturally inspired merchandise from over 50 countries. This merchandise is grouped in five categories: home furnishing, decorative accessories, housewares, bed and bath products, and seasonal items.

Prior to 1998, Pier 1 also had a sixth category, apparel, which generated approximately $70 million in sales. With the help of the JDA's Arthur, Pier 1 determined that apparel was not a growth business for it. Seeing increased demand for furniture and decorative accessories, Pier 1 wanted to proactively address this trend by investing more of its floor space, as well as inventory and advertising dollars, on these products. As a result, the company began to de-emphasize apparel in 1995 and discontinued this product category by the end of 1997.

It was able to replace the lost revenue from soft lines with increased sales from other product groups, plus Arthur helped it deal with the markdowns of the discontinued apparel line. It managed this major transition without taking focus away from its fast-turning merchandise assortments, which change 70 percent each year.

In 1997, with only 7 percent of sales from apparel, Pier 1 still achieved double-digit sales gains with no decrease in operating margin and just a slight increase in average inventory. By analyzing its overall business, buying smarter, and emphasizing high-demand product categories, it also achieved higher average-ticket sales as well as increased sales per average square foot of retail space.

Source: M. Deena Amato-McCoy, "More Sales with Less Inventory," *RT,* October 1999, pp. 51–53.

Monthly Sales Percent Distribution to Season (Line 1)

Line 1 of the plan projects what percentage of the total sales is expected to be sold in each month. Thus, in Exhibit 13–2, 21 percent of the six-month sales is expected to occur in January.

EXHIBIT 13–2

Six-Month
Merchandise
Budget Plan

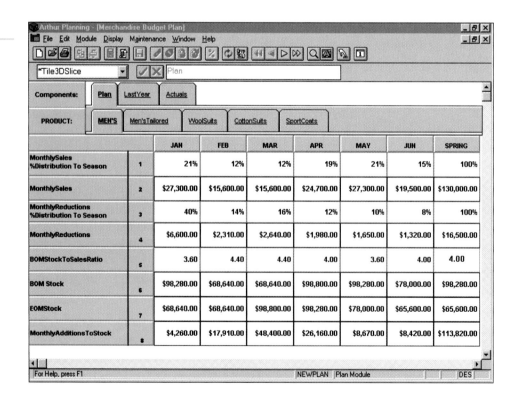

In the seven days before Christmas, retailers have marked peaks in sales that can amount to as much as 40 percent of their December sales figures. Vic Bider/Photo Edit

MonthlySales %Distribution To Season	1	21%	12%	12%	19%	21%	15%	100%

The starting point for determining the percent distribution of sales by month is historical records. The percentage of total sales that occurs in a particular month doesn't vary appreciably from year to year. Even so, it's helpful to examine each month's percentage over a few years to check for any significant changes. For instance, the merchandise planner realizes that the autumn selling season for men's tailored suits continues to be pushed further back into summer. Over time, this general shift toward earlier purchasing will affect the percent distribution of sales by month. The distribution may also vary due to changes in the planner or her competitors' marketing strategies. She must include special sales that didn't occur in the past, for instance, in the percent distribution of sales by month in the same way that they're built into the overall sales forecast.

Monthly Sales (Line 2) Monthly sales equal the forecast total sales for the six-month period (last column = $130,000) multiplied by each sales percentage by month (line 1). We discussed methods of determining the sales forecast in Chapter 12. In Exhibit 13–2, monthly sales for January = $130,000 × 21% = $27,300.

MonthlySales	2	$27,300.00	$15,600.00	$15,600.00	$24,700.00	$27,300.00	$19,500.00	$130,000.00

Monthly Reductions Percent Distribution to Season (Line 3) Reductions include markdowns, discounts, and shrinkage. To have enough merchandise every month to support the monthly sales forecast, the planner must consider factors that reduce the inventory level. Although sales are the primary reduction, the value of the inventory is also reduced by markdowns, shrinkage, and discounts to employees. The merchandise budget planning process builds in these additional reductions into the planned purchases. Otherwise, the retailer would always be understocked. Note that in Exhibit 13–2, 40 percent of the season's total reductions occur in January as a result of end-of-season sales.

MonthlyReductions %Distribution To Season	3	40%	14%	16%	12%	10%	8%	100%

Markdowns can be forecast fairly accurately from historical records. Of course, changes in markdown strategies—or changes in the environment, such as competition or general economic activity—must be taken into consideration when forecasting markdowns. (Chapter 15 discusses markdowns.)

Discounts to employees are like markdowns, except that they're given to employees rather than to customers. Cost of the employee discount is tied fairly closely to the sales level and number of employees. Thus, its percentage of sales and dollar amount can be forecast fairly accurately from historical records.

Shrinkage is caused by shoplifting by employees and/or customers, by merchandise being misplaced or damaged, or by poor bookkeeping. The planner measures shrinkage by taking the difference between (1) the inventory's recorded value based on merchandise bought and received and (2) the physical inventory in stores and distribution centers. (Physical inventories are typically taken semiannually.) Shrinkage varies by department and season. Typically shrinkage also varies directly with sales. So if sales of men's tailored suits rise 10 percent, then the planner can expect a 10 percent increase in shrinkage. Chapter 17 provides details on how retailers reduce inventory losses.

To reduce losses from internal theft, this sophisticated security device enables security personnel to monitor checkout lanes and sales transactions simultaneously.

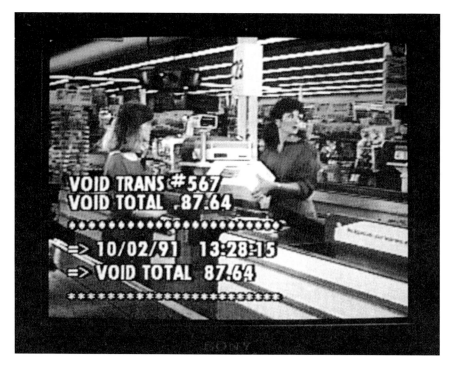

Monthly Reductions (Line 4)

The planner calculates the monthly reductions like she calculates monthly sales. She multiplies the total reductions by each percentage in line 3. In Exhibit 13–2,

MonthlyReductions	4	$6,600.00	$2,310.00	$2,640.00	$1,980.00	$1,650.00	$1,320.00	$16,500.00

January reductions = $16,500 \times 40\% = \$6,600$

BOM (Beginning-of-Month) Stock-to-Sales Ratio (Line 5)

This ratio specifies the amount of inventory that should be on hand at the beginning of the month to support the sales forecast and maintain the inventory turnover objective. The numerator is BOM inventory (specified at retail), while the denominator is the forecasted sales for the month. Thus, a stock-to-sales ratio of 2 means that we plan to have twice as much inventory on hand at the beginning of the month as we plan to sell for that month. The stock-to-sales ratio also represents the amount of months-of-supply on hand at the beginning of the month. A stock-to-sales ratio of 2 means we have two months of inventory, or approximately 60 days, on hand at the beginning of the month. A stock-to-sales ratio of 1/2 represents a half month's supply of merchandise or approximately 15 days, and so on.

As you will see in the next few paragraphs, there is a direct relationship between GMROI, the sales-to-stock ratio, inventory turnover, and the stock-to-sales ratio. Importantly, if inventory turnover is six times per year, on average you have a two-month supply of inventory, or a 60-day supply (360 days per year ÷ 6 turns = 60 days), and a BOM stock-to-sales ratio of 2! Likewise, a 24 inventory turn represents only a half month's supply (two per month), or 15-day supply (360 days per year ÷ 24 turns = 15 days), i.e., a BOM stock-to-sales ratio of 1/2.

The stock-to-sales ratios are calculated in four steps.

Step 1: Calculate Sales-to-Stock Ratio Begin with the planned GMROI, gross margin, and sales-to-stock ratio that was assigned to the category based on overall corporate financial objectives. (See Chapter 12.)

$$\text{GMROI} = \text{Gross margin \%} \times \text{Sales-to-stock ratio}$$
$$122.72\% = 45\% \times 2.727$$

Note that the sales-to-stock ratio is based on six-month rather than annual sales.

Step 2: Convert the Sales-to-Stock Ratio to Inventory Turnover As Chapter 12 said,

$$\text{Inventory turnover} = \text{Sales-to-stock ratio} \times (100\% - \text{Gross margin \%, expressed as a decimal})$$
$$1.5 = 2.727 \times .55$$

This adjustment is necessary since the sales-to-stock ratio defines sales at retail and inventory at cost, whereas inventory turnover defines both sales and inventory either at retail or at cost. This inventory turnover is based on a six-month period.

Step 3: Calculate Average Stock-to-Sales Ratio

$$\text{Average stock-to-sales ratio} = 6 \text{ months} \div \text{Inventory turnover}$$
$$4 = 6 \div 1.5$$

(If preparing a 12-month plan, the planner must divide 12 into the annual inventory turnover!) As with inventory turnover, both the numerator and denominator can be either at cost or at retail. Since Exhibit 13–2's merchandise budget plan is based on retail, it's easiest to think of the numerator as BOM (beginning-of-month) retail inventory and the denominator as sales for that month. Thus, to achieve a six-month inventory turnover of 1.5, on average, the planner must plan to have a BOM inventory that's four times the amount of sales for a given month.

Even a planner must be careful when thinking about the average stock-to-sales ratio. It can be easily confused with the sales-to-stock ratio. One isn't the inverse of the other, however. Sales are the same in both ratios. But stock in the sales-to-stock ratio is the average inventory at cost over all days in the period, whereas stock in the average stock-to-sales ratio is the average BOM inventory at retail. Also, the BOM stock-to-sales ratio is an average for all months. Adjustments are made to this average in line 5 to account for seasonal variation in sales.

Step 4: Calculate Monthly Stock-to-Sales Ratios The monthly stock-to-sales ratios in line 5 must average the BOM stock-to-sales ratio calculated above to achieve the planned inventory turnover. Generally, monthly stock-to-sales ratios vary in the opposite direction of sales. That is, in months when sales are larger, stock-to-sales ratios are smaller, and vice versa.

The merchandise planner must consider the seasonal pattern for men's tailored suits in determining her monthly stock-to-sales ratios. In the ideal situation, men's tailored suits arrive in the store the same day and in the same quantity that customers demand them. Unfortunately the real-life retailing world isn't this simple. Note in Exhibit 13–2 (line 8) that men's tailored suits for the spring season start arriving slowly in January, yet demand lags behind these arrivals until the weather starts getting warmer. Monthly sales then jump from 12 percent of annual sales in March to 19 percent in April (line 1). But the stock-to-sales ratio (line 5) decreased from 4.4 in March to 4.0 in April. Thus, in months when sales increase (e.g., April), beginning-of-month inventory also increases (line 6) but at a slower rate. This causes stock-to-sales ratios to decrease. Likewise, in months when sales decrease dramatically, like in June (line 1), inventory also decreases (line 6), again at a slower rate, causing stock-to-sales ratios to increase (line 5).

BOMStockToSalesRatio	5	3.60	4.40	4.40	4.00	3.60	4.00	4.00

How, then, should specific monthly stock-to-sales ratios be determined? When doing a merchandise budget plan for a classification that has accumulated history (like men's tailored suits), the planner examines previous stock-to-sales ratios. To judge how adequate these past ratios were, the planner determines if inventory levels were exceedingly high or low in any months. Then she makes minor corrections to adjust for a previous imbalance in inventory levels.

We must also make adjustments for changes in the current environment. For instance, assume the planner is planning a promotion for Groundhog Day. Since this promotion has never been done before, the stock-to-sales ratio for that February should be adjusted downward to allow for the expected increase in sales. Caution: Monthly stock-to-sales ratios don't change by the same percentage as the percent distribution of sales by month is changing. In months when sales increase, stock-to-sales ratios decrease, but at a slower rate. Since there's no exact method of making these adjustments, the buyer must make some subjective judgments.

BOM (Beginning-of-Month) Stock (Line 6)

The amount of inventory planned for the beginning of the month (BOM) equals

Monthly sales (line 2) × BOM stock-to-sales ratio (line 5)

When doing this multiplication, sales drops out of the equation, leaving BOM stock. In Exhibit 13–2,

BOM stock for January = $27,300 × 3.6 = $98,280

BOM Stock	6	$98,280.00	$68,640.00	$68,640.00	$98,800.00	$98,280.00	$78,000.00	$98,280.00

EOM (End-of-Month) Stock (Line 7)

The BOM stock from the current month is the same as the EOM (end-of-month) stock in the previous month. So, to derive line 7, the planner simply moves the BOM stock in line 6 down one box and to the left.

In Exhibit 13–2, the EOM stock for January is the same as the BOM stock for February, $68,640. We must forecast ending inventory for the last month in the plan.

EOMStock	7	$68,640.00	$68,640.00	$98,800.00	$98,280.00	$78,000.00	$65,600.00	$65,600.00

Monthly Additions to Stock (Line 8)

The monthly additions to stock is the amount to be ordered for delivery in each month, given turnover and sales objectives.

Additions to stock = Sales (line 2) + Reductions (line 4)
+ EOM inventory (line 7) – BOM inventory (line 6)

In Exhibit 13–2,

Additions to stock for January = $27,300 + 6,600 + 68,640 – 98,280 = $4,260

MonthlyAdditionsToStock	8	$4,260.00	$17,910.00	$48,400.00	$26,160.00	$8,670.00	$8,420.00	$113,820.00

This formula isn't particularly enlightening, so consider the following explanation. At the beginning of the month, the inventory level equals BOM stock. During the month, merchandise is sold and various reductions, such as markdowns, occur. So BOM stock minus monthly sales minus reductions equals EOM stock if nothing is purchased. But something must be purchased to get back up to the forecast EOM stock. The difference between EOM stock if nothing is purchased (BOM stock – sales–reductions) and the forecast EOM stock is the additions to stock.

Evaluating the Merchandise Budget Plan

GMROI, inventory turnover, and the sales forecast are used for both planning and control. The previous sections have described how they all fit together in planning the merchandise budget. A merchandise planner negotiates a GMROI, inventory turnover, and sales forecast goal based on the top-down/bottom-up planning process described in Chapter 12. This plan is used to purchase men's tailored suits for the upcoming season. Well in advance of the season, the planner purchases the amount of merchandise found in the last line of the merchandise budget plan to be delivered in those specific months—the monthly additions to stock.

After the selling season, the planner must determine how well she actually performed compared to the plan for control purposes. If the actual GMROI, turnover, and forecast are greater than those in the plan, then performance is better than expected. No performance evaluation should be based on any one of these measures, however. Several additional questions must be answered to evaluate her performance: Why did her performance exceed or fall short of the plan? Was the deviation from the plan due to something under her control? (For instance, was too much merchandise purchased? Did she react quickly to changes in demand by either purchasing more or having a sale? Was the deviation due to some external factor, such as a change in competitive level or economic activity?) Every attempt should be made to discover answers to these questions. Later in this chapter, we'll examine several additional tools used to evaluate merchandise performance.

OPEN-TO-BUY

The open-to-buy starts where the merchandise budget plan ends. That is, the merchandise budget provides the merchandise planner with a plan for purchasing merchandise to be delivered in a particular month. The **open-to-buy** system keeps track of merchandise flows while they're occurring. Specifically, open-to-buy records how much is spent each month (and therefore how much is left to spend).

Even if everything in the planner's merchandise budget for men's tailored suits goes according to plan, without careful attention to the record keeping performed in the open-to-buy, she'll fail. In the same way that you must keep track of the checks you write, the planner must keep careful records of the merchandise she purchases and when it's to be delivered. Otherwise she would buy too much or too little. Merchandise would be delivered in months when it wasn't needed, and would be unavailable when it was needed. Sales and inventory turnover would suffer, and the merchandise budget plan would be useless. Thus, the open-to-buy system presented here is a critical component of the merchandise management process.

For the merchandise budget plan to be successful (i.e., meet the sales, inventory turnover, and GMROI goals for a category), the merchandise planner attempts to buy merchandise in quantities and with delivery dates such that the actual EOM (end-of-month) stock for a month will be the same as the projected EOM stock. For example, at the end of June, which is the end of the spring season, the planner would like to be completely out of men's tailored suits so there will be room for the summer collection. Thus, the planner would want the projected EOM stock and the actual EOM stock to both equal zero.

Using the Arthur planning system, Exhibit 13–3 presents the six-month open-to-buy for the same category of men's suits discussed in the merchandise planning section earlier in the chapter. The first row of numbers for each entry represents the plan, whereas the second row represents what has actually occurred. So, for instance, in January our BOM (beginning-of-month) stock was

EXHIBIT **13-3**

Six-Month Open-to-Buy

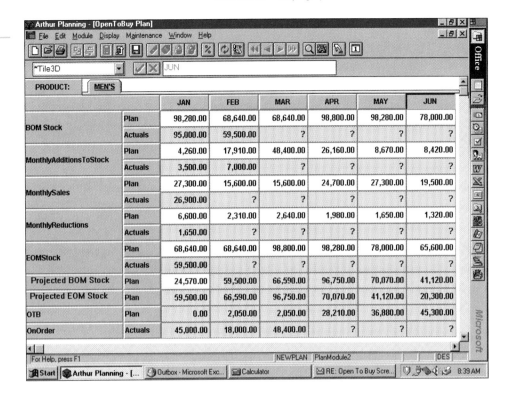

planned to be $98,280, but it was actually $95,000. Note also that the first five row entries also appear in the merchandise budget plan: BOM stock, monthly additions to stock, monthly sales, monthly reductions, and EOM stock.

Calculating Open-to-Buy for Past Periods

The way we view open-to-buy and how it is calculated vary depending on whether we're looking at a past period or at the current period. Let's start with a past period. We're now in the middle of February—January is over. Notice that there's an entry for actual January EOM stock ($59,500), but not one for February. The calculation of open-to-buy at the end of a period is easy. Since the month is over, we know that the planned EOM stock is equal to the actual EOM stock. Open-to-buy is zeroed out because there's no point in buying merchandise for a month that's already over. Thus,

$$\text{Planned EOM stock} = \text{Actual EOM stock}$$
$$\$59,500 = \$59,500$$
$$\text{Open-to-buy} = 0$$

Calculating Open-to-Buy for the Current Period

Now let's look at February, the current month. Notice that there is a BOM stock of $59,500, but not an EOM (end-of-month) stock because the month has started but it hasn't finished. When calculating the open-to-buy for the current month, the projected EOM stock comes into play. Think of the projected EOM stock as a new and improved estimate of the planned EOM stock from the merchandise budget plan. This new and improved version takes information into account that wasn't available when the merchandise budget plan was made. The formula for projected EOM stock is

Projected EOM stock =	$66,590 =
Actual BOM stock	59,500
+ Actual monthly additions to stock (what was actually received)	+ 7,000
+ Actual on order (what is on order for the month)	+ 18,000
– Plan monthly sales	– 15,600
– Plan reductions for the month	– 2,310

Although this formula may seem complicated, think of it this way: The projected EOM stock is equal to the inventory we have at the beginning of the month plus what we buy minus what we get rid of through sales or other inventory reductions.

The open-to-buy formula used during the current month is simply the difference between what you originally planned to end with from the merchandise budget plan (planned EOM stock) and what you think you will end with based on information collected during the month (projected EOM stock):

$$\text{Open-to-buy} = \text{Planned EOM stock} - \text{Projected EOM stock}$$
$$\$2,050 = \$68,640 - \$66,590$$

This means that we have $2,050 left to spend in February if we want to reach our planned EOM stock of $68,640.

As this section's example shows, the assortment planning process for fashion merchandise can be complicated. In an actual multistore chain, the process is even more complex than in our example. A good assortment plan requires a fine mix of subjective and experienced judgments, a good information system, and a systematic method of keeping historical records. Now let's look at buying systems for staple items.

STAPLE MERCHANDISE BUYING SYSTEMS

A very different, more mechanical system of inventory management is used for staple merchandise as opposed to the system for fashion merchandise. Staple merchandise buying systems are used for merchandise that follows a predictable order–receipt–order cycle. Most merchandise fits this criterion. These systems don't work well with fashion merchandise, however, because they use past history to predict sales for the future—and fashion merchandise has no history from previous seasons on specific SKUs. But most items found in food and discount stores are good candidates for these systems. So are categories in specialty and department stores like underwear, socks, and housewares.

Numerous inventory management systems for staple merchandise are currently available for both micro- and mainframe computers for retailers of all sizes. Let's explore the basics of these systems using E3's Slim system. Retailing View 13.4 describes how E3's SLIM system trimed the inventory system at Best Buy.

Most items in a hardware store are staples and can therefore utilize inventory management systems such as E3's SLIM system.

HAMPERED BY HOME-GROWN AND MANUAL SYSTEMS that could not keep pace with its rapid growth, electronics retailer Best Buy Co. has invested in new systems to control inventory, boosting inventory turns from four to more than six annually. For a $10 billion company, that amounts to millions of dollars of inventory that it doesn't have to carry. Product availability improved, thus increasing sales. Finally, gross margins increased because the faster inventory turnover resulted in fewer markdowns. While technology spending increased, gross profit margin exceeded the costs of these investments.

Best Buy utilized a staple merchandise buying system from E3 Corporation (Marietta, Georgia). E3 SLIM enables the store to perform economic analysis and simulations that balance the costs of acquiring and carrying inventory in order to maximize return on inventory investment. The system also allows Best Buy to evaluate forward buying opportunities offered by its vendors. A **forward buy** is an opportunity to purchase at an extra discount more merchandise than the retailer normally needs to fill demand. The E3 system determines how much merchandise should be purchased at the lower price by taking into consideration the additional inventory carrying costs.

Source: Joseph McKendrick, *Retail Info Systems News,* June 1999.

INTERNET EXERCISE   Go to (www.E3.com). How are E3 products being used by retailers today? Which retailers are using E3 products?

What the System Does

Staple merchandise buying systems contain a number of program modules that show how much to order and when. These systems assist merchandise planners by performing three functions:

- Monitoring and measuring average current demand for items at the SKU level.
- Forecasting future SKU demand with allowances made for seasonal variations and changes in trend.
- Developing ordering decision rules for optimum restocking.

The Inventory Management Report

The inventory management report provides information on sales velocity, inventory availability, the amount on order, inventory turnover, sales forecast, and, most important, the quantity to order for each SKU. Take a look at Exhibit 13–4, which shows an actual inventory management report for Rubbermaid, a large manufacturer of household plastic products. Note the last number of the second row for each SKU in parentheses. This is the suggested order quantity for each SKU—the end product of the inventory management process.

The retailer will have a prespecified schedule for each vendor. The schedule is determined by weighing the cost of carrying inventory versus the cost of buying and handling the inventory. The more they purchase at one time, the higher the carrying costs, but the lower the buying and handling costs.

Although each line has a prespecified schedule for ordering, each vendor's inventory status is checked daily. For instance, even though Rubbermaid may be scheduled to be purchased every five days, occasionally increased demand may dictate that several items need replenishment sooner. The combination of having a prespecified schedule based on the trade-off between inventory carrying and

EXHIBIT 13-4   Sample Inventory Management Report for Rubbermaid

STOCK NUMBER	DESCRIPTION	QUANTITY ON HAND (ON ORDER)	SALES LAST 12 WKS. (LAST 4 WKS.)	TURNOVER ACTUAL (PLAN)	PRODUCT AVAILABILITY (BACKUP STOCK)	FORECAST CURRENT 4 WKS. (NEXT 8 WKS.)	ORDER POINT (ORDER QTY.)
4050	RM bath mat avocado	6 (120)	215 (72)	9 (12)	96 (20)	94 (117)	167 (42)
4051	RM bath mat blue	0 (96)	139 (56)	5 (9)	100 (17)	58 (113)	110 (96)
4052	RM bath mat gold	1 (60)	234 (117)	9 (12)	95 (27)	42 (196)	200 (144)
4053	RM bath mat pink	2	41 (31)	5 (9)	95 (10)	41 (131)	58 (60)

Source: Banner Distributing Company, Denver, Colorado; used with permission.

ordering costs, and the flexibility to react to demand fluctuations, helps to ensure a profitable ordering strategy.

Basic Stock List   The first four columns of Exhibit 13–4 represent what many retailers call the basic stock list. The **basic stock list** describes each SKU and summarizes the inventory position. Specifically, it contains the stock number and description of the item, how many items are on hand and on order, and sales for the past 12 and 4 weeks. The basic stock list differs from the assortment plan used in the fashion-based systems in that it defines each SKU in precise rather than general terms.

Examine the first item: stock number 4050, a Rubbermaid bath mat in avocado green. There are 6 on hand and 120 on order. Thus, the quantity available is 126. (Quantity on hand + quantity on order = quantity available.) Sales for the past 12 and 4 weeks were 215 and 72 units, respectively.

The basic stock list is a necessary component of any inventory management system, yet many retailers go beyond the basic record keeping function. The last four columns of Exhibit 13–4 are needed too. Using this information, the inventory management part of the system manipulates the numbers in the basic stock list to arrive at sales forecasts and suggested order quantities. Now let's talk about the remaining entries in Exhibit 13–4 and how they fit into the system.

Inventory Turnover   Like the merchandise budget plan, a planned inventory turnover, based on overall financial goals, drives the inventory management system. The planner achieves an actual inventory turnover of 9 for the avocado bath mat, but the planned turnover was 12.

Product Availability   In Exhibit 13–4's avocado bath mat example, on average, out of every 100 customers wanting the item, 96 found it in stock. Determining the appropriate planned level of product availability for staple merchandise can be difficult and requires considerable managerial judgment.

Backup Stock   Backup stock, also known as safety stock or buffer stock, is inventory used to guard against going out of stock when demand exceeds forecasts or when merchandise is delayed. (See Chapter 12.) Backup stock for the avocado bath mat is 20 units.

Bricks-and-mortar and Internet retailers utilize E3 Corporation's inventory management solutions to identify seasonal and promotional effects on their inventory.

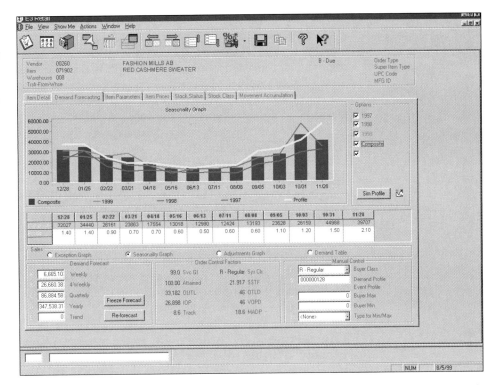

Forecast   Sales forecasts for staple items are fairly straightforward and mechanical compared to those for fashion merchandise. With fashion merchandise, past trends and other issues that help determine the future are examined. Forecasting sales of staple items entails extending sales trends from the past into the future.

Exponential smoothing is a forecasting technique in which sales in previous time periods are weighted to forecast future periods. To understand exponential smoothing, again consider the Rubbermaid avocado bath mat whose average sales forecast over the past few four-week periods is 100 units (not shown in Exhibit 13–4). But the sales total for the past four-week period was 72 units. To forecast the next four-week period, the planner wants to be responsive to the decrease in sales from 100 to 72, but doesn't want to overreact by ignoring the historical average since the decrease could be a random occurrence. The following formula takes into account the two sales forecasting objectives of being responsive and ignoring random occurrences:

New forecast = Old forecast + α (Actual demand – Old forecast)

The Greek letter alpha (α) is a constant between 0 and 1 that determines the influence of actual demand on the new forecast. When demand is increasing or decreasing sharply, high values of alpha, such as .5, cause the forecast to react quickly. Low values of alpha, such as .1, are appropriate when demand is changing very slowly. Let's continue the forecast for the bath mat using high and low alphas:

$$
\begin{array}{ccccc}
\text{New forecast} & = & \text{Old forecast} & + & \alpha \ (\text{Actual demand} \ - \ \text{Old forecast}) \\
94 & = & 96 & + & .1 \ (72 - 96) \\
84 & = & 96 & + & .5 \ (72 - 96)
\end{array}
$$

Alpha in Exhibit 13–4 is .1, indicating a forecast for the next four-week period of 94. Determining what alpha to use requires experimentation. If the planner believes the last period's decrease in demand represents a real shift rather than a random occurrence, the .5 alpha is more appropriate since it yields the much lower forecast of 84 bath mats. In general, if alpha is too high, an unstable forecasting process results because the forecasts overreact to random changes in demand. If alpha is too low, the forecast will always lag behind or ahead of the trend. Once the system is forecasting properly, the software will automatically adjust alpha when necessary.

Even staple items like bath mats have some seasonality—typically demand rises slightly around spring-cleaning time. The new forecast, which the planner calculated using exponential smoothing, is called the deseasonalized demand. **Deseasonalized demand** is forecast demand without the influence of seasonality. The season's influence is removed before making the calculations. To obtain the actual forecast of demand including the influence of seasonality, the inventory management system multiplies deseasonalized demand times a seasonality index in the same way that it was done in the first two lines in the merchandise budget plan in Exhibit 13–2. In the bath mat case, there was no seasonality for the example month.

Order Point   The **order point** is the amount of inventory below which the quantity available shouldn't go or the item will be out of stock before the next order arrives. The order point in the periodic system is defined as

Order point = [(Demand/Day) (Lead time + Review time)] + (Backup stock)

The lead time is the amount of time between recognition that an order needs to be placed and when it arrives in the store and is ready for sale. Assume demand per day is 1 and lead time is zero days. (This may be the case in a pharmacy receiving shipments from its wholesaler more than once a day.) Here the order point would be zero. The planner would wait until stock ran out, and then order and replenish the merchandise almost instantaneously.

With lead time of two weeks, there's some point below which the planner shouldn't deplete the inventory without ordering, or the retailer would start selling the backup stock before the next order arrived. Further, the planner only reviews the line once a week, and 20 units of backup stock are necessary to maintain a high service level. In this case, if demand is 7 units per day, then

Order point = [(7 units) × (14 + 7 days)] + (20 units) = 167 units

Here the planner orders if quantity available falls to 167 units or fewer.

Order Quantity   The question remains, how much should the planner order when the quantity available is less than the order point? He should order enough so the cycle stock isn't depleted and sales dip into backup stock before the next order arrives—this is the difference between the quantity available and the order point. Using the avocado bath mats in Exhibit 13–4, since quantity available is 126, the planner orders 41 units, because the order point is 167 (i.e., 167 – 126 = 41). The actual suggested order quantity is 42 since the bath mats are packed 6 to a carton, and the computer rounds up to the next whole carton.

EXHIBIT **13–5**

Breakdown by Store
of Traditional $35
Denim Jeans in
Light Blue

(1) TYPE OF STORE	(2) NUMBER OF STORES	(3) PERCENTAGE OF TOTAL SALES, EACH STORE	(4) SALES PER STORE (TOTAL SALES X COL. 3)	(5) SALES PER STORE TYPE (COL. 2 X COL. 4)	(6) UNIT SALES PER STORE (COL. 4/$35)
A	4	10.0%	$15,000	60,000	429
B	3	6.7	10,000	30,000	286
C	8	5.0	7,500	60,000	214
Total sales $150,000					

ALLOCATING MERCHANDISE TO STORES

Once the merchandise is purchased for either fashion or staple merchandise, it must be allocated to stores. Retailers utilize historical sales information, but pay close attention to current supply and demand situations to determine the proper inventory allocation. For instance, if a retailer is having difficulty meeting demand because a vendor is unable to deliver, or if actual sales are lagging behind the forecast, the retailer will have to adjust the historically derived allocation downward.

Exhibit 13–5 illustrates a traditional percent contribution method through which a planner allocates additions to stock of $150,000 among 15 stores to girls' traditional $35 denim jeans in light blue.

Chain stores traditionally classify their stores as A, B, or C stores based on their potential sales volume (column 1). This chain has four A stores, each of which is expected to sell 10 percent of the total, equaling $15,000 per store; three B stores, each expected to sell 6.7 percent, equaling $10,000 per store; and eight C stores, each expected to sell 5 percent, equaling $7,500 per store (columns 2, 3, and 4). The percentage breakdown (column 3) is based on historical records for similar merchandise for that chain.

Every chain's allocation of merchandise to stores is different. A **core assortment** is a relatively large proportion of the total assortment that is carried by each store in the chain, regardless of size. The core assortment is necessary to maintain the image of the chain. If the chain cut back the assortment too far in smaller stores, customers would perceive the smaller stores as having an inferior assortment. Hence, smaller stores require a higher-than-average stock-to-sales ratio. The opposite is true for stores with larger-than-average sales. For instance, one major department store chain allocates merchandise to stores as follows:[2]

	FEWER SALES, MORE INVENTORY					MORE SALES, LESS INVENTORY		
Percentage of total sales	1	1.5	2.5	3.5	4	6	8	12
Percentage of total inventory	1.5	2	3	4	4	4	6	10

This means that if a store generates 4 percent of the sales of a classification for the chain, it should also receive 4 percent of the inventory. Note that stores with sales below 4 percent require proportionally more inventory. For instance, the smallest store, which generates only 1 percent of sales, requires 1.5 percent of the total inventory—inventory equals 1½ times the level of sales. Even though

WALK INTO THE CHILLED AIR OF the cavernous Kmart Corp. store on the Western Pacific island of Guam and you feel as if you could be anywhere in the United States. Disembodied voices appeal to "Kmart shoppers," red-vested men and women punch a line of cash registers, and teenagers munch pizza at Little Caesar's.

But take a second look, and it's clear this isn't Kansas. Japanese in beach togs hover around stacks of Tengu-brand beef jerky, and Chomorro-speaking Pacific islanders trade food stamps for Spam. Guam, one of America's smallest territories, boasts one of Kmart's largest stores both in physical size and in the volume of cash running through its registers.

Developing an effective assortment strategy is particularly important and difficult in this and other remote locations. Kmart must maintain some corporate identify, while at the same time appealing to the local market and to Japanese visitors. Guam is a popular honeymoon destination for Japan's newlyweds, and the island still draws people who lost relatives there during World War II. Company surveys show that at least a quarter of all Japanese who come to Guam visit the store an average of two times during their stay—once upon arrival to stock up on snacks and beach gear, and once before they leave to buy presents and take cheap U.S.-brand clothes, toys, or even furniture home.

This complex market has made for a unique assortment strategy. Along with Kmart's usual stock of orange marshmallow peanuts and printed T-shirts, the store carries a large supply of Spam, which is favored by the local population. Guam's Kmart is also the world's largest single seller of Tengu beef jerky, a California-made snack. Tengu along with other snack foods are very popular in Japan. In all, the store has 50 linear feet of Japanese snack foods—and that's a lot of rice crackers.

Source: Craig S. Smith, "The Exotic Sound of Guam: 'Attention, Kmart Shoppers!'," *The Wall Street Journal*, July 12, 1999, pp. A17, A20; and Holly M. Werner, "From Globe Trotting to Galloping (Global Consolidation in the Retail Industry)," *HFN: The Weekly Newspaper for the Home Furnishings Network,* December 21, 1998.

---

this store has low sales, it still needs to stock an adequate assortment and backup stock. Customers must not feel that just because the store is small or has relatively low sales that it isn't well stocked.

At the other extreme, stores with sales greater than 4 percent require proportionally less inventory. The largest store, with sales of 12 percent, requires only 10 percent of the inventory allocation for the classification—here inventory equals 83 percent of sales. This store can boost inventory turnover by receiving more frequent shipments. Also, thanks to high sales, the largest store can present an aesthetically pleasing, well-stocked look with less inventory.

Sales per store (column 4 of Exhibit 13–5) is total sales multiplied by the percentage of total sales for each store. Thus, the four A stores are each expected to generate sales of $15,000.

Sales per store type (column 5) is the number of stores (column 2) times sales per store (column 4). Thus, combined sales for the four A stores is $60,000.

The jeans are expected to sell for $35. Therefore, unit sales per store is dollar sales per store (column 4) divided by $35. Thus, each A store is expected to sell 429 units.

The planner must also adjust the breakdown by store according to individual store differences. See Retailing View 13.5.

The process of allocating merchandise to stores that we just described is useful for fashion merchandise and new staple items. As merchandise sells, it must be replenished, either by the vendor or through distribution centers. As Chapter 11 said, retailers use either a pull or a push distribution strategy to replenish merchandise. With a pull distribution strategy, orders for merchandise are generated at the store level on the basis of demand data captured by point-of-sale terminals. With a push distribution strategy, merchandise is allocated to the stores based on

Refact Saks Fifth Avenue increases its assortment of long dresses in New Orleans at Mardi Gras. Sears sells diving watches in coastal communities and watches with easy to read numbers in Miami and Phoenix where there are a lot of retirees. Sears also sells suede vests and skirts during rodeo season in a few Texas stores.[3]

historical demand, the inventory position at the distribution center, as well as the needs of the stores. As Chapter 11 noted, a pull strategy is used by more sophisticated retailers because it's more responsive to customer demand.

ANALYZING MERCHANDISE PERFORMANCE

As part of the ongoing merchandise planning process, retailers should continually ask when to add or delete SKUs, vendors, classifications, or departments. Here we examine three procedures for analyzing merchandise performance. The first, known as ABC analysis, is a method of rank-ordering merchandise to make inventory stocking decisions. The second procedure, a sell-through analysis, compares actual and planned sales to determine whether early markdowns are required or whether more merchandise is needed to satisfy demand. The third approach is a method for evaluating vendors using the multiple-attribute (or multiattribute) model.

ABC Analysis

ABC analysis rank-orders merchandise by some performance measure to determine which items should never be out of stock, which items should be allowed to be out of stock occasionally, and which items should be deleted from the stock selection.[4] An ABC analysis can be done at any level of merchandise classification, from the SKU to the department. The SKU is the level of analysis discussed in this section.

ABC analysis utilizes the general 80–20 principle that implies that approximately 80 percent of a retailer's sales or profits come from 20 percent of the products. This means that retailers should concentrate on products that provide the biggest bang for their buck.

The first step in the ABC analysis is to rank-order SKUs using one or more criteria. The most important performance measure for this type of analysis is contribution margin:

Contribution margin = Net sales – Cost of goods sold – Other variable expenses

An example of an "other variable expense" in retailing is sales commissions. It's important to do ABC analyses using multiple performance measures since different measures give the planner different information. Other measures commonly used in ABC analysis are sales dollars, sales in units, gross margin, and GMROI (gross margin return on investment).

Some less profitable items, like portable appliances, may be high in sales dollars or units. Such items are often important because they draw people into the store. It may also be important to carry some low-profit/high-volume merchandise because such merchandise complements other items in the store. For instance, batteries may sell at a low price, but they're necessary to sell cameras, radios, and flashlights.

Sales or gross margin per square foot measures are also useful in ABC analyses. For instance, a line of sunglasses may not appear particularly profitable in comparison to other items on the basis of contribution margin, sales, or units. But the display also takes relatively little space. Thus, performance of the merchandise on a square-foot basis may be very high.

The next step is to determine how items with different levels of profit or volume should be treated differently. Consider the dress shirts for a chain of men's stores in Exhibit 13–6. Even though the exact distribution varies across products,

EXHIBIT 13–6

ABC Analysis for
Dress Shirts

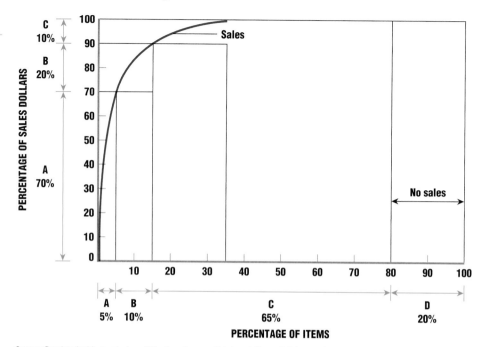

the general shape of the curve is the same for most types of products due to the 80–20 principle. Here the planner has defined the A, B, C, and D SKUs by rank-ordering each SKU by sales volume and examining the distribution of those sales.

The planner defines A items as those that account for 5 percent of items and represent 70 percent of sales. These items should never be out of stock. A items can be expensive to carry because they generally require high levels of backup stock to buffer against variations in demand and lead times. They include most sizes of long-and short-sleeve white and blue dress shirts.

Retailers should never be out of A items like these white and blue dress shirts. The shirt on the right, however is a D item. It had no sales during the past season. What should the retailer do with this shirt? Get rid of it!

EXHIBIT **13–7**

Sell-through Analysis
for Blouses

STOCK NUMBER		DESCRIPTION	WEEK 1			WEEK 2		
					ACTUAL-TO-PLAN			ACTUAL-TO-PLAN
			PLAN	ACTUAL	PERCENTAGE	PLAN	ACTUAL	PERCENTAGE
1011	Small	White silk V-neck	20	15	–25%	20	10	–50%
1011	Medium	White silk V-neck	30	25	–16.6	30	20	–33
1011	Large	White silk V-neck	20	16	–20	20	16	–20
1012	Small	Blue silk V-neck	25	26	4	25	27	8
1012	Medium	Blue silk V-neck	35	45	29	35	40	14
1012	Large	Blue silk V-neck	25	25	0	25	30	20

B items represent 10 percent of the SKUs and an additional 20 percent of sales. The store should pay close attention to the B items, which include some of the other better-selling colors and patterned shirts. Occasionally, however, it will run out of some SKUs in the B category because it's not carrying the same amount of backup stock as for A items.

C items account for 65 percent of SKUs but contribute only 10 percent of sales. The planner may plan to carry C items only in certain odd sizes (very small or very large), with special orders used to solve out-of-stock conditions.

Although the analysis is called ABC, there are also D items. D items, the remaining 20 percent of SKUs, had no sales whatsoever during the past season, having become out-of-date or shopworn. Not only is excess merchandise an unproductive investment, but it also distracts from the rest of the inventory and clutters the store. Most retailers with excess merchandise should have a simple decision strategy: Mark it down or give it away, but get rid of it.

Sell-through Analysis

A **sell-through analysis** is a comparison between actual and planned sales to determine whether early markdowns are required or whether more merchandise is needed to satisfy demand. Exhibit 13–7 shows a sell-through analysis for blouses for the first two weeks of the season. Because the blouses are a very high-fashion item, the planner believes that, if necessary, corrective action should be made to the buying plan after only two weeks.

Examine the week 1 column for the first SKU, the small white blouse. Planned sales were 20 units. The actual sales were 15 units. Therefore, the actual-to-plan percentage was –25 percent [(15 – 20) ÷ 20 = –25 percent]. This means that actual sales were 25 percent less than the planned sales. In fact, the actual-to-plan percentage is negative for all of the white blouses and positive for all of the blue blouses.

What should the planner do? There's no exact rule for determining when a markdown is necessary or when more merchandise should be ordered. The decision depends on experience with the merchandise in the past, whether the merchandise is scheduled to be featured in advertising, whether the vendor can reduce the planner's risk by providing markdown money (funds a vendor gives a retailer to cover lost gross margin dollars that result from markdowns), and other merchandising issues. In this case, however, it appears that the white blouses are selling significantly less than planned. Therefore, early markdowns are probably justified to ensure that the merchandise isn't left unsold at the end of the season.

The decision regarding the blue blouses isn't so clear, though. The small blue blouses are selling slightly ahead of the plan. The medium blue blouses are selling briskly. The large blue blouses are selling ahead of plan only in the second week. In this case, the planner may need to wait another week or two before a distinct sales pattern emerges. If actual sales stay significantly ahead of planned sales, a reorder should be made.

Multiple-Attribute Method

The multiple-attribute (or multiattribute) method for evaluating vendors uses a weighted average score for each vendor. This score is based on the importance of various issues and the vendor's performance on those issues.[5] This method is very similar to the multi-attribute approach that can be used to understand how customers evaluate stores and merchandise (discussed in Chapter 5) and the market attractiveness/competitive position matrix (examined in Chapter 6).

To illustrate the multiattribute method for evaluating vendors, either current or proposed, consider the example in Exhibit 13–8 for a vendor of men's tailored suits. A planner can evaluate vendors by using the following five steps:

1. Develop a list of issues to consider in the decision (column 1).[6] A balance should be made between having too short or too comprehensive a list of issues. Too short a list will ignore some relevant issues. Too long a list will be hard to use. Also, the list should be balanced so that one dimension of vendor performance doesn't receive too much attention. For instance, if there are three issues dealing with different aspects of a vendor's promotional package and only one with product characteristics, promotional considerations will receive too much attention in the overall evaluation.

2. Importance weights for each issue in column 1 should be determined by the planner in conjunction with the merchandise manager (column 2). Here we used

EXHIBIT 13–8

Evaluating a Vendor: A Weighted Average Approach

ISSUES (1)	IMPORTANCE EVALUATION OF ISSUES (I) (2)	PERFORMANCE EVALUATIONS OF INDIVIDUAL BRANDS ACROSS ISSUES			
		BRAND A (P_a) (3)	BRAND B (P_b) (4)	BRAND C (P_c) (5)	BRAND D (P_d) (6)
Vendor reputation	9	5	9	4	8
Service	8	6	6	4	6
Meets delivery dates	6	5	7	4	4
Merchandise quality	5	5	4	6	5
Markup opportunity	5	5	4	4	5
Country of origin	6	5	3	3	8
Product fashionability	7	6	6	3	8
Selling history	3	5	5	5	5
Promotional assistance	4	5	3	4	7
Overall evaluation = $\sum_{i=1}^{n} I_i * P_{ij}$		290	298	212	341

$\sum_{i=1}^{n}$ = Sum of the expression

I_i = Importance weight assigned to the ith dimension
P_{ij} = Performance evaluation for jth brand alternative on the ith issue
1   = Not important
10 = Very important

a scale of 1 to 10, where 1 equals not important and 10 equals very important. In developing these importance scores, be sure that all issues don't receive high (or low) ratings. For instance, the planner and her merchandise manager might believe that vendor reputation should receive a 9 since it's very important. Merchandise quality could receive a 5 since it's moderately important. Finally, a vendor's selling history is less important, so it could be rated 3.

3.   Make judgments about each individual brand's performance on each issue (the remaining columns). This procedure should also be a joint decision between the category and merchandise managers. Note that some brands have high ratings on some issues, but not on others.

4.   We can't evaluate the overall performance of the vendors without combining the importance and performance scores. We do this by multiplying the importance for each issue by the performance for each brand or its vendor. For instance, vendor reputation importance (9) multiplied by the performance rating (5) for brand A is 45. Vendor promotional assistance importance (4) multiplied by the performance rating (7) for vendor D is 28. This type of analysis illustrates an important point: It doesn't pay to perform well on issues that customers don't believe are very important. Although vendor D performed well on promotional assistance, the planner didn't rate this issue highly on importance so the resulting score was still low.

5.   To determine a vendor's overall rating, sum the product for each brand for all issues. In Exhibit 13–8, brand D has the highest overall rating (341) so D's the preferred vendor.

SUMMARY

This chapter (the second to deal with merchandise management) built on basic concepts and tools of assortment planning described in Chapter 12. The sales forecast and inventory turnover described in Chapter 12 work together to drive the merchandise budget plan for fashion merchandise. The sales forecast is broken down by month, based on historical seasonality patterns. It's necessary to purchase more in months when sales are forecast to be higher than average. Planned inventory turnover is converted to stock-to-sales ratios and used in the merchandise budget plan to determine the inventory level necessary to support sales. Monthly stock-to-sales ratios are then adjusted to reflect seasonal sales patterns. The end product of the merchandise budget planning process is the dollar amount of merchandise a planner should purchase each month for a category if the sales forecast and inventory turnover goals are to be met.

The open-to-buy system begins where the merchandise budget plan leaves off. It starts with the additions to stock from the merchandise budget plan and keeps track of how much merchandise is purchased for delivery in each month. Using an open-to-buy system, merchandise planners know exactly how much money they've spent compared to how much they plan to spend.

While the merchandise budget plan provides a spending plan in dollars, it doesn't specify the exact SKUs to purchase. The assortment plan described in Chapter 12 supplies the merchandising team with a general outline of what should be carried in a particular merchandise category for fashion merchandise. The selection of specific fashion items and the quantities to be purchased requires a blend of skill, style, and experience. Planners collect information on trends from vendors, customers, and competition.

Buying systems for staple merchandise are very different. They provide specific information on how much of a particular SKU to purchase.

Once the merchandise is purchased, merchandise planners in multistore chains must allocate the merchandise to stores. Not only must the planners look at the differences in sales potential among stores, they also must consider the differences in the characteristics of the customer base.

In the end, the performance of buyers, vendors, and individual SKUs must be determined. We examined three different approaches to evaluating merchandise performance. In ABC analysis, merchandise is rank-ordered from highest to lowest. The merchandising team uses this information to set inventory management policy. For example, the most productive SKUs should carry sufficient backup stock so as to never be out-of-stock. The second evaluation technique, sell-through analysis, is more useful for examining the performance of individual SKUs. The planner compares actual-to-planned sales to determine whether more merchandise needs to be ordered or whether the merchandise should be put on sale. Finally, the multiple-attribute method is most useful for evaluating vendors' performance.

The chapter concludes with two appendixes. In Appendix 13A, we examine the retail inventory method. Appendix 13B provides several alternatives to using the stock-to-sales ratio in the merchandise budget plan. Specifically, we discuss the week's supply method, the basic stock method, and the percentage variation method.

KEY TERMS

ABC analysis, *401*

basic stock list, *396*

core assortment, *399*

deseasonalized demand, *398*

forward buy, *395*

open-to-buy, *392*

order point, *398*

sell-through analysis, *403*

DISCUSSION QUESTIONS AND PROBLEMS

1. Inventory shrinkage can be a problem for many retailers. How does the merchandise budget planning process account for inventory shrinkage?

2. Using the following information, calculate additions to stock:

Sales	$24,000
EOM stock	$90,000
BOM stock	$80,000

3. Using the following information, calculate the average beginning-of-month stock-to-sales ratio for a six-month merchandise budget plan:

GMROI	150%
Gross margin	40%

4. Today is July 19. The merchandise planner is attempting to assess his current open-to-buy given the following information:

BOM stock for July	$50,000
Merchandise already received in July	25,000
Merchandise on order to be delivered in July	10,000
Planned monthly sales for July	30,000
Planned reductions	5,000
Planned EOM stock	65,000

What is the open-to-buy on July 19? What does this number mean to you?

5. Now it is July 31 and we need to calculate the open-to-buy for August given the following information:

Planned monthly sales	$20,000
Merchandise on order	40,000
Planned markdowns	5,000
Projected BOM stock	50,000
Planned EOM stock	30,000

Calculate open-to-buy and explain what the number means to you.

6. Typically, August school supplies sales are relatively low. In September, sales increase tremendously. How does the September stock-to-sales ratio differ from the August ratio?

7. Using the 80–20 principle, how can a retailer make certain that there's enough inventory of fast-selling merchandise and a minimal amount of slow-selling merchandise?

8. What's the order point, and how many units should be reordered if a food retailer has an item with a 7-day lead time, 10-day review time, and daily demand of 8 units? Say 65 units are on hand and the retailer must maintain a backup stock of 20 units to maintain a 95 percent service level.

9. A buyer at a sporting goods store in Denver receives a shipment of 400 ski parkas on October 1 and expects to sell out by January 31. On November 1, she still has 375 parkas left. What issues should she consider in evaluating the selling season's progress?

10. A buyer is trying to decide from which vendor to buy a certain item. The item can be purchased as either a manufacturer brand or private-label brand. Using the following information, determine which vendor the buyer should use.

		PERFORMANCE EVALUATIONS OF BRANDS	
ISSUES	**IMPORTANCE WEIGHT**	**MANUFACTURER BRAND**	**PRIVATE-LABEL BRAND**
Vendor reputation	8	5	5
Service	7	6	7
Meets delivery dates	9	7	5
Perceived merchandise quality	7	8	4
Markup opportunity	6	4	8
Demand-generating ability	5	7	5
Promotional assistance	3	6	8

SUGGESTED READINGS

Anderson, Barbara V. *The Art and Science of Computer Assisted Ordering.* Greenwood Publishing Group, 1996.

Beninati, Marie. "A Blueprint for Local Assortment Management." *Store Age Executive with Shopping Center Age,* February 1997, pp. 27, 28.

Combined Financial, Merchandising and Operating Results of Retail Stores, 1999 ed. Washington DC: National Retail Federation.

Donnellan, John. *Merchandise Buying and Management.* New York: Fairchild Publications, 1996.

Goodwin, David R. "The Open-to-Buy System and Accurate Performance Measurement." *International Journal of Retail and Distribution Management* 20, no. 2 (March 1992), pp. 16–27.

Kunz, Grace I. *Merchandising: Theory, Principles, and Practice.* New York: Fairchild Books, 1998.

Lambert, Douglas M., James R. Stock, Lisa M. Ellram, and Jim Stockdale. *Fundamentals of Logistics Management.* Burr Ridge, IL: Irwin/McGraw-Hill, 1997.

Powers, James T. *The Retail Inventory Method Made Practical.* New York: National Retail Federation, 1971.

Robeson, James F., and Robert G. House. *The Distribution Handbook.* New York: Free Press, 1985.

Smith, Stephen A., Narendra Agrawal, and Shelby H. McIntyre. "A Discrete Optimization Model for Seasonal Merchandise Planning." *Journal of Retailing* 74, no. 2 (Summer 1998), pp. 193–223.

Switzer, Gerald J. "A Modern Approach to Retail Accounting." *Management Accounting* 75, no. 8 (February 1994), pp. 55–64.

Taylor, Charles G. *Merchandise Assortment Planning.* New York: National Retail Federation, 1970.

Urban, Timothy L. "An Inventory-Theoretic Approach to Product Assortment and Shelf-Space Allocation." *Journal of Retailing* 74, no. 1 (Spring 1998), pp. 15–21.

Wild, Tony. *Best Practice in Inventory Management.* New York: John Wiley & Sons, 1998.

Retail Inventory Method (RIM)

Like firms in most industries, retailers can value their inventory at cost—and in fact, some retailers do so. Yet many retailers find significant advantages to the retail inventory method (RIM).[7] RIM has two objectives:

1. To maintain a perpetual or book inventory in terms of retail dollar amounts.
2. To maintain records that make it possible to determine the cost value of the inventory at any time without taking a physical inventory.

The Problem   Retailers generally think of their inventory at retail price levels rather than at cost. They take their initial markups, markdowns, and so forth as percentages of retail. (These terms are thoroughly defined in Chapter 15 and the Glossary.) When retailers compare their prices to competitors', they compare their retail prices. The problem is that when retailers design their financial plans, evaluate performance, and prepare financial statements, they need to know the cost value of their inventory. One way to keep abreast of their inventory cost is to take physical inventories. Anyone who has worked in retailing knows that this process is time-consuming, costly, and not much fun. So retailers usually only take physical inventories once or twice a year. By the time management receives the results of these physical inventories, it's often too late to make any changes.

Many retailers use POS terminals that easily keep track of every item sold, its original cost, and its final selling price. The rest of the retail world faces the problem of not knowing the cost value of its inventory at any one time. RIM can be used by retailers with either computerized or manual systems.

Advantages of RIM   RIM has five advantages over a system of evaluating inventory at cost.

- The retailer doesn't have to "cost" each time. For retailers with many SKUs, keeping track of each item at cost is expensive and time-consuming, and it increases the cost of errors. It's easier to determine the value of inventory with the retail prices marked on the merchandise than with unmarked or coded cost prices.
- RIM follows the accepted accounting practice of valuing assets at cost or market, whichever is lower. The system lowers the value of inventory when markdowns are taken but doesn't allow inventory's value to increase with additional markups.
- As a by-product of RIM, the amounts and percentages of initial markups, additional markups, markdowns, and shrinkage can be identified. This information can then be compared with historical records or industry norms.
- RIM is useful for determining shrinkage. The difference between the book inventory and the physical inventory can be attributed to shrinkage.
- The book inventory determined by RIM can be used in an insurance claim in case of a loss (e.g., due to fire).

Disadvantages of RIM   RIM is a system that uses average markup. When markup percentages change substantially during a period, or when the inventory on hand at a particular time isn't representative of the total goods handled in terms of markup, the resulting cost figure may be distorted. As with inventory turnover, merchandise budget planning, and open-to-buy, RIM should be applied on a category basis to avoid this problem.

The record keeping process involved in RIM is burdensome. Buyers must take care so that changes made to the cost and retail inventories are properly recorded.

Steps in RIM   Exhibit 13–9 is an example of RIM in action. The following discussion, which outlines the steps in RIM, is based on this exhibit.

Calculate Total Goods Handled at Cost and Retail   To determine the total goods handled at cost and retail:

1. *Record beginning inventory at cost* ($60,000) *and at retail* ($84,000). The initial markup is reflected in the retail inventory.
2. *Calculate net purchases* ($39,000 at cost and $54,600 at retail) by recording gross purchases ($50,000 at cost and $70,000 at retail) and adjusting for merchandise returned to vendor ($11,000 at cost and $15,400 at retail).

EXHIBIT 13–9

Retail Inventory
Method Example

TOTAL GOODS HANDLED	COST		RETAIL	
Beginning inventory		$60,000		$84,000
Purchases	$50,000		$70,000	
– Return to vendor	(11,000)		(15,400)	
Net purchases		39,000		54,600
Additional markups			4,000	
– Markup cancellations			(2,000)	
Net markups				2,000
Additional transportation		1,000		
Transfers in	1,428		2,000	
– Transfers out	(714)		(1,000)	
Net transfers		714		1,000
Total goods handled		$100,714		$141,600

REDUCTIONS	RETAIL	
Gross sales	$82,000	
– Customer returns and allowances	(4,000)	
Net sales		$78,000
Markdowns	6,000	
– Markdown cancellations	(3,000)	
Net markdowns		3,000
Employee discounts		3,000
Discounts to customers		500
Estimated shrinkage		1,500
Total reductions		$86,000

3. *Calculate net additional markups* ($2,000) by adjusting gross additional markups ($4,000) by any additional markup cancelations ($2,000). Note: These are recorded only at retail because markups affect only the retail value of inventory.

4. *Record transportation expenses* ($1,000). Here transportation is recorded at cost because it affects only the cost of the inventory.

5. *Calculate net transfers* ($714 at cost and $1,000 at retail) by recording the amount of transfers in and out. A transfer can be from one department to another or from store to store. Transfers are generally made to help adjust inventory to fit demand. For instance, a sweater may be selling well at one store but not at another. A transfer is, in effect, just like a purchase (transfer in) or a return (transfer out). Thus, it's recorded at both cost and retail.

6. *The sum is the total goods handled* ($100,714 at cost and $141,600 at retail).

Calculate Retail Reductions   Reductions are the transactions that reduce the value of inventory at retail (except additional markup cancelations, which were included as part of the total goods handled). Reductions are calculated as follows:

1. *Record net sales.* The largest reduction in inventory is sales. Gross sales ($82,000) are reduced to net sales ($78,000) by deducting customer returns and allowances ($4,000).

2. *Calculate markdowns.* Net markdowns ($3,000) are derived by subtracting any markdown cancelations ($3,000) from gross markdowns ($6,000).

3. *Record discounts to employees* ($3,000) *and customers* ($500).

4. *Record estimated shrinkage* ($1,500). Estimated shrinkage is used to determine the ending book inventory if the buyer is preparing an interim financial statement. The estimate is based on historical records and is presented as a percentage of sales. Estimated shrinkage wouldn't be included, however, if a physical inventory was taken at the time the statement was being prepared. In this case, the difference between physical inventory and book inventory would be the amount of shrinkage due to loss, shoplifting, and so forth.

5. *The sum is the total reductions* ($86,000).

Calculate the Cumulative Markup and Cost Multiplier   The cumulative markup is the average percentage markup for the period. It's calculated the same way the markup for an item is calculated:

$$\text{Cumulative markup} = \frac{\text{Total retail} - \text{Total cost}}{\text{Total retail}}$$

$$28.87\% = \frac{\$141,600 - \$100,714}{\$141,600}$$

The cumulative markup can be used as a comparison against the planned initial markup. If the cumulative markup is higher than the planned initial markup, then the category is doing better than planned.

The cost multiplier is similar to the cost complement.

$$\text{Cost multiplier} = (\$100\% - \text{Cumulative markup \%})$$
$$71.13\% = 100\% - 28.87\%$$

or

$$\frac{\text{Total cost}}{\text{Total retail}} = \frac{\$100,714}{\$141,600} = 71.13\%$$

The cost multiplier is used in the next step to determine the ending book inventory at retail.

Determine Ending Book Inventory at Cost and Retail

Ending book inventory at retail = Total goods handled at retail
− Total reductions

$55,600 = $141,600 − $86,000

The ending book inventory at cost is determined in the same way that retail has been changed to cost in other situations—multiply the retail times (100% − gross margin percentage). In this case,

Ending book inventory at cost = Ending book inventory at retail
× Cost multiplier

$39,548 = $55,600 × 71.13%

APPENDIX 13B

Alternatives to the Stock-to-Sales Ratio

The average BOM (beginning-of-month) stock-to-sales ratio was derived directly from the planned inventory turnover to determine monthly additions to stock in the merchandise budget plan in Chapter 13. This appendix looks at some retailers' similar methods of defining the relationship between inventory and sales.

Week's Supply Method   The week's supply method is the inventory management method most similar to the stock-to-sales method. The difference is that everything is expressed in weeks rather than months. The average BOM stock-to-sales ratio equals the number of months in the period divided by the planned inventory turnover for the period. For instance, if the plan is for 12 months and planned turnover is 6, the average BOM stock-to-sales ratio = 12 ÷ 6 = 2.

Using the week's supply method, 52 weeks are substituted for 12 months. Thus, 52 weeks ÷ 6 turns = 8.66 weeks of supply. This means the buyer is planning to have 8.66 weeks of supply at the beginning of the month. (Of course, 8.66 weeks is equivalent to two months.)

Basic Stock Method   The basic stock method is the inventory management method used to determine the BOM inventory by considering both the sales forecast for the month and the backup stock.

BOM inventory = Forecast monthly sales + Basic stock

So basic stock and backup stock are really the same thing. Like the stock-to-sales ratio and the week's supply methods, the basic stock method uses inventory turnover to calculate BOM inventory. Exhibit 13–10 illustrates the basic stock method.

1.   Given the monthly sales, the average sales for the period is $16,666 (total period sales ÷ number of months).

MONTH	SALES	BOM INVENTORY: BASIC STOCK METHOD	BOM INVENTORY: PERCENTAGE VARIATION METHOD
October	$15,000	$23,334	$23,750
November	$15,000	$23,334	$23,750
December	$20,000	$28,335	$27,500
Total	$50,000		
Average sales	$16,666		
Average inventory	$25,000		
Basic stock	$ 8,334		

2. Assuming inventory turnover for the three-month period is 2 (eight annual turns), average inventory for the period is $25,000.

$$\begin{aligned} \text{Average inventory} &= \text{Total period sales} \div \text{Inventory turnover} \\ \$25,000 &= \$50,000 \div 2 \end{aligned}$$

3. Basic stock = Average inventory − Average sales

$$\begin{aligned} \text{Basic stock} &= \text{Average inventory} - \text{Average sales} \\ \$8,334 &= \$25,000 - \$16,666 \end{aligned}$$

4. BOM inventory for October = Basic stock + Planned sales for October

$$\begin{aligned} \text{BOM inventory for October} &= \text{Basic stock} + \text{Planned sales for October} \\ \$23,334 &= \$8,334 + \$15,000 \end{aligned}$$

The basic stock method has some shortcomings. First, it won't work if inventory turnover is greater than 12 times a year. In this case, average inventory would be less than average monthly sales, causing basic stock to be negative. Further, the basic stock is the same for every month, no matter what the sales. By comparison, in the stock-to-sales method, monthly stock-to-sales ratios fluctuate with the forecast level of sales. This makes more sense for months with higher sales, where there's greater need for backup stock.

Percentage Variation Method The percentage variation method considers the same factors as the basic stock method. The formula used to calculate BOM inventory can be expressed as

$$\text{BOM inventory} = \text{Average inventory} \times \frac{1}{2}\left(1 + \frac{\text{Planned sales for the month}}{\text{Average monthly sales}}\right)$$

Using Exhibit 13–10's data, the BOM inventory for October is

$$\$25,000 \times \frac{1}{2}\left(1 + \frac{\$15,000}{\$16,666}\right) = \$23,750.45$$

November and December BOM inventories are calculated the same way.

Note the similarities between the BOM inventories in the basic stock and the percentage variation methods. In fact, the percentage variation gives the same results as the basic stock method when an annual inventory turnover of 6 is planned. When higher inventory turnovers are planned, however, the percentage variation method gives BOM inventories less than the basic stock method.[8] The percentage variation method has the same shortcomings as the basic stock method. In addition, the "1/2" in the formula is arbitrarily set.

Chris Manning
Buyer
Rich's Department Store

MY JOB FINDING FASHION trends is like surfing. Sometimes you catch a big wave (trend) and it's exhilarating and sometimes you think you've caught a good wave, and brown turns out not to be the color this season. But the real fun is getting the most out of the wave that you can. Let me give you an example of how I worked a big wave. • Last fall at the swimwear marts they started to show tankinis—womens' bathing suits with bikini bottoms and tank tops. My customers are women in their 40s who have a couple of kids. I thought they would really go for this new style because it had the advantages of a two-piece bathing suit, but wasn't much more revealing than a one-piece suit. I bought a wide color assortment—bright reds, yellows, pink, and black—and put them in our fashion-forward stores in January for a test. The initial sales were good but our customers thought they were a little too skimpy. Then I started to work the wave. I went back to the vendor and got them to recut the top so that the suit was less revealing and I placed a big order for the colors that were selling best. We launched an advertising campaign presenting the tankini as the suit of the season. Sales were so good that the other Federated Divisions picked up on it, but we rode the wave the longest and had the best swimwear sales of all of the Federated divisions. • I am the women's swimwear and casual weekend buyer for Rich's/Lazarus/Goldsmith's (RLG), a department store division of Federated Department Stores, headquartered in Atlanta. I started my retail career with Macy's, which is now a division of Federated, after graduating with a finance major from Michigan State University. • I feel like I am an entrepreneur running Chris Manning.com. The swimwear business at RLG is *my* business. I use my finance background to analyze investments in inventory, my management skills in supervising my assistant buyers and coordinating activities with our planner and the swimwear department managers in the stores, and my marketing knowledge to develop promotions and advertising for swimwear. The key to success in my business is speed and reaction. You need to move quickly. Everyday I come in, turn on the computer, and get a score card on how much we sold yesterday. I look over the trends, talk to people in the stores, and go to work on getting some more out of the wave.

14

Buying Merchandise

QUESTIONS

- What branding options are available to retailers?

- What issues should retailers consider when sourcing internationally?

- How and where do retailers meet with their vendors?

- What is the future of strategic partnerships when manufacturers compete directly with their retail customers over the Internet?

- What ethical and legal issues are associated with purchasing merchandise?

IN THE PRECEDING two chapters, we discussed the process that buyers go through to determine what and how much merchandise to buy. This chapter focuses on the process of buying merchandise: making branding and international sourcing decisions, meeting with vendors, establishing and maintaining strong vendor relationships, and ethical and legal issues.

Branding is one of the most important strategic merchandising decisions facing retailers. The types of brands a retailer chooses to carry are essential cues that customers use to evaluate a store. Brands influence consumers' loyalty to a store and image of it. The choice of brands also dictates margins and the degree of flexibility retailers have with their vendors.

The issue of branding goes hand in hand with international sourcing decisions, particularly for those retailers purchasing private-label merchandise. Not only does a product's country of origin denote its quality, it will also influence the merchandise cost and how long it takes to get. Recently, international sourcing decisions have been complicated with charges of human rights and child labor violations.

Whether the retailer decides to buy merchandise domestically or from an international source, it must "go to market" to view the merchandise and negotiate with vendors. It can meet vendors in a market center where there's a concentration of hundreds—or possibly thousands—of vendors. Or it can buy in its own office. A third alternative is to have a third party, called a resident buying office, prearrange meetings with potential vendors. Finally, many retailers are locating and communicating with vendors over the Internet.

As merchandise is purchased from the same vendors over and over, relationships develop. Developing strong relationships with vendors is a good way to achieve a sustainable competitive advantage. Simply buying from the same vendor, however, doesn't necessarily end in a competitive advantage. Both parties must agree to a strategic partnership based on trust, shared goals, and a strong financial commitment. Some of these strategic partnerships are threatened as manufacturers compete directly with their retail customers over the Internet.

Given the number of transactions between a retailer and each of its vendors, there are lots of opportunities for unethical and even illegal behavior. The ethical issues involved in purchasing merchandise are often subtle, yet they define the principles of conduct that govern the behavior of category managers and their employees. The law formalizes society's ethical concerns and dictates what, when, why, and how things are sold, and who may sell them. Failure to be aware of the impact of these issues can result in crippling, if not ruinous, consequences for a retailer. On the other hand, retailers that take a positive, proactive role can benefit financially and psychologically from the knowledge that they're doing the right thing.

We conclude this chapter with two appendixes. In the first, we provide tips for retailers negotiating with their vendors. Negotiations—a basic form of human interaction—are particularly important when making buying decisions. A good negotiator can easily make her yearly salary in one good negotiating session.

The second appendix examines the terms under which merchandise is purchased from vendors. Unfortunately, buying from vendors isn't as simple as when you buy from a store. Retailers must choose between several types of discount and payment date combinations. Although these discounts are relatively small compared to the total cost of an order, over a year they can become sizable. In fact, the discounts could make the difference between realizing a profit or a loss for small–gross-margin retailers like grocery stores.

BRANDING STRATEGIES

Think about the products that you've bought recently. Have you bought manufacturer brands like Levi's, Kellogg's, or Black & Decker? How about private labels like Gap jeans, America's Choice cookies from A&P, or Craftsman tools from Sears? As they develop their merchandise and assortment plans, buyers must also decide the mix of manufacturer versus private-label brands to buy. In this section, we examine the relative advantages of these branding decisions, which are summarized in Exhibit 14–1.

Manufacturer Brands

Manufacturer brands, also known as **national brands,** are products designed, produced, and marketed by a vendor. The manufacturer is responsible for developing the merchandise and establishing an image for the brand. In some cases, the manufacturer will use its name as part of

Retailers sell well-known manufacturer brands like Timex watches, Lee jeans, and Adidas sports shoes to increase store image and attract customers to their store.

EXHIBIT **14–1**

Relative Advantages
of Manufacturer
versus Private Brands

	TYPE OF VENDOR	
IMPACT ON STORE	**MANUFACTURER BRANDS**	**PRIVATE-LABEL BRANDS**
Store loyalty	?	+
Store image	+	+
Traffic flow	+	+
Selling and promotional expenses	+	–
Restrictions	–	+
Differential advantages	–	+
Margins	?	?

+ advantage to the retailer, – disadvantage to the retailer, ? depends on circumstances

the brand name for a specific product such as Kellogg's corn flakes. However, some manufacturers like Procter & Gamble (manufacturer of Tide, Cheer, and Ivory) don't associate their name with the brand. Exhibit 14–2 shows some of the most recognizable apparel and accessories brands.

EXHIBIT **14–2**

Most Recognized
Apparel and
Accessory Brands

RANK	BRAND	PRODUCT
	TOP 10 BRANDS	
1	L'Eggs	Legwear
2	Hanes	Legwear
3	Timex	Watches
4	Hanes Her Way	Daywear, underwear, bras, casualwear, socks, casual shoes
5	Levi Strauss	Jeans and sportswear
6	London Fog	Outerwear, rainwear
7	Lee	Jeans and sportswear
8	Nike	Activewear, athletic footwear, sporting goods, accessories
9	Victoria's Secret	Bras, underwear, sleepwear
10	Reebok	Activewear, athletic footwear, accessories
	PRIVATE-LABEL BRANDS IN TOP 100	
9	Victoria's Secret	Intimate apparel
20	Gap	Jeans, sportswear
29	Esprit	Sportswear, shoes, children's wear, accessories
32	Arizona (JCPenney)	Jeans, casual sportswear
36	Eddie Bauer	Outerwear, sportswear
37	Lands' End	Catalog/Internet retailer of sportswear, outerwear, accessories
41	Anne Klein	Sportswear, licensing
52	Jaclyn Smith (Kmart)	Sportswear, accessories
55	Frederick's of Hollywood	Bras, panties, daywear, shapewear, sleepwear, robes
78	J. Crew	Sportswear
79	Kathie Lee Collection (Wal-Mart)	Sportswear and ready-to-wear
87	Cartier	Fine jewelry, accessories
90	Tiffany	Fine jewelry, accessories

Source: "The Fairchild 100," *WWD*, November 1997, p. S9. Courtesy of Fairchild Publications.

Some retailers organize some of their categories around their most important national brands. For instance, buyers in department stores are responsible for brands, such as Clinique or Estée Lauder, rather than for products, such as lipstick and fragrances. Clothing is also often organized by manufacturer brand (e.g., Polo/Ralph Lauren, Levi's, Liz Claiborne, or DKNY). These brands often have their own boutique within stores. Managing a category by national brand, rather than a more traditional classification scheme, is useful so that merchandise can be purchased in a coordinated manner around a central theme.

Buying from vendors of manufacturer brands can help store image, traffic flow, and selling/promotional expenses. (See Exhibit 14–1.) Retailers buy from vendors of manufacturer brands because they have a customer following—people go into the store and ask for them by name. Loyal customers of manufacturer brands generally know what to expect from the products and feel comfortable with them.

Manufacturers devote considerable resources to creating demand for their products. As a result, relatively less money is required by the retailer for selling and promotional expenses for manufacturer brands. For instance, Guess? Inc., manufacturer of jeans and other casual clothing, attempts to communicate a constant and focused message to the consumer by coordinating advertising with in-store promotions and displays. But manufacturer brands typically have lower realized gross margins than private-label brands. These lower gross margins are due to the manufacturer assuming the cost of promoting the brand and increased competition among retailers selling these brands. Typically many retailers offer the same manufacturer brands in a market so customers compare prices for these brands across stores. Retailers often offer significant discounts on some manufacturer brands to attract customers to their stores.

Stocking national brands may increase or decrease store loyalty. If the manufacturer brand is available through a limited number of retail outlets (e.g., Lancôme cosmetics or Diesel jeans), customers loyal to the manufacturer brand will also become loyal to the store. If, on the other hand, manufacturer brands are readily available from many retailers in a market, customer loyalty may decrease because the retailer can't differentiate itself from competition. Another problem with manufacturer brands is that they can limit a retailer's flexibility. Vendors of strong brands can dictate how their products are displayed, advertised, and priced. Jockey underwear, for instance, tells retailers exactly when and how its products should be advertised.

Licensed Brands A special type of manufacturer brand is a **licensed brand,** in which the owner of a well-known brand name (licensor) enters a contract with a licensee to develop, produce, and sell the branded merchandise. The licensee may be either (1) the retailer that contracts with a manufacturer to produce the licensed product or (2) a third party that contracts to have the merchandise produced and then sells it to the retailer.

The use of the Green Bay Packer logo is licensed to the manufacturer of this sweatshirt by the Green Bay Packers football team.

Licensed brands' market share has grown increasingly large in recent years. Owners of trade names not typically associated with manufacturing have also gotten into the licensing business. For instance, the manufacturer of the sweatshirt or baseball cap emblazoned with your university's logo pays your school a

FOR THE STATUS-CONSCIOUS PERSON who can't honestly hang a Harvard diploma on his office wall, there's hope: Harvard, the brand—shoes, eyeglass frames, umbrellas, neckties, and briefcases, all embossed discreetly with the prestige of "Harvard University."

It's only a thought though, for these items, among others, are available only in selected stores in East Asia, mostly Japan. There, the status they confer doesn't come cheap. The eyeglass frames, for instance, start at about $90 a pair, and the briefcases can go for more than $100.

These aren't the typically logo-laden T-shirts, sweat shirts, and other memorabilia sold at the Harvard Coop. In fact, many Harvard University students and alumni are unaware that the merchandise exists. Nor are they aware that their school's name, when sewn into the lining of a blazer or etched into eyeglass frames, conveys the "American traditional" look, which has its fans in East Asia.

For years, Ivy League schools looked askance at the unashamedly self-promoting licensing operations that bring in as much as $3 million a year for some big state universities. Alumni of Texas A&M University, for example, can cut their lawns with "Aggie Backer Tractors" and go to their graves in caskets bearing their school's colors and shield.

But more recently, Harvard and other institutions known better for their academics than their athletics have been trying to snag a bigger piece of the $2.5 billion-a-year collegiate-licensing market. And like the American movie stars who hawk beer, cars, and other products on Japanese TV but shrink from such endorsements here, these hallowed institutions find they can rake in cash from overseas licensing without coming across as crassly commercial at home.

Source: Melinda Beck, "So You Didn't Go to Harvard; You Can Still Wear the Shoes," *The Wall Street Journal,* December 29, 1997, pp. A1–A2; and Michael D. White, "Know Yourself, Know Your Product," *World Trade,* March 1, 1999, p. 50.

licensing fee. If it didn't, it would be infringing on the university's logo (a trademark) and therefore be involved in counterfeiting. (Counterfeiting is discussed later in this chapter.) Retailing View 14.1 shows how some universities make big money on licensing.

The Internet offers licensors a great opportunity to sell merchandise directly to consumers. As a result, some licensors, particularly entertainment companies, are not allowing their licensees to sell to online retailers, ostensibly to keep more business for themselves. The major sports leagues appear to have a more liberal policy about who can sell their licensed products and where such items can be sold.[2]

Refact Macy's was among the very first department stores to pioneer the concept of private brands for fashion goods. In the 1890s, its "Macy's" and "Red Star" brands were the rage in New York.[3]

Private-Label Brands
Private-label brands (also called **store brands**) are products developed and marketed by a retailer. Refer back to Exhibit 14–2, which lists the most recognizable private-label brands. Note that Victoria's Secret is in the only private-label brand in the top 10. Exhibit 14–3 gives examples of more private-label brands. Typically, retail buyers or category managers develop specifications for the merchandise and then contract with a vendor to manufacture it. But the retailer, not the manufacturer, is responsible for promoting the brand.

Retailers' use of private labels was relatively small in the past for several reasons. First, national brands had been heavily advertised on TV and other media for decades, creating a strong consumer franchise. Second, it had been hard for retailers to gain the economies of scale in design and production necessary to compete against manufacturer brands. Third, many retailers weren't sophisticated enough to aggressively compete against manufacturer brands. Finally, private labels had a reputation of being inferior to manufacturer brands.

The Original Arizona Jean Company®

In recent years, private labels have assumed a new level of significance by establishing distinctive identities among retailers.[4] Some retailers such as The Gap and The Limited sell their own labels exclusively as an integral element of their distinctiveness. Other retailers, such as JCPenney and Sears, successfully mix manufacturer brands with their own retailer brands to project their unique image statement. Loblaw, a Canadian food retailer and distributor, has become so successful with its own retailer labels, now surpassing 5,000 items, that it even has begun supplying products for other retailers in Canada, Australia, Hong Kong, and the United States.

Private-branded products now account for an average of 20 percent of the purchases in U.S. grocery stores and as much as 50 percent in some product categories in drugstores. Private-label dollar volume in supermarkets, drug chains, and mass merchandisers is increasing at three times the rate of national brands.

Offering private labels provides a number of benefits to retailers, as Exhibit 14–1 shows. First, the exclusivity of strong private labels boosts store loyalty. For instance, I.N.C., described later in Retailing View 14.2, won't be found at a May Department Store. A second advantage of buying from private-label vendors is that they can enhance store image if the brands are high quality and fashionable. Third, like manufacturer brands, successful private-label brands can draw cus-

EXHIBIT **14–3**

Examples of Private-Label Brands

INDUSTRY	STORE	BRAND
Grocery stores	Safeway	Safeway Select
	Sobey's	Our Complements, Smartchoice
	A&P	Master Choice, American Choice
	Loblaw	President's Choice
	Wegman's	Wkids, Italian Classics
Chain stores	Kmart	Sesame Street, Martha Stewart, Benchtop
	Target	Merona, Sonia Kashuk, Honors, Michael Graves, Durabilt
	Wal-Mart	Sam's Choice, Popular Mechanics, Kathie Lee
	Sears	Kenmore, Diehard, Craftsman
	JCPenney	Arizona, St. John's Bay, Stafford, USA Olympic, Hunt Club, JCPenney Home Collection, Worthington, Jaqueline Ferrar
Department stores	May	Valerie Stevens, Karen Scott, Clairbrooke, Brandini
	Macy's	Charter Club
	Dillard's	Roundtree & York
	Nordstrom	Classiques Entier, Previews, Essentials, Premier, E-wear
Specialty stores	Neiman Marcus	Calerow, Will Swilly, Shelly Burton
	The Limited, Express	The Limited, Express
	Lowe's	Kobalt
	Home Depot	Husky

I.N.C. (PRONOUNCED INK) IS A WOMAN'S apparel label Macy's introduced in the early 1990s, one of several brands Federated has been quietly developing since acquiring Macy's several years ago. The roll-out of I.N.C. shops in many Federated stores marks a major move into vertical retailing for the chain.

Federated isn't the first department store chain to introduce its own private-label shops; JCPenney has been doing that successfully for years. But Penney does not carry the kind of designer shops Federated stores have long showcased. With I.N.C., Federated is going up against its own vendors, heavy hitters like Calvin Klein, Tommy Hilfiger, Ralph Lauren, and Donna Karan, whose shops surround the I.N.C. shops in many Macy's now.

I.N.C. shops offer merchandise of similar quality to those designers but at prices about 20 to 30 percent lower. It's a saving that Federated can offer, supposedly, due to bypassing the middleman other vendors must finance themselves. But then, those designers have begun bypassing the middleman themselves in recent years.

Source: Cathleen McCarthy, "Filling a Gap: Federated's Major Move into Vertical Retailing," *VM+SD*, May 1997, pp. 26–28.

---

tomers to the store. Fourth, retailers that purchase private-label brands don't have the same restrictions on display, promotion, or price that often encumber their strategy with manufacturer brands. Retailers purchasing private brands also have more control over manufacturing, quality control, and distribution of the merchandise. Talbot's, for instance, can contract with any vendor to manufacture its private-label sweaters. Finally, gross margin opportunities may be greater.

But there are drawbacks to using private-label brands. Although gross margins may be higher for private-label brands than for manufacturer brands, there are other expenses that aren't readily apparent. Retailers must make significant investments to design merchandise, create customer awareness, and develop a favorable image for their private-label brands. When private-label vendors are located outside the United States, the complications become even more significant, as we'll see in the next section. Sales associates may need additional training to help them sell private-label brands against better-known brands. If the private-label merchandise doesn't sell, the retailer can't return the merchandise to the vendor. These problems are most severe for high-fashion merchandise.

Private-Label Options   Retail branding strategies have run the gamut from closely imitating manufacturer-brand **trade dress** and products to distinct brand images, from low product quality and prices to premium positioning, and from nonexistent promotion and merchandising to intense activity.[5] We group private brands into four broad categories: bargain, copycat, premium, and parallel.

Bargain branding targets a price-sensitive segment by offering a no-frills product at a discount price. Known as **generic** or **house brands,** such unbranded, unadvertised merchandise is found mainly in drug, grocery, and discount stores. The bargain brand, frequently referred to as the "house brand," generally is perceived by the consumer as lower quality, and its trade dress identifies it as a brand of the retailer.

In the context of differentiating the retailer, bargain branding is primarily defensive. Its value comes from neutralizing competitors who may gain an advantage from discount pricing and by serving a secondary market segment whose patronage potentially leads to collateral sales.

Copycat branding imitates the manufacturer brand in appearance and trade dress, generally is perceived as lower quality, and is offered at a lower price. For example, knock-off brands abound in the fragrance market. By not drawing attention to the brand's origin, the copycat can confuse the consumer about the source of the product. Copycat branding is a risky private-branding alternative because close copies can violate trade dress and patent laws. Poor copies are ineffective.

Premium branding offers the consumer a private label at a comparable manufacturer-brand quality, usually with modest price savings. Safeway's Select brand in grocery products and JCPenney's Worthington brand in women's clothing are two examples. The premium brand attempts to match or exceed the product quality standard of the prototypical manufacturer brand in its category. There is no intention to duplicate the trade dress or to trade off the brand equity of a particular manufacturer brand. However, consumers frequently perceive the retailer premium labels as competing manufacturer brands.

Retailer premium brands, with the appearance of comparability, compete directly with manufacturer national brands. To succeed, the retailer must commit the resources in market research, product development, quality control, and promotion in its market area commensurate with its manufacturer-brand competitors. Consequently, development of a premium branding program precludes many retailers who have few resources from diverting to this strategy.

Parallel branding represents private labels that closely imitate the trade dress and product attributes of leading manufacturer brands but with a clearly articulated "invitation to compare" in its merchandising approach and on its product label. This "invitation to compare" on the product label was the basis for a recent legal action. Like copycat branding, parallel branding seeks to benefit from the brand equity of the manufacturer brand by closely imitating the national brand's trade dress and product qualities. However, the "invitation to compare" leaves little doubt that different manufacturers produce the two products. Consequently, the imitative trade dress does not constitute a trademark infringement. Nevertheless, patent considerations can be an issue if appropriate discretion is not used.

Parallel branding is a leveraging strategy used to bolster a retailer's private-brand sales. The closer two products are in form, logo, labeling, and packaging, the more they are perceived as substitutes. Parallel brands attempt to produce a product and trade dress so similar to the manufacturer brand that the only noticeable difference between the two is price. This promotes the view that the parallel brand provides better value for the consumer. Manufacturer brands produce store traffic and the parallel brand leverages this traffic into parallel brand sales through similar trade dress and aggressive store signage, displays, and shelf location.

Sometimes it's hard to distinguish a brand from a store and vice versa. See Retailing View 14.3.

INTERNATIONAL SOURCING DECISIONS

Take a look at what you are wearing to see if anything is made in the United States. Chances are your shirt or blouse was made in Hong Kong, your jeans were made in Italy, those beautiful new shoes are Brazilian, while those old sweat socks are from China. Your undergarments may be from Honduras. To top it off, your watch is probably from Japan or Switzerland.

THE DISTINCTION BETWEEN A STORE and a brand has become blurred in recent years. Some large retailers have developed strong private-label merchandise. Other retailers—like The Gap and its sister store, Banana Republic—have such a strong "brand name" that the average consumer cannot make a distinction between store and brand. The Gap has capitalized on its strong name recognition by widening the variety of merchandise offered at its stores. It now sells personal care products like perfume, lotion, and lip gloss. Brooks Brothers (the traditional clothing retailer) and Crate & Barrel (the upscale soft home store chain) only carry merchandise with their names on it.

A natural extension of the retailer's brand strategy is to exploit a strong retail name recognition by selling its products through channels other than its own stores. For instance, Tiffany's, the upscale jewelry store with its flagship store in Manhattan and other outlets around the country, now sells its products to other jewelry stores. Starbucks staged one of the most aggressive moves by a retailer to broaden its customer base. The coffee shop retailer that brought Middle America the "short, skinny, decaf latte" has teamed up with PepsiCo to market the Frappuccino, a coffee-and-milk blend sold through traditional grocery channels. Starbucks also is engaged in a joint venture with Dreyer's Grand Ice Cream to distribute Starbucks coffee-flavored ice cream. Late in 1998, Starbucks entered into a long-term licensing agreement with Kraft Foods, Inc., to accelerate the growth of the Starbucks brand into the grocery channel in the United States. Kraft handles all distribution, marketing, advertising, and promotions for Starbucks whole-bean and ground coffee in grocery, warehouse club, and mass merchandise stores.[6]

On the other side of the distribution spectrum, several firms that have traditionally been exclusively manufacturers have become retailers. Examples are Guess?, Calvin Klein, Ralph Lauren, Georgio Armani, Levi's, Harley-Davidson, Sony, and Nike. Why have these manufacturers chosen to become retailers? First, by becoming retailers they have total control over the way their merchandise is presented to the public. They can price, promote, and merchandise their line with a unified strategy. They don't have to worry about retailers cherry-picking certain items or discounting the price, for instance. Second, they can use these stores to test new merchandise and merchandising concepts. Based on these tests' results, they can better advise other retailers what to buy and how to merchandise their stores. Third, these manufacturers/retailers use their stores to showcase their merchandise to the public as well. The Sony and Nike stores, Ralph Lauren's flagship store in Manhattan, and Levi's flagship store in San Francisco have atmospheres that enhance the manufacturer's image as well as help to sell merchandise. Finally, although these stores often compete with stores that carry the same merchandise, some would argue that having a stronger retail presence creates a name recognition and synergy between the manufacturer and retailer that benefit both parties.

Refact The U.S. apparel industry has been in a state of decline. In 1998, China (including Hong Kong) accounted for about 18 percent, Mexico 13 percent, Dominican Republic 5 percent, and Honduras 4 percent of apparel sold in the United States. Cambodia has become the fastest-growing source of apparel imports into the United States.[7]

A decision that's closely associated with branding decisions, which we discussed in the previous section, is to determine where the merchandise is made. Retailers involved in private branding are faced with all of the issues that we'll examine in this section. Although retailers buying manufacturer brands usually aren't responsible for determining where the merchandise is made, a product's country of origin is often used as a signal of quality. Certain items are strongly associated with specific countries, and products from those countries, such as gold jewelry from Italy or cars from Japan, often benefit from those linkages.

In this section we'll first examine the cost implications of international sourcing decisions. Superficially, it often looks like retailers can get merchandise from foreign suppliers cheaper than from domestic sources. Unfortunately, there are a lot of "hidden" costs, including managerial issues, associated with sourcing globally that make this decision more complicated. We then examine the trend toward sourcing closer to home or actually reversing the trend toward international sourcing by buying "made in America." This section concludes by exploring ethical issues associated with retailers who buy from vendors engaged in human rights and child labor violations.

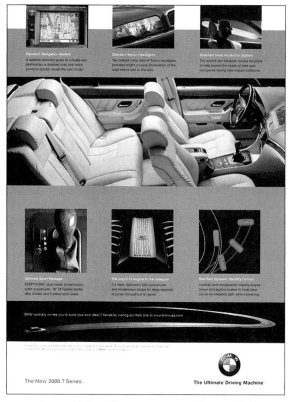

Some products, like watches from Switzerland and automobiles from Germany, have a high quality reputation just because of their country-of-origin effects.

Costs Associated with Global Sourcing Decisions

A demonstrable reason for sourcing globally rather than domestically is to save money. Retailers must examine several cost issues when making these decisions. The cost issues discussed in this chapter are country-of-origin effects, foreign currency fluctuations, tariffs, free trade zones, inventory carrying costs, and transportation costs.

Country-of-Origin Effects   The next time you're buying a shirt made in Western Europe (e.g., Italy, France, or Germany), notice that it's probably more expensive than a comparable shirt made in a developing country like Hungary, Ecuador, or Cambodia. These Western European countries have a reputation for high fashion and quality. Unfortunately for the U.S. consumer, however, the amount of goods and services that can be purchased from those countries with U.S. dollars is significantly less than amount of merchandise that can be purchased from developing countries for the same amount of money. When making international sourcing decisions, therefore, retailers must weigh the savings associated with buying from developing countries with the panache associated with buying merchandise from a country that has a reputation for fashion and quality.

Other countries might have a technological advantage in the production of certain types of merchandise and can therefore provide their products to the world market at a relatively low price. For example, Japan has always been a leader in the development of consumer electronics. Although these products often enter the market at a high (skimming) price, the price soon drops as manufacturers learn to produce the merchandise more efficiently.

Refact   Products made in the United States and U.S.-based retailers have special panache in other countries. Examples include McDonald's, Pizza Hut, TGI Friday's, Coca-Cola, Disney, Harley-Davidson, and Levi Strauss.[8]

Foreign Currency Fluctuations An important consideration when making global sourcing decisions is fluctuations in the currency of the exporting firm. Unless currencies are closely linked, for example, between the United States and Canada, changes in the exchange rate will increase or reduce the cost of the merchandise.

Suppose, for instance, that Service Merchandise is purchasing watches from Swatch in Switzerland for $100,000, which is equivalent to 120,000 Swiss francs (SFr) since the exchange rate is 1.2 SFr for each U.S. dollar. If the dollar falls to, say, 1.1 SFr before the firm has to pay for the watches, it would end up paying $109,090 (or 120,000 SFr ÷ 1.1).

Refact JCPenney buys its goods from suppliers spread across 50 countries.[9]

Tariffs A **tariff,** also known as a **duty,** is a tax placed by a government upon imports.[10] Import tariffs have been used to shield domestic manufacturers from foreign competition and to raise money for the government. In general, since tariffs raise the cost of imported merchandise, retailers have always had a strong incentive to reduce them. The General Agreement on Tariffs and Trade, the North American Free Trade Agreement, and foreign trade zones all reduce tariffs.

World Trade Organization The World Trade Organization (WTO) replaced GATT (The General Agreement on Tariffs and Trade) in 1996. With 135 member countries and 30 more that want to join, the WTO will be the global watchdog for free trade. The WTO will continue to push for tariff reductions on manufactured goods as well as liberalization of trade in agriculture and services.

North American Free Trade Agreement (NAFTA) The ratification of NAFTA on January 1, 1994, created a tariff-free market with 364 million consumers and a total output of $6 trillion.[11] NAFTA members are currently the United States, Canada, and Mexico. Other Latin American countries are anticipated to join in the next few years. NAFTA is expected to strengthen North America's position when negotiating with the European Union.

U.S. retailers stand to gain from NAFTA for two reasons. First, Mexican labor is relatively low-cost and abundant. Thus, retailers can either search for low-cost suppliers in Mexico or begin manufacturing merchandise there themselves. **Maquiladoras** (plants in Mexico that make goods and parts or process food for export to the United States) are plentiful, have lower costs than their U.S. counterparts, and are located throughout Mexico, particularly in border towns such as Nogales and Tijuana. Second, with the growing importance of quick response inventory systems, the time it takes to get merchandise into stores becomes ever more critical. Transit times are shorter and managerial control problems are reduced when sourcing from Mexico, compared to the Far East or Europe.

Maquiladores are manufacturing plants in Mexico that make goods and parts or process food for export to the United States. They are very popular because their costs are lower than those of their U.S. counterparts.

Foreign Trade Zones Retailers involved in foreign sourcing of merchandise can lower import tariffs by using foreign trade zones. A **foreign trade**

zone is a special area within a country that can be used for warehousing, packaging, inspection, labeling, exhibition, assembly, fabrication, or transshipment of imports without being subject to that country's tariffs.

To illustrate how a foreign trade zone can benefit retailers, consider how German cars are imported to a foreign trade zone in Guatemala for distribution throughout Central America. The duty for passenger vehicles is 100 percent of the landed cost of the vehicle. The duty for commercial vehicles, however, is only 10 percent. The German manufacturer imported commercial vans with no seats or carpeting, and with panels instead of windows. After paying the 10 percent import duty, it converted the vans to passenger station wagons in the foreign trade zone in Guatemala and sold them throughout Latin America.

Cost of Carrying Inventory   The cost of carrying inventory is likely to be higher when purchasing from suppliers outside the United States than from domestic suppliers.

$$\text{Cost of carrying inventory} = \text{Average inventory value (at cost)} \\ \times \text{Opportunity cost of capital}$$

The **opportunity cost of capital** is the rate available on the next best use of the capital invested in the project at hand.[12]

There are several reasons for the higher inventory carrying costs. Consider The Spoke bicycle store in Aspen, Colorado, which is buying Moots bicycles manufactured in Steamboat Springs, Colorado. The Spoke knows that the **lead time**—the amount of time between recognition that an order needs to be placed and the point at which the merchandise arrives in the store and is ready for sale—is usually two weeks, plus or minus three days. But if The Spoke is ordering bikes from Italy, the lead time might be three months plus or minus three weeks. Since lead times are longer, retailers must maintain larger inventories to ensure that merchandise is available when the customer wants it. Larger inventories mean larger inventory carrying costs.

It's also more difficult to predict exactly how long the lead time will be when sourcing globally. When the bicycle goes from Steamboat Springs to Aspen, the worst that could happen is getting caught in a snowstorm for a day or two. On the other hand, the bicycle from Italy might be significantly delayed because of multiple handlings at sea or airports, customs, strikes of carriers, poor weather, or bureaucratic problems. Similar to long lead times, inconsistent lead times require the retailer to maintain high levels of safety stock.

Transportation Costs   In general, the further merchandise has to travel, the higher the transportation cost will be for any particular mode of transportation. For instance, the cost of shipping a container of merchandise by ship from China to New York is significantly higher than the cost from Panama to New York.

Managerial Issues Associated with Global Sourcing Decisions

In the previous section we examined the specific costs associated with global sourcing decisions. In most cases, retailers can obtain hard cost information that will help them make their global sourcing decisions. The managerial issues discussed in this section—quality control and developing strategic alliances—are not as easily evaluated.

Quality Control   When sourcing globally, it's harder to maintain and measure quality standards than when sourcing domestically. Typically these problems are more pronounced in countries that are far away and underdeveloped. For instance, it's easier to address a quality problem if it occurs on a shipment of dresses from Costa Rica to the United States than if the dresses were shipped from Singapore because Costa Rica is much closer.

There are both direct and indirect ramifications for retailers if merchandise is delayed because it has to be remade due to poor quality. Suppose Banana Republic is having pants made in Haiti. Before the pants leave the factory, Banana Republic representatives find that the workmanship is so poor that the pants need to be remade. This delay reverberates throughout the system. Banana Republic could have extra safety stock to carry it through until the pants can be remade. More likely, however, it won't have advance warning of the problem, so the stores will be out of stock.

A more serious problem occurs if the pants are delivered to the stores without the problem having been detected. This could happen if the defect is subtle, such as inaccurate sizing. Customers can become irritated and question merchandise quality. Also, markdowns ensue because inventories become unbalanced and shopworn.

Building Strategic Alliances   The importance of building strategic alliances is examined later in this chapter. It is typically harder to build these alliances when sourcing globally, particularly when the suppliers are far away and in underdeveloped countries. Communications are more difficult. There is often a language barrier, and there are almost always cultural differences. Business practices—everything from terms of payment to the mores of trade practices such as commercial bribery—are different in a global setting. The most important element in building a strategic alliance—maintaining the supplier's trust—is more arduous in an international environment.

Source Close to Home or Buy "Made in America"   Some U.S. retailers are shifting suppliers from Asia and Europe to nearby Central American and Caribbean countries, or they're seeking products made in America. There are four reasons for this shift. First, it may be more profitable for all of the reasons that we detailed above.

Many retailers are increasing the amount of merchandise that is "Made in America." Sourcing closer to home is often more profitable, is consistent with Quick Response inventory systems, and is preferred by some cusotmer groups.

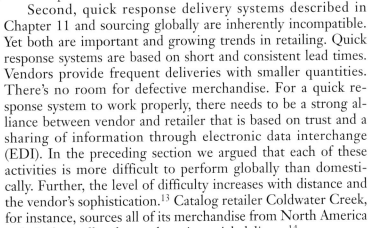

Second, quick response delivery systems described in Chapter 11 and sourcing globally are inherently incompatible. Yet both are important and growing trends in retailing. Quick response systems are based on short and consistent lead times. Vendors provide frequent deliveries with smaller quantities. There's no room for defective merchandise. For a quick response system to work properly, there needs to be a strong alliance between vendor and retailer that is based on trust and a sharing of information through electronic data interchange (EDI). In the preceding section we argued that each of these activities is more difficult to perform globally than domestically. Further, the level of difficulty increases with distance and the vendor's sophistication.[13] Catalog retailer Coldwater Creek, for instance, sources all of its merchandise from North America so it can purchase relatively small orders and receive quick delivery.[14]

The third reason why retailers are taking a close look at domestic sources of supply is that some of their customers prefer products that are "made in America." A national survey of consumers indicates that Americans purchase goods based first on quality, then features, followed by price, warranty, and country of origin. Importantly, American-made products are perceived as being superior in quality to foreign-made goods, especially tools, clothing, candy and confections, and toys.[15] Retailers are simply reacting to their customers' quality perceptions.

Retailers are searching for merchandise closer to home so they can police potential violations of human rights and child labor.

Refact The top garment imports from Latin America to the United States in 1998 were men's and women's intimate apparel, men's and boys' cotton pants, women's cotton pants, cotton knit T-shirts, and men's and boys' synthetic-fiber underwear. Production in Latin America represents particularly significant savings for labor-intensive articles such as jeans, wrinkle-free pants, and intimate apparel, all of which require a high degree of technical expertise and equipment to produce quickly at top quality and meet delivery dates.[17]

The fourth reason for sourcing closer to home is that it's easier to police potential violations of human rights and child labor. Sears, Wal-Mart, Ralph Lauren, the Gap, Nordstrom, J. Crew, The Limited, and others have had to publicly deflect allegations about human rights, child labor, or other abuses involving factories and countries where their goods are made.[16]

Some firms respond by promising an inquiry. They require their contractors to sign strict codes of conduct that threaten withdrawal of business if labor abuses occur. Many companies are asking their quality control people to look out for worker abuses while also watching that zippers are sewn on straight.

MEETING VENDORS

Now that we've examined the different branding decisions available to retailers and the issues surrounding global sourcing, we concentrate on how and where retailers meet with their vendors. Retailers "go to market" to see the variety of available merchandise and to buy. A market, from the retail buyer's perspective, is a concentration of vendors within a specific geographic location, perhaps even under one roof. These markets may be permanent wholesale market centers or temporary trade fairs. Retailers may also buy on their own turf, either in stores or at corporate headquarters. Resident buying offices prearrange opportunities for buyers to visit vendors in major market centers in the United States and abroad. Finally, buyers can use the Internet to find merchandise and buying services such as freight forwarders from around the world.

INTERNET EXERCISE   Go to www.inretail.com, www.market4retail.com, www.Asiansources.com, and www.hotoffthewire.com. If you were a buyer, which site would you use? Why?

Wholesale Market Centers For many types of merchandise, retailers can do much of their buying in established market centers. Wholesale market centers have permanent vendor sales offices retailers can visit throughout the year. Probably the world's most significant wholesale market center for many merchandise categories is in New York City. The Fashion Center, also known as the Garment District, is located from Fifth to Ninth avenues and from 35th to 41st streets. An estimated 22,000 apparel buyers visit every year for five market weeks and 65 annual related trade shows. The Garment District has 5,100 showrooms and 4,500 factories.[18]

The United States also has a number of regional wholesale market centers. The Dallas Market Center, the world's largest, is a 6.9 million–square-foot complex of six buildings. Over 26,000 manufacturers and importers display their international products in its 2,400 permanent showrooms and more than 2,000 temporary spaces. Some regional centers have developed into national markets for specific merchandise categories (for example, the Miami Merchandise Mart for swimwear).

Trade Shows Many wholesale market centers host **trade shows** (also known as **merchandise shows** or **market weeks**). Permanent tenants of the wholesale market centers as well as vendors leasing temporary space participate. Here retailers place orders and get a concentrated view of what's available in the marketplace. The Dallas Market Center hosts over 40 shows annually for products ranging from floor coverings to toys, apparel, jewelry, and gifts. Trade shows are also staged by convention centers not associated with wholesale market centers. McCormick Place in Chicago (the nation's largest convention complex with almost 2 million square feet) hosts over 65 meetings and trade shows per year, including the National Hardware Show, National Housewares Manufacturers Association International Exposition, and National Sporting Goods Association Market.

Buying on Their Own Turf Although buyers go to wholesale market centers and trade shows to search for new merchandise, place orders, and meet with vendors, vendors also work with buyers in their offices. Most buying activity in buyers' offices is for basic merchandise or rebuys on fashion merchandise.

Resident Buying Offices **Resident buying offices** are organizations located in major buying centers that provide services to help retailers buy merchandise. Doneger Group, Frederick Atkins, and Associated Merchandising are the three primary buying offices in the United States. As retailers have become larger and more sophisticated, the resident buying offices have become less important in recent years. Retailers simply perform the services formerly provided by these buying offices themselves.[19]

To illustrate how buying offices operate, consider how David Smith of Pockets Men's Store in Dallas utilizes his resident buying offices when he goes to market in Milan. Smith meets with market representative Alain Bordat of the Doneger Group. Bordat, an English-speaking Italian, knows Smith's store and his upscale customers, so in advance of Smith's visit he sets up appointments with Italian vendors he believes would fit Pockets' image.

When Smith is in Italy, Bordat accompanies him to the appointments and acts as translator, negotiator, and accountant. Bordat informs Smith of the cost of importing the merchandise into the United States, taking into account duty, freight, insurance, processing costs, and so forth.

INTERNET EXERCISE   Go to www.Doneger.com and click on Guests to learn more about this resident buying office.

Once the orders are placed, Bordat writes the contracts and follows up on delivery and quality control. The Doneger Group also acts as a home base for buyers like Smith, providing office space and services, travel advisors, and emergency aid. Bordat and his association continue to keep Smith abreast of what's happening on the Italian fashion scene through reports and constant communication. Without the help of a resident buying office, it would be difficult, if not impossible, for Smith to penetrate the Italian wholesale market.

Internet Buying Services   Sometimes it is not possible or practical to travel to market. It is time-consuming and expensive. Often a buyer can spend a whole day and end up with only a few purchases. Retail buyers are turning to the Internet to find new products and repurchase familiar products for the same reasons that shopping on the Internet is a convenient alternative to going to stores for you. Several sites are currently available to retailers to preview merchandise before going to market or find new merchandise.

ESTABLISHING AND MAINTAINING STRATEGIC PARTNERSHIPS WITH VENDORS

As we discussed in Chapter 6, maintaining strong vendor relationships is an important method of developing a sustainable competitive advantage. Meeting with vendors is only the first step in this process. In this section we examine how retailers can develop relationships with their vendors that can evolve into a strategic partnership. Like a good marriage, strategic partnerships require a lot of work. In this section we discuss several characteristics of a successful long-term relationship that, if present, should result in a strategic partnership. We conclude this section with a discussion of disintermediation, a major threat to strategic partnerships among manufacturers selling directly to consumers over the Internet and their traditional channel partners.

Establishing Strategic Partnerships   Relationships between retailers and vendors are often based on "splitting up a profit pie."[20] Both parties may be interested exclusively in their own profits and be unconcerned about the other party's welfare. These relationships are common when the products are commodities and have no major impact on the retailers' performance. This type of relationship is basically a "win–lose" relationship because when one party gets a larger portion of the pie, the other party gets a smaller portion. This type of arrangement does not have any of the qualities necessary to achieve a competitive advantage.

To develop a strategic partnership that will lead to a competitive advantage, the retailer and vendor must commit to a long-term business relationship in which partners make significant investments to improve both parties' profitability. In these relationships, it's important for the partners to "put their money where their mouth is." They've taken risks to "expand the pie"—to give the partnership a strategic advantage over other companies.

Benetton USA has a strategic partnership with Sears. They work together to maximize the profitability of this department.

Refact The population of Bentonville, Arkansas, the corporate headquarters for Wal-Mart, is 17,000 with 7,000 of these people working for Wal-Mart. Another 7,000 people representing vendors call on Wal-Mart every month. More than 100 companies that are suppliers to Wal-Mart have opened offices in Bentonville including Hewlett-Packard, Clorox, Nabisco, and Procter & Gamble.[22]

Thus a strategic partnership is a win–win relationship. Both parties benefit because the size of the pie has increased. Strategic partnerships are created explicitly to uncover and exploit joint opportunities.[21] Members in strategic partnerships depend on and trust each other heavily; they share goals and agree on how to accomplish those goals; and they're willing to take risks, share confidential information, and make significant investments for the sake of the relationship.

Wal-Mart has made great strides in developing strategic partnering relationships with its vendors. Wal-Mart and many of its suppliers have created cross-functional teams composed of individuals from various areas of the firm such as marketing, finance, operations, distribution, and management information systems. Wal-Mart's teams work closely with similar teams from Procter & Gamble, Kraft General Foods, James River, Black & Decker, and other companies to develop unique information systems and promotional programs tailored to markets served by Wal-Mart and its vendors.

Similarly, Levi Strauss teams worked with JCPenney to create a specially designed area for stores to display Docker merchandise. Then the teams developed sophisticated inventory control systems to make sure the stores were always stocked with strong-selling styles and sizes. As a result, JCPenney is now Levi's largest customer. Penney also increased its profits by offering customers a unique display and in-stock merchandise competing department stores lacked.

A strategic partnership is like a marriage. When businesses enter strategic partnerships, they're wedded to their partner for better or worse. For example, if the Levi Docker merchandise hadn't sold well, Penney and Levi would have lost money. Strategic partnerships are risky and reduce flexibility. Once Penney formed a true strategic partnership with Levi, it couldn't "date around" with Levi's competitors.

Now let's look at characteristics that are necessary to maintain strategic partnerships.

Maintaining Strategic Partnerships

Maintaining a strategic partnership accomplishes both parties' goals. Successful buyer–vendor relationships involve increasing the mutual benefits as the partners learn to trust and depend on each other more and more. Additionally, the buyer and vendor can resolve conflicts as they arise, settle differences, and compromise when necessary. The four foundations of successful strategic partnerships are mutual trust, open communication, common goals, and credible commitments.

Mutual Trust The key to developing a strategic partnership is trust. Lou Pritchett, former senior vice president of sales for Procter & Gamble, once said, "Cost reduction throughout the total system can be accomplished when trust replaces skepticism. Trusting suppliers, customers and employees is one of the most effective, yet most underutilized techniques available to management."[23]

Trust is a belief by one party that the other party will fulfill its obligations in a relationship.[24] When vendors and buyers trust each other, they're more willing to share relevant ideas, clarify goals and problems, and communicate efficiently. Information shared between the parties becomes increasingly comprehensive, accurate, and timely. There's less need for the vendor and buyer to constantly monitor and check up on each other's actions because each believes the other won't take advantage of him, given the opportunity.[25]

For example, an apparel manufacturer might want to develop quick response relationships with a retailer. (See Chapter 11.) To do so, it must get cooperation from the retailer. The manufacturer has a better chance of realizing its goal by approaching a retailer that (1) can visualize the benefits from working together with the manufacturer and (2) is willing to take the risks associated with altering its normal routines. If the manufacturer and retailer trust each other, they'll be more willing to try new and different ways of doing business because they know their partner is similarly committed to the relationship. Further, they believe that any gains and losses resulting from their partnership will even out over the long run so they aren't afraid to sustain a short-term loss for the sake of gaining a greater long-term advantage.

Vendors develop trust in buyers when the salespeople consistently take the buyers' needs and interests into account. A vendor who has a track record of consistent deliveries and reliable performance and who cultivates a positive, interpersonal relationship with the customer earns valuable trust.

Open Communication   Open, honest communication is a key to developing successful relationships. Buyers and vendors in a relationship need to understand what's driving each other's business, their roles in the relationship, each firm's strategies, and any problems that arise over the course of the relationship.

Common Goals   Vendors and buyers must have common goals for a successful relationship to develop. Shared goals give both members of the relationship incentive to pool their strengths and abilities, and to exploit potential opportunities between them. There's also assurance that the other partner won't do anything to hinder goal achievement within the relationship.

For example, if Johnson & Johnson (J&J) and Kmart commit to reducing out-of-stock occurrences at the store level, then they both must work toward this goal. J&J can't fall behind on its shipments and Kmart can't be lackadaisical about getting the product on the shelf in a timely manner. With a common goal, both firms have incentive to cooperate because they know that by doing so, each can boost sales.

Shared goals also help to sustain the partnership when expected benefit flows aren't realized. If one J&J shipment fails to reach a Kmart store on time due to an uncontrollable event like misrouting by a trucking firm, Kmart won't suddenly call off the whole arrangement. Instead, Kmart is likely to view the incident as a simple mistake and will remain in the relationship. This is because Kmart knows it and J&J are committed to the same goal in the long run.

Credible Commitments   Successful relationships develop because both parties make credible commitments to the relationship. Credible commitments are tangible investments in the relationship. They go beyond just making the hollow statement "I want to be a partner." Credible commitments involve spending money to improve the supplier's products or services provided to the customer.[26]

For example, a vendor may train sales associates, invest in special displays, and develop a special system to interface with the retailer's computer. These investments signal a partner's long-run commitment to the relationship.

Disintermediation   Disintermediation has become a topic of increasing intensity as e-retailing grows in importance. **Disintermediation** occurs when a manufacturer or wholesaler competes directly with its retailers. Disintermediation systems usually arise when a vendor decides to vertically integrate by starting retailing activities. Disintermediation can be illegal if it restrains competition either by systematically undercutting the retail price of the retailers it sells to or by making merchandise that is not otherwise available difficult to obtain.

Some manufacturers believe that selling over the Internet directly to the ultimate consumer is a way to increase their profit margins by bypassing their current retail channels, both Internet and bricks-and-mortar retailers. To these retailers, the Internet is just another channel from a competitive perspective—starting to use it is no different than opening a chain of factory outlet stores.

Other manufacturers, notably Levi Strauss, experimented with disintermediation and concluded that it was not worth the trouble for two important reasons. First, manufacturers are generally not set up to perform the fulfillment functions that are required to get merchandise from the factory to the customer. They are accustomed to manufacturing and shipping large quantities. They generally do not have the capability to store and ship items one at a time, promote or customize assortments at a local level, provide customer service to retail customers, collect money from individuals, or take care of returns from individuals.[27] Second, manufacturers do not want to anger their current retail customers by competing with them. Home Depot, for example, issued a warning to vendors suggesting that anyone attempting to sell direct will be treated as a competitor. In other words, Home Depot would cut them off.[28]

Manufacturers can take several approaches to appease their traditional retail customers if they intend to sell over the Internet. They can offer a selection of brands and products that's only available online. For instance, Procter & Gamble is selling a premium line of cosmetics directly to the consumer via the Internet. Its site, www.reflect.com, is a personalized beauty experience that suggests products based on individual skin tones, texture, color, and so on.[29] Other vendors are simply attempting to keep a low profile, are using higher price points over the Internet, or are leaving successful promotional events in the exclusive domain of traditional retailers.[30]

In the end, experts believe that the disintermediation issue will turn into a battle of the brands. Toys "R" Us needs Barbie dolls more than Home Depot needs Armstrong flooring. The channel partner with the strongest brand will be able to dictate whether disintermediation takes place or not.[31]

ETHICAL AND LEGAL ISSUES IN PURCHASING MERCHANDISE

As you can imagine, given the thousands of relationships and millions of transactions between retailers and their vendors, unethical or illegal situations may arise. In this section we'll view ethical and legal issues from both retailers' and vendors' perspectives. Retailers should not take advantage of their position of power in the marketing channel. In this regard, we'll examine slotting allowances, buybacks, chargebacks, and commercial bribery. To protect their customers' interests and their own reputation, retailers must be cognizant of whether the merchandise is counterfeit or from the diverted market (the gray market). From the vendor's perspective, they aren't likely to become legally entangled with their retailers so long as they sell to whomever wants to buy, sell whatever they want, and sell at the same price to all. In this regard, we'll look at exclusive territories, exclusive dealing agreements, tying contracts, and refusals to deal.

Slotting Allowances

Slotting allowances (also called **slotting fees** when viewed from the vendor's perspective) are fees paid by a vendor for space in a retail store.[32] Slotting allowances currently aren't illegal. Although government agencies, from the Federal Trade Commission and the U.S. Department of Justice to several state attorney general offices, are attempting to determine if they are illegal under antitrust laws.[33] You may decide, depending on your perspective, that they're unethical.

Here's an example. When General Foods or any other consumer package goods manufacturer wants to introduce a new product, it often pays a slotting allowance to grocery and discount store chains for the space (slot) on the shelf. The fee varies depending on the nature of the product and the relative power of the retailer. Products whose brand names command relatively low customer loyalty pay the highest slotting allowances. Likewise, large grocery chains can demand higher slotting allowances than small mom-and-pop stores can. Fees can be significant—estimates in the grocery industry alone are in excess of $9 billion or approximately 16 percent of all new product introduction costs.[34] The per-item store costs are estimated to be $5,000 to $25,000.[35] At that rate, it may cost $1 million or more to get national distribution of a new product!

Slotting fees are present not only in the food industry. They are becoming prevalent in other retail venues such as OTC drugs, apparel, magazines, and computer software. In the music industry, for instance, retailers regularly charge vendors for the right to display and sell their merchandise. Coconuts leases out its windows to the highest bidder. In a busy midtown Manhattan store, companies like Time Warner Inc. and Sony pay $200,000 per window per year! The top six companies in the music industry each pay at least $10 million a year to secure desirable locations in major cities.[36]

Some retailers argue that slotting allowances are a reasonable method for ensuring that their valuable space is used efficiently. Of course, manufacturers view slotting allowances as extortion.

As part of a program to develop strategic partnerships, some manufacturers avoid slotting allowances by working closely with retail stores and sharing the financial risk of new products. For instance, to avoid slotting allowances, Campbell Soup launched a "failure fee" program that guarantees each new Campbell item will achieve certain sales after six months or Campbell will pay the retailer a specified fee.

Buybacks

Similar to slotting allowances, the buyback (also known as a **stocklift,** or **lift-out**) is a strategy vendors and retailers use to get products into retail stores. Specifically, a **buyback** can occur under two scenarios. The first and most ethically troubling is when a retailer allows a vendor to create space for its goods by "buying back" a competitor's inventory and removing it from a retailer's system. In the second case, the retailer forces a vendor to buy back slow-moving merchandise.[37]

Consider the following buyback scenario.[38] At 100 Lowe's Home Improvement Warehouse stores, thousands of garden gloves manufactured by Wells Lamont vanished almost overnight. The empty shelves were restocked with gloves made by Wells Lamont's archrival, Midwest Quality Gloves Inc. Midwest made a deal with Lowe's to buy 225,000 pairs of Wells Lamont gloves and clear them all out so it could fill the shelves with its own product. The Wells Lamont gloves were probably dumped into a sprawling underground pipeline for resale by faraway, perhaps foreign, retailers. There are about a half-dozen companies that provide buyback-type liquidation services.

Buybacks are not limited to garden gloves. Power adaptors and leather cases for cellular phones, baby products, pet toys, humidifiers, flashlights, faucets, and glue are all targets.

Are buybacks illegal? Technically a company may violate federal antitrust laws if it stocklifts from a competitor so often as to shut it out of a market. But such cases brought under the Sherman Antitrust Act are difficult to prove.[39]

Chargebacks

A **chargeback** is a practice used by retailers in which they deduct money from the amount they owe a vendor. There are two reasons for a chargeback. The first, similar to a buyback, is when the retailer deducts money from an invoice because merchandise isn't selling. The second reason is vendor mistakes such as shoddy labeling, lost billings, wrong-size boxes or hangers, missing items, and late shipments.[40] Although often legitimate, chargebacks are frequently viewed as being unjustified by vendors. Retailers can use chargebacks as a profit center. For instance, one senior executive at a large department store chain was told to collect $50 million in chargebacks.[41] What makes chargebacks especially difficult for vendors is that once the money is deducted from an invoice, it is difficult to get it back.

Commercial Bribery

Commercial bribery occurs in retailing when a vendor or its agent offers to give or pay a retail buyer "something of value" to influence purchasing decisions. Say a sweater manufacturer takes a department store buyer to lunch at a fancy private club and then proposes a ski weekend in Vail. The buyer enjoys the lunch but graciously turns down the ski trip. These gifts could be construed as bribes or kickbacks, which are illegal. In fact, the Internal Revenue Service doesn't allow money paid for bribes to be deducted as a business expense. From an ethical perspective, there's a fine line between the social courtesy of a free lunch and an elaborate free vacation.

To avoid these problems, many companies forbid employees to accept any gifts from vendors. Kmart specifically forbids the taking of "bribes, commissions, kickbacks, payments, loans, gratuities or other solicitations, including any item of value from suppliers to the company."[42] But many companies have no policy against receiving gifts, and some unethical employees accept and even solicit gifts, even if their company has a policy against it. A good rule of thumb is to accept only limited entertainment or token gifts, such as flowers or a bottle of wine, for Christmas, birthdays, or other occasions. When the gift or favor is perceived to be large enough to influence a buyer's purchasing behavior, it's considered to be commercial bribery and therefore illegal.

Counterfeit Merchandise

Counterfeit merchandise includes goods made and sold without the permission of the owner of a trademark, a copyright, or a patented invention that is legally protected in the country where it is marketed. Trademarks, copyrights, and patents are all under the general umbrella of intellectual property. **Intellectual property** is intangible and is created by intellectual (mental) effort as opposed to physical effort. A **trademark** is any mark, word, picture, or design associated with certain merchandise (for instance, the crown on a Rolex watch and the GE on General Electric products). A **copyright** protects original work of authors, painters, sculptors, musicians, and others who produce works of artistic or intellectual merit. The copyright protects only the physical expression of the effort, not the idea. This book is copyrighted, so these sentences cannot be used by anyone without the consent of the copyright owner. However, anyone can take the ideas in this book and express them in different words. The owner of a **patent** controls the right to make, sell, and use a product for a period of 17 years or a design for 14 years.[43]

The nature of counterfeiting has changed over the past decade. Although manufacturers of high-visibility, strong–brand-name consumer goods are still tortured by counterfeiters, there's now a thriving business in counterfeit high-tech products such as software, CDs, and CD-ROMs. For instance, it is estimated that the software publishing and distribution industries lose over $12 billion a year.[44] Why is this type of merchandise so attractive to counterfeiters? It has a high unit value, is relatively easy to duplicate and transport, and has high consumer demand. For instance, suppose *Retailing Management* were available on a CD-ROM. It could be easily duplicated as a CD or reprinted as a book for a few dollars in a foreign country. Neither the publishers nor the authors would receive any money. In fact, it's likely that they wouldn't even know about the copyright infringement.

Retailers and their vendors have four avenues to pursue to protect themselves against the ravages of counterfeiting and intellectual property rights violations: product registration, legislative action, bilateral and multilateral negotiations, and measures taken by companies.[45]

With today's advanced technology, counterfeiting is almost as easy as photocopying. The labels can be the trickiest part. The counterfeiters who made these products allow the buyer to choose which brand name they want to use on a product.

online three months ago, the Germantown, Tennessee, homemaker has been snapping up designer wares at unbelievable discounts—a pair of Chanel sunglasses for $65, a pair of Oakley shades for $15, and three stylish Louis Vuitton accessories for as little as $53. There's just one thing she can't figure out: Are they fake? The answer, probably! Yet, she—and others—don't seem to care.

The Web presents special problems because online shoppers "can't touch or feel" what they are buying. Indeed, some knockoffs on the Internet are of such high quality that even manufacturers have a little trouble telling the difference.

Cyberspace is turning out to be the scourge of the luxury-goods industry. While everybody else is reveling in booming Internet sales, designer manufacturers see a dark side of e-retailing: an onslaught of cyberfakes. In 1999, online counterfeit sales were expected to total as much as $25 billion world wide, 10 percent of the total counterfeit market, according to the Counterfeiting Intelligence Bureau of the International Chamber of Commerce. That's about double the amount of legitimate online retail sales in the United States—and a major threat to an industry that lives and dies on brand identity.

Even if law enforcement gets more aggressive, the battle looks daunting. Unlike street vendors, who tend to congregate in certain areas, Internet counterfeiters are scattered around an estimated 5,000 sites and range from shady overseas manufacturers to school kids operating out of a basement. Another problem: Sellers who get caught can simply pick a new Internet address and jump back into business. "They're like roaches." When companies come across a cyberfeiter, they typically dispatch a cease-and-desist letter. Even if that doesn't shut the site down, it may prompt the operator to quit selling the product in question. But it doesn't solve the problem.

One reason the Internet is so worrisome is that online counterfeiters are generally more savvy about technology than their street-vendor counterparts. The Web also provides a vast new distribution channel for the crime syndicates and overseas gangs that federal authorities have been cracking down on for years.

Source: *The Wall Street Journal*, "Sleaze E-Commerce," Rebecca Quick and Ken Basinger, May 14, 1999, p. W1; permission conveyed through the Copyright Clearance Center.

Refact Counterfeit merchandise causes a significant drain in the world economy. It is estimated that 8 percent of all goods sold worldwide today are counterfeit.[46]

First, the product must be trademarked, copyrighted, and/or patented in the countries in which it's sold. Unfortunately, registration in the United States provides no protection in another country although treaties and other international agreements provide some protection outside the United States.

The second method of protection is through legislative action. Several laws protect businesses against counterfeiting. For instance, the Trademark Counterfeiting Act of 1984 made counterfeiting a criminal rather than a civil offense, and established stiff penalties for the practice.

Third, the U.S. government is engaged in bilateral and multilateral negotiations and education to limit counterfeiting. For instance, the WTO (World Trade Organization described earlier in this chapter) has rules on intellectual property protection.[47]

Finally, companies are aggressively taking steps to protect themselves. The International Anti-Counterfeiting Coalition is a group of 375 firms that lobbies for strong legal sanctions worldwide. Individual companies are also taking an aggressive stance against counterfeiting.

Retailing View 14.4 examines how retailing has given counterfeiters a great channel from which to cheat the public.

Gray-Market and Diverted Merchandise

A **gray-market good** possesses a valid U.S. registered trademark and is made by a foreign manufacturer but is imported into the United States without permission of the U.S. trademark owner. Gray-market merchandise is not counterfeit. This merchandise is the same quality and may actually be identical to merchandise brought into the country through normal channels.

Selling gray-market merchandise is legal in the United States. Recently, the Supreme Court ruled that American manufacturers cannot stop discount stores from buying U.S. products overseas and selling them domestically at reduced prices.[49]

Without realizing it, we see gray-market goods in the marketplace all the time. Some manufacturers of cars, jewelry, perfume, liquor, watches, cameras, crystal ware, ski equipment, tractors, baby powder, and batteries are all involved in gray marketing in the United States.

Here's an example of how the gray market for watches might work in the United States. To help create a prestigious image, to offset an unfavorable exchange rate, and to pad profit margins, Swiss watch manufacturers often charge a higher wholesale price in the United States than in Europe and other countries. A Swiss watchmaker such as Patek Philippe may sell 1,000 watches to a distributor in Egypt. But instead of shipping the watches to Egypt, the watchmaker sends the shipment to the free-trade zone in Panama. Gray Goods, Inc., in New York buys the entire shipment in Panama from the Egyptian distributor. It's then imported into the United States, where it's sold to a chain of discounters called Mel's Jewelry Stores. Mel can sell these watches at a significantly lower price than a traditional jewelry store can and still make an adequate profit margin.

Diverted merchandise is similar to gray-market merchandise except there need not be distribution across international boundaries. Suppose, for instance, fragrance manufacturer Givenchy grants an exclusive territory to all May Department Stores, including a Lord & Taylor store in Denver. A discount store in Denver purchases Givenchy products from a wholesale distributor in Las Vegas and sells it for 20 percent below the suggested retail price. The merchandise is diverted from its legitimate channel of distribution, and the wholesaler in this case would be referred to as a diverter.

Some discount store operators argue that customers benefit from the lack of restriction on gray-market and diverted goods because it lowers prices. Competition with retailers selling gray-market and diverted merchandise forces authorized dealers to cut their prices.

Traditional retailers, on the other hand, claim gray-market and diverted merchandise has a negative impact on the public. They believe that important service after the sale will be unavailable through retailers of gray-market or diverted goods. They also think that a less expensive gray-market or diverted product may hurt the trademark's image. Importantly, the gray-market product may be an out-of-date model or not work properly in a different country. For example, Philip Morris makes cartons of Marlboros in the United States earmarked for foreign markets where prices are lower. These cigarettes often carry warning labels that are different from the federally required surgeon general's message. Further, the packages and formulation may be different as well.[50]

Vendors wishing to avoid the gray-market problem have several remedies. First, they can require all of their retail and wholesale customers to sign a contract stipulating that they will not engage in gray marketing. If a retailer is found in violation of the agreement, the vendor will refuse to deal with it in the future. Another strategy is to produce different versions of products for different markets. For instance, a camera manufacturer could sell the same camera in the United States and the European Union but with different names and warranties. This strategy would not prevent the European product from being sold in the

United States. But distinctive packaging, design, instructions, and other features may dissuade its sale.

Exclusive Territories   Vendors often grant **exclusive geographic territories** to retailers so no other retailer in the territory can sell a particular brand. These territorial arrangements can benefit vendors by assuring them that "quality" retailers represent their products. In cases of limited supply, providing an exclusive territory to one retailer helps ensure that enough inventory can be carried to make a good presentation and offer the customer an adequate selection. If, for instance, the luxury Ferrari Automobile Company allowed its products to be distributed through all dealers that want to carry them, there wouldn't be enough Ferraris to go around, leading to customer confusion. Being granted exclusive territories helps retailers as well because it gives them a monopoly for the product—a strong incentive to push that vendor's products. They know there will be no competing retailers to cut prices so their profit margins are protected. The retailer with an exclusive territory has the incentive to carry more inventory; use extra advertising, personal selling, and sales promotions; provide special displays and display areas; and develop special services for customers.

The courts have tended to hold exclusive territories illegal when they restrict competition. Competition is restricted when other retailers have no access to similar products. For example, having exclusive Ferrari dealers wouldn't be a restraint of trade since other luxury cars are readily available to the public. On the other hand, if De Beers, the South African diamond cartel, granted exclusive territories to certain jewelry retailers, this would probably be seen as a restraint of trade because diamonds wouldn't be readily available through other sources.

> **Refact** Sporting goods manufacturer Nike signed an exclusive territorial agreement with Internet sporting goods and apparel retailer Fogdog Sports. Nike products (apparel, footwear, equipment, and accessories) were to be available on the www.fogdog.com site in return for a 12 percent equity stake in Fogdog and a seat on Fogdog's board of directors for the Nike chairman of the board. The deal stated that Nike agreed to not sell its product to any other pure Internet retailer for the six-month period.[51]

Exclusive Dealing Agreements   Exclusive dealing agreements occur when a manufacturer or wholesaler restricts a retailer into carrying only its products and nothing from competing vendors. The effect on competition determines these contracts' legality. For instance, suppose a retailer signs an agreement with Lee's to sell only its jeans. There's no real harm done to competition because other manufacturers have many alternative retail outlets, and Lee's market share isn't large enough to approach monopolistic levels.

On the other hand, in 1987, Hartz Mountain (which has a majority market share in the pet products market) was fined $1 million by a St. Louis federal court for attempting to monopolize the pet supplies market. The court ruled that Hartz had tried to draw retailers away from a wholesaler selling competing pet products.[52] The difference in the legal interpretations of these two cases is based on the relative impact on competition. Because Hartz Mountain has such a large market share, small competitors could be severely injured.

Tying Contracts   When a vendor and a retailer enter into an agreement that requires the retailer to take a product it doesn't necessarily desire (the "tied product") to ensure that it can buy a product it does desire (the "tying product"), a tying contract exists. Tying contracts are illegal if they may substantially lessen competition or tend to create a monopoly.

A vendor is entitled to create tying contracts to protect its goodwill and quality reputation. For instance, the Italian knitwear manufacturer Benetton may legally require its retail stores to purchase all their sweaters from Benetton since the legitimate purpose is to maintain the brand name's image. Alternatively, the

U.S. Court of Appeals for the District of Columbia held that no tying arrangement existed when Microsoft bundled its Internet browser, Internet Explorer, to the sale of its operating software, Windows 95, because the two programs were part of a single, "integrated" software product.[53]

Refusals to Deal The practice of refusing to deal (buy or sell to) can be viewed from both suppliers' and retailers' perspectives. Generally, both suppliers and retailers have the right to deal or refuse to deal with anyone they choose. But there are exceptions to this general rule when there's evidence of anticompetitive conduct.

A manufacturer may refuse to sell to a particular retailer, but it can't do so for the sole purpose of benefiting a competing retailer. Suppose Levi Strauss & Co. refuses to deal with any retailer ordering less than $10,000 worth of goods a year. The company argues that it's part of an effort to eliminate processes that aren't cost-effective. The courts would probably allow the situation in which Bob's Western Wear Store is cut from Levi's list of outlets because it can't make the minimum annual purchases. It would, however, be unlawful for a competitor of Bob's to pressure Levi into not selling to Bob, but from a practical perspective it's hard to prove such coercive influence.

In summary, anytime two parties interact, there's a potential for ethical and legal problems. Buyers face issues such as how much to charge a vendor for shelf space in their stores or whether they should accept a gift or favor from a vendor with "no strings attached." An eye toward fairness and the desire to maintain a strong relationship should dictate behavior in these areas. Retailers must also be concerned with the origin of their merchandise. Specifically, is it counterfeit or gray-market? Vendors encounter a different set of issues. In general, vendors need not worry about legal problems when selling to retailers so long as they sell whatever the retailers want, to whomever wants to buy, at the same price to all. But when vendors start making restrictions and exceptions, there may be legal violations.

SUMMARY This chapter examined issues surrounding vendor relations and purchasing merchandise. Simply put, retailers can't succeed without their vendors. To survive, they must be able to count on a predictable supply of merchandise at competitive prices and with sufficient promotional support.

Retailers can purchase either manufacturer's brands or private-label brands. Each type has its own relative advantages. Choosing brands and a branding strategy is an integral component of a firm's merchandise and assortment planning process.

A large percentage of the merchandise we buy is manufactured outside of the United States. The decision to buy from domestic manufacturers or source internationally is a complicated one. We examined the cost, managerial, and ethical issues surrounding global sourcing decisions.

Buyers and their merchandise managers have several opportunities to meet with vendors, view new merchandise, and place orders. They can visit their vendors at wholesale market centers such as New York, Paris, or Milan. Virtually every merchandise category has at least one annual trade show where retailers and vendors meet. Buyers often meet with vendors on their own turf—in the retail store or corporate offices. Finally, meetings with vendors are facilitated by resident buying offices. Market representatives of these resident buying offices facilitate merchandising purchases in foreign markets.

Retailers who can successfully team up with their vendors can achieve a sustainable competitive advantage. There needs to be more than just a promise to buy and sell on a regular basis. Strategic partnerships require trust, shared goals, strong communications, and a financial commitment. Disintermediation as a result of the growth of e-retailing is a potential threat to many strategic partnerships.

With thousands of annual transactions taking place between retailers and their vendors, there's plenty of room for ethical and legal problems. The issues of charging vendors for shelf space or taking bribes were discussed. We also examined problems associated with counterfeit and gray-market merchandise. We then looked at the issues (such as exclusive territories and tying contracts) that vendors face when selling to retailers. We concluded that care should be taken when making restrictions on which retailers they will sell to, what merchandise, how much, and at what price.

The chapter concludes with two appendixes. In Appendix 14A, we look at how a retailer should prepare for and conduct a negotiation with a vendor. Successful vendor relationships depend on planning for and being adept at negotiations. Appendix 14B reviews the purchase and payment terms given to retailers. Retailers face a plethora of discount/payment-date combinations. A working knowledge of these terms of purchase is essential for any person involved in merchandising. More importantly, the most advantageous application of the terms can make a significant impact on corporate profits.

KEY TERMS

bargain branding, *421*

buyback, *434*

chargeback, *435*

copycat branding, *421*

copyright, *436*

counterfeit merchandise, *436*

disintermediation, *433*

diverted merchandise, *438*

exclusive geographic territory, *439*

foreign trade zone, *425*

generic brand (house brand), *421*

gray-market good, *437*

intellectual property, *436*

lead time, *426*

licensed brand, *418*

manufacturer brand (national brand), *416*

maquiladoras, *425*

opportunity cost of capital, *426*

parallel branding, *422*

patent, *436*

premium branding, *422*

private-label brand (store brand), *419*

resident buying office, *429*

slotting allowance (slotting fee), *434*

stocklift (lift-out), *434*

tariff (duty), *425*

trade show (merchandise show, market week), *429*

trade dress, *421*

trademark, *436*

trust, *432*

DISCUSSION QUESTIONS AND PROBLEMS

1. Do retailers take advantage of their power positions by charging slotting fees, buybacks, and chargebacks?

2. Assume you have been hired to consult with The Gap on sourcing decisions for sportswear. What issues would you consider when deciding whether you should buy from Mexico or China, or find a source in the United States?

3. How would the decision to source outside the United States affect a retailer's need to carry safety stock?

4. Name several manufacturers that are involved in disintermediation. What do you expect to be the impact of disintermediation on their strategic partnerships with retailers?

5. What kinds of social courtesies or gifts (lunches, theater tickets, etc.) are appropriate and acceptable for buyers to accept from vendors?

6. Does your favorite clothing store have a strong private-brand strategy? Should it?

7. When setting goals for a negotiation session with a vendor, what issues should a buyer consider?

8. A $500 invoice is dated October 1, the merchandise arrives October 15, and the terms are 3/30, n/60 ROG.

   a. How many days does the retailer have to take advantage of the discount?

   b. What is the percentage of discount?

   c. How much is due November 10?

   d. What's the final date the retailer can pay the invoice without being considered late?

9. Suppose a warehouse club like Costco or Sam's are contemplating the purchase of some gray-market TV sets. What are the ramifications, both positive and negative, of such a purchase?

10. What factors should a buyer consider when deciding which vendors to develop a close relationship with?

SUGGESTED READINGS

Acuff, Frank L. *How to Negotiate Anything with Anyone, Anywhere around the World.* AMACOM, 1997.

Buzzell, Robert D., and Gwen Ortmeyer. "Channel Partnerships Streamline Distribution." *Sloan Management Review* 36, no. 3 (March 22, 1995), pp. 85–97.

Epprn, Gary, and Anath Iyer. "Backup Agreements in Fashion Buying—The Value of Upstream Flexibility." *Management Science* 43 (November 1997), pp. 1469–84.

Fisher, Roger, and William Ury. *Getting to Yes.* New York: Penguin, 1981.

Hulland, John S. "The Effects of Country-of-Brand and Brand Name on Product Evaluation and Consideration: A Cross-Country Comparison." *Journal of International Consumer Marketing*, January 1999, pp. 23–40.

Klein, Jill Gabrielle, Richard Ettenson, and Marlene D. Morris. "The Animosity Model of Foreign Product Purchase: An Empirical Test in the People's Republic of China." *Journal of Marketing*, January 1999, pp. 89+.

Li, Zhan G., and Rajiv P. Dant. "An Exploratory Study of Exclusive Dealing in Channel Relationships." *Journal of the Academy of Marketing Science* 25, no. 3 (1997), pp. 201–13.

Maltz, E., and R.K. Srivastava. "Managing Retailer–Supplier Partnerships with EDI: Evaluation and Implementation." *Long Range Planning* 30 (December 1997).

Quelch, John, and David Husling. "Brands vs. Private Labels: Fighting to Win." *Harvard Business Review* 74 (1996), pp. 99–111.

Richardson, Paul S., Arun K. Jain, and Alan S. Dick. "Household Store Brand Proneness: A Framework." *Journal of Retailing* 72, no. 2 (Summer 1996), pp. 159–86.

Yu, Haekyung, Ann Fairhurst, and Sharron Lennon. "Small Retail Stores' Buyers Response to Apparel Markets." *Journal of Small Business Management* 34 (October 1996), pp. 14–22.

APPENDIX 14A
Negotiating with Vendors

Negotiations are as basic to human nature as eating or sleeping.[54] A negotiation takes place any time two parties confer with each other to settle some matter. Negotiations take place between parents and their children about issues like allowances. People negotiate with their friends about what to do on the weekend.

Business negotiations occur almost daily. People negotiate for higher salaries, better offices, and bigger budgets. Negotiations are crucial in buyers' discussions with vendors.

No one should go into a negotiation without intensive planning. We first provide guidelines for planning negotiations with vendors. Then we discuss some tips for conducting the negotiation face-to-face.

Guidelines for Planning Negotiations with Vendors As a vehicle for describing how a buyer should prepare for and conduct a negotiation with a vendor, consider the hypothetical situation in which Carolyn Swigler, men's designer shirt buyer at Lord & Taylor, is preparing to meet with Dario Carnevale, the salesman from Tommy Hilfiger, in her office in New York. Swigler is ready to buy Tommy Hilfiger's spring line, but she has some merchandising problems that have yet to be resolved from last season. Let's go over seven general guidelines

for planning a negotiation session and seven for conducting a face-to-face negotiation session, all described in terms of Swigler's hypothetical situation.

KNOWLEDGE IS POWER! The more the buyer knows about the vendor,
the better his negotiating strategy will be.

Consider History Buyers need a sense of what has occurred between the retailer and the vendor in the past. Though Swigler and Carnevale have only met a
few times in the past, their companies have had a long, profitable relationship. A
sense of trust and mutual respect has been established, which may work to
Swigler's advantage in the upcoming meeting. An established vendor may be
more likely to take care of old problems and accept new demands if a long-term,
profitable relationship already exists.

Assess Where Things Are Today Although Tommy Hilfiger shirts have been
profitable for Lord & Taylor in the past, three patterns sold poorly last season.
Some vendors believe that once they've sold merchandise to the retailer, their responsibility ends. This is a short-term perspective, however. If the merchandise
doesn't sell, a good vendor, like Tommy Hilfiger, will arrange to share the risk of
loss. Swigler will ask Carnevale to let her return some merchandise. Or
Carnevale may provide markdown money—funds a vendor gives a retailer to
cover lost gross margin dollars due to markdowns and other merchandising issues—usually in the form of a credit to the Lord & Taylor account.

Set Goals Besides taking care of last season's leftover merchandise, the buyer
Swigler has set goals in six areas for the upcoming meeting: additional markup
opportunities, terms of purchase, transportation, delivery and exclusivity, communications, and advertising allowances.

Additional Markup Opportunities Vendors may have excess stock (manufacturers'
overruns) due to order cancelations, returned merchandise from retailers, or simply an overly optimistic sales forecast. To move this merchandise, vendors offer it
to retailers at lower than normal prices. Retailers can then make a higher than
normal gross margin and/or pass the savings on to the customer. Since Lord &
Taylor is noted as a fashion leader, it probably isn't interested in any excess inventory that Tommy Hilfiger has to offer. Off-price retailers such as T.J. Maxx
and Marshalls (both owned by TJX) or Internet retailer Bluefly.com specialize in
purchasing manufacturers' overruns. Another opportunity for additional
markups is with private-label merchandise, which we discussed earlier in this
chapter.

Terms of Purchase It's advantageous for buyers to negotiate for a long time period in which to pay for merchandise. Long terms of payment improve the firm's
cash flow position, lower its liabilities (accounts payable), and can cut its interest
expense if it's borrowing money from financial institutions to pay for its inventory. According to the Robinson-Patman Act, however, a vendor can't offer different terms of purchase or prices to different retailers unless the difference can
be cost-justified. But buyers would be remiss if they didn't ask for the best terms
of purchase available. (Terms of purchase are detailed in Appendix 14B to this
chapter.)

Transportation Transportation costs can be substantial, though this doesn't pose
a big problem with the Tommy Hilfiger shirts due to their high unit cost and
small size. Nonetheless, the question of who pays for shipping merchandise from

vendor to retailer can be a significant negotiating point. (Transportation issues are part of the terms of purchase discussed in this chapter's Appendix 14B.)

Delivery and Exclusivity   In retailing in general (and in fashion in particular), timely delivery is essential. Being the only retailer in a market to carry certain products helps a retailer hold a fashion lead and achieve a differential advantage. Swigler wants to be certain that her shipment of the new spring line arrives as early in the season as possible, and that some shirt patterns won't be sold to competing retailers.

Communications   Vendors and their representatives are excellent sources of market information. They generally know what is and isn't selling. Providing good, timely information about the market is an indispensable and inexpensive marketing research tool, so Swigler plans to spend at least part of the meeting talking to Carnevale about market trends.

Advertising Allowances   Retailers have the choice of advertising any product in the store. They can sometimes share the cost of advertising through a cooperative arrangement with vendors known as co-op advertising—a program undertaken by a vendor in which the vendor agrees to pay all or part of a pricing promotion. By giving retailers advertising money based on a percentage of purchases, vendors can better represent their product to consumers. (Chapter 16 describes cooperative advertising.) Under the Robinson-Patman Act, vendors are allowed to give advertising allowances on an equal basis—the same percentage to everyone—usually based on a percentage of the invoice cost. As a fashion leader, Lord & Taylor advertises heavily. Swigler would like Tommy Hilfiger to support a number of catalogs with a generous ad allowance.

Know the Vendor's Goals and Constraints   Negotiation can't succeed in the long run unless both parties believe they've won. By understanding what's important to Carnevale and Tommy Hilfiger, Swigler can plan for a successful negotiating session. Generally, vendors are interested in a continuous relationship, testing new items, communication, and a showcase.

A Continuous Relationship   Vendors want to make a long-term investment in their retailers. For seasonal merchandise like men's designer shirts, they have to plan their production in advance so it's important to Tommy Hilfiger that certain key retailers like Lord & Taylor will continue their support. Swigler plans to spend some time at the beginning of the meeting reviewing their mutually profitable past and assuring Carnevale that Lord & Taylor hopes to continue their relationship.

Testing New Items   There's no better way to test how well a new product will sell than to put it in a store. Retailers are often cautious with new items due to the risk of markdowns and the opportunity cost of not purchasing other, more successful merchandise. Yet vendors need their retailers to provide sales feedback for new items. Lord & Taylor has always been receptive to some of Tommy Hilfiger's more avant-garde styles. If these styles do well in certain Lord & Taylor stores, they'll likely succeed in similar stores around the country.

Communication   Just as Carnevale can provide market information to Swigler, she can provide sales information to him. Also, Swigler travels the world market. On one buying trip to England, she found an attractive scarf. She bought the scarf and gave it to Carnevale, who had it copied for a shirt. It was a big success!

Showcase   In certain urban centers—notably New York, Los Angeles, Dallas, London, Milan, and Paris—vendors use large stores to showcase their merchandise. For instance, many U.S. buyers go to market in New York. Most stop at Lord & Taylor to see what's new, what's selling, and how it's displayed. Thus Carnevale wants to make sure that Tommy Hilfiger is well represented at Lord & Taylor.

A good understanding of the legal, managerial, and financial issues that constrain a vendor will facilitate a productive negotiating session. For instance, Swigler should recognize from past experience that Tommy Hilfiger normally doesn't allow merchandise to be returned, but does provide markdown money. If Carnevale initially says that giving markdown money is against company policy, Swigler will have strong objective ammunition for her position.

Plan to Have at Least as Many Negotiators as the Vendor   There's power in numbers. Even if the vendor is more powerful, aggressive, or important in the marketplace, the retailer will have a psychological advantage at the negotiating table if the vendor is outnumbered. At the very least, the negotiating teams should be of equal number. Swigler plans to invite her merchandise manager into the discussion if Carnevale comes with his sales manager.

Choose a Good Place to Negotiate   Swigler may have an advantage in the upcoming meeting since it will be in her office. She'll have everything at her fingertips, such as information plus secretarial and supervisory assistance. From a psychological perspective, people generally feel more comfortable and confident in familiar surroundings. On the other hand, if the negotiation were to be in Carnevale's office Swigler would be able to learn a lot about Carnevale and his company. Further, Swigler might get more out of the negotiation if Carnevale feels comfortable.[55] In the end, the preferable location for a negotiation is a personal choice.

Be Aware of Real Deadlines   To illustrate the importance of deadlines, consider when labor strikes are settled. An agreement is often reached one minute before everyone walks out. There's always pressure to settle a negotiation at the last minute. Swigler recognizes that Carnevale must go back to his office with an order in hand since he has a quota to meet by the end of the month. She also knows that she must get markdown money or permission to return the unsold shirts by the end of the week or she won't have sufficient open-to-buy to cover the orders she wishes to place. Recognizing these deadlines will help Swigler come to a decisive closure in the upcoming negotiation.

Guidelines for Face-to-Face Negotiations   The most thoughtful plans can go astray if the negotiators fail to follow some important guidelines in the meeting. Here are seven tips for successful negotiations, including separating people from the problem, insisting on objective criteria, and inventing options for mutual gain.[56]

Separate People from the Problem   Suppose Swigler starts the meeting with "Carnevale, you know we've been friends for a long time. I have a personal favor to ask. Would you mind taking back $10,000 in shirts?" This personal plea puts Carnevale in an uncomfortable situation. Swigler's personal relationship with Carnevale isn't the issue here and shouldn't become part of the negotiation.

An equally detrimental scenario would be for Swigler to say, "Carnevale, your line is terrible. I can hardly give the stuff away. I want you to take back

$10,000 in shirts. After all, you're dealing with Lord & Taylor. If you don't take this junk back, you can forget about ever doing business with us again." This approach serves as a personal attack on Carnevale. Even if he had nothing to do with the shirts' design, Swigler is attacking his company. Reminding Carnevale that he's dealing with a large concern like Lord & Taylor is threatening and would probably further alienate him. Finally, threats usually don't work in negotiations; they put the other party on the defensive. Threats may actually cause negotiations to break down, in which case no one wins.

Conversely, if Carnevale takes a personal, aggressive, or threatening stance in the negotiations, what should Swigler do? Let him talk. If Swigler allows Carnevale to work through his aggression or anger, it will probably dissipate like a tropical storm going out to sea. Listen. Swigler may find that Carnevale's problem can be easily resolved. Finally, apologize if necessary. Even if Swigler doesn't believe she or Lord & Taylor did anything to cause Carnevale's anger, an apology that doesn't admit to any personal or corporate responsibility will probably calm him down.

Insist on Objective Criteria   The best way to separate people from the problem is to insist on objective criteria. Swigler must know exactly how many shirts need to be returned to Tommy Hilfiger or how much markdown money is necessary to maintain her gross margin.

If Carnevale argues from an emotional perspective, Swigler should stick to the numbers. For instance, suppose that after Swigler presents her position, Carnevale says that he'll get into trouble if he takes back the merchandise or provides markdown money. With the knowledge that Tommy Hilfiger has provided relief in similar situations in the past, Swigler should ask what Tommy Hilfiger's policy is regarding customer overstock problems. She should also show Carnevale a summary of Lord & Taylor's buying activity with Tommy Hilfiger over the past few seasons. Using this approach, Carnevale is forced to acknowledge that providing assistance on this overstock situation—especially if it has been done in the past—is a small price to pay for a long-term profitable relationship.

Invent Options for Mutual Gain   Inventing multiple options is part of the planning process, but knowing when and how much to give (or give up) requires quick thinking at the bargaining table.

Consider Swigler's overstock problem. Her objective is to get the merchandise out of her inventory without significantly hurting her gross margin. Carnevale's objective is to maintain a healthy yet profitable relationship with Lord & Taylor. Thus Swigler must invent options that could satisfy both parties. Her options are

- Sell the shirts to an off-price retailer at 10 cents on the retail dollar.
- Have Carnevale take back the shirts.
- Get Tommy Hilfiger to provide markdown money and put the shirts on sale.
- Return some of the shirts and get markdown money for the rest.

Clearly, selling the shirts to an off-price retailer would cause Swigler to take a loss. But from Carnevale's perspective, taking back the merchandise may be unacceptable because the styles are from last season and some shirts may be shopworn. Swigler could, however, present this option first with the knowledge that it will probably be rejected. Then she could ask for markdown money. Carnevale would believe he got off easy, and Swigler would have her problem solved.

In developing her plan for the meeting, Swigler followed some important rules of negotiation. She identified viable options for both parties. Then she determined which options would satisfy both parties' objectives. When presenting the options, she held back the one she believed would be most acceptable to Carnevale so he would think he was a winner.

Let Them Do the Talking   There's a natural tendency for one person to continue to talk if the other person involved in the conversation doesn't respond. If used properly, this phenomenon can work to the negotiator's advantage. Suppose Swigler asks Carnevale for special financial support on Lord & Taylor's Christmas catalog. Carnevale begins with a qualified no and cites all the reasons why he can't cooperate. But Swigler doesn't say a word. Although Carnevale appears nervous, he continues to talk. Eventually, he comes around to a yes. In negotiations, those who break the silence first, lose!

Know How Far to Go   There's a fine line between negotiating too hard and walking away from the table with less than necessary. If Swigler overnegotiates by getting the markdown money, better terms of purchase, and a strong advertising allowance, the management of Tommy Hilfiger may decide that other retailers are more worthy of early deliveries and the best styles. Carnevale may not be afraid to say no if Swigler is pushing him beyond a legal, moral, profitable relationship.

Don't Burn Bridges   Even if Swigler gets few additional concessions from Carnevale, she shouldn't be abusive or resort to threats. Professionally, Lord & Taylor may not wish to stop doing business with Tommy Hilfiger on the basis of this one encounter. From a personal perspective, the world of retailing is relatively small. Swigler and Carnevale may meet at the negotiating table again—both working for different companies. Neither can afford to be known in the trade as being unfair, rude, or worse.

Don't Assume   Many issues are raised and resolved in any negotiating session. To be certain there are no misunderstandings, participants should orally review the outcomes at the end of the session. Swigler and Carnevale should both summarize the session in writing as soon as possible after the meeting.

APPENDIX **14B**

Terms of Purchase

Now that we have chosen our merchandise, developed relationships with our suppliers, and considered the legal ramifications of our actions, we must negotiate the terms of purchase. There are two sides to the pricing equation. In Chapter 15 ("Pricing"), we'll examine the price at which merchandise is sold. In this section, we look at the price at which merchandise is purchased. When determining price, vendors must examine the different types of discounts they may offer. These discounts—referred to as the terms of purchase—include trade or functional discounts, chain discounts, quantity discounts, seasonal discounts, cash discounts, anticipation discounts, and shipping terms and conditions.

Trade Discounts (Functional Discounts)   Trade or functional discounts are reductions in a manufacturer's suggested retail price granted to wholesalers or retailers. For instance, suppose a TV's suggested retail price is $100. If the manufacturer sells to a wholesaler, the price is 50 percent off the suggested retail price, or $50. Alternatively, if the set is bought by the retailer, the cost is 33.3 percent off the suggested retail price, or $66.67.

Many issues come to mind when thinking about this rather quaint tradition in pricing. First, why is it called a trade or functional discount? It's because different prices are offered to different lines of trade (i.e., wholesalers versus retailers). It's also known as a functional discount since retailers and wholesalers often perform different functions in the channel of distribution.

Under the cost justification defense of the Robinson-Patman Act, vendors can offer different prices to wholesalers and retailers for the same merchandise and quantity if they can show that costs of manufacture, sale, or delivery are different. The costs of manufacture wouldn't often be different, but selling and delivery could be more expensive to retailers than to wholesalers. Because there are multiple retail outlets within a chain, a manufacturer's sales staff may expend more effort when selling to retailers than to wholesalers. The manufacturer may also incur larger transportation expenses due to multiple delivery points and smaller shipments to retailers.

In recent years, however, most large retailers have convinced some vendors to give them the lowest prices offered. These retailers argue that they perform all the functions that would otherwise be performed by an independent wholesaler, such as transportation from distribution centers to stores, price marking, and inventory management. Thus, they say, they should receive the lowest price.

Another question is, why would the manufacturer discount a suggested retail price rather than simply quoting a net cost? It's because retailers generally think of their merchandise in terms of retail rather than cost. By quoting prices as discounted suggested retail prices, the manufacturer's practice remains consistent with retailing thought. Further, by providing suggested retail prices, the manufacturer has some subtle influence on the retail price. Note, however, that manufacturers can influence retailers to maintain suggested retail prices only under certain circumstances. (See "Vertical Price Fixing" in Chapter 15.)

Chain Discounts   In some lines of trade—such as housewares and hardware—chain discounts are used. A chain discount is a number of different discounts taken sequentially from the suggested retail price. An example is 50–10–5 (spoken "fifty, ten, and five"). Using the previous example, if the TV set has a suggested retail price of $100, then the price is calculated as follows:

1. A 50 percent reduction is taken:

    $100 × .5 = $50.

2. An additional 10 percent reduction from the remaining $50 is taken:

    $50 – ($50 × .1) = $50 – $5 = $45.

3. A 5 percent discount from the remaining $45 is taken:

    $45 – ($45 × .05) = $45 – $2.25 = $42.75.

So, with a 50–10–5 chain discount on a $100 suggested retail item, the retailer pays $42.75. But note that the discounts can't be added! A 50–10–5 discount isn't the same as a 65 percent discount: $100 – (100 × .65) = $35.

Why do vendors and retailers use such an awkward pricing scheme? Simply because it's traditional. In the precalculator era, it was easier for people to calculate chain discount prices in their heads without having to resort to tedious computations.

Quantity Discounts   Quantity discounts are of two types: cumulative and noncumulative. Retailers earn cumulative quantity discounts by purchasing certain quantities over a specified period of time. For instance, a vendor may grant an additional discount to a retailer that purchases $100,000 worth of merchandise in one year. These discounts have the same effect as a year-end rebate. Vendors grant cumulative quantity discounts as an incentive to buy more merchandise and to encourage retailer loyalty. Under the Robinson-Patman Act, however, it's hard for a vendor to justify lower costs for higher quantities on a cumulative basis.[57] To justify cumulative quantity discounts, a vendor could show that having retailers commit to certain levels of purchases in advance allows the vendor to plan production more efficiently and thus cut costs. Cumulative quantity discounts could be easily justified in the garment industry, for instance, since garment manufacturers must commit to their cloth suppliers months in advance.

Noncumulative quantity discounts are offered to retailers as an incentive to purchase more merchandise on a single order. Larger, less frequent orders may save vendors order processing, sales, and transportation expenses. These expenses are often found in retailing and are more easily cost-justified than cumulative quantity discounts.[58]

Exhibit 14–4 presents a sample price list that combines trade/functional, chain, and noncumulative quantity discounts for an appliance manufacturer. The headings "Price to Wholesaler" and "Price to Retailer" illustrate trade/functional discounts. The "40–5%," "50–10," and "50–10–5" under "Price to Wholesaler, Discount" represent different chain discounts. Finally, the first column, "Quantity per Order," illustrates noncumulative quantity discounts.

Examine the columns under "Price to Retailer." At which price should the retailer buy? At first glance, the lowest price appears to be $54. But the lowest price isn't always the most profitable. If the dealer purchases 26 or more TV sets all at once, it may have more than a year's supply. Inventory turnover and the cost of carrying the inventory would be unsatisfactory. The merchandise may become shopworn, and the large quantity might even require more space than is available.[59]

Seasonal Discounts   A seasonal discount is an additional discount offered as an incentive to retailers to order merchandise in advance of the normal buying season. For instance, Black & Decker garden tools may be offered to retailers at a

---

EXHIBIT **14–4**

A Sample Price List

QUANTITY PER ORDER	PRICE TO WHOLESALER		PRICE TO RETAILER	
	DISCOUNT	PRICE	DISCOUNT	PRICE
1–10	40–5%	$57*	30%	$70
11–25	50–10	45	40	60
26+	50–10–5	42.75	40–10	54

*Based on a $100 suggested retail price

special price in January. Black & Decker can more easily plan its production schedules and lower its finished goods inventory if it can ship early in the season. Retailers, on the other hand, must consider the benefits of a larger gross margin from the discount versus the additional cost of carrying the inventory for a longer period of time.[60]

Cash Discounts   A cash discount is a reduction in the invoice cost for paying the invoice prior to the end of the discount period. It's applied after the functional/trade, chain, quantity, and seasonal discounts. An example is 1/30, n/60 (spoken as "one, thirty, net sixty"). This means the retailer can take a 1 percent discount if it pays on or before the 30th day after the date of invoice. Or the full invoice amount is due 60 days after the date of invoice.

Thus there are three components of a cash discount: the percentage of the discount, the number of days in which the discount can be taken, and the net credit period (when the full amount of the invoice is due). For example, a typical cash discount is 1/30, n/60. This means that if the invoice is dated on November 1, the retailer has 30 days (until December 1) to take the 1 percent discount. The full amount is due 60 days after the invoice date, on January 1. (If retailers really counted days, the full amount would be due on December 31 since there are 31 days in December. But retailers usually don't pay that much attention to the number of days in a month for the purpose of taking cash discounts.)

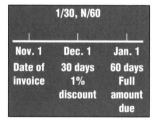

There are a number of variations on the basic cash discount format known as dating. The term *dating* refers to the dates on which discounts can be taken and full amounts are due in a cash discount pricing policy. Here are four examples of common forms of dating.

Receipt of Goods (ROG) Dating   Using ROG dating, the cash discount period starts on the day the merchandise is received. If the merchandise is shipped and invoiced on November 1, but doesn't arrive until November 15, using dating of 1/30, n/60, ROG, the cash discount can be taken until December 15, and the full amount is due January 15.

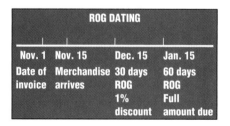

End-of-Month (EOM) Dating In EOM dating, the discount period starts at the end of the month in which the invoice is dated (except when the invoice is dated the 25th or later—as we'll discuss shortly). As in the previous example, if merchandise is invoiced on November 1, using dating of 1/30, n/60, EOM, the cash discount can be taken until January 1, and the full amount is due February 1. The retailer can pay 30 days later than the same terms without the EOM designation.

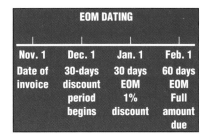

EOM Dating, Grace Period A grace period is often given when an invoice with EOM dating is dated after the 25th of the month. The vendor starts counting on the first of the next month. If the merchandise is invoiced on October 25, using the same dating of 1/30, n/60, EOM, the cash discount can still be taken until January 1, and the full amount is due February 1. This time the retailer gets 36 days longer to pay than without the EOM designation! So if the retailer wanted to maximize the length of time to pay for the merchandise and still take the cash discount, the merchandise would be ordered so that it would be invoiced as close to the 25th of the month as possible.

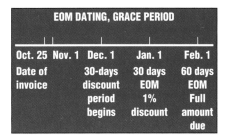

Extra Dating With extra dating, the retailer receives an extra amount of time to pay the invoice and still take the cash discount. Assume again that the merchandise is invoiced on November 1. Using dating of 1/30, n/60, EOM, 60 days extra (also written 60X or 60 ex.), the cash discount could be taken until March 1, with the net amount due April 1. That is, the discount period starts December 1, due to the EOM designation. The buyer gets 30 days for the regular discount period, plus an additional 60 days.

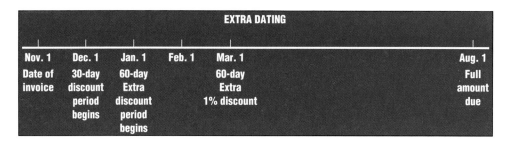

The rationale for offering extra dating is similar to that for the seasonal discount. The vendor may need to give the retailer an additional incentive to purchase risky or seasonal merchandise. Instead of giving the retailer a lower price (as is the case with the seasonal discount), the vendor grants the retailer a longer time in which to pay.

Anticipation Discounts   Under the previously discussed dating policies, a retailer has no incentive to pay earlier than the last day of the discount period. An anticipation discount provides this incentive. It's a discount offered in addition to the cash discount or dating if an invoice is paid before the end of the cash discount period. Let's say the dating is 1/30, n/60, EOM, with anticipation of 18 percent per year, and the invoice is dated November 1, the 30-day discount period ends at the end of December, but the retailer pays on December 1, 30 days earlier. Let's calculate the net cost on a $100 item.

Cash discount = $100 × .01 = $1
Invoice less discount = $100 − $1 = $99

Since the anticipation is 18 percent a year, but the retailer is paying 30 days early, we calculate the anticipation as

Anticipation = $99 × .18 × (30 days early ÷ 360 days per year) = $1.49
Net amount = $99.00 − $1.49 = $97.51

The retailer can earn an extra $2.49 (or $100 − $97.51) by paying early, taking the cash discount, and taking the anticipation.

Shipping Terms and Conditions   The last question in any terms of purchase policy is who (the retailer or the vendor) has responsibility for the different aspects of shipping the merchandise. Two basic issues must be agreed upon when designating the shipping terms and conditions: Who pays the freight charges, and who owns the merchandise while it's in transit?

Transportation costs for shipping merchandise from vendor to retailer can be substantial. If the retailer incurs this expense, it increases the cost of the merchandise.

The party owning the merchandise in transit is responsible for filing a claim with the transportation company in case of lost or damaged merchandise. This is a time-consuming, potentially expensive process. The party filing the claim may have to wait months before it's reimbursed for the loss or damage. Also, the party

EXHIBIT 14–5

Alternative Shipping
Terms and
Conditions

	PAYS FREIGHT CHARGES	OWNS MERCHANDISE IN TRANSIT AND FILES CLAIMS (IF ANY)
FOB origin, freight collect	Retailer	Retailer
FOB origin, freight prepaid	Supplier	Retailer
FOB destination, freight collect	Retailer	Supplier
FOB destination, freight prepaid	Supplier	Supplier

owning the merchandise while in transit may be responsible for paying insurance that might be needed above the liability of the transportation company to cover merchandise lost or damaged in transit.

Many forms of shipping terms and conditions are used. Exhibit 14–5 outlines the most common ones. The designation *freight prepaid* means freight is paid by the vendor; *freight collect* means the retailer pays the freight. The term *FOB (free on board) origin* means ownership of the merchandise changes hands at the location where the shipment originates. When the ownership changes hands, so does responsibility for filing claims and insurance in case of lost or damaged merchandise. Thus FOB origin is beneficial to the vendor. The term *origin* is often substituted for plant or factory. *FOB destination* means ownership of the merchandise changes hands at the store. So the term *destination* is often substituted for *store* or *retailer.*

Diane Paccione
Vice-President/GMM
Sears

MY RETAIL CAREER STARTED when I worked for Bloomingdale's while I was going to school at Queens College in New York City. After graduating with a BA in Spanish, I took a job as an assistant buyer for Bloomingdale's. Then I went to work for May Department Stores as an intimate apparel buyer and worked my way up to Divisional Vice President. I joined Sears' merchandising group in 1996 to help implement our strategic repositioning that places more emphasis on fashionable women's apparel. My group at Sears includes 40 buyers and assistant buyers and is responsible for $1.6 billion in merchandising sales. • Pricing is really important in merchandise management. If you set prices too high, the merchandise won't sell and if you set them too low you won't meet your margin goals. There are some magic price points for our target market for sportswear, like $19.95 for tops (blouses) or bottoms (pants and skirts). But shoppers today are looking for good value. We can set higher prices for merchandise that offers value. For example, our customers will pay $39.95 for a stylish, fully-lined, linen jacket. The challenge for our buyers is to find merchandise that can be priced to offer a good value and still meet our markup plan. • When I was a buyer, it was very gratifying for me to see the sales generated by the merchandise I bought. Each day I looked forward to turning on my computer and seeing how the merchandise I bought was selling. Sometimes, fortunately not too often, I made some poor decisions and had to markdown merchandise to clear it out of our stores so I could bring in new merchandise. But the nice thing for me is that it was my responsibility. It was very exciting and challenging. Something new was happening every day. It felt like I was an entrepreneur in control of my own destiny. If I met my goals, I got rewards, and it was my fault if I fell short. As a Vice-President, I still have that excitement and sense of ownership for my merchandise categories. The numbers are just bigger.

15

Pricing

QUESTIONS

- Why do some retailers have frequent sales while others attempt to maintain an everyday low price strategy?

- How is the Internet changing the way retailers price their merchandise?

- How do retailers set retail prices?

- Why are markdowns taken, and what are some guidelines for taking them?

- Under what circumstances can retailers' pricing practices get them into legal difficulties?

TODAY'S CUSTOMERS ARE looking for a good value in what they purchase. To some people, a good value means a low price. Many types of consumers have become much more price-sensitive. Others are willing to pay extra as long as they believe they're getting their money's worth in terms of product quality or service.

The growth of online Internet sales has complicated the pricing equation. Search engines like www.mysimon.com help customers find the lowest price in a particular product category. Other customers have turned to Internet auctions such as ebay.com and sothebys.amazon.com to find everything from computers to vintage Barbie dolls. Unlike the auctions, where the highest bidder takes the prize, customers seeking airline tickets, hotels, and other products and services can bid what they want to pay at online services like Priceline.com.

Retailers have responded to their customers' needs with retail formats that emphasize low prices as a means of creating a differential advantage. National discount store chains that offer everyday low prices (EDLP), such as Wal-Mart, dominate many markets in many product categories. A close competitor in the price-oriented market is the membership-only warehouse club, such as Sam's Warehouse Club and Costco. Another retail format is the off-price retailer (e.g., T. J. Maxx, Marshalls, and Bluefly.com), which purchases closeout and end-of-season merchandise at lower-than-normal prices and passes the savings on to the customer. (Chapters 2 and 4 describe these stores and trends.)

Some of the more mature retailing institutions have come to grips with these new forms of price competition in various ways. Dayton Hudson, for example,

Wal-Mart's Everyday Low Pricing (EDLP) strategy has helped make them the market leader in every market they enter, and the largest retailer in the world.

has expanded beyond its traditional department store boundaries to offer discounting (Target) and heavy price promotion (Mervyn's). Other retailers, from department stores to supermarkets, have taken on more of a price promotion orientation. Finally, many retailers—notably Dillard's and Nordstrom—have successfully maintained their market appeal by offering customers high-quality merchandise and service without attempting to offer the lowest prices on a particular product category.

In the middle of this price competition among national giants are the smaller retailers. Typically unable to purchase in large quantities to receive lower prices like their larger competitors, "ma-and-pa" retailers have either learned to use other strategies to compete or gone out of business. For instance, to compete with Wal-Mart's low prices, small retailers have developed niche strategies by providing a broader assortment of merchandise within a given product category and better service. Wal-Mart may have the lowest average price on the few water skis that it carries. A successful sporting goods specialty store, however, might have a larger assortment than Wal-Mart and be willing to special-order merchandise so that its customers could get exactly the water skis they're looking for. It could also give advice on the product itself as well as lessons.

This chapter begins by comparing everyday low pricing with high/low pricing. In addition, we describe several other pricing practices that retailers use to get a competitive edge. Then we explore two complementary methods of setting retail prices: cost-oriented and demand-oriented approaches. We conclude this chapter with a discussion of important legal issues involved in making price decisions.

PRICING STRATEGIES AND PRACTICES

Retailers have made the pricing problem interesting by adding various nuances to the basic process of adding a markup to the cost of merchandise. In today's retail market, two opposing pricing strategies prevail: everyday low pricing and high/low pricing.[1]

Everyday Low Pricing (EDLP)

Many retailers have adopted an **everyday low pricing (EDLP) strategy**. This strategy stresses continuity of retail prices at a level somewhere between the regular nonsale price and the deep discount sale price of the retailer's competitors. The term *everyday low pricing* is therefore somewhat of a misnomer. Low doesn't necessarily mean lowest. Although retailers using EDLP strive for low prices, they aren't always the lowest price in the market. At any given time, a sale price at a competing store or a special purchase at a wholesale club store may be the lowest price. A more accurate description of this strategy is therefore everyday stable prices because the prices don't have significant fluctuations. Several of the biggest U.S. retailers—Home Depot, Wal-Mart, Staples, and Amazon.com—have adopted EDLP.

Since it is difficult to always have the lowest prices, some retailers have adopted a **low price guarantee policy** in which they guarantee that they will have the lowest possible price for a product or a group of products. The guarantee usually promises to match or better any lower price found in the local market. The promise normally includes a provision to refund the difference between the seller's offer price and the lower price. Sun Television & Appliances in Ohio takes its low price guarantee policy one step further. If somebody beats Sun's price within 30 days of purchase, the customer automatically gets a check in the mail, along with a letter from the store that says something like, "We noticed that two weeks ago you bought a TV in our store for $3.12 more than Sears' price that week, and here is the difference." The customer doesn't lift a finger.[2]

High/Low Pricing

In a **high/low pricing strategy,** retailers offer prices that are sometimes above their competition's EDLP, but they use advertising to promote frequent sales. Like EDLP, the use of high/low strategies has become more intense in recent years. In the past, fashion retailers would mark down merchandise at the end of a season; grocery and drugstores would only have sales when their vendors offered them special prices or when they were overstocked. Today, many retailers respond to increased competition and a more value-conscious customer by promoting more frequent sales.

Deciding Which Strategy Is Best

An EDLP has five relative benefits in relation to high/low.

- *Reduced price wars.* Many customers are skeptical about initial retail prices. They have become conditioned to buying only on sale—the main characteristic of a high/low pricing strategy. A successful EDLP strategy enables retailers to withdraw from highly competitive price wars with competitors. Once customers realize that prices are fair, they'll buy more each time and buy more frequently.
- *Reduced advertising.* The stable prices caused by EDLP limit the need for weekly sale advertising used in the high/low strategy. Instead, retailers can focus on more image-oriented messages. Also, catalogs don't become obsolete as quickly since prices don't change as often.
- *Improved customer service.* Without sale-stimulated throngs of people, salespeople can spend more time with customers. Retailers that participate in high/low pricing can offer high levels of customer service during sales, but only if they hire additional salespeople during the sales.
- *Reduced stockouts and improved inventory management.* An EDLP reduces the large variations in demand caused by frequent sales with large markdowns. As a result, retailers can manage their inventory with more certainty. Fewer stockouts mean more satisfied customers, higher sales, and fewer rain checks. (**Rain checks** are given to customers when merchandise is out of stock; they're written promises to sell customers merchandise at the sale price when the merchandise arrives.) In addition, a more predictable customer demand pattern enables the retailer to improve inventory turnover by reducing the average inventory needed for special promotions and backup stock. (**Backup stock** is inventory used to guard against going out of stock when demand exceeds forecasts or when merchandise is delayed; see Chapter 12.)
- *Increased profit margins.* Even though prices are generally lower with EDLP, overall profit margins can increase since merchandise is no longer sold at large reductions as it is using a high/low strategy. Prices change much less often with EDLP. This lowers costs of (1) making price changes and (2) mistakenly charging customers sale prices on merchandise that's no longer on sale.

But EDLP policy isn't for every retailer. A high/low strategy has five relative strengths too.

- *The same merchandise appeals to multiple markets.* When fashion merchandise first hits the store, it's offered at its highest price. Fashion leaders, those who are less sensitive to price, and hard-to-fit customers often buy as soon as the merchandise is available. As the season progresses and markdowns are taken, more people enter the market. Finally, hard-core bargain hunters enter the market for the end-of-season deep-discount sales like the Neiman Marcus Last Call Sale at the end of each season—25 percent off merchandise that has already been marked down 33 to 50 percent. Grocery and drugstore customers react to high/low prices in a similar manner. Some customers pay little attention to the prices they pay, while others will wait for merchandise to go on sale and stockpile for future use.

- *It creates excitement.* A "get them while they last" atmosphere often occurs during a sale. Sales draw crowds, and crowds create excitement. Some retailers augment low prices and advertising with special in-store activities like product demonstrations, giveaways, celebrity appearances, and very-short–term special prices that last only a few minutes.

- *It moves merchandise.* All merchandise will eventually sell—the question is, at what price? Frequent sales enable retailers to move the merchandise, even though profits erode.

- *Emphasis is on quality or service.* A high initial price sends a signal to customers that the merchandise is high quality and/or excellent service is provided. When merchandise goes on sale, customers still use the original (or reference) price to gauge quality. An EDLP policy may send the wrong signal to customers. They may assume that since prices are low, quality or services may suffer.

- *It's hard to maintain EDLP.* EDLP is difficult for most retailers. Those who promote an EDLP policy must, in fact, have low prices on merchandise that customers can compare with that of the competition, such as national brands at a department store or commodity products, such as milk or sugar in a supermarket. Merchandise must be purchased frequently since customers are aware of these products' prices. Given these constraints, it's generally hard for certain types of retailers such as fashion or small retailers to implement an EDLP strategy.

Retailers using EDLP are eventually doomed if their prices are higher than competitors' but they still advertise EDLP. Home Depot, Wal-Mart, and others have succeeded in the long run by consistently offering everyday low prices.

Guidelines for EDLP and High/Low Pricing Strategies

Retailing is always in a state of flux. Retailers who've pioneered an everyday low pricing strategy (like Wal-Mart and Home Depot) are using frequent promotions, while retailers engaged primarily in a high/low strategy are attempting to stabilize their wild price fluctuations with more everyday low prices. Retailing View 15.1 tells how Dollar General has elevated EDLP to a higher plane.

INTERNET EXERCISE   Go to the websites for Bloomingdale's (www.bloomingdales.com) and Dillard's Department Stores (www.dillards.com). Which department store chain is using an everyday low pricing strategy and which is using a high/low strategy? How can you tell?

THE SUCCESS OF DOLLAR GENERAL according to CEO Cal Turner Jr., grandson of the founder, is simple. Based on strong religious values, Turner believes that people want to be a part of an organization that makes a difference and that values them. "There's a real ministry when you're dedicated to selling toilet paper and bleach cheaper than anybody in the business," Turner said.

Dollar General shares its profits with associates at all levels and goes beyond offering financially strapped consumers value-priced products. Efforts such as Dollar General's literacy referral program and learning center work programs at inner-city stores have made a real difference in customers' lives.

The predecessor to the first Dollar General store opened in 1939. Today there are over 3,000 stores in 24 states with sales in fiscal 1999 of $3.2 billion. Stores are located in small communities of less than 25,000 population and in urban areas with low-income demographics.

Understanding the needs of Dollar General's core customer is key to comprehending what makes the concept work.

Forty-nine percent of Dollar General customers have a gross household income of less than $20,000 and they "understand true everyday low price." Therefore, supplying consumables and apparel basics at low prices is paramount.

In 1998, Dollar General shifted its assortment to roughly 18 percent soft lines and 82 percent hard lines. It changed its apparel offerings to what Turner calls "consumable basics" (such as khakis, jeans, T-shirts, socks, and underwear) and culled more fashion-oriented items.

Pricing is also simple. "We'll clothe you from the waist up for 5 bucks and from the waist down for 10 bucks," he said. Core merchandise price points range from four for $1 up to $20. Noncore items go as high as $35.

Source: Debbie Howell, "The Right Reverend of EDLP," *Discount Store News*, May 24, 1999; and Jennifer Negley, "Taking Value to the Extreme," *Discount Store News*, April 19, 1999. Reprinted by permission from *Discount Store News*, April and May 1999. Copyright Lebhar-Friedman, Inc. 425 Park Avenue, New York, NY 10022.

We offer guidelines for how to deal with this basic pricing strategy.[3] First, EDLP should not be used for all product categories. Brands that enjoy high consumer loyalty and have a high market share in a category with relatively few players are likely to benefit from EDLP. Generally, it's hard for a brand that already has a relatively high market share to increase its share through promotions. For example, the profitability in the diaper category—where Procter & Gamble's Pampers and Luvs, along with Kimberly-Clark's Huggies, account for about 75 percent of total sales—should benefit from EDLP. People are more likely to respond to high levels of promotion in a product category like shampoos with lots of highly competitive products. Thus, retailers can adopt EDLP for some product categories and use price to promote others.

Second, some retailers have developed strategies to wean customers off high/low strategies.[4] Dayton Hudson Corp., for instance, has reduced the number of sales "events" at its department stores. Kmart has reduced the number of items featured in its newspaper sales circulars. Ann Taylor and others are trying to encourage customers to buy at full price by displaying fewer clothes. They assume that if customers believe the item is scarce, they are more likely to buy now (at full price) rather than take the chance of waiting for it to go on sale.

Third, those retailers who have embraced an EDLP strategy must convince their customers that they do, in fact, have low prices, even if they don't have the lowest price on every item. For instance, you may be able to find items that are lower priced than those at Wal-Mart, but the chain's loyal customers probably won't believe you. Promotions can play an important role in creating a perception of EDLP. For instance, Daffy's is an off-price clothing retailer that thrives on no advertised discount or sale, only an increasing perception that it's a great place to shop every day. (See the accompanying ad on the next page.)

Finally, retailers must recognize that they generally can't avoid sales altogether. Sure, if they don't buy enough merchandise or buy a narrow assortment, they can avoid sales. Unfortunately, they'll also pass up the chance to satisfy more customers by doing so. It's a tough trade-off.

Although retailers' basic pricing strategies lie along a continuum from everyday low pricing to high/low strategies, they use other practices too—coupons, rebates, leader pricing, price bundling, multiple-unit pricing, price lining, and odd pricing—in conjunction with their basic strategy. But before we look at these practices, let's see how the Internet has complicated retailers' pricing equation.

Pricing and the Internet

The Internet is a panacea for comparison shoppers who can click around looking for great prices or let Shopper.com, botspot.com, mysimon.com, bottomdollar.com, 20-20consumer.com, or shopping.yahoo.com find the lowest price for a specific item. But setting pricing strategy on the Internet can be hit-or-miss, with relatively few "correct" answers.

In the mid-1990s, when e-retailing was in its infancy, Internet retailers used low prices to attract customers and make them loyal. Clearly, price has always been the most vulnerable component of retail strategy for competition to meet. Many startup e-retail firms invested millions in this low-margin pricing strategy, never making a profit.

Today, many more customers are buying online. At the same time, the borders between Internet-only retailers and the traditional world of bricks-and-mortar stores have blurred. More traditional retailers have a strong Internet presence. Also, some manufacturers are bypassing their retailer partners and selling directly to the consumer. (See "Disintermediation" in Chapter 14.)

No longer the domain of wealthy collectors of art and other luxury goods, Internet auctions have gone from nowhere in the mid-1990s to big business today. The birth of retail phenomenon eBay began with a Pez obsession. At dinner one night in the spring of 1995, the founders talked about an online destination where they and other Pez lovers could discuss and trade their Plasticine candy dispensers. The rest is history. eBay, short for "electronic Bay," an homage to the company's California Bay Area location, has revolutionized the way many Web surfers spend their time and money.[5] It's also spawned a host of copycat trading/auction sites from such companies as Yahoo and

Refact In June 1999, at eBay, 2,272,518 items were up for sale in 1,627 categories. During the same period, eBay was logging more than 1.5 billion monthly page views. Rosie O'Donnell recently auctioned off a special Star Wars desk signed by George Lucas for over $28,000 on eBay.[6]

IN 1997 CONGRESS PASSED a three-year moratorium on Internet taxation and created an Advisory Commission on Electronic Commerce to come up with recommendations on handling tax issues associated with electronic commerce. The commission is to decide whether e-retailing should be taxed and, if so, how.

Many state, county, and local jurisdictions, fearful that the growth of e-retailing will decrease their tax revenues, argue that service to citizens will be reduced due to budget shortfalls.

Arguments against the tax, however, abound. First, some say that mail order firms don't charge sales tax unless the company has a "nexus" or a physical presence in a state. If a customer in Florida buys something from a catalog store in Maine, then the consumer generally doesn't have to pay taxes on the purchase. Why, then, should Internet operators have to collect taxes on sales from customers outside their states of operation?

Second, a corollary issue is that states shouldn't be allowed to tax other states' residents. To do so would result in taxation without representation. Of course, they could tax residents in the areas in which they operate, just like catalogs do.

Third, Internet purchases could be taxed in the area in which the purchaser resides. But this would force all e-retailers to be concerned about 30,000 or so sometimes overlapping jurisdictions. Small Internet businesses and mom-and-pop sales sites would be particularly affected by schemes of taxation that would require them to track transactions, ascertain the appropriate jurisdiction for each transaction, sift through thousands of pages of mind-boggling tax codes, and make innumerable tax filings with the various authorities. Such complexities would seriously hamper all but the largest firms from participating and flourishing in e-retailing.

Fourth, there is a concern about Internet privacy. Specifically, Internet taxation may violate consumers' privacy because some states and local jurisdictions may force e-retailers or third-party providers like credit card companies to disclose personal information for tax liability and collection purposes.

Congress definitely has its hands full attempting to make this decision.

Source: Frances B. Smith, "Internet Taxation Schemes Threaten Consumers' Privacy," *Consumers' Research Magazine*, October 1, 1999, p. 34; and McGregor McCance, "Internet Tax Commission Finds Bit of Harmony," *KRTBN Knight-Ridder Tribune Business News: Richmond Times-Dispatch–Virginia*, December 15, 1999.

Amazon.com. The traditional upscale auction house, Sotheby's, has found the potential of the Internet so enticing that it has become partners with Amazon at www.sothebys.amazon.com.

An unusual twist to the traditional "English" auction where the *highest* bidder takes the goods is the "Dutch" auction, typified by Mercata.com.[7] The site prenegotiates volume discounts with manufacturers. The more people who place a "bid" on a certain item, the *lower* the price gets. The price may drop a few cents or a few dollars. It may not be the lowest price available in the marketplace, but it will be lower than the customer's original bid.

Why leave the pricing decision up to the retailer at all? At www.Priceline.com, consumers post the price they want to pay for, say, an airline ticket from Los Angeles to Denver. Priceline then attempts to find a seller who will fulfill the request. The airline would rather sell the seat at a low price than have it go empty. So it may take the offer. Nothing is without its price, however. Priceline customers give up the flexibility of being able to travel exactly when they want. They also may have a layover or change of planes. High-ticket items worth a look at Priceline.com include hotels and other travel packages, automobiles, and home mortgages.

Finally, Internet retailers currently do not have to charge sales tax except in states in which they have a bricks-and-mortar store. Traditional retailers don't think it is fair that they have to collect sales tax, while their Internet competitors do not. See Retailing View 15.2 for more details.

Refact We've come full circle. Most retail transactions in the United States have used one-price buying for almost 150 years. R.H. Macy, founder of Macy's, was ahead of his time when he opened his first dry good store in 1858 and did away with bargaining over price by initiating one-price buying. He was the first to advertise these fixed prices in a newspaper. Priceline.com and others are trying to change the way customers view price.[8]

So, with all these new Internet business models, how will e-retailers price merchandise in the future? There is no need to stray far from the basics. Although the channel is different, the strategies that are successful for developing a sustainable competitive advantage in a bricks-and-mortar space should work in a virtual environment. E-retailers will specialize. Some will be low-cost providers. Others will offer more and better service. Still others may offer a better assortment—unique merchandise, deeper, broader, more specialized, whatever. Those who consistently exceed the expectations of their customers, whatever that may be, will be the winners. Importantly, those who have developed a strong brand, either because they had developed the brand prior to e-retailing (e.g., Landsend.com or barnesandnoble.com) or because they built their brand in the virtual world (e.g., Amazon.com), will have the ability to profitably compete on factors other than price.

INTERNET EXERCISE   Go to www.ebay.com, www.Priceline.com, and www. Mercata.com and shop for an airline ticket. Where do you think you will get the best deal? Which was the easiest site to navigate? Which company do you think will have the strongest market position in five years?

Coupons   **Coupons** are documents that entitle the holder to a reduced price or *x* cents off the actual purchase price of a product or service. Coupons are issued by manufacturers and retailers in newspapers, on products, on the shelf, at the cash register, and through the mail. Retailers' use of coupons is staggering. It's estimated that 292 billion coupons were issued in 1995. But only about 2 percent were redeemed, compared to about 4 percent in 1980. The decline is partly because manufacturers have cut the average time before expiration by more than half to limit their exposure.[11]

Coupons are thought to be an important sales promotional tool because they induce customers to try products for the first time, convert those first-time users to regular users, encourage large purchases, increase usage, and protect market share against competition.[12]

The evidence on couponing's overall profitability is mixed. Since coupons have the seemingly positive effect of encouraging larger purchases than without coupons, the coupon promotion may be stealing sales from a future period without any net increase in sales. For instance, if a supermarket runs a coupon promotion on sugar, households tend to buy a large quantity of sugar and stockpile it for future use. Thus, unless the coupon is used mostly by new buyers, the net impact on sales will be negligible, and there will be a negative impact on profits by the amount of the redeemed coupons and cost of the coupon redemption procedures. Unfortunately, it's very hard to isolate a market for new users without allowing current users to take advantage of the coupon promotion.[13]

Some believe that coupons annoy, alienate, and confuse consumers, and therefore do little to increase store loyalty.[14] Consider the following ad for a supermarket. The headline reads "Double Coupons," meaning the customer gets twice the face value of the coupon. Sounds good so far, but it's followed by these eight caveats:

1. No minimum purchase required.
2. Manufacturers' paper coupons only. Coupons with a face value over $1.00 will be redeemed at face value.

3. If doubled coupon value is greater than price of the product, you get it FREE!

4. The value of the double coupon is not to exceed the retail value of the product.

5. Tobacco, milk, pharmacy, and other coupons excluded by law will not be doubled.

6. Coupons identified as "ShopRite Super Coupon" or "Valuable ShopRite Coupon" in any ShopRite advertisement will not be doubled.

7. Check-out Coupons and Act Media Coupons will not be doubled.

8. The offer applies to manufacturers' paper coupons only (from newspapers, magazines, etc.). It does not include clipless coupons.

Rebates   A **rebate** is money returned to the buyer based on a portion of the purchase price. Generally, the customer sends a proof of purchase to the manufacturer, and the manufacturer sends the customer the rebate. Rebates are most useful when the dollar amount is relatively large. Otherwise, it's not worth the customer's time and postage to redeem the rebate. For instance, rebates are often offered on cars, major and portable appliances, computers, and electronic products.

From the retailer's perspective, rebates are more advantageous than coupons since they increase demand in the same way coupons may, but the retailer has no handling costs.

Manufacturers like rebates because many consumers never bother to redeem them, allowing manufacturers to offer, in effect, phantom discounts.[15] Many advertisements prominently proclaim low prices, noting the requirement to send in for rebates in microscopic letters. The consumer is drawn to the store, purchases the product, but only 5 to 10 percent claim the rebate. As a result, consumer advocates hate rebates.

Manufacturers also like rebates because they let them offer price cuts to consumers directly. With a traditional price cut, retailers can keep the price on the shelf the same and pocket the difference. Rebates can also be rolled out and shut off quickly. That allows manufacturers to fine-tune inventories or respond quickly to competitors without actually cutting prices. Finally, because buyers are required to fill out forms with names, addresses, and other data, rebates become a great way to build a customer data warehouse.

Leader Pricing   In **leader pricing,** certain items are priced lower than normal to increase customers' traffic flow and/or to boost sales of complementary products. Reasons for using leader pricing are similar to those for coupons. The difference is that with leader pricing, merchandise has a low price to begin with so customers, retailers, and vendors don't have to handle the coupons. Some retailers call these products loss leaders. In a strict sense, loss leaders are sold below cost. But a product doesn't have to be sold below cost for the retailer to be using a leader pricing strategy. The best items for leader pricing are products purchased frequently, primarily by price-sensitive shoppers. For instance, supermarkets typically use white bread, eggs, and milk as loss leaders. Price-sensitive customers take note of ads for these products because they're purchased weekly. The retailer hopes consumers will also purchase their weekly groceries while buying loss leaders. Toys "R" Us has successfully used a leader pricing strategy for disposable diapers. New parents get in the habit of shopping at Toys when their children are infants and become loyal customers throughout their parenting period.

Refact The average retail sale for almost every hard goods retailer including Staples, Office Depot, OfficeMax, Home Depot, Lowe's, Bed Bath & Beyond, and Linens N' Things, as well as Internet giants Amazon.com and eBay is only $40.[16] The average retail sale for catalogs, however, including Lands' End, Coldwater Creek, DM management, Corporate Express, Fingerhut, and Williams-Sonoma, is $176.[17]

Which ad is using price bundling and which is using multiple-unit pricing?

Price Bundling

Price bundling is the practice of offering two or more different products or services for sale at one price.[18] For instance, a travel agency may sell a tour that includes airfare, a cruise, and meals, all for $1,500. If purchased separately, the items might total $2,600. Price bundling is used to increase both unit and dollar sales by bringing traffic into the store. The strategy can also be used to move less desirable merchandise by including it in a package with merchandise in high demand.

INTERNET EXERCISE   Price bundling is very common in the travel and vacation industry. Go to the webpage for Sandals and see what you can get—all for one price (www.sandals.com/general/entry-why.html).

Multiple-Unit Pricing

Multiple-unit pricing is similar to price bundling, except the products or services are similar rather than different. For example, a convenience store may sell three liters of soda for $2.39 when the price per unit is 99 cents—a savings of 58 cents. Like price bundling, this strategy is used to increase sales volume. Depending on the type of product, however, customers

Dollar Tree stores make price lining easy— everything's $1.00 . . . everyday.

may stockpile for use at a later time. For example, although you typically purchase and consume one liter of soda a week, you may purchase several if you perceive a substantial cost savings. If customers stockpile, demand is shifted back in time with no long-term effect on sales.

Some retailers abuse price bundling and multiple-unit prices by implying a savings when there really isn't one (say, 49 cents each or two for 98 cents—or, even worse, 49 cents each or three for $1.59). This type of deceptive practice has received considerable attention from consumer groups.

Price Lining

In **price lining,** retailers offer a limited number of predetermined price points within a classification. For instance, a tire store may offer tires only at $29.99, $49.99, and $79.99. Both customers and retailers can benefit from such a strategy for several reasons:

- Confusion that often arises from multiple price choices is essentially eliminated. The customer can choose the tire with either the low, medium, or high price. (There need not be three price lines; the strategy can use more or fewer than three.)
- From the retailer's perspective, the merchandising task is simplified. That is, all products within a certain price line are merchandised together. Further, when going to market, the firm's buyers can select their purchases with the predetermined price lines in mind.
- Price lining can also give buyers greater flexibility. If a strict initial markup is required, there could be numerous price points. But with a price lining strategy, some merchandise may be bought a little below or above the expected cost for a price line. Of course, price lining can also limit retail buyers' flexibility. They may be forced to pass up potentially profitable merchandise because it doesn't fit into a price line.
- Although many manufacturers and retailers are simplifying their product offerings to save distribution and inventory costs and to make the choice simpler for consumers, price lining can be used to get customers to "trade up" to a more expensive model. Research indicates a tendency for people to choose the product in the middle of a price line. So, for example, if a camera store starts carrying a "super deluxe" model, customers will be more likely to purchase the model that was previously the most expensive. Retailers must decide whether it's more profitable to sell more expensive merchandise or save money by paring down their stock selection.[19]

Odd Pricing

Odd price refers to a price that ends in an odd number (such as 57 cents or 63 cents) or to a price just under a round number (such as $98 instead of $100). Odd pricing has a long history in retailing. In the 19th and early 20th centuries, odd prices were used to reduce losses due to employee theft. Because merchandise had an odd price, salespeople typically had to go to the cash register to give the customer change and record the sale. This

Does odd pricing—a price that ends in an odd number—really work?

reduced salespeople's chances to take money for an item from a customer, keep the money, and never record the sale. Odd pricing was also used to keep track of how many times an item had been marked down. After an initial price of $20, the first markdown would be $17.99, the second markdown $15.98, and so on.

While odd pricing originally had loss prevention and accounting functions, some retailers believe that odd pricing can increase sales. Most empirical studies, however, don't support this proposition.[20]

Nonetheless, many retailers use some rules of thumb regarding odd prices. Odd pricing may be less successful for products that require some thought. For instance, when purchasing a car, most customers wouldn't have to think long to realize that $17,995 is almost $18,000. Also, odd pricing seems to imply a low price. So retailers interested in maintaining an upscale image probably shouldn't use odd pricing. For instance, Tiffany's doesn't advertise diamond rings for $6,999. But if it put a ring on sale, it might use an odd price to signal a price reduction. Odd pricing, then, may be most successful for impulse purchases at lower-end retailers or on sale merchandise.

Service retailers face unique challenges that aren't as salient to merchandise retailers. See the More Information About box on page 467 for details.

CONTRASTING COST-ORIENTED, COMPETITION-ORIENTED, AND DEMAND-ORIENTED METHODS OF SETTING RETAIL PRICES

The previous section examined general strategies for setting retail prices. The following sections examine three distinct methods of setting retail prices: cost-oriented, competition-oriented, and demand-oriented. Under the **cost-oriented method,** the retail price is determined by adding a fixed percentage to the cost of the merchandise. For instance, Primrose Fashions, a family-owned women's specialty store in Dallas, uses the **keystone method** of setting prices in which it simply doubles the cost of the merchandise to obtain the original retail selling price. If a dress costs Primrose $50, the original selling price is $100. Using competition-oriented pricing, prices are based on competitions' prices. In the **demand-oriented method,** prices are based on what customers expect or are willing to pay. In this case, Primrose may have found a particularly good value at $50, but believe that the profit-maximizing price is $115.

Which method is best? The answer is all three! The cost-oriented method's strength is that it's designed to achieve target levels of profits. Also, it's quick, mechanical, and relatively simple to use.

The competition-oriented method should be considered to some degree. It is always important to keep in mind what competition is doing—after all, the customer does. The degree to which a retailer sets the market price or follows the market leader is, however, a complicated issue.

The demand-oriented method's strength is its consistency with the marketing concept. That is, it considers customers' wants and needs. Further, the

THE PRICING OF SERVICES can be more complicated than the pricing of goods for two reasons. First, it is more difficult for consumers to obtain accurate reference prices for services. A **reference price** is a price point in memory for a good or a service, and can consist of the price last paid, the price most frequently paid, or the average of all prices customers have paid for similar offerings.[21] Second, customers use price as an indicator of service quality more than they do the quality of goods.

Because services are intangible and are not created on a factory assembly line, service retailers have greater flexibility in the configurations of services they offer than do retailers of goods. As a result, it is difficult for customers to discern the reference price. Service retailers can conceivably offer an infinite variety of combinations and permutations, leading to complex and complicated pricing structures. As an example, consider how difficult it is to get comparable price quotes when buying life insurance. With the multitude of types (e.g. whole life versus term), features (different deductibles), and variations associated with customers (age, health risk, smoking or nonsmoking), few insurance companies offer exactly the same features and the same prices. Only an expert customer, one who knows enough about insurance to completely specify the options across providers, is likely to find prices that are directly comparable.

Another factor that results in the inaccuracy of reference prices is that individual customer needs vary. Some hair stylists' service prices vary across customers on the basis of length of hair, type of haircut, and whether a conditioning treatment and style are included. Therefore, if you were to ask a friend what a cut costs from a particular stylist, chances are that your cut from the same stylist may be a different price. In a similar vein, a service as simple as a hotel room will have prices that vary greatly: by size of room, time of year, type of room availability, and individual versus group rate.

Still another reason customers lack accurate reference prices for services is that customers feel overwhelmed with the information they need to gather. With most goods, retail stores display the products by category to allow customers to compare and contrast the prices of different brands and sizes. Rarely is there a similar display of services in a single outlet. If customers want to compare prices (for example, for dry cleaning), they must drive to or call individual outlets.

Another intriguing aspect of pricing of services is that buyers are likely to use price as an indicator of both service costs and service quality.[22] Customers' use of price as an indicator of quality depends on several factors, one of which is the other information available to them. When service cues to quality are readily accessible, when brand names provide evidence of a company's reputation, or when level of advertising communicates the company's belief in the brand, customers may prefer to use those cues instead of price. In other situations, however, such as when quality is hard to detect or when quality or price varies a great deal within a class of services, consumers may believe that price is the best indicator of quality. Many of these conditions typify situations that face consumers when purchasing services.[23]

Another factor that increases the dependence on price as a quality indicator is the risk associated with the service purchase. In high-risk situations, many of which involve credence services such as medical treatment or management consulting, the customer will look to price as a surrogate for quality.

Because customers depend on price as a cue to quality and because price sets expectations of quality, service prices must be determined carefully. In addition to being chosen to cover costs or match competitors, prices must be chosen to convey the appropriate quality signal. Pricing too low can lead to inaccurate inferences about the quality of the service. Pricing too high can set expectations that may be difficult to match in service delivery.

Source: Valarie A. Zeithaml and Mary Jo Bitner, *Services Marketing* (New York: Irwin/McGraw-Hill, 1996), pp. 486–87, 490–91.

---

demand-oriented method can determine profit-maximizing prices. But demand-oriented pricing is hard to implement, especially in a retailing environment with thousands of SKUs that require individual pricing decisions.

A combined demand-, competition-, and cost-oriented method is useful. The cost-oriented method would be the basis of the pricing strategy. The competitive-oriented method provides an outside check on the marketplace. The demand-oriented method, on the other hand, would be used for fine-tuning the strategy. Retailers would start with a price based on their profit goals, consider competition, and then perform tests to determine if it's the most profitable price. The initial retail price could then be changed according to the findings.

THE COST-ORIENTED METHOD OF SETTING RETAIL PRICES

This section shows how retail prices are set based on cost of the merchandise. Unfortunately, the process isn't always as simple as doubling the cost, which we described earlier. For instance, the retail price at which the product is originally sold may not be the same as the final retail selling price due to markdowns. So retailers have devised methods of keeping track of changes in the retail price so they can achieve their overall financial goals, as we discussed in Chapter 7.

Recall that the retailer's financial goals are set by top management in terms of a target return on assets. In the strategic profit model, return on assets is calculated as net profit margin multiplied by asset turnover. Pricing goals are determined primarily from net profit margin.

For pricing decisions, the key component of net profit margin is gross profit margin percentage (gross margin ÷ net sales). Retailers set initial prices high enough so that after markdowns and other adjustments (known as reductions) are made, they'll end up with a gross margin consistent with their overall profit goals.

First, we describe how retailers determine their initial selling price based on their gross margin goal. Then we examine various adjustments to the retail price such as markdowns and additional markups.

Determining the Initial Markup from Maintained Markup and Gross Margin

The performance measure usually used to evaluate pricing decisions is gross margin. Exhibit 15–1 summarizes its components. In Chapter 7, we used the traditional accounting definition of gross margin: net sales minus cost of goods sold. But retailers use an additional term called *maintained markup* that is similar to gross margin, but it considers two additional costs. The relationship can be expressed as

$$\text{Maintained markup percentage} = \frac{\text{Net sales} - \text{Costs of goods sold}}{\text{Net sales}}$$

$$\text{Gross margin percentage} = \frac{\text{Maintained markup} - \text{Workroom costs} + \text{Cash discounts}}{\text{Net sales}}$$

Thus, the only difference between the two terms is the workroom costs and cash discounts (given to the store by the vendor for paying invoices early). Why do retailers make this distinction between maintained markup and gross margin? In many retail organizations, workroom (or alteration) costs aren't controlled by the person who makes the pricing decision. For instance, the furniture buyer doesn't have control over costs associated with assembling a dining room table. In the same way, a buyer typically has no control over whether the accounting department takes the cash discounts offered to them from their vendors for paying their invoices early. But remember that conceptually, maintained markup and gross margin are very similar.

The term **maintained markup** is very descriptive. It's the amount of profit (markup) a retailer plans to maintain on a particular category of merchandise. For example, in Exhibit 15–1, planned maintained markup is $62,000 on sales of $120,000, or 51.67 percent ($62,000 ÷ $120,000). In other words, to meet its profit goals, this retailer must obtain a 51.67 percent maintained markup.

EXHIBIT 15–1

Sample Income
Statement Showing
Gross Margin

Net sales	**$120,000**
– Cost of goods sold	**58,000**
= Maintained markup	**62,000**
– Alteration costs + Cash discounts	**3,000**
= Gross margin	**$ 59,000**

A retailer's life would be relatively simple if the amount of markup it wanted to maintain (maintained markup) were the same as the initial markup.

Initial markup = Retail selling price *initially* placed on the merchandise –
Cost of goods sold

whereas,

Maintained markup = The *actual* sales that you get for the merchandise –
Cost of goods sold

Why is there a difference? A number of reductions to the value of retail inventory occur between the time the merchandise is originally priced (initial markup) and the time it's sold (maintained markup). Reductions include markdowns, discounts to employees and customers, and inventory shrinkage (due to shoplifting, breakage, or loss). Initial markup must be high enough so that after reductions are taken out, the maintained markup is left.

A few retail customers might feel slightly guilty when buying a product that has been drastically marked down. They shouldn't, however. Retailers that successfully plan their sales and markdowns also build the markdown into the initial price. Even though a customer may receive a very good price on a particular purchase, other people paid the premarkdown price. So, on average, the markup was maintained.

Retailers expect shrinkage and include this loss in the price customers pay. To illustrate, consider a TV campaign that ran a few years ago showing someone shoplifting. The message was "When you shoplift, you are ripping off your neighbor." If two retailers plan to achieve the same maintained markup, but one has a high percentage of shrinkage due to shoplifting, that store needs a higher initial markup if all other factors are held constant.

The relationship between initial markup and maintained markup is

$$\text{Initial markup} = \frac{\text{Maintained markup } + \text{ Reductions}}{\text{Net sales } + \text{ Reductions}}$$

or

$$\text{Initial markup} = \frac{\text{Maintained markup (as a \% of net sales)} + \text{Reductions (as a \% of net sales)}}{100\% + \text{Reductions (as a \% of net sales)}}$$

Using the information in Exhibit 15–1 and assuming that reductions of $14,400 here equal 12 percent of net sales,

$$\text{Initial markup} = \frac{\$62,000 + \$14,400}{\$120,000 + \$14,400} = 56.85\%$$

or

$$\text{Initial markup} = \frac{51.67\% + 12\%}{100\% + 12\%} = 56.85\%$$

Note that the same answer is obtained using both formulas. Also, initial markup is always greater than maintained markup so long as there are any reductions. Finally, initial markup is expressed either in dollars or as a percentage of retail price. This is because retailers using the retail inventory method (RIM) of inventory accounting (described in Appendix 13A) think of their inventory in "retail" rather than "cost" terms. Also, expressing initial markup as a percentage of retail price closely resembles the other accounting conventions of expressing net profit, gross margin, and maintained markup as percentages of net sales, which are, of course, at retail.

Determining the Initial Retail Price under Cost-Oriented Pricing

Continuing the preceding example, with the initial markup of 56.85 percent, assume that the suggested retail price of a certain item is $100. What are the dollar markup and the merchandise cost?

Retail	=	Cost	+	Markup
$100	=	Cost	+	(56.85% × Retail)
$100	=	Cost	+	$56.85
$100	=	$43.15	+	$56.85

The dollar markup is $56.85 and the merchandise cost is $43.15.

Here's another example. A salesperson comes into a buyer's office with a great new product that will cost $100. What will be the retail price if the initial markup is still 56.85 percent?

There are three ways to solve this problem. First, the buyer can convert the initial markup as a percentage of retail to initial markup as a percentage of cost using the formula[24]

$$\text{Initial markup as a \% of cost} = \frac{\text{Initial markup as a \% of retail}}{100\% - \text{Initial markup as a \% of retail}}$$

$$131.75\% = \frac{56.85\%}{100\% - 56.85\%}$$

Then the problem can be set up as before:

Retail	=	Cost	+	Markup
Retail	=	$100	+	(131.75% × Cost)
$231.75	=	$100	+	$131.75

The second way to solve this problem uses algebra. Let's say that R stands for the retail price.

Retail	=	Cost	+	Markup
Retail	=	$100	+	(56.85% × Retail)
R	=	$100	+	.5685 × R

By subtracting $.5685 \times R$ from both sides of the equation, the resulting initial retail price can be figured as follows:

$$4315 \times R = \$100$$
$$R = \$231.75$$

The third way to solve this problem uses the formula

$$\text{Retail} = \frac{\text{Cost}}{1 - \text{Markup}}$$

$$\$231.75 = \frac{\$100}{1 - .5685}$$

Adjustments to the Initial Retail Price

The initial retail price isn't always the price at which the merchandise is ultimately sold. The four adjustments to the initial retail price are markdowns, markdown cancelations, additional markups, and additional markup cancelations.

Markdowns   **Markdowns** are reductions in the initial retail price. Let's examine why retailers take markdowns, how to reduce the amount of markdowns, how large a markdown should be, the duration of the markdown period, how to liquidate markdown merchandise, and the mechanics of taking markdowns.

Reasons for Taking Markdowns   Retailers' many reasons to take markdowns can be classified as either clearance (to get rid of merchandise) or promotional (to generate sales).

Many retailers think of markdowns as mistakes. When merchandise is slow-moving, obsolete, at the end of its selling season, or priced higher than competitors' goods, it generally gets marked down for clearance purposes. This merchandise can become an eyesore and impair a store's image. Further, even if the merchandise can be sold in the following season, it may become shopworn or out of style. Also, cost of carrying inventory is significant. If a buyer has to carry $10,000 of unwanted inventory at cost for a year with an annual inventory carrying cost of 35 percent, the cost would be $3,500 (or $10,000 × .35)—not a trivial amount! Markdowns are part of the cost of doing business. As we've said, retailers plan their markdowns. They set an initial markup high enough so that after markdowns and other reductions are taken, the planned maintained markup is achieved. Thus, a retailer's objective shouldn't necessarily be to minimize markdowns. If markdowns are too low, the retailer is probably pricing the merchandise too low, not purchasing enough merchandise, or not taking enough risks with the merchandise being purchased.

Using a high/low pricing strategy described earlier in this chapter, retailers employ markdowns to promote merchandise to increase sales. A buyer may decide to mark down some merchandise to make room for something new. An additional benefit is that the markdown sale generates cash flow to pay for new merchandise. Markdowns are also taken to increase customers' traffic flow. Retailers plan promotions in which they take markdowns for holidays, for special events, and as part of their overall promotional program. (Chapter 16 gives details.) In fact, small portable appliances (such as toasters) are called traffic appliances because they're often sold at reduced prices to generate in-store traffic. Retailers hope that customers will purchase other products at regular prices while they're in the store. Another opportunity created by markdowns is to increase the sale of complementary products. For example, a supermarket's markdown on hot dog buns may be offset by increased demand for hot dogs, mustard, and relish—all sold at regular prices.

Reducing the Amount of Markdowns   Although retailers should expect and plan for a certain amount of markdowns, it's crucial not to have more than an optimal amount. The most important means to reduce potential markdowns is to have a good merchandise budget plan (detailed in Chapter 13). A good plan will ensure that the right amount of merchandise is on hand when the customer wants it. A number of other issues also affect the amount of markdowns.

Retailers should make sure that merchandise selections are coordinated. For example, a buyer for a traditional men's clothier wouldn't purchase avant-garde Italian neckwear to go with traditional button-down shirts.

Another means to reduce markdowns is to obtain timely deliveries. Although not often possible, the best plan is to purchase a small amount of a new product as a test. If it gets a favorable response, the retailer buys again. At the very least, retailers should try to avoid deliveries too early in the season. The fashion "season" seems to be pushed back further every year. It's not uncommon now to see newly arrived heavy winter coats for sale in July. By the time customers are ready to purchase, the merchandise may look shopworn. On the other hand, when merchandise arrives too late, retailers may have trouble selling the entire stock without taking markdowns. Quick response (QR) inventory systems (Chapter 11) are becoming increasingly popular with retailers. By reducing lead time for receiving merchandise, retailers can more closely monitor changes in trends and customer demand, thus reducing markdowns.

Retailers must work with their vendors. Vendors have a vested interest in retailers' success. Vendors who are knowledgeable of the market and competition can help with stock selections. Of course, a retailer must also trust its own taste and intuition; otherwise, its store will have the same merchandise as all other stores. Retail buyers can often obtain **markdown money**—funds a vendor gives the retailer to cover lost gross margin dollars that result from markdowns and other merchandising issues. For instance, assume a retailer has $1,000 worth of ties at retail that are given a 25 percent markdown. Thus, when the ties are sold, the retailer receives only $750. But if the vendor provides $250 in markdown money, the maintained markup remains. In this way, the vendor helps share the risk. Wal-Mart has informed some of its vendors that any markdown will be paid for by the vendors.[25] According to the Robinson-Patman Act, markdown money should be provided to all retailers on a proportionally equal basis—typically as a percentage of purchases. (Markdown money falls under the umbrella of price discrimination discussed later in this chapter.)

When to Take Markdowns   Retailers must keep good records. This means keeping track of (1) types of merchandise that required markdowns in the past and (2) what's not selling in the current season. If, for example, certain sizes required significant markdowns in the past, the retailer would cut purchases in those sizes for the current season. Part of keeping good records is doing sell-through analyses. Recall from Chapter 13 that **sell-through analysis** is a comparison between actual and planned sales to determine whether early mark-

Some retailers mark down merchandise for a limited time, just to generate sales.

downs are required or whether more merchandise is needed to satisfy demand.

Size of the Markdown and Duration of the Markdown Period Many retailers take some markdowns early in the season, when demand is still fairly active. By taking markdowns early, price reductions don't have to be as deep as those for markdowns taken late in the selling season. As noted above, early markdowns free up selling space for new merchandise and improve the retailer's cash flow position. And customer traffic rises due to marked-down merchandise.

Storewide clearance sales (late-markdown policy) are usually conducted twice a year (after the peak selling seasons of Christmas and the Fourth of July), although recently these sales have started earlier in the season. A late-markdown policy is commonly used by upscale department and specialty stores, though most retailers with seasonal merchandise also find this policy useful. In London, Harrod's after-Christmas sale, for instance, has become more of a national event than simply a way to get rid of end-of-season merchandise. One advantage is that a longer period is available to sell merchandise at regular prices. But it's likely that retailers using a late-markdown policy will need to offer large markdowns, 40 to 50 percent, to make sure the merchandise is sold. Also, as we discussed earlier in this chapter, frequent markdowns that are inherent in a high/low pricing strategy can destroy customer confidence in a store's regular pricing policy. Finally, clearance sales limit bargain hunting to twice a year.

The size of the markdown required to sell the merchandise is hard to determine. Highly perishable merchandise, like fresh meat and produce as well as fashion, typically requires more substantial markdowns than staple merchandise. A markdown's absolute dollar amount may be different for different products.[26] For instance, a 10 percent reduction on a $10,000 car would probably be viewed as a greater incentive than a 10 percent reduction on a $1 ice cream cone. Retailing View 15.3 describes how Dayton Hudson controls markdowns.

Liquidating Markdown Merchandise No matter what markdown strategy a retailer uses, some merchandise may still remain unsold. A retailer can use one of five strategies to liquidate this merchandise:

1. "Job-out" the remaining merchandise to another retailer.
2. Consolidate the marked-down merchandise.
3. Place the remaining merchandise on an Internet auction site like eBay or have a special clearance location on its own webpage.
4. Give the merchandise to charity.
5. Carry the merchandise over to the next season.

Selling the remaining marked-down merchandise to another retailer has been very popular among retailers. For instance, T.J. Maxx, Marshalls, and Bluefly.com purchase end-of-season merchandise from other retailers and sell it at

MANY STORES DETERMINE the amount of markdowns they can take based on their markdown budget. If a merchant had a $100,000 budget, she might mark the merchandise down 25 percent. If she had a bigger budget, she might go 40 percent. Such a strategy doesn't make much sense, does it?

Dayton Hudson (the parent company of Dayton's, Hudson's, Target, Marshall Field's, and Mervyn's California) with California's Santa Clara University developed a forecasting model that minimizes both the cost of taking markdowns and the time it takes to clear underperforming merchandise from its shelves.

Using two years of past promotional and markdown performance data on a specific item, the model determines how deep a markdown is necessary to sell all of the remaining merchandise by a specific date. The model is so robust that it can assign a different markdown strategy to different stores. For instance, stores in California's central valley may get a more severe markdown for bathing suits than stores in San Diego because their season ends sooner.

After using the model for some time, Dayton Hudson found that its first markdown was more drastic than in the past, and it was able to get rid of the merchandise after only one markdown. "If you have to take a second markdown, it's because the first markdown didn't do what you thought it was going to do," said Dale Achabal, a marketing professor at Santa Clara University.

Source: "Managing Markdown Madness," *Chain Store Age,* March 1999, pp. 118, 120; and Stephen A. Smith and Dale D. Achabal, "Clearance Pricing and Inventory Policies for Retail Chains," *Management Science* 44, no. 2 (February 1998).

deep discounts. (See Chapter 2 for details.) This strategy enables the retailer to have a relatively short markdown period, provides space for new merchandise, and at the same time eliminates the often unappealing sale atmosphere. The problem with this strategy is that the retailer can only recoup a small percentage of the merchandise's cost—often a mere 10 percent.

Marked-down merchandise can be consolidated in a number of ways. First, the consolidation can be made into one or a few of the retailer's regular locations. Second, marked-down merchandise can be consolidated into another retail chain or an outlet store under the same ownership. Saks Fifth Avenue (Off-Fifth) and Neiman Marcus (Last Call Outlet Center) use this strategy. Finally, marked-down merchandise can be shipped to a distribution center or a rented space such as a convention center (Barney's of New York and J. Crew) for final sale. Retailers that use these strategies condition customers to anticipate out-of-stock situations at locations that don't participate in the consolidation sales, since the merchandise is only at those locations for a relatively short time. This practice encourages a successful yet relatively short markdown period. Further, customers who shop during the consolidation sale enjoy a better selection than they'd find in the individual stores. But consolidation sales can be complex and expensive due to the extra transportation and record-keeping involved.

The Internet is expected to be increasingly useful for liquidating markdown merchandise. For example, an electronics store is partnering with eBay to sell goods it has received from

Neiman Marcus' Last Call Clearance Center is the last stop for merchandise that hasn't sold at sale prices at regular Neiman Marcus' or Bergdorf Goodman's stores.

trade-ins. J.Crew and many others have separate areas of their websites for clearance merchandise.

Giving clearance merchandise to charities is an increasingly popular practice. Charitable giving is always a good corporate practice. It is a way of giving back to the community and has strong public relations benefits. Also, the cost value of the merchandise can be deducted from income.[27]

The final liquidation strategy—to carry merchandise over to the next season—is used with relatively high-priced nonfashion merchandise, such as traditional men's clothing and furniture. Generally, however, it's not worth carrying over merchandise due to excessive inventory carrying costs.

Profit Impact of Adjustments to the Retail Price: The Use of Break-Even Analysis

Now that we've examined the mechanics of setting an initial retail price and taking markdowns, we must understand the profit impact of our actions. A useful analytical tool here is **break-even analysis,** which analyzes the relationship between total revenue and total cost to determine profitability at various sales levels. Break-even analysis has many applications in retailing. Just to name a few:

- Break-even volume and dollars of a new product, product line, department, store, and so on.
- Break-even sales change needed to cover a price change.
- Break-even sales to cover a target profit.
- Change in profit based on change in sales volume.

Let's look more closely at the first two: the break-even volume of a new private-label product and the break-even sales change needed to cover a price change.

Calculating Break-Even for a New Product Assume that a large retailer like The Gap is interested in developing a new private-label product—a ribbed sleeveless T-shirt for women. Cost of developing this shirt is about $300,000, including executives' and designers' salaries, rent on the design team's buildings, and warehousing. Since these costs are stable and don't change with the quantity of product that's produced and sold, they're known as fixed costs. Management plans to sell the T-shirt for $12—the unit price. Cost of the shirt is $5. In economic terms, this is known as the **variable cost**—the sum of the firm's expenses that vary directly with the quantity of product produced and sold. Variable costs often include direct labor and materials used in producing the product. But in this case, The Gap is purchasing the shirt from a third party. Thus, the only variable cost is the shirt's cost. The **break-even point (BEP)** is the quantity at which total revenue equals total cost, and beyond which profit occurs.

$$\text{BEP quantity} = \frac{\text{Fixed cost}}{\text{Unit price} - \text{Unit variable cost}}$$

In this example,

$$\text{BEP quantity} = \frac{\$300,000}{\$12 - \$5} = 42,857 \text{ units}$$

This means The Gap must sell 42,857 T-shirts to break even. To make things interesting, let's assume The Gap wishes to make a $100,000 profit. The break-even quantity now becomes

$$\text{BEP quantity} = \frac{\$300,000 + \$100,000}{\$12 - \$5} = 57,143 \text{ units}$$

If it decides to reduce the selling price to $10, we calculate the break-even quantity again:

$$\text{BEP quantity} = \frac{\$300,000 + \$100,000}{\$10 - \$5} = 80,000 \text{ units}$$

To convert the break-even quantity to break-even sales dollars, simply multiply the BEP quantity by the selling price: 80,000 units × $10 = $800,000.

Calculating Break-Even Sales   A closely related issue to the calculation of a break-even point is determining how much sales would have to increase to profit from a price cut, or how much sales would have to decline to make a price increase unprofitable.[28] Continuing with The Gap example, assume our break-even quantity is 57,142 units (based on the $300,000 fixed cost, the $100,000 profit, a selling price of $12, and a cost of $5). We want to know how many units we must sell to break even if we lower our selling price by 16.6 percent to $10. Using the formula

$$\text{\% break-even sales change} = \frac{-\text{\% price change}}{\text{\%CM} + \text{\% price change}} \times 100$$

where %CM stands for percent contribution margin. **Contribution margin** is gross margin less any expense that can be directly assigned to the merchandise. In this example, since there are no variable costs besides the cost of the shirt, the contribution margin is the same as the gross margin. Also, don't forget the minus sign in the formula's numerator.

CM   = Selling price – Variable costs
CM   = $12 – $5 = $7
%CM = (CM/Selling price) × 100
%CM = ($7/$12) × 100 = 58.33%

Substituting the %CM into the formula, we can calculate the break-even sales change:

$$\text{\% break-even sales change} = \frac{-(-16.6)}{58.33 + -(-16.6)} \times 100 = 39.78\%$$

Unit break-even sales change = 39.78% × 57,143 units = 22,731 units

Thus, if The Gap reduces its price to $10, it must sell an additional 22,731 units to break even. It should come as no surprise that when we add the break-even quantity at $12 to the break-even sales change to $10, we get 79,874 units (57,143 + 22,731)—almost the same break-even of 80,000 units that we obtained using the first formula. (The difference is due to rounding.) The same formula can be used to determine the sales change necessary to break even with a price increase.

As you'll see in the next section, the concepts of costs and revenues you've become familiar with in studying break-even analysis are useful when determining the initial retail price under demand-oriented pricing.

THE COMPETITION-ORIENTED METHOD OF SETTING RETAIL PRICES

As the name implies, when retailers use competition-oriented pricing, they set their prices based on their competition, rather than cost or demand considerations. Retailers can price either above, below, or at parity with competition. The chosen strategy must be consistent with the retailer's overall strategy and their relative market position. Consider, for instance, Wal-Mart and Tiffany and Co. as we did in Chapter 7. Wal-Mart's overall strategy is to be the low-cost provider of any market basket of goods in every market in which it competes. It tries to price below competition. Tiffany and Co., on the other hand, has significant equity in its brand name, which connotes high quality, unique merchandise, impeccable service, and elegant locations. Those little blue boxes and wonderful trinkets stamped TIFFANY & CO. can command more than market price.

Market leaders cannot, however, ignore their small competitors. Suppose that a sporting goods store in Norman, Oklahoma, consistently underprices Wal-Mart on fishing gear. Wal-Mart will adjust its prices to meet or even beat the competitor in that market.

What should small competitors do to compete with market leaders? A jewelry store could price at parity or below against Tiffany & Co. Additionally, it could strive for competitive advantages in assortment or service. A more difficult question is how a western wear store can compete against Wal-Mart's prices. It cannot compete head-to-head with Wal-Mart on every item. To do so would probably put it out of business because it cannot achieve the buying quantities of scale of Wal-Mart. Instead, it should pick items that are very visible to customers, and generate margin on items that customers cannot readily compare. If Wal-Mart is advertising Lee jeans at $19.99, then the western store should either carry another brand of jeans or bite the bullet and price with or below Wal-Mart.

THE DEMAND-ORIENTED METHOD OF SETTING RETAIL PRICES

Demand-oriented pricing should be used in conjunction with the cost-oriented method to determine retail prices. Using this method, retailers not only consider their profit structure but also pay close attention to price changes' impact on sales. For instance, if customers are extremely sensitive to price, then a price cut increases demand so much that profits actually increase. Alternatively, if customers are insensitive to price, raising the price also boosts profits, since sales don't decrease. Demand-oriented pricing seeks to determine the price that maximizes profits.

This section examines (1) factors that affect customers' sensitivity to price and (2) how to establish the initial retail price using the demand-oriented method.

Factors That Affect Customers' Sensitivity to Price

When retailers determine how to set initial retail prices, they must consider how sensitive customers are to price.[29] In general, retailers set relatively higher prices on products for which customers are less price-sensitive. Let's look at the factors that determine customers' price-sensitivity.

Substitute Awareness Effect   The substitute awareness effect occurs when customers become more sensitive to price because there are a lot of substitutes for a product or for a retailer. For instance, there are many options for purchasing electronic equipment on the Internet. Further, it is quick and easy to compare items. Thus, price competition is keen.

Total Expenditure Effect   Customers are more price-sensitive when the expenditure is large, both in dollars and as a percentage of income. Home improvement centers like Home Depot thus attempt to be very price-competitive on expensive products like major appliances. But for small purchases such as bulk nuts and bolts, customers will tolerate higher prices.

Difficult Comparison Effect   Customers are more sensitive to price when it's easy to compare competing offerings. A problem facing many retailers—notably fashion retailers, particularly department stores—is finding unique product offerings. Some manufacturer brands, like Levi's, are so strong that customers demand that they be stocked. As a result, customers can purchase Levis almost anywhere. Customers can easily compare similar products, making it hard for any one retailer to command higher prices.

To combat this problem and make product comparison more difficult, some retailers have developed their own private-label merchandise. **Private label** means that the brand name or logo identifying the product is owned by the retailer rather than the manufacturer. Chapter 14 discusses private labels.

Benefits/Price Effect   The benefits/price effect defines the relationship between people's perception of the benefits they receive from a product and its price.[30] For some "image" or "exclusive" products, customers are less sensitive to price—they feel they receive higher benefits from the product because it's more expensive. For example, a Polo/Ralph Lauren polo shirt may be priced twice as high as the same shirt of equal quality without the logo. The customer who purchases the Polo shirt values the recognition or ego gratification that comes from buying an image—and isn't as sensitive to price.

Most research indicates people use price as a cue for determining value only when little other information is available. For instance, people generally have a difficult time evaluating the quality of diamonds. Due to their relatively high price and people's lack of information and knowledge about them, customers perceive diamonds to be a risky purchase. They therefore equate high price with high quality. Zale jewelry stores found this human characteristic to be so strong that it developed an entire ad campaign around the concept. The campaign's theme was that customers should go to a jeweler they can trust because it's so hard to evaluate diamonds' quality. Of course, the trustworthy jewelry store is Zale!

Products can also be priced so low that consumers perceive a lack of quality. For instance, Pathmark's Premium All-Purpose Cleaner was packed like Fantastik, a top-seller in the category. Its chemical composition was the same as well. Best of all, Premium cost shoppers only 89 cents, compared with $1.79 for Fantastik. Unfortunately the product failed, probably because customers believed its low price meant it couldn't be high quality.[31]

Situation Effect   Driving down a country road, we spot an old store all by itself. Approaching the store, we see a sign: FINE ANTIQUES FOR SALE. Driving past the store, on the other side we see another sign: WE BUY JUNK. This story illus-

Why are people willing to pay $2.50 for popcorn that would cost about five cents if they made it themselves at home?

trates the situation effect—consumers' sensitivity to price can be different depending on the situation. Why are movie patrons willing to pay $2.50 for popcorn that would cost about five cents if they made it themselves at home? Eating popcorn is part of the overall movie-going experience. Also, people expect to pay a premium for merchandise purchased under certain situations.[32] Many restaurants also take advantage of the situation effect. Their lunches cost less than their dinners because people expect to pay less for lunch. Upscale fashion retailers also take advantage of the situation effect. Customers expect to pay extra in a plush atmosphere with attentive service. Alternatively, many off-price and warehouse stores maintain a sparse, utilitarian environment to create the "low-price" atmosphere customers expect when looking for bargains. Thus, understanding how to manipulate situations to impact customers' perception of price can influence overall corporate strategy and profitability.

Determining the Initial Retail Price under Demand-Oriented Pricing

To illustrate how an initial retail price is set using the demand-oriented method, we continue the hypothetical situation of The Gap's new ribbed sleeveless T-shirt for women. Recall that fixed cost of developing the product was $300,000 and variable cost was $5 each. One benefit of private-label merchandise is the flexibility of being able to set any retail price. The Gap decides to test the T-shirt in four markets at different prices. Exhibit 15–2 shows the pricing test's results. It's clear (from column 5) that a unit price of $10 is by far the most profitable ($450,000).

Unfortunately, determining the most profitable retail price isn't as simple as this example suggests. The primary difficulty is that most retailers carry so many products that these tests become a very expensive proposition. Also, a retailer must have multiple outlets to be able to manipulate prices in this manner.

A more sophisticated method of determining the most profitable price is a pricing experiment. In a pricing experiment, a retailer actually changes the price in a systematic manner to observe changes in purchases or purchase intentions. Exhibit 15–3 shows an example of a simple experiment—a classic before/after experiment with control group design. Two stores are similar in size and customer characteristics. Their weekly sales for a compact microwave oven are almost

EXHIBIT 15–2

Results of Pricing Test

MARKET	(1) UNIT PRICE	(2) MARKET DEMAND AT PRICE (IN UNITS)	(3) TOTAL REVENUE (COL. 1 × COL. 2)	(4) TOTAL COST OF UNITS SOLD ($300,000 FIXED COST + $5 VARIABLE COST)	(5) TOTAL PROFITS (COL. 3 − COL. 4)
1	$8	200,000	$1,600,000	$1,300,000	$300,000
2	10	150,000	1,500,000	1,050,000	450,000
3	12	100,000	1,200,000	800,000	400,000
4	14	50,000	700,000	550,000	150,000

EXHIBIT 15–3

A Pricing
Experiment

	BEFORE	AFTER
Store 1	10 units @ $100 Gross margin = $500	21 units @ $80 Gross margin = $630
Store 2 (control)	12 units @ $100 Gross margin = $600	13 units @ $100 Gross margin = $650

identical (10 and 12 units per week), and the ovens are selling at the same price, $100. Price at the first store is changed to $80, but the second store's price is left at $100. Thus, the second store is used as a control to make sure that any change in sales is due to the price change rather than to some outside force such as competition or weather. Now sales at the first store jump to 21 units per week, while sales at the control store hit 13 units. Barring any circumstances unknown to the retailer, the change in sales is due to the price cut. And, by the way, the $100 price is more profitable than the $80 price in the second store! Since product cost is $50, the $100 retail price provides a $650 gross margin [($100 – $50) × 13 units], whereas the $80 price provides a $630 gross margin [($80 – $50) × 21 units].

In the past, these pricing experiments weren't regularly applied due to the time and expense of administering them. But now any retailer with point-of-sale (POS) terminals can run large-scale experiments. Retailers can utilize the data warehouses derived from their loyalty programs in conjunction with sales and price data to run experiments. (See Chapter 11 for information on how these loyalty programs work.) These records cover what customers have purchased, prices paid, and conditions of sale (such as coupon usage and price specials). Various demographic information on the customer makes it possible to correlate price sensitivity with customer profiles.

Retailers and their vendors can also buy from private firms like InfoScan.[33] InfoScan purchases information from individual supermarket chains on price and promotion activity that has been scanned through their POS terminals; it then aggregates data by region, chain, or market area.

Now that we have looked at methods of setting retail prices, let's examine the legal ramifications of our decisions.

LEGAL ISSUES IN RETAIL PRICING

The legal environment surrounding retail pricing is complex. Let's examine legal issues surrounding the buying of merchandise (price discrimination and vertical price fixing) and legal issues affecting the customer (horizontal price fixing, predatory pricing, comparative price advertising, and bait-and-switch tactics).

Price Discrimination

Price discrimination occurs when a vendor sells the same product to two or more customers at different prices. Price discrimination can occur between vendors and retailers, or between retailers and their customers, although the legal ramifications are different in the two situations. We will first examine price discrimination between vendors and retailers, and then between retailers and their customers.

Although price discrimination between vendors and their retailers is generally illegal, there are three situations where it's acceptable. First, different retailers can be charged different prices as a result of differences in the cost of manufacture, sale, or delivery resulting from the differing methods or quantities in which such commodities are sold or delivered. Under what conditions may these differences exist?

It's often less expensive per unit to manufacture, sell, or deliver large quantities than small quantities. Manufacturers can achieve economies of scale through the longer production runs achieved with large quantities. Cost of selling to a customer also decreases as the quantity of goods ordered increases because it costs almost the same for a salesperson to write a small order as a large order. Finally, delivery or transportation expenses decrease on a per unit basis as quantities of goods ordered increase. These exceptions give rise to **quantity discounts,** the practice of lowering prices to retailers who buy in high quantities. (See Chapter 14.)

The differences in methods of sale that allow for differing prices refer specifically to the practice of granting **functional discounts** (also known as **trade discounts**). Functional discounts are different prices, or percentages off suggested retail prices, granted to customers in different lines of trade (e.g., wholesalers and retailers). Wholesalers often receive a lower price than retailers for the same quantity purchased. This is legal, for wholesalers perform more functions in the distribution process than do retailers. For instance, wholesalers store and transport merchandise, and they use salespeople for writing orders and taking care of problems in the stores. Essentially, manufacturers "pay" wholesalers for servicing retailers by giving the wholesalers a lower price.

With the growth of large chain retailers like Home Depot and Wal-Mart, functional discounts become more difficult to justify. Wal-Mart performs virtually all the functions an independent wholesaler provides. Therefore, Wal-Mart demands and should receive the same low prices as wholesalers. These lower prices make it hard for smaller retailers to compete.

The second exception to the no-price-discrimination rule is when the price differential is in response to changing conditions affecting the market for or the marketability of the goods concerned. The third exception is when the differing price is made in good faith to meet a competitor's equally low price. Suppose, for example, that Ben & Jerry's ice cream is experiencing severe price competition with a locally produced ice cream in Wisconsin. Ben & Jerry's is allowed to lower its price in this market below its price in other markets to meet the low price of local competition. In this case, market conditions have changed and Ben & Jerry's has reacted by meeting the competition's price.

Refact Twenty-five bookstores across the country have filed an antitrust lawsuit against their large competitors, Barnes & Noble and Borders Group, Inc. They charge that the nation's largest book retailers are in violation of the Robinson-Patman Act because they illegally use their buying clout with publishers to get special discounts and benefits not available to smaller rivals.[34]

Large retailers often benefit from subtle forms of price discrimination. For instance, book publishers have been accused of charging independent booksellers more than chain operators even though their individual orders are the same size. Many manufacturers take back merchandise that isn't selling at large retailers without penalty or give the retailers markdown money to help them defray the markdown cost—a perk not available to smaller stores.

Unless a particular situation comes within one of the exceptions just discussed, retailers should never ask a vendor for or accept a net price (after all discounts, allowances, returns, and promotional allowances) that they know—or experience tells them—won't be offered to their competitors on a proportional basis for similar merchandise to be purchased at about the same time.

The legal issue of price discrimination between retailers and their customers is not as clear. Different customers will receive different prices after negotiating for such items as cars, jewelry, or collectibles. Price discrimination becomes

IT'S WELL KNOWN THAT WOMEN often earn less than men in similar jobs, even when they have similar education and experience. It's also true that they pay more for products and services ranging from haircuts to cars. For the most part, trying to explain gender-differentiated prices is like trying to justify racial discrimination—it just doesn't cut it.

Why do women's haircuts cost more than men's? The "traditional" response is that it takes longer and more skill to cut more hair. But a survey in Pennsylvania found that 90 of 130 hair salons charged women more than men even though a state law prohibits price discrimination based on gender.

For years, dry cleaners have cited the same reasons for pricing women's services higher. They have argued that it's harder to press a woman's shirt with equipment designed for men's shirts. Although the Massachusetts Attorney General's office did a study and found this not to be the case.

Clothing merchants usually have different staff altering men's and women's clothing, so it's hard to make true comparisons based on job difficulty. However, the fact remains that many stores still offer most alterations free to men, but not to women.

Unlike alterations, dry cleaning, and haircuts, where the actual service provided to men and women may vary slightly, there is no comparable explanation why women pay more for cars. In some cases, salespeople simply don't offer women the same deals they offer men because they think they can get away with it. But women are less likely than men to bargain on car prices, partly because they're less knowledgeable about the process. Salespeople perceive that women are not comfortable about dickering on prices, and they take advantage of the situation. Gender-based price discrimination should decrease as more women educate themselves and purchase automobiles over the Internet.

In many businesses, however, the price women pay is not seriously challenged or addressed. Until women get fed up with paying more, they will continue to be taken to the cleaners.

Source: Dianna Marder, "Study Finds Gender Bias in Philadelphia Merchants Pricing," *The Philadelphia Inquirer,* March 5, 1999; and Gerry Myers, "Why Women Pay More," *American Demographics,* April 1996, pp. 40–41. For more details about gender and pricing, see Frances Cerra Whittelsey, *Why Women Pay More* (Washington, DC: Center for Study of Responsive Law).

illegal in many states, however, when different groups of people—such as men and women—systematically receive different prices. See Retailing View 15.4.

Vertical Price Fixing   **Vertical price fixing** involves agreements to fix prices between parties at different levels of the same marketing channel (e.g., retailers and vendors). The agreements are usually to set prices at the manufacturer's suggested retail price (MSRP). So pricing either above or below MSRP is often a source of conflict.

Refact A California survey found that gender-based price discrimination adds up to as much as $1,351 annually for each woman in the state for a total of nearly $15 billion a year more than men's expenditures for similar volumes of similar items.[35]

Resale price maintenance laws (fair trade laws) were enacted in the early 1900s to curb vertical price fixing, and have had a mixed history ever since. Initially, resale price maintenance laws were primarily designed to help protect small retailers by prohibiting retailers to sell below MSRP. Congress believed that these small, often family-owned, stores couldn't compete with large chain stores like Sears or Woolworth, which could buy in larger quantities and sell at discount prices. By requiring retailers to maintain manufacturers' suggested retail prices, however, prices to the consumer may have been higher than they would have been in a freely competitive environment. Due to strong consumer activism, the Consumer Goods Pricing Act (1975) repealed all resale price maintenance laws and enabled retailers to sell products below suggested retail prices. Congress's attitude was to protect customers' right to buy at the lowest possible free market price—even though some small retailers wouldn't be able to compete. For instance, in a 1996 decision, the Federal Trade Commission (FTC) ordered New Balance Athletic Shoe Co. to stop "fixing, controlling or maintaining prices at which retailers advertise" the company's products and refrain from "coercing any retailer to maintain or adopt any resale price."[36] Unfortunately, some vendors coerce retailers into maintaining the MSRP by delaying or canceling shipments.[37]

Some retailers, on the other hand, want to be able to price above MSRP.[38] For instance, Harley-Davidson motorcycles are so popular that some dealers have sold them over the manufacturers' suggested retail price. Large manufacturers and franchise companies are generally against pricing above MSRP. They argue that their brand's image can be damaged if retailers price above MSRP. Retailers like the extra profit potential and argue that competitive conditions may vary by locality. The Supreme Court ruled in 1997 that price ceilings would not necessarily violate federal antitrust laws. This was the first time the Court had carved an exception to the general ban on vertical price fixing. From now on, each case will be judged on whether it restricts competition.

Horizontal Price Fixing

Horizontal price fixing involves agreements between retailers that are in direct competition with each other to have the same prices. Consider the hypothetical case of two large discount stores, Mel's and KD's, that conspire to fix retail paint prices at an extremely low level. Big G, a small chain of three paint stores, can't compete with their low prices. Mel's and KD's can sell the paint as a loss leader. But Big G sells only paint. If the price fixing continues, Big G may have to close. With Big G out of the market, Mel's and KD's could raise their paint prices. Clearly, such behavior by Mel's and KD's is anticompetitive. Horizontal price fixing is always illegal since it suppresses competition while often raising the cost to the consumer.

As a general rule of thumb, retailers should refrain from discussing prices or terms or conditions of sale with competitors. Terms or conditions of sale may include charges for alterations, delivery, or gift wrapping, or the store's exchange policies. If a buyer or store manager needs to know a competitor's price on a particular item, it's permissible to "shop" at the competitor's store by going personally or sending an assistant to the store to examine the product. But the buyer or manager shouldn't call the competitor to get the information. Further, retailers shouldn't respond to any competitor's request to verify those prices. The only exception to the general rule is when a geographically oriented merchants association, such as a downtown area or a shopping center, is planning a special coordinated event. In this situation, the retailer may announce that merchandise will be specially priced during the event, but the specific merchandise and prices shouldn't be identified.

Predatory Pricing

Establishing merchandise prices to drive competition from the marketplace is called **predatory pricing.** It's illegal. A retailer can, however, sell the same merchandise at different geographic locations for different prices if its costs of sale or delivery are different. For instance, a national specialty store chain like The Limited may charge more for a dress in California than in Ohio, since the cost of shipping the dress from its distribution center in Columbus, Ohio, to California is higher than the cost of shipping it to a store in Ohio. A competing retailer in Ohio may not be able to meet The Limited's lower price on this dress. But because the lower price is due to The Limited's lower distribution cost rather than an attempt to drive the competitor out of business, the tactic is allowable.

It's also illegal to sell merchandise at unreasonably low prices—usually below their cost. However, a retailer generally may sell merchandise at any price so long as the motive isn't to destroy competition. For instance, independent retailers in small towns have long accused Wal-Mart of selling goods below cost to drive them out of business, and then boosting prices after seizing control of the local market. Wal-Mart maintains that it hasn't violated the law because it didn't intend to hurt competitors. But it admits it has sold some products below cost, as do other retailers. The chain claims its intent was only to provide the best everyday low price to customers. Wal-Mart's everyday low price strategy bases prices on local competition: More competition leads to lower prices, while less competition leads to higher prices. Wal-Mart's so-called predatory pricing strategy has been tested in the courts. After an earlier conviction in a lower court, the Arkansas Supreme Court ruled that the chain had no intent to destroy competition through its practice of selling a revolving selection of prescription and nonprescription drugs at less than cost.[39]

Comparative Price Advertising

A department store in Denver was selling two cutlery sets on "sale"—reduced from "original" or "regular" prices of $40 and $50. The true regular prices were $19.99 and $29.99. They sold few at the "original" price for two years. This common retailing practice, known as **comparative price advertising,** compares the price of merchandise offered for sale with a higher "regular" price or a manufacturer's list price. Consumers use the higher price, known as the reference price, as a benchmark for what they believe the "real" price of the merchandise should be.

This practice may be a good strategy, since it gives customers a price comparison point and makes the merchandise appear to be a good deal. Retailers, like the one in Denver, may use comparative price advertising to deceive the consumer, however. To avoid problems with the Federal Trade Commission and state governments that have been actively prosecuting violators, retailers should follow these guidelines:

- Have the reference price in effect at least one-third of the time the merchandise is on sale.
- Disclose how "sale" prices are set and how long they will be offered.
- Offer a "satisfaction-guaranteed policy" in which customers can return the merchandise for any reason for a full refund, with possible reasons including a customer feeling she was deceived. This strategy doesn't stop deception, but acts as a "good-faith" effort if the retailer gets caught.
- Be careful when using a manufacturer's suggested list price. Don't use it as the reference price unless it is the "regular" price.
- Use objective terms. *Special, valued at,* and *worth* are too subjective.
- If a retailer advertises that it has the lowest prices in town or that it will meet or beat any competitor's price, it should have proof that its prices are, in fact, the lowest in town before the ad is placed.
- If a retailer advertises that it will meet or beat any competitor's prices, the retailer must have a company policy that enables it to adjust prices to preserve the accuracy of its advertising claims.[40]

Bait-and-Switch Tactics   **Bait-and-switch** is an unlawful deceptive practice that lures customers into a store by advertising a product at a lower than usual price (the bait) and then induces the customer to switch to a higher-priced model (the switch). Bait-and-switch can occur in two ways. Suppose customer Smith is in the market for a new refrigerator. Smith checks the ads in the newspaper and finds a particularly attractively priced unit. At the store, however, Smith finds that the retailer has significantly underestimated demand for the advertised product and no longer has any available for sale. The person begins pushing a higher-priced model that's heavily stocked.

In the second bait-and-switch method, the retailer has the advertised model in stock but disparages its quality while highlighting the advantages of a higher-priced model. In both cases, the retailer has intentionally misled the customer.

To avoid disappointed customers and problems with the Federal Trade Commission, retailers should have sufficient quantities of advertised items. If they run out of stock on these items, they should offer customers a rain check. Finally, they should caution salespeople not to disparage the lower-priced advertised items with the intent of trading customers up to a higher-priced model.

In summary, retailers, wholesalers, and manufacturers should be aware that whenever they decide to sell the same merchandise for different prices at different locations, or to sell merchandise at extraordinarily low prices to attract customers, they may be susceptible to federal and state prosecution and to lawsuits from competitors. But as a practical matter, the length of time and the expense of acquiring sufficient data and legal assistance to prove injury by a competitor may be so great that the injured party may still lose its business.

SUMMARY   There's more to setting retail prices than just taking the manufacturer's suggestions. Everyday low pricing (EDLP), coupons, and rebates are popular alternatives to the frequent use of sales. The Internet has complicated the pricing strategy for bricks-and-mortar retailers and introduced new forms of pricing strategies into the marketplace. Leader pricing, price bundling, price lining, and odd pricing are also commonly used strategies for pricing product lines.

After examining the relative merits of the cost-, competition-, and demand-oriented methods of setting retail prices, we've concluded that a mix of the methods is best. Since the initial retail price isn't necessarily the price at which the merchandise is finally sold, you must understand how to use the cost-oriented method to adjust the initial retail price and how these adjustments affect profits. Specifically, we examined several issues regarding markdowns (such as reasons for taking markdowns and when to take markdowns) and break-even analysis.

Competition-oriented pricing should be easy to implement if the retailer is following competition. But if the retailer wants to strengthen its relative market position, determining prices vis-à-vis competition is complicated.

As for demand-oriented methods of setting retail prices, several qualitative factors affect customers' sensitivity to prices. Specifically, customers are more sensitive to price when there are many alternative stores from which to choose, when the total expenditure is large, when comparisons between existing brands are easy, and when it's hard to perceive special benefits from the products or retailers. Experiments and consumer panel data can help retailers determine initial retail prices using demand-oriented methods. Although all these approaches are useful, they're harder to use than the cost-oriented method, especially for small retailers.

Legal issues that impact pricing decisions come from two sides. Those that affect the buying of merchandise include price discrimination and vertical price fixing. The legal pricing issues that affect the consumer are horizontal price fixing, predatory pricing, comparative price advertising, and bait-and-switch.

KEY TERMS

backup stock, *457*

bait-and-switch, *485*

break-even analysis, *475*

break-even point, *475*

comparative price advertising, *484*

contribution margin, *476*

cost-oriented method, *466*

coupon, *462*

demand-oriented method, *466*

everyday low pricing (EDLP), *456*

functional discount (trade discount), *481*

high/low pricing strategy, *457*

horizontal price fixing, *483*

initial markup, *469*

keystone method, *466*

leader pricing, *463*

low price guarantee policy, *456*

maintained markup, *468*

markdown, *471*

markdown money, *472*

multiple-unit pricing, *464*

odd price, *465*

predatory pricing, *483*

price bundling, *464*

price discrimination, *480*

price lining, *465*

private label, *478*

quantity discount, *481*

rain check, *457*

rebate, *463*

reference price, *467*

resale price maintenance laws (fair trade laws), *482*

sell-through analysis, *472*

variable cost, *475*

vertical price fixing, *482*

DISCUSSION QUESTIONS AND PROBLEMS

1. What's the difference between initial markup and maintained markup? Can initial markup and maintained markup ever be the same?

2. Simple examination of markdowns could lead us to believe that they should be taken only when a retailer wants to get rid of merchandise that's not selling. What other reasons could a retailer have to take markdowns?

3. Do you know any retailers who have violated any of the legal issues discussed in this chapter? Explain your answer.

4. Which of the pricing strategies discussed in this chapter are used by your favorite retailer? Do you think they're used effectively? Can you suggest a more effective strategy?

5. A department's maintained markup is 38 percent, reductions are $560, and net sales are $28,000. What's the initial markup percentage?

6. Maintained markup is 39 percent, net sales are $52,000, alterations are $1,700, shrinkage is $500, markdowns are $5,000, employee discounts are $2,000, and cash discounts are 2 percent. What are gross margin in dollars and initial markup as a percentage? Explain why initial markup is greater than maintained markup.

7. Cost of a product is $150, markup is 50 percent, and markdown is 30 percent. What's the final selling price?

8. Manny Perez bought a tie for $9 and priced it to sell for $15. What was his markup on the tie?

9. What is the difference in the pricing strategies of ebay.com, priceline.com, and Mercata.com. Which firm do you think will be the strongest in 10 years? Why?

10. Mary White has one blouse in inventory marked to sell for $50. She wants to take a 25 percent markdown on the blouse. What price should she put on the blouse?

SUGGESTED READINGS

Berry, Leonard L., and Manjit S. Yadav. "Capture and Communicate Value in the Pricing of Services." *Sloan Management Review* 37, no. 4 (June 22, 1996), pp. 41–48.

Bitran, Gabriel R., and Susana V. Mondschein. "Periodic Pricing of Seasonal Products in Retailing." *Management Science* 43, no. 1 (January 1997), pp. 64–79.

Krishnan, Trichy V., and Ram C. Rao. "Double Couponing and Retail Pricing in a Couponed Product Category." *Journal of Marketing Research* 32 (November 1995), pp. 419–32.

Lal, Rajiv, and Ram Rao. "Supermarket Competition: The Case of Every Day Low Pricing." *Marketing Science* 16, no. 1 (1997), pp. 60–80.

Manning, Kenneth C., William O. Bearden, and Randall L. Rose. "Development of a Theory of Retailer Response to Manufacturers' Everyday Low Cost Programs." *Journal of Retailing* 74, no. 1 (March 1998), pp. 107+.

Monroe, Kent B. *Pricing: Making Profitable Decisions*, 2d ed. New York: McGraw-Hill, 1990.

Mulhern, Francis J., and Daniel T. Padgett. "The Relationship between Retail Price Promotions and Regular Price Purchases." *Journal of Marketing* 59, no. 4 (Fall 1995), pp. 83–91.

Nagle, Thomas T. *The Strategy and Tactics of Pricing.* Englewood Cliffs, NJ: Prentice-Hall, 1994.

Shankar, Venkatesh, and Ruth N. Bolton. "Dimensions and Determinants of Retailer Pricing Strategy and Tactics." *Marketing Science Institute—Report Summary*, working paper 99–101, 1999.

Sivakumar, K., and Robert E. Weigand. "Model of Retail Price Match Guarantees." *Journal of Business Research* 39 (1997), pp. 241–55.

Lora Kellogg
Vice-President
Marketing, Scotty's

SCOTTY'S IS A RETAIL CHAIN that has close to 150 stores in Florida, Georgia, and Alabama. For over 75 years, Scotty's has sold home improvement items in the Southeast. This year, Scotty's repositioned itself as Scotty's Bargain Outlet with five stores in one: a brand name Closeout Store, a Dollar Store, a Home Fashions Outlet, a Floor Store Outlet, and a Scotty's Hardware Outlet. • For the past year I have been part of the management team that developed and implemented the new marketing and sales strategies for Scotty's Bargain Outlet. Scotty's new Dollar Store has over 100,000 household items for just a buck. • Scotty's also added Scotty's Factory Closeout Store, where customers will find brand name closeouts, buybacks, overruns, and surplus items all at up to 70 percent off retail. You'll find luggage, sporting goods, appliances, giftware, electronics, and more all at rock-bottom prices. The third and fourth stores are the Home Fashions and Floor Store Outlets. These two stores already existed in Scotty's but were remerchandised to sell closeouts and special buys. You'll find everything from pillows to comforters to tile and carpet. • The fifth store is Scotty's Hardware Outlet, which includes lumber and building materials, as well as lawn and garden. Scotty's merchandising team downsized some of its traditional categories and products to create more space needed for the Bargain Outlet concept. • I graduated from the University of Florida in 1995 with a bachelor's degree in public relations. In the summer between my junior and senior years, I did an internship with Scotty's, which hired me to work in the advertising department when I graduated. At age 27, I was promoted to vice-president of marketing. • In the last five years, the two most exciting projects I have worked on have been implementing Scotty's Money in 1997, the company's most successful customer loyalty program ever, and this year, repositioning our company to Scotty's Bargain Outlet. The most exciting promotion I have done was dropping a quarter-million dollars in Scotty's Money from 40 helicopters all over the state of Florida one Saturday in 1997 to introduce Scotty's Money to the public. We brought out over 100,000 customers and made news on almost all-major radio and TV stations in Florida. I am responsible for promoting our new positioning and getting customers to visit the redesigned stores. I was responsible for the new exterior and interior signage of the Bargain Outlet stores as well as print, radio, news releases, and overall branding and marketing of the new Bargain Outlet stores. • I never would have dreamed I would be leading the Marketing and Advertising for a half billion dollar company five years after I graduated from college but I am. It's hard work, insanely stressful, incredibly challenging. I absolutely love it.

16

Retail Communication Mix

QUESTIONS

- What are the strengths and weaknesses of the different methods for communicating with customers?

- Why do retailers need to have an integrated marketing communication program?

- What steps are involved in developing a communication program?

- How do retailers establish a communication budget?

- How can you use the different elements in a communication mix to alter customers' decision-making processes?

- What factors should retailers consider when designing advertising and frequent shopper loyalty programs?

THE PRECEDING CHAPTERS described how retailers develop a merchandise budget plan and then buy and price merchandise. The next step in the retail management decision-making process is developing and implementing a communication program to attract customers to stores and Internet sites and encourage them to buy merchandise. The communication program informs customers about the retailer as well as the merchandise and services it offers.

In addition, retailers are using communication programs to build repeat business and store loyalty. For example, Gary Mead, a 34-year-old entrepreneur, uses database marketing to take on the giants: Domino's, Little Caesar's, and Pizza Hut. With a $5,000 computer system, he keeps track of the purchase history of customers patronizing his restaurant, Mi Amore Pizza & Pasta in Lompoc, California. If customers don't order for 60 days, the system spits out a postcard with a discount to lure them back. Other promotions encourage customers to try all of the dishes offered by suggesting pasta dishes to pizza lovers. The database has 8,500 customers in a town of 11,000; business has been increasing 25 to 30 percent each year.[1]

Retailers communicate with customers through five vehicles: advertising, sales promotion, publicity, store atmosphere and visual merchandising, and personal selling. This chapter focuses on the first three of these vehicles in the communication mix. In large retail firms, the communication mix is managed by the firm's marketing or advertising department and the buying organization. Store atmosphere and salespeople selling are managed by store personnel and are thus discussed in Section IV.

ROLE OF THE RETAIL COMMUNICATION PROGRAM

The ultimate goal of the retail communication program is to generate sales to customers in the retailer's target market. To accomplish this goal, retailers use a variety of methods to inform, persuade, and remind customers about the retailer. (See Exhibit 16–1.)

Tasks Performed by the Communication Program

In Chapter 5, we discussed how customers go through a number of stages as they decide which retailer to visit and what to purchase from the retailer. The retailer's communication program moves customers through the stages in the buying process outlined in Exhibit 5–1.

Refact Electronic retailers typically spend more than 25 percent of revenues on advertising, while store-based retailers spend 3 to 5 percent of revenues on advertising.[2]

Informing   The first task performed by the communication program is informing customers about the retailer and the merchandise and services it offers. For example, a carpet cleaning company places ads in the Yellow Pages to make customers aware of its services and telephone number. "Clicks-and-mortar" retailers tell customers about their website by putting their URLs in their storefront windows, on their shopping bags, and in their ads.

Persuading   The second task is motivating customers to visit the retailer and buy merchandise and services. For example, the department store salesperson described in Chapter 5 encouraged the college student to buy a suit for her upcom-

EXHIBIT 16–1

The Retail Promotion Mix

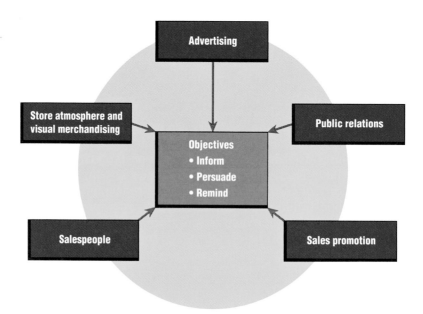

ing interviews. Mi Amore Pizza & Pasta, the restaurant described at the beginning of this chapter, sends out coupons offering discounts to motivate customers to order pizzas.

Reminding   As we discussed in Chapter 5, simply making a sale isn't enough. Although a customer may like a retailer, the retailer is vulnerable to appeals made by competitors. Retailers need to build repeat sales and loyalty by reminding customers about their offering and its benefits.

More and more retailers are using frequent shopper programs to perform this reminding task. **Frequent shopper programs** are reward-and-communication programs to encourage continued sales to the retailer's best customers. For example, many department chains identify their best customers, send them periodic newsletters announcing programs, invite the customers to special showings, assign personal shoppers to them, and offer special discounts. These programs are discussed in detail later in the chapter.

Methods for Communicating with Customers

Exhibit 16–2 classifies communication methods used by retailers to inform, persuade, and remind customers. The classification is based on whether the methods are impersonal or personal and paid or unpaid.

Paid Impersonal Communications   Advertising, sales promotions, store atmosphere, and websites are examples of paid impersonal communications. **Advertising** is a form of paid communication to customers using impersonal mass media such as newspapers, TV, radio, and direct mail.

Sales promotions offer extra value and incentives to customers to visit a store and/or purchase merchandise during a specific period of time. For example, Kmart's "blue-light specials" are a dramatic way to increase sales of specific items. They're announced over the store's public address system and a flashing blue light is placed near the item on sale. The sales last only 5 to 15 minutes. Since the stock of sale items is limited, customers rush to the merchandise to make sure they get it before it runs out or the sale ends. Besides increasing sales of specific items, blue-light specials reinforce Kmart's image of providing good value to its customers. The most common sales promotion is a sale. Other sales promotions involve special events, in-store demonstrations, coupons, and contests.

Refact The Christmas story about Rudolph the Red-Nosed Reindeer was developed by a Montgomery Ward copywriter in 1939 for a store promotion.[3]

Refact More than $125 million is spent on providing samples of merchandise for customers in stores.[4]

EXHIBIT **16–2**

Communications Methods

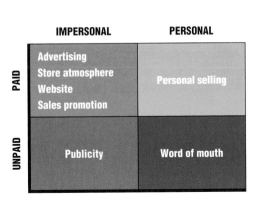

Albertson's holds special events in its stores like this Shrimp Fest that are tied to neighborhood activities. These events generate publicity for the store and generate traffic.

Merchandise Demonstrations and Sampling   Some retailers use in-store demonstrations and offer free samples of merchandise to build excitement in the store and stimulate purchases. In department stores, fashion shows and cooking demonstrations draw customers to the store and encourage impulse purchases.

Contests   **Contests** are promotional games of chance. They differ from price-off sales in that (1) only a few customers receive rewards and (2) winners are determined by luck. For example, fast-food restaurants frequently have contests associated with major films (such as *The Lion King*) or sports events (such as the Super Bowl).

Coupons   **Coupons** offer a discount on the price of specific items when they're purchased at a store. Coupons are the most common promotional tool used by supermarkets. Retailers distribute them in their newspaper ads and in direct-mail programs. For example, Publix, a Florida-based supermarket chain, targeted a promotion at affluent customers using a direct-mail piece that included recipes for a gourmet meal with coupons to purchase the products needed to prepare it.

INTERNET EXERCISE   Retailers and manufacturers now deliver coupons through the Internet rather than by mail or in free-standing inserts (FSIs.) Go to www.coolsavings.com or www.supercoups.com for coupons offered over the Internet. How does this coupon distribution system compare to more traditional distribution systems?

Refact Annually, manufacturers distributed 300 billion coupons in the United States valued at $175 billion, but less than 3.0 percent of the coupons are redeemed.[5]

Refact The first coupons were handwritten notes given by Asa Chandler, an Atlanta druggist, offering customers a free glass of his new soft drink, Coca-Cola, in 1895.[6]

Manufacturers also distribute coupons for their products that can be used at retailers that stock the products. To attract customers, some supermarkets accept coupons distributed by competing retailers. Another technique is for a retailer to offer double or triple the value of coupons distributed by manufacturers.

While sales promotions are effective at generating short-term interest among customers, they aren't very useful for building long-term loyalty. Customers attracted by sales promotions are interested in the promoted merchandise, not the retailer. But customers who participate in the promotion might learn more about a store and return to it. Unfortunately, when a specific promotion is effective for a retailer, competing retailers learn about it quickly and offer the same promotion, which prevents the innovating retailer from gaining any long-term advantage.

The retail store itself provides paid impersonal communications to its customers. **Store atmosphere** is the combination of the store's physical characteristics, such as architecture, layout, signs and displays, colors, lighting, temperature, sounds, and smells, which together create an image in the customer's mind. The atmosphere communicates information about the store's service, its

The Ultimate His-and-Hers Gift

THE NEIMAN MARCUS CHRISTMAS CATALOG IS perhaps the nation's best-known retail catalog. Its reputation is largely due to its annual tradition of ultraextravagant his-and-hers gifts. The Christmas catalog was first distributed in 1915 as a Christmas card inviting Neiman Marcus customers to visit the store during the holiday season. In the late '50s, customers were asking Neiman Marcus about unique gifts merchandise not available in the store or from other catalogs. The first unique gift was a pair of vicuña coats offered in 1951. In 1959, the gift of a black angus steer, delivered on the hoof or in steaks, generated a lot of publicity and elevated the catalog to national prominence.

The next year, Neiman Marcus offered the first his-and-hers gift—a pair of Beechcraft airplanes—and a tradition was born. His-and-hers gifts have included ermine bathrobes, hot-air balloons, Chinese junks, and a pair of camels. The most expensive gift was a set of his-and-hers diamonds priced at $2 million. Most of these gifts are actually sold. A highly publicized chocolate Monopoly set was purchased by Christie Hefner, president of Playboy Enterprises, for her father, Hugh Hefner, founder of *Playboy* magazine.

Neiman's his-and-her gift for the millennium was a donation to The Nature Conservancy to preserve, under the name of the donor, a tract of U.S. land that's critical to wildlife. "As we are reaching into the new millennium we wanted to do gifts that keep on giving," explained Sharen Jester Turney, president of NM Direct, the firm's catalog division. "It's all about giving back to the future." Neiman's lists a price of $200,000 to create a nature preserve, but land is available at a variety of costs in all states, according to Bill Weeks, executive director of the conservation group. The less affluent can get in on the act by paying $35 to conserve an acre of rain forest in Pantanal, Brazil. Plenty of expensive toys abound in the 1999 Christmas catalog, including a Boeing business jet with dining room, bedrooms, and full bath for $35 million and an interactive Venturer race-car and motorcycle simulator for $98,000.

Source: "Neiman's Chooses Conservation as Ultimate Christmas Gift," *DNR,* September 15, 1999, p. IFC; and Anne Dingus, "The Neiman Marcus Catalog," *Texas Monthly,* December 1996, p. 184.

---

pricing, and the fashionability of its merchandise.[7] Chapter 18 discusses elements of store atmosphere.

Finally, store-based retailers are increasing their emphasis on communicating with customers through their websites. Retailers' websites build their brand image; inform customers of store locations, special events, and the availability of merchandise in local stores; and sell merchandise and services.

Paid Personal Communications   Retail salespeople are the primary vehicle for providing paid personal communications to customers. **Personal selling** is a communication process in which salespeople assist customers in satisfying their needs through face-to-face exchange of information.

E-mail is another paid, personal communication vehicle. Electronic retailers use e-mail to inform customers of new merchandise, confirm the receipt of an order, and indicate when an order has been shipped.

Unpaid Impersonal Communications   The primary method for generating unpaid impersonal communication is publicity. **Publicity** is communication through significant unpaid presentations about the retailer (usually a news story) in impersonal media. Examples of publicity are the newspaper and TV coverage of Macy's Thanksgiving Day parade in New York and the Sears trophy for the national collegiate football championship. Retailing View 16.1 describes how Neiman Marcus creates a newsworthy event by offering unique gifts in its annual Christmas catalog.

Refact Macy's first Thanksgiving Day Parade was held in 1924.[8]

Most communications are directed toward potential customers. Publicity, however, is often used to communicate with employees and investors. Favorable news stories generated by publicity can build employee morale and help improve employee performance. Much of this publicity is provided by internal newsletters, magazines, bulletin board notices, handbooks, and inserts into pay envelopes. However, news about the retailer published in newspapers or broadcast over TV and radio can have a greater impact on employees than internally distributed information. Just like customers, employees place more credibility on information provided by news media than on information generated by the retailer. Similarly, stockholders, the financial community, vendors, and government agencies are influenced by publicity generated by retailers.

Unpaid Personal Communications   Finally, retailers communicate with their customers at no cost through **word of mouth** (communication between people about a retailer).[9] For example, retailers attempt to encourage favorable word-of-mouth communication by establishing teen boards composed of high school student leaders. Board members are encouraged to tell their friends about the retailer and its merchandise. On the other hand, unfavorable word-of-mouth communication can seriously affect store performance.

Refact People who have an unsatisfactory experience with retail service typically tell nine other people on average about their experience.[10]

Strengths and Weaknesses of Communication Methods

Exhibit 16–3 compares communication methods in terms of control, flexibility, credibility, and cost.

Control   Retailers have more control when using paid versus unpaid methods. When using advertising, sales promotions, websites, and e-mail, and store atmosphere, retailers determine the message's content and, and for advertising and sales promotions, they control the time of its delivery. Since each salesperson can deliver different messages, retailers have less control over personal selling than other paid communication methods. Retailers have very little control over the content or timing of publicity and word-of-mouth communications. Since unpaid communications are designed and delivered by people not employed by the retailer, they can communicate unfavorable as well as favorable information. For example, news coverage of food poisoning at a restaurant or racial discrimination at a hotel can result in significant declines in sales.

Flexibility   Personal selling is the most flexible communication method, because salespeople can talk with each customer, discover her specific needs, and

EXHIBIT 16–3

Comparison of Communication Methods

	CONTROL	FLEXIBILITY	CREDIBILITY	COST
Paid impersonal				
• Advertising	Highest	Lowest	Lowest	Modest
• Sales promotion	Highest	Low	N/A	Modest
• Store atmosphere	Highest	Low	N/A	Modest
• Website	Highest	Modest	Low	Modest
Paid personal				
• Salespeople	High	Highest	Low	High
Unpaid impersonal				
• Publicity	Low	Low	High	Low
Unpaid personal				
• Word of mouth	Low	Low	High	Lowest

Publicity is considered an unpaid approach for communicating with customers. But Circuit City incurs considerable costs for the publicity generated from sponsoring their NASCAR racing team.

develop unique presentations for her. Other communication methods are less flexible. For example, ads deliver the same message to all customers. However, websites can be tailored to individual visitors.

Credibility Because publicity and word of mouth are communicated by independent sources, their information is usually more credible than the information in paid communication sources. For example, customers see their friends and family as highly credible sources of information. Customers tend to doubt claims made by salespeople and in ads since they know retailers are trying to promote their merchandise.

Refact In 1998, Sears spent over $1.5 billion on advertising and was the fifth largest advertiser in the United States. McDonald's was 14th and JCPenney was 16th.[12]

Cost Publicity and word of mouth are classified as unpaid communication methods, but retailers do incur costs to stimulate them. Creating an event that merits significant news coverage can be costly for a retailer. For example, Circuit City incurs costs sponsoring a race car and team on the NASCAR circuit.[11]

Paid impersonal communications often are economical. For example, a full-page ad in the *Los Angeles Times* costs about two cents per person to deliver the message in the ad. In contrast, personal selling is more effective than advertising, but more costly. A 10-minute presentation by a retail salesperson paid $12 per hour costs the retailer $2—100 times more than exposing a customer to a newspaper, radio, or TV ad. While maintaining a website on a server is relatively inexpensive, it is costly to design and continuously update a site and promote the site to attract visitors.

Refact Amazon.com spends over 30 percent of its revenues on website development and promotion.[13]

Due to the differences just described, communication methods differ in their effectiveness in performing communication tasks. Typically, advertising, publicity, and store atmosphere are most cost-effective at building the retailer's image. Websites and advertising are effective for conveying information about a retailer's offerings. Personal selling and sales promotion are used to persuade customers to purchase merchandise. Remembering and repeat purchase are developed through image advertising, customer service, and frequent shopper promotional programs offered by sales associates.

Integrated Marketing Communications

As described previously, the communication methods vary in their effectiveness in performing tasks in the communication program. Rather than creating unique programs for sales associates, advertising, sales promotion, and direct mail, retailers need to coordinate these activities into an integrated marketing communication program. Without this coordination, the communication methods might work at cross-purposes. For example, the retailer's TV advertising campaign might attempt to build an image of exceptional customer service, but the firm's sales promotions might all emphasize low prices. If communication methods aren't used consistently, customers may become confused about the retailer's image and therefore may not patronize the store.

Integrated marketing communications is the strategic integration of multiple communication methods to form a comprehensive, consistent message. For example, Lane Bryant used an integrated approach to target the African American market. The focus of the program was a five-city mall tour coordinated by *Essence* magazine. Radio and TV ads were used to inform customers about the tour and the special mall event. Prior to the arrival of the tour, direct-mail announcements were sent to consumers in the city announcing the mall event and presenting Lane Bryant's offering for African American customers. Ads with discount coupons placed in the *Essence* issues distributed during the tour offered additional encouragement to visit Lane Bryant stores.[14]

INTERNET EXERCISE   Trader Joe's is an interesting retail concept, an off-price retailer selling food and wine. Go to www.traderjoes.com and see how the firm uses its Internet site to promote its retail offering. How effective do you think the site is in promoting the store?

Retailing View 16.2 describes how Zellers uses an integrated communication program to compete against Wal-Mart in Canada. The next section of this chapter is devoted to planning the communication program.

PLANNING THE RETAIL COMMUNICATION PROGRAM

Exhibit 16–4 illustrates the four steps in developing and implementing a retail communication program: setting objectives, determining a budget, allocating the budget, and implementing and evaluating the mix. The following sections detail each of these steps.

EXHIBIT 16–4

Steps in Developing a Retail Promotion Program

Establish objectives	Determine budget	Allocate budget	Implement and evaluate programs
• Positioning	• Marginal analysis		
• Sales goals	• Objective and task		
• Communication objectives	• Rules of thumb		

ZELLERS, A DIVISION OF THE HUDSON'S BAY COMPANY, is a chain of over 350 discount stores in Canada. When Wal-Mart entered the Canadian market, Zellers initially tried unsuccessfully to compete on price. Now Zellers has developed a retail strategy supported by an integrated marketing communication program to position the chain between Wal-Mart's low-cost image and the high-fashion, high-price image of department stores.

CEO George Heller emphasizes, "We're going after our target customer, mum. We are creating a pleasant shopping experience where we treat her as the CEO of the family." To communicate this new image, Zellers advertises its unique private brands, Cherokee and Martha Stewart Everyday, as brands that are fashion-right, not fashion-forward.

The store atmosphere was changed by removing large bins and pallets that made it difficult to get around the store. Improving sight lines and using uniform signage with color coding by category make it easier for customers to find what they are looking for. Merchandise is stacked low to increase accessibility. Benches placed in the aisles give customers a place to rest.

Zellers builds customer loyalty and emphasizes its value proposition through its Club Z programs. More than 11 million Club Z members participate in different programs including Advantage 60 for seniors, and Generation Z for children of Club Z members; Community Group programs enable associations and community organizations to redeem rewards. Purchases of merchandise and services at Zellers and its business partners earn loyalty points that can be redeemed for merchandise in a rewards catalog, discounts on store mer-

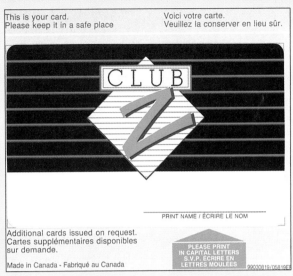

Over 11 million Canadians are members of Zellers' Club Z frequent shopper program.

chandise, or contributions to charitable organizations. Special rewards are available for Generation Z and Advantage 60 members. In-store bonus promotions enable club members to earn double Club Z points.

Source: Kelly Shermach, "Hudson's Bay Covers A to 'Club Z' in Developing Loyalty Programs," *Card Marketing*, March 1999, pp. 13–15; and Sunil Taneja, "Creating Mum's Store," *Chain Store Age*, January 1999, pp. 46–47.

Setting Objectives

Retailers establish objectives for promoting a program to provide (1) direction for people implementing the program and (2) a basis for evaluating its effectiveness. Some communication programs have a long-term objective, such as creating or altering customers' image of the retailer. Other communication programs focus on improving short-term performance, such as increasing store traffic on weekends.

Brand Building: A Long-Term Objective **Brand building,** also referred to as **positioning,** is the design and implementation of a retail communication program to create an image in the customer's mind of the retailer relative to its competitors.[15] As Chapter 6 said, a long-term competitive advantage can be developed through positioning.

A communication program with a brand building objective attempts to create associations in the customer's mind between the retailer and specific image-related characteristics such as

1. *Merchandise category.* The most common association objective is to link the retailer to a category of merchandise. For example, Circuit City is closely

related in consumers' minds with consumer electronics. Consumers view Circuit City as having any electronic item they might want in stock at all times.

2. *Price/quality.* Some retailers (such as Neiman Marcus) are associated with offering high prices and high fashion. Other retailers (such as Wal-Mart) are positioned as offering low prices, adequate merchandise and service, and good value.

3. *Specific attribute or benefit.* A retailer can link its stores to attributes such as convenience (7-Eleven) or service (Nordstrom).

4. *Lifestyle or activity.* Some retailers associate themselves with a specific lifestyle or activity. For example, The Nature Company, a retailer offering books and equipment to study nature, is linked to a lifestyle of interacting with the environment. Electronic Boutique is associated with home use of computer game software.

These strong associations influence consumer buying behavior. For example, when consumers think about camping, REI might immediately come to mind, stimulating a visit to an REI store or the REI website.

Sales Goals: Short-Term Objectives   A common short-term objective for a communication program is to increase sales during a specified time period. For example, retailers often have sales during which some or all merchandise is priced at a discount for a short time. Grocery stores usually place weekly ads with coupons that can be used to save money on purchases made during the week.

Communication Objectives   While retailers' overall objective is to generate long- and short-term sales and profits, they often use objectives related to the communication tasks discussed previously rather than sales objectives to plan and evaluate their communication programs. **Communication objectives** are specific goals related to the retail communication mix's effect on the customer's decision-making process. Retailing View 16.3 describes how electronic retailers focus their communication budgets on building awareness.

Retail advertising can be used to achieve long-term positioning goals and short-term goals. The Fashion Bug ad (left) is used to reinforce the retailer's image with its fashion-oriented target market. The Payless ad (right) builds sales for a short-term promotion.

Dot.Coms Have Problems Building Awareness

A MAJOR PROBLEM FACING ELECTRONIC RETAILERS is building awareness and traffic at their Internet sites. Building awareness is not as great a problem for store-based retailers. Customers become aware of stores when they drive by them or visit neighboring stores in a shopping center. These exposures offered by a storefront are relatively inexpensive. The $10,000 monthly rent for a mall location can expose the retailer to 1,000,000 mall visitors a month—a cost per thousand (CPM) of about one cent.

On the other hand, customers must know an electronic retailer's URL before they can visit its website. Initially electronic retailers attempted to build awareness and traffic by placing banner ads at popular websites such as Yahoo and AOL. For example, Ameritrade, DLJdirect, E∗Trade, and Waterhouse each paid $25 million to have a button on the brokerage center page in AOL's personal finance channel, enabling AOL subscribers to "click through" or hyperlink to the brokers' own websites. Electronic retailers are finding that these banners are not very effective at building traffic for their websites.

Rather than relying on banner ads to generate traffic, electronic retailers are using more traditional communication vehicles: television and radio, billboards, and publicity. For example, Garden.com is spending $20 million to construct living billboards, including a real garden. Pets.com entered a float in the Macy's Thanksgiving Day parade.

In addition, electronic retailers are developing **affiliate** or **associate programs** in which they are the permanent advertiser on a site. For instance, women's site iVillage.com has created an area on its site for Ford that asks visitors to design their dream car. Amazon.com has hundreds of partnership with affiliates. The affiliates provide hyperlinks embedded in their content so visitors can go to Amazon.com's site and buy books on the subject matter discussed on the affiliates' websites. In exchange for providing the hyperlinks, Amazon.com pays its affiliates a commission on all purchases resulting from the hyperlink.

Source: "New Media Goes Old Fashioned," *New Media Age,* January 20, 2000, pp. 26–27; Heather Green, "To the Victors Belong the Ads," *Business Week,* October 4, 1999, p. 39; Heather Green, "Portals Are Mortal After All," *Business Week,* June 21, 1999, p. 148; and Linda Frakes, "Through the Looking Glass," www.TheRetailSource.com, January 2000.

Electronic retailers like iVillage are focusing on generating traffic and revenue through affiliate program rather than banner ads. For example, iVillage has an affiliate with Amazon.com.

EXHIBIT 16–5

Communication
Objectives and
Stages in Consumers'
Decision-Making
Process

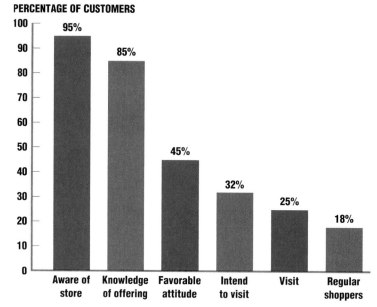

PERCENTAGE OF CUSTOMERS

Exhibit 16–5 shows hypothetical information about customers in the target market for a Safeway supermarket. This information illustrates goals related to stages in the consumer decision-making process outlined in Chapter 5. Note that 95 percent of the customers are aware of the store (the first stage in the decision-making process) and 85 percent know the type of merchandise it sells. But only 45 percent of the customers in the target market have a favorable attitude toward the store. Thirty-two percent intend to visit the store during the next few weeks; 25 percent actually visit the store during the next two weeks; and 18 percent regularly shop at the store.

In this hypothetical example, most people know about the store and its offering. The major problem confronting the Safeway supermarket is the big drop between knowledge and favorable attitude. Thus the store should develop a communication program with the objective of increasing the percentage of customers with a favorable attitude toward it.

To effectively implement and evaluate a communication program, objectives must be clearly stated in quantitative terms. The target audience for the communication mix needs to be defined along with the degree of change expected and the time period over which the change will be realized.

For example, the communication objective for the Safeway program might be to increase from 45 percent to 55 percent within three months the percentage of customers within a five-mile radius of the store who have a favorable attitude toward the store. This objective is clear and measurable. It indicates the task the program should address. The people who implement the program know what they're supposed to accomplish.

Exhibit 16–6 describes how the communication objectives and approaches used by vendors and retailers differ and how these differences can lead to conflicts.

Setting the Communication Budget

The second step in developing a retail communication program is determining a budget (as Exhibit 16–4 shows). The economically correct method for setting the communication budget is marginal analysis. Even though retailers usually don't have enough information to perform a complete marginal analysis, the method shows how managers should approach budget-setting programs.

LONG-TERM versus **SHORT-TERM GOALS**

Most communications done by vendors (manufacturers) are directed toward building a long-term image of their products. On the other hand, most retailer communications are typically used to announce promotions and special sales that generate short-term revenues.

PRODUCT versus **LOCATION**

When vendors advertise their branded products, they don't care where the customer buys them. On the other hand, retailers don't care what brands customers buy as long as they buy them in their store. Vendors want to sell their specific brands, while retailers want to sell the most profitable brands.

GEOGRAPHIC COVERAGE

Since people tend to shop at stores near their homes or workplaces, most retailers use local newspapers, TV, and radio to target their communications. On the other hand, most vendors sell their brands nationally and thus tend to use national TV and magazines.

BREADTH OF MERCHANDISE OFFERED

Typically, vendors have a relatively small number of products to advertise. They can devote a lot of attention to developing consistent communication programs for each brand they make. Since retailers offer a much broader set of products and often focus on building short-term sales, retail communications can easily confuse customers if they focus on different products and don't develop a consistent overall store image.

Marginal Analysis Method   **Marginal analysis** is based on the economic principle that firms should increase communication expenditures so long as each additional dollar spent generates more than a dollar of additional contribution. To illustrate marginal analysis, consider Diane West, owner-manager of a specialty store selling women's business clothing. Exhibit 16–7 shows her analysis to determine how much she should spend next year on her communication program.[16]

For 21 different communication expense levels (column 1), she estimated store sales (column 2), gross margin (column 3), and other expenses (columns 4 and 5). Then she calculated the contribution excluding expenses on communications (column 6) and the profit when the communication expenses are considered (column 7). To estimate the sales generated by different levels of communications, West could have simply relied on her judgment and experience, or she might have analyzed past data to determine the relationship between communication expenses and sales. Historical data also provide information about the gross margin and other expenses as a percentage of sales.

Notice that at low levels of communication expenses, an additional $5,000 in communication expenses generates more than a $5,000 incremental contribution. For example, increasing the communication expense from $15,000 to $20,000 increases contribution by $10,800 (or $48,400 – $37,600). When the communication expense reaches $65,000, further increases of $5,000 generate less than $5,000 in additional contributions. For example, increasing the budget from $65,000 to $70,000 generates only an additional $4,050 in contribution ($125,350 – $121,300).

In this example, West determined that the maximum profit would be generated with a communication expense budget of $65,000. But she noticed that expense levels between $55,000 and $70,000 all result in about the same level of profit. Thus, West might make a conservative decision and establish a $55,000 budget for communication expenses.

In most cases, it's very hard to do a marginal analysis because managers don't know the relationship between communication expenses and sales. Note that the numbers in Exhibit 16–7 are simply West's estimates; they may not be accurate.

EXHIBIT **16–7**   Marginal Analysis for Setting Diane West's Promotion Budget

	PROMOTION EXPENSES (1)	SALES (2)	GROSS MARGIN REALIZED (3)	RENTAL EXPENSE (4)	PERSONNEL EXPENSE (5)	CONTRIBUTION BEFORE PROMOTION EXPENSES (6) = (3) − (4) − (5)	PROFIT (7) = (6) − (1)
	$ 0	$240,000	$ 96,000	$44,000	$52,200	($200)	($200)
	5,000	280,000	112,000	48,000	53,400	10,600	5,600
	10,000	330,000	132,000	53,000	54,900	24,100	14,100
	15,000	380,000	152,000	58,000	56,400	37,600	22,600
	20,000	420,000	168,000	62,000	57,600	48,400	28,400
	25,000	460,000	184,000	66,000	58,800	59,200	34,200
Last year	30,000	500,000	200,000	70,000	60,000	70,000	40,000
	35,000	540,000	216,000	74,000	61,200	80,800	45,800
	40,000	570,000	228,000	77,000	62,100	88,900	48,900
	45,000	600,000	240,000	80,000	63,000	97,000	52,000
	50,000	625,000	250,000	82,500	63,750	103,750	53,750
	55,000	650,000	260,000	85,000	64,500	110,500	55,500
	60,000	670,000	268,000	87,000	65,100	115,900	55,900
Best profit	65,000	690,000	276,000	89,000	65,700	121,300	56,300
	70,000	705,000	282,000	90,500	66,150	125,350	55,350
	75,000	715,000	286,000	91,500	66,450	128,050	53,050
	80,000	725,000	290,000	92,500	66,750	130,750	50,750
	85,000	735,000	294,000	93,500	67,050	133,450	48,450
	90,000	745,000	298,000	94,500	67,350	136,150	46,150
	95,000	750,000	300,000	95,000	67,500	137,500	42,500
	100,000	750,000	300,000	95,000	67,500	137,500	37,500

Sometimes retailers do experiments to get a better idea of the relationship between communication expenses and sales. Say, for example, a catalog retailer selects several geographic areas in the United States with the same sales potential. The retailer then distributes 100,000 catalogs in the first area, 200,000 in the second area, and 300,000 in the third area. Using the sales and costs for each distribution level, he could go through an analysis like the one in Exhibit 16–7 to determine the most profitable distribution level. (Chapter 15 described the use of experiments to determine the relationship between price and sales.)

Some other methods that retailers use to set budgets are the objective-and-task method and rules of thumb, such as the affordable, percentage-of-sales, and competitive parity methods. These methods are less sophisticated than marginal analysis, but easier to use.

Objective-and-Task Method   The **objective-and-task method** determines the budget required to undertake specific tasks for accomplishing communication objectives. To use this method, the retailer first establishes a set of communication objectives. Then the necessary tasks and their costs are determined. The sum total of all costs incurred to undertake the tasks is the communication budget.

Exhibit 16–8 illustrates how Diane West used the objective-and-task method to complement her marginal analysis. West established three objectives: to increase the awareness of her store, to create a greater preference for her store

EXHIBIT **16–8**

Illustration of
Objective-and-Task
Method for Setting a
Promotion Budget

Objective: **Increase the percentage of target market (working women living and/or working within 10 miles of our store) who know of our store's location and that it sells women's business attire from 25 percent to 50 percent over the next 12 months.**	
Task: **480, 30-second radio spots during peak commuting hours (7:00 to 8:00 A.M. and 5:00 to 6:00 P.M.).**	**$12,300**
Task: **Sign with store name near entrance to mall.**	**4,500**
Task: **Display ad in the Yellow Pages.**	**500**
Objective: **Increase the percentage of target market who indicate that our store is their preferred store for buying their business wardrobe from 5 percent to 15 percent in 12 months.**	
Task: **Develop TV campaign to improve image and run 50, 30-second commercials.**	**$24,000**
Task: **Hold four "Dress for Success" seminars followed by a wine-and-cheese social.**	**8,000**
Objective: **Selling merchandise remaining at end of season.**	
Task: **Special event.**	**6,000**
Total budget	**$55,300**

among customers in her target market, and to promote the sale of merchandise remaining at the end of each season. The total communication budget she requires to achieve these objectives is $55,300.

Besides defining the objectives and tasks, West also rechecked the financial implications of the communication mix by projecting the income statement for next year using the communication budget. (See Exhibit 16–9.) This income statement includes an increase of $25,300 in communication expenses over last year. But West feels that this increase in the communication budget will boost annual sales from $500,000 to $650,000. Based on West's projections, the increase in communication expenses will raise store profits. The results of the marginal analysis and the objective-and-task methods suggest a communication budget between $55,000 and $65,000.

Rule-of-Thumb Methods   In the previous two methods, the communication budget is set by estimating communication activities' effects on the firm's future sales or communication objectives. The **rule-of-thumb methods** discussed in this section use the opposite logic. These methods use past sales and communication activity to determine the present communication budget.[17]

Affordable Method   When using the **affordable budgeting method,** retailers first forecast their sales and expenses excluding communication expenses during the budgeting period. The difference between the forecast sales and expenses plus desired profit is then budgeted for the communication mix. In other words, the affordable method sets the communication budget by determining what money is available after operating costs and profits are budgeted.

EXHIBIT **16–9**

Financial Implications
of Increasing the
Promotion Budget

	LAST YEAR	NEXT YEAR
Sales	**$500,000**	**$650,000**
Gross margin (realized)	**200,000**	**260,000**
Rental, maintenance, etc.	**70,000**	**85,000**
Personnel	**60,000**	**64,500**
Communications	**30,000**	**55,300**
Profit	**$ 40,000**	**$ 55,200**

The major problem with the affordable method is that it assumes that the communication expenses don't stimulate sales and profit. Communication expenses are just a cost of business, like the cost of merchandise. When retailers use the affordable method, they typically cut "unnecessary" communication expenses if sales fall below the forecast rather than increase communication expenses to increase sales.

Percentage-of-Sales Method   The **percentage-of-sales method** sets the communication budget as a fixed percentage of forecast sales. Retailers use this method to determine the communication budget by forecasting sales during the budget period and using a predetermined percentage to set the budget. The percentage may be the retailer's historical percentage or the average percentage used by similar retailers.

The problem with the percentage-of-sales method is that it assumes the same percentage used in the past, or by competitors, is still appropriate for your firm. Consider a retailer that hasn't opened new stores in the past but plans to open many new stores in the current year. It must create customer awareness for these new stores so the communication budget should be much larger in the current year than in the past.

Using the same percentage as competitors also may be inappropriate. For example, a retailer might have better locations than its competitors. Due to these locations, customers may already have a high awareness of the retailer's stores. Thus, the retailer may not need to spend as much on communications as competitors with poorer locations spend.

One advantage of both the percentage-of-sales method and the affordable method for determining a communication budget is that the retailer won't spend beyond its means. Since the level of spending is determined by sales, the budget will only go up when sales go up and the retailer generates more sales to pay for the additional communication expenses. When times are good, these methods work well because they allow the retailer to communicate more aggressively with customers. But when sales fall, communication expenses are cut, which may accelerate the sales decline.

Competitive Parity Method   Under the **competitive parity method,** the communication budget is set so that the retailer's share of communication expenses equals its share of the market. For example, consider a sporting goods store in a small town. To use the competitive parity method, the owner-manager would first estimate the total amount spent on communications by all of the sporting goods retailers in town. Then the owner-manager would estimate the store's market share for sporting goods and multiply the market share by the sporting goods stores' total advertising expenses to set its budget. Assume that the owner-manager's estimate of advertising for sporting goods was $5,000 and the estimate of the store's market share was 45 percent. Based on these estimates, the owner-manager would set the store's communication budget at $2,250 to maintain competitive parity.

Like the other rule-of-thumb methods, the competitive parity method doesn't allow retailers to exploit the unique opportunities or problems they confront in a market. If all competitors used this method to set communication budgets, their market shares would stay about the same over time (assuming that the retailers develop equally effective campaigns).

Evaluating a Specific Promotion Opportunity Many promotion opportunities undertaken by retailers are initiated by vendors. For example, Procter & Gamble might offer the following special promotion to Kroger: During a one-week period, Kroger can order Tide laundry detergent in the 48-ounce size at 15 cents below the standard wholesale price. However, if Kroger elects to buy Tide at the discounted price, the grocery chain must feature the 48-ounce container of Tide in its Thursday newspaper ad at $1.59 (20 cents off the typical retail price). In addition, Kroger must have an end-aisle display of Tide.

Before Kroger or any other retailer decides whether to accept such a trade promotion and then promote Tide to its customers, it needs to assess the promotion's impact on its profitability. Such a promotion may be effective for the vendor but not for the retailer.

To evaluate a trade promotion, the retailer considers

- The realized margin from the promotion.
- The cost of the additional inventory carried due to buying more than the normal amount.
- The potential increase in sales from the promoted merchandise.
- The potential loss suffered when customers switch to the promoted merchandise from more profitable unpromoted brands.
- The additional sales made to customers attracted to the store by the promotion.[19]

When Tide's price is reduced to $1.59, Kroger will sell more Tide than it normally would. But Kroger's margin on the Tide will be less because the required retail discount of 20 cents isn't offset by the wholesale discount of 15 cents. In addition, Kroger might suffer losses because the promotion encourages customers to buy Tide, which has a lower margin than Kroger's private-label detergent people might have bought. In fact, customers may stockpile Tide, buying several boxes, which will reduce sales of Kroger's private-label detergent for some time after the special promotion ends. On the other hand, the promotion may attract customers who don't normally shop at Kroger but who will visit to buy Tide at the discounted price. These customers might buy additional merchandise, providing a gain to the store that it wouldn't have realized if it hadn't promoted Tide.

Allocating the Promotion Budget

After determining the size of the communication budget, the third step in the communication planning process is allocating the budget. (See Exhibit 16–4.) In this step, the retailer decides how much of its budget to allocate to specific communication elements, merchandise categories, geographic regions, or long- and short-term objectives. For example, Dillard's must decide how much of its communication budget to spend in each area where it has stores: Arkansas, Texas, Florida, North Carolina, Arizona, and Ohio. Sears decides how much to allocate to appliances, hardware, and apparel. The sporting goods store owner-manager must decide how much of the store's $2,250 communication budget to spend on promoting the store's image versus generating sales during the year and how much to spend on advertising and special promotions.

Research indicates that allocation decisions are more important than the decision on the amount spent on communications.[20] In other words, retailers often

WHEN TJX, THE CORPORATION THAT OWNS T.J. Maxx, bought Marshalls, another off-price retail chain, the firm reduced Marshalls' ad budget by $28 million and eliminated Marshalls' "buy one, get one free" promotion program—and sales actually increased. Bernard Cammaratus, TJX's CEO, attributes the sales increase to a new communication strategy that "reestablished the true off-price mentality in the Marshalls organization and got the Marshalls shopper all excited again."

Prior to the acquisition by TJX, Marshalls' advertising frequently featured new shipments of clothing and products. An ad would say, "We just got in a boatload of Armani suits. Please come down and see us," or it would highlight prices of specific items, emphasizing the size of the discount off list price. Shoppers were attracted to the stores by these ads, but they just cherry picked the advertised items. (**Cherry picking** involves customers visiting a store and buying only merchandise sold at big discounts.)

Cammaratus believes that advertising is different for off-price retailers than for other retailers. Visiting an off-price retailer is like going on a treasure hunt. Shoppers can find apparel, glassware, and jewelry at 30 to 60 percent below department store prices. The chance of finding a real bargain keeps customers going through the merchandise until they find something to buy. But Marshalls' advertising told customers what was new and what were the good buys so it eliminated the adventure in the off-price shopping experience.

T.J. Maxx's advertising campaign stresses everyday low prices. One ad features a shopper named Marsha thinking out loud about what she might find at T.J. Maxx. The tagline is "Brand Names for Less Everyday."

Source: Chris Reidy, "Marshalls's Marsha More than 'Spokestoon,' " *The Boston Globe,* January 22, 1999, p. C3; and Joseph Pereira, "TJX Slashes Ad Budget to Revitalize Unit," *The Wall Street Journal,* October 8, 1996, p. B4.

can realize the same objectives by reducing the size of the communication budget, but allocating the budget more effectively. Retailing View 16.4 illustrates how T.J. Maxx cut its advertising budget and increased sales.

An easy way to make such allocation decisions is just to spend about the same in each geographic region or for each merchandise category. But this allocation rule probably won't maximize profits because it ignores the possibility that communication programs might be more effective for some merchandise categories or for some regions than for others. Another approach is to use rules of thumb such as basing allocations on the sales level or contribution for the merchandise category.

Allocation decisions, like budget-setting decisions, should use the principles of marginal analysis. The retailer should allocate the budget to areas that will yield the greatest return. This approach for allocating a budget is sometimes referred to as the high-assay principle. Consider a miner who can spend his time digging on two claims. The value of the gold on one claim is assayed at $10,000 per ton, while the assay value on the other claim is $5,000 per ton. Should the miner spend 2/3 of his time at the first mine and 1/3 third of his time at the other mine? Of course not! The miner should spend all of his time mining the first claim until the assay value of the ore mined drops to $5,000 a ton, at which time he can divide his time equally between the claims.

Similarly, a retailer may find that its customers have a high awareness and very favorable attitude toward its women's clothing but may not know much about the store's men's clothing. In this situation, a dollar spent on advertising men's clothing might generate more sales than a dollar spent on women's clothing.

Implementing and Evaluating the Mix

The final two stages in developing a retail communication program are implementation and evaluation. (See Exhibit 16–4.) At the end of this chapter we discuss some specific issues in implementing advertising and frequent shopper loyalty programs.

When evaluating communication programs, a retailer needs to compare the results of the program to the objectives developed during the first part of the planning process. Here's an example of the use of market research to evaluate a communication program.

South Gate West is one of several specialty import furniture stores competing for upscale shoppers in Charleston, South Carolina. The store has the appearance of both a fine antique store and a traditional furniture shop, but most of its merchandise is new Asian imports.[21]

The owner realized his communication budget was considerably less than the budget of the local Pier 1 store. (Pier 1 is a large national import furniture chain.) He decided to concentrate his limited budget on a specific segment and use highly distinctive copy and art in his advertising. His target market was experienced, sophisticated consumers of household furniture. His experience indicated the importance of personal selling for more seasoned shoppers because they (1) make large purchases and (2) seek considerable information before making a decision. Thus the owner spent part of his communication budget on training his sales associates.

The advertising program he developed stressed his store's distinctive image. The owner used the newspaper as his major vehicle. Competitive ads contained line drawings of furniture with prices. His ads emphasized the imagery associated with Asian furniture by featuring off-the-beaten-path scenes of Asian countries with unusual art objects. This theme was also reflected in the store's atmosphere.

To measure his campaign's effectiveness, the manager conducted an inexpensive tracking study. Telephone interviews were conducted periodically with a representative sample of furniture customers in his store's trading area. Communication objectives were assessed using the following questions:

COMMUNICATION OBJECTIVE	QUESTION
Awareness	What stores sell East Asian furniture?
Knowledge	Which stores would you rate outstanding on the following characteristics?
Attitude	On your next shopping trip for East Asian furniture, which store would you visit first?
Visit	Which of the following stores have you been to?

Here are the survey results over one year:

COMMUNICATION OBJECTIVE	BEFORE CAMPAIGN	SIX MONTHS AFTER	ONE YEAR AFTER
Awareness (% mentioning store)	38%	46%	52%
Knowledge (% giving outstanding rating for sales assistance)	9	17	24
Attitude (% first choice)	13	15	19
Visit (% visited store)	8	15	19

The results show a steady increase in awareness, knowledge of the store, and choice of the store as a primary source of East Asian furniture. This research provides evidence that the advertising is conveying the intended message to the target audience.

In the rest of this chapter we discuss specific issues in implementing advertising and frequent shopper loyalty programs.

This Target ad is used to build its image of a discount store that offers fashionable apparel.

IMPLEMENTING RETAIL ADVERTISING PROGRAMS

Retail advertising is used to develop and reinforce a firm's image, inform customers about merchandise and prices, and announce a sale. While some national retailers invest in image advertising, most retail advertising focuses on short-term objectives. Implementing an ad program involves developing the message, choosing the specific media to convey the message, and determining the frequency and timing of the message. Next we'll look at each of these decisions.

Developing the Advertising Message

Most retail advertising messages have a short life and are designed to have an immediate impact. This immediacy calls for a copy writing style that grabs the reader's attention. Exhibit 16–10 outlines specific suggestions for developing local newspaper ads.[23]

Assistance in Advertising   Cooperative (co-op) advertising is a program undertaken by a vendor. The vendor pays for part of the retailer's advertising. But the vendor dictates some conditions for the advertising. For example, Sony may have a co-op program that pays for half of a consumer electronics retailer's ads for Sony digital TVs.

EXHIBIT 16–10   Suggestions for Developing Local Ads

Have a dominant headline	The first question a consumer asks is, "What's in it for me?" Thus, retailers need to feature the principal benefit being offered in the headline along with a reason why the consumer should act immediately. The benefit can be expanded on in a subhead.
Use a dominant element	Ads should include a large picture or headline. Typically, photographs of real people attract more attention than drawings. Action photographs are very effective in getting readers' attention.
Stick to a simple layout	The ad's layout should lead the reader's eye through the message from the headline to the illustration and then to the explanatory copy, price, and retailer's name and location. Complex elements, decorative borders, and many different typefaces distract the reader's attention from the retailer's message.
Provide a specific, complete presentation	Ad readers are looking for information that will help them decide whether to visit the store. The ad must contain all of the information pertinent to this decision, including the type of merchandise, brands, prices, sizes, and colors. Consumers are unlikely to make a special trip to the store on the basis of vague information. Broadcast ads, particularly radio ads, tend to be very creative but often leave the consumer thinking, "Gee that was a clever ad, but what was it advertising?"
Use easily recognizable, distinct visuals	Consumers see countless ads each day. Thus, to get the consumers' attention, retailers must make their ads distinct from the competition's. Ads with distinctive art, layout, design elements, or typeface generate higher readership.
Give the store's name and address	The store's name and location are the two most important aspects of a retail ad. If consumers don't know where to go to buy the advertised merchandise, the retailer won't make a sale. The retailer's name and location must be prominently displayed in print ads and repeated several times in broadcast ads.

This Kmart free-standing insert (FSI) is supported by a co-op advertising program offered by Rubbermaid.

Co-op advertising enables a retailer to increase its advertising budget. In the previous example, Best Buy only pays for half of its expenses (for ads including Sony digital TVs). In addition to lowering costs, co-op advertising enables a small retailer to associate its name with well-known national brands and use attractive art work created by the national brand.

Co-op advertising programs are often used to support a vendor's effort to discourage retailers from discounting the vendor's products. For example, Estée Lauder might give its department store retailers 7 percent of sales for co-op advertising only if the retailers agree not to advertise a price below its suggested retail price.

Co-op advertising has other drawbacks. First, vendors want the ad to feature their products, while retailers are more interested in featuring their store's name, location, and assortment of merchandise and services offered. This conflict in goals can reduce co-op advertising's effectiveness from the retailer's perspective. In addition, ads developed by the vendor often are used by several competing retailers and may list the names and locations of all retailers offering their brands. Thus, co-op ads tend to blur any distinctions between retailers. Finally, restrictions the vendor places on the ad may further reduce its effectiveness for the retailer. For example, the vendor may restrict advertising to a period of time when the vendor's sales are depressed, but the retailer might not normally be advertising during this time frame.

Most large retailers have a department that creates advertising for sales and special events. Advertising agencies are often used by large retailers to develop ads for store image campaigns. Many small retailers use local agencies to plan and create their advertising. These local agencies are often more skilled in planning and executing advertising than the retailer's employees are. Agencies also work on other aspects of the communication programs, such as contests, direct mail, and special promotions.

Besides selling newspaper space and broadcast time, the advertising media offer services to local retailers ranging from planning an ad program to actually designing the ads. Media companies also do market research on their audiences and can provide information about shopping patterns in the local area.

Choosing the Most Effective Advertising Medium

After developing the message, the next step is deciding what medium to use to communicate the message. The media used for retail advertising are newspapers, magazines, direct mail, radio, TV, outdoor billboards, the Internet, shopping guides, and the Yellow Pages. Exhibit 16–11 summarizes their characteristics.

EXHIBIT **16-11**

Media Capability

MEDIA	TARGETING	TIMELINESS	INFORMATION PRESENTATION CAPABILITY	LIFE	COST
Newspapers	Good	Good	Modest	Short	Modest
Magazines	Poor	Poor	Modest	Modest	High
Direct mail	Excellent	Modest	High	Modest	Modest
Television	Modest	Modest	Low	Short	Modest
Radio	Modest	Good	Low	Short	Low

Internet
  Banner ads
  Website
	
	Excellent
	Excellent
		
		Excellent
		Excellent
			
			Low
			High
				
				Long
				Long
					
					High
					High

Outdoor billboards	Modest	Poor	Very low	Long	Modest
Shopping guides	Modest	Modest	Low	Modest	Low
Yellow Pages	Modest	Poor	Low	Long	Low

Refact Daily newspapers account for 37 percent of all advertising but 60 percent of retail advertising expenditures. A full 85 percent of newspaper revenues are generated by local retail advertising.[26]

Newspapers   Retailing and newspaper advertising grew up together over the past century. But the growth in retail newspaper advertising has slowed recently as retailers have begun using other media. Still, 16 of the nation's 25 largest newspaper advertisers are retailers.[25]

In addition to printing ads with their editorial content, newspapers distribute free-standing inserts. A **free-standing insert (FSI),** also called a **preprint,** is an ad printed at the retailer's expense and distributed as an insert in the newspaper.

Since newspapers are distributed in a well-defined local market area, they're effective at targeting retail advertising. Often the local market covered by a newspaper is similar to the market served by the retailer. Newspapers are beginning to offer opportunities for small retailers to target their advertising by developing editions for different areas of a city. For example, the *Los Angeles Times* has 11 special editions for regions of southern California, including editions for Ventura County, the desert cities, and San Diego County.

Newspapers also offer quick response. There's only a short time between the deadline for receiving the ad and the time that the ad will appear. Thus, newspapers are very useful for delivering messages on short notice.

Newspapers, like all print media, effectively convey a lot of detailed information. Readers can go through an ad at their own pace and refer back to part of the ad when they want to. In addition, consumers can save the ad and take it to the store with them. This makes newspaper ads very effective at conveying information about the prices of sale items. But newspaper ads aren't effective for showing merchandise (particularly when it's important to illustrate colors) because of the poor reproduction quality.

While newspapers are improving their printing facilities to provide better reproductions and color in ads, retailers continue to rely on preprints to get good reproduction quality. JCPenney uses FSIs extensively, distributing them to over 50 million newspaper readers weekly. However, FSIs are so popular that the insert from one retailer is lost among the large number of inserts in the newspaper. Walgreens has reduced its FSIs from two to one a week because of the clutter and because it has found that young people don't read newspapers as much as their parents. However, Walgreens is trying to increase the effectiveness of its FSIs by streamlining the message and using a better grade of paper.[27]

The life of a newspaper ad is short because the newspaper is usually discarded after it's read. In contrast, magazine advertising has a longer life since consumers tend to save magazines and read them several times during a week or month.

Finally, the cost of developing newspaper ads is very low, but the cost of delivering the message may be high if the newspaper's circulation is broader than the retailer's target market, thus requiring the retailer to pay for exposures that won't generate sales. Newspaper ads can be developed by less experienced people and don't require expensive color photography or typesetting.

Magazines   Retail magazine advertising is mostly done by national retailers such as Target and The Gap. But magazine advertising is increasing with the growth of local magazines and regional editions of national magazines. Retailers tend to use this medium for image advertising because the reproduction quality is high.[28] Due to the lead time (time between submitting the ad and publication), a major disadvantage is that the timing of a magazine ad is difficult to coordinate with special events and sales.

Direct Mail   Retailers frequently use data collected at POS terminals to target their advertising and sales promotions to specific customers using direct mail. (See Chapter 11.) For example, Neiman Marcus keeps a database of all purchases made by its credit card customers. With information on each customer's purchases, Neiman Marcus can target direct mail on a new perfume to customers with a history of purchasing such merchandise.

Retailers also can purchase a wide variety of lists for targeting consumers with specific demographics, interests, and lifestyles. For example, a home furnishings store could buy a list of subscribers to *Architectural Digest* in its trading area and then mail information about home furnishings to those upscale consumers. Finally, many retailers encourage their salespeople to maintain a preferred customer list and use it to mail personalized invitations and notes. While direct mail can be very effective due to the ability to personalize the message, it's also costly. Many consumers ignore direct-mail advertising and treat it as junk mail.

Television   TV commercials can be placed on a national network or a local station. A local commercial is called a **spot.** Retailers typically use TV for image advertising. They take advantage of the high reproduction quality and the opportunity to communicate through both visual images and sound. TV ads can also demonstrate product usage. For example, Eckerd Drug's TV ad program is built around the theme "It's Right at Eckerd." The ads summarize the advantages of shopping at Eckerd on many levels: convenient location, available parking, broad assortment, and fast, easy checkout. Lifestyle ads connect Eckerd as a vital link to an active, healthy, reduced-stress lifestyle. On the other hand, Walgreens' advertising campaign stresses its position as the leading national drugstore via the theme "The Pharmacy America Trusts."[29]

Besides high production costs, broadcast time for national TV advertising is expensive. Spots have relatively small audiences, but may be economical for local retailers. To offset the high production costs, many suppliers provide modular commercials, in which the retailer can insert its name or a "tag" after information about the vendor's merchandise.

Refact Americans spend 1,645 hours annually watching TV and only 175 hours a year reading newspapers.[30]

Radio   Many retailers use radio advertising because messages can be targeted to a specific segment of the market.[31] Some radio stations' audiences are highly loyal to their announcers. When these announcers promote a retailer, listeners are impressed. The cost of developing and broadcasting radio commercials is quite low.

One disadvantage of radio advertising is that listeners generally treat the radio broadcast as background, which limits the attention they give the message. As with all broadcast media, consumers must get the information from a radio commercial when it's broadcast. They can't refer back to the ad for information they didn't hear or remember.

 INTERNET EXERCISE   You can find more information about the use of radio as an advertising media at the Radio Advertising Bureau site, www.rab.com. Based on this information, what types of retail messages can be delivered most effectively by radio compared to other media?

Internet   Two uses of the Internet by retailers to communicate with customers are (1) banner ads and affiliate programs to generate awareness (see Retailing View 16.3) and (2) websites to provide information about merchandise and special events.[32] Banner ads and affiliate programs are very effective for targeting communication, but they are not cost effective for building awareness. Using information from a visitor's navigation and purchase behavior, and IP address, banner ads can be targeted to specific individuals. For example, Sportsline.com visitors who look at the box scores for Kansas City Royals baseball games are shown ads for Royals logo apparel and hats. Double Click, an Internet ad agency, downloads different banner ads from its server to host websites based on information it has on the specific visitor. However, Internet advertising is not cost-effective for building awareness because the large number of websites reduces the number of customers visiting a site and seeing a particular ad.

While the Internet is not effective for building awareness, it is an excellent vehicle for conveying information to customers. In addition to selling merchandise for a website, retailers can provide a wide array of information ranging from the store locations to the availability and pricing of merchandise in specific stores. The interactivity of the Internet gives customers the opportunity to quickly sift through a vast amount of information. For example, visitors to the Circuit City website can find detailed information on specific digital camera models and generate a table comparing a select group of cameras on features of importance to the customer.

Finally, retailers can use the Internet to send e-mails to customers informing them of special events and new merchandise.

Outdoor Billboards   Billboards and other forms of outdoor advertising are effective vehicles for creating awareness and providing a very limited amount of information to a narrow audience. Thus, outdoor advertising has limited usefulness in providing information about sales. Outdoor advertising is typically used to remind customers about the retailer or to inform people in cars of nearby retail outlets.[33]

Shopping Guides   **Shopping guides** are free papers delivered to all residents in a specific area. This medium is particularly useful for retailers that want to saturate a specific trading area. Shopping guides are very cost-effective and assure the local retailer of 100 percent coverage in a specific area. In contrast, subscription newspapers typically offer only 30 to 50 percent coverage. An extension of the shopping guide concept is the coupon book or magazine. These media contain coupons offered by retailers for discounts. Shopping guides and coupon books make no pretense about providing news to consumers. They're simply delivery vehicles for ads and coupons.

Yellow Pages   The Yellow Pages are useful for retailers because they have a long life. The Yellow Pages are used as a reference by consumers who are definitely interested in making a purchase and seeking information.

Factors in Selecting Media   To convey their message with the most impact to the most consumers in the target market at the lowest cost, retailers need to evaluate media in terms of coverage, reach, cost, and impact of the advertising messages delivered through the medium.

Coverage   **Coverage** refers to the number of potential customers in the retailer's target market that could be exposed to an ad in a given medium. For example, assume that the size of the target market is 100,000 customers. The local newspaper is distributed to 60 percent of the customers in the target market, 90 percent of the potential customers have a TV set that picks up the local station's signal, and 5 percent of the potential customers drive past a billboard. Thus, the coverage for newspaper advertising would be 60,000; for TV advertising, 90,000; and for the specific billboard, 5,000.

Reach   In contrast to coverage, **reach** is the actual number of customers in the target market exposed to an advertising medium. If on any given day, 60 percent of the potential customers who receive the newspaper actually read it, then the newspaper's reach would be 36,000 (or 60 percent of 60,000). Retailers often run an ad several times, in which case they calculate the **cumulative reach** for the sequence of ads. For example, if 60 percent of the potential customers receiving a newspaper read it each day, 93.6 percent (or $1 - .40 \times .40 \times .40$) of the potential customers will read the newspaper at least one day over the three-day period in which the ad appears in the paper. Thus, the cumulative reach for running a newspaper ad for three days is 56,160 (or 93.6 percent $\times$ 60,000), which almost equals the newspaper's coverage.

When evaluating Internet advertising opportunities, the measure used to assess reach is the number of unique visitors—the number of different people who access the webpage on which the ad is located.

Cost   The **cost per thousand (CPM)** measure is often used to compare media. Typically, CPM is calculated by dividing an ad's cost by its reach. Another approach for determining CPM is to divide the cost of several ads in a campaign by their cumulative reach. If, for instance, in the previous example, one newspaper ad costs $500 and three ads cost $1,300, the CPM using simple reach is $13.89 (or $500/36). Using cumulative reach, the CPM is $23.15 (or $1,300/56.16). Note that the CPM might be higher using cumulative reach rather than simple reach, but the overall reach is also higher, and many potential customers will see the ad two or three times.

EXHIBIT **16-12**   Effectiveness of Media on Communication Objectives

COMMUNICATION TASK	NEWSPAPER	MAGAZINE	DIRECT MAIL	TV	RADIO	INTERNET	OUTDOOR
Getting attention	Low	Medium	Medium	High	Low	Low	Medium
Identifying name	Medium	High	Low	Low	Low	Low	High
Announcing events	High	Low	High	High	Medium	Low	Low
Demonstrating merchandise	Low	Medium	High	High	Low	Highest	Low
Providing information	Low	High	High	Low	Low	Highest	Lowest
Changing attitudes	High	Medium	High	High	Medium	High	Low
Building brand image	Low	Medium	High	High	Low	High	Low

CPM is a good method for comparing similar-size ads in similar media, such as full-page ads in the *Los Angeles Times* and the *Orange County Register*. But CPM can be misleading when comparing the cost-effectiveness of ads in different types of media, such as newspaper and TV. A TV ad may have a lower CPM than a newspaper ad, but the newspaper ad may be much more effective at achieving the ad's communication objectives, such as giving information about a sale.

Impact **Impact** is an ad's effect on the audience. Due to their unique characteristics, different media are particularly effective at accomplishing different communication tasks. Exhibit 16–12 shows various media's effectiveness for different communication tasks. TV is particularly effective at getting an audience's attention, demonstrating merchandise, changing attitudes, and announcing events. Magazines are particularly appropriate for emphasizing the quality and prestige of a store and its offering, and for providing detailed information to support quality claims. Newspapers are useful for providing price information and announcing events. The Internet is particularly effective at demonstrating merchandise and providing information. Outdoor advertising is most effective at promoting a retailer's name and location.

Determining Ad Frequency and Timing

The frequency and timing of ads determine how often and when customers will see the retailer's message.

Frequency   **Frequency** is how many times the potential customer is exposed to an ad. When assessing frequency for Internet advertising, frequency is typically assessed by measuring the number of times a webpage with the ad is downloaded during a visit to the site.

The appropriate frequency depends on the ad's objective. Typically, several exposures to an ad are required to influence a customer's buying behavior. Thus, campaigns directed toward changing purchase behavior rather than creating awareness emphasize frequency over reach. Ads announcing a sale are often seen and remembered after one exposure. Thus, sale ad campaigns emphasize reach over frequency.

Timing   Typically, an ad should appear on, or slightly preceding, the days consumers are most likely to purchase merchandise. For example, if most consumers buy groceries Thursday through Sunday, then supermarkets should advertise on

Thursday and Friday. Similarly, consumers often go shopping after they receive their paychecks at the middle and the end of the month. Thus, advertising should be concentrated at these times.

Retailers should avoid advertising during periods of limited demand. Seasonal merchandise should only be advertised during periods when it's bought. Advertise lawn mowers at the beginning of summer and skimobiles at the beginning of winter. Advertising isn't very effective during bad weather because customers are reluctant to leave their homes to visit a store. But these might be good times for direct-mail retailers to advertise.

FREQUENT SHOPPER LOYALTY PROGRAMS

For most retailers, a small percentage of their customers account for most of their sales. For example, when Schultz Sav-O Stores analyzed the customer database for its Wisconsin Piggly Wiggly outlets, it discovered that 30 percent of its customers were responsible for 70 percent of its sales.[34] In addition, research indicated that it is much less costly to retain existing customers than to acquire new customers.[35] Thus many retailers are initiating frequent shopper programs to target special services and promotion to building loyalty among their best customers. The programs provide special benefits to the retailer's most important customers and motivate them to develop loyalty. Due to these programs' success, many retailers are shifting their expenditures from newspaper advertising and newspaper coupons to frequent shopper programs.

Refact When firms increase customer retention by 5 percent, they realize a 25 to 95 percent increase in net present value.[36]

Customer Benefits Offered by Frequent Shopper Programs

Service-oriented retailers such as Neiman Marcus typically offer their best customers specialized services. Customers who spend over $3,000 at Neiman's become members of the retailer's InCircle program. Members of the program receive a distinctive credit card; free gift wrapping; discounts and upgrades on services provided by affiliated airlines, hotels, and rental car firms; and $200,000 of free travel insurance. But the primary benefit is the individualized attention provided by the local store manager and sales associates. Store managers invite InCircle members to a free luncheon on their birthdays. Sales associates are encouraged to contact members and be creative in uncovering ways to help them. Annually, InCircle members are invited to sit on Neiman's InCircle Board and provide feedback and suggestions as to how Neiman's can continue to improve its customers' shopping. Through these boards Neiman's maintains an ongoing dialogue with best customers.[37]

On the other hand, self-service retailers such as supermarkets typically focus their frequent shopper programs on merchandise discounts. For example, Fresh Farm, a Norfolk, Virginia-based supermarket chain, has a frequent shopper program called the Gold Card program for its best customers. When Gold Card member Tina Williams enters the store, she "swipes" her card at a kiosk, and a high-speed printer provides a personalized shopping list with up to 25 deals. The deals offered are based on Tina's purchase history. For example, Tina's history shows she frequently purchases corn chips but does not buy dip. She'll get a deal on bean dip printed on her shopping list to encourage her to try a new product. If she passes up the deal this time in the market, the next time the value of the bean dip coupon will be automatically increased.[38]

Brian Woolf, the guru of frequent shopper programs, offers the following points for developing an effective program:[39]

* Price—Members of the program should receive lower prices than nonmembers.

* Purchases—The more you spend, the more rewards you should receive. For example, offer a free turkey at Thanksgiving if the customer spends x dollars during the previous six weeks.

* Points—Award points based on customer purchases. Then allow customers to use the points to buy what they like.

* Partners—Bring noncompetitive retailers into the program. For example, airline frequent flyer programs have partnerships with rental car companies, hotels, and restaurants. General merchandise retailers can team up with local restaurants, gas stations, banks, and movie theaters.

* Prizes—Big Y in New England ran a $1 million sweepstakes plus weekly prizes of $1,000 in cash for members of its frequent shopper club.

* Privileges—If you stay in a Disney hotel, you have the privilege of entering the park an hour early. Marks & Spencer in England has a special shopping evening before Christmas for only its best customers. As American Express says in its ads, "Membership has its privileges."

* Pro bono—Tie in with local charities. Have your best customers select a charity and donate 1 percent of their money from purchases to the charity.

* Personalization—When the frequent shopper card is scanned by the POS terminal, have the screen give the sales associate the opportunity to say "Good morning, Ms. Ramirez." A bakery in Ireland can tell the salesperson that the card holder's birthday is within a week and then the sales associate gets a free birthday cake for the customer.

* Participation—Involve your best customers in decisions. Ask them to participate in focus groups.

* Presto—Treat special customers like they're special. Empower sales associates to make favorable decisions for these customers.

Targeting Frequent Shoppers

To exploit the potential of frequent shopper programs, retailers need to develop and maintain a comprehensive customer database. The most basic customer database consists of the names, addresses, telephone numbers, and e-mail addresses of customers along with a record of how much they have purchased from the retailer. With this information, retailers can identify and target marketing programs such as the frequent shopper program to their best customers.

Developing this basic database is challenging for store-based retailers because they cannot easily link sales transactions with specific customers. For example, department store retailers know what customers have purchased using their proprietary credit card, but have no record of purchases these customers made with cash, checks, or bank credit cards. Many retailers issue frequent shopper cards as a method for creating a customer database rather increasing customer loyalty. When customers purchase merchandise, their frequent shopper cards are scanned along with the merchandise so that the transactions can be linked to the customers. Catalog and electronic retailers do not have this problem of relating transactions to specific customers because customer identifications are collected at the time of the transaction so the merchandise can be shipped to the customer.

In addition to the basic customer information, retailers collect information at the point of sale and also ask their customers to provide information when they apply for frequent shopper cards or place an initial order with an electronic retailer. Sophisticated customer databases include demographics (age, income, family members, birthdays), lifestyles (activities and interests), and detailed purchase histories including the items purchased and whether they were on sale. Fingerhut, a catalog retailer, has 1,400 pieces of information about each of its 30 million customers in its database.[40]

With this additional information, retailers can target communications and promotions to its customers. For example, Streamline, an electronic grocery retailer, sends e-mails to customers when its analysis of their purchase history suggests that they're about to stock out of products such as paper towels or soft drinks. The purchase history uncovers opportunities for cross-selling such as promoting kitty litter to customers who buy cat food.[41]

Privacy

Many consumers and consumer advocacy groups are concerned about retailers' potential misuse of detailed customer databases. These concerns are particularly acute for electronic retailers because many consumers do not realize the extensive amount of information that can be collected without their knowledge. In addition to collecting transaction data, electronic retailers can collect information by placing cookies on visitor's hard drives. **Cookies** are text files that identify visitors when they return to a website. Due to the data in the cookies, customers do not have to identify themselves and use passwords every time they visit a site. However, the cookies also collect information about other sites the person has visited and what pages they have downloaded.[42]

INTERNET EXERCISE   Go to the sites of some of the electronic retailers listed in the appendix to Chapter 3. Do the retailers post their privacy policies? How do the policies posted compare with each other?

Refact Of the top 100 retail websites, 87 percent use cookies to gather visitor information and 18 percent have no privacy policy stated on their sites.[43]

To address these concerns, many electronic retailers and other retailers that collect customer information have privacy policies. The Electronic Privacy Information Center (www.epic.org) recommends that privacy policies clearly state what information is collected from each visitor and how it will be used, give consumers a choice as to whether they give information, and allow them to view and correct any personal information held by an online retail site. Internet retailers should also ensure that consumer information is held securely and is not passed on to other companies without the permission of the customer.[44]

SUMMARY   Retailers communicate with customers through advertising, sales promotions, websites, store atmosphere, publicity, personal selling, and word of mouth. These elements in the promotion mix must be coordinated so customers will have a clear, distinct image of the retailer and won't be confused by conflicting information.

The communication program can be designed to achieve a variety of objectives for the retailer. Objectives include building a brand image of the retailer in the customer's mind, increasing sales and store traffic, providing information about the retailer's location and offering, and announcing special activities.

Many retailers use rules of thumb to determine the size of the promotion budget. Marginal analysis (the most appropriate method for determining how much must be spent to accomplish the retailer's objectives) should be used to determine whether the level of spending maximizes the profits that could be generated by the promotion mix.

The largest portion of a retailer's promotion budget is typically spent on advertising and sales promotions. A wide array of media can be used for advertising. Each medium has its pros and cons. Newspaper advertising is effective for announcing sales, while TV ads are useful for developing an image. Sales promotions are typically used to achieve short-term objectives, such as increasing store traffic over a weekend. Most sales promotions are supported in part by promotions offered to the retailer by its vendors. Publicity and word-of-mouth communications are typically low-cost but are very difficult for retailers to control.

Many retailers are using frequent shopper programs to build loyalty. The customer databases developed to support these programs can also be used for targeting special promotions. However, maintaining customers' privacy is a concern.

KEY TERMS

advertising, *491*

affiliate program (associate program), *499*

affordable budgeting method, *503*

brand building, *497*

cherry picking, *506*

communication objectives, *498*

competitive parity method, *504*

contest, *492*

cookies, *517*

cooperative (co-op) advertising, *508*

cost per thousand (CPM), *513*

coupon, *492*

coverage, *513*

cumulative reach, *513*

free-standing insert (FSI), *510*

frequency, *514*

frequent shopper program, *491*

impact, *514*

integrated marketing communications, *496*

marginal analysis, *500*

objective-and-task method, *502*

percentage-of-sales method, *504*

personal selling, *493*

positioning, *497*

preprint, *510*

publicity, *493*

reach, *513*

rule-of-thumb methods, *503*

sales promotion, *491*

shopping guide, *513*

spot, *511*

store atmosphere, *492*

word of mouth, *494*

DISCUSSION QUESTIONS AND PROBLEMS

1. How can advertising, personal selling, and promotion complement each other in an integrated marketing communications program?

2. Why do retailers use frequent shopper programs?

3. As a means of communicating with customers, how does advertising differ from publicity?

4. Why is the newspaper the favorite medium used by retailers for advertising? What are the advantages and disadvantages of newspaper advertising? Why is the use of newspaper decreasing and use of direct mail increasing?

5. Assume you are launching a website to sell merchandise with your university's logo. Develop a communication program to promote your new website.

6. What factors should be considered in dividing up the budget among a store's different merchandise areas? Which of the following should receive the highest advertising budget: fashionable women's clothing, men's underwear, women's hosiery, or kitchen appliances? Why?

7. Outline some elements in a promotion program to achieve the following objectives:
   a. Increase store loyalty by 20 percent.
   b. Build awareness of the store by 10 percent.
   c. Develop an image as a low-price retailer.

8. How would you determine whether the communication program met the objective?

9. Retailers use TV to build a brand image. TV advertisers have identified many types of markets based on the day, time, and type of show during which their ads may appear. During which days, times, and types of shows would retailers advertise fresh produce and meat, power drills, beer, and health club memberships? Why?

10. Some retailers direct their advertising efforts toward reaching as wide an audience as possible. Others try to expose the audience to an advertisement as many times as possible. When should a retailer concentrate on reach? When should a retailer concentrate on frequency?

11. A retailer plans to open a new store near a university. It will specialize in collegiate merchandise such as T-shirts, fraternity/sorority accessories, and sweatshirts. What specific advertising media should the new store use to capture the university market?

12. Cooperative (co-op) advertising is a good way for a retailer to extend an ad budget. Why isn't it always in a retailer's best interests to rely extensively on co-op advertising?

SUGGESTED READINGS

Belch, George, and Michael Belch. *Introduction to Advertising and Promotion Management*, 3d ed. Burr Ridge, IL: Irwin/McGraw-Hill, 1999.

Chen, Shih-Fen. "The Effects of Framing Price Promotion Messages on Consumers' Perceptions and Purchase Intentions." *Journal of Retailing* 74 (Fall 1998), pp. 353–55.

Dowling, Grahame, and Mark Uncles. "Do Customer Loyalty Programs Really Work?" *Sloan Management Review* 38 (November 1998), pp. 45–57.

Karande, Kiram, and V. Kumar. "The Effects of Brand Characteristics and Retailer Policies on Response to Retail Price Promotion: Implications for Retailers." *Journal of Retailing* 71 (Fall 1995), pp. 249–78.

Keller, Kevin. *Strategic Brand Management: Building, Measuring, and Managing Brand Equity.* Englewood Cliffs, NJ: Prentice Hall, 1997.

McArthur, David. "A Marketing Management View of Integrated Marketing Communications." *Journal of Advertising Research* 37 (September–October 1997), pp. 19–27.

Murphy, Patricia. "Effective Loyalty Programs Seen Catering to Individual Needs." *Stores*, February 1999, pp. 46–48.

Reda, Susan. "Measuring Marketing's ROI." *Stores*, May 1998, pp. 22–27.

Redman, Russell. "Selling the Image." *Supermarket News*, March 18, 1996, pp. 1–2.

Ryan, Ken. "The Internet Is a Flop in Retail Advertising." *HFN*, June 15, 1998, pp. 6–7.

Srinivasan, Srini, Robert Leone, and Francis Mulhern. "The Advertising Exposure Effect of Free Standing Inserts." *Journal of Advertising*, March 22, 1995, pp. 29–38.

Zeff, Robbin, and Brad Aronson. *Advertising on the Internet*, 2d ed. New York: Wiley, 1999.

Ziccardi, Donald, and David Moin. *Masterminding the Store: Advertising, Sales Promotion, and the New Marketing.* New York, Wiley, 1997.

SECTION IV

Store Management

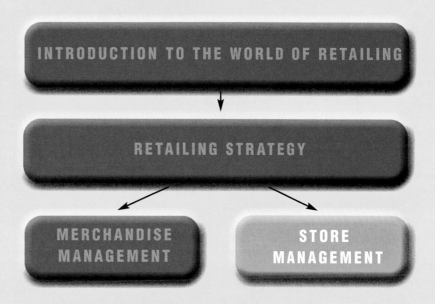

INTRODUCTION TO THE WORLD OF RETAILING

RETAILING STRATEGY

MERCHANDISE MANAGEMENT

STORE MANAGEMENT

SECTION IV FOCUSES on implementation issues associated with store management, including managing store employees and controlling costs (Chapter 17), presenting merchandise (Chapter 18), and providing service (Chapter 19). Traditionally, the issues concerning merchandise management were considered the most important retail implementation decisions, and buying was considered the best career path for achieving senior retail management positions. Developing a strategic advantage through merchandise management is becoming more and more difficult. Competing stores often have similar assortments of branded merchandise. Since customers can find the same assortments in a number of conveniently located retail outlets, store management issues have become a critical basis for developing strategic advantage. Retailers are increasing their emphasis on differentiating their offering from competitive offerings based on customer service, store design, and visual merchandising.

Juli Johnson
Store Manager
Walgreens

I REALLY LIKE BEING A STORE MANAGER. Sitting at a desk all day would really bore me. I need to walk around and talk to people. As a store manager, I get to work with a lot of different people—customers, store employees, people in our district office—and I do a lot of different things. In a single day I will be handling some personnel issues, talking with customers, deciding how we should display new merchandise, and reviewing the reports summarizing the store's financial performance. • When I was in college, I didn't know much about retailing. But for 10 weeks between my junior and senior years, I did an internship with Walgreens. The internship, arranged by the Retail Institute at Texas A&M, was a great management training experience. For 10 weeks during the summer, I was exposed to all of the facets of store management. I found it so interesting that I went back to work in the store the following Christmas and took a job as an assistant store manager when I graduated. After 16 months, I was promoted to store manager in Houston. My store has annual sales of $5.5 million and employs 100 people. • It's very rewarding for me to work with our employees. I get a lot of satisfaction helping them learn more about how our store and company operates, seeing them develop their skills, and eventually get promoted. I'm also getting more responsibilities. This year I helped our corporate recruiters at college career fairs and I started interviewing people for assistant manager positions in the company. • One thing I impress on my staff is that the customer is number one. We always need to provide the best service so that customers will keep on coming back. I am proud of the fact that my store went 148 days without receiving a complaint card from a customer. • My approach to getting the customer orientation in my store is creating a positive and exciting atmosphere for the employees. When one of them gets praised in a customer comment card, I post the card on the bulletin board to reward the employee and send a signal to others. I want them to feel responsible for making sure that customers love the store and have a great experience and will come back often. • Being a store manager at Walgreens is like running my own business—I get recognized and rewarded. But the rewards I get are more than money. I like to work with and help people. Walgreens is a great place for me to work because Walgreens cares about people, customers, and employees, just like I do.

17

Managing the Store

QUESTIONS

- What are the responsibilities of store managers?
- How should store managers recruit, select, motivate, train, and evaluate their employees?
- How should store managers compensate their salespeople?
- What legal and ethical issues must store managers consider in managing their employees?
- What can store managers do to increase productivity and reduce costs?
- How can store managers reduce inventory losses due to employee theft and shoplifting?

STORE MANAGERS ARE RESPONSIBLE for increasing the productivity of two of the retailer's most important assets: the firm's investments in its employees and real estate. Store managers are on the firing line in retailing. Due to their daily contact with customers, they have the best knowledge of customer needs and competitive activity. From this unique vantage point, store managers play an important role in formulating and executing retail strategy. Buyers can develop exciting merchandise assortments and procure them at low cost, but the retailer only realizes the benefits of the buyer's effort when the merchandise is sold. Good merchandise doesn't sell itself. Store managers must present the merchandise effectively and offer services that stimulate and facilitate customer buying decisions.

Even in national chains, store managers are treated as relatively independent managers of a business within the corporation. Some department store managers are responsible for $150 million in annual sales and manage over 1,000 employees. For example, James Nordstrom (CEO of Nordstrom) tells store managers, "This is your business. Do your own thing. Don't listen to us in Seattle, listen to your customers. We give you permission to take care of your customers." And Michele Love, manager of the Nordstrom store in Skokie, Illinois, responded by building a mammography center in the store without asking anyone. The center has been booked solid since it opened.[1]

EXHIBIT **17-1**

Responsibilities of
Store Managers

MANAGING STORE EMPLOYEES (Chapter 17)

Recruiting and selecting
Socializing and training
Motivating
Evaluating and providing constructive feedback
Rewarding and compensating

CONTROLLING COSTS (Chapter 17)

Increasing labor and productivity
Reducing maintenance and energy costs
Reducing inventory losses

MANAGING MERCHANDISE

Displaying merchandise and maintaining visual standards (Chapter 18)
Working with buyers
  Suggesting new merchandise
  Buying merchandise
  Planning and managing special events
  Marking down merchandise

PROVIDING CUSTOMER SERVICE (Chapter 19)

STORE MANAGEMENT RESPONSIBILITIES

The responsibilities of store managers are shown in Exhibit 17–1. These functions are divided into four major categories: managing employees, controlling costs, managing merchandise, and providing customer service. Issues concerning managing store employees and controlling costs are discussed in this chapter. The following chapters examine the store manager's responsibilities for presenting and managing merchandise and providing customer service.

An important function of store managers is increasing the productivity of store employees by recruiting and selecting effective people; improving their skills through training; motivating them to perform at higher levels; and then evaluating and rewarding them. Retailing View 17.1 describes the special issues that German retailers face increasing employee productivity.

In addition to increasing employee productivity, store managers also need to develop employees who can assume more responsibility and be promoted to higher-level management positions. By developing subordinates, managers help both their firm and themselves. The firm benefits from having more effective managers, and the manager benefits because the firm has a qualified replacement when the manager is promoted.[2]

Managers also increase their stores' profits by reducing costs. The major costs are the compensation and benefits of employees. But store managers also need to control maintenance and energy costs and inventory loss due to shoplifting and employee theft. These cost control issues are discussed at the end of the chapter.

The first portion of this chapter, focusing on the management of store employees, complements the strategic human resource management issues discussed in Chapter 10. Chapter 10 examined the organization of the tasks performed by the retailers and the general approaches for motivating retail employees and building their commitment to the firm. In this chapter, we discuss how store managers implement the retailer's human resource strategy.

Refact In supermarkets, which are largely self-service, wages account for 65 percent of stores' controllable expenses.[3]

MS. ANGIE CLARK AND MR. ANDREAS DRAUSCHKE have similar store management jobs with similar pay at two different department stores. However, Mr. Drauschke, in Germany, only works 37 hours a week (rarely at night or on weekends) and has six weeks of annual paid vacation. Ms. Clark, in the United States, works 44 hours a week (including evening and weekend shifts), frequently brings work home at night, and spends some off-time shopping the competitors. While Americans often marvel at German efficiency, Mr. Drauschke's workweek and benefits are typical in Germany, where workers are guaranteed five weeks paid vacation by law and stores rarely are open more than one night a week and only a half-day on Saturday.

German retail sales associates serve an apprenticeship for two or three years. During this time, they learn the business and the merchandise inside out. In contrast, sales associates in U.S. department stores typically receive only two or three days of training before they start to work with customers.

Keeping work hours short is an obsession in Germany and a goal of the country's powerful labor unions. When Germany introduced Thursday-night shopping in 1989, retail workers went on strike. Mr. Drauschke still finds it difficult to staff the extra two hours on Thursday even though employees are given an hour less work overall. In contrast, many American retail employees work a second job to send their children through college or save money for a house.

However, the long, irregular hours for U.S. retail managers take their toll. Turnover among U.S. retail managers is as high as 40 percent while turnover among German retail managers is negligible.

Source: Guy Raz, "Closed on Sunday? Shopkeepers Rebel," *The Christian Science Monitor*, August 12, 1999, p. 8; and Daniel Benjamin and Tony Horwitz, "German View: You Americans Work Too Hard and for What?" *The Wall Street Journal*, July 14, 1994, pp. B1, B6.

Exhibit 17–2 outlines the steps in the employee management process that impact store employees' productivity. These steps are discussed in the following sections.

RECRUITING AND SELECTING STORE EMPLOYEES

The first step in the employee management process is recruiting and selecting employees. To effectively recruit employees, store managers need to undertake a job analysis, prepare a job description, find potential applicants with the desired capabilities, and screen the best candidates to interview.[4] (Appendix 1A to Chapter 1 described the recruiting and selection process from the perspective of people interested in pursuing retail careers and applying for management trainee positions.)

EXHIBIT **17–2**   Steps in the Employee Management Process

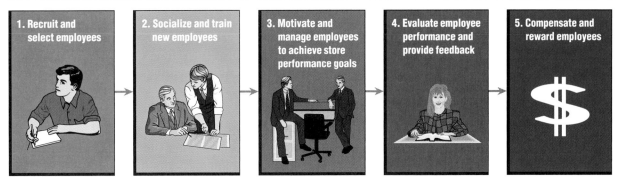

1. Recruit and select employees

2. Socialize and train new employees

3. Motivate and manage employees to achieve store performance goals

4. Evaluate employee performance and provide feedback

5. Compensate and reward employees

EXHIBIT **17–3**

Questions for
Undertaking
a Job Analysis

How many salespeople will be working in the department at the same time?
Do the salespeople have to work together in dealing with customers?
How many customers will the salesperson have to work with at one time?
Will the salesperson be selling on an open floor or working behind the counter?
How much and what type of product knowledge does the salesperson need?
Does the salesperson need to sell the merchandise or just ring up the orders and provide information?
Is the salesperson required to make appointments with customers and develop a loyal customer base?
Does the salesperson have the authority to negotiate price or terms of the sale?
Does the salesperson need to demonstrate the merchandise?
Will the salesperson be expected to make add-on sales?
Is the salesperson's appearance important? How should an effective salesperson look?
Will the salesperson be required to perform merchandising activities such as stocking shelves and setting up displays?
Who will the salesperson report to?
What compensation plan will the salesperson be working under?

Job Analysis   The objective of the **job analysis** is to identify essential activities and to determine the qualifications employees need to perform them effectively. For example, retail salespeople's responsibilities vary from company to company and from department to department within a store. Clothing salespeople work on an open floor and need to approach customers. Cosmetic and jewelry salespeople work behind a counter, so their customers approach them. Due to these differences, effective open-floor selling requires more aggressive behavior than counter selling.

Managers can obtain the information needed for a job analysis by observing employees presently doing the job and by determining the characteristics of exceptional performers. Exhibit 17–3 lists some questions that managers should consider in a job analysis for sales associates. Information collected in the job analysis is used to prepare a job description.

The job analysis can lead to redefining the employee's authority as well as responsibilities. As discussed in Chapter 10, retailers are attempting to improve customer service by empowering sales associates to make more decisions. For example, sales clerks at Target's Greatland store can take the customer's word for items priced below $20 if the merchandise can't be scanned; give customers the sale price even if the sale's week has ended; and offer the customer comparable merchandise at the sale price rather than a rain check for out-of-stock sale items.[5]

Job Description   A **job description** includes (1) activities the employee needs to perform and (2) the performance expectations expressed in quantitative terms. The job description is a guideline for recruiting, selecting, training, and eventually evaluating employees. The description must be in writing so it can be communicated accurately and consistently to present and prospective employees.

Locating Prospective
Employees   Staffing stores is a critical problem because changing demographics are reducing the size of the labor pool.[6] Here are some suggestions for recruiting employees in this tight labor market:

- Look beyond the retail industry. For example, a jewelry store owner recruited a waitress from a deli she frequented who was "unflappable and was paid next to nothing." Another jeweler hired a dance instructor whose artistic eye and charisma made her a very effective jewelry salesperson.[7] Use your employees as talent scouts. Ask employees if they know someone you could hire or if they have recently encountered a particularly good salesperson when purchasing any item.

- Provide incentives for employee referrals. For example, Professional Salon Concepts, a chain of beauty parlors, offers a referral bonus to its employees. Employees get $100 after a recommended recruit is on the job for 30 days, another $100 on the recruit's six-month anniversary, and $500 if the recruit works for the company for a year.[8]

- Recruit from minority and immigrant communities. Burger King aggressively pursues the growing number of immigrants as a source for new employees. Application forms are available in English and Spanish; prospective workers can bring a family member or friend to act as an interpreter during the interview. Training programs are developed for people who aren't familiar with U.S. business practices. For example, many foreign-born workers don't understand benefits like life insurance and are reluctant to report job-related injuries for fear of being fired.[9]

- Use your storefront creatively. Don't just post a HELP WANTED sign. Print one reading, "Thank you! Business is great. Because things are so good, we're hiring additional staff. Please stop in to discuss career opportunities."

Retailers are using the Internet to locate prospective employees. For example, The Olive Garden posts job openings on sites such as www.Restaurant Managers.com, www.RestaurantJobsNetwork.com, and www.RestaurantRecruit.com. It has found that applicants coming from these sites are better prepared for today's retail environment. Andy Snitz, director of employment at the Olive Garden, comments, "Fifteen years ago, if someone wrote 'computers and electronics,' under 'special interests,' we would have thought, 'What a nerd'. Today you can't survive in business unless you have computer skills. [These people] aren't going to be challenged by our point-of-sale systems or running a back office program."[10]

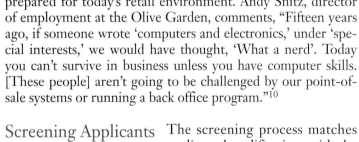

T.J. Maxx uses this ad to interest prospect employees in its entry-level positions as assistant store managers.

Screening Applicants to Interview

The screening process matches applicants' qualifications with the job description. Many retailers use automated prescreening programs as a low-cost method for identifying qualified candidates. Applicants call a toll-free telephone number and a computer program asks some basic questions that the applicants answer by pressing 1 for yes or 2 for no. Some questions are "Have you reached your 16th birthday?" and "Are you a resident of the United States?"

Other questions are tailored to the retailer's specific needs and environment. For example, Hot Topics, a mall-based chain selling music-themed merchandise, asks, "Would you work in environment where loud, alternative music is played?" The response time for answering the questions is monitored and follow-up questions are asked when the answers are unusually slow. When applicants pass this automated prescreen, additional information is collected using application forms, reference checks, and tests.[11]

Application Forms   **Job application forms** contain information about the applicant's employment history, previous compensation, reasons for leaving previous employment, education and training, personal health, and references. This information enables the manager to determine whether the applicant has the minimum qualifications and also provides information for interviewing the applicant.[12]

References   A good way to verify the application form's information is to contact the applicant's references. Contacting references is also helpful for collecting additional information from people who've worked with the applicant. In addition, store managers should check with former supervisors not listed as references. Due to potential legal problems, however, many companies have a policy of not commenting on past employees.[13]

Store managers generally expect to hear favorable comments from an applicant's references or even from previous supervisors who may not have thought highly of the applicant. One approach for reducing the positive bias is to ask the reference to rank the applicant relative to others in the same position. For example, the manager might ask, "How would you rate Pat's customer service skill in relation to other retail sales associates you have worked with?" Another approach is to use a positively toned scale ranging from "somewhat effective" to "extremely effective."

Testing   Intelligence, ability, personality, and interest tests can provide insights about potential employees. For example, intelligence tests yield data about the applicant's innate abilities and can be used to match applicants with job openings and to develop training programs. However, tests must be scientifically and legally valid. They can only be used when the scores have been shown to be related to job performance. It is illegal to use tests assessing factors that are not job-related or that discriminate against specific groups.

Due to potential losses from theft, many retailers such as Wal-Mart and Home Depot require applicants to take drug tests. Some retailers use tests to assess applicants' honesty and ethics. Paper-and-pencil honesty tests include questions to find out if an applicant has ever thought about stealing and if he believes other people steal ("What percentage of people take more than $1 from their employer?").[14]

The use of lie detectors in testing employees is prohibited. Retailers and other employers have been discouraged from HIV testing for prospective employees. But testing for illegal drug use isn't prohibited because drug users are violating the law.[16]

Realistic Job Preview   Turnover is reduced when the applicants understand both the attractive and unattractive aspects of the job. For example, PETsMART, a pet supply category specialist, has each applicant view a 10-minute video that begins with the advantages of being a company employee and then shows scenes of employees dealing with irate customers and cleaning up animal droppings.

Refact Seventy-two percent of retailers check references as part of the selection process; 34 percent do drug screening; and 33 percent use paper-and-pencil honesty tests.[15]

Refact A retailer incurs an additional $7,000 to 10,000 of expenses in medical costs, absences, turnover, and lost productivity when it hires a drug user.[17]

This type of job preview typically screens out 15 percent of the applicants who would most likely quit within three months if they were hired.[18]

Selecting Applicants

After screening applications, the selection process typically involves a personal interview. Since the interview is usually the critical factor in the hiring decision, the store manager needs to be well prepared and to have complete control over the interview.

Preparation for the Interview   The objective of the interview is to gather relevant information, not simply to ask a lot of questions. The most widely used interview technique, called the behavioral interview, asked candidates how they handle actual situations they encountered in the past—situations requiring skills outlined in the job description. For example, applicants applying for a job requiring them to handle customer complaints would be asked to describe a situation in which they were confronted by someone who was angry with something they had done. Candidates are asked to describe the situation, what they did, and what were the outcomes of their actions. These situations also can be used to interview references for the applicants.[19]

An effective approach to interviewing involves some planning by the managers but also allows some flexibility in selecting questions. Managers should develop objectives for what they want to learn about the candidate. Each topic area covered in the interview starts with a broad question, such as "Tell me about your last job," designed to elicit a lengthy response. The broad opening question is followed by a sequence of more specific questions, such as "What did you learn from that job?" or "How many subordinates did you have?" Finally, managers need to avoid asking questions that are discriminatory.[20]

Managing the Interview   Exhibit 17–4 shows questions the manager might ask. Here are some suggestions for questioning the applicant during the interview:

- Encourage long responses by asking questions like "What do you know about our company?" rather than "How familiar are you with our company?"
- Avoid asking questions that have multiple parts.
- Avoid asking leading questions like "Are you prepared to provide good customer service?"
- Be an active listener. Evaluate the information that is being presented and sort out the important comments from the unimportant ones. Some techniques for active listening are repeating or rephrasing information, summarizing the conversation, and tolerating silences.[21]

Some managers interview candidates while giving a candidate a tour through the store. When the manager sees a display that's out of order, he might say, "While we're talking, would you help me straighten this out?" Some candidates will stand back; others will jump right in and help out. (Hint: You want to hire candidates from the second group.)

Legal Considerations in Selecting and Hiring Store Employees

Heightened social awareness and government regulations emphasize the need to avoid discriminating against hiring the handicapped, women, minorities, and older workers. Title VII of the Civil Rights Act prohibits discrimination on the basis of race,

EXHIBIT 17–4   Intervierwing Questions

EDUCATION

What were your most favorite and least favorite subjects in college? Why?

What types of extracurricular activities did you participate in? Why did you select those activities?

If you had the opportunity to attend school all over again what, if anything, would you do differently? Why?

How did you spend the summers during college?

Did you have any part-time jobs? Which of your part-time jobs did you find most interesting? What did you find most difficult about working and attending college at the same time? What advice would you give to someone who wanted to work and attend college at the same time?

What accomplishments were you most proud of?

PREVIOUS EXPERIENCE

What's your description of the ideal manager? Subordinate? Co-worker?

What did you like most/least about your last job?

What kind of people do you find it difficult/easy to work with? Why?

What has been your greatest accomplishment during your career to date?

Describe a situation at your last job involving pressure. How did you handle it?

What were some duties on your last job that you found difficult?

Of all the jobs you've had, which did you find the most/least rewarding?

What is the most frustrating situation you've encountered in your career?

Why do you want to leave your present job?

What would you do if . . . ?

How would you handle . . . ?

What would you like to avoid in future jobs?

What do you consider your greatest strength/weakness?

What are your responsibilities on your present job?

Tell me about the people you hired on your last job. How did they work out? What about the people you fired?

What risks did you take in your last job and what were the results of those risks?

Where do you see yourself in three years?

What kind of references will your previous employer give?

What do you do when you have trouble solving a problem?

QUESTIONS THAT SHOULD NOT BE ASKED PER EQUAL EMPLOYMENT OPPORTUNITY GUIDELINES

Do you have plans for having children/a family? What are your marriage plans? What does your husband/wife do? What happens if your husband/wife gets transferred or needs to relocate? Who will take care of your children while you're at work? (Asked of men) How would you feel about working for a woman?

How old are you? What is your date of birth? How would you feel working for a person younger than you? Where were you born? Where were your parents born?

Do you have any handicaps? As a handicapped person, what help are you going to need to do your work? How severe is your handicap?

What's your religion? What church do you attend? Do you hold religious beliefs that would prevent you from working on certain days of the week?

Do you feel that your race/color will be a problem in your performing the job?
Are you of _____ heritage/race?

---

national origin, sex, or religion in company personnel practices. Discrimination is specifically prohibited in the following human resource decisions: recruitment, hiring, discharge, layoff, discipline, promotion, compensation, and access to training. In 1974, the act was expanded in the **Equal Employment Opportunity Commission (EEOC)** to allow employees to sue employers that violate the law. Several major retailers have been sued because they discriminated in hiring and promoting minorities and women.

The **Age Discrimination and Employment Act** makes it illegal to discriminate in hiring and termination decisions concerning people between the ages of 40 and 70. Finally, the **Americans with Disabilities Act (ADA)** opens up job opportunities for the disabled by requiring employees to provide accommodating work environments.[22]

SOCIALIZING AND TRAINING NEW STORE EMPLOYEES

After hiring employees, the next step in developing effective employees (as Exhibit 17–2 shows) is introducing them to the firm and its policies. Retailers want the people they hire to become involved, committed contributors to the firm's successful performance. On the other hand, newly hired employees want to learn about their job responsibilities and the company they've decided to join. **Socialization** is the set of steps taken to transform new employees into effective, committed members of the firm. Socialization goes beyond simply orienting new employees to the firm. A principle objective of socialization is to develop a long-term relationship with new employees to reduce turnover costs.[23]

A key factor in socializing new employees is to create a training and work environment that articulates the retailer's culture and strategy. For example, at Target the phrase "Fast, Fun, and Friendly" is used to explain its customer-service philosophy to its employees. Karen Grabow, Target's human resources VP, emphasizes that, "Everything must work around the culture; check everything against 'Fast, Fun, and Friendly.' You have to reiterate it with mind-numbing repetition, but more importantly you have to walk the talk."[25]

Refact The U.S. Department of Labor estimates that it costs a company one-third of a new hire's annual compensation to replace an employee.[24]

Orientation Program

Orientation programs are critical in overcoming entry shock and socializing new employees.[26] Even the most knowledgeable and mature new employees encounter some surprises. College students who accept management trainee positions often are quite surprised by the differences between student and employee roles. Retailing View 17.2 describes some of these differences.

Orientation programs can last from a few hours to several weeks. The orientation and training program for new salespeople might be limited to several hours during which the new salesperson learns the retailer's policies and procedures and how to use the POS terminal. On the other hand, the orientation program for a department or assistant store manager might take several weeks. For example, Burdines hires approximately 150 college students each year into its management training program. New trainees typically report to work at corporate headquarters in Miami. They're housed in a hotel for a four-week orientation during which they attend classes, meet company executives, and work on projects. After completing the orientation program, they begin their initial assignment as a department manager in a store.

Effective orientation programs need to avoid information overload and one-way communication. When new hires are confronted with a stack of forms and company policies, they get the impression the company is very bureaucratic. Large quantities of information are hard to absorb in a short period of time. New employees learn information best when it's parceled out in small doses.

Store managers need to foster two-way communication when orienting new employees. Rather than just presenting information about their firm, managers need to give newly hired employees a chance to have their questions and concerns addressed.

Disney overhauled its orientation program to emphasize emotion rather than company policies and procedures. The new program begins with current employees, referred to as cast members, discussing their earliest memories of Disney, their visions of great service, and their understanding of teamwork. Then trainers relate "magic moments" they have witnessed to emphasize that insignificant actions can have a big impact on a guest. For example, a four-year-old trips

MANY STUDENTS HAVE SOME DIFFICULTY ADJUSTING to the demands of their first full-time job, because student life and professional life are very different. Students typically "report" to three or four supervisors (professors). A student selects new "supervisors" every four months. On the other hand, management trainees have limited involvement, if any, in selecting the one supervisor they'll report to often for several years.

Student life has fixed time cycles, one-to-two–hour classes with a well-defined beginning and end. Retail managers are involved in a variety of activities with varied time horizons, ranging from a five-minute interaction with a customer to developing and implementing a merchandise budget over a season.

The decision making students encounter differs dramatically from the decision making retail managers encounter. For example, business students might make several major deci-sions a day when they discuss cases in class. These decisions are made and implemented in one class period and then a new set of decisions is made and implemented in the next class. In a retail environment, strategic decisions evolve over a long time period. Most decisions, such as those regarding merchandise buying and pricing, are made with incomplete information. The buyers in real life often lack the extensive information provided in many business cases studied in class. Finally, there are long periods of time when retail managers undertake mundane tasks associated with implementing decisions and no major issues are being considered. Students typically don't have these mundane tasks to perform.

Source: Daniel Feldman, *Managing Careers in Organizations* (Reading, MA: Addison-Wesley, 1989), pp. 45–52. From "Managing Careers in Organizations" by Daniel Feldman, © 1989. Reprinted by permission of Addison-Wesley Educational Publishers, Inc.

and falls, spilling his box of popcorn. The boy cries, the mother is concerned, and a costumed cast member, barely breaking stride, picks up the empty box, takes it to the popcorn stand for a refill, presents it to the child, and goes on his way.[27]

The orientation program is just one element in the overall training program. It needs to be accompanied by a systematic follow-up to ensure that any problems and concerns arising after the initial period are considered.

Training Store Employees

Effective training for new store employees includes both structured and on-the-job learning experiences.

Refact Annual spending by U.S. employers on training totals $200 billion, which is slightly more than annual public and private spending on elementary and secondary education.[28]

Structured Program   During the structured program, new employees are taught the basic skills and knowledge they'll need to do their job. For example, salespeople learn what the company policies are, how to use the point-of-sale terminal, and how to perform basic selling skills; stockroom employees learn procedures for receiving merchandise. This initial training might include lectures, audiovisual presentations, manuals, and correspondence distributed to the new employees. In large firms, structured training may be done at a central location (such as the corporate headquarters or district office) under the human resources department's direction.

The initial structured program should be relatively short so new employees don't feel they are simply back in school. Effective training programs try to bring new recruits up to speed as quickly as possible and then get them involved in doing the job for which they've been hired.[29]

On-the-Job Training   The next training phase emphasizes on-the-job training. New employees are assigned a job, given responsibilities, and coached by their supervisor. The best way to learn is to practice what has been taught. New employees learn by doing activities, making mistakes, and then learning how not to make those

The on-the-job training provided by the Hallmark manager gives the new employees an opportunity to make decisions and get constructive feedback.

mistakes again. Information learned through classroom lectures tends to be forgotten quickly unless it's used soon after the lecture.

For example, students can learn about developing a merchandise budget plan by reading Chapter 13 of this text or by listening to a lecture. But they typically don't acquire all the necessary information or remember the information from these sources. The actual hands-on experience of making a plan and getting feedback provides more complete and lasting knowledge.

Analyzing Successes and Failures
Every new employee makes mistakes. Unfortunately, some managers make new employees feel uncomfortable if they admit to making a mistake. When this happens, new employees have less opportunity to learn from their mistakes.

Store managers should provide an atmosphere in which salespeople try out different approaches for providing customer service and selling merchandise. Store managers must recognize that some of these new approaches are going to fail, and when they do, managers shouldn't criticize the individual salesperson. Instead, they should talk about the situation, analyze why the approach didn't work, and discuss how the salesperson could avoid the problem in the future.

Similarly, managers should work with employees to help them understand and learn from their successes. For example, salespeople shouldn't just consider a large multiple-item sale to be simply due to luck. They should be encouraged to reflect on the sale, identify their key behaviors that facilitated the sale, and then remember these sales behaviors for future use.

It's important to help salespeople assign the right kinds of reasons for their performance. For example, some salespeople take credit for successes and blame the company, the buyers, or the merchandise for their failures. This tendency to avoid taking responsibility for failures doesn't encourage learning. When salespeople adopt this reasoning pattern, they aren't motivated to change their sales behavior because they don't take personal responsibility for losing a sale.

Managers can help salespeople to constructively analyze their successes and failures by asking salespeople "why" questions that force them to analyze the reasons for effective and ineffective performance. To encourage learning, managers should get salespeople to recognize that they could have satisfied the customer if they had used a different approach or been more persistent. When salespeople accept such responsibility, they'll be motivated to search for ways to improve their sales skills.

INTERNET EXERCISE   Go to www.astd.org, the website for the American Society for Training and Development, and read one of the articles from the latest issue of *Training and Development*, a magazine published by the society. How would you suggest that a retailer use the information in this article to increase the effectiveness of its employees?

MOTIVATING AND
MANAGING STORE
EMPLOYEES

After employees have received their initial training, managers must work with them to help them meet their performance goals. (Refer back to Exhibit 17–2.)

Leadership

Leadership is the process by which one person attempts to influence another to accomplish some goal or goals. Store managers are leaders of their group of employees. Managers use a variety of motivational techniques to increase productivity by helping employees achieve personal goals consistent with their firm's objectives.[31]

Leader Behaviors   Leaders engage in task performance and group maintenance behaviors. **Task performance behaviors** are the store manager's efforts to make sure that the store achieves its goals. Task performance behaviors are planning, organizing, motivating, evaluating, and coordinating store employees' activities.

Group maintenance behaviors are activities store managers undertake to make sure that employees are satisfied and work well together. These activities include considering employees' needs, showing concern for their well-being, and creating a pleasant work environment.

Leader Decision Making   Store managers vary in how much they involve employees in making decisions. **Autocratic** store managers make all decisions on their own and then announce them to employees. They use the authority of their position to tell employees what to do. For example, an autocratic store manager determines who will work in each area of the store, when they'll take breaks, and what days they'll have off. On the other hand, a **democratic** store manager seeks information and opinions from employees and bases decisions on this information. Democratic store managers share their power and information with their employees. The democratic store manager asks employees where and when they want to work and makes a work schedule to accommodate employee desires.

Leadership Styles   Store managers tend to develop a specific leadership style. They emphasize either task performance or group maintenance behaviors. They range from autocratic to democratic in their decision-making style.

Tim O'Donnell (right rear), manager of the Sandy City, Utah, Shopko store, is a democratic leader who holds meetings to keep employees informed about company and store activities. He encourages suggestions for improving store performance.

Which leadership style is best for store managers? After 60 years of research, psychologists have concluded there's no one best style. Effective managers use all styles, selecting the style most appropriate for each situation. For example, a store manager might be autocratic and relations-oriented with an insecure new trainee, but be democratic and task-oriented with an effective, experienced employee.

Effective store managers must consider both their firm's objectives and their employees' needs. They must recognize that employees aren't all the same. For some employees, promotions are crucial. Others want more compensation, and

Sears builds morale and motivates its sales associates by holding "ready meetings" for each department before the store opens. At this meeting, the department manager discusses approaches for providing better customer service.

some simply want to be recognized for doing a good job. Some employees need to be motivated to work harder, while others need to be taught how to do their jobs effectively. Thus effective leaders use different approaches or styles for managing each employee.

Transformational Leaders The previous discussion and most of the chapter describe specific behaviors, activities, and programs store managers use to influence their employees. But the greatest leaders and store managers go beyond influencing employee behaviors to changing the beliefs, values, and needs of their employees. **Transformational leaders** get people to transcend their personal needs for the sake of the group or organization. They generate excitement and revitalize organizations.

Transformational store managers create this enthusiasm in their employees through their personal charisma. They're self-confident, have a clear vision that grabs employee attention, and communicate this vision through words and symbols. Finally, transformational leaders delegate challenging work to subordinates, have free and open communication with them, and provide personal mentoring to develop subordinates.[32]

Motivating Employees

Motivating employees to perform up to their potential may be store managers' most important and frustrating task.[33] The following hypothetical situation illustrates issues concerning employee motivation and evaluation.

After getting an associates degree at a local community college, Jim Taylor was hired for a sales position at the Foley's store in Denver's Cherry Creek Mall. The position offers firsthand knowledge of the firm's customers, managers, and policies. Taylor was told that if he did well in this assignment, he could become a management trainee.

His performance as a sales associate was average. After observing Taylor on the sales floor, his manager, Sally Rivera, felt he was effective only when working with customers like himself: young, career-oriented men and women. To encourage Taylor to sell to other types of customers, Rivera reduced his salary and increased his commission rate. She also reviewed Taylor's performance goals with him.

Taylor now feels a lot of pressure to increase his sales level. He's beginning to dread coming to work in the morning and is thinking about getting out of retailing and working for a bank.

In this hypothetical situation, Rivera focused on increasing Taylor's motivation by providing more incentive compensation. In discussing this illustration, we'll examine the appropriateness of this approach versus other approaches for improving Taylor's performance.

Setting Goals or Quotas Employee performance improves when employees feel that (1) their efforts will enable them to achieve the goals set for them by their managers and (2) they'll receive rewards they value if they achieve their goals. Thus managers can motivate employees by setting realistic goals and offering rewards employees want.[34]

For example, Sally Rivera set specific selling goals for Jim Taylor when he started to work in her department. Taylor, like all Foley's sales associates, had goals in five selling areas: sales per hour, average size of each sale, number of multiple-item (add-on) sales, number of preferred clients, and number of appointments made with preferred clients. (Preferred clients are customers whom salespeople communicate with regularly, send notes to about new merchandise and sales in the department, and make appointments with for special presentations of merchandise.) Besides the selling goals, salespeople are evaluated on the overall department shrinkage due to stolen merchandise, the errors they make in using the point-of-sale terminal, and their contribution to maintaining the department's appearance.

Rivera also developed a program for Taylor's development as a sales associate. The activities she outlined over the next six months involved Taylor's attending classes to improve his selling skills. Rivera needs to be careful in setting goals for Taylor. If she sets goals too high, he might become discouraged, feel the goals are unattainable, and thus not be motivated to work harder. On the other hand, if she sets goals too low, Taylor can achieve them easily and won't be motivated to work to his full potential.

Rather than setting specific goals for each salesperson, Foley's uses the average performance for all salespeople as its goal. However, goals are most effective at motivating employees when they're based on the employee's experience and confidence. Experienced salespeople have confidence in their abilities and should have "stretch" goals (high goals that will make them work hard). New salespeople need lower goals that they have a good chance of achieving. The initial good experience in achieving and surpassing goals builds new salespeople's cofidence and motivates them to improve their skills.[35] Later in the chapter we'll look at the use of rewards to motivate employees.

Maintaining Morale

Store morale is important in motivating employees. Typically morale goes up when things are going well and employees are highly motivated. But when sales aren't going well, morale tends to decrease and employee motivation declines. Here are some suggestions for building morale:

- Have storewide or department meetings prior to the store opening. Pass along information about new merchandise and programs and solicit opinions and suggestions from employees.
- Educate employees about the firm's finances, set achievable goals, and throw a pizza party when the goals are met.
- Divide the charity budget by the number of employees and invite the employees to suggest how their "share" should be used.
- Print stickers that tell customers that this sandwich was "wrapped by Roger" or this dress was "dry cleaned by Sarah."
- Give every employee a business card with the company mission printed on its back.[36]

Paula Hankins, a store manager for Pier 1 Imports, uses real-time sales data collected in her firm's information system (see Chapter 11) to build excitement among her employees. On the first day of the Christmas season, she wrote

$3,159 on a blackboard in the store. That was the store's sales during the first day of the Christmas season last year. She tells her sales associates that beating that number is not enough. She wants a 36 percent increase, the same sales increase the store achieved prior to the Christmas season.

By setting financial objectives and keeping sales associates informed of the up-to-the-minute results, an eight-hour shift of clock watchers is converted into an excited team of racers. All day, as customers come and go, sales associates take turns consulting the backroom computer recording sales from the store's POS terminals. David Self, Hankins' regional manager, emphasizes, "The more information you give the associates, the more ownership they feel in the store's performance."[37]

EVALUATING STORE EMPLOYEES AND PROVIDING FEEDBACK

The fourth step in the management process (refer back to Exhibit 17–2) is evaluating and providing feedback to employees. The evaluation process's objective is to identify employees who are performing well and those who aren't. Based on the evaluation, high-performing employees should be rewarded. Plans need to be developed to increase the productivity of employees performing below expectations. Should poor performers be terminated? Do they need additional training? What kind of training do they need?

Who Should Do the Evaluation?

In large retail firms, the evaluation system is usually designed by the human resources department. But the evaluation itself should be done by the employee's immediate supervisor—the manager who works most closely with the employee. For example, in a discount store, the department manager is in the best position to observe a salesperson in action and understand the reasons for the salesperson's performance. The department manager also oversees the recommendations that come out of the evaluation process. Inexperienced supervisors are often assisted by a senior manager in evaluating employees.

How Often Should Evaluations Be Made?

Most retailers evaluate employees annually or semiannually. Feedback from evaluations is the most effective method for improving employee skills. Thus, evaluation should be done more frequently when managers are developing inexperienced employees' skills. However, frequent formal evaluations are time-consuming for managers and may not give employees enough time to respond to suggestions. Managers should supplement these formal evaluations with frequent informal ones. For example, Sally Rivera should work with Jim Taylor informally and not wait for the formal six-month evaluation. The best time for Rivera to provide this informal feedback is immediately after she has obtained, through observations or reports, positive or negative information about Taylor's performance.

Format for Evaluation

Evaluations are only meaningful if employees know what they're required to do, what level of performance is expected, and how they'll be evaluated. Exhibit 17–5 shows The Gap's criteria for evaluating sales associates.

The Gap employee's overall evaluation is based on subjective evaluations made by the store manager and assistant managers. It places equal weight on

EXHIBIT 17–5   Factors Used to Evaluate Sales Associates at The Gap

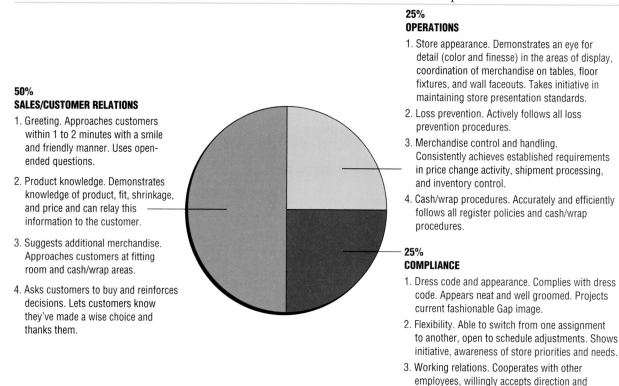

25%
OPERATIONS

1. Store appearance. Demonstrates an eye for detail (color and finesse) in the areas of display, coordination of merchandise on tables, floor fixtures, and wall faceouts. Takes initiative in maintaining store presentation standards.

2. Loss prevention. Actively follows all loss prevention procedures.

3. Merchandise control and handling. Consistently achieves established requirements in price change activity, shipment processing, and inventory control.

4. Cash/wrap procedures. Accurately and efficiently follows all register policies and cash/wrap procedures.

50%
SALES/CUSTOMER RELATIONS

1. Greeting. Approaches customers within 1 to 2 minutes with a smile and friendly manner. Uses open-ended questions.

2. Product knowledge. Demonstrates knowledge of product, fit, shrinkage, and price and can relay this information to the customer.

3. Suggests additional merchandise. Approaches customers at fitting room and cash/wrap areas.

4. Asks customers to buy and reinforces decisions. Lets customers know they've made a wise choice and thanks them.

25%
COMPLIANCE

1. Dress code and appearance. Complies with dress code. Appears neat and well groomed. Projects current fashionable Gap image.

2. Flexibility. Able to switch from one assignment to another, open to schedule adjustments. Shows initiative, awareness of store priorities and needs.

3. Working relations. Cooperates with other employees, willingly accepts direction and guidance from management. Communicates to management.

individual sales/customer relations activities and activities associated with overall store performance. By emphasizing overall store operations and performance, The Gap's assessment criteria motivate sales associates to work together as a team.

The criteria used at Foley's to evaluate Jim Taylor are objective sales measures based on point-of-sale data rather than the subjective measures used by The Gap. Exhibit 17–6 summarizes Taylor's formal six-month evaluation. The evaluation form lists for various factors (1) what's considered average performance for company salespeople and (2) Taylor's actual performance. His department has done better than average on shrinkage control, and he has done well on system errors and merchandise presentation. However, his sales performance is below average even though he made more than the average number of presentations to preferred customers. These results suggest that Taylor's effort is good but his selling skills may need improvement.

Evaluation Errors   Managers can make evaluation errors by first forming an overall opinion of the employee's performance and then allowing this opinion to influence the ratings of each performance factor (haloing). For example, a store manager might feel a salesperson's overall performance is below average and then rate the salesperson below average on selling skills, punctuality, appearance, and stocking. When an overall evaluation casts such a halo on specific

EXHIBIT **17–6**

Summary of Jim
Taylor's Six-Month
Evaluation

	AVERAGE PERFORMANCE FOR SALESPEOPLE IN THE COMPANY	JIM TAYLOR'S ACTUAL PERFORMANCE
Sales per hour	$75	$65
Average amount per transaction	$45	$35
Percent multiple transactions	55%	55%
Number of preferred customers	115	125
Number of preferred customer appointments	120	95
Departmental shrinkage	2.0%	1.8%
Systems errors	10	2
Merchandise presentation (10-point scale)	5	8

aspects of a salesperson's performance, the evaluation is no longer useful for identifying specific areas that need improvement.

In making evaluations, managers are often unduly influenced by recent events (recency) and by their evaluations of other salespeople (contrast). For example, a manager might remember a salesperson's poor performance with a customer the day before and forget the salesperson's outstanding performance over the past three months. Similarly, a manager might be unduly harsh in evaluating an average salesperson just after completing an evaluation of an outstanding salesperson.

Finally, managers have a natural tendency to attribute performance (particularly poor performance) to the salesperson and not to the environment the salesperson is working in (attributions). When making evaluations, managers tend to underemphasize effects of external factors such as merchandise in the department and competitors' actions.

The Foley's evaluation of sales associates (refer back to Exhibit 17–6's sample evaluation) avoids many of these potential biases because most ratings are based on objective data. In contrast, The Gap evaluation (Exhibit 17–5) considers a wider range of activities but uses more subjective measures of performance. Since subjective information about specific skills, attitudes about the store and customers, interactions with co-workers, enthusiasm, and appearance aren't used in the Foley's evaluation, performance on these factors may not be explicitly communicated to Jim Taylor. The subjective characteristics in The Gap evaluation are more prone to bias, but they also might be more helpful to salespeople as they try to improve their performance. To avoid bias when making subjective ratings, managers should observe performance regularly, record their observations, avoid evaluating many salespeople at one time, and remain conscious of the various potential biases.

COMPENSATING AND REWARDING EMPLOYEES

The fifth and final step in improving employee productivity in Exhibit 17–2 is compensating and rewarding employees. Store employees receive two types of rewards from their work: extrinsic and intrinsic. **Extrinsic rewards** are rewards provided by either the employee's manager or the firm—such as compensation, promotion, and recognition. **Intrinsic rewards** are rewards employees get personally from doing their job well. For example, salespeople often like to sell because they think it's challenging and fun. Of course, they want to be paid, but they also find it rewarding to help customers and make sales.[38]

SOME OF THE PROBLEMS OF DISSATISFIED employees and high turnover in retail are due to the generation gap between boomer store managers and Generation Xers who have entered the work force in the past few years. "A lot has been made of Generation Xers not having a strong work ethic," retail consultant Terri Kabachnick, notes. "I don't agree; it's just that it is a lot different. Boomers feel they have to work a lot of hours, while GenXer's ask, 'Why? Who are you trying to impress?' " Boomers emphasize that you need to work long and hard to get ahead, paying your dues before you get more responsibility and higher pay. The younger employee responds with "Get a life. I don't mind working hard, but what about my family, my happiness?"

Rather than getting regular performance reviews, Generation Xers want a pat on the back and recognition when they have accomplished something. They want flexibility in their work schedules and time for themselves, their interests, and priorities.

"They don't want time off to be sick; they want time off to be well," says Kabachnick. To address this need for flexibility, retailers are experimenting with sabbaticals—weeks or months off to think about how to do your job better—and time banks, where sick days, overtime, and/or vacation time can be deposited for use at some time in the future with no questions asked.

Retailers also consider personal needs by having pet and child care centers, on-site fitness centers, personnel to run personal errands such as dropping off and picking up laundry, and "relaxation rooms" where employees can go to sit, think, or nap. One company even provides back rubs at desks and workstations.

Source: David Schulz, "Generational Tensions Add to 'Quiet Rebellion' in Retail Workforce," *Stores,* March 11, 1999, pp. 61–62. Reprinted for *Stores* magazine, © NRF Enterprises, Inc. 1999.

Extrinsic Rewards Managers can offer a variety of extrinsic rewards to motivate employees. However, store employees don't all seek the same rewards. For example, some salespeople want more compensation; others strive for a promotion in the company or public recognition of their performance. Jim Taylor wants a favorable evaluation from his manager so he can enter the management training program. Part-time salespeople often take a sales job to get out of the house and meet people. Their primary work objective isn't to make money.

Because of these different needs, managers may not be able to use the same rewards to motivate all employees. Large retailers, however, find it hard to develop unique reward programs for each individual. One approach is to offer à la carte plans. For example, salespeople who achieve their goals could choose a cash bonus, extra days off, or a better discount on merchandise sold in the store. This type of compensation plan enables employees to select the rewards they want. Recognition is an important nonmonetary extrinsic reward for many employees. (Compensation and financial rewards are discussed later.) Telling employees they've done a job well is appreciated. However, it's typically more rewarding when good performance is recognized publicly. In addition, public recognition can motivate all store employees, not just the star performers, because it demonstrates management's interest in rewarding employees.

Most managers focus on extrinsic rewards to motivate employees. For example, a store manager might provide additional compensation if a salesperson achieves a sales goal. This emphasis on extrinsic rewards can make employees lose sight of their job's intrinsic rewards. They may feel that their only reason for working is to earn money and that the job isn't fun.

Retailing View 17.3 discusses how the differences between the goals and rewards sought by boomer managers and Generation X employees can cause problems.

Public recognition programs make employees feel they are appreciated and motivate them to improve their performance. For providing excellent customer service, the sales associates at the Mansfield, Ohio Limited store were recognized with a "Hero Award."

Intrinsic Rewards

Note that Sally Rivera tried to motivate Jim Taylor by using extrinsic rewards when she linked his compensation to how much he sold. This increased emphasis on financial rewards may be one reason Taylor now dreads to come to work in the morning. He might not think his job is fun anymore.

When employees find their jobs intrinsically rewarding, they're motivated to learn how to do them better. They act like a person playing a video game. The game itself is so interesting that the player gets rewards from trying to master it.

One approach to making work fun is to hold contests with relatively small prizes. Contests are most effective when everyone has a chance to win. Contests in which the best salespeople always win aren't exciting and may even be demoralizing. For example, consider a contest in which a playing card is given to a salesperson for each men's suit he sells during a two-week period. At the end of two weeks, the best poker hand wins. This contest motivates all salespeople during the entire period of the contest. A salesperson who sells only four suits can win with four aces. Contests should be used to create excitement and make selling challenging for everyone, not to pay the best salespeople more money.

Experienced employees often lose interest in their jobs. They no longer find them exciting and challenging. Extrinsic rewards, such as pay or promotion, might not be so attractive to them. They might be satisfied with their present income and job responsibilities.

More experienced employees can be motivated by providing intrinsic rewards through job enrichment. For example, they could be given responsibility for merchandising a particular area, training new salespeople, or planning and managing a special event.

Compensation Programs

The objectives of a compensation program are to attract and keep good employees, motivate them to undertake activities consistent with the retailer's objectives, and reward them for their effort. In developing a compensation program, the store manager must strike a balance between controlling labor costs and providing enough compensation to keep high-quality employees.[39]

Compensation plans are most effective for motivating and retaining employees when the employees feel the plan is fair and when their compensation is related to their efforts. In general, simple plans are preferred to complex plans. Simple plans are easier to administer and employees have no trouble understanding them.

Types of Compensation Plans   Retail firms typically use one or more of the following compensation plans: straight salary, straight commission, salary plus commission, and quota–bonus.

With **straight salary compensation,** salespeople or managers receive a fixed amount of compensation for each hour or week they work. For example, a salesperson might be paid $6 per hour, or a department manager $600 per week. This plan is easy for the employee to understand and for the store to administer.

Under a straight salary plan, the retailer has flexibility in assigning salespeople to different activities and sales areas. For example, salaried salespeople will undertake nonselling activities (such as stocking shelves) and won't be upset if they're transferred from a high–sales-volume department to a low–sales-volume department.

The major disadvantage of the straight salary plan is employees' lack of immediate incentives to improve their productivity. They know their compensation won't change, in the short run, whether they work hard or slack off. Another disadvantage for the retailer is that straight salary becomes a fixed cost the firm incurs even if sales decline.

Incentive compensation plans compensate employees based on their productivity. Many retailers now use incentives to motivate greater sales productivity. Under some incentive plans, a salesperson's income is based entirely on commission (straight commission). For example, a salesperson might be paid a commission based on a percentage of sales made minus merchandise returned. Normally, the percentage is the same for all merchandise sold (such as 7 percent). But some retailers use different percentages for different categories of merchandise (such as 4 percent for low-margin items and 10 percent for high-margin items). By using different percentages, the retailer provides additional incentives for its salespeople to sell specific items. Typically, compensation of salespeople selling high-priced items such as men's suits, appliances, and consumer electronics is based largely on their commissions.

Incentive plans may include a fixed salary plus a smaller commission on total sales or a commission on sales over a quota. For example, a salesperson might receive a salary of $200 per week plus a commission of 2 percent on all sales over $50 per hour.

Incentive compensation plans are a powerful motivator for salespeople to sell merchandise, but they have a number of disadvantages. For example, it's hard to get salespeople who are compensated totally by commission to perform nonselling activities. Understandably, they're reluctant to spend time stocking shelves when they could be making money by selling. Also, salespeople will concentrate on the more expensive, fast-moving merchandise and neglect other merchandise. Incentives can also discourage salespeople from providing services to customers. Finally, salespeople compensated primarily by incentive don't develop loyalty to their employer. Since the employer doesn't guarantee them an income, they feel no obligation to the firm.[39]

Under a 100 percent straight commission plan, salespeople's income can fluctuate from week to week, depending on their sales. Since retail sales are seasonal, salespeople might earn most of their income during the Christmas season and much less during the summer months. To provide a more steady income for salespeople under high-incentive plans, some retailers offer a drawing account. With a **drawing account,** salespeople receive a weekly check based on their estimated annual income. Then commissions earned are credited against the weekly payments. Periodically, the weekly draw is compared to the commission earned. If the draw exceeds earned commissions, the salespeople return the excess money they've been paid, and their weekly draw is reduced. If commissions earned exceed the draw, salespeople are paid the difference.

Quota–bonus plans have performance goals or objectives established to evaluate employee performance. Examples are sales per hour for salespeople and maintained margin and inventory turnover for buyers. For department store salespeople, selling quotas vary across departments due to differences in sales productivity. Quotas are often used with compensation plans. For example, in a quota–bonus plan, salespeople earn a bonus if their sales exceed their quota over a certain time period.

A quota–bonus plan's effectiveness depends on setting reasonable, fair quotas. Setting effective quotas can be hard. Usually, quotas are set at the same level for everyone in a department. But salespeople in the same department may have different abilities and face different selling environments. For example, in the men's department, salespeople in the suit area have much greater sales potential than salespeople in the accessories area. Newly hired salespeople might have a harder time achieving a quota than more experienced salespeople. Thus, a quota based on average productivity may be too high to motivate the new salesperson and too low to effectively motivate the experienced salesperson. Quotas should be developed for each salesperson based on her experience and the nature of the store area where she works.[40]

Group Incentives To encourage employees in a department or store to work together, some retailers provide additional incentives based on the performance of the department or store as a whole. For example, salespeople might be paid a commission based on their individual sales and then receive additional compensation based on the amount of sales over plan or quota generated by all salespeople in the store. The group incentive encourages salespeople to work together on nonselling activities and handling customers so the department sales target will be achieved.[41]

Designing the Compensation Program A compensation program's two elements are the amount of compensation and the percentage of compensation based on incentives. Typically, market conditions determine the amount of compensation. When economic conditions are good and labor is scarce, retailers pay higher wages. Retailers that hire inexperienced salespeople pay lower wages than those that recruit experienced salespeople with good skills and abilities. Incentives are most effective when a salesperson's performance can be measured easily and precisely. It's difficult to measure individual performance when salespeople work in teams or when they must perform a lot of nonselling activities. Retailers can easily measure a salesperson's actual sales, but it's hard to measure their customer service or merchandising performance.

When the salesperson's activities have a great impact on sales, incentives can provide additional motivation. For example, salespeople who are simply cashiers have little effect on sales and thus shouldn't be compensated with incentives. However, incentives are appropriate for salespeople who provide a lot of information and assistance about complex products such as designer dresses or stereo systems. Incentives are less effective with inexperienced salespeople because they inhibit learning. Inexperienced salespeople are less confident in their skills, and incentives can cause excessive stress.

Finally, compensation plans with too many incentives may not promote good customer service. Salespeople on commission become interested in selling anything they can to customers. They aren't willing to spend time helping customers buy the merchandise they need. They tend to stay close to the cash register or the dressing room exits so they can ring up a sale for a customer who's ready to buy.

Setting the Commission Percentage   Assume that a specialty store manager wants to hire experienced salespeople. To get the type of person she wants, she feels she must pay $12 per hour. Her selling costs are budgeted at 8 percent of sales. With compensation of $12 per hour, salespeople need to sell $150 worth of merchandise per hour ($12 divided by 8 percent) for the store to keep within its sales cost budget. The manager believes the best compensation would be one-third salary and two-thirds commission, so she decides to offer a compensation plan of $4 per hour salary (33 percent or $12) and a 5.33 percent commission on sales. If salespeople sell $150 worth of merchandise per hour, they'll earn $12 per hour ($4 per hour in salary plus $150 multiplied by 5.33 percent, which equals $8 per hour in commission).

LEGAL ISSUES AND COMPENSATION

The **Fair Labor Standards Act** of 1938 set minimum wages, maximum hours, child labor standards, and overtime pay provisions. Enforcement of this law is particularly important to retailers because they hire many low-wage employees and teenagers and have their employees work long hours.

The **Equal Pay Act,** now enforced by the EEOC, prohibits unequal pay for men and women who perform equal work or work of comparable worth. Equal work means that the jobs require the same skills, effort, and responsibility and are performed in the same working environment. Comparable worth implies that men and women who perform different jobs of equal worth should be compensated the same. Differences in compensation are legal when compensation is determined by a seniority system, an incentive compensation plan, or market demand.

Sexual harassment is an important issue confronting store managers. Managers must make sure that store employees avoid actions that are, or can be interpreted as, sexual harassment.

Sexual Harassment

An important issue in managing employees is sexual harassment. **Sexual harassment** includes unwelcome sexual advances, requests for sexual favors, and other verbal and physical conduct. Harassment isn't confined to requests for sexual favors in exchange for job considerations such as a raise or promotion. Simply creating a hostile work environment can be considered sexual harassment.[42]

Actions that are considered sexual harassment include lewd comments, gestures, joking, and graffiti as well as showing obscene photographs, staring at a co-worker in a sexual manner, alleging that an employee got rewards by engaging in sexual acts, and commenting on an employee's moral reputation. Managers must prevent such behaviors because they're both unethical and illegal.

Sexual harassment is not restricted just to supervisors and fellow employees. It's even more of a problem when the offender is a customer. For example, fe-

EXHIBIT **17–7**

Procedure for Sexual
Harrassment
Allegations

Step 1: Always treat an employee's complaint seriously.

Step 2: Get information from the alleged victim. Ask questions like
- **Tell me what happened. Who was involved?**
- **What did the harasser do and say?**
- **When did this happen? If this wasn't the first time, when has it happened before?**
- **Where did it happen?**
- **Were there any witnesses?**
- **Have you told anyone else about this or these instances?**
- **Has anyone else been the object of harassment?**
- **How did you react to the harasser's behavior?**
- **Would you care to speak with someone else: another member of management, the personnel department, or the company employment assistance plan person?**

Step 3: Review with the employee your company's sexual harassment policy.

Step 4: Document your meeting with the alleged victim.

Step 5: Inform your human resource department and/or the next higher level of company management.

Source: John Farr, "Sexual Harassment: Handling the 'He-Said–She-Said' Hot Potato," *Chain Store Age*, April 1998, pp. 56–59.

male pharmacists find that some male customers demand lengthy discussions when they buy condoms. The pharmacists may have difficulty dealing with these situations because they want to keep the person as a customer and also protect themselves from abuse. Managers will need to respond to these situations as pharmacists shift their responsibility from simply dispensing to providing face-to-face information to customers.[43]

An appropriate procedure for dealing with a sexual harassment allegation is outlined in Exhibit 17–7.

CONTROLLING COSTS

Labor scheduling, store maintenance, and energy management offer three opportunities for reducing store operating expenses. Retailing View 17.4 describes how a convenience store chain reengineered its operations to reduce cost and increase customer service.

Labor Scheduling

Using store employees efficiently is an important and challenging problem. Store employees provide customer service that can increase sales. On the other hand, employees are the largest store operating expense. **Labor scheduling** (determining the number of employees assigned to each area of the store) is difficult because of the multiple-shift and part-time workers needed to staff stores 12 hours a day, seven days a week. In addition, customer traffic varies greatly during the day and the week. Bad weather, holidays, and sales can dramatically alter normal shopping patterns and staffing needs.

Managers can spot obvious inefficiencies like long checkout lines and sales associates with nothing to do. But some inefficiencies are more subtle. For example, if 6 percent of a store's sales volume occurs between 2 and 3 P.M. and 9 percent of the total labor hours occur during this time period, the store might be overstaffed during this time period. Many stores use specially designed computer software to deal with the complexities of labor scheduling. Labor schedulers can reduce store payroll costs between 2 and 5 percent without affecting store sales.[44]

Refact Sixty percent of retailers use computer programs for merchandise planning, but only 37 percent use software for labor scheduling.[45]

SHEETZ, A 192-STORE CONVENIENCE store chain based in Altoona, Pennsylvania, started a series of detailed studies to determine how store-level tasks could be performed more efficiently. Charlie Campbell, a former store manager and now director of organizational efficiency, says, "We looked at everything from how the store manager closed out the day to how the staff emptied the trash." The results of the studies were implemented in 1997. Over the next two years the company saved $5.1 million in payroll costs alone.

Sheetz found that store managers were taking three to four hours to close out their sales day. Each day, they had to fill out 40 computer screens of information and would spend an hour looking for a $5 error. The time spent on closing was affecting customer service. Managers would do this paperwork during the morning of the following day, the busiest traffic time, when they should have been out in the stores managing. When Sheetz reexamined these practices, it eliminated over 160,000 hours annually of time the store managers were spending on nonproductive administrative tasks.

Sheetz also found that a lot of the information being sent to store managers was of questionable value. Campbell noted, "There were too many redundant reports. Two hundred and four reports were available on the store managers' computers. We've gotten that number down to 23."

Sheetz saved 55 employee-hours per week per store by reexamining its labor scheduling. Prior to the study, staffing for stores was based on sales. This approach did not consider that some stores generate a lot of sales from labor-intensive activities such as food service, while others derive sales from labor-free pay-at-the-pump transactions (called outside sales by convenience store operators). Some tasks performed in the store were eliminated. The company stopped tracking newspapers at the SKU. On some papers, Sheetz only make a two-cent margin. If store employees spend time receiving and tracking them by SKU, the firm loses money on each paper it sells.

Source: "Rap Sheetz," *Chain Store Age*, June 1999, pp. 78–82.

Efficient labor scheduling requires more than POS sales data by day and time of day. The manager also needs to know the traffic patterns and the impact of store employees on sales. For example, one store manager saw a downturn in sales during the hour before the store closed so she considered reducing the level of staffing. However, when traffic counters were installed, the manager discovered that the number of customers in the store did not decline during the last open hour. The manager then realized that employees were forsaking customer service and spending time preparing to close the store. Rather than reducing the staff, the manager extended the work hours so sales associates would realize the sales potential during the last hour.

INTERNET EXERCISE Bunyar Malenfant International (www.bmi.ca) sells systems that enable retailers to assess potential sales by counting the customers entering the stores and passing through areas. Campbell Software, a division of SAP (www.campbellsoft.com), is a leader in developing software for labor scheduling. Visit the home pages of these companies. What products and services are they selling? By looking at the comments in the discussion groups, decide what issues are of concern to retailers.

This output from Campbell Software labor scheduling system helps store managers improve their labor efficiency.

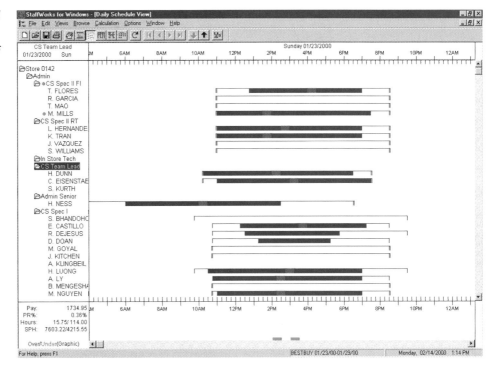

Store Maintenance

Store maintenance is the activities involved with managing the exterior and interior physical facilities associated with the store. The exterior facilities include the parking lot, the entrances to the store, and signs on the outside of the store. The interior facilities include the walls, flooring, ceiling, and displays and signs.

Store maintenance affects both the sales generated in the store and the cost of running the store. A store's cleanliness and neatness affect consumer perceptions of the quality of its merchandise. Maintenance is costly. Floor maintenance for a 40,000–square-foot home center is about $10,000 a year. Poor maintenance shortens the useful life of air conditioning units, floors, and fixtures.

Energy Management

Energy management is a major issue in store operations, especially in stores with special refrigeration needs such as supermarkets and restaurants. Wal-Mart has been very innovative in designing an energy-efficient store located in the City of Commerce, California. Rather than using individual energy-efficient systems for heating, air conditioning, and lighting, the store uses a systems approach that results in an annual energy savings of $75,000. To use more daylight, the store has 180 skylights. Photo sensors continuously monitor the light levels so that as the amount of daylight increases, the artificial lighting in the store is reduced automatically, reducing the heat generated by the artificial lighting and the need for air conditioning. Electronic sensors on faucets and toilets reduce water consumption in the store. Solar panels in the store's atrium provide 15 percent of the energy used in the store.[46]

Refact Energy costs in a typical supermarket are 1.0 to 1.4 percent of sales.[47]

REDUCING INVENTORY LOSS

An important issue facing store management is reducing inventory losses due to employee theft, shoplifting, mistakes and inaccurate records, and vendor errors. Examples of employee mistakes are failing to ring up an item when it's sold and miscounting merchandise when it's received or when physical inventories are taken. Inventory shrinkage due to vendor mistakes arises when vendor shipments contain less than the amount indicated on the packing slip.

Although shoplifting receives most of the publicity, employee theft accounts for about the same amount of inventory loss. A recent survey attributes 39 percent of inventory shrinkage to employee theft, 36 percent to shoplifting, 19 percent to mistakes and inaccurate records, and 6 percent to vendor errors.[48]

In developing a loss prevention program, retailers confront a trade-off between providing shopping convenience and a pleasant work environment and, on the other hand, preventing losses due to shoplifting and employee theft. The key to an effective loss prevention program is determining the most effective way to protect merchandise while preserving an open, attractive store atmosphere and a feeling among employees that they are trusted. Loss prevention requires coordination between store management, visual merchandising, and store design.

Refact Computer and software retailers attribute 64 percent of their inventory shrinkage to employee theft, while music stores attribute 66 percent of their shrinkage to shoplifting.[49]

Calculating Shrinkage

Shrinkage is the difference between the recorded value of inventory (at retail prices) based on merchandise bought and received and the value of the actual inventory (at retail prices) in stores and distribution centers divided by retail sales during the period. For example, if accounting records indicate inventory should be $1,500,000, the actual count of the inventory reveals $1,236,000, and sales were $4,225,000, the shrinkage is 6.7 percent [($1,500,000 − $1,236,000)/$4,225,000]. Reducing shrinkage is an important store management issue. Retailers' annual loss from shrinkage is between 1 and 5 percent of sales. Every dollar of inventory shrinkage translates into a dollar of lost profit.

Detecting and Preventing Shoplifting

Losses due to shoplifting can be reduced by store design, employee training, and special security measures.

Store Design   Security issues need to be considered when placing merchandise near store entrances, delivery areas, and dressing rooms. For example, easily stolen merchandise such as jewelry and other small, expensive items should never be displayed near an entrance. Dressing room entrances should be visible to store employees so they can easily observe customers entering and exiting with merchandise.[50]

Employee Training   Store employees can be the retailer's most effective tools against shoplifting. They should be trained to be aware, visible, and alert to potential shoplifting situations. Exhibit 17–8 outlines rules for spotting shoplifters. Perhaps the best deterrent to shoplifting is an alert employee who is very visible.

Security Measures   Exhibit 17–9 describes retailers' use of security measures. Department stores often chain expensive merchandise to fixtures. Another approach for deterring shoplifting is to embed dye capsules in the merchandise tags. If the tags aren't removed properly by a store employee, the capsules break and damage the merchandise.

EXHIBIT **17–8**

Spotting Shoplifters

DON'T ASSUME THAT ALL SHOPLIFTERS ARE POORLY DRESSED

To avoid detection, professional shoplifters dress in the same manner as customers patronizing the store. Over 90 percent of all amateur shoplifters arrested have either the cash, checks, or credit to purchase the merchandise they stole.

SPOT LOITERERS

Amateur shoplifters frequently loiter in areas as they build up the nerve to steal something. Professionals also spend time waiting for the right opportunity, but less conspicuously than amateurs.

LOOK FOR GROUPS

Teenagers planning to shoplift often travel in groups. Some members of the group divert employees' attention while others take the merchandise. Professional shoplifters often work in pairs. One person takes the merchandise and passes it to a partner in the store's restroom, phone booths, or restaurant.

LOOK FOR PEOPLE WITH LOOSE CLOTHING

Shoplifters frequently hide stolen merchandise under loose-fitting clothing or in large shopping bags. People wearing a winter coat in the summer or a raincoat on a sunny day may be potential shoplifters.

WATCH THE EYES, HANDS, AND BODY

Professional shoplifters avoid looking at merchandise and concentrate on searching for store employees who might observe their activities. Shoplifters' movements might be unusual as they try to conceal merchandise.

By placing convex mirrors at key locations, employees can observe a wide area of the store. Closed-circuit TV cameras can be monitored from a central location, but purchasing the equipment and hiring people to monitor the system can be expensive. Some retailers install nonoperating equipment that looks like a TV camera to provide a psychological deterrent to shoplifters.

While these security measures reduce shoplifting, they can also make the shopping experience more unpleasant for honest customers. The atmosphere of a fashionable department store is diminished when guards, mirrors, and TV cameras are highly visible. Customers may find it hard to try on clothing secured

Refact Retailers lose more than $29 billion annually due to shrinkage.[51]

EXHIBIT **17–9**

Use of Security Measures by Retailers

Live closed-circuit TV	**77%**
Observation mirrors	**60**
Cables, locks, and chains	**50**
Mystery and honesty shoppers	**50**
Secured displays	**46**
Plain-clothes detectives	**46**
Uniformed guards	**41**
EAS tags	**33**
Simulated closed-circuit TV	**31**
Ink/dye tags	**29**
Observation booths	**19**
Fitting room attendants	**16**

Source: Richard Hollinger, John Kane, and Read Hayes, *1998 National Retail Security Survey* (Gainesville, FL: Security Research Project, 1998), p. 24.

Retailers use electronic article surveillance systems (EAS) to reduce inventory loss. If the clothing tags (left) are not removed when the merchandise is purchased, the tags will be detected when a shoplifter passes through the sensor gates (right) at the store entrance.

with a lock-and-chain or an electronic tag. They can also be uncomfortable trying on clothing if they think they're secretly being watched via a surveillance monitor. Thus, when evaluating security measures, retailers need to balance the benefits of reducing shoplifting with the potential losses in sales.

Electronic article surveillance is a promising approach for reducing shrinkage with little effect on shopping behavior. In **electronic article surveillance (EAS) systems,** special tags are placed on merchandise. When the merchandise is purchased, the tags are deactivated by the POS scanner. If a shoplifter tries to steal the merchandise, the active tags are sensed when the shoplifter passes a detection device at the store exit and an alarm is triggered.

EAS tags do not affect shopping behavior because customers do not realize they're on the merchandise. Due to the effectiveness of tags in reducing shoplifting, retailers can increase sales by displaying theft-prone, expensive merchandise openly rather than behind a counter or in a locked enclosure.

Some large national retailers insist that vendors install EAS tags during the manufacturing process because the vendors can install the tags at a lower cost than the retailers. In addition, retail-installed tags can be removed more easily by shoplifters. Vendors are reluctant to get involved with installing EAS tags because industry standards have not been adopted. Without these standards, a vendor would have to develop unique tags and merchandise for each retailer.[52]

Prosecution   Many retailers have a policy of prosecuting all shoplifters. They feel a strictly enforced prosecution policy deters shoplifters. Some retailers also sue shoplifters in civil proceedings for restitution of the stolen merchandise and the time spent in the prosecution.[53]

Reducing Employee Theft

The most effective approach for reducing employee theft and shoplifting is to create a trusting, supportive work environment. When employees feel they're respected members of a team, they identify their goals with the retailer's goals. Stealing from their employer becomes equivalent to stealing from themselves or their family, and they go out of their way to prevent others from stealing from the "family." Thus retailers with a highly committed workforce and low turnover typically have low inventory shrinkage. Additional approaches for reducing employee theft are carefully screening employees, creating an atmosphere that encourages honesty and integrity, using security personnel, and establishing security policies and control systems.

Redner's Warehouse Markets, a chain in Reading, Pennsylvania, has one of the industry's lowest inventory shrinkages, 0.16 percent of retail sales. Redner's achieves this low shrinkage by educating its employees about the causes and effects of shrinkage on the business. Then it backs this message with incentives. It annually budgets 0.50 percent for shrinkage. If a store improves on this budgeted level, the difference is paid back to its employees. Employees earned $590,000 in annual bonuses for beating the budgeted shrinkage level.[54]

Screening Prospective Employees   Many retailers use paper-and-pencil honesty tests and make extensive reference checks to screen out potential employee theft problems. The major problem related to employee theft may be illegal drug use. Some retailers now require prospective employees to submit to drug tests as a condition of employment. Employees with documented performance problems, an unusual number of accidents, or erratic time and attendance records are also tested. Unless they're involved in selling drugs, employees who test positive are often offered an opportunity to complete a company-paid drug program, submit to random testing in the future, and remain with the firm.

Using Security Personnel   In addition to uniformed guards, retailers use undercover shoppers to discourage and detect employee theft. These undercover security people pose as shoppers. They make sure salespeople ring up transactions accurately.

Establishing Security Policies and Control Systems   To control employee theft, retailers need to adopt policies relating to certain activities that may facilitate theft.

- Randomly search containers such as trash bins where stolen merchandise can be stored.
- Require store employees to enter and leave the store through designated entrances.
- Assign salespeople to specific POS terminals and require all transactions to be handled through those terminals.
- Restrict employee purchases to working hours.
- Provide customer receipts for all transactions.
- Have all refunds, returns, and discounts cosigned by a department or store manager.
- Change locks periodically and issue keys to authorized personnel only.
- Have a locker room where all employee handbags, purses, packages, and coats must be checked.

In addition, computer software is available to detect unusual activity at POS terminals. For example, a POS terminal where shortages are frequently reported or return activity is unusually high can be located and then employees using the terminal can be monitored. Transactions can also be analyzed to identify employees who ring up a lot of no-receipt returns or void other employees' returns.

SUMMARY   Effective store management can have a significant impact on a retail firm's financial performance. Store managers increase sales by increasing labor productivity, decrease costs through labor deployment decisions, and reduce inventory loss by developing a dedicated workforce.

Increasing store employees' productivity is challenging because of the difficulties in recruiting, selecting, and motivating store employees. Employees typically have a range of skills and seek a spectrum of rewards. Effective store managers need to motivate their employees to work hard and to develop skills so they improve their productivity. To motivate employees, store managers need to understand what rewards each employee is seeking and then provide an opportunity to realize those rewards. Store managers must establish realistic goals for employees that are consistent with the store's goals and must motivate each employee to achieve them.

Store managers also must control inventory losses due to employee theft, shoplifting, and clerical errors. Managers use a wide variety of methods in developing loss prevention programs, including security devices and employee screening during the selection process. However, the critical element of any loss prevention program is building employee loyalty to reduce employee interest in stealing and increase attention to shoplifting.

KEY TERMS

ADA (Americans with Disabilities Act), *530*

Age Discrimination and Employment Act, *530*

autocratic leader, *534*

democratic leader, *534*

drawing account, *543*

EEOC (Equal Employment Opportunity Commission), *530*

electronic article surveillance (EAS) system, *550*

energy management, *547*

Equal Pay Act, *544*

extrinsic reward, *539*

Fair Labor Standards Act, *544*

group maintenance behavior, *534*

incentive compensation plan, *542*

intrinsic reward, *539*

job analysis, *526*

job application form, *528*

job description, *526*

labor scheduling, *545*

leadership, *534*

quota–bonus plan, *543*

sexual harassment, *544*

shrinkage, *548*

socialization, *531*

store maintenance, *547*

straight salary compensation, *542*

task performance behavior, *534*

transformational leader, *535*

DISCUSSION QUESTIONS AND PROBLEMS

1. How do on-the-job training and classroom training differ? What are the benefits and limitations of each approach?

2. Give examples of a situation in which a manager of a McDonald's fast-food restaurant must utilize different leadership styles.

3. Job descriptions should be in writing so employees clearly understand what's expected of them. But what are the dangers of relying too heavily on written job descriptions?

4. Name some laws and regulations that affect the employee management process.

5. What's the difference between extrinsic rewards and intrinsic rewards? What are the effects of these rewards on the behavior of retail employees? Under what conditions would you recommend that a retailer emphasize intrinsic rewards over extrinsic rewards?

6. Many large department stores such as JC Penney, Sears, and Macy's are changing their salespeople's reward system from a traditional salary to a commission-based system. What problems can incentive compensation systems cause? How can department managers avoid these problems?

7. When evaluating retail employees, some stores use a quantitative approach that relies on checklists and numerical scores similar to the form in Exhibit 17–6. Other stores use a more qualitative approach whereby less time is spent checking and adding and more time is devoted to discussing strengths and weaknesses in written form. Which is the best evaluation approach?

8. What are the different methods for compensating employees? Discuss which methods you think would be best for compensating a sales associate, store manager, and buyer.

9. Is training more important for a small independent retailer or a large national chain? Why? How does training differ between these two types of retailers?

10. Discuss how retailers can reduce shrinkage from shoplifting and employee theft.

SUGGESTED READINGS

Farr, John. "Loss Prevention." *Chain Store Age Executive,* January 1999, pp. 116–17.

"Getting the Best out of 'Em." *Sales & Marketing Management,* October 1997, pp. 34–36.

Hacker, Carol. *The Costs of Bad Hiring Decisions & How to Avoid Them,* 2d ed., Boca Raton, FL: St. Lucie Press, 1999.

Johnson, Gary. "Training as a Competitive Tool." *Chain Store Age,* April 1996, pp. 113–14.

Klinvex, Kevin, Matthew O'Connell, and Christopher Klinvex. *Hiring Great People.* New York: McGraw-Hill, 1999.

McAfee, R. Bruce. "Workplace Harassment: Employees vs. Customers." *Business Horizons* 42 (March–April 1999), pp. 79–85.

Pfeffer, Jeffrey. "Six Dangerous Myths about Pay." *Harvard Business Review,* May–June 1998, pp. 109–18.

"Retail Theft." *Discount Store News,* May 11, 1998, pp. 4, 6.

"A Roadmap for Retail Training." *WWD,* May 6, 1998, p. 9.

Sender, Isabelle. "Organized Labor: The Art of the Match—How Automated Solutions Are Helping Retailers." *Chain Store Age,* April 1, 1998, p. 68.

Toriello, Monica. "Making Training Pay Off—and Proving It." *National Home Center News,* April 19, 1999, p. 12.

Washburn, Dan. "Insider Stealing: How to Fight Employee Theft." *Home Improvement Market,* May 1997, pp. 40–44.

Kathie Greenwood
Director of Store Planning
Galyan's

WE ARE SHIFTING AWAY from the traditional interactive retailing—which consisted of large games such as golf simulators, hockey slapstick machines, and batting cages—to concepts that are easier to manage. The traditional interactivity was only entertaining to a small segment of our customers; and the modest increase in sales didn't justify the costs of devoting staff to the batting cage or having them sell merchandise. The staff opted for selling, not entertaining. Going forward, we will still include our 45-foot climbing wall. This wall attracts customers and provides an exciting experience in a safe environment. It also increases the time our customers stay in our building, in turn increasing their opportunity to buy products. In addition to the climbing wall, all stores will have simple interactive units, such as a hitting net and a putting green. It is more profitable to hire a golf pro to work with customers in a simple hitting net than to have a golf simulator for customers to play St. Andrews.   •   I am director of store planning at Galyan's, a retail chain selling sports and recreation equipment and apparel to people with an active lifestyle. Galyan's 19 stores range in size from 80,000 to 100,000 square feet. The stores are free-standing, in strip centers, and mall anchors. My five direct reports are responsible for store planning and merchandise presentation, purchasing, store design, construction, and specifications. Prior to assuming the responsibility for store planning, I worked in store management and buying for Galyan's—experience that enables me to integrate the variety of issues I need to deal with in developing a productive store design.   •   We're opening three to six new stores a year. We have created a model store to use as a template for all locations. The template is used when producing initial block layouts. However, each store has to be tweaked to mirror the demographics profile for that region. Our planning process for a new store starts with management setting an overall sales target for the stores and our budget for the building costs. Then we work with the buyers, analyzing the trading demographics to allocate the floor space to our 23 departments. This process is like a financial analyst developing a stock portfolio—we have to make trade-offs between the space allocated to a department and the sales that will be generated by the space.   •   Retailing is a competitive business, but I've met and worked with a lot of great supportive people. I have taken counsel from many of my peers who are further along their career path and they are always happy to provide assistance. For example, when I needed guidance in developing an organization chart for my growing department, Dave Lindsay, VP of store planning at Nordstrom's, was kind enough to offer his counsel.   •   You can take a virtual tour of a Galyan's store at www.galyans.com.

18

Store Layout, Design, and Visual Merchandising

QUESTIONS

- What are the critical issues in designing a store?
- What are the alternative methods of store layout?
- How is space assigned to merchandise and departments?
- What are the best techniques for merchandise presentation?

IN A TIME WHEN RETAILERS are finding it increasingly difficult to create a differential advantage on the basis of merchandise, price, promotion, and location, the store itself becomes a fertile opportunity for market differentiation. In fact, today's consumers have a multitude of shopping choices outside the store. For many there must be very compelling reasons to go to a store when the same merchandise is available over the Internet. They don't have to worry about hours of operation, parking, or getting large purchases home. Thus, even more than in the past, retailers must create an exciting store design with innovative merchandising techniques to make people want to get off their couches and go shopping.

Many retailers like to think of their store as a theater. The walls and floors represent the stage. The lighting, fixtures, and visual communications such as signs represent the sets. And the merchandise represents the show. Like the theater, the store design and all its components should work in harmony to support the merchandise, rather than competing with it. Booksellers, Borders, and Barnes & Noble have coffee bars and comfortable couches to encourage customers to browse and read—amenities that Amazon.com cannot provide. Outdoor equipment and apparel retailer REI in Seattle found that the installation of a climbing wall spurred sales so much that it is rolling out the concept in its other stores. Other stores like Restoration Hardware, Crate & Barrel, the Disney Store, The Gap, and Victoria's Secret don't have extraordinary features, but are entertaining nonetheless.

When designing or redesigning a store, managers must consider three objectives. First, the store's atmosphere must be consistent with the store's image and overall strategy. The second objective of a good store design is to help influence customers' buying decisions. Finally, when making design decisions, managers must bear in mind the productivity of the retail space—how many sales can be generated out of each square foot of space.

To meet the first objective, retail managers must define the target customer and then design a store that complements customers' needs. Is the shop traditional or trendy, masculine or feminine? To illustrate, consider the New York City Ducati motorcycle showroom. The Italian racing bike style is sleeker and more refined than Harley-Davidson's hogs. So Ducati designed a sophisticated space using graphically appealing, bold signage. Large black-and-white digital images of cool-looking riders as well as large three-dimensional Ducati logos adorn the walls. In contrast, think of the long gondola fixtures and bare fluorescent lighting that complement discount and warehouse stores' no-frills, low-price image. (A **gondola** is an island-type of self-service counter with tiers of shelves, bins, or pegs.) Customers would find it hard to accurately judge value if the physical environment were inconsistent with the merchandise or prices. Throughout this chapter, keep in mind the relationships between the overall retail strategy and the store's image as it's portrayed by the store layout, merchandise display, and atmospheric design elements such as signs, graphics, lighting, color, music, and scent. In Retailing View 18.1 we describe how two different target markets for bowling alleys require two different designs.

To meet the second design objective of influencing customer buying decisions, retailers concentrate on store layout and space-planning issues. Imagine a grocery store laid out like a women's specialty store, or an art gallery that looked like a tire store. Grocery stores are organized to facilitate an orderly shopping trip and to display as much merchandise as possible. Yet boutiques are laid out in a "free-form" design that allows customers to browse. Products are also located in certain areas to facilitate purchases. For instance, next time you visit a grocery or discount store, notice the merchandise displayed at the checkout area. **Impulse merchandise** (products purchased without prior planning such as candy, batteries, and the *National Enquirer*) are often located in these areas because people are often stuck in line with nothing else to do but buy.

Customers' purchasing behavior is also influenced by the store's atmosphere. Notice how your eye moves to an attractive, informative sign in a department store. On a more subtle level, have you ever been attracted to a Mrs. Fields Cookies store because of the chocolate chip cookie smell? Chances are the retailer planned this and other sensory experiences to get your attention. This chapter explores the methods retailers use to positively influence consumers' purchase behavior.

Each department in Joslins Park Meadows store is designed for the specific target customer that often result in great contrasts. For example, the men's department (left) is characterized by wide aisles, open space and refined finishes. The juniors and young men's area (right) is raw, industrial and merchandise is dense.

IN THE KANSAS CITY SUBURB of Olathe, Kansas, there are two bowling centers—Olathe Lanes East and Olathe Lanes West, located three miles apart. Olathe East burned to the ground, so the owners started the long process of rebuilding. The designers noticed two distinct groups were going to Olathe West, which was now accommodating both East and West leagues. Using Claritas's PRIZM clusters described in Chapter 9, researchers confirmed their suspicions and found substantial differences in the customers who bowl at the two facilities. As a result, the designers decided to create different designs appealing to each group. The customer base at Olathe Lanes East fell almost entirely into three upscale PRIZM clusters: Young Suburbia, Pools and Patios, and Furs and Station Wagons. Working with the demographic information, the designers selected an art deco motif for rebuilding the facility at East, a style popular in the area and seen in many Kansas City municipal structures. Art deco not only suggests a certain sophistication appealing to the target group, it also fits stylistically with bowling and echoes scheme of the sport's history. For example, it enabled the designers to work with black-and-white formats as well as a complex color scheme, involving teal and bordeaux, favored by upper-socioeconomic–status patrons.

Rather than using sharp edges and angles that suggest tension and motion, everything was softened to create a relaxing atmosphere. The icons of art deco lend themselves well to the shapes that create the best backdrop for an upper-scale customer profile. The cloud and circle shapes predominant in art deco design became curves and balls in the redesigned facility. From chair backs to curved walls, virtually every countertop and sign reflects the round smoothness of the bowling balls and pins themselves.

Some people equate higher noise levels with having more fun, but noise is not music to these particular lifestyle groups. Nine different decorative sound-refracting materials minimize the decibel level usually associated with noisy pinsetters. Newly designed Brunswick high-tech bowling equipment adds to the upscale look. Other structural elements include concourse skylights and floor-to-ceiling windows often seen in the homes of Young Suburbia and Furs and Station Wagons, their target market. These dispel the popular image of bowling alleys as dimly lit places, instead creating a personalized, open, active environment.

Following the grand reopening of Olathe Lanes East, the owners decided to redesign their West facility. Despite the fact that this bowling center draws business from essentially the same six-mile radius as the East lanes, the Furs and Station Wagons were replaced by four predominantly blue-collar groups: Blue Collar Nursery, Middle America, Blue Chip Blues, and Shotguns and Pickups.

The redone Lanes West features a folksy, outdoors style tied thematically to the Southwest. The predominant scheme is peach stucco with blue-green accents. The dark mahogany used in the East's center gave way to natural oak, and the East's soothing half-round shapes gave way to West's squares and energetic triangles.

Together, the two facilities, which the owners had considered extremely successful prior to the redesign, showed a substantial increase in total profitability. Each customer base favored its center's atmosphere over the other's.

Source: Barbara J. Eichhorn, of Lifecode® Design Marketing in Leawood, KS, "Selling by Design: Using Lifestyles Analysis to Revamp Retail Space," *American Demographics*, October 1996, pp. 44+.

Consistent with any retail decision, the third design objective is to consider the costs associated with each store design element versus the value received in terms of higher sales and profits. For instance, the free-form design found in many boutiques is much more costly than rows of gondolas in a discount store. Also, custom wood fixtures are more expensive than wire racks. Retailers must be aware of the financial ramifications of any store layout decision.

In Chapter 9 we examined the relative costs and space productivity associated with different store location decisions. Some issues examined there are relevant when determining where to locate certain departments and types of merchandise within a store. The best locations within a store are "worth" the most, so they're reserved for certain types of merchandise. For instance, many grocery stores place their produce near the store's entrance because it has a higher margin than other merchandise categories and it creates a nice atmosphere. Furniture and rugs are usually located off the beaten path in a department store because customers will

Refact It costs over $20 million to build a new department store and $7 to $10 million for a redo.

seek out this merchandise. Retailers have developed maps called planograms that prescribe the location of merchandise based on profitability and other factors.

Finally, when considering atmospheric issues of store design, retailers must weigh the costs along with the strategy and customer attraction issues. For instance, certain types of lighting used to highlight expensive jewelry and crystal cost more than rows of bare fluorescent bulbs.

This chapter is part of the store management section. In it, we examine the store design objectives that we've been discussing. First, we start with the big picture—how should the overall store be laid out? Then, we look at how retailers plan and evaluate the location of departments and, next, merchandise within departments. Finally, we explore very specific methods of altering a store's atmosphere.

STORE LAYOUT

To design a good store layout, store designers must balance many objectives—objectives that often conflict. First, the store layout should entice customers to move around the store to purchase more merchandise than they may have originally planned. One method is to expose the customer to a layout that facilitates a specific traffic pattern. Customers should be enticed to follow what amounts to a "yellow brick road."[1] For instance, Toys "R" Us uses a layout that almost forces customers to move through sections of inexpensive impulse-purchase products to get to larger, more expensive goods. It takes a very strong-willed parent to navigate through the balloons and party favors without making a purchase.

Another method of helping customers move through the store is to provide variety. The store should be filled with little nooks and crannies that entice shoppers to wander around. If the yellow brick road comes to a dead end, customers will stop shopping. A store designer need not be satisfied with flat spaces filled with long rows of racks and shelves. Multilevels and ramps add variety. If the floor must be flat, at least display heights can be varied to avoid a monotonous presentation.

A second objective of a good layout is to provide a balance between giving customers adequate space in which to shop and productively using this expensive, often scarce resource for merchandise. A store with lots of people creates a sense of excitement and, hopefully, increases buying. But a store with too many racks and displays causes customers to get confused or even lost. Some department store chains have chopped their stores into so many small boutiques that customers don't know where to find even a simple silk blouse. Finally, when laying out stores, retailers must consider the special needs of the disabled.

To meet these objectives, store designers decide about (1) alternative design types, (2) allocating space to feature and bulk-of-stock selling areas, and (3) making efficient use of walls. At the same time, retailers must attempt to make their stores flexible so adjustments can be easy and inexpensive. Retailing View 18.2 describes how computers are currently being used to create store layouts.

Types of Design

Today's modern retailers use three general types of store layout design: grid, racetrack, and free-form.

Grid   The **grid layout** is best illustrated by most grocery and drugstore operations. It contains long gondolas of merchandise and aisles in a repetitive pattern (Exhibit 18–1). The grid isn't the most aesthetically pleasing arrangement, but it's very good for shopping trips in which the customer plans to move throughout the entire store. For instance, when customers do their weekly grocery shopping, they weave in and out of the aisles with great agility, picking up similar products

A STORE MANAGER AND STORE DESIGNER are walking through their latest supermarket. The grocer remarks, "I think we should widen the aisles by another foot and put in four more doors in frozen foods. Also, move the deli from the left to the right side of the store." Minutes later, it is done! Of course we aren't talking about a real store. They're using a 3-D CAD (computer-aided–design) program that runs on their desktop computer.

Picture this: One by one, segments of a two-dimensional drawing begin to rise up from the computer screen's surface and assemble themselves into magical shapes. Wire-frame figures evolve into colorful three-dimensional forms.

This is where Alice would have ended up if she had followed a different rabbit. For retailers, 3-D animation is a powerful design, communication, and store-planning tool—one that is changing the way stores are designed. Existing on the realism scale somewhere between conceptual drawing and actual construction, an animated rendering has the ability to convey spatial ideas more dramatically and realistically than an artist's rendering, and it's far less expensive than building a prototype.

A store designer can create a lifelike, three-dimensional guided tour of any retail space using only her imagination and a desktop computer. Some of these systems run on mainstream Windows-based systems. You don't need to be a computer expert to run the program—just click the mouse and away you go.

Source: Len Lewis, "LED by Hand," *Progressive Grocer,* May 1997, pp. 133–34; and Sean O'Leary, "Revenge of the Sorcerer's Apprentice," *Visual Merchandising and Store Design,* December 1995, pp. 56–62.

every week. Since they know where everything is, they can minimize the time spent on a task that many don't especially enjoy. The grid layout is also cost-efficient. There's less wasted space with this design than with others because the aisles are all the same width and are designed to be just wide enough to accommodate shoppers and their carts. Since the grid design is used with long gondolas

EXHIBIT 18–1

Grid Store Layout

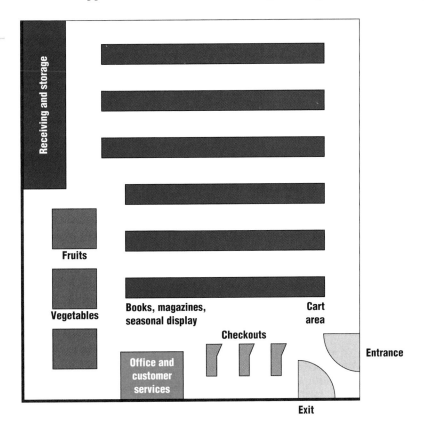

EXHIBIT 18–2   JCPenney Racetrack Layout at NorthPark Center in Dallas

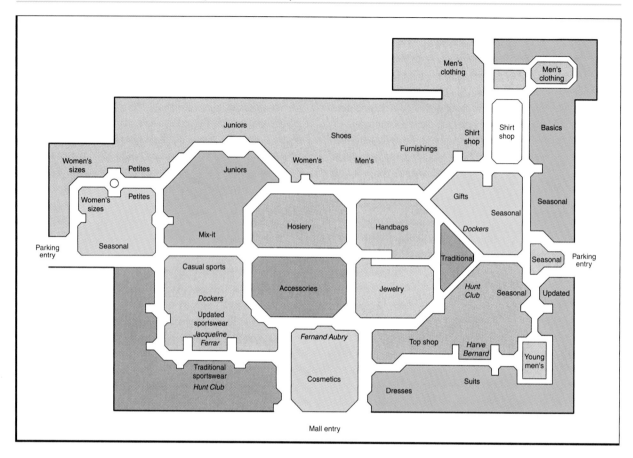

that have multiple shelf levels, the amount of merchandise on the floor can be significantly more than with other layouts. Thus, space productivity is enhanced. (Space productivity is discussed later in this chapter.) Finally, since the fixtures are generally standardized and repetitive, the fixturing cost is reduced.

Racetrack   One problem with the grid design is that customers aren't naturally drawn into the store. This isn't an issue in grocery stores, where most customers have a good notion of what they're going to purchase before they enter the store. But how can a store design pull customers through large shopping goods stores such as traditional department stores like Macy's or a discount store like Target?

The racetrack layout facilitates the goal of getting customers to visit multiple departments. The **racetrack layout** (also known as a **loop**) is a type of store layout that provides a major aisle to facilitate customer traffic that has access to the store's multiple entrances. This aisle "loops" through the store, providing access to **boutiques** (departments designed to resemble small, self-contained stores). The racetrack design encourages impulse purchasing. As customers go around the racetrack, their eyes are forced to take different viewing angles, rather than looking down one aisle as in the grid design.

Exhibit 18–2 shows the layout of JCPenney's store in the upscale NorthPark Center in Dallas, Texas. Since the store has multiple entrances, the loop design

Refact In 1936, Sylvan Goldman, owner of two Oklahoma City supermarkets, noticed that customers quit shopping when their wicker baskets got too full or too heavy. So he designed the first grocery cart.[2]

tends to place all departments on the "main aisle" by drawing customers through the store in a series of major and minor loops. To entice customers through the store, Penney's has placed some of the more important departments, like juniors, toward the rear of the store. The newest items are featured on the aisles to draw customers into departments and around the loop. To direct the customer through the store, the aisles must be defined by a change in surface or color. For instance, the aisle flooring is of marble-like tile, while the departments vary in material, texture, and color, depending on the desired ambiance.

Free-Form   A **free-form layout** (also known as **boutique layout**) arranges fixtures and aisles asymmetrically (Exhibit 18–3). It's successfully used primarily in small specialty stores or within the departments of large stores. In this relaxed environment, customers feel like they're at someone's home, which facilitates shopping and browsing. A pleasant atmosphere isn't inexpensive, however. For one thing, the fixtures are likely to be expensive custom units. Since the customers aren't naturally drawn around the store as they are in the grid and racetrack layouts, personal selling becomes more important. Also, since sales associates can't easily watch adjacent departments, theft is higher than with the grid design. Finally, the store sacrifices some storage and display space to create the more spacious environment. If the free-form layout is carefully designed, however, the increased costs can be easily offset by increased sales and profit margins because the customer feels at home.

To illustrate a free-form boutique within a racetrack layout, consider the Bloomingdale's I.C.B. boutique in the picture. The designers' objective was to create a simple, clear space that draws customers into the area. Fixtures with the latest

In this I.C.B. department at Bloomingdale's, fixtures with the latest garments are placed along the perimeter of the boutique to draw customers into the area. Flooring and lighting clearly delineate the area from adjacent departments and the walkway.

EXHIBIT **18–3**

Free-Form Store
Layout

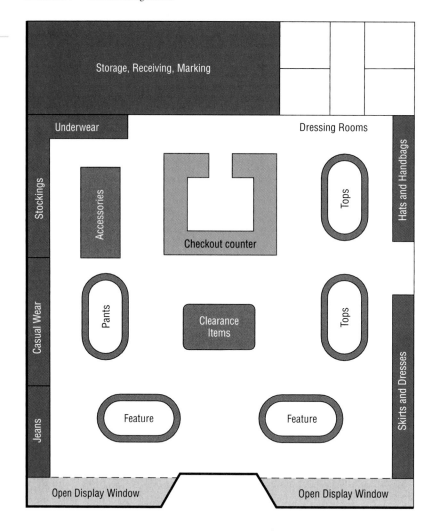

EXHIBIT **18–3**

Free-Form Store
Layout

garments are placed along the perimeter of the boutique. Yet the flooring and lighting clearly delineate the area from adjacent departments and the walkway.[3]

One would think that the issues to be considered when designing a bricks and mortar store would be very different than the design issues surrounding a virtual store. Think again, and see Retailing View 18.3.

The three types of display areas include feature areas, bulk-of-stock, and walls.

Feature Areas   **Feature areas** are designed to get the customer's attention. They include end caps, promotional aisles or areas, freestanding fixtures and mannequins that introduce a soft goods department, windows, and point-of-sale areas.

End caps are located at the end of an aisle. The last time Howard Marmon was shopping at his local Kroger food store, a large end cap display of Coca-Cola caught his attention. The Coca-Cola was located near the rest of the soft drinks but was on sale. It's not always necessary to use end caps for sales, however. Due to their high visibility, end caps can also be used to feature special promotional items, like beer and potato chips before the Fourth of July.

SUPERFICIALLY, NOTHING COULD BE more different. A webpage is virtual, and a store is physical. But good design components appear to transcend the physical world to the virtual world. Consider the following examples:

Simplicity matters. A good store design allows shoppers to move freely, unencumbered by clutter. There is a fine line between providing customers with a good assortment and confusing them with too much merchandise.

Similarly in a website, the spoke design, where every page is linked to every other page, leads to reduced usability. Further, it is not necessary to mention all the merchandise available at a site on each page. It is better to present a limited selection tailored to the customer's needs and then provide a few links to related merchandise and alternative assortments. It is also important to have a search feature on each page in case a customer gets lost. Note, the search feature in the virtual world is similar to having sales associates readily available in the physical world. Also, less is more. Having a small number of standard links on every page makes it more likely that users will learn the navigation scheme for the site.

Getting around. When a store is properly designed, customers should be able to easily find what they are looking for. The products that customers purchase together are merchandised together—umbrellas are with raincoats, soft drinks are with snack foods.

One way to help customers get around a website is by using *local links*—links that are internal to a website. Users rarely land directly at the desired page, especially when using a search engine. But they often get close. When establishing local links, websites should link:

- Products that are close in price, both higher and lower. If you link only to higher priced merchandise, you might lose customer trust.
- Complementary products
- Products that differ from the current product in some important dimension (for example, link to a color printer if the user is looking at a black-and-white printer)
- Different versions of the current product (for example, the same blouse in yellow)

Prioritize. Stores become annoying if everything jumps out at you as if to say, "buy me, no buy me." Other stores are so bland that the merchandise appears boring.

Setting priorities for merchandise displays and locations are just as important on the web as they are in a physical store. A common mistake on many Internet sites is that everything is too prominent: over-use of colors, animation, blinking, and graphics. If everything is equally prominent, then *nothing* is prominent. Being too bland is equally troublesome.

The site should be designed to advise the customer and guide them to the most important or most promising choices, while at the same time ensuring their freedom to go anywhere they please. Like a newspaper, the most important items or categories should be given the bigger headlines and more prominent placement.

Type of layout. Some stores are laid out to be functional like supermarkets and discount stores. They use a grid design to make it easy to locate merchandise. Other stores, like department or book stores use a more relaxed layout to encourage browsing. The trick is to pick the appropriate layout that matches the typical motives of the shopper.

Similarly, in the virtual world, stores have a similar trade-off. They can have a simple design that allows customers to easily find merchandise. Alternatively, they can employ complex graphics and animation that makes the site more entertaining, but increases download time and distracts shoppers from looking for specific information and merchandise. The nice thing about a virtual store, is the layout can be easily changed to reflect a change in strategy, while this can not be easily done in the real world.

Store designers also strive to make their stores different, to stand out in the crowd. A website, on the other hand, must strive for the balance between keeping the customer's interest and providing them with a comfort level based on convention. Users spend most of their time on *other* sites, so that's where they form their expectations for how the web works. So when trying to make a decision about website design, good website designers look at the most-visited sites on the Internet to see how they do it. If 90 percent or more of the big sites do things in a single way, then this is the de-facto standard.

Source: Jakob Nielsen's *Alertbox,* January 9, 2000, www.useit.com/alertbox/20000109.html; May 30, 1999, www.useit.com/alertbox/990530.html; October 3, 1999, www.useit.com/alertbox/991003.html; October 17, 1999, www.useit.com/alertbox/991017.html; November 14, 1999, www.useit.com/alertbox/991114.html.

A **promotional aisle** or **area** is used similarly to an end cap. Since Marmon was getting ready for the Christmas holidays, he stopped by a JCPenney store to stock up on ornaments. They were all in a special "trim-the-tree" department that seems to magically appear right after Halloween every year.

Freestanding fixtures and mannequins located on aisles are designed primarily to get customers' attention and bring them into a department. These fixtures often display and store the newest, most exciting merchandise in the department. (Reexamine the Bloomingdale's I.C.B. boutique in the picture on page 561.)

Although windows are clearly external to the store, they can be an important component of the store layout. Properly used, window displays can help draw customers into the store. They provide a visual message about the type of merchandise for sale in the store and the type of image the store wishes to portray. Window displays should be tied to the merchandise and other displays in the store. For instance, say Howard Marmon notices a window display of bath towels, which draws him into a local boutique. The bath towels should then be prominently displayed inside. Otherwise, the drawing power of the window display is lost. Finally, windows can be used to set the shopping mood for a season or holiday like Christmas or Valentine's Day.

Point-of-sale areas (also known as **point-of-purchase** or **POP areas**) can be the most valuable piece of real estate in the store, because the customer is almost held captive in that spot. While waiting in a long checkout line at Kmart, Marmon picked up some batteries, candy, razors, and a copy of *People Magazine*. Did he need these items? Not really, but the wait bored him, so he spent the extra time shopping.

Since retail space is often scarce and expensive, many retailers have successfully increased their ability to store extra stock, display merchandise, and creatively present a message by utilizing wall space.

Bulk-of-Stock Area The **bulk-of-stock area** contains the total assortment of merchandise. It is usually on gondolas in grocery and discount stores, and on freestanding fixtures for soft goods. This merchandise is usually introduced by a feature area. Presentation techniques for this merchandise are found later in this chapter.

Walls Since retail space is often scarce and expensive, many retailers have successfully increased their ability to store extra stock, display merchandise, and creatively present a message by utilizing wall space. Merchandise can be stored on shelving and racks. The merchandise can be coordinated with displays, photographs, or graphics featuring the merchandise. At Nike Town, for instance, a lot of merchandise is displayed relatively high on the wall. Not only does this allow the merchandise to "tell a story," but customers feel more comfortable because they aren't crowded by racks or other people, and they can get a perspective of the merchandise by viewing it from a distance.[4]

Flexibility of Store Design   As merchandise changes, so must a store's image. Thus, store planners attempt to design stores with maximum flexibility. Flexibility can take two forms: the ability to physically move store components and the ease with which components can be modified.

Most retailers have learned from the mistakes made by their predecessors following World War II. Stores during this period were often more like monuments, with inflexible wall-to-wall fixtures. The role of merchandise was almost an afterthought. Unfortunately, most of these architectural cathedrals quickly became outdated as tastes, attitudes, and the merchandise itself changed. Many of these landmark structures were made to last as long as the pyramids. Although they've long since closed for business, some still stand vacant as a sad tribute to what they once were, while others have been demolished. A few stores, like the Marshall Field's flagship store in Chicago, have been restored to their original splendor at a cost of millions of dollars.

Today, however, most stores are designed with flexibility in mind. For instance, IKEA, the Scandinavian furniture and home accessory retailer, has opened a small store in Manhattan called IKEA Marketing Outpost that is completely reset every two to three months. Outpost was originally designed with displays of selected merchandise with a common theme so as to inspire New York shoppers to visit IKEA's full-size stores. But the Outpost has also become a successful retail location in its own right. The design is remarkably flexible. The walls, video displays, merchandise, and signage can easily be reconfigured. For instance, when the store opened, the theme "IKEA Cooks" focused on the chain's line of kitchen cabinetry, cookware, and accessories. After two months,

Talk about flexibility, IKEA, the Scandinavian furniture store and home accessory retailer, has opened a small store in Manhattan called IKEA Marketing Outpost that is completely reset every two or three months.

the store closed for three days and reopened with an "IKEA plays" theme featuring juvenile furniture and toys.[5]

Recognizing the Needs
of the Disabled

A critical consideration in any store design or redesign decision is the Americans with Disabilities Act (ADA).[6] This landmark federal civil rights law protects people with disabilities from discrimination in employment, transportation, public accommodations, telecommunications, and the activities of state and local government. Since both the owner of a shopping center and the retailer are responsible for compliance, the lease may delineate responsibilities, although the lease relieves neither party from its legal obligation not to discriminate.

The requirements for compliance with the ADA are different depending on whether it's an existing facility, a newly built facility, or a facility undergoing remodeling. It's easiest to comply in an existing facility. In essence, barriers must be removed if doing so doesn't involve much difficulty or expense. The ADA insists on higher standards for larger facilities. For most stores and shopping centers, the ADA requires building ramps, adding grab bars, rearranging restroom stall dividers, adding a handrail to stairs, providing Braille elevator buttons, and other measures.

Requirements for newly built facilities or those undergoing remodeling are more stringent. For instance, if a shopping center has five or more stores, it must have an elevator even if it's a small building of under three stories or under 3,000 square feet per story.

SPACE PLANNING

Allocation of space to departments, categories, and finally items is one of store planners' and category managers' most complicated and difficult decisions. They must answer four questions:

1. What items, vendors, categories, and departments should be carried?
2. How much of each item should be carried?
3. How much space should the merchandise take?
4. Where should the merchandise be located?

Chapter 12's discussion of assortment planning gave procedures for answering the first two questions. Now let's examine the last two questions.

Store planners in conjunction with category managers typically start by allocating space based on sales productivity. For instance, if knit shirts represent 15 percent of the total expected sales for the men's furnishings department, it will initially get 15 percent of the space. Store planners must then adjust the initial estimate based on the following five factors.

1. *How profitable is the merchandise?* The marginal analysis approach for allocating promotional expenditures to merchandise (as Chapter 16 related) also works for allocating space. In this situation, a retailer allocates space to SKUs to maximize the merchandise category's profitability. Similar analyses can be performed for departments. Consider, for instance, allocating space for beer in a supermarket. At first glance, you might think that since Bud Light is the most profitable brand, it should get all the space. But if the store took this approach, it would lose sales on less profitable brands—and it might even lose customers who are loyal to other brands. Thus, the store should

experiment with different shelf space allocations until it finds a combination that maximizes profits for the category.

2. *How will the planned inventory turnover and the resulting stock-to-sales ratio affect how many SKUs will normally be carried in stock?* Recognize that (as in the merchandise budget plan) monthly inventory levels vary according to seasonal demands, holidays, and so on. Category managers and store planners must allocate space based on these seasonal needs rather than yearly averages. They must also estimate the proportion of merchandise kept on display versus backup stock. Merchandise kept as backup stock in a storage area takes much less room.

3. *How will the merchandise be displayed?* Merchandise and fixtures go hand in hand. Store planners design fixtures to go with the merchandise. But once the fixtures are in the store, category managers must consider the fixtures' physical limitations when assigning space to merchandise. Will the shirts be displayed on hangers or folded on tables? Customers can more easily examine merchandise on hangers, but this display method takes more space.

4. *What items does the retailer wish to emphasize?* The category managers have decided that this season will be particularly strong in knit shirts rather than woven shirts. They've bought accordingly, and planned additional advertising. As a result, knit shirts must also receive additional selling and display space.

5. *Will the location of certain merchandise draw the customer through the store, thus facilitating purchases?* Notice, for instance, the way the mannequins and fixtures are placed on the perimeter of the department in the Bloomingdale's I.C.B. boutique in the picture on page 561. Throughout this section, we examine how retailers locate departments and specific merchandise to facilitate purchases of impulse and complementary products.

We've discussed in general terms how store planners and buyers plan the space requirements for a category like knit shirts or beer. Similar decisions are made for larger groups of merchandise like classifications, departments, and even merchandise groups. Now let's examine how retailers decide where to locate departments and where to locate merchandise within departments.

Location of Departments

Sandy Williams recently went to Nordstrom for a haircut. On the way in, she stopped at the cosmetics counter to buy makeup. Then on the escalator, she spotted a red dress to examine on her way out. Before leaving the store, she stopped by the lingerie department to browse.

Did she simply take a random walk through the store? Probably not. The departments she shopped—like all Nordstrom departments—are strategically located to maximize the entire store's profits. The profit-generating abilities of various locations within a store aren't equal. (Remember the retail site selection techniques in Chapter 9.) The more traffic through a department, the better the location will be. Unfortunately, every department can't be situated in the best location. Retailers must consider additional demand-generating factors and the interrelations between departments when determining their locations.

Relative Location Advantages The best locations within the store depend on the floor location, the position within a floor, and its location relative to traffic aisles, entrances, escalators, and so on. In general, in a multilevel store, a space's value decreases the further it is from the entry-level floor. As we've said, men aren't generally avid shoppers for clothing. Thus, many large stores locate the men's department on the entry-level floor to make shopping as easy as possible.

The position within a floor is also important when assigning locations to departments. The best locations are those closest to the store's entrances, main aisles, escalators, and elevators. Sandy Williams spotted the red dress because she could see it from the escalator. Multilevel stores often place escalators so customers must walk around the sales floor to get to the next level. Also, most customers turn right when entering a store or floor, so the right side will be especially desirable space. Finally, most customers won't get all the way to the center of the store, so many stores use the racetrack design to induce people to move into the store's interior.[8]

Impulse Products   **Impulse products**—like fragrances and cosmetics in department stores and magazines in supermarkets—are almost always located near the front of the store, where they're seen by everyone and may actually draw people into the store. Sandy Williams didn't plan her makeup purchase, for example, but decided she wanted some once she saw the displays.

Demand/Destination Areas   Children's, expensive specialty goods, and furniture departments as well as customer-service areas like beauty salons, credit offices, and photography studios are usually located off the beaten path—in corners and on upper floors. Due to the exclusive nature of Steuben Glass, for instance, the department is typically located in a low-traffic area of high-end stores like Neiman Marcus. A purchase of one of these unique, expensive pieces requires thought and concentration. Sandy Williams would probably become distracted if the department were adjacent to a high-traffic area. Besides, customers looking for these items will find them no matter where they're located in the store. These departments are known as **demand/destination areas** because *demand* for their products or services is created before customers get to their *destination*. Thus, they don't need prime locations.

Seasonal Needs   Some departments need to be more flexible than others. For instance, it's helpful to locate winter coats near sportswear. Extra space in the coat department can be absorbed by sportswear or swimwear in the spring when the bulk of the winter coats have been sold.

Physical Characteristics of Merchandise   Departments that require large amounts of floor space, like furniture, are often located in the less desirable locations. Some departments (like curtains) need significant wall space, while others (like shoes) require accessible storage.

Adjacent Departments   After trying on the red dress, Sandy found a complementary scarf and stockings nearby. Retailers often cluster complementary products together to facilitate multiple purchases.

Some stores are now combining traditionally separate departments or categories to facilitate multiple purchases using market-basket analysis. Stores are laid out based on the way customers purchase merchandise, rather than based on traditional categories or departments. (See Chapter 11 for details.)

Evaluating a Departmental Layout   Paco Underhill and his company Envirosell have made a science out of determining the best ways to lay out a department or a store.[9] Although they utilize lots of hidden video cameras and other high-tech equipment, their most important research tool is a piece of paper

Why the Bread's in the Back of the Store

GROCERY SHOPPERS OF THE WORLD, UNITE! Supermarkets know everything about you. It's time you learned something about them.

The barricade is the first thing you notice when you enter a Winn-Dixie supermarket. Everything, from checkout stands to grocery bins, pushes you to the right.

Meanwhile, the items almost everyone buys—milk, eggs, butter, and bread—are in the back left-hand corner. To get to them, a shopper tending to turn right must travel half the store's perimeter and go past every aisle.

Most supermarkets steer shoppers immediately into the produce section. That's because they can see and feel and smell the food there, unlike the meat section, for instance, where items are hermetically sealed in plastic, or the snack section, where products are locked up in bags. The smell of fresh fruits and vegetables gets a shopper's mouth watering—

and any supermarket manager can tell you that the best customer is a hungry customer.

The first produce item you see is apples, and that's no accident either. The apple is by far the most popular item in produce, almost twice as popular as oranges, bananas, lettuce, and potatoes, the runners-up.

Supermarkets prefer store brands because they carry higher profit margins than name brands. So, stock clerks place the former to the right of the latter. Why? Because most people are right-handed and, to retrieve a name brand, will have to reach across the store brand to get it. Similarly, supermarkets display high-profit items on the right side of an aisle.

Source: Vince Staten, *Can You Trust a Tomato in January?* New York: Simon & Schuster, 1993. Reprinted with the permission of Simon & Schuster from "Can You Trust a Tomato in January?" by Vince Staten. Copyright © 1993 by Vince Staten.

called a track sheet in the hands of individuals they call trackers. Trackers follow shoppers and note everything they do. They also make inferences on consumer behavior based on what they've observed. Here are just a few of the things they have learned:

- Avoid the butt-brush effect. The butt-brush effect was discovered at New York City's Bloomingdale's. The researchers taped shoppers attempting to reach the tie rack while negotiating an entrance during busy times. They noticed that after being bumped once or twice, most shoppers abandoned their search for neckwear. The conclusion: Shoppers don't like to shop when their personal space is invaded.
- Place merchandise where their customers can readily access it. This sounds easy and obvious. But until little kids and old ladies were observed having difficulty reaching treats for their pets in a supermarket, they were typically stocked near the top of the shelf.
- Allow a transition zone. The first product encountered in a department isn't always going to have an advantage. Sometimes, just the opposite will happen. Allowing some space between the entrance of a store and a product gives it more time in the shopper's eye as he or she approaches it. For instance, cosmetics firms don't usually want to occupy the first counter inside the entrance of a department store because they know that women want a little privacy.

Next time you go grocery shopping, think about why things are located where they are. But first, read Retailing View 18.4.

Location of Merchandise within Departments: The Use of Planograms

To determine where merchandise should be located within a department, retailers of all types generate maps known as planograms. A **planogram** is a diagram created from photographs, computer output, or artists' renderings that illustrates exactly where every SKU should be placed. See photo on page 570. Technology for computer-generated planograms is readily available from commercial sources.[10]

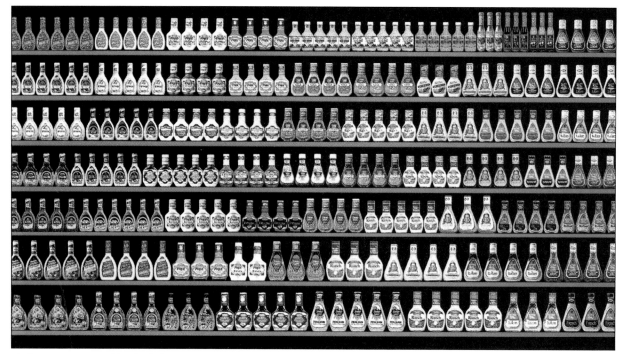

A planogram prepared by Apollo Space Management Systems for the salad dressing section of a grocery store.

Each planogram is accompanied by the following reports: a productivity report by SKU based on sales history; an ABC analysis by SKU (see Chapter 13); a space utilization report that describes the percentage of available space used in the planogram; and a comparison report that can describe productivity between any two retail spaces or between a current and a proposed space. (The comparison report is discussed in the next section.)

Electronic planogramming requires the user to input model numbers or UPC codes, product margins, turnover, sizes of product packaging or actual pictures of the packaging, and other pertinent information into the program. The computer plots the planogram based on the retailer's priorities. For instance, if the retailer wants prime shelf space given to products that produce the highest turns, the computer will locate those products in the best locations. If margins are more important, the computer will determine the shelf space priority and the optimal number of SKUs to stock in that space. Adjustments to the initial planogram can be made to see how additional space or different fixtures would affect the productivity measures.

Planograms are also useful for merchandise that doesn't fit nicely on gondolas in a grocery or discount store. The Gap and Banana Republic, for instance, provide their managers with photographs and diagrams of how merchandise should be displayed.

Recent advances in computer graphics and three-dimensional modeling allow planograms to be designed, tested with consumers, and changed, all in a "virtual" shopping environment.[12] A consumer can view merchandise on a computer screen that looks like a real store. The shopper can "pick up" a package by touching its image on the monitor. She can turn the package so it can be examined from all sides. If she wants, she can "purchase" the product. In the meantime, the computer tracks the time spent shopping and examining a particular product, and quantity purchased. Armed with this information, the retailer can "test" the effectiveness of different planograms.

In the next section, we describe how we use planograms to evaluate the productivity of space in a retail store.

Evaluating Space Productivity

Recall from Chapter 7 that a **productivity measure** (the ratio of an output to an input) determines how effectively a retailer uses a resource. Most retailers measure the productivity of space on a **sales-per-square-foot basis,** since rent and land purchases are assessed on a per-square-foot basis. But sometimes it's more efficient to measure profitability using **sales per linear foot.** For instance, in a grocery store, most merchandise is displayed on multiple shelves on long gondolas. Since the shelves have approximately the same width, only the length, or linear dimension, is relevant. Sales per cubic foot may be most appropriate for stores like wholesale clubs that use multiple layers of merchandise.

When allocating space to merchandise or a department, a retail manager must consider the profit impact on all departments. Remember, the objective is to maximize the profitability of the store, not just a particular department. Since cosmetics and drugs have a relatively high gross margin per square foot, should management give it more or less space? The answer depends on whether profitability of the entire store would increase if more space were allotted to this department. The department may be achieving its high productivity ratio because it's too small and has only a limited assortment. Conversely, a department may actually be too large—if so, almost as much profit could be generated with a smaller space. The buyer could buy smaller quantities more often, thereby making more productive use of a smaller space. If management decides to shrink cosmetics and the drugs department, more space would be available for, say, female apparel. If the departments' overall profitability would be increased by making this move, then the retailer should do it.[14]

Another way to evaluate the performance of retail space is to compare the productivity between any two retail spaces or between a current and a proposed space. Exhibit 18–4 compares the performance of the salad dressing planogram depicted earlier with one in which two Dunne dressings were added and two Kraft dressings were deleted. This report can be used to test different planograms and ask "what-if" questions. It provides information on gross margin per week, sales per week, unit sales per week, and inventory turnover for the current gondola and proposed gondola, and shows the net change between the two.

The revised gondola should improve gross margin by $5.54, sales by $36.75, unit sales by 35.00, and inventory turnover by .66. (See the last line of Exhibit 18–4.) The category manager or merchandise planner for salad dressing should try several alternative configurations before settling on a new planogram for this gondola.

Refact Median sales per square foot is $240 for high-profit department stores, compared to $214 for all department stores. At specialty stores, the median is $268 for high-profit stores, compared to $248.73 for all stores. Sales per square foot for department stores has been increasing from $148 in 1993 to $214 in 1997.[13]

MERCHANDISE PRESENTATION TECHNIQUES

Many methods are available to retailers for effectively presenting merchandise to the customer. To decide which is best for a particular situation, store planners must consider the following four issues.

EXHIBIT **18–4**

Financial
Comparison Report
for Existing and
Proposed Salad
Dressing Planogram

BRAND	GROSS MARGIN PER WEEK	SALES PER WEEK	UNIT SALES PER WEEK	INVENTORY TURNOVER
SECTION SALES DRESSING CURRENT				
1. 7SEAS	$50.33	$273.68	222.00	35.52
2. HV RANCH	$26.01	$165.13	90.80	22.59
3. KENS STK	$46.76	$330.14	266.00	27.61
4. KRAFT	$59.83	$336.42	238.00	23.48
5. NWMN OW	$32.63	$186.06	114.00	34.87
6. PRS CHOI	$27.88	$122.18	82.00	59.22
7. WLD FRMS	$20.80	$109.85	65.00	45.07
8. WSHBN	$102.76	$590.03	431.00	25.73
Totals	$367.00	$2,113.49	1,508.80	28.53
SECTION: SALAD DRESSING REVISED				
1. 7SEAS	$50.33	$273.68	222.00	35.52
2. DUNNE	$6.97	$46.20	44.00	26.00
3. HV RANCH	$26.01	$165.13	90.80	22.59
4. KENS STK	$46.76	$330.14	266.00	27.61
5. KRAFT	$58.40	$326.97	229.00	27.13
6. NWMN OW	$32.63	$186.06	114.00	34.87
7. PRS CHOI	$27.88	$122.18	82.00	59.22
8. WLD FRMS	$20.80	$109.85	65.00	45.07
9. WSHBN	$102.76	$590.03	431.00	25.73
Totals	$372.54	$2,150.24	1,543.80	29.19
NET CHANGE				
1. 7SEAS	$0.00	$0.00	0.00	0.00
2. DUNNE	$6.97	$46.20	44.00	26.00
3. HV RANCH	$0.00	$0.00	0.00	0.00
4. KENS STK	$0.00	$0.00	0.00	0.00
5. KRAFT	($1.43)	($9.45)	–9.00	3.64
6. NWMN OW	$0.00	$0.00	0.00	0.00
7. PRS CHOI	$0.00	$0.00	0.00	0.00
8. WLD FRMS	$0.00	$0.00	0.00	0.00
9. WSHBN	$0.00	$0.00	0.00	0.00
Totals	$5.54	$36.75	35.00	0.66

Source: Apollo Space Management System.

First, and probably most important, merchandise should be displayed in a manner consistent with the store's image. For instance, some traditional men's stores display dress shirts by size so all size 15½–34 shirts are together. Thus the customer can easily determine what's available in his size. This is consistent with a no-nonsense image of the store. Other stores keep all color/style combinations together. This presentation evokes a more fashion-forward image and is more aesthetically pleasing, but it forces the customer to search in each stack for his size.

Second, store planners must consider the nature of the product. Basic jeans can easily be displayed in stacks, but skirts must be hung so the customer can more easily examine the design and style.

Third, packaging often dictates how the product is displayed. Discount stores sell small packages of nuts and bolts, for example, but hardware stores still sell these products by the unit. Although the per-unit price is significantly higher for the packages, self-service operations don't have adequate personnel to weigh and bag these small items.

Finally, products' profit potential influences display decisions. For example, low-profit/high-turnover items like back-to-school supplies don't require the same elaborate, expensive displays as Parker fountain pens.

In this section, we'll examine some specific presentation techniques. Then we'll describe the fixtures used in these merchandise presentations.

Refact Fifty percent of women get their ideas for clothes from store displays or window shopping.[15]

Idea-Oriented Presentation

Some retailers successfully use an **idea-oriented presentation**— a method of presenting merchandise based on a specific idea or the image of the store. Women's fashions, for instance, are often displayed to present an overall image or idea. Also, furniture is combined in room settings to give customers an idea of how it would look in their homes. Individual items are grouped to show customers how the items could be used and combined. This approach encourages the customer to make multiple complementary purchases.

Manufacturers with strong consumer demand are often merchandised together in the boutique layout described earlier in this chapter. This technique is similar to the idea-oriented presentation in that merchandise made by the same vendor will tend to be coordinated. Some apparel manufacturers like Liz Claiborne and Jaeger coordinate both style and color to influence multiple purchases within the line and enhance the line's overall image.

Style/Item Presentation

Probably the most common technique of organizing stock is by style or item. Discount stores, grocery stores, hardware stores, and drugstores employ this method for nearly every category of merchandise. Also, many apparel retailers use this technique. When customers look for a particular type of merchandise, such as a sweater, they expect to find all items in the same location.

Arranging items by size is a common method of organizing many types of merchandise, from nuts and bolts to apparel. Since the customer usually knows the desired size, it's easy to locate items organized in this manner.

Color Presentation

A bold merchandising technique is by color. For instance, in winter months women's apparel stores may display all white cruisewear together to let customers know that store is the place to purchase clothing for their winter vacation.

Price Lining

Organizing merchandise in price categories, or **price lining** (when retailers offer a limited number of predetermined price points within a classification), was discussed in Chapter 15. This strategy helps customers easily find merchandise at the price they wish to pay. For instance, men's dress shirts may be organized into three groups selling for $30, $45, and $60.

Vertical Merchandising

Another common way of organizing merchandise is **vertical merchandising.** Here merchandise is presented vertically using walls and high gondolas. Customers shop much as they read a newspaper—from left to right, going down each column, top to bottom. Stores can effectively

This Diesel store uses vertical merchandising to display their jeans. Organized to follow the eye's natural movement, customers can search for what they want by going left to right, going down each column, top to bottom.

organize merchandise to follow the eye's natural movement. Retailers take advantage of this tendency in several ways. Many grocery stores put national brands at eye level and store brands on lower shelves because customers scan from eye level down. Finally, retailers often display merchandise in bold vertical bands of an item. For instance, you'll see vertical columns of towels of the same color displayed in a department store or a vertical band of yellow-and-orange boxes of Tide detergent followed by a band of blue Cheer boxes in a supermarket.

Tonnage Merchandising

As the name implies, **tonnage merchandising** is a display technique in which large quantities of merchandise are displayed together. Customers have come to equate tonnage with low price, following the retail adage "stock it high and let it fly." Tonnage merchandising is therefore used to enhance and reinforce a store's price image. Using this display concept, the merchandise itself is the display. The retailer hopes customers will notice the merchandise and be drawn to it. For instance, before many holidays, grocery stores use an entire end of a gondola (i.e., an end cap) to display six-packs of Pepsi.

Frontage Presentation

Often, it's not possible to create effective displays and efficiently store items at the same time. But it's important to show as much of the merchandise as possible. One solution to this dilemma is the **frontal presentation** (a method of displaying merchandise in which the retailer exposes as much of the product as possible to catch the customer's eye). Book manufacturers, for instance, make great efforts to create eye-catching covers. But bookstores usually display books exposing only the spine. To create an effective display and break the monotony, book retailers often face the cover out like a billboard to catch the customer's attention. A similar frontal presentation is achieved on a rack of apparel by simply turning one item out to show the merchandise.

Fixtures

The primary purposes of fixtures are to efficiently hold and display merchandise. At the same time, they must help define areas of a store and encourage traffic flow. Fixtures must be in concert with the other physical aspects of the store, such as floor coverings and lighting, as well as the

EXHIBIT **18–5**

Four Fixture Types

(A) Straight rack

(B) Rounder

(C) Four-way

(D) Gondola

overall image of the store. For instance, in stores designed to convey a sense of tradition or history, customers automatically expect to see lots of wood rather than plastic or metal fixtures. Wood mixed with metal, acrylic, or stone changes the traditional orientation. The rule of thumb is that the more unexpected the combination of textures, the more contemporary the fixture.

Fixtures come in an infinite variety of styles, colors, sizes, and textures, but only a few basic types are commonly used. For apparel, retailers utilize the straight rack, rounder, and four-way. The mainstay fixture for most other merchandise is the gondola.

The **straight rack** consists of a long pipe suspended with supports going to the floor or attached to a wall (Exhibit 18–5A). Although the straight rack can hold a lot of apparel, it's hard to feature specific styles or colors. All the customer can see is a sleeve or a pant leg. As a result, straight racks are often found in discount and off-price apparel stores.

A **rounder** (also known as a **bulk fixture** or **capacity fixture**) is a round fixture that sits on a pedestal (Exhibit 18–5B). Although smaller than the straight rack, it's designed to hold a maximum amount of merchandise. Since they're easy to move and they efficiently store apparel, rounders are found in most types of apparel stores. But, as with the straight rack, customers can't get a frontal view of the merchandise.

ELECTRONICS RETAILER CIRCUIT CITY has installed an in-store kiosk system enabling customers to order custom-configured computers directly from manufacturers. In an effort to increase sales per square foot, improve customer service, expand their PC selections, and ward off inroads from their Internet-based retail competitors and manufacturers, each of Circuit City's 520 locations now has a built-to-order kiosk. Customers can choose models from NEC, IBM, Compaq, and Hewlett-Packard, select the features they would like, and order directly from the manufacturer.

The system has several benefits for the customer over buying a ready-made computer at the store or ordering over the Internet. First, customers have an infinite array of choices. Second, they can easily compare products and costs across brands. Finally, they can have the computer delivered directly to their homes or to the store. Customers don't have to worry about UPS dropping a computer off at home when they aren't there.

From Circuit City's perspective, the kiosk can provide a great selection for their customers without having to invest in a huge inventory. Sales per square foot can be huge compared to a traditional computer department's. Also, almost anything Circuit City can do to preempt customers from shopping for a computer over the Internet is probably worthwhile.

Source: Ginger Koloszyc, "Innovative Kiosk System Helps Circuit City Offer Custom Computers," *Stores,* January 1999, pp. 36–40. Reprinted from *Stores* Magazine, © NRF Enterprises, Inc. 1999.

A **four-way fixture** (also known as a **feature fixture**) has two crossbars that sit perpendicular to each other on a pedestal (Exhibit 18–5C). This fixture holds a large amount of merchandise and allows the customer to view the entire garment. The four-way is harder to properly maintain than the rounder or straight rack, however. All merchandise on an arm must be of a similar style and color, or the customer may become confused. Due to their superior display properties, four-way fixtures are commonly utilized by fashion-oriented apparel retailers.

A gondola is an island type of self-service counter with tiers of shelves, bins, or pegs (Exhibit 18–5D). Gondolas are extremely versatile. They're used extensively, but not exclusively, in grocery and discount stores to display everything from canned foods to baseball gloves. Gondolas are also found displaying towels, sheets, and housewares in department stores. Folded apparel too can be efficiently displayed on gondolas, but, because the items are folded, it's even harder for customers to view apparel on gondolas than on straight racks.

A method of selling merchandise in a store without actually displaying it is with an interactive electronic kiosk. See Retailing View 18.5.

Refact An Office Depot has over 1,700 linear feet of fixtures. A 100,000–square-foot Burdines Department Store has about 1,000 fixtures—half are for hanging apparel.

ATMOSPHERICS

Atmospherics refers to the design of an environment via visual communications, lighting, colors, music, and scent to stimulate customers' perceptual and emotional responses and ultimately to affect their purchase behavior.[16] Many retailers have discovered the subtle benefits of developing atmospherics that complement other aspects of the store design and the merchandise. Now let's explore some basic principles of good atmospheric design and examine a few new, exciting, and somewhat controversial trends.

Visual Communications

Visual communications—comprising graphics, signs, and theatrical effects, both in the store and in windows—help boost sales by providing information on products and suggesting items or special purchases. Signs and graphics also help customers find a department or merchandise.

Adding to the atmospherics at Swatch's New York City flagship store, the Swatch Speed Reponse exhibit tests reflexes and coordination. The 4-foot watch face is dotted with colored buttons that customers whack as they light up in random sequence, racing the countdown clock.

Graphics (such as photo panels) can add personality, beauty, and romance to the store's image.

Retailers should consider the following seven issues when designing visual communications strategies for their stores.

Coordinate Signs and Graphics with the Store's Image   Signs and graphics should act as a bridge between the merchandise and the target markets. The colors and tone of the signs and graphics should complement the merchandise. Colors that aren't pleasing to the overall presentation will visually destroy a good display and detract from the merchandise. For example, a pastel pink sign in a store selling nautical supplies would not be as appropriate as bold red, white, and blue. Also, a formally worded black-and-white rectangular sign doesn't relate to a children's display as well as a red-and-yellow circus tent design does. Color combinations should appeal to specific target customers or highlight specific merchandise—primary colors for kids, hot vivid colors for teens, pastels for lingerie, brights for sportswear, and so forth. Wall posters should depict merchandise used by the appropriate target market. Posters of teenagers in jeans should be used in the young men's department, for example.

Inform the Customer   Informative signs and graphics make merchandise more desirable. For instance, Crate & Barrel, the upscale home furnishings retailer, has a small white placard with black descriptive copy and price as an integral part of each display. The sign is foremost a sales tool designed to appeal to specific customer needs and wants. For example, one sign may explain how a food processor works; another may announce that a particular flatware pattern was an award winner.

Alphabet Soup, a small Iowa-based chain of educational toy stores, imploys lively graphics in a unifying theme that is consistent with the store's image.

Large photo panels depicting the merchandise in use or in an actual home help shoppers visualize how the merchandise will function in their lives. As retailers know, customers aren't just worried about buying the product per se. They're concerned with the solution to a problem or with the gratification the product offers.

Use Signs and Graphics as Props   Using signs or graphics that masquerade as props (or vice versa) is a great way to unify theme and merchandise for an appealing overall presentation. For instance, images of fruit slices of watermelons, oranges, lemons, limes, or kiwis make colorful signs that tie in with all kinds of summer sales and promotions. A retailer could plan a storewide sale incorporating fruit slices into signage, posters, shopping bags, window displays, banners, and so forth. Sometimes, however, displays clutter stores and detract from sales. Retailing View 18.6 gives details.

Keep Signs and Graphics Fresh   Signs and graphics should be relevant to the items displayed and shouldn't be left in the store or in windows after displays are removed. Forgotten, faded, and fraught with water spots, such signs do more

"Wobblers" and "Danglers" Clutter Stores, Irk Retailers

IT'S THE GREATEST SHOW in the grocery store. Sales of Barnum's Animals jumped more than 15 percent in the past year—and half the cookies sold were munched even before people got to the checkout counter.

The reason? A 76-inch gorilla-shaped cardboard tower that greets supermarket shoppers right at the front door. The gorilla towers, along with their tiger and elephant predecessors, have prompted children to pester parents for Barnum's new cookie shapes, flavors, and back-of-the-box prizes.

All over the grocery store, food and beverage makers are laying eye-catching promotional traps to snare impulse purchases. Marketers insist that as much as 70 percent of all purchase decisions in grocery and drugstores are made on the spot, in store aisles. The goal is to intrude into the environment.

But the intrusion is raising merchants' hackles. Store aisles, ceilings, and refrigerator cases have become so cluttered with novelty displays that some retailers have drawn up strict rules about what kind of signs they'll accept. The backlash is forcing marketers to become more creative in staking out store turf.

The proliferation of in-store advertising come-ons has sparked a jargon all its own. Here is a glossary:

Aisle interrupter	Cardboard sign that juts into the middle of the aisle
Dangler	Sign hanging down from a shelf that sways when shoppers pass
Dump bin	Box-shaped display holding products loosely dumped inside
Glorifier	Small plastic "stage" that elevates one product above the rest
Lipstick board	Plastic surface on which messages are written with crayons
Necker	Coupon hanging on a bottle neck
Wobbler	A jiggling sign
Y.E.S. unit	"Your extra salesperson," a fact sheet that pulls down like a shade

Source: Yumiko Ono, " 'Wobblers' and 'Sidekicks' Clutter Stores, Irk Retailers," *The Wall Street Journal,* September 8, 1998, pp. B1, B4; permission conveyed through the Copyright Clearance Center.

---

to disparage a store's image than sell merchandise. Also, new signs imply new merchandise.

Limit the Copy of Signs Since a sign's main purpose is to catch attention and inform customers, the copy is important to its overall success. As a general rule, signs with too much copy won't be read. Customers must be able to quickly grasp the information on the sign as they walk through the store.

Use Appropriate Typefaces on Signs Using the appropriate typeface is critical to a sign's success. Different typefaces impart different messages and moods. For instance, carefully done calligraphy in an Old English script provides a very different message than a hastily written price-reduction sign.

Create Theatrical Effects Part of any theatrical set are special effects that transcend yet coordinate the other elements. To heighten store excitement and enhance store image, retailers have again borrowed from the theater. Theatrical effects may be simple extensions of more functional elements, like signs using colored fabric to identify a department. Or bold graphic posters or photographs can be hung from ceilings and walls to decorate, provide information, or camouflage less aesthetic areas, such as the ceiling structure.

Refact An effective sign in a window or just inside a doorway must be read in an instant—less than two seconds per customer—and should therefore contain only two or three words.[17]

Refact A typical category killer store has about 150 lighting fixtures, whereas a 100,000–square-foot department store has over 1,000.

Lighting Good lighting in a store involves more than simply illuminating space. Lighting is used to highlight merchandise, sculpt space, and capture a mood or feeling that enhances the store's image. Lighting can also be used to downplay less attractive features that can't be changed. European lighting designs are changing the look of U.S. boutiques.

From the parking lot, Joslin's Park Meadows' (Englewood, Colorado) customers are treated to an all-night computer-controlled light show with sequenced colored lighting focused on the store's atrium and facade.

Highlight Merchandise   A good lighting system helps create a sense of excitement in the store. At the same time, lighting must provide an accurate color rendition of the merchandise. A green silk tie should look the same color in the store as at the office. Similarly, lighting should compliment the customer. A department store's cosmetics area, for instance, requires more expensive lighting than the bare fluorescent lighting found in most grocery stores.

Another key use of lighting is called **popping the merchandise**—focusing spotlights on special feature areas and items. Using lighting to focus on strategic pockets of merchandise trains shoppers' eyes on the merchandise and draws customers strategically through the store.

Structure Space and Capture a Mood   When Greg Feffer was in The Broadway department store shopping for a suit, he noticed his mood changed as he moved from department to department and across aisles. Part of his mood change may have been due to the store planner's explicit lighting plan.

Downplay Features   Lighting can hide errors and outmoded store designs. Cavanaugh's shoe store, for example, has outgrown its space. To increase its storage, it has created a false ceiling of wooden rafters with overstock above. Careful lighting de-emphasizes this area, which could otherwise be an eyesore.

Euro Lighting Crosses the Atlantic   Traditionally U.S. specialty and department stores have employed incandescent lighting sources to promote a warm and cozy ambiance.[18] Overall lighting sources were reduced and accent lighting was pronounced to call attention to merchandise and displays. It was meant to feel like someone's home—dim lighting overall, with artwork and other areas of interest highlighted.

The European method of lighting can now be found in the most exclusive specialty stores of Rodeo Drive, Bal Harbour, and even some department stores like Bloomingdale's. European stores have long favored high light levels, cool colors, and little contrast or accent lighting. Lighting design has been more bold, stark, and minimal than in the United States.

The reason for the shift in lighting philosophies in the United States can be attributed to advances in lamps and fixtures, which makes the European bright look more aesthetically pleasing and economical.

Color   The creative use of color can enhance a retailer's image and help create a mood. Research has shown that warm colors (red and yellow) produce opposite physiological and psychological effects from cool colors (blue and green), which are opposite on the color spectrum.[19] For example, red and warm colors have been found to increase blood pressure, respiratory rate, and other physiological responses. As we translate these findings to a retail store environment, warm colors are thought to attract customers and gain attention, yet they can be distracting and even unpleasant.

In contrast, research has shown that cool colors, like blue or green, are relaxing, peaceful, calm, and pleasant. Thus, cool colors may be most effective for retailers selling anxiety-causing products, such as expensive shopping goods. Alternatively, warm colors may be more appropriate in stores that want to generate excitement.

Music Like color and lighting, music can either add or detract from a retailer's total atmospheric package. Unlike other atmospheric elements, however, music can be easily changed and adjusted with a mere change of tape or radio station. Seattle-based Muzak and AEI Music provides background music for many commercial enterprises, including retailing. It offers a service that allows retailers to automatically change their music throughout the day to reflect different customers' tastes. For instance, a store might use adult contemporary in the morning and switch to Top 40 when teens start coming in after school.

Other retailers use volume and tempo for crowd control. For instance, Dick Clark's American Bandstand Grills play faster and louder songs at times of the day when the restaurant wants to turn more tables.[20] But research in grocery stores indicates that music's tempo and volume don't significantly influence patrons' shopping time or purchase amount.[21]

Retailers can also use music to impact customers' behavior. Music can control the pace of store traffic, create an image, and attract or direct consumers' attention. For instance, Limited Too, a division of Limited Group, has created a signature sound to appeal to its target market—8- to 14-year-old girls. It is a mix of hip hop, R&B, pop, and swing featuring artists such as Brandy, Fastball, and Brian Setzer Orchestra.[22] The Disney Stores pipe in soundtracks from famous Disney movies that are tied directly to the merchandise.

Limited Too has created a signature sound to appeal to its target market—8- to 14-year-old girls. It's a mix of hip hop, R&B, pop, and swing.

Like variations in lighting, fixtures, and other store design elements, changing music in different parts of a store can help alter a mood or appeal to different markets. The new Joslins department store in Englewood, Colorado, has an environmental sound system with 10 different sound zones aimed at emotionally connecting with customers.[23] As customers move from one department to the other, the sounds quickly change from modern jazz in men's contemporary to big band in men's suiting, hip hop and rock in juniors, and classical in fragrance. Activewear brings the outdoors in with wind and bird sounds. The home area features campy 1930s and 40s music conjuring up Mom, the smells of the kitchen, and home. Each zone is treated to its own specialty store ambiance of sound.

Scent Most buying decisions are based on emotions. Of all the human senses, smell has the greatest impact on our emotions.[25] "Smell, more than any other sense, is a straight line to feelings of happiness, hunger, disgust, and nostalgia—the same feelings marketers want to tap."[26] Although particular smells may put customers in a better mood or make them linger in a store longer, there's mixed evidence among researchers that better smells lead to better sales. Nonetheless, retailers from Federated Department Stores to The Limited are experimenting with scents in their stores. Most of the "proof" is anecdotal. Consider, for instance, that in the Aventura Shoe Store in Chicago's Watertower Place, sales tripled after it introduced an aroma that combined leather, citrus, and baby powder.

Retailers must carefully plan the scents that they use, depending on their target market. Gender of the target customer should be taken into account in deciding on the intensity of the fragrance in a store. Research has shown that women have a better ability to smell than men. Age and ethnic background are also factors. As people get older, their sense of smell decreases. Half of all people over 65 and three-quarters over 80 have almost no smell at all. Korean Americans have the best ability to smell; blacks, whites, and Hispanics are in the middle; and Japanese have the worst sense of smell.[27]

How are these scents introduced into the store? Retailers can use time-release atomizers available through janitorial supply vendors, or computerized heating and air conditioning systems. But polymer pellets soaked in a fragrance and placed in ordinary light fixtures, where the lamp's heat activates the scent, are the most economical way to disperse fragrance.

Refact One of the Big Three automakers is spending a tidy sum to come up with a scent that can be sprayed on car salespeople to make them seem more honest.[24]

SUMMARY This chapter examined issues facing store designers, buyers, and merchandise planners. A good store layout helps customers find and purchase merchandise. Several types of layouts are commonly used by retailers. The grid design is best for stores in which customers are expected to explore the entire store, such as grocery stores and drugstores. Racetrack designs are more common in large upscale stores like department stores. Free-form designs are usually found in small specialty stores and within large stores' departments. Store planners also must carefully delineate different areas of the store. Feature areas, bulk of stock, and walls each have their own unique purpose but must also be coordinated to create a unifying theme.

There's more to assigning space to merchandise and departments than just determining where they'll fit. Departments' locations should be determined by the overall profitability and inventory turnover goals of the assortment, type of product, consumer buying behavior, the relationship with merchandise in other departments, and the physical characteristics of the merchandise. Planograms, both manual and computer-generated, are used to experiment with various space allocation configurations to determine the most productive use of space. When evaluating the productivity of retail space, retailers generally use sales per square foot.

Several tricks of the trade can help retailers present merchandise to facilitate sales. Retailers must attempt to empathize with the shopping experience and answer the following questions: How does the customer expect to find the merchandise? Is it easier to view, understand, and ultimately purchase merchandise when it's presented as a total concept or presented by manufacturer, style, size, color, or price? Ultimately, retailers must decide on the appropriate type of fixture to use for a particular purpose.

Retailers utilize various forms of atmospherics—graphics, signs, and theatrical effects—to facilitate the sale. Strategies involve lighting, colors, music, and scent.

KEY TERMS

atmospherics, *576*

boutique, *560*

bulk-of-stock area, *564*

demand/destination area, *568*

end cap, *562*

feature area, *562*

four-way fixture (feature fixture), *576*

free-form layout (boutique layout), *561*

freestanding fixture, *564*

frontal presentation, *574*

gondola, *556*

grid layout, *558*

idea-oriented presentation, *573*

impulse merchandise, *556*

impulse product, *568*

planogram, *569*

point-of-sale area (point-of-purchase area, POP area), *564*

popping the merchandise, *579*

price lining, *573*

productivity measure, *571*

promotional aisle (promotional area), *564*

racetrack layout (loop), *560*

rounder (bulk fixture, capacity fixture), *575*

sales per linear foot, *571*

sales per square foot, *571*

straight rack, *575*

tonnage merchandising, *574*

vertical merchandising, *573*

DISCUSSION QUESTIONS AND PROBLEMS

1. One of the fastest growing sectors of the population is the over-60 age group. But these customers may have limitations in their vision, hearing, and movement. How can retailers develop store designs with the older population's needs in mind?

2. Assume you have been hired as a consultant to assess a local discount store's space productivity. What analytical tools would you use to assess the situation? What suggestions would you make to improve the store's space productivity?

3. What are the different types of design that can be used in a store layout? Why are some stores more suited for a particular type of layout than others?

4. Generally speaking, departments located near entrances, on major aisles, and on the main level of multilevel stores have the best profit-generating potential. What additional factors help to determine the location of departments? Give examples of each factor.

5. A department store is building an addition. The merchandise manager for furniture is trying to convince the vice president to allot this new space to the furniture department. The merchandise manager for men's clothing is also trying to gain the space. What points should each manager use when presenting his or her rationale?

6. How would a retailer use information provided by a planogram?

7. Describe the ways in which designing a webpage is similar to and different from designing a store.

8. Which retailers are particularly good at presenting their "store as theater"? Why?

9. Lighting in a store has been said to be similar to makeup on a model. Why?

10. Why do supermarkets put candy, gum, and magazines at the front of the store?

SUGGESTED READINGS

Barr, Vilma, and Katherine Field. *Stores: Retail Display and Design*. PBC International, 1999.

Dube, Laurette, Jean-Charles Chebat, and Sylvia Morin. "The Effects of Background Music on Consumers' Desire to Affiliate in Buyer–Seller Interactions." *Psychology and Marketing* 12 (July 1995), pp. 305–20.

Herrington, J. Duncan, and Louis Capella. "Effects of Music in Service Environments: A Field Study." *Journal of Services Marketing* 10, no. 2 (1996), pp. 26–41.

Hui, Michael E., Laurette Dube, and Jean-Charles Chebat. "The Impact on Consumers' Reactions to Waiting for Services." *Journal of Retailing* 73, no. 1 (1997), pp. 87–104.

Israel, Lawrence J. *Store Planning/Design: History, Theory, Process*. New York: John Wiley & Sons, 1994.

Spangenberg, Eric R., Ayn E. Crowley, and Pamela W. Henderson. "Improving the Store Environment: Do Olfactory Cues Affect Evaluations and Behaviors?" *Journal of Marketing* 60, no. 2 (Spring 1996), pp. 67–80.

Staten, Vince. *Can You Trust a Tomato in January?* New York: Simon & Schuster, 1993.

Tai, Susan H.C., and Agnes M.C. Fung. "Application of Environmental Psychology Model to In-Store Buying Behavior." *International Review of Retail, Distribution and Consumer Research* 7, no. 4 (1997).

Underhill, Paco. *Why We Buy: The Science of Shopping*. New York: Simon & Schuster, 1999.

Urban, Timothy L. "An Inventory-Theoretic Approach to Product Assortment and Shelf-Space Allocation." *Journal of Retailing*, March 1998, pp. 15+.

Michelle Rupert
Store Manager
Home Depot

ALL THE HOME IMPROVEMENT center chains can build the same size stores, have the same selection of merchandise, and have the same prices. Customer service is the best opportunity for us to differentiate ourselves from the competition. Our approach to providing the best customer service is to hire the best people and take care of them. If we take care of our employees, they will take care of the customers. • After I received my MBA from the University of South Florida, I went to work for Home Depot in its management training program. In three years, I was promoted to store manager. I will start a new assignment in the Southeast Regional Training Center soon. • We are really picky about whom we hire. All applicants go through a computerized prescreening and then two interviews: one is with an assistant store manager and then I talk with all of the applicants. It's important for me to know all of our employees personally. During the interviews, I try to see if the candidates have good people skills by asking them to describe specific instances when they have worked with others and helped people. • To provide good service, you need to know how the products we sell are used. All of our new employees go through 24 hours of classroom-type training and then are paired with an experienced employee to learn the store systems and operations. • I reinforce Home Depot's service culture by being a role model. I am always on the floor working elbow to elbow with others in the store, helping customers solve their problems. A lot of our customers know my name even if I am not wearing my name tag. Sometimes people ask me where my office is and I tell them I really don't have one. • Everyone in our company focuses on the customers. When my district manager and other company executives come into the store, they all put on the orange apron and pitch in. • I always emphasize with our employees that we need to do everything we can to satisfy customers and keep them coming back. For example, today a customer purchased a dryer. We made sure he bought all of the material he needed to make the installation. When the dryer was delivered, he was very upset that the driver did not install it. Even though the customer did not pay for installation, I got one of our people who is a licensed electrician to go over to his house and do the installation. We should have made it clearer to the customer what he was buying and what he wasn't getting.

19

Customer Service

QUESTIONS

- What services do retailers offer customers?

- How can customer service build competitive advantage?

- How do customers evaluate a retailer's service?

- What obstacles hinder retailers in providing good service?

- How can retailers improve their customer service?

SUPPOSE YOU ARE surfing the Internet for a music CD. At www.cheapcds.com, a hypothetical site, you are asked to type in the name of a specific CD. Then a price with shipping charges is quoted and you are asked for your credit card number and a shipping address. In contrast, when you go to www.CDNOW.com, you can buy a specific CD or browse through descriptions of CDs organized by genre. CDNOW also offers other services to you including an electronic agent that suggests CDs based on your music preferences, e-mail notification when new CDs are available from artists you like, 30-second sound clips to preview CDs, reviews by critics and other customers, a privacy policy statement, and a money-back guarantee on merchandise returned in 30 days. Which of these electronic retailers would you prefer to shop at?

Customer service is the set of activities and programs undertaken by retailers to make the shopping experience more rewarding for their customers. These activities increase the value customers receive from the merchandise and services they purchase. All employees of a retail firm and all elements of the retailing mix provide services that increase the value of merchandise. For example, employees in the distribution center contribute to customer service by making sure that the merchandise is in stock. The employees in store location and design contribute by increasing the customer's convenience in getting to the store and finding merchandise in the store.

Exhibit 19–1 lists some of the services provided by retailers. Most of these services furnish information about the retailer's offering and make it easier for customers to locate and buy products and services. Services (such as alterations

EXHIBIT 19-1

Services Offered
by Retailers

	Department and specialty stores	Discount stores
Acceptance of credit cards	●	●
Alteration of merchandise	●	○
Assembling of merchandise	●	○
Bridal registry	●	○
Check cashing	●	◑
Child care facilities	○	○
Credit	●	◑
Delivery to home	○	○
Demonstrations of merchandise	●	◑
Displaying of merchandise	●	●
Dressing rooms	●	○
Extended store hours	○	●
Extensive signage to identify merchandise	○	●
Gift wrapping	●	●
Facilities for shoppers with special needs (physically handicapped, etc.)	○	○
Layaway plan	●	◑
Parking	●	●
Personal assistance in selecting merchandise	●	◑
Personal shoppers	○	○
Play areas for children	◑	◑
Presentations on how to use merchandise	◑	◑
Provisions for customers with special needs (wheelchairs, translators)	○	○
Repair services	○	○
Rest rooms	●	●
Return privileges	●	●
Rooms for checking coats and packages	○	○
Special orders	○	◑
Warranties	●	●

● Frequently   ◑ Occasionally   ○ Rarely

and the assembly of merchandise) actually change merchandise to fit the needs of a specific customer. Some of these services are derived from the website or store design or from policies established by the retailer. However, this chapter focuses on some of the most important personalized services provided by sales associates interacting directly with customers.

In the next section, we discuss retailers' opportunities to develop strategic advantage through customer service. Then we examine how retailers can take advantage of this opportunity by providing high-quality service.

STRATEGIC ADVANTAGE THROUGH CUSTOMER SERVICE

McDonald's, Nordstrom, Amazon.com, Disney World, and Marriott differentiate their retail offering, build customer loyalty, and develop a sustainable competitive advantage by providing excellent customer service. Good service keeps customers returning to a retailer and generates positive word-of-mouth communication, which attracts new customers.[1]

The quality of customer service is particularly important for electronic retailers. Using shopping bots, customers can easily compare the prices for branded merchandise from different electronic retailers. The branded items sold by these retailers are identical. Thus, the only way electronic retailers can differentiate their offering and increase their profit margin is through the addi-

Electronic retailers like Garden.com offer a number of services including a garden doctor to make suggestions for dealing with aphids in your garden.

tional services they provide their customers, services like those provided by CDNOW.[2]

Providing high-quality service is difficult. Automated manufacturing makes the quality of most merchandise consistent from item to item. For example, all Super Twist Skil™ electric screwdrivers look alike and typically perform alike. But the quality of retail service can vary dramatically from store to store and from salesperson to salesperson within a store because the most impactful services are performed by employees interacting with customers. It's hard for retailers to control the performance of employees who provide the service. Thus a salesperson may provide good service to one customer and poor service to the next customer.

In addition, most services provided by retailers are intangible—customers can't see or feel them. Clothing can be held and examined, but the assistance provided by a salesperson and electronic agent can't. Intangibility makes it hard to provide and maintain high-quality service because retailers can't count, measure, or check service before it's delivered to customers.

The difficulty of providing consistent high-quality service provides an opportunity for a retailer to develop a sustainable competitive advantage. Nordstrom devotes much time and effort to developing an organizational culture that stimulates and supports excellent customer service. Competing department stores would like to offer the same level of service, but find it hard to match Nordstrom's performance.[3]

Customer Service Strategies

Customization and standardization are two approaches retailers use to develop a sustainable customer service advantage. Successful implementation of the customized approach relies on the performance of sales associates or the degree to which electronic retailers personalize their offering. The standardization approach relies more on policy, procedures, and store and website design and layout.[4]

Customization Approach The **customization approach** encourages service providers to tailor the service to meet each customer's personal needs.[5] For example, sales associates are available in department stores to help customers locate appropriate apparel and accessories.

Some electronic retailers are introducing the human element to their websites. At Lands' End, customers can simply click on a button and exchange messages (referred to as instant messaging) with a service provider. Cameraworld.com found that 20 percent of its visitors who used the instant messaging service made a purchase compared to a 3 percent purchase rate for all visitors.[6]

Inspired by the Disney approach to customer service, Target launched its Guest Service program. Customers are treated as guests with store employees as their hosts. Stock clerks are taught that helping guests isn't an intrusion on their work. Several employees called guest ambassadors roam the store looking for customers who need assistance. Employees are also empowered to make sure that guests have a satisfying experience in the store. If the shelf price isn't on an item, checkout

The office supply center uses its signage as part of a standardized approach for providing customer service, while Target's (right) sales associates use a customized approach tailoring services to match each customer's needs.

Refact The word *service* is from the Latin term *servus,* meaning slave.[8]

clerks can take the customer's word for prices up to $20. The guest doesn't have to wait for the clerk to check the price with someone on the floor. When customers return merchandise without a receipt, employees at the Guest Service counter simply ask them how much they paid for the merchandise and give a refund.[7]

The customized approach typically results in customers' receiving superior service. But the service might be inconsistent because service delivery depends on the judgment and capabilities of the service providers. In addition, providing the customized service is costly since more well-trained service providers or complex computer software is required.

Refact Shopping carts were first introduced in 1937 in a Humpty Dumpty store in Oklahoma City.[9]

Standardization Approach   The **standardization approach** is based on establishing a set of rules and procedures and being sure that they are implemented consistently. By strict enforcement of these procedures, inconsistencies in the service are minimized. Through standardization, customers receive the same food and service at McDonald's restaurants across the globe. The food may not be exactly what customers want, but it's consistent and served in a timely manner at a low cost.

Store or website design and layout also play an important role in the standardization approach. In many situations, customers don't need the services employees provide. They know what they want to buy, and their objective is to find it in the store and buy it quickly. In these situations, retailers offer good service by providing a layout and signs that enable customers to locate merchandise easily, by having relevant information in displays, and by minimizing the time required to make a purchase.[10]

Retailing View 19.1 shows how IKEA uses a standardized service approach with some unique elements to attract customers expecting the traditional customized approach employed in furniture retailing.

Cost of Customer Service   As indicated previously, providing high-quality service, particularly customized service, can be very costly. For example, due to its outstanding service, the Savoy Hotel in London maintains a special place in the hearts of the world's elite. The Savoy's special mattress with "864 pocketed springs, two layers of pure cotton fleece, masses of the finest curled horse hair, and a generous layer of fleece wool" makes sure that guests get a good night's sleep.

IKEA Offers a Different Type of Service than Traditional Furniture Stores

IKEA IS A GLOBAL FURNITURE RETAILER based in Sweden. Its concept of service differs from the traditional furniture store. The typical furniture store has a showroom displaying some of the merchandise sold in the store. Complementing the inventory are books of fabric swatches, veneers, and alternative styles customers can order. Salespeople assist customers in going through the books. When the customer makes a selection, an order is placed with the factory, and the furniture is delivered to the customer's home in six to eight weeks. This system maximizes customization, but the costs are high.

In contrast, IKEA uses a self-service model based on extensive in-store displays. At information desks in the store, shoppers can pick up a map of the store plus a pencil, order form, clipboard, and tape measure. After studying the catalog and displays, customers proceed to a self-service warehouse and locate their selections using codes copied from the sales tags. Every product available is displayed in over 70 roomlike settings throughout the 150,000–square-foot warehouse store. Thus customers don't need a decorator to help them picture how the furniture will go together. Adjacent to the display room is a warehouse with ready-to-assemble furniture in boxes that customers can pick up when they leave the store.

Although IKEA uses a "customers do it themselves" approach, it does offer some services that traditional furniture stores do not, such as in-store child care centers and information on the quality of the furniture. Toddlers can be left in a supervised ballroom filled with 50,000 brightly colored plastic balls. There are changing rooms in each store complete with bottle warmers and disposable diaper dispensers. Displays cover quality of products in terms of design features and materials, with demonstration of testing procedures.

Source: "The New Consumers," *Business Week*, May 25, 1998, pp. 40–46; "Then and Now: IKEA," *Chain Store Age*, March 1, 1998, p. 114; and Michael Porter, "What Is Strategy?" *Harvard Business Review*, November–December 1996, pp. 61–73.

But the Savoy goes beyond providing a good night's sleep. Maids switch off vacuum cleaners and greet guests entering the hallway in the morning. Each floor has it own waiter on duty from 7 A.M. to 3 P.M. Guests can get cotton sheets instead of the standard Irish linen sheets if they wish. Preferred fruits are added to the complimentary fruit bowl in each room. Rooms are personally furnished for customers who regularly have extended stays at the hotel. For example, Kerry Packer, the Australian media magnate, hardly leaves home when he comes to the Savoy during the Australian winter. The hotel staff moves his furniture including personal pictures into his room when he arrives in April.

However, this high level of personal attention is very costly to provide. The Savoy employs about three people for each of its 200 rooms, about double the average for a London hotel. The corporation that owns the Savoy is concerned that the lack of profits may indicate that the Savoy is providing too much service.[11]

However, from a long-term perspective, good customer service can actually reduce costs and increase profits. A study by Anderson Consulting estimates that it costs 5 to 15 times more to acquire a new customer than to generate repeat business from present customers, and a 5 percent increase in customer retention can increase profits by 25 to 40 percent.[12] Thus it costs much less to keep your existing customers satisfied and sell more merchandise to them than it costs to sell merchandise to people who aren't buying from you now.

Retailers need to consider the costs and benefits of service policies. For example, many retailers are reconsidering their "no questions asked" return policy. Wal-Mart now sets a 90-day limit for returns to combat situations like a customer asking for a refund on a battered thermos that the supplier stopped manufacturing

Refact Product returns cost the consumer electronics industry more than $15 billion a year.[14]

in the 50s. Best Buy won't take back merchandise unless the customer has a receipt. This policy prevents customers from taking merchandise off the shelf and taking it to the return counter for a reimbursement, claiming they lost the receipt. Best Buy customers are also charged a 15 percent restocking charge.[13]

In the next section, we examine how customers evaluate service quality.

CUSTOMER EVALUATION OF SERVICE QUALITY

When customers evaluate retail service, they compare their perceptions of the service they receive with their expectations. Customers are satisfied when the perceived service meets or exceeds their expectations. They're dissatisfied when they feel the service falls below their expectations.[15]

Role of Expectations

Customer expectations are based on a customer's knowledge and experiences.[16] For example, customers do not expect to get an immediate response to a letter or even a telephone call, but expect to get a response to an e-mail the next time they turn on their computer.

This Wal-Mart employee greets customers when they enter the store and answers their questions. Since this service is unexpected in a discount store, it creates a favorable impression of Wal-Mart's customer service.

Expectations vary depending on the type of store. Customers expect a supermarket to provide convenient parking, to be open from early morning to late evening, to have a wide variety of fresh and packaged food that can be located easily, to display products, and to offer fast checkout. They don't expect the supermarket to have store employees stationed in the aisle to offer information about groceries or how to prepare meals. On the other hand, when these same customers shop in a department store, they do expect the store to have knowledgeable salespeople who can provide information and assistance.

Since expectations aren't the same for all types of retailers, a customer may be satisfied with low levels of actual service in one store and dissatisfied with high service levels in another store. For example, customers have low service expectations for self-service retailers such as discount stores and supermarkets. Wal-Mart provides an unusual service for a discount store: An employee stands at the entrance to each store, greeting customers and answering questions. Because this service is unexpected in a discount store, customers evaluate Wal-Mart's service positively, even though the actual level of service is far below that's provided by a typical department store.

Department stores have many more salespeople available to answer questions and provide information than Wal-Mart does. But customer service expectations are also higher for department stores. If department store customers can't locate a salesperson quickly when they have questions or want to make a purchase, they're dissatisfied.

Retailers can provide unexpected services to build customer satisfaction. These include

• A restaurant that sends customers who have had too much to drink home in a taxi and then delivers their cars in the morning.

- A men's store that sews numbered tags on each garment so the customer will know what goes together.
- A gift store that keeps track of important customer dates and suggests appropriate gifts.[17]

Customer service expectations vary around the world. Although Germany's manufacturing capability is world renowned, its poor customer service is also well known. People wait years to have telephone service installed. Many restaurants do not accept credit cards, and customers who walk into stores near closing time often receive rude stares. Customers typically have to bag merchandise they buy themselves. Because Germans are unaccustomed to good service, they don't demand it. But as retailing becomes global and new foreign competitors enter, German retailers are growing concerned.[18]

On the other hand, the Japanese expect excellent customer service. In the United States, it's said that "The customer is always right." In Japan the equivalent expression is *okyakasuma wa kamisama desu*, the customer is God. When a customer comes back to a store to return merchandise, he's dealt with even more cordially than when the original purchase was made. Customer satisfaction isn't negotiable. The customer is never wrong. Even if the customer misused the product, retailers feel they were responsible for not telling the customer how to use it properly. The first person in the store who hears about the problem must take full responsibility for dealing with the customer even if the problem involved another department.[19]

Perceived Service

Customers base their evaluations of store service on their perceptions. While these perceptions are affected by the actual service provided, service due to its intangibility is often hard to evaluate accurately. Exhibit 19–2 shows some cues customers use to evaluate services.

Employees can play an important role in customer perceptions of service quality.[20] Customer evaluations of service quality are often based on the manner in which store employees provide the service, not just the outcome. Consider the following situation: A customer goes to a store to return an electric toothbrush that isn't working properly. In one case, company policy requires the employee to ask the customer for a receipt, check to see if the receipt shows the toothbrush was bought at the store, examine the toothbrush to see if it really doesn't work properly, ask a manager if a refund can be provided, complete some paperwork, and finally give the customer the amount paid for the toothbrush in cash. In a second case, the store employee simply asks the customer how much he paid and gives him a cash refund. The two cases have the same outcome: The customer gets a cash refund. But the customer might be dissatisfied in the first case because the employee appeared not to trust the customer and took so much time providing the refund. In most situations, employees have a great effect on the process of providing services and, thus, on the customer's eventual satisfaction with the services.

Situations Producing Satisfactory and Unsatisfactory Experiences

Most experiences customers have with retailers are quite ordinary. Customers visit a store or website, select an item, pay for it, and take it home from the store or wait to have it delivered. These uneventful experiences may not stimulate customers to evaluate the service they received. But customers are motivated

Tangibles • Appearance of store or website • Display of merchandise • Appearance of salespeople	**Access** • Download speed of website • Short waiting lines • Convenient operating hours • Convenient store locations • Providing information on order status
Understanding and knowing customers • Providing individual attention • Personalization of website • Recognition of regular customers • Notes and e-mail sent to customers informing them of sales and new merchandise	**Competence** • Knowledge and skill of employees • Depth of information provided on website
Security • Feeling safe in parking lot • Describing security of Internet transactions • Stating policy about confidentiality of customer information	**Responsiveness** • Returning customer calls and e-mails • Giving prompt service
Trustworthiness • Reputation for honoring commitments • Guarantees and warranties • Return policy	**Reliability** • Accuracy in billing • Delivering merchandise when promised

Source: Adapted from Valarie Zeithaml, A. Parasuraman, and Leonard Berry, *Delivering Quality Service: Balancing Customer Perceptions and Expectations* (New York: Free Press, 1990), pp. 20–22; and A. Parasuraman, Valarie Zeithaml, and Leonard Berry, "A Conceptual Model of Service Quality and Its Implications for Future Research," *Journal of Marketing* 49 (Fall 1985), pp. 41–50.

to evaluate service quality when an unexpected or unusual event occurs—when they have a problem locating merchandise, when they need or request special attention, or when a store employee undertakes an unprompted or unsolicited action.[21] Exhibit 19–3 lists examples of situations that stimulate satisfactory or unsatisfactory service evaluations.

THE GAPS MODEL FOR IMPROVING RETAIL SERVICE QUALITY

The Gaps model (Exhibit 19–4) indicates what retailers need to do to provide high-quality customer service.[22] When customers' expectations are greater than their perceptions of the delivered service, customers are dissatisfied and feel the quality of the retailer's service is poor. Thus, retailers need to reduce the **service gap** (the difference between customers' expectations and perceptions of customer service) to improve customers' satisfaction with their service.

Four factors affect the service gap:

- **Knowledge gap:** The difference between customer expectations and the retailer's perception of customer expectations.
- **Standards gap:** The difference between the retailer's perceptions of customers' expectations and the customer service standards it sets.
- **Delivery gap:** The difference between the retailer's service standards and the actual service provided to customers.
- **Communication gap:** The difference between the actual service provided to customers and the service promised in the retailer's promotion program.

EXHIBIT **19–3**

Situations
Stimulating
Customers to
Evaluate Service
Quality

SITUATION	MORE SATISFYING EXPERIENCE	LESS SATISFYING EXPERIENCE
Unavailable service Customer enters name in bridal registry but discovers desired merchandise was never listed.	Manager apologizes for losing merchandise listing and offers to call people invited to wedding.	No explanation, no apology, and no assistance.
Employee response to slow service Customer waits two weeks to have table delivered when a two-day delivery was promised.	Employee apologizes and finally says retailer will give customer a free tablecloth for the table.	Employee says table will be delivered in two days every two days.
Employee response to service failure Customer finds a frayed cord on a lamp and returns it, asking for a replacement.	Employee provides a replacement cord.	Employee suggests cord wasn't frayed when customer left store with it; suggests customer damaged it and is trying to rip store off.
Response to a special need Customer brings a baby into store and has trouble shopping and taking care of baby.	Salesperson holds baby while customer tries on clothing.	Salesperson suggests customer return to store when someone can watch baby.
Response to admitted error Customer leaves charge card in store after making purchase.	Salesperson notifies customer and then delivers card to customer's home.	Salesperson waits until customer discovers charge card is missing and returns to store to get it.
Response to customer need Customer wants a toaster oven in a size not in stock in the store.	Salesperson locates toaster oven in another store and has it delivered to customer's home.	Salesperson suggests customer check with other store to see if toaster oven is available.
Attention paid to customer Customer walks into store and asks for some assistance.	Salesperson treats customer like royalty, finding merchandise, putting clothing together to make outfits, and accessorizing outfits.	Salesperson acts as if customer is a bother, provides short answers, and turns attention to setting up a display.

Reprinted with permission from the American Marketing Association. "The Service Encounter: Diagnosing Favorable and Unfavorable Incidents," by Mary Jo Bitner, Bernard Booms, and Mary Stanfield Tetreault, *Journal of Marketing* 54, January 1990, pp. 71–84.

These four gaps add up to the service gap. The retailer's objective is to reduce the service gap by reducing each of the four gaps. Thus, the key to improving service quality is to (1) understand the level of service customers expect, (2) set standards for providing customer service, (3) implement programs for delivering service that meets the standards, and (4) undertake communication programs to inform customers about the service offered by the retailer. The following sections describe these gaps and methods for reducing them.

KNOWING WHAT
THE CUSTOMER WANTS:
THE KNOWLEDGE GAP

The most critical step in providing good service is to know what the customer wants. Retailers often lack accurate information about what customers need and expect. This lack of information can result in poor decisions. For example, a supermarket might hire extra people to make sure the shelves are stocked so customers

EXHIBIT 19-4   The Gaps Model of Improving Service Quality

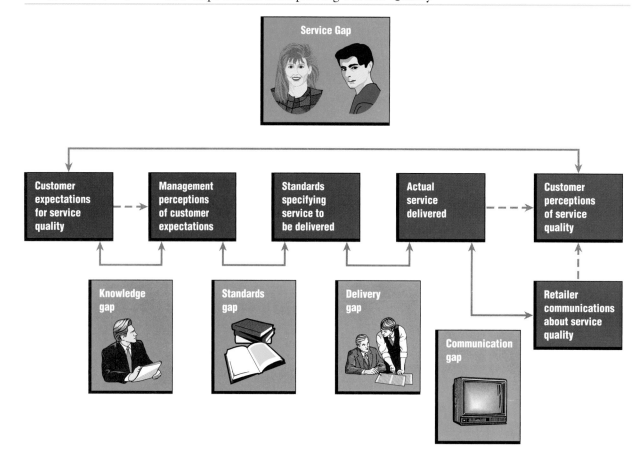

will always find what they want, but it may fail to realize that customers are most concerned about waiting at the checkout line. From the customer's perspective, the supermarket's service would improve if the extra employees were used to open more checkout lines rather than to stock shelves.

Retailers can reduce the knowledge gap and develop a better understanding of customer expectations by undertaking customer research, increasing interactions between retail managers and customers, and improving communication between managers and employees who provide customer service.

Refact Consumers report that the greatest burden on their time is waiting in lines.[23]

Researching Customer Expectations and Perceptions

Market research can be used to better understand customers' expectations and the quality of service provided by a retailer. Methods for obtaining this information range from comprehensive surveys to simply asking some customers about the store's service.

Comprehensive Studies   Some retailers have established programs for assessing customers' expectations and service perceptions. For example, every year JCPenney sales associates pass out questionnaires to shoppers in each store and its mall. Shoppers are asked about the service and merchandise offered by Penney and by competing department stores in the mall. Over 50,000 completed questionnaires

The first step in providing good customer service is understanding customer expectations. This sales associate is conducting a survey in a mall to assess customer expectations.

are collected and analyzed. Since the same questionnaire is used each year, Penney can track service performance, determine whether it's improving or declining, and identify opportunities for improving service quality. The importance Penney places on customer service is revealed by its using the annual customer service profile to evaluate store manager performance.

Gauging Satisfaction with Individual Transactions   Another method for doing customer research is to survey customers immediately after a retail transaction has occurred. For example, Sears employees who deliver and assemble furniture in homes ask customers to complete a short survey describing how helpful, friendly, and professional the employees were. Airlines periodically ask passengers during a flight to evaluate the ticket-buying process, flight attendants, in-flight service, and gate agents.

Customer research on individual transactions provides up-to-date information about customers' expectations and perceptions. The research also indicates the retailer's interest in providing good service. Since the responses can be linked to a specific encounter, the research provides a method for rewarding employees who provide good service and correcting those who exhibit poor performance.

INTERNET EXERCISE   Bizrate (www.bizrate.com) is a company that collects information about consumer shopping experiences with electronic retailers. Go to Bizrate's site and review the evaluations of different electronic retailers. How useful is this information to you? What could Bizrate do to make the information more useful?

Customer Panels and Interviews   Rather than surveying many customers, retailers can use panels of 10 to 15 customers to gain insights into expectations and perceptions. For example, some store managers might meet once a month for an hour with a select group of customers who are asked to provide information about their experiences in the stores and to offer suggestions for improving service.

To reduce the knowledge gap, some supermarket managers go through the personal checks they receive each day and select customers who've made large and small purchases. They call these customers and ask them what they liked and didn't like about the store. With small purchasers, they probe to find out why the customers didn't buy more. Could they find everything they wanted? Did they get the assistance they expected from store employees?

Pier 1 Imports, a home furnishing chain, has a Customer Advisory Board (CAB) composed of 1,200 preferred customers representing a cross-section of the retailer's customer base. CAB members complete questionnaires three to four times a year on subjects like holiday shopping problems, in-store signage, and service quality. In exchange for their inputs, members receive a $5 gift certificate.[24]

This customer service representative is empowered to resolve the problems the customer is having with a windbreaker purchased at the store.

Interacting with Customers   Owner-managers of small retail firms typically have daily contact with their customers and thus have accurate firsthand information about them. In large retail firms, managers often learn about customers through reports so they miss the rich information provided by direct contact with customers. Exhibit 19–5 lists common service complaints by customers.

Stanley Marcus, founder of Neiman Marcus, feels managers can become addicted to numbers and neglect the merchandise and customers. He uses suspenders as an example of how buyers can make poor decisions by only looking at the numbers. Originally, suspenders came in two sizes: short and long. By analyzing the numbers, buyers realized they could increase turnover by stocking one-size-only suspenders. The numbers looked good but the store had a lot of dissatisfied customers. With only one size, short men's pants fell down, while the fit was uncomfortable for tall men. "It comes back to the fact that the day is still only 24 hours long, and if you're a retailer, you've still got to spend some of those 24 hours with your customers and your products. You can't allow the computer to crowd them out as crucial sources of information."[26]

Customer Complaints   Complaints allow retailers to interact with their customers and acquire detailed information about their service and merchandise. Handling complaints is an inexpensive means to isolate and correct service problems.[27]

Catalog/electronic retailer L.L. Bean keeps track of all complaints and reasons for returned merchandise. These complaints and returns are summarized daily and given to customer service representatives so they can improve service. For example, a customer who returns a sweater might indicate the sweater was too large or the color tone differed from the picture in the catalog. With this information, customer service representatives can inform other customers who place an order for the sweater that it tends to be large and has a slightly different color than shown in the catalog. The information can also be used by buyers to improve vendor merchandise.

Miami's Baptist Hospital was very concerned when customer research found customer complaints among the city's growing Hispanic population were rising. "No one doubted the quality of the health care delivery," recalls Fred Messing, the hospital's CEO, "but there was a feeling we lacked sensitivity to cultural needs." Messing presented the problem to the hospital's Continuous Improvement Coordinating Committee, which developed Hispanic-friendly services like bilingual voice mail responses to outside calls, bilingual clinical brochures, additional translators in each department, and additional Hispanic dishes on patients' menus. "If you're truly committed to good customer service," says Messing, "you've got to know exactly where you are and be ready to move the instant you detect a problem."[29]

Although customer complaints can provide useful information, retailers can't rely solely on this source of market information. Typically, dissatisfied customers don't complain. To provide better information on customer service, retailers need to encourage complaints and make it easy for customers to provide feedback about their problems. For example, some retailers set up a complaint desk in a convenient location where customers can get their problems heard and solved quickly.

Feedback from Store Employees   Salespeople and other employees in regular contact with customers often have a good understanding of customer service ex-

Refact Ninety-one percent of customers dissatisfied with a firm's offering never buy from the firm again. These dissatisfied customers will tell nine other people, on average, about their unsatisfactory experience.[25]

Refact Less than 5 percent of consumers with problems actually complain to companies.[28]

EXHIBIT **19–5**

Common Service
Complaints

 TRUE LIES
Blatant dishonesty or unfairness, such as selling unneeded services.

 AUTOMATIC PILOT
Impersonal, no-eye-contact, emotionless, go-through-the-motion interactions with service providers.

 RED ALERT
Retailers who think customers are stupid and treat them disrespectfully.

 SUFFERING IN SILENCE
Employees who don't bother to respond to customers.

 BROKEN PROMISES
Service providers who don't show up.

 DON'T ASK
Sales associates who are put out by requests for assistance.

 I JUST WORK HERE
Powerless sales associates who lack the authority, or desire, to solve customer problems.

 LIGHTS ON, NO ONE AT HOME
Clueless sales associates who don't know the answers to commonly asked questions.

 THE BIG WAIT
Waiting in line because some of the checkout aisles are closed.

 MISPLACED PRIORITIES
Sales associates who visit with each other or conduct personal business while the customer waits.

pectations and problems. This information will improve service quality only if they're encouraged to communicate their experiences to high-level managers who can act on it.

Some retailers regularly survey their employees, asking questions like

- What is the biggest problem you face in delivering high-quality service to your customers?

- If you could make one change in the company to improve customer service, what would it be?

Using Customer Research   Collecting information about customer expectations and perceptions isn't enough. The service gap is reduced only when retailers use this information to improve service. For example, store managers should review the suggestions and comments made by customers daily, summarize the information, and distribute it to store employees and managers.

Feedback on service performance needs to be provided to employees in a timely manner. Reporting the July service performance in December makes it hard for employees to reflect on the reason for the reported performance.

Finally, feedback must be prominently presented so service providers are aware of their performance. For example, at Marriott, front desk personnel's performance feedback is displayed behind the front desk, while restaurant personnel's performance feedback is displayed behind the door to the kitchen.

SETTING SERVICE STANDARDS: THE STANDARDS GAP   After retailers gather information about customer service expectations and perceptions, the next step is to use this information to set standards and develop systems for delivering high-quality service. Service standards should be based on customers' perceptions rather than internal operations. For example, a supermarket chain might set an operations standard of a warehouse delivery every day to each store. But frequent warehouse deliveries may not result in more merchandise on the shelves or improve customers' impressions of shopping convenience.

To close the standards gap, retailers need to (1) commit their firms to providing high-quality service, (2) develop innovative solutions to service problems, (3) define the role of service providers, (4) set service goals, and (5) measure service performance.

Commitment to Service Quality

Service excellence occurs only when top management provides leadership and demonstrates commitment. Top management must be willing to accept the temporary difficulties and even the increased costs associated with improving service quality. This commitment needs to be demonstrated to the employees charged with providing the service. For example, a Lands' End poster prominently displays the following inscription for employees who process customer orders:

> What is a Customer? A Customer is the most important person in this office . . . in person or by mail. A Customer is not dependent on us . . . we are dependent on him. A customer is not an interruption in our work . . . he is the purpose of it. We are not doing him a favor by serving him . . . he is doing us a favor by giving us an opportunity to do so. A Customer is not someone to argue or match wits with.[30]

Top management's commitment sets service quality standards, but store managers are the key to achieving those standards. Store managers must see that their efforts to provide service quality are noticed and rewarded. Providing incentives based on service quality makes service an important personal goal. Rather than basing bonuses only on store sales and profit, part of store managers' bonuses should be determined by the level of service provided. For example, some retailers use results of customer satisfaction studies to determine bonuses.

Developing Solutions to Service Problems

Frequently, retailers don't set high service standards because they feel service improvements are either too costly or not achievable with available employees. This reflects an unwillingness to think creatively and to explore new approaches for improving service.

Innovative Approaches   Finding ways to overcome service problems can improve customer satisfaction and, in some cases, reduce costs. For example, when customers complained about the long wait to check out, many hotels felt they couldn't do anything about the problem. Marriott, however, thought of a creative approach to address this service problem. It invented Express Checkout, a system in which a bill is left under the customer's door the morning before checkout and, if the bill is accurate, the customer can check out by simply leaving the keys at the front desk and have the bill charged automatically to her credit card.

Parisian, a specialty department store division of Saks, holds a meeting before the Christmas season to identify and remove obstacles to improving customer service. At one meeting, store managers felt the policy of requiring a department manager's approval for personal checks over $250 was frustrating customers. During the hectic Christmas season, customers often had to wait 10 or 15 minutes while salespeople located their department managers. The vice president of stores suggested changing the policy and letting salespeople accept checks up to $5,000 without approval. The chief financial officer felt that changing the policy would increase the number of bad checks and reduce profits. But management decided that improving customer service was worth the risk. When the policy was implemented, the number of bad checks actually decreased because salespeople felt responsible and took time to verify the customers' identification. Previously, department managers had been so busy that they often just approved checks without looking closely at the identification.

The Container Store emphasizes the importance of flexibility, teamwork, and empowerment using the cartoon character known as Gumby®. A six-foot Gumby® character is prominently displayed at the entrance to the corporate headquarters, and small versions are on managers' desks. The frequent use of the phrase "We have to be Gumby®-like" reinforces the corporate culture of doing whatever needs to be done to provide service for customers and to help fellow employees complete tasks.[31]

Using Technology Retailers can use technology to simplify and improve customer service. Routine, repetitious tasks can be handled by a system, freeing employees to deal with more demanding customer requests and problems. For example, Pizza Hut uses a computer system to centralize its home delivery business. Operators at a central location take all calls for home delivery. By training operators who specialize in order taking, Pizza Hut has reduced to 17 seconds the time required to take orders and verify directions to the caller's house. After calls are completed, orders are transmitted via computers to a printer in the restaurant closest to the caller's location. The system reduces delivery time and eliminates situations in which customers place calls at the "wrong" restaurant.[32]

Standardizing routine activities can actually improve service to important customers. For example, Marriott developed its Honored Guest program to provide extra service to its best customers. Customers who stay frequently at Marriott hotels or resorts automatically receive a special guest room, a gift, and a note from the hotel manager when they check in and show their Honored Guest card. Thus, these customers receive standardized special treatment.[33]

Retailing View 19.2 describes how USAA, the most profitable insurance company in the United States, uses technology to provide outstanding customer service.

Defining the Role of Service Providers

Managers can tell service providers that they need to provide excellent service, but not clearly indicate what excellent service means. Without a clear definition of the retailer's expectations, service providers are directionless.

The Ritz-Carlton Hotel Company, winner of the Malcolm Baldrige National Quality Award, has its "Gold Standards" printed on a wallet-size card carried by all employees. The card contains the hotel's motto ("We Are Ladies and Gentlemen Serving Ladies and Gentlemen"), the three steps for high-quality service (warm and sincere greeting, anticipation and compliance with guests' needs, and fond farewell), and 20 basic rules for Ritz-Carlton employees including

- Any employee who receives a complaint "owns" the complaint.
- Instant guest gratification will be ensured by all. React quickly to correct problems immediately.
- "Smile. We are on stage." Always maintain positive eye contact.
- Escort guests rather than giving directions to another area of the hotel.[34]

Setting Service Goals

To deliver consistent, high-quality service, retailers need to establish goals or standards to guide employees. Retailers often develop service goals based on their beliefs about the proper operation of the business rather than the customers' needs and expectations. For example, a retailer might set a goal that all monthly bills are to be mailed five days before the end of the

BASED IN SAN ANTONIO, TEXAS, United Services Automobile Association (USAA) is the fastest growing and most profitable insurance company in the United States. Its strategy is providing insurance and other financial services to military officers and their dependents. The company, which is owned by its policy holders, provides coverage for 95 percent of the active-duty military officers. However, its market is shrinking. So USAA invested over $130 million in a paperless information system and database enabling its service providers to support the sales of a broader spectrum of financial services to its customers.

The system stores more than 65,000 documents a day electronically into a database containing over 150 million documents. The mail room in the auto and homeowners insurance area scans 20,000 documents each day. The originals are held for two to three weeks for legal reasons or to be sure a document was accurately scanned. Then the paper is destroyed.

The company has also streamlined its claims process by equipping its adjustors with laptop computers. An adjustor inspects a damaged automobile, uploads the information over a cellular phone to USAA's computer system, prints an estimate, and usually issues a check on a portable printer right on the spot. Adjustors have even been given digital cameras to photograph damaged cars, and the digital information is fed back through remote access lines into USAA's system. Using this system a USAA service representative can insure a member's new car, add a driver to the policy, shift investments from one mutual fund to another, and make a claim on a homeowner's policy. There are no callbacks or transfers needed. "In one five-minute phone call, you and our service representative have done all the work that used to take 55 steps, umpteen people, two weeks, and a lot of money," explains former CEO Robert McDermott.

Source: Don Peppers and Martha Rogers, "Lessons from the Front," *Marketing Tools*, January–February 1998, pp. 38–40; and "USAA: Conquering a Paper Mountain," *Forbes*, October 9, 1995, p. 56.

month. This goal reduces the retailer's accounts receivable but offers no benefit to customers. Research undertaken by American Express showed customer evaluations of its service were based on perceptions of timeliness, accuracy, and responsiveness. Management then established goals (such as responding to all questions about bills within 24 hours) related to these customer-based criteria.

Employees are motivated to achieve service goals when the goals are specific, measurable, and participatory in the sense that they participated in setting them. Vague goals—such as "Approach customers when they enter the selling area" or "Respond to e-mails as soon as possible"—don't fully specify what employees should do, nor do such goals offer an opportunity to assess employee performance. A better goal would be "All customers should be approached by a salesperson within 30 seconds after entering a selling area" or "All e-mails should be responded to in three hours." These goals are both specific and measurable.

Employee participation in setting service standards leads to better understanding and greater acceptance of the goals. Store employees resent and resist goals arbitrarily imposed on them by management. Chapter 17 says more on goal setting.

Measuring Service Performance Retailers need to continuously assess service quality to ensure that goals will be achieved.[35] Many retailers do periodic customer surveys to assess service quality. Many retailers are using mystery shoppers to assess their service quality. **Mystery shoppers** are professional shoppers who "shop" a store to assess the service provided by store employees. Some retailers use their own employees as mystery shoppers but most contract with a firm to provide the assessment. Information typically reported by the mystery shoppers includes (1) How long before a sales associate greeted you? (2) Did the sales associate act as if he wanted your business? (3) Was the sales associate knowledgeable about the merchandise?

Retailers typically inform salespeople that they have "been shopped" and provide feedback from the mystery shopper's report. Some retailers offer rewards to sales associates who receive high marks and schedule follow-up visits to sales associates who get low evaluations.[36]

MEETING AND EXCEEDING SERVICE STANDARDS: THE DELIVERY GAP

To reduce the delivery gap and provide service that exceeds standards, retailers must give service providers the necessary knowledge and skills, provide instrumental and emotional support, improve internal communications and reduce conflicts, and empower employees to act in the customers' and firm's best interests. Retailing View 19.3 describes how electronic retailers' chat rooms enable customers to provide services to others.

Giving Information and Training

Store employees need to know about the merchandise they offer as well as their customers' needs. With this information, employees can answer customers' questions and suggest products. This also instills confidence and a sense of competence, which are needed to overcome service problems.

In addition, store employees need training in interpersonal skills. Dealing with customers is hard—particularly when they're upset or angry. All store employees, even those who work for retailers that provide excellent service, will encounter dissatisfied customers. Through training, employees can learn to provide better service and to cope with the stress caused by disgruntled customers.[37]

Specific retail employees (salespeople and customer service representatives) are typically designated to interact with and provide service to customers. However, all retail employees should be prepared to deal with customers. For example, Walt Disney World provides four days of training for its maintenance workers, even though people can learn how to pick up trash and sweep streets in much less time. Disney has found that its customers are more likely to direct questions to maintenance people than to the clean-cut assistants wearing ASK ME, I'M IN GUEST RELATIONS buttons. Thus, Disney trains maintenance people to confidently handle the myriad of questions they'll be asked, rather than responding, "Gee, I dunno. Ask her."[38]

Toys "R" Us assesses customer satisfaction with checkout service by counting the number of abandoned shopping carts with merchandise left in the store because customers became impatient with the time required to make a purchase. After the firm noticed an alarming increase in abandoned carts, it developed a unique program to reduce customers' time in line waiting to pay. Cashiers' motions while ringing up and bagging merchandise were studied. Based on this research, a training program was developed to show cashiers how to use their right hand to record purchases on the POS terminal and their left hand to push merchandise along the counter. Counters were redesigned to have a slot line with shopping bags in the middle of the counter. As the cashier pushes the merchandise along the counter, it drops into a bag. After the customer pays for the merchandise, the cashier simply lifts the bag from the slot and hands it to the customer, and a new bag pops into place.

Refact Two-thirds of the customers who put merchandise into an electronic shopping cart at a website do not complete the transaction.[39]

To motivate cashiers to use the new system effectively, Toys "R" Us holds competitions in each store, district, and region to select the fastest cashiers. Regional winners receive a free vacation in New York City and participate in a competition at corporate headquarters to select a national champion.[40]

ELECTRONIC RETAILERS USE A VARIETY of techniques including message boards and chat rooms that provide a valuable service by enabling customers to communicate with each other. **Message boards** are locations in an Internet site at which customers can post comments, while **chat rooms** are locations at which customers can engage in interactive, real-time, text-based discussions. REI, the outdoor recreation retail chain, has message boards (www.rei.com/reihtml/LEARN_SHARE/camp/comfave.html0) on which customers can post information about favorite camping and hiking trips they have taken. Authors and visitors to www.Amazon.com post comments and book reviews. Visitors to electronic travel retail sites frequently post messages inquiring about hotels, restaurants, and tourist attractions at places they will be visiting. Other customers who are familiar with the places respond to these inquiries with their suggestions.

Many electronic retailers offer public chat rooms. At The Knot site (www.theknot.com) people can enter a public chat room and have a real-time discussion about their experiences planning their weddings, seven days a week, 24 hours a day. In addition to the public chat room, The Knot also offers moderated chat rooms in which a staff member leads an electronic discussion at specific times during the day. Electronic retailers also offer celebrity chat rooms. For example, Garden.com schedules well-known experts on various aspects of gardening to participate in a chat room at a specific time.

Offering this opportunity for customers to exchange information provides a valuable service. In many cases, the information provided by the respondents is more current and detailed than the retailer's information. In addition to providing information, message boards and chat rooms create loyalty to a retailer's website. Garden Escape found that customers who use chat rooms at its site are twice as likely to make purchases as customers who don't participate in a chat.

Source: Mary C. Hickey, "Click, Click, and a Way! *Business Week,* March 29, 1999, p. 188; Michelle Rafter, "Can We Talk?" *The Industry Standard,* February 8, 1999, pp. 53–54; and Cliff Figallo, *Hosting Web Communities* (New York: Wiley, 1998).

Electronic retailers like iVillage offer customers opportunities to interact and learn from other customers through electronic chat rooms.

Providing Instrumental and Emotional Support

Service providers need to have the **instrumental support** (the appropriate systems and equipment) to deliver the service desired by customers. For example, a hotel chain installed a computer system to speed up the checkout process. A study of the new system's effectiveness revealed that checkout time was not reduced because clerks had to wait to use the one stapler available to staple the customer's credit card and hotel bill receipts.

In addition to instrumental support, service providers need emotional support from their co-workers and supervisors. **Emotional support** involves demonstrating a concern for the well-being of others. Dealing with customer problems and maintaining a smile in difficult situations are psychologically demanding. For example, Ricky Anderson, a 20-year-old host at Disney's Tomorrowland, says, "Sometimes, you get hot in your costume, you get fed up dealing with angry guests who are tired of waiting in line. But then a kid asks you a question, you answer it, and she breaks into a smile. I realize that what I am doing is actually important and not to be taken for granted."[41] Service providers need to be in a supportive, understanding atmosphere to deal with these demands effectively.[42]

Improving Internal Communications and Reducing Conflict

When providing customer service, store employees must often manage the conflict between customers' needs and the retail firms' needs. For example, many retailers have a "no-questions-asked" return policy. Under this policy, the retailer will provide a refund at the customer's request even if the merchandise wasn't purchased at the store or was clearly used improperly. When JCPenney inaugurated this policy, some employees refused to provide refunds on merchandise that had been worn or damaged by the customer. They were loyal Penney employees and didn't want customers to take advantage of their firm.

Retailers can reduce such conflicts by having clear guidelines and policies concerning service and by explaining the rationale for these policies. Once Penney employees recognized that the goodwill created by the no-questions-asked policy generated more sales than the losses due to customers' abusing the policy, they implemented the policy enthusiastically.

Conflicts can also arise when retailers set goals inconsistent with the other behaviors expected from store employees. For example, if salespeople are expected to provide customer service, they should be evaluated on the service they provide, not just on the sales they make.

Finally, conflicts can also arise between different areas of the firm. Childress Buick, an auto dealer with an excellent customer service reputation, devotes considerable effort to reducing conflict by improving communication between its employees. The dealership holds a town hall in which employees feel free to bring up service problems. For example, Cheryl Pierson, a receptionist, discussed her frustration when she couldn't locate a sales rep for whom a customer had called. The customer finally said, "Well, I'll just take my business elsewhere." She used this example to emphasize that sales reps should tell her when they slip out to run an errand. Now no one forgets that the front desk is the nerve center for the dealership.[43]

Empowering Store Employees

Empowerment means allowing employees at the firm's lowest level to make important decisions concerning how service is provided to customers. When the employees responsible for providing service are authorized to make important decisions, service quality improves.

AMY'S ICE CREAM (a seven-store chain of premium–ice-cream shops in Austin and Houston, Texas) sells terrific products and gives excellent service. But that's where the similarity to other scoop shops ends. Visit an Amy's store and you'll see employees performing in a manner you won't forget. They juggle with their serving spades, toss scoops of ice cream to one another behind the counter, and break-dance on the freezer top. If there's a line out the door, they might pass out samples or offer free ice cream to any customer who'll sing or dance or recite a poem or mimic a barnyard animal, or who wins a 60-second cone-eating contest.

Amy Miller, the founder and CEO, obviously sells entertainment along with ice cream. To provide this atmosphere, she has to hire the right people and get them to be inventive. To identify employees who'll take the initiative, she uses the "white paper bag" test. Instead of an application form, prospective employees get a plain white paper bag along with the instructions to do anything they want with it and bring it back in a week. Those who just jot down a phone number will find that "Amy's isn't really for them," says Miller. But an applicant who produces "something unusual from a white paper bag tends to be an amusing person who would fit in with our environment." One job seeker turned his into an elaborate pop-up jack-in-the box and became a scooper at the Westbank Market store. That store's former manager painted an intricate green-and-blue sphere resembling the earth atop a waffle cone on his bag.

Source: John Case, "Corporate Culture," *Inc.*, November 1996, p. 42. Reprinted with permission, *Inc.*, November 1996. Copyright 1996 by Glodhirsh Group, Inc., 38 Commercial Wharf, Boston, MA 02110.

Service can be provided quickly without involving too many people. In our previous example, customer service improved when Parisian salespeople were given responsibility for authorizing customer checks without department managers' approval. Marshall Field's, a regional department store chain, empowered salespeople to make more decisions concerning returns when it trimmed its 36-page return policy to one page. Retailing View 19.4 shows how an ice cream parlor empowers employees to be creative.

Nordstrom provides an overall objective—satisfy customer needs—and then encourages employees to do whatever's necessary to carry out the objective. For example, a Nordstrom department manager bought 12 dozen pairs of hosiery from a competitor in the mall when her stock was depleted and the new shipment was delayed. Even though Nordstrom lost money on this hosiery, management applauded her actions to make sure customers found hosiery when they came to the store looking for it. Empowering service providers with only a rule like "Use your best judgment" can cause chaos. At Nordstrom, department managers avoid abuses by coaching and training salespeople. They help salespeople understand what "Use your best judgment" means.

However, empowering service providers can be difficult. Some employees prefer to have the appropriate behaviors clearly defined for them. They don't want to spend the time learning how to make decisions or assume the risks of making mistakes. For example, the First National Bank of Chicago found that when it empowered its tellers, the tellers were frightened to make decisions about large sums of money. The bank had to develop decision guideposts and rules until tellers felt more comfortable.[44]

In some cases, the benefits of empowering service providers may not justify the costs. For example, if a retailer uses a standardized service delivery approach like McDonald's, the cost of hiring, training, and supporting empowerment may not lead to consistent and superior service delivery.[45]

Providing Incentives As we discussed in Chapter 17, many retailers use incentives, like paying commissions based on sales, to motivate employees. But retailers have found that commissions on sales can decrease customer service and job satisfaction. Incentives can motivate high-pressure selling, which leads to customer dissatisfaction. However, incentives can be used effectively to improve customer service. For example, Kmart's "The Power to Please" program encourages sales associates to handle customer problems by providing hard-dollar rewards for successful customer service. Associates receive Knote bonuses from store and regional managers that convert into cash discounts. Kmart is also using nonmonetary forms of recognition such as the chairman's award and special certificates.[46]

COMMUNICATING THE SERVICE PROMISE: THE COMMUNICATIONS GAP

The fourth factor leading to a customer service gap is a difference between the service promised by the retailer and the service actually delivered. Overstating the service offered raises customer expectations. Then, if the retailer doesn't follow through, expectations exceed perceived service, and customers are dissatisfied. For example, if a store advertises that a customer will always be greeted by a friendly, smiling sales associate, customers may be disappointed if this doesn't occur. Raising expectations too high might bring in more customers initially, but it can also create dissatisfaction and reduce repeat business. The communication gap can be reduced by making realistic commitments and by managing customer expectations.

Realistic Commitments Advertising programs are typically developed by the marketing department, while the store operations division delivers the service. Poor communication between these areas can result in a mismatch between an ad campaign's promises and the service the store can actually offer. This problem is illustrated by Holiday Inn's "No Surprises" ad campaign. Market research indicated hotel customers wanted greater reliability in lodging so Holiday Inn's agency developed a campaign promising no unpleasant surprises. Even though hotel managers didn't feel they could meet the claims promised in the ads, top management accepted the campaign. The campaign raised customer expectations to an unrealistic level and gave customers who did confront an unpleasant surprise an additional reason to be angry. The campaign was discontinued soon after it started.[47]

Managing Customer Expectations How can a retailer communicate realistic service expectations without losing business to a competitor that makes inflated service claims? American Airlines' "Why Does It Seem Every Airline Flight Is Late?" ad campaign is an example of a communication program that addresses this issue. In print ads, American recognized its customers' frustration and explained some uncontrollable factors causing the problem: overcrowded airports, scheduling problems, and intense price competition. Then the ads described how American was improving the situation.

Information presented at the point of sale can be used to manage expectations. For example, theme park and restaurants indicate the waiting time for an attraction or a table. Electronic retailers tell their customers if merchandise is in stock and when customers can expect to receive it. Providing accurate information can increase customer satisfaction even when customers must wait longer than desired.[48]

Sometimes service problems are caused by customers. Customers may use an invalid credit card to pay for merchandise, may not take time to try on a suit and have it altered properly, or may use a product incorrectly because they failed to read the instructions. Communication programs can also inform customers about their role and responsibility in getting good service, and can give tips on how to get better service (such as the best times of the day to shop and the retailer's policies and procedures for handling problems).

Now that we've discussed how retailers can improve customer service by reducing the knowledge, standards, delivery, and communication gaps, let's focus on an important issue retailers deal with daily, recovering from service problems.

SERVICE RECOVERY

As we said, delivery of customer service is inherently inconsistent so service failures are bound to arise. Rather than dwelling on negative aspects of customer problems, retailers should focus on the positive opportunities they generate. Service problems and complaints are an excellent source of information about the retailer's offering (its merchandise and service). Armed with this information, retailers can make changes to increase customer satisfaction. Marriott Corporation makes it easy for customers to complain by maintaining a 24-hour hotline in its hotels.[49]

Service problems also enable a retailer to demonstrate its commitment to providing high-quality customer service. By encouraging complaints and handling problems, a retailer has an opportunity to strengthen its relationship with its customers.

Most retailers have standard policies for handling problems. If a correctable problem is identified, such as defective merchandise, many retailers will make restitution on the spot and apologize for inconveniencing the customer. The retailer will either offer replacement merchandise, a credit toward future purchases, or a cash refund.

In many cases, the cause of the problem may be hard to identify (did the salesperson really insult the customer?), uncorrectable (the store had to close due to bad weather), or a result of the customer's unusual expectations (the customer didn't like his haircut). In this case, service recovery might be more difficult. The steps in effective service recovery are (1) listen to the customer, (2) provide a fair solution, and (3) resolve the problem quickly.

Listening to the Customer

Customers can become very emotional over their real or imaginary problems with a retailer. Often this emotional reaction can be reduced by simply giving customers a chance to get their complaints off their chests.

Store employees should allow customers to air their complaints without interruption. Interruptions can further irritate customers who may already be emotionally upset. It's very hard to reason with or satisfy an angry customer.

Refact Less than 2 percent of the complaints made by customers are premeditated and fraudulent.[50]

Customers want a sympathetic response to their complaints. Thus, store employees need to make it clear they're happy that the problem has been brought to their attention. Satisfactory solutions rarely arise when store employees have an antagonistic attitude or assume that the customer is trying to cheat the store.

Employees also need to listen carefully to determine what the customer perceives to be a fair solution. For example, a hotel employee might assume that a customer who's irritated about a long wait to check in will be satisfied with an apology. But the customer might be expecting to receive a free drink as compensation for the wait. A supermarket employee may brusquely offer a refund for spoiled fruit, when the customer is also seeking an apology for the inconvenience of having to return to the store. Store employees shouldn't assume they know what the customer is complaining about or what solution the customer is seeking.

Providing a Fair Solution

When confronted with a complaint, store employees need to focus on how they can get the customer back, not simply how they can solve the problem.[51] Favorable impressions arise when customers feel they've been dealt with fairly. When evaluating the resolution of their problems, customers compare how they were treated in relation to others with similar problems. This comparison is based on observation of other customers with problems and/or on information about complaint handling learned from reading books and talking with others. Customers' evaluations of complaints' resolutions are based on distributive fairness and procedural fairness.

Distributive Fairness **Distributive fairness** is customers' perceptions of the benefits received compared to their costs (their inconvenience or loss). Customers want to get what they paid for. The customer's need can affect the perceived correspondence between benefits and costs. For example, one customer might be satisfied with a raincheck for a food processor that was advertised at a discounted price but was sold out. This customer feels the low price for the food processor offsets the inconvenience of returning to the store. But another customer may need the food processor immediately. A rain check won't be adequate compensation for him. To satisfy this customer, the salesperson must locate a store that has the food processor and have it delivered to the customer's house.

Customers typically prefer tangible rather than intangible resolutions to their complaints. Customers may want to let off steam, but they also want to feel the retailer was responsive to their complaint. A low-cost reward a free soft drink or a $1 discount communicates more concern to the customer than a verbal apology.

If providing tangible restitution isn't possible, the next best alternative is to let customers see that their complaints will have an effect in the future. This can be done by making a note, in front of the customer, to a manager about the problem or writing to the customer about actions taken to prevent similar problems in the future.

Procedural Fairness **Procedural fairness** is the perceived fairness of the process used to resolve complaints. Customers consider three questions when evaluating procedural fairness:

1. Did the employee collect information about the situation?
2. Was this information used to resolve the complaint?
3. Did the customer have some influence over the outcome?

Discontent with the procedures used to handle a complaint can overshadow the benefits of a positive outcome. For example, customers might be less satisfied with their refund for a clerk's mistake in ringing up groceries if they get no chance to talk about their other problems with the clerk.

Customers typically feel they're dealt with fairly when store employees follow company guidelines. Guidelines reduce variability in handling complaints and lead customers to believe they're being treated like everyone else. But rigid adherence to guidelines can have negative effects. Store employees need some flexibility in resolving complaints, or customers may feel they had no influence in the resolution.

Resolving Problems Quickly

Customer satisfaction is affected by the time it takes to get an issue resolved. To respond to customers quickly, Smith & Hawken, a garden supply mail order company, uses the telephone instead of the mail. The company feels that sending a letter is too time consuming and impersonal. Resolving complaints by phone can take minutes while sending letters can take weeks.

Retailers can minimize the time to resolve complaints by reducing the number of people the customer must contact, providing clear instructions, and speaking in the customer's language.[52]

Reducing the Number of Contacts As a general rule, store employees who deal with customers should be made as self-sufficient as possible to handle problems. Customers are more satisfied when the first person they contact can resolve a problem. When customers are referred to several different employees, they waste a lot of time repeating their story. Also, the chance of conflicting responses by store employees increases.

Giving Clear Instructions Customers should be told clearly and precisely what they need to do to resolve a problem. When American Express cardholders ask to have an unused airline ticket removed from their bill, they're told immediately that they must return the ticket to the airline or travel agency before a credit can be issued. Fast service often depends on providing clear instructions.

Speaking the Customer's Language Customers can become annoyed when store employees use company jargon to describe a situation. To communicate clearly, store employees should use terms familiar to the customer. For example, a customer would be frustrated if a salesperson told her the slacks in her size were located on a rounder to the right of the four-way.[53]

Resolving customer complaints increases satisfaction. But when complaints are resolved too abruptly, customers might feel dissatisfied because they haven't received personal attention. Retailers must recognize the trade-off between resolving the problem quickly and taking time to listen to and show concern for the customer.[54]

SUMMARY

Due to the inherent intangibility and inconsistency of service, providing high-quality customer service is challenging. However, customers also provide an opportunity for retailers to develop a strategic advantage. Retailers use two basic approaches for providing customer service; customization and standardization approaches. The customized approach relies primarily on sales associates. The standardized approach places more emphasis on developing appropriate rules and procedures and the store design.

Customers evaluate customer service by comparing their perceptions of the service delivered with their expectations. Thus, to improve service, retailers need to close the gaps between the service delivered and the customer's expectations. This gap is reduced by knowing what customers expect, setting standards to provide the expected service, providing support so store employees can meet the standards, and realistically communicating the service they offer to customers.

Due to inherent inconsistency, service failures are bound to arise. These lapses in service provide an opportunity for retailers to build even stronger relationships with their customers.

KEY TERMS

chat rooms, *602*	delivery gap, *592*	instrumental support, *603*	procedural fairness, *607*
communication gap, *592*	distributive fairness, *607*	knowledge gap, *592*	service gap, *592*
customer services, *585*	emotional support, *603*	message boards, *602*	standardization approach, *588*
customization approach, *587*	empowerment, *603*	mystery shopper, *600*	standards gap, *592*

DISCUSSION QUESTIONS AND PROBLEMS

1. For each of these services, give an example of a retailer for which providing the service is critical to its success. Then give an example of retailer for which providing the service is not critical:
   a. Personal shoppers.
   b. Delivery.
   c. Money-back guarantees.
   d. Credit.

2. Nordstrom and McDonald's are noted for their high-quality customer service. But their approaches to providing this quality service are different. Describe this difference. Why have the retailers elected to use these different approaches?

3. Is customer service more important for store-based retailers or electronic retailers? Why?

4. Providing customer service can be very expensive for retailers. When are the costs for providing high-quality services justified? What types of retailers find it financially advantageous to provide high-quality customer service? What retailers can't justify providing high-quality service?

5. Assume you're the department manager for menswear in a local department store that emphasizes empowering its managers. A customer returns a dress shirt that's no longer in the package it was sold in. The customer has no receipt, says that when he opened the package he found that the shirt was torn, and wants cash for the price the shirt is being sold at now. The shirt was on sale last week when the customer claims to have bought it. What would you do?

6. Citibank found that chat rooms were not an important service for customers of its electronic banking offering. However, Garden.com, an electronic retailer targeting gardeners, found that chat rooms are an important service for attracting customers. Why did these retailers have different experiences with the use of chat rooms?

7. How should store employees handle customer complaints?

8. Gaps analysis provides a systematic method of examining a customer service program's effectiveness. Kmart top management has told an information systems manager that customers are complaining about the long wait to pay for merchandise at the checkout station. How can the systems manager use Gaps analysis to analyze this problem and suggest approaches for reducing this time?

9. How could an effective customer service strategy cut a retailer's costs?

10. Employees play a critical role in customer perceptions of quality service. If you were hiring salespeople, what characteristics would you look for to assess their ability to provide good customer service?

SUGGESTED READINGS

Anderson, Kristin, and Ron Zemke. *Delivering Knock Your Socks Off Service.* New York: AMACOM, 1998.

Babin, Barry, and James Boles. "Employee Behavior in Service Environment: A Model and Test of Potential Differences between Men and Women." *Journal of Marketing* 62 (April 1998), pp. 77–91.

Berry, Leonard. *Discovering the Soul of Service.* New York: Free Press, 1999.

"Enhancing the Shopping Experience." *Discount Store News,* July 12, 1999, pp. 13, 15.

Joubert, Michelle. "Retailers Begin to Take Stock of Better Customer Service." *The Financial Times,* February 17, 1999, p. 10.

Karr, Albert. "A Hot New Job Is Chief of Customer Service for Internet Retailers." *The Wall Street Journal,* June 1, 1999, pp. A1, A8.

Reda, Susan. "Seven Keys to Better Service." *Stores,* January 1996, pp. 32–34.

Sterne, Jim. *Customer Service on the Internet: Building Relationships, Increasing Loyalty, and Staying Competitive.* New York: Wiley, 1996.

Whitt, Ward. "Improving Service by Informing Customers about Anticipated Delays." *Management Science* 45 (February 1999), pp. 192–217.

Winsted, Kathryn. "The Service Experience in Two Cultures." *Journal of Retailing* 73 (Fall 1997), pp. 337–60.

Zemke, Ron, and John Woods. *Best Practices in Customer Service.* New York: AMACOM, 1999.

Cases

CASE	1	2	3	4	5	6	7	8	9	10	11	12	13	14	15	16	17	18	19	C
1. Old Navy	P			S		S														
2. Blue Sky Surf Shop	P			S	S															
3. Cleveland Clinic	P	P				S														
4. Mustafa Center		P	S			S														
5. Online Grocers			P																	S
6. Garden.com			P																	P
7. Abercrombie & Fitch				P		S														
8. White Family Buys Bicycles					P															
9. Bloomingdale's				P	P															
10. Toys "R" Us			S	S		P														S
11. Winn-Dixie and Dillard						S	P													
12. Stephanie's Boutique						S		P												
13. Hutch									P											
14. Marriott										P							S			
15. The Computer Shoppe											P					S				
16. Merchandise Planning Problems												P	S							
17. McFadden's												S	P							
18. Nolan's Finest Foods												P	P							
19. Stan's Shirts															P					
20. Pricing Problems															P					
21. eBay			S			S									P					
22. Loyalty Wars in the UK																				
23. Advertising Plan																P				
24. Neiman Marcus																P				
25. Max Murphy																	P			
26. Borders																	P	S		
27. Best Display?																S	P			
28. Discmart																				
29. Starbucks				S														P	P	
30. Wolf Camera						S								S						P
31. Lindy's Bridal Shoppe						S										S				P
						S					S									P

P Primary Use
S Secondary Use
C Comprehensive

The Gap and Old Navy

DONALD FISHER AND WIFE launched the The Gap in 1969. Initially, The Gap stores were unique in offering every size and style of Levi's, arranged by size for convenience. When the teen-jean craze slowed in the mid-1970s, stores were repositioned for people interested in a fashionable, causal lifestyle. Donald Fisher, then CEO, and Mickey Drexler, then president, added other chains to the The Gap portfolio of specialty apparel stores: Banana Republic and Old Navy. Banana Republic is positioned at the high end of the quality/price spectrum that includes the moderately priced Gap and the company's newest chain, Old Navy, featuring the least expensive clothing.

For years, the flagship Gap stores, with $11.6 billion in sales and an estimated $1.1 billion in profits, made up more than a third of the entire company's profits. But in May 1999, Gap began to lose the edge it had enjoyed for several years. Other competitors such as Abercrombie & Fitch and American Eagle Outfitter were beginning their assault on the fashion market with trendier clothes and better, more aggressive advertising campaigns.

For six consecutive months, sales at Gap stores fell to all-time lows, taking the stock price down with them. The apparel market was in a transitional phase that favored either high-priced designer-name fashions or the low-end wear that has consistently sold well. This trend was reflected in large sales increases in the high- and low-end Gap chains—Banana Republic and Old Navy were selling very well. The challenge for Gap was that it needed a new marketing plan without disrupting the strong sales of its other stores. Drexler was well aware of this fact and brought with him new and innovative ideas that the company desperately needed. Drexler, the Gap's president since 1983, became the CEO in October 1999 when Robert Fisher, the president and son of the Gap founders, retired. The company's stock immediately rose 10 percent on the news of Drexler taking over.

Mickey Drexler developed the concept for the Old Navy chain to cater to the new lifestyle of teens and young adults who want fashion but do not have much to spend on clothing. He selected the name for the chain after seeing it on a building during a walk around Paris. Old Navy is consistent with the growing strength of discount stores in apparel retailing. Consumers were predicted to spend $40 billion—nearly a third of their apparel dollars—at discount department stores, off-pricers, and factory outlets in 1999. It is not only price that drives consumers into discount stores for apparel. The industry has made great efforts in assortment, quality, and fashion. Discount stores have also come a long way in improving display, borrowing ideas from regular stores. In 1999, the Old Navy, with 16 percent of the stores, accounted for 35 percent of the sales of Gap Inc.

The Old Navy Clothing Stores have the same kind of merchandise as The Gap stores, but will be able to keep prices low by using lighter-weight, less expensive fabrics in addition to scaled-down store decor and lower-priced locations in strip shopping malls. Old Navy stores have unique design elements featuring 1950 Chevies and merchandise piled on old freezers.

Although half of all Old Navy stores are within a mile of a Gap, they take only 5 to 10 percent of Gap's business, with all of the rest coming from elsewhere. As COO of Gap, Inc., John Wilson said, "It's a temporary hit, but the volume comes back; we'd rather cannibalize our own business than have the competition do it."

In April 1999, Jenny Ming was appointed president of Old Navy. Ming started her career at The Gap in 1986 as a buyer. Ming has a knack for predicting what hip-looking clothing will appeal to the masses and making big bets on producing large quantities to ensure that these items will be in stock. One of her early successes was dramatically increasing the sales of T-shirts by increasing the color assortment from six to a couple dozen and marketing them all year, instead of just in the summer. More recently she was the key force behind the explosive growth of fleece merchandise.

Old Navy's new, four-story, 100,000–square-foot flagship store in San Francisco is its largest ever built. This store is similar to its 80,000–square-foot showplace in New York, with a deejay booth where shoppers can create their own CDs and a lower-level, fashion-forward, off-price department.

Discussion Questions

1. How do you think the growth of Old Navy will affect the sales in The Gap chain?

2. In the next five years, where should Gap, Inc., place the greatest resources: Old Navy, Gap, or Banana Republic? Why?

3. In what ways could the Gap chain enhance customer appeal and loyalty?

Source: This case was prepared by Pirkko Peterson, University of Florida.

CASE *2*

Blue Sky Surf Shop— Twenty-One Years of Surfing and Still Going Strong

BLUE SKY SURF SHOP in St. Augustine, Florida, is owned and operated by husband and wife Dave and Nancy Macri. After surfing in St. Augustine for several years, the Macris, who are originally from the gulf side of Florida, decided to start their business in 1979 in what was then a small, low-key surfer's town. Located on Anastasia Blvd. (the main route through Anastasia Island and a direct road to the beach), the shop is not out of sight but is easily missed if one is not looking for it. This is not a disadvantage to the store because (unlike most businesses in tourist-dependent St. Augustine) Blue Sky relies on local surfers and word of mouth for 90 percent of its business. Surfers from Jacksonville, Gainesville, Daytona Beach, and the west coast of Florida flock to St. Augustine for the consistent waves, clean water, and wide open beaches, and all rely on Blue Sky for surf accessories.

Blue Sky receives most of its business from males between ages 10 and 25 as opposed to a lot of larger, more diversified surf shops that also carry camping, kayaking, and fishing equipment aimed at the adult and family markets. Unlike many surf shops that cater to multisport lifestyles, Blue Sky has remained true to the hardcore surfer by carrying products that are solely related to surfing and the lifestyle that accompanies it. This customer demographic demands very knowledgeable service and high-quality products. All the employees at Blue Sky are avid surfers; some are even past or presently sponsored by companies. This gives them a huge advantage with customers who know what they want and are very fast at spotting below-par products and service. A very large portion of the competition employs almost any teenager or young adult willing to work, many of whom have never surfed.

Customers entering Blue Sky, see surf videos constantly playing on a television monitor, over 200 brand new surfboards neatly displayed on floor racks, and the best brand name clothing. This quickly tells them they are in the best possible place to suit their needs. Just as back in 1979, when the store was a mere 600 square feet, it's dedicated to maximizing every inch for surfers needs. The store is now 1,800 square feet and Blue Sky consistently carries roughly 250 new and 60 used surfboards, more than any other shop in northeast Florida. Going into its 21st year of business, Blue Sky has perfected the concept of quality products and service while staying true to its original clientele, no matter what the rate of expansion.

Although the majority of surfers are male, Blue Sky has always been aware of the female surf market. However, unlike most of its competition, it does not waste space with hundreds of interchangeable bikinis and swimwear. It sells functional bathing suits, surf trunks, wetsuits, and anything else a female surfer could possibly need. Even though the female market may be smaller, Blue Sky is and always has been about supplying anyone that truly loves to surf.

With more and more surf shops popping up in St. Augustine, many of which have large advertising budgets, Blue Sky need not worry about losing customers; 21 years of solid no-frills service has built an extremely loyal customer base. You couldn't put a price tag on the store's word-of-mouth reputation. It does occasionally advertise in local newsletters and newspapers, but at a fraction of the cost of any competition. A very smart idea to further satisfy customers and to add to its exposure is Blue Sky's free surf report. Many other surf shops and companies have 1-900 telephone numbers that give you surf conditions, surf forecasts, water temperature, and tides, but most of these lines cost between fifty cents and a $1.25 per minute for their services. Blue Sky provides this valuable service absolutely free. This exemplifies the ability of Blue Sky to do small but highly effective things to evolve and satisfy, yet always keep in tune with the original philosophy of being the "surfer's surf shop."

Discussion Questions

1. What is the target market of Blue Sky Surf Shop?

2. What role has location played in the long-term success of Blue Sky?

3. How has Blue Sky achieved long-term success with minimal advertising?

Source: This case was written by Pirkko Peterson, University of Florida.

CASE 3

Cleveland Clinic

FOR YEARS, OHIO'S CLEVELAND CLINIC has ranked with the top world-class providers of medical care. It pioneered coronary bypass surgery and developed the first kidney dialysis machine. King Hussein of Jordan used the clinic, as does the royal family of Saudi Arabia.

Big-name health care institutions like the Cleveland Clinic are after new markets for their state-of-the-art medical care, and are posing a new threat to local physicians. The expansions are also disrupting traditional relationships between physicians and their patients, physicians and their hospitals, and physicians and their fellow physicians.

Like any business, the Cleveland Clinic keeps close tabs on its core market, and the outlook wasn't all that bright. Seven Midwestern states provided 90 percent of the clinic's business, though population growth in that region is expected to be flat through the year 2010. But not so southeastern Florida, where the population is still growing and, in many areas, is highly affluent. Southeastern Florida appeared to be a dream market. Yachts lining the canals of the Intracoastal Waterway and a ubiquitous building boom reflect wealth and growth so palpable that clinic officials have come to call it immaculate consumption. Moreover, about 20 percent of the 3.7 million residents in Dade, Broward, and Palm Beach counties are over 65 years old. About 50 percent of the population is over 45—a potential mother lode of patients. "We felt there was room for us," Dr. Kiser, CEO of Cleveland Clinic, said. "We decided to go on our own rather than wait to be invited."

When the Cleveland Clinic opened an outpatient clinic in South Florida, a war broke out. In a full-page advertisement in the *Miami Herald*, Dr.

Seropian, a local physician, pulled out the stops. He likened the clinic to dingoes (wild Australian dogs) that roam the bush, eating every kind of prey. The clinic filed suit in federal district court in Fort Lauderdale, charging, among other things, that some physicians had conspired to hamper its entry into Broward County.

Famous medical institutions like the Cleveland Clinic and Mayo are victims of their own success. Many of the once-exotic procedures that they invented are now routinely available across the country, reducing patients' need to travel to the medical meccas. For instance, the Cleveland Clinic might once have had a hold on coronary bypass surgery, but no more. In 2000, more than 350,000 patients had the operation at hospitals throughout the United States.

"These clinics used to be the court of last resort for complex medical cases," says Jeff Goldsmith, national health care advisor to Ernst & Young, the accounting firm. "Now, the flooding of the country with medical specialties and high technology equipment has forced them to adopt a different strategy."

Their expertise and reputation mean formidable competition for the local medical community. "On one level," says Jay Wolfson, a health policy expert at the University of South Florida in Tampa, "it's like bringing in a McDonald's. If you're a mom-and-pop sandwich shop on the corner, you could get wiped out."

Discussion Questions

1. Compare the Cleveland Clinic to traditional retailers.

2. What was its retail mix?

3. What factors in its environment resulted in it changing its retail mix?

Mustafa Center: Singapore's All-in-One Retailer

MUSTAFA CENTER IS A WELL-KNOWN RETAILER in Singapore that provides one-stop shopping. The breadth of product variety is truly amazing, covering a wide range including jewelry, watches, electronics, home appliances, apparel, cloth, personal computers, grocery and food items, hardware, gift items, and luggage. The store combines a department store, grocery store, pharmacy, hotel, and services retailers including currency exchange and travel agency.

Mustafa Center was established in 1971 in a part of Singapore known as Little India. From its original site of 500 square feet, it has now grown to cover 150,000 square feet in two adjacent locations, with over 90,000 SKUs. The company's sales revenue in 1999 was S$240 million. In addition to its retail outlets, it has a warehouse not far from Little India. The founder, Mr. Mustaq Ahmad, can often be seen serving customers, unrecognized by those whom he serves. Under his leadership, the company has achieved national recognition and was a winner of the Enterprise 50 awards in 1998.

On a normal weekday, 10,000 customers visit the store with the number increasing to between 15,000 and 20,000 on weekends. Prior to the Asian economic crisis that started in 1997, approximately 80 percent of its customers were tourists, and the rest were locals. The tourists were mainly from India, Pakistan, Bangladesh, and Sri Lanka, although those from Middle Eastern countries, North Asia, and Europe have also been increasing. This is a unique feature given that the majority (about 75 percent) of Singapore's population is of Chinese descent.

In terms of competition, Mustafa Center's unique positioning grants it much monopolistic power. Its closest competitors are the large department stores on Orchard Rd. (the major shopping stretch in Singapore), including CK Tang, Isetan, Robinson's, and Takashimaya. It also competes to some extent with the small sundry and provision stores in Little India. The large department stores on Orchard Rd. cannot compete with Mustafa on prices due to higher overheads, while the small stores in Little India cannot offer the same assortment and convenience provided by Mustafa.

Mustafa practices EDLP, providing fair value on its product assortment. Although it does not necessarily have the lowest prices in town, it is often perceived to be competitive by its customers. The gross margin on products is 15 percent on average, with the range at 10 to 30 percent, much lower than the department stores. For example, the markups in the supermarket do not exceed 15 percent, thus being very competitive with other grocery stores in Singapore.

In order to achieve EDLP, Mustafa is very scrupulous in its sourcing practices. Where it previously used only a few suppliers, it has now widened its purchasing network and buys goods from countries in the region including Malaysia, Thailand, Indonesia, and Hong Kong as well as further afield in India, China, Japan, and Europe. The store buyers are responsible for sourcing from the cheapest suppliers, bypassing all intermediaries. Parallel imports make up about 20 percent of all products.

Given its large product variety and limited space, the store layout at Mustafa is extremely cramped. Mr. Ahmad believes this actually works to his benefit, as most of his customers from the Indian subcontinent are familiar with cramped shopping conditions. He also believes that since only serious buyers frequent both stores, there is little need for a glamourous layout.

Mustafa mainly employs Muslim and Indian workers. However, as the store layout is quite cramped, most customers have to find the items they want by themselves, except for items such as jewelry and home appliances, where shop assistance is available.

Mustafa's communication efforts are limited. Although it does buy airtime on local TV and radio stations (mainly English-speaking and Tamil-speaking) and advertises in the local newspapers, it believes positive word-of-mouth communication is a more effective means of promotion. According to Mr. Ahmad, "We're not promoting any products, we are selling promoted products. So let someone else promote them and we'll do the selling."

A major concern is shoplifting. In order to reduce inventory shrinkage, security guards at all entrances of the stores use security tags to seal all bags that customers carry into the stores. Upon payment of purchases, the plastic bags are also sealed with tags, which cannot be opened unless they are cut. Bulky items are stuck with "item-paid" stickers.

In 1995, Mustafa Center set up its own website, www.mustafa.com.sg. The website is meant to replace its catalogs. The time taken to update, print, and bind new editions meant that by the time the catalogs were ready, many product listings were already outdated. From a static information site, the website has since grown to become fully functional, where customers can browse approximately 5,000 products online and also purchase them. The website received $50,000 worth of orders in April 1999, with the orders coming mainly from Indonesia, Pakistan, the United States, India, Brunei, Canada, and Israel. The Mustafa Online store uses the industry standard Secure Sockets Layer (SSL) technology to allow for the encryption of the user's name and address as well as critically sensitive information such as the credit card number. Credit card payments on the Mustafa site are handled using the SSL solution from the National Computer Systems Consumer Connect Service. This authenticates the security of the site.

In mid-1997, the Asian economic crisis struck. As with virtually all other retailers in town, Mustafa's business was adversely affected, although it was not as badly hit as some other retailers who suffered major losses. Its major customers, tourists, declined to only about 60 percent of its customers. Local customers who are trying to stretch their dollar increased slightly.

Founder Ahmad is now faced with the problems of how to expand his store operations and how to increase both online and physical store patronage. He is debating whether to open a new local outlet or one in India, where Mr. Ahmad believes much potential exists.

Discussion Questions

1. What do you think Mr. Ahmad should do in order to increase local store patronage?

2. Should Mustafa expand its operations by opening a new local store or one in India?

3. Visit Mustafa's website. Evaluate its potential for further growth.

4. Would a store offering the variety of Mustafa Center flourish in the United States? Why or why not?

Source: This case was written by Professors Hean Tat Keh and Vidya Sundari in the Department of Marketing, the NUS Business School at the National University of Singapore. © Hean Tat Keh. A longer version of this case is available from the first author by request to fbakehht@nus.edu.sg.

CASE 5

Online Grocers

THE LUXURY OF SITTING IN FRONT of your computer in your home or office while shopping and ordering groceries and various products online is an appealing idea to many people in today's fast-paced, no-time society. Online grocery services are attempting to accommodate these types of busy people through various strategies that they hope will catch on as the norm. Not only does this model appeal to the busy people of the world, but it also presents a great opportunity to those who dread grocery shopping and to those who are physically unable to conveniently travel to the grocery store. Online grocers are providing consumers with doorstep, and in some cases in-house, delivery of groceries and various other products and services.

The Internet and e-commerce are expanding at an astounding rate. Research by International Data Corporation indicates that there were about 63 million web users in the United States at the end of 1998; it believes that this number will reach about 177 million by the end of 2003. Forrester Research believes that the market for online grocery shopping in the United States will increase from $513 million in 1999 to $16.8 billion by 2004. These numbers, along with the logic of human nature, indicate a fit for the future of online grocers. Webvan, Peapod, HomeGrocer, and Streamline are four online retailers that believe that now is the time to penetrate the consumer direct, online grocery delivery market.

Webvan is an online retailer of grocery products and other merchandise. Its large selection of about 18,000 grocery and specialty products includes name brands, produce, meats, baked goods, seafood, nonperishables, nonprescription drugs, wines, cigars, and office products. Products may be browsed and purchased through Webvan's categorization structure, through keyword searches, or by personalized grocery lists. The website also offers various content features such as recipes and articles. The website is well organized, is easy to navigate, and provides in-depth product information.

Through its advanced and highly automated distribution center model, Webvan offers same-day delivery (sometimes within 30 minutes) for many products. The products are delivered to the end consumer via temperature-controlled trucks. The distribution centers are designed to manage large product volumes and a flexible inventory of more than 50,000 SKUs. The centers also host such features as food preparation facilities for meals that are ordered by customers. Webvan currently has one distribution center in Oakland, California, which serves the San Francisco Bay Area. It plans to duplicate this distribution center in various geographic markets. Webvan entered into an agreement with Bechtel Corporation in July 1999 to build as many as 26 new distribution centers over the following three years.

Webvan relies on its one-on-one customer service to build its brand name. Each courier is trained to speak with the customers and discuss the service to build awareness and gather feedback. Webvan believes that this development of long-term relationships with customers will encourage repeat purchases.

Webvan currently has strategic alliances with Kellogg, Pillsbury, Quaker Oats, Nestlé USA, SUPERVALU, and Fleming. The relationships are meant to exchange industry competencies. Webvan benefits from the manufacturers' supply chain, merchandising, and product knowledge. The relationships with SUPERVALU and Fleming provide Webvan with a national distribution source for grocery, frozen, and dairy products. In return, Webvan provides the businesses with online retailing expertise.

Webvan's objective is to be the leading retailer of same-day delivery for consumer products. Its growth strategy to reach this objective consists of building brand awareness and market share, providing superior customer service and operating performance, replicating distribution centers and delivery systems in various geographic markets, and expanding into new product markets.

Peapod is an online grocer and a provider of targeted media and research services. Peapod's company slogan is "Smart Shopping for Busy People®," which is meant to portray the practicality, convenience, and time savings offered through the company's services. Peapod carries name brands, meat, produce, deli products, baked goods, packaged foods, household items, and health and beauty products.

Peapod's national online network of member data provides various consumer goods companies with valuable information regarding consumer behavior and demographics. Businesses take advantage of this information through highly effective interactive advertising, electronic couponing, and product research.

Peapod stresses its importance of customer service through "The Peapod Promise" to ensure member satisfaction. Peapod's website provides consumers with a functional, personalized interface displaying extensive product information. Members have the option to shop by browsing, by using lists compiled of products that they frequently purchase, or through the product search engine using keywords or brand names. The products that customers select can then be sorted in various orders, such as by price or nutritional content. Peapod finds importance in upholding its customer service reputation through its website and by offering service to its members through e-mail and the telephone.

After exploring various business models for efficient order fulfillment, Peapod has concluded that a centralized distribution model is the most effective way to accommodate growing customer demand. Its current structure consists of order fulfillment through partnerships with existing retailers in each market. However, it is currently shifting over to a new centralized distribution model. The new centralized model is currently implemented in Long Island, New York and Chicago, Illinois, and will be used in all future locations.

Peapod's fulfillment applications are designed for both in-store and warehouse fulfillment, which allows for the highest quality of product and service to the end consumer. Peapod purchases its products through various suppliers and sometimes traditional retailers for the distribution centers.

The company's growth strategy includes success in providing superior customer service, an optimal model for fulfillment services, increasing membership and order volume, improving brand identity and awareness, building leadership in interactive marketing services, and leveraging local fulfillment infrastructure.

HomeGrocer is an online grocer offering over 11,000 products that include name brands, vegetables, fruit, dairy products, baked goods, meat, fish, household products, and nonperishables. In addition to a wide selection of food items, it offers flowers, beauty products, beer, wine, pet products, home office supplies, postage stamps, books, movies, and video games. Its pricing is comparable to traditional grocery stores and retailers. Its shopping website is graphically appealing, quick loading, customizable, and easy to use.

HomeGrocer offers next-day home delivery of all products. It has a partnership with Roadnet, a subsidiary of UPS, to utilize software for efficient package routing and scheduling. Roadnet also supplies a wireless communications technology that allows HomeGrocer to efficiently track shipments and communicate with delivery people. HomeGrocer stocks its own warehouses and delivers groceries by refrigerated trucks. Its inventory is purchased from national suppliers, premium specialty suppliers, and local sources.

HomeGrocer currently offers its service to three markets: Seattle, Washington; Portland, Oregon; and Orange County/Los Angeles, California. It plans to rapidly expand nationally into several additional metropolitan areas. It anticipates this to be a fairly smooth process since its customer fulfillment centers are designed for easy replication.

HomeGrocer currently has strategic marketing alliances with Amazon.com and America Online. Amazon.com (its largest shareholder) markets the grocery service to Amazon customers who reside within HomeGrocer's geographic market areas. HomeGrocer's service is also featured on America Online websites and affiliate sites.

Streamline is an online retailer that delivers groceries and various other products directly to the home on a weekly basis. Streamline actually arranges to drop the deliveries off in a secure area of the customer's home, such as the garage, so that customers can receive the goods even when they are not home. To accommodate the need for refrigeration of grocery products, Streamline provides the customer with the Streamline Box, (a refrigerator/freezer with a compact storage unit) to be located in the customer's desired secure area.

Streamline carries name brands, meats, seafood, baked goods, prepared meals, produce, dairy products, frozen foods, deli products, pet foods, beauty products, firewood, cleaning products, and more. Streamline also provides services such as package and dry cleaning pickup and delivery, clothing alteration and repair, bottle and can redemption, video and video game rental, shoe repair, film processing, and food and clothing drives. Streamline believes that these service offerings are excellent solutions for the busy suburban family. Streamline's customer service representatives are cross-trained to assist customers with product and service questions, delivery inquiries, and technical problems with the website.

Streamline plans to expand nationally into 20 high-potential markets. It believes that it will be able to centralize the majority of its operations, including order processing, customer service, customer acquisition, and general management and administration.

Streamline developed and sponsors an on-site research center designed to strengthen the knowledge of consumer behavior in the consumer direct industry. It is called the Consumer Learning Center and participants include companies such as Campbell Soup, Nestlé USA, Gillette, and Procter & Gamble. All participants are required to pay Streamline a membership fee. Streamline also has other types of strategic alliances with various e-commerce businesses to increase exposure.

Streamline wishes to become the leading national direct supplier of groceries and other related products and services to busy suburban families. It believes that it can achieve this objective by nationally replicating its business model, by developing and strengthening its customer acquisition capabilities, by increasing revenue per customer, by maximizing operational efficiency, and through relationships with consumer packaged goods companies, e-commerce companies, and strategic investors.

Though these businesses are experiencing some success in their strategies, there are currently some obstacles that they, and any other business entering the market, need to overcome. The first and biggest problem is that many consumers will be reluctant to use an online shopping format because they cannot feel and examine products before purchasing them. This is especially the case in the produce, meat, and seafood areas. Most of these types of companies assure customers that their grocery pickers will pick only the freshest, highest-quality items, but who knows if the customers would have picked what the picker did if they were actually the shopper. The best thing that these businesses can do is to really get the best products for their customers and hope that they build a trustful relationship so that they may continue to do their shopping for them.

Another important issue that the consumer experiences is the lack of variety in product selection that online grocers provide compared to that of traditional grocery stores. In order for these businesses to truly provide a better option to traditional grocery shopping, they will need to make their product lines more extensive.

Consumer perceptions that online delivery services are more expensive than traditional stores is a problem that needs to change before the real potential of the market can be realized. People believe that, since they are purchasing products over the Internet, having a person actually shop for the products, and then having items delivered to their house, this service will be significantly more expensive than traditional shopping. In some cases they are right. On the other hand, many consumers are willing to make the sacrifice.

Another obstacle that needs to be overcome is the immediacy that grocery consumers demand. The first business that can successfully implement a delivery system that will get the consumer any grocery product within 30 minutes will have a significant advantage in this industry. It is too easy for a person to decide to drive a few blocks to the store and purchase a product that he needs immediately rather than waiting a day or two to receive it.

Not only does the order need to get there quickly, it also needs to get there accurately. The difficult logistics of the distribution systems that these businesses use makes them vulnerable to confusing orders and routes. This can damage the reputation and approval of the business. The fact that customers' orders will be packed in a truck along with other customers' orders can also pose a problem of food damage and spoilage.

Finally, a problem plaguing every type of online retailer is the consumer's insecurity about the safety of online transactions. Internet hackers have been highly publicized for stealing entire databases of credit card information from insecure online retailers. This has greatly damaged consumers' perceptions of online security and privacy. Online grocers will need to assure and educate consumers of their security technology. They will need to let the customer know that they will accommodate the victim of credit card fraud if something were to happen through their website. They should also provide the option of payment by check or cash on delivery. What better way could these businesses build a relationship with their customers than through the mutual trust that would be developed through these types of options?

From an internal standpoint, these emerging online grocery companies are confronted with the difficult task of expanding nationally. The capital, time, and meticulous strategy needed to accomplish this task creates another large hindrance to this industry's success.

In conclusion, the online grocery market possesses incredible potential to take advantage of the need for consumers to get away from the drudgery and inconvenience of regularly walking the aisles of a grocery store. Webvan, Peapod, HomeGrocer, and Streamline are online businesses that have taken the plunge in order to try to get a jump on this impatient market. All of them have interesting, and in some cases unique, strategies that they believe will pave the road to success in this industry. In order for them to succeed, they must overcome the many difficult obstacles that are currently in their way.

Discussion Questions

1. What are the challenges of selling groceries over the Internet compared to books and CDs?

2. What unique benefits are offered by each of the online grocers?

3. What are the strategic advantages each of the four online supermarkets are attempting to develop?

Source: This case was prepared by William Walsch, University of Florida.

Garden.com

GARDEN.COM WAS FOUNDED in September 1995 by the current President/CEO Clifford A. Sharples, Lisa Sharples, James N. O'Neill, and Andrew R. Martin. Their innovative retail concept was stimulated by a course they had all taken at Northwestern University's Kellogg Graduate School of Management. In the course, "The Policies in Marketing Channels," Professor Louis Stern emphasized the difference between a supply chain and a marketing channel. Supply chains move products from producer to end user, while a marketing channel focuses on using the channel to satisfy consumer needs. Stern also emphasized that successful companies like Wal-Mart dominate their marketing channels by blocking competition, becoming superbrands in and of themselves.

THE GARDEN MARKET

The founders were attracted to the gardening industry because of its size and lack of dominant suppliers and retailers. Gardening is the most popular hobby in the United States with consumers spending over $45 billion a year on plants, tools, and services—more than twice the expenditures on books. The gardening industry is highly fragmented. No company in the industry accounts for more than 1 percent of the market. There are few national brands. Gardening is a regional, if not local, phenomenon due to important variations in climate and soil conditions. However, gardeners are affluent and willing to pay for quality products and expert advise.

Many baby boomers are involved in gardening. Cliff Sharples refers to this cohort as "the Pottery Barn generation"—people who are short on time, yet hungry for knowledge about how to do things in an artful way. "The interest is now about fashion, collection, and decoration," he says. "It's about designing your exterior space the way you would think about your interior space." However, retailers are not satisfying the needs of these time-pressured consumers who want to order ornamental fruit trees by mail and have them arrive, without fail, on Tuesday, because they are leaving on Wednesday for a three-day business trip.

MEMBERS

As of March 2000, Garden.com had over 600,000 members. Membership is free. Each member fills out a survey during the signup process to provide Garden.com with valuable marketing information. In addition to the information collected on a membership application form, Garden.com has extensive data about members from their purchases and uses of the website. The amount of information Garden.com has about its members can raise privacy concerns. However, Garden.com emphasizes the personalized services it can provide to its members with this information. As Lisa Sharples points out, "We now know what plants people have in their gardens. So we can tell them when to prune, when to divide them, when to fertilize them, and when to cover them." And with each of those advisories comes the chance to make another sale—and to find out just a little more about the buyer.

The website has 1.6 million visitors during March, the peak time of the gardening season. It currently attracts 10 million page views per month and a total of 450,000 unique visitors per month. Seventy percent of its users are female, and 30 percent are male. The age demographic is 35 to 54 years old, with an average household income level of $65,000 and up.

RETAIL OFFERING

Garden.com (www.garden.com) offers a one-stop shopping Internet site for gardeners. The website is extremely comprehensive and provides gardeners with vast amounts of information, products, and resources to assist them with their hobby. Features of the website include merchandise, information, community, and personalization.

- *Merchandise.* In the "shopping section," Garden.com offers over 16,000 products from 60 different suppliers. Product categories include plants, bulbs, organic solutions, tools and accessories, furniture and ornaments, books, seeds, watering, home decorating, and gifts. Detailed information about the products is provided with pictures. Free membership provides customers with an account so that they don't have to enter ordering information every time they would like to purchase a product. The products are shipped by the suppliers to the customer's doorstep usually no more than three days after placing the order.

- *Information.* The "magazine" sections offer general articles like those you would find in a traditional print magazine on gardening.

However, the interactivity of the Internet is exploited by linking the content of the articles to other sections of the Garden.com website. For example, when a plant or tool is mentioned in an article, a link is provided to offer members the opportunity to purchase the product. In the "regional gardening" section, there are articles and advice for different climatic regions of the United States. The editor-in-chief of the magazine section is Doug Jimerson, who previously spent 18 years as an editor and writer at *Better Homes and Gardens.*

- *Community.* In the "community" section of the website, customers have an opportunity to interact with other gardeners and gardening experts. A chat room allows members and guests to communicate with other members and guests who are logged on at the same time. Participants in the chat room can pose questions or trade ideas with other knowledgeable gardeners. Garden.com also hosts chats with celebrities (garden experts). Scheduled for specific times, they enable members to ask questions and learn new techniques. The "community" section also has a "garden doctor" feature where members can have specific questions answered. The "quiz of the week" feature is an area to test users' knowledge and expertise, which allows Garden.com to know what types of information might be good potential additions to the website. The "gardeners' forum" is a page devoted to displaying users' photos. For fun, the "send a postcard" feature lets the user send e-mail postcards with different floral themes on them. The "kids' gardening camp" lets children get involved with different types of gardening projects. The "plant a row for the hungry" feature is a charity that Garden.com hosts in which gardeners plant an extra row of food in their harvest to give to the needy.
- *Personalization.* Garden.com provides a special, personal folder on its website, in the "my stuff" section, where members can store information of interest to them. For example, using a software program in the "design a garden" section, members can select a template representing their garden and then select and position the types of plants they want to have

in the bed. They can store the plan, return and make changes, and, when the design is finalized, order all the plants with one click and have them shipped by overnight mail when they should be planted in the member's climate zone. The "my stuff" section is a central location for user-specific activity. In the "my stuff" section, members can find out the status for any orders as well as store articles that have been "clipped" and any notes that the user may have recorded during visits to the website.

SUPPLIERS

Garden.com's strategy is to find the best suppliers in each gardening category and sign them to exclusive contracts. It wants all of a supplier's online sales to go through Garden.com. In return, Garden.com will not sign up any direct competitors of that supplier. The company and its suppliers are tied together by a proprietary extranet integrated with Federal Express. It seems to the consumer as though everything came out of a warehouse in Texas, when, in fact, it was being drop shipped from multiple locations around the country. "The power is in the idea of tying all these niche growers together into a virtual store," says O'Neill. "I got the zen of that business model—and the customer reaction is awesome. A really well executed one-stop shop is an extremely powerful tool from the customer's standpoint."

Garden.com wants its brand to become a seal of approval for all its suppliers' products. A gardener who buys a bulb in October will pay a premium to ensure a healthy flower in the spring, O'Neill notes. "The quality of the plant material is incredibly important; most people don't realize that," he says. "It improves your chances of success. Otherwise, gardening can be a very frustrating hobby."

Discussion Questions

1. What benefits does Garden.com offer its customers? How do these benefits compare to those offered by a store-based retailer of garden supplies?

2. How can Garden.com build a competitive advantage over other store-based and electronic garden supply retailers?

Source: This case was prepared by William Walsch, University of Florida.

Abercrombie & Fitch

ABERCROMBIE & FITCH (A&F) was founded in 1892 as an eclectic sporting goods store. The chain was basically known in the past for selling most of its clothing to over-40–year-old Caucasians who were generally affluent. It outfitted customers like Ernest Hemingway and Teddy Roosevelt. However, over time its tweedy image became less attractive to consumers and the chain experienced a significant decline in sales and profits. In 1988, The Limited bought the chain for a bargain basement $47 million.

Michael Jeffries was hired in 1992 to revitalize the chain. His strategy was to provide apparel with classic American style targeted at young consumers. A&F's sales have skyrocketed from $165 million in 1994 to $1.06 billion in 1999; and its stores now total 230 in comparison to only 36 in 1992. Profits this year should reach an estimated $148.5 million. Jeffries has been successful in one of the most challenging retail assignments: selling consistently to the teenage and college set, a fickle market segment with significant disposable income.

Jeffries, age 55, revived Abercrombie by staying true to its East Coast roots but changing its focus and energy from the over-55 set to the 14-to-22–year-old consumer market. A&F still projects the aura of an exclusive, affluent lifestyle, just younger; magazines and television now carry its ads featuring beautiful twentysomething male and female models. To keep up with current trends, A&F merchandisers visit a different college campus every weekend to stay up to date on the products and styles their vast majority of consumers are wearing. Despite all of its recent success, A&F is still not doing as well on Wall Street as many people predicted. Many analysts, fearful of flash-in-the-pan versus long-term returns, pounded the stock in October 1999, saying that the company's 30 percent annual growth might be on the decline. However, CEO Jeffries started what he called a "magalog," a quarterly publication somewhere between a catalog and magazine. When the Christmas edition of the magalog, themed "Naughty or Nice," came out, sales rose 27 percent for the quarter. With its racy pictures and interview with a porn star, the issue quickly gained notoriety and word-of-mouth sales for A&F, further complimenting Michael Jeffries' ability to sell clothes and ease the worry of stockholders.

Discussion Questions

1. What is A&F's retail strategy?
2. What challenges does A&F face in satisfying the needs of the 14-to-22–year-old market?
3. What steps can it undertake to provide a retail mix appealing to this segment?

Source: This case was written by Pirkko Peterson at the University of Florida.

The White Family Buys Bicycles

THE WHITES LIVE IN RIVERSIDE, CALIFORNIA, west of Los Angeles. Terry is a physics professor at the University of California, Riverside. His wife Cheryl is a volunteer 10 hours a week at the Crisis Center. They have two children: Judy, age 10, and Mark, age 8.

In February, Cheryl's parents sent her $100 to buy a bicycle for Judy's birthday. They bought Judy her first bike when she was five. Now they wanted to buy her a full-size bike for her 11th birthday.

Even though Cheryl's parents felt every child should have a bike, Cheryl didn't think Judy really wanted one. Judy and most of her friends didn't ride their bikes often and she was afraid to ride to school because of traffic. So Cheryl decided to buy her the cheapest full-size bicycle she could find.

Since most of Judy's friends didn't have full-size bikes, she didn't know much about them and had no preferences for a brand or type. To learn more about the types available and their prices, Cheryl and Judy checked the JCPenney catalog. After looking through the catalog, Judy said the only thing she cared about was the color. She wanted a blue bike, blue being her favorite color.

Using the Yellow Pages, Cheryl called several local retail outlets selling bikes. To her surprise, she found that a department store actually had the best price for a 26-inch bicycle, even lower than Toys "R" Us and Wal-Mart.

Cheryl drove to the department store, went straight to the toy department, and selected a blue bicycle before a salesperson approached her. She took the bike to the cash register and paid for it. After making the purchase, the Whites found out that the bike was cheap in all senses. The chrome plating on the wheels was very thin and rusted away in six months. Both tires split and had to be replaced.

A year later, Cheryl's grandparents sent another $100 for a bike for Mark. Based on their experience with Judy's bike, the Whites by then realized that the lowest-priced bike might not be the least expensive option in the long run. Mark is very active and somewhat careless, so the Whites wanted to buy a sturdy bike. Mark said he wanted a red, 10-speed, lightweight imported bike with lots of accessories: headlights, special foot pedals, and so forth. The Whites were concerned that Mark wouldn't maintain an expensive bike with all these accessories.

When they saw an ad for a bicycle sale at Montgomery Ward, Cheryl and Terry went to the store with Mark. A salesperson approached them at an outdoor display of bikes and directed them to the sporting goods department inside the store. There they found row after row of red three-speed bikes with minimal accessories—the type of bike Cheryl and Terry felt was ideal for Mark.

A salesperson approached them and tried to interest them in a more expensive bike. Terry dislikes salespeople trying to push something on him and interrupted her in midsentence. He said he wanted to look at the bikes on his own. With a little suggestion, Mark decided he wanted one of these bikes. His desire for accessories was satisfied when they bought a wire basket for the bike. After buying a bike for Mark, Terry decided he'd like a bike for himself to ride on weekends. Terry had ridden bikes since he was five. In graduate school, before he was married, he'd owned a 10-speed. He frequently took 50-mile rides with friends. But he hadn't owned a bike since moving to Riverside 15 years ago.

Terry didn't know much about current types of touring bicycles. He bought a copy of *Touring* at a newsstand to see what was available. He also went to the library to read *Consumer Reports'* evaluation of touring bikes. Based on this information, he decided he wanted a Serrato. It had all the features he wanted: light weight, durable construction, and flexible setup. When Terry called the discount stores and bicycle shops, he found they didn't carry Serrato. He then decided he might not really need a bike. After all, he'd done without one for 15 years.

One day, after lunch, he was walking back to his office and saw a small bicycle shop. The shop was run down with bicycle parts scattered across the floor. The owner, a young man in grease-covered shorts, was fixing a bike. As Terry was looking around, the owner approached him and asked him if he liked to bicycle. Terry said he used to but had given it up when he moved to Riverside. The owner said that was a shame because there were a lot of nice places to tour around Riverside.

As their conversation continued, Terry mentioned his interest in a Serrato and his disappointment in not finding a store in Riverside that sold them. The owner said that he could order a Serrato for Terry but that they weren't very reliable. He suggested a Ross and showed Terry one he had in stock. Terry thought the $400 price was too high, but the owner convinced him to try it next weekend. They would ride together in the country. The owner and some of his friends took a 60-mile tour with Terry. Terry enjoyed the experience, recalling his college days. After the tour, Terry bought the Ross.

Discussion Questions

1. Outline the decision-making process for each of the Whites' bicycle purchases.

2. Compare the different purchase processes for the three bikes. What stimulated each of them? What factors were considered in making the store choice decisions and purchase decisions?

3. Construct a multiattribute model for each purchase decision. How do the attributes considered and importance weights vary for each decision?

Bloomingdale's

IN 1872, BROTHERS LYMAN AND JOSEPH BLOOMINGDALE OPENED their first retail outlet, the East Side Bazaar, in New York City. Bloomingdale's, now a division of Federated Department Stores, has grown into a national chain with 21 stores in Florida, Illinois, Maryland, Massachusetts, Minnesota, New York, New Jersey, Pennsylvania, and California.

With a reputation for quality, creativity, and uniqueness, Bloomingdale's has managed to stay at the forefront of retailing worldwide. The chain is known for its breadth of merchandise in all categories for women, men, children, and home as well as for its outstanding customer service.

Bloomingdale's is more committed than ever to increasing and perfecting customer service. Personal shopping services available by appointment or by phone give customers access to all of Bloomingdale's unique merchandise collections. Bridal registry, delivery services, coat and package checks, restaurants, and gift wrapping are just some of the complimentary services available at Bloomingdale's. The retailer has mandated that every employee's goal is to make shopping an easy and enjoyable experience for each customer.

Due to Bloomie's unique merchandise and service it has become a tourist destination. Foreign customers are from almost every country with a strong representation from Japan, the United Kingdom, Brazil, Argentina, Germany, Australia, and Canada. These international patrons are affluent, educated, and typically from 35 to 55 years old.

Bloomingdale's has an extensive marketing department with professionals who specifically target international customers. Patti Freeman Evans, senior manager of international marketing for Bloomingdale's, says, "The mission of our department is to communicate with both current and potential customers who do not live near a Bloomingdale's location. We want to make it easy for everyone to shop at Bloomingdale's." To accomplish this mission, the department has developed a number of programs.

The international marketing division offers numerous services: shopping assistance in various languages; assistance with shipping; delivery to local hotels; news and information regarding what's happening at Bloomingdale's; and appointments with in-store services such as personal shoppers, alterations, spas, and beauty services. There is also a staff of visitors center consultants to assist traveling customers with any special needs. Special discounts, service coupons, and other benefits for tourist customers are available.

The International Club is a special program for foreign customers. Membership is available to any customer visiting from abroad who signs up in a Bloomingdale's store. It entitles them to exclusive benefits not offered to the general public: special in-store offers, gifts, services, and savings; Bloomingdale's catalogs mailed directly to their homes; semiannual editions of Bloomingdale's *International Club Newsletter*; notification of special events; private invitations; and more.

Most Bloomingdale's stores have an International Service Desk/Visitors Center. When a foreign customer comes to this area and asks for shopping assistance in her native language, the consultant will find an associate who speaks that language. If the associate is working elsewhere in the store that day, he will be released from his normal responsibilities to accompany the customer for as long as he is needed. A considerable number of international customers take advantage of this service.

Discussion Questions

1. What are the unique needs of international customers and what services can Bloomingdale's offer to satisfy those needs?

2. Are international customers an attractive market to pursue? Why?

3. Will their needs vary depending on their nationality?

4. How can Bloomingdale's market its international services to attract more international customers?

Source: This case was prepared by Allison Karrh, University of Florida.

10

Toys "R" Us

"SANDY, WILL YOU AND JOHNNY PLEASE stop fighting. We're leaving as soon as we find Glamour Barbie for the birthday party you're going to tonight. I just don't understand why we can't find them. They should be here with the other dolls. Now we just need someone to help us find it. Finally I think I see a guy who works here."

"Excuse me. Could you tell me if you carry Glamour Barbie and, if so, where I can find it?"

"Ah, no. I just stock shelves, but I think maybe on aisle 10."

"Come on, kids. We'll just go to Wal-Mart and we can get everything we need in one stop."

Has this type of situation ever happened to you? Have you ever felt like you are the only customer in the store, yet when you do find an employee, he hasn't got a clue? This type of situation was becoming synonymous with Toys "R" Us. It was a big powerhouse that didn't have to rely on customer service to create sales. Instead, its toys practically sold themselves because it was the only big-store toy discounter of its kind for 16 years, and consumers were willing to search, on their own, through piles of toys to find what they wanted. But with retail discounters and superstores, such as Wal-Mart, Kmart, and Target, becoming increasingly competitive in the toy industry, Toys "R" Us had to implement a major restructuring of its organization. And after having to shut down 25 of its 650 U.S. stores, including 12 Kids "R" Us stores, Toys "R" Us realized it needed to revamp its business or prepare to surrender to the competitors.

Michael Goldstein, chief executive of Toys "R" Us, approved a $270 million restructuring plan for 1996 to get Toys "R" Us back on the right track. The main agenda was to expand and remodel its stores to better suit its customers' needs and wants and to take back its market share from competitors. First, Toys "R" Us introduced Babies "R" Us to compete directly with Baby Superstores and other baby-oriented stores. These stores offer parents a one-stop shopping trip for everything a baby needs from diapers and clothing to nursery furniture and baby food and formula. Each store provides more than 30,000 items for babies with a floor plan featuring panoramic viewing, wide aisles, and skylights. The first store opened in May 1996 in Westbury, Long Island, and the chain plans to launch nine more before the year's end.

Along with these new stores, Toys "R" Us has developed "Concept 2000," which will be unveiled in approximately 14 locations, three of which will be retrofits of existing stores. These are Toys "R" Us/Kids World superstores that combine all of the "R" Us concepts under one roof. Superstores are an advantage to Toys "R" Us because these stores only require 90,000 square feet, whereas dividing products into different stores requires more space. It is also an advantage to consumers not only because of lower prices, but also because they can pick up all their children's needs and wants in one place.

Although superstores are an advantage, they can also discourage consumers because of their large size. Therefore, Toys "R" Us is not focusing all of its efforts on these stores only. In addition to the Concept 2000 format, it's planning to open 35 new toy stores and 8 to 10 new Kids "R" Us stores in the United States this year. Internationally, it plans to add 55 new stores, including 20 franchise stores.

In 1999, Toys "R" Us's financial performance was declining as it faced increased competition from discount store chains such as Wal-Mart, Kmart, and Target as well as from electronic retailers like eToys and Amazon.com. Wal-Mart surpassed Toys "R" Us as the largest toy retailer by focusing on a limited assortment of the popular toys and offering them at low prices.

The increased pressure from competition forces Toys "R" Us to rethink its retail strategy. The consumers now have control of the steering wheel—they have the power to decide the future of Toys "R" Us. Parents have grown intolerant of the lack of attention and the haphazard arrangements at Toys "R" Us, especially when they can go right down the street to a retail discounter and purchase products for the same price—sometimes even lower. Toys "R" Us must now find new ways to attract customers who have become accustomed to price wars and their spoils, and who are always searching for fresh concepts and new merchandise. The "supermarket style" Toys "R" Us has been noted for, broad assortments plus crowded aisles, toys stacked so high they cannot be reached, and plain decor.

Toys "R" Us needs also to evaluate the potential impact of electronic toy retailers and what it needs to do to address this challenge.

Discussion Questions

1. What do you think of Toys "R" Us expanding internationally?

2. Do you think that Kids World superstores and Babies "R" Us will create a competitive edge for Toys "R" Us?

3. How can Toys "R" Us compete effectively against discount stores and electronic retailers?

Source: This case was prepared by Allison Karrh, University of Florida.

CASE **11**

Winn-Dixie and Dillard: Comparing Strategic Profit Models

ELLIS JACKSON WORKS IN THE FINANCE Department of Winn-Dixie Stores, Inc., a major food retailer with 1,159 stores in 13 southeastern and southwestern states and the Bahama Islands. Winn-Dixie has divisions in Jacksonville, Greenville, Montgomery, Tampa, Atlanta, Raleigh, Louisville, New Orleans, Charlotte, Orlando, Miami, and Fort Worth. It also has 12 subsidiaries.

His new boss, Sam Frogg, was hired from Dillard Department Stores, Inc., to be the chief financial officer. Dillard operates stores in Arkansas, Tennessee, Texas, New Mexico, Oklahoma, Missouri, Nebraska, Kansas, Louisiana, Nevada, Arizona, Illinois, Alabama, Ohio, North Carolina, South Carolina, Mississippi, Iowa, Utah, Florida, and Kentucky.

Frogg is concerned and somewhat confused about why the key financial ratios for Winn-Dixie are so different from those of Dillard. Specifically, executives at Dillard always stressed the importance of net profit margin, and Dillard's net profit margin percentage is significantly higher than Winn-Dixie's.

You may do the strategic profit models by hand by using the form accompanying this case or you may prepare the plan using the Integrated Interactive module on the disk accompanying the text. After installing the disks, go through the Strategic Profit Model Tutorial. Then, open Integrated Interactive, and plug in the numbers from the case.

On a separate sheet of paper, provide your explanation of why the ratios are different.

Discussion Questions

1. Construct strategic profit models using Exhibit 3 for Winn-Dixie and Dillard using data from the abbreviated income statements and balance sheets in Exhibits 1 and 2.

2. Explain, from a marketing perspective, why you would expect gross margin percentage, expenses-to-sales ratio, net profit margin, inventory turnover, and asset turnover to be different for a grocery store chain versus a department store chain.

3. Assess which chain has better overall financial performance.

EXHIBIT 1

Income Statements for Winn-Dixie Stores, Inc., and Dillard Department Stores, Inc.

	WINN-DIXIE (PERIOD ENDING 6/30/99)	DILLARD (PERIOD ENDING 1/30/99)
Net sales and other income	$14,255,369	$8,011,724
Less: Cost of goods sold	10,335,590	5,218,095
Gross margin	3,919,779	2,793,629
Less: Operating expenses	3,593,651	2,377,865
Less: Interest expenses	29,648	196,680
Total expenses	3,623,299	2,574,545
Net profit, pretax	296,480	219,084
Less: Taxes	114,145	83,825
Tax rate	38.50%	38.26%
Net profit after tax	$182,335	$135,259

Source: SEC 10K filings at www.sec.gov/edaux/searches.htm.

EXHIBIT 2

Balance Sheet Information for Winn-Dixie Stores, Inc.,
and Dillard Department Stores, Inc.

	WINN-DIXIE (PERIOD ENDING 6/30/99)	DILLARD (PERIOD ENDING 1/30/99)
Assets		
Current assets		
Accounts receivable	$ 188,314	$1,192,572
Merchandise inventory	1,425,098	2,157,010
Cash	24,746	72,401
Other current assets	159,832	15,728
Total current assets	1,797,990	3,437,711
Fixed assets		
Building, equipment, and other fixed assets, less depreciation	1,222,633	3,684,629
Other assets	128,524	1,055,219
Total assets	$3,149,147	$8,177,559

Source: SEC 10K filings at www.sec.gov/edaux/searches.htm.

EXHIBIT 3   Strategic Profit Model

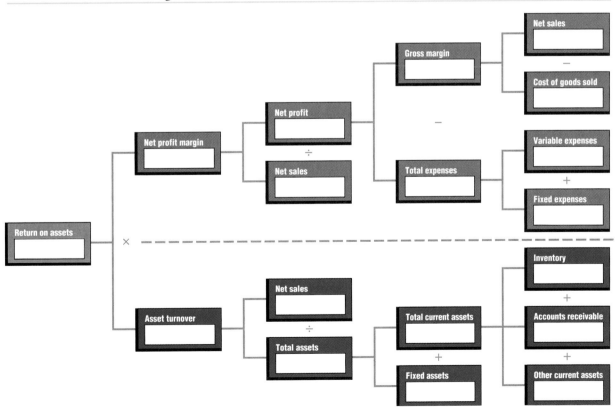

Stephanie's Boutique: Selecting a Store Location

STEPHANIE WILSON MUST DECIDE WHERE TO open a ready-to-wear boutique she's been contemplating for several years. Now in her late 30s, she's been working in municipal government ever since leaving college, where she majored in fine arts. She's divorced with two children (ages five and eight) and wants her own business, at least partly to be able to spend more time with them. She loves fashion, feels she has a flair for it, and has taken evening courses in fashion design and retail management. Recently she heard about a plan to rehabilitate an old arcade building in the downtown section of her midwestern city. This news crystallized her resolve to move now. She's considering three locations.

THE DOWNTOWN ARCADE

The city's central business district has been ailing for some time. The proposed arcade renovation is part of a master redevelopment plan, with a new department store and several office buildings already operating. Completion of the entire master plan is expected to take another six years.

Dating from 1912, the arcade building was once the center of downtown trade, but it's been vacant for the past 15 years. The proposed renovation includes a three-level shopping facility, low-rate garage with validated parking, and convention center complex. Forty shops are planned for the first (ground) floor, 28 more on the second, and a series of restaurants on the third.

The location Stephanie's considering is 30 feet square and situated near the main ground floor entrance. Rent is $20 per square foot, for an annual total of $18,000. If sales exceed $225,000, rent will be calculated at 8 percent of sales. She'll have to sign a three-year lease.

TENDERLOIN VILLAGE

The gentrified urban area of the city where Stephanie lives is nicknamed Tenderloin Village because of its lurid past. Today, however, the neat, well-kept brownstones and comfortable neighborhood make it feel like a yuppie enclave. Many residents have done the rehabilitation work themselves and take great pride in their neighborhood.

About 20 small retailers are now in an area of the Village adjacent to the convention center complex. Most of them are "ferns-and-quiche" restaurants. There are also three small women's clothing stores.

The site available to Stephanie is on the Village's main street on the ground floor of an old house. Its space is also about 900 square feet. Rent is $15,000 annually with no coverage clause. The landlord knows Stephanie and will require a two-year lease.

APPLETREE MALL

This suburban mall has been open for eight years. A successful regional center, it has three department stores and 100 smaller shops just off a major interstate highway about eight miles from downtown. Of its nine women's clothing retailers, three are in a price category considerably higher than what Stephanie has in mind.

Appletree has captured the retail business in the city's southwest quadrant, though growth in that sector has slowed in the past year. Nevertheless, mall sales are still running 12 percent ahead of the previous year. Stephanie learned of plans to develop a second shopping center east of town, which would be about the same size and character as Appletree Mall. But ground breaking is still 18 months away, and no renting agent has begun to enlist tenants.

The store available to Stephanie in Appletree is two doors from the local department store chain's mall outlet. At 1,200 square feet, it's slightly larger than the other two possibilities. But it's long and narrow—24 feet in front by 50 feet deep. Rent is $24 per square foot ($28,800 annually). In addition, on sales that exceed $411,500, rent is 7 percent of sales. There's an additional charge of 1 percent of sales to cover common-area maintenance and mall promotions. The mall's five-year lease includes an escape clause if sales don't reach $411,500 after two years.

Discussion Questions

1. Give the pluses and minuses of each location.

2. What type of store would be most appropriate for each location?

3. If you were Stephanie, which location would you choose? Why?

Source: This case was prepared by David Ehrlich, Marymount University.

Hutch: Locating a New Store

IN JUNE, AFTER RETURN-ING FROM A trip to the Bahamas, Dale Abell, vice president of new business development for the Hutch Corpora-tion, began a search for a good location to open a new store. After a preliminary search, Abell nar-rowed the choice to two locations, both in Geor-gia. He now faces the difficult task of thoroughly analyzing each location and determining which will be the site of the next store.

COMPANY BACKGROUND

The Hutch store chain was founded in 1952 by John Henry Hutchison, a musician and an ex-tremely successful insurance salesman. Hutchison established the headquarters in Richmond, Vir-ginia, where both the executive offices and one of two warehouse distribution centers are located. Hutch currently operates 350 popularly priced women's clothing stores throughout the Southeast and Midwest. Manufacturers ship all goods to these distribution centers. They are delivered "floor-ready" in that the vendor has attached price labels, UPC identifying codes, and source tags for security purposes, and has placed appropriate mer-chandise on hangers. Once at the distribution cen-ters, the merchandise is consolidated for reship-ment to the stores. Some staple merchandise, such as hosiery, is stored at these distribution centers. All Hutch stores are located within 400 miles of a distribution center. This way, as Abell explains, "A truck driver can deliver to every location within a 400-mile radius in two days."

Hutch Fashions

Hutch Fashions is considered one of the leading popular-priced women's fashion apparel chains in the Southeast. The stores carry trendy apparel se-lections in juniors', misses', and women's sizes, all at popular prices. The chain offers a complemen-tary array of accessories in addition to its main fea-tures of dresses, coats, and sportswear. Located mainly in strip centers and malls, these shops typi-cally require 4,000 to 5,000 square feet.

Hutch Extra

Hutch Extra stores are primarily located in strip centers and malls. They bear a strong resemblance to Hutch Fashions. The difference is that Hutch Extra stores require less space (from 2,000 to 3,000 square feet) and cater to women requiring large and half-size apparel. (Women who wear half-sizes require a larger size but are not tall enough to wear a standard large size. In other words, a size 18½ is the same as size 18 except that it is cut for a shorter woman.)

Hutch Fashions* Hutch Extra

Although Hutch Fashions and Hutch Extra stores selectively appear as separate entries, the corporate goal is to position both as a single entity. The com-bination store emerged in 1986 and is now used for all new stores.

The Hutch Fashions* Hutch Extra combina-tion occupies a combined space of 6,000 to 7,000 square feet with separate entrances for each en-tity. A partial wall separates the two frontal areas of the store but allows a combined checkout/cus-tomer service area in the rear. The new stores are primarily located in strip centers and can occa-sionally be found in malls. (Exhibit 1 shows a typ-ical layout.)

MARKETING STRATEGY

Customers

Hutch's target market is women between the ages of 18 and 40 who are in the lower-middle-to middle-income range. Abel explains, "We don't cater to any specific ethnic group, only to women who like to wear the latest fashions."

Product/Price

Hutch positions merchandise and price levels be-tween the mass merchandisers and the department stores. You won't find any blue-light specials or de-signer boutiques in a Hutch store. By avoiding di-rect competition for customers with the large discounters (Kmart and Wal-Mart) and the high-fashion department stores and specialty shops, Hutch has secured a comfortable niche for itself. "Our products must be priced at a level where our customers perceive our products to be elegant and fashionable but not too expensive," notes Abell.

Location

Hutch stores are located throughout the South-east and Midwest and must be within a 400-mile radius of a Hutch distribution center. Within this

EXHIBIT **1**

Layout of a Hutch
Fashions* Hutch
Extra Store

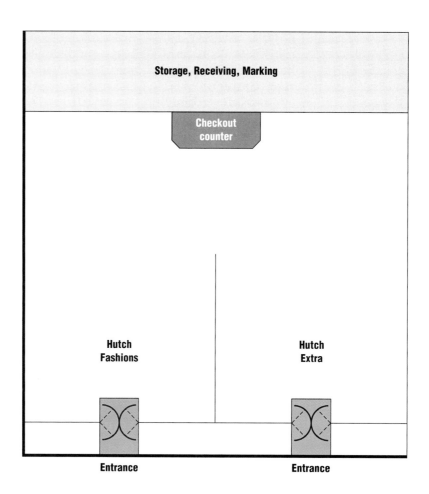

geographic area, Hutch stores are located in communities with a population range of 10,000 to 50,000 and a trade area of 50,000 to 150,000. These locations are characterized by a large concentration of people in the low- to middle-income brackets who work in agriculture and industry.

Hutch stores are primarily located in strip malls or strip centers—generally ones anchored by either a regional or national mass merchandiser (Wal-Mart or Kmart). In addition, these centers contain a mix of several nationally recognized and popular local tenants. Hutch stores are primarily located adjacent to the center's anchor. Mall locations must be on the main corridor as close to "center court," as economics (rent) will allow. Abell remarked, "We don't care if it's the only center in the country. If the only space available is at the end of the mall, we won't go in there. Our plan is to be a complement to the an-

chor and to feed off the traffic coming to it. We may have a reputation for being picky and having one of the toughest lease agreements in the business, but it's one of the main reasons for our continued success."

DATA SOURCES

Abell is using several reports generated by Claritas/UDS Data Service to help him decide which location to choose for the next Hutch store. He has chosen reports that describe the 10-mile ring around each of the proposed locations.

Exhibits 2 and 3 summarize these reports. They contain detailed population, household, race, income, education, and employment data plus figures on retail sales and number of establishments. The reports also provide information about women's apparel sales and give a market index that estimates the annual per-person spending potential

EXHIBIT 2

Population and
Competitive Profile,
10-Mile Ring from
Center of Dalton and
Hinesville, Georgia

		DALTON	HINESVILLE
Population	2005 projection	93,182	64,195
	1999 estimate	87,293	57,945
	1990 Census	79,420	49,853
	1980 Census	71,373	34,125
	% change, 1990–96	9.9%	16.2%
	% change, 1980–90	11.3%	46.1%
	In group quarters (military base)		
	1996	.9%	11.2%
Household	2005 projection	35,570	20,010
	1999 estimate	33,140	17,541
	1990 Census	29,340	14,061
	1980 Census	24,302	8,557
	% change, 1990–96	12.9%	24.7%
	% change, 1980–90	20.7%	64.3%
Families	1996 estimate	24,347	14,277
Race, 1999	White	92.0%	54.1%
	Black	4.9%	38.3%
	American Indian	0.2%	0.5%
	Asian or Pacific Islander	0.6%	3.1%
	Other	2.3%	4.0%
Age, 1999	0–20	31.2%	40.2%
	21–44	37.1%	47.0%
	45–64	21.7%	9.2%
	65+	9.9%	3.4%
	Median age, 1996	33.7	23.9
	Male	32.5	23.6
	Female	35.0	24.6
Household size, 1999	1 person	21.0%	15.2%
	2 persons	32.3%	26.6%
	3–4 persons	38.1%	45.7%
	5+ persons	8.7%	12.6%
Income, 1999	Median household income	$30,516	$23,686
	Average household income	$40,397	$28,677
Sex (% male)		49.1%	55.8%
Education, 1999	Population age 25+	49,298	22,455
	No high school diploma	41.0%	15.5%
	High school only	28.6%	41.2%
	College, 1–3 years	19.1%	29.7%
	College, 4+ years	11.3%	13.5%
Industry	Manufacturing: nondurable goods	42.3%	7.2%
	Retail trade	12.6%	23.3%
	Professional and related services	13.3%	21.4%
	Public administration	2.2%	20.0%
Retail sales (000)	Total	$706,209	$172,802
	General merchandise stores		
	Apparel stores	$26,634	$9,339
Retail establishments	General merchandise stores	12	3
	Women's apparel stores	21	8

EXHIBIT 3

	AREA SALES ($ Mil.)	AREA SALES PER CAPITA	U.S. SALES PER CAPITA	INDEX (AREA SALES ÷ U.S. SALES)
Dalton	$18.01	$206.26	$207.65	99
Hinesville	$8.97	$154.74	$207.65	75

for the trade area divided by the national average. (See Exhibit 3.) Dalton's 99 index means that the spending potential for women's clothing is slightly lower than the national average.

Finally, Abell is using Claritas/UDS's PRIZM™ lifestyle reports. These reports contain numeric figures and percentages on the population, households, families, sex, age, household size, and ownership of housing. An excerpt from the report is given in Exhibit 4. Some of the cluster group names are described in Exhibit 5.

THE POTENTIAL LOCATIONS

Dalton

Dalton produces most of the carpeting in the United States. Consequently, the carpet mills are the major employers in Dalton. Stain Master carpeting has been putting a strain on the City's water supply. Stain Master is said to require seven times the amount of water as regular carpeting and is rapidly becoming the largest proportion of carpeting produced. Expressing concern over market validity, Abell said, "If the Dalton area were ever to experience a severe drought, the carpet mills would be forced to drastically reduce production. The en-

suing layoffs could put half the population on unemployment."

The proposed site for the new store is the Whitfield Square shopping center located off the main highway approximately two miles from the center of town. (See Exhibit 6.) After meeting with the developer, Abell was pleased with several aspects of the strip center. He learned that the center has good visibility from the highway, will be anchored by both Kmart and Kroger (a large grocery chain), and has ample parking. Abell is also reasonably pleased with the available location within the center, which is one spot away from Kmart. However, he was displeased with the presence of two large out-parcels in front of the center that would reduce the number of parking spaces and direct visibility of the center. (An out-parcel is a freestanding structure at the front of a mall commonly a fast-food outlet, a bank, or a gas station.) Other tenants in the center include a nationally recognized shoe store, a beauty salon, two popular restaurants (Chinese and Mexican), and Little Caesar's Pizza at the end of the center, and a Century 21 real estate training school in the middle.

EXHIBIT 4

PRIZM CLUSTER	POPULATION, 1999	PERCENTAGE OF POPULATION
Dalton		
Big fish, small pond	4,727	5.4%
New homesteaders	6,030	6.9
Red, white & blues	31,123	35.7
Shotguns & pickups	8,881	10.2
Rural industrial	12,757	14.6
Mines & mills	7,694	8.8
Back country folks	4,293	4.9
Hinesville		
Military quarters	45,127	77.9
Scrub pine flats	3,476	6.0

EXHIBIT **5**   PRIZM Lifestyle Clusters

BIG FISH, SMALL POND

Small-town executive families; upper-middle incomes; age groups 35–44, 45–54; predominantly white. This group is married, family-oriented, and conservative. Their neighborhoods are older. Best described as captains of local industry, they invest in their homes and clubs, and vacation by car in the U.S.

RURAL INDUSTRIAL

Low-income, blue-collar families; lower-middle incomes; age groups <24, 25–34, predominantly white, high Hispanic. Once dependent on railroads and major markets, 18-wheelers freed light industry to go farther afield to seek the low-cost, nonunion labor found in this cluster, which is comprised of hundreds of blue-collar mill towns on American's rural backroads.

MINES & MILLS

Older families; mine and mill towns; poor; age groups 55–64, 65+; predominantly white. Down the Appalachians, across the Ozarks to Arizona, and up the Missouri, this cluster is exactly as its name implies. This older, mostly single population with a few children lives in the midst of scenic splendor.

SHOTGUNS & PICKUPS

Rural blue-collar workers and families; middle income; age groups 35–44, 45–54; predominantly white. This cluster is found in the Northeast, the Southeast, and in the Great Lakes and Piedmont industrial regions. They are in blue-collar jobs; most are married with school-age kids. They are churchgoers who also enjoy bowling, hunting, sewing, and attending car races.

BACK COUNTRY FOLKS

Older African-American farm families; lower-middle income; age groups 55–64, 65+; predominantly white. This cluster is centered in the Eastern uplands along a wide path from the Pennsylvania Poconos to the Arkansas Ozarks. Anyone who visits their playgrounds

in Branson, Missouri, or Gatlinburg, Tennessee, can attest that these are the most blue-collar neighborhoods in America. Centered in the Bible Belt, many back country folks are hooked on Christian and country music.

SCRUB PINE FLATS

Older African-American farm families; poor; age groups 55–64, 65+; predominantly black. This cluster is found mainly in the coastal flatlands of the Atlantic and Gulf states from the James to the Mississippi rivers. These humid, sleepy rural communities, with a mix of blacks and whites, live in a seemingly timeless, agrarian rhythm.

NEW HOMESTEADERS

Young middle-class families; middle income; age groups 35–44, 45–54; predominantly white. This cluster has above-average college education. Executives and professionals work in local service fields such as administration, communications, health, and retail. Most are married; the young have children, the elders do not. Life is homespun with a focus on crafts, camping, and sports.

RED, WHITE & BLUES

Small-town blue-collar families; middle income; age groups 35–54, 55–64; predominantly white, with skilled workers primarily employed in mining, milling, manufacturing, and construction. Geocentered in the Appalachians, Great Lakes industrial region, and Western highlands, these folks love the outdoors.

MILITARY QUARTERS

GIs and surrounding off-base families; lower-middle income; age groups under 24, 25–34; ethnically diverse. Since this cluster depicts military life with personnel living in group quarters, its demographics are wholly atypical because they are located on or near military bases; this skews toward our principal harbors and defense perimeters. Racially integrated, and with the highest index for adults under 35, "Military Quarters" likes fast cars, bars, and action sports.

Hinesville

Like Dalton, Hinesville has one major employer, the Fort Stuart army base. Abell recalls that popular-priced stores generally do very well in military towns. Additionally, Fort Stuart is a rapid-deployment force base. Even though the United States currently enjoys stable relations with the rest of the world, Abell is concerned with a comment by a Hinesville native, "If these guys have to ship out, this place will be a ghost town."

The location under consideration is the Kmart Plaza at the junction of State Route 119 and US Highway 82. (See Exhibit 7.) The center is anchored by Kmart and a grocery store that is part of a popular eastern chain. The two anchors are lo-

cated side by side in the middle of the center. The spot available in the center is a 6,800–square-foot combination of three smaller units immediately adjacent to Kmart. Other tenants in the center include a bookstore, a waterbed store, a shoe store, an electronics retailer, a yogurt store, a video store, and a movie theater.

Discussion Questions

1. How do the people living in the trade areas compare with Hutch's target customer?

2. How do the proposed locations, including the cities, tenant mix, and the locations within the malls, fit with Hutch's locational requirements?

3. Which location would you select? Why?

EXHIBIT **6**

Whitfield Square
Shopping Center,
Dalton, Georgia

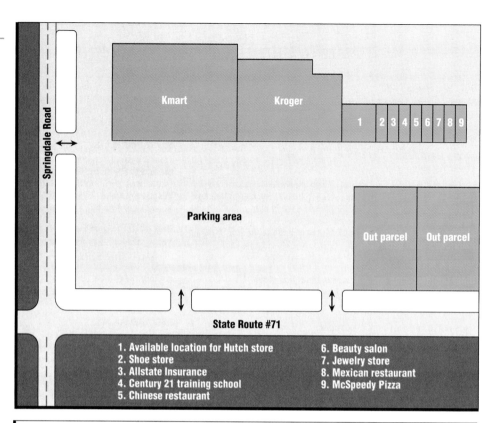

1. Available location for Hutch store
2. Shoe store
3. Allstate Insurance
4. Century 21 training school
5. Chinese restaurant
6. Beauty salon
7. Jewelry store
8. Mexican restaurant
9. McSpeedy Pizza

EXHIBIT **7**

Kmart Plaza,
Hinesville, Georgia

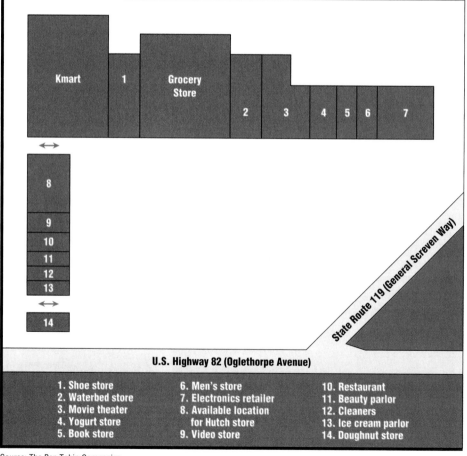

1. Shoe store
2. Waterbed store
3. Movie theater
4. Yogurt store
5. Book store
6. Men's store
7. Electronics retailer
8. Available location for Hutch store
9. Video store
10. Restaurant
11. Beauty parlor
12. Cleaners
13. Ice cream parlor
14. Doughnut store

Source: The Ben Tobin Companies.

14

Marriott's Success in Managing Human Resources to Create an Organizational Culture

IN OCTOBER 1993, THE MARRIOTT CORPORATION, known for its lodging services, divided into two separate companies: Marriott International and Host Marriott. Marriott International manages lodging service businesses and has operations in 28 countries with almost 200,000 employees and 1995 sales of more than $38 billion. The Host Marriott, formerly part of the Marriott Corporation, focuses on real estate ownership.

J. Willard (Bill) Marriott and his wife Alice started the Marriott Corporation in 1927 by operating a root beer stand in Washington, D.C. Thirty years later, the couple opened the Twin Bridges Marriott Motor Hotel in Arlington, Virginia, near National Airport. The hotel boasted 300 rooms and a drive-in registration. It was the largest of its kind at that time.

In 1996, Marriott International grew to include over 1,000 hotels across six established hotel brands throughout the world. The brands include the four- and five-star Marriott Hotels, Resorts and Suites properties; moderately priced Courtyard by Marriott hotels; economy-minded Fairfield Inn Hotels; Residence Inn properties for extended-stay travelers; Marriott Conference Centers; and Marriott Vacation Club International (time share properties). In 1995, Marriott also purchased 49 percent interest in the Ritz-Carlton Hotel Company.

Although Marriott has become a major player in the lodging business, it maintains that relationships are an integral part of the company's mission. J.W. Marriott, Jr. (son of Bill Marriott), serves as the chairman and president of Marriott International. He is committed to enhancing the relations with the company's associates, guests, franchisees, owners, and others. To assist in this, a positive and open environment is established in each location. Associates are valued, treated with respect, appreciated for their cultural and intellectual diversity, given opportunities to learn and develop, and encouraged to be candid and innovative. The hope is that this environment will foster exceptional service for the guests so that the company may grow and prosper.

Mr. Marriott viewed his organization in the same way he viewed his own family. The principles of cooperation, support, and openness are applied to both "families." Marriott, Jr., stated that his father felt that his employees should be looked after. "My father knew if he had happy employees, he would have happy customers and that would result in a good bottom line," said Marriott.

One way that Marriott is retaining its employees and increasing customer satisfaction is through "guest service associates" (GSAs). This program empowers its associates to perform almost all tasks that would assist a guest upon her check-in to a hotel. The usual scenario begins with a GSA meeting guests at their vehicles, picking up keys to the assigned rooms, and escorting the guests immediately to their rooms. If there is a problem with the room assignment, the GSA can address it instead of having to solicit the help of a desk clerk. A GSA also performs the duties of a concierge; the associate can acquire tickets or reservations upon a guest's request.

The benefits of this service are apparent on many levels. The GSA becomes involved with the guests for the duration of their stay. This gives the GSA a sense of ownership of the business and a stake in each guest's happiness. GSAs also have the opportunity to earn high tips from the guests.

The guests receive special attention from these GSAs, which is unique for today's consumers. Good, consistent customer service is increasingly hard to find. Customers seem to be grateful when they find extraordinary one-on-one treatment from any establishment. Marriott executives believe that taking care of its associates is the key to its success. This is to be done by treating people fairly, ethically, honestly, and in a caring manner. Also, opportunity for an individual to grow professionally is important to the company. An environment that is positive and generates teamwork and instills pride is important as well.

Discussion Questions

1. What problems could arise from such open and supportive work environments? How could a manager combat them?

2. Marriott International is quite large and has diverse lodging divisions. How do you think the corporate headquarters keeps each division employee-oriented?

Source: This case was prepared by Allison Karrh, University of Florida.

The Computer Shoppe: Database Retailing

IT WAS JULY 1, 2000, as Mr. Fred Webster sat at his desk in the back room of his Computer Shoppe franchise. On his lap was a thick printout of five years worth of customer information concerning past computer system purchasers. Although sales had picked up since he had moved into his new location within the mall, there was still much room for growth. Since Computer Shoppe franchisees had a lot of autonomy in the running of their local operations, Fred was wondering how he could leverage the data he had collected to increase sales.

THE COMPUTER SHOPPE

The Computer Shoppe's home computer channel consisted of retail stores selling personal computers, peripherals, TV games, software, calculators, and accessories. They were located in high-traffic areas, particularly in shopping malls, and catered to the family and home office/small business consumer. Computer Shoppe stores offered postsales technical support and services that were second to none in Canada. There were a total of 53 locations in Canada, with 24 in Alberta. Fred's store was the only Computer Shoppe in Calgary.

Computer Shoppe's parent company, Heathcliff, operated a number of computer product companies, of which the Computer Shoppe chain had the most outlets.

The Computer Shoppe franchisee agreement gave the store owner a great deal of autonomy and flexibility. Heathcliff did run a distributor, Micro Distributors, from which Computer Shoppe stores purchased most of their merchandise. However, they were not limited to buying from Micro Distributors and could potentially purchase as much as they pleased from any other distributor. In most cases, however, Micro Distributors offered the most competitive prices and the best support; thus it was in the store's best interest to deal exclusively with them. The franchisee was free to set prices for all products with the caveat that he or she was not running the business into the ground.

Each region received a certain level of marketing support from the head office in the form of newspaper inserts and flyers. Flyers were distributed to a number of postal code areas within the city, as chosen by the franchisee. Fred traditionally selected postal code areas surrounding the mall but never really measured which areas were most effective. Additional local marketing efforts, at the franchisee's expense, were expected. The head office would reimburse the franchisee up to 0.5 percent of sales for local advertising spending. In the past Fred had experimented with radio advertising and mall publication inserts with varying degrees of success. He was willing to devote 50 percent of his maximum advertising allowance to a new marketing approach. The type of advertising that could be claimed for reimbursement was a gray area but Fred was confident that direct marketing costs would be reimbursed. His concern was with the upfront cost of setting up a large customer database, which the head office would probably not deem advertising. However, he was willing to go beyond 0.5 percent of sales if necessary.

CALGARY'S COMPUTER MARKET

The retail computer market had been traditionally divided into two types of establishments: brand-name resellers and private-label clone (PLC) dealers. The brand-name resellers included retailers such as Computer Shoppe, Future Shop, Radio Shack, and Business Depot, which carried such computer brands as Compaq, IBM, Apple, and Toshiba. The PLC dealers built their own computer systems and marketed them under their own names. This gave the PLC dealers more flexibility in building systems to customer specifications, versus preconfigured systems from name-brand manufacturers, but sacrificed quality and postsales support. Recently, the distinction between these retailers had begun to blur as PLC dealers began to sell some name-brand products and some traditional name-brand resellers carried built-to-order systems.

Direct competitors to the Computer Shoppe in the Calgary market were currently Future Shop, Business Depot, and Electronics Boutique. Both Future Shop and Business Depot carried very similar lines of products to the Computer Shoppe, including hardware, software, and computer-related accessories. However, only Electronics Boutique, a software-only retailer, could match Computer Shoppe's breadth of computer and game system software. Computer Shoppe and Electronics Boutique were strictly located within malls and shopping centres, while Future Shop and Business Depot were big box retailers.

Fred's store was located within the largest north Calgary mall, Stonehedge Mall, near the food court. There were two other retailers within the mall that carried computer-related products: Radio Shack and Adventure Electronics. However, these retailers had a very limited selection of merchandise and were not considered a threat. Diagonally opposite the Stonehedge Mall was Hylands Plaza, which housed a Business Depot and Calgary's only other Future Shop. Also in the vicinity were two PLC dealers selling hardware and software products.

FRED'S DATA COLLECTION

Exhibit 1 shows the data entry screen for a typical computer system sale. Only during computer purchases did a screen come up allowing *all* purchaser information to be entered. Once customer infor-

mation had been entered, the program had to be told to save the information to a customer database file, which each employee was told to do for computer purchases. Otherwise the customer information was included in the invoices database. For software or accessory sales, a name would be entered only if payment was by credit card. An address was never entered and there was no option to save the information into the customer database. For this reason, only computer system information was kept. The customer database file contained all the fields seen in Exhibit 1 and could be sorted or parsed accordingly. There were over 400 system purchases in his database.

FRED'S COMPUTER SHOPPE

Over the past few years, Fred had tried to differentiate Computer Shoppe not on price, but on the basis of salespeople's knowledge and service. Staff was not commissioned individually; instead a bonus was distributed to all employees based on hours worked if the sales target for the month was met. To become familiar with software titles, employees were encouraged to borrow and evaluate software. The store was neat in appearance with four to five computer systems on display, a glass enclosure

---

EXHIBIT **1**

Sample of Customer
Information Screen

Date: 05/06/00		Time: 13:42:00		Invoice #:A4584	
Qty:	**SKU:**	**Description:**		**Price:**	**Total:**
1	453452	Compaq 526 CDS		$2499.99	$2499.99
1	324999	Canon BJ-200		$ 299.88	$ 299.88
1	857304	16′ Printer Cable		$ 19.88	$ 19.88
1	384932	500 Sheets Husky Paper		$ 5.99	$ 5.99
	PST:				$ 226.06
	GST:				$ 197.80
	Total:				$3253.60

Name:	Mr. George Bothwell
Address:	34 College Rd.
City:	Calgary
Province:	AB
Postal Code:	T2J 5P7
Payment Method:	VISA
Card Number:	4535-454-454-454
Expiry Date:	12/02
Phone Number: (403) 596–8743	

showcasing handheld electronics, and software and accessories arranged on shelving along the walls and in an aisle rack.

According to company averages, based on the size of Fred's store, his annual sales should reach $1.5 million with a high near $1.8 million. Unfortunately, even though sales had grown from last year, he estimated 2000 sales would reach only $1.2 million. His revenues were broken down as follows: 35 percent hardware, 35 percent software, and 30 percent accessories. (Accessories included replacement cartridges for printers, paper, diskettes, cleaning supplies, disk cases, and stands.) Most profits, however, came from software, 55 percent, followed by accessories, 35 percent, and lastly hardware, 10 percent. Hardware was certainly the least attractive product in terms of gross margin, but Fred deemed it was a way to differentiate his store and to present cross-selling opportunities.

FUTURE MARKETING POSSIBILITIES

Fred felt there was a lot of room for growth within his business and wondered if he could somehow utilize this customer database to achieve that growth. His primary goals were to increase profitability and sales. Traffic creation was not a main concern for Fred since that was one of the responsibilities of the mall. He was positioned well in a high-traffic area near the food court. Since the business was currently profitable, Fred was fairly conservative in his choices.

Fred had not done much analysis of the information he had collected on system purchasers (Exhibit 1). He wondered what sort of analysis might be helpful and even if he was collecting the right information. He also wondered whether it would be worth the trouble of collecting information about other purchases made in his store. He thought he could use the lists he had to undertake direct-mail or telemarketing programs, but then again he was considering a loyalty rewards program and he knew he couldn't do all of these on his limited budget.

Discussion Questions

1. What would you recommend Fred do?

Source: Matt Brudzynski, Loretta Lo, and Patrick Spence prepared this case under the supervision of Professor Michael Pearce, Eaton/NSERC/SSHRC chair in retailing, Richard Ivey School of Business, the University of Western Ontario. © Richard Ivey School of Business.

CASE 16

Merchandise Planning Problems

1. Clothes for Men casuals has $20 million net sales. Average inventory at retail is $17 million. What is Clothes for Men's inventory turnover?

2. What is inventory turnover of a pet shop chain with annual sales of $20 million, average inventory at cost of $6 million, and a gross margin of 40 percent?

3. What is the GMROI for each of the following merchandise categories in a bookstore?

	TEXTBOOKS	GENERAL READING	REFERENCE BOOKS	NEWSPAPERS MAGAZINES
Annual sales	$800,000	$450,000	$600,000	$100,000
Average inventory (at cost)	$70,000	$110,000	$250,000	$10,000
Gross margin	10%	25%	40%	12%

Which of these categories is most profitable for the bookstore? Should the bookstore eliminate the least profitable category?

4. What is the annual inventory turnover for a retailer with the following monthly sales levels?

MONTH	SALES	BOM INVENTORY
January	$14,000	$40,000
February	13,000	38,000
March	13,000	39,000
April	17,000	41,000
May	16,000	40,000
June	14,000	38,500
July		40,000

5. What are the retail and cost inventory values of Sound Music at the end of the month of October based on the following accounting information?
   a. Beginning-of-month (BOM) inventory worth $200,000 at cost and $300,000 at retail.
   b. Purchases made during the month worth $250,000 at cost and $350,000 at retail.
   c. $14,000 paid for freight charges.
   d. $260,000 net sales of retail, with a cost of goods sold at $180,000.
   e. $10,000 total markdowns.
   f. $300 in employee discounts.
   g. $4,800 allowance for shrinkage.

6. Crafts and Things had sales of $102,000 during June. Its end-of-month (EOM) stock was $300,000 and its BOM stock was $270,000. What was its additions to stock during June?

7. The annual sales of Harry's Stereo chain was $56,000,000. The average inventory at cost was $40,000,000 and the gross margin was 43 percent. What were the chain's GMROI, inventory turnover, and average stock-to-sales ratio?

8. A tennis shop has developed the following merchandise plan:

Planned EOM stock	$45,000
Projected BOM stock	$35,000
Actual on order (what is on order for the month)	$25,000
Plan monthly sales	$10,000
Plan reductions for the month	$2,000

9. Gifts, Etc., a small gift-and-craft store, has the following plan for April:

Sales	$35,000
BOM stock	$100,000
EOM stock	$97,500
Planned reductions	$1,250
Planned gross margin	40%

What are the planned purchases for the store at retail and at cost?

10. Based on the following information from the merchandise budget plan for a women's accessory department in a specialty store, what is the open-to-buy as of April 1?

Planned monthly sales	$124,000
BOM inventory	$150,000
EOM inventory	$160,000
April merchandise already received	$90,000
April merchandise on order	$36,000
Planned reductions	$25,000

11. Forecast the sales for the next sales period for a retailer using exponential smoothing and the following information:

Old forecast	=	100 units
Actual demand	=	67 units
Alpha	=	.08

12. What is the order point, and how many units should be ordered if a food retailer has an item with a 10-day lead time, 3-day review time, and daily demand of 15 units? A total of 75 units are on hand and the retailer must take a safety stock of 50 units to maintain a 95 percent service level.

McFadden's Department Store: Preparation of a Merchandise Budget Plan

MCFADDEN'S DEPART-MENT STORE HAS BEEN a profitable family-owned business since its beginning in 1910. Last year's sales volume was $180 million. More recently, however, many of its departments have been losing ground to national stores moving into the area. To complicate this problem, the National Retail Federation (NRF) predicts recession. The NRF estimates a 6.5 percent drop in sales in the coming year for the Pacific Coast, where McFadden's operates.

Department 121 has one of the more profitable departments in the store, maintaining a gross margin of 55 percent. Its basic merchandise is young men's clothing. Last year sales reached $2,780,750 for the July–December season. The highest sales period is the back-to-school period in August, when autumn fashions are supported by strong promotional advertising. Reductions (including markdowns, discounts to employees, and shrinkage) typically run 20 percent of sales. The percentage of reductions are spread throughout the season as follows:

JULY	AUG.	SEPT.	OCT.	NOV.	DEC.
10	20	15	10	10	35

By month the percentage of annual sales for Department 121 within this six-month period had been distributed as follows:

	JULY	AUG.	SEPT.	OCT.	NOV.	DEC.
1996	3.6	10.1	9.2	6.4	4.8	9.1
1997	3.5	10.3	9.6	6.8	5.3	8.6
1998	3.5	10.5	9.6	6.2	5.5	8.2
1999	3.0	10.3	9.8	6.6	5.5	8.0

A pre-Christmas sale has been planned in an attempt to counterbalance the slackened sales period following the first of the year. The buyer has decided to bring in some new merchandise for the sale to go along with the remaining fall fashion merchandise. The buyer expects that this will increase December's percentage of annual sales to 30 percent above what it would be without the sale. Top management has stressed that the department achieve a gross margin return on investment (GMROI) of 250 percent. Forecasted ending stock level in December is $758,000.

Additional information is available on the historical stock-to-sales ratio for this type of department. This information is taken from a similar department in another store that happens to have a lower average stock-to-sales ratio.

JULY	AUG.	SEPT.	OCT.	NOV.	DEC.
3.0	1.9	2.1	2.4	2.5	2.2

In essence, this is the information that the manager of Department 121 has available for the preparation of his merchandise plan.

Assignment

Your task is to prepare a merchandise budget plan. You may do the plan by hand by using the form in Exhibit 1 or you may prepare the plan using the Excel spreadsheet on the disk accompanying the text. You will have to prepare some intermediate calculations before inputting your answers onto the spreadsheet. After installing the disks, open the Integrated Tutorial and go through the merchandise budget plan segment. Then, open Interactive Merchandise Budget, and plug in the numbers from the case. On a separate sheet of paper, explain how you determined the sales forecast, percentage of sales per month, and the monthly stock-to-sales ratios.

Source: This case was prepared by Michael Levy, Babson College, and Harold Koenig, Oregon State University.

EXHIBIT 1   Form for Merchandise Budget Plan

McFadden's Merchandise Budget

Planning Data

SALES FORECAST $

$$\text{Planned GMROI} = \frac{\text{Gross Margin}}{\text{Net Sales}} \times \frac{\text{Net Sales}}{\text{Inventory Costs}}$$

$$= \frac{\$ \quad}{\$ \quad} \times \frac{\$ \quad}{\$ \quad}$$

$$\frac{\text{Sales}}{\text{Inventory Costs}} \times (100\% - GM\%) = \text{Inventory Turnover}$$

$$\boxed{} \times \boxed{\quad \% \quad} = \boxed{}$$

$$12 \div \text{Inventory Turnover} = \text{B.O.M. Stock/Sales}$$

$$\boxed{} + \boxed{} = \boxed{}$$

Forecasted Ending Inventory $\boxed{\$ \quad}$

	%
Markdowns	$
Discounts	$
Shortages	$
Total Reductions	$

The Plan

		Jan	Feb	Mar	Apr	May	Jun	Jul	Aug	Sept	Oct	Nov	Dec	Total (Average)	Remarks
% Distribution of Sales by Month	1													100.0%	History/Projection
Monthly Sales	2														Step (1) × Net Sales
% Distribution of Reductions/Mo	3													100.0%	History/Projection
Monthly Reductions	4														Step (3) × Net Sales
B.O.M. Stock/Sales Ratios	5														Adjusted by Mo. Sales Fluctuations
B.O.M. Stock ($000)	6												(Forecasted End Inventory)		Step (2) × Step (5)
E.O.M. Stock ($000)	7														EOM Jan = BOM Feb
Monthly Additions to Stock ($000)	8														Steps 2 + 4 + 7 − 6 Sales + Reductions + EOM − BOM

CASE 18

Nolan's Finest Foods: Category Management

NOLAN'S FINEST FOODS IS A FULL-SERVICE retailer that offers shoppers the convenience of one-stop shopping at its high-end food-and-drug combo stores in the San Francisco Bay area. The chain features a variety of high-quality products at competitive prices but uses promotional pricing as well. Historically, Nolan's has enjoyed great success in its markets and had led the region for several years. However, on this winter morning Roberto Ignacio, the director of strategic planning, had a more immediate concern. The wire services had reported a few weeks ago that the Valumart grocery chain had announced plans for the construction of 10 new food-and-drug combo centers throughout Nolan's markets. After pouring over current research and financial results, a decision had been made to examine category management as a defense against the encroachment of Valumart.

To date Nolan's did not have any experience with category management. A decision was also made to pilot test category management in some test categories before implementing a systemwide rollout. One of the categories chosen for the test was shampoo. Roberto's immediate assignment was to review the product category and report back to management with an initial report. As Roberto looked out of his window at the scenic sunset over the San Francisco Bay, he reviewed the events of the past few weeks and the information that he had obtained on the shampoo category. He had obtained several third-party reports (Exhibits 1, 2, and 3) that provided background information about national trends in the shampoo category and trends in supermarkets. Another report (Exhibit 4) provided him with information on how Nolan's shampoo sales compared to the rest of the market. However, these reports did not provide Roberto with information on how Nolan's stacked up against the competition in terms of its assortment and pricing. After some checking around, Roberto found that he could order reports from third-party vendors that would provide him with an analysis of Nolan's and the competition on product mix and pricing. He had placed an urgent order for these

EXHIBIT 1

Total U.S. Supermarket Dynamics: Shampoo—Aeorsol, Liquid, Lotion, and Powder

52 WEEKS	# ACTIVE UPCs	% NEW UPCs	# UPCs HANDLED	UPC DOLLAR VELOCITY
Category	1,974	15%	235	$1.64
Brands	1,714	16	229	1.65
Private label	241	12	5	1.33
Generic	19	—	1	1.00

Source: *Nielsen Marketing Research, Nielsen Highlights, Category Performance Report.* Copyright 1992, *Nielsen Marketing Research.*

EXHIBIT 2

Shampoo Dollar Share

TRADE CHANNEL	12 MONTHS LAST YEAR	12 MONTHS THIS YEAR
Food	51.7%	50.5%
Drug	25.6	25.0
Mass merchant	22.7	24.5

Source: *Nielsen Marketing Research: Procision.*

EXHIBIT 3

Shampoo Growth

TRADE CHANNEL	DOLLAR SALES % CHANGE VERSUS A YEAR AGO
Food	0.9%
Drug	4.2
Mass merchant	8.1

Source: *Nielsen Marketing Research: Procision.*

EXHIBIT 4

Dollar Sales: Percent Change versus A Year Ago

	MARKET		NOLAN'S FINEST	
	13 WEEKS	52 WEEKS	13 WEEKS	52 WEEKS
Total dollar sales	+.1	+1.2	−10.6	−4.5
HBA department	+1.5	+4.2	−8.5	−4.3
Shampoo category	−3.5	+.7	−19.6	−9.7

Source: *Nielsen Marketing Research, SCAN*FACT PC for Retailers.*

analyses, which had arrived this morning through courier (Exhibits 5, 6, and 7).

UPC	Supermarket terminology for SKU (stockkeeping unit)
UPCs handled	Average number of UPCs stocked by food stores
UPC dollar velocity	Revenue per UPC per store per week
HBA	Health and beauty aids
Market	All food stores
Remaining market	All food stores excluding Nolan's

EXHIBIT **5**

Competitive Price Comparison for Shampoo: Counts of Items Showing Differences from the Base Zone (Nolan's Finest Foods)

	NOLAN'S	FOOD #1	MASS MERCH.	CHAIN DRUG	FOOD #2
Competition is higher	0	87	0	101	0
Competition is same	103	0	0	0	59
Competition is lower	0	16	103	2	44
Competition does not carry	0	0	0	0	0

Source: *Nielsen Marketing Research, Nielsen Retail Price Simulator.*

Here are explanations of a few terms in the analyses: After reviewing these reports he concluded that there were several possible courses of action.

As Roberto headed for the water cooler, feeling upbeat in the thought that he had a handle on the shampoo category, he ran into Hal Jeffreys, who was a longtime veteran of Nolan's and a vice president of information systems. Knowing that Hal had at one time managed Health and Beauty Aids at Nolan's, Roberto mentioned his review of the shampoo category and the category management initiative. Hal mentioned that for years he had a simple approach for "category management." He would begin by generating a list of slow sellers in the category and then try to replace these slow sellers with new products or by increasing the shelf space for existing products. With the new information systems that Nolan's had installed in the past year, generating a slow seller list was very easy. To prove his point Hal walked back with Roberto to his office and, using his PC, generated a slow seller report for the shampoo category (Exhibit 8). "See, technology has made this a real cinch," said Hal and wondered whether the expense and effort of category management would produce net improvements over and above this very simple "knock off the slow seller" approach. "I'll try to come to your presentation tomorrow," said Hal as he left Roberto's office.

As Hal left his office, Roberto sank back into his chair with a knot in his stomach. He felt that he had jumped the gun in thinking that he had a

EXHIBIT **6**   Brand Importance Report for Shampoo: Nolan's Foods versus Remaining Market for 13 Weeks

DESCRIPTION	CHAIN SALES	CHAIN RANK	REM. MKT. RANK	REM. MKT. SALES	CHAIN MKT. SHARE	CHAIN CATEGORY IMPT.	REM. MKT. CAT. IMPT.
Clean & Soft	$108,826	1	1	$ 512,345	17.5%	14.5	13.0
1st Impressions	77,672	2	3	370,341	17.3	10.3	9.4
Mane Tame	64,446	3	4	244,160	20.9	8.6	6.2
Bargain Bubbles	56,864	4	2	433,300	11.6	7.6	11.0
Silky Style	43,198	5	6	147,773	22.6	5.8	3.7
Elegance	30,869	6	5	181,075	14.6	4.1	4.6

Source: *Nielsen Marketing Research, SCAN*FACT PC for Retailers.*

EXHIBIT 7 Product Mix Summary Report: Shampoo Dollar Sales—13 Weeks

	CLEAN & SOFT	1ST IMPRESSIONS	MANE TAME	BARGAIN BUBBLES	SILKY STYLE	ELEGANCE	PRIVATE LABEL
ITEMS CARRIED							
Nolan's	25	25	15	21	13	5	7
Rem. mkt.	25	39	28	42	20	16	28
SIZES CARRIED							
Nolan's	6	6	6	2	4	1	4
Rem. mkt.	7	10	11	3	5	4	6
TYPES CARRIED							
Nolan's	6	7	6	19	4	5	6
Rem. mkt.	6	10	8	32	5	7	21

Source: *Nielsen Marketing Research, SCAN*FACT PC for Retailers.*

EXHIBIT 8   Slow Mover Report: Shampoo for Nolan's Foods, 13 Weeks versus A Year Ago

ITEM	CHAIN SALES	CHAIN MKT. SHR.	CHAIN SUBCAT IMPT.	REM. MKT. GROWTH	CHAIN GROWTH	CHAIN AVG. % STORES SELLING
Golden JJB Lq T 3 oz.	$ 3	9.9%	.0	−51.2-	−50.0	0%
1st Imprs. DF ND Lot. 11 oz.	10	.7	.0	−59.4	−99.4	0
Gentle GLD Lq. 11 oz.	11	100.0	.0	−100.0	9.6	0
Golden AV Lq. T 3 oz.	12	22.4	.0	13.2	−69.2	1
Suds PB Lq. 8 oz.	14	6	.0	107.1	2.9	0
Silky Style X-B Lq. 18 oz.	14	1.6	.0	−65.6	−99.5	0

Source: *Nielsen Marketing Research, SCAN*FACT PC for Retailers.*

handle on the shampoo category. Things seemed to be more complicated than they had appeared earlier in the day. Roberto wondered whether the shampoo category seemed so difficult because it was the first attempt at category management. In any case his immediate concern was to prepare for his presentation tomorrow. Since Hal Jeffreys would be in the audience, he knew that he would have to address the "knock out the slow sellers" perspective.

Discussion Questions

1. What are the national sales trends in the shampoo category?

2. What are the differences in shampoo sales trends at Nolan's compared to the national trends?

3. What could be causing these differences?

4. Suggest a plan of action.

Source: This case was written by Professor Kirthi Kalyanam, Retail Management Institute, Santa Clara University. © Dr. Kirthi Kalyanam.

Stan's Shirts

STAN SOPER HAS A 600-SQUARE-FOOT T-shirt store in a good mall location. He has all colors and sizes plus hundreds of designs for heat-embossing onto the shirts. Every shirt sells for $10. In his area, Stan estimates he has about a steady 12 percent share of a 100,000-units-per-year customized T-shirt market. Stan has found this to be a nonseasonal business. Sales hardly vary from one month to the next.

Stan's costs are

Store lease	$1,400 a month
T-shirts	$4 each
Embossing decals	$.50 each
Embossing equipment	$24,000
Store fixtures	$14,400
Telephone, postage, and so on	$125 per month

Stan's advertising budget is $200 per month. He pays one store assistant $240 per week ($1,040 a month) and draws a salary for himself of $300 per week ($1,300 a month). His waste (T-shirts spoiled by a poor or misapplied decal) runs around 2 percent of T-shirts sold.

Discussion Questions

1. What's the unit contribution for the T-shirts?
2. What is Stan's monthly break-even point?
3. What market share does he need to break even?
4. What is his monthly profit?
5. Because of some new fashion announcements he has just received, Stan expects T-shirt sales in his area to increase to about 144,000 next year. He's considering raising his advertising budget by $800 per month.
   - a. If the advertising budget is raised, how many T-shirts must he sell to break even?
   - b. How many T-shirts must he sell per month to get the same profit as this year?
   - c. What must his market share be next year to get the same profit as this year?
   - d. What must his market share be for him to have a monthly profit of $3,000?

Source: This case was prepared by William R. Swinyard, Brigham Young University.

Pricing Problems

SOME OF THESE PROBLEMS CAN BE solved using the computer disks accompanying the text. After installing the disks, open the Integrated Tutorial and go through the pricing and breakeven segments. Then, open Integrated Interactive and select either the Cost/Retail Markup page, Maintained Markup page, or Breakeven page, and plug in the numbers from the case.

Questions

1. The cost of a new CD album is $8.75. The buyer plans to make an initial markup of 25 percent on the retail price. What should the retail price be?
2. The initial selling price for a blouse is $25. The cost was $14. What was the initial markup on retail?
3. A belt was originally priced at $17 and put on sale for $12. What was the markdown percentage on retail?
4. The cost of a bicycle is $200. The initial markup on retail is 40 percent. After offering the bicycle at the initial selling price, the bicycle was marked down by 20 percent and it sold at that price.
   - a. What was the eventual selling price for the bicycle?
   - b. What was the maintained markup?
5. A woman's dress suit was originally priced at $250. The first markdown was 20 percent on retail; the second markdown was an additional 30 percent. What is the selling price of the suit after the second markdown?
6. A buyer for men's ties wants to have a maintained markup of 40 percent. The buyer forecasts that the reduction as a percentage of sales will be 13 percent.
   - a. What should the initial markup be?
   - b. If the cost of each tie is $12, what would be the initial selling price?

7. A buyer orders 500 cotton sweaters at a cost of $20 per sweater.

    a. What is the cost for all of the sweaters when they are sold?

    b. If the buyer wants to have a maintained markup of 50 percent, what total sales dollars must be generated by the sale of all 500 sweaters?

    c. The buyer sets the sweaters' initial selling price at $45. Two hundred sweaters are sold at that price. How many sales dollars were generated by the sales of the initial 200 sweaters?

    d. How many sales dollars must be generated by the remaining 300 sales to achieve a maintained markup of 50 percent?

    e. Sales of the sweaters are slowing so the buyer is going to mark them down. At what price does he need to sell each of the remaining 300 sweaters to realize 50 percent maintained markup?

    f. How much of a markdown on retail can the buyer take to realize a 50 percent maintained markup on the sales of all 500 sweaters?

8. A buyer for women's hosiery is planning to buy merchandise to be sold during the summer season that will generate retail sales of $150,000. The buyer wants to have a maintained markup of 34 percent on retail for summer hosiery sales. Reductions will be very small and can be ignored. The buyer has already spent $53,250 for merchandise that will generate $75,450 at retail. What markup does the buyer need to have on the remainder of the planned purchases to realize the overall markup of 34 percent?

9. A buyer has purchased 100 handbags at $18 each. Some will be sold at $28 retail; others will be sold at $36 retail. How many handbags should be put at each price point to realize a maintained markup of 40 percent, assuming no reductions?

10. A retailer is considering the development of a collection of private-label men's ties. The ties, which will retail for $65 each, will incur an expense to the retailer that includes $15,000 in fixed costs and $19.50 per tie in variable costs. What is the retailer's breakeven point expressed in both units and dollars?

C A S E **21**

eBay

THE CONCEPT FOR EBAY WAS BORN during a conversation between Pierre Omidyar and his wife, an avid Pez™ collector. (She currently has a collection of more than 400 dispensers.) She commented to Pierre how great it would be if she were able to collect Pez dispensers and interact with other collectors over the Internet. As an early Internet enthusiast, Pierre felt that many people like him needed a place to buy and sell unique items and to meet other users with similar interests. He started eBay in 1995 to fulfill this need.

Luckily for Pierre Omidyar, he was living in Silicon Valley when he got the idea for eBay. If Omidyar's family had stayed in France, his idea never would have gotten off the ground. It's not a lack of venture capital or Internet audience in France that would have stopped him. It's the law. Under French regulations, only a few certified auctioneers are allowed to operate. eBay hasn't even opened for business in its founder's homeland even though it operates auctions in Germany and the UK now.

OFFERING TO CONSUMERS

eBay pioneered online person-to-person trading by developing a web-based community in which buyers and sellers are brought together in an efficient and entertaining auction format to buy and sell personal items such as antiques, coins, collectibles, computers, memorabilia, stamps, and toys. The eBay service permits sellers to list items for sale and enables buyers to bid on items of interest. All eBay users can browse through listed items in a fully automated, topically arranged, intuitive, and easy-to-use online service that is available 24 hours a day, seven days a week. However, even with the automated bidding feature, participating in an online auction is more work than buying fixed-price goods, and once the auction is over, most buyers have to send a check or money order, then getting the merchandise up to two weeks later.

Since its founding, 50 million items have changed hands through its auctions. From Civil War to Star Wars items, from baby clothes to Beanie Babies, chances are that you'll find it among eBay's 2,000 categories. "If you can't sell it on eBay, you might as well open up the window and throw it out in the backyard because it ain't worth a damn," says Bob Watts, an antique dealer in Fairfield, Virginia. In 1999, eBay had over 4 million registered users. These members spend an average of 130 minutes a month browsing through its listings of more than 2 million items.

eBay is one of the stickiest Internet sites with a large number of loyal users. Users often refer to eBay as a community—a group of people with similar interests. For example, Dr. Michael Levitt by day is a distinguished medical researcher at the Minneapolis Veterans Medical Center, but at night he is an eBay warrior. Levitt is a collector of antique California Perfume Company bottles. Every night he logs on to eBay to see if anything new is being offered. He has purchased hundreds of bottles through eBay simply because it's the most convenient way to connect with sellers.

Buyers and sellers can check the "reputation" of anyone using eBay. A Feedback Forum is provided where eBay users can leave comments about their buying and selling experiences. If you're a bidder, you can check your seller's Feedback Profile before you place a bid to learn about her reputation with previous buyers. If you're a seller, do the same with your bidders.

But eBay has had some significant technical problems delivering its service. In June 1999, the site suffered an outage that lasted nearly 24 hours—the second major outage in as many days. It was, as one disgruntled seller put it, "The day eBay stood still." While the company attributed the outage to a bug in the Sun Microsystems software used to power the site, many of the eBay faithful were less than satisfied with the explanation. "We are all trying to hang in there," wrote another disenchanted regular, "but how many days of no eBay, stupidly slow response times, and 'unscheduled down times' can one take?"

BUSINESS MODEL

Unlike most e-commerce companies, eBay has been profitable from the very beginning. In 1999, its net profits were $10.8 million on net revenues of $225 million. Most of the company's revenues come from fees and commissions (between 1.25 and 5.0 percent of the sale price) associated with online and traditional offline auction services. Online revenues come from placement and success fees paid by sellers. eBay does not charge fees to buyers. Sellers pay a nominal placement fee and by paying additional fees, sellers can have items featured in various ways. Sellers also pay a success fee based on the final purchase price. Online advertising on eBay has not made significant contributions to net revenues, and no significant revenue from advertising is expected in the near future. Additional revenues come from auction-related services including bidder registration fees and appraisal and authentication.

eBay's online business model is significantly different from electronic retailers. Because individual sellers, rather than eBay, sell the items listed, the company has no procurement, carrying, or shipping costs and no inventory risk. The company's expenses are just personnel, advertising and promotion, and depreciation on site hardware and software.

COMPETITION

Due to the popularity of auctions with consumers, a number of e-businesses have entered the market. Some competing Internet auctions offering a broad range of products are Onsale, UBid.com, and Firstauction. In addition to these multicategory sites, there are vertical auction sites specializing in a single category of merchandise such as stamps or baseball cards.

Perhaps the most significant competitor is Amazon.com, which launched an auction site in 1999. Amazon has a well-known and highly regarded brand name and has substantial traffic on its website. (Amazon is the most widely known e-business with eBay ranking third in brand awareness.) When Amazon launched its auction site, it offered some unique benefits to customers including a no-deductible, no-haggle, no third-party money-back guarantee for purchases up to $250 and a feature called Going, Going, Gone that extends the auction for 10 minutes if a bid is made in the last 10 minutes before closing. On eBay, it is common for items to be picked off in the closing minutes by vigilant consumers who make the last bid.

Amazon is known for the usability of its site. In response to Amazon's entry, eBay took steps to make buying and selling easier. eBay now offers 300 new categories of products, a Personal Shopper program that searches out specified products, and a gift program.

Finally, some Internet businesses have arisen that simply search and display summary information from many auction sites to enable comparison shopping. eBay sued one such site and has used technology to block access of another site to prevent it from gathering and displaying eBay auction data.

Discussion Questions

1. What are the advantages and disadvantages from the consumer's perspective of buying merchandise through Internet auctions like eBay?

2. Will a significant amount of retail sales be made through Internet auctions like eBay in the future? Why or why not?

3. What are eBay's competitve advantages? Will it be able to withstand the competition from other auction sites, vertical auctions, and Amazon? Why or why not?

CASE *22*

Loyalty Wars in the British Supermarket Industry

IN FEBRUARY 1995, TESCO—THE NUMBER two UK supermarket chains—launched Clubcard, the first loyalty card in the UK supermarket scene, after a trial of one year in 14 stores. Shoppers could collect one point for every £5 (five pounds) spent over a minimum of £10 per shopping trip. Every three months, these points could be converted into money-off vouchers sent to the customer's home. The value of the vouchers represented a reward rate of about 1 percent. In addition to the vouchers, customers would receive supplier-funded coupons in their quarterly Clubcard mailing.

Sir Ian MacLaurin, chairman of Tesco, explained the positioning of the Clubcard: "In Tesco we work hard to develop a close relationship with our customers, in order to serve them well. The Clubcard is a way of thanking them for shopping with us. At the same time, the technology gives us a clearer picture of their likes and dislikes, which helps us to give them an even better service."

Operating costs of the Tesco Clubcard were estimated at £10 million, the costs of the money-off vouchers at £50 million. Tesco would have to make an increase in like-for-like sales of 1.5 to 2 percent for the scheme to pay for itself.

UK GROCERY ENVIRONMENT

In the 1985–95 period, UK supermarket results were fed by sales from new outlets. In 1995, the market became saturated, and supermarkets were faced with the problem of static sales. With stricter planning legislation, the traditional route of opening new stores to create impressive sales growth slowed. Instead, supermarkets now had to increase sales from existing stores in order to keep shareholders satisfied. In addition to the problem of stifled consumer spending, there was an increasing pressure on the margins of the supermarket as discounters—such as Kwick Save, Aldi, and Netto—were luring customers away with lower prices.

THE PLAYERS

There were four major players on the grocers battlefield: Sainsbury's, Tesco, Argyll (which owned Safeway supermarkets), and Asda. All four endeavored to distinguish themselves from the others, trying to introduce new ways of pleasing the customer that would remain uncopied for at least a few months. These players are described in the following paragraphs. (Exhibit 1 provides financial and marketing information.)

Sainsbury's

Sainsbury's had been doing very well for the previous five years with continuously growing sales and profits. It had opened around 14 new stores a year. Sainsbury's had been a public company since 1973, but it had kept the company culture of a family-

EXHIBIT **1**   Facts and Figures of the Top Four Grocers, 1994–95

	STORE			
	SAINSBURY'S	**TESCO**	**ARGYLL/SAFEWAY**	**ASDA**
Sales	£10,719**	£10,120	£6,218	£5,683
Operating profit	£859**	£589	£383	£251
Market share, food and toiletries, December 1994	12.6%	11.7%	7.8%	6.9%
Turnover from loyal customers*, 8 2/3 March 1995	66%	65%	56%	67%
Share of own brand, 1995, for package grocery/toiletry goods	53.4%	45.2%	41.2%	38.6%

Source: Company annual reports, Institute of Grocery Distribution in Watford, AGB Superpanel.

* Loyal customers are here defined as customers who spend more than 70 percent of their total grocery money at one store.

** Sainsbury's sales and profits include revenues from nongrocery business units such as do-it-yourself and furniture outlets.

owned and-run business. As a retail analyst at Société Générale Strauss Trunbull described Sainsbury's, "It is like the Civil Service—if it is not broken don't fix it. Historically, they have never had any new people coming from the outside into the top jobs, so they never had any new ideas."

Despite this view of the company, Sainsbury's had always been the number one UK grocer, holding the largest share of the food market. It claimed to have the highest number of customers with the highest spending. Sainsbury's' 355 food store locations ranged from the middle-of-town sites to large edge-of-town shopping centers. Sainsbury's had an impressive operating margin of 8.1 percent, which testified to its operating efficiency. Its own-label brand represented more than half of Sainsbury's' product range, and its sales per square foot (£18.53/week) were unrivaled. The efficiency at the stores might have had a downside to it, as customer surveys dating as far back as 1993 had started to reveal that customers experienced the stores as a bit cold and unfriendly. David Sainsbury, chairman, conceded, "The message that came over loud and clear was that staff were so busy running the stores that they couldn't find time for the customers."

After acknowledging this consumer verdict, Sainsbury's implemented several service initiatives, ranging from improving "wonky trolleys" to decreasing the checkout scanning speed of 22 items a minute to 18 items a minute, so staff would have time for a "Hello" and a smile at the counter. Managers and staff were retrained to make the store environment warmer and friendlier. Feedback systems—such as anonymous questionnaires—were put in place to solicit employees' opinions on store management, and store managers had to make action plans for improvement. In early 1995, Sainsbury's was not communicating these initiatives as loudly as its competitors, as it wanted to get all the elements in place first to make sure it could deliver on promises. According to David Sainsbury, not delivering on promises was one of the fastest ways to lose customers.

Tesco

Tesco had been the second largest UK supermarket chain from 1985 to 1995. It had experienced continuous growth in sales and operating profits, adding new stores at an average rate of 17 a year. In 1995, it had a total of 545 stores in the UK, with an average size—comparable to Sainsbury's—of 25,600 square feet. Tesco's sales of £17.00 per square foot per week and its operating margin of 5.7 percent were considerably lower than Sainsbury's.

In response to the pressure from the discounters, Tesco—like all nondiscount retailers—had to come up with initiatives that would justify its higher prices. It introduced a campaign under the banner "Every Little Bit Helps." The initiatives included a First Class Customer Service program where staff were encouraged to go that little bit further in helping customers, Value Lines (low-priced basic products) that catered to the price-minded customer, and the building of new store formats. With regard to store formats, the chain could be described as an innovative performer. It responded to consumers' varying shopping patterns and to changes in national and local planning policies by introducing store formats like Tesco-Metro (high street concept) and its stand-alone petrol forecourt with attached convenience store.

Like Sainsbury's, Tesco had asked its customers what they wanted. The answers were clear: no sweets at the checkout, shorter queues, more staff to help out, and trolleys that steered well. So Tesco took the sweets away from the checkouts and promised to open a new checkout as soon as more than one other customer waited in line. New trolleys were brought in, with a special shallow model for people who had difficulty in bending down. Other services included baby changing facilities, with free nappies so shopping parents did not even have to bring any themselves. Tesco also claimed it had the widest choice of own-label and branded products of all food retailers. It set up its own Food Technology Center that researched food and the best ways of handling it. Tesco communicated this extensively with its "Quality Guarantee" labels in the stores.

Argyll/Safeway

Argyll was the third largest food retailer in the UK. From 1990 to 1995, it had had increasing sales and fluctuating profits. In the last two years, Argyll's sales growth had come predominately from new stores. Argyll added around 23 superstores a year while it decreased the number of smaller stores. After divesting small and underperforming outlets, Argyll had a total of around 547 outlets by 1995. These outlets included supermarkets that operated under the Presto name. Presto had an average store sales area of 6,100 square feet, compared to Safeway's 21,900 square feet. Argyll was in the process of increasing the number of Safeways and decreasing the number of Presto outlets by either converting them into Safeways or closing them altogether.

Argyll also wanted to adopt the "Safeway culture" for its whole business. The Safeway culture involved a "value-added" approach with in-store post offices, dry cleaning services, and frequent consultation of customer panels. Specialist departments such as delicatessens, bakeries, pharmacies, and coffee shops appeared in more and more of the stores, the latest service being photo processing in five of the Safeway stores. The chain paid extra attention to families as customers, with, for example, special parking areas for parents with children and

in-store crèches. Next to its regular own-brand products, Safeway also had a value-for-money line, the Safeway Savers Range. It initiated a program in 1994—the range review program—that sought a balance between economical, standard, and premium products that customers said they wanted.

The chain could be regarded as a forerunner in technology applications with advanced scanning and ordering systems. In March 1995, it introduced a self-scanning system in a test shop, the first such system in use in the UK supermarket business. In addition to offering its customers facilities that would make shopping more efficient, Safeway was using technology to help improve its sales per square foot per week, which, at £12.86, was considerably lower than Sainsbury's' or Tesco's.

Asda

Asda was the number four with a market share of 6.9 percent in December 1994. The company had been through turbulent times, with a near bankruptcy in 1991. In 1995, the situation looked much brighter. Asda's like-for-like sales growth was the highest of the four superstores in 1994–95 due to a company renewal program lead by Archie Norman, chief executive since 1991. Asda did not increase sales by adding new stores, although it did increase its total sales area slightly by adapting existing stores. Instead, Asda reemphasized its old reputation of value for money with share pricing. Prices—5 to 7 percent below its competitors'—were important, as 75 percent of the Asda stores were in areas whose populations had an average or below-average income.

But Asda was not only attracting customers with low prices. It had also introduced new customer service initiatives like diaper changing rooms, five types of shopping carts (like the gold-plated one for large-quantity shoppers), and extra checkout counters. Asda's customer service initiatives were supported by extensive employee training and motivational campaigns. Employees were called colleagues and could buy share options on the same terms as those available to the top executives.

Asda's own-brand share was the lowest of the four at 38.6 percent, but the company was working on 1,300 new Asda products in 1995 in order to increase the percentage. It had 203 outlets, nearly all superstore format. With an average store size of

40,000 square feet, Asda stores were almost as big as the average Tesco, Sainsbury's, or Safeway store.

THE OTHER FOOD RETAILERS

More than 60 percent of the packaged groceries and toiletries market was shared among smaller supermarkets, local convenience stores, specialty stores, and discounters. The largest other chains were Somerfield, a supermarket with 4.5 percent market share, Kwik Save, a discounter with 4.1 percent market share, and Marks & Spencer, a mixed retailer whose share of the grocery market was 3.3 percent (all with own-brand products). Kwik Save and Somerfield had more than 600 outlets. Marks & Spencer had more than 290 outlets. In addition to these chains, co-ops accounted for 7.8 percent of the market. All other outlets held less than 2.5 percent of the total market.

THE GROCERS DELIBERATE

Initially, reactions to the launch of Tesco's Clubcard in February 1995 were diverse, but the most unambiguous reaction came from David Sainsbury, chairman and chief executive of Sainsbury's: "Tesco's Clubcard is a marketing gimmick and no more than electronic Green Shield stamps."

Despite Sainsbury's reaction, in the first weeks more than a million customers signed up for Tesco's Clubcard. It was too early to say whether these were Tesco's own customers or those from competing chains.

Discussion Questions

1. Should the chains, especially Sainsbury's—the market leader—react or just wait?

2. If they decide to react, should it be with traditional pricing, merchandising, promotional, and service initiatives or with a loyalty program of their own?

3. In case they decide to adopt loyalty programs, how should they make them attractive for their customers? What should the accrual system be like? Should they target specific groups of customers, and, if so, what kind of rewards would these customers want?

4. In addition to making the programs attractive, how should they limit the costs?

Source: This case was prepared by Research Associate Els van Weering under the supervision of Professor Nirmalya Kumar, International Institute of Management, Lausanne, Switzerland©.

CASE 23

Advertising Plan for a Rug Sale

A MAJOR DEPARTMENT STORE in the Washington, D.C., area is planning a big rug sale in its suburban Virginia warehouse over the three-day Washington's Birthday weekend (Saturday through Monday). On sale will be nearly $2 million worth of rugs, assembled both from the company's inventory and from various market purchases. The average sale price of each rug is approximately $300. The company hopes to realize at least $900,000 in sales during the three days. This is the first time the store has sold rugs from its warehouse, but previous experience with coats and furniture has been good. Two factors in particular were common to the previous events:

1. The first day's sales were 50 percent of the total. The second day's were 35 percent, and the last day's, 15 percent.

2. One of every two customers who came made a purchase.

It's known further that large numbers of people always flock to such sales, some driving as far as 50 miles. They come from all economic levels, but are all confirmed bargain hunters. You're the assistant to the general merchandise manager, who has asked you to plan the event's campaign. The following information is at your disposal:

1. A full-page *Washington Post* ad costs $10,000; a half-page ad costs $6,000, and a quarter-page ad costs $3,500. To get the maximum value from a newspaper campaign, it's company policy to always run two ads (not necessarily the same size) for such events.

2. The local Northern Virginia paper is printed weekly and distributed free to some 15,000 households. It costs $700 for a full page and $400 for a half page.

3. To get adequate TV coverage, at least three channels must be used, with a minimum of eight 30-second spots on each at $500 per spot, spread over three or more days. Producing a TV spot costs $3,000.

4. The store has contracts with three radio stations. One appeals to a broad general audience aged 25 to 34. One is popular with the 18-to-25 group. A classical music station has a small but wealthy audience. Minimum costs for a saturation radio campaign (including production) on the three stations are $8,000, $5,000, and $3,000, respectively.

5. To produce and mail a full-color flyer to the store's 80,000 charge customers costs $10,000.

When the company used such a mailing piece before, about 3 percent responded.

Discussion Questions

1. Knowing that the company wants a mixed-media ad campaign to support this event, prepare an ad plan for the general merchandise manager that costs no more than $40,000.

2. Work out the daily scheduling of all advertising.

3. Work out the dollars to be devoted to each medium.

4. Justify your plan.

Source: This case was prepared by David Ehrlich, Marymount University.

C A S E 24

Neiman Marcus's Preferred Customer Program

DALLAS-BASED DEPART-MENT STORE RETAILER NEIMAN MARCUS (NM) began the first preferred customer program, In-Circle, in 1984. In such a program, purchases can only be completed with either the Neiman Marcus credit card, American Express Card, cash, or check. This retailer utilizes its own card to reward and provide incentives for its customers.

Customers must spend $3,000 on their Neiman Marcus charge in one calendar year to become eligible for the InCircle program. People qualifying for the program are the top 2 percent of Neiman Marcus's customers. Once a part of this program, shoppers receive one InCircle point for each dollar charged to their Neiman Marcus card. These points must be redeemed at the end of the calendar year for everything from a bottle of Dom Perignon to a new Jaguar or a Caribbean cruise for two. In keeping with the high standards of Neiman Marcus's customer service, a full-time travel coordinator and assistant are on staff to personalize the trips earned by the InCircle customers.

The rewards for InCircle membership include invitations to exclusive shopping events, a quarterly newsletter, free gift wrapping for purchases of $25 or more, and double points on birthdays. All In-Circle customers are invited to private shopping parties where they generally earn double points for their purchases. These dates, times, and locations are printed in the newsletter.

In 1995, the customer programs division of Neiman Marcus developed different levels and programs within InCircle. Once an InCircle member has accumulated 1,500 points in a calendar year, she is extended an offer to become a Neiman Marcus Gold Card holder for a $50 annual fee. This status allows the member to earn double points for each dollar spent (up to $1,500). Other bonuses are given to the customer upon "earning" her Gold Card status, including a $50 American Airlines certificate for travel, a complimentary magazine subscription, free credit protection for charge cards, bonus InCircle points for certain events, and travel benefits.

The Platinum Card is offered to InCircle members who have accumulated 3,000 or more points. The $500 annual fee allows a customer to earn double points for the first $30,000 in purchases each year. Charter Platinum status is maintained by those who earn a minimum of 100,000 points yearly. Special gifts are available only to platinum members. They include restaurant gift certificates to exclusive establishments, such as Charlie Trotter's in Chicago. American Airlines travel certificates and unlimited Four Season's Hotel upgrades are also part of the platinum perks.

InCircle not only benefits its members, it rewards its sales professionals too. Loyalty will bring customers into Neiman Marcus to make more purchases, as the promise of the coveted points will also. This means more sales for a store's staff. The sales staff also have access to the purchase history of InCircle customers and are encouraged to contact these customers personally.

InCircle members are given the opportunity to present Exceptional Service Awards to deserving NM associates. These awards are in the form of a sticker and enclosed with each member's InCircle card. A sticker brings the member bonus points when it is presented to the associate, and the associate's name is entered into a quarterly prize drawing.

Other department stores have patterned preferred customer or valued customer programs after Neiman's InCircle. In a recent survey 28 percent of the department store chains have preferred customer programs. These programs offer customers a combination of hard benefits (points, rewards, discounts) and soft benefits (recognition and preferential treatment).

Discussion Questions

1. How does InCircle build loyalty for Neiman Marcus versus other upscale retailers like Saks and Lord & Taylor?

2. How effective is the InCircle program in developing customer loyalty?

3 What obstacles might InCircle professionals face in further developing their program?

4. If all of Neiman Marcus's customers were ranked in terms of their annual purchases from the store, to which group should Neiman Marcus target its frequent shopper program? The top 10 percent? The second decile? The bottom 10 percent? Why?

5. Should Neiman Marcus emphasize hard or soft benefits?

Source: This case was prepared by Allison Karrh, University of Florida.

CASE **25**

Max Murphy and the Tardy Trainee

THE METRO-DAY DEPARTMENT STORE IN DOWNTOWN Seattle specializes in well-made clothing plus up-to-the-minute kitchen items and home furnishings. Of the six Metro-Day stores around the country, it's ranked number one in terms of sales volume and store standards. It's also the home of the company's Executive Training Program for future store managers.

A rising star with Metro-Day, Max Murphy had graduated from the training program only two years ago and had performed well with his first two assignments at other Metro locations. When an opening arose in the Seattle store, Max jumped at the chance. Not only would he be getting a promotion to sales manager of the Kitchen and Home Furnishings Department, he'd also get to teach that section of the training program. Max had done well in the training program and had gained the reputation of being a sharp, creative manager at both assignments prior to the Seattle promotion.

His first few months of managing the new department went smoothly. Max had gotten most of the usual personnel gripes under control and had familiarized and remerchandised the stock in his area to boost sales 20 percent over last year's figures. The first batch of two trainees came through the program with high marks, singing Max's praises. He was not only a smart merchant, but also a fair, honest, caring trainer.

Four people (twice the normal number) were going through the second training program. One of them, Sue Baker, presented Max with concerns. Sue would often show up late or work on written homework when she was supposed to be managing sections of the sales floor with the other trainees. Max knew he needed to sit down and talk with Sue after two weeks of working with her, but whenever he had a chance to talk with her, she was either absent (she was sick often) or somewhere other than the department. With three other trainees plus Christmas preparations, Max was very busy.

Max finally cornered Sue and spoke to her about her performance, highlighting his concerns. She seemed to take the conversation very personally. She said that Max didn't understand that she

653

had car problems and allergies and that, not being a parent himself, he wouldn't understand her responsibilities when her two children were sick. She claimed that when she was on the sales floor, he wasn't around. Max tried to be sympathetic to Sue's situation, but made it clear that she had responsibilities to the store. The conversation ended with both parties agreeing to try to do better.

Midway through the program, all trainees were to turn in progress sheets for Max to initial and rate. All did so but Sue. Max asked Sue for the report twice, but she never seemed to get it to him. By the end of the program, Max turned in a final report on all trainees. Now Sue came through with her midway review sheets as well. Both reports would need passing marks for the trainee to move on to the next section of the store. Sue's work on the second half was passable, but just barely. Looking over the review sheet for the first part of the program with so much time passing in the interim, not to mention the problems with Sue's attendance and work performance, made it almost impossible, in Max's mind, to evaluate Sue fairly.

Max was befuddled. He honestly didn't believe that Sue had successfully completed the program, and he couldn't fairly evaluate her on the first half. But he felt partly responsible for her failure since he hadn't pushed her harder to get her work turned in, though he had pushed her twice as hard as the other trainees. To further complicate matters, the program was a "self-motivated" one and the trainees knew from the start that Max wasn't there to baby-sit them.

Discussion Question

What should Max do?

Source: This case was prepared by Laura Bliss, Stephens College.

C A S E 26

Borders Bookstore: A Merchandise Display Problem

MICHAEL CHAIM, GENERAL MANAGER of the Borders Bookstore in Madison, Wisconsin, was proud of his store. Located in a city that has one of the highest levels of book purchases per capita, Mr. Chaim felt Borders' selection, services, and location near the 40,000-student university served the community well. Even with competitive pressure from the newly opened Barnes & Noble on the west side of town, his bookstore/cafe was often a busy place.

Michael was taken aback when an article in a widely read alternative newspaper criticized the bookstore's merchandise arrangement as prejudiced. The store carries a large selection of literature and poetry, but separates some specialty categories, such as African American literature, gay and lesbian literature, and feminist literature, from the general literature and poetry sections. In part, this arrangement reflects Borders' college town roots in Ann Arbor, Michigan, where specialty collections were established to match course offerings.

The article described this arrangement as "ghettoizing" authors who were not white males, although some female authors were in the general literature and poetry sections. The article and some follow-up letters to the newspaper's editor derided Borders for the few "nontraditional" authors who made it into the general literature collection. They felt that these African American, homosexual, Native American, and other nontraditional writers probably would have been separated from the general collection, had the management known the literature better. While Madison is known as a very liberal community, Michael thought the accusation was very unfair. He strongly believed that he was doing his customers a service in highlighting authors and literary genres that might be overlooked in a large, nondifferentiated collection. More immediately, he knew that he should respond to the article's accusations.

Discussion Questions

1. What should Michael Chaim do?

2. One option is to duplicate the titles that could be shelved in either the general literature section or in a specialty collection. What are the advantages and disadvantages of this tactic?

Source: This case was prepared by Jan Owens, University of Wisconsin, Parkside.

Picking the Best Display

A MAJOR DEPARTMENT STORE RECOGNIZED THAT its first-floor selling fixtures had become outmoded so it set aside funds to renovate. The main floor had not been changed appreciably since the store was built in the 1920s. There were a number of handsome mahogany-paneled counter islands, which had always given the store an aura of tasteful elegance.

Jim Lewis, director of store fixturing, was debating the merits of several possible display systems. The selling departments that would be affected by the renovation were cosmetics; fine and costume jewelry; women's handbags, scarves, and belts; men's shirts, ties, and furnishings; women's sweaters; and gifts.

As Lewis saw it, the two major issues surrounding his decision were incompatible. On the one hand, the store wanted to make merchandise as accessible to customers as possible; on the other hand, experience had indicated that open-selling fixtures inevitably lead to more shoplifting. As an experiment, the store had tried substituting self-service fixtures in its upstairs sweater department a year earlier. Sales jumped 30 percent, but inventory shrinkage in the department had gone from 2 to almost 5 percent.

A further consideration was that the size and quality of the staff on the selling floor had declined dramatically. In 1929, there were always two salespeople behind every counter, and customers could count on never having to wait for service. However, selling costs had since escalated, and the store's staff was less than half what it had been then. Furthermore, the store had instituted modern point-of-sale cash registers that enabled every salesperson to ring up a sale from any department in the store at any register. Most of the clerks were minimum-wage individuals who were only working there until something better turned up. Although some were able to provide useful selling information to the public, most could do little more than ring up sales.

The kind of open-selling fixtures Lewis was considering were contemporary and very attractive. They allowed the customer to pick up, un-

fold, or unpackage merchandise; try it on if appropriate; and then return it to the fixture. Such fixtures would unquestionably lead to more sales, especially since the customer could merely look for any salesperson or perhaps go to a central cashier to pay. However, it was equally unquestionable that such easy access to merchandise, especially to small goods, would encourage shoplifting and would increase the need for ongoing stock keeping.

Another disadvantage to the new type of fixturing was that, in addition to being contemporary, it was somewhat trendy, which would lead to the need to replace it in a few years, thereby adding to capital costs.

An alternative system would be to retain the old counter islands, or a portion of them, but to put more goods on the countertops to encourage a measure of self-service. The disadvantage here, of course, would be the blocking of sight lines. Salespeople could not see customers, customers could not see salespeople, and the store security personnel could not see either. There would also need to be more policing by the store's display and merchandising staff to be sure the countertops looked inviting at all times. Manufacturers often contribute countertop displays to stores as part of the merchandise buying, and many of them might not be in harmony with the store's overall appearance.

Lewis recognized that he would have to make some compromises. Every affected department has its own peculiarities, and his job was to minimize those differences, rather than allow them to get out of hand. Some merchandise, such as fine jewelry, would obviously have to remain behind glass, but other departments would probably do much better by opening up their stocks to the public.

Discussion Questions

1. What display system would you recommend? Why?

2. Would you make the same recommendation for each of the affected departments? Why?

Source: This case was prepared by David Ehrlich, Marymount University.

A Stockout at Discmart: Will Substitution Lead to Salvation?

ROBERT HONDA, THE MANAGER OF A DISCMART STORE (a discount retailer similar to Kmart and Wal-Mart) in Cupertino, California, was surveying the Sunday morning activity at his store. Shoppers were bustling around with carts; some had children in tow. In the front side of the store a steady stream of shoppers were heading through the checkout counters. Almost all the cash registers that he could see from his vantage point were open and active. The line in front of register 7 was longer than the other lines, but other than that things seemed to be going quite smoothly.

The intercom beeped and interrupted his thoughts. A delivery truck had just arrived at the rear of the store. The driver wanted to know which loading dock to use to unload merchandise. Robert decided to inspect the available space before directing the driver to a specific loading dock. As he passed the cash registers on his way to the rear of the store, Robert noticed that the line at register 7 had gotten a little bit longer. The light over the register was flashing, indicating that the customer service associate (CSA) had requested assistance. (At Discmart all front-line personnel who interact with customers are called customer service associates.) As he passed by the register he could not help overhearing the exchange between what seemed to be a somewhat irate customer and the CSA. The customer was demanding that another item should be substituted for an item that was on sale but currently out of stock, and the CSA was explaining the store policy to the customer. Normally, during a busy time like this, Robert would have tried to help the CSA resolve the situation, but he knew that the truck driver was waiting to unload merchandise that was needed right away on the floor. Hence he quickly walked to the rear of the store.

After assigning the truck to a docking bay for unloading, Robert headed back toward the front of the store. On the way back, he ducked into the break room to get a coke and noticed that Sally Johnson, the CSA who was at register 7, was on a break. Sally had been on the Discmart team for about a year and was considered a very capable employee who always kept the store's interests at heart.

Robert: Hi Sally, I noticed that you had quite a line in front of your register earlier today.

Sally: Hi Robert. Yes, I had a very irate customer and it took us a while to resolve the issue.

Robert: Oh really! What was he irate about?

Sally: We are out of stock on the 100-ounce Tide Liquid Detergent that was advertised in our flyer and was on sale at 20 percent off. I offered the customer a raincheck or the same discount on the same size of another brand, but the customer kept insisting that he wanted us to substitute a 200-ounce container of Tide Liquid Detergent at the same discount. Apparently Joe Chang (the assistant manager) had told the customer that we would substitute the 200-ounce size.

Robert: Did you point out to the customer that our sale prices are valid only while supplies last?

Sally: I did mention this to the customer, but he thought it was strange that we ran out of stock on the morning of the first day of the sale.

Robert: Well, I guess you should have gone ahead and given him what he wanted.

Sally: As you know, our point-of-sale systems allow me to make adjustments only on designated items. Since the 200-ounce sizes were not designated as substitutes, I had to request a supervisor to help me.

Robert: I am glad that you got it resolved.

Sally: Well, the customer got tired of waiting for the supervisor, who was busy helping another customer, so he decided to take a rain check instead. He seemed quite dissatisfied with the whole episode and mentioned that we should stop running these TV ads claiming that we are always in stock and that we guarantee satisfaction.

Robert: I do hate it when they run these ad campaigns and we have to take the heat on the floor, trying to figure out what those cowboys in marketing promised the customer.

Sally: Well, my break is nearly over. I have to get back.

Robert pondered the encounter that Sally had with the customer. He wondered whether to discuss this issue with Joe Chang. He remembered talking to Joe about inventory policies a couple of days ago. Joe had indicated that their current inventory levels were fairly high and that any further increases would be hard to justify from a financial perspective. He mentioned some market research that had surveyed a random sample of customers who had redeemed rain checks. The results of the survey indicated that customers by and large were satisfied with Discmart's rain check procedures. Based on this finding, Joe had argued that current inventory levels supplemented with a rain check policy would keep customers satisfied.

Discussion Questions

1. Why did this service breakdown occur?
2. How was this service gap related to the other gaps (standards, knowledge, delivery, and communications) described in the GAPS Model in Chapter 19?

Source: This case was prepared by Dr. Kirthi Kalyanam, Retail Management Institute, Santa Clara University ©.

CASE 29

Starbucks Coffee Company

BY 1999, STARBUCKS WAS THE LEADING retailer of specialty coffee beverages and beans and related food and merchandise. Its annual sales were $1.68 billion with a profit of $102 million. Starbucks owned and operated 2,200 retail stores and licensed an additional 300 airport stores in the United States, Japan, and Great Britain. In addition to its direct retailing activities, Starbucks had formed strategic alliances with Dreyer's Grand Ice Cream, Barnes & Noble Booksellers, Capitol Records, PepsiCo, and Nordstrom to expand its product and distribution portfolios. Howard Schultz, (chairman and CEO) and his senior management team were focusing on how to sustain their phenomenal growth and maintain their market leadership position.

THE COFFEE MARKET

The commercial market for coffee began in 1000 AD when Arab traders brought the coffee tree from its native Ethiopia to the Middle East. Over the next 200 years coffee drink spread through the Arab world and was eventually introduced in Europe in the 1500s by Italian traders. By 1650, coffee houses emerged as popular meeting places in England and France. Well-known public figures would frequent London coffee houses to discuss political and literary issues.

Coffee consumption flourished in the mid-20th century, aided by developments in manufacturing and cultivation. By 1940, large coffee processors such as Nestlé (Hills Bros.), Kraft General Foods (Maxwell House brand), and Procter & Gamble (Folgers brand) developed instant and decaffeinated coffee varieties in addition to their staple regular ground. Supermarkets emerged as the primary distribution channel for traditional coffee sales.

In the late 1980s, per capita coffee consumption fell slowly and steadily as consumers turned to soft drinks, bottled water, juices, and iced teas. The three major manufacturers—Procter & Gamble, Nestlé, and Kraft—fought for market share in a stagnant market. All of the major coffee brands were unprofitable. In an effort to regain profitability, the majors decreased historically high expenditures on image, increased the use of robusta beans (as opposed to the high-quality arabica beans) to further reduce cost, and converted from 16-ounce cans to 13-ounce cans, claiming that the contents produced the same amount of coffee. Coupons and in-store promotions dominated manufacturer marketing plans as price warfare continued.

THE STARBUCKS COFFEE COMPANY: BACKGROUND

Inspiration for the present Starbucks concept came to Howard Schultz when he went to Italy on a buying trip in 1983. While wandering through the ancient piazzas of Milan, Schultz took particular note of the many cheerful espresso bars and cafes he passed. Italians, he felt, had captured the true romance of the beverage. Coffee drinking was an integral part of the Italian culture. Italians started their day at the espresso bar and returned there later on. "There's such a strong sense of community in those coffee bars," he mused. "People come together every single day and in many cases they

657

don't even know each other's names. In Italy, coffee is the conduit to the social experience."

Schultz realized that Americans lacked the opportunity to savor a good cup of coffee while engaging good conversation in a relaxed atmosphere. He returned to the United States convinced that Americans would find the Italian coffee house culture attractive. In 1987, Schultz bought Starbucks.

GROWING THE COMPANY: THE INITIAL YEARS

Retail Offering

Starbucks offers more than a cup of coffee. Scott Bedbury, the VP of marketing, elaborates:

> Our product is not just that which resides in the cup. The product is the store and the service you get in the store. We need to help people appreciate at a higher level why that coffee break feels the way it does, why it's worth the time it takes to prepare a good cup of coffee. I like to think that Starbucks is not so much *food* for thought, but *brewed* for thought. Coffee has for centuries been for thought. I have sometimes thought to myself, "Get out of this chair. You hit the wall." It's that private time for me between 2 and 3 PM when I walk down the Commons area here and make myself an Americano and think something through. I think that's maybe what Starbucks has to offer people: that safe harbor, that place to kind of make sense of the world. In the long run, what distinguishes us from our customers, what is the most enduring competitive advantage we have, is that we are able to give our customers an experience at the store level . . . better than any competitor out there, even the small ones.
> Starbucks should be a place, an experience, tied up in inspired thought.

While designs vary in any particular store to match the local market, the typical Starbucks store works around a planned mix of organic and manufactured components: light wood tones at the counters and signage areas, brown bags, polished dark marble counter tops, glass shelves, thin modern white track lighting, and pure white cups. Even the logo delivers the double organic/modern message: The Starbucks icon is earthy looking, yet rendered in a modern abstract form, in black and white with a band of color around the center only. The colors of the lamps, walls, and tables mimic

coffee tones, from green (raw beans) to light and darker browns. Special package and cup designs are coordinated to create livelier, more colorful tones around holidays. Starbucks also keeps its look lively with rotating in-store variations based on timely themes.

Starbucks stores are spacious so that customers can wander around the store, drinking their coffee and considering the purchase of coffee paraphernalia ranging from coffee beans to brushes for cleaning coffee grinders to $1,000 home cappuccino machines. Retail sales are composed of coffee beverages (58 percent), whole bean coffee by the pound (17 percent), food items (16 percent), and coffee-related equipment (9 percent). Although coffee beverages are standardized across outlets, food offerings vary from store to store.

At Starbucks, espresso is brewed precisely 18 to 23 seconds and thrown away if it is not served within 10 seconds of brewing. Coffee beans are donated to charities seven days after coming out of their vacuum-sealed packs. Drip coffee is thrown away if it is not served within an hour of making it. Throughout the store there exists a keen attention to aroma: Employees are not allowed to wear colognes, stores use no scented cleaning products, and smoking is *verboten*.

Human Resource Management

The company, recognizing that its front-line employees are critical to providing "the perfect cup," has built an organizational culture based on two principles: (1) strict standards for how coffee should be prepared and delivered to customers and (2) a laid-back, supportive, and empowering attitude toward its employees.

All new hires, referred to as partners, go through a 24-hour training program that instills a sense of purpose, commitment, and enthusiasm for the job. New partners are treated with the dignity and respect that goes along with their title as *baristas* (Italian for bartender). To emphasize their responsibility in pleasing customers, baristas are presented with scenarios describing customers complaining about beans that were ground incorrectly. The preferred response, baristas learn, is to replace the beans on the spot without checking with the manager or questioning the complaint.

Baristas learn to customize each espresso drink and to explain the origins of different coffees, and claim to be able to distinguish Sumatran from Ethiopian coffees by the way it "flows over the tongue."

Holding on to their motivated, well-trained employees is important so all are eligible for health benefits and a stock option plan called "Bean Stock." Each partner is awarded stock options worth 12 percent of his annual base pay. (Starbucks now allows options at 14 percent of base pay in light of "good profits.") Employees are also given a free pound of coffee each week and a 30 percent discount on all retail offerings. Baristas know about and are encouraged to apply for promotion to store management positions. Every quarter the company has open meetings at which company news, corporate values, and financial performance data are presented and discussed.

Due to the training, empowerment, benefits, and growth opportunities, Starbucks' turnover is only 60 percent, considerably less the 150 to 200 percent turnover at other firms in the food service business. "We treat our employees like true partners and our customers like stars," comments Schultz.

And stars they are. The average Starbucks customer visits the store 18 times a month; 10 percent visit twice a day. "I don't know of any retailer or restaurant chain that has that kind of loyalty," Schultz says.

Location Strategy

Starbucks' retail expansion strategy was sequential, based on conquering one area of a city or region at a time. Centralized cities served as hubs or regional centers for roll-out expansion into nearby markets (e.g., Chicago as a hub for the Midwest). "Clustering" was also central to the strategy—major markets were saturated with stores before new markets were entered. For example, there were over 100 Starbucks outlets in the Seattle area before the company expanded to a new region. Having several stores in close proximity to each other generally increased overall revenues, though slowed growth in comparable store sales in saturated markets suggested sales were at the expense of cannibalization of existing businesses.

Traffic was the major determinant in selecting cities and locations. "We want to be in highly visible locations," Senior VP of Real Estate Jim Rubin explains, "with access to customers that value quality and great coffee. You want a store in the path of people's weekly shopping experience, their route to work, their way home from a movie. You want to be America's porch that no longer exists."

PHASE II GROWTH STRATEGY
Product Strategy

Starbucks has introduced a number of new products designed to capitalize on the company's strong brand name. "My plan is to bring the company and consequently the brand closer to consumers, and to help unlock a greater potential for the brand while keeping its soul and integrity intact," explains Bedbury.

- *Blue Note Blend.* Blue Note Blend was introduced in conjunction with Capitol Records and its Blue Note label for jazz. "The combination of jazz music and coffees was consistent with the atmosphere of Starbucks," explained Bedbury.

- *Frappuccino©.* The frappuccino beverage is a sweet, cold, creamy drink that combines milk, coffee, and ice. The product was very successful when introduced to cafes in 1995, so Starbucks entered a joint venture with PepsiCo to bottle a ready-to-drink (RTD) version. This product was in test market in early 1997, with plans to take the brand national by early Fall. While canned or bottled coffee beverages had not been marketed in the United States, they were popular in Japan and other parts of the world. Coca-Cola was experimenting with a Nescafe RTD coffee beverage.

- *MAZAGRAN™.* MAZAGRAN is a carbonated coffee RTD beverage. The product is manufactured, bottled, and distributed by PepsiCo, but Starbucks shared in the R&D and set flavor standards. Starbucks was currently test marketing the beverage in supermarkets and convenience stores in the Southeast.

- *Dreyer's Grand Ice Cream.* Dreyer's Grand Ice Cream agreed to produce a line of premium ice cream products flavored with Starbucks coffee. The first products in this line, five coffee-flavored gourmet ice creams, were sold under the Starbucks name and distributed through supermarket outlets. As of 1997, Starbucks ice cream was the leading brand of gourmet coffee ice cream on the market. Chocolate-covered ice cream novelties and Frappuccino ice cream bars were under consideration.

- *Redhook Ale Brewery.* Seattle-based Redhook Ale Brewery was making a dark brewed beer with coffee, called Double Black Stout, with the Starbucks name on every bottle.
- *Other products.* Starbucks managers debated whether the company should integrate backward into food preparation for additional profits, considering muffins, pastries, scones, desserts, and chocolates. Some thought the housewares collection could be expanded. Product ideas included coffee perfumes and scented candles, and coffee liquor. Additional partnerships with food and beverage manufacturers were being brainstormed as the company sought further leverage from its brand name.

Distribution Strategy

Retail expansion remained a major company goal. Three hundred additional stores were planned for the United States, Canada, Japan, and Great Britain. Starbucks was also considering alternative distribution channels to strengthen its competitive position and increase sales. Several alternative channels had already been established including the sale of whole beans through Nordstrom department stores and the sale of coffee by the cup in the cafes of Barnes & Noble bookstores. Additional channels under consideration included distribution through service providers like Holland America Cruise Lines, United Airlines, and Sheraton and Westin Hotels. The company was also exploring opportunities for selling its branded coffee beans through supermarkets, which still commanded 80 percent of all coffee sales and generated nearly $3 billion in revenues annually. The company designed a line of specialty coffees just for supermarkets and opened Starbucks-operated kiosks in selected grocery chains.

Communication Strategy

Starbucks historically invested very little in advertising—less than $100 million in its entire history. Explains Bedbury, "Our brand is at its best in the store."

LOOKING TO THE FUTURE

Schultz is considering developing partnerships with gourmet food sellers like Harry and David and home furnishing companies like Williams-Sonoma to launch a lifestyle Internet portal. The portal would offer access to a wide variety of products, services, and information sought by the typical Starbucks customer.

Discussion Questions

1. What is Starbucks' retail strategy? What is its target market and how does it try to develop an advantage over its competition?

2. Describe Starbucks' retail mix: location, merchandise assortment, pricing, advertising and promotion, store design and visual merchandising, customer service, and personal selling. How does its retail mix support its strategy?

3. What factors in the environment provided the opportunity for Starbucks to develop a new, successful retail chain? What demand and supply conditions prevailed in the U.S. coffee market when Howard Schultz purchased Starbucks in 1987? What insight did Schultz have that other players in the coffee market did not?

4. What were the principal drivers behind Starbucks' success in the marketplace? What does the Starbucks brand mean to consumers?

5. What are the major challenges facing Starbucks as it goes forward? Is the brand advantage sustainable going forward? Can Starbucks defend its position against other specialty coffee retailers?

Wolf Camera

RETURNING FROM A VA-CATION IN POLAND and Russia, a Delta Air Lines attendant recognized Chuck Wolf. Charles R. (Chuck) Wolf, long regarded as one of the most successful leaders and entrepreneurs in the retail photography industry, is the president and CEO of Wolf Camera. The flight attendant thanked him for opening a photo store in Macon, Georgia, where she lives. In return, Wolf gave her a coupon for free processing of a roll of film. The gesture is telling. Atlanta-based Wolf Camera & Video is successful because its founder knows how to make customers feel wanted. "He deserves some attention for what he does," said Kenneth Bernhardt, a marketing professor at Georgia State University. "He's bringing in new customers, and once he gets them in the door, he's got the programs in place to keep them there."

Wolf Camera was founded in 1974, when Wolf swapped his stock in Ritz Camera for nine stores in Atlanta, Georgia and Charlotte, North Carolina. Wolf's growth has been the result of a steadfast commitment to customer satisfaction, providing the best selection of photo and video products and accessories, followed by the best service at the lowest possible prices.

Photography retailing, including film sales and processing and equipment sales, has evolved along two tracks. Major retailers, such as discounters, drugstores, and supermarkets, set aside a corner of their floor space for photography. Stores that focus exclusively on photography are generally individual outlets or in small chains. In between are Wolf and Ritz Camera Centers. Both companies are busily building national chains of photo stores.

Wolf is one of about 5,000 specialty photo retailers, a rapidly shrinking market that numbered about 12,000 in the early 90s. While other independents sold out or closed shop, Wolf began a period of expansion that tripled the company's store count in the 90s and landed it in second place behind Ritz Camera, an 810-store chain. Most recently, Wolf has agreed to acquire Eastman Kodak's 450-store Fox Photo chain, which will more than double the retailer's size at the outset and catapult it to a near tie with the country's largest specialty photo retailer.

"This is the most exciting news for Wolf Camera since our founding 24 years ago," said Mr. Wolf. "We used to say we were a coast-to-coast company, but the addition of the Fox, CPI, and Proex stores will make Wolf Camera a truly national photo retailer, with nearly 800 stores in 35 states and the District of Columbia." Indeed, the combination of the two companies will form a powerful new alliance in Wolf's continuing effort to be the nation's premier photography store.

In 1974, 10 percent of Wolf's revenue was from photofinishing, compared to nearly 40 percent today. Wolf does not try to compete negative-for-negative on price with discounters. It sells quality instead. Every Wolf Camera store has one-hour 35mm photofinishing, and more than 100 stores offer on-site 24mm APS one-hour processing as well. Unlike at most supermarkets and drugstores, film at Wolf Camera never leaves the store.

Wolf claimed, "We have found our niche. And our niche is not only having very competitive prices, but having service that exceeds our customers' expectations. And the quality of our product, which is the photofinishing product, we feel is far above anything else." This has allowed Wolf to attract and retain regular loyal customers who use their Wolfpack frequent user benefits to save money on processing related services. The Wolfpack Club, which offers discounts on film processing, now has 600,000 members and has been a successful way to encourage repeat business. While the average consumer turns in five rolls of film a year, Wolfpack members typically process a dozen rolls annually. "It's separated us from our competition," said Wolf about the WolfPack. "I have a great name, and I might as well use it."

In TV commercial spots, Wolf places broccoli in a grocery cart and picks a box of aspirin off a shelf. The message: You don't buy those products at Wolf Camera, so why take your film processing to a grocery or drugstore? "They're in a tough business, because it's price sensitive and they get hit from the one-hour places on one side and the mass merchants on the other side," said Cynthia Cohen, a Miami-based retail consultant. "This is a business that years ago was a mom-and-pop operation," explained David Herskovits, head of the retail practice at Deloitte & Touche. "Chuck has taken this thing and really grown it, especially in the last five years, because he understands people and marketing."

To separate Wolf from the stand-alone one-hour lab, the hard-goods-only camera store, or the mass merchant, Wolf maintains a two-core business: film processing and the sale of cameras, camcorders, and the latest innovations to serve their customers. Film processing is, however, the most profitable part of the business.

Over the years, processing has evolved with technology. For example, Wolf welcomed the Advanced Photo System with open arms. "The first year was a little rocky from the manufacturers," Chuck Wolf remarked. "It was a new technology we had to teach our customers. The versatility—small film cassettes, smaller cameras, three different print sizes and index prints—is the greatest innovation in photography since color film." Additionally, Wolf Camera now provides photo-to-floppy-disk transfers so customers can view their pictures on their home computers. Wolf can upload consumers' images to the Wolf Photonet from their photography center, which delivers images on the Internet.

The introduction of digital cameras, because they are linked to a computer, has also opened up a whole new area of competition. "We are embracing it; we're not fighting it," said Wayne Freedman, vice president of marketing. First, the company is selling "a ton" of digital cameras. Then, it is preparing to be able to offer processing for digital cameras that will far exceed the quality of home equipment, he said. One research analyst said that he does not expect an impact on specialty photo processing chains for another two years or so, until digital cameras get below $500 for an easy-to-use camera that produces quality prints. Then there will only be a modest impact, predicted Ron Tussy of International Data Corp. "People will buy a digital camera and still not

want to mess with it," he said. Photos still need to be color corrected, sharpened, and output to print, so many people will still pay to have it done, he said.

Despite the new competition, 35mm cameras seem unlikely to fade away soon, as camera manufacturers continue to produce and promote them. Digital technology is "not better than 35mm, it's different," Freedman said. "35mm is still the quality standard; it still gives the best results for the least amount of money."

Outside of film processing, the equipment business also poses challenges with the whims of technology. Wolf has always embraced any new developments in the industry, including digital imaging and Internet scanning services. Wolf was one of the first to try one-hour photo labs. "We dive in as soon as we can," Wolf said. "New technology gets people into the store."

"When Chuck sees a new product, he can tell if it's going to be successful," said Jerry Johnson, vice president and general manager of Eastman Kodak's consumer imaging division. "He's truly a merchant at heart. He has the unique ability to find consumer applications." For example, consumers can bring creased and faded photos into a Wolf store and have them refurbished. There have been a few duds, though. Wolf admits that video rentals, radios, and cellular phones were ill-fated tests.

New technology aside, Wolf has no plans to abandon his niche in film processing, which he stated is relatively recession proof in the picture snapping needs of consumers. "If there's a downturn, they may not take European vacations, but they'll still take a weekend trip," he said. "And people will still get married and have children regardless."

The future of the photo industry, in terms of growth, is not so much with people who are already taking lots of pictures and know about and love photography. It lies more with the people who are not taking pictures and might be a bit intimidated by photography. Wolf is trying to cement photography as an activity and position itself as the family photography store.

Wolf Camera has found several avenues to work with children to promote ongoing public relations and marketing campaigns. During the last five years, more than 500 schools throughout the country have been involved in Wolf's Kids-n-

Kodak camera program, which gives youngsters a chance to learn photography and put their skills to use. Wolf Camera estimates that more than 4,000 students will participate this year.

The program, which teams Wolf with Kodak, provides participating students with a 12-exposure Kodak disposable camera. A special curriculum is given to the teachers, and everyone sees how photofinishing is done. Each student gets a processing certificate and a temporary Wolfpack discount card for parents. The public relations effort tied to this program has helped Wolf gain significant media exposure.

In 1996, Wolf launched a Focus on Kids program designed to allow schools to earn free photography, video, and imaging equipment. The promotions had two goals: to bring media attention to Wolf and to help schools by donating needed equipment. Children from participating schools collect original receipts for products and services purchased at any Wolf Camera store. Once a school has accumulated various total amounts, it can redeem them for merchandise prizes. By using five redemption levels, Wolf Camera hopes to interest small schools that might otherwise find the program unrealistic. Persuading the media to assume much of the burden in spreading the word about the program permits Wolf Camera to devote 95 percent of the funds allocated to the program to equipment premiums while spending only 5 percent on administration and printed materials for participating schools.

Wolf Camera does not stop there. In its continuing efforts to draw children into the hobby of photography, it has several other programs started and in the planning stages. Kids are computer literate, and they know how to scan and manipulate photos, so Wolf offers kids and their families the opportunity to put their pictures on its online magazine for kids, TCFG (*Too Cool for Grown-Ups*). All the kids have to do is bring their film into a Wolf Camera store for developing and mention *TCFG*. Wolf will then put their pictures on the Wolf Photonet website, free of charge. Other programs on Wolf Photonet include photo contests, a pen pal area where kids can exchange e-mail, and pictures, film, and cameras for a "Day in the Life of Kids at School" projects.

Discussion Questions

1. What is Wolf Camera's retail strategy?
2. What are the key factors in Wolf Camera's success in the photography marketplace?
3. What are Wolf Camera's strengths and weaknesses? Threats and opportunities?
4. What does Wolf Camera need to do to continue its success?

CASE 31

Lindy's Bridal Shoppe

LOCATED IN LAKE CITY (population 80,000), Lindy's Bridal Shoppe, a small bridal store, sells bridal gowns, prom gowns, accessories, and silk flowers. It also rents men's formal wear and performs various alteration services.

Lindy Armstrong, age 33, has owned the store since its founding in March 1997. She's married to a high school teacher and is the mother of three young children. A former nurse, she found the demands of hospital schedules left too little time for her young family. An energetic, active woman with many interests, she wanted to continue to work but also have time with her children.

The silk flowers market enabled Lindy to combine an in-home career with child rearing. She started Lindy's Silk Flowers with $75 of flower inventory in Vernon, a small town of about 10,000 people 10 miles from Lake City. Working out of her home, she depended on word-of-mouth communication among her customers (mainly brides) to bring in business. As Lindy's Silk Flowers prospered, a room was added onto the house to provide more space for the business. Lindy was still making all the flowers herself. Her flower-making schedule kept her extremely busy. Long hours were the norm.

Lindy was approached by a young photographer named Dan Morgan, who proposed establishing a one-stop bridal shop. In this new business,

Dan would provide photography, Lindy would provide silk flowers, and another partner, Karen Ross (who had expertise in the bridal market), would provide gowns and accessories. The new store would be located in Vernon in a rented structure. Shortly before the store was to open, Dan and Karen decided not to become partners and Lindy became the sole owner. She knew nothing about the bridal business. Having no merchandise or equipment, Lindy was drawn to an ad announcing that a bridal store in a major city was going out of business. She immediately called and arranged to meet the owner. Subsequently she bought all his stock (mannequins, racks, and carpet) for $4,000. The owner also gave her a crash course in the bridal business.

From March 1994 to December 1996, Lindy Armstrong owned and operated a bridal gown and silk flowers store named Lindy's Bridal Shoppe in Vernon. The location was chosen primarily because it was close to her home. While Vernon is a very small town, Lindy felt that location wasn't a critical factor in her store's success. She maintained that people would travel some distance to make a purchase as important as a bridal gown. Rent was $250 per month plus utilities. Parking was a problem.

During this period, Lindy's Bridal Shoppe grew. Bridal gowns and accessories as well as prom gowns sold well. As the time approached for Lindy to renew her lease, she wondered about the importance of location. A move to Lake City might be advisable.

A much larger town than Vernon, Lake City is the site of a state university. Lindy decided to move.

GENERAL BUSINESS DESCRIPTION

The majority of Lindy's Bridal Shoppe's current sales are made to individuals who order bridal gowns from the rack or from the catalogs of three major suppliers. At the time of the order, the customer pays a deposit (usually half of the purchase price). The balance is due in 30 days. Lindy would like payment in full at the time of ordering regardless of the delivery date. But payment is often delayed until delivery. Once ordered, a gown must be taken and the bill paid when delivered.

No tuxedos are carried in the store so customers must order from catalogs. Fitting jackets and shoes are provided to help patrons size their purchases. Lindy's Bridal Shoppe rents its men's formal wear from suppliers. Payment from the customer is due on delivery.

Certain times of the year see more formal events than others. Many school proms are held during late April and May, while June, July, and August are big months for weddings. Since traditional dates for weddings are followed less and less closely, Lindy believes that the business is becoming less seasonal, though January and February are quite slow.

PROMOTION PRACTICES

Lindy's Bridal Shoppe engages in various promotional activities but is constrained by its limited financial ability. The firm has no operating budget, which prevents any formal appropriation for advertising expenses.

Newspaper ads constitute the primary promotional medium, though radio is occasionally used. Ads for prom gowns are run only during prom season. These ads usually feature a photograph of a local high school student in a Lindy's Bridal Shoppe gown plus a brief description of the student's activities.

Other promotional activities include bridal shows at a local mall. Lindy feels these have been very successful, though they're a lot of work. A recent prom show in a local high school used students as models. This proved to be an excellent way to stimulate sales. Lindy hopes to go into several other area high schools during the next prom season though this will demand much planning.

PERSONNEL

Lindy Armstrong (the sole owner and also the manager of the firm) finds it hard to maintain a capable workforce. A small company, Lindy's Bridal Shoppe can't offer premium salaries for its few positions. There's one full-time salesperson. The part-time staff includes a salesperson, alterations person, bookkeeper, and custodian.

Lindy handles all the paperwork. Her responsibilities include paying bills, ordering merchandise and supplies, hiring and firing personnel, fitting customers, and selling various items. She makes all the major decisions that directly affect the firm's operations. She also makes all the silk flowers herself. It's time consuming, but she isn't satisfied with how anyone else makes them.

MERCHANDISE OFFERINGS

Lindy's Bridal Shoppe's major product lines are new wedding, prom, and party gowns. No used gowns are sold. Discontinued styles or gowns that have been on the rack for a year are sold at reduced prices, primarily because discoloration is a major problem. Gowns tend to yellow after hanging on the racks for a year.

A wide variety of accessories are provided. Lindy believes it's important that her customers not have to go anywhere else for them. These accessories include shoes, veils, headpieces, jewelry, and foundations. Slips may be rented instead of purchased.

One room of Lindy's Bridal Shoppe is used only to prepare silk flowers.

SERVICE OFFERINGS

Lindy's Bridal Shoppe's major service offering is fitting and alteration. Most gowns must be altered, for which there's a nominal charge. Lindy Armstrong feels that personal attention and personal service set her apart from her competitors. Stressing customer satisfaction, she works hard to please each customer. This isn't always easy. Customers can be picky, and it takes time to deal with unhappy people.

LOCATION

Lindy's Bridal Shoppe is located at the end of Lake City's main through street. Initially Lindy didn't think location was important to her bridal store's success, but she's changed her mind. Whereas business was good in Vernon, it's booming in Lake City. Vehicular traffic is high, and there's adequate, if not excess, parking.

Lindy's Bridal Shoppe has a 12-year lease. Rent ($1,800 per month) includes heat and water, but Lindy's Bridal Shoppe must pay for interior decoration. The physical facility is generally attractive, with open and inviting interior display areas. But some areas both inside and outside the store have an unfinished look.

Some storage areas require doors or screens to enhance the interior's appearance. The fitting room ceilings are unfinished, and the carpeting inside the front door may be unsafe. One other interior problem is insufficient space. There seems to be inadequate space for supporting activities such as flower preparation, customer fittings, and merchandise storage, which gives the store a cluttered look.

Several external problems exist. The signs are ineffective, and there's a strong glare on the front windows. This detracts from the effectiveness of the overall appearance and interior window displays. The parking lot needs minor maintenance. Parking lines should be painted and curbs must be repaired. Much should be done to add color and atmosphere through basic landscaping.

COMPETITION

Lindy's Bridal Shoppe is the only bridal shop in Lake City. Lindy believes she has four main competitors. Whitney's Bridal Shoppe is 30 miles from Lake City; Ender's Brides, a new shop with a good operation, is in Spartan City, 50 miles away; Carole's is a large, established bridal shop in Smithtown, 70 miles distant; and Gowns-n-Such is in Andersonville, 75 miles away. A new store in Yorktown (15 miles away) is selling used gowns and discontinued styles at very reduced prices. Lindy watches this new-and used-gown store closely.

Some of her potential customers are buying wedding gowns from electronic retailers such as The Knot (www.theknot.com) and The Wedding Channel (www.weddingchannel.com). While these electronic retailers are making significant sales in her trading area now, Lindy is concerned that some of the services offered by these electronic retailers (such as gift registries, e-mail notices, wedding planning, and wedding picture displays) will attract her customers.

FINANCIAL CONSIDERATIONS

Basic financial information includes

1. Markup: 50 percent.
2. 1999 sales: $200,000 (estimated).
3. Average inventory: $70,000.
4. Turnover: 3.0 (approximately).
5. Annual expenses are
    Rent: $19,200.
    Labor: $24,000.
    Utilities: $7,000.
    Supplies: $12,000.
    Equipment: $4,000.
    Miscellaneous: $4,000.

6. Estimated total costs ($200,000 sales): $170,200.

7. Implied profit including owner's salary: $29,800.

8. Capital invested (equipment, $8,000; inventory, $70,000): $78,000.

9. ROI: $5,800/$78,000 = 7.4 percent. (Assume owner salary of $24,000 per year.)

THE FUTURE

Lindy Armstrong is uncertain about the future. She enjoys the business but feels that she's working very hard and not making much money. During all the years of Lindy's Bridal Shoppe's operation, she hasn't taken a salary. She works 60 hours or more a week. Business is excellent and growing, but she's tired. She has even discussed selling the business and returning to nursing.

Discussion Questions

1. Could Lindy change the emphasis of her merchandise mix to increase her sales?

2. Which products should have more emphasis? Which should have less?

3. What personnel decisions must Lindy face to improve her business?

4. How could someone like Lindy Armstrong balance the demands of her family and her business?

5. If one of Lindy's competitors were to offer her $150,000 for her business, should she sell?

Source: This case was prepared by Linda F. Felicetti and Joseph P. Grunewald, Clarion University of Pennsylvania.

ABC analysis an analysis that rank-orders SKUs by a profitability measure to determine which items should never be out of stock, which should be allowed to be out of stock occasionally, and which should be deleted from the stock selection.

abilities the aptitude and skills of an employee.

accessibility the degree to which customers can easily get into and out of a shopping center.

accessories merchandise in apparel, department, and specialty stores used to complement apparel outfits. Examples include gloves, hosiery, handbags, jewelry, handkerchiefs, and scarves.

accordion theory a cyclical theory of retailer evolution suggesting that changes in retail institutions are explained in terms of depth versus breadth of assortment. Retail institutions cycle from high-depth/low-breadth to low-depth/high-breadth stores and back again.

account opener a premium or special promotion item offered to induce the opening of a new account, especially in financial institutions and stores operating on an installment credit basis.

accounts payable the amount of money owed to vendors, primarily for merchandise inventory.

accounts receivable the amount of money due to the retailer from selling merchandise on credit.

accrued liabilities liabilities that accumulate daily but are paid only at the end of a period.

acquisition a strategic growth activity in which one firm acquires another firm, usually resulting in a merger. See also **leveraged buyout.**

actionability means that the definition of a market segment must clearly indicate what the retailer should do to satisfy its needs.

activity-based costing (ABC) a financial management tool in which all major activities within a cost center are identified, calculated, and then charged to cost objects, such as stores, product categories, product lines, specific products, customers, and suppliers.

adaptive selling an approach to personal selling in which selling behaviors are altered based on information about the customer and the buying situation.

additional markup an increase in retail price after and in addition to original markup.

additional markup cancelation the percentage by which the retail price is lowered after a markup is taken.

additional markup percentage the addition of a further markup to the original markup as a percentage of net sales.

administered vertical marketing system a form of vertical marketing system designed to control a line of classification of merchandise as opposed to an entire store's operation. Such systems involve the development of comprehensive programs for specified lines of merchandise. The vertically aligned companies, even though in a nonownership position, may work together to reduce the total systems cost of such activities as advertising, transportation, and data processing. (See also **contractual vertical marketing system** and **corporate vertical marketing system.**)

advanced shipping notice (ASN) an electronic document received by the retailer's computer from a supplier in advance of a shipment.

advertising paid communications delivered to customers through nonpersonal mass media such as newspapers, television, radio, and direct mail.

advertising manager a retail manager who manages advertising activities such as determining the advertising budget, allocating the budget, developing ads, selecting media, and monitoring advertising effectiveness.

advertising reach the percentage of customers in the target market exposed to an ad at least once.

affiliate program communications programs electronic retailers are developing in which they are the permanent advertiser on a site. Also called **associate programs.**

affinity marketing marketing activities that enable consumers to express their identification with an organization. An example is offering credit cards tied to reference groups like the consumer's university or an NFL team.

affordable budgeting method a budgeting method in which a retailer first sets a budget for every element of the retail mix except promotion and then allocates the leftover funds to a promotional budget.

Age Discrimination and Employment Act a federal act that makes it illegal to discriminate in hiring and termination decisions concerning people between the ages of 40 and 70.

agent (1) a business unit that negotiates purchases, sales, or both but does not take title to the goods in which it deals. (2) a person who represents the principal (who, in the case of retailing, is the store or merchant) and who acts under authority, whether in buying or in bringing the principal into business relations with third parties.

aging   the length of time merchandise has been in stock.

all-purpose revolving account   a regular 30-day charge account that, if paid in full within 30 days from date of statement, has no service charge, but when installment payments are made, a service charge is made on the balance at the time of the next billing.

alteration costs   expenses incurred to change the appearance or fit, to assemble, or to repair merchandise.

Americans with Disabilities Act (ADA)   a federal act that opens up job opportunities for the disabled by requiring employees to provide accommodating work environments.

analog approach   a method of trade area analysis also known as the "similar store" or "mapping" approach. The analysis is divided into four steps: (1) describing the current trade areas through the technique of customer spotting, (2) plotting the customers on a map, (3) defining the primary, secondary, and tertiary area zones, and (4) matching the characteristics of stores in the trade areas with the potential new store to estimate its sales potential.

anchor store   a large, well-known retail operation located in a shopping center or Internet mall and serving as an attracting force for consumers to the center.

ancillary services   services such as layaway, gift wrap, and credit that are not directly related to the actual sale of a specific product within the store.

anticipation discount   a discount offered by a vendor to a retailer in addition to the cash discount or dating, if the retailer pays the invoice before the end of the cash discount period.

anticompetitive leasing arrangement   a lease that limits the type and amount of competition a particular retailer faces within a trading area.

antitrust legislation   a set of laws directed at preventing unreasonable restraint of trade or unfair trade practices. Aim is to foster a competitive environment. See also **restraint of trade.**

application form   a form used for information on a job applicant's education, employment experience, hobbies, and references.

artificial barriers   in site evaluations for accessibility, barriers such as railroad tracks, major highways, or parks.

asset turnover   net sales divided by total assets.

assets   economic resources (such as inventory or store fixtures) owned or controlled by an enterprise as a result of past transactions or events.

associate programs   see **affiliate programs.**

assortment   the number of SKUs within a merchandise category.

assortment plan   a list of merchandise that indicates in very general terms what should be carried in a particular merchandise category.

assortment providing   a function performed by retailers that enables customers to choose from a selection of brands, designs, sizes, and prices at one location.

atmospherics   the design of an environment via visual communications, lighting, colors, music, and scent to stimulate customers' perceptual and emotional responses and ultimately to affect their purchase behavior.

auction   a market in which goods are sold to the highest bidder; usually well publicized in advance or held at specific times that are well known in the trade. Auctions are becoming very popular over the Internet.

autocratic method of store management   when managers make all decisions on their own and then announce them to employees.

automatic reordering system   a system for ordering staple merchandise using a predetermined minimum quantity of goods in stock. An automatic reorder can be generated by a computer on the basis of a perpetual inventory system and reorder point calculations.

average BOM stock-to-sales ratio   the number of months in the period divided by planned inventory turnover for the period.

average inventory   the sum of inventory on hand at several periods in time divided by the number of periods.

baby boomer   the generational cohort of people born between 1946 and 1964.

back order   a part of an order that the vendor has not filled on time and that the vendor intends to ship as soon as the goods in question are available.

backup stock   the inventory used to guard against going out of stock when demand exceeds forecasts or when merchandise is delayed.

backward integration   a form of vertical integration in which a retailer owns some or all of its suppliers.

bait-and-switch   an unlawful deceptive practice that lures customers into a store by advertising a product at lower than usual prices (the *bait*), then inducing the customers to switch to a higher-price model (the *switch*).

balance sheet   the summary of a retailer's financial resources and claims against the resources at a particular date; indicates the relationship between assets, liabilities, and owners' equity.

bank card   credit card issued by a bank, such as Visa and MasterCard.

bar code   see **Universal Product Code (UPC).**

bargain branding a branding strategy that targets a price sensitive segment by offering a no-frills product at a discount price.

bargaining power of vendors a competitive factor that makes markets unattractive when a few vendors control the merchandise sold in it. In these situations, vendors have an opportunity to dictate prices and other terms, reducing retailer's profits.

barriers to entry conditions in a retail market that make it difficult for firms to enter the market.

base stock see **cycle stock.**

basic merchandise see **staple merchandise.**

basic stock list the descriptive and recordkeeping function of an inventory control system; includes the stock number, item description, number of units on hand and on order, and sales for the previous periods.

basic stock method an inventory management method used to determine the beginning-of-month (BOM) inventory by considering both the forecast sales for the month and the safety stock.

benchmarking the practice of evaluating performance by comparing your performance with that of other retailers using a similar retail strategy.

benefit segmentation a method of segmenting a retail market based on similar benefits sought in merchandise and/or services.

benefits the customer's specific needs that are satisfied when the customer buys a product.

benefits/price effect the condition that arises when customers' price sensitivity increases because they cannot perceive special benefits from a product.

black market the availability of merchandise at a high price when it is difficult or impossible to purchase under normal market circumstances; commonly involves illegal transactions.

blue laws laws prohibiting retailers from being open two consecutive days of the weekend—ostensibly to allow employees a day of rest or religious observance. Most states no longer have blue laws.

bonus additional compensation awarded periodically, based on a subjective evaluation of the employee's performance.

book inventory system see **retail inventory method.**

bottom-up planning when goals are set at the bottom of the organization and filter up through the operating levels.

boutique departments in a store designed to resemble small, self-contained stores.

boutique layout see **free-form layout.**

brand a distinctive grouping of products identified by corporate name, logo, design, symbol, or trademark.

brand building the design and implementation of a retail communication program to create an image in the customer's mind of the retailer relative to its competitors. Also called **positioning.**

brand loyal term for customers who like and consistently buy a specific brand in a product category.

brand loyalty an example of habitual decision making that occurs when consumers like and consistently buy a specific brand in a product category.

breadth of merchandise see **variety.**

break-even analysis a technique that evaluates the relationship between total revenue and total cost to determine profitability at various sales levels.

break-even point the quantity at which total revenue equals total cost, and beyond which profit occurs.

breaking bulk a function performed by retailers or wholesalers in which they receive large quantities of merchandise and sell them in smaller quantities.

breaking sizes running out of stock on particular sizes.

broker a middleman that serves as a go-between for the buyer or seller; assumes no title risks, does not usually have physical custody of products, and is not looked upon as a permanent representative of either the buyer or seller.

buffer stock merchandise inventory used as a safety cushion for cycle stock so the retailer won't run out of stock if demand exceeds the sales forecast. Also called **safety stock.**

building codes legal restrictions describing the size and type of building, signs, type of parking lot, and so on that can be used at a particular location.

bulk fixture see **rounder.**

bulk-of-stock area the store area in which the total assortment of merchandise is placed. Usually contains gondolas in grocery and discount stores and freestanding fixtures for soft goods in other types of stores.

buyback a strategy vendors and retailers use to get products into retail stores, either when a retailer allows a vendor to create space for goods by "buying back" a competitor's inventory and removing it from a retailer's system, or when the retailer forces a vendor to buy back slow-moving merchandise.

buyer's market market occurring in economic conditions that favor the position of the retail buyer (or merchandiser) rather than the vendor; in other words, economic conditions are such that the retailer can demand and usually get concessions from suppliers in terms of price, delivery, and other market advantages. Opposite of a seller's market.

buyer's report   information on the velocity of sales, availability of inventory, amount of order, inventory turnover, forecast sales, and, most important, the quantity that should be ordered for each SKU.

buying behavior   the activities customers undertake when purchasing a good or service.

buying calendar   a plan of a store buyer's market activities, generally covering a six-month merchandising season based on a selling calendar that indicates planned promotional events.

buying committee   a committee that has the authority for final judgment and decision making on such matters as adding or eliminating new products.

buying power   the customer's financial resources available for making purchases.

buying process   the stages customers go through to purchase merchandise or services.

buying situation segmentation   a method of segmenting a retail market based on customer needs in a specific buying situation such as a fill-in shopping trip versus a weekly shopping trip.

call system   a system of equalizing sales among salespersons—for example, some stores rotate salespeople, giving each an equal opportunity to meet customers.

capacity fixture   see **rounder.**

career path   the set of positions to which management employees are promoted within a particular organization as their careers progress.

cart   a retail facility that offers the simplest presentation, is mobile, and is on wheels.

cash   money on hand.

cash discounts   reductions in the invoice cost that the vendor allows the retailer for paying the invoice prior to the end of the discount period.

catalog retailer   a nonstore retailer that communicates directly with customers using catalogs sent through the mail.

catalog showroom   a type of retailer that uses a showroom to display merchandise combined with an adjacent warehouse; typically specializes in hard goods such as housewares.

category   an assortment of items (SKUs) the customer sees as reasonable substitutes for each other.

category captain   a supplier that forms an alliance with a retailer to help gain consumer insight, satisfy consumer needs, and improve the performance and profit potential across the entire category.

category killer   a discount retailer that offers a complete assortment in a category and thus dominates a category from the customers' perspective.

category life cycle   a merchandise category's sales pattern over time.

category management   the process of managing a retail business with the objective of maximizing the sales and profits of a category.

category specialist   a discount store that offers a narrow variety but deep assortment of merchandise.

caveat emptor   Latin term for "let the buyer beware."

census tracts   subdivisions of a **Metropolitan Statistical Area (MSA),** with an average population of 4,000.

central business district (CBD)   the traditional downtown business area of a city or town.

central market   see **market.**

central place   a center of retailing activity such as a town or city.

central place theory   Christaller's theory of retail location suggesting that retailers tend to locate in a central place. As more retailers locate together, more customers are attracted to the central place. See also **central place.**

centralization   the degree to which authority for making retail decisions is delegated to corporate managers rather than to geographically dispersed regional, district, and store management.

centralized buying   a situation in which a retailer makes all purchase decisions at one location, typically the firm's headquarters.

chain   see **retail chain.**

chain discount   a number of different discounts taken sequentially from the suggested retail price.

channel of distribution   see **distribution channel.**

chargeback   a practice used by retailers in which they deduct money from the amount they owe a vendor.

chat room   location in an Internet site at which customers can engage in interactive, real-time, text-based discussions.

checking   the process of going through goods upon receipt to make sure that they arrived undamaged and that the merchandise received matches the merchandise ordered.

cherry picking   customers visiting a store and buying only merchandise sold at big discounts.

classic   a fashion that has both a high level and a long duration of acceptance.

classification   a group of items or SKUs for the same type of merchandise, such as pants (as opposed to jackets or suits), supplied by different vendors.

classification dominance an assortment so broad that customers should be able to satisfy all of their consumption needs for a particular category by visiting one retailer.

classification merchandising divisions of departments into related types of merchandise for reporting and control purposes.

Clayton Act (1914) an act passed as a response to the deficiencies of the **Sherman Act;** it specifically prohibits price discrimination, tying arrangements, and exclusive dealing contracts that have the effect of limiting free trade, and it provides for damages to parties injured as a result of violations of the act.

clearance sale an end-of-season sale to make room for new goods; also pushing the sale of slow-moving, shop-worn, and demonstration model goods.

close-out an offer at a reduced price to clear slow-moving or incomplete stock; also, an incomplete assortment, the remainder of a line of merchandise that is to be discontinued and so is offered at a low price to ensure immediate sale.

close-out retailer off-price retailer that sells a broad but inconsistent assortment of general merchandise as well as apparel and soft home goods, obtained through retail liquidations and bankruptcy proceedings.

cocooning a term that describes a behavioral pattern of consumers who increasingly turn to the nice, safe, familiar environment of their homes to spend their limited leisure time.

COD (collect on delivery) purchase terms in which payment for a product is collected at the time of delivery.

collaboration, planning, forecasting, and replenishment (CPFR) an inventory management system in which a retailer will send information to a manufacturer and the manufacturer will use the data to construct a computer-generated replenishment forecast that will be shared with the retailer before it's executed.

combination store food-based retailer between 30,000 and 100,000 square feet in size with over 25 percent of its sales from nonfood merchandise such as flowers, health and beauty aids, kitchen utensils, photo developing, prescription drugs, and videotape rentals.

commercial bribery a vendor's offer of money or gifts to a retailer's employee for the purpose of influencing purchasing decisions.

commission compensation based on a fixed formula, such as percentage of sales.

committee buying the situation whenever the buying decision is made by a group of people rather than by a single buyer. A multiunit operation is usually the type of firm that uses this procedure.

common stock the type of stock most frequently issued by corporations. Owners of common stock usually have voting rights in the retail corporation.

communication gap the difference between the actual service provided to customers and the service promised in the retailer's promotion program. This factor is one of the four factors identified by the GAPS model for improving service quality.

communication objectives specific goals for a communication program related to the effects of the communication program on the customer's decision-making process.

community center shopping center that typically includes a discount store, specialty department store, super drugstore, home improvement center, and other convenience and shopping goods stores.

comparative price advertising a common retailing practice that compares the price of merchandise offered for sale with a higher "regular" price or a manufacturer's list price.

comparison shopping a market research method in which retailers shop at competitive stores, comparing the merchandise, pricing, visual display, and service to their own offering.

compensation monetary payments including salary, commission, and bonuses; also, paid vacations, health and insurance benefits, and a retirement plan.

competitive-oriented pricing a pricing method in which a retailer uses competitors' prices (rather than demand or cost considerations) as guides.

competitive parity method an approach for setting a promotion budget so that the retailer's share of promotion expenses is equal to its market share.

competitive rivalry the frequency and intensity of reactions to actions undertaken by competitors.

competitor analysis an examination of the strategic direction that competitors are likely to pursue and their ability to successfully implement their strategy.

composite segmentation a method of segmenting a retail market using multiple variables including benefits sought, lifestyles, and demographics.

computerized checkout see **point-of-sale (POS) terminal.**

conditional sales agreement an agreement that passes title of goods to the consumer, conditional on full payment.

conditions of sale see **terms of sale.**

conflict of interest a situation in which a decision maker's personal interest influences or has the potential to influence his or her professional decision.

congestion the amount of crowding of either cars or people.

consideration set the set of alternatives the customer evaluates when making a merchandise selection.

consignment goods items not paid for by the retailer until they are sold. The retailer can return unsold merchandise; however, the retailer does not take title until final sale is made.

consumer cooperative customers own and operate this type of retail establishment. Customers have ownership shares, hire full-time managers, and share in the store's profits through price reductions or dividends.

Consumer Goods Pricing Act (1975) the statute that repealed all resale price maintenance laws and made it possible for retailers to sell products below suggested retail prices.

consumerism the activities of government, business, and independent organizations designed to protect individuals from practices that infringe upon their rights as consumers.

contest promotional activity in which customers compete for rewards through games of chance. Contests can also be used to motivate retail employees.

contract distribution service company firm that performs all of the distribution functions for retailers or vendors, including transportation to the contract company's distribution center, merchandise processing, storage, and transportation to retailers.

contractual vertical marketing system a form of vertical marketing system in which independent firms at different levels in the channel operate contractually to obtain the economies and market impacts that could not be obtained by unilateral action. Under this system, the identity of the individual firm and its autonomy of operations remain intact. See also **administered vertical marketing system** and **corporate vertical marketing system.**

contribution margin gross margin less any expense that can be directly assigned to the merchandise.

convenience center a shopping center that typically includes such stores as a convenience market, a dry cleaner, or a liquor store.

convenience goods products that the consumer is not willing to spend the effort to evaluate prior to purchase, such as milk or bread.

convenience store a store that provides a limited variety and assortment of merchandise at a convenient loca-

tion in a 2,000- to 3,000–square-foot store with speedy checkout.

conventional supermarket a self-service food store that offers groceries, meat, and produce with limited sales of nonfood items, such as health and beauty aids and general merchandise.

cooperative an establishment owned by an association of customers. In general, the distinguishing features of a cooperative are patronage dividends based on the volume of expenditures by the members and a limitation of one vote per member regardless of the amount of stock owned.

cooperative (co-op) advertising a program undertaken by a vendor in which the vendor agrees to pay all or part of a promotion for its products.

cooperative buying when a group of independent retailers work together to make large purchases from a single supplier.

copy the text in an advertisement.

copycat branding a branding strategy that imitates the manufacturer brand in appearance and trade dress, but generally is perceived as lower quality and is offered at a lower price.

copyright a regulation that protects original works of authors, painters, sculptors, musicians, and others who produce works of artistic or intellectual merit.

core assortment a relatively large proportion of the total assortment that is carried by each store in the chain, regardless of size.

corporate vertical marketing system a form of vertical marketing system in which all of the functions from production to distribution are at least partially owned and controlled by a single enterprise. Corporate systems typically operate manufacturing plants, warehouse facilities, and retail outlets. See also **administered vertical marketing system** and **contractual vertical marketing system.**

corporation a firm that is formally incorporated under state law and that is a different legal entity from stockholders and employees.

cost code the item cost information indicated on price tickets in code. A common method of coding is the use of letters from an easily remembered word or expression with nonrepeating letters corresponding to numerals. For example,

y o u n g b l a d e

1 2 3 4 5 6 7 8 9 0

cost complement the percentage of net sales represented by the cost of goods sold.

cost method of accounting a method in which retailers record the cost of every item on an accounting sheet or include a cost code on the price tag or merchandise container. When a physical inventory is conducted, the cost of each item must be determined, the quantity in stock is counted, and the total inventory value at cost is calculated. See **retail inventory method.**

cost multiplier   the cumulative markup multiplied by 100 percent minus cumulative markup percentage.

cost-oriented method   a method for determining the retail price by adding a fixed percentage to the cost of the merchandise; also known as *cost-plus pricing.*

cost per thousand (CPM)   a measure that is often used to compare media. CPM is calculated by dividing an ad's cost by its reach.

counterfeit merchandise   goods that are made and sold without permission of the owner of a trademark, a copyright, or a patented invention that is legally protected in the country where it is marketed.

coupon   documents that entitle the holder to a reduced price or *x* cents off the actual price of a product or service.

courtesy days   the days on which stores extend to credit customers the privilege of making purchases at sale prices in advance of public sale.

coverage   the theoretical number of potential customers in the retailer's target market that could be exposed to an ad in a given medium.

credible commitment   tangible investment in a relationship between retailer and vendor.

credit   money placed at a consumer's disposal by a retailer or financial or other institution. For purchases made on credit, payment is due in the future.

credit limit   the quantitative limit that indicates the maximum amount of credit that may be allowed to be outstanding on each individual customer account.

cross-docking   when merchandise is delivered to one side of a warehouse by vendors, is unloaded, and is immediately reloaded onto trucks that deliver merchandise to the stores. With cross-docking, merchandise spends very little time in the warehouse.

cross-selling   when sales associates in one department attempt to sell complementary merchandise from other departments to their customers.

cross-shopping   a pattern of buying both premium and low-priced merchandise or patronizing expensive, status-oriented retailers and price-oriented retailers.

culture   the meaning and values shared by most members of a society.

cumulative attraction   the principle that a cluster of similar and complementary retailing activities will generally have greater drawing power than isolated stores that engage in the same retailing activities.

cumulative markup   the average percentage markup for the period; the total retail price minus cost divided by retail price.

cumulative quantity discounts   discounts earned by retailers when purchasing certain quantities over a specified period of time.

cumulative reach   the cumulative number of potential customers that would see an ad that runs several times.

current assets   cash or any assets that can normally be converted into cash within one year.

current liabilities   debts that are expected to be paid in less than one year.

current ratio   current assets divided by current liabilities; indicates the firm's ability to meet current debt with current assets.

customer allowance   an additional price reduction given to the customer.

customer buying process   the stages a customer goes through in purchasing a good or service. Stages include need recognition, information search, evaluation and choice of alternatives, purchase, and postpurchase evaluation.

customer loyalty   customers' commitment to shopping at a store.

customer returns   the value of merchandise that customers return because it is damaged, doesn't fit, and so forth.

customer service   the set of retail activities that increase the value customers receive when they shop and purchase merchandise.

customer service department   the department in a retail organization that handles customer inquiries and complaints.

customer spotting   a technique used in trade area analysis that "spots" (locates) residences of customers for a store or shopping center.

customization approach   an approach used by retailers to provide customer service that is tailored to meet each customer's personal needs.

cycle stock   inventory that results from the replenishment process and is required to meet demand when the retailer can predict demand and replenishment times (lead times) perfectly.

cyclical theories   theories of institutional change based on the premise that retail institutions change on the basis of cycles. See also **wheel of retailing** and **accordion theory.**

DAGMAR (defining advertising goals for measured advertising results)   a method for setting advertising goals based on communication objectives.

data warehouse   a computerized file of customer profiles and purchase patterns.

databased retailing   the development and implementation of retailing programs to build store loyalty utilizing a computerized file (data warehouse) of customer profiles and purchase patterns.

dating   a process that determines when discounts can be taken and when the full invoice amount is due.

deal period   a limited time period allowed by manufacturers to purchase merchandise at a special price.

debit card   a card that resembles a credit card but allows the retailer to automatically subtract payments from a customer's checking account at the time of sale.

decentralization   when authority for retail decisions is made at lower levels in the organization.

deceptive advertising   any advertisement that contains a false statement or misrepresents a product or service.

deferred billing   an arrangement that enables customers to buy merchandise and not pay for it for several months, with no interest charge.

delivery gap   the difference between the retailer's service standards and the actual service provided to customers. This factor is one of the four factors identified by the GAPS model for improving service quality.

demalling   the activity of revitalizing a mall by demolishing a mall's small shops, scrapping its common space and food courts, enlarging the sites once occupied by department stores, and adding more entrances into the parking lot.

demand/destination area   department or area in a store in which demand for the products or services offered is created before customers get to their destination.

demand-oriented method   a method of setting prices based on what the customers would expect or be willing to pay.

democratic method of store management   when a store manager seeks information and opinions from employees and bases decisions on this information.

demographic segmentation   a method of segmenting a retail market using demographic characteristics of consumers.

demographics   vital statistics about populations such as age, sex, and income.

department   a segment of a store with merchandise that represents a group of classifications the consumer views as being complementary.

department store   a retailer that carries a wide variety and deep assortment, offers considerable customer services, and is organized into separate departments for displaying merchandise.

departmentalization   an organizational design in which employees are grouped into departments that perform specific activities to achieve operating efficiencies through specialization.

depth interview   an unstructured personal interview in which the interviewer uses extensive probing to get individual respondents to talk in detail about a subject.

depth of merchandise   see **assortment**.

deseasonalized demand   the forecast demand without the influence of seasonality.

destination store   a retail store in which the merchandise, selection, presentation, pricing, or other unique feature acts as a magnet for customers.

dialectic theory   an evolutionary theory based on the premise that retail institutions evolve. The theory suggests that new retail formats emerge by adopting characteristics from other forms of retailers in much the same way that a child is the product of the pooled genes of two very different parents.

difficult comparison effect   the condition that arises when customers' price sensitivity increases because they find it difficult to compare existing brands.

direct investment   the investment and ownership by a retail firm or a division or subsidiary that builds and operates stores in a foreign country.

direct-mail catalog retailer   a retailer offering merchandise and/or services through catalogs mailed directly to customers.

direct-mail retailer   a nonstore retailer that communicates directly with customers using letters and brochures sent through the mail.

direct marketing   a form of nonstore retailing in which customers are exposed to merchandise through print or electronic media and then purchase the merchandise by telephone, mail, or over the Internet.

direct product profitability (DPP)   the profit associated with each category or unit of merchandise. DPP is equal to the per-unit gross margin less all variable costs associated with the merchandise such as procurement, distribution, sales, and the cost of carrying the assets.

direct response advertising   advertisements on TV and radio that describe products and provide an opportunity for customers to order them.

direct retailers   nonstore retailers that sell merchandise through salespeople who contact consumers directly or by telephone at home or place of work.

direct retailing   see **nonstore retailing**.

direct selling   a retail format in which a salesperson, frequently an independent distributor, contacts a customer directly in a convenient location (either at a customer's home or at work) and demonstrates merchandise benefits, takes an order, and delivers the merchandise to the customer.

disclosure of confidential information an unethical situation in which a retail employee discloses proprietary or confidential information about the firm's business to anyone outside the firm.

discount a reduction in the original retail price granted to store employees as special benefits or to customers under certain circumstances.

discount-anchored center a shopping center that contains one or more discount stores and smaller retail tenants.

discount-oriented center see **promotional center.**

discount store a general merchandise retailer that offers a wide variety of merchandise, limited service, and low prices.

disintermediation when a manufacturer sells directly to consumers, thus competing directly with its retailers.

dispatcher a person who coordinates deliveries to the distribution center.

display stock merchandise placed on various display fixtures for customers to examine.

distribution see **logistics.**

distribution center a warehouse that receives merchandise from multiple vendors and distributes it to multiple stores.

distribution channel a set of firms that facilitate the movement of products from the point of production to the point of sale to the ultimate consumer.

distribution intensity the number of retailers carrying a particular category.

distributive fairness the customers' perceptions of the benefits received compared to their costs, their inconvenience, or loss.

diversification opportunity a strategic investment opportunity that involves an entirely new retail format directed toward a market segment not presently being served.

diversionary pricing a practice sometimes used by retailers in which low price is stated for one or a few goods or services (emphasized in promotion) to give the illusion that the retailer's prices are all low.

diverted merchandise merchandise that is diverted from its legitimate channel of distribution similar to gray-market merchandise except there need not be distribution across international boundaries.

diverter a firm that buys unwanted merchandise from retailers and manufacturers and then resells the merchandise to other retailers.

double-coupon redemption a retail promotion that allows the customer to double the face value of a coupon.

drawing account a method of sales compensation in which salespeople receive a weekly check based on their estimated annual income.

drugstore specialty retail store that concentrates on pharmaceuticals and health and personal grooming merchandise.

dual distribution when a manufacturer or wholesaler uses multiple channels of distribution to reach ultimate consumers.

duty see **tariff.**

economic order quantity (EOQ) the order quantity that minimizes the total cost of processing orders and holding inventory.

electronic article surveillance system (EAS) a loss-prevention system in which special tags placed on merchandise in retail stores are deactivated when the merchandise is purchased. The tags are used to discourage shoplifting.

electronic data interchange (EDI) the computer-to-computer exchange of business documents from retailer to vendor, and back.

electronic retailing a retail format in which the retailer and customer communicate with each other through an interactive electronic network.

emotional support supporting retail service providers with the understanding and positive regard to enable them to deal with the emotional stress created by disgruntled customers.

employee discount a discount from retail price offered by most retailers to employees.

employee productivity output generated by employee activities. One measure of employee productivity is the retailer's sales or profit divided by its employee costs.

empowerment the policy of allowing employees at the firm's lowest level to make important decisions on how service is provided to customers.

empty nest a stage in a family life cycle where children have grown up and left home.

empty nester household where all children are grown and have left home.

end cap display fixture located at the end of an aisle.

end-of-month (EOM) dating a method of dating in which the discount period starts at the end of the month in which the invoice is dated (except when the invoice is dated the 25th or later).

energy management   the coordination of heating, air-conditioning, and lighting to improve efficiencies and reduce energy costs.

environmental apparel   merchandise produced with few or no harmful effects on the environment.

Equal Employment Opportunity Commission (EEOC)   a federal commission that was established for the purpose of taking legal action against employers that violate Title VII of the Civil Rights Act. Title VII prohibits discrimination in company personnel practices.

Equal Pay Act   A federal act enforced by the **Equal Employment Opportunity Commission (EEOC)** that prohibits unequal pay for men and women who perform equal work or work of comparable worth.

escape clause   a clause in a lease that allows the retailer to terminate its lease if sales don't reach a certain level after a specified number of years or if a specific co-tenant in the center terminates its lease.

ethics   a system or code of conduct based on universal moral duties and obligations that indicate how one should behave.

evaluation of alternatives   the stage in the buying process in which the customer compares the benefits offered by various retailers.

everyday-low-price strategy (EDLP)   a pricing strategy that stresses continuity of retail prices at a level somewhere between the regular nonsale price and the deep discount sale price of the retailer's competitors.

evolutionary theories   theories of institutional change based on the premise that retail institutions evolve. See **dialectic theory** and **natural selection.**

exclusive dealing agreement   restriction a manufacturer or wholesaler places on a retailer to carry only its products and no competing vendors' products.

exclusive geographical territory   a policy in which only one retailer in a certain territory is allowed to sell a particular brand.

exclusive use clause   a clause in a lease that prohibits the landlord from leasing to retailers selling competing products.

executive training program (ETP)   a training program for retail supervisors, managers, and executives.

expenses   costs incurred in the normal course of doing business to generate revenues.

experiment   a research method in which a variable is manipulated under controlled conditions.

expert system   computer program that incorporates knowledge of experts in a particular field. Expert systems are used to aid in decision making and problem solving.

exponential smoothing   a sales forecasting technique in which sales in previous time periods are weighted to develop a forecast for future periods.

express warranty   a guarantee supplied by either the retailer or the manufacturer that details the terms of the warranty in simple, easily understood language so customers know what is and what is not covered by the warranty.

extended problem solving   a buying process in which customers spend considerable time at each stage of the decision making process because the decision is important and they have limited knowledge of alternatives.

external source   information provided by the media and other people.

extra dating   a discount offered by a vendor in which the retailer receives extra time to pay the invoice and still take the cash discount.

extranet   a collaborative network that uses Internet technology to link businesses with their suppliers, customers, or other businesses.

extrinsic reward   reward (such as money, promotion, and recognition) given to employees by their manager or the firm.

factoring   a specialized financial function whereby manufacturers, wholesalers, or retailers sell accounts receivable to financial institutions, including factors for banks, and sales finance companies.

factory outlet store   outlet store owned by a manufacturer.

fad   a merchandise category that generates a lot of sales for a relatively short time—often less than a season.

Fair Labor Standards Act   a federal law, enacted in 1938, that sets minimum wages, maximum hours, child labor standards, and overtime pay provisions.

fair trade laws   see **resale price maintenance laws.**

fashion   a type of product or way of behaving that is temporarily adopted by a large number of consumers because the product or behavior is considered to be socially appropriate for the time and place.

fashion-oriented shopping center   shopping center usually containing a high-quality department store as well as small boutiques.

feature area   area designed to get the customer's attention that includes end caps, promotional aisles or areas, freestanding fixtures and mannequins that introduce a soft goods department, windows, and point-of-sale areas.

feature fixture   see **four-way fixture.**

features   the qualities or characteristics of a product that provide benefits to customers.

Federal Trade Commission Act (1914) the congressional act that created the Federal Trade Commission (FTC) and gave it the power to enforce federal trade laws.

financial leverage a financial measure based on the relationship between the retailer's liabilities and owners' equity that indicates financial stability of the firm.

fixed assets assets that require more than a year to convert to cash.

fixed expenses expenses that remain constant for a given period of time regardless of the sales volume.

fixed-rate lease a lease that requires the retailer to pay a fixed amount per month over the life of the lease.

flattening the organization a reduction in the number of management levels.

flexible pricing a pricing strategy that allows consumers to bargain over selling prices.

flextime a job scheduling system that enables employees to choose the times they work.

floor-ready merchandise merchandise received at the store ready to be sold, without the need for any additional preparation by retail employees.

FOB (free-on-board) destination a term of sale designating that the shipper owns the merchandise until it is delivered to the retailer and is therefore responsible for transportation and any damage claims.

FOB (free-on-board) origin a term of sale designating that the retailer takes ownership of the merchandise at the point of origin and is therefore responsible for transportation and any damage claims.

focus group a marketing research technique in which a small group of respondents is interviewed by a moderator using a loosely structured format.

foreign trade zone a special area within a country that can be used for warehousing, packaging, inspection, labeling, exhibition, assembly, fabrication, or transshipment of imports without being subject to that country's tariffs.

forward buy an opportunity to purchase at an extra discount more merchandise than the retailer normally needs to fill demand.

forward integration a form of vertical integration in which a manufacturer owns wholesalers and/or retailers.

four-way fixture a fixture with two cross bars that sit perpendicular to each other on a pedestal.

franchisee the owner of an individual store in a franchise agreement.

franchising a contractual agreement between a franchisor and a franchisee that allows the franchisee to operate a retail outlet using a name and format developed and supported by the franchisor.

franchisor the owner of a franchise in a franchise agreement.

free-form layout a store design, used primarily in small specialty stores or within the boutiques of large stores, that arranges fixtures and aisles asymmetrically. Also called **boutique layout.**

freestanding fixture fixtures and mannequins located on aisles that are designed primarily to get customers' attention and bring them into a department.

freestanding insert (FSI) an ad printed at a retailer's expense and distributed as a freestanding insert in the newspaper. Also called a **preprint.**

freestanding retailer a retailer that is not connected to other retailers by location.

freestanding site a retail location that is not connected to other retailers.

freight collect when the retailer pays the freight.

freight prepaid when the freight is paid by the vendor.

frequency the number of times a potential customer is exposed to an ad.

frequent shopper program a reward and communication program used by a retailer to encourage continued purchases from the retailer's best customers. See **loyalty program.**

fringe trade area see **tertiary trade zone.**

frontal presentation a method of displaying merchandise in which the retailer exposes as much of the product as possible to catch the customer's eye.

full warranty a guarantee provided by either the retailer or manufacturer to repair or replace merchandise without charge and within a reasonable amount of time in the event of a defect.

full-line discount store a retailer that offers a broad variety of merchandise, limited service, and low prices. It offers national brands, but these brands are typically less fashion-oriented than brands in department stores.

full-line forcing when a supplier requires a retailer to carry the supplier's full line of products if the retailer wants to carry any part of that line.

functional discount see **trade discount.**

functional needs the needs satisfied by a product or service that are directly related to its performance.

functional product grouping categorizing and displaying merchandise by common end uses.

functional relationships a series of one-time market exchanges linked together over time.

future dating a method of dating that allows the buyer additional time to take advantage of the cash discount or to pay the net amount of the invoice.

GAPS model a conceptual model that indicates what retailers need to do to provide high-quality customer service. When customers' expectations are greater than their perceptions of the delivered service, customers are dissatisfied and feel the quality of the retailer's service is poor. Thus, retailers need to reduce the service gap— the difference between customers' expectations and perceptions of customer service to improve customers' satisfaction with their service.

general merchandise discount store a discount store that carries a broad variety of general merchandise.

general merchandise retailer a retailer selling merchandise that is not refrigerated or perishable.

Generation X the generational cohort of people born between 1965 and 1976.

Generation Y the generational cohort of people born between 1977 and 1995.

generational cohort people within the same generation who have similar purchase behaviors because they have shared experiences and are in the same stage of life.

generic brand unbranded, unadvertised merchandise found mainly in drug, grocery, and discount stores.

gentrification a process in which old buildings are torn down or are restored to create new offices, housing developments, and retailers.

geographic information system (GIS) a computerized system that enables analysts to visualize information about their customers' demographics, buying behavior, and other data in a map format.

geographic segmentation segmentation of potential customers by where they live. A retail market can be segmented by countries, states, cities, and neighborhoods.

glass ceiling an invisible barrier that makes it difficult for minorities and women to be promoted beyond a certain level.

gondola an island type of self-service counter with tiers of shelves, bins, or pegs.

graduated lease a lease that requires rent to increase by a fixed amount over a specified period of time.

gray-market goods merchandise that possesses a valid U.S. registered trademark and is made by a foreign manufacturer, but is imported into the United States without permission of the U.S. trademark owner.

green marketing a strategic focus by retailers and their vendors to supply customers with environmentally friendly merchandise.

greeter a retail employee who greets customers as they enter a store and who provides information and/or assistance.

grid layout a store design, typically used by grocery stores, in which merchandise is displayed on long gondolas in aisles with a repetitive pattern.

gross margin the difference between the price the customer pays for merchandise and the cost of the merchandise (the price the retailer paid the supplier of the merchandise). More specifically, gross margin = net sales – cost of goods sold (= maintained markup) – alteration cost + cash discounts.

gross margin return on investment (GMROI) gross margin dollars divided by average (cost) inventory.

gross profit see **gross margin.**

gross sales the total dollar revenues received from the sales of merchandise and services.

group boycott a concerted refusal by either retailers or vendors to deal with a particular business.

group maintenance behaviors activities store managers undertake to make sure that employees are satisfied and work well together.

habitual decision making a purchase decision involving little or no conscious effort.

high/low pricing strategy a strategy in which retailers offer prices that are sometimes above their competition's everyday low price, but they use advertising to promote frequent sales.

historical center a shopping center located in a place of historical interest.

home improvement center a category killer offering equipment and material used by do-it-yourselfers and construction contractors to make home improvements.

horizontal price fixing an agreement between retailers in direct competition with each other to charge the same prices.

house brand see **generic brand.**

Huff's model a trade area analysis model used to determine the probability that a customer residing in a particular area will shop at a particular store or shopping center.

human resource management management of a retailer's employees.

hypermarket a very large retail store that offers low prices and combines a discount and a superstore food retailer in one warehouse like building.

idea-oriented presentation a method of presenting merchandise based on a specific idea or the image of the store.

impact an ad's effect on the audience.

implied warranty of merchantability a guarantee that accompanies all merchandise sold by a retailer, assuring customers that the merchandise is up to standards for the ordinary purposes for which such goods are used.

impulse buying a buying decision made by customers on the spot after seeing the merchandise.

impulse merchandise see **impulse products.**

impulse products products that are purchased by customers without prior plans. These products are almost always located near the front of the store, where they're seen by everyone and may actually draw people into the store.

impulse purchase an unplanned purchase by a customer.

in-house credit system see **proprietary store credit card system.**

incentive compensation plan a compensation plan that rewards employees based on their productivity.

income statement a summary of the financial performance of a firm for a certain period of time.

infomercial a TV program that mixes entertainment with product demonstrations and solicits orders placed by telephone from consumers.

information search the stage in the buying process in which a customer seeks additional information to satisfy a need.

infringement unauthorized use of a registered trademark.

ingress/egress the means of entering/exiting the parking lot of a retail site.

initial markup the retail selling price initially placed on the merchandise less the cost of goods sold.

input measures performance measures used to assess the amount of resources or money used by the retailer to achieve outputs.

installment credit plan a plan that enables consumers to pay their total purchase price (less down payment) in equal installment payments over a specified time period.

institutional advertisement an advertisement that emphasizes the retailer's name and positioning rather than specific merchandise or prices.

instrumental support support for retail service providers such as appropriate systems and equipment to deliver the service desired by customers.

integrated marketing communications the strategic integration of multiple communication methods to form a comprehensive, consistent message.

intellectual property property that is intangible and is created by intellectual (mental) effort as opposed to physical effort.

intelligent agent a computer program that locates and selects alternatives based on some predetermined characteristics.

interactive electronic retailing a system in which a retailer transmits data and graphics over cable or telephone lines to a consumer's TV or computer terminal.

interactive kiosk a vending machine enabling consumers to interactively see the merchandise in use, have information about the merchandise, and use their credit cards to make a purchase.

interest the amount charged by a financial institution to borrow money.

internal sources information in a customer's memory such as the names, images, and past experiences with different stores.

Internet a worldwide network of computers linked to facilitate communications between individuals, companies, and organizations.

intertype competition competition between retailers that sell similar merchandise using different formats, such as discount and department stores.

intranet a secure communication system that takes place within one company.

intratype competition competition between the same type of retailers (e.g., Kroger versus Safeway).

intrinsic rewards nonmonetary rewards employees get from doing their jobs.

inventory goods or merchandise available for resale.

inventory management the process of acquiring and maintaining a proper assortment of merchandise while keeping ordering, shipping, handling, and other related costs in check.

inventory shrinkage see **shrinkage.**

inventory turnover net sales divided by average retail inventory; used to evaluate how effectively managers utilize their investment in inventory.

invoice cost the actual amount due for the merchandise after both trade and quantity discounts are taken.

item price removal the practice of marking prices only on shelves or signs and not on individual items.

job analysis identifying essential activities and determining the qualifications employees need to perform them effectively.

job application form a form a job applicant completes that contains information about the applicant's employment history, previous compensation, reasons for leaving previous employment, education and training, personal health, and references.

job description a description of the activities the employee needs to perform and the firm's performance expectations.

job sharing when two or more employees voluntarily are responsible for a job that was previously held by one person.

joint venture an entity formed when the entering retailer pools its resources with a local retailer to form a new company in which ownership, control, and profits are shared.

junk bond bond that offers investors a higher-risk/higher-yield investment than conventional bonds.

key items the items that are in greatest demand. Also referred to as *best-sellers*.

keystone method a method of setting retail prices in which retailers simply double the cost of the merchandise to obtain the original retail selling price.

kickback same as **commercial bribery.**

kiosk selling spaces typically found in mall common areas.

knowledge gap the difference between customer expectations and the retailer's perception of customer expectations. This factor is one of four factors identified by the GAPS model for improving service quality.

labor scheduling the process of determining the number of employees assigned to each area of the store at each hour the store is open.

latchkey children children in homes where both parents work.

layaway a method of deferred payment in which merchandise is held by the store for the customer until it is completely paid for.

lead time the amount of time between recognition that an order needs to be placed and the point at which the merchandise arrives in the store and is ready for sale.

leader pricing a pricing strategy in which certain items are priced lower than normal to increase the traffic flow of customers and/or to increase the sale of complementary products.

leadership the process by which a person attempts to influence another to accomplish some goal or goals.

leased department an area in a retail store leased or rented by an independent company. The leaseholder is typically responsible for all retail mix decisions involved in operating the department and pays the store a percentage of its sales as rent.

less-than-carload-lot (LCL) the transportation rate that applies to less than full carload shipments.

lessee the party signing the lease.

lessor the party owning a property that is for rent.

level of support see **service level.**

leveraged buyout (LBO) a financial transaction in which a buyer (the firm's management or an outside individual or group) acquires a company by borrowing money from a financial institution or by issuing junk bonds using its assets as collateral. See also **merger** and **acquisition.**

liabilities obligations of a retail enterprise to pay cash or other economic resources in return for past, present, or future benefits.

licensed brand brand for which the licensor (owner of a well-known name) enters a contractual arrangement with a licensee (a retailer or a third party). The licensee either manufactures or contracts with a manufacturer to produce the licensed product and pays a royalty to the licensor.

lifestyle the manner in which individual consumers or families (households) live and spend their time and money, the activities they pursue, and their attitudes and opinions about the world they live in.

lifestyle retailing development of a retail format based on consumer living patterns.

lifestyle segmentation a method of segmenting a retail market based on how consumers live, how they spend their time and money, what activities they pursue, and their attitudes and opinions about the world they live in.

lift-out see **buyback.**

limited problem solving a purchase decision process involving a moderate amount of effort and time. Customers engage in this type of buying process when they have some prior experience with the product or service and their risk is moderate.

limited warranty a type of guarantee in which any limitations must be stated conspicuously so that customers are not misled.

lines of authority and responsibility the organizational principle that employees should be given the authority to accomplish the responsibilities assigned to them.

local links a way to help customers get around a website on the Internet by using links that are internal to a website.

logistics an organization process of managing the flow of merchandise from the source of supply—the vendor, wholesaler, or distributor—through the internal processing functions—warehouse and transportation—until the merchandise is sold and delivered to the customer.

long-term liabilities debts that will be paid after one year.

loop layout see **racetrack layout.**

loss leader an item priced near or below cost to attract customer traffic into the store.

low-price guarantee policy a policy that guarantees that the retailer will have the lowest possible price for a product or group of products, and usually promises to match or better any lower price found in the local market.

loyalty program a program set up to reward customers with incentives such as discounts on purchases, free food, gifts, or even cruises or trips in return for their repeated business.

mail order retailer see **direct-mail catalog retailer.**

Main Street the central business district located in the traditional shopping area of smaller towns, or a secondary business district in a suburb or within a larger city.

maintained markup the amount of markup the retailer wishes to maintain on a particular category of merchandise; net sales minus cost of goods sold.

maintenance-increase–recoupment lease a provision of a lease that can be used with either a percentage or straight lease. This type of lease allows the landlord to increase the rent if insurance, property taxes, or utility bills increase beyond a certain point.

mall a shopping center with a pedestrian focus where customers park in outlying areas and walk to the stores.

management by objectives a popular method for linking the goals of a firm to goals for each employee and providing information to employees about their role.

managing diversity a set of human resource management programs designed to realize the benefits of a diverse workforce.

manufacturer brand a brand that is produced and controlled by and that carries the name of a manufacturer; also known as a **national brand.**

manufacturer's agent an agent who generally operates on an extended contractual basis; often sells within an exclusive territory; handles noncompeting but related lines of goods; and possesses limited authority with regard to prices and terms of sale.

manufacturer's outlet store a discount retail store owned and operated by a manufacturer.

mapping see **analog approach.**

maquiladoras manufacturing plants in Mexico that make goods and parts or process food for export to the United States.

marginal analysis a method of analysis used in setting a promotional budget or allocating retail space, based on the economic principle that firms should increase expenditures as long as each additional dollar spent generates more than a dollar of additional contribution.

markdown the percentage reduction in the initial retail price.

markdown cancelation the percentage increase in the retail price after a markdown is taken.

markdown money funds provided by a vendor to a retailer to cover decreased gross margin from markdowns and other merchandising issues.

market a group of vendors in a concentrated geographic location or even under one roof; also known as a **central market.**

market attractiveness–competitive position matrix a method for analyzing opportunities that explicitly considers the capabilities of the retailer and the attractiveness of retail markets.

market basket analysis analysis in which a retailer uses data mining techniques to determine what predominant categories individual customers are buying.

market development see **market penetration opportunity.**

market exchange a short-term transaction between a buyer and vendor who do not expect to be involved in future transactions with each other.

market expansion opportunity a strategic investment opportunity that employs the existing retailing format in new market segments.

market penetration opportunity an investment opportunity strategy that focuses on increasing sales to present customers using the present retailing format.

market positioning see **positioning.**

market research the systematic collection and analysis of information about a retail market.

market share a retailer's sales divided by the sales of all competitors within the same market.

market week see **trade show.**

marketing segmentation the process of dividing a retail market into homogeneous groups. See **retail market segment.**

markup the increase in the retail price of an item after the initial markup percentage has been applied but before the item is placed on the selling floor.

marquee a sign used to display a store's name and/or logo.

mass customization the production of individually customized products at costs similar to mass-produced products.

Mazur plan a method of retail organization in which all retail activities fall into four functional areas: merchandising, publicity, store management, and accounting and control.

media coverage   the theoretical number of potential customers in a retailer's market who could be exposed to an ad.

memorandum purchases   items not paid for by a retailer until they are sold. The retailer can return unsold merchandise; however, the retailer takes title on delivery and is responsible for damages. See **consignment goods.**

mentoring program   the assigning of higher-level managers to help lower-level managers learn the firm's values and meet other senior executives.

merchandise budget plan   a plan used by buyers to determine how much money to spend in each month on a particular fashion merchandise category, given the firm's sales forecast, inventory turnover, and profit goals.

merchandise category   see **category.**

merchandise classification   see **classification.**

merchandise group   a group within an organization managed by the senior vice presidents of merchandise and responsible for several departments.

merchandise management   the process by which a retailer attempts to offer the right quantity of the right merchandise in the right place at the right time while meeting the company's financial goal.

merchandise show   see **trade show.**

merchandising   see **merchandise management.**

merger   a financial strategy in which one larger firm acquires a smaller firm. This term is used interchangeably with **acquisition.** See also **leveraged buyout.**

message board   location in an Internet site at which customers can post comments.

Metropolitan Statistical Area (MSA)   a city with 50,000 or more inhabitants or an urbanized area of at least 50,000 inhabitants and a total MSA population of at least 100,000 (75,000 in New England).

mission statement   a broad description of the scope of activities a business plans to undertake.

mixed-use development (MXD)   development that combines several uses in one complex—for example, shopping center, office tower, hotel, residential complex, civic center, and convention center.

model stock list   a list of fashion merchandise that indicates in very general terms (product lines, colors, and size distributions) what should be carried in a particular merchandise category; also known as *model stock plan.*

monthly additions to stock   the amount to be ordered for delivery in each month, given the firm's turnover and sales objectives.

motivation   the drive within people to expend effort to achieve goals.

multiattribute attitude model   a model of customer decision making based on the notion that customers see a retailer or a product as a collection of attributes or characteristics.

multiattribute method   see **multiple-attribute method.**

multilevel direct selling   a form of direct selling in which people sell directly to customers, serve as master distributors, and recruit other people to become distributors in their network. The master distributors either buy merchandise from the firm and resell it to their distributors or receive a commission on all merchandise purchased by the distributors in their network.

multiple-attribute method   a method for evaluating a retailer, product, or vendor that uses a weighted average score based on the importance of various issues and the performance on those issues.

multiple-unit pricing   practice of offering two or more similar products or services for sale at one price.

mystery shopper   professional shopper who "shops" a store to assess the service provided by store employees.

national brand   see **manufacturer brand.**

natural barrier   a barrier, such as a river or mountain, that impacts accessibility to a site.

natural selection   those institutions best able to adapt to changes in customers, technology, competition, and legal environments have the greatest chance for success.

needs   the basic psychological forces that motivate customers to act.

negligence   a product liability suit that occurs if a retailer or a retail employee fails to exercise the care that a prudent person usually would.

negotiation   an interaction between two or more parties to reach an agreement.

neighborhood center   a shopping center that includes a supermarket, drugstore, home improvement center, or variety store. Neighborhood centers often include small stores, such as apparel, shoe, camera, and other shopping goods stores.

net invoice price   the net value of the invoice or the total invoice minus all other discounts.

net lease   a lease that requires all maintenance expenses such as heat, insurance, and interior repairs to be paid by the retailer.

net profit   a measure of the overall performance of a firm; revenues (sales) minus expenses and losses for the period.

net sales   the total number of dollars received by a retailer after all refunds have been paid to customers for returned merchandise.

net worth see **owners' equity.**

network direct selling see **multilevel direct selling.**

never-out list a list of key items or best-sellers that are separately planned and controlled. These items account for large sales volume and are stocked in a manner so they are always available. These are A items in an **ABC analysis.**

noncumulative quality discount discount offered to retailers as an incentive to purchase more merchandise on a single order.

nondurable perishable product consumed in one or a few uses.

nonstore retailing a form of retailing to ultimate consumers that is not store-based. Nonstore retailing is conducted through computer interfaces, vending machines, mail, direct selling, and direct marketing.

notes payable current liabilities representing principal and interest the retailer owes to financial institutions (banks) that are due and payable in less than a year.

objective-and-task method a method for setting a promotion budget in which the retailer first establishes a set of communication objectives and then determines the necessary tasks and their costs.

observation a type of market research in which customer behavior is observed and recorded.

odd price a price ending with an odd number (such as 57 cents or 63 cents) or just under a round number (such as $98 instead of $100).

off-price retailer a retailer that offers an inconsistent assortment of brand-name, fashion-oriented soft goods at low prices.

off-price shopping centers centers that specialize in off-price retail tenants such as T.J. Maxx or Burlington Coat Factory.

off-the-job training training conducted in centralized classrooms away from the employee's work environment.

on-the-job training a decentralized approach in which job training occurs in the work environment where employees perform their jobs.

one hundred percent location the retail site in a major business district that has the greatest exposure to a retail store's target market customers.

one-price policy a policy that, at a given time, all customers pay the same price for any given item of merchandise.

one-price retailer a store that offers all merchandise at a single fixed price.

open-to-buy the plan that keeps track of how much is spent in each month (and how much is left to spend).

opinion leader person whose attitudes, opinions, preferences, and actions influences those of others.

opportunity cost of capital the rate available on the next-best use of the capital invested in the project at hand. The opportunity cost should be no lower than the rate at which a firm borrows funds, since one alternative is to pay back borrowed money. It can be higher, however, depending on the range of other opportunities available. Typically, the opportunity cost rises with investment risk.

optical character recognition (OCR) an industry-wide classification system for coding information onto merchandise; enables retailers to record information on each SKU when it is sold and to transmit the information to a computer.

option credit account a revolving account that allows partial payments without interest charges if a bill is paid in full when due.

option-term revolving credit a credit arrangement that offers customers two payment options: (1) pay the full amount within a specified number of days and avoid any finance charges or (2) make a minimum payment and be assessed finance charges on the unpaid balance.

order form when signed by both parties, a legally binding contract specifying the terms and conditions under which a purchase transaction is to be conducted.

order point the amount of inventory below which the quantity available shouldn't go or the item will be out of stock before the next order arrives.

organization chart a graphic that displays the reporting relationships within a firm.

organization structure a plan that identifies the activities to be performed by specific employees and determines the lines of authority and responsibility in the firm.

organizational culture a firm's set of values and customs that guide employee behavior.

outlet center typically features stores owned by retail chains or manufacturers that sell excess and out-of-season merchandise at reduced prices.

outlet store off-price retailer owned by a manufacturer or a department or specialty store chain.

outparcel a building or kiosk that is in the parking lot of a shopping center, but isn't physically attached to a shopping center.

output measure measure that assesses the results of retailers' investment decisions.

outshopping customers shopping in other areas because their needs are not being met locally.

outsourcing obtaining a service from outside the company that had previously been done by the firm itself.

overstored　an area having so many stores selling a specific good or service that some stores will fail.

owners' equity　the amount of assets belonging to the owners of the retail firm after all obligations (liabilities) have been met; also known as **net worth.**

pallet　a platform, usually made of wood, that provides stable support for several cartons. Pallets are used to help move and store merchandise.

parallel branding　a branding strategy that represents a private label that closely imitates the trade dress and product attributes of leading manufacturer brands but with a clearly articulated "invitation to compare" in its merchandising approach and on its product label.

parasite store　a store that does not create its own traffic and whose trade area is determined by the dominant retailer in the shopping center or retail area.

partnership　an ongoing, mutually beneficial relationship with each party having concern for the other party's well-being.

party plan system　salespeople encourage people to act as hosts and invite friends or co-workers to a "party" at which the merchandise is demonstrated. The host or hostess receives a gift or commission for arranging the meeting.

patent　a law that gives the owner of a patent control of the right to make, sell, and use a product for a period of 17 years (14 years for a design).

penetration　a low pricing strategy for newly introduced categories.

perceived risk　the level of risk a consumer believes to exist regarding the purchase of a specific good or service.

percentage lease　a lease in which rent is based on a percentage of sales.

percentage lease with specified maximum　a lease that pays the lessor, or landlord, a percentage of sales up to a maximum amount.

percentage lease with specified minimum　the retailer must pay a minimum rent no matter how low sales are.

percentage-of-sales method　a method for setting a promotion budget based on a fixed percentage of forecast sales.

percentage variation method　an inventory planning method wherein the actual stock on hand during any month varies from average planned monthly stock by only half of the month's variation from average estimated monthly sales.

periodic reordering system　an inventory management system in which the review time is a fixed period (e.g., two weeks), but the order quantity can vary.

perpetual book inventory　see **retail inventory method.**

perpetual ordering system　the stock level is monitored perpetually and a fixed quantity, known as **EOQ (economic order quantity),** is purchased when the inventory available reaches a prescribed level.

personal selling　a communication process in which salespeople assist customers in satisfying their needs through face-to-face exchange of information.

physical inventory　a method of gathering stock information by using an actual physical count and inspection of the merchandise items.

pick ticket　a document that tells the order filler how much of each item to get from the storage area.

pilferage　the stealing of a store's merchandise. See also **shoplifting.**

planogram　a diagram created from photographs, computer output, or artists' renderings that illustrates exactly where every SKU should be placed.

PM　see **push money.**

point-of-purchase (POP) area　see **point-of-sale area.**

point-of-sale area　an area where the customer waits at checkout. This area can be the most valuable piece of real estate in the store, because the customer is almost held captive in that spot.

point-of-sale (POS) terminal　a cash register that can electronically scan a **UPC code** with a laser and electronically record a sale; also known as **computerized checkout.**

polygon　trade area whose boundaries conform to streets and other map features rather than being concentric circles.

popping the merchandise　focusing spotlights on special feature areas and items.

population density　the number of people per unit area (usually square mile) who live within a geographic area.

positioning　the design and implementation of a retail mix to create in the customer's mind an image of the retailer relative to its competitors. Also called brand building.

postpurchase behavior　a customer's further purchases and/or reevaluation based on a purchase.

postpurchase evaluation　the evaluation of merchandise or services after the customer has purchased and consumed them.

poverty of time　a condition in which greater affluence results in less, rather than more, free time because the alternatives competing for customers' time increase.

power retailer   see **category killer** or **category specialist.**

power shopping center   an open-air shopping center with the majority of space preleased to several well-known anchor retail tenants—category killers—with high credit ratings.

predatory pricing   a method for establishing merchandise prices for the purpose of driving competition from the marketplace.

preferred client   customers salespeople communicate with regularly, send notes to about new merchandise and sales in the department, and make appointments with for special presentations of merchandise.

premarking   marking of the price by the manufacturer or other supplier before goods are shipped to a retail store. Also called **prepricing.**

premium   merchandise offered at a reduced price, or free, as an incentive for a customer to make a purchase.

premium branding   a branding strategy that offers the consumer a private label at a comparable manufacturer-brand quality, usually with a modest price savings.

prepricing   see **premarking.**

preprint   an advertisement printed at the retailer's expense and distributed as a freestanding insert in a newspaper. Also called **freestanding insert (FSI).**

press conference   a meeting with representatives of the news media that is called by a retailer.

press release   a statement of facts or opinions that the retailer would like to see published by the news media.

prestige pricing   a system of pricing based on the assumption that consumers will not buy goods and services at prices they feel are too low.

price bundling   the practice of offering two or more different products or services for sale at one price.

price comparison   a comparison of the price of merchandise offered for sale with a higher "regular" price or a manufacturer's list price.

price discrimination   an illegal practice in which a vendor sells the same product to two or more retailers at different prices.

price elasticity of demand   a measure of the effect a price change has on consumer demand; percentage change in demand divided by percentage change in price.

price fixing   an illegal pricing activity in which several marketing channel members establish a fixed retail selling price for a product line within a market area. See **vertical price fixing** and **horizontal price fixing.**

price guarantee   a term of purchase that protects retailers against price declines. In the event that a retailer cannot sell merchandise at a given price, the manufacturer pays the retailer the difference between the planned retail and the actual retail selling price.

price lining   a pricing policy in which a retailer offers a limited number of predetermined price points within a classification.

pricing experiment   an experiment in which a retailer actually changes the price of an item in a systematic manner to observe changes in customers' purchases or purchase intentions.

primary data   marketing research information collected through surveys, observations, and experiments to address a problem confronting a retailer.

primary trade zone   the geographic area from which a store or shopping center derives 60 to 65 percent of its customers.

private label   a designation that means the brand name or logo identifying the product is owned by the retailer rather than the manufacturer.

private-label brand   products developed and marketed by a retailer. Also called **store brand.**

private-label store credit-card system   a system in which credit cards have the store's name on them, but the accounts receivable are sold to a financial institution.

PRIZM (potential rating index for ZIP markets)   a database combining census data, nationwide consumer surveys, and interviews with hundreds of people across the country into a geodemographic segmentation system.

procedural fairness   the perceived fairness of the process used to resolve customer complaints.

product attributes   characteristics of a product that affect customer evaluations.

product availability   a measurement of the percentage of demand for a particular SKU that is satisfied.

product liability   a tort (or wrong) that occurs when an injury results from the use of a product.

product line   a group of related products.

productivity measure   the ratio of an output to an input determining how effectively a firm uses a resource.

profit margin   net profit after taxes divided by net sales.

profitability   a company's ability to generate revenues in excess of the costs incurred in producing those revenues.

prohibited use clause   a clause in a lease that keeps a landlord from leasing to certain kinds of tenants.

promotion   activities undertaken by a retailer to provide consumers with information about a retailer's store and its retail mix.

promotion from within a staffing policy emphasizing that employees are only hired for low-level positions, while promotions to higher levels are given to employees of the firm rather than outsiders.

promotion mix a communication program made up of advertising, sales promotions, websites, store atmosphere, publicity, personal selling, and word of mouth.

promotional advertising advertising intended to inform prospective customers of special sales; it announces the arrival of new and seasonal goods; and it features, creates, and promotes a market for the merchandise items in regular stock.

promotional aisle or area aisle or area of a store designed to get the customer's attention. An example might be a special "trim-the-tree" department that seems to magically appear right after Halloween every year for the Christmas holidays.

promotional allowance an allowance given by vendors to retailers to compensate the latter for money spent in advertising a particular item.

promotional center a type of specialty shopping center that contains one or more discount stores plus smaller retail tenants. Also called **discount-oriented center.**

promotional department store a department store that concentrates on apparel and sells a substantial portion of its merchandise on weekly promotion.

promotional stock a retailer's stock of goods offered at an unusually attractive price in order to obtain sales volume; it often represents special purchases from vendors.

proprietary EDI system electronic data interchange system that is owned and operated by either a retailer, a vendor, or a third-party provider known as a **value added network (VAN).**

proprietary store credit card system a system in which credit cards have the store's name on them and the accounts receivable are administered by the retailer; also known as **in-house credit system.**

psychographic segmentation see **lifestyle segmentation.**

psychographics see **lifestyle.**

psychological needs needs associated with the personal gratification that customers get from shopping or from purchasing and owning a product.

public warehouse warehouse that is owned and operated by a third party.

publicity communications through significant unpaid presentations about the retailer (usually a news story) in impersonal media.

puffing an advertising or personal selling practice in which a retailer simply exaggerates the benefits or quality of a product in very broad terms.

pull logistics strategy strategy in which orders for merchandise are generated at the store level on the basis of demand data captured by point-of-sale terminals.

purchase visibility curve a display technique in which the retailer tilts low shelves so more merchandise is in direct view.

push logistics strategy strategy in which merchandise is allocated to stores based on historical demand, the inventory position at the distribution center, as well as the stores' needs.

push money (PM) an incentive for retail salespeople provided by a vendor to promote, or push, a particular product; also known as **spiff.**

quantity discount the practice of granting low prices to retailers who buy in high quantities.

quick-response (QR) delivery system system designed to reduce the lead time for receiving merchandise, thereby lowering inventory investment, improving customer service levels, and reducing distribution expenses; also known as *just-in-time inventory management system.*

quotas bonus plan compensation plan that has a performance goal or objective established to evaluate employee performance, such as sales per hour for salespeople and maintained margin and turnover for buyers.

racetrack layout a type of store layout that provides a major aisle to facilitate customer traffic that has access to the store's multiple entrances. Also known as a **loop layout.**

rain check when sale merchandise is out of stock, a written promise to customers to sell them that merchandise at the sale price when it arrives.

reach the actual number of customers in the target market exposed to an advertising medium. See **advertising reach.**

rebate money returned to the buyer in the form of cash based on a portion of the purchase price.

receipt of goods (ROG) dating a dating policy in which the cash discount period starts on the day the merchandise is received.

receiving the process of filling out paperwork to record the receipt of merchandise that arrives at a store or distribution center.

recruitment activity performed by a retailer to generate job applicants.

reduction markdown; discount to employees and customers; and inventory shrinkage due to shoplifting, breakage, or loss.

reference group one or more people whom a person uses as a basis of comparison for his beliefs, feelings, and behaviors.

reference price a price point in the consumer's memory for a good or service that can consist of the price last paid, the price most frequently paid, or the average of all prices customers have paid for similar offerings. A benchmark for what consumers believe the "real" price of the merchandise should be.

refusal to deal a legal issue in which either a vendor or a retailer reserves the right to deal or refuse to deal with anyone it chooses.

region in retail location analysis, refers to the part of the country, a particular city, or **Metropolitan Statistical Area (MSA).**

regional center a shopping center that includes up to three department stores plus shopping or specialty stores rather than convenience stores. Superregionals are similar but have at least four department stores.

Reilly's law a model used in trade area analysis to define the relative ability of two cities to attract customers from the area between them.

related diversification opportunity a diversification opportunity strategy in which the retailer's present offering and market share something in common with the market and format being considered.

relational partnership long-term business relationship in which the buyer and vendor have a close, trusting interpersonal relationship.

remarking the practice of changing the price label or identification tag on merchandise due to price changes, lost or mutilated tickets, or customer returns.

reorder point the stock level at which a new order is placed.

resale price maintenance laws laws enacted in the early 1900s to curb **vertical price fixing.** These laws were designed to help protect small retailers by prohibiting retailers to sell below manufacturer's suggested retail price. Also called **fair trade laws.**

resident buying office office that either is an independent organization or is directly associated with particular retailers and that offers a number of services associated with the procurement of merchandise.

restraint of trade any contract that tends to eliminate or stifle competition, create a monopoly, artificially maintain prices, or otherwise hamper or obstruct the course of trade and commerce as it would be carried on if left to the control of natural forces; also known as *unfair trade practices.*

retail accordion theory see **accordion theory.**

retail audit see **situation audit.**

retail chain a firm that consists of multiple retail units under common ownership and usually has some centralization of decision making in defining and implementing its strategy.

retail format the retailers' type of retail mix (nature of merchandise and services offered, pricing policy, advertising and promotion program, approach to store design and visual merchandising, and typical location).

retail format development opportunity an investment opportunity strategy in which a retailer offers a new retail format—a format involving a different retail mix—to the same target market.

retail information system system that provides the information needed by retail managers by collecting, organizing, and storing relevant data continuously and directing the information to the appropriate managers.

retail inventory method (RIM) an accounting procedure whose objectives are to maintain a perpetual or book inventory in retail dollar amounts and to maintain records that make it possible to determine the cost value of the inventory at any time without taking a physical inventory; also known as **book inventory system** or **perpetual book inventory.**

retail market a group of consumers with similar needs (a market segment) and a group of retailers using a similar retail format to satisfy those consumer needs.

retail market segment a group of customers whose needs will be satisfied by the same retail offering because they have similar needs and go through similar buying processes.

retail merchandising unit (RMU) a relatively new and sophisticated location alternative that offers the compactness and mobility of a cart, but the more sophisticated features of a kiosk. It can also be locked or enclosed, so it can serve as a display when closed for business.

retail mix the combination of factors used by a retailer to satisfy customer needs and influence their purchase decisions; includes merchandise and services offered, pricing, advertising and promotions, store design and location, and visual merchandising.

retail-sponsored cooperative an organization owned and operated by small, independent retailers to improve operating efficiency and buying power. Typically, the retail-sponsored cooperative operates a wholesale buying and distribution system and requires its members to concentrate their purchases from the cooperative whole-sale operation.

retail strategy   a statement that indicates (1) the target market toward which a retailer plans to commit its resources, (2) the nature of the retail offering that the retailer plans to use to satisfy the needs of the target market, and (3) the bases upon which the retailer will attempt to build a sustainable competitive advantage over competitors.

retailer   a business that sells products and services to consumers for their personal or family use.

retailing   a set of business activities that adds value to the products and services sold to consumers for their personal or family use.

retailing concept   a management orientation that holds that the key task of a retailer is to determine the needs and wants of its target markets and to direct the firm toward satisfying those needs and wants more effectively and efficiently than competitors do.

retained earnings   the portion of owners' equity that has accumulated over time through profits but has not been paid out in dividends to owners.

return on assets   net profit after taxes divided by total assets.

return on owners' equity   net profit after taxes divided by owners' equity; also known as *return on net worth*.

reverse logistics   a flow back of merchandise through the channel, from the customer to the store, distribution center, and vendor, for customer returns.

review time   the period of time between reviews of a line for purchase decisions.

revolving credit   a consumer credit plan that combines the convenience of a continuous charge account and the privileges of installment payment.

ribbon center   see **strip center.**

road condition   includes the age, number of lanes, number of stoplights, congestion, and general state of repair of roads in a trade area.

road pattern   a consideration used in measuring the accessibility of a retail location via major arteries, freeways, or roads.

Robinson–Patman Act (1946)   the Congressional act that revised Section 2 of the **Clayton Act** and specifically prohibits price discrimination.

role clarity   the degree to which employees know what their duties and responsibilities are.

role conflict   the degree to which employees receive mixed messages about the scope of their activities.

rounder   a round fixture that sits on a pedestal. Smaller than the straight rack, it is designed to hold a maximum amount of merchandise. Also known as a **bulk** or **capacity fixture.**

routine decision making   see **habitual decision making.**

rule-of-thumb method   a type of approach for setting a promotion budget that uses past sales and communication activity to determine the present communications budget.

safety stock   see **buffer stock.**

sale–leaseback   the practice in which retailers build new stores and sell them to real estate investors who then lease the buildings back to the retailers on a long-term basis.

sales associate   the same as a salesperson. The term is used to recognize the importance and professional nature of the sales function and avoids the negative image sometimes linked with the term *salesperson*.

sales consultant   see **sales associate.**

sales per cubic foot   a measure of space productivity appropriate for stores such as wholesale clubs that use multiple layers of merchandise.

sales per linear foot   a measure of space productivity used when most merchandise is displayed on multiple shelves of long gondolas, such as in grocery stores.

sales per square foot   a measure of space productivity used by most retailers since rent and land purchases are assessed on a per-square-foot basis.

sales promotions   paid impersonal communication activities that offer extra value and incentives to customers to visit a store and/or purchase merchandise during a specific period of time.

satisfaction   a postconsumption evaluation of the degree to which a store or product meets or exceeds customer expectations.

saturated trade area   a trade area that offers customers a good selection of goods and services, while allowing competing retailers to make good profits.

scale economies   cost advantages due to the size of a retailer.

scanning   the process in point-of-sale (service) systems wherein the input into the terminal is accomplished by passing a coded ticket over a reader or having a hand-held wand pass over the ticket.

scrambled merchandising   the offering of merchandise not typically associated with the store type, such as clothing in a drugstore.

search engine computer programs that simply search for and provide a listing of all Internet sites selling a product category and/or brand with the price of the merchandise offered. Also called **shopping bots.**

seasonal discount discount offered as an incentive to retailers to place orders for merchandise in advance of the normal buying season.

seasonal merchandise inventory whose sales fluctuate dramatically according to the time of the year.

secondary data market research information previously gathered for purposes other than solving the current problem under investigation.

secondary trade zone the geographic area of secondary importance in terms of customer sales, generating about 20 percent of a store's sales.

security an operating unit within a retail organization that is responsible for protecting merchandise and other assets from pilferage (internal or external). Those working in security may be employees or outside agency people.

self-analysis an internally focused examination of a business's strengths and weaknesses.

self-service retailer a retailer that offers minimal customer service.

sell-through analysis a comparison of actual and planned sales to determine whether early markdowns are required or whether more merchandise is needed to satisfy demand.

selling agent an agent who operates on an extended contractual basis; the agent sells all of a specified line of merchandise or the entire output of the principal, and usually has full authority with regard to prices, terms, and other conditions of sale. The agent occasionally renders financial aid to the principal.

selling process a set of activities that salespeople undertake to facilitate the customer's buying decision.

selling space the area set aside for displays of merchandise, interactions between sales personnel and customers, demonstrations, and so on.

seniors the generational cohort of people born before 1946.

service gap the difference between customers' expectations and perceptions of customer service to improve customers' satisfaction with their service.

service level a measure used in inventory management to define the level of support or level of product availability; the number of items sold divided by the number of items demanded. Service level should not be confused with customer service. See **customer service.**

services retailer retailing organization that offers consumers services—rather than merchandise. Examples include banks, hospital, health spas, doctors, legal clinics, entertainment firms, and universities.

sexual harassment unwelcome sexual advances, requests for sexual favors, or other verbal or physical conduct with sexual elements.

Sherman Antitrust Act (1890) the act protecting small businesses and consumers from large corporations by outlawing any person, corporation, or association from engaging in activities that restrain trade or commerce.

shoplifting the act of stealing merchandise from a store by customers or people posing as customers.

shopping bots computer programs that simply search for and provide a listing of all Internet sites selling a product category and/or brand with the price of the merchandise offered. Also called **search engines.**

shopping center a group of retail and other commercial establishments that is planned, developed, owned, and managed as a single property.

shopping goods products for which consumers will spend time comparing alternatives.

shopping guide free paper delivered to all residents in a specific area.

shopping mall generally more planned than a strip center and with more pedestrian activity, it can be either open-air or enclosed.

shortage see **shrinkage.**

shrinkage the difference between the recorded value of inventory (at retail) based on merchandise bought and received and the value of actual inventory in stores and distribution centers divided by retail sales during a time period. Shrinkage is caused by employee theft, by customer shoplifting, and by merchandise being misplaced, damaged, or mispriced.

single-price retailer close-out stores that sell all their merchandise at a single price, typically $1.

situation audit an analysis of the opportunities and threats in the retail environment and the strengths and weaknesses of the retail business relative to its competitors.

skimming a high pricing strategy for newly introduced categories.

SKU see **stock keeping unit.**

sliding scale a part of some leases that stipulates how much the percentage of sales paid as rent will decrease as sales go up.

slotting allowance fee paid by a vendor for space in a retail store. Also called *slotting fee.*

socialization   the steps taken to transform new employees into effective, committed members of the firm.

sole proprietorship   an arrangement in which an unincorporated retail firm is owned by one person.

source tag   a very small electronic device that is unobtrusively affixed to merchandise to prevent shoplifting and provide retailers with merchandise movement information.

span of control   the number of subordinates reporting to a manager.

specialization   the organizational structure in which employees are typically responsible for only one or two tasks rather than performing all tasks. This enables employees to develop expertise and increase productivity.

specialty center   see **promotional** or **discount-oriented center** and **fashion-oriented shopping center.**

specialty department store   a store with a department store format that focuses primarily on apparel and soft home goods (such as Neiman Marcus or Saks Fifth Avenue).

specialty product   a product for which the customer will expend considerable effort to buy.

specialty store   store concentrating on a limited number of complementary merchandise categories and providing a high level of service in an area typically under 8,000 square feet.

spiff   see **push money.**

split shipment   a vendor ships part of a shipment to a retailer and back orders the remainder because the entire shipment could not be shipped at the same time.

spot   a local television commercial.

spot check   used particularly in receiving operations when goods come in for reshipping to branch stores in packing cartons. Certain cartons are opened in the receiving area of the central distribution point and spot-checked for quality and quantity.

spotting techniques   see **analog approach.**

staging area   area in which merchandise is accumulated from different parts of the distribution center and prepared for shipment to stores.

standardization   involves requiring service providers to follow a set of rules and procedures when providing service.

standardization approach   an approach used by retailers to provide customer service by using a set of rules and procedures so that all customers consistently receive the same service.

standards gap   the difference between the retailer's perceptions of customers' expectations and the customer service standards it sets. This factor is one of four factors identified by the GAPS model for improving service quality.

staple merchandise   inventory that has continuous demand by customers over an extended period of time. Also known as **basic merchandise.**

stock balance   trade-offs associated with determining variety, assortment, and product availablity.

stock keeping unit (SKU)   the smallest unit available for keeping inventory control. In soft goods merchandise, an SKU usually means size, color, and style.

stock overage   the amount by which a retail book inventory figure exceeds a physical ending inventory.

stock-to-sales ratio   the beginning-of-month (BOM) inventory divided by sales for the month. The average stock-to-sales ratio is 12 divided by planned inventory turnover. This ratio is an integral component of the merchandise budget plan.

stockholders' equity   see **owners' equity.**

stocklift   see **buyback.**

store atmosphere   the combination of the store's physical characteristics (such as architecture, layout, signs and displays, colors, lighting, temperature, sounds, and smells), which together create an image in the customers' mind. See **atmospherics.**

store brand   see **private-label brand.**

store image   the way a store is defined in a shopper's mind. The store image is based on the store's physical characteristics, its retail mix, and a set of psychological attributes.

store loyalty   a condition in which customers like and habitually visit the same store to purchase a type of merchandise.

store maintenance   the activities involved with managing the exterior and interior physical facilities associated with the store.

store visibility   see **visibility.**

straight lease   a type of lease in which the retailer pays a fixed amount per month over the life of the lease.

straight rack   a type of fixture that consists of a long pipe suspended with supports going to the floor or attached to a wall.

straight salary compensation   a compensation plan in which salespeople or managers receive a fixed amount of compensation for each hour or week they work.

strategic alliance   collaborative relationships between independent firms. For example, a foreign retailer might enter an international market through direct investment but develop an alliance with a local firm to perform logistical and warehousing activities.

strategic partnership long-term relationship in which partners make significant investments to improve both parties' profitability.

strategic profit model (SPM) a tool used for planning a retailer's financial strategy based on both margin management (net profit margin), asset management (asset turnover), and financial leverage management (financial leverage ratio). Using the SPM, a retailer's objective is to achieve a target return on owners' equity.

strategic retail plan a grand design or blueprint indicating the retail strategy and the steps for implementing the plan.

strategic retail planning process the steps a retailer goes through to develop a strategic retail plan. It describes how retailers select target market segments, determine the appropriate retail format, and build sustainable competitive advantages.

strengths-and-weaknesses analysis a critical aspect of the situation audit in which a retailer determines its unique capabilities—its strengths and weaknesses relative to its competition.

strict product liability a product liability suit in which the injury to the customer may not have been intentional or under the retailer's control.

strip center a shopping center that usually has parking directly in front of the stores and does not have enclosed walkways linking the stores.

style the characteristic or distinctive form, outline, or shape of a product.

subculture a distinctive group of people within a culture. Members of a subculture share some customs and norms with the overall society but also have some unique perspectives.

subjective employee evaluation assessment of employee performance based on a supervisor's ratings rather than on objective measures such as sales per hour.

substitute awareness effect a condition in which customers become more price-sensitive because they can find a lot of substitutes for a product or for a retailer.

supercenter a retail format combining a superstore (a large supermarket) and a full-line discount store in stores ranging from 150,000 to 200,000 square feet.

supermarket see **conventional supermarket.**

superstore a large supermarket between 20,000 and 50,000 square feet in size.

supply chain management the integration of business processes from end user through original suppliers that provides products, services, and information that add value for customers.

survey a method of data collection, using telephone, personal interview, mail, or any combination thereof.

sustainable competitive advantage a distinct competency of a retailer relative to its competitors that can be maintained over a considerable time period.

sweepstake a promotion in which customers win prizes based on chance.

tall wall unit retail facility that is a six-to-seven–foot selling space placed against a wall in a mall instead of in the middle of an aisle as a cart or kiosk would be.

target market the market segment(s) toward which the retailer plans to focus its resources and retail mix.

target segment see **target market.**

tariff a tax placed by a government upon imports.

task performance behaviors planning, organizing, motivating, evaluating, and coordinating store employees' activities.

television home shopping retailing a retail format in which customers watch a TV program demonstrating merchandise and then place orders for the merchandise by phone.

terms of purchase conditions in a purchase agreement with a vendor that include the type(s) of discounts available and responsibility for transportation costs.

terms of sale conditions in a sales contract with customers including such issues as charges for alterations, delivery, or gift wrapping, or the store's exchange policies.

tertiary trade zone the outermost ring of a trade area; includes customers who occasionally shop at the store or shopping center.

theme center a shopping center that tries to replicate a historical place and typically contains tenants similar to those in specialty centers, except there usually is no large specialty store or department store as an anchor. See **historical center.**

third-party logistics company firm that facilitates the movement of merchandise from manufacturer to retailer, but is independently owned.

thrift store a retail format offering used merchandise.

ticketing and marking procedures for making price labels and placing them on the merchandise.

tie-in an approach used to attract attention to a store's offering by associating the offering with an event.

tonnage merchandising a display technique in which large quantities of merchandise are displayed together.

top-down planning one side of the process of developing an overall retail strategy where goals are set at the top of the organization and filter down through the operating levels.

total expenditure effect a condition in which customer price sensitivity increases when the total expenditure is large.

trade area a geographic sector that contains potential customers for a particular retailer or shopping center.

trade discount reduction in a retailer's suggested retail price granted to wholesalers and retailers; also known as a **functional discount.**

trade dress a product's physical appearance, including its size, shape, color, design, and texture. For instance, the shape and color of a Coca-Cola bottle is its trade dress.

trade show a temporary concentration of vendors that provides retailers opportunities to place orders and view what is available in the marketplace; also known as a **merchandise show** or **market week.**

trademark any mark, work, picture, or design associated with a particular line of merchandise or product.

traffic appliance small portable appliance.

traffic flow the balance between a substantial number of cars and not so many that congestion impedes access to the store.

transformational leader a leader who gets people to transcend their personal needs for the sake of realizing the group goal.

transportation cost the expense a retailer incurs if it pays the cost of shipping merchandise from the vendor to the stores.

travel time contours used in trade area analysis to define the rings around a particular site based on travel time instead of distances.

triple-coupon promotion a retail promotion that allows the customer triple the face value of the coupon.

trust a belief by one party that the other party will fulfill its obligations in a relationship.

turnover the number of employees occupying a set of positions during a period (usually a year) divided by the number of positions.

tying contract an agreement between a vendor and a retailer requiring the retailer to take a product it does not necessarily desire (the *tied product*) to ensure that it can buy a product it does desire (the *tying product*).

ultimate consumers individuals who purchase goods and services for their own personal use or for use by members of their household.

undercover shopper person hired by or working for a retailer who poses as a customer to observe the activities and performance of employees.

understored trade area an area that has too few stores selling a specific good or service to satisfy the needs of the population.

unit pricing the practice of expressing price in terms of both the total price of an item and the price per unit of measure.

unity of command the appropriate relationship between managers and their subordinates.

Universal Product Code (UPC) the black-and-white bar code found on most merchandise; used to collect sales information at the point of sale using computer terminals that read the code. This information is transmitted computer-to-computer to buyers, distribution centers, and then to vendors, who in turn quickly ship replenishment merchandise.

unrelated diversification diversification in which there is no commonality between the present business and the new business.

UPC code see **Universal Product Code.**

URL (uniform resource locator) the standard for a page on the World Wide Web (e.g., www.nrf.org).

utility the consumer's perception of the benefits of the product and services offered by the retailer.

value added network a third-party logistics company that facilitates **electronic data interchange (EDI)** by making computer systems between vendors and retailers compatible.

value pricing setting prices based on fair value for both the service provider and the consumer.

variable direct costs costs that vary with the level of sales and that can be applied directly to the decision in question.

variety the number of different merchandise categories within a store or department.

vending machine retailing A nonstore format in which merchandise or services are stored in a machine and dispensed to customers when they deposit cash or use a credit card.

vendor any firm from which a retailer obtains merchandise.

vertical integration an example of diversification by retailers involving investments by retailers in wholesaling and/or manufacturing merchandise.

vertical merchandising a method whereby merchandise is organized to follow the eye's natural up-and-down movement.

vertical price fixing agreements to fix prices between parties at different levels of the same marketing channel (for example, retailers and their vendors).

video kiosk see **interactive kiosk.**

virtual community a network of members that communicate with each other electronically over the Internet.

virtual mall   a group of retailers and service providers that can be accessed over the Internet at one location.

visibility   the customers' ability to see the store and enter the parking lot safely.

visual communications   the act of providing information to customers through graphics, signs, and theatrical effects—both in the store and in windows—to help boost sales by providing information on products and by suggesting items or special purchases.

want book   information collected by retail salespeople to record out-of-stock or requested merchandise. Similar to a *want slip*.

warehouse club   a retailer that offers a limited assortment of food and general merchandise with little service and low prices to ultimate consumers and small businesses.

warehouse store   a discount food retailer that offers merchandise in a no-frills environment.

website   a page or series of pages on the Internet, identified by a unique address (**URL**), that can provide information and/or facilitate electronic commerce.

week's supply method   an inventory management method most similar to the **stock-to-sales method.**

The difference is that everything is expressed in weeks rather than months.

wheel of retailing   a cyclical theory of retail evolution whose premise is that retailing institutions evolve from low-price/service to higher-price/service operations.

wholesale-sponsored voluntary cooperative group   an organization operated by a wholesaler offering a merchandising program to small, independent retailers on a voluntary basis.

wholesaler   a merchant establishment operated by a concern that is primarily engaged in buying, taking title to, usually storing, and physically handling goods in large quantities, and reselling the goods (usually in smaller quantities) to retailers or to industrial or business users.

word of mouth   communications between people about a retailer.

WWW (World Wide Web)   the user-friendly area of the Internet that consists of linked pages containing graphics, text, sound, and video.

zoning   the regulation of the construction and use of buildings in certain areas of a municipality.

NOTES

Chapter 1

1. "Sphere of Influence," *Progressive Grocer*, May 1998, p. 33.

2. See Pattie Maes, Robert Guttman, and Alexandros Moukas, "Agents That Buy and Sell," *Communications of the ACM* 42 (March 1999), pp. 81–99; John Blackford, "Staying One-Up Online," *Computer Shopper*, June 1, 1999, pp. 86–87; and Jim O'Brien, "Hot off the Wire," *Computer Shopper*, February 1999, pp. 421–23.

3. Jennifer Steinhauer, "The Teach and Sell of School of Retailing," *The New York Times*, February 28, 1998, pp. B1+; and Cyndee Miller, "Surreal Is Latest to Make Retailing Entertaining," *Marketing News*, June 23, 1997, pp. 1, 20.

4. Edwin McDowell, "America's Hot Tourist Spots," *The New York Times*, May 26, 1996, pp. 1, 17.

5. S.A. Mcgurr and T. Devaney, "Predicting Business Failure of Retail Firms: An Analysis Using Mixed Industry Models," *Journal of Business Research* 43 (October 1998), pp. 323–35; and John Watson and Jim Everett, "Do Small Businesses Have Higher Failure Rates? Evidence from Australian Retailer," *Journal of Small Business Management* 34 (October 1996), pp. 45–62.

6. For a more detailed discussion of distribution channels, see Louis Stern, Adel El-Ansary, and James Brown, *Management in Marketing Channels*, 3d ed. (Englewood Cliffs, NJ: Prentice Hall, 1996).

7. Roy Larke, "Japanese Retailing: Fascinating, but Little Understood," *International Journal of Retail & Distribution Management*, January–February 1992, pp. 3–15.

8. Census of Retail Trade, U.S. Dept. of Commerce.

9. *Retailing: Mirror on America* (New York: National Retail Federation, 1999), p. 5.

10. Retail Industry Indicators. National Retail Institute, Washington, DC, May 1998, pp. 7, 10.

11. Census of Retail Trade, U.S. Dept. of Commerce.

12. A. Raucher, "Dime Store Chains: The Making of Organization Men 1880–1940," *Business History Review* 65 (Spring 1991), pp. 130–63.

13. Robert Hoff, "Amazon.Com: The Wild World of E-Commerce," *Business Week*, December 14, 1998, pp. 106–9; and Justin Hibbard, "Amazon.Com v. Wal-Mart: The Inside Story," *Information Week*, February 22, 1999, p. 27.

14. Carolyn Walkup, "David Thomas: Founder of Wendy's International," *Nation's Restaurant News*, February 12, 1996, p. 162; and Louise Kramer, "Pioneer of the Year: Dave Thomas," *Nation's Restaurant News*, October 9, 1995, p. 152.

15. Kramer, ibid.

16. Forest Reinhardt, "Environmental Product Differentiation: Implications for Corporate Strategy," *California Management Review* 40 (June 1998), pp. 43–64; "Patagonia Comes of Age," *Industry Week*, April 3, 1995, pp. 42–44; and "Retail Entrepreneurs of the Year," *Chain Store Age Executive*, December 1994, pp. 46–47.

17. Susan Caminiti, "Will Old Navy Fill the Gap?" *Fortune*, March 18, 1996, pp. 59–64.

18. Ibid., p. 60.

19. Michael Porter, "What Is Strategy?" *Harvard Business Review*, November–December 1996, pp. 61–78; and Shelby Hunt and Robert Morgan, "The Comparative Advantage Theory of Competition," *Journal of Marketing*, 59 (April 1995), pp. 1–15.

20. See Stanley Hollander and Glenn Omura, "Chain Store Development and Their Political, Strategic, and Social Interdependence," *Journal of Retailing* 65 (Fall 1989), pp. 299–326.

21. "Rating the Stores," *Consumer Reports*, November 1994, p. 714.

22. Leslie Kaufman, "Can J.C. Penney Evolve?" *The New York Times*, June 26, 1999, pp. B1, B14; and William Davidson, Daniel Sweeney, and Ronald Stampfl, "J.C. Penney (A): Marketing and Financial Strategy," in *Retail Management*, 6th ed. (New York: Wiley, 1988).

23. "Back to the Future," *The New York Times Magazine*, April 6, 1997, pp. 48–49.

24. *Whole Foods Market 1999 Annual Report*; Adam Blair, "Whole Foods Expands Frequent Shopper Program," *Supermarket News*, November, 1997, p. 15; and Wendy Zellner, "Love, Peace, and the Bottom Line," *Business Week*, December 7, 1998, pp. 79–80.

Chapter 2

1. *1998 Census of Retail Trade* (Washington, DC: U.S. Dept. of Commerce, Bureau of the Census).

2. "Bye, SICs! NAICS Is the New Industry Nomenclature," *Purchasing Magazine*, March 12, 1998, p. 25; and Michael Mandel, "Vital Statistics for the Real-Life," *Business Week*, December 29, 1997, p. 43.

3. Sandra Sutton, "Drug Chains' Solid Performances Rack Up $80 Billion Year," *Drug Store News*, May 17, 1999, p. 35; and Barbara Beliveau and Eldon Bernstein, "Struggling to Survive: The Case of Independent Pharmacy," *Journal of Business and Entrepreneurship* 9 (October 1997), pp. 36–49.

4. "Markets in Motion," in "66th Annual Report of the Grocery Industry," *Progressive Grocer*, April 1999, p. 31.

5. "Consolidation Continues," The DSN Annual Industry Report, *Discount Store News*, July 12, 1999, p. 67; and

Martin Tosh, "Forever Changed," 66th Annual Report of the Grocery Industry Supplement, *Progressive Grocer*, April 1999, pp. 31–32.

6. "Markets in Motion," in "66th Annual Report of the Grocery Industry," *Progressive Grocer*, April 1999, p. 31.

7. William Woodard, "In Global Retailing, The Game's the Same but the Rules Can Be Different," *Chain Store Age*, December 1996, section 3, p. 9B.

8. A.C. Samli, "The Status of Global Sourcing as a Critical Tool of Strategic Planning: Opportunistic versus Strategic Dichotomy," *Journal of Business Research* 43 (October 1998), pp. 123–34.

9. David Appel, "The Supermarket: Early Development of an Institutional Innovation," *Journal of Retailing* 48 (Spring 1972), pp. 39–53; and Arieh Goldman, "Stages in the Development of the Supermarket," *Journal of Retailing* 51 (Winter 1975–76), pp. 49–64.

10. "Roaring 20's Ends in Depression," *Chain Store Age Executive*, June 1994, p. 49.

11. Greg Jacobson, "Big Year for Food Lion," *MMR*, March 8, 1999, p. 5.

12. "Markets in Motion," in "66th Annual Report of the Grocery Industry," *Progressive Grocer*, April 1999, p. 9.

13. "The DSN Annual Industry Report," *Discount Store News*, July 12, 1999, p. 58.

14. "Consumers Are Skeptical Again," in "63rd Annual Report on the Grocery Industry," *Progressive Grocer Supplement*, April 1996, p. 42.

15. Joanne Frederick, "Supercenters: The Threat du Jour," *Grocery Marketing*, March 1995, pp. 14–17.

16. Ibid.

17. "A Short History of the Convenience Store Industry," at www.cstorecentral.com.

18. 1998 Convenience Store Industry Annual Report at www.cstorecentral.com.

19. "Spending Slide Continues," in "63rd Annual Report of the Grocery Industry," *Progressive Grocer*, April 1996, p. 15.

20. Rachel Weissman, "Guess Who's Not Coming to Dinner," *American Demographics*, June 1999, pp. 30–34.

21. Debbie Howell, "FMI Report: Shoppers Want Healthier, Easier Food," *Discount Store News*, May 3, 1999, p. 19; Shelly Reese, " 'Meal Solutions' Pose Complex Issues for Supermarket Operations," *Stores*, February 1998, pp. 43–47; Rosanne Harper, "Prepared Food Revolution," *Supermarket News*, September 9, 1996, p. 37; and Wendy Bounds, "As Big as Kodak Is in Rochester, N.Y., It Still Isn't Wegman's," *The Wall Street Journal*, December 27, 1994, pp. A1, A6.

22. Len Lewis, "Markets in Motion," in "66th Annual Report of the Grocery Industry," *Progressive Grocer Supplement*, April 1999, p. 10.

23. "The EatZi's Solution," *MMR*, January 12, 1998, pp. 21–22. See also Glenn Collins, "Proliferation of Gourmet Shops Creates a Manhattan Feeding Frenzy," *The New York Times*, June 13, 1999, p. 39.

24. Frederick, "Supercenters," pp. 14–17.

25. "The Battle Royal," in "63rd Annual Report of the Grocery Industry," *Progressive Grocer*, April 1996, p. 30.

26. The *Census of Retail Trade* published by the U.S. Bureau of the Census adopts a much broader definition of department stores, a definition that is not consistent with practice in the retail industry. To be classified as a department store for the census, a store must employ more than 25 people; sell dry goods, household items, family apparel, home furnishings, furniture, appliances, and TV sets; and have no more than 80 percent of its sales from one category of merchandise or have sales over $1 million in the smallest two categories. Using this definition, the *Census of Retail Trade* considers traditional department stores such as Macy's, May Company, and Burdines to be in the same category as discount stores such as Wal-Mart and Kmart.

27. "Top 100 Retailers," *Stores*, July 1999, p. S14. Sears and Penney are occasionally referred to as mass merchants rather than department stores because they were the first broad-line national retailers. However, these firms view themselves as department stores using the same retail mix as other department chains such as Federated Department Stores and May Company that now also have stores across the U.S.

28. David Moin, "Department Stores: The Issues," *WWD Infotracs*, June 1997, pp. 4–6.

29. "How to Lure Diverse Groups without Alienating Either," *Discount Store News*, June 3, 1996, p. 28.

30. Moin, "Department Stores: The Issues" and Arthur Friedman, "A Consumer Critique of Big Anchor Stores," *WWD Infotracs*, June 1997, pp. 14–15.

31. "Retail Perspectives," *Women's Wear Daily*, September 26, 1996, p. 21.

32. "The DSN Annual Industry Report," *Discount Store News*, July 12, 1999, p. 58.

33. Larry Greenberg, "Hudson's Bay Faces Challenge from Southern Rival," *The Wall Street Journal*, May 24, 1996, p. B4.

34. Tim Moran, "Kmart Corp.'s Billion-Dollar 'Brand-Aid' Is Martha Stewart," *HFN*, May 24, 1999, p. 1,; "This Year, It's Chic to Shop Cheap," *Business Week*, November 16, 1998, p. 215; "Brand Management," *Chain Store Age State of the Industry Supplement*, August 1998, p. 24A–25A; and "Kmart, Target Proceed Cautiously," *MMR*, May 17, 1999, p. 20.

35. "Top 100 Retailers," *Stores*, July 1999, p. S12.

36. Tracie Rozhon, "Main Street's Latest Threat," *The New York Times*, June 14, 1999, A25; "Annual Report of Categories," *Drug Store News*, May 17, 1999; and "Annual Report on Drug Chains," *Drug Store News*, April 26, 1999.

37. Susan Reda, "Redefining Pharmacy's Role," *Stores*, April 1997, pp. 34–36.

38. Ibid., p. 35.

39. "Top 100 Retailers," *Stores*, July 1999, p. S16.

40. "Lowe's Widens Its Growth Focus," *National Home Center News*, September 8, 1997, p. 7.

41. Mike Duff, "Home Depot Debuts New Format," *Discount Store News*, July 12, 1999, pp. 1, 80; Margaret Pressler, "The High End Gets Higher; Home Depot's Luxury Stores Ride a Trend of Rising Expectations—and Spending," *The Washington Post*, July 11, 1999, p. H01; and James Hagerty, "Gilding the Drill Bit? Hardware Giants Go High End," *The Wall Street Journal*, July 28, 1998, pp. B1, B5.

42. "The DSN Annual Industry Report," *Discount Store News*, July 12, 1999, pp. 58–59.

43. "Back to the Future," *The New York Times Magazine*, April 6, 1997, pp. 48–49.

44. "The DSN Annual Industry Report," *Discount Store News*, July 12, 1999, pp. 60–62.

45. Ibid., pp. 61–62.

46. "Sorting Out the Stores: Clothing Stores Survey/Report," *Consumer Reports*, November 1998, pp. 12–16.

47. Sharon Edelson, "Once a Poor Relation, Outlets Go Legit and Trouble Looms," *Women's Wear Daily*, April 4, 1995, pp. 1, 8.

48. *Statistical Abstract of the United States*, 119th ed. (Washington, DC: U.S. Government Printing Office, 1999).

49. Jennifer Porter, "Supermarket Banker Personifies the New Way in Bank Sales," *Bank Marketing*, October 1996, pp. 8–10; Jeffrey Westegren, "The New Bank Marketing," *Bank Marketing*, July 1996, pp. 7–8; and Beverly Wayne and Curtis Wayne, "Tailoring Retailing to Fit Banking," *Bank Marketing*, February 1996, pp. 43–47.

50. Valarie Zeithaml, A. Parasuraman, and Leonard Berry, "Problems and Strategies in Services Marketing," *Journal of Marketing* 49 (Spring 1985), pp. 33–46.

51. *Dun and Bradstreet Corporate Starts* (New York: Dun and Bradstreet, 1998), p. 74.

52. James Hagerty, "Home Depot Raises the Ante, Targeting Mom and Pop Rivals," *The Wall Street Journal*, January 23, 1999, pp. A1, A10.

53. S.J. Arnold, J. Handelman, and D.J. Tigert, "The Impact of a Market Spoiler on Consumer Preference Structures (or, What Happens When Wal-Mart Comes to Town)," *Journal of Retailing and Consumer Services* 5 (November 1997), pp. 323–54; and Nora Barnes, Allicon Connell, Lisa Hermengildo, and Lucinda Mattson, "Regional Differences in the Economic Impact of Wal-Mart," *Business Horizon* 39 (July–August 1996), pp. 21–25.

54. Stanley Hollander, "Clio Goes Shopping," *Anderson Retailing Issues Letter*, Center for Retailing Studies, Texas A&M University, September 1998.

55. Stanley Hollander, "The Wheel of Retailing: What Makes Skilled Managers Succumb to the 'Prosper, Mature, and Decay' Pattern?" *Marketing Management*, Summer 1996, pp. 63–65; Stephen Brown, "Postmodernism, the Wheel of Retailing, and Will to Power," *The International Review of Retail, Distribution, and Consumer Research*, July 1995, pp. 387–412; and Arieh Goldman, "Institutional Change in Retailing: An Updated Wheel of Retailing," in *Foundations of Marketing Channels*, ed. A. Woodside, J. Sims, D. Lewison, and I. Wilkenson (Austin, TX: Lone Star, 1978), pp. 193–201.

56. Stanley C. Hollander, "Notes on the Retail Accordion," *Journal of Retailing* 42 (Summer 1966), pp. 20–40, 54.

57. Thomas J. Maronick and Bruce J. Walker, "The Dialectic Evolution of Retailing," in *Proceedings: Southern Marketing Association*, ed. Barnett Greenberg (Atlanta: Georgia State University, 1974), p. 147.

58. A.C.R. Dreesmann, "Patterns of Evolution in Retailing," *Journal of Retailing* (Spring 1968) pp. 81–96; and Murray Forester, "Darwinian Theory of Retailing," *Chain Store Age*, August 1995, p. 8.

Chapter 3

1. See also Connie Bauer and John Miglautsch, "A Conceptual Definition of Direct Marketing," *Journal of Direct Marketing* 6 (Spring 1992), pp. 7–17.

2. Cynthia Crossen and Ellen Graham, "Pressed for Time or Pressed for Money?" *The Wall Street Journal*, March 8, 1996, p. B4; George Milne and Mary Ellen Gordon, "A Segmentation Study of Consumers' Attitudes toward Direct Mail," *Journal of Direct Marketing* 8 (Spring 1994), pp. 45–52.

3. Andy Reinhardt. "As the Web Spins," *Business Week*, May 24, 1999, p. 30; Russ Mitchell, "Why Big Pipes Rock," *U.S. News & World Report*, February 1, 1999, pp. 40–41; and Jerry Bowles, "The Future Internet: Faster, Smarter, Mobile, Scarier," *Newsweek*, November 16, 1998, pp. 12–13.

4. "Retailing: Confronting the Challenges That Face Bricks-and-Mortar Stores," *Harvard Business Review*, July–August 1999, pp. 159–173; Nanette Byrnes and Paul Judge, "Internet Anxiety," *Business Week*, June 28, 1999, pp. 78–88; and "In the Balance: The Net Changes Location Analysis," *Chain Store Age*, May 1999, pp. 79–83.

5. Valerie Seckler, "E-Tailing Sales: Data Privacy Is Seen as Key," *WWD*, August 25, 1999, p. 5.

6. Everett Rogers, *Diffusion of Innovations*, 4th ed. (New York: The Free Press, 1995).

7. "Amount of Women Holiday Shoppers to Surge," Rochester, NY: Harris Interactive, August 27, 1999.

8. *Meeting Generation Y*. Nua, July 19, 1999; and *Young Consumers Have Internalised the Net* (Forrester Research, August 11, 1999).

9. Rebecca Quick, "New Websites Let Kids Shop, Like, without Credit Cards," *The Wall Street Journal*, June 14, 1999, pp. B1, B4.

10. Joanne Cleaver, "Surfing for Seniors," *Marketing News*, July 19, 1999, pp. 1, 7; and Justina Gapper, "The Rise of

the New Media Greys," *New Media Age*, January 29, 1998, pp. 10–12.

11. Ibid.

12. Thomas Weber, "Who, What, Where: Putting the Internet in Perspective," *The Wall Street Journal*, April 16, 1998, p. B12.

13. John Tagliabue, "Foie Gras and Chips, Anyone?" *The New York Times*, March 27, 1999, pp. B1, B5.

14. Warren Caragata, "An Overview of Electronic Commerce," *Prism*, July 12, 1999, pp. 32–38.

15. *Consumers in 21st Century* Washington, DC; National Consumers League (May 1999).

16. This section is based on Joseph Alba, John Lynch, Barton Weitz, Chris Janiszewski, Richard Lutz, Alan Sawyer, and Stacy Woods, "Interactive Home Shopping: Consumer, Retailer, and Manufacturers Incentives to Participate in Electronic Markets," *Journal of Marketing* 61 (July 1997), pp. 38–53.

17. Lorrie Grant, "Grocery Chore No More," *USA Today*, July 21, 1999, pp. B1–B2.

18. Reid Claxton, "Customer Safety: Direct Marketing's Undermarketed Advantage," *Journal of Direct Marketing* 9 (Winter 1995), pp. 67–78.

19. William Wilkie and Peter R. Dickson, "Consumer Information Search and Shopping Behavior," working paper (Cambridge, MA: Management Science Institute, 1985).

20. Phil Patton, "Nuy Here, and We'll Teach You What You Like," *The New York Times*, Electronic Commerce Special Section, September 22, 1999, p. 5; and Pattie Maes, "Smart Commerce: The Future of Intelligent Agents in Cyberspace," *Journal of Interactive Marketing* 3 (Summer 1999), pp. 66–76.

21. James Peltier, John Schibrowsky, and John Davis, "Using Attitudinal and Descriptive Database Information to Understand Interactive Buyer–Seller Relationships," *Journal of Interactive Marketing* 12 (Summer 1998), pp. 32–45; and John Eighmey, "Adding Value in the Information Age: Uses and Gratifications of Sales on the World-Wide Web," *Journal of Business Research* 41 (March 1998), pp. 34–45.

22. Wilkie and Dickson, "Consumer Information Search and Shopping Behavior."

23. Jared Sandberg, "It Isn't Entertainment That Makes the Web Shine: It's Dull Data," *The Wall Street Journal*, July 20, 1998, pp. A1, A6.

24. John Verity and Robert Hof, "The Internet: How Will It Change the Way You Do Business?" *Business Week*, November 14, 1994, pp. 80–88.

25. Michael Hartnett, "Not All Items Prosper in On-Line Sales Arena," *Discount Store News*, April 20, 1998, pp. 16–17.

26. *The State of Online Retailing 2.0* (Silver Spring, MD: Shop.org, July 1999).

27. Timothy Mullaney, "Taking in the Travel Sites," *Business Week*, July 26, 1999, p. EB68; "Travel Special Report," *The Industry Standard*, June 14, 1999, pp. 52–74; and "E-Comm Fly with Me," *New Media Age*, March 11, 1999, pp. 12–14.

28. Andrew Osterland, "Nothing but Net," *Business Week*, August 2, 1999, p. 72; Bill Orr, "E-banks or E-branches?" *ABA Banking Journal*, July 1999, pp. 32–42; Alex Sheshunoff, "The Wait Is Over for Internet Banking," *ABA Banking Journal*, June 1999, pp. 18–20; "Financial Services On-Line," *The Industry Standard*, May 17, 1999, pp. 44–80; and "Banking in Cyberspace," *International Journal of Retail & Distribution Management* 26 (February–March 1998), pp. 128–30.

29. Michelle Rafter, "Cheap, Cheaper, Cheapest," *The Industry Standard*, January 11, 1999, pp. 50–52; and George Anders, "Comparison Shopping Is the Web's Virtue–Unless You're a Seller," *The Wall Street Journal*, July 23, 1998, pp. A1, A8.

30. Rebecca Quick, "Web's Robot Shoppers Don't Roam Free," *The Wall Street Journal*, September 3, 1998, pp. B1, B8.

31. Valerie Seckler, "E-Tailing Sales: Data Privacy Is Seen as Key," *WWD*, August 25, 1999, p. 5.

32. Joanne Cleaver, "The Garden Spot," *Marketing News*, May 10 1999, pp. 15–16; Albert Karr, "A Hot New Job Is Chief of Customer Service for Internet Retailers," *The Wall Street Journal*, June 1, 1999, p. A1; Stewart Alsop, "You Can Trust Me on This—Really, *Fortune*, March 15, 1999, pp. 175–76; and John Hammond, "Give Customers a Little Love; They'll Need It in Cyberland," *Do-It-Yourself Retailing*, February 1999, p. 8.

33. *The State of Online Retailing 2.0.*

34. Ibid.

35. Study conducted by Mary Cullen at Georgetown University. (www.msb.edu/faculty/culnanm/gippshome.html.)

36. Ibid.

37. John Hagel and Arthur Armstrong, *Net Gain: Expanding Markets through Virtual Communities* (Boston: Harvard Business School Press, 1998).

38. Edward Welles, "Perfect Internet Business, *Inc.*, September 1999, pp. 71–75; and Carol Chapman, "In Full Flower," *Texas Monthly*, June 1999, pp. 20–21.

39. Mark Bergen, Shantanu Dutta, and Steven M. Shugan, "Branded Variants: A Retail Perspective," *Journal of Marketing Research* 33 (February 1996), pp. 9–19.

40. Gerald Lohse and Peter Spiller, "Electronic Shopping," *Communications of the ACM* 41 (July 1998), pp. 81–88; and Donna Hoffman and Thomas Novak, "Marketing in Hypermedia Computer-Mediated Environments: Conceptual Foundations," *Journal Of Marketing* 60 (Summer 1996), pp. 50–63.

41. Ginger Koloszyc, "Internet-Only Retailers Struggle to Improve Product Return Process," *Stores*, July 1999,

pp. 54–59; and David Schulz, "Growth of Direct-to-Customer Channels Reshapes Retail Distribution," *Stores*, March 1999, pp. 48–51.

42. George Anders, "Virtual Reality: Web Firms Go on Warehouse Building Boom," *The Wall Street Journal*, September 8, 1999, pp. B1, B9.

43. J.C. Herz, "Web Sales Fill Gap Left by Software Store," *The New York Times*, July 23, 1998, p. D4.

44. Dana Canedy, "Need Asparagus? Just Click It," *The New York Times*, September 10, 1999, pp. C1, C18; Cecile Corral, "On-Line Grocery Shopping Heats Up despite Concerns over Big Issues," *Discount Store News*, July 12, 1999, pp. 18, 20; Linda Himelstein, "Can You Sell Groceries Like Books?" *Business Week*, July 26, 1999, p. EB44; and Frank Britt, "Building a Lifestyle Brand: The Unfolding Story of Streamline, Inc." *Anderson Retailing Issues Letter*, Center for Retailing Studies, Texas A&M University, July 1998.

45. Company documents.

46. Lisa Vincenti, "Retailers Eye Internet, Global Market," *HFN*, January 25 1999, p. 6.

47. Valerie Seckler, "A Warning to Stores: Get Online or Risk Loss of Share to Net," *WWD*, August 4, 1999, pp. 1, 144; "Net Effects," *Chain Store Age*, section two, September 1999, pp. 3A–7A; and Emily Nelson, "As Web Retailing Surges, Where's Wal-Mart?" *The Wall Street Journal*, May 17, 1999, pp. B1, B4.

48. Katrina Brooker, "Toys Were Us," *Fortune*, September 27, 1999, pp. 145–48; and Bernard Warner and Miguel Helft, "How Culture Clash Sank the Toys 'R' Us Deal," *The Industry Standard*, August 30, 1999, pp. 28, 30.

49. "Most Recognized E-Commerce Names," *Discount Store News*, September 6, 1999, p. 4.

50. Faye Brookman, "Drugstores Face New Rival," *WWD*, March 5, 1999, p. 16.

51. James Frederick, "Walgreen's Gears for Opening of Its Own Internet Pharmacy," *Drug Store News*, July 19, 1999, pp. CP1–CP4; and "State of the Industry: Drug Stores: Chain Drug Stores Provide Rx for Whole Health," *Chain Store Age State of the Industry Supplement*, August 1999, pp. 21A–24A.

52. Megan Barnett, "Why Macys.com Won't Sell Levi's," *The Industry Standard*, November 30, 1998, p. 22.

53. "Mail-Order Shopping: Which Catalogs Are Best?" *Consumer Reports*, October 1994, p. 622.

54. *1999 Statistical Fact Book* (New York: Direct Marketing Association, 1999), pp. 30, 72.

55. Ibid., p. 101.

56. "Mail-Order Shopping: Which Catalogs Are Best?" pp. 622–23.

57. Jill Roth, "The Good, the Bad, and the Uncertain," *American Printer*, August 1999, pp. 3–5.

58. *1999 Direct Selling Growth and Outlook Survey* (Washington, DC: Direct Selling Associations, 1999).

59. Ibid.; and Valarie Retiman, "In Japan's Car Market, Big Three Face Rivals Who Go Door to Door," *The Wall Street Journal*, September 28, 1994, pp. A1, A6.

60. Mary Ann Eastwick and Mengmeng Lui, "The Influence of Store Attitudes and Other Nonstore Shopping Behaviors on Patronage of Television Shopping Programs," *Journal of Direct Marketing* 11 (Summer 1997), pp. 14–24.

61. "Home Shopping: Home Alone?" *Economist*, October 12, 1996, pp. 67–68.

62. "State of the Industry: Nonstore Retailing Gains Favor with Consumers," *Chain Store Age State of the Industry Supplement*, August 1999, p. 31A; and "Dinosaurs Still Stalk the Earth," *The Economist*, November 8, 1997, p. 67.

63. "1999 State of the Vending Industry Report," *Automatic Merchandiser*, August 1999, pp. S1–S20.

64. Alan Gilbert, "Three Years Later, Wireless Communication May Find Its Place," *Automatic Merchandiser*, August 1999, pp. 32, 34.

Chapter 4

1. John Hoeffel, "The Next Baby Boom," *American Demographics*, October 1995, pp. 22–31.

2. Cynthia R. Cohen, "The Next Generation of Consumers: Will They Incite Revolution or Evolution," speech presented at the National Retail Federation's 87th annual convention, January 20, 1997.

3. Cyndee Miller, "Teens Seen as the First Truly Global Consumers," *Marketing News*, March 27, 1995, p. 9.

4. James U. McNeal, "Tapping the Three Kids' Markets," *American Demographics*, April 1998, pp. 37–41.

5. Lisa Bannon, "As Children Become More Sophisticated, Marketers Think Older," *The Wall Street Journal*, October 13, 1998, pp. A1, A6, based on research by Professor James U. McNeal, Texas A&M University.

6. McNeal, "Tapping the Three Kids' Markets."

7. Bannon, "As Children Become More Sophisticated, Marketers Think Older"; Mike Duff, "Zellers Loyalty Program Cultivates Young Consumers, Rewards Parents," *Discount Store News*, October 26, 1998, p. 19.

8. Cynthia R. Cohen, "The Next Generation of Consumers."

9. Ibid.

10. Johanna Omelia, "Understanding Generation Y: A Look at the Next Wave of US Consumers," *Drug & Cosmetic Industry*, December 1998, pp. 90–91, as reported in *Teen Market Report*.

11. Ibid.

12. Ibid.

13. Ibid.

14. Ibid.

15. "Retailers at Play," *Design Forum Ideations* 3, no. 1 (January–February 1996).

16. Molly O'Neill, "Feeding the Next Generation," *The New York Times*, March 14, 1998, pp. B1+.

17. J. Walker Smith and Ann Clurman, *Rocking the Ages: The Yankelovich Report on Generational Marketing.* (Harperbusiness, 1998).

18. "In Marketing to Xers Retailers Are Novices," *Discount Store News*, October 26, 1998, p. 72.

19. "Demographics Don't Support New-Store Boom," *Chain Store Age*, May 1998, pp. 104–10, based on research by Richard Green, University of Wisconsin, Madison.

20. Cheryl Russell, *The Master Trend—How the Baby Boom Generation Is Remaking America* (New York: Plenum, 1993), cited in Patricia Braus, "The Baby Boom at Mid-Decade," *American Demographics*, April 1995, pp. 40–45.

21. Susan Reda, "Reaching the Aging Boomers," *Stores*, March 1998, pp. 22–26.

22. Ibid, pp. 22–24; Keith Naughton and Bill Vlasic, "The Nostalgia Boom," *Business Week*, March 23, 1998, pp. 58–59; and Michael Hartnett, "The 'Gold' in Oldies Is Yet to Come," *Discount Store News;* February 23, 1998, p. 17–18.

23. Braus, "The Baby Boom at Mid-Decade."

24. Shannon Dortch, "Rise and Fall of Generations." *American Demographics*, July 1996, pp. 6–7, 43.

25. Mary Ellen Kelly, "Discounters Grow Wiser to Seniors' Spending Potential," *Discount Store News*, May 18, 1992, pp. 113–14; attributed to Professor George Moschis of Georgia State University.

26. Mike Duff, "The Customer Connection, Seniors," *Discount Store News*, October 26, 1998, pp. 102, 104.

27. "As Seniors Multiply, An Opportunity Arises," *Discount Store News*, October 26, 1998.

28. Ann D'Innocenzio, "Moderate Firms Push Fashion Limit Past 55; Others Ride the Break," *Women's Wear Daily*, June 4, 1997, pp. 1, 14.

29. "Immigration's Impact on Real Estate and Retailing," *Chain Store Age*, October 1996, pp. 68–74; and "Minority Customers to Become a Major Marketing Target," *Discount Store News*, May 18, 1992, p. 100.

30. Tom Maguire, "Ethnics Outspend in Areas," *American Demographics*, December 1998, pp. 12–16, based on research by New American Strategies Group and Demographic Corporation.

31. "African-Americans Grow, Seek Big-Ticket Purchases," *Discount Store News*, October 26, 1998; Marcia Mogelonsky, "Meet the Inner-City Shopper," *American Demographics*, December 1998, pp. 38–41; and Christy Fisher, "Black, Hip, and Primed (to Shop)," *American Demographics*, September 1996, pp. 52–58.

32. "Surging Hispanic Market Draws Interest at Retail," *Discount Store News*, October 26, 1998, p. 112.

33. "Marketing to Hispanics: Beyond the Obvious," *Discount Merchandiser*, July 1, 1998, pp. 25–27. Research attributed to Joe Musser, senior vice president of client services for Newport Beach, CA-based Mendoza Dillon, an advertising agency involved in Sears' Hispanic marketing efforts.

34. Susan Reda, "Beyond Discounting," *Stores*, May 1996, pp. 24–28; statistics taken from the U.S. Bureau of the Census and Kurt Salmon Associates.

35. Rebecca Piirto Heath, "Life on Easy Street," *American Demographics*, April 1997, p. 32.

36. Jennifer Steinhauser, "The Stores That Cross Class Lines," *The New York Times*, March 15, 1998, Sec. 3, pp. 1, 11.

37. Amy Barrett, "French Discounter Takes Cheap Chic World-Wide," *The Wall Street Journal*, May 27, 1998, pp. B1, B8.

38. Reda, "Beyond Discounting"; statistics attributed to MIT economist Lester Thurow.

39. Michael P. Niemira, "Are the Fortunes of Retailers That Appeal to Lower-Income Groups about to Change?" *Chain Store Age*, April 1996, p. 24.

40. www.intelliquest.com/products/mbt/wwits.html, and www.intelliquest.com/press/release78.asp

41. www.headcount.com/globalsource/ecommerce/ ?id=6&choice=The+US

42. www.cyberatlas.com/market/retailing/gender.html www.cyberatlas.internet.com/big_picture/demographics/ gender.html

43. www.cyberatlas.com/market/retailing/gender.html

44. www.gvu/gatech.edu/user_surveys/survey-1998- 10/graphs/use/q30.htm

45. www.cyberatlas.internet.com/big_picture/demographics/ roper.html

46. "The Devotion Cycle," *Chain Store Age*, January 1999, pp. 52–70, based on research by Kurt Salmon Associates.

47. Adapted from Laura Liebeck, "Shoppers Need Ways to Beat the Clock," *Discount Store News*, May 6, 1996, pp. 88–94.

48. Douglas A. Blackmon, "Forget the Stereotype: America Is Becoming a Nation of Culture," *The Wall Street Journal*, September 17, 1998, pp. A1, A8.

49. Ibid., data from League of American Theaters and Producers and the Theater Communications Group in New York.

50. "Shopper Loyalty May Flag if Euro Lowers Prices," *The Wall Street Journal Europe*, November 10, 1998, based on an interview with Professor Erin Anderson, INSEAD, France, p. 6.

51. Teri Agins, "Why Cheap Clothes Are Getting More Respect," *The Wall Street Journal*, October 16, 1995, pp. B1, B3.

52. Nancy Ten Kate, "Lose the Suit," *American Demographics*, April 1998, pp. 31–32.

53. Mark Manoff, "Smart Companies Capitalize on Corporate Dress-Down Policies," *Ernst & Young's Retail News*, Fall 1995, pp. 4–6.

54. Nancy Ten Kate, "Lose the Suit," based on research by Dan Chew, consumer marketing director at Levi Strauss.

Chapter 5

1. "Coldwater Creek Rises to the Top," *Chain Store Age*, November 1997, pp. 41–43.

2. For a detailed discussion of customer behavior, see J. Paul Peter and Jerry C. Olson, *Consumer Behavior and Marketing Strategy*, 5th ed. (Burr Ridge, IL: Irwin/McGraw-Hill, 2000). See also Jagdish Sheth, "An Integrative Theory of Patronage Preference and Choice," in William Darden and Robert Lusch, eds., *Patronage Theory and Retail Management* (New York: North-Holland, 1989), pp. 9–28.

3. "Working Women: $50 Billion in Sales," *WWD*, May 8, 1996, section II, p. 14.

4. Francis Piton, "Defining Impulse Purchasing," in R. Hillman and M. Houston, eds., *Advances in Consumer Research*, vol. 19 (Provo, UT: Association for Consumer Research, 1990), pp. 509–14; and Dennis Rock, "The Buying Impulse," *Journal of Consumer Research*, September 1987, pp. 189–99.

5. Kevin Armata, "Signs that Sell," *Progressive Grocer*, October 1996, p. 21.

6. Sharon Beatty and M. Elizabeth Ferrell, "Impulse Buying: Modeling Its Precursors," *Journal of Retailing* 74 (Summer 1998), pp. 169–91; and John Willman, "Parting a Fool from His Money," *The Financial Times*, August 10, 1998, p. 9. See Alison Smith, "A Grab for Impulse Shoppers," *The Financial Times*, September 18, 1998, p. 12, for a discussion of how Internet retailers are trying to encourage impulse shopping.

7. Joel Urbany, Peter Dickson, and Rosemary Kalapurakai, "Price Search in the Retail Grocery Market," *Journal of Marketing* 60 (April 1996), pp. 91–111; and Peter Dickson and Alan Sawyer, "The Prince Knowledge and Search of Supermarket Shoppers," *Journal of Marketing*, July 1991, pp. 49–59.

8. "Consumer Buying Patterns: Beyond Demographics," *Progressive Grocer*, May 1995, p. 136.

9. Pamela Sebastian, " 'Aspirational Wants' Form the Basis of a Modern Retailing Strategy," *The Wall Street Journal*, October 15, 1998, p. A1; and Barry Babin, William Darden, and Mitch Griffin, "Work and/or Fun: Measuring Hedonic and Utilitarian Shopping Value," *Journal of Consumer Research* 20 (March 1994), pp. 644–56.

10. This hierarchical structure of needs is based on Abraham Maslow, *Motivation and Personality* (New York: Harper & Row, 1954).

11. "Why Do You Shop?" *WWD*, July 22, 1997, pp. 44–46; "Shop, Shop, Shop," *Advertising Age*, August 22, 1994, p. 3; Betsy Morris, "As a Favored Pastime, Shopping Ranks High with Most Americans," *The Wall Street Journal*, July 30, 1987, pp. 1, 113; Robert A. Westbrook and William C. Black, "A Motivational-Based Shopper Typology," *Journal of Retailing* 61 (Spring 1985), pp. 78–103; and Scott Dawson, Peter Dawson, and Nancy Ridgeway, "Shopping Motives, Emotional States, and Retail Outcomes," *Journal of Retailing* 66 (Winter 1990), pp. 408–27.

12. Jacquelyn Bivens, "Fun and Mall Games," *Stores*, August 1989, p. 35; Peter Block, Nancy Ridgeway, and Scott Dawson, "The Shopping Mall as Consumer Habitat," *Journal of Retailing* 70 (Winter 1994), pp. 23–42.

13. Stephen Grove and Raymond Fisk, "The Impact of Other Customers on Service Experiences: A Critical Incident Examination of Getting Along," *Journal of Retailing* 73 (Spring 1997), pp. 63–86; Dale Duhan, Scott Johnson, James Wilcox, and Gilbert Harrell, "Influence on Consumer Use of Word-of-Mouth Recommendation Sources," *Journal of the Academy of Marketing Science* 25 (Fall 1997), pp. 283–95; Kenneth Evans, Tim Christiansen, and James Gill, "The Impact of Social Influence and Role Expectations on Shopping Center Patronage Intentions," *Journal of the Academy of Marketing Science* 24 (Summer 1996), pp. 208–18; and Yong-Soon Kang and Nancy Ridgeway, "The Importance of Consumer Market Interactions as a Form of Social Support for Elderly Consumers," *Journal of Public Policy & Marketing* 15 (Spring 1996), pp. 108–17.

14. Susan Caminiti, "Ralph Lauren: The Emperor Has Clothes," *Fortune*, November 11, 1996, p. 82.

15. David Mick, Michelle DeMoss, and Ronald Faber, "A Projective Study of Motivations and Meanings of Self-Gift," *Journal of Retailing*, Summer 1992, pp. 112–44.

16. Gordon Burner and Richard Pomazal, "Problem: Recognition: The Crucial First State of the Consumer Decision Process," *Journal of Consumer Marketing*, Summer 1987, pp. 59–66.

17. Lisa Gubernick, "Through a Glass, Brightly," *Forbes*, August 11, 1986, p. 34.

18. Philip Titus and Peter Everett, "The Consumer Retail Search Process: A Conceptual Model and Research Agenda," *Journal of the Academy of Marketing Science* 23 (Spring 1995), pp. 106–19; and Paul Bloom and James Pailin, "Using Information Situations to Guide Marketing Strategy," *Journal of Consumer Marketing* 12 (Spring 1995), pp. 19–28.

19. Sanjay Putrevu and Brian T. Ratchford, "A Model of Search Behavior with an Application to Grocery Shopping," *Journal of Retailing* 73 (Winter 1997), pp. 463–87; Sridhar Moorthy, Brian Ratchford, and Debabrata Talukdar, "Consumer Information Search Revisited: Theory and Empirical Analysis," *Journal of Consumer Research*, 23 (March 1997), pp. 263–78; and Jeffrey Schmidt and Richard Prend, "A Proposed Model of Consumer External Information Search," *Journal of the Academy of Marketing Sciences* 24 (Summer 1996), pp. 246–56.

20. Arch Woodside and Eva Thelen, "Accessing Memory and Customer Choice: Benefit-to-Store Retrieval Models That Predict Purchase," *Marketing & Research Today* 24 (November 1996), pp. 260–88.

21. Lawrence Feick, Linda Prie, and Robie Higie, "People Who Use People: The Other Side of Opinion Leadership," in R. Lutz, ed., *Advances in Consumer Research* (Provo, UT: Association of Consumer Research, 1986), pp. 10–12.

22. George Russell, "Where the Customer Is Still King," *Time*, February 2, 1987, pp. 56–57.

23. Adam Finn and Jordan Louviere, "Shopping Center Image, Considerations, and Choice: Anchor Store Contribution," *Journal of Business Research* 35 (1996), pp. 241–51; and Don James, Richard Durand, and Robert Dreves, "The Use of a Multi-Attribute Attitude Model in a Store Image Study," *Journal of Retailing* 52 (Summer 1976), pp. 23–32.

24. Robert Hansen and Terry Deutscher, "An Empirical Investigation of Attribute Importance in Retail Store Selection," *Journal of Retailing* 53 (Winter 1978), pp. 59–72.

25. Patrich Van Kenhove, Walter Van Waterschoot, and Kristoff De Wulf, "The Impact of Task Definition on Store-Attribute Saliences and Store Choice," *Journal of Retailing* 75 (Spring 1999), pp. 125–36.

26. William L. Wilkie and Edgar D. Pessimier, "Issues in Marketing's Use of Multi-Attribute Attitude Models," *Journal of Marketing Research*, November 1973, pp. 428–41; and Richard J. Lutz and James R. Bettman, "Multi-Attribute Models in Marketing: A Bicentennial Review," in A.G. Woodside, J.N. Sheth, and P.D. Bennett, eds., *Consumer and Industrial Buying Behavior* (New York: Elsevier–North Holland, 1977), pp. 13–50.

27. Eric Johnson and Robert Meyer, "Compensatory Models of Non-Compensatory Choices Processes: The Effect of Varying Context," *Journal of Consumer Research* 5 (June 1984), pp. 52–58.

28. David Bell, Tech-Hua Ho, and Christopher Tang, "Determining Where to Stop: Fixed and Variable Costs of Shopping," *Journal of Marketing Research* 35 (August 1998), pp. 352–70. For a discussion of the different decision rules customers use, see James R. Bettman, *An Information Processing Theory of Consumer Choice* (Reading, MA: Addison-Wesley, 1979).

29. Richard Brand and Joseph Cronin, "Consumer-Specific Determinants of the Size of Retail Choice Sets: An Empirical Comparison of Physical Good and Service Providers," *Journal of Services Marketing* 11 (January–February 1997), pp. 19–39; and Ronald LeBlanc and L.W. Turley, "Retail Influence on Evoked Set Formation and Final Choice of Shopping Goods," *International Journal of Retail & Distribution Management* 22 (1994), pp. 10–17.

30. Wayne Hoyer and Steven Brown, "Effects of Brand Awareness of Choice for a Common, Repeat-Purchase Product," *Journal of Consumer Research*, September 1990, pp. 141–49.

31. Susan M. Broniarczyk, Wayne D. Hoyer, and Leigh McAlister, "Consumers' Perceptions of the Assortment Offered in a Grocery Category: The Impact of Item Reduction," *Journal of Marketing Research* 35 (May 1998), pp. 166–77.

32. Masaaki Kiotabe, "The Return of 7-Eleven . . . from Japan: The Vanguard Program," *Columbia Journal of World Business* 30 (Winter 1995), pp. 70–81; and Kevin Helliker, "Some 7-Elevens Try Selling a New Image," *The Wall Street Journal*, October 25, 1991, pp. B1–B2.

33. Richard J. Lutz, "Changing Brand Attitudes through Modification of Cognitive Structure," *Journal of Consumer Research* 1 (March 1975), pp. 49–59.

34. Roger Bennett, "Queues, Customer Characteristics and Policies for Managing Waiting-Lines in Supermarkets," *International Journal of Retail & Distribution Management* 26 (February 1998), pp. 78–86; M. Kostecki, "Waiting Lines as a Marketing Issue," *European Management Journal* 14, no. 3 (1996), pp. 295–303; M.K. Hui and D.K. Tsi, "What to Tell Consumers in Waits of Different Lengths: An Integrative Model of Service Evaluation," *Journal of Marketing* 60, no. 2 (1996), pp. 81–90; K.L. Katz, B.M. Larson, and R.C. Larson, "Prescriptions for Waiting in Line Blues: Entertain, Enlighten, and Enrage," *Sloan Management Review* 32, no. 4 (1991), pp. 44–53; S. Taylor, "The Effects of Filled Waiting Time and Service Provider Control over the Delay on Evaluation of Service," *Journal of the Academy of Marketing Science* 23 (1995), pp. 38–48.

35. "How to Turn Away Shoppers," *WWD*, June 10, 1997, p. 8.

36. Jagdip Singh, "A Typology of Consumer Dissatisfaction Response Styles," *Journal of Retailing*, Spring 1990, pp. 57–58; and Richard Oliver and Wayne DeSarbo, "Response Determinants in Satisfaction Judgments," *Journal of Consumer Research* 15 (March 1988), pp. 495–507.

37. Josee Bloemer and Ko de Ruyter, "On the Relationship between Store Image, Store Satisfaction and Store," *European Journal of Marketing* 32 (May–June 1998), pp. 499–514; Eugene Anderson, "Customer Satisfaction and Word-of-Mouth," *Journal of Services Research* 1 (August 1998), pp. 13–21; Richard Oliver, Roland Rust, and Sajeev Varki, "Customer Delight: Foundations, Findings, and Managerial Insights," *Journal of Retailing* 73 (Fall 1997), pp. 311–36; and Richard L. Oliver, "Measurement and Evaluation of Satisfaction Processes in a Retail Setting," *Journal of Retailing* 57 (Fall 1981), pp. 26–31.

38. Conway Lachman and John Lanasa, "Family Decision-Making Theory: An Overview and Assessment," *Psychology & Marketing* 10 (March–April 1993), pp. 81–94; Robert Boutlier, "Pulling the Family Strings," *American Demographics*, August 1993, pp. 44–48; Irene Foster and Richard Olshavsky," An Exploratory Study of Family Decision Making Using a New Taxonomy of Family Role Structure," in T. Srull, ed., *Advances in Consumer Research* (Provo, UT: Association for Consumer Research, 1989), pp. 665–700.

39. Jean Darian, "Parent–Child Decision Making in Children's Clothing Stores," *International Journal of Retail & Distribution Management* 26 (October 1998), pp. 421–32; Kay Palanand and Robert Wilkes, "Adolescent–Parent Interaction in Family Decision Making," *Journal of Consumer Research*, 24 (September 1997), pp. 159–71; Christy Fisher, "Kidding Around Makes Sense," *Advertising Age*, June 27, 1994, pp. 34, 37; Sharon Beatty and Salil Talpade, "Adolescent Influence in Family Decision Making: A Replication with Extension," *Journal of Consumer Research* 31 (September 1994), pp. 332–41; and Ken Wells, "Hotels and Resorts Are Catering to Kids: Day Care and Activities Programs Help Welcome the Traveling Family," *The Wall Street Journal*, August 11, 1988, p. 25.

40. Sharen Kindal, "They May Be Small, but They Shop Big," *Adweek*, February 10, 1992, p. 38.

41. Dianne Pogoda, "It's a Matter of Time: Stores Keep Traffic Moving, Cash Flowing," *Women's Wear Daily*, April 9, 1996, pp. 1, 8.

42. Ibid.

43. Hiroshi Tanaka and Miki Iwamura, "Gift Selection Strategy of Japanese Seasonal Gift Purchasers," Association for Consumer Research Conference, Boston, 1994; and Terrence Witkowski and Yoshito Yamamoto, "Omiyage Gift Purchasing by Japanese Travelers to the US," in *Advances in Consumer Research*, vol. 18 (Provo, UT: Association of Consumer Research, 1991), pp. 123–28.

44. Soyeon Shim and Mary Ann Eastwick, "The Hierarchical Influence of Personal Values on Mall Shopping Attitudes and Behaviors," *Journal of Retailing* 74 (Spring 1998), pp. 139–60.

45. Cyndee Miller, "Top Marketers Take a Bolder Approach in Targeting Gays," *Marketing News*, July 4, 1994, pp. 1–2.

46. Geng Cui, "The Different Faces of the Chinese Consumer," *China Business Review*, July 1997, pp. 34–42.

47. www.dreyers.com; and Florence Fabricant, "The Geography of Taste," *New York Times Magazines*, March 10, 1996, pp. 40–41.

48. Robert Verdisco, "Gender-Specific Shopping," *Chain Store Age*, February 1999, pp. 26–28; Matthew Klein, "He Shops, She Shops," *American Demograhics*, March, 1998, pp. 34–40; Suein Hwang, "From Choices to Checkout, the Genders Behave Very Differently in Supermarkets," *The Wall Street Journal*, March 22, 1994, pp. A1, A4.

49. For additional information about fashion and the fashion industry, see Giannino Malossi, ed., *The Style Engine: Spectacle, Identity, Design and Business: How the Fashion Industry Uses Style to Create Wealth* (New York: Monacelli Press, 1998); Jeannette Jarnow and Kitty G. Dickerson, *Inside the Fashion Business*, 6th ed. (Upper Saddle River, NJ: Merrill, 1997); and Mike Easey, ed. *Fashion Marketing* (Oxford, England: Blackwell, 1995).

50. "Millennium Timeline: Ideas," *The Wall Street Journal*, January 11, 1999, p. R14.

51. Ibid.

52. "The Fashion Innovators," *WWD*, March 20, 1997, p. 2.

53. Veronica Chambers and Alisha Davis, "Direct from Paris . . . to the Mall," *Newsweek*, April 13, 1998, p. 64.

54. Rich Marin and Sarah Van Boven, "The Buzz Machine," *Newsweek*, July 27, 1998, p. 22.

55. J. Freedom du Lac, "Entering the World of Goth," *Sacramento Bee*, March 9, 1999, p. C1; and "Dressed to Express & Impress," *Women's Wear Daily Echo Boomers Supplement*, February 19, 1998, pp. 26–27.

Chapter 6

1. See A. Coskun Samli, *Strategic Marketing for Success in Retailing* (Westport, CT: Quorum Books, 1998); and David Aaker, *Strategic Market Management*, 5th ed. (New York: John Wiley, 1998).

2. Roger Evered, "So What Is Strategy?" *Long Range Planning* 16 (Fall 1983), p. 120.

3. Michael Porter, "What Is Strategy?" *Harvard Business Review*, November–December 1996, pp. 61–78; and Barton Weitz and Robin Wensley, "What Is Marketing Strategy?" working paper, College of Business Administration, University of Florida, Gainesville.

4. Kevin Keller, "Managing Brands for the Long Run: Effective Brand Reinforcement and Revitalization Strategies," *California Management Review* 41 (March 1999), pp. 102–21, and "Starbucks Rides the Caffeine Wave," *Chain Store Age*, April 1996, pp. 80–81.

5. Susan Reda, "Fingerhut Conquers Mountain of Customer Data with Power of Parallel Processing," *Stores*, July 1999, pp. 46–48; Wendy Bounds and Calmetta Coleman, "A Retail Marriage of Mass and Class," *The Wall Street Journal*, February 12, 1999, p. B1; Joseph Cahill, "Credit Companies Find Tough Rival at Bottom of Consumer Market," *The Wall Street Journal*, December 1998, pp. A1, A4; and David Pearson, "Marketing for Survival," *CIO*; April 15, 1998, pp. 44–48.

6. Bounds and Coleman, "A Retail Marriage of Mass and Class."

7. "Auto Chain Report," *Aftermarket Business*, January 1999, pp. 22–32; Howard Rudnitsky, "Keeping the Family Buggy on the Road," *Forbes*, March 11, 1996, pp. 52–53; and John Wirebach, "Autozone Strikes the Heartland," *Automotive Marketing*, October 1996, pp. 19–21.

8. Leonard Berry, *Discovering the Soul of Service* (New York: Free Press, 1999); and "Ukrop's Journey, Outward and Inward," *Progressive Grocer*, October 1997, pp. 12–14.

9. Anthony Boardman and Aidan Vining, "Defining Your Business Using Product–Customer Matrices," *Long Range Planning* 29 (February 1996), pp. 38–48; and R.L. Rothschild, *How to Gain and Maintain Competitive Advantage in Business* (New York: McGraw-Hill, 1984). Chapter 2 gives other examples of this approach to mapping competitive markets.

10. Cynthia Montgomery, "Creating Corporate Advantage," *Harvard Business Review*, May–June 1998, pp. 71–80; Shelby Hunt and Robert Morgan, "The Comparative Advantage Theory of Competition," Journal of Marketing 59 (April 1995), pp. 1–15; Kathleen Conner and C.K. Prahalad, "A Resource-Based Theory of the Firm: Knowledge versus Opportunism," *Organizational Science* 7 (September–October 1996), pp. 477–501; David Collins and Cynthia Montgomery, "Competing on Resources: Strategy for the 1990s," *Harvard Business Review* 73 (July–August 1995), pp. 118–28; and William Werther and Jeffrey Kerr, "The Shifting Sands of Competitive Advantage," *Business Horizons* 38 (May–June 1995), pp. 11–17.

11. Gerrard Macintosh and Lawrence Lockshin, "Retail Relationships and Store Loyalty: A Multi-Level Perspective," *International Journal of Research in Marketing* 14 (1997), pp. 487–97.

12. D. Lee Carpenter, "Return on Innovation—The Power of Being Different," *Anderson Retailing Issues Letter*, Center for Retailing Studies, Texas A&M University, May 1998; Kathleen Seiders and Douglas Tigert, "Impact of Market Entry and Competitive Structure on Store Switching/Store Loyalty," *International Review of Retail, Distribution and Consumer Research* 7, no.3 (1997), pp. 234–56; and Niren Sirohi, Edward McLaughlin, and Dick Wittink, "A Model of Consumer Perceptions and Store Loyalty Intentions for a Supermarket Retailer," *Journal of Retailing* 74 (June 1998), pp. 223–47.

13. "NDP: May Co. Tops Loyalty List," *WWD*, June 3, 1999, p. 22.

14. Richard Czerniawski and Michael Maloney, *Creating Brand Loyalty: The Management of Power Positioning and Really Great Advertising* (New York: AMACOM, 1999); S. Chandrasekhar, Vinod Sawhney, Rafique Malik, S. Ramesh Kumar, and Pranab Dutta, "The Case of Brand Positioning," *Business Today*, June 7, 1999, pp. 131–40; and Bernd Schmitt, Alex Simonson, and Joshua Marcus, "Managing Corporate Image and Identity," *Long Range Planning* 28 (October 1995), pp. 82–92.

15. For examples of this type of research, see James Mammarella, "Value Rules Apparel Decisions as Battle for Share Sharpens," *Discount Store News*, October 7, 1996, pp. 21–25; and Mary R. Zimmer and Linda L. Golden, "Impressions of Retail Stores: A Content Analysis of Consumer Images," *Journal of Retailing* 64 (Fall 1988), pp. 266–93.

16. "Understanding Customer Loyalty," *Stores*, June 1998, p. 16.

17. Nancy Brumback, "Sears Revising 'Softer Side'," *WWD*, February 18, 1999, p. 18; Susan Reda, "Goodbye Bloomingdale's . . . Hello Sears," *Discount Store News*, September 16, 1996, pp. A64–A65; and Scott McMurray, "Sears Fashions a New Future for Itself," *US News and World Report*, June 15, 1996, p. 61.

18. Leonard Berry, "Relationship Marketing of Services Growing Interest: Emerging Perspectives," *Journal of the Academy of Marketing Sciences* 23 (Fall 1995), pp. 236–45; and Mary Jo Bitner, "Building Service Relationships: It's All about Promises," *Journal of the Academy of Marketing Sciences* 23 (Fall 1995), pp. 246–51.

19. Stanley Marcus, *Minding the Store* (Boston: Little, Brown, 1974), p. 81.

20. Susan Greco, "The Road to One to One Marketing," *Inc.*, October 1995, pp. 56–58; Leslie Wines, "Know Thy Customer: Lessons in Value," *Journal of Business Strategy* 16 (November–December 1995), pp. 13–15; and Rashi Glazer, "Marketing in an Information Intensive Environment: Strategic Implications of Knowledge as an Asset," *Journal of Marketing* 55 (October 1991), pp. 1–19.

21. See Dhruv Grewal, R. Krishnan, Julie Baker, and Norm Borin, "The Effect of Store Name, Brand Name and Price Discounts on Customers' Evaluations and Purchase Intentions," *Journal of Retailing* 74 (September 1998), pp. 331–62; Kevin Keller, *Strategic Brand Management: Building, Measuring and Managing Brands* (Upper Saddle River, NJ: Prentice Hall, 1998); Andrew Wileman and Michael Jary, *Retail Power Plays: From Trading to Brand Leadership: Strategies for Building Retail Brands* (Washington Square, NY: New York University Press, 1997); and David Aaker, *Building Strong Brands* (New York: Free Press, 1996).

22. S.A. Shaw and J. Gibbs, "Procurement Strategies of Small Retailers Faced with Uncertainty: An Analysis of Channel Choice and Behaviour," *International Review of Retail, Distribution and Consumer Research* 9, no. 1 (1999), pp. 61–75.

23. Clinton Wilder, "A Thousand Points of Service—IT Is Helping Retailers Offer Better Shopping Experiences Both Online and in the Store," *InformationWeek*, September 14, 1998, p. 235.

24. Jeffrey Pfeffer, *The Human Equation: Building Profits by Putting People First* (Boston: Harvard Business School Press, 1998); and Jeffrey Pfeffer, *Competitive Advantage through People: Unleashing the Power of the Work Force* (Boston: Harvard Business School Press, 1994).

25. "Profiles of Excellence," *Progressive Grocer*, November 1997, p. 55; Debra Chanil, "A Year of Change," *Discount Merchandiser*, January 1996, pp. 10–12ff; and "Family Dollar," 1998, *Annual Report*.

26. William Werther and Jeffrey Kerr, "The Shifting Sands of Competitive Advantage," *Business Horizons* 38 (May–June 1995), pp. 11–17.

27. H. Igor Ansoff, *Corporate Strategy* (New York: McGraw-Hill, 1965); and Roger Kerin, Vijay Mahajan, and P. Rajan Varadarajan, *Contemporary Perspectives on Strategic Market Planning* (Boston: Allyn & Bacon, 1990), chapter 6. See also Susan Mudambi, "A Topology of Strategic Choice in Retailing," *International Journal of Retail & Distribution Management*, 1994, pp. 22–25.

28. Ian Murphy, "Marketers Ponder P-O-P in Stores of the Future," *Marketing News*, May 26, 1997, p. 2.

29. David Aaker, "Should You Take your Brand to Where the Action Is?" *Harvard Business Review*, September–October, 1997, pp. 135–44; and Linda Himelstein, "The World According to the Gap," *Business Week*, January 27, 1997, p. 72.

30. Erin Anderson and Barton Weitz, "Make-or-Buy Decisions: Vertical Integration and Marketing Productivity," *Sloan Management Review* 28 (Spring 1986), p. 319.

31. Rebecca Mead, "Brooks Brothers A Go-Go," *New Yorker Magazine*, March 22, 1999, p. 88.

32. "Global Powers of Retailing," *Store Supplement*, February 1999; "Global Retailing: Global Uncertainties," *Chain Store Age*, December 1998, pp. 132–41; "Sphere of Influence," *Progressive Grocer*, May 1998, pp. 33–37; David Moln, "World View: A Guide to Going Global," *WWD*, July 21, 1998, pp. 22–24; Erik Gordon, "Taking the Plunge?" *Chain Store Age Supplement*, December 1997, pp. 14–23; "Retailing's Great Global Gold Rush," *Chain*

Store Age Supplement, December 1997, pp. 1–13; and Eithel Simpson and Dayle Thorpe, "A Conceptual Model of Strategic Considerations for International Retail Expansion," *Service Industries Journal*, October 1995.

33. Gordon, "Taking the Plunge?" p. 15.

34. Bernard Wysocki Jr., "In Developing Nations, Many Youth Are Big Spenders," *The Wall Street Journal*, June 26, 1997, pp. A1, A11.

35. David Woodruff, "For French Retailers, A Weapon against Wal-Mart," *The Wall Street Journal*, September 27, 1999, pp. B1, B4; David Woodruff, "Carrefour is Mounting a Push into Japanese Markets," *The Wall Street Journal*, June 15, 1999, p. B7.

36. "Retailers Are Trying to Go Global," *The Economist Newspaper* (U.S. ed.), June 19, 1999, p. 1; Jay Johnson, "The Globe Trotters: Retail's Multinationals," *Discount Merchandiser*, September 1995, pp. 40–41; and Moln, "World View," pp. 22–23.

37. Mark Carr, Arlene Hostrop, and Daniel O'Connor, "Global Expansion: The Era of Global Retailing," *Journal of Business Strategy*, May–June 1998, p. 145; and Moln, "World View."

38. Gordon, "Taking the Plunge?"

39. Lisa Penaloza and Mary Gilly, "Marketer Acculturation: The Changer and the Changed," *Journal Of Marketing* 63 (Summer 1999), pp. 84–95.

40. Yumiko Ono, "Pizza in Japan Is Adapted to Local Tastes," *The Wall Street Journal*, June 4, 1993, p. B1.

41. "Sphere of Influence," *Progressive Grocer*, May 1998, p. 33.

42. Gordon, "Taking the Plunge?"; and "Shopping the World," *The Economist Newspaper*, June 18, 1999, pp 1–2.

43. "Shopping the World," *The Economist Newspaper*, June 18, 1999, pp 1–2.

44. "What's the Best Way to Set Up Shop?" *Chain Store Age Global Retailing Supplement*, December 1997, pp. 32–35.

45. William Woodward, "In Global Retailing, The Game's the Same, but the Rules Can Be Different," *Chain Store Age*, December 1996, section 3, p. 11B.

46. "Retailing's Great Global Gold Rush," *Chain Store Age Supplement*, December 1997, p. 4.

47. See Steve Weinstein, "How Retailers Set Goals and Reach Them," *Progressive Grocer*, April 1990, pp. 155–60; William Rothschild, *Putting It All Together: A Guide to Strategic Thinking* (New York: AMACON, 1976); Donald Lehman and Russell Winer, *Analysis for Marketing Planning*, 4th. ed. (Burr Ridge, IL: Irwin McGraw-Hill, 1998); and Myron Gable and Martin Topol, "Planning Practices of Small-Scale Retailers," *American Journal of Small Business*, Fall 1987, pp. 19–32.

48. Andrew Campbell, "Mission Statements," *Long Range Planning* 30 (December 1997), pp. 931–33.

49. Alfred Rappaport, *Creating Shareholder Value: The New Standard for Business Performance* (New York: Wiley, 1988).

50. See Linda Gatley and David Clutterbuck, "Superdrug Crafts a Mission Statement," *International Journal of Retail & Distribution Management* 26 (October–November 1998), pp. 10–11, for an interesting example of the process used by a UK drugstore chain to develop a mission statement.

51. Adam Finn, "Characterizing the Attractiveness of Retail Markets," *Journal of Retailing* 63 (Summer 1987), pp. 129–62.

52. Michael Porter, *Competitive Strategy* (New York: Free Press, 1980).

53. See "Reaching for Prestige," *Women's Wear Daily*, June 1, 1990, pp. 12–13.

54. James Lang, Roger Calantone, and Donald Gudmundson, "Small Firm Information Seeking as a Response to Environmental Threats and Opportunities," *Journal of Small Business Management*, January 1997, pp. 11–29; Masoud Yasai-Ardekani and Paul Nystrom, "Designs for Environmental Scanning Systems: Tests of a Contingency Theory," *Management Science* 42 (February 1996), pp. 187–204; and P. Rajan Varadarajan, Terry Clark, and William Pride, "Controlling the Uncontrollable: Managing Your Market Environment," *Sloan Management Review* 33 (Winter 1992), pp. 39–47.

55. "Mail-Order Shopping: Which Catalogs Are Best?" *Consumer Reports*, October 1994, pp. 622–23.

56. George Day and Robin Wensley, "Assessing Advantage: A Framework for Diagnosing Competitive Superiority," *Journal of Marketing* 52 (April 1988), pp. 1–20; C.K. Prahalad and Gary Hamel, "The Core Competencies of the Corporation," *Harvard Business Review* 68 (May–June 1970), pp. 79–97; G. Stalk, "Competing on Capabilities: The New Rules of Corporate Strategy," *Harvard Business Review*, March–April 1992, pp. 51–69; and Donna Cartwright, Paul Boughton, and Stephen Miller, "Competitive Intelligence Systems: Relationships to Strategic Orientation and Perceived Usefulness," *Journal of Managerial Issues* 7 (Winter 1995), pp. 420–34.

57. Robert Buzzed, Bradley Gale, and Ralph Sultan, "Market Share Key to Profitability," *Harvard Business Review* 55 (January–February 1975), pp. 97–106; and Robert Jacobson and David Aaker, "Is Market Share All That It's Cracked Up to Be?" *Journal of Marketing* 49 (Fall 1985), pp. 11–22.

58. Cindy Guier, "Cosmic Bowling Strikes at Whole New Audience," *Amusement Business*, May 18, 1998, pp. 20–24.

59. Henry Mintzberg, "Crafting Strategy," *Harvard Business Review* 65 (July–August 1987), pp. 66–79; Henry Mintzberg, "What Is Planning Anyway?" *Strategic Management Journal* 2 (1981), pp. 319–24; and James Brian Quinn, "Strategic Goals: Process and Politics," *Sloan Management Review*, Fall 1977, pp. 21–35.

60. See Kerin, Mahajan, and Varadarajan, *Contemporary Perspectives*, chapter 3. Another matrix that is often used in strategic planning is the Boston Consulting Group (BCG) market growth/market share matrix. Rather than considering all of the factors that determine market

attractiveness and competitive position, the BCG matrix focuses on jut two factors: market growth and market share. Research indicates that concentrating on these two factors may result in poor strategic decisions. See Robin Wensley, "Strategic Marketing: Betas, Boxes, and Basics," *Journal of Marketing* 45 (Summer 1981), pp. 173–82, for a critical analysis of these approaches.

61. "Global Retailing: Asian Assignment," *Chain Store Age Executive*, January 1995, section 2, p. 5.

Chapter 7

1. "Harper's Index," *Harpers*, February 1994, p. 13.

2. www.chainstorage.com, "Top 100 Companies," 1999.

3. Average retail inventory is estimated from the balance sheet inventory. Assume the end-of-year inventory on the balance sheet is average cost inventory. Average retail inventory = average cost inventory/1 – gross margin percent (expressed as decimal).

4. *Change Store Age Executive*, January 1996, section II, p. 23A.

5. Although the use of asset turnover presented here is helpful for gaining appreciation of the performance ratio, capital budgeting or present value analyses are more appropriate for determining long-term return of a fixed asset.

6. All categories of stock (including preferred, paid-in capital, and treasury stock) are included with common stock for simplicity.

7. B.S. Chakravarthy, "Measuring Strategic Performance," *Strategic Management Journal* 7 (1986), pp. 437–58; R.A. D'Aveni, "The Aftermath of Organizational Decline: A Longitudinal Study of the Strategic and Managerial Characteristics of Declining Firms," *Academy of Management Journal* 32, no. 3 (1989), pp. 577–605; D.C. Hambrick and R.A. D'Aveni, "Large Corporate Failures as Downward Spirals," *Administrative Science Quarterly* 33 (1988), pp. 1–23; R. Rust and D.C. Schmittlein, "A Bayesian Cross-Validated Likelihood Method for Comparing Alternative Specifications of Quantitative Models," *Marketing Science* 4, no. 1 (1985), pp. 20–28; and S. Sharma and V. Mahajan, "Early Warning Indicators of Business Failure," *Journal Marketing*, Fall 1980, pp. 80–89.

8. www.edgar-online.com.

9. Average retail inventory is estimated from the balance sheet inventory. Assume the end-of-year inventory on the balance sheet is average cost inventory. Average retail inventory = average cost inventory/1 – gross margin percent (expressed as a decimal).

10. *Activitiy Based Costing for Food Wholesalers and Retailers* (Ernst & Young LLP and the Joint Industry Project on Efficient Consumer Response, 1994), p. 53. See also Robin Cooper and Robert S. Kaplan, "Profit Priorities from Activity-Based Costing," *Harvard Business Review*, May–June 1991, pp. 130–35; Ted R. Compton, "Implementing Activity-Based Costing," *The CPA Journal*, March 1996, pp. 20–27; Robin Cooper and Robert S. Kaplan, "Activity-Based Systems: Measuring the Costs of Resource Usage," *Accounting Horizons*, September 1992, pp. 1–13; Charles D. Mecimore and Alice T. Bell, "Are We Ready for Fourth-Generation Activity-Based Costing?" *Management Accounting*, January 1995, pp. 22–26; Michael D. Woods, "Economic Choices with Activity Based Costing," *Management Accounting*, December 1992, pp. 53–57; Harper A. Roehm, Melissa A. Critchfield, and Joseph F. Castellano, "Yes, Activity Based Costing Works with Purchasing Too," *Journal of Accountancy*, November 1992, pp. 59–62; and Kenneth H. Manning, "Distribution Channel Profitability," *Management Accounting*, January 1995, pp. 44–48.

Chapter 8

1. Personal communication, John Konarski III, PhD, director of research, International Council of Shopping Centers, January 1999.

2. Sarah Raper, "Gap's Tour de Force," *WWD*, July 1, 1999, p. 3.

3. Debra Hazel, "Cityscape Retail: The Last Frontier?" *Chain Store Age Executive*, September 1994, pp. 21–28.

4. Sunil Taneja, "Inner-City Opportunity Knocks," *Chain Store Age*, October 1998, pp. 177–180, based on research by Initiative for a Competitive Inner City (ICIC), Boston, in conjunction with The Boston Consulting Group.

5. Cynthia Cohen, president of Strategic Mindshare, in a speech at the National Retail Federation's annual convention, New York City, January 20, 1999.

6. Ibid.

7. "Streets Paved with Gold," *Chain Store Age*, May 1998, p. 132. Research attributed to Equis.

8. Joanne Gordon, "Saks Appeal," *Chain Store Age*, May 1998, p. 85–90; and Tara Weingarten, "Main Street vs. the Mall: Part II, the Comeback," *Newsweek*, June 8, 1998, p. 12.

9. Stephanie Anderson Forest, "Look Who's Thinking Small," *Business Week*, May 17, 1999, pp. 66, 70.

10. This section draws from *The ICSC Research Quarterly*, no. 1 (1994).

11. The definitions and exhibit are meant to be guidelines for understanding major differences between the basic types of shopping centers. They are not meant to encompass the operating characteristics of every center.

12. John McCloud, "Power Center Development Explodes across U.S.," *Shopping Center World*, August 1994, pp. 34–41.

13. "Back to the Future," *The New York Times Magazine*, April 6, 1997, pp. 48–49.

14. "Malls Losing Popularity with Shoppers," *Marketing News*, May 26, 1997, p. 10.

15. "Back to the Future," *The New York Times Magazine*, April 6, 1997, pp. 48–49.

16. "Consolidate or Bust," *The Economist*, March 4, 1995, p. 11; Debra Hazel, "At Long Last, The Megamall," *Chain Store Age Executive*, September 1992, pp. 53–55; and Paul Doocey, "Mall of America Fallout," *Stores*, May 1993, pp. 44–47.

17. Kevin Kenyon, "Mall of America Turns Trash into Cash," *Shopping Centers Today*, October 1997, pp. 5–6.

18. "Back to the Future," *The New York Times Magazine*, April 6, 1997, pp. 48–49.

19. Bill Levine, "Survival of the Fittest," *Chain Store Age*, May 1998, pp. 92–96.

20. Christina Duff, "Brighter Lights, Fewer Bargains: Outlets Go Upscale," *The Wall Street Journal*, April 11, 1994, p. B1.

21. "Developers Bring Value Closer to Shoppers," *Chain Store Age*, September 1998, pp. 168–70.

22. Leslie Kaufman, "Outlets Slipping out of Fashion," *The New York Times*, January 17, 1999, p. C1.

23. Edmund Mander, "For Outlets, Europe a Boon and a Bear," *Shopping Centers Today*, March 1998, p. 32.

24. "Developers Bring Value Closer to Shoppers," *Chain Store Age*.

25. Bill Levine, "The Store Stands Alone," *Chain Store Age*, April 1998, pp. 107–8, research attributed to F.W. Dodge/The McGraw-Hill Cos., Lexington, Kentucky.

26. Russel Redman, "Drugstore Chains Alter Site Strategy," *Shopping Centers Today*, April 1995, pp. 12, 14.

27. Ibid.

28. Jennifer Steinhauser, "It's a Mall . . . , It's an Airport," *The New York Times*, June 10, 1998, pp. C1, C4.

29. Emily Nelson, "Wal-Mart Puts Coffee to Test in Indiana Stores," *The Wall Street Journal*, April 2, 1999, p. B1.

30. John McCloud, "The World Beckons American Retail," *Shopping Center World*, May 1998, pp. 23–34.

31. Corporate sources, The Ben Tobin Companies.

32. Lisa Holton, "Policies Protect Tenants, Developers from Unseen Environmental Risks," *Stores*, February 1996, p. 64.

Chapter 9

1. See Michael E. Porter, *The Competitive Advantage of Nations* (New York: Free Press, 1990).

2. Connie Gentry, "Revisit Your Site-Selection Processes," *Chain Store Age*, July 1998, pp. 137–39.

3. Robert W. Buckner, *Site Selection: New Advancements in Methods and Technology* (New York: Lebhar-Friedman Books, 1998), p. 18.

4. Sevgin Eroglu and Gilbert D. Harrell, "Retail Crowding: Theoretical and Strategic Implications," *Journal of Retailing* 62 (Winter 1996), pp. 346–63.

5. See Buckner, *Site, Location*, pp. 31–32, for more information about using these techniques.

6. R.L. Polk, and Co., 26955 Northwestern Highway, Southfield, MI 48034, 248-728-7000.

7. GIS vendors include
   Autodesk Inc. (www.autodesk.com.gis)
   Caliper Corp. (www.caliper.com)
   Cypress Geo-Resources Inc. (www.cyp.com)
   Decisionmark Corp. (www.decisionmark.com)
   ERDAS Inc. (www.erdas.com)
   ESRI Inc. (www.esri.com)
   Genasys (www.genasys.com)
   GeoResearch Inc. (www.georesearch.com)
   GeoSystems Global Corp. (www.mapquest.com)
   The IDRISI Project (www.idrisi.clarku.edu)
   Insurance Services Office Inc. (www.iso.com)
   Intergraph Corp. (www.intergraph.com)
   MAPCOM Systems Inc. (www.mapcom.com)
   MapInfo Corp. (www.mapinfo.com)
   MatchWare Technologies Inc. (www.matchware.com)
   Northwood Geoscience Ltd. (www.northwoodgeo.com)
   Object/FX Corp. (www.objectfx.com)
   Qualitative Marketing Software Inc. (www.qmsoft.com)
   SAS Institute Inc. (www.sas.com)
   Scan/US Inc. (www.scanus.com)
   Sites USA (www.sitesusa.com)
   Tactician Corp. (www.tactician.com)
   Tetrad Computer Applications (www.tetrad.com)
   Total Systems Inc. (www.totalsystemsinc.com)
   Visio Corp. (www.visio.com)

   Source: Gilbert H. Castle, "Internet Resources," *Business Geographics*, August 1998, pp. 29–30; also in Gilbert H. Castle, *GIS in Real Estate* (The Appraisal Institute, 1998).

8. National Decision Systems and Claritas are now "sister" companies. National Decision Systems specializes in retail location analysis. National Decision Systems, 1-800-866-6510, www.natdecsys.com.

   Claritas Inc., 53 Brown Road, Ithaca, NY 14850-1262, (607) 257-5757, fax: (607) 266-0425, www.claritas.com

9. ESRI (Environmental Systems Research Institute Inc), 380 New York St., Redlands, CA 92373-8100, Telephone (909) 793-2853, www.esri.com.

10. Buckner, *Site Location*, Chapter 15; and Christian Harder, *GIS Means Business* (Redlands, CA: Environmental Systems Research Institute, Inc., 1997).

11. Harder, *GSIS Means Business*, p. 1.

12. A list of regional planning commissions is available through the National Association of Regional Councils, 1700 K St. NW, Washington, DC 20006.

13. *Demographics USA 1998* is published by Market Statistics (800-685-7828 or 212-592-6246).

14. Buckner, *Site Location*.

15. G.L. Drummey, "Traditional Methods of Sales Forecasting," in R.L. Davies and D.S. Rogers, eds., *Store Location and Store Assessment Research* (New York: John Wiley & Sons, 1984), pp. 279–99.

16. We illustrated Mr. I's trade area in Exhibit 9–4 by defining the drive times to the store. To simplify this analysis, we've defined its primary trade area as the three-mile circle around the store rather than the drive time polygons described earlier.

17. Susan Mitchell, "Birds of a Feather," *American Demographics*, February 1995, pp. 40–48. PRIZM is available from Claritas, 201 North Union St., Alexandria, VA 22314, telephone 1-800-284-4868. Other major cluster systems are ACORN from CACI Marketing Systems, 1100 North Glebe Rd., Arlington, VA 22201, telephone 1-800-292-2224; ClusterPLUS 2000 from Strategic Mapping, Inc., 70 Seaview Ave., Stamford, CT 06192-0058, telephone (203) 353-7500; and MicroVision from Equifax National Decision Systems, 5375 Mira Sorrento Place, Suite 400, San Diego, CA 92121, telephone 1-800-866-6510.

18. See Buckner, *Site Location*, Chapter 8, for more information.

19. John S. Thompson, *Site Selection* (New York: Lebhar-Friedman, 1982), pp. 13–40.

20. David L. Huff, "Defining and Estimating a Trade Area," *Journal of Marketing* 28 (1964), pp. 34–38; D.S. Rogers, "Modern Methods of Sales Forecasting," in *Store Location*, ed. Davies and Rogers, pp. 319–31; C. Samuel Craig, Avijit Ghosh, and Sara McLafferty, "Models of the Retail Location Process: A Review," *Journal of Retailing* 60, no. 1 (Spring 1981), p. 536; M. Nakanishi and L.G. Cooper, "Parameter Estimate for Multiplicative Interaction Choice Model: Least Squares Approach," *Journal of Marketing Research* 11 (1974), pp. 303–11; A.K. Jain and V. Mahajan, "Evaluating the Competitive Environment in Retailing Using Multiplicative Competitive Interactive Models, in *Research in Marketing*, ed. J. Sheth (Greenwich, CT: JAI) 1 (1979), pp. 217–35.

21. W.J. Reilly, *The Laws of Retail Gravitation* (New York: Knickerbocker Press, 1931).

22. P.D. Converse, "New Laws of Retail Gravitation," *Journal of Marketing* 14 (1949), pp. 379–84.

23. Walter Christaller, *Central Places in Southern Germany*, 1935, trans. Carlisle W. Baskin (Englewood Cliffs, NJ: Prentice-Hall, 1966).

24. For specifics, see Buckner, *Site Location*, Chapter 15.

Chapter 10

1. Michael Losey, "Mastering the Competencies of HR Management," *Human Resource Management* 38 (Summer 1999), pp. 99–103; and Terri Kabachink, "The Strategic Role of Human Resources," *Anderson Retailing Newsletter*, Texas A&M University, January 1999.

2. *Merchandising and Operations Costs Report* (New York: Fairchild Publications, 1999).

3. Michael Bergdal, "Our 'People' Culture is a Major Competitive Asset," *Stores*, April 1999, pp. 114–15; Raphael Amit, "Human Resources Management Processes: A Value-Creating Source of Competitive Advantage," *European Management Journal*, April 1999, pp. 174–82; Tim Ambler, "Valuing Human Assets," *Business Strategy Review* 10 (Spring 1999), pp. 57–58; Tony Grundy, "How Are Corporate Strategy and Human Resources Strategy Linked?" *Journal of General Management* 23 (Spring 1998), pp. 49–73; and Gerard Farias, "High Performance Work Systems: What We Know and What We Need to Know," *Human Resource Planning* 21 (June 1998), pp. 50–55.

4. Jeffrey Pfeffer, *The Human Equation* (Boston: Harvard Business School Press, 1998), pp. 26–28.

5. John Burdett and Lawson Mardon, "A Template for Organization Design," *Busines Quarterly*, Summer 1992, p. 40.

6. *Census of Retail Trade* (U.S. Department of Commerce, Bureau of the Census, 1999), p. 15.

7. "Business Antiquities," *The Wall Street Journal*, November 17, 1999, p. B1.

8. *1999 Corporate Fact Book* (Cincinnati, OH: Federated Department Stores, 1999).

9. Paul M. Mazur, *Principles of Organization Applied to Modern Retailing* (New York: Harper & Brothers, 1927).

10. *1999 Corporate Fact Book* (Cincinnati, OH: Federated Department Stores, 1999).

11. Walter Loeb, "Unbundling or Centralize: What Is the Answer?" *Retailing Issues Letter* (College Station: Center for Retailing Studies, Texas A&M University, May 1992).

12. Susan Reda, "American Drug Stores Custom Fits Each Market," *Stores*, September 1994, pp. 22–24.

13. Bill Saporito, "A Week aboard the Wal-Mart Express," *Fortune*, August 24, 1992, pp. 77–84.

14. "Penney's at the Crossroads: A Retailer Reorients Its Course," *DNR*, May 5, 1999, p. 2; Seanna Browder, "Great Service Was Not Enough," *Business Week*, April 19, 1999, p. 126; and "Branching Out," *Chain Store Age Executive*, May 1999, p. 51.

15. Marc Singer, "Unbundling the Corporation," *Harvard Business Review*, March–April 1999, pp. 133–40; "The Advantages of Outsourcing," *Chain Store Age*, July 1999, p. 106; and Isabelle Sender, "Outsourcing Requires Long-Term Vision," *Chain Store Age*, September 1998, pp. 116–17.

16. "Outsourcing," *Chain Store Age*, September 1996, pp. 22B–24B; and Susan Reda, "Bringing a Sense of Passion to Vital Housekeeping Needs," *Stores*, August 1996, pp. 79–80.

17. Denise Power, "Penney's Human Resources Goes Self-Service," *WWD*, June 23, 1999, p. 13.

18. *Retailing: Mirror on America* (Washington, DC: National Retailer Federation, 1999).

19. JoAnn Greco, "America's Changing Workforce," *Journal of Business Strategy* 19 (March–April 1998), pp. 43–47.

20. Manfred Krafft, "An Empirical Investigation of the Antecedents of Sales Force Control Systems," *Journal of*

Marketing 63 (Summer 1999), pp. 120–34; Bernard Jaworski, "Toward a Theory of Marketing Control: Environmental Context, Control Types, and Consequences," *Journal of Marketing* 52 (July 1988), pp. 23–39; and William Ouchi, "A Conceptual Framework for the Design of Organizational Control Mechanisms," *Management Science* 25 (September 1979), pp. 833–49.

21. Louise Longman, "Pick of the Perks," *Supermarketing*, July 30, 1999, pp. 20–21; and Jules Abend, "A Bonus Does Pay Off," *Stores*, July 1987, pp. 69–73.

22. Patrica Sellers, "Can Home Depot Fix Its Sagging Stock?" *Fortune*, March 4, 1996, pp. 139–45; and Bob Ortega, "What Does Wal-Mart Do If Stock Drop Cuts into Workers' Morale?" *The Wall Street Journal*, January 4, 1995, pp. A1, A5.

23. Jeffrey Pfeffer, "Six Dangerous Myths about Pay," *Harvard Business Review*, May–June 1998, pp. 109–29.

24. William Bliss, "Why Is Corporate Culture Important?" *Workforce* 78 (February 1999), pp. W8–10; W. Matthew Juechter, "Five Conditions for High-Performance Cultures," *Training & Development* 52 (May 1998), pp. 63–68; and Andrew Chan, "Corporate Culture of a Clan Organization," *Management Decision*, January–February 1997, pp. 94–100.

25. David Boje, "Stories of the Story Telling Organization: A Post Modern Analysis of Disney as 'Tamara-Land'," *Academy of Management Journal*, August 1995, pp. 997–1015; and Charles O'Reilly, "Corporations, Culture, and Commitment: Motivation and Social Control in Organizations," *California Management Review* 31 (Summer 1989), pp. 9–25.

26. Daniel Roth, "My Job at The Container Store," *Fortune*, January 10, 2000, p. 76.

27. See Beverly Kaye, "True Tales and Tall Tales: The Power of Organizational Storytelling," *Training & Development* 53 (March 1999), pp. 44–51; and Nancy Breuer, "The Power of Storytelling," *Workforce* 77 (December 1998), pp. 36–42.

28. Hal Lancaster, "Herb Kelleher Has One Strategy: Treat Employees Well," *The Wall Street Journal*, August 31, 1999, p. B1; John Huey, "The Jack and Herb Show," *Fortune*, January 11, 1999, pp. 163–64; Ronald Lieber, "Why Employees Love These Companies," *Fortune*, January 12, 1998, pp. 72–75; and Dan Reed, "Flying Like a Madman," *Sales & Marketing Management*, October 1996, pp. 92–97.

29. This section is based on Chapter 3 in Jeffrey Pfeffer, *The Human Equation* (Boston: Harvard Business School Press, 1998).

30. "Workers Are Seeking Employers of Choice," *Chain Store Age*, October 1998, p. 72.

31. Frank Hammel, "Tackling Turnover" *Supermaket Business*, October 1995, pp. 103–8.

32. Gary Desller, "How to Earn Your Employees' Commitment," *Academy of Management Executive* 13 (May 1999), pp. 58–59; Deb McCusker, "Loyalty in the Eyes of Employers and Employees," *Workforce*, November 1998, pp. 23–28; David L. Stum, "Five Ingredients for an Employee Retention Formula," *HR Focus*, September 1998, pp. S9–11; and Kal Lifson, "Turn Down Turnover to Turn Up Profits," *Stores*, November 1, 1996, pp. 65–66.

33. M. Youndt, S. Snell, J. Dean, and D. Lepak, "Human Resource Management, Manufacturing Strategy, and Firm Performance," *Academy of Management Journal* 39 (1996), pp. 836–66; and M. Huselid, "The Impact of Human Resource Management Practices on Turnover, Productivity, and Corporate Financial Performance," *Academy of Management Journal* 38 (1995), pp. 635–72.

34. Ling Sing Chee, "Singapore Airlines: Strategic Human Resource Initiatives," in *International Human Resource Management: Think Globally and Act Locally*, ed. Derek Torrington (New York: Prentice Hall, 1994).

35. "State of the Industry Operational Management," *Chain Store Age*, August 1, 1998, p. 17A.

36. Michael Hartnett, "Men's Wearhouse Tailors Employee Support Programs," *Stores*, August 1996, pp. 46–49.

37. Catherine Yang, "Low Wage Lessons," *Business Week*, November 11, 1996, pp. 108–16.

38. Martin Beirne, "Managing to Empower? A Healthy Review of Resources and Constraints," *European Management Journal*, April 1999, pp. 218–26; and Mohammed Rafiq, "A Customer-Oriented Framework for Empowering Service Employees," *Journal of Services Marketing* 12 (May–June 1998), pp. 379–97.

39. Shankar Ganesan and Barton Weitz, "The Impact of Staffing Policies on Retail Buyer Job Attitudes and Behaviors," *Journal of Retailing*, Spring 1996, pp. 231–45.

40. Leslie Faught, "At Eddie Bauer You Can Work and Have a Life," *Workforce*, April 1997, pp. 83–88; Davan Maharaj, "A Suitable Schedule: Flextime Gains as Employers Agree There's More to Life than Work," *Los Angeles Times*, July 10, 1998, p. D2; and Maureen Conroy, "Flextime Revisited: The Need for a Resurgence of Flextime," *Journal of Compensation and Benefits*, November–December 1997, pp. 36–40.

41. Kerry Dolan, "When Money Isn't Enough," *Forbes*, November 18, 1996, pp. 164–70; and Keith Hammonds, "Balancing Work and Family," *Business Week*, September 16, 1996, pp. 74–79.

42. R. Roosevelt Thomas, "From Affirmative Action to Diversity," *Harvard Business Review*, March–April 1990, pp. 107–17; and "Race in the Workplace: Is Affirmative Action Working?" *Business Week*, July 8, 1991, pp. 50–61.

43. T. Cox and S. Blake, "Managing Cultural Diversity: Implications for Organizational Competitiveness," *Academy of Management Executive* 5 (August 1991), pp. 45–56.

44. "Diversity Programs Become Valuable Tools for Increased Profitability," *Black Enterprise*, July 1998, pp. 120–21.

45. Parshotam Dass, "Strategies for Managing Human Resource Diversity: From Resistance to Learning," *Academy of Management Executive* 13 (May 1999), pp. 68–69; Philip Rosenzweig, "Strategies for Managing Diversity," *The Financial Times*, March 6, 1998, pp. FTS2–3; Marianne Wilson, "JCPenney Embraces Diversity," *Chain Store Age Executive*, June 1995, pp. 19–25; and Steve Weinstein, "Managing Diversity," *Progressive Grocer*, April 1996, pp. 28–30.

46. Max Messmer, "Mentoring: Building Your Company's Intellectual Capital," *HR Focus*, September 1998, pp. S11–13; and Erik Van Slyke, "Mentoring: A Results-Oriented Approach," *HR Focus*, February 1998, pp. 14–15.

47. "80 Most Influential People in Sales and Marketing," *Sales & Marketing Management*, October 1998, p. 78.

48. Sheila Wellington, "Cracking the Ceiling," *Time*, December 7, 1998, p. 187; Alison Maitland, "Cracks Appear in Glass Ceiling," *The Financial Times*, April 8, 1999, p. 22; and Tammy Reiss, "More Cracks in the Glass Ceiling," *Business Week*, August 10, 1998, p. 6.

Chapter 11

1. The Global Supply Chain Forum, Douglas M. Lambert, director, The Ohio State University and University of North Florida.

2. Alan R. Simon, *Data Warehousing for Dummies*, (Foster City, CA: IDG Books Worldwide, 1997), p. 12.

3. There are four main processes used to extract information from the data warehouse: basic querying and reporting (reporting what is happening), OLAP (online analytical processing—reporting what happened and why, including some data manipulation), data mining (reporting what may be happening or something interesting), and EIS (executive information systems—reporting lots of things to people who are too busy to look for them). Each of these processes requires successively more sophisticated analyses and techniques. For instance, only the most sophisticated retailers are able to use the artificial intelligence and neural network techniques inherent in data mining. For more information on each of these processes, see ibid.

4. Emily Nelson, "Why Wal-Mart Sings, 'Yes, We Have Bananas!'" *The Wall Street Journal*, October 6, 1998, pp. B1, B4.

5. "Williams-Sonoma Refines Mailings with Data Management," *Business Geographics*, May 1997, p. 28.

6. Laurie Freeman, "Marketing the Market: Savvy Grocers Reach Out to Their Super Customers," *Marketing News*, March 2, 1998, p. 1.

7. Frederick F. Reichheld, "Learning from Customer Defections," *Harvard Business Review*, March–April 1996, pp. 56–61.

8. Thomas J. Peters, *Thriving on Chaos: Handbook for a Management Revolution* (New York: HarperCollins Publishers, 1987).

9. Thomas J. Peters, "Quality Equals Respect," *The Journal for Quality and Participation* 11 (March 1988), pp. 44–48.

10. Frederick F. Reichheld and W. Earl Sasser, Jr., "Zero Defections: Quality Comes to Services," *Harvard Business Review*, September–October 1990, pp. 301–11, and Frederick F. Reichheld, "Loyalty and the Renaissance of Marketing," *Marketing Management*, 1994, pp. 10–16.

11. James L. Heskett, W. Earl Sasser, Jr., and Leonard A. Schlesinger, *The Services Profit Chain: How Leading Companies Link Profit and Growth to Loyalty, Satisfaction, and Value* (New York: The Free Press, 1997).

12. Susan Albert, "Customer Loyalty Programs, Rewards for Customers and Retailers," *Business Geographics*, October 1997, pp. 20–24.

13. "Growing Lifetime Value," *Chain Store Age*, May 1999, p. 143.

14. Patricia A. Murphy, "Effective Loyalty Programs Seen Catering to Individual Needs," *Stores*, February 1999, pp. 46–48.

15. Matt Nannery, "ASNs Prove a Hot Topic at the UCCs' EDI User's Group," *Chain Store Age*, December 1997, pp. 143–44.

16. Marc Andreessen, Netscape creator, October 1996. Extranet security and privacy could be obtained either by ensuring that transmission lines were privately owned or leased, by tunneling through the Internet, or by using the Internet with special forms of security protection and password authorization.

17. Ginger Koloszyc, "Supplier/Buyer Extranet Simplifies Global Sourcing Process," *Stores*, January 1999, pp. 28–30.

18. Liz Parks, "Transforming the Supply Chain with Technology," *Drug Store News*, July 19, 1999, p. 10.

19. Bob Tedeschi, "The Net's Real Business Happens .com to .com," *The New York Times*, April 19, 1999, pp. C1, C6.

20. "Internet Revolutionizes EDI," *Impact*, May 1999, pp. 3–6.

21. Susan Reda, "Internet–EDI Initiatives Show Potential to Reinvent Supply Chain Management," *Stores*, January 1999, pp. 26–27.

22. Liz Parks, "Transforming the Supply Chain with Technology," *Drug Store News*, July 19, 1999, p. 10; and James A Cooke, "VMI: Very Mixed Impact?" *Logistics Management & Distribution Report*, December 31, 1998, p. 51.

23. Charles Batchelor, "Moving up the Corporate Agenda," *Financial Times*, December 1, 1998, p. 1, data from Michigan State University/Geologistics.

24. Martha C. Cooper, Douglas M. Lambert, and Janus D. Pagh, "Supply Chain Management: More than a New Name for Logistics," *The International Journal of Logistics Management* 8, no. 1 (1997), pp. 1–14.

25. Susan Reda, "Crossdocking: Can Supermarkets Catch Up?" *Stores*, February 1998, pp. 20–24.

26. "Flow-Through DC Yields Savings for Fred Meyer," *Chain Store Age*, October 1995, pp. 64–66; quote by Mary Sammons, senior vice president, Fred Meyer.

27. Kurt Salmon Associates, Inc., *Efficient Consumer Response: Enhancing Consumer Value in the Grocery Industry* (Washington, DC: Food Marketing Institute, January 1993).

28. Julie Ritzer Rose, "New Study Finds Major Gains from Quick Response," *Stores*, March 1997, p. 46.

29. Georgia Lee, "Wal-Mart's Tool: Data for Vendors," *Women's Wear Daily*, December 5, 1995, p. 10.

30. Paul F. Christ and Jack Gault, "The Benefits, Costs and Strategic Implications of Quick Response Systems," *1995 AMA Summer Educators' Conference Proceedings* (Chicago: American Marketing Association), pp. 485–91.

31. Laurie Joan Aron, "Deliverying on E-Commerce," *Chain Store Age*, June 1999, pp. 130–31.

32. Ibid.

33. Kim Ann Zimmermann, "Saks Fifth Avenue's Scorecard on Vendors," *Women's Wear Daily*, November 12, 1997, p. 14.

34. "Sea–Air: Cheap and Fast," *Global Trade*, February 1992, pp. 16–18, taken from Michael R. Czinkota and Ilkka A. Ronkainen, *Global Marketing* (Orlando, FL: Harcourt Brace, 1996), p. 486.

35. Douglas M. Lambert, James R. Stock, and Lisa M. Ellram, *Fundamentals of Logistics Management* (Burr Ridge, IL: Irwin/McGraw-Hill, 1998), p. 230.

Chapter 12

1. "The Categorical Imperative: Learning from Consumer Behavior," *Transformations*, Spring 1999.

2. Faye Brookman, "Category Management: A New Way of Life," *Women's Wear Daily*, June 1995, pp. 36–37. The concept of category management began in the grocery business, but has spread rapidly to general merchandise, home furnishings, books, and recordings. In fact, the Food Marketing Institute (FMI), the primary trade organization in the grocery industry, has published a book on the subject. (Robert C. Blattberg and Edward J. Fox, *Category Management* [Washington, DC: Food Marketing Institute and the Center for Retail Management, Northwestern University, 1995]). Also, The National Association of Convenience Stores has published the *NACS Category Management Handbook*, which is available through it at (703) 684-3600.

3. Brookman, "Category Management."

4. Arthur Friedman, "KSA's Guide to Managing a Category," *Women's Wear Daily*, March 6, 1996, p. 12.

5. www.cstorecentral.com, Category Management Executive Summary, March 1998.

6 Daniel J. Sweeney, "Improving the Profitability of Retail Merchandising Decisions," *Journal of Marketing*, January 1973, pp. 60–68.

7. The rationale behind this equation is as follows: The sales-to-stock ratio is expressed with the numerator at retail and the denominator at cost. To get inventory turnover, both numerator and denominator must be at either retail or cost. 100% – gross margin % is the percentage of net sales represented by the cost of goods sold (also known as the cost complement). By multiplying the sales-to-stock ratio by the cost complement we, in essence, convert the numerator (sales) to the cost of goods sold and therefore have numerator and denominator both expressed at cost.

8. To illustrate, suppose net sales = $50,000 and average inventory at retail = $10,000; inventory turnover = $50,000 ÷ $10,000 = 5. To convert inventory turnover expressed at retail to turnover at cost, we multiply by the cost complement, which is the percentage of net sales represented by the cost of goods sold. If the gross margin is 40 percent, the cost complement is 60 percent (100% – 40%). By multiplying the numerator and denominator by 60 percent, the result is cost of goods sold ÷ the average inventory at cost.

Thus, inventory turnover is 5 whether it is calculated using retail or cost figures.

9. This section is adapted from William R. Davidson, Daniel J. Sweeney, and Ronald W. Stampfl, *Retailing Management*, 5th ed. (New York: John Wiley & Sons, 1984).

10. Rajiv Chandrasekaran, "Revolution Is at Hand for Use of the Handheld Computer," *Star–Tribune Newspaper of the Twin Cities*, June 13, 1999, p. 7D.

11. Prices based on Boston to New York.

12. Teri Agins and Kathryn Kranhold, "Coat Peddlers Are Using Forecasters to Beat the Heat," *The Wall Street Journal*, February 18, 1999, pp. B1, B13.

13. *Demographics USA 1998* is published by Market Statistics (telephone 1-800-685-7828 or 212-592-6246).

14. PRIZM is available from Claritas, 201 North Union St., Alexandria, VA 22314, telephone 1-800-284-4868.

15. David Steward and Prem Shamdasani, *Focus Groups: Theory and Practice* (Newbury Park, CA: Sage, 1990); Gloria E. Bader and Catherin A. Rossi, *Focus Groups: A Step-By-Step Guide* (The Bader Group, 1998); and Holly Edmonds, *The Focus Group Research Handbook* (NTC Business Books, 1999).

16. Rusty Williamson, "Penney's Labels, Online Getting Push this Year," *WWD*, March 12, 1999.

17. David Moin, "Macy's Web Site Gets a Major Apparel Upload," *WWD*, November 19, 1998.

18. Mark Kingdom, "Consumer Enhancement & Development," *Chain Store Age*, January 1996, section 3, p. 5.

19. Cristina Lourosa-Ricardo, "E-Commerce (A Special Report): The Basics—Picking the Product," *The Wall Street Journal*, November 22, 1999, p. R8.

Chapter 13

1. "Robbery, Employee Theft, Leading Causes of Supermarket Losses," *Chain Store Age*, August 1998, p. 84, based on the Food Marketing Institute's annual security survey.

2. The department store chain wishes to remain anonymous. The allocation of inventory to stores is based on each store's standard deviation of sales. Larger stores will have a proportionally smaller standard deviation, causing the backup stock to be proportionally smaller.

3. Sharon Edelson, "Micromerchandising: When Retailers Grow by Thinking Small," *Women's Wear Daily*, May 1, 1997, pp. 1, 12.

4. See James R. Stock and Douglas M. Lambert, *Strategic Logistics Management*, 3d ed. (Burr Ridge, IL: Richard D. Irwin, 1993), pp. 419–21; and Lynn E. Gill, "Inventory and Physical Distribution Management," in *The Distribution Handbook*, ed. James F. Robeson and Robert G. House (New York: Free Press, 1988), pp. 664–67.

5. For a review of multiattribute decision models, see Kenneth R. MacCrimmon, "An Overview of Multiple Objective Decision Making," in *Multiple Criteria Decision Making*, ed. J.L. Cochrane and M. Zeleny (Columbia: University of South Carolina Press, 1973), pp. 18–44. For other attitudinal approaches to vendor evaluation, see John S. Berens, "A Decision Matrix Approach to Supplier Selection," *Journal of Retailing* 47, no. 4 (1971–72), pp. 47–53; Elizabeth C. Hirschman, "An Exploratory Comparison of Decision Criteria Used by Retail Buyers," in *Retailing Patronage Theory*, ed. Robert F. Lusch and William R. Darden (Norman: Center for Economic and Management Research, University of Oklahoma, 1981), p. 15; Elizabeth C. Hirschman and David Mazursky, "A Trans-Organizational Investigation of Retail Buyers' Criteria and Information Sources," New York University Institute of Retail Management working paper 1982, pp. 82–88; Rom J. Markin, *Retail Management: A Systems Approach* (New York: Macmillan, 1971); William F. Massey and Jim D. Savvas, "Logical Flow Models for Marketing Analysis," *Journal of Marketing* 28 (January 1964), pp. 30–37; and Janet Wagner, Richard Ettenson, and Jean Parrish, "Vendor Selection among Retail Buyers: An Analysis by Merchandise Division," *Journal of Retailing* 65, no. 1 (Spring 1989), pp. 58–79.

6. These issues were taken from Wagner, Ettenson, and Parrish, "Vendor Selection."

7. For a thorough treatment of the retail inventory method, see James T. Powers, *The Retail Inventory Method Made Practical* (New York: National Retail Merchants Association, 1971).

8. Robert F. Lusch and Patrick Dunne, *Retail Management* (Cincinnati: South-Western, 1990), p. 356.

Chapter 14

1. Jane Bainbridge, "The World's Biggest Brands: Consistent Brand Building Is the Key to This Year's Success Stores as Brand Consultancy Interbrand Reveals," *Marketing*, June 24, 1999, p. 22.

2. "Fear of Uncharted Waters Still Rules Many Licensors' Attitudes toward E-commerce," *Licensing Letter*, June 7, 1999.

3. www.federated-fds.com/home.asp.

4. Michael Harvey and Jack J. Kasulis, "Retailer Brands—The Business Distinction," *Arthur Andersen Retailing Issues Letter* 10, no. 1 (January 1998), pp. 1–4.

5. Ibid.

6. *Starbucks 1998 Annual Report.*

7. Michael P., Niemira "The Ever-Growing Appetite for Imported Apparel," *Chain Store Age*, February 1999, p. 24.

8. Sherrie E. Zhan, "Made in the USA," *World Trade*, April 1, 1999, pp. 32–46.

9. "Change at the Checkout," *The Economist*, March 4, 1995.

10. Export tariffs are used in some less developed countries to generate additional revenue. For instance, the Argentine government may impose an export tariff on wool that is exported. An export tariff actually lowers the competitive ability of domestic manufactures, rather than protecting them, as is the case with import tariffs.

11. "The Likely Impact on the United States of a Free Trade Agreement with Mexico" (Washington, DC: U.S. International Trade Commission, 1991).

12. The opportunity cost of capital should be no lower than the rate at which a firm borrows funds, since one alternative is to pay back borrowed money. But it can be higher, depending on the range of other opportunities available. Typically, this rate rises with the investment's risk. So, if average inventory is $100,000 and the cost of borrowing money is 10 percent per year, the inventory carrying cost is $10,000.

13. Stanley E. Fawcett and Laura M. Birou, "Exploring the Logistics between Global and JIT Sourcing," *International Journal of Physical Distribution & Logistics Management* 22, no. 1 (1992), pp. 3–14.

14. Marianne Wilson, "Coldwater Creek Is Still at the Top," *Chain Store Age*, November 1998, pp. 74–75.

15. "Asia's Fertile Fields." Women's Wear Daily, May 1, 1996, pp. 8–9.

16. Steven Greenhouse, "18 Major Retailers and Apparel Makers Are Accused of Using Sweatshops," *The New York Times*, January 14, 1999, pp. A9.

17. Rocio Maria Winger and Eva Martinez-Fornos, "Exports 1998: Analysis of a Regional Success," *Apparel Industry Magazine*, September 1, 1999, p. SS2.

18. "The Fashion Center," *Women's Wear Daily*, Advertising Supplement, September 1995, p. 4.

19. Isadore Barmash, "Buying Offices: Once a Staple, Now Few Exist," *Retailing Today*, May 1997, pp. 76, 86.

20. Sandy Jap and Barton Weitz, "A Taxonomy of Long-Term Relationships," working paper, College of Business Administration, University of Florida, Gainesville, 1994; and F. Robert Dwyer, Paul Shurr, and Sejo Oh, "Developing Buyer–Seller Relationships," *Journal of Marketing* 51 (April 1987), pp. 11–27.

21. Robert Krapel, Deborah Salmond, and Robert Spekman, "A Strategic Approach to Managing Buyer–Seller Relationships," *European Journal of Marketing* 25 (1991), pp. 22–37; B.G. Yovovich, "Dos and Don'ts of Partnering," *Business Marketing*, March 1992, pp. 38–39; and "Smart Selling: How Companies Are Winning Over Today's Tough Customers," *Business Week*, August 3, 1992, pp. 46–52.

22. Jim Yardley, "Vendorville," *The New York Times Magazine*, March 8, 1998, p. 62.

23. "Pritchett on Quick Response," *Discount Merchandiser*, April 1992, p. 64.

24. John Swan and Johannah Nolan, "Gaining Customer Trust: A Conceptual Guide for the Salesperson," *Journal of Personal Selling and Sales Management*, November 1985, pp. 39–48; and John Swan, I. Fred Trawick, David Rink, and Jenney Roberts, "Measuring Dimensions of Purchaser Trust of Industrial Salespeople," *Journal of Personal Selling and Sales Management*, May 1988, pp. 1–9.

25. Erin Anderson and Barton Weitz, "The Use of Pledges to Build and Sustain Commitment in Distribution Channels," *Journal of Marketing Research* 29 (February 1992), pp. 18–34.

26. Ibid.

27. Kris Frieswick, "Changing Channels (Adopting a Direct-Sales Model)," *CFO, The Magazine for Senior Financial Executives*, February 1, 1999.

28. "Home Depot Tells Vendors to Stay off the 'Net," *Industrial Distribution*, September 1, 1999, p. 21.

29. Ibid, p. 47.

30. David Merrefield, "CONSUMER DIRECT. (Internet Is Increasingly Used to Market Consumer Products)," *Supermarket News*, February 1, 1999.

31. Aram Rubinson and Brett Levy, *E-Commerce Navigator: An Anthology of Web Thoughts* (PaineWebber, October 1999, p. 39).

32. Similar types of fees charged to vendors are display fees (paid for special merchandising and display of products) and pay-to-stay fees (paid to continue stocking and displaying a product).

33. Paul N. Bloom, Joseph P. Cannon, and Gregory T. Gundlach, "Slotting Allowances and Fees: Schools of Thought and the Views of Practicing Managers," *Journal of Marketing*, forthcoming; Russell Redman, "FTC Hearing Newsprogram Focus on Slotting Allowance," *Supermarket News* 45, no. 27 (1995), p. 4; and Leslie Hansen Harps and Warren Thayer, "FTC Is Investigating 'Exclusive Dealing'," *Frozen Food Age* 45, no. 10 (1997), pp. 8, 78.

34. Deloitte & Touche, *Managing the Process of Introducing and Deleting Products in the Grocery and Drug Industry* (Washington, DC: Grocery Manufacturers of America, 1990).

35. Allison Lucas, "Shelf Wars," *Sales & Marketing Management* 148, no. 3 (1996), p. 121.

36. Jeffrey A. Trachtenberg, "Record Stores Lease Out Windows, Walls, Whatever," *The Wall Street Journal*, April 19, 1995, p. B1.

37. Michael Hartnett, "Shelf-Space Wars Increase Use of Buy-Back Liquidation Strategies," *Stores*, August 1999, pp. 54, 56.

38. Yumiko Ono, "Inventory Switch—Where Are the Gloves? They Were Stocklifted by a Rival Producer," *The Wall Street Journal*, May 15, 1998, p. A1.

39. Ibid.

40. Thomas J. Ryan, "Errors Invite Charges," *WWD*, June 1, 1998, p. 17.

41. Thomas J. Ryan, "Financial Forum: Chargeback Debate Roars On as Practice Remains Fact of Life," *WWD*, June 1, 1998, pp. 14, 16.

42. Read Hayes, "Retailers Toughen Ethics Codes to Curb Employee Abuses," *Stores*, July 1996, pp. 83–84.

43. Edward J. Conry, Gerald R. Ferrera, and Karla H. Fox, *The Legal Environment of Business* (Boston: Allyn & Bacon, 1993), pp. 185–91.

44. "Software Piracy Continues to Plague Industry," *Business Software Alliance*, April 27, 1994.

45. This section draws from Michael R. Czinkota and Ilkka A. Ronkainen, *International Marketing* (Dryden Press, 1998).

46. Michael Kessler, "Counterfeiting Hurts Reputations," *Discount Store News*, July 17, 1998, p. 13.

47. "Intellectual Property . . . Is Theft," *The Economist*, January 22, 1993, pp. 72–73.

48. "Gray Goods Cleared by Court," *Chain Store Age*, April 1988, p. 34.

49. Ibid.

50. Suein L. Hwant, "Tobacco: As Cigarette Prices Soar, a Gray Market Booms," *The Wall Street Journal*, January 28, 1999, p. B1.

51. Melonee McKinney, "Nike Deal with Fogdog Sign of Things to Come, Internet Retailers May Have to Share Equity to Secure Leading Brands," *Daily News Record*, September 29, 1999, p. 13.

52. "Hartz Mountain Gets Knocked," *Sales & Marketing Management*, April 1987, p. 4.

53. David K. Lam, "Revisiting the Separate Products Issue," *Yale Law Journal*, April 1, 1999, p. 1441.

54. This section was developed with the assistance of Howard Kreitzman.

55. Hal Lancaster, "You Have to Negotiate for Everything in Life, so Get Good at It," *The Wall Street Journal*, January 27, 1998, p. B1.

56. These quidelines are based on Roger Fisher and William Ury, *Getting to Yes* (New York: Penguin, 1981).

57. Itzhak Sharav, "Cost Justification under the Robinson-Patman Act," *Management Accounting*, July 1978, pp. 15–22.

58. For different perspectives on determining a quantity discount pricing policy, see Abel P. Jeuland and Steven M. Shugan, "Managing Channel Profits," *Marketing Science* 2 (Summer 1983), pp. 239–72; Rajiv Lal and Richard Staelin, "An Approach for Developing an Optimal Discount Pricing Policy," *Management Science* 30 (December 1984), pp. 1524–39; Michael Levy, William Cron, and Robert Novack, "A Decision Support System for Determining a Quantity Discount Pricing Policy," *Journal of Business Logistics* 6, no. 2 (1985), pp. 110–41; James Monahan, "A Quantity Discount Pricing Model to Increase Vendor Profits," *Management Science* 30 (June 1984), pp. 720–27; Kent B. Monroe and Albert J. Della Bitta, "Models for Pricing Decisions," *Journal of Marketing Research* 15 (August 1990), pp. 413–28; James B. Wilcox, Roy D. Howell, Paul Kuzdrall, and Robert Britney, "Price Quantity Discounts: Some Implications for Buyers and Sellers," *Journal of Marketing* 51, no. 3 (July 1987), pp. 60–71; and Pinhas Zusman and Michael Etgar, "The Marketing Channel as an Equilibrium Set of Contracts," *Management Science* 27 (March 1981), pp. 284–302.

59. Michael Levy and Michael van Breda, "A Fininical Perspective on the Shift of Marketing Functions," *Journal of Retailing* 60, no. 4 (Winter 1984), pp. 23–42.

60. Ibid.

Chapter 15

1. Alan Sawyer and Peter Dickson, "Everyday Low Prices vs. Sale Price," *Retailing Review* 1, no. 2 (1993), pp. 1–2, 8; and Gwen Ortmeyer, John A. Quelch, and Walter Salmon, "Restoring Credibility to Retail Pricing," *Sloan Management Review* 33, no. 1 (Fall 1991), pp. 55–56.

2. Anne Fisher, "Best Practices the Latest Weapon in the Price Wars," *Fortune*, July 7, 1997, p. 200.

3. Andrew Shore, Gary Giblen, and Margaret Lenahan, "Household Products and Cosmetics: Everyday Low (or 'Value') Pricing: An Idea Whose Time Has Come," *PaineWebber*, October 13, 1992.

4. Laura Bird, "Apparel Stores Seek to Cure Shoppers Addicted to Discounts," *The Wall Street Journal*, May 29, 1996, pp. A1, A10.

5. Kipp Cheng, "Ebay Best Viral Marketing," *Brandweek*, June 28, 1999 p. IQ/42.

6. Ibid.

7. Jennifer Tanaka. "The Never-Ending Search for the Lowest Price," *Newsweek*, June 7, 1999, p. 86.

8. "80 Most Influential People in Sales and Marketing," *Sales & Marketing Management*, October 1998, p. 78.

9. John Godfrey, "Survey Says Two-Thirds of Americans Favor Tax for Online Sales," *KRTBN Knight-Ridder Tribune Business News: The Washington Times—Washington, DC*, December 15, 1999.

10. Zachary Schiller, "First Green Stamps. Now, Coupons?" *Business Week*, April 22, 1996.

11. Ibid. Information provided by coupon processor, NCH Promotional Services in Lincolnshire, IL.

12. William O. Bearden, Donald R. Lichtenstein, and Jesse E. Teel, "Comparison Price, Coupon, and Brand Effects on Consumer Reactions to Retail Newspaper Advertisements," *Journal of Retailing* 60, no. 2 (Summer 1984), pp. 11–34.

13. Kapil Bawa and Robert W. Shoemaker, "The Coupon-Prone Consumer: Some Findings Based on Purchase Behavior across Product Classes," *Journal of Marketing* 51 (October 1987), pp. 99–110; and Jesse E. Teel, Robert H. Williams, and William O. Bearden, "Correlates of Consumer Susceptibility to Coupons in New Grocery Product Introductions," *Journal of Advertising* 9, no. 3 (1980), pp. 31–35.

14. Tony Lisanti, "The Almighty Coupon, Redux," *Discount Store News*, September 21, 1998, p. 13.

15. William M. Bulkeley, "Rebates' Big Appeal: Many People Neglect to Redeem Them," *The Wall Street Journal*, February 10, 1998, pp. B1–B2.

16. "Web Thought: The $40 Ticket," PaineWebber, April 13, 1999.

17. "Web Thought: Average Order Size Matters," PaineWebber, April 13, 1999.

18. See Joseph P. Guiltinan, "The Price Bundling of Services: A Normative Framework," *Journal of Marketing* 51 (April 1987), pp. 74–85; Rockney G. Walters, "Assessing the Impact of Retail Price Promotions on Product Substitution, Complementary Purchase, and Interstore Sales Displacement," *Journal of Marketing* 55, no. 2 (1991), pp. 17–28; and Francis J. Mulhern and Robert Leone, "Implicit Price Bundling of Retail Products: A Multiproduct Approach to Maximizing Store Profitability," *Journal of Marketing* 55, no. 4 (October 1991), pp. 63–76.

19. Itamar Simonson, "Shoppers Easily Influenced Choices," *The New York Times*, November 6, 1994, based on research by Itamar Simonson and Amos Tversky.

20. Robert Blattberg and Kenneth Wisniewski, "How Retail Price Promotions Work: Empirical Results," Marketing Working Paper no. 42 (Chicago: University of Chicago, December 1987). This study indicated that odd pricing increases sales. The following studies don't support this proposition, however: Robert M. Schindler and Thomas Kibarian, "Testing Perceptual Underestimation of 9-Ending Prices," *Advances in Consumer Research* 11 (Association for Consumer Research, 1993), pp. 580–85; Zarrel V. Lambert, "Perceived Prices as Related to Odd

and Even Price Endings," *Journal of Retailing* 51 (Fall 1975), pp. 13–22; Robert M. Schindler and Alan R. Wiman, "Consumer Recall of Odd and Even Prices," Working Paper (Boston: Northeastern University, 1983); Robert Schindler, "Consumer Recognition of Increases in Odd and Even Prices," *Advances in Consumer Research* 11 (Association for Consumer Research, 1983), pp. 459–62; and Eli Ginzberg, "Customary Prices," *American Economic Review* 26 (1936), p. 296. For recent research in this area, see Robert M. Schindler and Patrick N. Kirby, "Patterns of Rightmost Digits Used in Advertised Prices: Implications for Nine-Ending Effects," *Journal of Consumer Research* 24 (September 1997), pp. 192–201; and Mark Stiving and Russell S. Winer, "An Empirical Analysis of Price Endings with Scanner Data," *Journal of Consumer Research* 24 (June 1997), pp. 57–67.

21. Kent Monroe, "The Pricing of Services," in *Handbook of Services Marketing*, ed. Carole A. Congram and Margaret L. Friedman (New York: AMACOM, 1989), pp. 20–31.

22. Ibid.

23. Valarie A. Zeithaml, "The Acquisition, Meaning, and Use of Price Information by Consumers of Professional Services," in *Marketing Theory: Philosophy of Science Perspectives*, ed. R. Bush and S. Hunt (Chicago: American Marketing Association), 1982, pp. 237–41.

24. In some rare situations, retail price and initial markup as a percentage of cost are known, and the retailer is seeking to determine the cost. In this case the following formula applies:

$$\text{Initial markup as a \% of retail} = \frac{\text{Initial markup as a \% of cost}}{100\% + \text{Initial markup as a \% of cost}}$$

25. "Wal-Mart's New Policy Makes Suppliers Pay," *Discount Store News*, May 20, 1996, p. 1.

26. Peter Cooper, "Subjective Economics: Factors in Psychology of Spending," and "The Begrudging Index and the Subjective Value of Money," in *Pricing Strategy*, ed. Bernard Taylor and Gordon Wills (Princeton, NJ: Brandon/Systems, 1970), pp. 112–31; and Steward Henderson Britt, "How Weber's Law Can Be Applied to Marketing," *Business Horizons*, February 1975, pp. 21–29.

27. Corporations (except for the Subchapter-S corporation, which is taxed differently from the normal garden-variety type of corporation) can deduct, as charitable contributions, the lower of the fair market value or the adjusted basis of inventory given to charity. Thus, if the fair market value is greater, then the deduction is limited to the lower adjusted basis of the inventory contributed (subject to some important exceptions where more than the adjusted basis, but not as much as the fair market value, can be deducted). Keep in mind also that, in any given year, the total deduction for charitable contributions is limited to 10 percent of the corporation's taxable income after certain adjustments are made to the taxable income. What can't be deducted in the current year because of the 10 percent limitation is eligible for a five-year carryover, subject to the same 10 percent limitation in the years of carryover. Thanks to Professor Donald B. Rotfort of Babson College for his insight on this issue.

28. This section is based on Thomas T. Nagle, *The Strategy and Tactics of Pricing* (Englewood Cliffs, NJ: Prentice-Hall, 1987), pp. 30–31.

29. This section draws from Nagle, *The Strategy and Tactics of Pricing*.

30. Kent B. Monroe, *Pricing: Making Profitable Decisions*, 2d ed. (New York: McGraw-Hill, 1990); Kent B. Monroe and William B. Dodds, "A Research Program for Establishing the Validity of the Price–Quality Relationship," *Journal of the Academy of Marketing Science* 16 (Spring 1990), pp. 151–68; Akshay R. Rao and Kent B. Monroe, "The Effect of Price, Brand Name, and Store Name on Buyers' Perceptions of Product Quality: An Integrative Review," *Journal of Marketing Research* 26 (August 1990), pp. 351–57; Valarie A. Zeithaml, "Consumer Perceptions of Price, Quality, and Value: A Means–End Model and Synthesis of Evidence," *Journal of Marketing* 52 (July 1988), pp. 2–22; and Gerald J. Tellis, "Consumer Purchasing Strategies and the Information in Retail Prices," *Journal of Retailing* 63, no. 3 (Fall 1987), pp. 279–97.

31. Alix M. Freedman, "A Price That's Too Good May Be Bad," *The Wall Street Journal*, November 15, 1988, p. 1B.

32. Richard Thaler, "Mental Accounting and Consumer Choice," *Marketing Science* 4 (Summer 1985), pp. 199–214.

33. InfoScan is available through Information Resources Inc., 150 N. Clinton St., Chicago, IL 60661, telephone (312) 726-1221.

34. "Booksellers Swear Anti-trust," *Discount Store News*, April 6, 1998, p. 8; and John Accola, "Tattered Cover Takes Aim," *Rocky Mountain News*, March 19, 1998, p. B1.

35. Dianna Marder, "Study Finds Gender Bias in Philadelphia Merchants Pricing," *The Philadelphia Inquirer*, March 5, 1999.

36. Ken Rankin, "Let's Hear Some Balance in Price-Fixing Cases," *Discount Store News*, October 7, 1996, p. 14.

37. Melody Petersen, "Treading a Contentious Line," *The New York Times*, January 13, 1999, pp. C1–C2.

38. Suan B. Garland, "You'll Charge What I Tell You to Charge: Will the Supreme Court Allow Manufacturer-Set Price Ceilings?" *Business Week*, October 6, 1997, pp. 118, 120; and "Justices: Suppliers Can Cap Retailer Prices," *The Miami Herald*, November 5, 1997, p. 9A.

39. Bob Ortega, "Suit over Wal-Mart's Pricing Practices Goes to Trial Today in Arkansas Court," *The Wall Street Journal*, August 23, 1993, p. A3; and Pete Hisey, "Ark. Supreme Court Rules Wal-Mart's No Predator: Lack of Proof Overturns Price Conviction," *Discount Store News*, February 6, 1995, pp. 3, 89.

40. Larry D. Compeau, Dhruv Grewal, and Diana S. Grewal, "Adjudicating Claims of Deceptive Advertised Reference Prices: The Use of Empirical Evidence," *Journal of Public*

Policy & Marketing 14 (Fall 1994); Dhruv Grewal, Diana S. Grewal, and Larry D. Compeau, "States' Crackdown on Deceptive Price Advertising: Retail and Public Policy Implications," *Pricing Strategy & Practice: An International Journal* 1, no. 2 (1993), pp. 33–40; Dhruv Grewal and Larry D. Compeau, "Comparative Price Advertising: Informative or Deceptive?" *Journal of Public Policy and Marketing* 11 (Spring 1992), pp. 52–62; Robert N. Corley and O. Lee Reed, *The Legal Environment*, 7th ed. (New York; McGraw-Hill, 1987); Teri Agins, "Low Prices or Low Practice? Regulators Cast Wary Eye on Retailers' Many Sales," *The Wall Street Journal*, February 13, 1990, pp. B1, B7; and *Do's and Don'ts in Advertising Copy* (Council of Better Business Bureaus, 1987).

Chapter 16

1. "Cooking Up a Deep-Dish Database," *Business Week*, November 20, 1995, p. 160.

2. "Nonstore Retailing: Nonstore Retailing Gains Favor with Consumers," *Chain Store Age State of the Industry Supplement*, August 1999, p. 29A.

3. "The Man Who Created Rudolph from an Idea That Almost Didn't Fly," *Chicago Tribune*, December 13, 1990, p. 1C.

4. Gabriella Stern, "With Sampling, There Is Too a Free Lunch," *The Wall Street Journal*, March 11, 1994, p. B1.

5. Raju Narisetti, "Move to Drop Coupons Puts Procter & Gamble in a Sticky PR Situation," *The Wall Street Journal*, April 17, 1997, pp. A1, A10.

6. Ibid., p. A1.

7. See A. Coskun Samli, "Store Image Definition, Dimensions, Measurement, and Management," in *Retail Market Strategy*, ed. A. Samli (New York: Quorum, 1989).

8. "Back to the Future," *The New York Times Magazine*, April 6, 1997, pp. 48–49.

9. W. Glynn Mangold, Fred Miller, and Gary Brockway, "Word-of-Mouth Communication in the Service Marketplace," *Journal of Services Marketing* 13 (January–February 1999), pp. 73–77. "Word of Mouth Still Works," *Discount Store News*, June 22, 1998, p. 17; George Silverman, "How to Harness the Awesome Power of Word of Mouth," *Direct Marketing*, November 1997, pp. 32–38; and Chip Walker, "Word of Mouth," *American Demographics*, July 1995, pp. 38–43.

10. Frederick Reichheld, "Loyalty-Based Management," *Harvard Business Review*, March–April 1993, p. 65.

11. Keith Dunnavant, "NASCAR: Unsafe at the Speed?" *Business Week*, November 1, 1999, p. 90.

12. "Top 100 Advertisers," *Advertising Age*, September 17, 1999, p. 16.

13. *Amazon.com 8K Quarterly Report*, October 28, 1999.

14. "Eyeing the Ethnic Market," *Body Fashions Intimate Apparel*, April 1999, p. 14; and Janet Smith, "Integrated Marketing," *Marketing Tools*, November–December 1995, pp. 62–65.

15. Kevin Keller, *Strategic Brand Management: Building, Measuring, and Managing Brand Equity* (Englewood Cliffs, NJ: Prentice Hall, 1997); and David Aaker, *Building Strong Brands* (New York: Free Press, 1995).

16. Stephen Smith, Narendra Agrawal, and Shelby McIntyre, "A Discrete Optimization Model for Seasonal Merchandise Planning," *Journal of Retailing* 74 (Summer 1998), pp. 193–222; Scott Neslin and John Quilt, "Developing Models for Planning Retailer Sales Promotions: An Application to Automobile Dealerships," *Journal of Retailing* 63 (Winter 1987), pp. 333–64; and Arthur Allaway, J. Barry Mason, and Gene Brown, "An Optimal Decision Support Model for Department-Level Promotion Mix Planning," *Journal of Retailing* 63 (Fall 1987), pp. 216–41.

17. Leonard Lodish, *Advertisers and Promotion Challenge: Vaguely Right or Precisely Wrong* (New York: Oxford University Press, 1986).

18. Erik Gordon, *Financial and Operating Results of Department & Specialty Stores in 1999* (Washington, DC: National Retail Federation, 1999), p. 17.

19. Ronald Curhan and Robert Kopp, "Obtaining Retailer Support for Trade Deals; Key Success Factors," *Journal of Advertising Research* 27 (December 1987–January 1988), pp. 51–60.

20. Giles D'Souza and Arthur Allaway, "An Empirical Investigation of the Advertising Spending Decision of a Multiproduct Retailer," *Journal of Retailing* 71 (Fall 1995), pp. 279–96.

21. This example is adapted by William R. Swinyard, professor of business management, Brigham Young University, from "Overseas Airlines Service" case.

22. Gary Witkin, "Effective Use of Retail Data Bases," *Direct Marketing*, December 1995, pp. 32–35.

23. Donald Ziccardi and David Moin, *Master Minding the Store: Advertising, Sales Promotion, and the New Marketing Reality* (New York: Wiley, 1997); John McCann, Ali Tadlaqui, and John Gallagher, "Knowledge Systems in Merchandising: Advertising Design," *Journal of Retailing*, Fall 1990, pp. 257–77; and Meryl Gardner and Michael Houston, "The Effects of Visual and Verbal Components of Retail Communications," *Journal of Retailing*, Summer 1986, pp. 65–78.

24. "Top 100 Advertisers," *Advertising Age*, September 17, 1999, p. 16.

25. Ibid., p. 31.

26. Ibid., p. 16.

27. James Fredrick and Allene Symons, "Building an Image," *Drug Store News*, November 18, 1996, p. 9.

28. Ibid., p. 9.

29. Ibid., pp. 9–10.

30. Tony Case, "A Rocky Road Predicted for Newspaper Advertising," *Editor & Publisher*, September 23, 1995, p. 27.

31. "Maximizing the Potential of Audio Advertising," *Chain Store Age*, March 1995, p. B13.

32. Susan Reda, "Retailers Use Affiliate Programs to Drive Internet Traffic and Sales," *Stores*, May 1998, pp. 46–49; Greg Notess, "Intricacies of Advertisement Information on the Web," *Online Magazine*, November 1999, pp. 79–81; and Retooling for Interactivity," *Response*, November 1999, pp. 28–31.

33. Cyndee Miller, "Outdoors Gets a Makeover," *Marketing News*, April, 10, 1995, pp. 1, 26; and Teresa Andreoli, "From Retailers to Consumers: Billboards Drive the Message Home," *Discount Store News*, September 19, 1994, p. 14.

34. Laurie Freeman, "Marketing the Market: Savvy Grocers Reach Out to Their Super Customers," *Marketing News*, March 2, 1998, p. 1.

35. Frederick Reichheld and W. Earl Sasser, "Zero Defections: Quality Comes to Services," *Harvard Business Review* 68 (September–October 1990), pp. 105–11; and Claes Fornell and Birger Wernerfelt, "Defensive Marketing Strategy by Customer Complaint Management," *Journal of Marketing Research* 24 (November 1987), pp. 337–46.

36. Frederick Reichheld, *The Loyalty Effect*, (Boston, MA: Harvard Business School Press, 1996).

37. "State of the Industry: Customer Management," *Chain Store Age*, August 1998, p. 20A; and Ira Scheiderman, "More Major Stores Offer Loyalty Programs," *DNR*, April 27, 1998, p. 2.

38. "The Future Is in the Cards," *Promo*, August 1995, p. S5.

39. Murray Raphael, "Customer Specific Marketing," *Direct Marketing*, June 1996, pp. 22–27; Brian Woolf, "Differentiate or Die," *Progressive Grocer*, May 1996, pp. 71–73; and "Select Few," *Marketing Week*, March 29, 1996, pp. 53–56.

40. Eric Malmborg, "Improve Customer Information—A Key to Catalog Success," *Direct Marketing*, June 1999, pp. 67–70; and "Customer Relationship Management—Leading the Data Warehousing Boom," *UK Retail Report*, September 1999, p. 89.

41. Heather Green, "The Information Gold Mine," *Business Week*, July 26, 1999, p. EB10; Sam Koslowsky, "Reducing Your Risk: What's Happening in Retail Database Marketing," *Direct Marketing*, January 1999, pp. 40–44; Patricia Murphy, "Effective Loyalty Programs Seen Catering to Individual Needs," *Stores*, February 1999, pp. 46–48; and Robert Blattberg, "Managing the Firm Using Lifetime-Customer Value," *Chain Store Age Executive*, January 1998, pp. 46–50.

42. Dan Scheraga, "Courting the Customer," *Chain Store Age*, January 2000, p. 88; Ro Panepinto, "Preventative Customer Care," *Response*, October 1999, pp. 46–53; and Steve Larsen, "Personalization without Privacy Won't Sell: Build Trust by Keeping Customers Informed," *Internet Retailer*, November 1999, p. 70

43. "Surfer Beware III: Privacy Policies without Privacy Protection," Electronic Privacy Information Center, December 1999 (www.epic.org/reports/surfer-beware3.html).

44. Ibid.

Chapter 17

1. Seth Lubovek, "Don't Listen to the Boss, Listen to the Customers." *Forbes*, December 4, 1995, pp. 45–46.

2. Joseph Carideo, "Developing Retail Talent," *Discount Merchandiser*, May 1993, pp. 117–18.

3. Steve Weinstein, "Motivating Forces," *Progressive Grocer*, September 1996, p. 32

4. Doug Donaldson, "Smart Hiring," *Do-It-Yourself Retailing*, January 1999, pp. 49–55; Herbert Heneman III, Timothy Judge, and Robert Heneman, *Staffing Organizations*, 3d ed. (Boston: Irwin/McGraw-Hill, 2000).

5. "Delivering Customer Satisfaction," *Chain Store Age Executive*, January 1994, p. 25.

6. Jennifer Steinhauer, "For U.S. Retailers, Grinch Brings a Tight Job Market," *The New York Times*, November 15 1997, p. A1; and Frank Hammel, "The Coming Crunch: Dealing with the Growing Labor Shortage," *Supermarket Business*, June 1996, p. 93.

7. Jessica Diamond, "New Strategies for Finding a High-Powered Staff," *Jewelers' Circular–Keystone*, September 1999, pp. 86–87.

8. Michael Cronin, "Turning Employees into Headhunters," *Inc.*, June 1992, pp. 112–13.

9. Charlene Solomon, "Managing Today's Immigrants," *Personnel Journal*, July 1993, pp. 57–65.

10. Ron Ruggles, "Internet Seen as an Effective Way to Recruit New Employees," *Nation's Restaurant News*, October 18, 1999, p. 80; and David Schulz, "Internet Emerging as Major Vehicle for Mid-Level Retail Recruiting," *Stores*, June 1999, pp. 70–73.

11. Ginger Koloszyc, "Tight Labor Market Spurs High-Tech Employment Screening," *Stores*, July 1998, pp. 77–81; David Schulz, "Small Retailers Turn to Pre-Employment Screening Services," *Stores*, May 1998, pp. 72–74; and George Kirk, Patrick Dunne, and James Wilson, "Pre-Employment Screening Devices: Are Retailers Using Them Correctly?" in Robert King, ed., *Retailing: Theories and Practices for Today and Tomorrow*, Proceedings of the Fourth Triennial National Retailing Conference, Richmond, VA, 1995, pp. 106–11.

12. Sarah Fister, "Separating Liars from Hires," *Training*, July 1999, pp. 22–24.

13. Jane Bahls, "Available upon Request," *HRMagazine*, January 1999, pp. S2–S7.

14. John Bernardin and Donna Cooke, "Validity of an Honesty Test in Predicting Theft among Convenience Store Employees," *Academy of Management Journal* 36 (October 1993), pp. 1097–109.

15. Richard Hollinger, *1998 National Retail Security Survey* (Gainsville, FL: Security Research Project, Department of Sociology, University of Florida, 1998), p. 17.

16. Jane Easter Bahls, "Dealing with Drugs: Keep It Legal," *HRMagazine*, March 1998, pp. 104–11.

17. John McKinnon, "Retailers Beware!" *Florida Trend*, June 1996, pp. 20–21.

18. Kal Lifson, "Turn Down Turnover to Turn Up Profits," *Chain Store Age*, November 1, 1996, pp. 64–66.

19. Paul Taylor, "Providing Structure to Interviews and Reference Checks," Workforce Tools Supplement, *Workforce*, May 1999, pp. S11–S55; and Allen Huffcutt and David Woehr, "Further Analysis of Employment Interview Validity: A Quantitative Evaluation of Interviewer-Related Structuring Methods," *Journal of Organizational Behavior* 20 (July 1999), pp. 549–56.

20. John Bible, "Discrimination in Job Applications and Interviews," *Supervision*, November 1998, pp. 9–12; Laura Williamson, James Campion, Mark Roehling, Stanley Malos, and Michael Campion, "Employment Interview on Trial: Linking Interview Structure with Litigation Outcomes," *Journal of Applied Psychology* 82 (December 1997), pp. 900–13; and Peter Burgess, "How Those 'Innermost Thoughts' Are Revealed," *Grocer*, March 9, 1996, pp. 60–62.

21. Lucette Comer and Tanya Drollinger, "Active Empathetic Listening and Selling Success: A Conceptual Framework," *Journal of Personal Selling and Sales Management* 9 (Winter 1999), pp. 15–29; C. David Sheppard, Stephen Castleberry, and Rick Ridnour, "Linking Effective Listening with Sales Performance: An Exploratory Investigation," *Journal of Business & Industrial Marketing* 12 (1997), pp. 315–21; and Stephen Castleberry and C. David Sheppard, "Effective Interpersonal Listening and Personal Selling," *Journal of Personal Selling & Sales Management*, Winter 1993, pp. 35–50.

22. Timothy Bland, "Build a Legal Employment Application," *HRMagazine*, March 1999, pp. 129–34; and Wayne Barlow and Edward Hane, "A Practical Guide to the Americans with Disabilities Act," *Personnel Journal*, June 1992, pp. 53–60.

23. Cheri Young and Craig Lundberg, "Creating a First Day on the Job," *Cornell Hotel and Restaurant Administration Journal*, December 1996, pp. 26–29.

24. Gerald White, "Employee Turnover: The Hidden Drain on Profits," *HR Focus*, January 1995, pp. 5–8.

25. "Workers Are Seeking Employers of Choice," *Chain Store Age Executive*, October 1998, pp. 72, 74.

26. Alice Starcke, "Building a Better Orientation Program," *HRMagazine*, November 1996, pp. 107–13.

27. Robert Henkoff, "Finding, Training, and Keeping," *Fortune*, October 3, 1994, p. 118.

28. "Education," *The Wall Street Journal*, February 9, 1991, p. R5.

29. Roy Canning, "Enhancing the Quality of Learning in Human Resource Development," *Journal of European Industrial Training* 20 (February 1996), pp. 3–11; Joy Riggs, "Faster, Shorter, Cheaper Drives Training Today," *Personnel Journal*, May 1996, pp. S1–S4; and Karen West, "Effective Training for a Revolving Door," *Training & Development*, September 1996, pp. 50–53.

30. "The 100 Best Companies to Work For," *Fortune*, January 10, 2000, p. 82.

31. Chris Roebuck, *Effective Leadership* (New York: AMACOM, 1999); and John Kotter, *John Kotter on What Leaders Really Do* (Boston: Harvard Business School Press, 1999).

32. Alan Coad and Anthony Berry, "Transformational Leadership and Learning Orientation," *Leadership & Organization Development Journal* 19 (March–April 1998), pp. 164–73; and Richard Koonce, "Do You Have a Transformational Leadership Style?" *Bank Marketing*, August 1997, pp. 5–6.

33. Donald McNermey, "Creating a Motivated Workforce," *HR Focus*, August 1996, pp. 1–8.

34. John Donovan and David Radosevich, "The Moderating Role of Goal Commitment on the Goal Difficulty–Performance Relationship: A Meta-Analytic Review and Critical Reanalysis," *Journal of Applied Psychology* 83 (April 1998), pp. 308–16; and M. Watson, "Designing a Goal Setting System to Enhance Performance: A Practical Guide," *Organizational Dynamics*, Summer 1998, pp. 69–78.

35. Thomas W. Lee, Edwin A. Locke, and Soo H. Phan, "Explaining the Assigned Goal-Incentive Interaction: The Role of Self-Efficacy and Personal Goals," *Journal of Management* 23 (July–August 1997), pp. 541–60; and M.E. Gist, "Self-Efficacy: Implications of Organizational Behavior and Human Resource Management," *Academy of Management Review* 12, no. 3 (1990), pp. 472–85.

36. Frank Hammel, "Becoming the Employer of Choice," *Supermarket Business*, June 1996, pp. 98–106.

37. Kevin Helliker, "Pressure at Pier 1: Beating the Sales Numbers of a Year Earlier Is a Storewide Obsession," *The Wall Street Journal*, December 7, 1995, pp. B1–B2.

38. Theodore Kinni, "Why We Work," *Training*, August 1998, pp. 34–40; and Nora Wood, "What Motivates Best?" *Sales & Marketing Management*, September 1998, pp. 71–72.

39. Richard McBain, "Pay, Performance, and Motivation," *Journal of General Management*, Autumn 1998, pp. S20–S32.

40. William Liccione, "Effective Goal Setting: A Prerequisite for Compensation Plans with Incentive Value," *Compensation & Benefits Management*, Winter 1997, pp. 19–26.

41. Parbudyal Singh, "Organizational Rewards for a Changing Workplace: An Examination of Theory and Practice," *International Journal of Technology Management* 16 (September–October 1998), pp. 225–39; and Haig

Nalbantian, "Productivity under Group Incentives: An Experimental Study," *American Economic Review* 87 (June 1997), pp. 314–42.

42. Susan Long, "The Changing Face of Sexual Harassment," *HR Focus*, October 1999, p. S1; Monica Ballard, "Avoid Unwanted Harassment Charges by Educating Workers, Responding to Claims," *Nation's Restaurant News*, August 31, 1998, pp. 34–35; and Michael Barrier, "Sexual Harassment," *Nation's Business*, December 1998, p. 14.

43. Carol Ukens, "Job Hazard," *Drug Topics*, May 29, 1996, p. 10.

44. Julie Ross, "Changes in Scheduling Software Target Improved Retail Performance," *Stores*, August 1997, pp. 85–88; "Retailers See Quick ROI in Automated Labor Scheduling," *Chain Store Age*, October 1996, pp. 78–82; and Bill Copeland, "The Latest and Greatest in People Planning," *Discount Merchandiser*, October 1995, pp. T66–T67.

45. "Frugal Retailers Splurge on IS," *Chain Store Age*, January 1, 1997, p. 146.

46. Jennifer Pellet, "Wal-Mart's Rush for California Green," *Discount Merchandiser*, February 1996, pp. 62–63; and Marianne Wilson, "Cutting Costs with Energy-Efficient HVAC," *Discount Store News*, February 1996, p. 53.

47. "Budget-Minded Retailers Maximize Dollars," *Chain Store Age Executive*, July 1993, pp. 56–61.

48. Hollinger, *1998 National Retail Security Survey*, p. 13.

49. Ibid.

50. Tracy Dougherty, "Loss Prevention: Winning the War against Theft," *VM + SD*, October 1993, pp. 44–49; and Timothy Crowe, "The Secure Store: A Clean, Well-Lighted Place," *Security Management*, March 1992, pp. 22A–24A.

51. "Retail Theft," *Discount Store News*, May 11, 1998, p. 4.

52. Ginger Koloszyc, "Supermarkets Find Growing Payoff in EAS Anti-Shoplifting Systems," *Stores*, February 1999, pp. 28–30; and "Sales Up, Shrink Down with Source Tagging," *Chain Store Age Executive*, August 1998, p. 84.

53. Read Hayes, "The Civil Recovery Side of Shoplifting," *Security Management*, March 1992, pp. 30A–32A.

54. Denise Zimmerman, "Theft Deterrents at Work," *Supermarket Business*, January 15, 1996, p. 21.

Chapter 18

1. "Enticing Shoppers to Follow the Yellow Brick Road," *Chain Store Age Executive*, August 1994, pp. 60–61.

2. Vince Staten, *Can You Trust a Tomato in January?* (New York: Simon & Schuster, 1993).

3. "International Interior Store Design Competition," *Visual Merchandising and Store Design*, February 1996, pp. 35–76.

4. "Enticing Shoppers to Follow the Yellow Brick Road."

5. "IKEA Holds Manhattan Outpost with Flexible Store Design," *Stores*, February 1996, pp. 65–66.

6. Marilyn Golden, "The Americans with Disabilities Act—Its Impact on Retailers," *Retail Business Review*, January 1993, pp. 14–19.

7. "Back to the Future," *The New York Times Magazine*, April 6, 1997, pp. 48–49.

8. Adapted from Dale M. Lewison, *Retailing*, 4th ed. (New York: Macmillan, 1991), pp. 287–88.

9. Paco Underhill, *Why We Buy: The Science of Shopping* (New York: Simon & Schuster, 1999).

10. Four of the most popular planogram programs are APOLLO (Information Resource Inc., Waltham, MA, 1-617-890-1100 or 1-617-290-0652), PEGMAN (MarketWare Inc., Norcross, GA, 1-404-246-1700, fax 1-404-246-1750), SPACEMAX (MarketMax Inc., Danvers, MA, 1-508-777-0057, fax 1-508-777-0195), and SPACEMAN III (Nielsen Marketing Research, Northbrook, IL, 1-708-498-6300).

11. Barbara J. White-Sax, "Store-Level Execution: Chains' Biggest Unrealized Opportunity," *Drug Store News*, April 26, 1999, p. 14.

12. Raymond R. Burke, "Virtual Shopping: Breakthrough in Marketing Research," *Harvard Business Review*, March–April 1996, pp. 120–34; and Lynn Fancher Canavan and Sean O'Leary, "Space Happens," *Visual Merchandising and Store Design*, October 1996, pp. 80–84.

13. Alexandra Moran, ed., *FOR/MOR 1998 Edition: The Combined Financial, Merchandising & Operating Results of Retail Stores in 1997*, 73d ed. (Washington, DC: National Retail Federation, 1998). High-profit stores are those in the top half as measured by operating earnings as a percentage of net sales.

14. See Heikki Rinne, Michael Geurts, and J. Patrick Kelly, "An Approach to Allocating Space to Departments in a Retail Store," *International Journal of Retailing* 2, no. 2 (1987), pp. 27–41; M. Corstjens and P. Doyle, "A Model for Optimizing Retail Space Allocations," *Management Science* 27, no. 7 (July 1981), pp. 822–33; and M. Corstjens and P. Doyle, "A Dynamic Model for Strategically Allocating Retail Space," *Journal of the Operational Research Society* 34, no. 10 (1983), pp. 943–52.

15. "The Need for Speed," *WWD*, November 5, 1998, p. 2.

16. The concept of atmospherics was introduced by Philip Kotler in "Atmosphere as a Marketing Tool," *Journal of Retailing* 49 (Winter 1973), pp. 48–64. The definition is adapted from Richard Yalch and Eric Spangenberg, "Effects of Store Music on Shopping Behavior," *The Journal of Service Marketing* 4, no. 1 (Winter 1990), pp. 31–39.

17. Underhill, *Why We Buy: The Science of Shopping*, p. 65.

18. Earl Print, "Euro Lighting," *VM&SD*, May 1999, pp. 38, 40.

19. For a review of this research, see Joseph A. Bellizzi and Robert E. Hite, "Environmental Color, Consumer Feelings, and Purchase Likelihood," *Psychology and Marketing* 9, no. 5 (September–October 1992), pp. 347–63.

20. Andrea Petersen, "Restaurants Bring In da Noice to Keep Out da Nerds," *The Wall Street Journal*, December 30, 1997, pp. B1, B2.

21. J. Duncan Herrington and Louis Capella, "Effects of Music in Service Environments: A Field Study," *Journal of Services Marketing* 10, no. 2 (1996), pp. 26–41.

22. Jennifer Markley, "Stay (Just a Little Big Longer)," *VM&SD*, November 1998, pp. 22–26.

23. Stacey Witt Toevs, "Three Stories One Mile High," *VM&SD*, November 1997, pp. 30–35.

24. Susan Reda, "Dollars and Scents," *Stores*, August 1994, pp. 38–39.

25. Ibid.; and Cathleen McCarthy, "Aromatic Merchandising: Leading Customers by the Nose," *Visual Merchandising and Store Design*, April 1992, pp. 85–87.

26. Maxine Wilkie, "Scent of a Market," *American Demographics*, August 1995, pp. 40–49.

27. McCarthy, "Aromatic Merchandising."

Chapter 19

1. Valarie Zeithaml, Leonard Berry, and A. Parasuraman, "The Behavioral Consequences of Service Quality," *Journal of Marketing* 60 (April 1996), pp. 31–46.

2. Susan Reda, "Internet Merchants Seek Ways to Improve On-Line Customer Service," *Stores*, August 1998, pp. 62–65.

3. Robert Spector and Patrick McCarthy, *The Nordstrom Way: The Inside Story of America's #1 Customer Service Company* (New York: John Wiley, 1999).

4. Benjamin Schneider and David Bowen, *Winning the Service Game* (Boston: Harvard Business School Press, 1995); and Rikard Larsson and David Bowen, "Organization and Customer: Managing Design and Coordination of Services," *Academy of Management Review* 14 (1989), pp. 213–33.

5. Banwari Mittal and Walfried Lassar, "The Role of Personalization in Service Encounters," *Journal of Retailng* 72 (Spring 1996), pp. 95–109.

6. Timothy Mullaney, "Needed: The Human Touch," *Business Week*, December 13, 1999, p. EB52; and Ellen Jovin and Jennifer Lach, "Online with the Operator," *American Demographics*, February 1999, p. 36.

7. "Workers Are Seeking Employers of Choice," *Chain Store Age Executive*, October 1998, pp. 72, 74; and Pete Hisey, "Customer Satisfaction Linked to Employee Training," *Discount Store News*, April 18, 1994, p. 41.

8. Murray Raphael, "Tell Me What You Want and the Answer Is Yes," *Direct Marketing*, October 1996, p. 22.

9. "Retailers Join the War Effort," *Chain Store Age Executive*, June 1994, p. 15.

10. Roger Bennett, "Queues, Customer Characteristics and Policies for Managing Waiting-Lines in Supermarkets," *International Journal of Retail & Distribution Management* 26 (February–March 1998), pp. 78–88; and Julie Baker and Michaelle Cameron, "The Effects of the Service Environment on Affect and Consumer Perceptions of Waiting Time: An Integrative Review and Research Propositions," *Journal of the Academy of Marketing Science* 24 (Fall 1996), pp. 338–49.

11. Janet Guyon, "Can the Savoy Cut Costs and Be the Savoy?" *The Wall Street Journal*, October 25, 1994, pp. B1, B5. See also Melissa Dowling, "Can We Afford Superior Service?" *Catalog Age*, July 1996, pp. 129–30.

12. William Parsons, "Give the Lady What She Wants," *Chain Store Age*, November 1995, pp. 86–87.

13. Louise Lee, "Retailers' Returns Policies Eyeballed," *HFN*, September 21, 1998 p. 49; and "Without a Receipt, You May Get Charged for That Ugly Scarf," *The Wall Street Journal*, November 1996, pp. A1, A6. See also Dowling, "Can We Afford Superior Service?"

14. Lee, "Retailers' Returns Policies Eyeballed."

15. Kenneth Clow, David Kurtz, and John Ozment, "A Longitudinal Study of the Stability of Consumer Expectations of Services," *Journal of Business Research* 42 (May 1998), pp. 63–74; Valerie Taylor and Anthony Miyazaki, "Assessing Actual Service Performance: Incongruities between Expectations and Evaluative Criteria," in Frank Kardas and Mitt Sujan, eds., *Advances in Consumer Research* 22 (Provo, UT: Association of Consumer Research, 1995), pp. 594–605; and A. Parasuraman, Leonard Berry, and Valarie Zeithaml, "Understanding Customer Expectations of Service," *Sloan Management Review*, Spring 1991, pp. 39–48.

16. Kenneth Clow, David Kurtz, John Ozment, and Beng Soo Ong, "The Antecedents of Consumer Expectations of Services: An Empirical Study across Four Industries," *The Journal of Services Marketing* 11 (May–June 1997), pp. 230–48; and Ann Marie Thompson and Peter Kaminski, "Psychographic and Lifestyle Antecedents of Service Quality Expectations," *Journal of Services Marketing* 7 (1993), pp. 53–61.

17. Bill Pearson, "Customer Service . . . Expect the Unexpected," *Stores*, March 1994, p. 58.

18. Greg Steinmetz, "Customer-Service Era Is Reaching Germany Late, Hurting Business," *The Wall Street Journal*, June 1, 1995, pp. A1, A8. See also Peter Maass, "Service with a Snarl," *The Washington Post*, August 17, 1993, p. 42.

19. Alain Genestre, Paul Herbig, and Alan Shao, "What Does Marketing Really Mean in Japan?" *Marketing Intelligence & Planning* 13, no. 9 (1995), pp. 16–27.

20. Michael Hartline and O.C. Ferrell, "The Management of Customer-Contact Service Employees: An Empirical Investigation," *Journal of Marketing* 60 (October 1996), pp. 52–70; and Lois Mohr and Mary Jo Bittner, "The Role of Employee Effort in Satisfaction with Service Transactions," *Journal of Business Research* 32 (March 1995), pp. 239–52.

21. Mona Fitzsimmons, *New Service Development: Creating Memorable Experiences* (Thousand Oaks, CA: Sage, 1999).

22. The following discussion of the Gaps model and its implications is based on Deon Nel and Leyland Pitt, "Service Quality in a Retail Environment: Closing the Gaps," *Journal of General Management* 18 (Spring 1993), pp. 37–57; Valarie Zeithaml, A. Parasuraman, and Leonard Berry, *Delivering Quality Customer Service* (New York: Free Press, 1990); and Valarie Zeithaml, Leonard Berry, and A. Parasuraman, "Communication and Control Processes in the Delivery of Service Quality," *Journal of Marketing* 52 (April 1988), pp. 35–48.

23. Cynthia Crossen, "Americans Have It All, but It Is Not Enough," *The Wall Street Journal*, September 29, 1996, p. R4.

24. Leonard Berry, *On Great Customer Service: A Framework for Action* (New York: Free Press, 1996), p. 44.

25. Thomas Peters and Nancy Austin, *A Passion for Excellence* (New York: Random House, 1985), p. 84.

26. "Merchant Prince: Stanley Marcus," *Inc.*, June 1987, pp. 41–44.

27. Jagdip Singh and Robert Wilkes, "When Customers Complain: A Path Analysis of Key Antecedents of Customer Complaint Response Analysis," *Journal of the Academy of Marketing Science* 24 (Fall 1996), pp. 350–65. For an illustration of the importance of stimulating customer complaints, see Claus Fornell and B. Wernerfelt, "Defensive Marketing Strategy by Customer Complaint Management," *Journal of Marketing Research* 24 (November 1987), pp. 337–46.

28. Ron Zemke and Dick Schaaf, *The Service Edge: 101 Companies That Profit from Customer Care* (New York: Plume, 1990), pp. 319–21.

29. David Villano, "Secrets of Service," *Florida Trend*, September 1996, pp. 48–54.

30. Peters and Austin, *A Passion for Excellence*, p. 95.

31. Daniel Roth, "My Job at the Container Store," *Fortune*, January 10, 2000, p. 76.

32. "Mr. Winchester Orders a Pizza," *Fortune*, November 14, 1996, p. 134.

33. Malcolm Fleschner and Gerhard Gschwandtner, "The Marriott Miracle," *Selling Power*, September 1994, pp. 17–23.

34. Berry, *On Great Customer Service*, pp. 73–74.

35. See Chuck Chakrapani, *How to Measure Service Quality and Customer Satisfaction: The Informal Field Guide for Tools and Techniques* (Chicago: American Marketing Association, 1998).

36. "Mystery Shopping's Lightweight Reputation Undeserved," *International Journal of Retail & Distribution Management* 27 (February–March 1999), pp. 114–17; Rachel Miller, "Undercover Shoppers," *Marketing*, May 28, 1998, pp. 27–30; and Jennifer Steinhauer, "The Undercover Shoppers," *The New York Times*, February 4, 1998, p. D1.

37. "New Developments in Customer Service Training," *International Journal of Retail & Distribution Management* 24 (Summer 1996), pp. 12–15.

38. Chip Bell and Ron Zemke, "Do Service Procedures Tie Employees' Hands," *Personnel Journal*, September 1988, p. 79.

39. T. Mullaney, "Needed: The Human Touch."

40. See Michael Hui and David Tse, "What to Tell Consumers in Waits of Different Length: An Integrated Model of Service Evaluation," *Journal of Marketing* 60 (April 1996), pp. 81–90; and Gail Tom and Scott Lucey, "Waiting Time Delays and Customer Satisfaction in Supermarkets," *Journal of Services Marketing* 9, no. 5 (1995), pp. 20–29.

41. Ronald Henkoff, "Finding, Training, and Keeping the Best Service Workers," *Fortune*, October 3, 1994, p. 120.

42. Mara Adelman and Aaron Ahuvia, "Social Support in the Service Sector: The Antecedents, Processes, and Consequences of Social Support in an Introductory Service," *Journal of Business Research* 32 (March 1995), pp. 273–82; and Arlie Russell Hochschild, *The Managed Heart: Commercialization of Human Feelings* (Berkeley, CA: University of California Press, 1983).

43. "The Informers," *Inc.*, March 1995, pp. 50–61.

44. Linda Cooper, "Polishing the Trophy: Enhancing the Service Commitment," *International Service Association Journal*, April 1991, pp. 25–28.

45. David Bowen and Edward Lawler, "The Empowerment of Service Workers: What, Why, How, and When?" *Sloan Management Review*, Spring 1992, pp. 32–44.

46. Alan Gilman, "Smart Compensation and Smart Selling," *Chain Store Age Executive*, September 1992, p. 134; and Pete Hisey, "Who Satisfies CE Shoppers Most: Commissioned or Noncommissioned Help?" *Discount Store News*, May 3, 1993, pp. 70–71.

47. William George and Leonard Berry, "Guidelines for the Advertising of Services," *Business Horizons*, May–June 1991, pp. 52–56.

48. Piyush Kumar, Manohar Kalawani, and Makbool Dada, "The Impact of Waiting Time Guarantees on Customers' Waiting Experiences," *Marketing Science* 16, no. 4, 1999, pp. 676–785.

49. Tibbett Speer, "They Complain because They Care," *American Demographics* 18 (May 1996), pp. 13–14; and Fredrick Reichheld, "Learning from Customer Defections," *Harvard Business Review*, March–April 1996, pp. 56–67.

50. "Improving Services Doesn't Always Require a Big Investment," *The Service Edge*, July–August 1990, p. 3.

51. Linda Lash, "Complaints as a Marketing Strategy," *The Marketing Strategy Letter*, February 1993, p. 3; John F. Sherry, Jr., Mary Ann McGrath, and Sidney J. Levy, "The Disposition of the Gift and Many Unhappy Returns," *Journal of Retailing*, Spring 1992, pp. 40–65; and Doris Kincade, Ann Redwine, and Gregory Hancock, "Apparel

Product Dissatisfaction and the Post-Complaint Process," *International Journal of Retail & Distribution Management*, September–October 1992, pp. 15–22.

52. Patricia Sellers, "Building Loyalty: Keeping the Buyers You Already Have," *Fortune*, November 22, 1993, pp. 56–58.

53. Richard Garfein, "Guiding Principles for Improving Customer Service," *Journal of Services Marketing* 2 (Spring 1988), pp. 37–41.

54. Stephen Tax, Stephen Brown, and Murali Chandrashekaran, "Customer Evaluations of Service Complaint Experience: Implications for Relationship Marketing," *Journal of Marketing* 62 (April 1998), pp. 60–76; Amy Smith and Ruth Bolton, "An Experimental Investigation of Customer Reactions to Service Failures and Recovery Encounters: Paradox or Peril?" *Journal of Services Research* 1 (August 1998), pp. 23–36; and Cynthia Webster and D.S. Sundaram, "Service Consumption Criticallity in Failure Recovery," *Journal of Business Research* 41 (February 1998), pp. 153–59.

CREDITS

Chapter 1

6 Courtesy liquidaudio.com 6 Mark Lewis/Stone 7 © Mark Graham 7 Rex Rystedt 7 Courtesy Nike 10 Courtesy Home Depot 11 Jonathon Johnson: AP/Wide World Photos 17 Courtesy Laura Phillips 18 © 1998, 1999 Patagonia, Inc., used with permission, all rights reserved 20 Courtesy Albertson's 20 Courtesy Albertson's 24 Courtesy JCPenney Co. 24 Courtesy JCPenney Co. 26 Courtesy Whole Foods Market

Chapter 2

40 Walter Hodges/Stone 40 Courtesy Toys "R" Us, Inc. 43 © 1999 Michael Bowles 47 © Stephen Begleiter 47 Stephen Begleiter 46 Courtesy Wal-Mart Stores, Inc. 50 Bruce Forster/Stone 54 Courtesy Radio Shack 56 © Todd Buchanan 59 Yvan Deweerdt/Gamma Liaison 62 © Arthur Tilley/FPG International 62 Bob Barrett/Unicorn Stock Photos 67 © Rex Rystedt

Chapter 3

78 Michael Keller/The Stock Market 81 Courtesy mustardstore.com 84 Courtesy etoys.com 88 Courtesy mysimon.com 89 Courtesy Bluefly, Inc. 90 Courtesy Circuit City Stores, Inc. 92 Courtesy perfumania.com 95 Courtesy garden.com 95 Courtesy garden.com 96 Courtesy The Knot, Inc. 99 Reprinted with permission by Lands End, Inc. 100 Courtesy Walgreens 103 Courtesy Gooseberry Patch Catalog 105 © Tom McCarthy/Photo Edit 104 Courtesy Dudley Products, Inc.

Chapter 4

114 © Mitch O'Connell 115 Courtesy Delia's 116 Myrleen Ferguson/Photo Edit 117 © Scott Willis 118 Lisa Quinones/Black Star 122 Courtesy South DeKalb Mall 123 Courtesy TJ MAXX 124 Courtesy Hammacher Schlemmer 127 Michael Newman/PhotoEdit 128 Courtesy Merck & Co.

Chapter 5

139 Courtesy Auto-By-Tel Corporation 140 © Michael Newman/PhotoEdit 140 David Young-Wolff/PhotoEdit 140 Jeff Greenberg/Unicorn Stock Photos 143 Steve Goldstein 150 Courtesy Public Technologies Multimedia, Inc. 152 Courtesy JCPenney Co. 154 Michael Newman/PhotoEdit 163 Michael Newman/PhotoEdit 163 Paul Fenton/Shooting Star 165 Courtesy Wet Seal, Inc.

Chapter 6

172 Michael Newman/PhotoEdit 175 Courtesy Ukrops Super Markets, Inc. 181 Courtesy The Container Store 183 © Andrew Garn 183 © Michael J Hruby 184 Courtesy Circuit City Stores, Inc. 186 © Munshi Ahmed 186 © Ed Kashi 192 Courtesy ABT Electronics & Appliances 197 Courtesy Brunswick Indoor Recreation Group

Chapter 7

207 Jon Riley/Stone 207 Don Smetzer/Stone 209 Courtesy Wal-Mart Stores, Inc. 211 © Stephen Begleiter 214 © Betts Anderson/Unicorn Stock Photos 215 © Ed Pritchard/Stone 216 Margaret Finefrock/Unicorn Stock Photos 226 Paul Conklin/PhotoEdit

Chapter 8

236 Wide World Photos 239 © Michael J. Hruby 240 North Wind Picture Archives 242 © Robert Burroughs 243 © Alice Prescott/Unicorn Stock Photos 248 © Bridget Barrett 249 © Stephen Begleiter 252 Courtesy Mr. I's photos by Erica N. Sanders

Chapter 9

260 © Michael J. Hruby 265 © Michael J. Hruby 265 © Michael J. Hruby 269 © Michael J. Hruby 271 Courtesy of The United States Department of Commerce 276 © Dale Durfee/Stone 278 © Steven Peters/Stone 279 © Ken Fisher/Stone

Chapter 10

288 Courtesy Taco Bell Corporation 290 Courtesy Sears Roebuck & Co 292 © Frank Herholdt/Stone 297 Courtesy Federated Department Stores 301 © Jon Riley/Stone 302 Courtesy JCPenney Co. 307 Courtesy JCPenney Co. 308 Courtesy Southwest Airlines 309 Courtesy Singapore Airlines 311 Michael Newman/PhotoEdit

Chapter 11

326 © Stephen Begleiter 329 From The Wall Street Journal-Permission, Cartoon Features Syndicate 331 Courtesy SuperValu 333 © David Strick/Corbis Outline 337 © Charles Gupton/Stone 338 Courtesy Sensoramatic

Chapter 12

349 © The Image Bank **352** © Jim Shipper/Unicorn Stock Photos **355** Rhoda Sidney/PhotoEdit **355** © Tom McCarthy/PhotoEdit **358** © Amy C. Etra/PhotoEdit **362** Steve Cohen/Stone **363** Tom McCarthy/Unicorn Stock Photos **363** © Michael J. Hruby **368** Courtesy Strategic Weather Services **370** Courtesy Shikatani Lacroix Design, Inc.

Chapter 13

388 Courtesy Pelco **394** Don Smetzer/Stone **397** Courtesy E3 Corporation **403** Michael Newman/PhotoEdit **403** Michael Newman/PhotoEdit

Chapter 14

416 Courtesy Timex Corporation **416** Courtesy Lee Apparel Co. **416** Courtesy Adidas **418** © Barry Yee **420** Courtesy The Great Atlantic & Pacific Company **420** Courtesy Sears Roebuck & Co. **424** © 2000 Rolex Watch USA, Inc. **420** Courtesy JCPenney Co. **424** © 2001 BMW of North America, Inc. Used with permission. The BMW name and logo are registered trademarks. **425** Jeff Greenberg/PhotoEdit **427** © Brent Jones **428** Superstock International **431** © Josh McHug **436** Mark Richards/Contact Press Images, Inc.

Chapter 15

456 © Jose Carrillo/PhotoEdit **460** Courtesy Daffy's **464** © David Young-Wolff/PhotoEdit **464** Michael Newman/PhotoEdit **465** © Andrew Garn **466** © Tony Freeman/PhotoEdit **476** Sears Roebuck & Co. **474** Courtesy Neiman-Marcus

Chapter 16

492 © Jeff Baker **495** Allsport **497** Courtesy Zellers **498** Courtesy of Fashion Bug **498** Courtesy Payless ShoeSource **499** Courtesy ivillage, Inc. **508** Courtesy Target Stores **509** Courtesy Kmart Properties, Inc.

Chapter 17

527 Courtesy TJ MAXX **533** © Michael Newman/PhotoEdit **534** Courtesy Shopko Stores, Inc. **535** Courtesy Sears Roebuck & Co., photography by Mark Joseph **541** Courtesy The Limited, Inc. **544** Frank Garner/The Stock Market **547** Courtesy SAP/Campbell Software Courtesy Sensormatic **550** Courtesy Sensormatic

Chapter 18

557 © Dick Loesch Cam-Tech Photography **557** © Dick Loesch Cam-Tech Photography **561** © Paul Warchol/Warchol Photogrpahy **564** © Tony Freeman/PhotoEdit **565** Courtesy of Jericho Promotions **570** Courtesy of Information Resources **574** Courtesy Diesal U.S.A., Inc. **575** © Sharon Hoogstraten **577** Courtesy of Planet Theory, Inc. **577** Courtesy Sayles Graphics Design **579** © Ron Forth Photography **580** Courtesy TOO Incorporated

Chapter 19

587 Courtesy garden.com **588** Courtesy Miller/Zell **588** Discount Store News **590** Courtesy Will and Deni McIntryre **595** © Bob Daemmrich/Stock Boston **596** Bruce Forster/Stone **601** Courtesy ivillage, Inc.

www.amazon.com   www.gap.c

www.circuitcity.com   www.tesc

www.bluelight.com   www.fingerhut.c

www.sears.com   www.cdno

www.officedepot.com   www.t

www.jcpenney.com   www.etoys

www.garden.com   w

www.toysrus.com   www.botto

www.wholefoods.com   www.ec

www.marks-and-spencer.co.uk   www.wal-mart.co

www.bn.co

www.traderjoes.com

www.nordstrom.com   www.bn.com   www.car